Great Britain

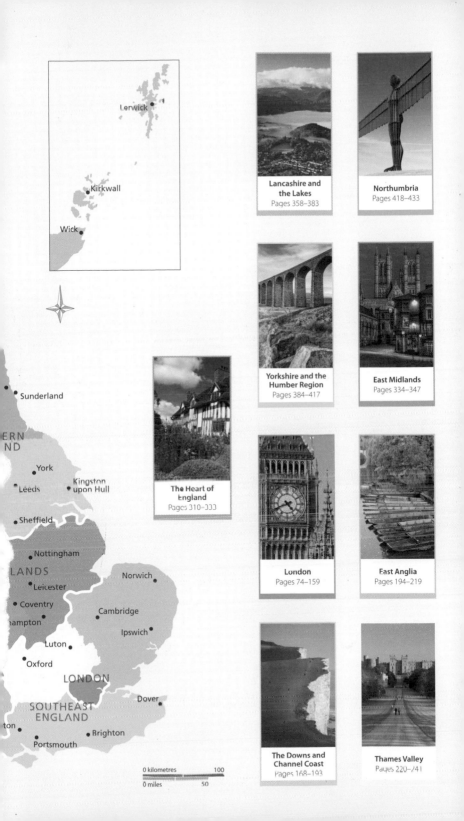

Lerwick

Kirkwall

Wick

Sunderland

ERN
ND

York

Leeds · Kingston
upon Hull

Sheffield

Nottingham

LANDS
· Leicester

· Coventry

hampton

Luton

Oxford

LONDON

SOUTHEAST
ENGLAND

ton

Portsmouth · Brighton

Norwich

Cambridge

Ipswich

Dover

**Lancashire and
the Lakes**
Pages 358–383

Northumbria
Pages 418–433

**Yorkshire and the
Humber Region**
Pages 384–417

East Midlands
Pages 334–347

**The Heart of
England**
Pages 310–333

London
Pages 74–159

East Anglia
Pages 194–219

**The Downs and
Channel Coast**
Pages 168–193

Thames Valley
Pages 220–241

0 kilometres   100
0 miles   50

DK EYEWITNESS TRAVEL

Great Britain

Main Contributor **Michael Leapman**

DK | Penguin Random House

Art Editor Stephen Bere
Project Editor Marian Broderick
Editors Carey Combe, Sara Harper,
Elaine Harries, Kim Inglis, Ella Milroy,
Andrew Szudek, Nia Williams
Designers Susan Blackburn, Elly King,
Colin Loughrey, Andy Wilkinson

Contributors Josie Barnard,
Christopher Catling, Juliet Clough,
Lindsay Hunt, Polly Phillimore,
Martin Symington, Roger Thomas

Maps Jane Hanson, Phil Rose,
Jennifer Skelley (Lovell Johns Ltd),
Gary Bowes (Era-Maptec Ltd)

Photographers Joe Cornish, Paul Harris,
Rob Reichenfeld, Kim Sayer

Illustrators Gary Cross, Richard Draper,
Jared Gilby (Kevin Jones Assocs), Paul Guest,
Roger Hutchins, Chris Orr & Assocs,
Maltings Partnership, Ann Winterbotham,
John Woodcock

Printed and bound in China

First published in the UK in 1995 by
Dorling Kindersley Limited
80 Strand, London WC2R 0RL, UK

18 19 20 21 10 9 8 7 6 5 4 3 2 1

Reprinted with revisions 1996, 1997,
1998, 1999, 2000, 2001, 2002, 2003,
2004, 2005, 2006, 2008, 2009, 2010,
2011, 2013, 2014, 2016, 2018
Copyright 1995, 2018 © Dorling
Kindersley Limited, London
A Penguin Random House Company

ISBN 978-0-2413-0623-9

Floors are referred to throughout in
accordance with British usage;
ie, the "first floor" is above ground level.

MIX
Paper from
responsible sources
FSC™ C018179
www.fsc.org

Introducing Great Britain

Discovering
Great Britain **10**

Putting Great Britain
on the Map **18**

A Portrait of
Great Britain **24**

The History of
Great Britain **42**

Great Britain
Through the Year **66**

London

Introducing London **76**

West End and
Westminster **80**

South Kensington and
Hyde Park **98**

Regent's Park and
Bloomsbury **106**

The City and
Southwark **112**

Further Afield **126**

London Street Finder **131**

Southeast England

Introducing
Southeast England **162**

The Downs and
Channel Coast **168**

East Anglia **194**

Thames Valley **220**

The West Country

Introducing the
West Country **244**

Wessex **250**

Devon and Cornwall **276**

Jurassic coastline at Durdle Door, Dorset

◀ **Title page** River Manifold Valley near Ilam, Peak District National Park, Derbyshire **Front cover image** The River Wye as seen from
Symonds Yat, Herefordshire **Back cover image** The striking Seven Sisters chalk cliffs, Eastbourne

Contents

The Midlands

Introducing
the Midlands **302**

The Heart of England **310**

East Midlands **334**

Wales

Introducing Wales **436**

North Wales **444**

South and Mid-Wales **460**

Travellers' Needs

Where to Stay **556**

Where to Eat and
Drink **574**

Shopping in Britain **610**

Entertainment in
Britain **612**

Specialist Holidays and
Outdoor Activities **614**

Blea Tarn near Little Langdale, the Lake District

Northern England

Introducing Northern
England **350**

Lancashire and
the Lakes **358**

Yorkshire and the
Humber Region **384**

Northumbria **418**

Scotland

Introducing
Scotland **482**

The Lowlands **494**

The Highlands
and Islands **528**

Survival Guide

Practical Information **620**

Travel Information **632**

General Index **644**

Culzean Castle, the
Lowlands, Scotland

HOW TO USE THIS GUIDE

This guide helps you to get the most from your stay in Great Britain. It provides both detailed practical information and expert recommendations. *Introducing Great Britain* maps the country and sets it in its historical and cultural context. The six regional chapters, plus *London*, describe important sights, using maps, pictures and illustrations. Features cover topics from houses and famous gardens to sport. Hotel, restaurant and pub recommendations can be found in *Travellers' Needs*. The *Survival Guide* has practical information on everything from travel information to public transport and personal security.

London at a Glance

The centre of London has been divided into four sightseeing areas. Each has its own chapter, which opens with a list of the sights described. The last section, *Further Afield*, covers the most attractive suburbs. All sights are numbered and plotted on an area map. Information on each sight is easy to locate as the entries follow the numbering used on the map.

1 Area Map
For easy reference, the sights in each area are numbered and located on an area map. The central sights are also marked on the London Street Finder maps on pages 131–151.

All pages relating to London have the same colour thumb tabs.

A locator map shows you where you are in relation to surrounding areas.

Numbered circles pinpoint all the listed sights on the area map.

Stars indicate the sights that no visitor should miss.

2 Street-by-Street Map
This gives a bird's-eye view of the heart of each sightseeing area. The numbering of the sights ties in with the area map and the fuller descriptions on the pages that follow.

A suggested route for a walk takes in the most attractive and interesting streets in the area.

3 Detailed information
The sights in London are described individually. Addresses, telephone numbers, opening hours, information on admission charges, tours and wheelchair access are also provided, as well as public transport links.

1 Introduction

The landscape, history and character of each region is outlined here, showing how the area has developed over the centuries and what it has to offer the visitor today.

Great Britain Area by Area

Apart from London, Great Britain has been divided into 14 regions, each of which has a separate chapter. The most interesting towns and places to visit have been numbered on a *Regional Map*.

Each area of Great Britain can be identified quickly by its colour coding; the key is on the inside front cover.

2 Regional Map

This shows the main road network and gives an illustrated overview of the whole region. All entries are numbered and there are also useful tips on getting around the region by car, train and other forms of transport.

3 Detailed information on each sight

All important sights in each area are described in depth in this section. They are listed in order, following the numbering on the *Regional Map*. Practical information on opening hours, telephone numbers, websites, admission charges and facilities available is given for each sight. The key to the symbols used can be found on the back flap.

Story boxes explore related topics.

The Visitors' Checklist provides the practical information you will need to plan your visit.

4 Great Britain's major sights

These are given two or more full pages in the sightseeing area in which they are found. Historic buildings are dissected to reveal their interiors; and museums and galleries have colour-coded floorplans to help you find important exhibits.

INTRODUCING GREAT BRITAIN

Discovering Great Britain   10–17

Putting Great Britain
  on the Map   18–23

A Portrait of Great Britain   24–41

The History of Great Britain   42–65

Great Britain
  Through the Year   66–73

DISCOVERING GREAT BRITAIN

The tours on the following pages have been designed to take in as many of Britain's myriad highlights as possible, while keeping long-distance travel to a minimum. First comes a two-day taste of London; this connects with the week-long tour of the Southeast that follows. The latter, in turn, links with a seven-day circuit through the West Country, and there are three further seven-day trips covering the North, Scotland, and Wales and the West. Scotland and the North can be easily combined into a fortnight-long drive. Each itinerary comes with extra suggestions for travellers who wish to extend their stay. Pick, combine and follow your favourite tours, or simply dip in and out and be inspired.

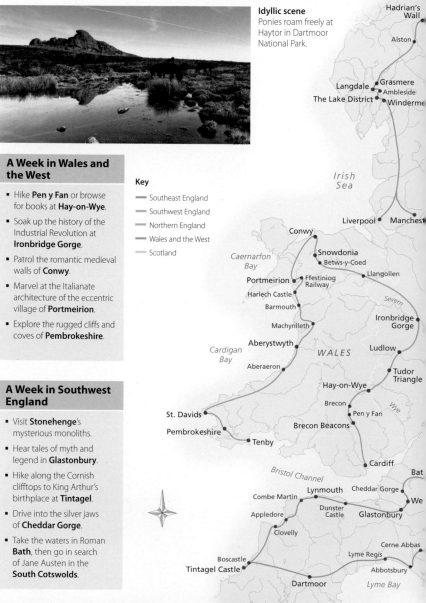

Idyllic scene
Ponies roam freely at Haytor in Dartmoor National Park.

A Week in Wales and the West

- Hike **Pen y Fan** or browse for books at **Hay-on-Wye**.
- Soak up the history of the Industrial Revolution at **Ironbridge Gorge**.
- Patrol the romantic medieval walls of **Conwy**.
- Marvel at the Italianate architecture of the eccentric village of **Portmeirion**.
- Explore the rugged cliffs and coves of **Pembrokeshire**.

A Week in Southwest England

- Visit **Stonehenge's** mysterious monoliths.
- Hear tales of myth and legend in **Glastonbury**.
- Hike along the Cornish clifftops to King Arthur's birthplace at **Tintagel**.
- Drive into the silver jaws of **Cheddar Gorge**.
- Take the waters in Roman **Bath**, then go in search of Jane Austen in the **South Cotswolds**.

Key
- Southeast England
- Southwest England
- Northern England
- Wales and the West
- Scotland

Hadrian's Wall
Alston
Langdale • Grasmere
Ambleside
The Lake District • Windermere

Irish Sea

Liverpool • Manches

Conwy
Snowdonia
Betws-y-Coed
Caernarfon Bay
Portmeirion • Ffestiniog Railway
Harlech Castle
Barmouth
Llangollen
Severn
Machynlleth
Ironbridge Gorge
Aberystwyth
WALES
Ludlow
Cardigan Bay
Aberaeron
Hay-on-Wye
Tudor Triangle
Brecon
Pen y Fan
St. Davids
Wye
Pembrokeshire
Brecon Beacons
Tenby
Cardiff
Bristol Channel
Bat
Lynmouth
Cheddar Gorge
Combe Martin
Dunster Castle
We
Appledore
Glastonbury
Clovelly
Cerne Abbas
Lyme Regis
Boscastle
Tintagel Castle
Abbotsbury
Dartmoor
Lyme Bay

Hastings (1810), an unfinished sketch by J M W Turner

A Week in Scotland

- Investigate Sherlock Holmes, Jekyll and Hyde and other literary legends in **Edinburgh**.
- Visit **Royal Deeside**, the royal family's summer retreat.
- Cross the mighty **Cairngorm Mountains**.
- Go in search of the Loch Ness monster on a cruise through the Great Glen from **Inverness**.
- Visit the art galleries of revitalized **Glasgow**.

Travelling in style
This horse-drawn carriage up the Long Walk at Windsor Castle travels at a relaxed pace.

A Week in Northern England

- Catch up with the latest in contemporary art at **Tate Liverpool**.
- Hike the sensational scenery of the **Lake District**.
- Watch archaeologists dig up real Roman history beside the remarkable 2nd-century ramparts of **Hadrian's Wall**.
- Ride back in time on a vintage tram to a working pit village at **Beamish**.
- Eat Britain's best fish and chips on the bustling harbour at **Whitby**.
- Come face to face with the Vikings in **York**, and wander along streets barely changed since medieval times.

A Week in Southeast England

- Take the sea air in buzzing Georgian **Brighton**.
- Examine King Arthur's legendary Round Table in historic **Winchester**.
- Soak up idyllic riverside views on a cruise along the Thames to **Henley**.
- Visit **Windsor Castle**, then take a stately carriage ride in Windsor Great Park.
- Explore England's oldest university in **Oxford**.
- Watch a play at the Royal Shakespeare Theatre in **Stratford-upon-Avon**.

Two Days in London

Offering a small taste of this great city, this itinerary scoops up the very best of London's history, pageantry and art.

- **Arriving** London's main international airport is Heathrow, 14 miles (22 km) west of the city centre and served by the Heathrow Express train, which connects in 15 minutes with London underground at Paddington Station. (In May 2018, Crossrail services will begin between Paddington and Heathrow Terminal 4.)

- **Moving on** An extensive rail network links London to provincial towns and cities. Coach connections are generally cheaper (and slower); many depart from Victoria Coach Station.

The London Eye on the South Bank, offering great views across the city

Day 1

Morning Begin where London did, beside the surviving chunk of Roman wall outside Tower Hill underground station. It's a 5-minute walk from here to the **Tower of London** *(pp122–3)*, where 2 hours should be enough to take in an enthralling guided tour with a Beefeater, and drop in on either the Tudor weaponry in the White Tower or the Crown Jewels. Stop at the Tower's Armoury Café for a snack, then walk 10 minutes west to **Monument** *(p121)*, Sir Christopher Wren's 17th-century column, to learn the history of the Great Fire of London. The view (via 311 spiral steps) over the City of London includes the dome of St Paul's Cathedral, the Gherkin and the Shard. Next, cross London Bridge for an iconic photo of **Tower Bridge** *(p120)*, peek into **Southwark Cathedral** *(p124)*, and forage for lunch among the cosmopolitan food stalls at **Borough Market** *(p124)* (open Mon–Sat). The charismatic **George Inn** *(p124)* is a great alternative: an authentic coaching tavern from 1676, it serves hearty pub meals.

Afternoon Spend the afternoon on Bankside, choosing between the colossal (and free) modern art installations in the Turbine Hall at **Tate Modern** *(p125)* and an entertaining auditorium tour at the spectacularly recreated **Shakespeare's Globe** *(p124)* next door. Better still, do both. Cross the Millennium Bridge for a look at **St Paul's Cathedral** *(pp118–19)*, and perhaps have dinner at the One New Change complex nearby, where celebrity chefs Jamie Oliver and Gordon Ramsay both have restaurants. Take in a play at the Globe, or board an evening riverboat cruise from Bankside Pier (Apr–Oct).

Day 2

Morning Start the day either by mingling with some of Britain's famous monarchs (and seeing where William and Kate were married) on a self-guided tour around **Westminster Abbey**

A street entertainer in the bustling Piazza, Covent Garden

(pp96–7) or by crossing Westminster Bridge and taking a panoramic spin on the **London Eye** *(pp84–5)*. To beat the crowds, book the first ride on the Eye (10 or 11am, depending on the month). Next, wander through Parliament Square into serene St James's Park, and skirt the lakeside to reach Horse Guards Parade, where mounted sentries trot in at 11am (10am on Sun) for the Changing of the Guard. Stroll through Trafalgar Square into the West End, and join the queue for half-price theatre tickets at the official booth in Leicester Square.

Afternoon After a dim sum lunch in Chinatown, visit the **National Gallery** *(pp86–7)*, packed with masterpieces. The neighbouring **National Portrait Gallery** *(p85)* is a fine place to enjoy an English high tea – its third-floor restaurant is knee-high with Nelson's Column. If there is time before the show, walk 10 minutes east to **Covent Garden** *(pp82–3)* for supper or a drink in the Piazza while watching the area's celebrated street entertainers.

> **To extend your trip...**
> Devote a third day to a scenic stroll in **Kensington Gardens** *(p105)*, dropping in to visit the area's titanic trio of museums: the **Natural History Museum** *(p104)*, the **Science Museum** *(p104)* and the **Victoria and Albert Museum** *(pp102–3)*. All offer free admission.

A Week in Southeast England

- **Airports** Heathrow is the main hub in the Southeast, a 90-minute drive from Brighton. However, Gatwick Airport is closer, just 45 minutes away. The nearest major airport to Cambridge is Stansted.
- **Transport** A car is necessary to cover this tour in full, although main cities and towns are linked by rail.

Day 1: Brighton

Popularized two centuries ago by the Prince Regent, **Brighton** (pp178–9) was Britain's first sea-bathing resort and retains a certain glamour. Tour the **Royal Pavilion** (pp182–3), with its onion domes, then stroll along the Victorian pier or head to the Lanes for some shopping. Next, drive east along the coast road to Seaford, gateway to one of England's most iconic viewpoints: along the chalk cliffs of the **Seven Sisters** (p184).

Day 2: Winchester

The drive west to Winchester winds through some of southern England's most bucolic countryside. Stop off at **Steyning** (p104), with its chequered church tower and tipsy Tudor houses, or at **Petworth House** (p176), whose treasure trove of art runs from Greek sculpture to Gainsborough. The Horse Guards Inn, in nearby Tillington, is lovely for lunch. Upon reaching **Winchester** (pp174–5), ancient capital of the Saxons, drop into the Great Hall to see King

Arthur's (alleged) Round Table, then tour the Norman cathedral and find Jane Austen's grave.

Day 3: Touring the Thames

Workaday Reading is the starting point for a day along a lazy stretch of the **River Thames** (pp238–9). Take a cruise to the town of Henley, whose River & Rowing Museum celebrates the famous Henley Regatta. Back in the car, drive on to riverside Marlow for lunch at one of the many excellent restaurants here. Other highlights include Cookham, with its gallery showcasing the art of Stanley Spencer, and the National Trust gardens at **Cliveden** (p239). End the day in **Windsor** (p239).

Day 4: Windsor and Eton

Windsor Castle (pp240–41) is the favourite weekend retreat of the Queen – and the world's oldest occupied royal abode. Storm its Round Tower and swoon over the State Apartments, then take a carriage ride (weather permitting) in adjacent Windsor Great Park. Across the river is **Eton College** (p239), England's most exclusive school, whose former pupils include princes William and Harry. It is open for tours in the summer months.

Day 5: Oxford and Blenheim

Home to England's oldest university, **Oxford** (pp226–31) demands a full day. Visit **Christ Church** (p230), where *Alice in Wonderland* was written and *Harry Potter* filmed. Next, take a tour of the **Bodleian Library** (p231), climb one of the famous dreaming spires at **St Mary the Virgin Church** (p229) or hire a

Punting on the River Cam past King's College Chapel, Cambridge

punt at Magdalen Bridge. It's a 20-minute drive north to stately **Blenheim Palace** (pp232–3), the birthplace of Winston Churchill.

Day 6: The Cotswolds and Stratford

Spend the morning exploring classic Village England with the **Midlands Garden Tour** (pp324–5), in the North Cotswolds. Stanton, Snowshill and Chipping Campden are especially idyllic, with good lunching pubs. Then it's on to **Stratford-upon-Avon** (pp328–31). Join the throng for a look around Shakespeare's Birthplace museum, and take in a play at the Royal Shakespeare Theatre – be sure to book in advance.

Day 7: Cambridge

The week ends in **Cambridge** (pp214–19), more compact than Oxford, and with one standout attraction – a chauffeured punting ride along **The Backs** (p214), to peek into the back gardens of a parade of majestic colleges, including **King's College** (pp218–19), with its 500-year-old chapel. The city's other highlights include the **Fitzwilliam Museum** (p218), for its mummies and Old Masters.

> **To extend your trip…**
> From Cambridge, continue east into East Anglia, heading north to the beautiful **Norfolk Coast** (pp200–201) via **Ely** (pp198–9), or south to the civilized Suffolk coast at **Southwold** (p206) via **Constable country** (p208).

The promenade and Palace Pier in Brighton

A Week in Southwest England

- **Airports** Many overseas visitors to Southwest England will arrive at London Heathrow, but the provincial airports at Bristol and Exeter are in the region.
- **Transport** A car is necessary for this tour.

Day 1: Stonehenge and Salisbury

Journey back 5,000 years at **Stonehenge** *(pp266–7)*, the grandest gathering of prehistoric stones in Europe. Allow a full morning for the visitor centre and the stones themselves. Spend the afternoon in nearby **Salisbury** *(pp268–9)*, home to England's tallest cathedral. Don't miss a roof tour, up to a viewing gallery under the famous spire.

Day 2: Wessex

Aim southwest and tour ancient Wessex, immortalized in the novels of Thomas Hardy. The market town of **Dorchester** *(p273)*, the setting for *The Mayor of Casterbridge*, is hemmed by a countryside of stone villages and soft-focus hills. Essential stops include the rather lewd **Cerne Abbas** giant *(p273)* and **Hardy's Cottage** *(p273)* at Higher Bockhampton. Head west to **Abbotsbury** *(p272)*, with its medieval Swannery and gardens, then follow the coast to **Lyme Regis** *(p274)*, where you can relax by eating ice cream on the quayside and looking for fossils along the beach.

Day 3: Dartmoor and Tintagel

Rise early for a long drive west into Devon. It's worth it, especially with a diversion for lunch on **Dartmoor** *(pp298–9)*, a landscape of brooding moorlands, woods and waterfalls, pierced by romantic granite tors. The Rock Inn at Haytor Vale is well placed for a clamber on **Haytor Rocks** *(p298)*. Spend the afternoon sampling the craggy Cornish coast at **Boscastle** *(p289)* – from there it's a 4-mile (6-km) hike along the Southwest Coast Path to the cliff-hanging ruins of **Tintagel Castle** *(p289)*, said to be the birthplace of King Arthur.

Day 4: The Exmoor Coast

Exmoor *(pp254–5)* is Dartmoor's softer sister, where heathery hills tumble to meet the sea in a succession of pretty villages. Break your journey with a cream tea in the cobbled alleyways of **Clovelly** *(p290)* or among the charming fishermen's nooks in **Appledore** *(p291)*. Paddle in the cove at **Combe Martin** *(p292)*; trundle up the cliffs on the water-powered funicular railway at **Lynmouth** *(p292)*; and walk the ramparts at romantic **Dunster Castle** *(p254)*.

Day 5: Glastonbury and Wells

Now known for its music festival, **Glastonbury** *(p257)* has been a tourist magnet since the Middle Ages, when the local monks enticed pilgrims with tales of King Arthur and the Holy Grail. Climb Glastonbury Tor for breezy views across the Somerset Levels. Spend the afternoon in **Wells** *(pp256–7)*, dominated by a vast cathedral and busy with independent shops. If there's time, drive on to **Cheddar Gorge** *(p258)*, a great silver ravine gouging through the Mendip Hills.

Day 6: Bath

Bath *(pp262–5)* is an irresistibly beautiful city founded by the Romans; a visit to the restored open-air **baths** *(pp264–5)* is an engrossing window on life in Roman Britain in the 1st century. Those who wish to bathe in the thermal waters can do so at nearby **Thermae Bath Spa** *(p265)* – turn up and swim, or pre-book treatments. Today's townscape, lined with Palladian terraces and crescents, looks much as it did when Jane Austen lived here between 1801 and 1806.

Day 7: The South Cotswolds

Follow Jane Austen east to discover **Lacock** and **Corsham** *(p259)*, two Cotswold villages so impeccably unspoilt that they often star in costume-drama adaptations of Austen's work, as well as the BBC series *Poldark*. Both Lacock's Rising Sun and the Methuen Arms, in Corsham, are great lunch choices. Spend your final afternoon driving the Wiltshire Downs to **Avebury** *(p267)*, a village surrounded by a stone circle and dotted with prehistoric remains.

> **To extend your trip…**
> Continue west from Dartmoor into deepest Cornwall, and visit the **Eden Project** *(pp286–7)* and the arty seaside enclave of **St Ives** *(p281)*. Or top off your tour with a day in cosmopolitan **Bristol** *(pp260–61)*.

Stonehenge – Britain's most famous and dramatic prehistoric monument

A misty scene at Rydal Water in the Lake District

A Week in Northern England

- **Airports** This itinerary begins and ends at Manchester Airport, but flying out from Newcastle or Leeds-Bradford may increase flexibility.

- **Transport** A car is necessary for this tour.

Day 1: Liverpool
Both **Manchester** (pp376–9) and **Liverpool** (pp380–83) jostle for a full day's attention. If time is tight, choose the latter. Begin beside the Mersey at **Albert Dock** (p381) where the Victorian warehouses have been rescued from dereliction and filled with contemporary art at Tate Liverpool, history at the Merseyside Maritime Museum, and music at the kitschy but fun Beatles Story. Pop pilgrims will want a picture on stage at the Cavern Club, still a live music venue today.

Day 2: The Lake District
England's most spectacular national park deserves to be lingered over. Start with **Windermere** (p371), the largest of the district's many lakes, for a steamboat tour or a lazy hour feeding the swans. Skip the touristy lakeside town of Bowness and take a car-ferry over the water to the picture-postcard village of Hawkshead. Stop en route to look for bunny rabbits in the rustic gardens at **Hill Top** (p371), once home to Beatrix

Potter, now a National Trust property open to the public.

Day 3: Langdale and Grasmere
It's a short drive north to **Ambleside** (p370), gateway to some of the area's most rugged mountain scenery. Pick up a picnic at Lucy's Deli in Church Street and press on into **Langdale** (p369). For a taste of the area's walking possibilities, hike south from quaint **Elterwater** (p369) to view the lake of the same name; then wander beside nearby **Grasmere** (p370), home of the Romantic poet William Wordsworth.

Day 4: Hadrian's Wall
Cross the Pennines to visit **Hadrian's Wall** (pp426–7). Break the drive in Alston, 304 m (1,000 ft) up in the hills, which claims to be the nation's highest

Whitby Harbour and St Mary's Church, Yorkshire

market town. The best surviving stretch of Emperor Hadrian's 2nd-century Roman rampart lies in the lonely countryside between Housesteads Fort and Vindolanda, where in summer it is possible to watch a live archaeological dig unfold.

Day 5: Durham
Newcastle (pp428–9) is enjoying a renaissance, especially around its vibrant quayside, overlooked by the **Baltic Centre for Contemporary Art** (p428) in Gateshead. Follow the **North Pennines Tour** (p431) via Stanhope to reach the 1,000-year-old university town of **Durham** (pp432–3), with its striking Norman castle and cathedral on the River Wear. The reimagined 1913 colliery town at **Beamish Open Air Museum** (pp428–9) offers an unusual diversion en route.

Day 6: Whitby and the Moors
Whitby (p400) is a charismatic seaside town, its red-roofed fishermen's cottages huddled around a busy quayside. Breeze along the beach, explore the Captain Cook Museum, and climb the 199 steps to Whitby Abbey, with its spooky Dracula connections. After a fish-and-chip lunch at the Magpie Café, drive across the beautiful **North York Moors** (p399) to Grosmont for a scenic steam-train ride.

Day 7: York
The tangled alleyways of the Shambles quarter in **York** (pp408–13) have changed little since medieval times. Walk the city walls, delve beneath the streets to discover the old Viking city at the **Jorvik Viking Centre** (p410), then soak up the sacred history of **York Minster** (pp412–13), the grandest medieval Gothic cathedral in northern Europe.

> **To extend your trip...**
> Link this itinerary with a week in **Scotland** (see p17) or, with an extra day or two, drive further north into Northumberland for beautiful unspoilt beaches and **Alnwick Castle** (p424).

A Week in Wales and the West

- **Airports** Cardiff Airport is the largest in Wales, but Bristol, Birmingham and Manchester are also viable starting points for this tour.
- **Transport** A car is essential.

Day 1: Cardiff

A century ago, **Cardiff** (pp474–7) was the world's busiest coal port; today, it offers a rich seam of attractions, from the Neo-Gothic **castle** (pp476–7) and art-filled **National Museum** (p475) to the impressive **Principality Stadium** (p474), home to the Welsh national rugby team. Down in bustling Cardiff Bay, consider capping the day with a show at the magnificent **Wales Millennium Centre** (p474).

Day 2: Brecon Beacons

This wild and wonderful **Brecon Beacons National Park** (pp472–3) has the highest mountain in southern Britain, **Pen y Fan** (p473), which dominates the drive north along the A470. The Georgian market town of Brecon is worth an hour's investigation, or stop off at the nearby Felin Fach Griffin pub, for lunch on the lawn. While away the afternoon in **Hay-on-Wye** (p465), a bucolic border town in the Black Mountains that is famous for its 30 or so bookshops.

Day 3: Ludlow and Ironbridge

Drive onward into the Welsh Marches, diverting, if there's time, to go through the famed "Tudor triangle" west of **Leominster**

(p317). Weobley, Pembridge and Eardisland are the standout villages here. Have lunch in **Ludlow** (pp316–17), pinned to a hilltop by its storybook Norman castle and known for its sophisticated dining: the Green Café, beside the tumbling River Teme, is a great choice. Nearby **Ironbridge Gorge** (pp318–19), once the crucible of the Industrial Revolution, is now an attractive living museum.

Day 4: Snowdonia

North Wales is all about the slatey scenery of Snowdonia. On a drive towards the mountains, pause in the canal town of **Llangollen** (p454), for a boat ride through the sky across the spectacular 38-m (124-ft) arches of Pontcysyllte Aqueduct, built by Thomas Telford (p451) in 1805. The best base in the national park is **Betws-y-Coed** (p454), hemmed in by tall peaks – a walk through the wooded glen to Swallow Falls makes an inspiring outing. If you have more time, continue north to **Conwy** (pp450–51), guarded from the sea by its imperious 13th-century fortress and ring of medieval walls.

Day 5: Portmeirion

Perhaps Britain's most extravagant folly, **Portmeirion** (pp458–9) is a madcap Italian-style village on a peninsula above Tremadog Bay. Eccentric and elegant in equal parts, it's a charming place to fritter away a morning. Not far south, **Harlech Castle** (p458) commands a crag-top spot above the ocean – but those tired of medieval masonry may prefer to head to the panoramic **Ffestiniog Railway** instead (pp456–7).

Buildings and boats lining the shore at the seaside resort of Tenby

Day 6: The Cardigan Coast

The roads swerving south alongside Cardigan Bay constitute some of Britain's greatest scenic drives: en route, there is Barmouth for beaches, **Machynlleth** (p466) for Welsh revolutionary history, and **Aberystwyth** (pp466–7) for pubs and partying, activities. Conclude the coastal tour in **Aberaeron** (p467), with its pastel-painted Georgian town houses lined up prettily around the harbour.

Day 6: Pembrokeshire

This southwest corner of Wales is a honeypot for summer holiday-makers, and no wonder: the rugged cliffs, endless white beaches and cute seaside villages are packed with promise. Those who prefer history to beaches can make for **St Davids** (pp468–9) – its grand 12th-century cathedral and Bishop's Palace were built to honour the province's patron saint, born nearby. But the coastline west of **Tenby** (p470) is loveliest of all, a fittingly dramatic finale to this tour.

> **To extend your trip...**
> The Wye Valley around **Tintern** (p479) is a wooded wonderland, especially beautiful in autumn. Or, in the north, there's the town of **Chester** (pp314–15), with its Roman walls.

Cardiff Bay, with the iconic red-brick Pierhead building

A Week in Scotland

- **Airports** This itinerary starts at Edinburgh Airport. Glasgow Airport, an hour away, is an alternative.
- **Transport** A car is best for touring in Scotland.

Day 1: Edinburgh

Scotland's capital, **Edinburgh** (pp508–15) is a powerhouse of the arts, and it spills over with world-class theatre, music and comedy at the **Edinburgh Festival** (p513) every August. The medieval Old Town clusters chaotically around hilltop **Edinburgh Castle** (pp510–11), while below, the **National Gallery of Scotland** (p508) shows off world-class art. Stroll down the famous **Royal Mile** (pp512–15) to visit the **Palace of Holyroodhouse** (p514); climb the city's extinct volcano, Arthur's Seat; or take a late night literary tour in search of Sherlock Holmes and Jekyll and Hyde.

Day 2: Stirling

The grand Renaissance halls of **Stirling Castle** (pp500–501) rise romantically atop vertiginous cliffs, and there's more than enough pomp and history to fill a morning. Afterwards, wander the cobbles of Stirling's Old Town, its bagpipe shops and bars still protected by 16th-century walls. If there's time, continue north to **Doune Castle** (p502), an intact Stuart stronghold famously featured in the film *Monty Python and the Holy Grail*.

Day 3: Royal Deeside

Get ready for a majestic drive north, pausing perhaps in **Dunkeld** (p545) or **Pitlochry** (p545), both swaddled in woodland; Dunkeld features in Shakespeare's *Macbeth*, while Pitlochry offers beautiful walks along pine-lined Loch Faskally. Don't linger, however: the target for the day is the baronial estate at Balmoral, summer home of the Windsors and the undisputed highlight of the **Royal Deeside Tour** (pp544–5).

Day 4: The Cairngorms

Climbing across the **Cairngorms** (pp548–9), the A939 road is packed with drama all the way to Speyside. The latter is a great place to sample whisky, Scotland's most famous export, ideally at the Glenlivet Distillery (tours Mar–Oct). The **Inverness Museum and Art Gallery** (p540) gives a fine primer on Highland history and exhibits a tress of Bonnie Prince Charlie's hair (p535). To see where his attempt on power perished, drive to nearby **Culloden** (p541), the moorland site of this 1746 battle.

Day 5: The Great Glen

Slicing through Scotland's most spectacular mountains, the Great Glen is perhaps best seen on a morning cruise from Inverness. Afterwards, gaze out in search of Nessie, the mythical Loch Ness monster, from the lochside road en route to the **Loch Ness Centre and Exhibition** (p540) and the romantically ruined **Urquhart Castle** (p540). The view of Ben Nevis is the best thing about Fort William, so keep going into gorgeous **Glencoe** (p547), where hill-walking options range from gentle to gargantuan, and the Clachaig Inn serves up near-legendary Highland hospitality.

Day 6: Loch Lomond

An awe-inspiring coastal road follows Loch Linnhe to Connel,

then head inland to **Loch Awe** (p551), where lightning-blasted Kilchurn Castle decays delectably beside the water. It's south from here to **Inveraray** (p552), where a rather grander castle is still home to Clan Campbell. Tour the family portrait collection and vicious-looking weaponry in the Armoury Hall, then head east to **Loch Lomond** (p498), Britain's largest freshwater lake. The best views are from the top of Ben Lomond, on its eastern banks.

Day 7: Glasgow

Scotland's biggest city, **Glasgow** (pp520–25) was built on Victorian industry, but it offers plenty for the 21st-century visitor. The well-to-do West End district is particularly busy with bars and restaurants and home to two art galleries, the **Hunterian** (p523) and the **Kelvingrove** (p524–5). Quirkier attractions include the **Tenement House** (p522), a working-class time capsule from Edwardian Glasgow, and Charles Rennie Mackintosh's **Willow Tea Room** (p522), a glamorous interior from 1904.

> **To extend your trip...**
> For more wild scenery and a salty scent of the islands, take the **Road to the Isles Tour** (pp550–51) from Fort William, and cast off for the **Isle of Skye** (pp534–5) and the **Western Isles** (p533).

Edinburgh Castle in all its glory

Putting Great Britain on the Map

Lying in northwestern Europe, Great Britain is bounded by the Atlantic Ocean, the North Sea and the English Channel. The island's landscape and climate are varied, and it is this variety that even today affects the pattern of settlement. The remote shores of the West Country peninsula and the inhospitable mountains of Scotland and Wales are less populated than the relatively flat and fertile Midlands and Southeast, where the vast majority of the country's 64 million people live. Due to this population density, the south is today the most built-up part of the country.

Key

- ▬▬ Motorway
- ▬▬ Major road
- - - Ferry route
- ⋯⋯ Channel Tunnel
- ▬▬ National border

For keys to symbols *see back flap*

Regional Great Britain: London, the South, the Midlands and Wales

Great Britain has airline connections with most cities in the world. London is the main transport hub with three major international airports, including Heathrow, the world's busiest. The most populous area, southern Britain, is divided within this book into four regions – Southeast England, the West Country, Wales and the Midlands – with a separate chapter for London. Road and rail links to the north and Scotland *(see pp22–3)* are plentiful, as are links between all main towns.

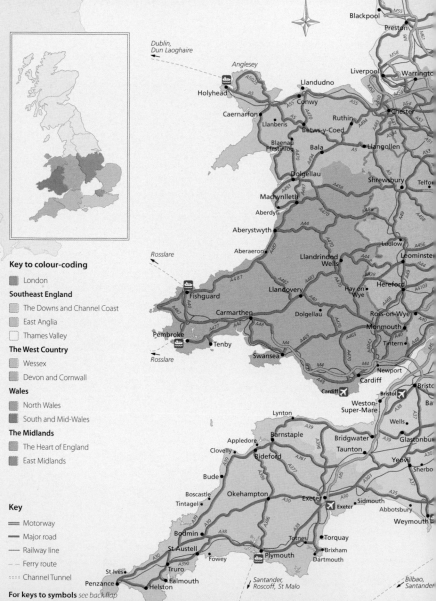

Key to colour-coding

- London

Southeast England
- The Downs and Channel Coast
- East Anglia
- Thames Valley

The West Country
- Wessex
- Devon and Cornwall

Wales
- North Wales
- South and Mid-Wales

The Midlands
- The Heart of England
- East Midlands

Key

- Motorway
- Major road
- Railway line
- Ferry route
- Channel Tunnel

For keys to symbols *see back flap*

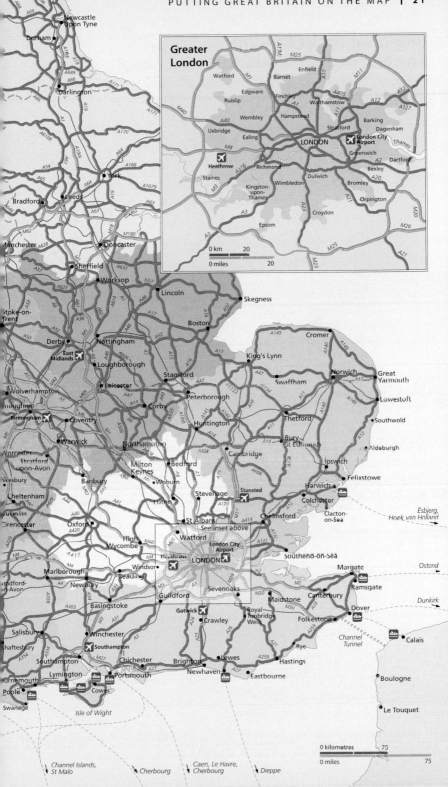

Regional Great Britain: The North and Scotland

This part of Great Britain is divided into two sections in this book – Northern England and Scotland. Although it is far less populated than the southern sector of the country, there are good road and rail connections, and ferry services link the islands with the mainland.

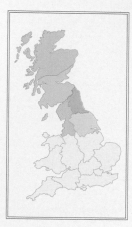

Key to colour-coding

Northern England

- Lancashire and the Lakes
- Yorkshire and Humber Region
- Northumbria

Scotland

- The Lowlands
- The Highlands and Islands

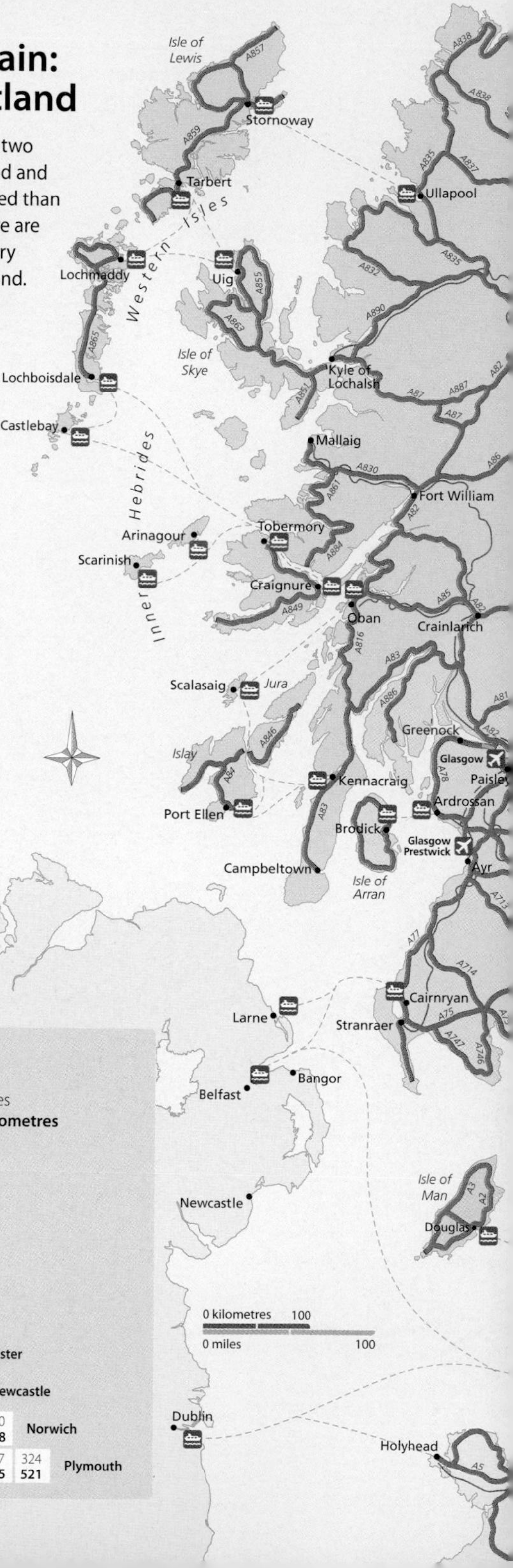

Isle of Lewis
Stornoway
Tarbert
Western Isles
Lochmaddy
Uig
Ullapool
Isle of Skye
Kyle of Lochalsh
Lochboisdale
Castlebay
Mallaig
Inner Hebrides
Fort William
Tobermory
Arinagour
Scarinish
Craignure
Oban
Crainlarich
Scalasaig
Jura
Islay
Greenock
Glasgow
Paisley
Kennacraig
Port Ellen
Ardrossan
Brodick
Glasgow Prestwick
Ayr
Campbeltown
Isle of Arran
Cairnryan
Stranraer
Larne
Belfast
Bangor
Newcastle
Isle of Man
Douglas
Dublin
Holyhead
A857
A859
A838
A835
A837
A865
A855
A863
A832
A890
A851
A87
A887
A830
A861
A82
A86
A884
A849
A85
A816
A83
A886
A846
A846
A84
A81
A78
A713
A77
A714
A75
A747
A746
A3
A2
A5
0 kilometres 100
0 miles 100

Distance Chart

Distance in miles
Distance in kilometres

	London	Birmingham	Cardiff	Dover	Edinburgh	Glasgow	Inverness	Manchester	Newcastle	Norwich
Birmingham	111 / **179**									
Cardiff	150 / **241**	102 / **164**								
Dover	74 / **119**	185 / **298**	228 / **367**							
Edinburgh	372 / **599**	290 / **467**	373 / **600**	442 / **711**						
Glasgow	389 / **626**	292 / **470**	374 / **602**	466 / **750**	45 / **72**					
Inverness	529 / **851**	448 / **721**	530 / **853**	600 / **966**	158 / **254**	167 / **269**				
Manchester	184 / **296**	81 / **130**	173 / **278**	257 / **414**	213 / **343**	214 / **344**	371 / **597**			
Newcastle	274 / **441**	204 / **328**	301 / **484**	343 / **552**	107 / **172**	145 / **233**	265 / **426**	131 / **211**		
Norwich	112 / **180**	161 / **259**	235 / **378**	167 / **269**	360 / **579**	383 / **616**	517 / **832**	185 / **298**	260 / **418**	
Plymouth	212 / **341**	206 / **332**	152 / **261**	287 / **462**	427 / **784**	426 / **785**	545 / **1038**	250 / **451**	427 / **655**	324 / **521**

For keys to symbols *see back flap*

Orkney and Shetland Islands

Shetland Islands

Unst

Yell

Mainland

Foula

Lerwick

Fair Isle

Westray

Sanday

Mainland

Stronsay

Stromness

Kirkwall

Orkney Islands

Hoy

Scrabster

Thurso

Wick

Aberdeen

Stromness

Scrabster
Thurso
Wick

Kirkwall, Lerwick

Thurso
Scrabster
Wick

Elgin
Fraserburgh
Peterhead
Aberdeen
Aberdeen
Braemar
Forfar
Montrose
Arbroath
Dundee
Perth
St Andrews
Kirkcaldy
Stirling
Dunfermline
Edinburgh
Edinburgh
Berwick-upon-Tweed
Holy Island
Galashiels
Peebles
Bamburgh
Farne Islands
Hawick
Jedburgh
Alnwick
Warkworth
Dumfries
Morpeth
Amsterdam
Hexham
Newcastle
Upon Tyne
Newcastle
Sunderland
Durham
Carlisle
Hartlepool
Cockermouth
Penrith
Barnard Castle
Middlesbrough
Keswick
Appleby-in-Westmorland
Darlington
Whitby
Grasmere
Hawkshead
Richmond
Scarborough
Windermere
Kendal
Helmsley
Barrow-in-Furness
Thirsk
Flamborough Head
Heysham
Ripon
Bridlington
Lancaster
Skipton
Harrogate
York
Beverley
Blackpool
Leeds Bradford
Leeds
Kingston upon Hull
Preston
Burnley
Bradford
Southport
Blackburn
Halifax
Wakefield
Scunthorpe
Grimsby
Bolton
Rochdale
Huddersfield
Wigan
Manchester
Barnsley
Doncaster
Liverpool
Manchester
Sheffield
Liverpool
Stockport
Chester
Lincoln

Key

Motorway
Major road
Railway line
Ferry route

Rotterdam, Zeebrugge

A PORTRAIT OF GREAT BRITAIN

Britain is proud of its traditions and history yet is much more than a country clinging to its past. Modern Britain is a dynamic place, the most culturally diverse in Europe, its capital one of the great cities of the world and its people reflecting a truly global heritage. It retains much of what makes it different – from red double-decker buses to village-green cricket matches.

Britain's character has been shaped by the country's geographical position as an island and by the legacy of having presided over the largest empire in history. Since 1066 it has not been successfully invaded, yet for many centuries it invaded and colonized countries around the world and, since the end of World War II, has experienced high levels of immigration from former colonies.

The expansion of the European Union in 2004 led to significant numbers of immigrants from Central and Eastern Europe coming to work and settle in Britain, and this influx became one of the central issues in the EU referendum held here in 2016. The British population voted, by a narrow majority, to leave the European Union, but the country remains one of the most ethnically diverse and multicultural in the world, and broadly speaking, most Brits see this as a positive thing.

As profound as any influence on Britain's early heritage was the Roman invasion of AD 43, which lasted 350 years. Roman culture and language were then overlain with those of the Northern European settlers who followed. Ties with Europe were loosened, however, in the 16th century when the Catholic Church was replaced by a less dogmatic Anglican Church. These seismic cultural shifts are all reflected in the rich mix of historic castles, cathedrals, monuments and stately homes and parklands across Britain.

The real twist with Great Britain is that it is several different countries within a single nation. Scotland and Wales are separate countries from England, with their own distinct identities and histories, as well as their own contemporary political institutions. They both have their own legislative assemblies, and Scotland has its own legal

The River Avon in summertime, Bath

◄ A cricket match played at Charterhouse School, Godalming, Surrey

Widecombe-in-the-Moor, a Devon village clustered round a church

and education systems and may even have broken away from Great Britain and the United Kingdom altogether in 2014, when a referendum on Scottish independence was held. The Scottish people voted to remain part of the UK, but having voted overwhelmingly to remain a part of the EU in 2016, in contrast to much of Wales and England, there is once again talk of independence and a second referendum.

Scotland and Wales are also among the various parts of Britain where languages other than English survive. Scots and Welsh Gaelic languages have their own radio and TV networks, while Manx and Cornish, from the Isle of Man and Cornwall respectively, have experienced small revivals over the past couple of decades. Throughout the country, English is spoken in a colourful

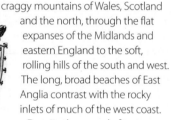

Scottish coat of arms at Edinburgh Castle

variety of dialects and accents, some of them identifiable with just a single city, as is the case with Liverpool and Newcastle.

The landscape is varied, too, from the craggy mountains of Wales, Scotland and the north, through the flat expanses of the Midlands and eastern England to the soft, rolling hills of the south and west. The long, broad beaches of East Anglia contrast with the rocky inlets of much of the west coast.

Despite the spread of towns and cities over the past 200 years, rural Britain flourishes. Nearly three-quarters of Britain's land is used for agriculture. The main commercial crops are wheat, barley, sugar beet and potatoes, though what catches the eye in early summer are fields of bright yellow rape or slate-blue flax.

The countryside is dotted with farms and charming villages, with picturesque cottages and lovingly tended gardens – a British passion. A typical village is built around an ancient church and a small, friendly pub. Here the pace of life slows. To drink a pint of ale in a cosy, village inn and relax before a fire is a time-honoured British custom. Strangers will be welcomed cordially, though perhaps with caution; for even if strict formality is a thing of the past, the British have a tendency to be reserved.

Lake and gardens at Petworth House, Sussex

In the 19th and early 20th centuries, trade with the extensive British Empire, fuelled by abundant coal supplies, spurred manufacturing and created wealth. Hundreds of thousands of people moved from the countryside to towns and cities near mines, mills and factories. By 1850 Britain was the world's strongest industrial nation. Now many of these old industrial centres have declined, and today manufacturing employs only 10 per cent of the labour force, while 75 per cent work in the service sector. These service industries are located mainly in the southeast, close to London, while what remains of the manufacturing sector is still concentrated in its traditional heartlands, the Midlands and the north.

Bustling Chinatown in Soho, London

Society and Politics

In contrast to rural areas, most British cities are ethnically diverse places. While around 80 per cent of the population describe themselves as white British, this figure drops below 50 per cent in London and is just above 50 per cent in Birmingham, while in Manchester around a quarter of the population describe themselves as black or Asian. Some of the most significant British

Asian communities, with roots primarily in India, Pakistan and Bangladesh, are in the old industrial cities of the Midlands and the north, notably Bradford, Oldham, Leicester and Wolverhampton.

With large numbers of British people in urban areas whose parents or grandparents came from other former British colonies in the Caribbean, Africa and the Middle East, the overall picture in Britain's cities is a multicultural mix that boasts a wide range of music, art, food and religion. Of course, this picture is not always a harmonious one, and racial tension certainly exists in Britain. Race was a factor in the urban riots that broke out across England in 2011 following the death of Mark Duggan, a black man, at the hands of the police in Tottenham in London. However, much of the tension had as much to do with the uneven distribution of wealth as it does with race.

Britain's class structure still intrigues and bewilders many visitors, based as it is on a subtle mixture of heredity and wealth. Even though many of the great inherited fortunes no longer exist, some old landed families still live on their large estates, and many now open them to the public. Class divisions are further entrenched by the education system. While more than 90 per cent of children are educated free by the state, richer parents often opt for private schooling, and the products of these

Priest in the Close at Winchester Cathedral

private schools are disproportionately represented in the higher echelons of government and business.

The monarchy's position highlights the dilemma of a people seeking to preserve its most potent symbol of national unity in an age that is suspicious of inherited privilege. Without real political power, though still head of the Church of England, the Queen and her family are subject to increasing public scrutiny and some citizens advocate the abolition of the monarchy.

Afternoon tea on the back lawn at the Thornbury Castle Hotel, Avon

Democracy has deep foundations in Britain: there was even a parliament of sorts in London in the 13th century. Yet with the exception of the 17th-century Civil War, power has passed gradually from the Crown to the people's elected representatives. A series of Reform Acts between 1832 and 1884 gave the vote to all male citizens, though women were not enfranchised on an equal basis until 1928. Margaret Thatcher – Britain's first woman Prime Minister – held office for 12 years from 1979. Since the late 20th century, the Labour (left wing) and Conservative (right wing) parties have, during their periods in office, favoured a mix of public and private ownership for industry and ample funding for the state health and welfare systems.

The House of Lords, in Parliament

Culture and the Arts

Britain has a famous theatrical tradition stretching back to the 16th century and William Shakespeare. His plays have been performed on stage almost continuously since he wrote them, and the works of 17th- and 18th-century writers are also frequently revived. Contemporary British playwrights such as Tom Stoppard, Alan Ayckbourn and David Hare draw on this long tradition with their vivid language and by using comedy to illustrate serious themes. The British affiliation with the theatre has created countless British film actors of international renown whose careers started on the stage – from Laurence Olivier, Ian McKellan and Judi Dench, to current Hollywood favourites such as Benedict Cumberbatch, David Oyelowo and Eddie Redmayne.

While London is the focal point of British theatre, fine drama is to be seen in many other parts of the country. The Edinburgh Festival and its Fringe are the high point of Great Britain's cultural calendar with theatre and music to suit all tastes. Dozens more music festivals are held across the country, chiefly in summer, while there are annual festivals of literature at Hay-on-Wye and Cheltenham. Poetry has had an enthusiastic following since Chaucer wrote the *Canterbury Tales* in the 14th century: poems from all eras can even be read on the London Underground, where they are interspersed with the advertisements in the carriages and on the station platforms.

In the visual arts, Britain has a strong tradition in portraiture, caricature, landscape and watercolour. Modern British artists David Hockney and Lucian Freud, and sculptors Henry Moore and Barbara Hepworth, have enjoyed worldwide

An array of fruit and vegetables for sale at London's Borough Market

recognition. British architects including Christopher Wren, Inigo Jones, John Nash and Robert Adam all created styles that define British cities; and today, Norman Foster and Richard Rogers carry the standard for Post-Modernism. Britain is famous for its innovative fashion designers, such as Vivienne Westwood and Matthew Williamson, many of whom show their spring and autumn collections in Paris.

The British are avid newspaper readers. There are nine national newspapers published from London on weekdays: the standard of the serious newspapers, such as *The Independent* and *The Guardian*, is very high, and *The Times* is read the world over because of its reputation for strong reporting. The best selling, however, are the tabloids, which are packed with celebrity gossip, crime and sport.

British television is famous for the quality of its news, current affairs and drama programmes. The publicly funded British Broadcasting Corporation (BBC) has numerous television channels and radio stations, as well as a variety of online services. The indigenous film industry has produced highly rated international hits such as *The Queen* and *Slumdog Millionaire*, though blockbusters such as the Harry Potter films are often backed by the US. Acclaimed British film directors include Danny Boyle and Mike Leigh.

The British are great sports fans, and favour football, rugby, cricket and golf. Nationwide, fishing is the most popular sporting pastime, and the British make excellent use of their national parks as keen walkers.

British food used to be derided for its lack of imagination, but many chefs – such as Heston Blumenthal and Angela Hartnett – are revitalizing the nation's standing, combining top-notch traditional ingredients with a variety of culinary influences and techniques from around the world. Furthermore, there is a great appetite for Indian, Spanish, Chinese, Italian and Thai food, among many others.

In this, as in other respects, the British are doing what they have done for centuries: accommodating their own traditions to influences from other cultures, while keeping elements of their national character intact.

Whitby harbour and St Mary's Church, Yorkshire

Gardens Through the Ages

Gardens were an integral part of the villas and palaces of Roman Britain, establishing a pattern of enclosed formal areas that continued with the monastic gardens of the Middle Ages. The Elizabethan knot garden became more elaborate in Jacobean times as the range of plants greatly increased. The 18th century brought a taste for large-scale "natural" landscapes with lakes, woods and meadows, creating a distinctly English style. Since then, debate has raged between supporters of natural and formal gardens, developing into the eclecticism of the 20th century when "garden rooms" in differing styles became popular.

Monumental column

A grotto and cascade brought romance and mystery.

"Capability" Brown (1715–83) was Britain's most influential garden designer, favouring the move away from formal gardens to man-made pastoral settings.

Blackthorn

Classical temples were a feature of many 18th-century gardens and were often exact replicas of buildings that the designers had seen in Greece.

Elaborate parterres
These formal gardens were a feature of aristocratic gardens of the 17th century, when the fashion spread from Europe. This is the Privy Garden at Hampton Court Palace.

Maple

Ideal Landscape Garden

Classical Greece and Rome inspired the grand gardens of the early 18th century, such as Stourhead and Stowe. Clumps of trees played a critical part in the serene landscapes.

Winding paths were carefully planned to allow changing vistas to open out as visitors strolled around the garden.

Design and Formality

A flower garden is a work of artifice, an attempt to tame nature rather than to copy it. Growing plants in rows or regular patterns, interspersed with statues and ornaments, imposes a sense of order. Designs change to reflect the fashion of the time and the introduction of new plants.

Medieval gardens usually had a herber (a turfed sitting area) and a vine arbour. A good reconstruction is Queen Eleanor's Garden, Winchester.

Tudor gardens featured edged borders and sometimes mazes. The Tudor House Garden, Southampton, also has beehives and heraldic statues.

Herbaceous borders
Full of lush plants, these are the glory of the summer garden. Gertrude Jekyll (1843–1932), was high priestess of the mixed border, with her eye for pretty colour combinations.

VISITORS' CHECKLIST

Practical Information
The National Garden Scheme (ngs.org.uk), founded in 1927, publishes *The Yellow Book*, an annual guide to gardens that are open to the public.

Cedar of Lebanon   Yew

Development of the Modern Pansy

All garden plants derive from wild flowers, bred over the years to produce qualities that appeal to gardeners. The story of the pansy, one of Britain's most popular flowers, is typical.

The wild pansy (Viola tricolor) native to Britain is commonly known as heartsease. It is a small-flowered annual which can vary considerably in colour.

The mountain pansy (Viola lutea) is a perennial. The first cultivated varieties resulted from crossing it with heartsease in the early 19th century.

The Show Pansy was bred by florists after the blotch appeared as a chance seedling in 1840. It was round in form with a small, symmetrical blotch.

The Fancy Pansy, developed in the 1860s, was much larger. The blotch covered all three lower petals save for a thin margin of colour.

Modern hybrids of pansies, violas and violettas, developed by selective breeding, are varied and versatile, in a wide range of vibrant colours.

The Palladian bridge was a favourite feature, often decorative rather than practical.

Rhododendron

Knot Gardens
These formal gardens, in vogue in the 1500s, saw intersecting lines of lavender or box filled with flowers, herbs or vegetables, as in this restoration.

17th-century gardening was more elaborate. Water gardens like those at Blenheim were often combined with parterres of exotic foreign plants.

Victorian gardens, their formal beds a mass of colour, were a reaction to the landscapes of "Capability" Brown. Alton Towers has a good example.

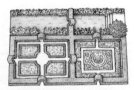

20th-century gardens mix historic and modern styles, as at Hidcote Manor, Gloucestershire. Growing wild flowers is a popular choice.

Stately Homes

The grand country house reached its zenith in the 18th and 19th centuries, when the old landed families and the new captains of industry enjoyed their wealth, looked after by a retinue of servants. The earliest stately homes date from the 14th century, when defence was paramount. By the 16th century, when the opulent tastes of the European Renaissance spread to England, houses became centres of pleasure and showcases for fine art *(see pp306–7)*. The Georgians favoured Classical architecture with rich interiors, the Victorians flamboyant Gothic. Due to 20th-century social change many stately homes have been opened to the public, some administered by the National Trust.

The saloon, a domed rotunda based on the Pantheon in Rome, was designed to display the Curzon family's Classical sculpture collection to 18th-century society.

The Marble Hall
This is where balls and other social functions took place among Corinthian columns of pink alabaster.

The Drawing Room, the main room for entertaining, contains the most important pictures and some exquisite plasterwork.

The Family Wing is a self-contained "pavilion" of private living quarters; the servants lived in rooms above the kitchen. The Curzon family still live here.

The Music Room is decorated with musical themes. Music was the main entertainment on social occasions.

1650	1700	1750

Colen Campbell (1676–1729) designed Burlington House *(see p85)*

William Kent (1685–1748) built Holkham Hall *(see p201)* in the Palladian style

John Carr (1723–1807) designed the Palladian Harewood House *(see p414)*

Robert Adam (1728–92), who often worked with his brother James (1730–94), was as famous for decorative details as for buildings

Henry Holland (1745–1806) designed the Neo-Classical south range of Woburn Abbey *(see p234)*

Sir John Vanbrugh *(see p403)* was helped by **Nicholas Hawksmoor** (1661–1736) on Blenheim Palace *(see pp232–3)*

Castle Howard (1702) by Sir John Vanbrugh

Adam fireplace, Kedleston Hall, adorned with Classical motifs

National Trust

National Trust oak leaf design

At the end of the 19th century, there were real fears that burgeoning factories, mines, roads and houses would obliterate much of Britain's historic landscape and finest buildings. In 1895 a group that included the social reformer Octavia Hill formed the National Trust, to preserve the nation's valuable heritage. The first building acquired by the trust was the medieval Clergy House at Alfriston in Sussex, in 1896 *(see p185)*. Today the National Trust is a charity that runs many historic houses and gardens, and vast stretches of countryside and coastline *(see p622)*. It is supported by more than two million members nationwide.

A corridor links the kitchen to the main house.

The 13th-century church is all that is left of Kedleston village, moved in 1760 to make way for the new house and its grounds.

Kedleston Hall

This Derbyshire mansion (see p340) is an early work of the influential Georgian architect Robert Adam, who was a pioneer of the Neo-Classical style derived from ancient Greece and Rome. It was built for the Curzon family in the 1760s.

Life Below Stairs by Charles Hunt (c.1890)

Life Below Stairs

A large community of resident staff was essential to run a country house smoothly. The butler was in overall charge, ensuring that meals were served on time. The housekeeper supervised uniformed maids who made sure the place was clean. The cook ran the kitchen, using fresh produce from the estate. Ladies' maids and valets acted as personal servants.

1800	1850	
Norman Shaw (1831–1912) was an exponent of Victorian Gothic, as in Cragside (below), and a pioneer of the Arts and Crafts movement	**Philip Webb** (1831–1915) was a leading architect of the influential Arts and Crafts movement, whose buildings favoured the simpler forms of an "Old English" style, instead of flamboyant Victorian Gothic	**Sir Edwin Lutyens** (1869–1944) designed the elaborate Castle Drogo in Devon *(see p299)*, one of the last grand country houses

Dining Room, Cragside, Northumberland

Standen, West Sussex (1891–94), by Philip Webb

Heraldry and the Aristocracy

The British aristocracy has evolved over the centuries from the feudal obligations of noblemen towards the Norman kings, who conferred privileges of rank and land in return for armed support. Subsequent monarchs bestowed titles and property on their supporters, establishing new aristocratic dynasties. The title of "earl" dates from the 11th century; that of "duke" from the 14th century. Soon the nobility began to choose their own symbols, partly to identify a knight concealed by his armour: these were often painted on the knight's coat (hence the term "coat of arms") and also copied onto his shield.

The College of Arms, London: housing records of all coats of arms and devising new ones

Royal Coat of Arms

The most familiar British coat of arms is the sovereign's. It appears on the royal standard, or flag, as well as on official documents and on shops that enjoy royal patronage. Since the 12th century, various monarchs have made modifications. The quartered shield in the middle displays the arms of England (twice), Scotland and Ireland. Surrounding it are other traditional images including the lion and unicorn, topped by the crown and the royal helm (helmet).

Edward III (1327–77) was the founder of the chivalric Order of the Garter. The garter, bearing the motto *Honi soit qui mal y pense* ("evil be to him who thinks of evil"), goes round the central shield.

The lion is the most common beast in heraldry.

The red lion is the symbol of Scotland.

The unicorn is a mythical beast, generally regarded as a Scottish royal beast in heraldry.

Henry II (1154–89) formalized his coat of arms to include three lions. This was developed by his son Richard I to become the "Gules three lions passant guardant or" seen on today's arms.

The royal helm with gold protective bars was introduced to the arms by Elizabeth I (1558–1603).

Dieu et mon droit (God and my right) has been the royal motto since the reign of Henry V (1413–22).

Henry VII (1485–1509) devised the Tudor rose, joining the white and red roses of York and Lancaster.

Admiral Lord Nelson

When people are ennobled they may choose their own coat of arms if they do not already have one. Britain's naval hero (1758–1805) was made Baron Nelson of the Nile in 1798 and a viscount in 1801. His arms relate to his life and career at sea; but some symbols were added after his death.

A seaman supports the shield.

The motto means "Let him wear the palm (or laurel) who deserves it".

A tropical scene shows the Battle of the Nile (1798).

The San Joseph was a Spanish man o'war that Nelson daringly captured.

Tracing Your Ancestry

For records of births, deaths and marriages in England and Wales since 1837, contact the General Register Office (0300 123 1837; www.gro.gov.uk); and in Scotland, contact the National Records of Scotland (0131 334 0380; www. nrscotland.gov.uk). For help in tracing family history, consult the Society of Genealogists, 14 Charterhouse Bldgs, London EC1 (020 7251 8799).

Inherited titles

usually pass to the eldest son or the closest male relative, but some titles may go to women if there is no male heir.

The Duke of Edinburgh (born 1921), husband of the Queen, is one of several dukes who are members of the Royal Family.

The Marquess of Salisbury (1830–1903), Prime Minister three times between 1885 and 1902, was descended from the Elizabethan statesman Robert Cecil.

Earl Mountbatten of Burma (1900–79) was ennobled in 1947 for diplomatic and military services.

Viscount Montgomery (1887–1976) was raised to the peerage for his military leadership in World War II.

Lord Byron (1788–1824), the Romantic poet, was the 6th Baron Byron: the 1st Baron was an MP ennobled by Charles I in 1625.

Peers of the Realm

There are nearly 1,200 peers of the realm. In 1999 the process began to abolish the hereditary system in favour of life peerages that expire on the death of the recipient *(see left and below)*. Ninety-two hereditary peers are entitled to sit in the House of Lords, including the Lords Spiritual – archbishops and senior bishops of the Church of England – and the Law Lords. In 1958 the Queen expanded the list of life peerages to honour people who had performed notable public service. From 1999 the system of "peoples peerages" began to replace inherited honours.

Key to the Peers

- 25 dukes
- 35 marquesses
- 175 earls and countesses
- 98 viscounts
- 800+ barons and baronesses

The Queen's Honours List

Twice a year several hundred men and women nominated by the Prime Minister and political leaders for outstanding public service receive honours from the Queen. Some are made dames or knights; a few receive the prestigious OM (Order of Merit); far more receive honours such as OBEs, CBEs or MBEs (Officers, Commanders or Members of the Most Excellent Order of the British Empire).

Mother Teresa received the OM in 1983 for her work in India.

Chris Hoy, Olympic gold medal cyclist, was knighted in 2009 for his services.

Elton John was given a CBE in 1995 and was knighted in 1998.

Rural Architecture

For many, the essence of British life is found in villages. Their scale and serenity nurture a way of life envied by those who live in towns and cities. The pattern of British villages dates back some 1,500 years, when the Saxons cleared forests and established settlements, usually centred on a green or pond. Most of today's English villages existed at the time of the *Domesday Book* in 1086 *(see p52)*, though few actual buildings survive from then. The settlements evolved organically around a church or manor; the cottages and gardens were created from local materials. Today, a typical village will contain structures of various dates, from the Middle Ages onward. The church is usually the oldest, followed perhaps by a tithe barn, manor house and cottages.

Abbotsbury, in Dorset – a typical village built up around a church

A steep-pitched roof covers the whole house.

Timbers are of Wealden oak.

Eaves are supported by curved braces.

Wealden Hall House in Sussex is a medieval timber-framed house, typically found in southeast England. It has a tall central open hall flanked by bays of two floors and the upper floor is "jettied", overhanging the ground floor.

A tiled roof keeps the grain dry.

The entrance is big enough for ox-wagons.

Holes let in air – and birds.

Walls and doors are weatherboarded.

The medieval tithe barn stored produce for the clergy – each farmer was required to donate one tenth (tithe) of his annual harvest. The enormous roofs may be supported by crucks, large curved timbers extending from the low walls.

The Parish Church

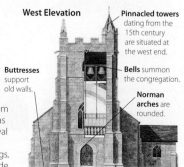

The church is the focal point of the village and, traditionally, of village life. Its tall spire could be seen – and its bells heard – by travellers from a distance. The church is also a chronicle of local history: a large church in a tiny village indicates a once-prosperous settlement. A typical church contains architectural features from many centuries, occasionally as far back as Saxon times. These may include medieval brasses, wall paintings, misericords *(see p345)*, and Tudor and Stuart carvings. Many sell informative guide books inside.

Slender spire from the Georgian era

West Elevation

Pinnacled towers dating from the 15th century are situated at the west end.

Buttresses support old walls.

Bells summon the congregation.

Norman arches are rounded.

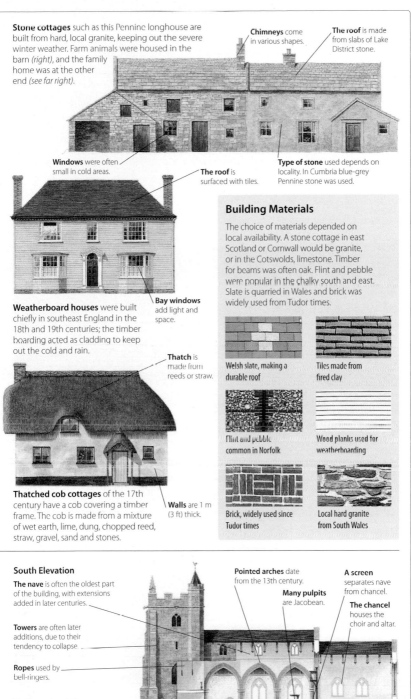

Stone cottages such as this Pennine longhouse are built from hard, local granite, keeping out the severe winter weather. Farm animals were housed in the barn *(right)*, and the family home was at the other end *(see far right)*.

Chimneys come in various shapes.

The roof is made from slabs of Lake District stone.

Windows were often small in cold areas.

The roof is surfaced with tiles.

Type of stone used depends on locality. In Cumbria blue-grey Pennine stone was used.

Weatherboard houses were built chiefly in southeast England in the 18th and 19th centuries; the timber boarding acted as cladding to keep out the cold and rain.

Bay windows add light and space.

Thatch is made from reeds or straw.

Thatched cob cottages of the 17th century have a cob covering a timber frame. The cob is made from a mixture of wet earth, lime, dung, chopped reed, straw, gravel, sand and stones.

Walls are 1 m (3 ft) thick.

Building Materials

The choice of materials depended on local availability. A stone cottage in east Scotland or Cornwall would be granite, or in the Cotswolds, limestone. Timber for beams was often oak. Flint and pebble were popular in the chalky south and east. Slate is quarried in Wales and brick was widely used from Tudor times.

Welsh slate, making a durable roof

Tiles made from fired clay

Flint and pebble common in Norfolk

Wood planks used for weatherboarding

Brick, widely used since Tudor times

Local hard granite from South Wales

South Elevation

The nave is often the oldest part of the building, with extensions added in later centuries.

Towers are often later additions, due to their tendency to collapse.

Ropes used by bell-ringers.

The font, where babies are baptized, is often a church's oldest feature.

Pointed arches date from the 13th century.

Many pulpits are Jacobean.

A screen separates nave from chancel.

The chancel houses the choir and altar.

The Countryside

For its size, Britain contains an unusual variety of geological and climatic conditions that have shaped diverse landscapes – from treeless windswept moorland and the wildness of the Scottish Highlands, to boggy marshes and small hedged cattle pastures. Each terrain nurtures its typical wildlife and displays its own charm through the seasons. With the reduction in farming and the creation of footpaths and nature reserves, the countryside is becoming more of a leisure resource.

Indigenous Animals and Birds

There are no large or dangerous wild animals in Britain but a wealth of small mammals, rodents and insects inhabit the countryside, and the rivers and streams are home to many varieties of fish. For bird-watchers there is a great range of songbirds, birds of prey and seabirds.

Livestock graze on low pastures.

Trees provide shelter and protection for wildlife.

Higher land is uncultivated.

Bushes and trees grow between rocks.

The highest ground is often covered in snow until spring.

Streams flow over a stony bed from mountain springs.

Wooded Downland

Chalk downland, seen here at Ditchling Beacon on the Downs *(see p185)*, has soil of low fertility and is grazed by sheep. However crops are sometimes grown on the lower slopes. Distinctive wild flowers and butterflies thrive here, while beech and yew predominate in the woods.

Spear thistle has pink heads in summer that attract several species of butterfly.

The dog rose is one of Britain's best-loved wild flowers; its pink single flower is widely seen in hedgerows.

Hogweed has robust stems and leaves with large clusters of white flowers.

Wild Hillside

Large tracts of Britain's uplands remain wild terrain, unsuitable for crops or forestry. Purple heather is tough enough to survive in moorland, the haunt of deer and game birds. The highest craggy uplands, such as the Cairngorms *(see pp548–9)* in Scotland, pictured here, are the habitat of birds of prey, such as the golden eagle.

Ling, a low-growing heather with tiny pink bell-flowers, adds splashes of colour to peaty moors and uplands.

Tormentil has small yellow flowers. It prefers moist, acid soil and is found near water on heaths and moors in summer.

Meadow cranesbill is a wild geranium with distinctive purple flowers.

Swallows, swifts and house martins are all summer visitors.

Kestrels are small falcons that prey on mammals such as voles.

Rabbits are often spotted feeding at the edge of fields or near woods.

Robins, common in gardens and hedgerows, have distinctive red breast feathers.

Foxes, little bigger than domestic cats, live in hideaways in woods, near farmland.

Cereal crops ripen in small fields.

Hedgerows provide refuge for wildlife.

Small mixed woods break up the field pattern.

Sheep graze on salty marshes.

Culverts drain water from the field.

Reed beds edge the water.

Traditional Fields

The patchwork fields here in the Cotswolds (see p308) reflect generations of small-scale farming. A typical farm would produce silage, hay and cereal crops, and keep a few dairy cows and sheep in enclosed pastures. The tree-dotted hedgerows mark boundaries that may be centuries old.

Marshland

Flat and low-lying wetlands, crisscrossed with dykes and drainage canals, provide the scenery of Romney Marsh (see pp186–7) as well as much of East Anglia. Some areas have rich, peaty soil for crops, or salty marshland for sheep, but there are extensive uncultivated sections, where reed beds shelter wildlife.

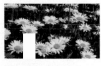

The oxeye daisy is a larger relative of the common white daisy, found in grassland from spring to late summer.

Orchids are among the rarer wild flowers. This species is the Common Spotted Orchid.

Cowslips belong to the primrose family. In spring they are often found in the grass on open meadowlands.

Sea lavender is a saltmarsh plant that is tolerant of saline soils. It flowers in late summer.

Poppies glow brilliant red in cornfields.

Buttercups are among the most common wild flowers. They brighten meadows in summer.

Walkers' Britain

Walkers of all levels of ability and enthusiasm are well served in Britain. There is an unrivalled network of long-distance paths through some spectacular scenery, which can be tackled in stages with overnight stays en route, or dipped into for a single day's walking. For shorter walks, Britain is dotted with signposts showing public footpaths across common or private land. You will find books of walk routes in local shops and a large map will keep you on track. Choose river routes for easy walking or take to the hills for a greater challenge.

The West Highland Way is an arduous 95-mile (153-km) route from Milngavie, near Glasgow, to north of Fort William, across mountainous terrain with fine lochs and moorland scenery *(see p498)*.

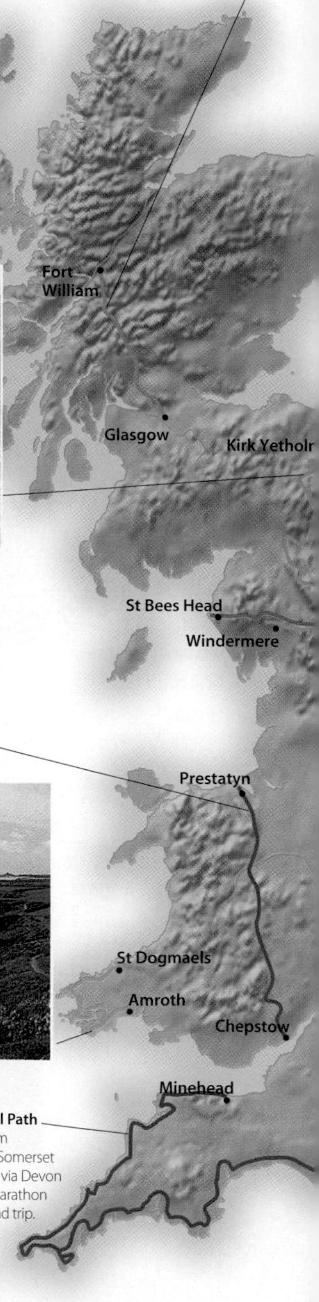

The Pennine Way
This is Britain's first designated long-distance path. The 268-mile (431-km) route from Edale in Derbyshire to Kirk Yetholm on the Scottish border is a challenging upland hike, with long, lonely stretches of moorland. It is only for experienced hill walkers.

Offa's Dyke Footpath
Following the boundary between Wales and England, this 168-mile (270-km) path goes through the beautiful Wye Valley in the Welsh borders.

Pembrokeshire Coastal Path
A 186-mile (299-km) path of rugged clifftop walking from Amroth on Carmarthen Bay to the west tip of Wales at Cardigan.

Ordnance Survey Maps

The best maps for walkers are published by the Ordnance Survey, the official mapping agency (08456 050505). Out of a wide range of maps, the most useful are the Explorer series, which include the more popular regions and cover a large area, on a scale of 1:25,000, and the Landranger series, on a scale of 1:50,000.

The Southwest Coastal Path offers varied scenery from Minehead on the north Somerset coast to Poole in Dorset, via Devon and Cornwall – in all a marathon 630-mile (1,014-km) round trip.

Fort William

Glasgow

Kirk Yetholm

St Bees Head

Windermere

Prestatyn

St Dogmaels

Amroth

Chepstow

Minehead

Signposts

Long-distance paths are well signposted, some of them with an acorn symbol (or with a thistle in Scotland). Many shorter routes are marked with coloured arrows by local authorities or hiking groups. Local councils generally mark public footpaths with yellow arrows. Public bridleways, marked by blue arrows, are paths that can be used by both walkers and horse riders – remember, horses churn up mud. Signs appear on posts, trees and stiles.

Tips for Walkers

Be prepared: The weather can change very quickly: dress for the worst. Always take a compass, a proper walking map and get local advice before undertaking any ambitious walking. Pack some food and drink if the map does not show a pub en route.

On the walk: Always keep to the footpath and close gates behind you. Never feed or upset farm animals, leave litter, pick flowers or damage plants.

Where to stay: The Hostelling International (see p623) has a network of hostels which cater particularly for walkers. Bed-and-breakfast accommodation is also available near most routes (see p557).

Further information: The Ramblers' Association (020 7339 8500; www.ramblers.org.uk) is a national organization for walkers, with a guide to accommodation.

The Coast to Coast Walk

A 190-mile (306-km) route that crosses the Lake District, Yorkshire Dales and North York Moors, this demanding walk covers a spectacular range of northern landscapes. All cross-country routes are best walked from west to east to take advantage of the prevailing wind.

Robin Hood's Bay

Dales Way runs from Ilkley in West Yorkshire to Bowness-on-Windermere in the Lake District, 81 miles (130 km) of delightful flat riverside walking and valley scenery.

Ilkley

Edale

The Ridgeway

This fairly easy ancient path follows an ancient track once used by cattle drovers. Starting near Avebury (see p267), it covers 85 miles (137 km) to Ivinghoe Beacon.

Peddars Way and the Norfolk Coast Path together make 94 miles (151 km) of easy lowland walking, from Thetford north to the coast then east to Cromer.

Sheringham
Thetford

Ivinghoe

Icknield Way, the most ancient prehistoric road in Britain, is 105 miles (168 km) long and links the Ridgeway to Peddars Way.

Kemble

Avebury

London

Farnham

Dover

inchester
Eastbourne

ole Harbour

The Thames Path follows the river for 213 miles (341 km) from central London to Kemble, its source in Gloucestershire.

The South Downs Way

This 101-mile (162-km) walk from Eastbourne (see p184) on the south coast to Winchester (see pp174–5) can be completed in a week.

The Isle of Wight Coastal Path circles the entire island on an easy 65-mile (105-km) footpath.

The North Downs Way is an ancient route through 141 miles (227 km) of low lying hills from Farnham in Surrey to Dover or Folkestone in Kent.

THE HISTORY OF GREAT BRITAIN

Britain began to assume a cohesive character as early as the 7th century, with the Anglo-Saxon tribes absorbing Celtic and Roman influences and finally achieving supremacy. They suffered repeated Viking incursions and were overcome by the Normans at the Battle of Hastings in 1066. Over centuries, the disparate cultures of the Normans and Anglo-Saxons combined to form the English nation, a process nurtured by Britain's position as an island. The next 400 years saw English kings involved in military expeditions to Europe, but their control over these areas was gradually wrested from them. As a result they extended their domain over Scotland and Wales. The Tudor monarchs consolidated this control and laid the foundations for Britain's future commercial success. Henry VIII recognized the vital importance of sea power and under his daughter, Elizabeth I, English sailors ranged far across the world, often coming into conflict with the Spanish.

The total defeat of the Spanish Armada in 1588 confirmed Britain's position as a major maritime power. The Stuart period saw a number of internal struggles, most importantly the Civil War in 1641. But by the time of the Act of the Union in 1707 the whole island was united and the foundations for representative government had been laid. The combination of this internal security with continuing maritime strength allowed Britain to seek wealth overseas. By the end of the Napoleonic Wars in 1815, Britain was the leading trading nation in the world. The opportunities offered by industrialization were seized, and by the late 19th century, a colossal empire had been established across the globe. Challenged by Europe and the rise of the US, and drained by its leading role in two world wars, Britain's influence waned after 1945. By the 1970s almost all the colonies had become independent Commonwealth nations.

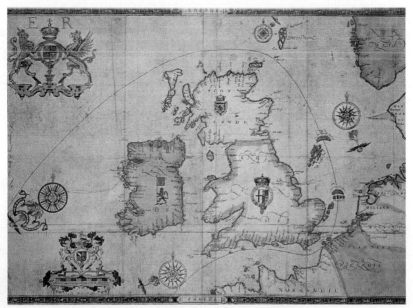

Contemporary map showing the defeat of the Armada (1588), which made Britain into a world power

◄ Henry VIII, founder of the British navy, seen here with his son, Edward, and wife Jane Seymour

Kings and Queens

All English monarchs since the Norman Conquest in 1066 have been descendants of William the Conqueror. Scottish rulers, until James VI and the Union of Crowns in 1603 *(see pp486–7),* have been more diverse. When the Crown passes to someone other than the monarch's eldest son, the name of the ruling family usually changes. The rules of succession, until 2015, strongly favoured men over women, but Britain has still had six queens since 1553. In Norman times the monarchy enjoyed absolute power, but today the position is largely symbolic.

1413–22 Henry V

1509–47 Henry VIII

1399–1413 Henry IV

1485–1509 Henry VII

1553–8 Mary I

1483–5 Richard III

1066–87 William the Conqueror

1087–1100 William II

1100–35 Henry I

1135–54 Stephen

1327–77 Edward III

1050	1100	1150	1200	1250	1300	1350	1400	1450	1500	1.
Norman		Plantagenet					Lancaster	York	Tudor	
1050	1100	1150	1200	1250	1300	1350	1400	1450	1500	1.

1154–89 Henry II

1189–99 Richard I

1199–1216 John

1216–72 Henry III

1307–27 Edward II

1272–1307 Edward I

1461–70 and 1471–83 Edward IV

1547–53 Edward VI

1422–61 and 1470–71 Henry VI

1377–99 Richard II

Matthew Paris's 13th-century chronicle showing clockwise from top left Richard I, Henry II, John and Henry III.

1483 Edward V

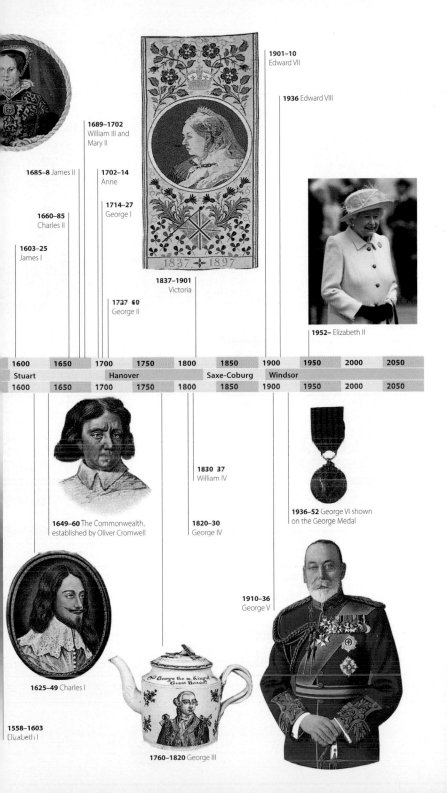

1901–10 Edward VII

1936 Edward VIII

1689–1702 William III and Mary II

1685–8 James II

1702–14 Anne

1714–27 George I

1660–85 Charles II

1603–25 James I

1837–1901 Victoria

1727–60 George II

1952– Elizabeth II

1600	1650	1700	1750	1800	1850	1900	1950	2000	2050
Stuart		Hanover			Saxe-Coburg	Windsor			
1600	1650	1700	1750	1800	1850	1900	1950	2000	2050

1830–37 William IV

1936–52 George VI shown on the George Medal

1649–60 The Commonwealth, established by Oliver Cromwell

1820–30 George IV

1910–36 George V

1625–49 Charles I

1558–1603 Elizabeth I

1760–1820 George III

Prehistoric Britain

Britain was part of the European landmass until
the end of the last Ice Age, around 6000 BC,
when the English Channel was formed by
melting ice. The earliest inhabitants lived in
limestone caves: settlements and farming skills
developed gradually through the Stone Age.
The magnificent wooden and stone henges and
circles are masterworks from around 3000 BC,
but their significance is a mystery. Flint mines
and ancient pathways are evidence of early
trading and many burial mounds (barrows)
survive from the Stone and Bronze Ages.

Axe Heads
Stone axes, like this
one found at Stone-
henge, were used
by Neolithic men.

Cup and ring marks
were carved on standing
stones, such as this one
at Ballymeanoch.

Mapping the Past

*Monuments from the Neolithic (New Stone),
Bronze and Iron Ages, together with artifacts
found from these periods, provide a wealth of
information about Britain's early settlers,
before written history began with the Romans.*

Neolithic Tools
Antlers and bones were
made into Neolithic leather-
working tools. These were
found at Avebury *(see p267).*

Pottery Beaker
The Beaker People, who came
from Europe in the early
Bronze Age, take their name
from these drinking cups often
found in their graves.

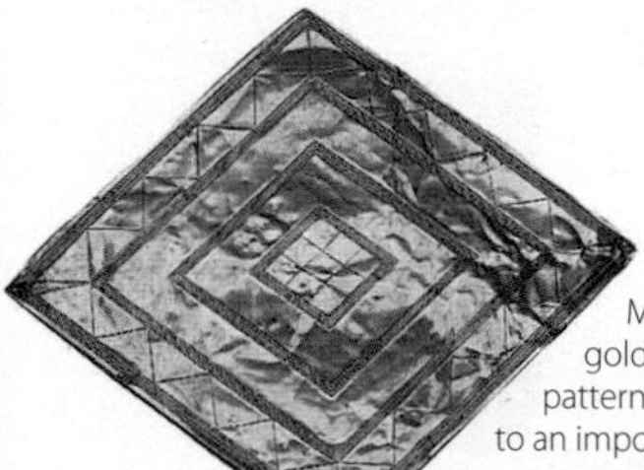

Gold Breast Plate
Made by Wessex
goldsmiths, its spectacular
pattern suggests it belonged
to an important chieftain.

Pentre Ifan, an impressive
Neolithic burial chamber in
South Wales, was once covered
with a huge earth mound.

Mold Cape
Gold was mined in Wales and
Cornwall in the Bronze Age.
This intricately worked
warrior's cape was buried in a
grave at Mold, Clwyd.

This gold cup, found
in a Cornish barrow, is
evidence of the wealth
of Bronze Age tribes.

6000–5000 As the Ice Age
comes to an end, sea levels
rise, submerging the land-
link between Britain and
the Continent

*Neolithic
flint axes*

6000 BC	5500 BC	5000 BC	4500 BC	4000 BC	3500 BC

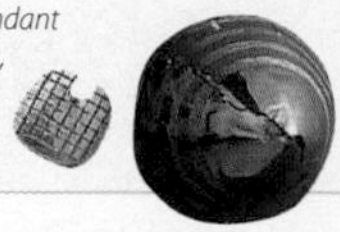

*A gold pendant
and button (1700 BC),
found in Bronze
Age graves*

3500 Neolithic Age
begins. Long
barrows and
stone circles built
around Britain

Skara Brae Is a Neolithic village of about 2500 BC (see p532).

Maiden Castle
An impressive Iron Age hill fort in Dorset, its concentric lines of ramparts and ditches follow the contours of the hilltop (see p273).

Iron Age Brochs, round towers with thick stone walls, are found only in Scotland.

Iron Age Axe
The technique of smelting iron came to Britain around 700 BC, brought from Europe by the Celts.

Castlerigg Stone Circle is one of Britain's earliest Neolithic monuments (see p365).

Uffington White Horse
Thought to be 3,000 years old, the shape has to be "scoured" to keep grass at bay (see p225).

Where to See Prehistoric Britain

Wiltshire, with Stonehenge (see pp266–7) and Avebury (see p267), has the best Neolithic monuments, and the Uffington White Horse is nearby (see p225). The Scottish islands have many early sites and the British Museum (see pp110–11) has a huge collection of artifacts.

A circular bank with over 180 stones encloses the Neolithic site at Avebury (see p267).

A chalk figure, thought to be a fertility goddess, was found at Grimes Graves (see pp198–9).

This bronze Celtic helmet (50 BC) was found in the River Thames, London.

Snettisham Torc
A torc was a neck ring worn by Celtic men. This one, found in Norfolk, dates from 50 BC and is made from silver and gold.

Stonehenge was begun around 5,000 years ago (see pp266–7).

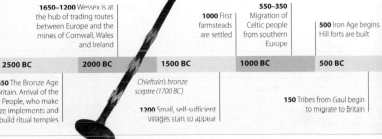

2500 Temples, or henges, are built of wood or stone	**1650–1200** Wessex is at the hub of trading routes between Europe and the mines of Cornwall, Wales and Ireland		**1000** First farmsteads are settled	**550–350** Migration of Celtic people from southern Europe	**500** Iron Age begins. Hill forts are built
3000 BC	**2500 BC**	**2000 BC**	**1500 BC**	**1000 BC**	**500 BC**
	2100–1650 The Bronze Age reaches Britain. Arrival of the Beaker People, who make bronze implements and build ritual temples	Chieftain's bronze sceptre (1700 BC) **1200** Small, self-sufficient villages start to appear			**150** Tribes from Gaul begin to migrate to Britain

Roman Britain

Throughout the 350-year Roman occupation, Britain was ruled as a colony. After the defeat of rebellious local tribes, such as Boudica's Iceni, the Romans remained an unassimilated occupying power. Their legacy is in military and civil construction: forts, walls, towns and public buildings. Their long, straight roads, built for easy movement of troops, are still a feature of the landscape.

Cavalry Sports Helmet
Found in Lancashire, it was used in tournaments by horsemen. Cavalry races and other sports were held in amphitheatres near towns.

Main baths

Silver Jug
This 3rd-century jug, the earliest known silver item with Christian symbols, was excavated near Peterborough.

Entrance hall

Fishbourne Palace was built beside a natural harbour, so ships could moor nearby.

Hadrian's Wall
Started in AD 120 as a defence against the Scots; it marked the northern frontier of the Roman Empire and was guarded by 17 forts housing over 18,500 foot- soldiers and cavalry (see pp426–7).

Mithras
This head of the god Mithras was found on the London site of a temple devoted to the cult of Mithraism. The sect demanded of its Roman followers loyalty and discipline.

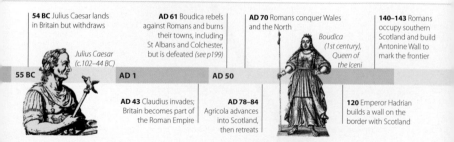

54 BC Julius Caesar lands in Britain but withdraws

Julius Caesar (c.102–44 BC)

AD 61 Boudica rebels against Romans and burns their towns, including St Albans and Colchester, but is defeated (see p199)

AD 70 Romans conquer Wales and the North

Boudica (1st century), Queen of the Iceni

140–143 Romans occupy southern Scotland and build Antonine Wall to mark the frontier

55 BC	AD 1	AD 50

AD 43 Claudius invades; Britain becomes part of the Roman Empire

AD 78–84 Agricola advances into Scotland, then retreats

120 Emperor Hadrian builds a wall on the border with Scotland

Flavian Mosaic
Roman floors of the 1st
century used patterns in black
and white stone. More
mosaics survive at
Fishbourne than at any
other British site.

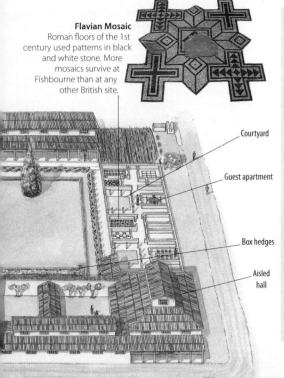

Courtyard

Guest apartment

Box hedges

Aisled
hall

Where to See
Roman Britain

Many of Britain's main towns
and cities were established by
the Romans and have Roman
remains, including York *(see
pp408–13)*, Chester *(see pp314–15)*,
St Albans *(see pp236–7)*, Colchester
(see p209), Bath *(see pp262–5)*,
Lincoln *(see pp344–5)* and London
(see pp74–159). Several Roman
villas were built in southern
England, favoured for its mild
climate and close proximity
to Europe.

The Roman baths in Bath
(see pp264–5), known as Aquae
Sulis, were built between the
1st and 4th centuries around
a natural hot spring.

Fishbourne Palace

*Built in the late 1st century for Togidubnus,
a pro-Roman king, the palace (here
reconstructed) featured advanced technology
such as underfloor heating and indoor
plumbing for baths (see p175).*

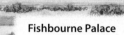

Chi-Rho Symbol
This early Christian
symbol is from a
3rd-century fresco
at Lullingstone
Roman villa in Kent.

Battersea Shield
Found in the Thames
near Battersea, the shield
bears Celtic symbols and
was probably made at
about the time of the
first Roman invasion.
Archaeologists suspect
it may have been lost by
a warrior while crossing
the river, or offered as
a sacrifice to one of the
many river gods. It is now
at the British Museum
(see pp110–11).

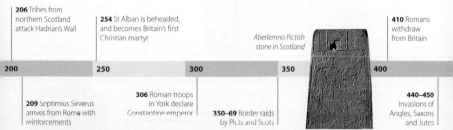

206 Tribes from northern Scotland attack Hadrian's Wall

254 St Alban is beheaded, and becomes Britain's first Christian martyr

Aberlemno Pictish stone in Scotland

410 Romans withdraw from Britain

200 | 250 | 300 | 350 | 400

209 Septimius Severus arrives from Rome with reinforcements

306 Roman troops in York declare Constantine emperor

350–69 Border raids by Picts and Scots

440–450 Invasions of Angles, Saxons and Jutes

Anglo-Saxon Kingdoms

By the mid-5th century, Angles and Saxons from
Germany had started to raid the eastern shores of
Britain. Increasingly they decided to settle, and within
100 years Saxon kingdoms, including Wessex, Mercia
and Northumbria, were established over the entire
country. Viking raids throughout the 8th and 9th
centuries were largely contained, but in 1066, the
last invasion of England saw William the Conqueror
from Normandy defeat the Anglo-Saxon King Harold
at the Battle of Hastings. William then went on to
assume control of the whole country.

Viking Axe
The principal weapons of
the Viking warriors were spear,
axe and sword. They were
skilled metal-workers with
an eye for decoration, as
seen in this axe head from
a Copenhagen museum.

Vikings on a Raiding Expedition
Scandinavian boat-building
skills were in advance of
anything known in Britain.
People were terrified
by these large, fast
boats with their
intimidating
figureheads, which
sailed up the
Thames and along
the coasts.

Anglo-Saxon Calendar

*These scenes from a chronicle of seasons,
made just before the Norman invasion, show
life in late Anglo-Saxon Britain. At first people
lived in small farming communities, but by
the 7th century towns began to spring up
and trade increased. Saxon kings were
supported by nobles but most of the
population were free peasants.*

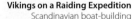

St Augustine (d.604)

c.470–495 Saxons
and Angles settle
in Essex, Sussex
and East Anglia

c.556 Saxons move
across Britain and set
up seven kingdoms

635 St Aidan
establishes a
monastery on
Lindisfarne

730–821 Supremacy
of Mercia, whose king,
Offa (d.796), builds
a dyke along the
Mercia–Wales border

| 450 | 500 | 550 | 600 | 650 | 700 | 7 |

450 Saxons first
settle in Kent

563 St Columba
lands on Iona

597 St Augustine sent
by Rome to convert
English to Christianity

617–85 Supremacy
of Northumbrian
kingdom

*Mercian coin which bears
the name of King Offa*

Ox-drawn plough for tilling

Alfred Jewel
This 9th-century gold ornament in the Ashmolean Museum (see p228) has the inscription: "Alfred ordered me made". This may refer to the Saxon King Alfred.

Where to See Anglo-Saxon Britain

The best collection of Saxon artifacts is from a burial ship unearthed at Sutton Hoo (see p207) in Suffolk in 1938 and now on display at the British Museum (see pp110–11). There are fine Saxon churches at Bradwell (see p213) in Essex and Bosham (see p175) in Sussex. In York the Viking town of Jorvik has been excavated (see p410) and actual relics are shown alongside models of people and dwellings.

The Saxon church of St Laurence (see p259) was built in the late 8th century.

Minstrels entertaining at a feast

Edward the Confessor
In 1042, Edward – known as "the Confessor" because of his piety – became king. He died in 1066 and William of Normandy claimed the throne.

Hawks, used to kill game

Harold's Death
This 14th-century illustration depicts the victorious William of Normandy after King Harold was killed by an arrow in his eye. The Battle of Hastings (see p185) was the last invasion of Britain.

Legend of King Arthur
Arthur is thought to have been a chieftain who fought the Saxons in the early 6th century. Legends of his knights' exploits were first popularized in 1139 (see p289).

An invading Norman ship

802–839 After the death of Cenwulf (821), Wessex gains control over most of England

867 Northumbria falls to the Vikings

878 King Alfred defeats Vikings but allows them to settle in eastern England

1016 Danish King Canute (see p175) seizes English crown

800	850	900	950	1000	1050	1100

843 Kenneth McAlpin becomes king of all Scotland

c.793 Lindisfarne sacked by Viking invaders; first Viking raid on Scotland about a year later

926 Eastern England, the Danelaw, is reconquered by the Saxons

1042 The Anglo-Saxon Edward the Confessor becomes king (d.1066)

1066 William of Normandy claims the throne, and defeats Harold at the Battle of Hastings. He is crowned at Westminster

The Middle Ages

Remains of Norman castles on English hilltops bear testimony to the military might used by the invaders to sustain their conquest – although Wales and Scotland resisted for centuries. The Normans operated a feudal system, creating an aristocracy that treated native Anglo-Saxons as serfs. French was spoken by the ruling class until the 13th century, when it mixed with the Old English used by the peasants. The medieval church's power is shown in the cathedrals that grace British cities today.

Magna Carta
To protect themselves and the church from arbitrary taxation, the powerful English barons compelled King John to sign a "great charter" in 1215 *(see p239)*. This laid the foundations for an independent legal system.

Craft Skills
An illustration from a 14th-century manuscript depicts a weaver and a copper-beater – two of the trades that created a wealthy class of artisans.

Becket is received into heaven.

Henry II's knights murder Becket in Canterbury Cathedral.

Murder of Thomas Becket

The struggle between church and king for ultimate control of the country was brought to a head by the murder of Becket, the Archbishop of Canterbury. After Becket's canonization in 1173, Canterbury became a major centre of pilgrimage.

Ecclesiastical Art
Nearly all medieval art had religious themes, such as this window at Canterbury Cathedral *(see pp190–91)* depicting Jeroboam.

Black Death
A plague swept Britain and Europe several times in the 14th century, killing millions of people. This illustration, in a religious tract produced around 100 years later, shows death taking its heavy toll.

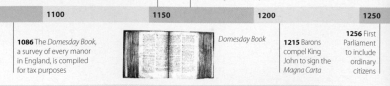

1071 Hereward the Wake, leader of the Anglo-Saxon resistance, defeated at Ely

1154 Henry II, the first Plantagenet king, demolishes castles, and exacts money from barons instead of military service

1170 Archbishop of Canterbury Thomas Becket is murdered by four knights after quarrelling with Henry II

1100 **1150** **1200** **1250**

1086 The *Domesday Book*, a survey of every manor in England, is compiled for tax purposes

Domesday Book

1215 Barons compel King John to sign the *Magna Carta*

1256 First Parliament to include ordinary citizens

Battle of Agincourt
In 1415, Henry V took an army to France to claim its throne. This 15th-century chronicle depicts Henry beating the French army at Agincourt.

This casket (1190), in a private collection, is said to have contained Becket's remains.

Becket takes his place in Heaven after his canonization.

Two clergymen look on in horror at Becket's murder.

Where to See Medieval Britain
The university cities of Oxford (see pp226–31) and Cambridge (see pp214–19) contain the largest concentrations of Gothic buildings. Magnificent cathedrals rise high above many historic cities, among them Lincoln (see pp344–5) and York (see pp408–13). Both cities still retain at least part of their ancient street pattern. Military architecture is best seen in Wales (see pp442–3) with the formidable border castles of Edward I.

All Souls College in Oxford (see p230), which only takes graduates, is a superb blend of medieval and later architecture.

Richard III
Richard, shown in this 16th-century painting, became king during the Wars of the Roses: a bitter struggle for power between two factions of the royal family – the houses of York and Lancaster.

John Wycliffe (1329–84)
This painting by Ford Madox Brown (1821–93) shows Wycliffe with the Bible he translated into English to make it accessible to everyone.

Castle Life
Every section of a castle was allotted to a baron whose soldiers helped defend it. This 14th-century illustration shows the coats of arms (see p34) of the barons for each area.

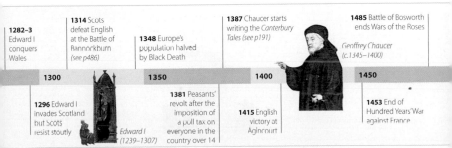

1282–3 Edward I conquers Wales

1314 Scots defeat English at the Battle of Bannockburn (see p486)

1348 Europe's population halved by Black Death

1387 Chaucer starts writing the Canterbury Tales (see p191)

1485 Battle of Bosworth ends Wars of the Roses

Geoffrey Chaucer (c.1345–1400)

1300 **1350** **1400** **1450**

1296 Edward I invades Scotland but Scots resist stoutly

Edward I (1239–1307)

1381 Peasants' revolt after the imposition of a poll tax on everyone in the country over 14

1415 English victory at Agincourt

1453 End of Hundred Years' War against France

Tudor Renaissance

After years of debilitating civil war, the Tudor monarchs established peace and national self-confidence, reflected in the split from the Church of Rome – due to Henry VIII's divorce from Catherine of Aragon – and the consequent closure of the monasteries. Henry's daughter, Mary I, tried to re-establish Catholicism but under her half-sister, Elizabeth I, the Protestant Church secured its position. Overseas exploration began, provoking clashes with other European powers seeking to exploit the New World. The Renaissance in arts and learning spread from Europe to Britain, with playwright William Shakespeare adding his own unique contribution.

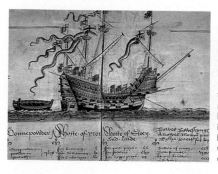

Sea Power
Henry VIII laid the foundations of the powerful English navy. In 1545, his flagship, the *Mary Rose* *(see p173)*, sank before his eyes in Portsmouth harbour on its way to do battle with the French.

Theatre
Some of Shakespeare's plays were first seen in purpose-built theatres such as the Globe *(see p124)* in south London.

The globe signifies that the queen reigns supreme far and wide.

Monasteries
With Henry VIII's split from Rome, England's religious houses, like Fountains Abbey *(see pp394–5)*, were dissolved. Henry seized their riches and used them to finance his foreign policy.

1497 John Colet denounces the corruption of the clergy, supported by Erasmus and Sir Thomas More

1533–4 Henry VIII divorces Catherine of Aragon and is excommunicated by the Pope. He forms the Church of England

1542–1567 Mary, Queen of Scots rules Scotland

1490

1510

1530

1497 John Cabot *(see p260)* makes his first voyage to North America

1513 English defeat Scots at Flodden *(see p486)*

1535 Act of Union with Wales

1536–40 Dissolution of the Monasteries *(see p355)*

1549 First Book of Common Prayer introduced

Henry VIII (1491–1547)

Mary, Queen of Scots

As great-granddaughter of Henry VII, she laid claim to the English throne in 1559. But in 1567, Elizabeth I had her imprisoned for 20 years until her execution for treason in 1587.

Jewels symbolize triumph.

Where to See Tudor Britain

Hampton Court Palace (see p177) has been altered over the centuries but remains a Tudor showpiece. Part of Elizabeth I's former home at Hatfield (see p235) still survives. In Kent, Leeds Castle (see p192), Knole (see pp192–3) and Hever Castle (see p193) all have connections with Tudor royalty. Burghley House (see pp346–7) and Hardwick Hall (see p306), both Midlands mansions, retain their 16th-century character.

This astronomical clock at Hampton Court (see p177), with its intriguing zodiac symbols, was installed in 1540 by Henry VIII.

Defeat of the Armada

Spain was England's main rival for supremacy on the seas, and in 1588 Philip II sent 100 powerfully armed galleons towards England, bent on invasion. The English fleet – under Lord Howard, Francis Drake, John Hawkins and Martin Frobisher – sailed from Plymouth and destroyed the Spanish navy in a famous victory. This commemorative portrait of Elizabeth I by George Gower (d.1596) celebrates the triumph.

Protestant Martyrs
Catholic Mary I reigned from 1553 to 1558. Protestants who opposed her rule were burned, such as these six churchmen at Canterbury in 1555.

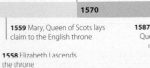

William Shakespeare (1564–1616)

1570 Sir Francis Drake's first voyage to the West Indies

1584 Sir Walter Raleigh tries to colonize Virginia after Drake's first unsuccessful attempt

1591 First play by Shakespeare performed

1600 East India Company founded, beginning British involvement on the Indian subcontinent

1550	1570	1590

1553 Death of Edward VI; throne passes to the Catholic Mary I

1559 Mary, Queen of Scots lays claim to the English throne

1558 Elizabeth I ascends the throne

1587 Execution of Mary, Queen of Scots on the orders of Elizabeth I

1588 Defeat of the Spanish Armada

Sir Walter Raleigh (1552–1618)

1603 Union of Crowns. James VI of Scotland becomes James I of England

Stuart Britain

The end of Elizabeth I's reign signalled the start of internal turmoil. The throne passed to James I, whose belief that kings ruled by divine right provoked clashes with Parliament. Under his son, Charles I, the conflict escalated into Civil War that ended with his execution. In 1660 Charles II regained the throne, but after his death James II was ousted for Catholic leanings. Protestantism was reaffirmed with the reign of William and Mary, who suppressed the Catholic Jacobites.

Science
Sir Isaac Newton (1642–1727) invented this reflecting telescope, laying the foundation for a greater understanding of the universe, including the law of gravity.

Charles I stayed silent at his trial.

Oliver Cromwell
A strict Protestant and a passionate champion of the rights of Parliament, he led the victorious Parliamentary forces in the Civil War. He became Lord Protector of the Commonwealth from 1653 to 1658.

The headless body kneels by the block.

On the way to his death, the king wore two shirts for warmth, so onlookers should not think he was shivering with fright.

Execution of Charles I

Cromwell was convinced there would be no peace until the king was dead. At his trial for treason, Charles refused to recognize the authority of the court and offered no defence. He faced his death with dignity on 30 January 1649, the only English king to be executed. His death was followed by a republic known as the Commonwealth.

Theatre
After the Restoration in 1660, when Parliament restored the monarchy, theatre thrived. Plays were performed on temporary outdoor stages.

1605 "Gunpowder Plot" to blow up Parliament thwarted

1614 "Addled Parliament" refuses to vote money for James I

1620 Pilgrim Fathers sail in the *Mayflower* to New England

1642 Civil War breaks out

1653–8 Cromwell rules as Lord Protector

1600

1625

1650

1611 New translation of Bible published, known as the King James Version

James I (1566–1625)

1638 Scots sign National Covenant, opposing Charles I's Catholic leanings

1649 Charles I executed outside Banqueting House and Commonwealth declared by Parliament

1660 Restoration of the monarchy under Charles II

Restoration of the Monarchy

This silk embroidery celebrates the fact that Charles II escaped his father's fate by hiding in an oak tree. There was joy at his return from exile in France.

The axeman holds the severed head of Charles I.

Plague
Bills of mortality showed the weekly deaths as bubonic plague swept London in 1665. Up to 100,000 Londoners died.

Onlookers soaked up the king's blood with their handkerchiefs to have a memento.

Where to See Stuart Britain

The best work of the two leading architects of the time, Inigo Jones and Christopher Wren, is in London, and includes St Paul's Cathedral (*see pp118–19*). In the south-east two classic Jacobean mansions are Audley End (*see p212*) and Hatfield House (*see p235*). The Palace of Holyroodhouse (*see p514*), in Edinburgh, is another example.

Hatfield House (*p235*) is a splendid Jacobean mansion.

Anatomy
By dissecting corpses, physicians began to gain an understanding of the working of the human body – a crucial step towards modern surgery and medicine.

Pilgrim Fathers
In 1620 a group of Puritans sailed to America. They forged good relations with the native Indians; here they are shown being visited by the chief of the Pokanokets.

1665–6
Great Plague

1666 Great Fire of London

The Great Fire of London

1688 The Glorious Revolution: Catholic James II deposed by Parliament

1675

1690 Battle of the Boyne: William's English/Dutch army defeats James II's Irish/French army

1692 Glencoe Massacre of Jacobites (Stuart supporters) by William III's forces

1700

1707 Act of Union with Scotland

William III (1689–1702)

Georgian Britain

The 18th century saw Britain, now recovered from the trauma of its Civil War, develop as a commercial and industrial powerhouse. London became a centre of banking, and a mercantile and professional class grew up. Continuing supremacy at sea laid the foundations of an empire; steam engines, canals and railways heralded the Industrial Revolution. Growing confidence was reflected in stately architecture and elegant fashions but, as cities became more crowded, conditions for the underclass grew worse.

Slate became the preferred tile for Georgian buildings. Roofs became less steep to achieve an Italian look.

A row of sash windows is one of the most characteristic features of a Georgian house.

Oak was used in the best dwellings for doors and stairs, but pine was standard in most houses.

The saloon was covered in wallpaper, a cheaper alternative to hanging walls with tapestries or fabrics.

The drawing room was richly ornamented and used for entertaining visitors.

The dining room was used for all family meals.

Steps led to the servants' entrance in the basement.

Battle of Bunker Hill
In 1775 American colonists rebelled against British rule. The British won this early battle in Massachusetts, but in 1783 Britain recognized the United States of America.

Watt's Steam Engine
The Scottish engineer James Watt (1736–1819) patented his engine in 1769 and then developed it for locomotion.

Lord Horatio Nelson
Nelson *(see p35)* became a hero after his death at the Battle of Trafalgar fighting the French.

1720 "South Sea Bubble" bursts: many speculators ruined in securities fraud

1746 Bonnie Prince Charlie *(see p535)*, Jacobite claimant to the throne, defeated at the Battle of Culloden

1700	1715	1730	1745	1760

1714 George, Elector of Hanover, succeeds Queen Anne, ending the Stuart dynasty and giving Britain a German-speaking monarch

1721 Robert Walpole (1646–1745) becomes the first Prime Minister

George I (1660–1727)

Satirical engraving about the "South Sea Bubble", 1720

1757 Britain's first canal completed

Canal Barge (1827)
Canals were a cheap way to carry the new industrial goods but were gradually superseded by railways during the 19th century.

The attics were where children and servants slept.

The master bedroom often had a mahogany four-poster bed.

Chippendale Armchair (1760)
Thomas Chippendale (1710–79) designed elegant furniture in a style still popular today.

Furniture was often carved, depicting animal heads and legs.

Georgian Town House

Tall, terraced dwellings were built to house wealthy families. The main architects of the time were Robert Adam (see p32) and John Nash.

The servants lived and worked in the basement during the day.

Kitchen

Where to See Georgian Britain

Bath *(see pp262–5)* and Edinburgh *(see pp508–15)* are two of Britain's best-preserved Georgian towns. The Royal Crescent in Bath *(see p262 and p264)* typifies Georgian architecture and Brighton's Royal Pavilion *(see pp182–3)* is a Regency extravaganza by John Nash.

Charlotte Square *(see p508)* in Edinburgh has fine examples of Georgian architecture.

Hogarth's Gin Lane
Conditions in London's slums shocked William Hogarth (1697–1764), who made prints like this to urge social reform.

1788 First convict ships are sent to Australia

1776 American Declaration of Independence

1811–17 Riots against growing unemployment

1805 The British, led by Lord Nelson, beat Napoleon's French fleet at Battle of Trafalgar

1815 Duke of Wellington beats Napoleon at Waterloo

Caricature of Wellington (1769–1852)

| 1775 | 1790 | 1805 | 1820 |

1783 Steam-powered cotton mill invented by Sir Richard Arkwright (1732–92)

1807 Abolition of slave trade

1825 Stockton to Darlington railway opens

1811 Prince of Wales made Regent during George III's madness

1829 Catholic Emancipation Act passed

Silver tureen, 1774

Victorian Britain

When Victoria became Queen in 1837, she was only 18. Britain was in the throes of its transformation from an agricultural country to the world's most powerful industrial nation. The growth of the Empire fuelled the country's confidence and opened up markets for Britain's manufactured goods. The accelerating growth of cities created problems of health and housing and a powerful Labour movement began to emerge. But by the end of Victoria's long and popular reign in 1901, conditions had begun to improve as more people got the vote and universal education was introduced.

Florence Nightingale (1820–1910)
Known as the Lady with the Lamp, she nursed soldiers in the Crimean War and pioneered many improvements in army medical care.

Glass walls and ceiling

Prefabricated girders

Newcastle Slum (1880)
Rows of cheap houses were built for an influx of workers to the major industrial cities. The awful conditions spread disease and social discontent.

As well as silk textiles exhibits included carriages, engines, jewels, glass, plants, cutlery and sculptures.

Union Banner
Trade unions were set up to protect industrial workers against unscrupulous employers.

Ophelia by Sir John Everett Millais (1829–96)
The Pre-Raphaelite painters chose Romantic themes, reflecting a desire to escape industrial Britain.

1832 Great Reform Bill extends the vote to all male property owners

1841 London to Brighton railway makes resort accessible

Vase made for the Great Exhibition

1851 Great Exhibition

1867 Second Reform Act gives the vote to all male householders in towns

1830	1840	1850	1860

1834 Tolpuddle Martyrs transported to Australia for forming a union

1833 Factory Act forbids employment of children for more than 48 hours per week

1854–6 Britain victorious against Russia in Crimean War

1863 Opening of the London Underground

Triumph of Steam and Electricity

This picture from the *Illustrated London News* (1897) sums up the feeling of optimism engendered by industrial advances.

Elm trees were incorporated into the building along with sparrows, and sparrow hawks to control them.

Where to See Victorian Britain

The industrial cities of the Midlands and the north are built around grandiose civic, commercial and industrial buildings. Notable Victorian monuments include Manchester's Museum of Science and Industry *(see p378)* and, in London, the Victoria and Albert Museum *(see pp102–3)* and St Pancras railway station *(see 109)*.

St Pancras International station *(see p109)*, London, is known for its Victorian architecture.

Great Exhibition of 1851

The brainchild of Prince Albert, Victoria's consort, the exhibition celebrated industry, technology and the expanding British Empire. It was the biggest of its kind held up until then. Between May and October, six million people visited Joseph Paxton's lavish Crystal Palace, in London's Hyde Park. Nearly 14,000 exhibitors brought 100,000 exhibits from all over the world. In 1852 it was moved to south London where it burned down in 1936.

Cycling Craze
The bicycle, invented in 1865, became immensely popular with young people, as illustrated by this photograph of 1898.

1872 The Ballot Act introduces secret voting

1874 Benjamin Disraeli becomes Prime Minister

1884 Telephones introduced

1893 Gladstone's Irish Home Rule Bill defeated

Cartoon of Gladstone, Vanity Fair (1869)

1901 Queen Victoria dies

1870

1880

1890

1900

1877 Queen Victoria becomes Empress of India

1892 First Labour MP elected

1899–1902 Britain defeats South African Dutch settlers in Boer War

1870 Education Act makes school compulsory for children up to the age of 11

Early telephone

Britain from 1900 to 1950

When Queen Victoria's reign ended in 1901, British society threw off many of its 19th-century inhibitions, and an era of gaiety and excitement began. This was interrupted by World War I. The economic troubles that ensued, which culminated in the Depression of the 1930s, brought misery to millions. In 1939 the ambitions of Germany provoked World War II. After emerging victorious from this conflict, Britain embarked on an ambitious programme of social, educational and health reform.

Welwyn Garden City
was based on the Utopian ideals of Sir Ebenezer Howard (1850–1928), founder of the garden city movement.

Wireless
Invented by Guglielmo Marconi, radios brought news and entertainment into homes for the first time.

Suffragettes
Women marched and chained themselves to railings in their effort to get the vote; many went to prison. Women over 30 won the vote in 1919.

The Roaring Twenties
Young flappers discarded the rigid social codes of their parents and instead discovered jazz, cocktails and the Charleston.

New Towns
A string of new towns was created on the outskirts of London, planned to give residents greenery and fresh air. Welwyn Garden City was originally founded in 1919 as a self-contained community, but fast rail links turned it into a base for London commuters.

World War I
British troops in Europe dug into deep trenches protected by barbed wire and machine guns, only metres from the enemy, in a war of attrition that cost the lives of 17 million.

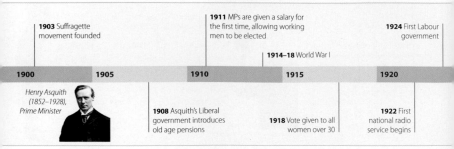

1903 Suffragette movement founded

1911 MPs are given a salary for the first time, allowing working men to be elected

1924 First Labour government

1914–18 World War I

| 1900 | 1905 | 1910 | 1915 | 1920 |

Henry Asquith (1852–1928), Prime Minister

1908 Asquith's Liberal government introduces old age pensions

1918 Vote given to all women over 30

1922 First national radio service begins

Garden cities all
had trees, ponds
and open spaces.

WYN
N CITY

TO LET
O PER ANNUM
AL PURCHASE TERMS

EN CITY HERTS
PAVEMENT. E.C.2.

Cheap housing and
the promise of a cleaner
environment attracted
many people to these
new towns.

Marching for Jobs
These men were
among thousands who
marched for their jobs
after being put out
of work in the 1920s.
The stock market
crash of 1929 and the
ensuing Depression
caused even more
unemployment.

World War II
German night-time air
raids targeted transport,
military and industrial
sites and cities, such as
Sheffield, in what was
known as the "Blitz".

Family Motoring
By the middle of the
century, more families
could afford to buy mass
produced automobiles,
like the 1950s Hillman
Minx pictured in this
advertisement.

Modern Homes
Labour-saving devices, such as
the vacuum cleaner, invented
by William Hoover in 1908, were
very popular. This was due to
the virtual disappearance of
domestic servants, as women
took jobs outside the home.

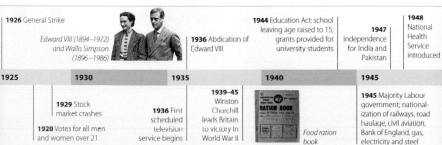

1926 General Strike

*Edward VIII (1894–1972)
and Wallis Simpson
(1896–1986)*

1936 Abdication of
Edward VIII

1944 Education Act: school
leaving age raised to 15;
grants provided for
university students

1947
Independence
for India and
Pakistan

1948
National
Health
Service
introduced

1925   1930   1935   1940   1945

1929 Stock
market crashes

1936 First
scheduled
television
service begins

1939–45
Winston
Churchill
leads Britain
to victory in
World War II

*Food ration
book*

1945 Majority Labour
government; national-
ization of railways, road
haulage, civil aviation,
Bank of England, gas,
electricity and steel

1920 Votes for all men
and women over 21

Modern Britain

Postwar Britain saw rapid cultural and social changes, with the emergence of youth culture and immigration from newly independent colonies. Membership of the European Community in 1973 and the privatization of several industries in the 1980s led to economic prosperity.

Soon after the millennium, Britain became part of an international effort against terrorism, joining the invasion of Afghanistan and Iraq. Since 2008 and the global recession, Britain has been going through a period of austerity. The nation's spirits were lifted with the 2012 London Olympic Games, but this was superseded by the divisions created by the 2016 referendum when the country voted, by a narrow majority, to leave the European Union.

1982 British troops set sail to drive the Argentinians from the British-owned Falkland Islands

1970s The outlandish clothes, hair and make-up of Punk Rockers shock the country

1960s The miniskirt takes British fashion to new heights of daring – and Flower Power arrives from California

1981 Charles, Prince of Wales, marries Lady Diana Spencer in "fairy-tale" wedding at St Paul's Cathedral

1951 Winston Churchill comes back as Prime Minister as Conservatives win general election

1965 Death penalty is abolished

1950	1960	1970	1980

1950	1960	1970	1980

1953 Elizabeth II crowned in first televised Coronation

1963 The Beatles pop group from Liverpool captures the spirit of the age with numerous chart-topping hits

1975 Drilling begins for North Sea oil

1984 Year-long miners' strike fails to stop pit closures and heralds decline in trade union power

1951 Festival of Britain lifts postwar spirits

1959 First full-length motorway, the M1, built from London to the Midlands

VOTE !

...GET BRITAIN OUT

1957 First immigrants arrive from the Caribbean by boat

1973 After years of negotiation, Britain joins the European Community

1979 The "Iron Lady" Margaret Thatcher becomes Britain's first woman Prime Minister; her right-wing Conservative government privatizes several state-owned industries

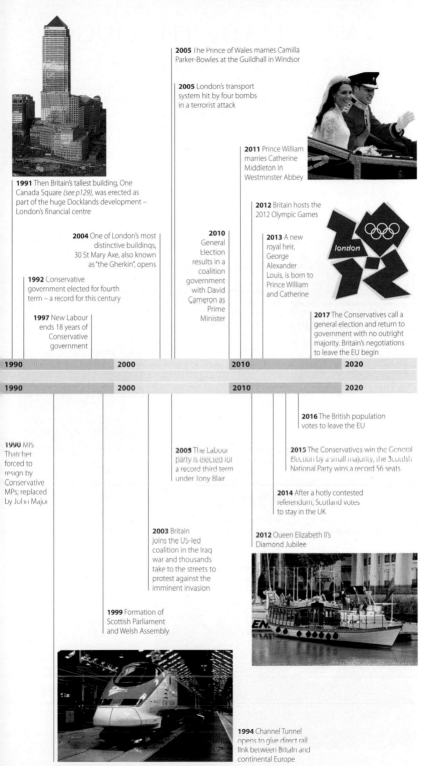

1991 Then Britain's tallest building, One Canada Square *(see p129)*, was erected as part of the huge Docklands development – London's financial centre

2005 The Prince of Wales marries Camilla Parker-Bowles at the Guildhall in Windsor

2005 London's transport system hit by four bombs in a terrorist attack

2011 Prince William marries Catherine Middleton in Westminster Abbey

2012 Britain hosts the 2012 Olympic Games

2004 One of London's most distinctive buildings, 30 St Mary Axe, also known as "the Gherkin", opens

2010 General Election results in a coalition government with David Cameron as Prime Minister

2013 A new royal heir, George Alexander Louis, is born to Prince William and Catherine

1992 Conservative government elected for fourth term – a record for this century

1997 New Labour ends 18 years of Conservative government

2017 The Conservatives call a general election and return to government with no outright majority. Britain's negotiations to leave the EU begin

1990	2000	2010	2020

1990	2000	2010	2020

2016 The British population votes to leave the EU

1990 Mrs Thatcher forced to resign by Conservative MPs; replaced by John Major

2005 The Labour party is elected for a record third term under Tony Blair

2015 The Conservatives win the General Election by a small majority, the Scottish National Party wins a record 56 seats

2014 After a hotly contested referendum, Scotland votes to stay in the UK

2003 Britain joins the US-led coalition in the Iraq war and thousands take to the streets to protest against the imminent invasion

2012 Queen Elizabeth II's Diamond Jubilee

1999 Formation of Scottish Parliament and Welsh Assembly

1994 Channel Tunnel opens to give direct rail link between Britain and continental Europe

GREAT BRITAIN THROUGH THE YEAR

Every British season has its particular charms. Most major sights are open all year round, but many secondary attractions may be closed in winter. The weather is changeable in all seasons and the visitor is as likely to experience a crisp, sunny February day as to be caught in a cold, heavy shower in July. Long periods of adverse weather and extremes of temperature are rare. Spring is characterized by daffodils and bluebells, summer by roses and autumn by the vivid colours of changing leaves. In wintertime, country vistas are visible through the bare branches of the trees. Annual events and ceremonies, many stemming from age-old traditions, reflect the attributes of the seasons.

Bluebells in spring in Angrove woodland, Wiltshire

Spring

As the days get longer and warmer, the countryside starts to come alive. At Easter many stately homes and gardens open their gates to visitors for the first time, and during the week before Whit Sunday, or Whitsun (the seventh Sunday after Easter), the Chelsea Flower Show takes place. This is the focal point of the gardening year and spurs on the nation's gardeners to prepare their summer displays. Outside the capital, many music and arts festivals mark the middle months of the year.

March
Ideal Home Show *(second week)*, Olympia, London. New products and ideas for the home.
Crufts Dog Show *(second week)*, National Exhibition Centre, Birmingham.
St Patrick's Day *(17 Mar)*. Musical events in major cities celebrate the feast day of Ireland's patron saint.
Oxford and Cambridge Boat Race *(late Mar or early Apr)*, River Thames, London.

April
Maundy Thursday *(Thursday before Easter)*. The Queen gives money to pensioners.
St George's Day *(23 April)*. English patron saint's day.

La Linea Latin Music Festival *(last 2 wks)*, London. Rising and established stars from the Latin music world perform at venues around the capital.
Antiques for Everyone *(last week Apr; also Jul & Nov)*, National Exhibition Centre, Birmingham. Largest art and antiques fair in the UK.

Water garden exhibited at the Chelsea Flower Show

May
Furry Dance Festival *(8 May)*, Helston, Cornwall. Spring celebration *(see p284)*.
Well Dressings *(Ascension Day)*, Tissington, Derbyshire *(see p341)*.
Chelsea Flower Show *(May)*, Royal Hospital, London.
Brighton Festival *(last 3 weeks)*. Performing arts.
Glyndebourne Festival Opera Season *(mid-May–end Aug)*, near Lewes, East Sussex. Opera productions.
Atholl Gathering and Highland Games *(last weekend)*, Blair Atholl, Scotland. The opening Highland Games event of the season, with classic competitions including the caber toss and hammer throw.

Yeomen of the Guard conducting the Maundy money ceremony

Bath International Music Festival *(late May)*, various venues. Arts events around the city.

Hay Festival *(end May–early Jun)*, Hay-on-Wye, Wales. A ten-day family-friendly literature and music festival.

Summer

Life moves outdoors in the summer months. Cafés and restaurants place tables on the pavements and pub customers take their drinks outside. The Queen holds garden parties for privileged guests at Buckingham Palace while, more modestly, village fêtes – which include traditional games and local stalls – are organized. Beaches and swimming pools become crowded and office workers picnic in city parks at lunch. The rose, England's national flower, bursts into bloom in millions of gardens. Cultural treats include open-air theatre performances, outdoor concerts and film screenings, a variety of music festivals, the Proms in London, the National Eisteddfod in Wales and Edinburgh's festival of the performing arts.

Deck chair at Brighton

Glastonbury music festival, a major event attracting thousands of people

June

Royal Academy of Arts Summer Exhibition *(Jun–Aug)*. Large and varied London show of new work by many artists.

Trooping the Colour *(Sat closest to 10 Jun)*, Whitehall, London. The Queen's official birthday parade.

Isle of Wight Music Festival *(mid-Jun)*. International headlining pop stars and rock groups perform at this historic music festival.

Aldeburgh Festival *(second and third weeks)*, Suffolk. Arts festival with concerts and opera.

Royal Highland Show *(third week)*, Ingliston, near Edinburgh. Agricultural show.

Glastonbury Festival *(late Jun)*, Somerset. A legendary five-day festival of contemporary music and performing arts *(see p257)*.

Leeds Castle Classical Concert *(last week Jun–early Jul)*, Leeds Castle, Kent. Open-air concerts in a picturesque setting.

Glasgow Jazz Festival *(last weekend Jun–early Jul)*, various venues. Hosts some of the biggest names in jazz.

Henley Royal Regatta *(late Jun–Jul)*, Henley-on-Thames. Rowing regatta on the Thames.

The Championships, Wimbledon *(late Jun–early Jul)*, London. The world's most prestigious tennis tournament.

July

International Eisteddfod *(first week)*, Llangollen, North Wales. International music and dance competition *(see p454)*.

Hampton Court Flower Show *(early Jul)*, Hampton Court Palace, Surrey. The world's largest flower show, with flower-filled marquees and demonstrations.

Cambridge Folk Festival *(last weekend)*. Music festival attracting top international artists.

Royal Welsh Show *(last weekend)*, Builth Wells, Wales. Agricultural show.

Sidmouth FolkWeek *(late Jul–early Aug)*, Sidmouth, Devon. A festival of traditional music, dance and craft *(see p293)*.

August

Royal National Eisteddfod *(early Aug)*. Traditional arts competitions, in Welsh *(see p439)*. Various locations.

Henry Wood Promenade Concerts *(mid-Jul–mid-Sep)*, Royal Albert Hall, London. Famous concert series popularly known as the Proms.

Edinburgh International Festival *(mid-Aug–mid-Sep)*. The largest festival of theatre, dance and music in the world *(see p513)*.

Edinburgh Festival Fringe. Alongside the festival, there are 400 shows a day.

Brecon Jazz *(mid-Aug)*, Brecon, Wales.

International Beatleweek *(last weekend)*, Liverpool. Music and entertainment related to the Fab Four *(see p381)*.

Notting Hill Carnival *(last weekend)*, London. A West Indian street carnival featuring floats, bands, Caribbean food and stalls.

Reveller in bright costume at the Notting Hill Carnival

Baskets filled with several varieties of apple from the autumn harvest

Autumn

After the heady escapism of summer, the start of the new season is marked by the various party political conferences held in October and the royal opening of Parliament. All over the country on 5 November, bonfires are lit and fireworks let off to celebrate the foiling of an attempt to blow up the Houses of Parliament by Guy Fawkes and his co-conspirators in 1605. Cornfields become golden, trees turn fiery yellow through to russet and orchards are heavy with apples and other fruits. In churches throughout the country, thanks-giving festivals mark the harvest. The shops stock up for the run-up to Christmas, their busiest time of the year.

Shot putting at Braemar

September
Blackpool Illuminations *(Sep–end Oct)*. A 5-mile (8-km) spectacle of lighting along Blackpool's seafront.
Braemar Gathering *(first Sat)*, Braemar, Scotland. One of the most prestigious of the various Highland Games. Kilted clansmen from all over the country toss cabers, shot put, dance and play the bagpipes. The royal family usually attends.
International Sheepdog Trials *(Jul–Sep)*, all over Britain, with venues changing from year to year.
Autumn Flower Show *(mid-Sep)*, Harrogate, Yorkshire. Displays by nurserymen and national flower organizations.
St Ives Festival *(second and third weeks)*, Cornwall. Open studios, exhibitions, live music, poetry and theatre take place in civic buildings, galleries, pubs and the streets of this picturesque and historic fishing village and artists' community.

October
Harvest Festivals *(whole month)*, all over Britain especially in farming areas.
Horse of the Year Show *(6–10 Oct)*, NEC, Birmingham.

Nottingham Goose Fair *(first week)*. One of Britain's oldest traditional fairs now has a funfair.
Canterbury Festival *(second and third weeks)*. Music, drama and the arts.
Brighton Early Music Festival *(end Oct)*, Sussex. Choral performances in venues across Brighton and Hove.
State Opening of Parliament *(Oct or Nov)*. The Queen goes from Buckingham Palace to Westminster in a state coach, to open the new parliamentary session.
London Film Festival *(end Oct–early Nov)*. Forum for new films, various venues.

Procession leading to the state opening of Parliament

November
Lord Mayor's Show *(second Sat)*, London. A full day of pageantry and parades, with a fireworks demonstration to round things off.
London to Brighton Veteran Car Rally *(first Sun)*. A 7am start from Hyde Park, London to Brighton, in Sussex.
Guy Fawkes Night *(5 Nov)*, fireworks and bonfires all over the country.
Remembrance Day *(second Sun)*. Services and parades at the Cenotaph in Whitehall, London, and all over Britain.
London Jazz Festival *(mid-Nov)*. A ten-day international jazz festival in venues all over the capital.
Regent Street Christmas Lights *(mid-Nov)*, London. Crowds of people gather to see the lights switched on.

Fireworks over Edinburgh at Hogmanay

Winter landscape in the Scottish Highlands, near Glencoe

Winter

Brightly coloured fairy lights and Christmas trees decorate Britain's principal shopping streets, and Christmas markets are held in many towns and cities. Carol services are held in churches across the country, and pantomime, a traditional entertainment for children deriving from the Victorian music hall, fills theatres in major towns.

Many offices close between Christmas and the New Year. Shops often reopen for the January sales on 26 December – a paradise for bargain-hunters.

Brightly lit Christmas tree at the centre of Trafalgar Square

December

Christmas Tree *(first Thu)*, Trafalgar Square, London. The tree is donated by the people of Norway and is lit by the Mayor of Oslo; this is followed by carol singing.
Carol concerts *(whole month)*, all over Britain.
Harrods Christmas Parade *(early Dec)*, London. Parade with floats to celebrate myth of Santa Claus.
The Burning of the Clocks *(21 Dec)*, Brighton, Sussex. Parades and fireworks on Brighton beach celebrating the winter solstice.
Midnight Mass *(24 Dec)*, in churches everywhere around the country.

Sprig of holly

Public Holidays

New Year's Day (1 Jan).
2 Jan (Scotland only).
Easter weekend (Mar or Apr). In England it begins on **Good Friday** and ends on **Easter Monday**; in Scotland there is no Easter Monday holiday.
May Day (usually first Mon in May).
Late Spring Bank Holiday (last Mon in May).
Bank Holiday (first Mon in Aug, Scotland only).
August Bank Holiday (last Mon in Aug, except Scotland).
Christmas and Boxing Day (25–26 Dec).

January

Hogmanay and **New Year** *(31 Dec, 1 Jan)*, Scottish celebrations.
Burns Night *(25 Jan)*. Scots everywhere celebrate poet Robert Burns' birth with poetry, feasting and drinking.

February

Chinese New Year *(late Jan or early Feb)*. Lion dances, firecrackers and processions in Chinatown, London.

Morris dancing on May Day in Midhurst, Sussex

The Sporting Year

Many of the world's major competitive sports, including football, cricket and tennis, were invented in Britain. Originally devised as recreation for the wealthy, they have since entered the arena of mass entertainment. Some, however, such as the Royal Ascot race meeting and Wimbledon tennis tournament, are still valued as much for their social prestige as for the sport itself. Other delightful sporting events in Britain take place at a local level: village cricket, point-to-point racing and the Highland Games are all popular amateur events.

Royal Ascot is the four day social highlight of the horse-racing year. The high class of the thoroughbred is matched by the high style of the fashions, with royalty attending

Oxford and Cambridge Boat Race, first held in 1829 at Henley, has become a national event, with the two university eights now battling it out between Putney and Mortlake on the Thames.

The FA Cup Final is the apex of the football season.

Derby Day horse races, Epsom

January	February	March	April	May	June

Cheltenham Gold Cup steeplechase *(see p332)*

Grand National steeplechase, Aintree, Liverpool *(see p616)*

Rugby League Cup Final, Wembley

Embassy World Snooker Championships, Sheffield

Wimbledon Lawn Tennis Tournment is the world's most prestigious lawn tennis championship.

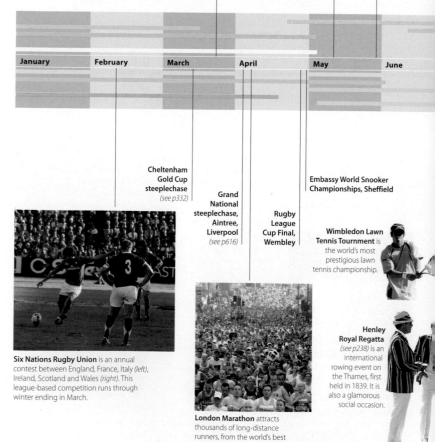

Six Nations Rugby Union is an annual contest between England, France, Italy *(left)*, Ireland, Scotland and Wales *(right)*. This league-based competition runs through winter ending in March.

London Marathon attracts thousands of long-distance runners, from the world's best to fancy-dressed fundraisers.

Henley Royal Regatta *(see p238)* is an international rowing event on the Thames, first held in 1839. It is also a glamorous social occasion.

British Grand Prix, held at Silverstone, is Britain's round of the Formula One World Championship.

British Open Golf Championship, a major golf event, is held at one of several British courses. Here, Luke Donald swings.

Tickets and Touts

For many big sporting events, the only official source of tickets is the club concerned. Booking agencies may offer hard to get tickets though often at high prices. Unauthorized touts may lurk at popular events but their expensive tickets are not always valid. Check carefully.

Tickets for the Grand Prix

The Twenty20 cricket final is played in September, marking the end of the season for this fast-paced variant of the sport.

Oxford versus Cambridge rugby union, Twickenham

Cowes Week, a yachting festival on the Isle of Wight.

Horse of the Year Show brings together top showjumpers to compete on a tough indoor course (see p68).

July	August	September	October	November	December

European Show Jumping Championships at Hickstead

Braemar Gathering (see p68)

British Figure Skating and Ice Dance Championships are a feast of elegance on ice (various venues).

Winmau World Masters Darts Championships

Gold Cup Humber powerboat race, Hull

Cartier International Polo, at the Guards Club, Windsor, is one of the main events for this peculiarly British game, played mainly by royalty and army officers.

Key to Sport Seasons

- Cricket
- River fishing
- Football (soccer)
- Hunting and shooting
- Rugby (union and league)
- Flat racing
- Jump racing
- Athletics – track and field
- Road running and cross-country
- Polo

The Climate of Great Britain

Britain has a temperate climate. No region is far from the sea, which exerts a moderating influence on temperatures. Seldom are winter nights colder than -15°C, even in the far north, or summer days warmer than 30°C in the south and west: a much narrower range than in most European countries. Despite Britain's reputation, the average annual rainfall is quite low – 108 cm (42 inches) – and heavy rain is rare. The Atlantic coast is warmed by the Gulf Stream, making the west slightly warmer, though wetter, than the east.

The Highlands
and Islands

The
Lowland

Lancashire
and
the Lakes

North
Wales

South
and
Mid-
Wales

Wessex

Devon and
Cornwall

LANCASHIRE AND THE LAKES

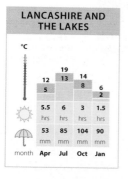

month	Apr	Jul	Oct	Jan
°C (max)	12	19	14	6
°C (min)	5	13	8	2
sunshine	5.5 hrs	6 hrs	3 hrs	1.5 hrs
rainfall	53 mm	85 mm	104 mm	90 mm

THE HEART OF ENGLAND

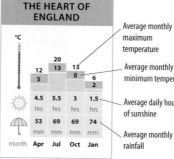

month	Apr	Jul	Oct	Jan
°C (max)	12	20	13	6
°C (min)	5	13	8	2
sunshine	4.5 hrs	5.5 hrs	3 hrs	1.5 hrs
rainfall	53 mm	69 mm	69 mm	74 mm

Average monthly
maximum
temperature

Average monthly
minimum temperature

Average daily hours
of sunshine

Average monthly
rainfall

SOUTH AND MID-WALES

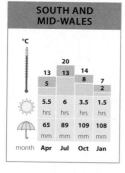

month	Apr	Jul	Oct	Jan
°C (max)	13	20	14	7
°C (min)	5	13	8	2
sunshine	5.5 hrs	6 hrs	3.5 hrs	1.5 hrs
rainfall	65 mm	89 mm	109 mm	108 mm

NORTH WALES

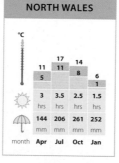

month	Apr	Jul	Oct	Jan
°C (max)	11	17	14	6
°C (min)	5	11	8	1
sunshine	3 hrs	3.5 hrs	2.5 hrs	1.5 hrs
rainfall	144 mm	206 mm	261 mm	252 mm

DEVON AND CORNWALL

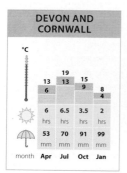

month	Apr	Jul	Oct	Jan
°C (max)	13	19	15	8
°C (min)	6	13	9	4
sunshine	6 hrs	6.5 hrs	3.5 hrs	2 hrs
rainfall	53 mm	70 mm	91 mm	99 mm

WESSEX

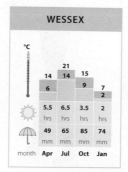

month	Apr	Jul	Oct	Jan
°C (max)	14	21	15	7
°C (min)	6	14	9	2
sunshine	5.5 hrs	6.5 hrs	3.5 hrs	2 hrs
rainfall	49 mm	65 mm	85 mm	74 mm

THAMES VALLEY

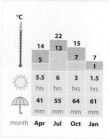

month	Apr	Jul	Oct	Jan
°C (max)	14	22	15	7
°C (min)	5	13	7	1
sunshine	5.5 hrs	6 hrs	3 hrs	1.5 hrs
rainfall	41 mm	55 mm	64 mm	61 mm

THE HIGHLANDS AND ISLANDS

°C				
	11	17	13	7
	3	10	7	1
☀	4.5 hrs	3.5 hrs	2 hrs	1 hrs
☂	111 mm	137 mm	215 mm	200 mm
month	Apr	Jul	Oct	Jan

THE LOWLANDS

°C				
	11	19	14	6
	4	11	7	1
☀	5 hrs	5.5 hrs	3 hrs	1.5 hrs
☂	38 mm	69 mm	56 mm	47 mm
month	Apr	Jul	Oct	Jan

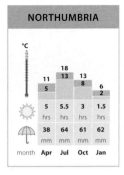

NORTHUMBRIA

°C				
	11	18	13	6
	5	13	8	2
☀	5 hrs	5.5 hrs	3 hrs	1.5 hrs
☂	38 mm	64 mm	61 mm	62 mm
month	Apr	Jul	Oct	Jan

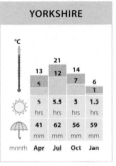

YORKSHIRE

°C				
	13	21	14	6
	5	12	7	1
☀	5 hrs	5.5 hrs	3 hrs	1.5 hrs
☂	41 mm	62 mm	56 mm	59 mm
month	Apr	Jul	Oct	Jan

EAST MIDLANDS

°C				
	13	21	14	6
	4	12	6	0
☀	5 hrs	5.5 hrs	3 hrs	1.5 hrs
☂	38 mm	58 mm	56 mm	56 mm
month	Apr	Jul	Oct	Jan

Northumbria
- Newcastle upon Tyne

Yorkshire
- York

Manchester

East Midlands

Birmingham
Heart of England

Norwich

Cambridge

East Anglia

Thames Valley

Oxford

London

Downs and Channel Coast

Dover

Portsmouth

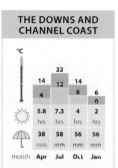

THE DOWNS AND CHANNEL COAST

°C				
	14	22	14	6
	4	12	6	0
☀	5.8 hrs	7.3 hrs	4 hrs	2 hrs
☂	38 mm	58 mm	56 mm	56 mm
month	Apr	Jul	Oct	Jan

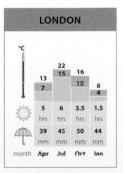

LONDON

°C				
	13	22	16	8
	7	15	10	4
☀	5 hrs	6 hrs	3.5 hrs	1.5 hrs
☂	39 mm	45 mm	50 mm	44 mm
month	Apr	Jul	Oct	Jan

EAST ANGLIA

°C				
	14	22	15	7
	4	12	6	1
☀	5 hrs	6 hrs	3.5 hrs	2 hrs
☂	37 mm	58 mm	51 mm	49 mm
month	Apr	Jul	Oct	Jan

LONDON

Introducing London   **76–79**

West End and Westminster   **80–97**

South Kensington and
  Hyde Park   **98–105**

Regent's Park and
  Bloomsbury   **106–111**

The City and Southwark   **112–125**

Further Afield   **126–130**

London Street Finder   **131–151**

Shops and Markets   **152–155**

Entertainment   **156–159**

London at a Glance

The largest city in Europe, London is home to over eight million people and covers 625 sq miles (1,600 sq km). The capital was founded by the Romans in the first century AD as a convenient administrative and communications centre and a port for trade with Continental Europe. For a thousand years it has been the principal residence of British monarchs as well as the centre of business and government, and it is rich in historic buildings and treasures from all periods. In addition to its diverse range of museums, galleries and churches, London is an exciting contemporary city, packed with a vast array of entertainments and shops. The attractions on offer are virtually endless but this map highlights the most important of those described in detail on the following pages.

Buckingham Palace *(pp90–91)* is the London home and office of the monarchy. The Changing of the Guard takes place on the palace forecourt.

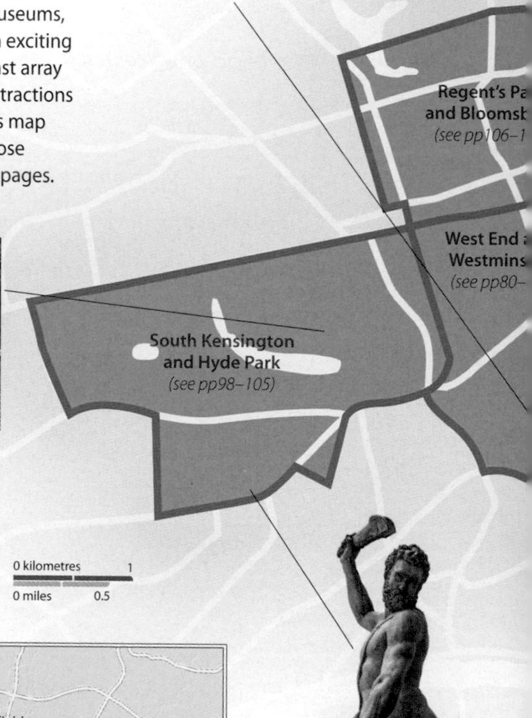

Regent's Pa and Bloomsb *(see pp106–1*

West End a Westmins *(see pp80–*

South Kensington and Hyde Park *(see pp98–105)*

Hyde Park *(p105)*, the largest central London park, was opened to the public in the early 17th century. It features restaurants, an art gallery, Speakers' Corner and the Princess Diana Memorial Fountain. The highlight of the park is the Serpentine Lake.

0 kilometres   1

0 miles   0.5

Greater London

Watford

Enfield

Barnet

Harrow

Wembley   Hampstead

Hackney   **London City Airport**

Romford

Ealing

Acton   **LONDON**

Heathrow Airport

Richmond

Greenwich

Dulwich

Dartford

Kingston upon Thames   Wimbledon

Beckenham

Bromley

Sutton   Croydon

Epsom

Thames

0 kilometres   15

0 miles   15

The Victoria and Albert Museum *(pp102–3)* is the world's largest museum of decorative arts. This marble sculpture (c.1560) is by Giambologna.

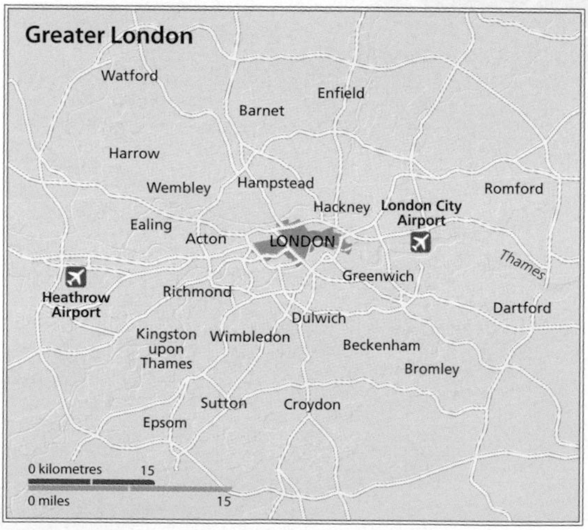

◀ Tower Bridge over the River Thames, with the Shard in the background

The British Museum's
(pp110–11) vast collection of antiquities from all over the world includes this Portland Vase from the 1st century BC.

The National Gallery's *(pp86–7)* world-famous collection of paintings includes works such as *Venus and Mars* (c.1485) by Sandro Botticelli.

The City and Southwark
(see pp112–125)

River Thames

St Paul's *(pp118–19)* huge dome is the cathedral's most distinctive feature. Three galleries around the dome give spectacular views of London.

Westminster Abbey *(pp96–7)* has glorious medieval architecture and has tombs and monuments to some of Britain's greatest public figures.

The Tower of London *(pp122–3)* is most famous as the prison where enemies of the Crown were executed. The Tower houses the Crown Jewels, including the Imperial State Crown.

Tate Britain *(p95)* displays an outstanding collection of British art ranging from stylized Elizabethan portraiture, such as *The Cholmondeley Ladies*, to cutting-edge installation and film.

London's Parks and Gardens

Whether it's a tree-filled square in Bloomsbury or one of the large Royal Parks, you are never far from a green space in London. Some are ancient Crown lands, and some are commons (land historically owned by the general public). Others were created from the gardens of private houses or disused land. All have their own particular charm and character, from the intimacy of the Chelsea Physic Garden to the rolling acres of Hampstead Heath. Londoners make the most of these open spaces – for exercise, entertainment or simply escaping the bustle of the city streets.

Holland Park
This haven of green in busy west London offers visitors acres of peaceful woodland, an open-air theatre and a café *(see pp126–7)*.

Kew Gardens
The world's premier botanic garden, Kew has an amazing variety of plants from all over the world. The living collections are complemented by Victorian glasshouses, a pagoda and a treetop walk *(see p130)*.

0 kilometres 1
0 miles 0.5

Historic Cemeteries

In the late 1830s, a ring of private cemeteries was established around London to ease the pressure on the monstrously overcrowded and unhealthy burial grounds of the inner city. Today the cemeteries, notably Highgate *(see p128)*, Kensal Green and Abney Park, are well worth visiting for their grand monuments and mausoleums.

Memorial to Robert William Siever, Kensal Green

Richmond Park
London's largest royal park, Richmond is designated a national nature reserve and features roaming deer and magnificent river views *(see p130)*.

Hampstead Heath is a breezy open space embracing a variety of landscapes (see p128).

Regent's Park

Surrounded by John Nash's graceful buildings, this is one of London's most civilized retreats. It is home to a large boating lake, an open-air theatre and ZSL London Zoo (see p108).

St James's Park

In the heart of the West End, this park is a popular escape for office workers. It is also a reserve for wildfowl.

Battersea Park is a pleasant riverside spot with a man made boating lake.

Green Park, with its shady trees and benches, offers a cool, restful spot bordering Buckingham Palace.

Greenwich Park

Home to the National Maritime Museum and the Queen's House, Greenwich Park has fine views from the Old Royal Observatory on the hilltop (see p129).

Hyde Park and Kensington Gardens Hyde Park features a recreational lake, while neighbouring Kensington Gardens is home to the Albert Memorial (see p105).

London Squares

From the 17th to the late 19th century, many houses in the more exclusive areas of central London, such as Bloomsbury, were laid out as squares, with a railed off piazza or garden in the centre, surrounded by roads and buildings. Many of these squares still exist today, and most are open to the public. Beautifully maintained, they provide small green oases for visitors and passersby alike.

Trees in bloom in Russell Square Gardens, Bloomsbury

WEST END AND WESTMINSTER

The West End is the city's social and cultural centre and the London home of the royal family. Stretching from the edge of Hyde Park to Covent Garden, the district bustles all day and late into the night. Whether you're looking for art, history, street life or café culture, it is the most rewarding area in which to begin an exploration of the city. Westminster has been at the centre of political and religious power for a thousand years. In the 11th century, King Canute founded Westminster Palace and Edward the Confessor built Westminster Abbey, where all English monarchs since 1066 have been crowned. As modern government developed, the great offices of state were established in the area.

Sights at a Glance

Historic Streets and Buildings
1 Covent Garden Piazza and Central Market
3 Royal Opera House
9 Piccadilly Circus
11 Ritz Hotel
13 The Mall
14 *Buckingham Palace pp90–91*
16 Royal Mews
17 Churchill War Rooms
18 Downing Street
19 Banqueting House
20 *Houses of Parliament p94*

Museums and Galleries
2 London Transport Museum
4 Somerset House

7 *National Gallery pp86–7*
8 National Portrait Gallery
10 Royal Academy of Arts
15 The Queen's Gallery
22 Tate Britain

Churches
12 Queen's Chapel
21 *Westminster Abbey pp96–7*

Attractions
5 London Eye
6 London Dungeon

See also Street Finder maps 10, 11, 18, 19

For keys to symbols *see back flap*

Street-by-Street: Covent Garden

Until 1973, Covent Garden was an area of decaying streets and warehouses, which only came alive after dark when the fruit and vegetable market traders packed up for the day. Since then the Victorian market and elegant buildings nearby have been converted into stylish shops, restaurants, bars and cafés, creating an animated district which attracts a lively young crowd, night and day.

Seven Dials is a replica of a 17th-century monument marking the crossroads.

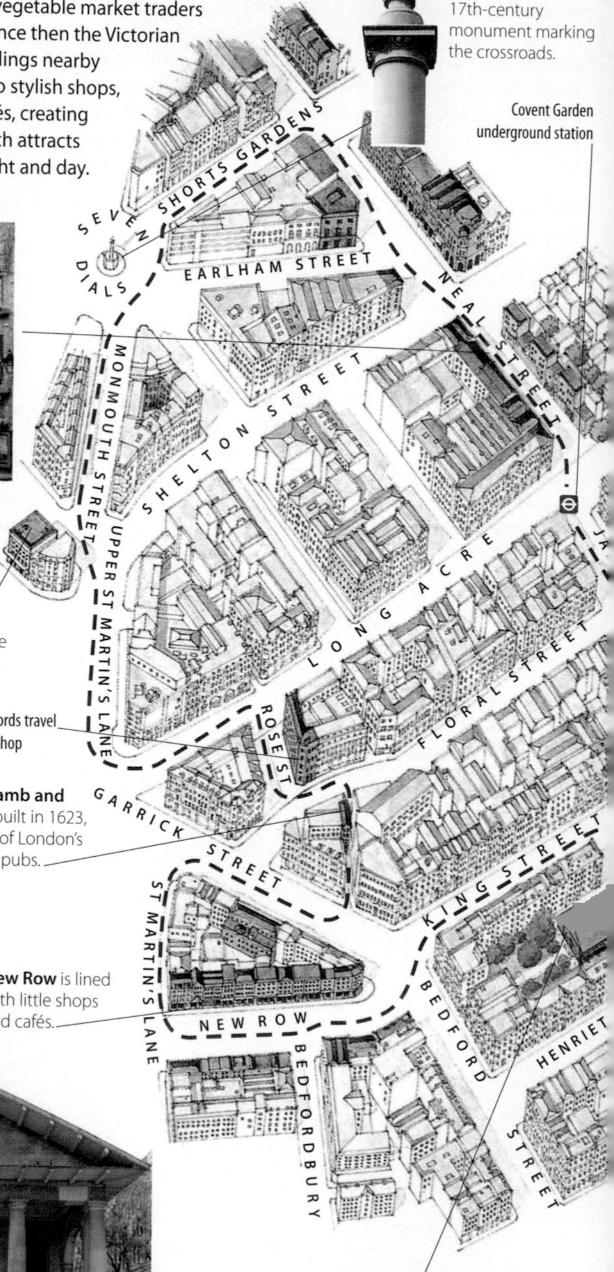

Covent Garden underground station

SEVEN DIALS

SHORTS GARDENS

EARLHAM STREET

NEAL STREET

MONMOUTH STREET

SHELTON STREET

UPPER ST MARTIN'S LANE

LONG ACRE

FLORAL STREET

ROSE ST

GARRICK STREET

ST MARTIN'S LANE

KING STREET

BEDFORD STREET

NEW ROW

BEDFORDBURY

HENRIET

STREET

Neal Street and Neal's Yard are lined with many specialist shops converted from former warehouses.

St Martin's Theatre *(see p157)* is home to the world's longest running play, *The Mousetrap*.

Stanfords travel bookshop

The Lamb and Flag, built in 1623, is one of London's oldest pubs.

New Row is lined with little shops and cafés.

St Paul's Church was designed in 1633 by Inigo Jones *(see p57)*, in the style of the Italian Renaissance architect, Andrea Palladio. Jones also designed the original Covent Garden Piazza.

For hotels and restaurants in this area see p560 and pp582–3

3 Royal Opera House Some of the world's greatest opera singers and ballet dancers have performed at the Royal Opera House.

Locator Map
See Street Finder map 11

Key

— Suggested route

0 metres 100
0 yards 100

2 London Transport Museum
This museum's intriguing collection brings to life the history of the city's tubes, buses and trains. It also has fine examples of 20th-century commercial art.

1 ★ Covent Garden Piazza and Central Market
Shops and cafés fill the piazza and market.

Jubilee Market

● Covent Garden Piazza and Central Market

Covent Garden WC2. **Map** 11 C2.
● Covent Garden. cobbled streets. Street performers in the Piazza: 10am–dusk daily. **coventgarden.london**

The 17th-century architect Inigo Jones (see p57) originally planned the Piazza in Covent Garden as an elegant residential square, modelled on the piazza in the Tuscan town of Livorno, which he had seen under construction during his travels in Italy. For a brief period, the Piazza became one of the most fashionable addresses in London, but it was superseded by the even grander St James's Square (see p89), which lies to the southwest. Today, the buildings on and around the Piazza are almost entirely Victorian.

The covered central market was designed by Charles Fowler in 1833 for fruit and vegetable wholesalers, the glass and iron roof anticipating the giant rail termini built later in the century – for instance, St Pancras (see p109) and Waterloo. The market soon outgrew its new home, and in 1973 it moved to a new site in south London, and over the next two decades Covent Garden was redeveloped. The covered market now makes a magnificent shell for an array of small shops selling designer clothes, books, arts, crafts, decorative items and antiques, surrounded by bustling market stalls that continue south in the neighbouring Jubilee Hall, which was built in 1903.

The colonnaded Bedford Chambers, on the north side, gives a hint of Inigo Jones's plan, although even they are not original: they were rebuilt and partially modified in 1879.

Street entertainment is a well-loved tradition in the area; in 1662, diarist Samuel Pepys wrote of watching a Punch and Judy show under the portico of St Paul's Church. This, along with the many shops, cafés, restaurants and market stalls, means Covent Garden remains one of London's liveliest districts.

METRO-LAND

PRICE TWO-PENCE

Poster by Michael Reilly (1929),
London Transport Museum

❷ London Transport Museum

Covent Garden Piazza WC2.
Map 11 C2. **Tel** 020 7379 6344.
🚇 Covent Garden. **Open** 10am–
6pm Sat–Thu, 11am–6pm Fri. 🎦
🎟 phone in advance. ♿ 🖥
🌐 **ltmuseum.co.uk**

This collection of buses, trams
and underground trains ranges
from the earliest horse-drawn
omnibuses to a present-day
Hoppa bus. Housed in the
Victorian Flower Market of
Covent Garden built in 1872,
the museum is particularly
good for children, who can sit
in the driver's seat of a bus or
an underground train, operate
signals and chat to an actor
playing a 19th-century tube-
tunnel miner.

London's bus and train
companies have long been

prolific patrons of artists,
and the museum holds a
fine collection of 19th- and
20th-century commercial art.
Copies of some of the best
works by distinguished artists,
such as Paul Nash and Graham
Sutherland, are on sale in the
shop. Original works can be
seen at the museum's depot
in Acton.

❸ Royal Opera House

Covent Garden WC2. **Map** 11 C2.
Tel 020 7304 4000. 🚇 Covent Garden.
Open for performances and guided
tours (phone to check). 🎦 ♿ 🎟 🎦
🌐 **roh.org.uk**

The first theatre on this site was
built in 1732, and staged plays
as well as concerts. However,
the building was destroyed by
fire in 1808 and again in 1856.
The present structure was
designed in 1858 by E M Barry.
John Flaxman's portico frieze,
depicting tragedy and comedy,
survived from the previous
building of 1809.

The Opera House is home
to the Royal Opera and Royal
Ballet companies. After two
years of renovation the
building reopened in the new
millennium, complete with a
second auditorium and new
rehearsal rooms. Backstage
tours are available, and once a
month visitors can watch the
Royal Ballet rehearse.

❹ Somerset House

Strand WC2. **Map** 11 D2. **Tel** 020 7845
4600. 🚇 Temple. Most areas: **Open**
10am–6pm daily; check website for
more specific info. **Closed** 1 Jan, 24–
26 Dec. 🌐 **somersethouse.org.uk**
Ice rink: **Open** two months in winter.
🎦 🖥 Courtauld Institute of Art
Gallery: **Tel** 020 7848 2777. ♿
🖊 🖥 🎦 🌐 **courtauld.ac.uk**
Tom's Kitchen: **Tel** 020 7845 4646.

Designed in 1770 by William
Chambers, Somerset House
presents London's most prestigious collection of Impressionist
art in the **Courtauld Gallery** and
excellent temporary exhibitions
in the **Embankment Galleries**.

The courtyard forms an
attractive piazza (which
becomes an ice rink in winter),
and the riverside terrace has a
café. Tom's Kitchen is also highly
regarded, and Tom's Deli is a
great spot for lunch. Located
in Somerset House but famous
in its own right is the Courtauld
Institute of Art Gallery, which
includes important Impressionist
and Post-Impressionist works by
artists such as Manet, Renoir and
Cézanne. In 2008 the riverside
Embankment Galleries were
opened. Occupying 750 sq m
(900 sq yd) of exhibition space
on the two lower floors, the
changing programme covers
a broad range of contemporary
arts, including photography,
design, fashion and architecture.

❺ London Eye

Jubilee Gardens, South Bank SE1.
Map 12 D4. **Tel** 0870 990 8883 (information); 0871 781 3000 (booking –
recommended in summer as tickets
sell out days in advance). 🚇 Waterloo,
Westminster. 🚌 11, 24, 211. **Open**
Apr–Sep: 10am–8:30pm daily (to
9:30pm on select days); Oct–Mar:
11am–6pm daily. **Closed** mid-Jan
(for maintenance), 25 Dec. 🎦 Pick up
tickets at County Hall (adjacent to Eye)
at least 30 mins before boarding time.
♿ 🖥 🎦 🌐 **londoneye.com**

The London Eye is a 135-m
(443-ft) observation wheel that
was installed on the South Bank
to mark the Millennium. Its
enclosed passenger capsules
offer a gentle, 30-minute ride as

Soho and Chinatown

Lion dancer in
February's Chinese
New Year celebrations

Soho has been renowned for pleasures of the
table, the flesh and the intellect ever since it
was first developed in the late 17th century.
At first a fashionable residential area, it declined
when high society shifted west to Mayfair and
immigrants from Europe moved into its narrow
streets. Furniture-makers and tailors set up shop
here and were joined in the late 19th century by
pubs, nightclubs, restaurants and brothels. In the
1960s, Hong Kong Chinese moved into the area
around Gerrard and Lisle streets and they created
an aromatic Chinatown, packed with many
restaurants and food shops. Soho's raffish reputation has long attracted
artists and writers, ranging from the 18th-century essayist Thomas de
Quincey to poet Dylan Thomas and painter Francis Bacon. Although
strip joints and peep shows remain, Soho has enjoyed something of
a renaissance, and today is full of stylish and lively bars and restaurants.

the wheel makes a full turn, with breathtaking views over London and for up to 26 miles (42 km) around. Towering over one of the world's most familiar riverscapes, it has understandably captured the hearts of Londoners and visitors alike, and is one of the city's most popular attractions. Trips on the wheel are on the hour and half-hour.

The London Eye, towering over the capital's South Bank

❻ London Dungeon

Riverside Building, County Hall, Westminster Bridge Rd SE1. **Map** 11 C5. **Tel** 0871 423 2240. ⊖ Waterloo, Westminster. **Open** 10am–5pm Mon–Fri (from 11am Thu), 10am–6pm Sat & Sun; open till later at holiday times. **Closed** 25 Dec. 🎟 book in advance to avoid queues. 🚻 one wheelchair user per tour. 🌐 thedungeons.com/london

This museum is a great hit with adults and children, illustrating many of the most bloodthirsty events in 1,000 years of London's history within a 110-minute tour. Guy Fawkes's attempt to blow up the Houses of Parliament, Jack the Ripper's reign of terror, and Great Plague-carrying rats are all covered. There are also two state-of-the-art thrill rides. Henry's Wrath is a boat trip towards execution, as ordered by a virtual Henry VIII; and Drop Dead sees visitors plunged three storeys in the pitch dark.

❼ National Gallery

See pp86–7.

❽ National Portrait Gallery

2 St Martin's Place WC2. **Map** 11 B3. **Tel** 020 7306 0055. ⊖ Charing Cross, Leicester Sq. **Open** 10am–6pm Sat–Wed, 10am–9pm Thu & Fri. **Closed** 24–26 Dec. 🎟🚻📷📖📷 🌐 npg.org.uk

This museum celebrates Britain's history through portraits, photographs and sculptures; subjects include the royal family, artists, musicians, politicians and writers. The top-floor restaurant has fabulous views over Trafalgar Square.

❾ Piccadilly Circus

W1. **Map** 11 A3. ⊖ Piccadilly Circus.

Dominated by neon billboards, Piccadilly Circus is a hectic traffic junction surrounded by shops and restaurants. It began as an early 19th-century crossroads between Piccadilly and John Nash's Regent Street. It was briefly an elegant space, edged by stucco façades, but by 1910 the first electric advertisements had been installed. For years people have congregated at its centre, beneath the iconic winged statue of the Shaftesbury Memorial Fountain, often mistakenly called Eros, which was erected in 1892.

❿ Royal Academy of Arts

Burlington House, Piccadilly W1. **Map** 10 F3. **Tel** 020 7300 8000. ⊖ Piccadilly Circus, Green Park. **Open** 10am–6pm Sat–Thu, 10am–10pm Fri. **Closed** Good Fri, 24–26 Dec. 🎟📷 free, usually noon–1pm Tue–Sun. 🎟🚻 📷📖 🌐 royalacademy.org.uk

Founded in 1768, the Royal Academy is best known for

its summer exhibition, which is an annual event and comprises a rewarding mix of around 1,200 new works by established and unknown painters, sculptors and architects. In 2018, the Royal Academy celebrated the event's 250th anniversary. During the rest of the year, the gallery shows prestigious touring exhibitions from around the world, and the courtyard in front of Burlington House, one of the West End's few surviving mansions from the early 18th century, is often filled with people waiting to get in.

An exceptional permanent collection (not all on display) includes one work by each current and former Academician; the highlights are displayed in the Madejski Rooms.

⓫ Ritz Hotel

Piccadilly W1. **Map** 10 F3. **Tel** 020 7493 8181. ⊖ Green Park. 🚻 📷 See Where to Stay p560. 🌐 theritzlondon.com

César Ritz, the Swiss hotelier who inspired the word "ritzy", had virtually settled down to a quiet retirement by 1906 when this hotel was built and named after him. The colonnaded front of the château-style building was erected to suggest just the merest whiff of Paris, where the grandest hotels were to be found at the turn of the century. It still maintains its Edwardian air of fin de siècle opulence and sophisticated grandeur, and is a popular venue for afternoon tea (reservations are required). A touch of soigné danger may be found in the casino.

The courtyard in front of the Royal Academy of Arts

❼ National Gallery

The National Gallery is London's leading art museum, with over 2,300 paintings, most on permanent display. It has flourished since 1824, when the House of Commons agreed to purchase 38 major paintings. The collection comprises paintings in the Western European tradition from late medieval times to the early 20th century by artists including Botticelli, Leonardo da Vinci, Titian, Rembrandt, Velázquez, Monet, and van Gogh. To the left of the main gallery is the Sainsbury Wing, financed by the family behind the supermarket chain and completed in 1991. It houses the Early Renaissance collection.

Samson and Delilah (c.1609–10)
This stunning, dramatic painting is by Peter Paul Rubens (1577–1640).

The Annunciation
This refined work of the early 1450s, by Fra Filippo Lippi, forms part of the gallery's exceptional Italian Renaissance collection.

The Arnolfini Portrait
Jan van Eyck (c.1385–1441), one of the pioneers of oil painting, shows his mastery of colour, texture, and minute detail in this portrait of 1434.

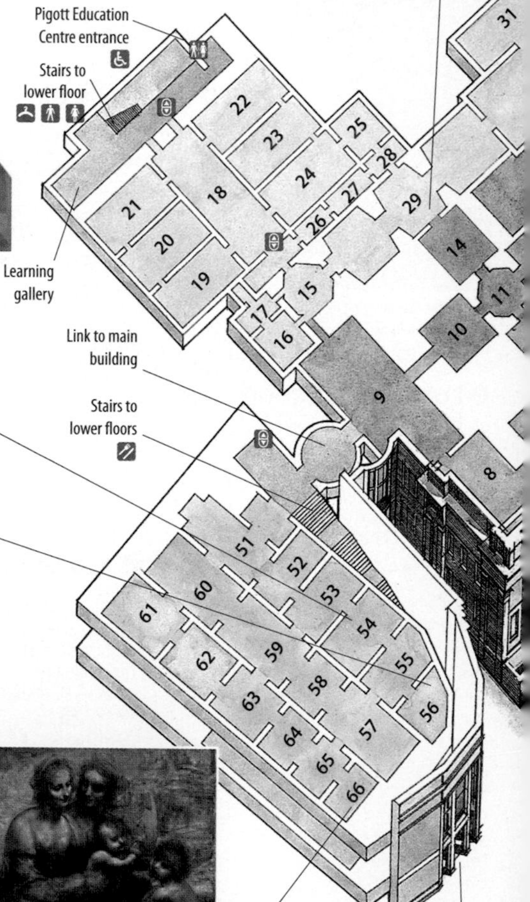

Pigott Education Centre entrance

Stairs to lower floor

Learning gallery

Link to main building

Stairs to lower floors

Entrance to Sainsbury Wing

Key to floorplan

- ▢ 13th- to 15th-century paintings
- ▢ 16th-century paintings
- ▢ 17th-century paintings
- ▢ 18th- to early 20th-century paintings
- ▢ Special exhibitions
- ▢ Non-exhibition space

★ **"The Burlington House Cartoon" (c.1499–1500)**
This composition by Leonardo da Vinci depicts the Virgin and Child, St Anne and St John the Baptist.

For hotels and restaurants in this area see p560 and pp582–3

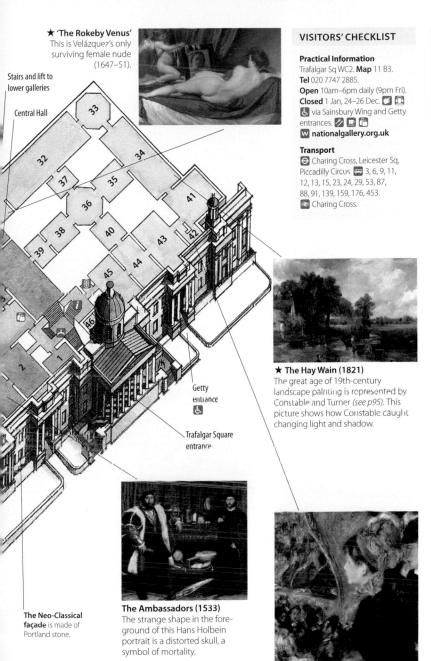

★ **'The Rokeby Venus'**
This is Velázquez's only surviving female nude (1647–51).

Stairs and lift to lower galleries

Central Hall

★ **The Hay Wain (1821)**
The great age of 19th-century landscape painting is represented by Constable and Turner (see p95). This picture shows how Constable caught changing light and shadow.

Getty entrance ♿

Trafalgar Square entrance

The Neo-Classical façade is made of Portland stone.

The Ambassadors (1533)
The strange shape in the foreground of this Hans Holbein portrait is a distorted skull, a symbol of mortality.

At the Theatre (1876–7)
Renoir was one of the greatest painters of the Impressionist movement. The theatre was a popular subject among artists of the time.

Gallery Guide

Most of the collection is housed on one floor. The paintings hang chronologically, with the earliest works, 1250–1500, in the Sainsbury Wing. Lesser paintings of all periods are displayed on the lower floor of the main building. There is a restaurant on the first floor in the Sainsbury Wing.

Street-by-Street: Piccadilly and St James's

As soon as Henry VIII built St James's Palace in the 1530s, the surrounding area became the centre of fashionable court life. Today Piccadilly is a bustling commercial street full of shopping arcades, eateries and cinemas, contrasting with St James's, to the south, which is still the domain of the wealthy and the influential.

St James's Church was designed by Sir Christopher Wren in 1684.

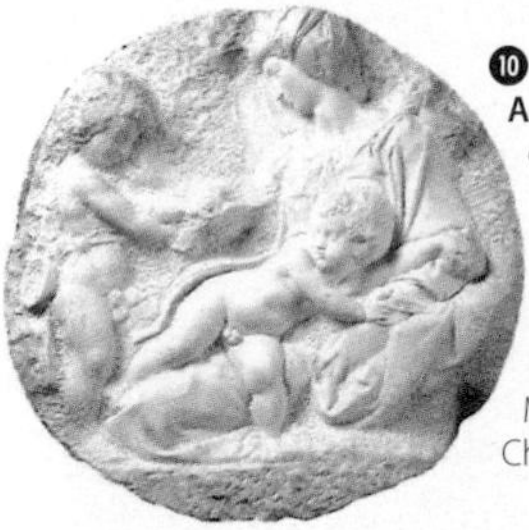

⑩ ★ Royal Academy of Arts
The permanent art collection here includes this Michelangelo relief of the Madonna and Child (1505).

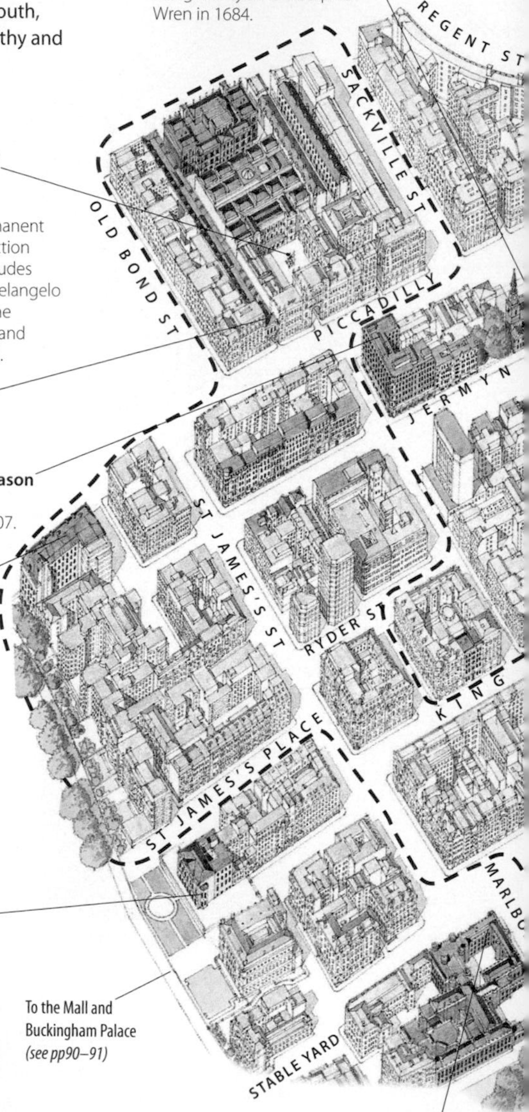

Burlington Arcade, an opulent covered walk, has fine shops and beadles on patrol.

Fortnum & Mason
(see p152) was founded in 1707.

⑪ The Ritz
César Ritz founded one of London's most famous hotels in 1906.

Spencer House, restored to its 18th-century splendour, contains fine period furniture and paintings. This Palladian palace was completed in 1766 for the 1st Earl Spencer, an ancestor of the late Princess of Wales.

To the Mall and Buckingham Palace
(see pp90–91)

St James's Palace was built on the site of a leper hospital.

OLD BOND ST
REGENT ST
SACKVILLE ST
PICCADILLY
JERMYN
ST JAMES'S ST
RYDER ST
KING
ST JAMES'S PLACE
MARLBO
STABLE YARD

9 ★ Piccadilly Circus

The crowds and dazzling neon lights make this the West End's focal point.

Locator Map

See Street Finder maps 10, 11

Key

— Suggested route

| 0 metres | 100 |
| 0 yards | 100 |

Piccadilly underground station

Jermyn Street has elegant shops selling antiques, unusual gifts and men's clothing.

Pall Mall is a street of gentlemen's clubs, which admit only members and their guests.

St James's Square has long been the most fashionable address in London.

12 Queen's Chapel

This was the first Classical church in England.

Royal Opera Arcade is lined with quality shops. Designed by John Nash, it was completed in 1818.

12 Queen's Chapel

Marlborough Rd SW1. **Map** 11 A4.
Tel 020 7930 4832. 🚇 Green Park.
Open to the public for Sun services (except Aug & Sep): 8:30am, 11:15am. ♿

The sumptuous Queen's Chapel was designed by Inigo Jones for the Infanta of Spain, the intended bride of Charles I *(see pp56–7)*. Work started in 1623 but ceased when the marriage negotiations were shelved. The chapel was completed in 1627 for Charles's eventual queen, Henrietta Maria. It was the first church in England to be built in a Classical style, with a coffered ceiling based on a reconstruction by Palladio of an ancient Roman temple.

Queen's Chapel, built as a private place of worship for Charles I's Catholic queen

13 The Mall

SW1. **Map** 11 A4. 🚇 Charing Cross, Green Park.

This broad triumphal approach from Trafalgar Square to Buckingham Palace was created by Aston Webb when he redesigned the front of the palace and the Victoria Monument in 1911. The spacious tree-lined avenue follows the course of an old path at the edge of St James's Park. The path was laid out in the reign of Charles II, when it became London's most fashionable and cosmopolitan promenade. The Mall is used for royal processions on special occasions. Flagpoles down both sides fly the national flags of foreign heads of state during official visits. The Mall is closed to traffic on Sundays.

⑭ Buckingham Palace

The British monarch's official London home and office is an extremely popular attraction. Architect John Nash began converting the 18th-century Buckingham House into a palace for George IV in 1826 but was dismissed in 1831 for overspending his budget. The first monarch to live in the palace was Queen Victoria, after she came to the throne in 1837. The palace tour takes visitors up the grand staircase and through the State Rooms, but not into the royal family's private apartments.

Music Room
State guests are presented and royal christenings take place in this room, which boasts a beautiful, original parquet floor by John Nash.

The Queen's Gallery
Masterpieces from the royal collection, such as Vermeer's *The Music Lesson* (c.1660), are displayed here in a series of changing exhibitions.

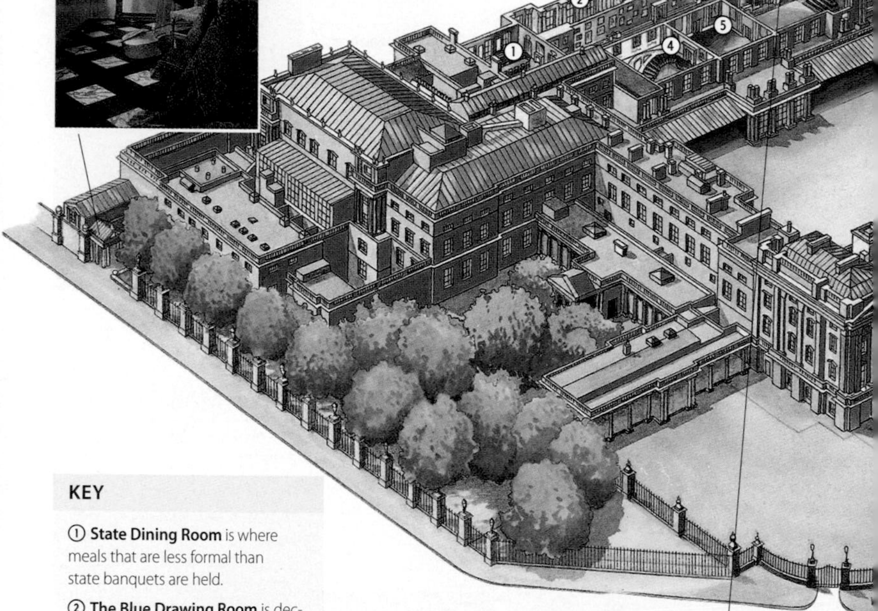

KEY

① **State Dining Room** is where meals that are less formal than state banquets are held.

② **The Blue Drawing Room** is decorated with imitation onyx columns.

③ **The White Drawing Room** is where the royal family assemble before passing into the State Dining Room or Ballroom.

④ **Grand Staircase**

⑤ **The Green Drawing Room** is the first of the large and magnificent state rooms entered by guests of the Queen at royal functions.

⑥ **The Royal Standard** flies while the Queen is in residence.

Throne Room
In a room lit by seven magnificent chandeliers stand the thrones used by the Queen and the Duke of Edinburgh during her coronation. The Queen carries out many formal ceremonial duties here.

View over the Mall
On special occasions the royal family wave to crowds from the balcony.

VISITORS' CHECKLIST

Practical Information
SW1. **Map** 10 F5. **Tel** 020 7766 7300. State Rooms: **Open** end Jul–Aug: 9:30am–7:30pm daily; Sep: 9:30am–6:30pm daily (last adm: 2 hr 15 mins before closing). Timed tickets sold in Ambassador's Court (also online or by phone). Or buy a Royal Day Out. call first. **W** royalcollection.org.uk Changing of the Guard: 11:30am daily (Aug–Mar: irregular times & alternate days). Subject to change; check the website. **W** house holddivision.org.uk.

Transport
St James's Park, Victoria. 11, 16, 24, 25, 28, 36, 38, 52, 73, 135, C1. Victoria.

⑮ The Queen's Gallery

Buckingham Palace Rd SW1. **Map** 10 F5. **Tel** 020 7766 7300. St James's Park, Victoria. **Open** 10am–5.30pm daily (Aug & Sep: from 9:30am; last adm: 4:15pm). **Closed** 25 & 26 Dec and other days through the year; visit the website for more details. **W** royalcollection.org.uk

The royal collection is one of the finest and most valuable art collections in the world, rich in the works of Old Masters such as Rembrandt and Leonardo. The gallery hosts changing exhibitions, enabling the year-round display of many masterpieces, drawings and decorative arts from the Queen's collection.

Detail: The Gold State Coach (1762), Royal Mews

⑯ Royal Mews

Buckingham Palace Rd SW1. **Map** 10 E5. **Tel** 020 7766 7300. Victoria. **Open** Feb–Mar, Nov & Dec: 10am–4pm Mon–Sat (last adm: 3:15pm); Apr–Oct: 10am–5pm daily (last adm: 4:15pm). Subject to closure at short notice. **Open** 9:30am–5pm daily all year. **Closed** 25 & 26 Dec. **W** royalcollection.org.uk

Lovers of horses and royal pomp should not miss this working stable and coach house. Designed by John Nash in 1825, it houses horses and state coaches used on official occasions. Among them is the glass coach used for royal weddings and foreign ambassadors. The star exhibit is the ornate gold state coach built for the Queen to celebrate her Diamond Jubilee in 2012. The shop sells interesting merchandise.

The Changing of the Guard

Dressed in brilliant scarlet tunics and tall furry hats called bearskins, the palace guards stand in sentry boxes outside the palace. Crowds gather to watch the colourful and musical military ceremony as the guards march from Wellington Barracks to Buckingham Palace, parading for 45 minutes while the palace keys are handed by the old guard to the new.

Street-by-Street: Whitehall and Westminster

The broad avenues of Whitehall and Westminster are lined with imposing buildings that serve the historic seat of both government and the established church. On weekdays the streets are crowded with members of the civil service who work in the area, while at weekends they take on a different atmosphere with a steady flow of tourists, visiting some of London's most famous sights.

⑱ Downing Street
Sir Robert Walpole was the first Prime Minister to live here in 1732.

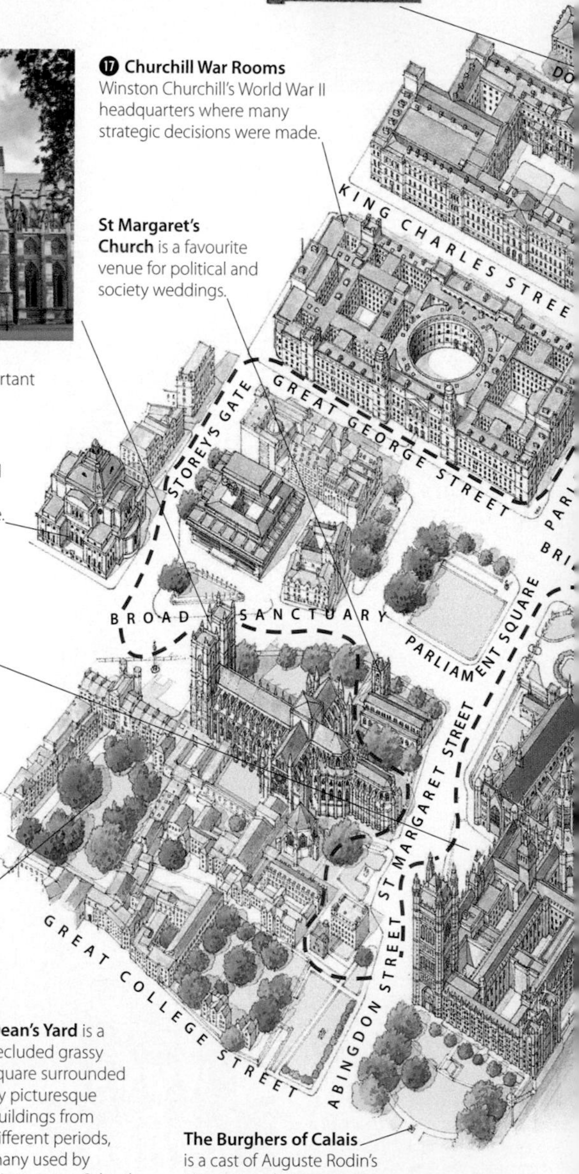

⑰ Churchill War Rooms
Winston Churchill's World War II headquarters where many strategic decisions were made.

St Margaret's Church is a favourite venue for political and society weddings.

㉑ ★ Westminster Abbey
The abbey is London's most important church and the largest in Britain.

Central Hall
(1911) is a florid example of the Beaux Arts style.

Richard I's Statue is an 1860 depiction of the king, killed in battle in 1199.

Dean's Yard is a secluded grassy square surrounded by picturesque buildings from different periods, many used by Westminster School.

The Burghers of Calais is a cast of Auguste Rodin's 1886 original in France.

KING CHARLES STREET

STOREY'S GATE

GREAT GEORGE STREET

PARLIAMENT SQUARE

BRI

PARL

BROAD SANCTUARY

ST MARGARET STREET

GREAT COLLEGE STREET

ABINGDON STREET

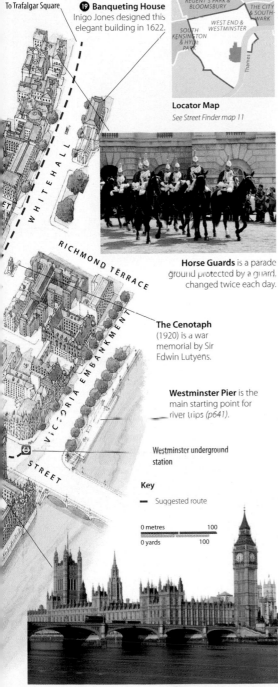

⑲ Banqueting House Inigo Jones designed this elegant building in 1622.

To Trafalgar Square

WHITEHALL

Locator Map
See Street Finder map 11

Horse Guards is a parade ground protected by a guard, changed twice each day.

RICHMOND TERRACE

The Cenotaph (1920) is a war memorial by Sir Edwin Lutyens.

VICTORIA EMBANKMENT

Westminster Pier is the main starting point for river trips (p641).

Westminster underground station

Key

— Suggested route

| 0 metres | 100 |
| 0 yards | 100 |

⑳ ★ Houses of Parliament
The seat of government is dominated by the clock tower, holding the 14-tonne bell Big Ben, hung in 1858. Its deep chimes are broadcast daily on BBC radio.

⑰ Churchill War Rooms

Clive Steps, King Charles St SW1.
Map 11 B5. **Tel** 020 7930 6961.
🚇 Westminster. **Open** 9:30am–6pm daily (last adm: 5pm).
Closed 24–26 Dec. ♿ 🏛 ♿
💻 📷 🅦 iwm.org.uk

This intriguing slice of 20th-century history is a warren of cellars below a government office building north of Parliment Square. It was here that the War Cabinet – first under Neville Chamberlain, then Winston Churchill from 1940 – met during World War II when German bombs were falling on London. The rooms include living quarters for ministers and military leaders and a Cabinet Room, where strategic decisions were taken. They are laid out as they were when the war ended, complete with Churchill's desk, communications equipment, and maps for plotting battles and strategies. The Churchill Museum records and illustrates Churchill's life and career.

Telephones in the Map Room, Churchill War Rooms

⑱ Downing Street

SW1. **Map** 11 B4. 🚇 Westminster.
Closed to the public.

Number 10 Downing Street has been the official residence of the British Prime Minister since 1732. It contains a Cabinet Room in which government policy is decided, an impressive State Dining Room and a private apartment; outside is a well-protected garden.

Next door at No. 11 is the official residence of the Chancellor of the Exchequer, who is in charge of the nation's financial affairs. In 1989, iron gates were erected at the Whitehall end of Downing Street for security purposes.

⑲ Banqueting House

Whitehall SW1. **Map** 11 B4. **Tel** 020 3166 6154. ⊖ Charing Cross. **Open** 10am–1pm daily (sometimes later). **Closed** public hols & for functions. Call in advance. 🐾 📷 ♿ partial. 📷 **w hrp.org.uk**

Completed by Inigo Jones *(see p57)* in 1622, this was the first building in central London to embody the Palladian style of Renaissance Italy. In 1629 Charles I commissioned Rubens to paint the ceiling with scenes exalting the reign of his father, James I. They symbolize the divine right of kings, disputed by the Parliamentarians, who executed Charles I outside the building in 1649 *(see p56)*.

Panels from the Rubens ceiling (1629–34), Banqueting House

⑳ Houses of Parliament

SW1. **Map** 11 C5. **Tel** 020 7219 3003. ⊖ Westminster. Visitors' Galleries: **Tel** 020 7219 4114 to book tours (Sat year-round and most weekdays during parliamentary recesses); 020 7219 4272 for details on attending debates. **Open** Check website for times. UK residents can apply to their local MP for gallery tickets for Question Time. **Closed** frequently for parliamentary recesses. 🎧 ♿ 📷 **w parliament.uk/visiting**

There has been a Palace of Westminster here since the 11th century, though very little remains from that time, most notably Westminster Hall. The present Neo-Gothic structure by Sir Charles Barry was built after the old palace was destroyed by fire in 1834. Since the 16th century it has housed the two Houses of Parliament, the Lords and the Commons. The House of Commons consists of elected Members of Parliament (MPs) of different political parties.

The party (or coalition of parties) with most MPs forms the government, and its leader becomes prime minister. MPs from other parties make up the Opposition. The House of Lords comprises mainly appointed life peers, but also hereditary peers and Church of England bishops.

The House of Commons' original chamber was destroyed by a bomb in 1941.

Central Lobby

Victoria Tower

Royal Gallery

Visitor entrance, Cromwell Green

The House of Lords is a lavishly decorated Gothic Hall designed by Pugin in 1836–7.

Entrance to Westminster Hall

Westminster Hall

Big Ben has kept exact time for the nation almost continuously since 1859.

㉑ Westminster Abbey

See pp96–7.

㉒ Tate Britain

Millbank SW1. **Map** 19 B2. **Tel** 020 7887 8888. 🚇 Pimlico. 🚌 87, 88, C10. 🚆 Victoria, Vauxhall. 🚤 to Tate Modern every 40 mins. **Open** 10am–6pm daily (to 10pm on select Fridays). **Closed** 24 26 Dec. 📷 for major exhibitions. 🎫 🛍 ♿ Atterbury St. 🚻 🖥 📷 **w** **tate.org.uk**

The First Marriage (A Marriage of Styles I) (1962) by David Hockney

Tate Britain is the national gallery of British art, and includes works from the 16th to the 21st centuries. Displays draw on the huge Tate Collection, which also includes the international modern art seen at Tate Modern (*p125*). A boat service runs between the two galleries.

The collection is arranged chronologically, giving an overview of the art being produced at any one historical moment. It also allows fascinating juxtapositions to emerge – for example, a Gainsborough landscape hangs side by side with Hogarth's satires; Alma Tadema's frolicking female nudes of *A Favourite Custom* (1909) are seen next to Walter Sickert's gritty modernist icon *La Hollandaise* (1906). There are also permanent galleries devoted to several of the greatest figures in British art: William Blake, Henry Moore,

Recumbent Figure (1938) by Henry Moore

John Constable and J M W Turner. Located in the Clore Gallery are works from the Turner Bequest (*see below*).

The section on the years 1500 to 1800 covers a period of dramatic change in British history, from the Tudors and Stuarts through to the age of Thomas Gainsborough.

The years 1800 to 1900 saw dramatic expansion and change in the arts in Britain. This section shows the new themes that began to emerge. Included are the "Victorian Narrative" painters such as William Powell Frith, and the work of the Pre-Raphaelites, such as John Everett Millais and Dante Gabriel Rossetti. The period 1900 to 1960 includes the work of Jacob Epstein, that of Wyndham Lewis and his Vorticist group, and the celebrated modernist works of Henry Moore, Barbara Hepworth, Ben Nicholson, Francis Bacon and Lucian Freud.

The displays in the outstanding collection of British art from 1960 to the present are changed on a regular basis. From the 1960s, Tate's funding for the purchase of works began to increase substantially, while artistic activity continued to pick up speed, encouraged by public spending. As a result, Tate Britain's collection is particularly rich in this period. Works range from the 1960s Pop artists David Hockney, Richard Hamilton and Peter Blake, through the works of Gilbert and George and the landscape artist Richard Long, to the 1980s paintings of Howard Hodgkin and R B Kitaj.

The Turner Bequest

The Turner Bequest comprises some 300 oil paintings and 20,000 watercolours and drawings, received by the nation from the great landscape painter J M W Turner some years after his death in 1851. Turner's will had specified that a gallery be built to house his pictures and this was finally done in 1987 with the opening of the Clore Gallery. Most of the oils are on view in the main galleries, and the watercolours are the subject of changing displays.

Shipping at the Mouth of the Thames (c.1806–7)

㉑ Westminster Abbey

Westminster Abbey has been the burial place of Britain's monarchs since the 11th century and the setting for many coronations and royal weddings. It is one of the most beautiful buildings in London, with an exceptionally diverse array of architectural styles, ranging from the austere French Gothic of the nave to the astonishing complexity of Henry VII's chapel. Half national church, half national museum, the abbey aisles and transepts are crammed with an extraordinary collection of tombs and monuments honouring some of Britain's greatest public figures, ranging from politicians to poets.

North Entrance
The mock-medieval stonework is Victorian.

★ Nave
At a height of 31 m (102 ft), the nave is the highest in Britain. The ratio of height to width is 3:1.

Coronation Chair
Constructed in 1301, this chair has been used at every coronation since 1308.

KEY

① **Statesmen's Aisle**

② **Flying buttresses** are external supports that help redistribute the great weight of the roof.

③ **The Sanctuary** was built by Henry III and has been the scene of 38 coronations.

④ **Entrance to the Queen's Diamond Jubilee Galleries**

⑤ **The Pyx Chamber** is where the coinage was tested in medieval times.

Coronation

The coronation ceremony is over 1,000 years old and since 1066, with the crowning of William the Conqueror on Christmas Day, the abbey has been its sumptuous setting. The coronation of Queen Elizabeth II, in 1953, was the first to be televised.

★ Lady Chapel
The chapel, built in 1503–19, has superb late Perpendicular vaulting and choir stalls dating from 1512, as well as two stained-glass windows installed in 2013.

WILLIAM SHAKESPEARE 1564–1616
BURIED AT STRATFORD-ON-AVON

Poets' Corner
A host of great poets are honoured here, including Shakespeare, Chaucer and T S Eliot.

VISITORS' CHECKLIST

Practical Information
Broad Sanctuary SW1.
Map 11 B5. **Tel** 020 7222 5152.
Abbey (Royal Chapels, Poets' Corner, Choir, Statesmen's Aisle, Nave): **Open** 9:30am–4:30pm Mon–Fri (to 7pm Wed), 9:30am–2:30pm Sat (last adm: 1 hr before closing). Chapter House, Pyx Chamber & Museum and College Garden: **Open** times vary; call ahead or check website for details. Evensong 5pm Mon–Fri (evening prayers Wed), 3pm Sat & Sun. **w** westminster-abbey.org

Transport
Westminster. 3, 11, 12, 24, 29, 53, 70, 77, 87, 88, 109, 159, 170. Victoria. Westminster Pier.

★ Chapter House
A beautiful octagonal room, remarkable for its 13th-century tile floor. It is lit by six huge stained-glass windows showing scenes from the abbey's history.

Cloisters
Built mainly in the 13th and 14th centuries, the cloisters link the abbey church with the other buildings.

Historical Plan of the Abbey

The first abbey church was established as early as the 10th century, but the present French-influenced Gothic structure was begun in 1245 at the behest of Henry III. Because of its unique role as the coronation church, the abbey escaped Henry VIII's onslaught on Britain's monastic buildings (see p355).

Key

- Built between 1055 and 1272
- Added 1376–1420
- Built between 1500 and 1512
- Completed 1745
- Restored after 1850

SOUTH KENSINGTON AND HYDE PARK

This exclusive district embraces one of London's largest parks and some of its finest museums, shops, restaurants and hotels. Until the mid-19th century it was a genteel, semi-rural backwater of large houses and private schools, lying to the south of Kensington Palace. In 1851, the Great Exhibition, then the largest arts and science event ever staged *(see pp60–61)*, was held in Hyde Park, transforming the area into a celebration of Victorian learning and self-confidence. The brainchild of Queen Victoria's husband, Prince Albert, the exhibition was a massive success and the profits were used to buy 35 ha (87 acres) of land in South Kensington. Here, Prince Albert championed the construction of a concert hall, museums and colleges devoted to the applied arts and sciences; most of them survive. The neighbourhood soon became fashionable, full of flamboyant red-brick mansion blocks, garden squares and the elite shops still to be found in Knightsbridge.

Sights at a Glance

Historic Buildings
⑧ Kensington Palace

Churches
② Brompton Oratory

Shops
① Harrods

Parks and Gardens
⑦ Hyde Park and
   Kensington Gardens

Museums and Galleries
③ *Victoria and Albert Museum pp102–3*
④ Science Museum
⑤ Natural History Museum

Concert Halls
⑥ Royal Albert Hall and
   Albert Memorial

See also Street Finder maps 8, 9, 16, 17

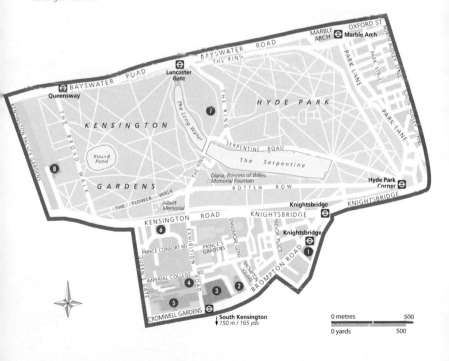

◀ Hintze Hall, the magnificent central hall of the Natural History Museum

For keys to symbols *see back flap*

Street-by-Street: South Kensington

The numerous museums and colleges
created in the wake of the Great Exhibition
of 1851 *(see pp60–61)* continue to give this
neighbourhood an air of leisured culture.
Visited as much by Londoners as tourists,
the museum area is liveliest on Sundays
and on summer evenings during the Royal
Albert Hall's famous season of classical
"Prom" concerts *(see p67).*

❻ The Royal Albert Hall
Opened in 1871,
this concert venue
was modelled
on Roman
amphitheatres.

**The Memorial to the Great
Exhibition** is surmounted by
a bronze statue of its instigator,
Prince Albert.

**The Royal College
of Music**, founded
in 1882, exhibits
historic musical
instruments such
as the harpsichord
dating from 1531.

❹ ★ Science Museum
Visitors can experiment
with over a thousand
interactive displays.

KENSIN

PRINCE CONS

IMPERIAL COLLEGE ROAD

EXHIBITI

CROMWELL ROAD

Entrance to South Kensington
underground station

**❺ ★ Natural
History Museum**
The Creepy Crawlies
exhibition has proved
highly popular.

Key

— Suggested route

0 metres	100
0 yards	100

CROMWE

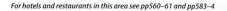

6 **The Albert Memorial** was built in memory of Queen Victoria's husband, who died in 1861.

Locator Map
See Street Finder maps 8, 16, 17

3 ★ **Victoria and Albert Museum**
The museum has a fine collection of applied arts and photography from around the world.

2 **Brompton Oratory**
This ornate Baroque church is famous for its splendid musical tradition.

Brompton Square (1821)

To Knightsbridge and Harrods →

Harrods Food Hall, offering a vast array of luxury foodstuffs

1 Harrods

87–135 Brompton Rd SW1. **Map** 9 C5. **Tel** 020 7730 1234. 🚇 Knightsbridge. **Open** 10am–9pm Mon–Sat, 11:30am–6pm Sun. ♿ 🚻 📷 *See Shops and Markets pp152–5.* 🖥 **harrods.com**

In 1849 Henry Charles Harrod opened a small grocery shop on Brompton Road, which soon became famous for its impeccable service and quality. The store moved into these extravagant premises in Knightsbridge in 1905.

2 Brompton Oratory

Brompton Rd SW7. **Map** 17 A1. **Tel** 020 7808 0900. 🚇 South Kensington. **Open** 6am–8pm daily. ♿ 📷 🖥 **bromptonoratory.co.uk**

The Italianate Oratory is a lavish monument to the 19th-century English Catholic revival. It was established as a base for a community of priests by John Henry Newman (later Cardinal Newman), who introduced the Oratorian movement to England in 1848. The church was opened in 1884, and the dome and façade added in the 1890s.

The interior holds many fine monuments. The 12 huge 17th-century statues of the apostles are from Siena Cathedral, the Baroque Lady Altar (1693) is from the Dominican church at Brescia, and the 18th-century altar in St Wilfred's Chapel is from Rochefort in Belgium.

● Victoria and Albert Museum

The Victoria and Albert Museum (the V&A) contains one of the world's widest collections of art and design, ranging from early Christian devotional objects and the mystical art of southeast Asia to cutting-edge furniture design. Originally founded in 1852 as the Museum of Manufactures to inspire students of design, it was renamed by Queen Victoria in 1899 in memory of Prince Albert. A staggering 145 galleries, dedicated to fashion, photography, ceramics, furniture and many other areas, house items spanning 5,000 years of art. The Europe galleries alone span three levels.

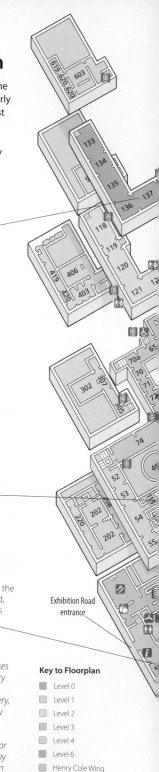

Ceramic galleries
The museum has the most comprehensive collection of ceramics in the world. This 16th-century Italian earthenware plate is one of the pieces on display in these stunning galleries.

★ British galleries
The Great Bed of Ware has been a tourist attraction since 1601, when Shakespeare sparked interest in it by making reference to it in *Twelfth Night*.

★ Fashion gallery
In this gallery, European fashion, fabrics and accessories from 1750 to the present day are displayed, such as these floral 1920s Lilley & Skinner shoes.

Exhibition Road entrance

Gallery Guide

The V&A has a 7-mile (11-km) layout spread over six levels. Level 1 houses the China, Japan and South Asia galleries, as well as the Fashion gallery and the Western Cast Court. The British Galleries are on levels 2 and 4. Level 3 contains the 20th Century galleries and displays of silver, jewellery, ironwork, paintings, photography and works of 20th- and 21st-century design. The glass display is on level 4, next to the architectural displays. The Ceramics and Furniture galleries are on level 6. European galleries from 300 to 1800 are on levels 0, 1 and 2. On the ground floor, to the rear beyond the courtyard, are the beautiful café rooms, featuring designs by William Morris. The Sainsbury Gallery, located underneath the museum on level 0, hosts major temporary exhibitions.

Key to Floorplan
- Level 0
- Level 1
- Level 2
- Level 3
- Level 4
- Level 6
- Henry Cole Wing
- Non-exhibition space

For hotels and restaurants in this area see pp560–61 and pp583–4

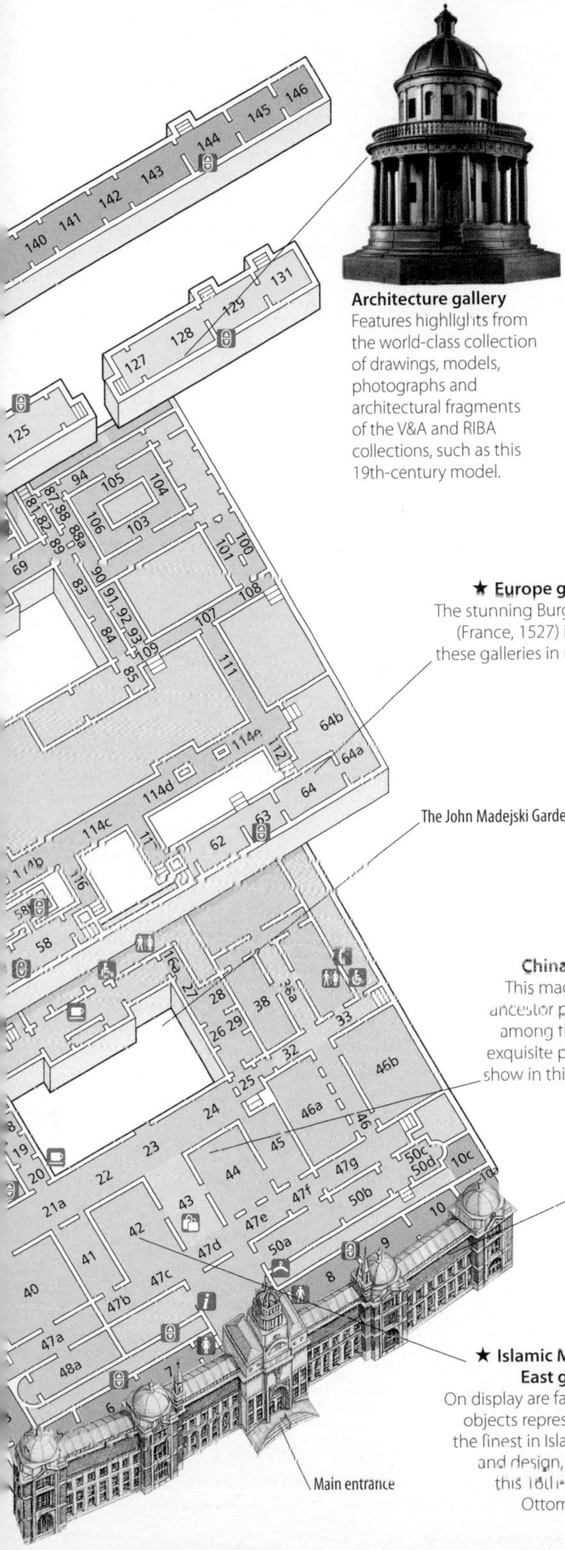

Architecture gallery
Features highlights from
the world-class collection
of drawings, models,
photographs and
architectural fragments
of the V&A and RIBA
collections, such as this
19th-century model.

★ Europe galleries
The stunning Burghley Nef
(France, 1527) is located in
these galleries in rooms 62–4.

The John Madejski Garden

China gallery
This magnificent
ancestor portrait is
among the many
exquisite pieces on
show in this gallery.

Aston Webb's façade
(1909) is decorated with
32 sculptures of English
craftsmen and designers.

**★ Islamic Middle
East gallery**
On display are fantastic
objects representing
the finest in Islamic art
and design, such as
this 18th-century
Ottoman table.

Main entrance

Inside the impressive Science Museum, unmissable for enquiring minds

❹ Science Museum

Exhibition Rd SW7. **Map** 17 A1. **Tel** 0870 870 4868. ⊖ South Kensington. **Open** 10am–6pm daily (last adm: 5:15pm). **Closed** 24–26 Dec. 🎦 for IMAX, special exhibitions and simulators only. 📷 ♿ 🖥 🏛 📶 **sciencemuseum. org.uk**

Centuries of continuing scientific and technological development lie at the heart of the Science Museum's massive collections. The hardware displayed is magnificent: from steam engines to aeroengines; spacecraft to the very first mechanical computers. Equally important is the social context of science – what discoveries and inventions mean for day-to-day life – and the process of discovery itself. There are many interactive and hands-on displays which are very popular with children.

The museum is spread over seven floors and includes the high-tech Wellcome Wing at the west end of the museum. The basement features excellent hands-on galleries for children, including The Garden. The Energy Hall dominates the ground floor, and is dedicated to steam power, with the still-operational Harle Syke Mill Engine of 1903. Here too are Exploring Space and Making the Modern World, a highlight of which is the display of the scarred Apollo 10 spacecraft, which carried three astronauts to the moon and back in May 1969. In Challenge of Materials, located on the first floor, our expectations of materials are confounded by exhibits such as a bridge made of glass and a steel wedding dress.

The Flight gallery on the third floor is packed with early flying contraptions, fighter planes, aeroplanes and the Launchpad.

The Wellcome Wing offers four floors of interactive technology, including "Who Am I?" (first floor), a fascinating exhibition exploring the science of you. With an IMAX 3D Cinema and the SimEx simulator ride, it is a breathtaking addition to the museum.

❺ Natural History Museum

Cromwell Rd SW7. **Map** 17 A1. **Tel** 020 7942 5000. ⊖ South Kensington. **Open** 10am–5:50pm daily (to 10:30pm last Fri of month). **Closed** 24–26 Dec. 📷 🏛 ♿ ⚜ 🖥 📶 **nhm.ac.uk**

This cathedral-like building's richly sculpted stonework conceals an iron and steel frame; this construction technique was revolutionary when the museum opened in 1881. The imaginative displays tackle fundamental issues such as the ecology and evolution of the planet, the origin of species and the development of human beings – all explained through the latest technology, interactive techniques and traditional displays.

The central Hintze Hall has various displays that showcase the museum's collections and explore humanity's relationship with the planet. But the main highlight is the huge suspended skeleton of a blue whale.

The museum is divided into four sections: the Blue Zone, Green Zone, Red Zone and the Orange Zone. In the Blue Zone, the Ecology exhibition explores the complex web of the natural world through a replica of a moonlit rainforest buzzing with the sounds of insects. One of the most popular exhibits is the Dinosaur Gallery, which includes animatronic models of dinosaurs. The Vault, in the Green Zone, contains a dazzling collection of gems, crystals, metals and meteorites from around the world. The Darwin Centre is the largest curved structure in Europe. The eight-storey-high cocoon houses a vast collection of insects and plants.

❻ Royal Albert Hall and Albert Memorial

Kensington Gore SW7. **Map** 8 F5. **Tel** 020 7589 8212 (box office). ⊖ South Kensington. **Open** for performances daily. Box office: 9am–9pm daily. **Closed** 24–26 Dec. 📷 guided tours from 9:30am daily. 🏛 ⚜ 🖥 🏛 📶 **royalalberthall. com** Albert Memorial: Kensington Gdns W2. **Tel** 030 0061 2000. **Open** 6am–dusk. 📷 📶 **royalparks.org.uk**

The vast oval hall named after Prince Albert was opened in 1871 and has mainly functioned as a concert venue, but it has hosted a wide variety of other

Joseph Durham's statue of Prince Albert (1858) in front of the Royal Albert Hall

Statue of the young Queen Victoria outside Kensington Palace, sculpted by her daughter, Princess Louise

events over the years. Today, it is probably most famous for the summer Proms (see p67).

A short walk north of Albert Hall, in Kensington Gardens, is the grandiose Albert Memorial. Designed by leading Victorian architect George Gilbert Scott and unveiled in 1876, it is made up of a vast decorative Gothic canopy within which sits a gilded statue of Prince Albert sculpted by John Foley.

A sculptural frieze at the base celebrates 169 great artistic figures. Eight large allegorical sculptures stand at the corner of the memorial and at the base of the steps leading up to it four representing industry; the other four the Empire.

❼ Hyde Park and Kensington Gardens

W2. **Map** 9 B3. **Tel** 0300 061 2000.
Hyde Park: 🚇 Hyde Park Corner,
Knightsbridge, Lancaster Gate, Marble
Arch. **Open** 5am–midnight daily. ♿📷
📷 Kensington Gardens: **Tel** 0300 061
2000. 🚇 Queensway, Lancaster Gate.
Open 6am–dusk daily. ♿📷
Diana, Princess of Wales Memorial
Playground: **Open** 10am–dusk daily.
📷 🌐 royalparks.org.uk

The ancient manor of Hyde was part of the lands of Westminster Abbey seized by Henry VIII at the Dissolution of the Monasteries in 1536 (see p355). James I opened the park to the public in the early 17th century, and it was soon one of the city's most fashionable public spaces.

Unfortunately it also became popular with duellists and highwaymen, and consequently William III had 300 lights hung along Rotten Row, the first street in England to be lit up at night. In 1730, the Westbourne River was dammed by Queen Caroline in order to create the Serpentine, an artificial lake that is today used for boating and swimming; Rotten Row is used for horse riding. South of the Serpentine is the Princess Diana Memorial Fountain. The park is also a rallying point for political demonstrations, while at Speaker's Corner, in the northeast, anyone has had the right to address the public since 1872. Sundays are particularly lively, with many budding orators and a number of eccentrics revealing their plans for the betterment of humanity.

Adjoining Hyde Park is Kensington Gardens, the former grounds of Kensington Palace. Three great attractions for children are the innovative Diana, Princess of Wales Memorial Playground, the bronze statue of J M Barrie's fictional Peter Pan (1912) by George Frampton, and the Round Pond where people sail model boats. Also worth seeing is the dignified Orangery (1704), once used by Queen Anne as a "summer supper house", now an elegant café.

Detail of the Coalbrookdale Gate, Kensington Gardens

❽ Kensington Palace

Kensington Gdns W8. **Map** 8 D4.
Tel 020 3166 6000. 🚇 High St
Kensington, Queensway. **Open** Nov–
Feb: 10am–4pm daily; Mar–Oct:
10am–6pm daily (last adm: 1 hr before
closing). **Closed** 1 Jan, 24–26 Dec. 📷
♿📷📷📷 🌐 hrp.org.uk

Kensington Palace was the principal residence of the royal family from the 1690s until the 1830s, when the court moved to Buckingham Palace. Over the years it has seen a number of important royal events. In 1714 Queen Anne died here from a fit of apoplexy brought on by overeating and, in June 1837, Princess Victoria of Kent was woken to be told that her uncle William IV had died and she was now queen – the beginning of her 64-year reign. After the death of Princess Diana in 1997, the palace became a focal point for mourners who gathered in their thousands at its gates and turned the area into a field of bouquets.

Half of the palace still holds royal apartments, but the other half is open to the public. Among the highlights are the 18th-century state rooms with ceilings and murals by William Kent (see p32) – the King's Staircase is particularly impressive. Another exhibit examines the life of Queen Victoria.

REGENT'S PARK AND BLOOMSBURY

Regent's Park, fringed by cream stuccoed Georgian terraces, is the busiest of the royal parks and is home to ZSL London Zoo, an open-air theatre, boating lake, rose garden, cafés and London's largest mosque. Bloomsbury, an enclave of attractive garden squares and Georgian brick terraces, was one of the most fashionable areas of the city until the mid-19th century, when the arrival of large hospitals and railway stations persuaded many of the wealthier residents to move west to Mayfair, Knightsbridge and Kensington. Home to the British Museum since 1753 and the University of London since 1828, Bloomsbury has long been the domain of artists, writers and intellectuals, including the Bloomsbury

Group *(see p167)*, George Bernard Shaw, Charles Dickens and Karl Marx. Traditionally a centre for the book trade, it remains a good place for literary browsing. Just beyond Bloomsbury's northern border, on the other side of the congested Euston Road, stands the red-brick British Library, one of the largest public buildings in the country, and the magnificent St Pancras International station, perhaps the finest example of Victorian Gothic architecture in the city. The station stands on the edge of the still expanding King's Cross quarter, an exciting, pedestrian-friendly district of public squares, restaurants, parkland, shops, galleries and other cultural institutions, carved out of a previously bleak industrial landscape.

Sights at a Glance

Historic Streets and Buildings
6 Bloomsbury
7 British Library
8 St Pancras International

Museums and Galleries
1 Madame Tussaud's
2 Sherlock Holmes Museum

4 Wallace Collection
5 *British Museum pp110–11*

Parks and Gardens
3 Regent's Park

See also Street Finder
maps 1, 2, 3, 10, 11

0 metres 300
0 yards 500

◀ The striking ceiling over the Great Court at the British Museum

❶ Madame Tussauds

Marylebone Rd NW1. **Map** 2 D5.
Tel 0871 894 3000. ⊖ Baker St.
Open daily, but times vary according
to time of year and other factors, so
check website for latest information.
Closed 25 Dec. 🚲 ♿ phone first.
📱 📷 🌐 **madametussauds.com**

Madame Tussaud began her
wax-modelling career making
death masks of victims of the
French Revolution. She moved
to England and in 1835 set up
an exhibition of her work in
Baker Street, near the present
site, where today's guests can
have photos taken with some of
the world's most famous faces.
The exhibition is divided into
around a dozen areas, including
the Party area where you can
find A-list celebrities, areas for
film stars, royals and figures
from the world of pop music,
and a *Star Wars* exhibit where
iconic scenes from the movie
series have been recreated.

The Marvel Super Heroes 4D
Experience, an exclusive short
film complete with water, wind
and vibration effects, puts you
right in the heart of the action.
In the Spirit of London finale,
visitors travel in stylized taxi-
cabs through the city's history
to "witness" events from the
Great Fire of 1666 to the
Swinging 1960s. Ticket prices
also include entry to temporary
exhibitions featuring media
icons of the moment.
Educational tours are also
available for groups.

Wax figure of Queen Elizabeth II (2012) at
Madame Tussauds

Conan Doyle's fictional detective
Sherlock Holmes

❷ Sherlock Holmes Museum

221b Baker St NW1. **Map** 1 C4. **Tel** 020
7224 3688. ⊖ Baker St. **Open** 9:30am–
6pm daily. **Closed** 25 Dec. 🚲 📷
🌐 **sherlock-holmes.co.uk**

Sir Arthur Conan Doyle's fictional
detective was supposed to live at
221b Baker Street, which did not
exist. The museum, labelled 221b,
actually stands between Nos. 237
and 239, and is the only surviving
Victorian lodging house in the
street. There is a reconstruction
of Holmes's front room, and
passionate memorabilia from the stories
decorate every room. Visitors can
buy plaques, Holmes hats, Toby
jugs and meerschaum pipes.

❸ Regent's Park

NW1. **Map** 1 C2. **Tel** 0300 061 2300.
⊖ Regent's Park, Baker St, Great
Portland St. **Open** 5am–dusk daily. ♿
🖥 Open Air Theatre: *See Entertainment
p157.* Sports facilities. 🌐 **royalparks.
org.uk**. ZSL London Zoo: **Map** 2 D2.
Open 10am–6pm daily (Sep–Mar: to
5:30pm; last adm: 1 hr before closing).
🚲 ♿ 🖥 📷 🌐 **zsl.org**

This land became enclosed as a
park in 1812. Designer John Nash
originally envisaged a kind of
garden suburb, with 56 villas in
a variety of Classical styles and a
pleasure palace for the Prince
Regent. In the event only eight
villas – and no palace – were
built (three survive round the
edge of the Inner Circle).

The boating lake has many
varieties of water birds and
is marvellously romantic.

Queen Mary's Gardens are a
mass of wonderful sights and
smells in summer, when visitors
can also enjoy outdoor theatre,
including Shakespeare, musicals
and children's plays, at the **Open
Air Theatre** nearby.

The park is also the site for a
lot of amateur sports leagues
and competitions, including
football, cricket and running, and
as the home of **ZSL London Zoo**,
one of London's biggest tourist
attractions and a major research
and conservation centre.
Opened in 1828, the zoo houses
more than 600 species, including
Sumatran tigers, as well as
Asiatic lions in a recreation
of an Indian national park.

❹ Wallace Collection

Hertford House, Manchester Sq W1.
Map 10 D1. **Tel** 020 7563 9500.
⊖ Bond St, Baker St. **Open** 10am–
5pm daily. **Closed** 24–26 Dec.
♿ phone first. 📷 🚫 📷
🌐 **wallacecollection.org**

One of the world's finest private
collections of European art, it
has remained intact since 1897.
The product of passionate
collecting by four generations
of the Seymour-Conway family,
who were Marquesses of
Hertford, it was bequeathed to
the state on the condition that it
would go on permanent public
display with nothing added or
taken away. Hertford House still
retains the atmosphere of a
grand 19th-century house, and
the Centenary Project in 1997
created more gallery space
and a stunning high-level
glass roof for the central

A 16th-century Italian majolica dish
from the Wallace Collection

courtyard, which now contains a sculpture garden and an elegant restaurant.

The 3rd Marquess (1777–1842), a flamboyant London figure, used his Italian wife's fortune to buy works by Titian and Canaletto, along with numerous 17th-century Dutch paintings including works by Van Dyck. The collection's particular strength is 18th-century French painting, sculpture and decorative arts, acquired by the 4th Marquess (1800–70) and his natural son, Sir Richard Wallace (1818–90). The Marquess had a taste for lush romanticism, and notable among his acquisitions are Watteau's *Les Champs Élisées* (c.1720–21), Fragonard's *The Swing* (c.1767–8) and Boucher's twin paintings *The Setting of the Sun* (1752) and *The Rising of the Sun* (1753).

Other highlights of the Wallace Collection include Rembrandt's *Titus, the Artist's Son* (c.1657), Titian's *Perseus and Andromeda* (1554–6) and Hals's famous *Laughing Cavalier* (1624). There is also an important collection of Renaissance armour, and superb examples of Sèvres porcelain and Italian majolica.

❺ British Museum

See pp110–11.

❻ Bloomsbury

WC1. **Map** 3 B4. 🚇 Russell Sq, Holborn, Tottenham Court Rd. Charles Dickens Museum: 48 Doughty St WC1. **Tel** 020 7405 2127. **Open** 10am–5pm Tue–Sun.
🅿 💻 📷 **W** dickensmuseum.com

Home to numerous writers and artists, Bloomsbury is a traditional centre of the book trade. It is dominated by the British Museum and the University of London and characterized by several fine Georgian squares. These include **Russell Square**, where the poet T S Eliot (1888–1965) worked for a publisher for 40 years; **Queen**

Square, which contains a statue of Queen Charlotte, wife of George III; and **Bloomsbury Square**, laid out in 1661. A plaque here commemorates members of the Bloomsbury Group *(see p167)*. One of London's best-preserved 18th-century oases is **Bedford Square**. Charles Dickens *(see p192)* lived at 48 Doughty Street during a brief but critical stage in his career, and it was here that he wrote *Oliver Twist* and *Nicholas Nickleby*, both completed in 1839.

His former home is now the **Charles Dickens Museum**, which has rooms laid out as they were in Dickens's time, with objects taken from his other London homes, and first editions of many of his works.

Queen Charlotte (1744–1818)

❼ British Library

96 Euston Rd NW1. **Map** 3 B3. **Tel** 01937 546 060. 🚇 King's Cross St Pancras. Building including Entrance Hall Gallery: **Open** 9:30am–8pm Mon–Sat (to 6pm Fri, 5pm Sat), 11am–5pm Sun. Treasures Gallery: **Open** 9:30am–6pm Mon & Fri, 9:30am–8pm Tue–Thu, 9:30am–5pm Sat, 11am–5pm Sun. PACCAR Gallery: **Open** 9:30am–6pm daily (to 8pm Tue, 5pm Sat, 11pm Sun). Regular events. 📷 for some special exhibitions. ⏱ twice daily; pre-booking advised.
✉ ♿ ⌨ 💻 📷 **W** bl.uk

This late 20th-century building houses the national collection of books, manuscripts and maps, as

well as the British Library Sound Archive. Designed in red brick by Sir Colin St John Wilson, it opened in 1997 after nearly 20 years of construction and is widely admired.

A copy of nearly every printed book in the UK is held here – more than 25 million – and can be consulted by those with a reader's ticket. Open to all are the temporary exhibitions in the Entrance Hall and PACCAR Galleries and, housing some of the library's most precious items, the Treasures Gallery, where, among other highlights, are the Lindisfarne Gospels, a Gutenberg Bible and Shakespeare's First Folio.

❽ St Pancras International

Euston Rd NW1. **Map** 3 B3. **Tel** 020 7843 7688. 🚇 King's Cross St Pancras. *See Travel Information p633.*
W stpancras.com

St Pancras, the London terminal for Eurostar rail services to continental Europe, is easily the most spectacular of the three rail termini along Euston Road, thanks to the extravagant front age, in red-brick ginger-bread Gothic, of the former Midland Grand Hotel, opened in 1874 as one of the most sumptuous hotels of its time. By 1935, now too expensive to run, it became office space. It was threatened with demolition in the 1960s but saved by a campaign led by the poet John Betjeman (there is a statue of him on the upper level of the station concourse). The hotel has since been restored.

The red-brick Gothic exterior of St Pancras International station

❺ British Museum

The oldest national public museum in the world, the British Museum was established in 1753 to house the collections of the physician Sir Hans Sloane (1660–1753). Sloane's collection has been added to by gifts and purchases from all over the world, and the museum now contains objects spanning millennia. The main part of the building (1823–50) is by architect Robert Smirke, but the architectural highlight is the modern Great Court, with the old Reading Room at its centre.

★ Egyptian Mummies
Animals such as this cat (30 BC) were preserved alongside humans by the ancient Egyptians.

Upper floors

Bronze Figure Shiva Nataraja
This statue of the Hindu God Shiva Nataraja (c.1100) from South India forms part of the fine collection of Oriental art.

Montague Place entrance

★ Parthenon Sculptures
These reliefs from the Parthenon in Athens were brought to London by Lord Elgin around 1802 and are housed in a special gallery.

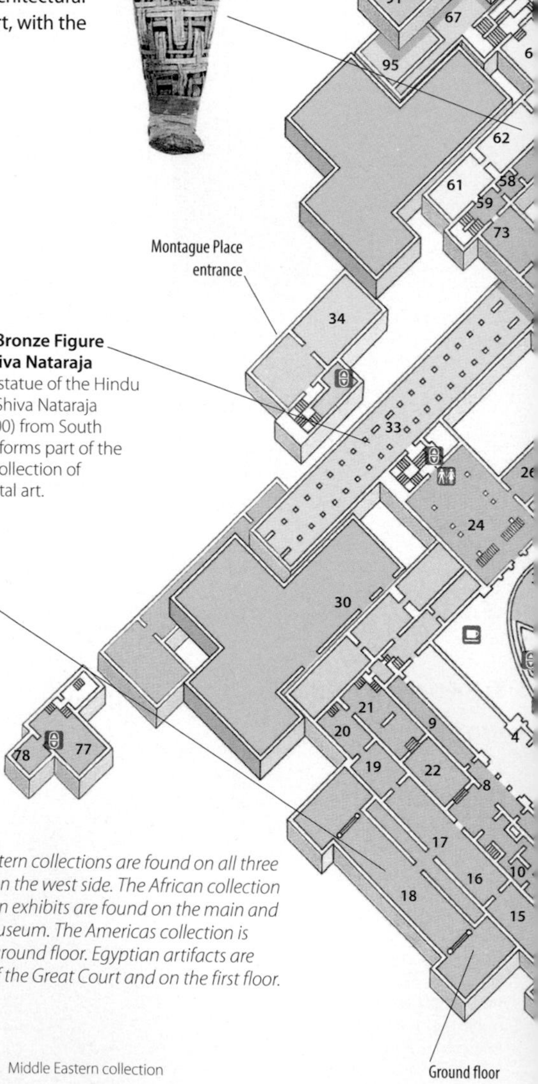

Gallery Guide

The Greek and Roman, and Middle Eastern collections are found on all three levels of the museum, predominantly on the west side. The African collection is located on the lower floor, while Asian exhibits are found on the main and upper floors on the north side of the museum. The Americas collection is located in the northeast corner of the ground floor. Egyptian artifacts are found in the large gallery to the west of the Great Court and on the first floor.

Ground floor

Key to floorplan

- Asian collection
- Enlightenment
- Coins and medals
- Greek and Roman collection
- Egyptian collection
- Middle Eastern collection
- Europe collection
- Africa, Oceania and the Americas
- Temporary exhibitions
- Non-exhibition space

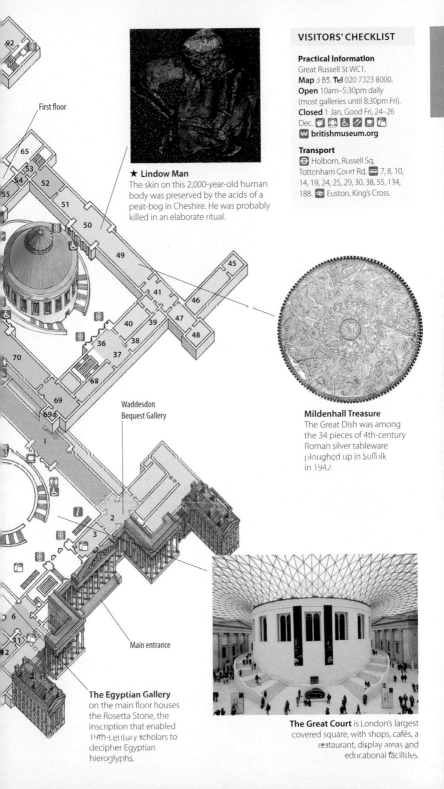

★ Lindow Man
The skin on this 2,000-year-old human body was preserved by the acids of a peat-bog in Cheshire. He was probably killed in an elaborate ritual.

VISITORS' CHECKLIST

Practical Information
Great Russell St WC1.
Map 3 B5. **Tel** 020 7323 8000.
Open 10am–5:30pm daily
(most galleries until 8:30pm Fri).
Closed 1 Jan, Good Fri, 24–26
Dec. 🎥 🏛 ♿ ✏ 🖥 📷
w britishmuseum.org

Transport
🚇 Holborn, Russell Sq,
Tottenham Court Rd. 🚌 7, 8, 10,
14, 19, 24, 25, 29, 30, 38, 55, 134,
188. 🚆 Euston, King's Cross.

First floor

92

65
53
54 52
55 51
50
49
45
41 46
47
40 39
36 38 48
37
70
68
69
69a

Waddesdon
Bequest Gallery

Mildenhall Treasure
The Great Dish was among the 34 pieces of 4th-century Roman silver tableware ploughed up in Suffolk in 1942.

i
2
3

6
11
2

Main entrance

The Egyptian Gallery
on the main floor houses the Rosetta Stone, the inscription that enabled 19th-century scholars to decipher Egyptian hieroglyphs.

The Great Court is London's largest covered square, with shops, cafés, a restaurant, display areas and educational facilities.

THE CITY AND SOUTHWARK

Dominated today by glossy office blocks, the City is the oldest part of the capital. When the Great Fire of 1666 obliterated four-fifths of its buildings, Sir Christopher Wren (see p119) rebuilt much of it, and many of his churches survived World War II. Commerce has always been the City's lifeblood, and the power of its merchants and bankers secured it a degree of autonomy from state control. The area hums with activity through the day and night.

In the Middle Ages Southwark, on the south bank of the River Thames, was a refuge for pleasure-seekers, prostitutes, gamblers and criminals. Even after 1550, when the area fell under the jurisdiction of the City, its brothels and taverns thrived. There were also several bear-baiting arenas in which plays were staged until the building of theatres such as the Globe (1598), where many of Shakespeare's works were first performed. Relics of old Southwark are mostly on the waterfront, which has been imaginatively redeveloped and provided with a pleasant walkway.

Sights at a Glance

Historic Sights and Buildings
- ❸ Temple
- ❼ Lloyd's Building
- ❽ Sky Garden
- ❾ Monument
- ❿ Tower of London pp122–3
- ⓫ Tower Bridge
- ⓬ City Hall
- ⓭ HMS Belfast
- ⓯ The Old Operating Theatre
- ⓳ Shakespeare's Globe

Pub
- ⓰ George Inn

Museums and Galleries
- ❹ Sir John Soane's Museum
- ❻ Museum of London
- ⓮ The Shard
- ⓴ Tate Modern

Market
- ⓱ Borough Market

Churches and Cathedral
- ❶ St Stephen Walbrook
- ❷ St Paul's Cathedral pp118–19
- ❺ St Bartholomew-the-Great
- ⓲ Southwark Cathedral

See also Street Finder maps 12, 13, 14

| 0 metres | 500 |
| 0 yards | 500 |

◀ Shakespeare's Globe theatre at dusk

For keys to symbols *see back flap*

Street-by-Street: The City

This is the financial heart of London and has been ever since the Romans set up a trading post here 2,000 years ago. For years it was London's main residential area but today very few people live here. The City was severely bombed in World War II and the main clues to its past are streets named after vanished inns and markets. Its numerous churches, many built after the Great Fire of 1666 by the architect Sir Christopher Wren *(see p119)*, are now dwarfed by lavish banks and post-modern developments.

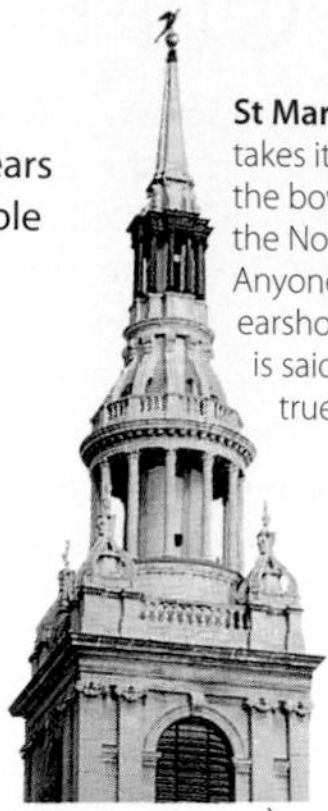

St Mary-le-Bow
takes its name from the bow arches in the Norman crypt. Anyone born within earshot of its bells is said to be a true Cockney.

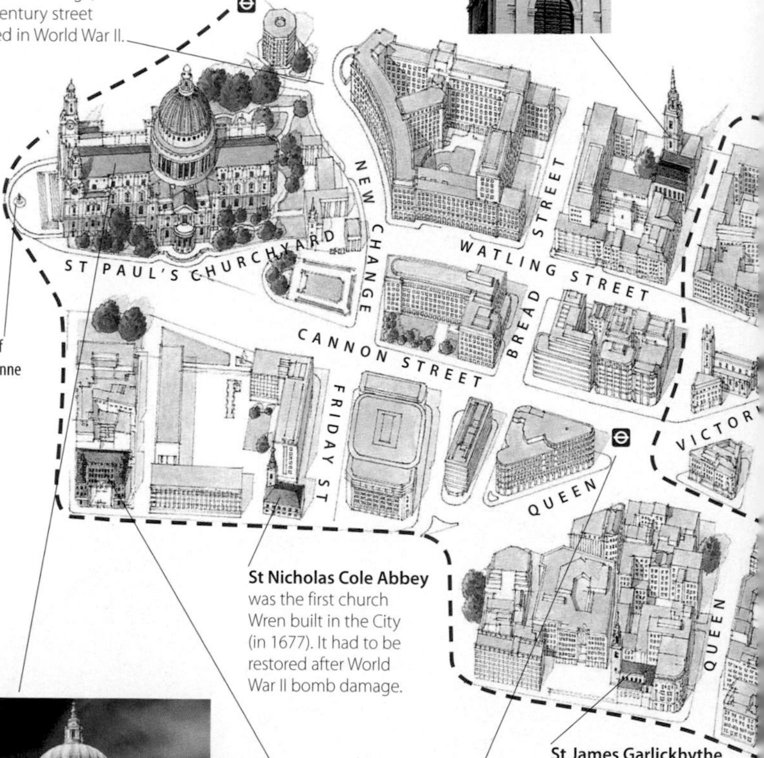

New Change
replaces Old Change, a 13th-century street destroyed in World War II.

St Paul's underground station

Statue of Queen Anne

ST PAUL'S CHURCHYARD

NEW CHANGE

WATLING STREET

BREAD STREET

CANNON STREET

FRIDAY ST

QUEEN

VICTORI

QUEEN

St Nicholas Cole Abbey
was the first church Wren built in the City (in 1677). It had to be restored after World War II bomb damage.

St James Garlickhythe
contains unusual sword rests and hat stands, beneath Wren's elegant spire of 1717.

Mansion House underground station

COLLEGE · OF · ARMS

2 ★ **St Paul's Cathedral**
Built after the Great Fire, Wren's cathedral is a masterpiece of Baroque design.

The College of Arms is the official repository of the coats of arms and pedigrees of British families *(see p34)*. It was rebuilt here, on its former site, in the 1670s after the Great Fire.

Mansion House (1753), designed by George Dance the Elder, is the official home of the Lord Mayor. The Palladian façade is a familiar City landmark.

Locator Map
See Street Finder map 13

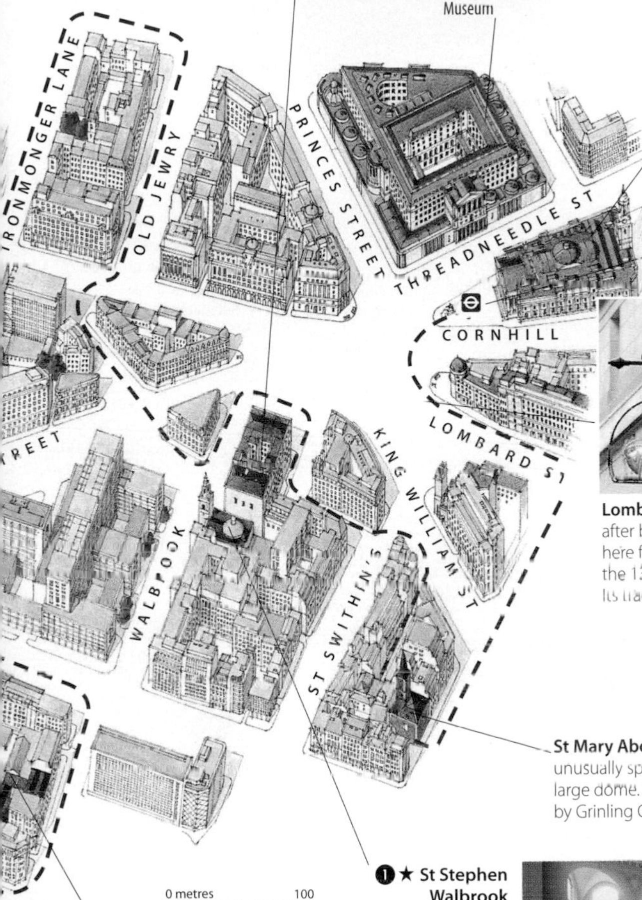

The Royal Exchange was founded in 1565 by Sir Thomas Gresham as a centre for commerce. The current building dates from 1844.

Bank of England Museum

Bank underground station

Lombard Street, named after bankers who came here from Lombardy in the 13th century, retains its traditional banking signs.

Key

— Suggested route

St Mary Abchurch owes its unusually spacious feel to Wren's large dome. The altar carving is by Grinling Gibbons.

❶ ★ St Stephen Walbrook
This fine Wren church contains a striking white stone altar by Henry Moore.

0 metres 100
0 yards 100

Skinners' Hall is an 18th-century Italianate building constructed for the ancient guild that controlled trade in fur and leather.

❶ St Stephen Walbrook

39 Walbrook EC4. **Map** 13 B2. **Tel** 020 7626 9000. 🚇 Bank, Cannon St. **Open** 10am–4pm Mon–Fri (11am–3pm Wed). **Closed** public hols. 🕐 12:45pm Thu. 🌐 **ststephenwalbrook.net**

The Lord Mayor's parish church was built by Sir Christopher Wren in the 1670s and is among the finest of all his City churches. The bright, airy interior is flooded with light by a huge dome that appears to float above the eight columns and arches that support it. The dome, deep and coffered with ornate plasterwork, was a forerunner of St Paul's. Original fittings, such as the highly decorative font cover and pulpit canopy, contrast with the stark simplicity of Henry Moore's massive white stone altar (1987). The best time to see the church is during one of its free organ recitals from 12:30 to 1:30pm on Fridays or chamber-music recitals at 1pm on Tuesdays (except Aug).

❷ St Paul's Cathedral

See pp118–19.

The altar at Temple Church, with stained-glass windows above

❸ Temple

Map 12 E2. 🚇 Temple. Inner Temple: King's Bench Walk EC4. **Tel** 020 7797 8250. **Open** 6am–8pm Mon–Fri, all day Sat & Sun (grounds only). 🚻 Middle Temple Hall: Middle Temple Ln EC4. **Tel** 020 7427 4800. **Open** for lunch (book ahead). 🚻 🌐 **middletemple hall.org.uk**. Temple Church: **Tel** 020 7353 3470. **Open** 11am–1pm & 2–4pm Mon–Fri; Sun service. 📷 book ahead.

A cluster of atmospheric squares form the Inner and Middle

Temples, two of London's four Inns of Court, where law students are trained. The name Temple derives from the medieval Knights Templar, a religious order which protected pilgrims to the Holy Land and was based here until 1312. Marble effigies of knights lie on the floor of the circular Temple Church, part of which dates from the 12th century. Middle Temple Hall has a fine Elizabethan interior.

❺ St Bartholomew-the-Great

West Smithfield EC1. **Map** 4 F5. **Tel** 020 7600 0440. 🚇 Barbican, St Paul's. **Open** 8:30am–5pm Mon–Fri (4pm in winter), 10:30am–4pm Sat, 8:30am–8pm Sun. **Closed** 1 Jan, 25 & 26 Dec. 📷 🚻 by appt. 🚻 📷 📷 🌐 **greatstbarts.com**

The historic area of Smithfield has witnessed a number of bloody events over the years, among them the execution of rebel peasant leader Wat Tyler in 1381 and, in the reign of Mary I (1553–58), the burning of scores of Protestant martyrs.

❹ Sir John Soane's Museum

13 Lincoln's Inn Fields WC2. **Map** 12 D1. **Tel** 020 7405 2107. 🚇 Holborn. **Open** 10am–5pm Tue–Sat, 6–9pm 1st Tue of month. **Closed** public hols, 24 Dec. 📷 see website for details. 🚻 call ahead of your visit. 🌐 **soane.org**

One of the most eccentric museums in London, this house was left to the nation by Sir John Soane in 1837, with a stipulation that nothing should be changed. The son of a bricklayer, Soane became one of Britain's leading late Georgian architects, developing a restrained Neo-Classical style of his own. After marrying the niece of a wealthy builder, whose fortune he inherited, he bought and reconstructed No. 12 Lincoln's Inn Fields. In 1813 he and his wife moved into No. 13 and in 1824 he rebuilt No. 14, adding a picture gallery and the mock medieval Monk's Parlour. Today, true to Soane's wishes, the

collections are much as he left them – an eclectic gathering of beautiful, instructional and often simply peculiar artifacts. There are casts, bronzes, vases, antique fragments, paintings and a selection of bizarre trivia which ranges from a giant fungus from Sumatra to a scold-bridle, a device designed to silence nagging wives. Highlights include the sarcophagus of Seti I, Soanes's own designs, including those for the Bank of England, models by leading Neo-Classical sculptors and the *Rake's Progress* series of paintings (1734) by William Hogarth, which Mrs Soane bought for £570.

The building itself is full of architectural surprises and illusions. In the main ground floor room, cunningly placed mirrors play tricks with light and space, while an atrium stretching from the basement to the glass-domed roof allows light on to every floor. Audio tours can be downloaded from the website.

A glass dome lets light on to all the floors.

A vast sarcophagus (1300 BC) stands on the floor of the crypt.

Hidden in a quiet corner behind Smithfield meat market (central London's only surviving wholesale food market), this is one of London's oldest churches. It once formed part of a priory founded in 1123 by a monk, Rahere, whose tomb is here. He was Henry I's court jester until he dreamed that St Bartholomew had saved him from a winged monster.

The 13th-century arch, now topped by a Tudor gatehouse, used to be the entrance to the church until the old nave was pulled down during the Dissolution of the Monasteries (see p355). The painter William Hogarth was baptized here in 1697. The church featured in the films *Four Weddings and a Funeral* and *Shakespeare in Love*.

St Bartholomew's gatehouse atop the original 13th-century archway

Delft plate made in London 1600, Museum of London

❻ Museum of London

150 London Wall EC2. **Map** 13 A1.
Tel 020 7001 9844. 🚇 Barbican, St Paul's. **Open** 10am–6pm daily.
Closed 24–26 Dec. 🚻 ♿ 🚫 🖥 📷
W museumoflondon.org.uk

This museum traces 450,000 years of life in London from prehistoric times to the present day. Displays of archaeological finds, including the remains of the Shepperton Woman, thought to be between 5,100 and 5,640 years old, and domestic objects alternate with reconstructed street scenes and interiors to bring the many incarnations of the city to life. Highlights include a working model of the Great Fire of 1666 in the London's Burning section and the brightly coloured 2nd-century fresco from a Southwark bathhouse in the Roman London gallery.

The Sackler Hall, at the heart of the musem, has a bank of computers where visitors can find out more the objects on display as well as changing exhibitions showcasing London talent.

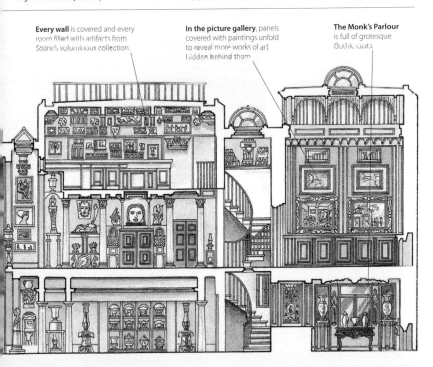

Every wall is covered and every room filled with artifacts from Soane's voluminous collection.

In the picture gallery, panels covered with paintings unfold to reveal more works of art hidden behind them.

The Monk's Parlour is full of grotesque Gothic casts.

❷ St Paul's Cathedral

The Great Fire of London in 1666 left the medieval cathedral of St Paul's in ruins. Wren was commissioned to rebuild it, but his design for a church on a Greek Cross plan (where all four arms are equal) met with considerable resistance. The authorities insisted on a conventional Latin cross, with a long nave and short transepts, which was believed to focus the congregation's attention on the altar. Despite the compromises, Wren created a magnificent Baroque cathedral, which was built between 1675 and 1710 and has since formed the lavish setting for many state ceremonies.

★ **West Front and Towers**
Inspired by the Italian Baroque architect, Borromini, the towers were added by Wren in 1707.

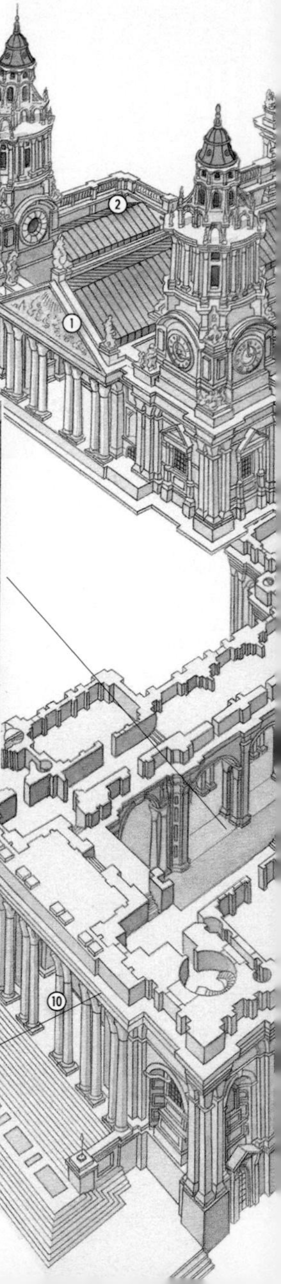

KEY

① **The West Portico** consists of two storeys of coupled Corinthian columns, topped by a pediment carved with reliefs showing the Conversion of St Paul.

② **The balustrade** along the top was added in 1718, against Wren's wishes.

③ **The lantern** weighs 700 tonnes.

④ **The Golden Gallery** has splendid views over London.

⑤ **The oculus** is an opening through which the cathedral floor can be seen.

⑥ **Stone Gallery**

⑦ **The High Altar** canopy was constructed in the 1950s, after the cathedral was bombed in World War II, and is based on designs by Wren.

⑧ **Entrance to crypt**, which has many memorials to the famous.

⑨ **The South Portico** was inspired by the porch of Santa Maria della Pace in Rome.

⑩ **West Porch**

The Nave
An imposing succession of massive arches and saucer domes open out into the vast space below the cathedral's main dome.

Main entrance approached from Ludgate Hill

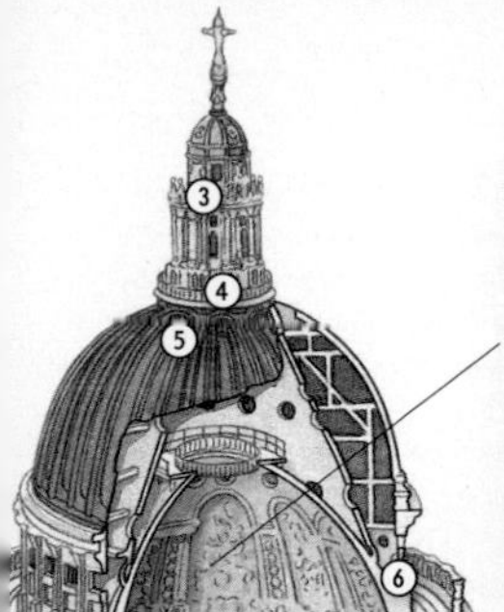

VISITORS' CHECKLIST

Practical Information
Ludgate Hill EC4. **Map** 13 A2.
Tel 020 7236 4128. **Open** 8:30am–
4:30pm Mon–Sat (last adm: 4pm).
Closed for sightseeing Sun; check
website for closures of all or part
of the cathedral. 🖼 includes
audio guide. 🎧 🏛 🚻 ♿
🍴 11am Sun. 🔔 📷 🏛
🌐 **stpauls.co.uk**

Transport
🚇 St Paul's, Mansion House.
🚌 4, 11, 15, 17, 23, 25, 76, 172.
🚃 City Thameslink.

★ Dome
At 111 m (365 ft),
the elaborate
dome is one of
the highest in
the world.

★ Whispering Gallery
The dome's unusual acoustics mean that words
whispered against the wall can be heard clearly
on the opposite side.

Quire
Jean Tijou, a
Huguenot refugee,
created much of the
fine wrought iron-
work in Wren's time,
including these
quire screens.

Entrance to
Golden, Whispering
and Stone galleries

Quire Stalls
The 17th-century quire stalls
and organ case were made by
Grinling Gibbons (1648–1721),
a wood-carver from Rotterdam.
He and his team of craftsmen
worked on these intricate carvings
for two years.

Christopher Wren

Trained as a scientist, Sir Christopher
Wren (1632–1723) began his impressive
architectural career at the age of 31. He
became a leading figure in the rebuilding
of London after the Great Fire of 1666,
building a total of 52 new churches. Although
Wren never visited Italy, his work was influenced by Roman,
Baroque and Renaissance architecture, as is apparent in his
masterpiece, St Paul's Cathedral.

Richard Rogers' Lloyd's building, as seen by night, illuminated by floodlights

❼ Lloyd's Building

1 Lime St EC3. **Map** 13 C2. **Tel** 020 7327 1000. 🚇 Monument, Bank, Aldgate.

Lloyd's was founded in the late 17th century and soon became the world's main insurer, issuing policies on everything from oil tankers to Betty Grable's legs.

The present building, designed by Richard Rogers, dates from 1986. Its exaggerated stainless-steel external piping and high-tech ducts echo Rogers' forceful Pompidou Centre in Paris. Lloyd's is well worth seeing floodlit at night. The interior is open to visitors once a year, during Open House London.

❽ Sky Garden

20 Fenchurch St EC3. **Map** 13 C2. **Tel** 020 7337 2344. 🚇 Bank, Monument. **Open** 10am–6pm Mon–Fri, 11am–9pm Sat & Sun (last adm: 1 hr earlier). Advance booking essential. Bars and restaurants: **Open** 7am–midnight. 🚹 **W** **skygarden.london**

Completed in 2014, the Rafael Viñoly-designed 20 Fenchurch Street skyscraper is commonly known as the "Walkie-Talkie",

thanks to its unusual shape. It has been the most controversial of London's modern towers, in part because its shape and position makes it particularly obtrusive on the skyline. However, it's one of the few with free, simple public access: book a ticket online to the Sky Garden, a large three-level viewing deck at the top of the building. Tickets are released three weeks in advance, and go quickly for popular times. There is also the Sky Pod bar (pre-booking advised) and some pricey restaurants. The Sky Garden is a perfect place from which to view London's other mega-structures: to the south, the Shard; and north, Tower 42, the immediately recognizable "Gherkin", and the "Cheesegrater" or Leadenhall Building. On Bishopsgate is Heron Tower, currently the tallest building in the City.

⓫ Tower Bridge

SE1. **Map** 14 D3. **Tel** 020 7403 3761. 🚇 Tower Hill. The Tower Bridge Exhibition: **Open** 10am–6pm daily (Oct–Mar: 9:30am–5:30pm; last adm: 1 hr before closing). **Closed** 24–26 Dec. 🚹 📷 pre-book (020 7407 9191). ♿ access lift. 🏠 **W** **towerbridge.org.uk**

This flamboyant piece of Victorian engineering, designed by Sir

Horace Jones, was completed in 1894 and soon became a symbol of London. Its two Gothic towers contain the mechanism for raising the roadway to permit large ships to pass through. The towers are made of a steel framework clad in stone, linked by two high-level walkways which were closed between 1909 and 1982 due to their popularity with

suicides and prostitutes. The bridge houses the Tower Bridge Exhibition, with interactive displays bringing the bridge's history to life. There are fine river views from the walkways, including through the glass floor, and a look at the steam engine room that powered the lifting machinery until 1976, when the system was electrified.

Walkways, open to the public, give panoramic views over the Thames and London.

The roadway, when raised, creates a space 40 m (135 ft) high and 60 m (200 ft) wide, big enough for large cargo ships.

Engine room

South Bank

Lifts and 300 steps lead to the top of the towers.

The Victorian winding machinery was originally powered by steam.

Entrance

North Bank

❾ Monument

Monument St EC3. **Map** 13 C2.
Tel 020 7626 2717. 🚇 Monument.
Open Apr–Sep: 9:30am–6pm; Oct–
Mar: 9:30am–5:30pm (last adm: 5pm).
Closed 1 Jan, 24–26 Dec. 🚭
w themonument.info

This Doric column, designed
by Wren to commemorate the
Great Fire of London that devastated the original walled city in
September 1666, was, in 1681,
the tallest isolated stone column
in the world. Topped with a
bronze flame, the Monument is
62 m (205 ft) high; the exact distance west to Pudding Lane,
where the fire is believed to
have started. Reliefs around the
base show Charles II restoring
the city after the tragedy.

The now restored column has
311 tightly spiralled steps that
lead to a tiny viewing platform.
(In 1842, it was enclosed with an
iron cage to prevent suicides.)
The steep climb is well worth
the effort as the views from the
top are spectacular and visitors
are rewarded with a certificate.

❿ Tower of London

See pp122–3.

⓫ Tower Bridge

See p120.

⓬ City Hall

The Queen's Walk SE1. **Map** 14 D4.
Tel 020 7983 4000. 🚇 London Bridge.
Open 8:30am–6pm Mon–Thu, 8:30am–
5:30pm Fri. 🛗 🖥 **w** london.gov.
uk/city-hall

The Norman Foster-designed
domed glass building near
Tower Bridge is the headquarters
for London's Mayor and the
Greater London Authority.
Anyone can visit the building
and look in on the assembly
chamber, or sit in on Mayor's
Question Time when assembly
members interrogate the mayor
on London issues (check website
for dates). On the lower ground
floor are temporary exhibitions
and a café. Outside, the stone
amphitheatre known as the
Scoop hosts free summer events.

The Shard dominating the skyline

⓭ HMS Belfast

The Queen's Walk SE1. **Map** 13 C3.
Tel 020 7940 6300. 🚇 London Bridge,
Tower Hill. **Open** 10am–6pm daily
(Nov–Feb: to 5pm; last adm: 1 hr
before closing). **Closed** 24–26 Dec.
🚭 🎧 🛗 limited. 🖥 🎦
w iwm.org.uk/visits/hms-belfast

Originally launched in 1938 to
serve in World War II, the 11,500-
ton warship HMS *Belfast* was
instrumental in the destruction
of the German battle cruiser
Scharnhorst in the battle of North
Cape, and also played a key role
in the Normandy Landings.
After the war, it was sent to work
for the United Nations in Korea.
The ship remained in service
with the Royal Navy until 1965.

Since 1971, *Belfast* has been a
floating museum. Some of it has
been recreated to show how the
ship was in 1943, when it partici-
pated in sinking the German
battle cruiser. Other displays
portray life on board during
World War II, and there are also
general exhibits which relate to
the history of the Royal Navy.

As well as being a great family
day out, on selected weekends
children can participate in
activities and events on board.

The naval gunship HMS *Belfast* on
the River Thames

⓮ The Shard

London Bridge St SE1. **Map** 13 C4.
Tel 0844 499 7111 (bookings).
🚇 London Bridge. **Open** Apr–Oct:
10am–10pm daily; Nov–Mar: 10am–
7pm Sun–Wed, 10am–10pm Thu–Sat
(last adm: 1 hr before closing.)
Closed 25 Dec. 🚭 🎦 🛗 🎦
w theviewfromtheshard.com

Designed by Italian architect
Renzo Piano, the Shard is one of
the tallest buildings in Western
Europe. At 310 m (1,016 ft) tall, it
dominates the London skyline,
its appearance changing with
the weather due to the crystalline
façade that reflects the sky. The
building's 95 floors are home to
offices, apartments, the five-star
Shangri-La hotel, and observation
gallery The View, which allows
visitors 360-degree panoramas
covering 40 miles (64 km). Top
floors have multimedia displays.

⓯ The Old
Operating Theatre

9a St Thomas St SE1. **Map** 13 B4.
Tel 020 7188 2679. 🚇 London
Bridge. **Open** 10:30am–5pm daily.
Closed 15 Dec–5 Jan. 🚭 🎦
🛗 partial. **w** thegarret.org.uk

St Thomas's Hospital stood here
from its foundation in the 12th
century until it was moved west
in 1862. At this time most of its
buildings were demolished to
make way for the railway. The
women's operating theatre (The
Old Operating Theatre Museum
and Herb Garret) survived only
because it was away from the
main buildings. It lay, bricked up
and forgotten, until the 1950s.
Britain's oldest operating theatre,
dating back to 1822, it has now
been fitted out as it would have
been in the early 19th century

⑩ Tower of London

Soon after William the Conqueror became king in 1066, he built a fortress here to guard the entrance to London from the Thames Estuary. In 1097 the White Tower was completed in sturdy stone; other fine buildings have been added over the centuries. The tower has served as a royal residence, armoury, treasury and, most famously, as a prison. Some were tortured here and among those who met their death were the "Princes in the Tower", the sons and heirs of Edward IV. Today the tower is a popular attraction, housing the Crown Jewels and other exhibits, including a display on the Peasants' Revolt of 1381, the only time the tower's walls were breached. The most celebrated residents are the ravens; legend has it that the kingdom will fall if they desert the tower. All guided tours are led by the colourful Beefeaters.

★ Jewel House
Among the magnificent Crown Jewels is the Sceptre with the Cross (1660), which contains the world's biggest diamond.

Beauchamp Tower
Many high-ranking prisoners were held here, often with their own retinues of servants. The tower was built by Edward I around 1281.

Queen's House
This Tudor building is the sovereign's official residence at the tower.

Main entrance from Tower Hill

KEY

① **Two 13th-century curtain walls** protect the tower.

② **Tower Green** was the execution site for favoured prisoners, away from crowds on Tower Hill, where many had to submit to public execution. Ten people died here, including two of Henry VIII's six wives, Anne Boleyn and Catherine Howard.

The Crown Jewels

The world's best-known collection of precious objects, displayed in a splendid exhibition room, includes the gorgeous regalia of crowns, sceptres, orbs and swords used at coronations and other state occasions. Most date from 1661, when Charles II commissioned replacements for regalia destroyed by Parliament after the execution of Charles I *(see pp56–7)*. Only a few older pieces survived, hidden by royalist clergymen until the Restoration – notably Edward the Confessor's sapphire ring, said to be incorporated into the Imperial State Crown *(see p77)*. The crown was made for Queen Victoria in 1837 and has been used at every coronation since.

The Sovereign's Orb (1661), a hollow gold sphere encrusted with jewels

"Beefeaters"
Thirty-seven Yemen Warders guard the Tower and live here. Their uniforms date back to Tudor times.

★ White Tower
When the tower was finished in 1097, it was the tallest building in London at 27 m (90 ft) high.

★ Chapel of St John
This austerely beautiful Romanesque chapel is a particularly fine example of Norman architecture

Traitors' Gate
The infamous entrance was used for prisoners brought from trial in Westminster Hall.

Bloody Tower
A permanent display explores the mysterious disappearance of Edward IV's two sons, who were put here by their uncle, Richard of Gloucester (later Richard III), after their father died in 1483. The princes disappeared, and Richard was crowned later that year. In 1674 the skeletons of two children were found nearby.

The George Inn, owned by the National Trust

⑯ George Inn

77 Borough High St SE1. **Map** 13 B4.
Tel 020 7407 2056. ⊖ London
Bridge, Borough. **Open** 11am–11pm
daily. **Closed** 25 & 26 Dec. 🖉 🛅
W nationaltrust.org.uk/george-inn

Dating from the 17th century,
this building is the only traditional
galleried coaching inn left in
London and is mentioned in
Dickens' *Little Dorrit*. It was rebuilt
after the Southwark fire of 1676
in a style that dates back to the
Middle Ages. There were three
wings around a courtyard, where
plays were staged in the 17th
century. In 1889, the north and
east wings were demolished, so
there is only one wing remaining.
    The inn is still a popular
pub with a comfortable atmosphere, perfect on a cold, damp
day. In the summer, the yard fills
with picnic tables, and patrons
are occasionally entertained
by actors and morris dancers.
The house bitter is highly
recommended.

⑰ Borough Market

8 Southwark St SE1. **Map** 13 B4.
Tel 020 7407 1002. ⊖ London Bridge.
Open 10am–5pm Mon–Thu (fewer
stalls & shops Mon & Tue), 10am–6pm
Fri, 8am–5pm Sat. **W** borough
market.org.uk

Borough Market was once an
exclusively wholesale fruit and
vegetable market, which had its
origins in medieval times, and
moved to its current position

beneath the railway tracks in 1756.
This hugely popular fine-food
market has now become well
established, selling gourmet
foods from Britain and abroad, as
well as quality fruit and vegetables, to locals and tourists alike.

Shakespeare memorial window (1954),
Southwark Cathedral

⑱ Southwark Cathedral

Montague Close SE1. **Map** 13 B3.
Tel 020 7367 6700. ⊖ London Bridge.
Open 8am–6pm daily (from 8:30am Sat
& Sun); limited access during services.
📷 ♿ 🚻 🖼 📷 **W** cathedral.
southwark.anglican.org

Although some parts of this
building date back to the 12th
century, it became a cathedral
only in 1905. Many original
features remain, notably the
tomb of the poet John Gower
(c.1325–1408), a contemporary
of Chaucer *(see p191)*. There is a
monument to Shakespeare,
carved in 1912, and a memorial
window installed in 1954.

⑲ Shakespeare's Globe

21 New Globe Walk SE1.
Map 13 A3. **Tel** 020 7902 1400.
Box office: 020 7401 9919.
⊖ Southwark, London Bridge.
Exhibition: **Open** 9am–5pm daily.
Closed 24 & 25 Dec. 🖉 🖋 every
30 mins, 9:30am–12:30pm daily
(to 11:30am Sun, 5pm Mon)
Performances: late Apr–mid-Oct.
♿ limited. 🖉 📷 🖼
W shakespearesglobe.com

Opened in 1997, this circular
building is a faithful reproduction of an Elizabethan
theatre, close to the site of the
original Globe where many of
Shakespeare's plays were first
performed. It was built using
handmade bricks and oak laths,
fastened with wooden pegs
rather than metal screws, and its
thatched roof is the first to have
been allowed in London since
the Great Fire of 1666. Open
to the elements (although
the seating area is covered),
the main theatre offers one of
the most stimulating theatrical
experiences in London but
operates only in the summer.
A second theatre, the Sam
Wanamaker Playhouse, is a
splendidly atmospheric
reproduction of a Jacobean
indoor candlelit theatre, with
performances all year round.
    Beneath the theatre,
Shakespeare's Globe Exhibition
is open all year and covers many
aspects of Shakespeare's work
and times. Groups of 15 or more
may book to see the foundations
of the nearby Rose Theatre.

Shakespeare's *Henry IV* (performed at the
Globe Theatre around 1600)

⑳ Tate Modern

Holland St SE1. **Map** 13 A3. **Tel** 020 7887 8888. Ⓔ Blackfriar's, Southwark. 🚢 to Tate Britain every 40 mins. **Open** 10am–6pm Sun–Thu, 10am–10pm Fri & Sat. **Closed** 24–26 Dec. 🎫 major exhibitions. 🅿️ ♿ ✏️ 📷 🎞️
Ⓦ **tate.org.uk/visit/tate-modern**

Looming over the southern bank of the Thames, Tate Modern occupies the converted Bankside power station, a dynamic space for one of the world's premier collections of contemporary art. Tate Modern draws its main displays from the expansive Tate Collection, also shown at the other Tate galleries: Tate St Ives (p281), Tate Liverpool (p381) and Tate Britain (p95). The displays change frequently, and works are sometimes moved temporarily, loaned out or removed for restoration. Works shown on these pages are examples of what might be on display. A river boat service transports visitors between Tate Modern and Tate Britain.

A massive new 11-storey extension, the Switch House, topped with a fantastic viewing platform, opened in 2016, increasing the size of Tate Modern by 60 per cent. This was accompanied by a complete rehang of the collection in the original building, now known as the Boiler House, with the

The Turbine Hall is used for temporary exhibitions of large-scale work

gigantic Turbine Hall at its heart. The first works of art to occupy this huge space, when the gallery opened in 2000, were the gargantuan spider sculpture *Maman* by Louise Bourgeois and her three steel towers *I Do*, *I Undo*, and *I Redo*. Each year a new installation is commissioned, attracting much debate and interest. In 2010, Ai Weiwei's *Sunflower Seeds* filled part of the Turbine Hall with 100 million hand-crafted porcelain seeds. The parallel basement level in the Switch House is home to the Tanks, industrial concrete spaces that are dedicated to live art – from performance and film, to installations and interactive sculptures.

The main collection is housed on levels 2, 3 and 4 of both buildings, and the gallery has continued its unconventional policy of organizing its displays by theme rather than chronology or school – a practice that cuts across movements and mixes up media. The best place to start is Level 2 of the Boiler House, designed for first-time visitors. It provides a kind of taster for the whole collection, featuring iconic works by Henri Matisse and Wassily Kandinsky while introducing lesser-known modern masters and key contemporary artists, like Olafur Eliasson and Gerhard Richter. From here you can explore modern art from

Fish (1926) by Constantin Brancusi

1900 to the present through the themed displays in the Boiler House or follow the development of new kinds of art since 1960 in the Switch House, charting how the roles of the artist, audience and the works of art themselves have changed over the past 50 years.

Across the collection are iconic works from key movements in 20th-century art history including Cubism, Surrealism, Abstract Expressionism, Constructivism and Minimalism. Among them are paintings such as *The Snail* by Matisse and *Quattro Stagioni* by Cy Twombly; sculpture, including *Fish* by Constantin Brancusi; and other important pieces by the likes of Pablo Picasso and Mark Rothko. To complement its permanent collection, Tate Modern presents a dynamic programme of temporary exhibitions, including three large-scale shows per year, and major live events inspired by the collection.

Bankside Power Station

This forbidding fortress was designed in 1947 by Sir Giles Gilbert Scott, the architect of Battersea Power Station, Waterloo Bridge and London's famous red telephone boxes. The power station is of a steel-framed brick skin construction, comprising over 4.2 million bricks. The Turbine Hall was designed to accommodate huge oil-burning generators and three vast oil tanks are still in situ, now converted into striking gallery spaces in the new Switch House. The power station itself was converted by Swiss architects Herzog and de Meuron, who designed the two-storey glass box, or lightbeam, which runs the length of the building. This serves to flood the upper galleries with light and also provides wonderful views of London.

The façade, chimney and light beam of Tate Modern

FURTHER AFIELD

Over the centuries London has steadily expanded to embrace the scores of villages that surrounded it, leaving the City as a reminder of London's original boundaries. Although now linked in an almost unbroken urban sprawl, many of these areas have maintained their old village atmosphere and character. Hampstead and Highgate are still distinct enclaves, as are artistic Chelsea and literary Islington. Greenwich, Chiswick and Richmond have retained features that hark back to the days when the Thames was an important artery for transport and commerce, while just to the east of the City the wide expanses of the former docks have been imaginatively rebuilt as new commercial and residential areas.

Sights at a Glance

① Chelsea
② Holland Park
③ Notting Hill and Portobello Road
④ Hampstead
⑤ Hampstead Heath
⑥ Highgate
⑦ Camden and Islington
⑧ East End and Docklands
⑨ Greenwich
⑩ Chiswick
⑪ Richmond and Kew

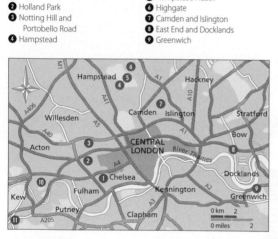

Key

▨ Main sightseeing areas
▢ Greater London
▢ Parks
━ Motorway
━ Major road
═ Minor road

① Chelsea

SW3. 🚇 Sloane Square. **Map** 18 D2.

Riverside Chelsea has been fashionable since Tudor times when Sir Thomas More, Henry VIII's Lord Chancellor, lived here. The river views attracted

Statue of Sir Thomas More (1478–1535), Cheyne Walk

artists, and the arrival of the historian Thomas Carlyle and essayist Leigh Hunt in the 1830s began a literary connection. Blue plaques on the houses of **Cheyne Walk** celebrate former residents such as J M W Turner *(see p95)* and writers George Eliot, Henry James and T S Eliot.

Chelsea's artistic tradition is maintained by its galleries and antique shops, many of them scattered among the clothes boutiques on **King's Road**. This begins at **Sloane Square**, named after the physician Sir Hans Sloane, who bought the manor of Chelsea in 1712. Sloane expanded the **Chelsea Physic Garden** (1673) along Swan Walk to cultivate plants and herbs.

Wren's **Royal Hospital**, on Royal Hospital Road, was built in 1692 as a retirement home for old soldiers and still houses 400 Chelsea Pensioners.

② Holland Park

W8, W14. 🚇 Holland Park. **Map** 7 B5.

This park is more intimate than the large royal parks such as Hyde Park *(see p105)*. It was opened in 1952 on the grounds of **Holland House**, a centre of social and political intrigue in its 19th-century heyday. Adjoining the park on the south side is the **Design Museum** in the striking modernist Commonwealth Institute Building, showcasing contemporary design, from architecture and fashion to graphics and household goods.

Around the park are some magnificent late Victorian houses. Previously known as Linley Sambourne House, **18 Stafford Terrace**, built in about 1870 remains much as Sambourne furnished it, in the Victorian manner, with china ornaments and heavy velvet drapes. He was a political cartoonist for the satirical magazine *Punch* and any of his drawings adorn the walls.

Leighton House, built for the Neo-Classical painter Lord Leighton in 1866, has been preserved as an extraordinary monument to the Victorian Aesthetic movement. Stuffed with *objets d'art* and paintings, some by Leighton himself, the highlight is the Arab Hall, which was added in 1879 to house Leighton's stupendous collection of 13th- to 17th-century Islamic tiles.

Georgian house, Hampstead

▥ Design Museum
224–238 Kensington High St W8. **Tel** 020 7940 8790. ☻ High St Ken, Earls Crt, Holland Pk. **Open** 10am–6pm daily (last adm: 5pm). **Closed** 25 & 26 Dec. ♿ ▢ ▣ ▢ design museum.org

▦ 18 Stafford Terrace
W8. **Tel** Mon–Fri: 020 7602 3316; Sat & Sun: 020 7938 1295. ☻ High St Ken. **Open** Wed, Sat & Sun (tours only 11am–12:15pm; open access 2–5:30pm). ▣ ▣ ▢ ▢ rbkc.gov.uk

▦ Leighton House
12 Holland Park Rd W14. **Tel** 020 7602 3316. ☻ High St Ken. **Open** 10am–5:30pm Wed–Mon (8:30pm on select evenings). **Closed** public hols. ▣ ▢ Wed & Sun. ▢ ▢ ▢ rbkc.gov.uk

❺ Notting Hill and Portobello Road

W11. ☻ Notting Hill Gate. **Map** 7 C3.

In the 1950s and 60s, Notting Hill became a centre for the Caribbean community and today it is a vibrant cosmopolitan part of London. It is also home to Europe's largest street carnival *(see p67)*, which began in 1965 and takes over the entire area on the August bank holiday week-end, when costumed parades run through the crowded streets.

Nearby, Portobello Road market *(see p153)* has a bustling atmosphere with hundreds of stalls and shops selling a variety of collectables.

❹ Hampstead

NW3, N6. ☻ Hampstead. ☷ Hampstead Heath.

On a high ridge north of the metropolis, Hampstead is essentially a Georgian village with many perfectly maintained mansions and houses. It is one of London's most desirable residential areas, home to a community of artists and writers since Georgian times.

Situated in a quiet Hampstead street, **Keats House** (1816) is an evocative tribute to the life and work of the poet John Keats (1795–1821). Keats lived here for two years before his tragic death from consumption at the age of 25, and it was under a plum tree in the garden that he reputedly wrote his celebrated *Ode to a Nightingale.* Mementos of Keats and of Fanny Brawne, the neighbour to whom he was engaged, are on show. Extensive displays include paintings, prints, artifacts and the engagement ring that Keats gave to Fanny.

The **Freud Museum**, which opened in 1986, is dedicated to the dramatic life of Sigmund Freud (1856–1939), the founder of psychoanalysis. At the age of 82, Freud fled from Nazi persecution in Vienna to this Hampstead house where he lived and worked for the last year of his life. His daughter Anna, pioneer of child psychoanalysis, continued to live here until her death in 1982. Inside, Freud's rich Viennese-style consulting rooms remain unaltered, and 1930s home movies show moments of Freud's life, including scenes of the Nazi attack on his home in Vienna.

▦ Keats House
Keats Grove NW3. **Tel** 020 7332 3868. ☻ Hampstead, Belsize Pk. **Open** Mar–Oct: 11am–5pm Wed–Sun; Nov–Feb: 11am–5pm Fri–Sun. **Closed** Christmas week. ▣ 3pm when house is open. ♿ partial. ▢ ▢ keatshouse.cityof london.gov.uk

▦ Freud Museum
20 Maresfield Gdns NW3. **Tel** 020 7435 2002. ☻ Finchley Rd. **Open** noon–5pm Wed–Sun (Aug & Sep: also Mon). **Closed** 1 Jan, 25 & 26 Dec. ▣ ▢ ♿ limited. ▢ ▢ freud.org.uk

Antique shop on Portobello Road

Hampstead Heath with views of nearby Highgate

➎ Hampstead Heath

N6. 🚇 Hampstead, Highgate.
🚃 Hampstead Heath.

Separating the hilltop villages of Hampstead and Highgate, the open spaces of Hampstead Heath are a precious retreat from the city. There are meadows, lakes and ponds for bathing and fishing, and fine views over the capital from **Parliament Hill**, to the east.

Situated in landscaped grounds high on the edge of the Heath is the magnificent **Kenwood House**. The house was remodelled by Robert Adam *(see p32)* in 1764 and most of his interiors have survived, the highlight of which is the library. The mansion is filled with Old Master paintings, such as works by Van Dyck, Vermeer, Turner *(see p95)* and Romney; the star attraction is Rembrandt's self-portrait of 1663. The Brew House Café has a beau-tiful terrace outside, surrounded by lush plants and flowers.

🏛 **Kenwood House**
Hampstead Lane NW3. **Tel** 020 8348 1286. **Open** 10am–5pm daily. 🚻 💷
🅿 **EH** 🆆 english-heritage.org.uk

➏ Highgate

N6. 🚇 Highgate, Archway.

A settlement since the Middle Ages, Highgate became a fashionable aristocratic retreat in the 16th century. Today, it still has an exclusive rural feel, aloof from the urban sprawl below, with a Georgian high street and many expensive houses.

Highgate Cemetery *(see p79)*, with its monuments and hidden corners, has an extraordinary, magical atmosphere. Tour guides (daily in summer, weekends in winter) recount the many tales of intrigue, mystery and vandalism connected with the cemetery since it opened in 1839. In the eastern section is the tomb of Victorian novelist George Eliot (1819–80) and that of the cemetery's most famous incumbent, Karl Marx (1818–83).

🏛 **Highgate Cemetery**
Swains Lane N6. **Tel** 020 8340 1834.
🚇 Archway, Highgate. **Open** Eastern Cemetery: 10am–5pm daily (from 11am Sat & Sun); Western Cemetery: daily by guided tour only (see website). **Closed** during burials, 25 & 26 Dec. 🅿
📷 🚻 🆆 highgatecemetery.org

➐ Camden and Islington

NW1, N1. Camden: 🚇 Camden Town, Chalk Farm. Islington: 🚇 Angel, Highbury & Islington.

Camden is a lively area packed with restaurants, shops and a busy **market** *(see p153)*. Thousands of people come here each weekend to browse among the stalls or simply to soak up the atmosphere of the lively cobbled area around the canal, which is enhanced by buskers and street performers.

Neighbouring Islington was once a fashionable spa but the rich moved out in the late 18th century and the area deteriorated rapidly. In the 20th century, writers such as Evelyn Waugh, George Orwell and Joe Orton lived here. Rediscovered in the 1980s, the area was one of the first in London to become "gentrified", with many residents renovating the old houses.

➑ East End and Docklands

E1, E2, E14. East End: 🚇 Aldgate East, Liverpool St, Bethnal Green, Stratford (for Queen Elizabeth Park). Docklands: 🚇 Canary Wharf.

In the Middle Ages the East End was full of craftsmen practising noxious trades such as brewing, bleaching and vinegar-making, which were banned within the City. The area has also been home to numerous immigrant communities since the 17th century, when French Huguenots, escaping religious persecution, moved into Spitalfields and made it a silk-weaving centre. Textiles continued to dominate in the 1880s, when Jewish tailors and furriers set up workshops here, and in the 1950s, when Bengali machinists worked in cramped conditions.

To enjoy the East End, explore its Sunday street markets *(see p153)* and sample freshly baked bagels and spicy Indian food. By way of contrast, anyone interested in contemporary architecture should visit **Docklands**, an ambitious redevelopment of disused docks, dominated by One Canada Square. Other attractions include the **V&A Museum of Childhood**, a toy museum with lots of activities; **Dennis Severs' House**, which takes a journey from the 17th to the 19th centuries; and the **Museum of London Docklands**, which explores the history of London's river and port.

The East End also hosted the 2012 Olympics. The **Queen Elizabeth Park** in Stratford, home to the aquatics centre, velodrome and impressive Arcelormittal Orbit, an 80-m (262-ft) high sculpture with an observation deck, is a great place to visit and relive the games.

Royal Naval College framing the Queen's House, Greenwich

🔲 **Queen Elizabeth Park**
E20 2ST. **Tel** 080 0072 2110.
Open daily (check website for further details). 🆆 **queenelizabeth olympicpark.co.uk**

❾ Greenwich

SE10. 🚆 Greenwich, Maze Hill.
🚈 Cutty Sark (DLR).

The world's time has been measured from the **Royal Observatory Greenwich** (now housing a museum) since 1884. The area is full of maritime and royal history, with Neo-Classical mansions, a park, antique shops and markets *(see p153)*. The **Queen's House**, designed by Inigo Jones for James I's wife, was completed in 1637 for Henrietta Maria, the queen of Charles I. Its highlights include the perfectly cubic main hall and the spiral "tulip staircase"

The adjoining **National Maritime Museum** has exhibits that range from primitive canoes, through Elizabethan galleons, to modern ships. The **Old Royal**

One Canada Square, Canary Wharf

Naval College was designed by Christopher Wren *(see p119)* in two halves so that the Queen's House kept its river view. The Rococo chapel and the 18th-century *trompe l'oeil* Painted Hall are open to the public.

The majestic **Cutty Sark** was built in 1869 as a tea carrier and made its final voyage in 1938.

Environs
In North Greenwich, **The O2** (formerly the Millennium Dome) is one of London's largest concert venues. It also houses bars, restaurants, a cinema and the smaller IndigO2 venue. You can don safety gear and climb to the top of the outside on a long, bouncy walkway for great views. Nearby, the Emirates Air Line Cable Car connects the Royal Victoria Dock and The O2; the journey takes 5 minutes and offers spectacular views.

🏛 **Royal Observatory Greenwich**
Greenwich Park SE10. **Tel** 020 8858 4422.
Open 10am–5pm daily. **Closed** 24–26 Dec. 📷 🆆 **rog.nmm.ac.uk**

🏛 **Queen's House and National Maritime Museum**
Romney Rd SE10. **Tel** 020 8858 4422.
Open 10am–5pm daily. **Closed** 24–26 Dec ♿ 🖥 📷 🆆 **nmm.ac.uk**

🏛 **Old Royal Naval College**
King William Walk SE10. **Tel** 020 8269 4799. **Open** 10am–5pm daily. **Closed** public hols. 📷 🖥 📷

🏛 **Cutty Sark**
King William Walk SE10. **Tel** 020 8858 4422. **Open** 10am–5pm daily (last adm: 4:15pm). **Closed** 25 & 26 Dec. 📷♿🖥📷

The O2
North Greenwich SE10. **Tel** 020 8463 2000 or 0844 856 0202 (tickets). 🚇 North Greenwich. **Open** 9am–late. Up at The O2 (climbing): **Tel** 020 8463 2680. ♿ 📷 🖥 🆆 **theo2.co.uk**

🏛 **V&A Museum of Childhood**
Cambridge Heath Rd E2. **Tel** 020 8983 5200. **Open** 10am–5:45pm daily. **Closed** 1 Jan, 25 & 26 Dec. ♿ 🖥 📷 🆆 **vam.ac.uk/moc**

🏛 **Dennis Severs' House**
18 Folgate St E1. **Tel** 020 7247 4013. **Open** noon–2pm Mon; 5–9pm Mon, Wed & Fri, noon–4pm Sun. 📷 🔲 🆆 **dennis severshouse.co.uk**

🏛 **Museum of London Docklands**
No.1 Warehouse, West India Quay E14. **Tel** 020 7001 9844. 🚇 Barbican, St Paul's. **Open** 10am–6pm daily. **Closed** 24–26 Dec. ♿ 📷 🖥 📷 🆆 **museumoflondon. org.uk/docklands**

⑩ Chiswick

W4. 🔵 Chiswick.

Chiswick is a pleasant suburb of London, with pubs, cottages and a variety of birdlife, such as herons, along the picturesque riverside. One of the main reasons for a visit is **Chiswick House**, a magnificent country villa inspired by the Renaissance architect Andrea Palladio. It was designed in the early 18th century by the 3rd Earl of Burlington as an annexe to his larger house (demolished in 1758), so he could display art works and entertain friends.

Heron

🏛 Chiswick House

Burlington Lane W4. **Tel** 020 8995 0508. **Open** Mar: 10am–4pm Sat & Sun; Apr–Oct: 10am–6pm Sun–Wed & bank hols (to 5pm Oct). Garden: **Open** dawn–dusk daily. 🎫 for house. ♿ call ahead. ▢ 🏠 **w** chgt.org.uk

⑪ Richmond and Kew

SW15. 🔵 🚉 Richmond.

The attractive village of Richmond took its name from a palace built by Henry VII (the former Earl of Richmond in Yorkshire) in 1500; the remains can be seen off the green. Nearby is expansive **Richmond Park**, once Charles I's royal hunting ground. In summer, boats sail down the Thames from Westminster Millennium Pier, making a pleasant day's excursion from central London.

The nobility continued to favour Richmond after royalty had left, and some of their mansions have survived. The Palladian villa **Marble Hill House** was built in 1724–9 for the mistress of George II and has been restored to its original appearance. On the opposite side of the Thames, **Ham House**, built in 1610, had its heyday later that century when it became the home of the Duke and Duchess of Lauderdale. Elizabeth Countess of Dysart inherited the house from her father, who had been Charles I's "whipping boy" – meaning that he was punished whenever the future king misbehaved. He was rewarded as an adult by being given a peerage and the lease of Ham estate.

North of here, a little downstream, **Syon House** has been inhabited by the Dukes and Earls of Northumberland for over 400 years. Numerous attractions include a butterfly house and a spectacular conservatory built in 1830. The lavish Neo-Classical interiors of the house, created by Robert Adam in the 1760s *(see p32)*, remain the highlight.

On the riverbank to the south, **Kew Gardens** *(see p78)*, the world's most complete botanic gardens, feature examples of nearly every plant that can be grown in Britain. Conservatories display thousands of exotic tropical blooms.

Brewers Lane, a historic narrow lane in Richmond

🏛 Marble Hill House

Richmond Rd, Twickenham. **Tel** 020 8892 5115. **Open** booked tours only: 10:30am & noon Sat; 10:30am, noon, 2:15pm & 3:30pm Sun. 🎫 ♿ ltd. ▢ 🏠 **w** englishheritage.org.uk

🏛 Ham House

Ham St, Richmond. **Tel** 020 8940 1950. **Open** Jan–Mar: guided tour only, hourly noon–3pm daily (to 4pm Sat & Sun); Apr–Dec: noon–4pm daily. Gardens: **Open** daily. 🎫 ♿ ▢ 🏠 NT **w** nationaltrust.org.uk/ham-house

🏛 Syon House

London Rd, Brentford. **Tel** 020 8560 0882. House: **Open** mid-Mar–Oct: 11am–5pm Wed, Thu, Sun & pub hols (last adm: 4pm). Gardens: **Open** daily (winter: Sat & Sun only). 🎫 🎁 ♿ gardens only. ▢ 🏠 **w** syonpark.co.uk

🌿 Kew Gardens

Royal Botanic Gdns, Kew Green, Richmond. **Tel** 020 8332 5655. **Open** from 10am daily (see website for closing times). **Closed** 1 Jan, 24 & 25 Dec. 🎫 🎁 ♿ ⌀ ▢ 🏠 **w** kew.org

Chiswick House

LONDON STREET FINDER

The map references given with the sights, hotels, restaurants, shops and entertainment venues based in central London refer to the following four maps. All the main places of interest within the central area are marked on the maps, in addition to useful practical information, such as tube, railway and coach stations. The key map below shows the area of London that is covered by the Street Finder. The four main city-centre areas (colour-coded in red) are shown in more detail on the inside back cover.

The London skyline across the River Thames, with Waterloo Bridge in the foreground

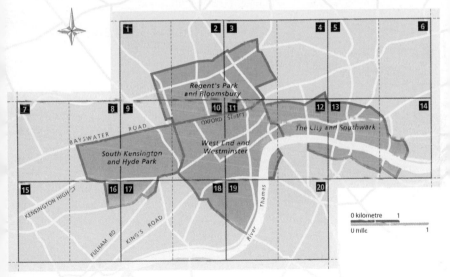

Key

■ Major sight	🏛 Police station
■ Other sight	✝ Church
■ Other building	✡ Synagogue
🚇 Underground station	=== Railway line
🚆 Railway station	▬ Motorway
🚌 Coach/bus station	▬ Pedestrian street
🚢 River boat boarding point	«56 House number (main street)
🅸 Tourist information	
✚ Hospital with casualty unit	

Scale of Map Pages 1:11,000

0 metres 200
0 yards 200

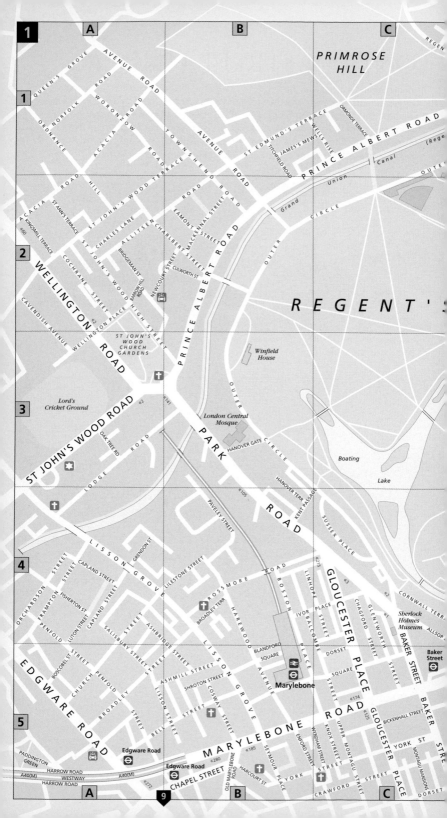

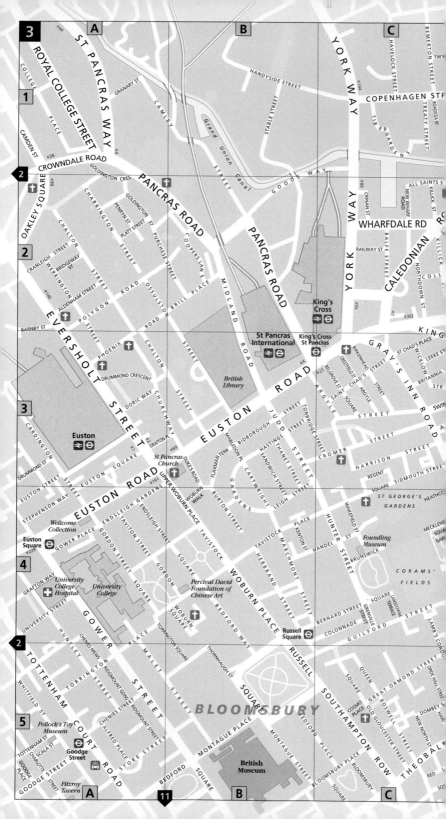

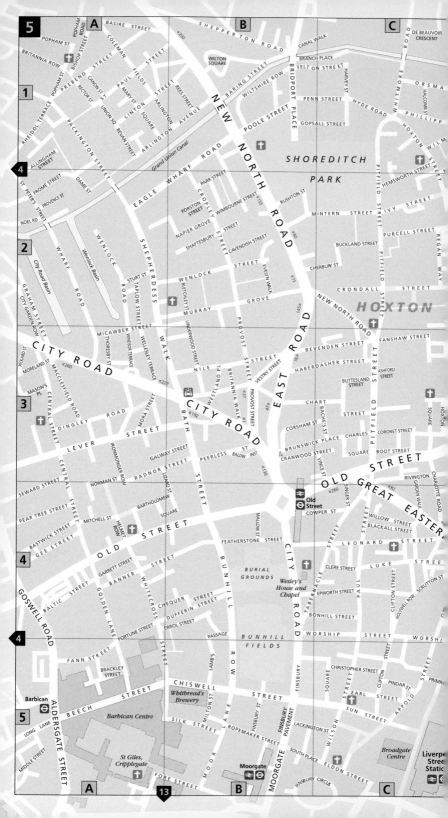

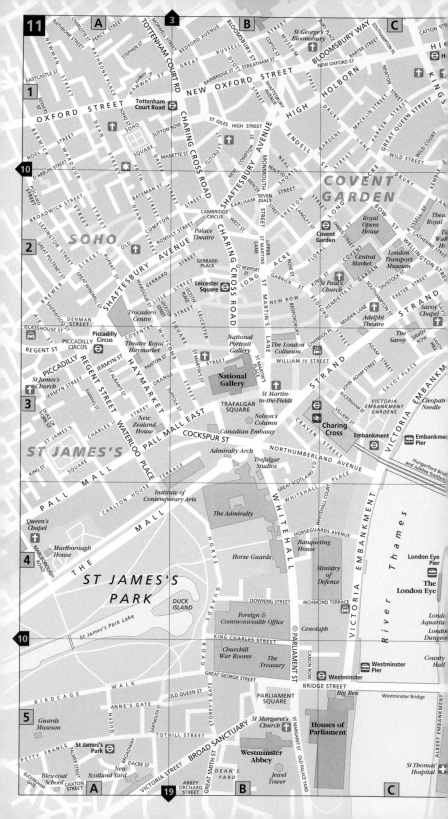

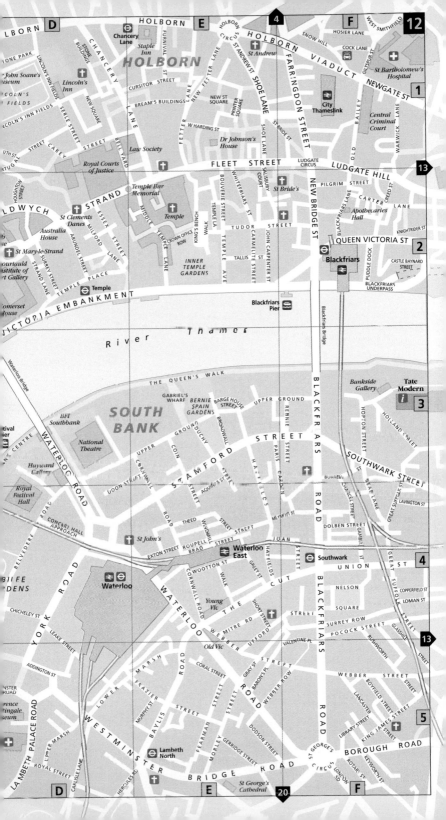

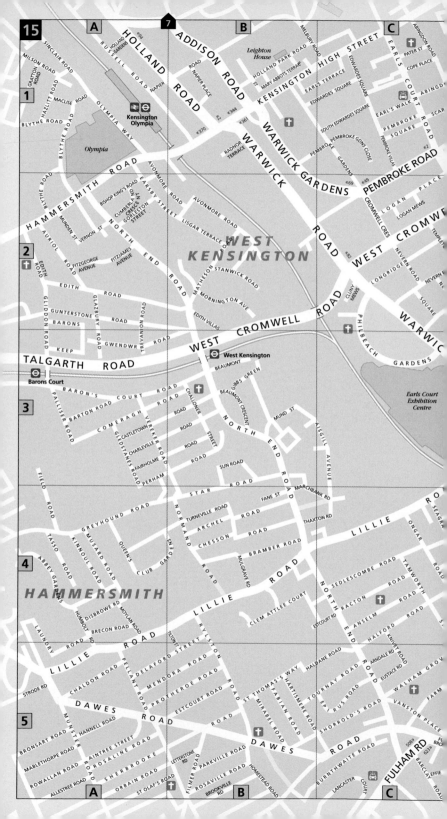

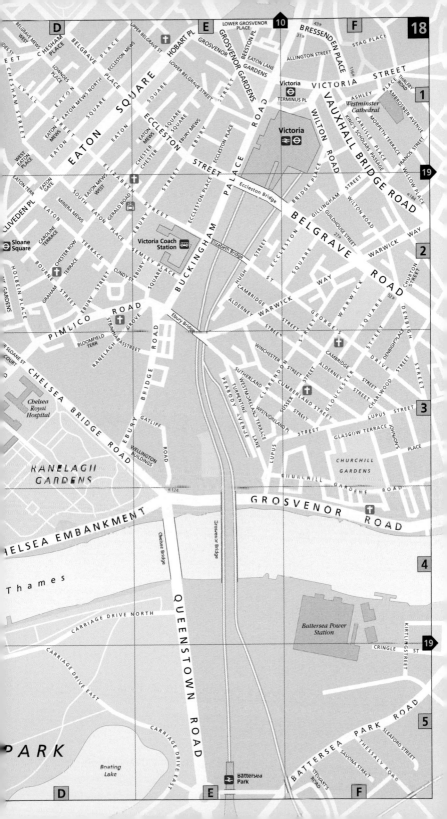

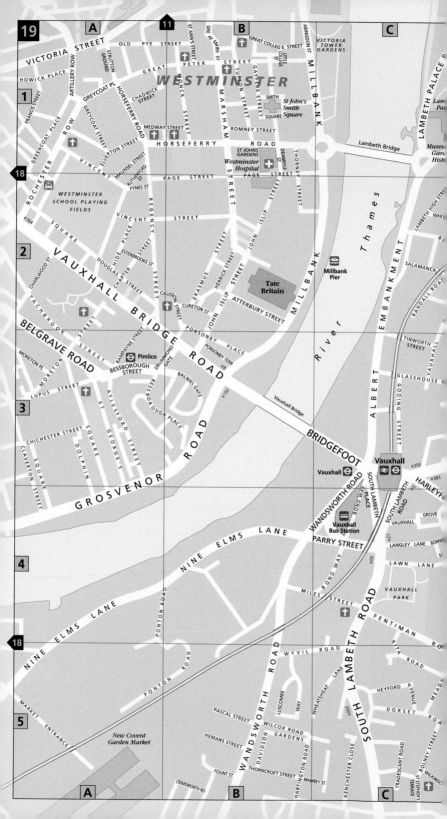

SHOPS AND MARKETS

London is one of the great shopping cities of Europe, with bustling, lively street markets, world-famous department stores and eclectic shops selling clothes, antiques, crafts and more. Whatever you are looking for, there is a place to find it. At the top end, head to the designer shops of Knightsbridge with their stunning window displays, or indulge in the luxurious shopping experience provided by the stores on Regent Street, where ultra-modern shops sit comfortably alongside the old-fashioned emporia. Oxford Street boasts a plethora of stores showcasing the latest in high-street fashion: Topshop's flagship branch is definitely worth a visit. For more bespoke finds, head to Notting Hill and Covent Garden. The vibrant markets of Covent Garden, Berwick Street and Brick Lane are also popular, and bargain hunters will find a wealth of inexpensive goods. Pick up a vintage piece in Camden Market, or browse for bric-a-brac or handmade jewellery on legendary Portobello Road. The city is best known, however, for its huge range of clothes shops selling everything from traditional tweeds to the latest designs from the ever-changing fashion world.

When to Shop

In central London, most shops stay open from 10am to at least 6pm Monday to Saturday. Many department stores, however, have longer hours. "Late night" shopping until 9 or 10pm is on Thursday in Oxford Street and the rest of West End; and on Wednesday in Knightsbridge and Chelsea. Some shops in tourist areas, such as Covent Garden, are open until 7pm or later every day, including Sunday. Some street markets and the majority of highstreet shops are usually open on Sundays as well, though the latter open for reduced hours.

Twice-Yearly Sales

The traditional sale season is from January to February and from June to July, when shops slash prices and sell off leftover stock. The department stores have some of the best reductions – queues for the famous Harrods sale start to form long before it opens.

Department Stores

Harrods is the king of the city's department stores with over 300 departments and a staff of 5,000. The spectacular food hall, decorated with Edwardian tiles, displays fish, cheese, fruit and vegetables. Other specialities include fashion, china and glass, kitchenware and electronics.

Londoners also often head for the nearby **Harvey Nichols**, which stocks the best of everything. The clothing department is particularly strong, with an emphasis on talented British, European and American names. The food hall, opened in 1992, is one of London's most stylish.

Selfridges, on Oxford Street, has arguably the widest choice of fashion labels, a great lingerie department and a section devoted to emerging designers. It also has a food hall that features delicacies from all over the world.

Originally a drapery, **John Lewis** still has a good selection of fabrics and haberdashery. Its china, glass and household items make this store and its Sloane Square partner, **Peter Jones**, equally popular with Londoners.

Liberty, near Carnaby Street, has been famous ever since 1875 for its beautiful silks and other Oriental goods. Don't forget to check out the famous scarf department.

Fortnum & Mason is best known for its ground-floor food department. It has everything from Fortnum's tins of biscuits and tea to cured meats and lovely wicker hampers. In fact, these exquisite delicacies are so engrossing that the upper floors filled with classic fashion and luxury items often remain free of crowds.

Harrods at night, illuminated by 11,500 lights

Markets

Whatever you're looking for, it's definitely worth visiting one of London's colourful markets. Many of them mix English traditions with those of more recent immigrants, creating an exotic atmosphere and a truly fascinating array of merchandise. At some, the seasoned hawkers have honed their sales patter to an entertaining art, which reaches fever pitch just before closing, when the plummeting prices at the end of the day are announced. Keep your wits about you, your hand on your purse and join in the fun.

Among the best of the West End markets are **Grays Antiques** and **Jubilee and Apple** markets in Covent Garden. Although it is somewhat touristy, **Piccadilly Crafts** is also very popular. In Soho, **Berwick Street** combines the vestiges of the traditional street market selling fresh fruit, vegetables and household goods with newer foodie stalls.

In the East End, **Petticoat Lane** is probably the most famous of London's street markets. Those in search of

Sprawling Borough Market, where all manner of goods and food can be found

the latest street fashions make a beeline for **Old Spitalfields**, while **Brick Lane** is massively popular due to its trendy location. Here you can find everything from shellfish to trainers. Nearby, on Sundays **Columbia Road** plays host to a vast flower market.

South of the river, **East Street** also has a flower market, but the majority of its traders sell clothes. **Bermondsey Market** is a gathering point for London's antiques traders. Collectors set off early to scrutinize the fine paintings and old jewellery. **Borough Market** *(see p124)* caters to the restaurant trade

with its fine food and farmer's market. **Brixton Market** stocks a superb assortment of Afro-Caribbean foods, often to the pounding beat of reggae music.

In north London, **Camden Lock Market** offers a vibrant atmosphere and stalls selling everything from vintage clothes to lovely crafts. In nearby Islington, **Camden Passage** is a quiet cobbled street where charming cafés nestle among quaint antiques shops.

In Notting Hill, **Portobello Road** is actually a bunch of markets rolled into one, and an entire afternoon can be spent browsing there.

DIRECTORY

Department Stores

Fortnum & Mason
181 Piccadilly W1. **Map 11** A3. **Tel** 020 7734 8040.

Harrods
87–135 Brompton Rd SW1. **Map** 9 C5. **Tel** 020 7730 1234.

Harvey Nichols
109–125 Knightsbridge SW1. **Map** 9 C5. **Tel** 020 7235 5000.

John Lewis
278–306 Oxford St W1. **Map** 10 E1. **Tel** 020 7629 7711.

Liberty
210–20 Regent St W1. **Map** 10 F2. **Tel** 020 7734 1234.

Peter Jones
Sloane Sq, SW1. **Map** 17 C2. **Tel** 020 7730 3434.

Selfridges
400 Oxford St W1. **Map** 10 D2. **Tel** 0800 123 400.

Markets

Bermondsey Market
Long Lane & Bermondsey St SE1. **Map** 13 C5. **Open** 6am–2pm Fri.

Berwick Street
Berwick St W1. **Map** 11 A2. **Open** 8am–6pm Mon–Sat.

Borough Market
8 Southwark St SE1. **Map** 13 B4. **Open** 10am–5pm Mon–Thu (fewer stalls and shops Mon & Tue), 10am–6pm Fri, 8am–5pm Sat.

Brick Lane
Brick Lane E1. **Map** 6 E5. **Open** 9am–5pm Sun.

Brixton Market
Electric Ave SW9. **Open** 8am–6pm Mon–Sat (to 3pm Wed).

Camden Lock Market
Chalk Farm Rd NW1. **Open** 10am–6pm daily.

Camden Passage
Camden Passage N1. **Map** 4 F1. **Open** 9am–6pm Wed & Sat, 10am–6pm Fri, 11am–6pm Sun.

Columbia Road
Columbia Rd E2. **Map** 6 D3. **Open** 8am–3pm Sun.

East Street
East St SE17. **Open** 8am–5pm Tue–Sun (to 6:30pm Sat and 2pm Sun).

Grays Antiques
58 Davies St, Mayfair. **Map** 10 E2. **Open** 10am–6pm Mon–Fri, 11am–5pm Sat.

Greenwich
College Approach SE10. **Open** 10am–5:30pm daily.

Jubilee and Apple
Covent Gdn Piazza WC2. **Map** 11 C2. **Open** 5am–5pm Mon (Antiques/ Vintage), 10.30am–7pm Tue–Fri (General), 10am–6pm Sat & Sun (Arts/Crafts).

Old Spitalfields
Commercial St E1. **Map** 6 D5. **Open** 10am–5pm Sun–Fri, 11am–5pm Sat (Sun–Wed General; Thu Antiques & Vintage; Fri Fashion & Art; Sat varies).

Petticoat Lane
Middlesex St E1. **Map** 14 D1. **Open** 9am–4pm Mon–Fri (to 2pm Thu).

Piccadilly Crafts
St James's Church, Piccadilly W1. **Map** 11 A3. **Open** 11am–5pm Mon & Tue (Food); 10am–6pm Wed–Sat (Arts/Crafts).

Portobello Road
Portobello Rd W10. **Map** 7 C3. **Open** daily (main market 9am–7pm Sat).

Clothes

British tailoring and fabrics are world-renowned for their high quality. **Henry Poole & Co**, **H Huntsman & Sons** and **Gieves & Hawkes** are among the most highly respected tailors on Savile Row.

A new generation of trend-conscious tailors who specialize in modern cuts and fabrics has firmly established itself on the fashion scene. The line-up includes **Richard James** and **Ozwald Boateng**. Several stalwarts of classic British style have also reinvented themselves as fashion labels. **Burberry** is the best example, although it still does a brisk trade in its famous trenchcoats, and distinctive accessories. **Crombie**, a world-renowned British brand, makes classic, quality garments and accessories for men. Designers **Margaret Howell** and **Nicole Farhi** create trend-setting versions of British country garments for men and women.

London designers are known for their eclectic, irreverent style. *Grande dames* of fashion, Zandra Rhodes and **Vivienne Westwood** have been on the scene since the 1970s. Many other British designers of international stature also have their flagship stores in the capital, including **Stella McCartney** and the late **Alexander McQueen**. Designer clothes, however, are not just the preserve of the rich. If you want a bit of British design but can't afford the prices, it's worth visiting **Debenhams**, which has harnessed the talents of numerous leading designers. Cheaper versions of all the latest styles appear in the shops almost as soon as they have been sashayed down the catwalk. **Topshop** and **Oasis** have both won celebrity fans for their up-to-the-minute ensembles of hip and youthful fashions for women; young professionals head to **French Connection**. The up-market chains **Jigsaw** and **Whistles** are more expensive, with their emphasis on beautiful fabrics and shapes. Fashion-conscious young men can turn to **Paul Smith** and **Ted Baker** for trendy clothing.

Exterior of Harrods department store *(see p152)*

Shoes

Some of the most famous names in the footwear industry are based in Britain. If you can spare a few thousand pounds, you can have a pair custommade by the Royal Family's shoemaker, **John Lobb**. Readymade, traditional brogues and Oxfords are the mainstay of **Church's Shoes**. **Oliver Sweeney** gives classics a contemporary edge. **The British Boot Company** in Camden has the widest range of funky Dr Martens, appropriated by rock'n'rollers and the grunge set. **Jimmy Choo** and **Manolo Blahnik** are two all-time favourites of fashionable women all over the world. Less expensive, yet good quality designs can be found in **Hobbs**, **Dune** or **Clarks**, while **Jones Bootmaker** and **Office** turn out young, voguish styles.

Gifts and Souvenirs

The market in Covent Garden Piazza stocks uniquely British pottery, knitwear and other crafts, and **Neal's Yard Remedies** sells organic health and beauty treats. To buy all your gifts under one roof, visit Liberty *(see p152)*, where all kinds of exquisite items can be found in every department.

Leading museums such as the Victoria and Albert *(see pp102–3)*, Natural History and Science Museums *(see p104)* sell unusual mementos. Try **Hamley's** for gifts and toys.

Books and Magazines

The bookshops in London rank among its most illustrious specialities. Charing Cross Road is a treasure-trove for those hunting for antiquarian, secondhand and new volumes. It is the home of **Foyles**, famous for its massive stock. Large branches of chains such as **Waterstones** co-exist with many specialist stores. **Hatchards** in Piccadilly is the city's oldest bookshop and one of its finest, offering an extensive and varied choice of titles.

Vintage Magazines in Soho stocks publications dating back to the early 1900s.

Art and Antiques

Art and antiques shops abound across London, and you are sure to find something of beauty and value that is within your means.

Cork Street is the centre of Britain's contemporary art world. **Waddington Custot Galleries** is the best-known, while **Redfern Art Gallery** and **Flowers** exhibit unusual modern art.

Visit **Roger's Antiques Galleries** and Grays Antiques *(see p153)* for striking vintage jewellery and objets d'art.

The cutting-edge **White Cube Gallery** has several sites dotted around the city.

For photography, visit the **Photographers' Gallery**, which has the largest collection of originals for sale in Britain. **Hamiltons Gallery** also hosts interesting exhibitions.

DIRECTORY

Clothes

Alexander McQueen
4–5 Old Bond St W1.
Map 10 F3.
Tel 020 7355 0088.

Burberry
21–23 New Bond St W1.
Map 10 F2.
Tel 020 7980 8425.
One of several branches.

Crombie
48 Conduit St W1.
Map 10 F2.
Tel 020 7434 2886.

Debenhams
334–348 Oxford St W1.
Map 10 E2.
Tel 08445 616 161.
One of several branches.

French Connection
10 Argyll St W1.
Map 10 F2.
Tel 020 7287 2046.
One of several branches.

Gieves & Hawkes
1 Savile Row W1.
Map 10 F3.
Tel 020 7432 6403.

H Huntsman & Sons
11 Savile Row W1.
Map 10 F3.
Tel 020 7734 7441.

Henry Poole & Co
15 Savile Row W1.
Map 10 F3.
Tel 020 7734 5985.

Jigsaw
6 Duke of York Sq,
Kings Rd SW3.
Map 17 C2.
Tel 020 7730 4404.
One of several branches.

Margaret Howell
34 Wigmore St W1.
Map 10 E1.
Tel 020 7009 9009.

Nicole Farhi
25 Conduit St W1.
Map 10 F2.
Tel 020 7499 8368.
One of several branches.

Oasis
12–14 Argyll St W1.
Map 10 F2.
Tel 020 7434 1799.
One of several branches.

Ozwald Boateng
30 Savile Row W1.
Map 10 F3.
Tel 020 7437 2030.

Paul Smith
Westbourne House
122 Kensington Park Rd
W11.
Map 7 B2.
Tel 020 7727 3553.
One of several branches.

Richard James
29 Savile Row W1.
Map 10 F2.
Tel 020 7434 0605.

Stella McCartney
30 Bruton St W1.
Map 10 E3.
Tel 020 7518 3100.

Ted Baker
9–10 Floral St WC2.
Map 11 C2.
Tel 020 7836 7808.
One of several branches.

Topshop
Oxford Circus W1.
Map 10 F1.
Tel 08448 487 487.
One of several branches.

Vivienne Westwood
44 Conduit St W1.
Map 10 F2.
Tel 020 7439 1109

Whistles
12–14 St Christopher's Pl
W1. **Map** 10 D1.
Tel 020 7487 4484.
One of several branches.

Shoes

The British Boot Company
5 Kentish Town Rd NW1.
Map 2 F1.
Tel 020 7485 8505.

Church's Shoes
201 Regent St W1.
Map 10 F2.
Tel 020 7734 2438.
One of several branches.

Clarks
203 Regent St W1.
Map 10 F2.
Tel 0844 499 9021.
One of several branches.

Dune
28 Argyll St W1.
Map 10 F2.
Tel 020 7287 9010.
One of several branches.

Hobbs
112–115 Long Acre WC2.
Map 11 C2.
Tel 020 7836 0625.
One of several branches.

Jimmy Choo
27 New Bond St W1.
Map 10 F2.
Tel 020 7493 5858.

John Lobb
88 Jermyn St SW1.
Map 10 F3.
Tel 020 7930 8089.

Jones Bootmaker
84 Old Broad St EC2.
Map 13 C1.
Tel 020 7256 7309.
One of several branches.

Manolo Blahnik
49–51 Old Church St,
Kings Road SW3.
Map 17 A4.
Tel 020 7352 8622.

Office
57 Neal St WC2.
Map 11 B1.
Tel 020 7379 1896.
One of several branches.

Oliver Sweeney
5 Conduit St W1.
Map 10 F2.
Tel 020 7491 9126.
One of several branches.

Gifts and Souvenirs

Hamley's
188–196 Regent St W1.
Map 10 F2.
Tel 0871 704 1977.

Neal's Yard Remedies
15 Neal's Yard WC2.
Map 11 B1.
Tel 020 7379 7222.

Books and Magazines

Foyles
107 Charing Cross Rd
WC2.
Map 11 B1.
Tel 020 7437 5660.
One of several branches.

Hatchards
187 Piccadilly W1.
Map 10 F3.
Tel 020 7439 9921.

Vintage Magazines
39–43 Brewer St W1.
Map 11 A2.
Tel 020 7439 8525.

Waterstones
203–205 Piccadilly W1.
Map 11 A3.
Tel 020 7851 2400.
One of several branches.

Art and Antiques

Flowers
21 Cork St W1
Map 10 F3.
Tel 020 7439 7766.

Hamiltons Gallery
13 Carlos Place W1.
Map 10 E3.
Tel 020 7499 9493.

Photographers' Gallery
16–18 Ramillies St W1.
Map 10 F2.
Tel 0207 087 9300.

Redfern Art Gallery
20 Cork St W1.
Map 10 F3.
Tel 020 7734 1732.

Roger's Antiques Galleries
65 Portobello Road W11.
Map 7 A1.
Tel 07887 527 523.

Waddington Custot Galleries
11 Cork St W1.
Map 10 F3.
Tel 020 7851 2200.

White Cube Gallery
144–152 Bermondsey
Street SE1 & 25–26
Mason's Yard SW1.
Map 13 C5 & 10 F3.
Tel 020 7930 5373.

ENTERTAINMENT

London is one of the great entertainment capitals of the world. Awash with theatres, cinemas, concert venues, sports stadiums and two of the greatest arts and performance hubs in Europe at the South Bank and the Barbican, there is a bewildering choice whatever your tastes and preferences. Since the 16th century, when Shakespeare's plays were first performed, the city's theatre scene has remained almost unrivalled internationally. In the Royal Opera House, London has one of the world's most fabled stages for opera and ballet, and at other renowned venues, notably Sadler's Wells, for contemporary dance. Live music fans are even better catered for, with every possible kind of

venue – from basement jazz clubs and pubs, to converted old cinemas and huge arenas like Wembley and The O2, where pop and rock megastars perform. There are over a dozen stadiums that host professional football and a plethora of other world-class sports venues for rugby, cricket, athletics, tennis and more.

Time Out, published every Tuesday, is a free comprehensive guide to what's on in London, with detailed weekly listings and reviews. *The Evening Standard* and *The Guardian* (Saturday) also have reviews and information on events. There are countless ticket agencies, but Ticketmaster and TKTS are among the most established.

Poster (1898) for the Palace Theatre, known for staging hit shows

West End and National Theatres

The glamorous, glittering world of West End Theatreland, emblazoned with the names of world-famous performers, offers an extraordinary range of entertainment.

West End theatres (see Directory for individual theatres) survive on their profits and rely on financial backers, known as "angels". Consequently, they tend to stage commercial productions with mass appeal: musicals, classics, comedies

and plays by bankable contemporary playwrights.

The state-subsidized **National Theatre** is based in the Southbank Centre *(see p158)*. It has three auditoriums – the large, open-staged Olivier, the proscenium-arched Lyttelton, and the small studio space of the Dorfman.

The **Royal Shakespeare Company** (RSC) regularly stages Shakespeare plays, but its repertoire also includes Greek tragedies, Restoration comedies and modern works. Based at Stratford-upon-Avon *(see pp329–31)*, its major productions are staged at London West End theatres and the Barbican. The RSC ticket hotline has information. **The Old Vic** was rejuvenated by Kevin Spacey, who held the role of director from 2003 to 2015, and has an exciting programme of drama attracting wide audiences.

Theatre tickets generally cost from £20 to £100 (for a top price West End show) and can be bought direct from box offices, by telephone or post. The "tkts" discount theatre ticket booth in Leicester Square sells tickets for a wide range of shows on the day of performance. It is open Monday to Saturday (10am–7pm) for matinees and evening shows, and Sundays (noon–3pm) for matinees only.

Off-West End and Fringe Theatres

Off-West End theatre is a middle category bridging the gap between West End and Fringe theatre. It includes venues that, regardless of location, have a permanent management team and often provide the opportunity for established directors and actors to turn their hands to more adventurous works in a smaller, more intimate environment. Fringe theatres, on the other hand, are normally venues hired out to visiting companies. Both offer innovative productions, serving as an outlet for new, often experimental writing.

Venues (see newspaper listings) range from tiny theatres or rooms above pubs such as the Gate, which produces neglected European classics, to theatres such as the Donmar Warehouse, which attracts major directors and actors.

The Old Vic, the first home of the National Theatre from 1963

A full house for a matinée performance at Regent's Park's Open Air theatre

Open-Air Theatre

In summer, a performance of one of Shakespeare's airier creations, such as *A Midsummer Night's Dream*, takes on an atmosphere of enchantment among the green vistas of Regent's Park (0870 060 1811, openairtheatre. com). Lavish summer opera shows are staged at Holland Park (020 3846 6222, www.opera hollandpark.com). Shakespeare's Globe (*see p124*) offers open-air performances in a beautifully recreated Elizabethan theatre.

Cinemas

The West End abounds with multiplex cinema chains (Odeon, Vue, Cineworld) which show big budget Hollywood films, usually in advance of the rest of the country, although release dates tend to lag well behind the US and many other European countries.

The Odeon Marble Arch has the largest commercial screen in Europe, while the Odeon Leicester Square boasts London's biggest auditorium with almost 2,000 seats.

Londoners are well-informed cinema-goers and even the larger cinema chains include some low-budget and foreign films in their repertoire. The majority of foreign films are subtitled, rather than dubbed. Curzon and Picturehouse are both excellent independent London chains with loyal followings among the capital's serious film buffs.

The largest concentration of cinemas is in and around Leicester Square although there are local cinemas in most areas. Just off Leicester Square,

the Prince Charles is the West End's cheapest cinema. Elsewhere you can expect to pay £10–15 for a ticket, and more for a performance in 3D.

The BFI Southbank, at the Southbank Centre, is London's flagship repertory cinema. Subsidized by the British Film Institute, it screens a wide range of films, old and new, from all around the world. Nearby at Waterloo is the BFI IMAX, with one of the world's largest screens.

In summer, outdoor screenings take place in parks, upon rooftops and in other inspired locations, such as Somerset House.

BFI IMAX Cinema, at Waterloo

DIRECTORY

Theatres

Adelphi
Strand. Map 11 C3.
Tel 020 3725 7060.

Aldwych
Aldwych. Map 11 C2.
Tel 0845 200 7981.

Apollo
Shaftesbury Ave. Map 11 B2. Tel 0844 482 9671.

Cambridge
Earlham St. Map 11 B2.
Tel 0844 412 4652.

Criterion
Piccadilly Circus. Map 11 A3. Tel 020 7839 8811.

Dominion
Tottenham Court Rd. Map 11 B1. Tel 0844 847 1775.

Duchess
Catherine St. Map 11 C2.
Tel 0844 482 9672.

Duke of York's
St Martin's Lane. Map 11 B2. Tel 0044 071 7627.

Fortune
Russell St. Map 11 C2.
Tel 0844 871 7626.

Garrick
Charing Cross Rd. Map 11 B2. Tel 0844 482 9673.

Gielgud
Shaftesbury Ave. Map 11 B2. Tel 0844 482 5130.

Harold Pinter
Panton St. Map 11 A3.
Tel 0844 871 7627.

Her Majesty's
Haymarket. Map 11 A3.
Tel 0844 412 4653.

Lyceum
Wellington St. Map 11 C2.
Tel 0844 871 7627.

Lyric
Shaftesbury Ave. Map 11 B2. Tel 0844 482 9674.

National Theatre
South Bank. Map 12 D3.
Tel 020 7452 3000.

New London
Drury Lane. Map 11 C1.
Tel 0844 412 4654.

Noel Coward
St Martin's Lane. Map 11 B2. Tel 0844 482 5141.

Novello
Aldwych. Map 12 D2.
Tel 0844 482 5171.

The Old Vic
Waterloo Rd SE1. Map 12 E4. Tel 0844 871 7628.

Palace
Cambridge Circus W1.
Map 11 B2. Tel 0330 333 4813.

Phoenix
Charing Cross Rd. Map 11 B2. Tel 0844 871 7629.

Piccadilly
Denman St. Map 11 A2.
Tel 0844 412 6666.

Prince Edward
Old Compton St.
Map 11 A2.
Tel 0844 482 5151.

Prince of Wales
Coventry St. Map 11 A3.
Tel 0844 482 5115.

Queen's
Shaftesbury Ave. Map 11 B2. Tel 0844 482 5160.

Shaftesbury
Shaftesbury Ave. Map 11 B2. Tel 020 7379 5399.

St Martin's
West St. Map 11 B2.
Tel 0844 499 1515.

Theatre Royal: Drury Lane
Catherine St. Map 11 C2.
Tel 0844 412 4660.

Theatre Royal: Haymarket
Haymarket. Map 11 A3.
Tel 020 7930 8800.

Vaudeville
Strand. Map 11 C3.
Tel 0844 482 9675.

Wyndham's
Charing Cross Rd. Map 11 B2. Tel 0844 482 5120.

The orchestra at the Royal Festival Hall, South Bank Centre

Classical Music, Opera and Dance

London is one of the world's great centres for classical music, with five symphony orchestras, internationally renowned chamber groups such as the Academy of St-Martin-in-the-Fields and the English Chamber Orchestra, and a number of contemporary groups. There are performances virtually every week by major international orchestras and artists, reaching a peak during the summer Proms season at the **Royal Albert Hall** *(see p67 and pp104–5)*. **Wigmore Hall** has excellent acoustics and is a fine setting for chamber music, as is the converted Baroque church (1728) of **St John's Smith Square**. The church of **St Martin-in-the-Fields** hosts concerts, sometimes held in the evenings by candlelight.

Although televised and outdoor performances by major stars have greatly increased the popularity of opera, prices at the **Royal Opera House** *(see p84)* are still aimed at corporate entertainment but the policy now is to keep a few cheaper seats. The refurbished building is elaborate and productions are often extremely lavish. English National Opera, based at the **London Coliseum**, has more adventurous productions, appealing to a younger audience (nearly all operas are sung in English). Tickets range from £12 to £200 and it is advisable to book in advance.

The Royal Opera House is also home to the Royal Ballet, and the London Coliseum to the English National Ballet, the two leading classical ballet companies in Britain. Visiting ballets also perform in both. There are numerous young contemporary dance companies, and **The Place** is a dedicated contemporary dance theatre where many companies perform. Other major dance venues are **Sadler's Wells**, the **ICA**, the **Peacock Theatre** and the **Chisenhale Dance Space**.

The **Barbican Concert Hall** and **Southbank Centre** (comprising the Royal Festival Hall, Queen Elizabeth Hall and Purcell Room) host an impressive variety of events ranging from touring opera and classical music performances to free foyer concerts.

Elsewhere in London many outdoor musical events take place in summer. Events to look out for are the Greenwich and Docklands International Festival in late June and early July, a large and groundbreaking festival of performing arts including dance, and contemporary dance festival Dance Umbrella (October) – *see Time Out* and newspaper listings.

Rock, Pop, Jazz and Clubs

London features scores of concerts, ranging from rock and pop to jazz, Latin, world, folk and reggae. Among the city's largest venues are **The O2** *(see p129)* and the Royal Albert Hall; smaller venues include **Brixton Academy** and **The Forum**.

There are a number of live jazz venues. Best of the old crop is **Ronnie Scott's**, although the **100 Club**, **Jazz Café** and **Vortex Jazz Club** have good reputations. The **Hippodrome** (on Leicester Square) also hosts jazz as well as cabaret nights.

London has a packed calendar of summer music festivals, most of them held in the parks that dot the capital. Two of the biggest are Lovebox in Victoria Park and Wireless in Finsbury Park; both take place over weekends in July and attract crowds to see some of the biggest names in contemporary urban, dance and alternative pop music.

London's club scene is one of the most innovative in Europe. It is dominated by big-name DJs, who host different nights in different clubs (see *Time Out* and newspaper listings). The West End venues **Ruby Blue** and the **Café de Paris** are glitzy, expensive and very much on the tourist circuit. The New York-style **Ministry of Sound**, the trendy Shoreditch clubs **333** and **Cargo**, and a host of other venues ensure that you will never be short of choice. Alternatives are the great laser and light shows at gay club **Heaven**, the hip super-club **Fabric**, or the live music venue **Koko** in Camden, which also hosts a variety of club nights. Heaven and the **Royal Vauxhall Tavern** are among the most popular of London's gay clubs.

Opening times are usually 10pm–3am, but on weekends many clubs open until 6am.

Booth selling discounted tickets in Leicester Square

Sports

An impressive variety of public sports facilities are to be found in London. Swimming pools, squash courts, gyms and sports centres, with an assortment of exercise classes, can be found in most districts, and tennis courts hired in most parks.

Watersports, ice skating and golf are among the variety of activities on offer. Spectator sports range from football and rugby at various club grounds to cricket at **Lord's** or the **Oval**, and tennis at the **All England Lawn Tennis Club**, Wimbledon (see p67). Tickets for the most

popular matches can often be hard to come by (see p71). Other traditional sports include polo at **Guards**, croquet at **Hurlingham** (private members only) and medieval "real tennis" at **Queen's Club**. See pages 614–617 for more on sporting activities.

DIRECTORY

Classical Music, Opera and Dance

Barbican Concert Hall
Silk St EC2.
Map 5 A5.
Tel 020 7638 8891.
W barbican.org.uk

Chisenhale Dance Space
64–84 Chisenhale Rd E3.
Tel 020 8981 6617.
W chisenhaledance
space.co.uk

ICA
The Mall SW1.
Map 11 A4.
Tel 020 7930 3647.
W ica.org.uk

London Coliseum
St Martin's Lane WC2.
Map 11 B3.
Tel 020 7845 9300.
W eno.org

Peacock Theatre
Portugal St WC2.
Map 12 D1.
Tel 020 7863 8222.
W peacocktheatre.com

The Place
17 Duke's Rd WC1.
Map 3 B3.
Tel 020 7121 1100.
W theplace.org.uk

Royal Albert Hall
Kensington Gore SW7.
Map 8 F5.
Tel 020 7589 8212.
W royalalberthall.com

Royal Opera House
Floral St WC2.
Map 11 C2.
Tel 020 7304 4000.
W roh.org.uk

Sadler's Wells
Rosebery Ave EC1.
Tel 020 7863 8198.
W sadlerswells.com

Southbank Centre
SE1. **Map** 12 D3.
Tel 020 7960 4200.
W southbankcentre.
co.uk

St John's Smith Square
Smith Sq SW1. **Map** 19 B1. **Tel** 020 7222 1061.
W sjss.org.uk

St Martin-in-the-Fields
Trafalgar Sq. **Map** 11 B3
Tel 020 7766 1100.
W stmartin-in-the-
fields.org

Wigmore Hall
Wigmore St W1.
Map 10 D1.
Tel 020 7935 2141.
W wigmore-hall.org.uk

Rock, Pop, Jazz and Clubs

100 Club
100 Oxford St W1.
Map 10 F1.
Tel 020 7636 0933.
W the100club.co.uk

333
333 Old St EC1.
Tel 020 7739 1800.
W 333oldstreet.com

Brixton Academy
211 Stockwell Rd SW9.
Tel 0844 477 2000.
W o2academy
brixton.co.uk

Café de Paris
3 Coventry St W1.
Map 4 D5.
Tel 020 7734 7700.
W cafedeparis.com

Cargo
83 Rivington St EC2.
Tel 020 7739 3440.
W cargo-london.com

Fabric
77a Charterhouse St EC1.
Tel 020 7336 8898
W fabriclondon.com

The Forum
9–17 Highgate Rd NW5.
Tel 020 7428 4080.
W academymusic
group.com

Heaven
Under the Arches, Villiers St WC2. **Map** 11 C3.
Tel 020 7930 2020.
W heavennightclub-
london.com

Hippodrome
Cranbourn St WC2.
Map 11 B2.
Tel 020 7769 8888.
W hippodromecasino.
com

Jazz Café
3–5 Parkway NW1.
Tel 020 7485 6834.
W thejazzcafelondon.
com

Koko
1A Camden High St NW1
Tel 020 7358 3222
W koko.uk.com

Ministry of Sound
103 Gaunt St SE1.
Tel 020 7740 8600.
W ministryofsound.
com

Ronnie Scott's
47 Frith St W1.
Map 11 A2.
Tel 020 7439 0747.
W ronniescotts.co.uk

Royal Vauxhall Tavern
372 Kennington Lane
SE11. **Tel** 020 7820 1222.
W vauxhalltavern.com

Ruby Blue
Leicester Sq WC2.
Map 11 B3.
Tel 020 7287 8050.
W rubybluebar.co.uk

The O2
Peninsula Square SE10.
Tel 020 8463 2000.
W theo2.co.uk

Vortex Jazz Club
11 Gillett Sq N16.
Tel 020 7254 4097.
W vortexjazz.co.uk

Sports

All England Lawn Tennis Club
Church Rd,
Wimbledon SW19.
Tel 020 8944 1066.

Guards Polo Club
Windsor Great Park.
Tel 01784 434212.

Hurlingham Club
Ranelagh Gardens SW6.
Map 18 D3.
Tel 020 7610 7400.

Lord's Cricket Ground
St John's Wood NW8.
Tel 020 7432 1000.

Oval Cricket Ground
Kennington SE11.
Tel 020 7820 5700.

Queen's Club
Palliser Rd W14.
Tel 020 7386 3400.

SOUTHEAST ENGLAND

Introducing Southeast
England   162–167

The Downs and
Channel Coast   168–193

East Anglia   194–219

Thames Valley   220–241

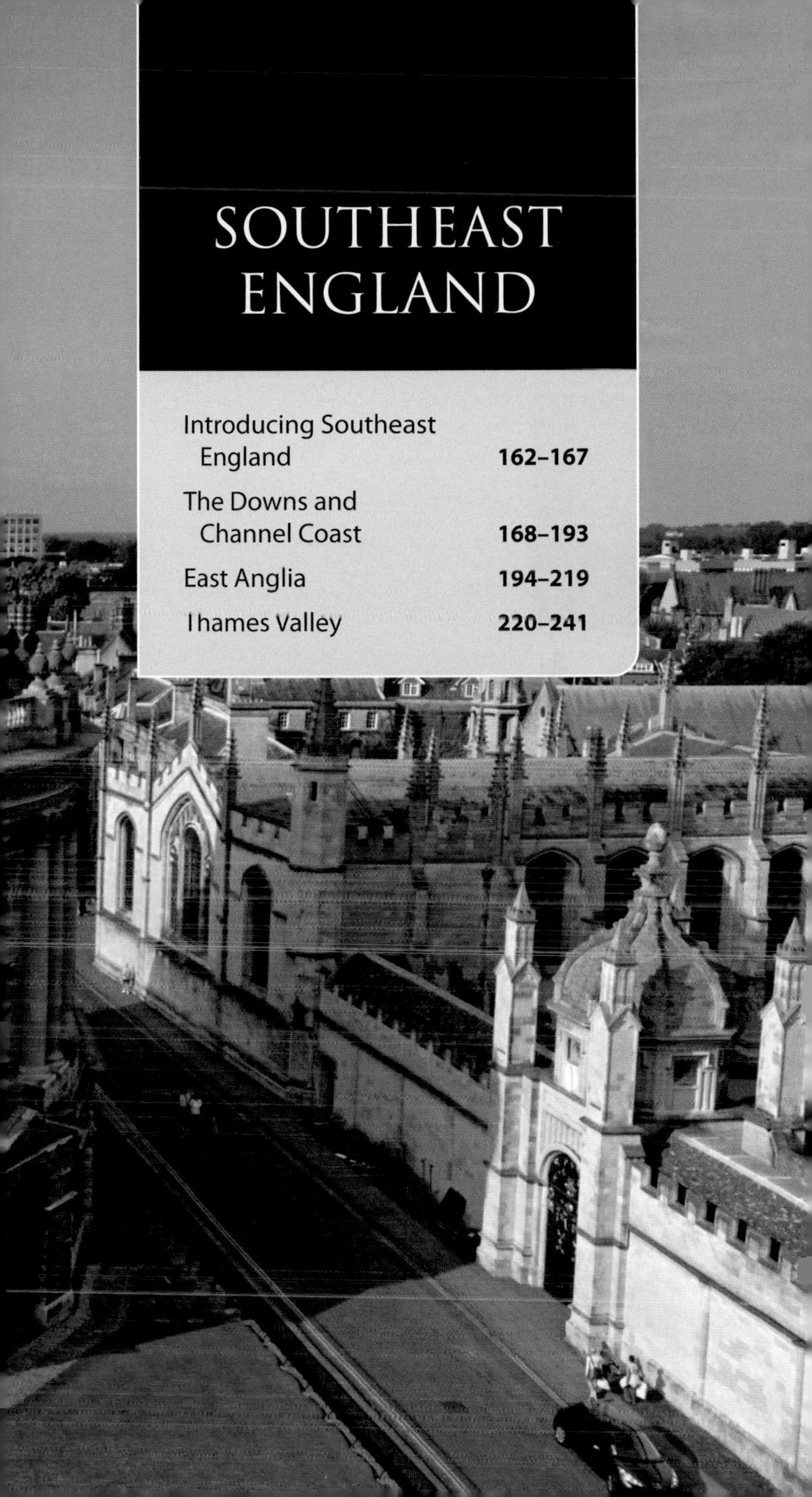

Southeast England at a Glance

The old Saxon kingdoms covered the areas surrounding London, and today, while their accessibility to the capital makes them a magnet for commuters, each region retains a character and history of its own. The attractions include England's oldest universities, royal palaces, castles, stately homes and cathedrals, many of which played critical roles in the nation's early history. The landscape is soft, with green and rounded hills levelling out to the flat fertile plains and fens of East Anglia, fringed by broad, sandy beaches.

Blenheim Palace *(see pp232–3)* is a Baroque masterpiece. The Mermaid Fountain (1892) is part of the spectacular gardens.

Oxford University's *(see pp226–31)* buildings amount to a textbook of English architecture from the Middle Ages to the present. Christ Church College (1525) is the largest in the university.

Bedfor
Banbury
BEDFC SHIR
BUCKINGHAM-SHIRE Lut
THAMES VALLEY
Oxford   *(See pp220–41)*
Wat
OXFORD-SHIRE High Wycombe
BERKSHIRE Windsor
Reading
Newbury
Su
Basingstoke   Guildford
HAMPSHIRE
THE DOWNS A CHANNEL CO
Winchester   *(See pp168–93)*
WEST SUSSE
Southampton   Chiche
Portsmouth
Lymington

Windsor Castle *(see pp240–41)* is Britain's oldest royal residence. The Round Tower was built in the 11th century when the palace guarded the western approaches to London.

Winchester Cathedral *(see pp174–5)* was begun in 1097 on the ruins of a Saxon church. The city has been an important centre of Christianity since the 7th century. The cathedral's northwest door is built in a characteristic medieval style.

◀ The Radcliffe Camera, Oxford

Ely Cathedral's *(see pp198–9)* south transept contains some of the finest stone carving in Britain. The octagonal corona was added in the 14th century when the Norman tower collapsed; the replacement tower dominates the surrounding flat fenland.

Cambridge University's *(see pp214–19)* buildings are enhanced by the quiet college gardens, the Backs and the public commons. King's College Chapel is the outstanding example of late medieval architecture in the city.

Canterbury Cathedral *(see pp190–91)* is the spiritual home of the Church of England. It contains some of the country's most exquisite medieval stained glass, for example in the nave's west window. It also has some well-preserved 12th-century wall paintings.

Brighton's Royal Pavilion *(see pp182–3)* was built for the Prince Regent and is one of the most lavish buildings in the land. Its design by John Nash is based on Oriental themes, and it has been restored to its original splendour.

0 kilometres 25

0 miles 25

The Garden of England

With its fertile soil, mild climate and regular rainfall, the Kentish countryside has flourished as a fruit-growing region ever since its first orchards were planted by the Romans. Wine-making has also been established here, as the vine-covered hillsides around Lamberhurst show, and several vineyards may be visited. The orchards are dazzling in the blossom season, and in the autumn the branches sag with ripening fruit – a familiar sight which inspired William Cobbett (1762–1835) to describe the area as "the very finest as to fertility and diminutive beauty in the whole world". Near Faversham, the fruit research station of Brogdale is open to the public, offering orchard walks, tastings and informative displays.

Hops and Hop-Picking

A family enjoying a break from hop-picking

Oast houses, topped with distinctive angled cowls, are a common feature of the Kentish landscape, and many have now been turned into houses. They were originally built to dry hops,

Seasonal Fruit

This timeline shows the major crops in each month of the farming year. The first blossoms may appear when the fields are still dusted with snow. As the petals fall, fruit appears among the leaves. After ripening in the summer sun, the fruit is harvested in the autumn.

Orchards are used to grow plums, pears and apples. The last (blossoming above) remain Kent's most important orchard crop.

Raspberries are a luscious soft fruit. Many growers allow you to pick your own from the fields, and then pay by weight.

Peach blossom is usually to be found on south-facing walls, as its fruit requires warm conditions.

March	April	May	June	July

Sour cherry blossom is the earliest flower. Its fruit is used for cooking.

Pear blossom has creamy white flowers which appear two or three weeks before apple blossom.

Cherry plum blossom is one of the most beautiful blossoms; the plant is grown more for its flowers than its fruit.

Strawberries are Britain's favourite and earliest soft fruit. New strains allow them to be picked all summer.

Gooseberries are not always sweet enough to eat raw, though all types are superb in pies and other desserts.

an ingredient in brewing beer *(see pp578–9)*. Many are still used for that, for although imports have reduced domestic hop-growing, 1,000 ha (2,500 acres) are devoted to hops, divided between Kent and the East Midlands.

In summer, the fruiting plants can be seen climbing the rectangular wire frames in fields by the roadside. Until the middle of the 20th century thousands of families from London's East End would move to the Kentish hop fields every autumn for working holidays harvesting the crop and camping in barns. The advance of the use of machinery, however, has meant the tradition has faded.

The cowls turn in the wind, providing air which is controlled by trapdoors below.

Oast House

Hops are dried above a fan which blows hot air from the underlying radiators.

After drying, the hops are cooled and stored.

A press packs the hops into bags, ready for the breweries.

Cherries are the sweetest of Kent's fruit: two popular varieties are Stella (top) and Duke.

Plums are often served stewed, in pies, made into jam or dried into prunes. The Victoria plum ripens in August and is the classic English dessert plum. It is also sweet enough to be eaten raw.

Greengages are green plums. They have a distinctive taste and can be made into jam.

Bramley Seedling is one of the best cooking apples, but it is not sweet enough to eat raw.

Pears, such as the William (left), should be eaten at the height of ripeness. The Conference keeps better.

August	September	October	November

Currants are among the most assertively flavoured fruit and are used in desserts and jams.

Peaches, grown in China 4,000 years ago, came to England in the 19th century.

Dessert apples, such as Cox's Orange Pippin (right), are some of England's best-loved fruits. The Discovery variety is easier to grow.

The Kentish cob, a variety of hazelnut, is undergoing a revival, having been eclipsed by European imports. Unlike many nuts, it is best picked fresh from the tree.

Vineyards are now a familiar sight in Kent (as well as Sussex and Hampshire). Most of the wine produced is white.

Houses of Historical Figures

Visiting the homes of artists, writers, politicians and royalty is a rewarding way of gaining an insight into their private lives. Southeast England boasts many historic houses that have been preserved as they were when their illustrious occupants were alive. All these houses, from large mansions such as Lord Mountbatten's Broadlands to the more modest dwellings, like Jane Austen's House, contain exhibits relating to the lives of the famous people who lived there.

Florence Nightingale (1820–1910), the "Lady with the Lamp", was a nurse in the Crimean War *(see p60)*. She stayed at Claydon House, Winslow, with her sister, Lady Verney.

Nancy Astor (1879–1964) was the first woman to sit in Parliament, in 1919. She lived at Cliveden House, near Maidenhead, until her death.

The Duke of Wellington (1769–1852) was given Stratfield Saye, Basingstoke, by the nation in 1817, as thanks for leading the British to victory at Waterloo *(see p59)*.

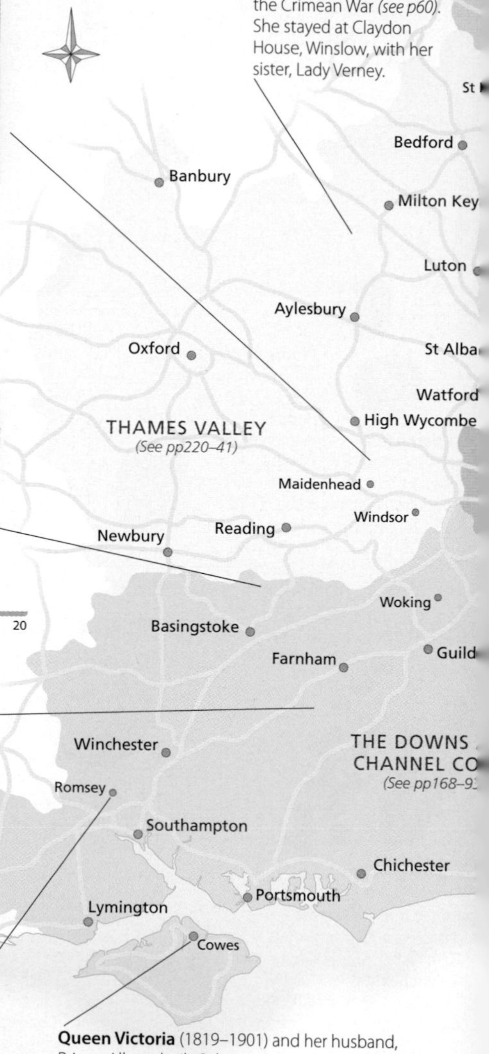

Jane Austen (1775–1817) wrote three of her novels, including *Emma*, and revised the others at a house in Chawton, where she lived for 8 years until shortly before her death *(see p176)*.

Lord Mountbatten (1900–79), a British naval commander and statesman, was the last Viceroy of India in 1947. He lived at Broadlands, near Southampton, all his married life and remodelled the original house considerably.

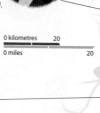

Queen Victoria (1819–1901) and her husband, Prince Albert, built Osborne House on the Isle of Wight *(see p172)* in 1855 as a seaside retreat for their family; they never truly warmed to the Royal Pavilion in Brighton.

St

Bedford

Milton Key

Banbury

Luton

Aylesbury

St Alba

Oxford

Watford

High Wycombe

THAMES VALLEY
(See pp220–41)

Maidenhead

Windsor

Newbury

Reading

Woking

0 kilometres 20
0 miles 20

Basingstoke

Guild

Farnham

Winchester

**THE DOWNS
CHANNEL CO**
(See pp168–9)

Romsey

Southampton

Chichester

Lymington

Portsmouth

Cowes

Bloomsbury Group

A circle of avant-garde artists, designers and writers, many of them friends as students, began to meet at a house in Bloomsbury, London, in 1904, and soon gained a reputation for their Bohemian lifestyle. When Duncan Grant and Vanessa Bell moved to Charleston in 1916 *(see p184)*, it became a Sussex outpost of the celebrated group. Many of the prominent figures associated with the circle, such as Virginia Woolf, E M Forster, Vita Sackville-West and J M Keynes paid visits here. The Bloomsbury Group was also known for the Omega Workshops, which made innovative ceramics, furniture and textiles.

Vanessa Bell at Charleston by Duncan Grant (1885–1978)

Thomas Gainsborough (1727–88), one of Britain's greatest painters, was born in a house in Lavenham *(see p210)*. He was best known for his portraits, such as this one of *Mr and Mrs Andrews*.

Charles Darwin (1809–82), who developed the theory that man and apes have a common ancestor, wrote his most famous book, *On the Origin of Species*, while living at Down House, Downe.

Charles Dickens (1812–70), the prolific and popular Victorian novelist *(see p192)*, had many connections with Kent. He took holidays in Broadstairs, at Bleak House, later named after his famous novel.

Winston Churchill (1874–1965), Britain's inspirational Prime Minister in World War II, lived at Chartwell *(see p193)*, in Westerham, for 40 years until his death. He relaxed by rebuilding parts of the house.

Vanessa Bell (1879–1961), artist and member of the Bloomsbury Group, lived at Charleston, in Lewes, until her death in 1961. The 18th-century farmhouse reflects her decorative ideas and is filled with murals, paintings and painted furniture *(see p184)*.

Rudyard Kipling (1865–1936), the poet and novelist, was born in India but lived at Batemans, in Burwash, near Hastings, for 34 years until his death. His most famous works include *Kim*, the two *Jungle Books* and the *Just So Stories*.

Map labels: Bury St Edmunds, nbridge, Ipswich, Saffron Walden, Sudbury, Halstead, Harwich, evenage, Bishop's Stortford, Colchester, EAST ANGLIA (See pp194–219), Clacton-on-Sea, Harlow, Chelmsford, Basildon, Southend-on-Sea, ONDON pp74–159, Margate, Chatham, Sevenoaks, Maidstone, Canterbury, Dover, awley, Royal Tunbridge Wells, Folkestone, Rye, Lewes, hton, Hastings, Eastbourne

THE DOWNS AND CHANNEL COAST

Hampshire · Surrey · East Sussex · West Sussex · Kent

England's southeast coast has been the first point of call for newcomers throughout history. The sandy beaches and natural harbours, fertile soil and proximity to the capital city have made this region an ideal base for settlers and tourists alike.

The Romans built fortifications along the Channel Coast in the 1st century, later incorporated into Dover Castle and Portchester Castle, and built towns and villas inland. Fishbourne Palace near Chichester is a fine example. Inland, the moated Bodiam in East Sussex and Leeds in Kent deliver the ideal of the romantic castle. In the 6th century, St Augustine came to Kent to convert the Anglo-Saxons to Christianity and made Canterbury the centre of the Anglican church, which it still is today. Other cathedrals – such as Winchester, Chichester and Rochester – all have their individual appeal.

As London consolidated its status as the focus and capital of the country, the counties between the city and the coast became favoured places for the monarchs and the nobility to show their wealth and prestige, and a number of lavish mansions arose. Hampton Court, close to London, was the favourite palace of Henry VIII; Knole in Kent acquired the vast number of 365 rooms; and like many other grand houses of the time, Petworth employed "Capability" Brown to design its deer park and grounds. The Royal Pavilion at Brighton, built for George IV in 1822, is embellishment taken to excess.

Seaside resorts, sandy beaches and white cliffs characterize the coast, which is also home to the working ports of Southampton and Portsmouth. The chalk ridges of the North and South Downs extend across Sussex as far as the New Forest in Hampshire. Below them is the lower-lying Weald of Kent, known as the "Garden of England" due to its fruitfulness and the beauty of its gardens – from the world-famous Sissinghurst, to small gems such as Ightham Mote.

The elegant Privy Garden at Hampton Court, Surrey

◄ People walking on the clifftop near Beachy Head, East Sussex

Exploring the Downs and Channel Coast

The southeastern wedge of the country is one of the most densely populated parts of England, but the countryside, especially on the South Downs, offers peaceful and secluded spaces. Here, and in the New Forest in Hampshire, there are wonderful opportunities for walking. The region also offers historic towns, castles and impressive mansions. Brighton, Canterbury and Winchester are excellent bases for exploring, as are smaller towns such as Chichester or Rye. Seaside places from cosmopolitan Brighton to genteel Eastbourne and buzzing Margate offer a choice of atmospheres. You can also find spectacular landscapes at Beachy Head, Dungeness and Romney Marshes.

Colourful wooden beach huts on the seafront in Brighton, Sussex

The Isle of Wight's famous chalk Needles and Trinity Lighthouse

Sights at a Glance

1. Isle of Wight
2. Beaulieu
3. New Forest
4. Southampton
5. Portsmouth
6. *Winchester pp174–5*
7. Chichester
8. Arundel Castle
9. Petworth House
10. Guildford
11. *Hampton Court p177*
12. *Brighton pp178–83*
13. Steyning
14. Lewes
15. Eastbourne
16. The Downs
17. Hastings
18. Bodiam Castle
19. *Rye pp188–9*
20. Romney Marsh
21. Dover
22. Margate
23. *Canterbury pp190–91*
24. Leeds Castle
25. Rochester
26. Knole
27. Hever Castle
28. Royal Tunbridge Wells

Getting Around

The area is well served by a network of motorways and A roads from London to the major towns. The A259 is a scenic coast road which offers fine views over the English Channel. Bus and rail transport is also good, with a number of coach companies providing regular tours to the major sites. A train service runs to all the major towns.

Leeds Castle, in Kent, seen from across its exceptionally broad moat

Key

- Motorway
- Major road
- Secondary road
- Minor road
- Scenic route
- Main railway
- Minor railway
- △ Summit

For keys to symbols see back flap

The Victorian Osborne House, Isle of Wight

❶ Isle of Wight

Isle of Wight. 🏠 140,000. 🚢 from Lymington, Southampton, Portsmouth. 🛈 The Guildhall, High St, Newport (01983 521555). 🌐 **visitisleofwight. co.uk**

A visit to **Osborne House**, the favoured seaside retreat of Queen Victoria and Prince Albert *(see p166),* is alone worth the ferry ride from the mainland. Furnished much as they left it, the house provides a marvellous insight into royal life and is dotted with family mementos.

The **Swiss Cottage** was built for the royal children to play in. It is now a museum attached to Osborne House. Adjacent to it you can see the bathing machine used by the queen to preserve her modesty while taking her to the edge of the sea.

The other main sight on the island is **Carisbrooke Castle**, built in the 11th century. A walk on its outer wall and the climb to the top of its keep offers spectacular views. It was here that Charles I *(see pp56–7)* was held prisoner in 1647; an attempt to escape was foiled when he got stuck between the bars of a window.

The island is a base for ocean sailing, especially during Cowes Week *(see p71).* The scenic highlight is the **Needles** – three towers of rock jutting out of the sea at the island's western end. This is only a short walk from Alum Bay, famous for its multi-coloured cliffs and sand.

🏛 Osborne House
East Cowes. **Tel** 01983 200022. **Open** 10am–5pm (4pm winter) daily (Nov–Mar: check website). 🅿 ♿ limited. 🚫 🖼 (also in Swiss Cottage Apr–Oct only). 🏠 EH

🏰 Carisbrooke Castle
Newport. **Tel** 01983 522107. **Open** 10am–5pm daily (to 4pm winter; Nov–Mar: check website). **Closed** 1 Jan, 24–26 Dec. 🅿 🚫 ♿ limited. 🖥 in summer. 🏠 EH

❷ Beaulieu

Brockenhurst, Hampshire. **Tel** 01590 612345. 🚊 Brockenhurst then taxi. **Open** 10am–5pm daily (to 6pm summer). **Closed** 25 Dec. 🅿 ♿ 🚫 🏠 🌐 **beaulieu.co.uk**

Palace House, once the gatehouse of Beaulieu Abbey, has been the home of Lord Montagu's family since 1538. It now contains the finest collection of vintage cars in the country at the **National Motor Museum**, along with boats used in the James Bond films.

There is also an exhibition of monastic life in the ruined ancient **abbey**, founded in 1204 by King John for Cistercian monks. The original refectory now serves as the parish church.

Environs
Just south is the maritime museum at **Buckler's Hard**, telling the story of shipbuilding in the 18th century. The yard employed 4,000 men at its peak but declined when steel began to be used. Boat trips are available.

🏛 Buckler's Hard
Beaulieu. **Tel** 01590 616203. **Open** daily. **Closed** 25 Dec. 🅿 ♿ limited. 🖥 🏠 🌐 **bucklershard.co.uk**

❸ New Forest

Hampshire. 🚊 Brockenhurst. 🚌 Lymington then bus. 🛈 St Barbe Museum, New St, Lymington (01590 676969). **Open** 10am–4pm Mon–Sat. **Closed** 1 Jan, 24–26 Dec. 🌐 **thenewforest.co.uk**

This unique expanse of heath and woodland is, at 145 sq miles (375 sq km), the largest area of unenclosed land in southern Britain.

Despite its name, this is one of the few primeval oak woods in England. It was a popular hunting ground of Norman kings, and in 1100 William II was fatally wounded here in a hunting accident.

Today it is enjoyed by up to seven million visitors a year, who share it with the New Forest ponies, unique to the area, and over 1,500 fallow deer.

❹ Southampton

Hampshire. 🏠 255,000. ✈ 🚊 🚌 🚢 🌐 **discoversouthampton.co.uk**

For centuries this has been a flourishing port. The *Mayflower* sailed from here via Plymouth

A 1909 Rolls-Royce Silver Ghost at Beaulieu's National Motor Museum

The luxurious liner the *Titanic*, which sank in 1912

to America in 1620 with the Pilgrim Fathers, as did the *Titanic* on its maiden and ultimately tragic voyage in 1912.

SeaCity Museum's galleries focus on the lives and times of those who have sailed from the port of Southampton over the past 2,000 years.

A well-marked walk runs around the remains of the city walls, which include, at the head of the High Street, **Bargate**, the most elaborate gate to survive in England. It still has its 13th-century drum towers and is decorated with intricate, 17th-century armorial carvings.

SeaCity Museum
Havelock Rd. **Tel** 023 8083 3007. **Open** 10am–5pm daily. **seacitymuseum.co.uk**

5 Portsmouth

Hampshire. 210,000. The Hard Interchange (023 9282 6722). Thu–Sat. **visitportsmouth.co.uk**

Once a vital naval port, this vibrant waterfront city has a fascinating naval history.

Portsmouth Historic Dockyard is the hub of the city's most important sights. Among these is the hull of the *Mary Rose*, the favourite of Henry VIII *(see p54)*, which capsized on its maiden voyage as it left to fight the French in 1545. It was recovered from the sea bed in 1982 and has been reunited, in the **Mary Rose Museum**, with many of the 19,000 16th-century objects that have been raised from the wreck in a museum that opened in 2013.

Nearby is the dockyard's most famous exhibit, HMS *Victory*, the English flagship on which Admiral Nelson was killed at Trafalgar *(see p35)*. Here visitors get a vivid idea of life at sea in the age of sail. You can also visit the National Museum of the Royal Navy, which deals with naval history from the 16th century to the Falklands War, the 19th-century HMS *Warrior*, and galleries telling the story of Nelson.

Portsmouth's other military memorial is the **D-Day Museum**. This is centred on the *Overlord Embroidery*, a masterpiece of needlework commissioned in 1968 from the Royal School of Needlework, depicting the World War II Allied landing in Normandy in 1944.

Portchester Castle, on the north edge of the harbour, was fortified in the third century and is the best example of Roman sea defences in northern Europe. The Normans later used the Roman walls to enclose a castle – only the keep survives – and a church. Henry V used the castle as a garrison before the Battle of Agincourt *(see p53)*. In the 18th and 19th centuries it was a prisoner-of-war camp.

The figurehead on the bow of HMS *Victory* at Portsmouth

Among less warlike attractions is the **Charles Dickens Birthplace Museum**, the house where the author was born in 1812 *(see p192)*.

The striking **Spinnaker Tower** rises to 170 m (558 ft) above Portsmouth; the views over the harbour and beyond are quite magnificent.

A wild pony and her foal roaming freely in the New Forest

Portsmouth Historic Dockyard
Victory Gate, HM Naval Base. **Tel** 023 9283 9766. **Open** 10am–5:30pm daily (Nov–Mar: to 5pm). **Closed** 24–26 Dec. partial.

Mary Rose Museum
Portsmouth Historic Dockyard. **Tel** 023 9281 2931. **Open** daily (last tickets: 4pm). **Closed** 24–26 Dec.

D-Day Museum
Museum Rd. **Tel** 023 9282 6722. **Open** daily. **Closed** 24–26 Dec.

Portchester Castle
Church Rd, Porchester. **Tel** 023 9237 8291. **Open** Apr–Oct: daily; Nov–Mar: Sat & Sun. **Closed** 1 Jan, 24–26 Dec.

Charles Dickens Birthplace Museum
393 Old Commercial Rd. **Tel** 023 9282 1879. **Open** Apr–Sep: Fri–Sun; also 7 Feb (Dickens' birthday).

Spinnaker Tower
Gunwharf Quays. **Tel** 023 9285 7520. **Open** daily.

❻ Winchester

Hampshire. 🅐 45,000. 🚆 🚌 🅵
Guildhall, High St (01962 840500). 🅰
Wed–Sat. 🆆 visitwinchester.co.uk

Capital of the ancient kingdom of Wessex, the city of Winchester was also the headquarters of the Anglo-Saxon kings until the Norman Conquest *(see p51)*.

William the Conqueror built one of his first English castles here. The only surviving part of the castle is the **Great Hall**, erected in 1235 to replace the original. It is now home to the legendary Round Table. The story behind the table is a mix of history and myth. King Arthur *(see p289)* had it shaped so no knight could claim precedence. It was said to have been built by the wizard Merlin but was actually made in the 13th century.

The **Westgate Museum** is one of the two surviving 12th-century gatehouses in the city wall. The room (once a prison) above the gate has a 16th-century painted ceiling, which was moved here from Winchester College, England's oldest fee-paying, or "public" school.

Winchester has been an ecclesiastical centre for many

The 13th-century Round Table, Great Hall, Winchester

centuries. **Wolvesey Castle** (built around 1110) was the home of the cathedral's bishops after the Conquest.

Winchester Cathedral

The first church was built here in 648, but the present building was begun in 1079. Originally a Benedictine monastery, much of the Norman architecture remains despite continual modifications until the early 16th century.

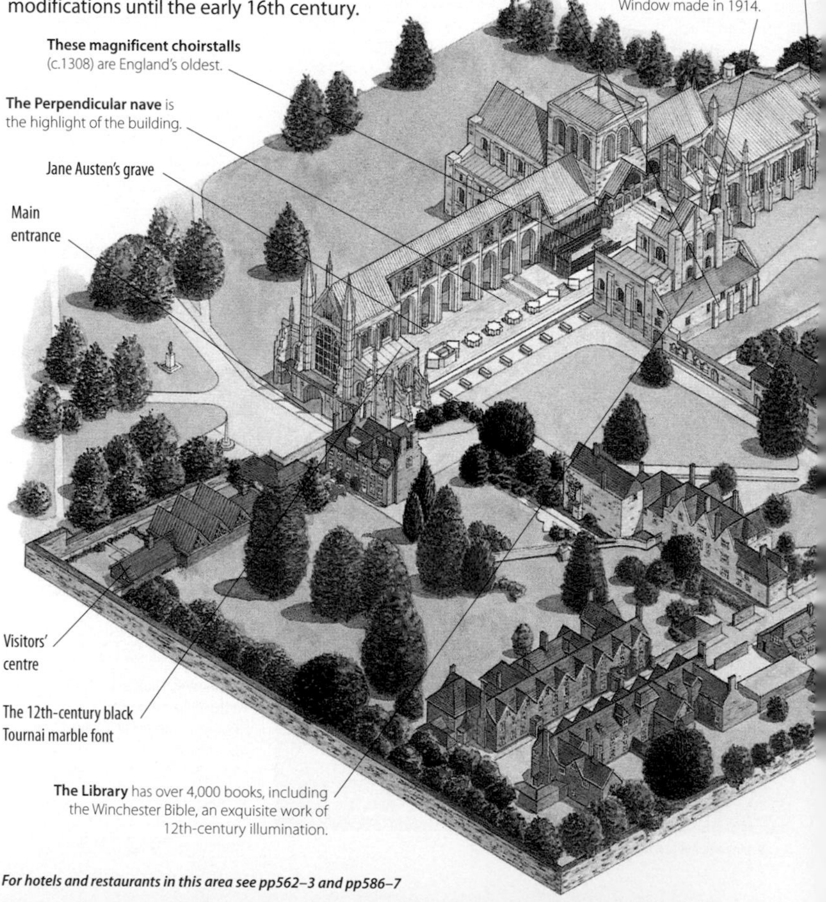

The Norman chapterhouse ceased to be used in 1580. Only the Norman arches survive.

The Lady Chapel was rebuilt by Elizabeth of York (c.1500) after her son was baptized in the cathedral.

Author Izaac Walton (1593–1683) is depicted in the stained-glass Anglers' Window made in 1914.

These magnificent choirstalls (c.1308) are England's oldest.

The Perpendicular nave is the highlight of the building.

Jane Austen's grave

Main entrance

Visitors' centre

The 12th-century black Tournai marble font

The Library has over 4,000 books, including the Winchester Bible, an exquisite work of 12th-century illumination.

The **Hospital of St Cross** is an almshouse built in 1446. Weary strangers may claim the "Wayfarer's Dole", a horn (cup) of ale and bread, given out since medieval times.

🏛 Great Hall
Castle Ave. **Tel** 01962 846476.
Open daily. **Closed** 25 & 26 Dec. ♿

🏛 Westgate Museum
High St. **Tel** 01962 869864.
Open mid-Feb–Oct: Sat & Sun. 📷

🏛 Hospital of St Cross
St Cross Rd. **Tel** 01962 851375.
Open Mon–Sat (daily in summer).
Closed Good Fri, 25 Dec. 📷 ♿
🌐 stcrosshospital.co.uk

VISITORS' CHECKLIST

Practical Information
The Close. **Tel** 01962 857200.
Open daily. 📷 🎫 ♿ 🚻 🖥
📷 🌐 winchester-cathedral.org.uk

Prior's Hall

The Close
originally contained the domestic buildings for the monks of the Priory of St Swithun – the name before it became Winchester Cathedral. Most of the buildings, such as the refectory and cloisters, were destroyed during the Dissolution of the Monasteries (see p355).

❼ Chichester

West Sussex. 🅰 27,000. 🚆 🚌 ℹ
The Novium, Tower St (01243 775888).
🍴 Wed, alternate Fri (Farmers' market), Sat. 🌐 visitchichester.org

This wonderfully preserved market town, with an elaborate early 16th-century market cross at its centre, is dominated by its **cathedral**, consecrated in 1108. The cathedral's graceful spire peers over the town and is said to be the only English cathedral spire visible from the sea. Also of interest is the cathedral's unique detached bell tower, dating from 1436.

There are two carved stone panels in the choir, dating from 1140. Modern works include paintings by Graham Sutherland (1903–80) and a stained-glass window by Marc Chagall (1887–1985).

Environs

Just west at Bosham is the Saxon **Holy Trinity Church**, thought to have been used by King Canute (see p51). Myth has it that this was where Canute failed to stop the incoming tide and so proved to his courtiers that his powers had limits. The church appears in the *Bayeux Tapestry*, held in France, because Harold heard mass here in 1064 before he was shipwrecked off Normandy and then rescued by William the Conqueror.

The refurbished **Fishbourne Roman Palace** (see pp48–9), between Bosham and Chichester, is the largest Roman villa in Britain. It covers 3 ha (7 acres) and was discovered in 1960 by a workman. Constructed from AD 75, it was destroyed by fire in 285. The north wing has some of

Chagall's stained-glass window (1978), Chichester Cathedral

the finest mosaics in Britain, including one of Cupid.

To the north is the 18th-century **Goodwood House**. Its magnificent art collection features works by Canaletto (1697–1768) and Stubbs (1724–1806). Home to the Earl of March, it has a motor racing circuit, where the popular Festival of Speed is held in July, and a horse-racing course on the Downs.

🏛 Chichester Cathedral
West St. **Tel** 01243 782595.
Open daily. 🎫 ♿ 🚻 📷
🌐 chichestercathedral.co.uk

🏛 Fishbourne Roman Palace
Roman Way. **Tel** 01243 785859.
Open Feb–mid-Dec: daily; mid- to end Dec: Sat & Sun. 📷 🎫 ♿ 🖥
📷 🌐 sussexpast.co.uk

🏛 Goodwood House
Goodwood. **Tel** 01243 755000.
Open mid-Mar–mid-Oct: Sun–Mon (pm); Aug: Sun–Thu (pm)
Closed special events, last-minute closures. Call ahead. 📷 ♿ 🖥 📷

William Walker

At the beginning of the 20th century, Winchester cathedral's east end seemed certain to collapse unless its foundations were underpinned. But because the water table lies only just below the surface, the work had to be done underwater. From 1906 to 1911, Walker, a deep-sea diver, worked 6 hours a day laying sacks of cement beneath the unsteady walls until the building was safe.

William Walker in his diving suit

The medieval Arundel Castle, West Sussex

❽ Arundel Castle

Arundel, West Sussex. **Tel** 01903 882173. 🚆 Arundel. **Open** Apr–Oct: 10am–5pm Tue–Sun & pub hols (Aug: daily; last adm: 4pm). 🚐 ♿ 🅿 ☐ 🏠 W **arundelcastle.org**

Dominating the small riverside town below, this vast, grey hilltop castle, surrounded by castellated walls, was originally built by the Normans.

During the 16th century it was acquired by the powerful Dukes of Norfolk, the country's senior Roman Catholic family, whose descendants still live here. They rebuilt it after the original was virtually destroyed by Parliamentarians in 1643 *(see p56)*, and then again in the 19th century.

In the castle grounds is the parish church of **St Nicholas**. The small Catholic Fitzalan chapel (c.1380) was built into its east end by the castle's first owners, the Fitzalans, and can only be entered from the grounds.

❾ Petworth House

Petworth, West Sussex. **Tel** 01798 342207. 🚆 Pulborough then bus. House: **Open** Mar–Oct: daily; Nov–Feb: see website. Park: **Open** daily. 🚐 ♿ limited. 🚫 🏠 **NT**

This late 17th-century house was immortalized in a series of famous views by the painter J M W Turner *(see p95)*. Some of his best paintings are on display here and are part of Petworth's outstanding art collection, which also includes works by Titian (1488–1576),

Van Dyck (1599–1641) and Gainsborough *(see p167)*. Also well represented is ancient Roman and Greek sculpture, notably the 4th-century BC *Leconfield Aphrodite*, widely thought to be by Praxiteles.

The Carved Room is decorated with intricately carved wood panels of birds, flowers and musical instruments, by Grinling Gibbons (1648–1721).

The large deer park includes some of the earliest work of "Capability" Brown *(see p30)*.

The Restoration clock on the Tudor Guildhall, Guildford

❿ Guildford

Surrey. 🅰 63,000. 🚆 🚌 ℹ 155 High St (01483 444333). 🏠 Fri, Sat. W **guildford.gov.uk**

The county town of Surrey, settled since Saxon times, incorporates the remains of a small refurbished Norman **castle**. The high street is lined with Tudor buildings, such as the impressive

Guildhall, and the huge red-brick cathedral, completed in 1954, dominates the town's skyline.

Environs

Guildford stands at the end of the North Downs, a range of chalk hills that are popular for walking *(see p41)*. The area also has two famous beauty spots: **Leith Hill** – the highest point in southeast England – and **Box Hill**. The view from the latter is well worth the short, steep climb from West Humble.

To the north of Guildford is **RHS Wisley** with 97 ha (240 acres) of beautiful gardens. To the southwest is **Loseley House**, a fine mansion, set in extensive gardens and unchanged since 1562. Lavishly decorated, it includes an elaborate fireplace and work by Grinling Gibbons.

Further southwest is Chawton, where **Jane Austen's House** *(see p166)* is located. This red-brick house is where Austen wrote most of her popular, witty novels, including *Pride and Prejudice*, exploring middle-class manners in Georgian England.

🏛 **RHS Wisley**
Off A3. **Tel** 0845 260 9000. **Open** daily. 🚐 ♿ 🚫 ☐ 🏠 W **rhs.org.uk**

🏛 **Losely Park**
Surrey. **Tel** 01483 304440. **Open** May–Aug: Sun–Thu pm (gardens from 11am). 🚐 🅿 ♿ ground floor. ☐ 🏠

🏛 **Jane Austen's House**
Alton, Hants. **Tel** 01420 83262. **Open** Jan–mid-Feb: Sat & Sun; mid-Feb–Dec: daily. **Closed** 24–26 Dec. 🚐 ♿ limited. 🏠 W **jane-austens-house-museum.org.uk**

⓫ Hampton Court

East Molesey, Surrey. **Tel** 020 3166 6000. 🚋 Hampton Court. **Open** daily (last adm: 3:30pm). **Closed** 24–26 Dec. 🅿️ 🍽️ 🏛️ ♿ 🚻 📷 **W** hrp.org.uk

The powerful chief minister and Archbishop of York to Henry VIII, Cardinal Wolsey leased a small manor house in 1514 and transformed it into a magnificent country residence. In 1528, to retain royal favour, Wolsey gave it to the king. After the royal takeover, Hampton Court was extended twice, first by Henry himself and in the 1690s by William and Mary, who used Christopher Wren (see p119) as the architect. From the outside the palace is a harmonious blend of Tudor and English Baroque; inside there is a striking contrast between Wren's Classical royal rooms, which include the King's Apartments, and Tudor architecture, such as the Great Hall. The Cumberland Art Gallery contains many paintings from the Royal Collection, including works by Rembrandt and Canaletto. The Baroque gardens, with their radiating avenues of majestic limes, collections of rare plants and formal plant beds, have been painstakingly restored.

Ceiling decoration, Hampton Court

The Baroque maze is one of the garden's most famous features; visitors often become lost in it.

The Queen's Apartments, including the Presence Chamber and Bedchamber, are arranged around the north and east sides of Fountain Court.

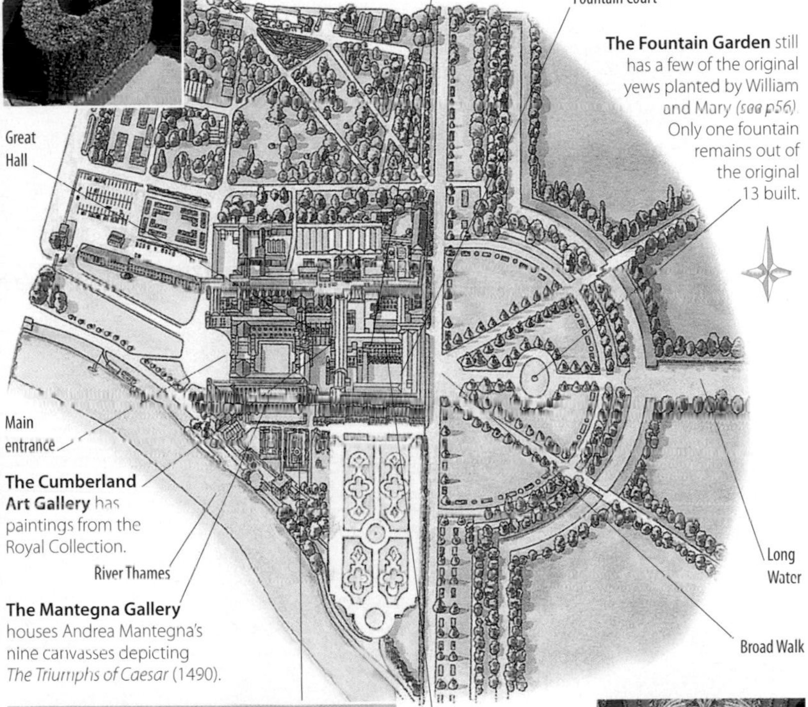

Fountain Court

The Fountain Garden still has a few of the original yews planted by William and Mary (see p56). Only one fountain remains out of the original 13 built.

Great Hall

Main entrance

The Cumberland Art Gallery has paintings from the Royal Collection.

River Thames

The Mantegna Gallery houses Andrea Mantegna's nine canvasses depicting *The Triumphs of Caesar* (1490).

Long Water

Broad Walk

The Pond Garden, a sunken water garden, was part of Henry VIII's elaborate designs. The small pond in the middle contains a single-jet fountain.

The Tudor Chapel Royal was completed by Henry VIII. But the superb woodwork, including the massive reredos by Grinling Gibbons, all date from a major refurbishment by Queen Anne (c 1711).

⑫ Street-by-Street: Brighton

As the nearest South Coast resort to London, Brighton is perennially popular, but has always been more sophisticated than brash neighbours such as Margate. Brighton has famously attracted actors and artists, and the spirit of the Prince Regent lives on, not only in the magnificence of his Royal Pavilion, but in the city's buzzing nightlife, unusual shops, thriving gay community and progressive politics – Brighton has Britain's only Green Member of Parliament.

The Old Ship Hotel, built in 1559, was later bought by Nicholas Tettersells with the money given to him by Charles II as a reward for helping him escape to the safety of France during the Civil War.

i360

Inaugurated in 2016, this breathtaking "vertical cable car" is a sleek glass pod that rises 137 m (450 ft) up a giant silver needle to provide superb 360° vistas. At the foot of the needle is a fine beachside restaurant, and inside the pod is the "Skybar", where visitors can enjoy an array of locally sourced drinks. The Skybar is also open at night for a unique view of the stars over the sea.

Brighton's i360 observation tower

Brighton Museum and Art Gallery
This lovely museum and art gallery has wonderfully varied exhibits ranging from seaside souvenirs to refined modern art.

★ **Brighton Pier**
Opened in 1899, this typical Victorian seaside pier now caters for modern visitors with arcade games, restaurants and great funfair rides.

| 0 metres | 100 |
| 0 yards | 100 |

Key
— Suggested route

The Theatre Royal, one of England's most historic theatres, opened in 1807. It often presents first performances of new plays before they move to the West End in London.

Brighton Museum and Art Gallery

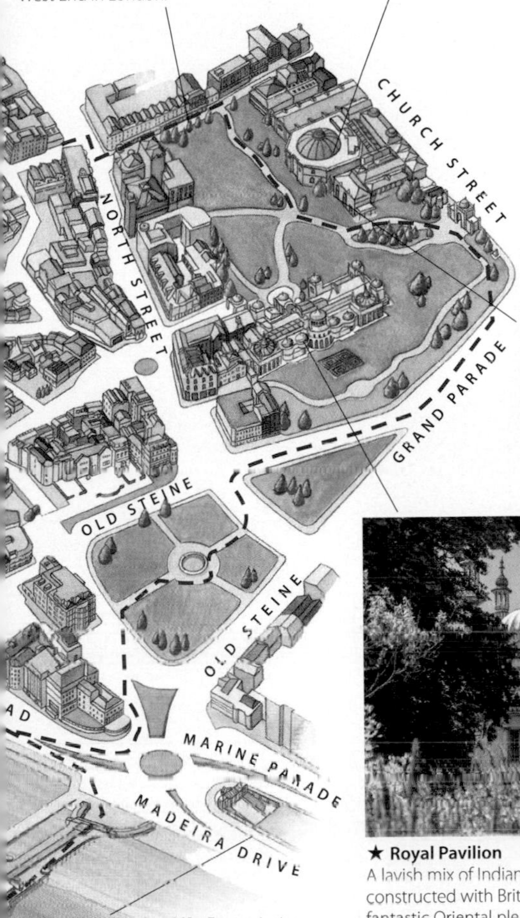

CHURCH STREET

NORTH STREET

GRAND PARADE

OLD STEINE

OLD STEINE

MARINE PARADE

MADEIRA DRIVE

The Sea Life Centre is the oldest continually operating aquarium in the world. It first opened in 1872, and now hosts modern exhibits on marine life, including a shark pool.

VISITORS' CHECKLIST

Practical Information
Brighton, East Sussex.
⚏ 280,000. 🛈 Brighton Centre, King's Rd (01273 290337). ✉
🎭 International Arts Festival: May.
🌐 **visitbrighton.com**

Transport
🚆 Brighton. 🚌 Pool Valley.

Brighton Dome
Built as the stables of the Royal Pavilion, this Indian-style domed building is now a concert hall and arts venue.

★ Royal Pavilion
A lavish mix of Indian, Islamic and Chinese styles, constructed with British materials, the Prince Regent's fantastic Oriental pleasure palace helped make Brighton a fashionable resort.

The Lanes
A maze of independent shops today, the Lanes were the original streets of the fishing village of Brighthelmstone.

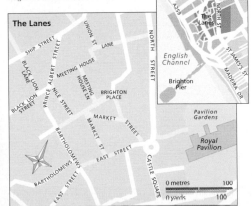

The Lanes

SHIP STREET · UNION ST · LANE · BLACK LION LANE · PRINCE ALBERT STREET · MEETING HOUSE LANE · MEETING HOUSE LN · BLACK LION STREET · NILE STREET · BRIGHTON PLACE · NORTH STREET · MARKET STREET · BARTHOLOMEWS · MARKET ST · STREET · EAST STREET · CASTLE SQUARE · BARTHOLOMEWS · EAST STREET

A259 · The Lanes · NORTH ST · ST JAMES'S ST · English Channel · MADERA DR · Brighton Pier · Pavilion Gardens · Royal Pavilion

0 metres 100
0 yards 100

Brighton: Royal Pavilion

As sea bathing became fashionable in the mid-18th century, Brighton was transformed into England's most fashionable seaside resort. Its gaiety soon appealed to the rakish Prince of Wales, who became George IV in 1820. When, in 1785, he secretly married Mrs Fitzherbert, it was here that they conducted their liaison. He moved to a lodging house near the shore and had it enlarged by Henry Holland *(see p32)*. In 1815, George employed John Nash to transform the house into a lavish Oriental palace, the expansions reflecting the change in his status from Prince of Wales to Regent to King. Completed in 1823, the exterior has remained largely unaltered. Queen Victoria sold the Pavilion to the town of Brighton in 1850.

★ Banqueting Room
Fiery dragons feature in many of the interior schemes. A particularly colourful one dominates the centre of the Banqueting Room's extraordinary ceiling, and has a huge crystal chandelier suspended from it.

★ Great Kitchen
The Prince's epic banquets required a kitchen of huge proportions. The vast ranges and long shelves of gleaming copper pans were used by famous chefs of the day.

KEY

① **The exterior**, partly built in Bath stone, is a mix of Indian, Islamic and European styles.

② **Eight original torchères**, oil lamps supported by a vertical base, decorate the the Banqueting Room. Made of Spode china stoneware, they are adorned with dragons, dolphins and lotus flowers.

③ **The banqueting table**, which seats 24 people, is laid for a splendid feast.

④ **Banqueting Room Gallery**

⑤ **South Gallery**

⑥ **The eastern façade**

⑦ **Queen Victoria's bedroom** is decorated with an exquisite hand-painted chinoiserie wallpaper.

⑧ **The central Dome** is an imposing onion dome decorated with delicate tracery. Nash drew heavily from Islamic buildings such as the Taj Mahal, but called this design his "Hindu style".

⑨ **Music Room Gallery**

⑩ **Yellow Bow Rooms**

⑪ **Cast iron domes**

Saloon
The original farmhouse that stood on the site was transformed into a villa by architect Henry Holland. The saloon, decorated with Chinese wallpaper, was the central room of the villa.

◀ Early evening at Brighton Pier, Brighton

Prince of Wales and Mrs Fitzherbert

The Prince of Wales was only 23 years old when he fell in love with Maria Fitzherbert, a 29-year-old Catholic widow, and secretly married her. They lived in the farmhouse that later became the Pavilion, and were the toast of Brighton society until George's official marriage took place to Caroline of Brunswick in 1795. Mrs Fitzherbert moved into a small house nearby, and stayed in Brighton for another 40 years.

Portrait of Maria Fitzherbert

VISITORS' CHECKLIST

Practical Information
Old Steine, Brighton. **Tel** 03000 290900. **Open** Apr–Sep: 9:30am–5:45pm; Oct–Mar: 10am–5:15pm daily (last adm: 45 mins before closing). **Closed** 25 & 26 Dec.
🅿 📷 💷 ♿ limited. 🏠 🎁
Ⓦ **brightonmuseums.org.uk**

Long Gallery
Mandarin figures, which can nod their heads, line the pink and blue walls of this 49 m (162 ft) gallery.

The Music Room
A 70-piece orchestra played for the Prince's guests in this exquisitely decorated room with crimson and gold murals.

Plan of the Royal Pavilion

Both Holland and Nash made additions and changes to the original farmhouse. The upper floor contains bedrooms, such as the Yellow Bow Rooms, which George's brothers used.

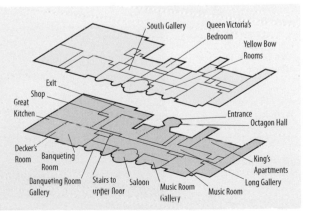

South Gallery
Queen Victoria's Bedroom
Yellow Bow Rooms
Exit
Shop
Great Kitchen
Entrance
Octagon Hall
Decker's Room
Banqueting Room
King's Apartments
Long Gallery
Banqueting Room Gallery
Stairs to upper floor
Saloon
Music Room Gallery
Music Room

Key to Floorplan
☐ First Floor
▨ Ground Floor

⑬ Steyning

West Sussex. 👥 6,000 🚌
ℹ️ 9 Causeway, Horsham (01403 211661).

This lovely little town in the lee of the Downs is packed with timber-framed houses from the Tudor period and earlier, with some built of flint and others in sandstone.

In Saxon times, Steyning was an important port and ship-building centre on the River Adur: King Ethelwulf, father of King Alfred *(see p51)*, was buried here in 858; his body was later moved to Winchester. The *Domesday Book (see p52)* records that Steyning had 123 houses, making it one of the largest towns in the south. The 12th-century church is spacious and splendid, evidence of the area's ancient prosperity; the tower, of chequered stone and flint, was added around 1600.

In the 14th century the river silted up and changed course away from the town, putting an end to its days as a port. Later it became an important coaching stop on the south coast road: the **Chequer Inn** recalls this prosperous period, with its unusual 18th-century flint and stone façade.

Environs
The remains of a **Norman castle** can be visited at Bramber, east of Steyning. This small, pretty village also contains the timber-framed **St Mary's House** (1470). It has fine panelled rooms, including the Elizabethan *trompe l'oeil* Painted Room, and one of the oldest trees in the country, a *Ginkgo biloba*.

Chanctonbury Ring and **Cissbury Ring**, on the hills west of Steyning, were Iron Age forts and the latter has the remains of a Neolithic flint mine.

Worthing is the resort where Oscar Wilde (1854–1900) wrote *The Importance of Being Earnest.*

🏛 **St Mary's House**
Bramber. **Tel** 01903 816205.
Open May–Sep: Sun pm, Thu pm, public hols pm (Aug: also Wed pm).
♿ 🖥 📷

View across the rooftops of Lewes, including the church spire

⑭ Lewes

East Sussex. 👥 17,000. 🚆 ℹ️ 187 High St (01273 483448). 🎵 Glyndebourne Festival: May–Aug. 🌐 **staylewes.info**

The ancient county town of Sussex was a vital strategic site for the Saxons because of its high vantage point over the coastline. William the Conqueror built a wooden castle here in 1067 but this was soon replaced by a large stone structure whose remains can be visited today.

In 1264 it was the site of a critical battle in which Simon de Montfort and his barons defeated Henry III, enabling them to establish the first English Parliament, though this victory was shortlived.

The Tudor **Anne of Cleves House** is a museum of local history, although Anne of Cleves, Henry VIII's fourth wife, never actually lived here.

On Guy Fawkes Night *(see p68)* lighted tar barrels are rolled to the river and various effigies, including of the Pope and Guy Fawkes, are burned. This commemorates the town's 17 Protestant martyrs burnt at the stake by Mary I *(see p55).*

Environs
Nearby are the 16th-century **Glynde Place**, a fine courtyard house, and the art-filled **Charleston**, home to the Bloomsbury Group *(see p167).*

🏛 **Anne of Cleves House**
Lewes. **Tel** 01273 474610.
Open Mar–Nov: daily. 📷 📷

🏛 **Glynde Place**
Lewes. **Tel** 01273 858224. **Open** May–Jun: Wed pm, Thu pm, Sun pm (May & Aug: also pub hols pm). 📷 📷 🖥
📷 🌐 **glynde.co.uk**

🏛 **Charleston**
Lewes. **Tel** 01323 811626. **Open** Apr–Oct: Wed–Sun pm, pub hols pm. 📷
📷 🖥 📷 🌐 **charleston.org.uk**

⑮ Eastbourne

East Sussex. 👥 100,000. 🚆 🚌
ℹ️ Cornfield Rd (01323 415415).
🛒 Wed. 🌐 **visiteastbourne.com**

With its pier and beachside promenade, Eastbourne is a classic Victorian seaside resort. It is also the starting point of the South Downs Way *(see p41)* and an excellent base for touring the South Downs. The path begins at **Beachy Head**, the spectacular 163-m (536-ft) chalk cliff just on the outskirts of the town. From here it is a bracing walk to

The lighthouse (1902) at the foot of Beachy Head, Eastbourne

The meandering River Cuckmere flowing through the South Downs to the beach at Cuckmere Haven

the clifftop at Birling Gap, with views to the **Seven Sisters**, the chalk hills that end abruptly as they meet the sea.

Environs
To the west of Eastbourne is **Seven Sisters Country Park**, an area of chalk cliffs and Downland marsh that is open all year. The **Park Visitor's Centre** contains information on the local area, history and geology.

Just north is the pretty village of **Alfriston**, with an ancient market cross and a 15th-century inn, **The Star**, in its quaint main street. Near the church is the 14th-century **Clergy House** that, in 1896, became the first National Trust property (see p33). To the east is the huge prehistoric chalk carving, the **Long Man of Wilmington** (see p225).

Park Visitor's Centre
Exceat, Seaford. **Tel** 0345 608 0193. **Open** Apr–Oct: daily; Mar & Nov: Sat & Sun. **Closed** Dec–Feb. **W** sevensisters.org.uk

Clergy House
Alfriston. **Tel** 01323 871961. **Open** Mar–Oct: Sat–Wed.

⑯ The Downs

East Sussex. Eastbourne, Petersfield, Chichester & others. Cornfield Rd, Eastbourne (01323 415415). **W** southdowns.gov.uk

The North and South Downs are parallel chalk ridges that run from east to west all the way across Kent, Sussex and Surrey, separated by the lower-lying and fertile Kent and Sussex Weald.

The South Downs were given National Park status in 2011. The area features great biodiversity and encompasses a multitude of bustling towns and villages.

The smooth Downland hills are covered with springy turf, kept short by grazing sheep, making an ideal surface for walkers. The hill above the precipitous Devil's Dyke, just north of Brighton, offers spectacular views across the Downs. The legend is that the Devil cut the gorge to let in the sea and flood the countryside, but was foiled by divine intervention. The River Cuckmere runs through one of the most picturesque parts of the South Downs.

Located at the highest point of the Downs is **Uppark House**, a neat, square National Trust-owned building that has been meticulously restored to its mid-18th-century appearance.

⑰ Hastings

East Sussex. 90,000. Aquila House, Breeds Place (01424 451111). **W** visit1066country.com

This fascinating seaside town was one of the first Cinque Ports

(see p186) and is still a thriving fishing port, as illustrated by the unique tall wooden "net shops" on the beach, where for hundreds of years fishermen have stored their nets. In the 19th century, the area to the west of the Old Town was built up as a seaside resort, which left the narrow, characterful streets of the old fishermen's quarter intact. There are two cliff railways and smugglers' caves displaying where contraband used to be stored (see p284).

Environs
Seven miles (11 km) from Hastings is the small town of Battle, whose central square is dominated by the gatehouse of **Battle Abbey**. William the Conqueror built this on the site of his great victory, reputedly placing the high altar where Harold fell, but the abbey was destroyed in the Dissolution (see p355). There is an evocative walk around the actual battlefield.

Battle Abbey
High St, Battle. **Tel** 01424 775705. **Open** Apr–Oct: daily; Nov–Mar: Sat & Sun. **Closed** 1 Jan, 24–26 Dec.

Small fishing boats and wooden net huts on Hastings' shingle beach

Battle of Hastings

In 1066, William the Conqueror's (see p51) invading army from Normandy landed on the south coast, aiming to take Winchester and London. Hearing that King Harold and his army were camped just inland from Hastings, William confronted them. He won the battle after Harold was mortally wounded by an arrow to the eye. This last successful invasion of England is depicted on the Bayeux Tapestry in Normandy, France.

King Harold's death, Bayeux Tapestry

The fairy-tale 14th-century Bodiam Castle surrounded by its moat

⑱ Bodiam Castle

Nr Robertsbridge, E Sussex. **Tel** 01580 830196. ⧩ Robertsbridge then taxi. **Open** daily. **Closed** 24–26 Dec. 🅿 🅰 limited. 💻 📷 NT

Surrounded by its wide, glistening moat, this late 14th-century castle, with its wooden portcullis, spiral staircases and battlements, is one of the most romantic in England.

It was previously thought to have been built as a defence against French invasion, but is now believed to have been intended as a home for a Sussex knight. The castle saw action during the Civil War in 1642–51 *(see p56)*, when it was damaged in an assault by Parliamentary soldiers. They removed the roof to restrict its use as a base for Charles I's troops.

It has been uninhabited since, but its grey stone has proved indestructible. With the exception of the roof, it was restored in 1919 by Lord Curzon, who gave it to the nation.

Environs

To the east is **Great Dixter**, a 15th-century manor house restored by Sir Edwin Lutyens in 1910. The late Christopher Lloyd created a magnificent garden with a blend of terraces and borders, and a great nursery, too.

🏛 **Great Dixter**
Northiam, Rye. **Tel** 01797 252878. **Open** Apr–Oct: Tue–Sun pm & public hols pm. 🅿 🅰 📷
W **greatdixter.co.uk**

⑲ Rye

See pp188–9.

⑳ Romney Marsh

Kent. ⧩ Ashford. 🚌 Ashford, Hythe. 🛈 Dymchurch Rd, New Romney (01797 369487). Visitor Centre: **Open** Easter–Oct: Thu–Mon; Nov–Easter: Fri–Mon. W **theromneymarsh.net**

Until Roman times Romney Marsh and its southern neighbour Walland Marsh were entirely covered by the sea at high tide. The Romans drained the Romney section, and Walland Marsh was gradually reclaimed during the Middle Ages. Together they formed a large area of fertile land, particularly suitable for the Romney Marsh sheep bred for the quality of their wool.

Dungeness, a desolate and lonely spot at the southeastern tip of the area, is dominated by a lighthouse and a nuclear power station. It is also the

Coastal Defence and the Cinque Ports

Before the Norman Conquest *(see pp50–51)*, national government was weak and, with threats from Europe, it was important for the Saxon kings to keep on good terms with the Channel ports. So, in return for keeping the royal fleet supplied with ships and men, five ports – Hastings, Romney, Hythe, Sandwich and Dover – were granted the right to levy taxes; others were added later. "Cinque" (pronounced "sink") came from the French word for five. The privileges were revoked during the 17th century. In 1803, in response to the growing threat from France, 74 fixed defences were built along the coast. Only 24 of these Martello towers still exist.

The clifftop position of Dover Castle

A Martello tower, built as part of the Channel's defences

...hern terminus of the popular **...mney, Hythe and Dymchurch ...ght Railway**, which was opened in 1927. During the summer this takes passengers 14 miles (23 km) up the coast to Hythe on trains a third the conventional size. For more information, visit www.rhdr.org.uk.

Fourteen medieval churches, some of them completely isolated, are scattered over the Marsh. Their vaults proved ideal storage places for contraband in the days of smuggling.

The Kent Wildlife Trust Visitor Centre explores the history of the Marsh and its wildlife. For more information visit www.kentwildlifetrust.org.uk.

㉑ Dover

Kent. 32,000. 🚉 🚌 ⛴ ℹ️ Dover Museum, Market Sq (01304 201066). 🛒 Tue. **W** whitecliffscountry.org.uk

Its proximity to the European mainland makes Dover the leading port for cross-Channel travel. Its famous white cliffs exert a strong pull on returning travellers.

Dover's strategic position and large natural harbour has meant the town has had an important role to play in the nation's defences.

Built on the original site of an ancient Saxon fortification, **Dover Castle**, helped defend the town from 1198, when Henry II first built the keep, right up to World War II, when it was used as the command post for the Dunkirk evacuation. Exhibits in the castle and in

The magnificent face of the iconic white cliffs of Dover

the labyrinth of tunnels beneath made by prisoners in the Napoleonic Wars *(see p59)* cover all these periods.

Environs

One of the most significant sites in England's early history is the ruin of **Richborough Roman Fort**. Now a large grassy site 2 miles (3 km) inland, this was where, in AD 43, Claudius's Roman invaders *(see p48)* made their first landing. For hundreds of years afterwards, Rutupiae, as it was known, was one of the most important ports of entry and military bases in the country.

🏰 **Dover Castle**
Castle Hill. **Tel** 01304 211067.
Open daily (Nov–Jan: Sat & Sun only).
Closed 1 Jan, 24–26 Dec. 🅿️ 📷 of the tunnels. ♿ 🚻 📷 EH

🏰 **Richborough Roman Fort**
Richborough. **Tel** 01304 612013.
Open Apr–Oct: daily; Nov–Mar: Sat & Sun. 🅿️ ♿ 📷 EH

㉒ Margate

Kent. 55,000. 🚉 🚌 ℹ️ The Droit House, Stone Pier (01843 577577).
W visitthanet.co.uk

A classic seaside resort on the Isle of Thanet, Margate is a draw not only for its amusement park, Dreamland, but also for **Turner Contemporary**. This spectacular modern building celebrates the town's connections with J M W Turner and hosts adventurous exhibitions.

Environs

Just south is a 19th-century gentleman's residence, **Quex Park**, with two unusual towers in its grounds. The adjoining **Powell-Cotton Museum** has a fine collection of predominantly African art and artifacts, as well as unique wildlife dioramas. To the west is a Saxon church, built within the remains of the bleak Roman coastal fort of **Reculver**. Dramatic twin towers, known as the Two Sisters, were added to the church in the 12th century. The church now stands at the centre of a very pleasant, if rather windy, 37-ha (91-acre) campsite.

🏛️ **Turner Contemporary**
Rendezvous. **Tel** 01843 233000.
Open Tue–Sun. ♿ 🚻 📷
W turnercontemporary.org

🏛️ **Quex Park & Powell-Cotton Museum**
Birchington. **Tel** 01843 842168.
Open Tue–Sun (House: pm only).
🅿️ ♿ 🚻 📷 **W** quexpark.co.uk

🏰 **Reculver Towers and Fort**
Reculver. **Tel** 01227 862162.
Open daily (exterior only). EH

Margate seafront as seen from the harbour wall, with its beach and steps at low tide

⑲ Street-by-Street: Rye

This ancient and charming fortified town was
added to the original Cinque ports *(see p186)*
in the 12th–13th century. A huge storm in 1287
diverted the River Rother so that it met the sea at
Rye, and for more than 300 years it was one of the
most important Channel ports. However, in the
16th century the harbour began to silt up and
the town is now 2 miles (3 km) inland. Rye was
frequently attacked by the French, culminating
in 1377 when it was burned to the ground.

★ **Mermaid Street**
This delightful cobbled street, its huddled
houses jutting out at unlikely angles, has
hardly altered since it was rebuilt in the
14th century.

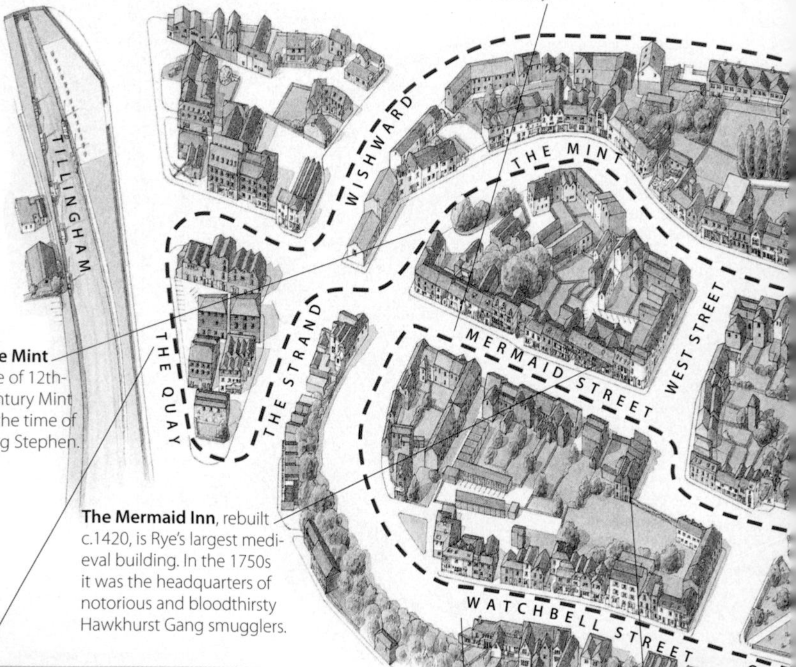

The Mint
Site of 12th-
century Mint
in the time of
King Stephen.

The Mermaid Inn, rebuilt
c.1420, is Rye's largest medieval building. In the 1750s
it was the headquarters of
notorious and bloodthirsty
Hawkhurst Gang smugglers.

Strand Quay
The brick and timber
warehouses survive from
the prosperous days when
Rye was a thriving port.

View over the
River Tillingham

Lamb House
This fine Georgian
house was built in 1722.
George I stayed here
when stranded in a
storm, and author
Henry James (1843–
1916) lived here.

St Mary's Church
The turret clock (1561) is claimed to be the oldest working clock in the country.

VISITORS' CHECKLIST

Practical Information
East Sussex. 🅰 4,500.
ℹ Strand Quay (01797 226696).
🗓 Wed, Thu. 🎭 Rye Festival: Sep.
🌐 visit1066country.com/rye

Transport
🚆 🚌 Station Approach.

Environs
Just 2 miles (3 km) to the south of Rye is the small town of **Winchelsea**. At the behest of Edward I, it was moved to its present position in 1288, when most of the old town on lower land to the southeast was drowned by the same storm that diverted the River Rother in 1287.

Winchelsea is probably Britain's first coherently planned medieval town. Although not all of it was built as originally planned, its rectangular grid survives today, as does the **Church of St Thomas Becket** (begun c.1300) at its centre. Several raids by the French during the 14th century damaged the church and burned down scores of houses. The church has three tombs, and there are also two well-preserved medieval tombs in the chantry. The three windows (1928–33) in the Lady Chapel were designed by Douglas Strachan as a memorial to those who died in World War I. Just beyond the edges of present-day Winchelsea are the remains of three of the original gates – showing just how big a town was first envisaged. The beach below is one of the finest on the southeast coast.

Camber Sands, to the east of the mouth of the Rother, is another excellent beach. Once used by fishermen, it is now popular with swimmers and edged with seaside bungalows and a bustling holiday camp. Camber Sands is also a favourite spot for kite- and windsurfing.

The ruins of **Camber Castle** are west of the beach, near Brede Lock, Rye. This was one of the forts built along this coast by Henry VIII when he feared an attack by the French. At the time of building, the castle was on the edge of the sea, but it was abandoned in 1642 when it became stranded inland as the river silted up.

🏛 **Camber Castle**
Camber, Rye. **Tel** 01797 227784.
Open Jul–Sep: 1st Sat of month (pm) for tours only. 🇪🇭

↖ Hastings and railway station

CINQUE PORT STREET

Land Gate
Built in the 14th century, this is the only survivor of the old fortified town's four gates.

TOWER STREET

CONDUIT HILL

HIGH STREET

HILDERS CLIFF

EAST STREET

MARKET STREET

The 16th-century Flushing Inn

This cistern was built in 1735; horse-drawn machinery was used to raise water to the highest part of the town.

Gun Garden, Ypres Tower

Key
— Suggested route

0 metres	50
0 yards	50

★ Ypres Tower
Built as a castle in 1250, it was turned into a house in 1430. It is now used as the museum.

Bronze sculpture of Christ on Christ Church Gate, Canterbury Cathedral

㉓ Canterbury

Kent. 🗺 51,000. 🚋 🚌 ℹ The Beaney House of Knowledge, 18 High St (01227 862162). 🛒 Wed, Fri. 🌐 canterbury.co.uk

Its position on the London to Dover route meant Canterbury was an important Roman town even before the arrival of St Augustine in 597, sent by the pope to convert the Anglo-Saxons to Christianity. The town soon became the centre of the Christian Church in England.

With the building of the cathedral and the martyrdom of Thomas Becket *(see p52)*, Canterbury's future as a religious centre was assured. Today, the town is a UNESCO World Heritage Site.

Adjacent to the ruins of St Augustine's Abbey, destroyed in the Dissolution *(see p355)*, is St Martin's Church, the oldest in England, where St Augustine first worshipped. It has impressive Norman and Saxon work.

The Westgate Towers, built in 1381, make for an imposing medieval gatehouse.

For a glimpse into the city's ancient past, visit the **Canterbury Roman Museum**.

The Poor Priests' Hospital, founded in the 1100s, is now the **Canterbury Heritage Museum**.

🏛 **Canterbury Roman Museum**
Longmarket, Butchery Lane. **Tel** 01227 785575. **Open** 10am–5pm daily. 🚻
♿ 🌐 canterbury-museums.co.uk

🏛 **Canterbury Heritage Museum**
Stour St. **Tel** 01227 475202.
Open 10am–5pm Wed–Sun. 🚻 📷
🌐 canterbury-museums.co.uk

Canterbury Cathedral

To match Canterbury's growing ecclesiastical rank as a major centre of Christianity, the first Norman archbishop, Lanfranc, ordered a new cathedral to be built on the ruins of the Anglo-Saxon cathedral in 1070. It was enlarged and rebuilt many times and as a result embraces examples of all styles of medieval architecture. The most poignant moment in its history came in 1170 when Thomas Becket was murdered here *(see p52)*. Four years after his death a fire devastated the cathedral and the Trinity Chapel was built to house Becket's remains. The shrine quickly became an important religious site and until the Dissolution *(see p355)* the cathedral was one of Christendom's chief places of pilgrimage.

Nave
At 60 m (188 ft), this extended aisle makes Canterbury Cathedral one of the world's longest medieval churches.

Main entrance

KEY

① **The South West Porch** (1426) may have been built to commemorate the victory at Agincourt *(see p53)*.

② **Great Cloister**

③ **Chapter House**

④ **The circular Corona Chapel**

⑤ **Trinity Chapel**

⑥ **St Augustine's Chair**

⑦ **The quire** (choir), completed in 1184, is one of the longest in England.

⑧ **The Great South Window** has four stained-glass panels (1958) by Erwin Bossanyi.

★ **Medieval Stained Glass**
This depiction of the 1,000-year-old Methuselah is a detail from the southwest transept window.

Geoffrey Chaucer

Considered to be the first great English poet, Geoffrey Chaucer (c.1345–1400), a customs official by profession, wrote a rumbustious and witty account of a group of pilgrims travelling from London to Becket's shrine in 1387 in the *Canterbury Tales*. The pilgrims represent a cross-section of 14th-century English society and the tales remain one of the greatest and most entertaining works of early English literature.

Wife of Bath, Canterbury Tales

VISITORS' CHECKLIST

Practical Information
11 The Precincts, Canterbury.
Tel 01227 762862. **Open** 9am–5:30pm Mon–Sat (to 5pm winter), 12:30–2:30pm Sun. Call ahead.
Closed for services & concerts; Good Friday, 24 & 25 Dec.
🅿 🚻 📷 ♿ 🚻 8am daily; 5:30pm Mon–Fri; 3:15pm Sat & Sun; 11am Sun. 📷
W canterbury-cathedral.org

Bell Harry Tower
The central tower was built in 1498 to house a bell donated by Henry of Eastry 100 years before. The fan vaulting is a superb example of the late Perpendicular style.

★ Site of the Shrine of St Thomas Becket
This Victorian illustration (anon) portrays Becket's canonization. The Trinity Chapel was built to house his tomb, which stood here until it was destroyed in 1538. The spot is now marked by a lighted candle.

★ Black Prince's Tomb
This copper effigy is on the tomb of Edward III's son, who died in 1376.

Rochester Castle and Cathedral as seen from across the River Medway

㉔ Leeds Castle

Maidstone, Kent. **Tel** 01622 765400.
🚆 Bearsted then bus. **Open** 10:30am–
5:30pm (Apr–Sep: to 6pm; Oct–Mar:
to 5pm) daily. **Closed** 1st w/e Nov &
25 Dec. 🅿 ♿ ✏ 🎫 📷 🔲 **leeds-
castle.com**

Surrounded by a lake that
reflects the warm buff stone
of its crenellated turrets, Leeds
is often considered to be the
most beautiful castle in England.
Begun in the early 12th century, it
has been continuously inhabited
and its present appearance is a
result of centuries of rebuilding
and extensions, most recently
in the 1930s. Leeds has royal
connections going back to 1278,
when it was given to Edward I
by a courtier seeking favour.
Henry VIII loved the castle and
visited it often to escape the
plague in London. It contains a
life-sized bust of Henry from the
late 16th century. Leeds passed
out of royal ownership when
Edward VI gave it to Sir Anthony
St Leger in 1552 as a reward for
helping to pacify the Irish.

㉕ Rochester

Kent. 🅰 27,000. 🚆 🚌 ℹ 95 High
Street (01634 338141).

Clustered at the mouth of the
River Medway are the towns
of Rochester, Chatham and
Gillingham, all rich in naval
history, but none more so than
Rochester, which occupied a
strategic site on the London
to Dover road.
England's tallest Norman keep
is at **Rochester Castle**, worth
climbing for the views over the
Medway. The town's medieval
history is still visible, with the
original city walls – which
followed the lines of the Roman
fortifications – on view in the
High Street, as well as some
well-preserved wall paintings
in the **cathedral**, built in 1088.

Environs

In Chatham, the **Historic
Dockyard** is now a museum of
shipbuilding and nautical crafts.
Fort Amherst nearby was built in
1756 to protect the dockyard and
river entrance from attack, and

has 1,800 m (5,570 ft) of tunnels
to explore that were hewn by
Napoleonic prisoners of war.

🏰 Rochester Castle
Castle Hill. **Tel** 01634 335882. **Open**
10am–4pm (Apr–Sep: to 6pm) daily
(last adm: 45 mins before closing).
Closed 1 Jan, 24–26 Dec. 🅿 🎫 ♿
grounds. 📷 EH

🏛 Historic Dockyard
Dock Rd, Chatham. **Tel** 01634 823800.
Open mid-Feb–Nov: daily. 🅿 ♿ ✏
🔲 📷 🔲 **thedockyard.co.uk**

🏰 Fort Amherst
Dock Rd, Chatham. **Tel** 01634 847747.
Open daily. 🅿 🔲 🔲 **fortamherst.com**

㉖ Knole

Sevenoaks, Kent. **Tel** 01732 462100.
🚆 Sevenoaks then taxi. Showrooms:
Open Mar–Oct: Tue–Sun pm & public
hols pm. Park: **Open** daily. 🅿 ✏ ♿
ltd to Great Hall and park. 🔲 📷 NT

This huge Tudor mansion was
built in the late 15th century, and
was seized by Henry VIII from the
Archbishop of Canterbury at
the Dissolution (see p355). In
1566 Queen Elizabeth I gave it
to her cousin Thomas Sackville.
His descendants have lived here
ever since, including the writer
Vita Sackville-West (1892–1962).
The house is well known for its
17th-century furniture, such as
the elaborate bed made for
James II. The 405-ha (1,000-acre)
park has deer and lovely walks.

Environs
Ightham Mote, east of Knole,
is the most complete medieval
manor house in England, with

Charles Dickens

Charles Dickens (1812–70) is considered the
greatest novelist of the Victorian era. He was
born in Portsmouth, but moved to Chatham
aged 5. He set many of his stories – especially
Great Expectations – in the Rochester area.
Although he later moved to London, Dickens
kept up his Kent connections and spent his last
years at Gad's Hill, near Rochester. The town
celebrates the famous connection with an
annual Dickens festival each June.

parts dating back to the 1320s. Its stone-and-timber building has over 70 rooms and a grand courtyard. Rooms are decorated in a range of styles from across the centuries, including a 15th-century chapel with an ornate 16th-century painted oak ceiling, and a drawing room with hand-painted 18th-century Chinese wallpaper. The house is surrounded by a placid moat, crossed by three bridges, and is set in beautifully manicured gardens.

At **Sissinghurst Castle Garden** are gardens created by Vita Sackville-West and her husband Harold Nicolson in the 1930s.

Ightham Mote
Ivy Hatch, Sevenoaks. **Tel** 01732 810 378. **Open** Mar–Oct & Dec: daily; Nov: Sat & Sun.

Sissinghurst Castle Garden
Cranbrook. **Tel** 01580 710700. **Open** Mar–Dec: daily. limited.

❷ Hever Castle

Edenbridge, Kent. **Tel** 01732 865224. Edenbridge Town. **Open** Jan–Mar & Nov: noon–4:30pm Wed–Sun; Apr–Oct & Dec: noon–6pm daily. limited.
w hevercastle.co.uk

This small, moated castle was the 16th-century home of Anne Boleyn, the doomed wife of Henry VIII, executed for adultery. She lived here as a young woman, and the king often visited her while staying at Leeds Castle. In 1903 Hever was bought by William Waldorf Astor, who began a restoration programme, building a Neo-Tudor village alongside it for guests and servants. The moat and gatehouse date from around 1270.

Inside the house, visitors can see Anne Boleyn's bedroom and many other apartments, while the lovely gardens are filled with sculptures, grottoes and imaginative topiary.

Environs

To the northwest of Hever is **Chartwell**, the family home of Sir Winston Churchill (*see p63*). Before he became prime minister in 1940, he expended a lot of his

The façade of Chartwell, Winston Churchill's home

energy on improving Chartwell, and with Lady Churchill he created a magnificent garden, with lakes, a rose garden and gorgeous views over the Kent Weald. His greatest hobby was painting, and his studio is lined with beautiful landscapes and portraits he painted at Chartwell and on his international travels.

After he died, Lady Churchill left the house almost immediately, and the main rooms are still preserved very much as they left them. Enormously atmospheric, they are full of books, photos, cigar stubs, letters, memorabilia and gifts from various world figures, giving a rich sense of Sir Winston's life and personality.

Chartwell
Westerham, Kent. **Tel** 01732 868381. House. **Open** Mar–Oct: daily. Gardens & exhibitions: times vary, phone for details. limited.

❷ Royal Tunbridge Wells

Kent. 56,000. The Corn Exchange, The Pantiles (01892 515675). 2nd & 4th Sat. **w** visittunbridge wells.com

Helped by royal patronage, the town became a popular spa in the 17th and 18th centuries after mineral springs were discovered in 1606. The Pantiles – the colonnaded and paved promenade – was laid out in the 1700s.

Environs

Nearby manor house **Penshurst Place**, built in the 1340s, has an 18-m- (60-ft-) high Great Hall.

Penshurst Place
Tonbridge, Kent. **Tel** 01892 870307. **Open** mid-Feb–Mar: Sat & Sun; Apr–Oct: daily (House: **Open** noon–4pm; Gardens. **Open** 10:30am–6pm; Toy Museum: **Open** noon–4pm). limited.

An early 18th-century astrolabe to measure the stars, Hever Castle garden

EAST ANGLIA

Norfolk · Suffolk · Essex · Cambridgeshire

The bulge of land between the Thames Estuary and the Wash, flat but far from featureless, sits aside from the main north–south axis through Britain, and for that reason it has succeeded in maintaining and preserving its distinctive architecture, traditions and rural character in both cities and countryside.

East Anglia's name derives from the Angles, the people from northern Germany who settled here during the 5th and 6th centuries. East Anglians have long been a breed of plain-spoken and independent people. Two prominent East Anglians – Queen Boudica in the 1st century and Oliver Cromwell in the 17th century – were famous for their stubbornness and their refusal to bow to constituted authority. The region is also referred to as the Fens, meaning swampy marshes. After these wetlands were drained in the 17th century, the peaty soil proved ideal for arable farming, and today East Anglia grows about a third of Britain's vegetables. The villages and towns, and even the cities, feel embedded in the countryside and are small in scale. The cities of Norwich and Ely, with their notable cathedrals, are easily explored, as is the university town of Cambridge, which is home to King's College, one of the finest Gothic buildings in Europe.

The royal family traditionally spends Christmas at Sandringham House in Norfolk, but the dry and sunny climate also draws summer visitors to the long stretches of sandy beaches, the charming seaside resorts of Southwold and Wells-next-the-Sea, and the atmospheric town of Aldeburgh. Wildlife lovers will feel the pull of the Broads, home to some of Great Britain's rarest animal and plant species.

Lavender fields in full bloom in July, Heacham, Norfolk

◀ Punts lined up along the River Cam, Cambridge

Exploring East Anglia

As you move away from London, you soon reach the countryside immortalized by the painter Constable (see p208), scattered with churches, windmills and medieval barns. Nature lovers will find it fruitful territory, especially north Norfolk with its bird reserves, seal colonies and the unique landscape of the watery Broads, best seen by boat or bike. The distinctive pink-washed cottages in Suffolk, flint cottages in Norfolk and thatched roofs dotted around the region evoke a time gone by.

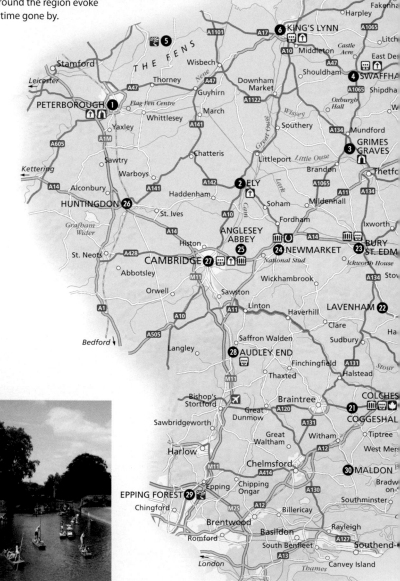

Punting on the River Cam in Cambridge

For hotels and restaurants in this area see pp563–4 and pp587–8

Key

— Motorway
— Major road
— Secondary road
····· Minor road
— Scenic route
···· Main railway
— Minor railway

Getting Around

The region's more isolated sights can be very difficult to reach by public transport and so car rental may be a cheaper and more efficient method of travelling around. The M11 motorway runs from London to Cambridge. The coast road from Aldeburgh to King's Lynn takes you through some of the most appealing countryside in the area. There are frequent mainline trains to Norwich, Ipswich and Cambridge, although local trains are more sporadic. There are international and domestic airports at Stansted *(see p634)* and Norwich.

Beach huts on Wells-next-the-Sea beach, north Norfolk

Sights at a Glance

1 Peterborough
2 Ely
3 Grimes Graves
4 Swaffham
5 The Fens
6 King's Lynn
7 Sandringham
9 Blickling Hall
10 *Norwich pp204–5*
11 The Broads
12 Great Yarmouth
13 Lowestoft
14 Southwold
15 Dunwich
16 Aldeburgh
17 Framlingham Castle
18 Ipswich
20 Colchester
21 Coggeshall
22 Lavenham
23 Bury St Edmunds
24 Newmarket
25 Anglesey Abbey
26 Huntingdon
27 *Cambridge pp214–19*
28 Audley End
29 Epping Forest
30 Maldon

Walks and Tours

8 *North Norfolk Tour pp200–201*
19 *Constable Walk p208*

0 kilometres 10
0 miles 10

For keys to symbols *see back flap*

● Peterborough

Cambridgeshire. 🚹 195,000.
🚆 🚌 **ⓘ** 41 Bridge Street
(01733 452336). 🛒 Tue–Sat.
w visitpeterborough.com

Although one of the oldest
settlements in Britain, Peterborough was designated a
New Town in 1967, and is now a
mixture of ancient and modern.

The city centre's main feature
is the 12th-century **St Peter's
Cathedral**, which gave the
city its name. The interior of
this classic Norman building,
with its vast, simple nave, was
badly damaged by Cromwell's
troops *(see p56)*, but its unique
painted wooden ceiling (1220)
has survived intact. Catherine
of Aragon, the first wife of
Henry VIII, is buried here,
although Cromwell's troops
also destroyed her tomb. In
the visitor centre there is a
fascinating exhibition that
explores the cathedral's history.

Environs

The oldest wheel in Britain (1300
BC) was found preserved in peat
at **Flag Fen**, a Bronze Age site.
The site's visitor centre provides
a glimpse into prehistory.

🏛 Flag Fen Bronze Age Centre
The Droveway, Northey Rd.
Tel 01733 864468. **Open** Apr–Sep:
daily. 🅿 🧥 🛗 🖥 **w** vivacity-
peterborough.com

❷ Ely

Cambridgeshire. 🚹 20,000. 🚆
ⓘ 29 St Mary's St (01353 662062).
Open daily. 🛒 Thu (general), Sat
(craft & antiques); farmers' market
every 2nd & 4th Sat. **w** visitely.org.uk

Built on a chalk hill, this small
city is thought to be named after
the eels in the nearby River Ouse.
The hill was once an inaccessible
island in the then marshy and
treacherous Fens *(see p200)*.
It was also the last stronghold

of Anglo-Saxon resistance under
Hereward the Wake *(see p52)*,
who hid in the cathedral until the
Normans crossed the Fens in 1071.

Today this small prosperous
city, dominated by the huge
cathedral dubbed the "Ship
of the Fens", is the market
centre for the rich agricultural
area surrounding it.

❸ Grimes Graves

Lynford, Norfolk. **Tel** 01842 810656.
🚌 Brandon then taxi. **Open** Easter–
Sep: daily; Oct: Wed–Mon. 🅿
🛗 exhibition area only. 🏛 **EH**

One of the most important
Neolithic sites in England,
this was once an extensive
complex of flint mines – 433
shafts have been located –
dating from before 2000 BC.

Using antlers as pickaxes,
Stone Age miners hacked
through the soft chalk to extract
the hard flint below to make

Ely Cathedral

Begun in 1083, the cathedral took 268 years to complete.
It survived the Dissolution *(see p355)* but was closed for
17 years by Cromwell *(see p56)*, who lived in Ely for a time.

The lantern's glass
windows admit
light into the
dome.

Stained-glass
museum

The huge cathedral dominates
the flat Fens countryside
surrounding Ely.

**This painted
wooden angel** is one
of hundreds of bosses
that were carved all
over the south and
north transepts
in the 13th and
14th centuries.

Area of cutaway

The Octagon was built in
1322 when the Norman tower
collapsed. Its roof, the lantern,
took an extra 24 years to build
and weighs 200 tonnes.

The tomb is that of Alan
de Walsingham, designer
of the unique Octagon.

Oxburgh Hall, surrounded by its medieval moat

weapons and tools. The flint may have been transported long distances around England on the prehistoric network of paths. You can descend 9 m (30 ft) by ladder into one of the shafts and see the galleries where the flint was mined. During excavations, unusual chalk models of a fertility goddess *(see p47)* and a phallus were discovered.

VISITORS' CHECKLIST

Practical Information
Ely. **Tel** 01353 667735. **Open** daily.
Closed special events. 🎧 📷 ♿
📖 📷 ⓦ elycathedral.org

Painted ceiling (19th century)

The south aisle has 12 classic Norman arches at its foot, with pointed Early English windows above.

The Prior's Door (c.1150)

Environs

Nearby, at the centre of the once fertile plain known as the Breckland, is the small market town of **Thetford**.

Once a prosperous trading town, its fortunes dipped in the 16th century, when its priory was destroyed *(see p355)*, and the surrounding land deteriorated due to excessive sheep grazing. The area was later planted with pine trees. A mound in the city marks the site of a pre-Norman castle.

The revolutionary writer and philosopher Tom Paine, author of *The Rights of Man*, was born here in 1737.

❻ Swaffham

Norfolk. 🚹 7,000. 🚌 🛈 4 London St (01760 722255). 🛒 Sat. ⓦ around **swaffham.co.uk**

The best-preserved Georgian town in East Anglia and a fashionable resort during the Regency period, Swaffham is at its liveliest on Saturdays

when a market is held in the square, around the market cross of 1783. In the centre of the town is the 15th-century **Church of St Peter and St Paul**, with a small spire added in the 19th century. It has a magnificent Tudor north aisle, said to have been paid for by John Chapman, the Pedlar of Swaffham. He is depicted on the two-sided town sign near the marketplace. Myth has it that he went to London and met a stranger who told him of hidden treasure at Swaffham. He returned, dug it up and used it to embellish the church.

Environs

Castle Acre, north of the town, has the remains of a massive Cluniac **priory**. Founded in 1090, its stunning Norman front still stands.

A short drive south is **Oxburgh Hall and Garden**, built by Sir Edmund Bedingfeld in 1482. The hall, entered through a huge 24-m (80-ft) fortified gatehouse, displays the velvet Oxburgh Hangings, embroidered by Mary, Queen of Scots *(see p515)*.

🏛 **Castle Acre Priory**
Castle Acre. **Tel** 01760 755394.
Open daily (Nov–Mar: Sat & Sun).
Closed 1 Jan, 24–26 Dec. 🎧
♿ limited. 📷 🇪🇭

🏠 **Oxburgh Hall & Garden**
Oxborough. **Tel** 01366 328258.
🚉 Downham Market then taxi.
Open mid-Feb–Oct: Mon–Wed & Fri–Sun; Nov–mid-Feb: Sat & Sun.
🎧 ♿ limited. 🎫 📷 🇳🇹

Boudica and the Iceni

When the Romans invaded Britain, the Iceni, the main tribe in East Anglia, joined forces with them to defeat the Catuvellauni, a rival tribe. But the Romans then turned on the Iceni, torturing Queen Boudica (or Boadicea). In AD 61, she led a revolt against Roman rule: her followers burned down London, Colchester and St Albans. The rebellion was put down and the queen took poison rather than submit. At Cockley Cley, near Swaffham, an Iceni camp has been excavated.

Illustration of Queen Boudica leading her Iceni followers

A windmill on Wicken Fen, England's most well-known fen

❺ The Fens

Cambridgeshire/Norfolk. 🚋 Ely.
ℹ 29 St Mary's St, Ely (01353 662062).
🆆 visitely.org.uk

This is the open, flat, fertile expanse that is encircled by Lincoln, Cambridge and Bedford.

Up until the 17th century it was a swamp, and settlement was possible only on "islands", such as Ely (see p198).

Through the 17th century, speculators, recognizing the value of the peaty soil for farmland, brought in Dutch experts to drain the fens. However, as the peat dried, it contracted, and the fens have slowly been getting lower. Powerful electric pumps now keep it drained.

Nine miles (14 km) from Ely is Wicken Fen, 254 ha (630 acres) of undrained fen providing a habitat for a wide range of water life, wildfowl and wild flowers. It is one of Europe's most important wetlands.

Trinity Guildhall, King's Lynn

❻ King's Lynn

Norfolk. 🚹 42,000. 🚋 🚌
ℹ Custom House, Purfleet Quay (01553 763044). 🏪 Tue.
🆆 visitwestnorfolk.com

Formerly Bishop's Lynn, its name was changed at the Reformation to reflect political reality. In the Middle Ages it was one of England's most prosperous ports, shipping local grain and wool to Europe. There are still a few surviving warehouses and merchants' houses by the River Ouse from this period. At the north end of the town, **True's Yard Fisherfolk Museum** contains a fisherfolk yard, with two cottages and a

---

❽ North Norfolk Coastal Tour

This tour takes you through some of the most beautiful areas of East Anglia; nearly all of the north Norfolk coast has been designated an Area of Outstanding Natural Beauty. The sea has dictated the character of the area. With continuing deposits of silt, once busy ports are now far inland and the shingle and sand banks that have been built up are home to a huge variety of wildlife. Do bear in mind when planning your journey that this popular route can get congested during summer.

Tips for Drivers

Tour length: 28 miles (45 km).
Stopping-off points: Holkham Hall makes a pleasant stop for a picnic lunch. There are some good pubs in Wells-next-the-Sea. (See also pp636–7.)

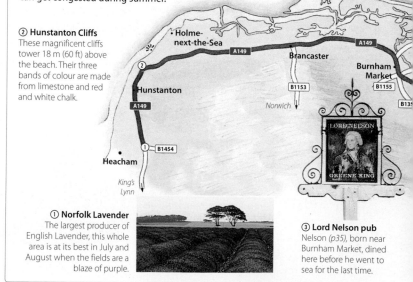

② **Hunstanton Cliffs**
These magnificent cliffs tower 18 m (60 ft) above the beach. Their three bands of colour are made from limestone and red and white chalk.

① **Norfolk Lavender**
The largest producer of English Lavender, this whole area is at its best in July and August when the fields are a blaze of purple.

③ **Lord Nelson pub**
Nelson (p35), born near Burnham Market, dined here before he went to sea for the last time.

smokehouse, the last remnants of the fishing community.

Saturday Market Place is surrounded by historic sites and buildings. The **Trinity Guildhall** dates back to the 15th century and was formerly a prison. **St Margaret's Church** dates from 1101; inside there is a fine Elizabethan screen.

The handsome **Custom House**, overlooking the river, was built in the 17th century as a merchant exchange. The first floor houses an exhibition dedicated to the town's colourful maritime history.

🏛 **True's Yard Fisherfolk Museum**
North St. **Tel** 01553 770479.
Open Tue–Sat. **Closed** 24 Dec–mid-Jan. 🗓 📷 🎫 .

🏛 **Custom House**
Purfleet Quay. **Tel** 01553 763044.
Open daily.

Sandringham, where the Royal Family spend every Christmas

❼ Sandringham

Norfolk. **Tel** 01485 545408.
🚌 from King's Lynn. **Open** Easter–Oct: daily. **Closed** 1 week Jul. 🗓
🎫 ♿ 🎫 all year. 📷 all year.
🌐 **sandringhamestate.co.uk**

This sizable Norfolk estate has been in royal hands since 1862, when it was bought by the Prince of Wales, who later became Edward VII. The 18th-century house was elaborately embellished and refurbished by the prince and retains an appropriately Edwardian atmosphere.

The large stables are now a museum and contain several trophies that relate to hunting, shooting and horse racing – all favourite royal activities. One popular feature is the display of royal motor cars spanning nearly a century. In the park there are scenic nature trails.

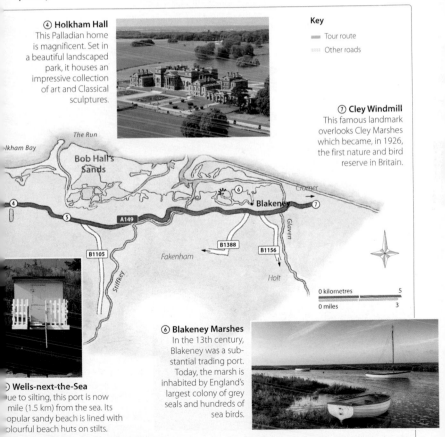

④ **Holkham Hall**
This Palladian home is magnificent. Set in a beautiful landscaped park, it houses an impressive collection of art and Classical sculptures.

Key
━━ Tour route
┅┅ Other roads

⑦ **Cley Windmill**
This famous landmark overlooks Cley Marshes which became, in 1926, the first nature and bird reserve in Britain.

The Run

lkham Bay

Bob Hall's Sands

Cromer

Blakeney ⑦

④

⑤ A149

B1105 *Stiffkey*

B1388 *Fakenham*

B1156

Glaven

Holt

0 kilometres   5
0 miles   3

⑥ **Blakeney Marshes**
In the 13th century, Blakeney was a substantial trading port. Today, the marsh is inhabited by England's largest colony of grey seals and hundreds of sea birds.

Wells-next-the-Sea
Due to silting, this port is now mile (1.5 km) from the sea. Its popular sandy beach is lined with colourful beach huts on stilts.

For keys to symbols *see back flap*

The symmetrical red-brick façade of the 17th-century Blickling Hall

❾ Blickling Hall

Aylsham, Norfolk. **Tel** 01263 738030.
🚂 Norwich, then bus. House:
Open Mar–Oct: daily; Nov–Feb:
check website. Garden: **Open** daily.
Park: **Open** daily. 🅿️ ♿ 🖥️ 🏠 NT
W nationaltrust.org.uk

Approached from the east, its symmetrical Jacobean front framed by trees and flanked by two yew hedges, Blickling Hall offers one of the most impressive vistas of any country house in the area.

Anne Boleyn, Henry VIII's tragic second queen, spent her childhood here, but very little of the original house remains. Most of the present structure dates from 1628, when it was home to James I's Chief Justice Sir Henry Hobart. Later, in 1767, the 2nd Earl of Buckinghamshire, John Hobart, celebrated the Boleyn connection with reliefs in the Great Hall depicting Anne and her daughter, Elizabeth I. The Long Gallery is the most spectacular room to survive

from the 1620s. Its ceiling depicts symbolic representations of learning.

The Peter the Great Room marks the 2nd Earl's service as ambassador to Russia and was built to display a huge spectacular tapestry (1764) of the tsar on horseback, a gift from Catherine the Great. It also has portraits (1760) of the ambassador and his wife by Gainsborough (*see p167*).

❿ Norwich

See pp204–5.

⓫ The Broads

Norfolk. 🚂 Hoveton, Wroxham.
🚌 Norwich, then bus. ℹ️ Station Rd,
Hoveton (01603 782281) Apr–Oct,
or Whitlingham Country Park, Trowse
(01603 617332). W **broads-authority.gov.uk**

These shallow lakes and waterways south and northeast of Norwich, joined by six rivers – the Bure, Thurne, Ant, Yare,

Waveney and Chet – were once thought to have been naturally formed, but in fact they are medieval peat diggings that flooded when the water level rose in the 13th century.

In summer the 125 miles (200 km) of open waterways, uninterrupted by locks, teem with thousands of boating enthusiasts. You can either hire a boat yourself or take one of the many trips on offer to view the plants and wildlife of the area. Look out for Britain's largest butterfly, the swallowtail. Wroxham, the unofficial capital of the Broads, is the starting point for many of these excursions.

The waterways support substantial beds of strong and durable reeds, much in demand for thatching (*see p37*). They are cut in winter and carried to shore in motorized "baking trays".

For a more detailed look at the origins of the Broads and their varied wildlife, visit the **Norfolk Wildlife Trust** – a large thatched floating information centre on Ranworth Broad, with displays on all aspects of the area, and a bird-watching gallery.

In the centre of Ranworth is **St Helen's Church**, which has a magnificent painted medieval screen, a well-preserved 15th-century illuminated manuscript and spectacular views over the entire area from its tower.

🏛️ **Norfolk Wildlife Trust**
Norwich. **Tel** 01603 270479.
Open Apr–Oct: daily. ♿ 🏠

Sailing boat, Wroxham Broad, Norfolk

⑫ Great Yarmouth

Norfolk. 🚗 97,000. 🚅 🚌
ℹ Marine Parade (01493 846346).
🗓 Wed, Fri (summer), Sat.
🌐 great-yarmouth.co.uk

Herring fishing was once the major industry of this port, with 1,000 boats engaged in it just before World War I. Over-fishing led to a depletion of stocks and, for the port to survive, it started to earn its living from servicing container ships and North Sea oil rigs.

It is also the most popular seaside resort on the Norfolk coast and has been since the 19th century, when Dickens (*see p192*) gave it useful publicity by setting part of his novel *David Copperfield* here.

The **Elizabethan House Museum** has a large, eclectic display which illustrates the social history of the area.

In the old part of the town, around South Quay, are a number of charming houses including the 17th-century **Old Merchant's House**. It retains its superb plaster ceiling, oak panelling and a collection of wall anchors, rescued from nearby houses destroyed in

Great Yarmouth's South Quay, with the historic town hall building

Word War II. The house across the court has been furnished as it was in 1942. You can also see the remains of the 13th-century Greyfriars Cloister.

🏛 **Elizabethan House Museum**
4 South Quay. **Tel** 01493 855746.
Open Apr–Oct: 10am–6pm Sun–Fri.
🐾 🏠 NT

🏛 **Old Merchant's House**
South Quay. **Tel** 01493 857900.
Open Apr–Sep: Mon–Fri. 🐾 🎫 🏠 EH

⑬ Lowestoft

Suffolk. 🚗 58,000. 🚅 🚌 🚌 Tue–Sat. 🌐 lovelowestoft.co.uk

The most easterly town in Britain was long a rival to Great Yarmouth, both as a holiday resort and a fishing port. The coming of the railway in the 1840s gave the town an advantage over other resorts, and the solid Victorian and Edwardian boarding houses are evidence of its popularity. The town's fishing industry has declined, and there are now only a few small fishing boats operating.

Lowestoft Museum, in a 17th-century house, has a good display of the fine porcelain made here in the 18th century, as well as exhibits on local archaeology and domestic life.

Environs
Somerleyton Hall is built in Jacobean style on the founda-tions of a smaller mansion. Its gardens are a real delight, and there is a genuinely baffling yew hedge maze.

🏛 **Lowestoft Museum**
Oulton Broad. **Tel** 01502 511457.
Open Apr–Oct: 1–4pm daily (from 2pm Sun). 🎫 by appt. 🦽 ltd. 🏠
🌐 lowestoftmuseum.org

🏛 **Somerleyton Hall**
On B1074. **Tel** 08712 224244.
Open Easter Sun–Sep: Tue–Thu & pub hols. 🐾 🎫 🦽 🛒 🏠
🌐 somerleyton.co.uk

Corn mill at Saxtead Green, near Framlingham

Herringfleet Smock Mill, near Lowestoft

Windmills on the Fens and Broads

The flat, open countryside and the stiff breezes from the North Sea made windmills an obvious power source for East Anglia well into the 20th century, and today they are an evocative and recurring feature of the landscape. On the Broads and Fens, some were used for drainage, while others, such as that at Saxtead Green, ground corn. On the boggy Fens they were not built on hard foundations, so few survived, but elsewhere, especially on the Broads, many have been restored to working order. The seven-storey Berney Arms Windmill is the tallest on the Broads. The Wind Energy Museum at Repps with Bastwick has a collection of mills both ancient and modern.

⑩ Norwich

In the heart of the fertile East Anglian countryside, Norwich, one of the best-preserved cities in Britain, is steeped in a relaxed provincial atmosphere. The city was first fortified by the Saxons in the 9th century and still has the irregular street plan of that time. With the arrival of Flemish settlers in the early 12th century and the establishment of a textile industry, the town soon became a prosperous market and was the second city of England until the Industrial Revolution in the 19th century *(see pp60–61)*.

One of over a thousand carved bosses in the cathedral cloisters

The quaintly cobbled medieval street of Elm Hill

Exploring Norwich

The oldest parts of the city are Elm Hill, one of the finest medieval streets in England, and Tombland, the old Saxon marketplace by the cathedral. Both have well-preserved medieval buildings, which are now incorporated into pleasant areas of small shops.

With a trading history spanning hundreds of years, the colourful market in the city centre is well worth a visit. A good walk meanders around the surviving sections of the 14th-century flint city wall.

🏛 Norwich Cathedral

The Close. **Tel** 01603 218300.
Open daily. Donations. 🎧 ♿
✏️ 📷 **W** cathedral.org.uk

This magnificent building was founded in 1096 by Bishop Losinga and built with stone from Caen in France and Barnack.

The precinct originally included a monastery, and the surviving cloister is the most extensive in England. The thin cathedral spire was added in the 15th century, making it, at 96 m (315 ft), the second tallest in England after Salisbury *(see pp268–9)*. In the majestic nave, soaring Norman pillars and arches support a 15th-century vaulted roof whose stone bosses, many of which illustrate well-known Bible stories, have been beautifully restored.

Easier to appreciate at close hand is the elaborate wood carving in the choir – the canopies over the stalls and the misericords beneath the seats, one showing a small boy being smacked. Not to be missed is the 14th-century Despenser Reredos in St Luke's Chapel. It was hidden for years under a carpenter's table to prevent its destruction by Puritans.

Two gates to the cathedral close survive: **St Ethelbert's**, a 13th-century flint arch, and the **Erpingham Gate** at the west end, built by Sir Thomas Erpingham, who led the triumphant English archers at the Battle of Agincourt in 1415 *(see p53)*.

Beneath the east outer wall is the grave of Edith Cavell, the Norwich-born nurse who was arrested and executed in 1915 by the Germans for helping Allied soldiers escape from occupied Belgium.

🏛 Castle Museum

Castle Meadow. **Tel** 01603 493625.
Open daily (Sun pm only). **Closed** 1 Jan, 25 & 26 Dec. 🎧 🅿 ♿ 🖥 📷
W museums.norfolk.gov.uk

The brooding keep of this 12th-century castle has been a museum since 1894, when it ended 650 years of service as a prison. The most important Norman feature

Norwich Cathedral's spire and tower as seen from the southeast

Colman's Mustard

It was said of the Colmans that they made their fortune from what diners left on their plate. In 1814 Jeremiah Colman started milling mustard at Norwich because it was at the centre of a fertile plain where mustard was grown. Today at 15 Royal Arcade a shop sells mustard and related items, while a small museum illustrates the history of the company.

It's nicer with **MUSTARD**   A 1950s advertisement for Colman's Mustard

VISITORS' CHECKLIST

Practical Information
Norfolk. 135,000.
The Forum, Millennium Plain (01603 213999).
Mon–Sat.
visitnorwich.co.uk

Transport
Thorpe Road.
Surrey St.

is a carved door that used to be the main entrance.

Exhibits include significant archaeology, natural history and fine art collections, as well as the world's largest collection of British ceramic teapots.

The art gallery is dominated by works from the Norwich School of painters. This group of early 19th-century landscape artists painted directly from nature, getting away from the stylized studio landscapes that had been fashionable up to then. Chief among the group were John Crome (1768–1821), whom many compare with Constable *(see p208),* and John Sell Cotman (1782–1842), known for his watercolours. There are also regular exhibitions held here.

🏠 Church of St Peter Mancroft
Chantry Rd. **Tel** 01603 610443.
Open 10am–4pm Mon–Sat (to 3:30pm in winter); Sun (services only). Donations. stpetermancroft. org.uk

This imposing Perpendicular church, built around 1455, so dominates the city centre that many visitors assume it is the cathedral. John Wesley *(see p283)* wrote of it, "I scarcely ever remember to have seen a more beautiful parish church".

The large windows make the church very light, and the dramatic east window still has most of its 15th-century glass. The roof is unusual in having wooden fan tracery – it is normally in stone – covering the hammerbeam construction. The famous peal of 13 bells rang out in 1588 to celebrate

the defeat of the Spanish Armada *(see p55)* and is still heard every Sunday.

Its name derives from the Latin *magna crofta* (great meadow), which described the area in pre-Norman times.

🏛 Museum of Norwich
Bridewell Alley. **Tel** 01603 629127.
Open 10am–4:30pm Tue–Sat.

One of the oldest houses in Norwich, this 14th-century flint-faced building was used for years as a jail for women and beggars. It now houses an exhibition of local industries, including the textile, shoe, chocolate and mustard trades, with displays of old machines and reconstructed shops.

🏛 Strangers' Hall
Charing Cross. **Tel** 01603 493625.
Open hours vary, check website for timings. **Closed** 24 Dec–mid-Feb.
museums.norfolk.gov.uk

This 14th-century merchant's house gives a glimpse into English domestic life through the ages. The house was inhabited by immigrant weavers – the "strangers". It has a fine 15th-century Great

Hall and a maze of rooms showing domestic life from Tudor to Victorian times.

🏛 Guildhall
Gaol Hill. **Tel** 01603 629364.
Above the city's ancient marketplace is the imposing 15th-century flint and stone Guildhall with its gable of checkered flushwork (now the Britannia Café).

🏛 The Sainsbury Centre for Visual Arts
University of E Anglia (on B1108).
Tel 01603 593199. **Open** 10am–6pm Tue–Fri, 10am–5pm Sat & Sun. **Closed** 23 Dec–2 Jan, around Easter (see website).
scva.ac.uk

This important art gallery was built in 1978 to house the collection of Robert and Lisa Sainsbury given to the University of East Anglia in 1973. The collection's strength is in its modern European paintings, including works by Modigliani, Picasso and Bacon, and in its sculptures by Giacometti and Moore. There are also displays of ethnographic art from Africa, the Pacific and the Americas.

The centre, designed by Lord Norman Foster, one of Britain's most innovative architects, was among the first to display its steel structure openly.

Back of the New Mills (1814) by John Crome of the Norwich School

Purple heather in flower on Dunwich Heath

⓮ Southwold

Suffolk. 🚉 3,900. 🚌 ⓘ The Library, North Green (01502 722519). 🗓 Fri am. Ⓦ **eastsuffolk.gov.uk/visitors**

This picture-postcard seaside resort, with its charming whitewashed villas clustered around small greens, has, largely by historical accident, remained unspoiled. The railway line which connected it with London was closed in 1929, which effectively isolated this Georgian town from an influx of day-trippers.

This was also once a large port, as testified to by the size of the 15th-century **St Edmund King and Martyr Church**, worth a visit for the 16th-century painted screens. On its tower is a small figure dressed in the

Jack o'the Clock, Southwold

uniform of a 15th-century soldier, known as Jack o'the Clock. **Southwold Museum** tells the story of the Battle of Sole Bay, which was fought offshore between the English and Dutch navies in 1672.

Environs

The pretty village of **Walberswick** lies across the creek. By road it is a long detour and the only alternatives are a rowing-boat ferry across the harbour (summer only) or a footbridge across the river half a mile inland. Further inland at Blythburgh, the 15th-century **Holy Trinity Church** dominates the surrounding land. In 1944 a US bomber blew up over the church, killing Joseph Kennedy Jr, brother of the future American president.

🏛 **Southwold Museum**
9–11 Victoria St. **Tel** 01502 726097. **Open** Easter–Oct: 2–4pm daily. 🅿 ♿ Ⓦ **southwoldmuseum.org**

⓯ Dunwich

Suffolk. 🚉 70.

This tiny village is all that remains of a "lost city" consigned to the sea by erosion. In the 7th century Dunwich was the seat of the powerful East Anglian kings. In the 13th century it was still the biggest port in Suffolk and some 12 churches were built. But the land was being eroded at about a metre (3 ft) a year, and the last original church collapsed into the sea in 1919.

Dunwich Heath, to the south, runs down to a sandy beach and is an important nature reserve. **Minsmere Reserve** has observation hides for watching a huge variety of birds.

🌿 **Dunwich Heath**
Nr Dunwich. **Tel** 01728 648501. **Open** dawn–dusk. ♿ 🚻 🏠 NT

🌿 **Minsmere Reserve**
Minsmere, Westleton. **Tel** 01728 648281. **Open** daily. **Closed** 25 & 26 Dec. 🅿 ♿ 🚻 🏠 Ⓦ **rspb.org.uk**

⓰ Aldeburgh

Suffolk. 🚉 2,800. 🚌
Ⓦ **visit-aldeburgh.co.uk**

Best known today for the music festivals at Snape Maltings, Aldeburgh has been a port since Roman times (the Roman area is underwater). Erosion has resulted in the fine Tudor **Moot**

Intricate carving on the exterior of the Tudor Moot Hall, Aldeburgh

For hotels and restaurants in this area see pp563–4 and pp587–8

Hall, once far inland, today being close to the beach. Its ground floor is now **Aldeburgh Museum**. The large timbered court room above can only be reached by the original outside staircase.

The **church**, also Tudor, had a large stained-glass window installed in 1979 as a memorial to composer Benjamin Britten. **The Red House** was Britten's home from 1957 to 1976.

🏛 **Aldeburgh Museum**
Moot Hall, Market Cross Pl. **Tel** 01728 454666. **Open** Apr–Oct: daily pm. (Redevelopment is planned for 2019.)
 w aldeburghmuseum online.co.uk

🏛 **The Red House**
Golf Lane. **Tel** 01728 451700. **Open** Feb & Mar: 1–4pm Tue–Fri; Apr–Oct: 1–5pm Tue–Sat

---

🔴 Aldeburgh Music Festival

Composer Benjamin Britten (1913–76), born in Lowestoft, Suffolk, moved to Snape in 1937. In 1945 his opera *Peter Grimes* – inspired by the poet George Crabbe (1754–1832), once a curate at Aldeburgh – was performed in Snape. Since then the area has become the centre of musical activity. In 1948, Britten began the Aldeburgh Music Festival, held every June (*see p67*). He acquired the Maltings at Snape and converted it into a music venue opened by the Queen in 1967. It has since become the focus of an annual series of East Anglian musical events in churches and halls throughout the entire region.

Benjamin Britten in Aldeburgh

⓱ Framlingham Castle

Framlingham, Suffolk. **Tel** 01728 724189. 🚆 Wickham Market then taxi. **Open** daily (Nov–Mar: Sat & Sun). **Closed** 1 Jan, 24–26 Dec.
♿ partial. **EH**

Perched on a hill, the small village of Framlingham has long been an important strategic site, even before the present castle was built in 1190 by the Earl of Norfolk.

Little of the castle from that period survives except the powerful curtain wall and its towers; walk round the top of it for fine views of the town.

Mary Tudor, daughter of Henry VIII, was staying here in 1553 when she heard she was to become queen.

Environs
To the southeast, on the coast, is the 27 m (90-ft), 16-sided keep of **Orford Castle**, built for Henry II as a coastal defence at around the same time as Framlingham. A short climb to the top of the castle gives fantastic views.

🏰 **Orford Castle**
Orford. **Tel** 01394 450472. **Open** daily (Nov–Mar: Sat & Sun). **Closed** 1 Jan, 24–26 Dec. **EH**

⓲ Ipswich

Suffolk. 🚇 140,000. 🚆 🚌
ℹ St Stephen's Lane (01473 258070).
📅 Tue, Thu–Sat. **w** allabout ipswich.com

Suffolk's county town has a largely modern centre but several buildings remain from earlier times. It rose to prominence after the 13th century as a port for the rich Suffolk wool trade (*see p211*).

The **Ancient House** in Buttermarket has a superb example of pargeting – the ancient craft of ornamental façade plastering. The town's museum and art gallery, **Christchurch Mansion**, is a Tudor house from 1548, where Elizabeth I stayed in 1561. It also boasts the best collection

of Constable's paintings outside London, including four marvellous Suffolk landscapes, as well as paintings by Gainsborough (*see p167*).

In the centre of the town is **St Margaret's**, a 15th-century church built in flint and stone with a double hammerbeam roof and 17th century painted ceiling panels. **Wolsey's Gate**, a Tudor gateway of 1527, provides a link with Ipswich's most famous son, Cardinal Wolsey. He started to build an ecclesiastical college in the town, but fell from royal favour before it was finished.

Environs
To the east lies **Sutton Hoo**, site of a fabulous horde of Anglo-Saxon silver. The museum houses a reconstructed burial mound and replicas of the treasure, as the originals are in the British Museum (*see pp110–11*).

🏛 **Christchurch Mansion**
Soane St. **Tel** 01473 433554. **Open** 10am–5pm Tue–Sun. **Closed** 1 Jan, Good Fri, 24–27 Dec. by appt. ♿ ltd.

🏛 **Sutton Hoo**
Tranmer House, Sutton Hoo. 🚆 Melton or Woodbridge, then taxi. **Tel** 01394 389700. **Open** daily (Nov–mid-Feb: Sat & Sun).

Pargeting on the Ancient House in Ipswich

⑲ Constable Walk

This walk in Constable country follows one of the most picturesque sections of the River Stour. The route taken would have been familiar to the landscape painter John Constable (1776–1837). Constable's father, a wealthy merchant, owned Flatford Mill, which was depicted in many of the artist's paintings. Constable claimed to know and love "every stile and stump, and every lane" around East Bergholt.

The River Stour, used as a backdrop for Constable's *Boatbuilding* (1814)

Tips for Walkers

Starting point: Park off Flatford Lane, East Bergholt (charge to park). 01206 297200; Bridge Cottage (01206 298260). NT
Getting there: A12 to East Bergholt, then follow signs to Flatford. Manningtree is within walking distance of Flatford. from Ipswich or Colchester.
Stopping-off point: Dedham.
Length: 3 miles (5 km).
Difficulty: Flat trail along river-side footpath with kissing gates.

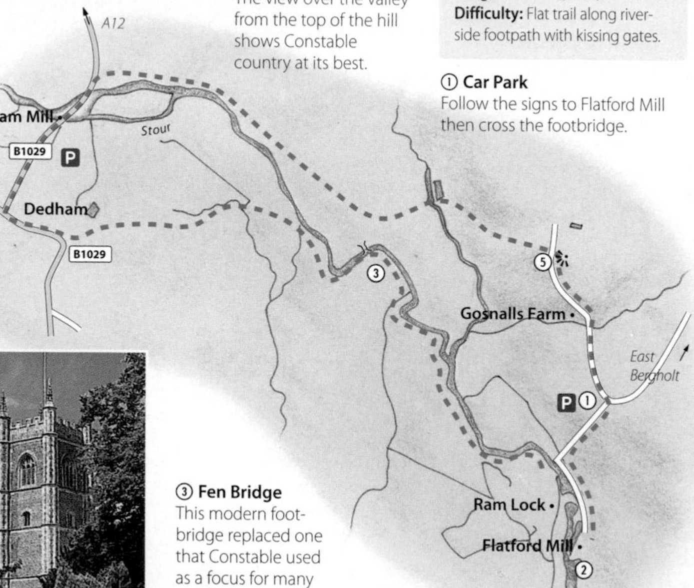
A12
Dedham Mill
Stour
B1029
P
Dedham
④
B1029
③
⑤
Gosnalls Farm
East Bergholt
P ①
Ram Lock
Flatford Mill
②

⑤ Viewpoint
The view over the valley from the top of the hill shows Constable country at its best.

① Car Park
Follow the signs to Flatford Mill then cross the footbridge.

③ Fen Bridge
This modern foot-bridge replaced one that Constable used as a focus for many of his paintings.

④ Dedham Church
The tall church tower appears in many of Constable's pictures, including the *View on the Stour near Dedham* (1822).

0 metres 500
0 yards 500

Key
Route
Secondary road
Minor road

② Willy Lott's Cottage
This cottage remains much the same as it did when featured in Constable's painting *The Hay Wain* (*see p87*).

⓴ Colchester

Essex. 180,000. Hollytrees Museum, Castle Park (01206 282920). Fri, Sat. **visitcolchester.com**

The oldest recorded town in Britain, Colchester was the effective capital of southeast England when the Romans invaded in AD 43, and it was here that the first permanent Roman colony was established.

After Boudica *(see p199)* burnt the town in AD 60, a 2-mile (3-km) wall was built, 3 m (10 ft) thick and 9 m (30 ft) high, to deter future attackers. You can still see these walls and the surviving Roman town gate, the largest in Britain.

During the Middle Ages Colchester developed into an important weaving centre. In the 16th century, a number of immigrant Flemish weavers settled in an area west of the castle, known as the **Dutch Quarter**, which still retains its original tall houses and steep, narrow streets.

Colchester was besieged for 11 weeks during the Civil War *(see p56)* before being captured by Cromwell's troops.

Hollytrees Museum

Castle Park. **Tel** 01206 282940. **Open** Mon–Sat. **Closed** 1 Jan, 24–27 Dec. **cimuseums.org.uk**

This elegant Georgian town house was built in 1719. Now a charming museum of social history, it records the day-to-day lives of Colchester people and changing technology over 300 years. Clock-making was an important craft in Colchester, as celebrated in displays here.

Young visitors especially will enjoy exploring the miniature world of the doll's house, and learning about the origin of the famous nursery rhyme "Twinkle, twinkle, little star", which was written in Colchester.

Castle Museum

Castle Park. **Tel** 01206 282939. **Open** 10am–5pm daily (from 11am Sun). **Closed** 1 Jan, 24–27 Dec. **cimuseums.org.uk**

This is the oldest and largest Norman keep still standing in

The Norman keep of the Castle Museum, Colchester

England. Twice the size of the White Tower at the Tower of London *(see pp122–3)*, it was built in 1076 on the platform of a Roman temple dedicated to Claudius *(see p48)*, using stones and tiles from other Roman buildings. The museum's displays relate the story of the town from prehistoric times to the Civil War. There is also a medieval prison here.

Layer Marney Tower

Off B1022. **Tel** 01206 330784. **Open** Apr–Sep: Wed & Sun (Jul & Aug: Sun–Thu). limited. **layermarneytower.co.uk**

This remarkable Tudor gatehouse is the tallest in Britain: its pair of six-sided, eight-storey turrets reach to 24 m (80 ft). It was intended to be part of a larger complex, but the designer, Sir Henry Marney, died before it was completed. The brickwork and terracotta ornamentation around the roof and windows are models of Tudor craftsmanship.

Beth Chatto Garden

Elmstead Market. **Tel** 01206 822007. **Open** Mar–Oct: 9am–5pm daily (from 10am Sun); Nov–Feb: 9am–4pm daily (from 10am Sun). **Closed** 22 Dec–5 Jan. **bethchatto.co.uk**

One of Britain's most eminent gardening writers, Beth Chatto began this experiment in the 1960s to test her belief that it is possible to create a garden in the most adverse conditions. The dry and windy slopes, boggy patches, gravel beds and wooded areas support an array of plants best suited to that particular environment.

㉑ Coggeshall

Essex. 5,000. Thu. **visitessex.com**

This town has two of the most important medieval and Tudor buildings in the country. Dating from 1140, **Coggeshall Grange Barn** is the oldest surviving timber-framed barn in Europe. Inside is a display of historic farm wagons. The half-timbered merchant's house, **Paycocke's**, was built around 1500 and has a beautifully panelled interior and fine display of Coggeshall lace.

Coggeshall Grange Barn

Grange Hill. **Tel** 01376 562226. **Open** Apr–Oct: from 11am Wed–Sun & public hols. **Closed** Good Fri. NT

Paycocke's

West St. **Tel** 01376 561305. **Open** Apr–Oct: Wed–Sun & public hols. **Closed** Good Fri. NT

Beth Chatto Garden, Colchester, in full summer bloom

For hotels and restaurants in this area see pp563–4 and pp587–8

㉒ Lavenham

Suffolk. 🚗 1,700. 🏛 Lady St (01787 248207). 🌐 **discoverlavenham.com**

Often considered the most perfect of all small English towns, Lavenham is a treasure trove of beautiful timber-framed houses ranged along streets whose pattern is virtually unchanged from medieval times. For 150 years, between the 14th and 16th centuries, it was the prosperous centre of the Suffolk wool trade. No fewer than 350 of the town's well-preserved buildings are Grade II listed, including the fine **Little Hall** in Market Place.

Environs
Gainsborough's House, the birthplace of the artist, has a splendid collection of his paitings, drawings and prints (see p167).

🏛 **Little Hall**
Market Place **Tel** 01787 247019. **Open** Mon am; Tue–Sun pm. 🅿
🌐 **littlehall.org.uk**

🏛 **Gainsborough's House**
Sudbury. **Tel** 01787 372958. **Open** daily. **Closed** 24 Dec–2 Jan, Good Fri.
🅿 ♿ 🖥 📷 🌐 **gainsborough.org**

Little Hall

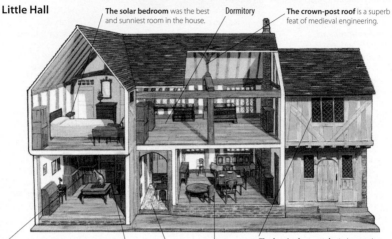

The solar bedroom was the best and sunniest room in the house.

Dormitory

The crown-post roof is a superb feat of medieval engineering.

Bronze of Egyptian Cat Goddess Bastet   Library   Entrance   Dining room

The herringbone-style timber on the exterior was common in the 14th century.

㉓ Bury St Edmunds

Suffolk. 🚗 47,000. 🚆 🚌 🏛 The Apex, Charter Square (01284 764667). 🛒 Wed, Sat. 🌐 **visit-burystedmunds.co.uk**

St Edmund was the last Saxon king of East Anglia, decapitated by Danish raiders in 870. Legend has it that a wolf picked up the severed head – an image that appears in a number of medieval carvings. Edmund was canonized in 900 and buried in Bury, where in 1014 King Canute (see p175) built an **abbey** in his honour, the wealthiest in England until its destruction in the Dissolution of the Monasteries (see p355). The abbey ruins lie in the town centre.

Nearby are two large 15th-century churches, built when the wool trade made the town wealthy. **St James's** was designated a cathedral in 1914. The best features of **St Mary's** are the north porch and the hammer-beam roof over the nave. A stone slab in the northeast corner marks the tomb of Mary Tudor (see p55).

Illustration of St Edmund

Just below the **market cross** in Cornhill – remodelled by Robert Adam (see p32) in 1714 – stands the large 12th-century **Moyse's Hall**, a merchant's house that serves as the local history museum.

Environs
Three miles (5 km) southwest of Bury is the late 18th-century **Ickworth House**. This eccentric Neo-Classical mansion features

The 18th-century rotunda of Ickworth House, Bury St Edmunds

For hotels and restaurants in this area see pp563–4 and pp587–8

an unusual rotunda with a domed roof flanked by two huge wings. Its art collection includes works by Reynolds and Titian. There are also fine displays of silver, porcelain and sculpture, for example John Flaxman's (1755–1826) moving *The Fury of Athamas*. The house is set in a large park.

🏛️ Moyse's Hall
Cornhill. **Tel** 01284 706183. **Open** daily (last adm: 4pm, Sun: 3pm). **Closed** public hols, 24 Dec. 🅿️ 👍 📷

🏠 Ickworth House
Horringer. **Tel** 01284 735270. **Open** Mar–Oct: Thu–Tue. 🅿️ 👍 ✏️ 📷 NT

㉔ Newmarket

Suffolk. 🚗 17,000. 🚆 🚌 🏢 Tue, Sat. 🌐 **visitcambridge.org**

A walk down the short main street tells you all you need to know about this busy and wealthy little town. The shops sell horse feed and all manner of riding accessories; the clothes on sale are tweeds, jodhpurs and the soft brown hats rarely worn by anyone except racehorse trainers.

Newmarket has been the headquarters of British horse racing since James I decided that its open heaths were ideal for testing the mettle of his fastest steeds against those of his friends. The first ever recorded horse race was held

The stallion unit at the National Stud, Newmarket

here in 1622. Charles II shared his grandfather's enthusiasm and after the Restoration *(see p57)* would move the whole court to Newmarket, every spring and summer, for the sport – he is the only British king to have ridden a winner.

The modern racing industry began to take shape here in the late 18th century. There are now over 2,500 horses in training in and around the town, and two racecourses staging regular race meetings from around April to October *(see pp70–71)*. Training stables are occasionally open to the public but you can view the

A horse being exercised on Newmarket Heath

horses being exercised on the heath in the early morning. Tattersall's, the auction house for thoroughbreds, is in the centre of Newmarket.

The **National Stud** can also be visited. You will see the five or six stallions on stud, mares in foal, and if you are lucky a newborn foal – most likely in April or May.

The National Horseracing Museum, housed in the restored palace and stables built by Charles II in 1651, comprises the **National Heritage Centre for Horseracing and Sporting Art** and a racing yard where ex-racehorses are retrained.

🔵 National Stud
Newmarket **Tel** 0344 748 9200. **Open** mid-Feb–Oct: tours only. 🅿️ 🚻 👍 🛒 📷 🌐 **nationalstud.co.uk**

🏛️ National Heritage Centre for Horseracing and Sporting Art
Palace House, Palace St. **Tel** 01638 667314 **Open** 10am–5pm daily. **Closed** 25 Dec. 🅿️ 🚻 👍 🛒 📷 🌐 **palacehousenewmarket.co.uk**

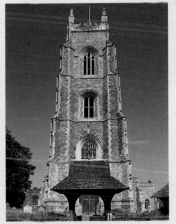
St Mary's Church, Stoke-by-Nayland, southeast of Bury St Edmunds

The Rise and Fall of the Wool Trade

Wool was a major English export from the 13th century and by 1310 some ten million fleeces were exported every year. The Black Death *(see p52)*, which swept Britain in 1348, perversely provided a boost for the industry: with labour in short supply, land could not be cultivated and was grassed over for sheep. Around 1350 Edward III decided it was time to establish a home-based cloth industry and encouraged Flemish weavers to come to Britain. Many settled in East Anglia, particularly Suffolk, and their skills helped establish a flourishing trade. This time of prosperity saw the construction of the sumptuous churches, such as the one at Stoke-by-Nayland, that we see today – East Anglia has more than 2,000 churches. The cloth trade here began to decline in the late 16th century with the development of water-powered looms. These were not suited to the area, which never regained its former wealth. Today's visitors are the beneficiaries of this decline, because wool towns such as Lavenham and Bury St Edmunds never became rich enough to destroy their magnificent Tudor halls and houses and construct new buildings.

The façade of Anglesey Abbey, a Jacobean-style manor house

㉕ Anglesey Abbey

Lode, Cambridgeshire. **Tel** 01223 810080. 🚆 Cambridge or Newmarket, then bus. House: **Open** Apr–Oct: Tue–Sun; Garden: **Open** daily year round. 🅿 ♿ limited. 🚫 📷 🎫 NT

The original abbey was built in 1135 for an Augustinian order. But only the crypt – also known as the monks' parlour – with its vaulted ceiling on marble and stone pillars, survived the Dissolution (see p355).

This was later incorporated into a manor house whose treasures include furniture from many periods and a rare seascape by Gainsborough (see p167). The superb garden was created in the 1930s by Lord Fairhaven as an ambitious landscape of trees, sculptures and borders.

㉖ Huntingdon

Cambridgeshire. 🅰 24,000. 🚆 🚌 🚍 Wed, Sat.

More than 300 years after his death, Oliver Cromwell (see p56) still dominates this small town. Born here in 1599, a record of his baptism and marriage can be seen in Huntingdon County Records Office. **Cromwell Museum**, his former school, traces his life with pictures and mementos, including his death mask.

Cromwell remains one of the most controversial figures in British history. An MP before he was 30, he became embroiled in the disputes between Charles I and Parliament over taxes and religion. In the Civil War (see p56) he proved an inspired general and, after refusing the title of king, was made Lord Protector in 1653, four years after the King was beheaded. Just two years after his death the monarchy was restored by popular demand, and his body was taken out of Westminster Abbey (see pp96–7) to hang on gallows.

The museum was also the former school of diarist Samuel Pepys (see p217), who lived at nearby Bampton.

There is a 14th-century bridge across the River Ouse which links Huntingdon with Godmanchester, the part of Ermine Street, the Roman road that led from London to York.

🏛 **Cromwell Museum**
Grammar School Walk. **Tel** 01480 375830. **Open** Tue–Sun (Nov–Mar: pm only except Sat). **Closed** 1 Jan, 24–27 Dec, some public hols. ♿ 📷

㉗ Cambridge

See pp214–19.

㉘ Audley End

Saffron Walden, Essex. **Tel** 01799 522842. 🚆 Audley End then taxi. House: **Open** Apr–Oct: pm daily. Garden: **Open** Apr–Oct: daily; Nov–Mar: Sat & Sun. **Closed** 24 Dec–Jan. 🅿 🚫 ♿ limited. 🚌 🎫 EH 🌐 english-heritage.org.uk

This was the largest house in England when built in 1603–14 for Thomas Howard, Lord Treasurer and 1st Earl of Suffolk. James I joked that Audley End was too big for a king but not for a Lord Treasurer. Charles II, his grandson, disagreed and bought it in 1667. He seldom went there, however, and in 1701 it was given back to the Howards, who demolished two thirds of it.

What remains is a Jacobean mansion, retaining its original hall and many fine plaster ceilings. Robert Adam (see p32) remodelled some of the interior in the 1760s, and these rooms have been restored to his original designs. At the same time, "Capability" Brown (see p30) landscaped the magnificent 18th-century park.

Stained-glass window, installed in 1771, depicts the Last Supper.

Jacobean wooden screen (c.1605)

The Chapel was completed in 1772 to a Gothic design. The furniture was made to complement the wooden pillars and vaulting which are painted to imitate stone.

Main entrance

The Great Hall, hung with family portraits, is the highlight of the house, with the massive oak screen and elaborate hammerbeam roof surviving in their Jacobean form.

㉙ Epping Forest

Essex. Chingford. Loughton, Theydon Bois. High Beach, Loughton (020 8508 0028); Highbridge St, Waltham Abbey (01992 660336); The View, Chingford (020 7332 1911).
W cityoflondon.gov.uk

As one of the largest open spaces near London, the forest is popular with walkers, just as, centuries ago, it was a favourite hunting ground for kings and courtiers – the word "forest"

A depiction of the Battle of Maldon (991) on the *Maldon Embroidery*

denoted an area for hunting. Henry VIII had a lodge built in 1543 on the edge of the forest. His daughter Elizabeth I often used the lodge and it soon became known as **Queen Elizabeth's Hunting Lodge**.

This three-storey timbered building has been renovated and now houses an exhibition of the lodge's history and the forest.

The tracts of open land and woods interspersed with a number of lakes make an ideal habitat for a variety of plant, bird and animal life: deer roam the northern part, many of a special dark strain introduced by James I. The Corporation of

Epping Forest contains oaks and beeches up to 400 years old

London bought the forest in the mid-19th century to ensure it remained open to the public.

Queen Elizabeth's Hunting Lodge
Rangers Rd, Chingford. **Tel** 020 7332 1911. **Open** daily. **Closed** 25 Dec & sometimes on Tue. limited.

㉚ Maldon

Essex. 14,000. Chelmsford then bus. Wenlock Way (01621 856503). Thu, Sat. **W** visitmaldondistrict.co.uk

This delightful old town on the River Blackwater, its High Street lined with shops and inns from the 14th century on, was once an important harbour. It is perhaps best known for its production of Maldon sea salt, panned in the traditional way.

A fierce battle here in 991, when Viking invaders defeated the Saxon defenders, is told in *The Battle of Maldon*, one of the earliest known Saxon poems. The battle is also celebrated in the *Maldon Embroidery* on display in the **Maeldune Centre**. This 13-m- (42-ft-) long embroidery, designed by a local artist, depicts the history of Maldon from 991 to 1991 and took 86 women three years to complete.

Environs

East of Maldon at Bradwell-on-Sea is the sturdy Saxon church of **St Peter's-on-the-Wall**, a simple stone building that stands isolated on the shore. It was built in 654, from the stones of a former Roman fort, by St Cedd, who used it as his cathedral. It was restored in the 1920s.

Maeldune Centre
Market Hill. **Tel** 01621 851628. **Open** mid-Feb–Dec: 11am–4pm daily.
W maelduneheritagecentre.co.uk

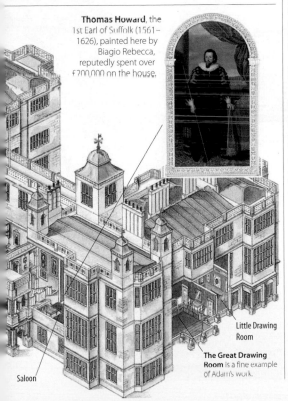

Thomas Howard, the 1st Earl of Suffolk (1561–1626), painted here by Biagio Rebecca, reputedly spent over £200,000 on the house.

Little Drawing Room

The Great Drawing Room is a fine example of Adam's work.

Saloon

㉗ Street-by-Street: Cambridge

Cambridge has been an important town since Roman times, as it was sited at the first navigable point on the River Cam. In the 11th century religious orders began to be established in the town and, in 1209, a group of religious scholars broke away from Oxford University (see pp226–31) after academic and religious disputes and came here. Student life dominates the city but it is also a thriving market centre serving a rich agricultural region.

Round Church
The 12th-century Church of the Holy Sepulchre has one of the few round naves in the country. Its design is based on the Holy Sepulchre in Jerusalem.

Newmarket ←

BRIDGE STREET

ST JOHN'S STR

Magdalene Bridge carries Bridge Street across the Cam from the city centre to Magdalene College.

St John's College has superb Tudor and Jacobean architecture.

Kitchen Bridge

TR

★ **Bridge of Sighs**
Built in 1831 and named after its Venetian counterpart, it is best viewed from the Kitchen Bridge.

Trinity College

Trinity Bridge

| 0 metres | 75 |
| 0 yards | 75 |

Key

— Suggested route

Clare College

Clare Bridge

Grantchester ↘

The Backs
This is the name given to the grassy strip lying between the backs of the big colleges and the banks of the Cam – a good spot to enjoy this classic view of King's College Chapel.

For hotels and restaurants in this area see pp563–4 and pp587–8

Great St Mary's Church
This clock is over the west door of the university's official church. Its tower offers fine views.

1679

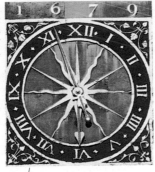

VISITORS' CHECKLIST

Practical Information
Cambridgeshire. 124,000.
The Guildhall, Peas Hill (01223 791500). 01223 791501.
daily. Folk Festival: Jul; Strawberry Fair: Jun.
visitcambridge.org

Transport
Stansted. Station Rd.
Drummer St.

Gonville and Caius
(pronounced "keys"), founded in 1348, is one of the oldest colleges.

★ King's College Chapel
This late medieval masterpiece took 70 years to build *(see pp218–19)*.

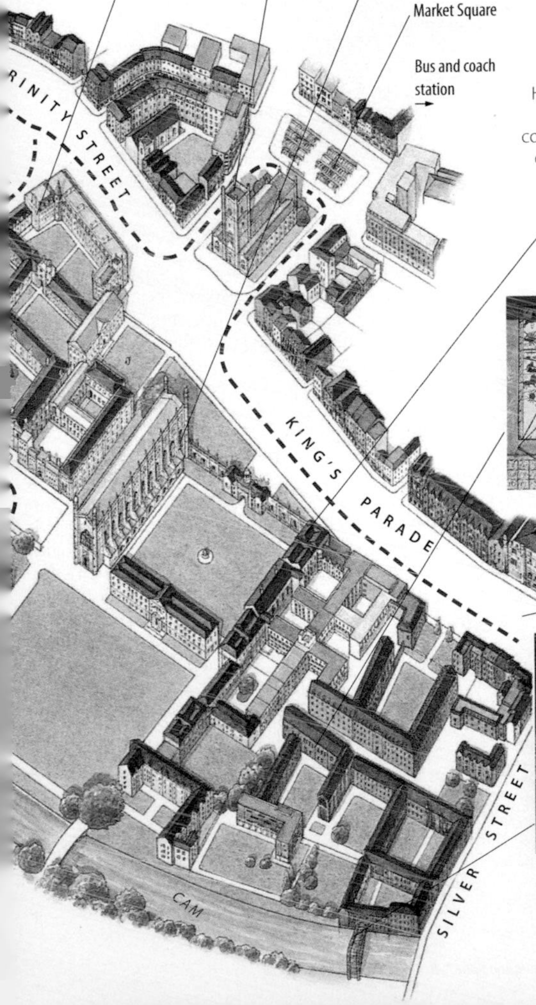

Market Square
Bus and coach station
TRINITY STREET
KING'S PARADE
Corpus Christi College
To Fitzwilliam Museum, railway station and London
SILVER STREET
CAM

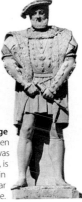

King's College
Henry VIII, king when the chapel was completed in 1515, is commemorated in this statue near the main gate.

Queens' College
Its Tudor courts are among the university's finest. This 18th-century sundial is over the old chapel – now a reading room.

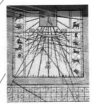

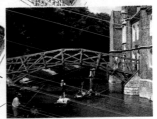

Mathematical Bridge
It is a myth that this bridge over the Cam at Queens' College was first built without nuts or bolts.

Exploring Cambridge University

Cambridge University has 31 colleges, the oldest being Peterhouse (1284) and the newest being Robinson (1979). Clustered around the city centre, many of the older colleges have peaceful gardens backing onto the River Cam, which are known as the "Backs". The layout of the older colleges, as at Oxford (see pp230–31), derives from their early connections with religious institutions, although few escaped heavy-handed modification in the Victorian era. The college buildings are generally grouped around squares called courts and offer an unrivalled mix of over 600 years of architecture from the late medieval period through Wren's masterpieces and up to the present day.

The nave of the Wren Chapel at Pembroke College

The imposing façade of Emmanuel College

Emmanuel College
Built in 1677 on St Andrew's Street, Sir Christopher Wren's (see p119) chapel is the highlight of the college. Some of the intricate interior details, particularly the plaster ceiling and Amigoni's altar rails (1734), are superb. Founded in 1584, the college has a Puritan tradition. One notable graduate was the clergyman John Harvard, who emigrated to America in 1636 and left all his money to the Massachusetts college that now bears his name.

Senate House
King's Parade is the site of this Palladian edifice (built 1722–30), which is used primarily for university ceremonies. It was designed by James Gibbs in 1722 as part of a grand square of university buildings – which was never completed.

Corpus Christi College
Just down from Senate House, this was founded in 1352 by the local trade guilds, anxious to ensure that education was not the sole prerogative of church and nobility. Its Old Court is remarkably well

preserved and looks today much as it would have done when built in the 14th century.

The college is connected by a 15th-century gallery of red brick to St Bene't's Church (short for St Benedict's), whose large Saxon tower is the oldest structure in Cambridge.

King's College
See pp218–19.

Pembroke College
The college chapel was the first building completed by Wren (see p119). A formal classical design, it replaced a 14th-century chapel that was turned into a library. The college, just off Trumpington Street, also has fine gardens.

Jesus College
Although established between 1496 and 1516, some of its buildings on Jesus Lane are older, as the college took over St Radegond's nunnery, built in the 12th century. There are traces of Norman columns, windows and a well-preserved hammerbeam roof in the college dining hall.

The chapel keeps the core of the original church but the stained-glass windows are modern and contain work by William Morris (see pp224–5).

Queens' College
Built in 1446 on Queens' Land, the college was endowed in 1448 by Margaret of Anjou, queen of Henry VI, and again in 1465 by Elizabeth Woodville, queen of Edward IV, which explains the position of the apostrophe. Queens' has a

Punting by the King's College "Backs"

Punting on the Cam

Punting captures the essence of carefree college days: a student leaning on a long pole, lazily guiding the flat-bottomed river craft along, while passengers stretch out and relax.

Punting is still popular with both students and visitors, who can hire punts from boatyards along the river – with a chauffeur if required. Punts do sometimes capsize, and novices should prepare for a dip.

marvellous collection of Tudor buildings, notably the half-timbered President's Gallery, built in the mid-16th century on top of the brick arches in the charming Cloister Court. The Principal Court is 15th-century, as is Erasmus's Tower, named after the Dutch scholar.

Pepys Library in Magdalene College

The college has buildings on both sides of the Cam, linked by the Mathematical Bridge, built in 1749. Though the bridge appears to be an arch, it is built entirely of straight timbers using a complicated engineering design.

Magdalene College

Pronounced "maudlin" – as is the Oxford college (see p230) – the college, on Bridge Street, was established in 1482. The diarist Samuel Pepys (1633–1703) was a student here and left his large library to the college on his death. The 12 red-oak bookcases hold over 3,000 books. Magdalene was the last all-male Cambridge college: it started admitting women students only in 1988.

St John's College

Sited on St John's Street, the imposing turreted brick and stone gatehouse of 1514, with its colourful heraldic symbols, provides a fitting entrance to the second largest Cambridge college and its rich store of 16th- and 17th-century buildings. Its hall, most of it Elizabethan, has portraits of the college's famous alumni, such as the poet William Wordsworth (see p370) and the statesman Lord Palmerston. St John's spans the Cam and boasts two bridges, one built in 1712 and the other, the Bridge of Sighs, in 1831, based on its Venetian namesake.

Peterhouse

The first Cambridge college, on Trumpington Street, is also one of the smallest. The hall still has original features from 1284 but its best details are later – a Tudor fireplace which is backed with 19th-century tiles by William Morris (see pp224–5). A gallery connects the college to the 12th-century church of St Mary the Less, which used to be called St Peter's Church – hence the college's name.

William Morris tiles, Peterhouse

Trinity College

The largest college, situated on Trinity Street, was founded by Henry VIII in 1546 and has a massive court and hall. The entrance gate, with statues of Henry and James I (added later), was built in 1529 for King's Hall, an earlier college incorporated into Trinity. The Great Court features a late Elizabethan fountain – at one time the main water supply. The chapel, built in 1567, has life-size statues of college members, notably Roubiliac's statue of the scientist Isaac Newton (1755).

University Botanic Garden

A delightful place for a leisurely stroll, just off Trumpington Street, as well as an important academic resource, the garden has been on this site since 1846. It has a superb collection of trees and a sensational water garden. The winter garden is one of the finest in the country.

The Bridge of Sighs over the River Cam, linking the buildings of St John's College

🏛 Fitzwilliam Museum

Trumpington St. **Tel** 01223 332900.
Open Tue–Sun; public hols. **Closed**
1 Jan, Good Fri, 24–27 Dec. Donation.
⏰ 2:30pm Sat. ♿ 📷 🔲
🌐 fitzmuseum.cam.ac.uk

Part of the University of
Cambridge, this is one of
Britain's oldest public museums,
this massive Neo-Classical
building contains some exceptional works of art, particularly
paintings and ceramics.

The core of the collection
was bequeathed in 1816 by
the 7th Viscount Fitzwilliam.
Other gifts have since greatly
added to the exhibits.

Works by Titian (1488–1576)
and the 17th-century Dutch
masters, including Hals, Cuyp and
Hobbema, stand out among the
paintings. French Impressionist
gems include Monet's *Le
Printemps* (1866) and Renoir's *La
Place Clichy* (1880), while Stanley
Spencer's *Self-Portrait with Patrica
Preece* (1937) is a notable modern
work. There are also pieces by
important British artists, such
as Hogarth in the 18th century,
Constable in the 19th and Ben
Nicholson in the 20th.

A collection of miniatures
includes the earliest surviving
depiction of Henry VIII. In the
same gallery are some dazzling
illuminated manuscripts, notably
the 15th-century *Metz Pontifical,*
a French liturgical work.

The impressive Glaisher
collection of European
earthenware and stoneware
includes a unique display of
English delftware from the
16th and 17th centuries.

Handel's bookcase contains
folios of his work, and nearby
is Keats' original manuscript for
Ode to a Nightingale (1819).

Portrait of Richard James (c.1740s)
by William Hogarth

Cambridge: King's College

Henry VI founded this college in 1441. Work on the
chapel – one of the most important examples of late
medieval English architecture – began five years later,
and took 70 years to complete. Henry himself decided
that it should dominate the city and gave specific
instructions about its dimensions: 88 m (289 ft) long,
12 m (40 ft) wide and 29 m (94 ft) high. The detailed
design is thought to have been by master stonemason
Reginald Ely, although it was altered in later years.

★ Fan Vaulted Ceiling
This awe-inspiring ceiling,
supported by 22 buttresses,
was built by master stonemason John Wastell in 1515.

KEY

① **The Fellows' Building** was
designed in 1724 by James Gibbs,
as part of an uncompleted design
for a Great Court.

② **One of four octagonal turrets**

③ **Side chapels**

④ **The massive 17th-century
organ** case above the screen
is decorated with two angels
playing trumpets.

⑤ **The screen** is a superb example
of Tudor woodwork and divides the
chapel into antechapel and choir.

⑥ **Gothic gatehouse**
(19th-century)

⑦ **Henry VI's bronze statue**
was erected in 1879.

**Crown and
Tudor Rose**
This detail of Tudor
heraldry on the
west door of the
chapel reflects
Henry VII's vision o
English supremac

King's College Choir

When he founded the chapel, Henry VI stipulated that a choir of six lay clerks and 16 boy choristers – educated at the College school – should sing daily at services. This still happens in term time, but the choir also performs all over the world. Its broadcast service of Nine Lessons and Carols has become a much-loved Christmas tradition.

Choristers in King's College Chapel

VISITORS' CHECKLIST

Practical Information
King's Parade. **Tel** 01223 331212.
Open daily (Sat–Mon during term time). **Closed** for events; ring first. 🅿 📷 ♿ 🚻 term time: 5:30pm Mon–Sat, 10:30am & 3:30pm Sun. W **kings.cam. ac.uk**

Stained-Glass Windows
The 16th-century windows in the chapel all depict biblical scenes. This one shows Christ baptizing his followers.

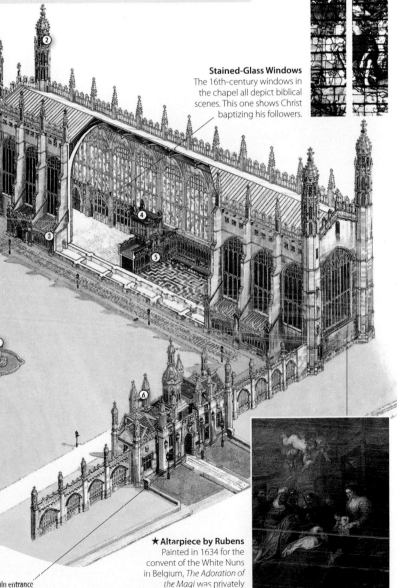

★**Altarpiece by Rubens**
Painted in 1634 for the convent of the White Nuns in Belgium, *The Adoration of the Magi* was privately donated to King's in 1961.

Main entrance

THAMES VALLEY

*Buckinghamshire · Oxfordshire · Berkshire
Bedfordshire · Hertfordshire*

The mighty tidal river on which Britain's capital city was founded begins its journey as a trickle in the hills of Gloucestershire, then meanders through lush green countryside towards London. Almost entirely agricultural land in the 19th century, the Thames Valley maintains its pastoral beauty despite the incursion of modern industry and commuter homes.

The pleasant countryside of the Chiltern Hills and of the Thames Valley itself appealed to aristocrats who built stately homes close to London, and many of these are among the grandest in the country. The area also abounds with royal connections. Windsor Castle has been a residence of kings and queens since William the Conqueror chose this strategic site above the Thames and began building in 1070. It played a critical role in 1215, when King John set out from here to sign the *Magna Carta* at Runnymede on the Thames. Further north, Queen Anne had Blenheim Palace built for her military commander, the 1st Duke of Marlborough. Elizabeth I spent part of her childhood at Hatfield House, and part of the Tudor palace still stands.

These royal residences had impressive parks and gardens, as do the other stately homes of the region – Classical Stowe, French-inspired Waddesdon, and Woburn Abbey and Safari Park.

Around these great houses grew picturesque villages, with half-timbered buildings and, as you move towards the Cotswolds, houses built in attractive buff-coloured stone. That the area has been inhabited for thousands of years is shown by the number of prehistoric remains, including a remarkable chalk hillside figure, the White Horse of Uffington.

Nearer to London is St Alban's, a city steeped in Roman history, and the Warner Bros Studios, which is a draw for all Harry Potter fans.

The River Thames at Marlow, Buckinghamshire

◀ Autumn view of the Long Walk, Windsor Castle, Berkshire

Exploring the Thames Valley

The area bordering the Thames is very well populated but still offers idyllic places to explore, especially the loop from Maidenhead to Reading through Cookham and Henley on Thames. There are delightful walks and gentle boat rides, with a wealth of waterside pubs, garden tea rooms and first-class restaurants. To the west beyond the Chiltern Hills is Oxford, the region's principal city, where the foundations of Britain's first university were laid in 1167. Further west still are the limestone hills of the Cotswolds and their characteristic honey-coloured villages.

Sights at a Glance

1. Great Tew
2. Burford
3. Kelmscott
4. Vale of the White Horse
5. Oxford pp226–31
6. Blenheim Palace pp232–3
7. Stowe
8. Woburn Abbey
9. Waddesdon Manor
10. Roald Dahl Museum
11. ZSL Whipsnade Zoo
12. Knebworth House
13. Hatfield House
14. St Albans pp236–7
15. Gardens of the Rose
16. Warner Bros. Studio Tour –
    The Making of Harry Potter
18. Windsor pp239–41

Walks and Tours

17. Touring the Thames
    pp238–9

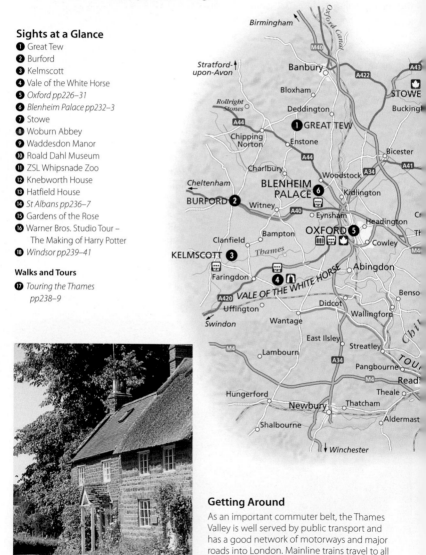

A thatched cottage, Upper Swarford, Banbury

Getting Around

As an important commuter belt, the Thames Valley is well served by public transport and has a good network of motorways and major roads into London. Mainline trains travel to all the major towns and there are many coach services that run from London to the major sights and attractions.

For hotels and restaurants in this area see p564 and pp588–9

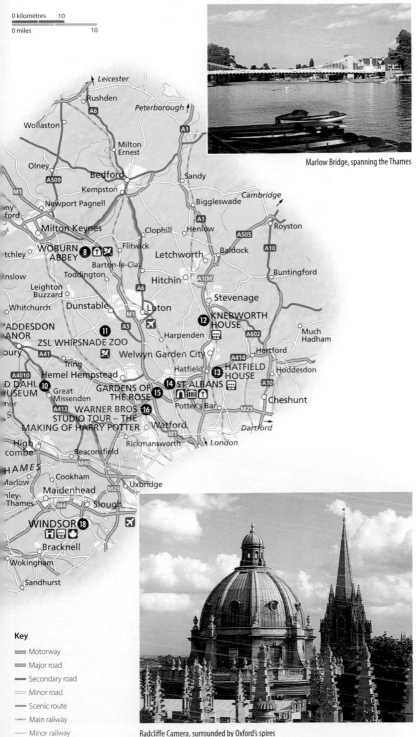

0 kilometres 10

0 miles 10

Marlow Bridge, spanning the Thames

Leicester

Rushden
A6
Peterborough
Wollaston
A1
Olney
Milton
Ernest
A509
Bedford
Sandy
Kempston
Biggleswade
Cambridge
Newport Pagnell
A1
Milton Keynes
Clophill
Henlow
Royston
WOBURN 8
ABBEY
Flitwick
Letchworth
A505
Baldock
A10
Barton-le-Clay
Buntingford
Toddington
Hitchin
A1(M)
Leighton
Buzzard
A6
Stevenage
Whitchurch
Dunstable
M1
Luton
KNEBWORTH 12
HOUSE
A602
Much
Hadham
ADDESDON
MANOR
11
A5
ZSL WHIPSNADE ZOO
Harpenden
Welwyn Garden City
Hertford
A414
A41
Tring
Hatfield
13 HATFIELD
HOUSE
Hoddesdon
A4010
Hemel Hempstead
14 ST ALBANS
A10
D DAHL
USEUM
10
Great
Missenden
GARDENS OF
THE ROSE 15
Cheshunt
A413
WARNER BROS.
STUDIO TOUR – THE
MAKING OF HARRY POTTER
16
Potter's Bar
M25
Watford
High
combe
Beaconsfield
Rickmansworth
Dartford
London
M1
M40
HAMES
Marlow
Cookham
M25
Uxbridge
nley-
Thames
Maidenhead
M4
Slough
WINDSOR 18
Bracknell
Wokingham
Sandhurst

Radcliffe Camera, surrounded by Oxford's spires

Key

━━ Motorway

━━ Major road

━━ Secondary road

┄┄ Minor road

━━ Scenic route

╌╌ Main railway

── Minor railway

For keys to symbols *see back flap*

❶ Great Tew

Oxfordshire. 🗺 150. 🚆 Oxford or Banbury then taxi. 🚹 Castle Quay Shopping Centre, Banbury (01295 753752). 🆆 **oxfordshire cotswolds.org**

This secluded village of ironstone was founded in the 1630s by Lord Falkland for estate workers. It was heavily restored between 1809 and 1811 in the Gothic style. Thatched cottages stand in gardens with clipped box hedges, and in the village centre is a 16th-century pub, the **Falkland Arms**, complete with flagstone floors and oak beams.

Environs

Five miles (8 km) west are the **Rollright Stones**, three Bronze Age monuments: the King's Men, a circle of 77 stones, about 30 m (100 ft) in diameter; the remains of a burial chamber called the Whispering Knights; and the solitary King Stone.

Further north is **Banbury**, known for its spicy flat cakes and its market cross, immortalized in the nursery rhyme "Ride a Cock-horse to Banbury Cross".

The original medieval cross was destroyed, but it was replaced in 1859.

🏠 **Falkland Arms Pub**
Great Tew. **Tel** 01608 683653. **Open** daily. **Closed** 25 Dec. ♿

The 19th-century Banbury Cross

❷ Burford

Oxfordshire. 🗺 1,400. 🚹 33a High St (01993 823558). 🆆 **oxfordshire cotswolds.org**

A charming small town, Burford has hardly changed since Georgian times, when it was an important coach stop between Oxford and the West Country. Cotswold stone houses, inns and shops, many built in the 16th century, line its main street.

The Tolsey is a former Tudor market house and now a museum. It is on the corner of Sheep Street, itself a reminder of the important medieval wool trade *(see p211)*.

St John the Baptist, at the end of High Street, is one of the Cotswolds' largest wool churches. It contains a monument to Henry VIII's barber surgeon, Edmund

Harman, depicting South American Indians, possibly their first representation in Britain.

Environs

Six miles (9 km) east of Burford are the ruins of **Minster Lovell Hall**, a 15th-century manor house with an unusual dovecote.

A few miles south of Burford is **Cotswold Wildlife Park**, home to a diverse collection of mammals, reptiles and birds.

🏠 **Minster Lovell Hall**
Minster Lovell. **Open** daily. EH

🦋 **Cotswold Wildlife Park**
Burford. **Tel** 01993 823006. **Open** daily. **Closed** 25 Dec. ♿ 🔋 ✏ 📷
🆆 **cotswoldwildlifepark.co.uk**

❸ Kelmscott

Oxfordshire. 🗺 100. 🚹 The Pump House, 5 Market Place, Faringdon (01367 242191). 🆆 **faringdontown council.gov.uk**

The designer, writer and publisher William Morris lived in this pretty Thameside village from 1871 until his death in 1896. He shared his house, the classic Elizabethan **Kelmscott Manor**, with fellow painter Dante Gabriel Rossetti (1828–82), who left after an affair with Morris's

Cotswold stone houses, Burford, Oxfordshire

The formal entrance of the Elizabethan Kelmscott Manor

wife Jane – the model for many Pre-Raphaelite paintings. Morris and his followers in the Arts and Crafts movement were attracted by the medieval feel of the village and several cottages were later built in Morris's memory.

Today Kelmscott Manor has works of art by members of the movement, including some William de Morgan tiles. Morris is buried in the village churchyard, with a tomb designed by Philip Webb.

Two miles (3 km) to the east is **Radcot Bridge**, thought to be the oldest bridge still standing over the Thames. Built in the 13th century from local Taynton stone, it was a strategic river crossing, and in 1387 was damaged in a battle between Richard II and his barons.

🏛 **Kelmscott Manor**
Kelmscott. **Tel** 01367 252486.
Open Apr–Oct: Wed & Sat (house & garden). 🎫 🚻 limited. 🔲 📷
W sal.org.uk/kelmscott-manor

❶ Vale of the White Horse

Oxfordshire. 🚃 Didcot. 🛈 Roysse Court, The Guildhall, Abingdon (01235 522711); 19 Church St, Wantage (01235 760176).

This lovely valley gets its name from the huge chalk horse, 100 m (350 ft) from nose to tail, carved into the hillside above Uffington. It is believed to be Britain's oldest hillside carving and has sparked many legends: some say it was cut by the Saxon leader Hengist (whose name means "stallion" in German), while others believe it is to do with Alfred the Great,

thought to have been born nearby. It is, however, a great deal older than either of these stories suggest, having been dated at around 1000 BC.

Nearby are the Celtic earth ramparts of the Iron Age hill fort, **Uffington Castle**. A mile (1.5 km) west along the Ridgeway, an ancient trade route *(see p41)*, is an even older

monument, a large Stone Age burial mound that is known as **Wayland's Smithy**. This is immersed in legends that Sir Walter Scott *(see p516)* used in his novel *Kenilworth*.

The best view of the horse is to be had from Uffington village, which is also worth visiting for the **Tom Brown's School Museum**. This 17th-century school house contains exhibits devoted to the author Thomas Hughes (1822–96). Hughes set the early chapters of his Victorian novel, *Tom Brown's Schooldays*, here. The museum also contains material about excavations on White Horse Hill.

🏛 **Tom Brown's School**
Broad St, Uffington. 🛈 01367 820978.
Open Easter–Oct: Sat pm, Sun pm & public hols pm. 🚻 limited. 📷
W museum.uffington.net

Hillside Chalk Figures

It was the Celts who first saw the potential for creating large-scale artworks on the chalk hills of southern England. Horses – held in high regard by both the Celts and later the Saxons, and the objects of cult worship – were often a favourite subject, but people were also depicted, notably at Cerne Abbas, Dorset *(see p273)*, and the Long Man of Wilmington *(see p185)*. The figures may have served as religious symbols or as landmarks by which tribes identified their territory. Many chalk figures have been obliterated, because without any attention they are quickly overrun by grass. Uffington is "scoured", to prevent encroachment by grass, a tradition once accompanied by a fair and other festivities. There was a second flush of hillside carving in the 18th century, especially in Wiltshire. In some cases – for instance at Bratton Castle near Westbury – an 18th-century carving has been superimposed on an ancient one.

Britain's oldest hillside carving, the White Horse of Uffington

⑤ Street-by-Street: Oxford

Oxford has long been a strategic point on the western routes into London – its name describes its position as a convenient spot for crossing the river (a ford for oxen). The city's first scholars, who founded the university, came from France in 1167. The development of England's first university created the spectacular skyline of tall towers and "dreaming spires".

Museum of the History of Science
This museum is housed in the Old Ashmolean, a resplendent building designed in 1683.

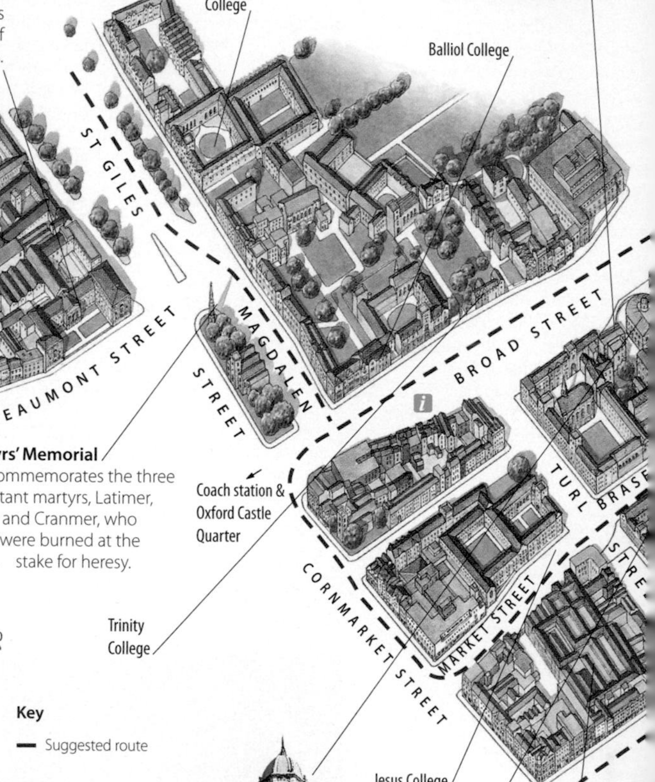

The Ashmolean Museum
displays one of Britain's foremost collections of fine art and antiquities.

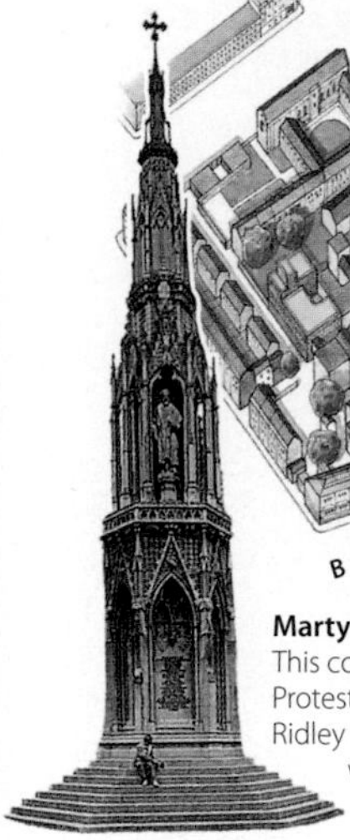

St John's College

Balliol College

ST GILES

MAGDALEN STREET

BEAUMONT STREET

BROAD STREET

TURL

BRASE

Martyrs' Memorial
This commemorates the three Protestant martyrs, Latimer, Ridley and Cranmer, who were burned at the stake for heresy.

Coach station & Oxford Castle Quarter

CORNMARKET STREET

MARKET STREET

0 metres   100
0 yards   100

Trinity College

Key

— Suggested route

Jesus College

Lincoln College

Railway station

ST ALD

Covered market

Percy Bysshe Shelley

Shelley (1792–1822), one of the Romantic poets, attended University College, Oxford, but was expelled after writing a revolutionary pamphlet, "The Necessity of Atheism". Despite that disgrace, the college has put up a memorial to him from his daughter-in-law.

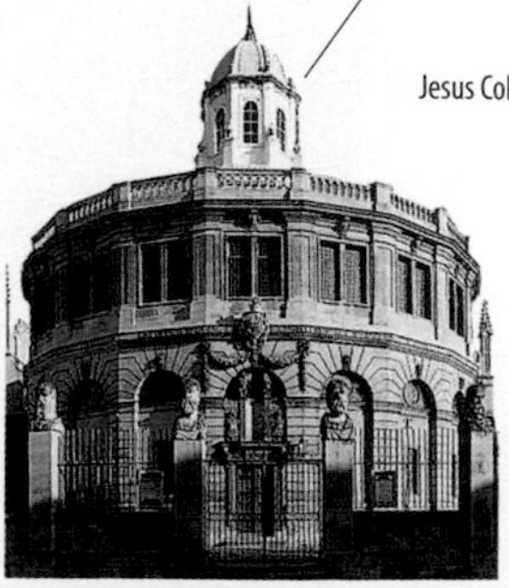

Sheldonian Theatre
The first building designed by Wren (see p119) is the scene of Oxford University's traditional graduation ceremonies.

Museum of Oxford

★ Radcliffe Camera
This Neo-Classical rotunda, Oxford's most distinctive building, is now a reading room of the Bodleian. It was one of the library's original buildings *(see p231)*.

Bridge of Sighs
Resembling the steeply arched bridge in Venice of the same name, this picturesque landmark was built in 1914 and joins the old and new buildings of Hertford College.

New College

St Mary the Virgin Church

QUEEN'S LANE

Queen's College

All Souls College

London

University College

Lincoln College Library

LOGIC LANE

Botanic Garden and Magdalen College

HIGH STREET

MAGPIE LANE

Oriel College

ORIEL STREET

MERTON STREET

Merton College

BEAR LANE

DEAD MAN'S WALK

Corpus Christi College

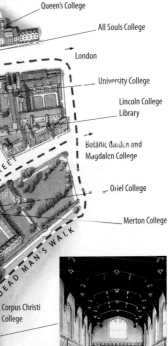

★ Christ Church
Students still eat at long tables in all the college halls. Senior academics sit at the high table and grace is almost always said in Latin.

Exploring Oxford

Oxford is more than just a university city; it has one of Britain's most important car factories in the suburb of Cowley. Despite this, Oxford is dominated by institutions related to its huge academic community: like Blackwell's bookshop which has over 20,000 titles in stock. The two rivers, the Cherwell and the Isis (the name given to the Thames as it flows through the city), provide lovely riverside walks, or you can hire a punt and spend an afternoon on the Cherwell.

🏛 Ashmolean Museum
Beaumont St. **Tel** 01865 278000.
Open Tue–Sun & public hols.
Closed 24–26 Dec. 🎬 Tue–Sat. 🔊
♿ ✏ 🖥 📷 🅦 ashmolean.org

One of the best British museums outside London, the Ashmolean is based on a collection known as The Ark, put together in the 17th century by two John Tradescants, father and son. On their death, their cabinet of curiosities was acquired by the antiquarian Elias Ashmole, who donated it to the university. He housed it in a purpose-built museum (1683) – the Old Ashmolean, now the Museum of the History of Science – and from here it was transferred to the University Galleries, a Neo-Classical building of 1845 that is now the Ashmolean.

In 2009, the museum building was greatly extended to include spacious new galleries that lead off a striking atrium and staircase.

Here, objects are displayed according to the theme "Crossing Cultures, Crossing Time", which imaginatively makes connections through different periods of history. Galleries in the older part of the building show Greek, Roman and Indian artifacts, Egyptian mummies, Anglo-Saxon treasures and modern Chinese painting, all of world-class standard.

Today, paintings and the applied arts overshadow the original curio collection. Highlights include the world's greatest collection of drawings by Raphael (1483–1520), Bellini's *St Jerome Reading in a Landscape* (late 15th century), Turner's *Venice: The Grand Canal* (1840), Picasso's *Blue Roofs* (1901) and a large group of Pre-Raphaelites including Rossetti and Millais. The second-largest coin collection in Britain is also housed here. One of the most notable pieces is a rare Oxford crown, minted in Oxford during the Civil War in 1644.

Perhaps the most famous item is the small, gold, enamelled ornament known as the Alfred Jewel, which dates from the 9th century. Also of interest is the shell-encrusted mantle of Powhatan, father of Pocahontas, and the lantern that belonged to Guy Fawkes.

A spectacular rooftop restaurant is open during the day and in the evenings at the weekend.

The entrance to the Ashmolean Museum

⬆ Museum of the History of Science
Broad St. **Tel** 01865 277280.
Open Tue–Sun. 🎬 ♿ 📷

Located in the Old Ashmolean, this museum has an outstanding collection of early scientific and mathematical instruments. The museum's permanent exhibitions are spread over three floors. Amid the astrolabes and quadrants are Lewis Carroll's camera box and the blackboard used by Einstein in a lecture on the theory of relativity.

An iron gate in the 17th-century Botanic Garden

🔲 The University of Oxford Botanic Garden
Rose Lane. **Tel** 01865 286690. **Open** daily. **Closed** Sep–May: Mon am; Good Fri, 25 Dec. 🐾 🎬 ♿
🅦 botanic-garden.ox.ac.uk

Britain's oldest botanic garden was founded in 1621 – one ancient yew tree survives from that period. The entrance gates were designed by Nicholas Stone in 1633 and paid for by the Earl of Danby. This delightful garden has an original walled garden, a rock garden, and an insectivorous plant house.

⬆ Carfax Tower
Carfax Sq. **Tel** 01865 792653. **Open** daily. **Closed** 1 Jan, 25 & 26 Dec. 🐾 📷

The tower is all that remains of the 14th-century Church of St Martin, demolished in 1896 so that the adjoining road could be widened. You can climb the 99 steps to the top for panoramic views. Carfax was the crossing point of the original north–south and east–west routes through Oxford: its name derives from the Latin *quadrifurcus* (four-forked).

🏛 Holywell Music Room

Holywell St. **Tel** 01865 276125.
Open concerts only. 🅿 ♿
This was the first building in
Europe designed, in 1752,
specifically for public musical
performances. The room is
regularly used for contemporary
and classical concerts.

🏛 Museum of Oxford

St Aldates. **Tel** 01865 252351.
Open 10am–5pm Mon–Sat.
Closed 1 Jan, 24–26 & 31 Dec. 📷
A well-organized display in the
Victorian town hall illustrates
the long history of Oxford and
its university. Exhibits include
a Roman pottery kiln. The main
feature is a series of well-recon-
structed rooms, including one
from an Elizabethan inn and an
18th-century student's room.

🏛 Martyrs' Memorial

Magdalen St.
This commemorates the three
Protestants burned at the stake
on Broad Street – Bishops
Latimer and Ridley in 1555, and
Archbishop Cranmer in 1556. On
the accession of Queen Mary in
1553 *(see p55)*, they were committed to the Tower of London,
then sent to Oxford to defend
their views before the doctors of
divinity who, after the hearing,
condemned them as heretics.
   The memorial was designed
in 1843 by George Gilbert
Scott and based on the Eleanor
crosses erected in 12 English
towns by Edward I (1239–1307).

🏛 Oxford Castle Quarter

44–46 Oxford Castle. **Tel** 01865
201657. **Open** daily. ♿ 🖥 📷
Following a £40-million development, this 1,000-year-old
castle forms part of the Oxford
Castle Quarter, an urban space
that also includes shops,
restaurants and a hotel.

🏛 Oxford Castle Unlocked

44–46 Oxford Castle. **Tel** 01865
260666. **Open** daily. **Closed**
24–26 Dec. 🅿 ♿ partial. 🖥 📷
The secrets of the castle are
revealed in this exhibition that
looks at the site's turbulent past.
Climb St George's Tower for
great views over the city.

🏛 Sheldonian Theatre

Broad St. **Tel** 01865 277299.
Open see website. **Closed** public
hols, Easter, Christmas period.
🅿 ♿ limited. 🆆 admin.ox.
ac.uk/ sheldonian

Completed in 1669,
this was designed
by Christopher
Wren *(see p119)*,
and paid for by
Gilbert Sheldon,
the Archbishop
of Canterbury,
as a location for
university degree
ceremonies. The
design of the D-shaped building
is based on the Theatre of
Marcellus in Rome. The octagonal cupola built in 1838 boasts
a famous view from its huge
Lantern. The theatre's painted
ceiling shows the triumph of
religion, art and science over
envy, hatred and malice.

🏛 St Mary the Virgin Church

High St. **Tel** 01865 279111. **Open**
daily. **Closed** Good Fri, 25 & 26 Dec. 📷
📷 🆆 university-church.ox.ac.uk
This, the official university church,
is said to be the most visited
parish church in England. The
oldest parts date from the early
13th century and include the
tower, from which there are
fine views. Its Convocation
House served as the
university's first library
until the Bodleian was
founded in 1488 *(see
p231)*. The church is

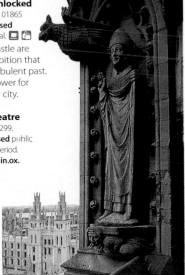

Thomas Cranmer statue, St Mary the Virgin Church

where the three Oxford Martyrs
were pronounced heretics in
1555. An architectural highlight
is the Baroque south porch.

🏛 Oxford University Museum of Natural History

Parks Rd. **Tel** 01865 272950.
Open 10am–5pm daily. **Closed** 25
Dec. ♿ 🖥 📷 🆆 oum.ox.ac.uk
Two of Oxford's most interesting
museums adjoin each other.
The first is a museum of natural
history with dinosaur relics, as
well as a stuffed dodo. This
flightless bird has been extinct
since the 17th century but was
immortalized by Lewis Carroll
(an Oxford mathematics lecturer)
in his book *Alice in Wonderland*.

🏛 Pitt Rivers Museum

Parks Rd. **Tel** 01865 270927. **Open**
10am–4:30pm Tue–Sun (noon–4:30pm
Mon). **Closed** 25 Dec. 🕑 2:30 & 3:15pm
Tue & Wed. ♿ 📷 🆆 prm.ox.ac.uk

Next to the Museum of
Natural History is the Pitt
Rivers Museum. This has
an extensive ethnographic
collection – masks and
totems from Africa
and the Far East – and
archaeological displays,
including exhibits collected by the explorer
Captain Cook.

The impressive frontage of the Oxford University Museum of Natural History

Exploring Oxford University

Many of the 38 colleges that make up the university were founded between the 13th and 16th centuries and cluster around the city centre. As scholarship was then the exclusive preserve of the Church, the colleges were designed along the lines of monastic buildings but were often surrounded by beautiful gardens. Although most colleges have been altered over the years, many still incorporate a lot of their original features.

The spectacular view of All Souls College from St Mary the Virgin Church

All Souls College
Founded in 1438 on the High Street by Henry VI, the chapel on the college's north side has a classic hammerbeam roof, unusual misericords *(see p345)* on the choir stalls and 15th-century stained glass.

Christ Church
The best way to view the largest of the Oxford colleges is to approach through the meadows from St Aldate's. Christ Church dates from 1525, when Cardinal Wolsey founded it as an ecclesiastical college to train cardinals. The upper part of the tower in Tom Quad – a rectangular courtyard – was built by Wren *(see p119)* in 1682 and is the largest in the city. When its bell, Great

Tom, was hung in 1648, the college had 101 students, which is why the bell is rung 101 times at 9:05pm, to mark the curfew for students (which has not been enforced since 1963). The odd timing is because Oxford is technically 5 minutes behind Greenwich Mean Time. Christ Church has produced 13 British prime ministers in the last 200 years. The Renaissance magnificence of Christ Church's Hall inspired the film-makers of the Harry Potter series. Beside the main quad is the 12th-century Christ Church Cathedral, one of the smallest in England.

Lincoln College
One of the best-preserved of the medieval colleges, it was

founded in 1427 on Turl Street, and the front quad and façade are 15th-century. The hall still has its original roof, including the gap where smoke used to escape. The Jacobean chapel is notable for its stained glass. John Wesley *(see p283)* was at college here, and his room off the front quad can be viewed.

New College
One of the grandest colleges, it was founded by William of Wykeham in 1379 to educate clergy to replace those killed by the Black Death of 1348 *(see p52)*.

Highlights of its magnificent chapel on New College Lane, restored in the 19th century, are the 14th-century misericords and El Greco's (1541–1614) painting of *St James*.

Queen's College
Most of the college buildings date from the 18th century and represent some of the finest work from that period in Oxford. The superb library was built in 1695 by Henry Aldrich (1647–1710). The front screen with its bell-topped gatehouse is a feature of the High Street.

Magdalen College
At the end of the High Street is perhaps the most iconic and beautiful Oxford college. Its 15th-century quads in contrasting styles are set in a park by the Cherwell, crossed by Magdalen Bridge. Every May Day at 6am, the college choir sings from the top of Magdalen's bell tower (1508) – a 16th-century custom to mark the start of summer.

Magdalen Bridge spanning the River Cherwell

Student Life
Students belong to individual colleges and usually live in them for the duration of their course. The university gives lectures, sets exams and awards degrees, but much of the students' tuition and social life is

based around their college. Many university traditions date back hundreds of years, like the graduation ceremonies at the Sheldonian, which are still held in Latin.

Graduation at the Sheldonian *(see p229)*

Merton College seen from Christ Church Meadows

St John's College

The impressive frontage on St Giles dates from 1437, when it was founded for Cistercian scholars. The library has lovely 17th-century bookcases and stained glass, and the college owns a magnificent collection of early embroidered vestments.

Trinity College

The oldest part of the college on Broad Street, Durham Quad, is named after the earlier college of 1296, which was incorporated into Trinity in 1555. The late 17th century chapel has a magnificent reredos and wooden screen.

Corpus Christi College

The whole of the charming front quad on Merton Street dates from 1517, when the college was founded. The quad's sundial, topped by a pelican – the college symbol – bears an early 17th-century calendar. The chapel has a rare 16th-century eagle lectern.

Merton College

Off Merton Street, this is the oldest college (1264) in Oxford. Much of its hall is original, including a sturdy decorated door. The chapel choir contains allegorical reliefs representing music, arithmetic, rhetoric and grammar. Merton's Mob Quad served as a model for the later colleges.

Bodleian Library

Founded in 1320, the library was expanded in 1426 by Humphrey, Duke of Gloucester (1391–1447) and brother of Henry V, when his collection of manuscripts would not fit into the old library. It was refounded in 1602 by Thomas Bodley, a wealthy scholar, who insisted on strict rules: the keeper was forbidden to marry. The library is one of the six copyright deposit libraries in the country – it is entitled to receive a copy of every book published in Britain

The Radcliffe Camera (1748), a domed Baroque rotunda, was built by James Gibbs as a library funded by a bequest from the Yorkshire physician Dr John Radcliffe (1650–1714).

Main entrance

This extension was built in 1630.

The Divinity School (1488)

One of the country's finest Gothic interiors, the Divinity School has a unique vaulted ceiling with 455 carved bosses representing biblical scenes and both mythical and real beasts.

Duke Humphrey's Library
This has ceiling panels that carry the university crest and Latin motto *Dominus Illuminatio Mea* – the Lord is my Light.

❻ Blenheim Palace

After John Churchill, the 1st Duke of Marlborough, defeated the French at the Battle of Blenheim in 1704, Queen Anne gave him the Manor of Woodstock and had this palatial house built for him. Designed by Nicholas Hawksmoor and Sir John Vanbrugh *(see p403)*, it is a Baroque masterpiece. It was also the birthplace of Winston Churchill in 1874. The palace is the only British historic house to be named a World Heritage Site.

Water Terraces
These magnificent gardens were laid out in the 1920s by French architect Achille Duchêne in 17th-century style, with patterned beds and fountains.

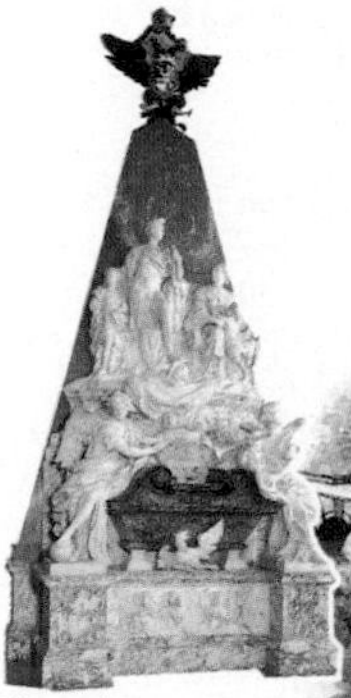

Chapel
The marble monument to the 1st Duke of Marlborough and his family was sculpted by Michael Rysbrack in 1733.

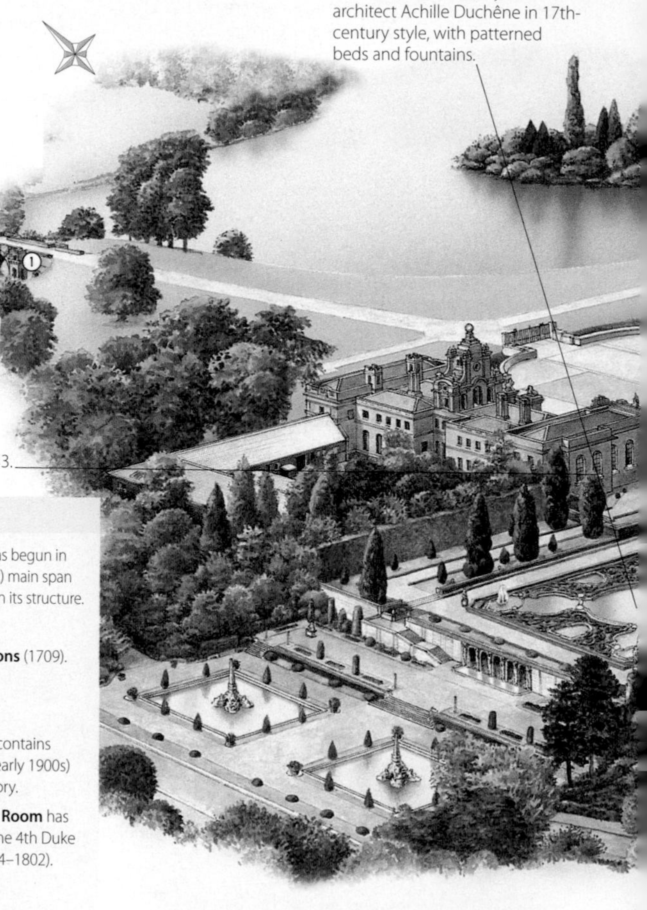

KEY

① **The Grand Bridge** was begun in 1708. It has a 31-m (101-ft) main span and contains rooms within its structure.

② **Great Court**

③ **Grinling Gibbons lions** (1709).

④ **Clock tower**

⑤ **East gate**

⑥ **The Italian Garden** contains the Mermaid Fountain (early 1900s) by US sculptor Waldo Story.

⑦ **The Green Drawing Room** has a full-length portrait of the 4th Duke by George Romney (1734–1802).

⑧ **Red Drawing Room**

⑨ **Green Writing Room**

⑩ **First State Room**

⑪ **Second State Room**

⑫ **Third State Room**

⑬ **The Great Hall** has a splendid ceiling by Thornhill (1716), showing the 1st Duke of Marlborough presenting his plan for the Battle of Blenheim to Britannia.

⑭ **Blenheim Palace: The Untold Story** exhibition

Winston Churchill (1874–1965), Britain's World War II leader

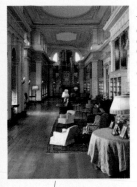

★ Long Library
This 55-m (183-ft) room was designed by Vanbrugh as a picture gallery. The portraits include one of Queen Anne by Sir Godfrey Kneller (1646–1723). The stucco on the ceiling is by Isaac Mansfield (1725).

VISITORS' CHECKLIST

Practical Information
Woodstock, Oxfordshire. **Tel** 0199 381 0530. Palace & Gardens: **Open** 10:30am–5:30pm daily. Park: **Open** 9am–5pm daily. **Closed** 25 Dec. The Private Apartments. partial. **blenheimpalace.com**

Transport
Oxford. S3 from Oxford train station.

Entrance
5
4
3
2
6
14
13
9
8
7
10
12
11

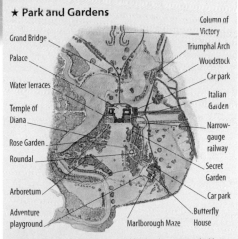

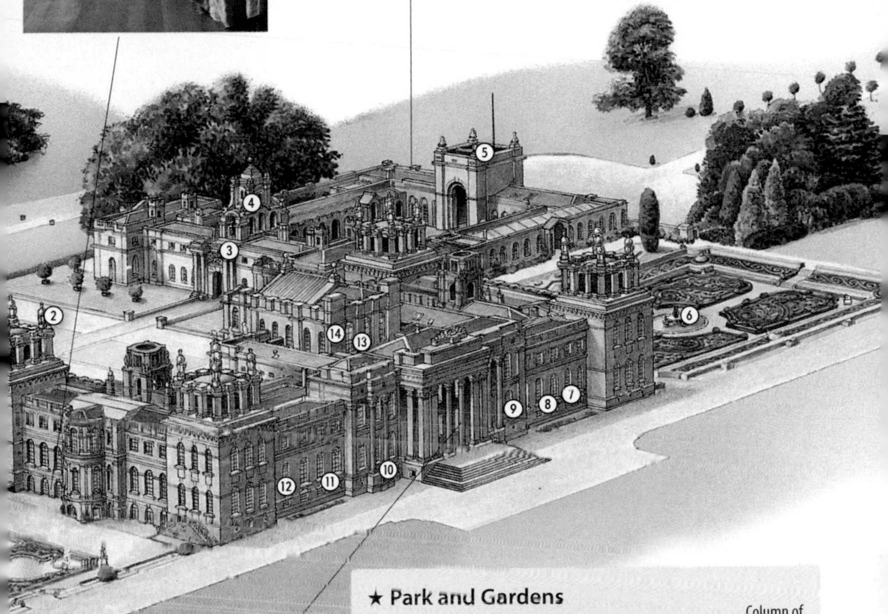

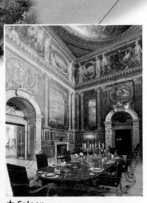

★ Saloon
French artist Louis Laguerre (1663–1721) painted the detailed scenes on the walls and ceiling.

★ Park and Gardens

Column of Victory
Grand Bridge
Triumphal Arch
Palace
Woodstock
Car park
Water Terraces
Italian Garden
Temple of Diana
Narrow-gauge railway
Rose Garden
Roundal
Secret Garden
Arboretum
Car park
Adventure playground
Butterfly House
Marlborough Maze

A house fit for a victorious general had to be surrounded by a park with suitably heroic monuments. They were kept when "Capability" Brown (see p30) re-landscaped the park (1764–74) and created the lake.

Canaletto's *Entrance to the Arsenal* (1730) hangs at Woburn Abbey

❼ Stowe

Buckingham, Buckinghamshire.
Tel 01280 817156. 🚆 Milton Keynes
then bus. **Open** daily. 🅿️ ♿ 🖥️ 🏠 NT

One of the most ambitious
landscaped gardens in Britain,
Stowe is also a fine example of the
18th-century passion for improving
on nature to make it conform to
fashionable notions of taste.

In the space of nearly 100 years
the original garden, first laid out
around 1680, was enlarged and
transformed by the addition of
monuments, Greek and Gothic
temples, grottoes, statues,
ornamental bridges, artificial
lakes and "natural" tree plantings.

Most of the leading designers
and architects of the period
contributed to the design,
including Sir John Vanbrugh and
"Capability" Brown *(see p30)*. Brown
was also married here and lived
in one of the Boycott Pavilions.

From 1593 to 1921 the property
was owned by the Temple and
Grenville families – later the
Dukes of Buckingham – until the
large Palladian house, **Stowe
House**, at its centre was converted into an elite boys' school.

The family were soldiers and
politicians in the liberal tradition,
and many of the garden's buildings and sculptures symbolize
Utopian ideals of democracy
and freedom. Some features
deteriorated in the 19th
century but a major restoration
programme has returned much
of the statuary to its former glory.

🏛️ **Stowe House**
Tel 01280 818002. **Open** during school
term for guided tours only; for other
days, check website. 🅿️ ♿ 🖥️ during
school hols. NT 🌐 stowe.co.uk/house

❽ Woburn Abbey

Woburn, Bedfordshire. **Tel** 01525
290333. 🚆 Flitwick then taxi.
Open Easter–Oct: daily. Garden & Deer
Park: **Open** daily (Fri–Sun in winter).
🅿️ ♿ gardens, house limited. 🖊️ 🏠
🌐 **woburnabbey.co.uk**

The Dukes of Bedford have
lived here since the 1620s and,
in 1955, were among the first
owners of an English stately
home to open their house
to the public.

The abbey was built in the
mid-18th century on the foundations of a large 12th-century
Cistercian monastery. Its mix of
styles include those of Henry
Flitcroft and Henry Holland
(see p32). The grounds are also
popular for their 142-ha (350-
acre) safari park and attractive
deer park, home to nine species,
including the Manchurian Sika
deer from China.

Woburn's magnificent state
apartments house an impressive
private art collection which
includes Gower's *Armada Portrait*
of Queen Elizabeth I (1588) and
works by Reynolds (1723–92)
and Canaletto (1697–1768).

❾ Waddesdon Manor

Nr Aylesbury, Buckinghamshire.
Tel 01296 653226. 🚆 Aylesbury
then taxi. House: **Open** late Mar–
Oct: Wed–Sun & pub hols.
Grounds: **Open** late Mar–Oct:
10am–5pm Wed–Sun; see website
for winter hours. 🅿️ ♿ 🖊️ 🖥️ 🏠
🌐 **waddesdon.org.uk**

Waddesdon Manor was built
in 1874–89 by Baron Ferdinand
de Rothschild and designed
by French architect Gabriel-
Hippolyte Destailleur in the
style of a French 16th-century
chateau. The manor houses one
of the world's finest collections
of French 18th-century
decorative art, as well as
Savonnerie carpets and Sèvres
porcelain. The garden, originally
laid out by French landscape
gardener Elie Lainé, is renowned
for its seasonal displays.

❿ Roald Dahl Museum

81–83 High St, Great Missenden,
Buckinghamshire. **Tel** 01494 892192.
🚆 Great Missenden. **Open** 10am–
5pm Tue–Fri, 11am–5pm Sat & Sun.
🅿️ ♿ 🖥️ 🏠 🌐 roalddahl.com/
museum

The magical world of Roald
Dahl's stories comes to life in
this award-winning museum.
A series of biographical galleries
explores the life and work of the
children's writer, while the Story
Centre's interactive exhibits
allow children to make their
own animated film, record
dreams in a "dream bottle" or try
their hand at creative writing.

The 17th-century Palladian bridge over the Octagon Lake in Stowe Park

Hatfield House, one of the largest Jacobean mansions in the country

⑪ ZSL Whipsnade Zoo

Nr Dunstable, Bedfordshire. **Tel** 01582 872171. ⊟ Hemel Hempsted or Luton then bus. **Open** daily **Closed** 25 Dec. 🐾 📷 ♿ 🅿 w zsl.org

The rural branch of London Zoo, this was one of the first zoos to minimize the use of cages, confining animals safely but without constriction.

At 240 ha (600 acres), it is one of Europe's largest conservation parks, with more than 2,500 species. You can drive through some areas or hop aboard a steam train. Popular attractions are the elephants, chimps and Hullahazoo Farm, the Cheetah Rock exhibit and the Butterfly House.

⑫ Knebworth House

Knebworth, Hertfordshire. **Tel** 01438 812661. ⊟ Stevenage then taxi. **Open** Sat, Sun; 2 weeks at Easter & Jul–Aug: daily. 🐾 📷 ♿ limited. 🅿 🏠 w knebworthhouse.com

Home of the Lytton family since 1490, this Tudor mansion, with a beautiful Jacobean banqueting hall, was remodelled in the early 19th-century into a Gothic structure. The eldest son of Lord Lytton, the 1st Earl of Lytton was Viceroy of India, and exhibits recall the Delhi Durbar of 1877, when Queen Victoria became Empress of India.

A visit includes the house, gardens, park, and a dinosaur trail for children.

⑬ Hatfield House

Hatfield, Hertfordshire. **Tel** 01707 287010. ⊟ Hatfield. **Open** Easter–Sep: Wed–Sun & public hols. 🐾 ♿ 📷 🏠 w hatfield-house.co.uk

One of England's finest Jacobean houses, Hatfield House was built between 1607 and 1611 for the powerful statesman Robert Cecil.

Its chief historical interest, though, lies in the surviving wing of the original Tudor Hatfield Palace, where Queen Elizabeth I (see pp54–5) spent much of her childhood. She held her first Council of State here when she was crowned in 1558. The palace was partly demolished in 1607 to make way for the new house, which contains mementos of her life, including the *Rainbow* portrait painted around 1600 by Isaac Oliver.

Originally laid out by Robert Cecil with help from John Tradescant, the gardens have been restored to reflect their Jacobean origins. The grounds host regular farmers' and antiques markets.

Famous Puritans

Three major figures connected with the 17th-century Puritan movement are celebrated in the Thames area. John Bunyan (1628–88), who wrote the allegorical tale *The Pilgrim's Progress*, was born at Elstow, near Bedford. A passionate Puritan orator, he was jailed for his beliefs for 17 years. The Bunyan Museum in Bedford is a former site of Puritan worship. William Penn (1644–1718), founder of the American colony of Pennsylvania, lived, worshipped and is buried at Jordans, near Beaconsfield.

18th-century engraving of John Bunyan

At Chalfont St Giles is the cottage where the poet John Milton (1608–74) stayed to escape London's plague. There he completed his greatest work, *Paradise Lost*. The house is now a museum based on his life and works.

William Penn, founder of Pennsylvania

John Milton painted by Pieter van der Plas

⑭ St Albans

Today a thriving market town and a base for London commuters, St Albans was for centuries at the heart of some of the most stirring events in English history. A regional capital of ancient Britain, it became a major Roman settlement and then a key ecclesiastical centre – so important that during the Wars of the Roses *(see p53)*, two battles were fought for it. In 1455 the Yorkists drove King Henry VI from the town and six years later the Lancastrians retook it.

One of the oldest surviving pubs in England

Exploring St Albans

Part of the appeal of this ancient and fascinating town, little more than an hour's drive from London, is that its 2,000-year history can be traced vividly by visiting a few sites within easy walking distance of one another. There is a large car park within the walls of the Roman city of Verulamium, between the museum and St Michael's Church and across the road from the excavated theatre. From there it is a pleasant lakeside walk across the park, passing more Roman sites, Ye Olde Fighting Cocks inn, the massive cathedral and the historic High Street. Marking the centre of the town, the High Street is lined with several Tudor buildings and there's a clock tower dating from 1412, from which the curfew bell used to ring at 4am in the morning and 8:30pm at night. The striking 19th-century Town Hall has been transformed into a history and cultural museum.

🏛 Verulamium

Just outside the city centre are the walls of Verulamium, one of the first British cities the Romans established after their invasion of Britain in AD 43. Boudica *(see p199)* razed it to the ground during her unsuccessful rebellion against the Romans in AD 62, but its position on Watling Street, an important trading route, meant that it was quickly rebuilt on an even larger scale and the city flourished until 410.

🏛 Verulamium Museum

St Michael's St. **Tel** 01727 751810. **Open** daily. **Closed** 1 Jan, 25 & 26 Dec. 🎟 🅿 ♿ 🅿 🅦 **stalbansmuseums.org.uk**

This excellent museum tells the story of the city, but its main attractions are the well-preserved Roman artifacts, notably some breathtaking mosaic floors, including one depicting the head of a sea god, and another of a scallop shell. Other finds include burial urns and lead coffins.

On the basis of excavated plaster fragments, a Roman room has been recreated, its walls painted in bright colours and geometric patterns.

Between here and St Albans Cathedral are a hypocaust with a mosaic, remnants of the ancient city wall and one of the original gates.

🍺 Ye Olde Fighting Cocks

Abbey Mill Lane. **Tel** 01727 869152. **Open** daily. ♿

Believed to be England's oldest surviving pub, Ye Olde Fighting Cocks is certainly, with its octagonal shape, one of the most unusual. It originated as the medieval dovecote of the old abbey and was moved here after the Dissolution *(see p355)*.

🏛 Roman Theatre

Bluehouse Hill. **Tel** 01727 835035. **Open** daily. **Closed** 1 Jan, 25 & 26 Dec. 🎟 🅿 🅦 **gorhamburyestate.co.uk**

Just across the road from the museum are the foundations of the open-air theatre, first built around AD 140 but enlarged several times. It is one of only six known to have been built in Roman Britain. Alongside it are traces of a row of Roman shops and a house, from which many of the museum's treasures – such as a bronze statuette of Venus – were excavated in the 1930s.

🏛 St Michael's Church

St Michael's. **Tel** 01727 835037. **Open** Apr–Sep: phone for details. ♿

This church was founded during the Saxon reign and is built partly with bricks taken from Verulamium, which by then was in decline. Numerous additions have been made since then, including a truly splendid Jacobean pulpit.

The church contains an early 17th-century monument to the statesman and writer Sir Francis Bacon; his father owned nearby Gorhambury, a large Tudor house, now in ruins.

A scallop shell, one of the mosaic floors at the Verulamium Museum

VISITORS' CHECKLIST

Practical Information
Hertfordshire. 141,000.
i Alban Arena Civic Centre
(01727 864511). Wed, Sat.
W enjoystalbans.com

Transport
Luton. St Albans City,
St Albans Abbey.

St Albans Cathedral
Sumpter Yard. **Tel** 01727 860780.
Open daily. 11:30am & 2:30pm.
W stalbanscathedral.org

This outstanding example of
medieval architecture has some
classic features, such as the 13th-
and 14th-century wall paintings
on the Norman piers.

It was begun in 793, when King
Offa of Mercia founded the abbey
in honour of St Alban, Britain's first
Christian martyr, put to death by
the Romans in the 3rd century for
sheltering a priest. The oldest parts,
which still stand, were first built in
1077 and are easily recognizable
as Norman by the round-headed
arches and windows. They form
part of the 84-m (276-ft) nave –
the longest in England.

The pointed arches further east
are Early English (1200s), while
the decorated work of the 14th
century was added when some
of the Norman arches collapsed.

Beyond the choir is the Shrine
of St Alban, covered by a red and
gold canopy and containing
remains of his shoulder-blade.
Monks kept guard from the
nearby Watching Loft.

It was at the cathedral that the
English barons drafted the *Magna
Carta* document *(see p52)*, which
King John was then forced to sign.

The splendour of the Gardens of the Rose in June

⑮ Gardens of the Rose

Chiswell Green, Hertfordshire.
Tel 08458 334344. St Albans
then bus. **Open** mid-Jun–early Aug,
but always call ahead.
W rnrs.org.uk

The 5-ha (12-acre) garden
of the Royal National Rose
Society, with over 30,000
plants and 1,700 varieties,
is at its peak in late June. The
gardens trace the history of
the flower as far back as the
white rose of York, the red
rose of Lancaster *(see p53)* and
the Rosa Mundi – named by
Henry II for his mistress Fair
Rosamond after she was
poisoned by Queen Eleanor
in 1177. Highlights include
roses in a garden setting,
demonstrating different styles
of planting.

⑯ Warner Bros. Studio Tour – The Making of Harry Potter

Leavesden, Hertfordshire.
Tel 03450 840900. Watford
Junction then shuttle bus. **Open** daily.
Closed 25 & 26 Dec.
W wbstudiotour.co.uk

Visitors to the Warner Bros. Studio
can see original scenery, costumes
and props from all eight Harry
Potter movies. Among the sets
are the iconic Great Hall and
Diagon Alley. The self-guided
tour offers glimpses into the off-
camera world of the film-makers,
including how animatronics and
green-screen effects brought to
life the monsters and marvels of
Harry's world. Children can even
ride broomsticks here. Tickets
must be booked in advance.

George Bernard Shaw

Although a controversial playwright the
Irish-born George Bernard Shaw (1856–
1950) was a man of settled habits. He
lived near St Albans in a house at Ayot
St Lawrence, now called Shaw's Corner,
for the last 44 years of his life, working
until his last weeks in a summer-house
at the bottom of his large garden. His
plays, combining wit with a powerful
political and social message, still
seem fresh today. One of the most
enduring is *Pygmalion* (1913), on
which the musical *My Fair Lady* is
based. The house and garden are
now a museum of his life and works.

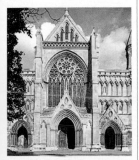
The imposing west side of
St Albans Cathedral

⑰ Touring the Thames

The Thames between Pangbourne and Eton is leafy and romantic and best seen by boat. If time is short travel by car: the road keeps close to the riverbank for much of the way. Swans glide gracefully below ancient bridges and elegant herons stand impassive at the river's edge. Huge beech trees overhang the banks, which are lined with fine houses, their gardens sloping to the water. This tranquil scene has inspired painters and writers through the ages.

⑥ Hambledon Mill
The white weather-boarded mill, which was operational until 1955, is one of the largest on the Thames as well as one of the oldest in origin. There are traces of the original 16th-century mill.

① Beale Park
The philanthropist Gilbert Beale (1868–1967) created a 10-ha (25-acre) park to preserve this beautiful stretch of river intact and breed endangered birds like owls, ornamental waterfowl, pheasants and peacocks.

⑤ Henley
This lovely old river town boasts houses and churches dating from the 15th and 16th centuries and an important regatta, first held in 1829 (see p70).

④ Sonning Bridge
The 18th-century bridge is made up of 11 brick arches of varying width.

② Pangbourne
Kenneth Grahame (1859–1932), author of *The Wind in the Willows*, lived here. Pangbourne was used as the setting by artists Ernest Shepard in 1908 and Arthur Rackham in 1951 to illustrate the book.

Tips for Drivers

Tour length: 50 miles (75 km).
Stopping-off points: The picturesque town of Henley has a large number of riverside pubs which will make good stops for lunch. If you are boating you can often moor your boat alongside the river bank. (See also pp636–7.)

③ Whitchurch Mill
This charming village, linked to Pangbourne by a Victorian toll bridge, has a picturesque church and one of the many disused watermills that once harnessed the power of this stretch of river.

⑦ Cookham

This is famous as the home of Stanley Spencer (1891–1959), one of Britain's leading 20th-century artists. The former Methodist chapel, which Spencer attended as a child, has been converted into a gallery that contains some of his paintings and equipment. This work, entitled *Swan Upping* (1914–19), recalls a Thames custom.

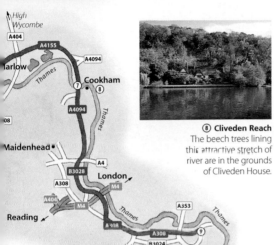

⑧ Cliveden Reach
The beech trees lining this attractive stretch of river are in the grounds of Cliveden House.

Key

━━ Tour route

━━ Other roads

0 kilometres   10

0 miles   5

⑨ Eton College
Founded by Henry VI in 1440, Eton is Britain's most famous public school. It has a superb Perpendicular chapel (1441) decorated with a series of very fine grisaille wall paintings (1479–88).

Boat Tours

In summer, scheduled river services run between Henley, Windsor, Runnymede and Marlow. Several companies operate from towns along the route. You can hire boats by the hour or the day or, for a longer tour, you can rent cabin cruisers and sleep on board *(see also p641)*. Ring Salter's Steamers on 01865 243421 for more information.

Salter Bros hire boats, moored at Henley

⑱ Windsor

Berkshire. 🅜 31,000. ⚏ 🅸 Thames St (01753 743900). 🆆 windsor.gov.uk

The town of Windsor is dwarfed by the enormous **castle** *(see pp240–41)* on the hill above – in fact its original purpose was to serve the castle's needs. The town is full of quaint Georgian shops, houses and inns. The most prominent building on the High Street is the **Guildhall** completed by Wren *(see p119)* in 1689, where Prince Charles and Camilla Parker-Bowles were married in 2005. **Eton College**, the most prestigious school in Britain, lies just a short walk away.

The huge 1,940-ha (4,800-acre) **Windsor Great Park** stretches from the castle three miles (5 km) to Snow Hill, where there is a statue of George III.

Environs

Four miles (7 km) to the south-east is the grassy meadow of **Runnymede**. This is one of England's most historic sites, where in 1215 King John was forced by his rebellious barons to sign the *Magna Carta (see p52)*, thereby limiting his royal powers. The dainty memorial pavilion at the top of the meadow was erected in 1957.

⌂ Eton College
Tel 01753 370100. **Open** for guided tours only; see website for details. 🆆 etoncollege.com

King John signing the *Magna Carta*, Runnymede

Windsor Castle

The oldest continuously inhabited royal residence in Britain, the castle, walled in timber, was built by William the Conqueror in around 1080 to guard the western approaches to London. He chose the site as it was on high ground and just a day's journey from his base in the Tower of London. Successive monarchs have made alterations that render it a remarkable monument to royalty's changing tastes. King George V's affection for it was shown when he chose Windsor for his family surname in 1917. The castle is used for state visits and banquets, and the Queen spends most of her weekends here.

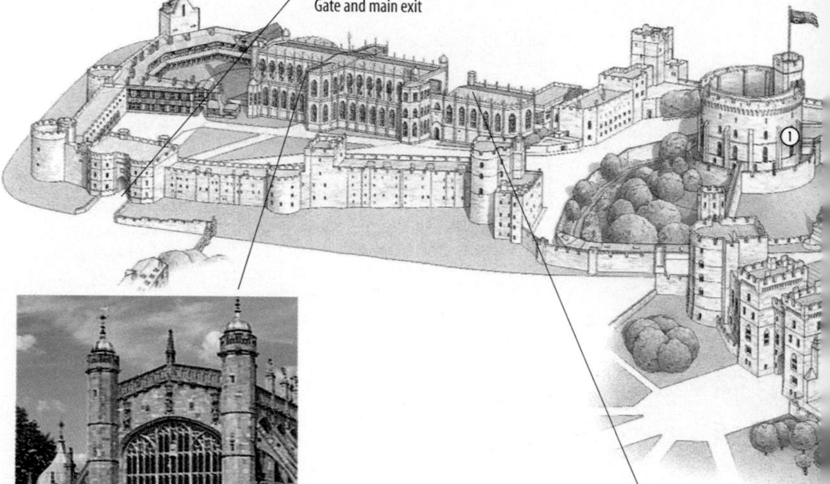

King Henry VIII
Gate and main exit

★ St George's Chapel
The architectural highlight of the castle, it was built between 1475 and 1528 and is one of England's outstanding Perpendicular Gothic churches. Ten monarchs are buried here.

Albert Memorial Chapel
First built in 1240, it was rebuilt in 1485 and finally converted into a memorial for Prince Albert in 1863.

KEY

① **The Round Tower** was first built by William the Conqueror. In 1170 it was rebuilt in stone by Henry II *(see p52)*. It now houses the Royal Archives and Photographic Collection.

② **Statue of Charles II**

③ **The Audience Chamber** is where the Queen greets her guests.

④ **The Queen's Ballroom**

⑤ **The Drawings Gallery** contains various pieces, including works by Holbein, Michelangelo and Leonardo da Vinci, though the artworks

and artists on display change from time to time.

⑥ **Queen Mary's Doll's House**, designed by Sir Edwin Lutyens, was given to Queen Mary in 1924. The wine cellar contains genuine vintage wine.

⑦ **A fire in 1992** destroyed the ceiling, roof and end wall of St George's Chapel, which has since been rebuilt.

⑧ **Brunswick Tower**

⑨ **The East Terrace Garden** was created by Sir Jeffry Wyatville for King George IV in the 1820s. It has views of the castle's east façade.

★ State Apartments
These rooms contain many treasures, such as this 18th-century bed in the King's State Bedchamber, hung in its present splendour for the visit in 1855 of Napoleon III.

VISITORS' CHECKLIST

Practical Information
Castle Hill. **Tel** 020 7766 7304.
Open 9:30am–5:30pm (Nov–Feb: to 4:15pm; last adm: 1 hr 15 mins before closing). **Closed** Good Fri, 25 & 26 Dec. 🅿 🚻 ♿ 🚻 daily services at St Georges Chapel. 📷
🌐 royalcollection.org.uk

Waterloo Chamber
This banqueting hall was created as part of Charles Long's brief for the remodelling of the castle in 1823.

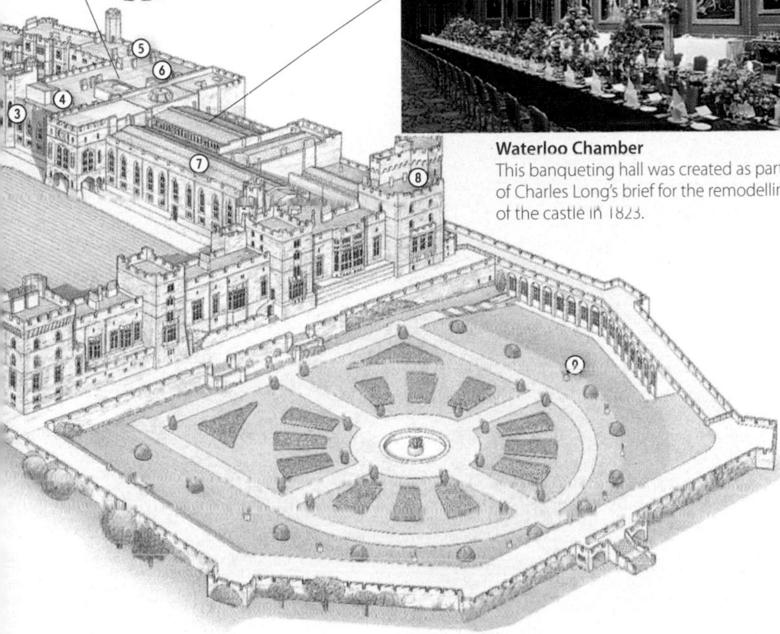

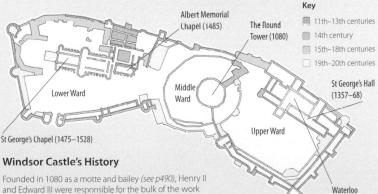

Key
🟦 11th–13th centuries
🟫 14th century
🟩 15th–18th centuries
⬜ 19th–20th centuries

Albert Memorial Chapel (1485)

The Round Tower (1080)

St George's Hall (1357–68)

Lower Ward

Middle Ward

Upper Ward

St George's Chapel (1475–1528)

Waterloo Chamber (1820s)

Windsor Castle's History

Founded in 1080 as a motte and bailey *(see p490)*, Henry II and Edward III were responsible for the bulk of the work until the castle was remodelled by George IV in 1823.

THE WEST COUNTRY

Introducing the
    West Country   244–249
Wessex   250–275
Devon and Cornwall   276–299

The West Country at a Glance

The West Country forms a long peninsula bounded by the Atlantic to the north and the English Channel to the south, tapering down to Land's End, mainland Britain's westernmost point. Whether exploring the great cities and cathedrals, experiencing the awesome solitude of the moors and their prehistoric monuments, or simply enjoying the miles of coastline and mild climate, this region has an enduring appeal for holiday-makers.

Exmoor's *(see pp254–5)* heather-clad moors and wooded valleys, grazed by wild ponies and red deer, lead down to some of Devon and Somerset's most dramatic cliffs and coves.

St Ives *(see p281)* has a branch of the Tate Gallery that shows modern works by artists associated with the area. Patrick Heron's bold coloured glass (1993) is on permanent display.

Lynton

Mi

Barnstaple

Appledore

Clovelly   Bideford

Tiverton

Bude

DEVON

Okehampton

Exeter

DEVON AND CORNWALL
(See pp276–99)

Padstow

Bodmin

Torq

Newquay   CORNWALL

Totnes   Brix

St Austell   Fowey   Plymouth

Dartmout

Truro

St Ives

Penzance   Falmouth

Helston

Dartmoor *(see pp298–9)* is a wilderness of great natural beauty covering an area of 365 sq miles (945 sq km). Stone clapper bridges, picturesque villages and weathered granite tors punctuate the landscape.

◀ Summer rainstorm over Exmoor National Park, viewed from Selworthy Beacon

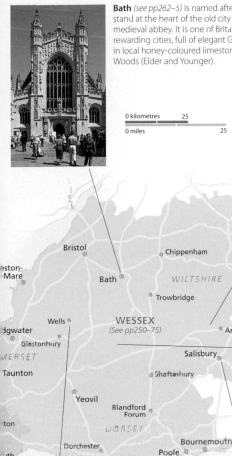

Bath *(see pp262–5)* is named after the Roman baths that stand at the heart of the old city next to the splendid medieval abbey. It is one of Britain's liveliest and most rewarding cities, full of elegant Georgian terraces, built in local honey-coloured limestone by the two John Woods (Elder and Younger).

```
0 kilometres    25
0 miles             25
```

Stonehenge *(see pp266–7)*, the world-famous prehistoric monument, was built in several stages from around 3000 BC. Moving and erecting its massive stones was an extraordinary feat for its time. It is likely that this magical stone circle was a place of worship to the sun.

Bristol
Chippenham
eston-Mare
Bath
WILTSHIRE
Trowbridge
Wells
WESSEX
(See pp250–75)
Amesbury
dgwater
Glastonbury
Salisbury
MERSET
Taunton
Shaftesbury
Yeovil
Blandford Forum
ton
DORSET
Bournemouth
Dorchester
Poole
uth
Weymouth
Swanage

Stourhead garden *(see pp270–71)* was inspired by the paintings of the French artists Claude and Poussin. Created in the 18th century, the garden is itself a work of art. Contrived vistas, light and shade and a mixture of landscape and gracious buildings, such as the Neo-Classical Pantheon at its centre, are vital to the overall effect.

Wells *(see pp256–7)* is a charming town nestling at the foot of the Mendip Hills. It is famous for its exquisite three-towered cathedral with an ornate west façade, featuring an array of statues. Alongside stand the moated Bishop's Palace and the 15th-century Vicar's Close.

Salisbury's *(see pp268–9)* cathedral with its soaring spire was the inspiration for one of John Constable's best-loved paintings. The picturesque Cathedral Close has a number of fine medieval buildings.

Coastal Wildlife

The long and varied West Country coastline, ranging from the stark, granite cliffs of Land's End to the pebble-strewn stretch of Chesil Beach, is matched with an equally diverse range of wildlife. Beaches are scattered with colourful shells, while rock pools form miniature marine habitats teeming with life. Caves are used by larger creatures, such as grey seals, and cliffs provide nest sites for birds. In the spring and early summer, an astonishing range of plants grow on the foreshore and cliffs, which can be seen at their best from the Southwest Coastal Path *(see p40)*. The plants in turn attract numerous moths and butterflies.

Cliff-tops of Land's End with safe ledges for nesting birds

Chesil Beach is an unusual ridge of pebbles *(see p272)* stretching 18 miles (29 km) along the Dorset coast. The bank was created by storms and the pebbles increase in size from northwest to southeast due to varying strengths of coastal currents. The bank encloses a lagoon called the Fleet, habitat of the Abbotsbury swans, as well as a large number of wildfowl.

The Painted Lady, often seen on cliff-top coastal plants, migrates to Britain in the spring.

High tides wash up driftwood and shells.

Clifftop turf contains many species of wild flowers.

Thrift, in hummocks of honey-scented flowers, is a familiar sight on cliff ledges in spring.

Yellowhammers are to be seen perched on clifftop bushes.

Marram grass roots help hold back sand against wind erosion.

Grey seals come on land to give birth in autumn. They can be spotted on remote beaches.

A Beachcomber's Guide

The best time to observe the natural life of the seashore is when the tide begins to roll back, before the scavenging seagulls pick up the stranded crabs, fish and sandhoppers, and the seaweed dries up. Much plant and marine life can be found in the secure habitat provided by rock pools.

Durdle Door was formed by waves continually eroding the weaker chalk layers of this cliff *(see p274)* in Dorset, leaving the stronger oolite to create a striking arch, known in geology as an eyelet.

Collecting Shells

Most of the edible molluscs, such as scallops and cockles, are classed as bivalves; others, such as whelks and limpets, are classed as gastropods.

Great scallop

Common cockle

Common whelk

Common limpet

Seaweed, such as bladder wrack, can resemble coral or lichen when in water.

Rocks are colonized by clusters of barnacles, mussels and limpets.

Oystercatchers have a distinctive orange beak. They hunt along the shore, feeding on all kinds of shellfish.

Starfish can be aggressive predators of shellfish. The light-sensitive tips of their tentacles help them to "see" the way.

Mussels are widespread and can be harvested for food.

Rock pools teem with crabs, mussels, shrimps and plant life.

The Velvet Crab, often found hiding in seaweed, is covered with fine downy hair all over its shell.

Grey mullet, when newly hatched, can often be seen in rock pools.

West Country Gardens

Gardeners have long been attracted to the West Country. Its mild climate is perfect for growing tender and exotic plants, many of which were brought from Asia in the 19th century. As a result, the region has some of England's finest and most varied gardens, covering the whole sweep of garden styles and history *(see pp30–31)*, from the clipped formality of Elizabethan Montacute to the colourful and crowded cottage-garden style of East Lambrook Manor.

Lanhydrock's *(see p288)* clipped yews and low box hedges frame a blaze of colourful annuals.

Trewithen *(see p285)* is renowned for its rare camellias, rhododendrons and magnolias, grown from seed collected in Asia. The huge garden is at its most impressive in March and June.

Cotehele *(see p297)* has a lovely lush valley garden.

Lost Gardens of Heligan *(see p285)* are glorious gardens recreated from 19th-century decay.

Trelissick *(see p285)* has memorable views over the Fal Estuary through shrub-filled woodland.

Glendurgan *(see p285)* is a plant-lover's paradise set in a steep, sheltered valley.

DEVON AND CORNWALL *(See pp276–99)*

Lynton
Barnsta
Bideford
Bude
Bodmin
St Austell
Truro
Plymouth
Tot

Mount Edgcumbe *(see p296)* preserves its 18th-century French, Italian and English gardens.

Penzance
Falmouth
Helston

Trengwainton *(see p280)* has a fine stream garden, whose banks are crowded with moisture-loving plants, beneath a lush canopy of New Zealand tree ferns.

Overbecks (near Salcombe) enjoys a spectacular site overlooking the Salcombe Estuary. There are secret gardens, terraces and rocky dells.

Creative Gardening

Gardens are not simply collections of plants; they rely for much of their appeal on man-made features. Whimsical topiary, ornate architecture, fanciful statuary and mazes help to create an atmosphere of adventure or pure escapism. The many gardens dotted around the West Country offer engaging examples of the vivid imagination of designers.

Mazes were created in medieval monasteries to teach patience and persistence. This laurel maze at Glendurgan was planted in 1833.

Fountains and flamboyant statuary have adorned gardens since Roman times. Such eye-catching embellishments add poetic and Classical touches to the design of formal gardens, such as Mount Edgcumbe.

Knightshayes Court *(see p293)* is designed as a series of formal garden "rooms", planted for scent, colour or seasonal effect.

East Lambrook Manor (near South Petherton) is a riot of colours, as old-fashioned cottage plants grow without restraint.

Bristol

Marlborough

Weston-Super-Mare

Bath

WESSEX
(See pp250–75)

Glastonbury

Bridgwater

Taunton

Salisbury

Shaftesbury

Yeovil

Stourhead *(see pp270–71)* is a magnificent example of 18th-century landscape gardening.

Honiton

Bournemouth

eter

Poole

Athelhampton's *(see p273)* gardens make use of fountains, statues, pavilions and columnar yews.

Weymouth

Swanage

quay

Montacute House *(see p272)* has pavilions and a centuries-old yew hedge, and is renowned for its collection of old roses.

0 kilometres   25

0 miles   25

Parnham (near Beaminster), like many West Country gardens, has several parts devoted to different themes. Here conical yews complement the formality of the stone balustrade; elsewhere there are woodland, kitchen, shade and Mediterranean gardens.

Many garden buildings are linked by an element of fantasy; while country houses had to conform to everyday practicalities, the design of many smaller buildings gave more scope for imagination. This fanciful Elizabethan pavilion on the forecourt at Montacute House was first and foremost decorative, but sometimes served as a lodging house.

Topiary can be traced back to the Greeks. Since that time the sculpting of trees into unusual, often eccentric shapes has been developed over the centuries. The yew topiary of 1920s Knightshayes features a fox being chased by a pack of hounds. The figures form a delightful conceit and come into their own in winter when little else is in leaf.

WESSEX

Wiltshire · Somerset · Dorset

The Wessex region stretches from the Somerset coast, bordered by the Bristol Channel in the north to the Dorset coast and the English Channel in the south. Between the long sandy beaches of Bournemouth and the rugged expanses of Exmoor are the apple orchards of Somerset, rounded heaths of Dorset and historic cities of Bristol and Bath.

This sleepy rural region has a rich history. Three thousand years ago, the downs of the Salisbury Plain were home to the settlers who created the mysterious stone circles at Stonehenge and Avebury and other prehistoric sites. Later, the Celts founded strongholds such as Dorchester's vast Maiden Castle, followed by the Romans who built England's first spa resort at Bath. In the 6th century the area became a stronghold of Celtic resistance against the Saxons. However, the Anglo-Saxon King Alfred was the first to unite the area as the kingdom of Wessex.

In the early 1700s, Bristol, the area's largest city, became a transatlantic port, and the grand buildings bear witness to the wealth acquired from the subsequent slave, tobacco and wine trades. At the same time, the building of the Georgian terraces and circuses of Bath made the town supremely fashionable. George III's regular visits to Weymouth set it on the map as a seaside resort, and with the introduction of the railway line in the 19th century, Bournemouth became popular. The long Dorset beaches, particularly around Studland, and the waters and natural harbours of the Solent appeal to summer visitors and sailors alike. Inland are the glorious medieval cathedrals of Wells and Salisbury and the mansions of later aristocrats set in stunning gardens and parks, such as at Stourhead, Montacute and Longleat, with its own safari park.

Somerset is known for its cider orchards and Cheddar cheese, which is aged in the caves of the dramatic Cheddar Gorge.

Abbey Mill, set on the banks of the river at Bradford-on-Avon, Wiltshire

◀ A winding road through Cheddar Gorge

Exploring Wessex

From the rolling chalk plains around Stonehenge to the rocky cliffs of Cheddar Gorge and the heather-covered uplands of Exmoor, Wessex is a scenically varied microcosm of England. Reflecting the underlying geology, each part of Wessex contributes its own distinctive architecture, with the honey-coloured limestone buildings of Bath giving way to the mellow brick and timber of Salisbury and the thatched flint-and-chalk cottages of the Dorset landscape.

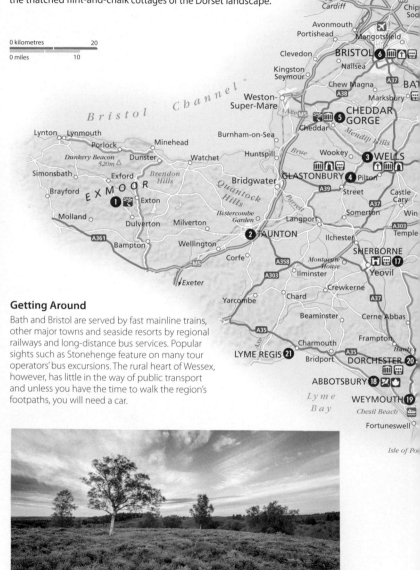

0 kilometres   20

0 miles   10

Getting Around

Bath and Bristol are served by fast mainline trains, other major towns and seaside resorts by regional railways and long-distance bus services. Popular sights such as Stonehenge feature on many tour operators' bus excursions. The rural heart of Wessex, however, has little in the way of public transport and unless you have the time to walk the region's footpaths, you will need a car.

Heather in bloom in the New Forest

For hotels and restaurants in this area see pp564–6 and pp589–91

Sights at a Glance

1. *Exmoor pp254–5*
2. Taunton
3. *Wells pp256–7*
4. Glastonbury
5. *Cheddar Gorge p258*
6. *Bristol pp260–61*
7. *Bath pp262–5*
8. Bradford-on-Avon
9. Corsham
10. Lacock
11. *Stonehenge pp266–7*
12. Avebury
13. *Salisbury pp268–9*
14. Longleat House
15. *Stourhead pp270–71*
16. Shaftesbury
17. Sherborne
18. Abbotsbury
19. Weymouth
20. Dorchester
21. Lyme Regis
22. Corfe Castle
23. Isle of Purbeck
24. Poole
25. Wimborne Minster
26. Bournemouth

Key

━━━ Motorway

━━━ Major road

━━━ Secondary road

┅┅┅ Minor road

━━━ Scenic route

━╍━ Main railway

─── Minor railway

△ Summit

The Cobb, the iconic harbour wall at Lyme Regis, Dorset

For keys to symbols

❶ Exmoor National Park

The majestic cliffs plunging into the Bristol Channel along Exmoor's northern coast are interrupted by lush, wooded valleys carrying rivers from the high moorland down to sheltered fishing coves. Inland, wild rolling hills are grazed by sturdy Exmoor ponies, horned sheep and the local wild red deer. Buzzards are also a common sight wheeling over the bracken-clad terrain looking for prey. For walkers, Exmoor offers 1,000 km (620 miles) of wonderful public paths and varied, dramatic scenery, while the tamer perimeters of the National Park offer less energetic attractions – everything from traditional seaside entertainments to picturesque villages and ancient churches.

Looking east along the Southwest Coastal Path

Heddon's Mouth
A 3-km (2-mile) walk through woodland and meadows leads down to this attractive point on the coast, where the River Heddon meets the sea.

The Valley of Rocks
A short walk west of Lynton, the Valley of Rocks is a dry gorge some 152 m (500 ft) above the sea. It is home to a series of sandstone outcrops, eroded into fantastical shapes, characterize this natural gorge.

KEY

① **The village of Simonsbath** is a good starting point for walkers.

② **Combe Martin** is home to the Pack o'Cards Inn *(see p292)*.

③ **Parracombe's church** has a Georgian interior with boxed pews, a wooden pulpit and a carved screen.

④ **Watersmeet**, set in a beautifully wooded valley, is spot where the East Lyn Hoar Oak Water join

together in a tumbling cascade. There is also a tearoom with a pretty garden.

⑤ **Oare's church** commemorates the writer R D Blackmore, whose romantic novel *Lorna Doone* (1869) is set in the area.

⑥ **Culbone church**, a mere 10.6 m (35 ft) in length, claims to be Britain's smallest parish church.

⑦ **Selworthy** is a picturesque village of thatched cottages.

⑧ **Minehead** is a major resort built around a pretty quay. A West Somerset Railway from here all the way to Bishop's Lydeard.

⑨ **Dunster** is a medieval village with an ancient castle and an unusual octagonal Yarn Market (c.1609), where local cloth was once sold.

⑩ **Tarr Steps** is an ancient "clapper" bridge built of stone slabs.

and restaurants in this area see pp564–6 and pp589–91

Lynmouth
Above the charming fishing village of Lynmouth stands hilltop Lynton. The two villages *(see p292)* are connected by a cliff railway. Since the early 19th century, this water-powered funicular railway has shuttled 263 m (862 ft) up a steep bank. The short ride offers fabulous views of the spectacular Jurassic Coast.

Porlock
This flower-filled village has a historic charm, with winding streets, thatched houses and a lovely old church.

Dunkery Beacon
Rising to a height of 519 m (1,703 ft), the summit of Dunkery Beacon is Exmoor's highest point. On a clear day, the views stretch as far as Wales to the north and Dartmoor to the south.

For keys to symbols *see back flap*

Key
— Main road
═ Secondary road
═ Minor road
- - - South West Coast Path
△ Peak

❷ Taunton

Somerset. 🗺 67,000. 🚊 🚌 ℹ️
Market House, Fore St (01823 340470).
🛒 Thu (farmers'). 🌐 visitsomerset.
co.uk

Taunton lies at the heart of a fertile region famous for its apples and cider, but it was the wool industry that financed the huge church of **St Mary Magdalene** (1488–1514) with its glorious tower. Taunton's **castle** was the setting for the notorious Bloody Assizes of 1685, when "Hanging" Judge Jeffreys dispensed harsh retribution to those involved in an uprising against King James II. The castle now houses the **Museum of Somerset**. A star exhibit is the Roman mosaic from a villa at Low Ham.

Environs
Hestercombe Garden is one of Sir Edwin Lutyens and Gertrude Jekyll's great masterpieces.

🏛 Museum of Somerset
Castle Green. **Tel** 01823 255088.
Open Tue–Sat & bank hol Mons. ♿
📷 🌐 museumofsomerset.org.uk

🌷 Hestercombe Garden
Cheddon Fitzpaine. **Tel** 01823 413923.
Open daily. **Closed** 25 Dec. 📷 ♿
🛒 📷 🌐 hestercombe.com

❸ Wells

Somerset. 🗺 11,000. 🚌 ℹ️ Cathedral
Green (01749 671770). 🛒 Wed, Sat.
🌐 wellssomerset.com

Wells is named after St Andrew's Well, the sacred spring that bubbles up from the ground near the 13th-century **Bishop's Palace**, residence of the Bishop of Bath and Wells. A tranquil city, Wells is famous for its magnificent cathedral, which was begun in the late 1100s. Penniless Porch, where beggars once received alms, leads from the bustling marketplace to the calm of the cathedral close. **Wells & Mendip Museum** has prehistoric finds from nearby Wookey Hole and other caves.

Somerset Cider

Somerset is one of the few English counties where real farmhouse cider, known as "scrumpy", is still made using the traditional methods. Cider once formed part of the farm labourer's wages and local folklore has it that various unsavoury additives, such as iron nails, were added to give strength. Cidermaking can be seen at **Sheppy's** farm, on the A38 near Taunton.

Scrumpy cider

Wells Cathedral and the Bishop's Palace

Wells has maintained much of its medieval character with its cathedral, Bishop's Palace and other buildings around the close forming a harmonious group. The cathedral was begun in the late 1100s, and is famous for its elaborate West Front and the "scissor arches" installed in 1338 to support the tower.

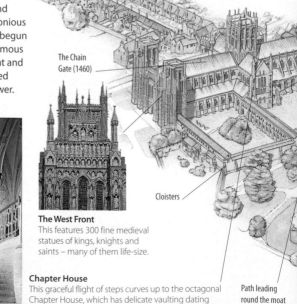

The Vicars' Close was built in the 14th century for the Vicars' Choir. It is one of the oldest complete streets in Europe.

The Chain Gate (1460)

Cloisters

Path leading round the moat

The West Front
This features 300 fine medieval statues of kings, knights and saints – many of them life-size.

Chapter House
This graceful flight of steps curves up to the octagonal Chapter House, which has delicate vaulting dating from 1306. The 32 ribs fanning from the central column create a beautiful palm-tree effect.

Environs
To the northeast of Wells lies the impressive cave complex of **Wookey Hole**, which has a wide range of popular attractions.

🏛 **Wells & Mendip Museum**
8 Cathedral Green. **Tel** 01749 673477. **Open** Mon–Sat. **Closed** 24 Dec–2 Jan. 🅿 ♿ limited. 📷 🌐 **wellsmuseum. org.uk**

🞕 **Wookey Hole**
Off A371. **Tel** 01749 672243. **Open** daily. **Closed** Dec & Jan: Mon–Fri. 🅿 🍴 🛍 📷 🌐 **wookey.co.uk**

❹ Glastonbury

Somerset. 🚗 9,000. 🚌 ℹ Tribunal, High St (01458 832954). 🛒 Tue. 🌐 **glastonburytic.co.uk**

Shrouded in Arthurian myth and rich in mystical association, the town of Glastonbury was once one of the most important destinations for pilgrims in England.

Glastonbury Abbey, left in ruins in 1539 after the Dissolution

Now thousands flock here for the annual rock festival *(see p67)* and for the summer solstice on Midsummer's Day (21 June).

Over the years history and legend have become intertwined, and the monks who founded **Glastonbury Abbey**, around AD 700, found it profitable to encourage the association between Glastonbury and the mythical "Blessed Isle" known as Avalon – alleged to be the last resting place of King Arthur and the Holy Grail *(see p289)*.

The great abbey was left in ruins after the Dissolution of the Monasteries *(see p355)*. Even so, some magnificent relics survive, including parts of the vast Norman abbey church, the unusual Abbot's Kitchen, with its octagonal roof, and the Victorian farmhouse, now the **Somerset Rural Life Museum**.

In the abbey grounds is a hawthorn grown from the famous Glastonbury thorn which is said to have miraculously sprouted from the staff of St Joseph of Arimathea. According to myth, he was sent around AD 60 to convert England to Christianity. The English hawthorn flowers at Christmas and in May.

The **Lake Village Museum** has some interesting finds from the Iron Age settlements that once fringed the marshlands around **Glastonbury Tor**. Visible for miles around, the Tor is a hill crowned by St Michael's Tower. The tower is all that remains of a 14th-century church that once stood here.

🏛 **Somerset Rural Life Museum**
Chilkwell St. **Open** Tue–Sun (Nov–Easter: Tue–Sat & pub hols). ♿ 🛍 📷 🌐 **somersetrurallifemuseum.org.uk**

🏛 **Lake Village Museum**
Tribunal, High St. **Tel** 01458 832954. **Open** Mon–Sat. **Closed** 23 Dec–3 Jan. 🅿 📷

Bishops' Tombs
The tombs of past bishops circle the chancel. This marble tomb, in the south aisle is that of Bishop Lord Arthur Hervey, who was Bishop of Bath and Wells 1869 to 1894.

VISITORS' CHECKLIST

Practical Information
The Close. **Tel** 01749 988111. **Open** daily. ♿ limited. Bishop's Palace: **Open** early Jan–late Dec: daily. 🅿 🍴 ♿ 📷 🌐 **wellscathedral.org.uk**

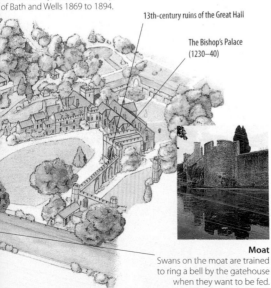
13th-century ruins of the Great Hall

The Bishop's Palace (1230–40)

Moat
Swans on the moat are trained to ring a bell by the gatehouse when they want to be fed.

❺ Cheddar Gorge

Described as a "deep frightful chasm" by novelist Daniel Defoe in 1724, Cheddar Gorge is a spectacular ravine cut through the Mendip plateau by fast-flowing streams during the interglacial phases of the last Ice Age. Cheddar has given its name to a rich cheese that originates from here and is now produced worldwide. The caves in the gorge provide the perfect environment of constant temperature and high humidity for storing and maturing the cheese.

VISITORS' CHECKLIST

Practical Information
On B3135, Somerset. Cheddar
Caves & Gorge: **Tel** 01934 742343.
Open daily. **Closed** 24 & 25 Dec.
🅿 entry with a Gorge & Caves
day ticket only. 🔲 🔲 🔲 🔲
W cheddargorge.co.uk
Cheddar Gorge Cheese Co.:
Tel 01934 742810. **Open** daily.
🔲 🔲 🔲 W cheddar
gorgecheeseco.co.uk

Transport
🚌 from Wells and Weston-super-Mare.

The Cheddar Gorge Cheese Company is the only working Cheddar dairy in Cheddar. Visitors can see Cheddar being made, and taste and buy cheese in the store.

The B3135 road winds round the base of the 3-mile (5-km) gorge.

The gorge is a narrow, winding ravine with limestone rocks rising almost vertically on either side to a height of 140 m (460 ft).

"Cheddar Man", a 9,000-year-old skeleton, is on display at Cheddar Caves and Gorge. The museum looks at the prehistoric world of our ancestors.

A footpath follows the top of the gorge on its southern edge.

Gough's Cave is noted for its cathedral-like proportions.

Cox's Cave contains unusually shaped stalactites and stalagmites.

A flight of 274 steps leads to the top of the gorge.

Lookout Tower has far-reaching views over the area to the south and west.

The rare Cheddar Pink is among the astonishing range of plant and animal life harboured in the rocks.

Bristol

See pp260–61.

❼ Bath

See pp262–5.

Typical Cotswold-stone architecture in Bradford-on-Avon

❽ Bradford-on-Avon

Wiltshire. 🅰 9,500. 🚆 🅸 St Margaret St (01225 865797). 🛒 Thu.
🅆 bradfordonavon.co.uk

This lovely Cotswold-stone town is full of flamboyant houses built by wealthy wool and cloth merchants in the 17th and 18th centuries. One fine Georgian example is **Abbey House**, on Church Street. Further along, **St Laurence Church** is a remarkably complete Saxon building founded in the 8th century *(see p51)*. Converted to a school and cottage in the 1100s, it was rediscovered in the 19th century when a vicar recognized the characteristic cross-shaped roof.

At one end of the medieval **Town Bridge** is a small stone cell, built as a chapel in the 13th century but later used as a lock-up for 17th-century vagrants. A short walk away, near converted mill buildings and a stretch of the Kennet and Avon Canal, is the spectacular 14th-century **Tithe Barn** *(see p36)*. There are several teashops in the town and canoe trips down the canal are popular.

🏚 **Tithe Barn**
Pound Lane. **Open** daily. **Closed** 25 & 26 Dec. ♿ EH

❾ Corsham

Wiltshire. 🅰 13,000. 🅸 31 High St (01249 714660). 🅆 **corsham.gov.uk**

The streets of Corsham are lined with stately Georgian houses in Cotswold stone. **St Bartholomew's Church** has an elegant spire and the lovely carved alabaster tomb (1960) of Lady Methuen, whose family founded Methuen publishers. The family acquired **Corsham Court** in 1745 with its picture gallery and a remarkable collection of Flemish, Italian and English paintings, including works by Van Dyck, Lippi and Reynolds. Peacocks wander through the grounds, adding their colour and elegance to the façade of the Elizabethan mansion.

🏚 **Corsham Court**
off A4. **Tel** 01249 701610. **Open** Apr–Sep: Tue–Thu pm, Sat & Sun pm; Oct–Mar: Sat & Sun pm. **Closed** Dec. 🎟
♿ 🅆 corsham-court.co.uk

Old historical cemetery in the churchyard at Corsham

❿ Lacock

Wiltshire. 🅰 1,000.

Maintained in its pristine state by the National Trust, the picturesque village of Lacock has provided the backdrop to numerous costume dramas, including *Downton Abbey*. The meandering River Avon forms the boundary to the north side of the churchyard, while humorous stone figures look down from **St Cyriac Church**. Inside the 15th-century church is the splendid Renaissance-style tomb of Sir William Sharington (1495–1553). He acquired **Lacock Abbey** after the Dissolution of the

Monasteries *(see p355)*, but it was a later owner, John Ivory Talbot, who had the buildings remodelled in the Gothic Revival style, in vogue in the early 18th century. The abbey is famous for the window (in the south gallery) from which his descendant William Henry Fox Talbot, an early pioneer of photography, took his first picture in 1835. A 16th-century barn at the abbey gates has been converted to the **Fox Talbot Museum**, which has displays on his experiments.

Environs
Designed by Robert Adam *(see p32)* in 1769, **Bowood House** includes the laboratory where Joseph Priestley discovered oxygen in 1774, and a rich collection of sculpture, costumes, jewellery and paintings. Italian-ate gardens surround the house while the lake-filled grounds, landscaped by "Capability" Brown *(see p30)*, contain a Doric temple, grotto, cascade and an adventure playground.

🏚 **Lacock Abbey**
Lacock. **Tel** 01249 730459.
Open daily (Nov–Feb: Sat & Sun).
Closed Good Fri. 🎟 ♿ limited. 🗐
📷 NT 🅆 nationaltrust.org.uk

🏛 **Fox Talbot Museum**
Lacock. **Tel** 01249 730459. **Open** daily.
Closed 1 Jan, 25 Dec. 🎟 ♿ NT

🏚 **Bowood House**
Derry Hill, nr Calne. **Tel** 01249 812102.
Open Apr–Oct: daily. 🎟 ♿ limited.
🎟 🗐 📷 🅆 bowood.org

William Henry Fox Talbot (1800–77)

⑥ Bristol

It was in 1497 that John Cabot sailed from Bristol on his historic voyage to North America. The city, at the mouth of the Avon, became the main British port for transatlantic trade, pioneering the era of the ocean-going steam liner with the construction of Brunel's SS *Great Britain*. The city flourished as a major trading centre, growing rich on the distribution of wine, tobacco and, in the 17th century, slaves.

Because of its docks and aero-engine factories, Bristol was heavily bombed during World War II. In 2008, a multimillion-pound development programme was completed with the opening of Cabot Circus, a vast shopping centre. The old dock area has been brought back to life with bars, cafés, restaurants and art galleries lining the waterside.

Christmas Steps, a historic lane in Bristol's city centre

Exploring Bristol

The oldest part of the city lies around Broad, King and Corn streets, known as the Old Quarter. The lively St Nicholas covered market, part of which occupies the **Corn Exchange**, was built by John Wood the Elder *(see p262)* in 1743. Outside are the Bristol Nails, four bronze 16th- to 17th-century pedestals which Bristol merchants used as tables when paying for goods – hence the expression "to pay on the nail". **St John's Gate**, at the head of Broad Street, has medieval statues of Bristol's two mythical founders, King Brennus

Bow of Brunel's SS *Great Britain*

and King Benilus. Between Lewins Mead and Colston Street, **Christmas Steps** is a steep lane lined with specialist shops and cafés. The **Chapel of the Three Kings** at the top was founded in 1504.

A group of buildings on the cobbled King Street include the 17th-century timber-framed **Llandoger Trow** inn. It is here that Daniel Defoe is said to have met Alexander Selkirk, whose true-life island exile served as the inspiration for Defoe's novel *Robinson Crusoe* (1719). Just up from here is the **Theatre Royal**, built in 1766 and home to the famous Bristol Old Vic.

Not far away, the renowned **Arnolfini** Arts Centre, on Narrow Quay, is a showcase for contemporary art, drama, dance and cinema.

On the Harbourside, **At-Bristol** (www.at-bristol.org.uk) combines an exciting, interactive science centre with a planetarium.

Above the Harbourside, elegant **Clifton** revels in ornate Regency crescents. **Clifton Observatory**, fitted with a camera obscura in 1829, gives panoramic views over the steep Avon Gorge and Suspension Bridge. **Bristol Zoo Gardens** houses over 400 exotic and endangered species set in stunning gardens.

Interior of the 14th-century church St Mary Redcliffe

⬆ St Mary Redcliffe

Redcliffe Way. **Tel** 0117 231 0060. **Open** daily. 📷 by arrangement. ♿ 🖥 🌐 **stmaryredcliffe.co.uk**

This magnificent 14th-century church was claimed by Queen Elizabeth I to be "the fairest in England". The church owes much to the generosity of William Canynge the Elder and Younger, both famous mayors of Bristol. Inscriptions on the tombs of merchants and sailors tell of lives devoted to trade. Look out for the Bristol maze roof boss in the north aisle.

🏛 M-Shed

Princes Wharf, Harbourside. **Tel** 0117 352 6600. **Open** Tue–Sun. 📷 temp exhibits only. ♿ 🖥 📷 🌐 **bristolmuseums.org.uk**

This museum in a 1950s harbourside transit shed focuses on the city's history. The story is told through film, photographs, objects and personal accounts. Temporary exhibitions take place regularly. There are also several historic vessels moored in the Wharf.

🏛 Brunel's SS Great Britain

Gas Ferry Rd. **Tel** 0117 926 0680. **Open** daily. **Closed** 24 & 25 Dec. 📷 ticket valid for one year. 📷 by appt. ♿ 🖥 📷 🌐 **ssgreatbritain.org**

Designed by Isambard Kingdom Brunel, this was the world's first large iron passenger ship. Launched in 1843, she travelled 32 times round the world before being abandoned in the Falkland Islands in 1886. The ship, set in a glass sea, has been imaginatively restored.

🔯 Bristol Cathedral

College Green. **Tel** 0117 926 4879.
Open daily. Donation. 🅿️ ♿ limited.
📧 W bristol-cathedral.co.uk

Bristol's cathedral, begun in
1140, took a long time to build.
Between 1298 and 1330 the
inventive choir was rebuilt;
the transepts and tower were
finished in 1515; and the Victorian
architect G E Street built the nave
in the 1860s. Humorous medieval
carvings abound – a snail crawl-
ing across the stone foliage in
the Berkeley Chapel, musical
monkeys in the Elder Lady
Chapel. There is also a fine set of
wooden misericords in the choir.

🏛 Georgian House

7 Great George St. **Tel** 0117 921
1362. **Open** Apr–Dec: Sat–Tue.
W bristolmuseums.org.uk

Life in a wealthy 1790s Bristol
merchant's house is reimagined
in rooms including the drawing
room and the servants' area.

🏛 Bristol Museum and Art Gallery

Queen's Rd. **Tel** 0117 922 3571. **Open**
Tue–Sun. **Closed** 24 & 25 Dec. ♿ ltd.
📧 📷 W bristolmuseums.org.uk

Varied collections include
Egyptology, dinosaur fossils,
Roman tableware, Chinese glass
and a fine collection of European
paintings with works by Renoir
and Bellini. Bristol artists include
Sir Thomas Lawrence, Francis
Danby and the celebrated
graffiti artist Banksy.

🌉 Clifton Suspension Bridge

ℹ️ Leigh Woods. **Tel** 0117 974 4664.
Open 10am–5pm daily. **Closed** 1 Jan,
24 & 25 Dec. 🅿️ ♿ 📷 W clifton
bridge.org.uk

The defining symbol of Bristol,
the Clifton Suspension Bridge
was designed by Isambard
Kingdom Brunel, who won
the commission at the age
of 23. Completed in 1864, the

bridge spans the dramatic
Avon Gorge from Clifton to
Leigh Woods. The visitor centre
provides an interesting and
entertaining background to
its history.

The impressive Clifton Suspension Bridge, crossing the Avon Gorge and River Avon

Bristol City Centre

① St Mary Redcliffe
② M-Shed
③ Brunel's SS *Great Britain*
④ Bristol Cathedral
⑤ Georgian House
⑥ Bristol Museum and Art Gallery

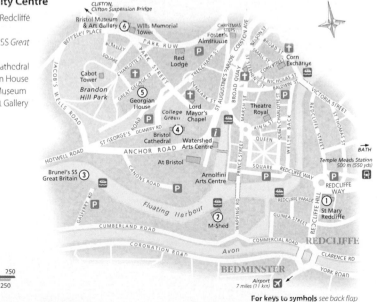

0 metres   250
0 yards   250

For keys to symbols *see back flap*

❼ Street-by-Street: Bath

Bath owes its magnificent Georgian townscape to the bubbling pool of water at the heart of the Roman Baths. The Romans transformed Bath into England's first spa resort and it regained fame as a spa town in the 18th century. At this time the two John Woods (Elder and Younger), both architects, designed the city's Palladian-style buildings. Many houses bear plaques recording the numerous famous people who have resided here.

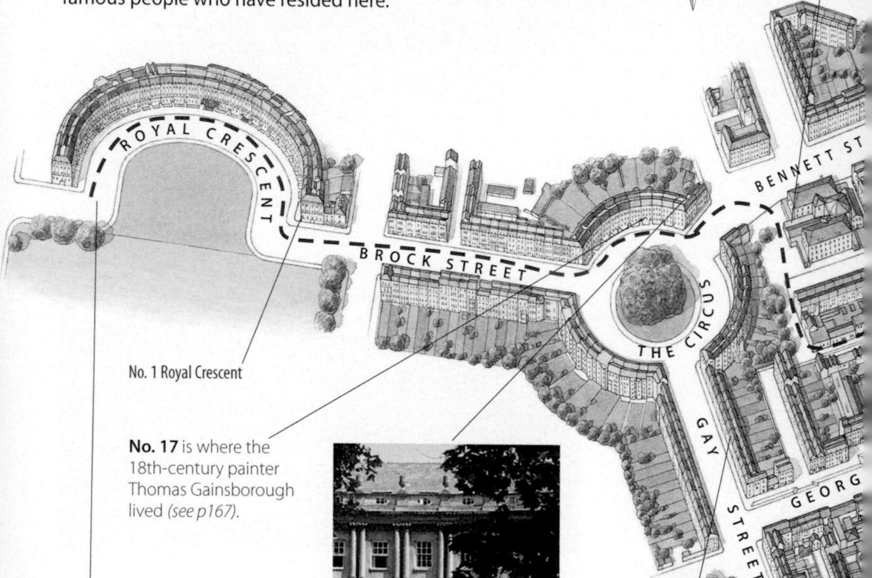

Assembly Rooms and Fashion Museum

ROYAL CRESCENT

BROCK STREET

BENNETT ST

THE CIRCUS

GAY STREET

GEORG

No. 1 Royal Crescent

No. 17 is where the 18th-century painter Thomas Gainsborough lived *(see p167).*

The Circus
This is a daring departure from the typical Georgian square, by John Wood the Elder (1705–54).

| 0 metres | 100 |
| 0 yards | 100 |

QUEEN

SQUARE

BARTON

BEAUFORD SQUARE

Jane Austen Centre
(see p264), a permanent exhibition of film, costumes and books, tells the story of the author's time in Bath.

Key

— Suggested route

Milsom Street and New Bond Street contain some of Bath's most elegant shops.

★ Royal Crescent
Hailed the most majestic street in Britain, this graceful arc of 30 houses (1767–74) is the masterpiece of John Wood the Younger. West of the Royal Crescent, Royal Victoria Park (1830) is the city's largest open space.

Theatre Royal (1805)

Pulteney Bridge

This charming bridge (1769–74), designed by Robert Adam, is lined with shops and links the centre with the magnificent Great Pulteney Street. Look out for a rare Victorian pillar box on the east bank.

Museum of Bath Architecture

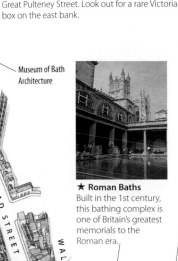

★ Roman Baths

Built in the 1st century, this bathing complex is one of Britain's greatest memorials to the Roman era.

★ Bath Abbey

The splendid abbey stands at the heart of the old city in the Abbey Church Yard, a paved courtyard enlivened by buskers. Its unique façade features stone angels climbing Jacob's Ladder to heaven.

Holburne Museum

Parade Gardens

Courting couples came to this pretty riverside park for secret liaisons in the 18th century.

Pump Rooms These tearooms once formed the social hub of the 18th-century spa community.

Sally Lunn's House (1482) is one of Bath's oldest houses.

Rail & coach stations

Exploring Bath

The beautiful and compact city of Bath is set among the rolling green hills of the Avon valley, and wherever you walk you will enjoy splendid views of the surrounding countryside. The traffic-free heart of this lively city is full of street musicians, museums, cafés and enticing shops, while the elegant honey-coloured Georgian houses, so characteristic of Bath, form an elegant backdrop to city life.

Bath Abbey, at the heart of the old city, begun in 1499

🏠 Bath Abbey

Abbey Churchyard. **Tel** 01225 422462. **Open** daily. **Closed** during services. Donation. 🚻 📷
W bathabbey.org

This splendid abbey was supposedly designed by divine agency. According to legend, Bishop Oliver King dreamed of angels going up and down to heaven, which then inspired the ladders carved on the façade of the west front. The bishop began work in 1499, rebuilding a church that had been founded in the 8th century. Memorials cover the walls and the varied Georgian inscriptions make fascinating reading. The spacious interior is remarkable for the fan vaulting of the nave, an addition made by Sir George Gilbert Scott in 1874.

🏛 National Trust Assembly Rooms and Fashion Museum

Bennett St. **Tel** 01225 477789. **Open** daily. **Closed** 25 & 26 Dec. 🚻 🚻 📷 **W** fashionmuseum. co.uk

The Assembly Rooms were built by Wood the Younger in 1769, as a meeting place for the elite and as a backdrop for glittering balls. Jane Austen's novel *Northanger Abbey* (1818) describes the gossip and flirtation that went on here. In the basement is a collection of costumes from the 1500s to the present day.

🏛 Jane Austen Centre

40 Gay St. **Tel** 01225 443000. **Open** daily. **Closed** 1 Jan, 24–26 Dec. 🚻 🚻 📷 **W** janeausten.co.uk

This site houses an exhibition about the author's life and her living in Bath affected her work.

🏛 No. 1 Royal Crescent

Royal Crescent. **Tel** 01225 428126. **Open** daily. **Closed** 25 & 26 Dec. 🚻 📷 **W** no1royalcrescent.org.uk

This handsome museum lets you inside the first house of this beautiful Georgian crescent, giving a glimpse of what life was like for 18th-century aristocrats, such as the Duke of York, who stayed here. You can also see the servants' quarters, the spit turned by a dog wheel and Georgian mousetraps.

🏛 Holburne Museum of Art

Great Pulteney St. **Tel** 01225 388569. **Open** daily. **Closed** Good Friday, 24–26 Dec. 🚻 🚻 📷 📷 **W** holburne.org

This historic building is named after William Holburne of Menstrie (1793–1874), whose collections form the nucleus of the display of fine and decorative arts, including superb silver and porcelain. Paintings by British artists such as Gainsborough and Stubbs are on show.

Roman Baths

Entrance in Abbey Churchyard. **Tel** 01225 477785. **Open** daily. **Closed** 25 & 26 Dec. 🚻 🚻 limited. **W** romanbaths.co.uk

According to legend, Bath owes its origin to the Celtic King Bladud who discovered the curative properties of its natural hot springs in 860 BC. Cast out from his kingdom as a leper, Bladud cured himself by imitating his swine and rolling in the hot mud at Bath.

In the first century, the Romans built baths around the spring, as well as a temple dedicated to the goddess Sulis Minerva, who combined the attributes of the Celt water goddess Sulis and the Roman goddess Minerva. Among the Roman relics is a bronze head of the goddess.

Medieval monks of Bath Abbey also exploited the springs' properties, but it was when Queen Anne visited in 1702 that Bath reached its zenith as a fashionable watering place.

For hotels and restaurants in this area see pp564–6 and pp589–91

🛁 Thermae Bath Spa

Hot Bath St. **Tel** 01225 331234.
Open 9am–9:30pm daily (last adm:
7pm). **Closed** 1 Jan, 25 & 26 Dec.
🚫 under-16s not permitted. ♿
📷 ♿ **W** thermaebathspa.com

Tourists have bathed in the
warm, mineral-rich waters
of the spa town of Bath since
Roman times and the opening
of the Thermae Bath Spa, in
2006, once again made Bath
a popular day-spa destination.
There are three pools fed by
natural thermal waters:
the New Royal Bath
has two baths including
an open-air rooftop pool
with superb views over the
city; across the road, the oval
Cross Bath is a more intimate
open-air bath, ideal for shorter
sessions. The spa also offers
scented steam rooms, footbaths
and an array of treatments,
bookable in advance. The
signature therapy is watsu, a
water-based version of the
shiatsu massage.

🏛 American Museum

Claverton Manor, Claverton Down.
Tel 01225 460503. **Open** mid-Mar–
Oct: Tue–Sun (Aug: daily). 🚫 ♿
limited. 📷 ♿ **W** american
museum.org

Founded in 1961, this was the
first American museum to be
established in Britain. The rooms
in the 1820 manor house are
decorated in many styles, from
the rudimentary
dwellings
of the first
settlers to
the opulent
style of 19th-
century
homes. The
museum has
special sections
on Shaker furniture,
quilts and Native
American art, and
a replica of George
Washington's
Mount Vernon
garden of
1785.

**A 19th-century
Native American
weathervane**

Richard "Beau" Nash (1674–1762)

Elected in 1704 as Master
of Ceremonies, "Beau"
Nash played a crucial role
in transforming Bath into
the fashionable centre of
Georgian society. During
his long career, he devised
a never-ending round
of games, balls and
entertainment (including
gambling) that kept the idle
rich amused and ensured a
constant flow of visitors.

The Great Bath

*The open-air Great Bath, which stands at the heart of the Roman
spa complex, was not discovered until the 1870s. Leading off this
magnificent pool were various bathing chambers which became
increasingly sophisticated over the four centuries the Romans
were here. The baths fell into ruin, but extensive
excavations have revealed the remarkable
skill of Roman engineering.*

The dome (1897) is based on St Stephen
Walbrook church in London (*see p116*).

Around the edges of the
bath are the bases of piers
that once supported a
barrel-vaulted roof.

York Street

**A late 19th-
century terrace** bears
statues of famous Romans
such as Julius Caesar.

The sacred spring was
a focal point for worship
in the Roman period.
The reservoir was later
named the King's Bath,
and niches were added
for bathers to sit in.

The water
flows from
the spring into the
corner of the bath at a
constant temperature
of 46° C (115° F).

**Steps, column bases and
paving stones** around the
edge of the bath date from
Roman times.

⑪ Stonehenge

Built in several stages from about 3000 BC, Stonehenge is Europe's most famous pre-historic monument. We can only guess at the rituals that took place here, but the alignment of the stones leaves little doubt that the circle is connected with the sun and the passing of the seasons. Despite popular belief, the circle was not built by the Druids, an Iron Age priestly cult that flourished from around 250 BC.

The Heel Stone casts a long shadow straight to the heart of the circle on Midsummer's Day.

The Avenue forms a ceremonial approach to the site.

The Slaughter Stone, named by 17th-century antiquarians who believed Stonehenge to be a place of human sacrifice, was in fact one of a pair marking the entrance to the interiors.

The Outer Bank, dug around 3000 BC, is the oldest known phase of Stonehenge.

Stonehenge as it is today

Reconstruction of Stonehenge
This illustration shows what Stonehenge probably looked like about 4,000 years ago.

Building of Stonehenge
Stonehenge's monumental scale is more impressive given that the only tools available were made of stone, wood and bone. Its builders must have been able to command immense resources and vast numbers of people to transport and erect the stones. One method is explained here.

A sarsen stone was moved on rollers and levered into a pit.

With levers supported by timber packing, it was slowly raised.

The stone was then pulled upright by about 200 men hauling on ropes.

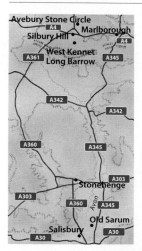

Avebury Stone Circle
Silbury Hill
Marlborough
West Kennet Long Barrow
A4
A4
A345
A361
A342
A342
A360
A345
A303
A303
Stonehenge
A360
A345
Avon
Old Sarum
Salisbury
A30
A30

Wiltshire's Other Prehistoric Sites
The open countryside of the Salisbury Plain made this area an important centre of pre-historic settlement, and today it is covered in many ancient remains. Ringing the horizon around Stonehenge are scores of circular barrows, or burial mounds, where members of the ruling class were honoured with burial close to the temple site. Ceremonial bronze weapons and other finds excavated around Stonehenge and the other local prehistoric sites can be seen in the visitor centre at Stonehenge and the museum at Salisbury *(see pp268–9).*

Silbury Hill

Silbury Hill is Europe's largest prehistoric earthwork, but despite extensive excavations its purpose remains a mystery. Built out of chalk blocks around 2750 BC, the hill covers 2 ha (5 acres) and rises to a height of 40 m (131 ft). Nearby **West Kennet Long Barrow** is the biggest chambered tomb in

The Sarsen Circle was erected around 2500 BC and is capped by lintel stones held in place by mortise and tenon joints.

The Bluestone Circle was built around 2500 BC out of some 80 slabs quarried in the Preseli Hills in south Wales.

VISITORS' CHECKLIST

Practical Information
Off A303, Wilts. **Tel** 0870 333 1181.
Open Apr & May: 9:30am–7pm; Jun–Aug: 9am–8pm; Sep–mid-Oct: 9:30am–7pm; mid-Oct–Mar: 9:30am–5pm (Stone Circle Access visit available outside these hours); Book ahead. **Closed** 20–22 Jun, 24 & 25 Dec. 🅿 🎦 ♿ 🖥 🏠 **EH** **w** english-heritage.org.uk

Transport
🚆 Salisbury then Stonehenge tour bus.

Horseshoe of Sarsen Trilothons

Horseshoe of Bluestones

The weight of the lintel was supported by a timber platform.

pit around the was packed y with stones halk.

Alternate ends of the lintel were levered up.

The lintel was then levered sideways on to the uprights.

Three of the stones that form part of the Avebury Stone Circle

⑫ Avebury

Wiltshire. 🚗 500. 🚆 Swindon then bus. ℹ Green St (01672 539250). **Open** daily. ♿ 🖥 🏠 **EH** **NT** **w** nationaltrust.org.uk

Built around 2500 BC, the **Avebury Stone Circle** surrounds the village of Avebury and was probably once some form of religious centre. Although the stones used are smaller than those at Stonehenge, the circle itself is larger. Superstitious villagers smashed many of the stones in the 18th century, believing the circle to have been a place of pagan sacrifice.

The original form of the circle is best appreciated by a visit to the **Alexander Keiller Museum** to the west of the site, which illustrates in detail the construction of the circle. There is also an exhibition explaining Avebury's changing landscape and Keiller's background, as well as an interactive zone for children.

St James's Church has a Norman font carved with sea monsters, and a rare 15th-century choir screen.

Environs
A few minutes' drive east, **Marlborough** is an attractive town with a long and broad High Street lined with colonnaded Georgian shops.

🏛 **Alexander Keiller Museum**
Off High St. **Tel** 01672 538016.
Open daily. **Closed** 1 Jan, 24 & 25 Dec. 🅿 ♿ 🎫 🖥 🏠 **NT**
w nationaltrust.org.uk

England, with numerous stone-lined "rooms" and a monumental entrance. Built as a communal burial site around 3250 BC, it was in use for several centuries – old bodies were taken away to make room for newcomers.

Old Sarum is set within the massive ramparts of a 1st-century Romano-British hill fort. The Norman founders of Old Sarum built their own motte and bailey castle inside this ready-made fortification, and the remains of this survive along with the foundations of the huge cathedral of 1075. Above ground nothing remains of the town that once sat within the ramparts. The town's occupants moved to the fertile river valley site that became Salisbury during the early 12th century (*see pp268–9*).

🏰 Old Sarum
Castle Rd. **Tel** 01722 335398.
Open daily. **Closed** 1 Jan, 24–26 Dec. 🅿 ♿ limited. 🏠 **EH**

The chambered tomb of West Kennet Long Barrow (c.3250 BC)

⓮ Salisbury

The "new" city of Salisbury was founded in 1220, when the hilltop settlement of Old Sarum *(see p267)* was abandoned – being too arid and windswept – in favour of a new site among the lush water meadows where the rivers Avon, Nadder and Bourne meet. Locally sourced Purbeck marble and Chilmark stone were used for the construction of a new cathedral, which was built mostly in the early 13th century, over the remarkably short space of 38 years. Its magnificent landmark spire – the tallest surviving in England – was an inspired afterthought added in 1280–1310.

Bishop's Walk and a sculpture by Elisabeth Frink (1930–93), Cathedral Close

Exploring Salisbury

The spacious and tranquil **Close**, with its schools, almshouses and clergy housing, makes a fine setting for Salisbury's cathedral. Among the numerous elegant buildings here are the **Matrons' College**, built in 1682 as a home for widows and unmarried daughters of the clergy, and 13th-century **Malmesbury House** with its splendid early Georgian façade (1719), fronted by lovely wrought-iron gates. Other buildings of interest include the **Medieval Hall**, the **Wardrobe**, now home to a regimental museum, and the **Cathedral School**, housed in the 13th-century Bishop's Palace and famous for the quality of the choristers who sing there.

Salisbury Cathedral

The cathedral was mainly built between 1220 and 1258. It is a fine example of Early English Gothic architecture, typified by tall, sharply pointed lancet windows.

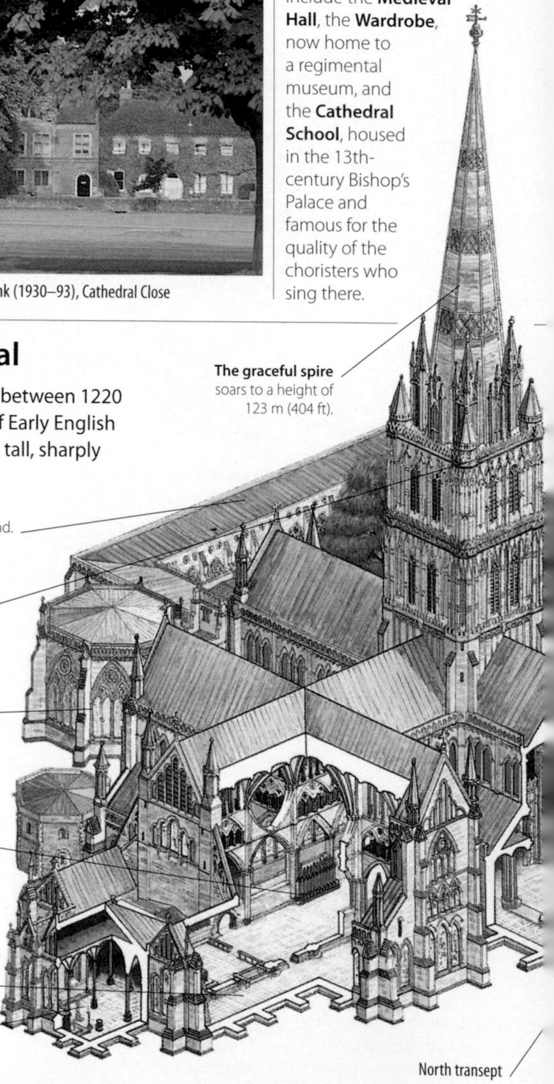

The graceful spire soars to a height of 123 m (404 ft).

The Cloisters are the largest in England. They were added between 1263 and 1284 in the Decorated style.

A roof tour takes visitors up to an external gallery at the base of the spire with views of the town and Old Sarum.

The Chapter House has an original of the *Magna Carta (see p52)*. Its walls have stone friezes showing scenes from the Old Testament.

Choirstalls

Bishop Audley's Chantry, a magnificent 16th-century monument was built to honour a former bishop, is one of several chapels around the altar.

The Trinity Chapel contains the tomb of St Osmund, who was bishop of Old Sarum from 1078 to 1099.

North transept

Double Cube room, designed by Inigo Jones in 1653, in Wilton House

Beyond the walls of the Cathedral Close, Salisbury developed its chessboard layout, with areas devoted to different trades, perpetuated in street names such as Fish Row and Butcher Row. Leaving the Close through **High Street Gate**, you reach the busy High Street leading to the 13th-century **Church of St Thomas**, which has a lovely carved timber roof (1450), and a late 15th-century Doom painting, showing Christ seated in judgment and demons seizing the damned. Nearby in Silver Street, **Poultry**

Cross was built in the 14th century as a covered poultry market. An intricate network of alleys with a number of fine timber-framed houses fans out from this point. In the large bustling **Market Place** the **Guildhall** is an unusual cream stone building built in 1787–95, used for civic functions. More attractive are the brick and tile-hung houses on the north side of the square, many with Georgian façades concealing medieval houses.

🏛 Mompesson House

The Close. **Tel** 01722 335659.
Open mid-Mar–Oct: daily.
🅿 🚹 limited. 🖼 **NT** 🔲 **national trust.org.uk**

Built by a wealthy Wiltshire family in 1701, the handsomely furnished rooms of this house give an indication of life for the Close's inhabitants in the 18th century. The delightful garden, bounded by the north wall of the Close, has fine herbaceous borders.

🏛 Salisbury Museum

The Close. **Tel** 01722 332151.
Open Mon–Sat (Apr–Oct: Sun pm).
🅿 🚹 limited. 🖼 🔲 **salisbury museum.org.uk**

In the medieval King's House, this museum explores the history and archaeology of Salisbury and South Wiltshire. It has displays on early man, Stonehenge and nearby Old Sarum *(see p267)*. There is also a fascinating Victorian ceramics and glass collection.

Environs

The town of Wilton is renowned for its carpet industry, founded by the 8th Earl of Pembroke using French Huguenot refugee weavers. The town's ornate **church** (1844) is a brilliant example of Neo-Romanesque architecture, incorporating genuine Roman columns, Flemish Renaissance woodwork, German and Dutch stained glass and Italian mosaics.

Wilton House has been home to the Earls of Pembroke since it was converted from a nunnery after the Dissolution *(see p355)*. The house, largely rebuilt by Inigo Jones in the 17th century, includes one of the original Tudor towers, a fine collection of art and a landscaped park with a Palladian bridge (1737). The Single and Double Cube State Rooms have magnificently frescoed ceilings and gilded stucco work, and were designed to hang a series of family portraits by Van Dyck.

🏛 Wilton House

Wilton. **Tel** 01722 746700.
Open Easter weekend, May–Aug; Sun–Thu, bank hol Sat. 🅿 🚹 🖋 🏛
🔲 wiltonhouse.co.uk

The West Front
The stunning façade is decorated by rows of symbolic figures and saints in niches.

The nave is divided into ten bays by columns of polished Purbeck marble.

Numerous stained-glass windows depict stories from the Bible.

The clock, dating from 1386, is the oldest working clock in Europe.

The Longleat Tree tapestry (1980) depicting a 400-year history

⓮ Longleat House

Warminster, Wiltshire. **Tel** 01985 844400. 🚌 Frome then taxi. House & Safari Park: **Open** mid-Feb–mid-Mar: Fri–Mon; mid-Mar–Oct: daily. 🌂 📷 ♿ 🚻 🍴 📷
Ⓦ longleat.co.uk

The architectural historian John Summerson coined the term "prodigy house" to describe the exuberance and grandeur of Elizabethan architecture that is so well represented at Longleat. The house was started in 1540, when John Thynne bought the ruins of a priory on the site for £53. Over the centuries subsequent owners have added their own touches. The present owner, the 7th Marquess of Bath, is renowned for his erotic murals. Less controversial are the Breakfast Room and Lower Dining Room (dating from the 1870s), modelled on the Venetian Ducal Palace. Today, the Great Hall is the only remaining room which belongs to Thynne's time.

In 1949, the 6th Marquess was the first landowner in Britain to open his stately home to the public, in order to fund the maintenance and preservation of the house and its estate. Parts of the grounds, landscaped by "Capability" Brown *(see p30)*, were turned into an expansive safari park in 1966, where lions, tigers and other wild animals roam freely. This, along with further additions such as enclosures for smaller animals, a large hedge maze, a Jungle Express mini-train and an Adventure Castle, have made Longleat one of England's most popular estates.

⓯ Stourhead

Stourhead is among the finest examples of 18th-century landscape gardening in Britain *(see pp30–31)*. The garden was begun in the 1740s by Henry Hoare (1705–85), who inherited the estate and transformed it into a breathtaking work of art. He created the lake, surrounding it with rare trees and plants, and Neo-Classical Italianate temples, grottoes and bridges. The Palladian-style house, built by Colen Campbell *(see p32)*, dates from 1724.

Pantheon
Modelled on the Pantheon in Rome, this elegant temple was designed by architect Henry Flitcroft (1679–1769) in 1753. It was intended as a visual centre-point for the garden and a place for the Hoare family to entertain their guests.

KEY

① **Turf Bridge**

② **A walk** of 2 miles (3 km) around the lake provides artistically contrived vistas.

③ **Iron Bridge**

④ **Gothic Cottage** (1806)

⑤ **The Grotto** is an artificial cave with a pool and a life-size statue of the guardian of the River Stour, sculpted by John Cheere in 1748.

⑥ **The Temple of Flora** (1744) is dedicated to the Roman goddess of flowers

⑦ **Stourton village** was incorporated into Hoare's overall design.

⑧ **Pelargonium House** contains a collection of over 100 species of the pelargonium plant and its cultivars.

⑨ **The reception** has a helpful visitor information centre.

★ **Temple of Apollo**
Inspired by Italian originals and dedicated to the sun god Apollo, this circular temple was architect Henry Flitcroft (1679–1769).

The Lake
Stourhead's famous lake was created by damming the River Stour in the 1750s. The path around it evokes the journeys of Aeneas in Virgil's *Aeneid*.

Colourful Shrubs and Trees
Fragrant rhododendrons bloom in the spring, and azaleas explode into colour later in the summer. There are also many fine cypresses, Japanese pines and other exotic trees.

St Peter's Church
The parish church contains monuments to the Hoare family. The medieval Bristol Cross, nearby, was brought from Bristol in 1765.

Entrance and car park

★ **Stourhead House**
Reconstructed after a fire in 1902, the house contains fine Chippendale furniture. The art collection reflects Henry Hoare's Classical tastes and includes *The Choice of Hercules* (1637) by Nicolas Poussin.

Picturesque cottages on a cobbled street at Gold Hill, in Shaftesbury

⑯ Shaftesbury

Dorset. 🚋 8,000. 🚌 ℹ️ 8 Bell St
(01747 853514). 🅿️ Thu.
🌐 shaftesburytourism.co.uk

Hilltop Shaftesbury, with its
cobbled streets and 18th-
century cottages, is often used
as a setting for films to give
a flavour of Old England.
Picturesque **Gold Hill** is lined
on one side by a wall of the
demolished **abbey**, founded
by King Alfred in 888. Only
the excavated remains of the
abbey church survive, with
many masonry fragments
displayed in the local museum.

⑰ Sherborne

Dorset. 🚋 9,500. 🚆🚌 ℹ️ Digby Rd
(01935 815341). 🅿️ Thu, Sat.
🌐 visit-dorset.com

Few other towns in Britain
have such a wealth of unspoilt
medieval buildings. Edward VI
founded the famous Sherborne
School in 1550, thereby saving
the splendid **Abbey Church**
and other monastic buildings
that might otherwise have
been demolished in the

The Almshouse (1437) adjoining the Abbey
Church, Sherborne

Dissolution *(see p355)*. Remains
of the Saxon church can be seen
in the abbey's façade, but the
most striking feature is the
15th-century fan-vaulted ceiling.
  Sherborne Castle, built by Sir
Walter Raleigh *(see p55)* in 1594,
is a wonderfully varied building
that anticipates the flamboyant
Jacobean style. Raleigh also
lived briefly in the early 12th-
century **Old Castle**, which now
stands in ruins, demolished
during the Civil War *(see p56)*.

Environs
West of Sherborne, past Yeovil,
is the magnificent Elizabethan
Montacute House *(see p249)*, set
in 120 ha (300 acres) of grounds.
It is noted for tapestries, and for
the Tudor and Jacobean portraits
in its vast Long Gallery.

🏠 **Sherborne Castle**
Off A30. **Tel** 01935 812027. Castle and
grounds: **Open** Apr–Oct: Tue–Thu, Sat,
Sun & public hols (pm). 🈂️ 📷 ♿
🌐 **sherbornecastle.com**

🏠 **Old Castle**
Off A30. **Tel** 01935 812730.
Open Easter–Oct: daily. 🈂️ ♿ 📷 EH

🏛️ **Montacute House**
Montacute. **Tel** 01935 823289. House:
Open Mar–Oct: daily; Nov–Feb: Sat &
Sun. Grounds: **Open** Mar–Oct: daily;
Nov–Feb: Wed–Sun. 🈂️ ⚫ 📷 NT

⑱ Abbotsbury

Dorset. 🚋 500. ℹ️ West Yard Barn,
West St (01305 871130).
🌐 abbotsbury-tourism.co.uk

The name Abbotsbury recalls
the town's 11th-century

Benedictine abbey, of which
little but the huge tithe barn,
built around 1400, remains.
  Nobody knows when the
Swannery here was founded,
but the earliest records date to
1393. Mute swans come to nest
in the breeding season, attracted
by the reed beds along the Fleet,
a brackish lagoon protected
from the sea by a high ridge of
pebbles called **Chesil Beach** *(see
p246)*. Its wild atmosphere makes
an appealing contrast to the
south coast resorts, although
strong currents make swimming
too dangerous. **Abbotsbury
Sub-Tropical Gardens** are
the frost-free home to many
new plants, discovered by
botanists travelling in South
America and Asia.

🦢 **Swannery**
New Barn Rd. **Tel** 01305 871858.
Open mid-Mar–Oct: daily.
🈂️ ♿ 📷 📷

🌿 **Abbotsbury Sub-Tropical
Gardens**
Off B3157. **Tel** 01305 871387.
Open daily. **Closed** late Dec. 🈂️
♿ limited. 📷 📷

The Swannery at Abbotsbury

⑲ Weymouth

Dorset. 🚋 55,000. 🚆🚌🚌🅿️ Thu.
🌐 visit-dorset.co.uk

Weymouth's popularity as a
seaside resort began in 1789,
when George III paid the first
of many summer visits here.
His statue is a prominent feature
on the seafront. Here gracious
Georgian terraces look across
to the beautiful expanse of
Weymouth Bay. Different in
character is the old town

around Custom House Quay with its boats and old seamen's inns. In 1944 the town played host to over 500,000 troops in advance of the D-Day Landings; **Nothe Fort** has displays of World War II memorabilia.

🏛 Nothe Fort
Barrack Rd. **Tel** 01305 766626. **Open** Apr–Sep: daily; Oct, Nov, Feb & Mar: Sun. 🐾 ♿ limited. 🖼 📷

⑳ Dorchester

Dorset. 🚉 19,000. 🚆 ℹ The Library, Charles St (01305 267992). 🛒 Wed. 🌐 visit-dorset.com

Dorchester, the county town of Dorset, is still recognizably the town in which Thomas Hardy based his novel *The Mayor of Casterbridge* (1886). Here, among the many 17th- and 18th-century houses lining the High Street, is the **Dorset County Museum**, where the original manuscript of the novel is displayed.

Dorchester has the only example of a **Roman town house** in Britain. The remains reveal architectural details including a fine mosaic. There are also finds from Iron Age and Roman sites on the outskirts of the town. **Maumbury Rings** (Weymouth Avenue) is a Roman amphitheatre, originally a Neolithic henge. To the west, many Roman graves have been

Hardy's statue, Dorchester

found below the Iron Age hill fort, **Poundbury Camp**.

Environs

Just southwest of Dorchester, **Maiden Castle** *(see p47)* is a massive monument dating from around 100 BC. In AD 43 it was the scene of a battle when the Romans fought the Iron Age people of southern England.

To the north lies the charming village of **Cerne Abbas** with its magnificent medieval tithe barn and monastic buildings. The huge chalk figure of a giant on the hillside here is a fertility figure thought to represent either the Roman god Hercules or an Iron Age warrior.

East of Dorchester are the churches, thatched villages and rolling hills immortalized in Hardy's novels. Picturesque **Bere Regis** is the Kingsbere of *Tess of the D'Urbervilles*, where the tombs of the family whose name inspired the novel may be seen in the Saxon **church**. **Hardy's Cottage** is where the writer was born and **Max Gate** is the house he designed and lived in from 1885 until his death. His heart is buried with his family at **Stinsford** church – his body was given a public funeral at Westminster Abbey *(pp96–7)*.

There are beautiful gardens *(see p249)* and a magnificent medieval hall at 15th-century **Athelhampton House**.

🏛 Dorset County Museum
High West St. **Tel** 01305 262735. **Open** Mon–Sat. **Closed** 25 & 26 Dec. 🐾 ♿ limited. 🖼 📷 🌐 dorsetcountymuseum.org

🏠 Hardy's Cottage
Higher Bockhampton. **Tel** 01305 262366. **Open** Mar–Oct: daily; Nov–Feb: Thu–Sun. 🐾 ♿ 📷 NT

🏠 Max Gate
Alington Ave, Dorchester. **Tel** 01305 262538. **Open** Mar–Oct: daily; Nov–Feb: Thu Sun. 🐾 ♿ 📷 NT

🏠 Athelhampton House
Athelhampton. **Tel** 01305 848363. **Open** Sun–Thu (Nov–Feb: Sun). 🐾 📷 ♿ gardens only. 🍴 📷 🌐 athelhampton.co.uk

A 55-m (180-ft) giant carved on the chalk hillside, Cerne Abbas

㉑ Lyme Regis

Dorset. 🚹 3,600. 🚻 Church St
(01297 442138). 🅦 lymeregis.org

Lyme Regis is the most picturesque resort of the Jurassic Coast, which runs from near Exmouth in Devon to near Swanage in Dorset (95 miles/ 153 km) and is the only natural site in Britain to hold UNESCO World Heritage status. The town and its neighbour Charmouth are known for their fossils. The Victorian pioneer fossil-hunter Mary Anning unearthed the first complete Ichthyosaurus and Plesiosaurus here, and you can see her story in the **Lyme Regis Museum**. Encircling the harbour is the famous Cobb breakwater, which gives great views along the coast and to the Georgian houses along the seafront.

🏛 **Lyme Regis Museum**
Bridge St. **Tel** 01297 443370. **Open** Easter–Oct: daily; Nov–Easter: Wed–Sun. **Closed** 25 & 26 Dec. 🅿 🔥 ltd. 🏠 🅦 lymeregismuseum.co.uk

㉒ Corfe Castle

Dorset. **Tel** 01929 481294. 🚆 Wareham then bus. **Open** daily. **Closed** 25 & 26 Dec. 🔲 🏠 🎫 🅦 nationaltrust.org.uk

The spectacular ruins of Corfe Castle romantically crown a jagged pinnacle of rock above the charming unspoilt village that shares its name. The castle has dominated the landscape

The ruins of Corfe Castle, dating mainly from Norman times

since the 11th century, first as a royal fortification, then as the dramatic ruins seen today. In 1635 the castle was purchased by Sir John Bankes, whose wife and her retainers – mostly women – courageously held out here against 600 Parliamentary troops in a six-week siege during the Civil War *(see pp56–7)*. The castle was eventually taken through treachery and in 1646 Parliament voted to have it "slighted" – deliberately blown up to prevent it being used again. From the ruins there are far-reaching views over the Isle of Purbeck and its coastline.

㉓ Isle of Purbeck

Dorset. 🚆 Wareham. 🚤 Shell Bay, Studland. 🚻 Swanage (01929 422885). 🅦 swanage.gov.uk

The Isle of Purbeck, which is in fact a peninsula, is the source of the grey shelly limestone,

known as Purbeck marble, from which the castle and surrounding houses were built. The geology changes to the southwest at **Kimmeridge**, where the muddy shale is rich in fossils and oil reserves. The Isle, a World Heritage site, is fringed with unspoilt beaches. **Studland Bay**, with its white sand and its sand-dune nature reserve, rich in birdlife, has been rated one of Britain's best beaches. Sheltered **Lulworth Cove** is almost encircled by white cliffs, and there is a fine clifftop walk to Durdle Door *(see p247)*, a natural chalk arch.

The main resort in the area is **Swanage**, the port where Purbeck stone was transported by ship to London, to be used for everything from street paving to church building. Unwanted masonry from demolished buildings was shipped back and this is how Swanage got its wonderfully ornate **town hall** façade, designed by Wren around 1668.

㉔ Poole

Dorset. 🚹 150,000. 🚆 🚌 🚤 🚻 4 High St (01202 262600). 🅦 pooletourism.com

Situated on one of the largest natural harbours in the world, Poole is an ancient, still thriving seaport. The quay is lined with old warehouses, modern apartments and a marina, overlooking a safe sheltered bay. The **Poole Museum**, partly housed in 15th-century cellars alongside the quay, has four floors of galleries.

Chapman's Pool anchorage on the Isle of Purbeck

Nearby **Brownsea Island** (reached by boat from the quay) is given over to a woodland nature reserve with egrets, herons and red squirrels. The fine views of the Dorset coast add to the appeal.

🏛 Poole Museum
High St. **Tel** 01202 262600. **Open** Apr–Oct: daily; Nov–Mar: Tue–Sun. **Closed** 1 Jan, 25 & 26 Dec. 🔾

🦑 Brownsea Island
Poole. **Tel** 01202 707744. **Open** mid-Mar–Oct: daily (boat trips leave the quayside every 30 mins during the season). 🔾🔾🔾🔾🔾🔾

㉕ Wimborne Minster

Dorset. 🔾 7,000. 🔾 🔾 29 High St (01202 886116). 🔾 Fri–Sun. 🔾 wimborne.info

The fine collegiate church of Wimborne's **Minster** was founded in 705 by Cuthburga, sister of King Ina of Wessex. It fell prey to marauding Danish raiders in the 10th century, and the imposing grey church of today dates from the refounding by Edward the Confessor *(see p51)* in 1043. Stonemasons made use of the local Purbeck marble, carving beasts, biblical scenes, and a mass of zig-zag decoration.

The 16th-century **Priest's House Museum** has rooms furnished in the style of different periods and an enchanting hidden garden.

Environs

Designed for the Bankes family after the destruction of Corfe Castle, **Kingston Lacy** was acquired by the National Trust in 1981. The estate has always been farmed by traditional methods and is astonishingly rich in wildlife, rare flowers and butterflies. This quiet, forgotten corner of Dorset is grazed by rare Red Devon cattle and can be explored using paths that date back to "green lanes" that date back to Roman and Saxon times. The fine 17th-century house on the estate contains an outstanding collection of paintings, including works by Rubens, Velázquez and Titian.

🏛 Priest's House Museum
High St. **Tel** 01202 882533. **Open** Mon–Sat. **Closed** 24 Dec–2Jan. 🔾🔾 limited. 🔾 🔾

🔾 Kingston Lacy
On B3082. **Tel** 01202 883402. House: **Open** daily. Gardens: **Open** daily. 🔾🔾🔾 limited. 🔾 🔾 🔾

㉖ Bournemouth

Dorset. 🔾 195,000. 🔾 🔾 🔾 🔾 Pier Approach (01202 451734). 🔾 bournemouth.co.uk

Bournemouth's popularity as a seaside resort is due to an almost unbroken sweep of sandy beach, extending from the mouth of Poole Harbour to Hengistbury Head. Most of the seafront is built up, with large seaside villas and exclusive hotels. To the west there are numerous clifftop parks and gardens, interrupted by beautiful wooded river ravines, known as "chines". The varied and colourful garden of **Compton Acres** was conceived as a museum of garden styles.

In central Bournemouth the amusement arcades, casinos, nightclubs and shops cater for the city's many visitors. In the summer, pop groups, TV comedians and the highly regarded Bournemouth Symphony Orchestra perform at various venues in the city. The **Russell-Cotes Art Gallery and Museum**, housed in a late Victorian villa, has an extensive collection, with many fine Oriental and Victorian artifacts.

Environs

The magnificent **Christchurch Priory**, east of Bournemouth, is 95 m (310 ft) in length – one of the longest churches in

Marchesa Maria Grimaldi by Sir Peter Paul Rubens (1577–1640), Kingston Lacy

England. It was rebuilt between the 13th and 16th centuries and presents a sequence of different styles. The original nave, from around 1093, is an impressive example of Norman architecture, but the highlight is the intricate stone reredos, which features a Tree of Jesse, tracing the lineage of Christ. Next to the Priory are the ruins of a Norman **castle**.

Between Bournemouth and Christchurch, **Hengistbury Head** is well worth climbing for grassland flowers, butterflies and sea views, while **Stanpit Marsh**, to the west of Bournemouth, is an excellent spot for viewing herons and other wading birds.

🔾 Compton Acres
Canford Cliffs Rd. **Tel** 01202 700778. **Open** daily. **Closed** 25 & 26 Dec. 🔾 🔾🔾🔾🔾 comptonacres.co.uk

🏛 Russell-Cotes Art Gallery and Museum
Eastcliff. **Tel** 01202 451858. **Open** Tue–Sun. **Closed** 25 Dec. 🔾 🔾 🔾 🔾 russellcotes.com

Bournemouth's sandy beach and pier

DEVON AND CORNWALL

Devon · Cornwall

Miles of magnificently varied coastline dominate this magical corner of Britain. Popular seaside resorts alternate with secluded coves and unspoilt fishing villages rich in maritime history. In contrast there are lush, exotic gardens and the wild terrain of the moorland interior, dotted with tors and historic remains.

Geographical neighbours, the counties of Devon and Cornwall are very different in character. Celtic Cornwall, with its numerous villages named after early Christian missionaries, is mostly stark and treeless at its centre. In many places it is still scarred by the remains of tin and copper mining that has played an important part in the economy for some 4,000 years. Yet this does not detract from the beauty and variety of the coastline dotted with lighthouses and tiny coves, and penetrated by deep tidal rivers.

Devon, by contrast, is a land of lush pasture divided into a patchwork of tiny fields and threaded with narrow lanes, whose banks support a mass of flowers from the first spring primroses to summer's colourful mixture of campion, foxglove, oxeye daisies and blue cornflowers. The leisurely pace of rural life here, and in Cornwall, contrasts with life in the bustling cities. Exeter with its magnificent cathedral, historic Plymouth, elegant Truro and Elizabethan Totnes are urban centres brimming with life and character.

The spectacular coastline and the mild climate of the region attract families, boating enthusiasts and surfers. For those in search of solitude, the Southwest Coastal Path provides access to the more tranquil areas. There are fishing villages and harbours whose heyday was in the buccaneering age of Drake and Raleigh *(see p55)*, and inland the wild moorland of Bodmin and Dartmoor, which provided inspiration for countless romantic tales. Many of these are associated with King Arthur *(see p289)* who, according to legend, was born at Tintagel on Cornwall's dramatically contorted north coast.

Beach huts on the seafront at Paignton, near Torquay

◀ The picturesque seaside town of St Ives, Cornwall

Exploring Devon and Cornwall

Romantic moorland dominates the inland parts of Devon and
Cornwall, ideal walking country with few roads and magnificent
views stretching for miles. By contrast the extensive coastline is
indented by hundreds of sheltered river valleys, each one seemingly
isolated from the rest of the world – one reason why Devon and
Cornwall can absorb so many visitors and yet still seem uncrowded.
Wise tourists get to know one small part of Devon or Cornwall
intimately, soaking up the atmosphere of the region, rather than
rushing to see everything in the space of a week.

Key

━━━ Motorway
━━━ Major road
━━━ Secondary road
═══ Minor road
━━━ Scenic route
╍╍╍ Main railway
──── Minor railway
△ Summit

Sights at a Glance

② St Ives
③ Penzance
④ *St Michael's Mount pp282–3*
⑤ Helston and the
    Lizard Peninsula
⑥ Falmouth
⑦ Truro
⑧ St Austell
⑨ *Eden Project pp286–7*
⑩ Fowey
⑪ Bodmin
⑫ Padstow
⑬ Tintagel
⑭ Bude
⑮ Clovelly
⑯ Bideford
⑰ Appledore
⑱ Barnstaple
⑲ Lynton and Lynmouth
⑳ *Exeter pp292–3*
㉑ Torbay
㉒ Dartmouth
㉓ Totnes
㉔ Buckfastleigh
㉕ Burgh Island
㉖ Plymouth
㉗ Buckland Abbey
㉘ Cotehele
㉙ Morwellham Quay
㉚ *Dartmoor National Park pp298–9*

Walks and Tours

① *Penwith Tour*
   p280

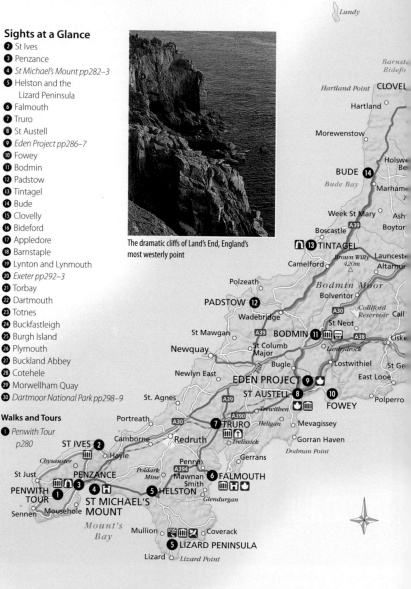

The dramatic cliffs of Land's End, England's
most westerly point

Subtropical gardens at Torquay, the popular seaside resort

Getting Around

Large numbers of drivers, many towing caravans (trailers), travel along the M5 motorway and A30 trunk road from mid-July to early September and travel can be slow, especially on Saturdays. Once in Devon and Cornwall, allow ample time if you are travelling by car along the region's narrow and high-banked lanes.

Regular train services, running from Paddington to Penzance, along Brunel's historic Great Western Railway, stop at most major towns. Aside from this, you are dependent on taxis or infrequent local buses.

Typical thatched, stone cottages, Buckland-in-the-Moor, Dartmoor

For keys to symbols *see back flap*

❶ Penwith Tour

This tour passes through a spectacular, remote Cornish landscape, dotted with relics of the tin mining industry, picturesque fishing villages and many prehistoric remains. The magnificent coastline varies between gentle rolling moorland in the north and the rugged, windswept cliffs that characterize the dramatic south coast. The beauty of the area, combined with the clarity of light, has attracted artists since the late 19th century. Their work can be seen in Newlyn, St Ives and Penzance.

Tips for Drivers

Tour length: 31 miles (50 km).
Stopping-off points: There are pubs and cafés in most villages. Sennen Cove makes a pleasant midway stop. (See also pp636–7.)

① Zennor
The carved mermaid in the church recalls the legend of the mermaid who lured the local squire's son to her ocean lair.

② Lanyon Quoit
One of many prehistoric monuments, this chambered tomb is visible on the left from the road to Madron.

⑧ Botallack Mine
Derelict engine-houses clinging to the cliffside are a vivid reminder of the region's former industry of tin mining.

③ Trengwainton
These gardens are noted for their exotic plants and trees (see p248).

⑦ Land's End
England's most westerly point is noted for its dramatic and wild landscape. A local exhibition reveals its history, geology and wildlife.

④ Newlyn
Cornwall's largest fishing port gave its name to a school of artists founded in the 1880s (see p282). Examples of their work can be seen in the art gallery here.

⑤ Merry Maidens
This Bronze Age stone circle is said to be 19 girls turned to stone for dancing on Sunday.

⑥ Minack Theatre
This Ancient Greek-style theatre (1923) overlooks the magical bay of Porthcurno. It forms a magnificent backdrop for productions in summer.

Map labels: St Ives, Morvah, B3306, B3306, B3318, St Just, B3306, Sennen Cove, A30, B3315, Porthcurno, Madron, A3071, A30, Penzance, A30, B3283, B3315, Mousehole, B3283, Lamorna, B3315

Key
— Tour route
--- Other roads

0 kilometres   3
0 miles   2

For keys to symbols see back flap

Porthminster Beach and the picturesque town of St Ives

❷ St Ives

Cornwall. 🚉 11,000. 🚆 🚌
ℹ️ Street-an-Pol (09052 522250).
🌐 visitstives.org.uk

With its whitewashed cottages, flower-filled gardens and sandy beaches, St Ives combines traditional seaside pleasures with a prestigious artistic heritage. The town is famous for the clarity of its light, which attracted a group of artists to set up a colony here in the 1920s. Their work is celebrated at the **Barbara Hepworth Museum and Sculpture Garden** and **Tate St Ives**. The former presents the sculptor's work in the house and garden where she lived and worked for many years. Tate St Ives reminds visitors of the natural surroundings that inspired the art on display within.

Popular taste rules in the many other art galleries tucked down winding alleys with names such as Teetotal Street, a legacy of the town's Methodist heritage. Many galleries are converted cellars and lofts where fish was once salted and packed.

The best beaches include Porthgwidden, which is great for children, and Porthmeor, good for surfing. The star, though, is sweeping Porthminster.

🏛️ **Barbara Hepworth Museum and Sculpture Garden**
Barnoon Hill. **Tel** 01736 796226.
Open daily (Nov–Feb: Tue–Sun).
Closed 24–26 Dec. 🎫 ♿ by appt. 📷

🏛️ **Tate St Ives**
Porthmeor Beach. **Tel** 01736 796226.
Open daily (Nov–Feb: Tue–Sun).
Closed 24–26 Dec; occasional rehanging – phone to check. 🎫 ♿ 📷
🌐 tate.org.uk/visit/tate-st-ives

St Ives Artists of the 20th Century

In the 1920s, St Ives, together with Newlyn, became a magnet for aspiring artists. Ben Nicholson and Barbara Hepworth formed the nucleus of a group of artists that made a major contribution to the development of abstract art in Europe. Other prolific artists associated with the area include the potter Bernard Leach and the painter Patrick Heron, whose Coloured Glass Window dominates the Tate St Ives entrance. Much of the art on display at Tate St Ives is abstract and illustrates new responses to the rugged Cornish landscape, the human figure and the ever-changing patterns of sunlight on sea.

Bernard Leach (1887–1979) became fascinated with *raku* pottery while living in Japan. On his return to England in 1920, he founded the Leach Pottery, a celebrated ceramic studio. A museum at the studio celebrates his life and work.

Barbara Hepworth (1903–75) was one of the foremost abstract sculptors of the 20th century. *Two Forms (Divided Circle)* (1969), a bronze sculpture created just six years before her death, is considered one of her most famous works.

Ben Nicholson's (1894–1982) work shows a change in style from simple scenes, such as the view from his window, to a pre-occupation with shapes – as seen in this painting *St Ives Cornwall* (1943–5).

❸ Penzance

Cornwall. 🚇 38,000. 🚌 🚂 🛳
ℹ️ Station Approach (01736 335530).
NT **W** lovepenzance.co.uk

Penzance is a bustling resort with a climate so mild that palm trees and subtropical plants grow happily in the lush **Morrab Gardens**. The town commands fine views of St Michael's Mount and a great sweep of clean sandy beach.

The main road through the town is Market Jew Street, at the top of which stands the magnificent domed Market House (1837), fronted by a statue of Sir Humphrey Davy (1778–1829). Davy, who came from Penzance, invented the miner's safety lamp, which detected lethal gases.

Chapel Street is lined with curious buildings, none more striking than the flamboyant **Egyptian House** (1835), with its richly painted façade and lotus bud decoration. Just as curious is **Admiral Benbow Inn** (1696) on the same street, which has a pirate perched on the roof looking out to sea. The **Penlee House Gallery and Museum** has pictures by the Newlyn School of artists.

Environs

A short distance south of Penzance, **Newlyn** *(see p280)* is Cornwall's largest fishing port, and has given its name to the local school of artists founded by Stanhope Forbes (1857–1947). They painted outdoors, aiming to capture the fleeting impressions of wind, sun and sea. Continuing south, the coastal road ends at **Mousehole** (pronounced Mowzall), a pretty,

The Egyptian House (1835)

popular village with a tiny harbour, tiers of cottages and a maze of narrow alleys.

North of Penzance, overlooking the magical Cornish coast, **Chysauster** is a fine example of a Romano-British village. The site has

❹ St Michael's Mount

According to Roman historians, the mount was the island of Ictis, an important centre for the Cornish tin trade during the Iron Age. It is dedicated to the archangel St Michael, who is said to have appeared here in AD 495.

When the Normans conquered England in 1066 *(see pp50–51)*, they were struck by the island's resemblance to their own Mont-St-Michel, whose Benedictine monks were then invited to build an abbey here. The abbey was absorbed into a fortress during the Dissolution *(see p355)*, when Henry VIII set up coastal defences to counter an attack from France. In 1659, St Michael's Mount was bought by Colonel John St Aubyn, whose descendants turned the fortress into a magnificent house.

Rocky Slopes
These slopes are planted with subtropical trees and shrubs.

Access to the island is by boat from Marazion or on foot by a cobbled causeway at low tide.

Harbourside village

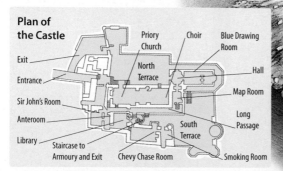

Plan of the Castle

- Exit
- Entrance
- Sir John's Room
- Anteroom
- Library
- Staircase to Armoury and Exit
- Priory Church
- North Terrace
- Chevy Chase Room
- Choir
- South Terrace
- Blue Drawing Room
- Hall
- Map Room
- Long Passage
- Smoking Room

remained almost undisturbed since it was abandoned during the 3rd century.

From Penzance, regular boat services depart for the **Isles of Scilly**, an enchanting archipelago forming part of the same granite mass as Land's End, Bodmin Moor and Dartmoor. Along with tourism, flower-growing is the main source of income here – fields of scented narcissi and pinks only add to the exceptional wild beauty of the Isles of Scilly.

Penlee House Gallery and Museum
Morrab Rd. **Tel** 01736 363625. **Open** Apr–Oct: 10am–5pm Mon–Sat; Nov–Mar: 10am–4:30pm Mon–Sat. **Closed** 1 Jan, 25 & 26 Dec.
w penleehouse.org.uk

Chysauster
Off B3311. **Tel** 07831 757934.
Open Apr–Oct: daily.

The Growth of Methodism

The hard-working and independent mining and fishing communities of the West Country had little time for the established Church, but they were won over by the new Methodist religion, with its emphasis on hymn singing, open-air preaching and regular or "methodical" Bible reading. When John Wesley, the founder of Methodism, made the first of many visits to the area in 1743, sceptical Cornishmen

John Wesley (1703–91)

pelted him with stones. His persistence, however, led to many conversions and by 1762 he was preaching to congregations of up to 30,000 people. Simple places of worship were built throughout the county; one favoured spot was the amphitheatre Gwennap Pit, at Busveal, south of Redruth. Methodist memorabilia can be seen in the Royal Cornwall Museum in Truro (*see p285*).

Castle entrance

Priory Church
Rebuilt in the late 14th century, this church at the summit of the island has lovely rose windows.

The Armoury displays military trophies brought back by the St Aubyn family from various wars.

The Chevy Chase Room takes its name from a frieze (1641) depicting hunting scenes.

The South Terrace forms the roof of the large Victorian wing.

The Blue Drawing Room
This room is decorated in Rococo Gothic style and features fine plaster work, furniture and paintings by Thomas Gainsborough and Joshua Reynolds.

Pinnacles of serpentine rock at Kynance Cove, Lizard Peninsula

❺ Helston and the Lizard Peninsula

Cornwall. 🚌 from Penzance.
🅆 visithelston.com

The attractive town of Helston makes a good base for exploring the windswept coastline of the Lizard Peninsula. The town is famous for its Furry Dance, which welcomes spring with dancing through the streets *(see p66)*; the **Helston Museum** explains the history of this ancient custom. The Georgian houses and inns of Coinagehall Street are a reminder that Helston was once a thriving stannary town where tin ingots were brought for weighing and stamping before being sold. Locally mined tin was brought down-river to a harbour at the bottom of this street until access to the sea was blocked in the 13th century by a shingle bar that formed across the estuary. The bar created the freshwater lake, Loe Pool, and an attractive walk skirts its wooded shores. In 1880, Helston's trade was taken over by a new harbour created to the east on the River Helford, at Gweek. Today, Gweek is the home of the **Cornish Seal Sanctuary**, where sick seals are nursed before being returned to the sea.

Cornwall's tin mining industry, from Roman to recent times, is covered at **Poldark Mine**, where underground tours show the working conditions of 18th-century miners. Another attraction is **Flambards Experience**, with its rides and recreations of a Victorian village and of Britain during the Blitz.

Further south is Britain's most southerly tourist attraction, the **Lizard Lighthouse Heritage Centre**. Built in 1619, the tower was automated in 1998. Interactive displays describe the workings of a lighthouse.

Local shops sell souvenirs carved from serpentine, a soft greenish stone which forms the unusual-shaped rocks that rise from the sandy beach at picturesque **Kynance Cove**.

🏛 **Helston Museum**
Market Place, Helston. **Tel** 01326 564027. **Open** Mon–Sat.
Closed Christmas week. ♿ ♿
📷 🅆 helstonmuseum.co.uk

🦭 **Cornish Seal Sanctuary**
Gweek. **Tel** 01326 221361. **Open** daily.
Closed 25 Dec. ♿ ♿ 🖬 📷
🅆 sealsanctuary.co.uk

🏛 **Poldark Mine**
Wendron. **Tel** 01326 573173.
Open Feb–mid-Jul, Oct: times vary; mid-Jul–Sep: daily. 📷 🖬 📷
🅆 poldarkmine.org.uk

🏛 **Flambards Experience**
Culdrose Manor, Helston. **Tel** 01326 573404. **Open** Jul & Aug: daily; times vary in other months. ♿ ♿ ✎ ♿
🅆 flambards.co.uk

🏛 **Lizard Lighthouse Heritage Centre**
Helston. **Tel** 01326 290202. **Open** Apr–Oct: Sun–Thu. ♿ 📷 📷

Cornish Smugglers

In the days before income tax was invented, the main form of government income came from tax on imported luxury goods, such as brandy and perfume. Huge profits were to be made by evading these taxes, which were at their height during the Napoleonic Wars (1780–1815). Remote Cornwall, with its coves and rivers penetrating deep into the mainland, was prime smuggling territory; estimates put the number of people involved, including women and children, at 100,000. Some notorious families resorted to deliberate wrecking, setting up deceptive lights to lure vessels onto the sharp rocks, in the hope of plundering the wreckage.

❻ Falmouth

Cornwall. 🅰 22,000. 🚊 🚌 🚌
🛈 11 Market Strand (01326 741194).
🚢 Tue. 🅆 falmouth.co.uk

Falmouth stands at the point where seven rivers flow into a long stretch of water called the **Carrick Roads**. The drowned river valley is so deep that huge ocean-going ships can sail up almost as far as Truro. Numerous creeks are ideal for boating excursions to view the varied scenery and birdlife.

Falmouth has the third largest naturally deep harbour after Sydney and Rio de Janeiro, and it forms the most interesting part of this seaside resort. On the harbour waterfront stands the **National Maritime Museum Cornwall**, part of a large waterside complex that includes cafés, shops and restaurants. The museum is dedicated to the great maritime tradition of Cornwall and contains Britain's finest public collection of historic and contemporary small craft. The hanging flotilla overhead in the Main Hall makes a great start to the five floors of exhibits.

The many old houses on the harbour include the **Customs House** and the chimney alongside, known as the "King's Pipe" because it was used for burning contraband tobacco seized from smugglers in the 19th century. **Pendennis Castle** and St Mawes Castle, opposite, were built by King Henry VIII. Towards the town centre is the **Falmouth Art Gallery**, with one of Cornwall's most important art collections.

Environs
To the south, **Glendurgan** (see p248) and **Trebah** gardens are both set in sheltered valleys leading down to delightful sandy coves on the Helford River.

IIII National Maritime Museum Cornwall
Discovery Quay, Falmouth. **Tel** 01326 313388. **Open** daily. **Closed** 25 & 26 Dec. ▨ ▤ ▦ ▦ **W** nmmc.co.uk

🏠 Pendennis Castle
The Headland. **Tel** 01326 316594. **Open** Apr–Oct: daily; Nov–Mar: Sat & Sun. **Closed** 1 Jan, 24–26 Dec ▨ ▦ ▦ limited. ▤ ▦ **EH**

Truro Cathedral, designed by J L Pearson and completed in 1910

IIII Falmouth Art Gallery
The Moor. **Tel** 01326 313863. **Open** Mon–Sat. **Closed** 1 Jan, 25 & 26 Dec. **W** falmouthartgallery.com

🌳 Glendurgan
Mawnan Smith. **Tel** 01326 252020. **Open** mid-Feb–Oct: Tue–Sun & public hols (Aug: daily). **Closed** Good Fri. ▨ ▤ ▦ **NT**

🌳 Trebah
Mawnan Smith. **Tel** 01326 252200. **Open** daily. ▨ ▦ ▤ ▦ **W** trebahgarden.co.uk

❼ Truro

Cornwall. ▨ 20,000. ⇌ ▦
ℹ Boscawen St (01872 274555). ▦ Wed & Sat (farmers' market). **W** visittruro.org.uk

Once a market town and port, Truro is now the administrative capital of Cornwall. Truro's many gracious Georgian buildings reflect its prosperity during the tin mining boom of the 1800s. In 1876 the 16th-century parish church was rebuilt to create the first new **cathedral** to be built in England since Wren built St Paul's (see pp118–19) in the 17th century. With its central tower, lancet windows and spires, the cathedral is an exuberant building that looks more French than English.

The **Royal Cornwall Museum** provides an excellent introduction to the history of the county with displays on tin mining, Methodism (see p283) and smuggling. Two of Cornwall's lush gardens (see p248) – **Trewithen** (to the east) and **Trelissick** (to the south) – are very close to the city.

IIII Royal Cornwall Museum
River St. **Tel** 01872 272205. **Open** Mon–Sat. **Closed** 1 Jan, 25 & 26 Dec. ▦ ▤ ▦ **W** royalcornwall museum.org.uk

🌳 Trewithen
Grampound Rd. **Tel** 01726 883647. **Open** Mar–Jun: daily; Jun–Sep: Mon–Sat. ▨ ▦ by arrangement. ▦ ▤ ▦ **W** trewithengardens. co.uk

🌳 Trelissick
Feock. **Tel** 01872 862090. **Open** daily. **Closed** 25 & 26 Dec. ▨ ▦ ▨ ▦ **NT**

The "Cornish Alps": china-clay spoil tips north of St Austell

❽ St Austell

Cornwall. ▨ 20,000. ⇌ ▦ **ℹ** Texaco Service Station, Southbourne Rd (01726 879500). ▦ Wed, Sat, Sun. **W** staustellbay.co.uk

The busy industrial town of St Austell is the capital of the local chinaclay industry, which rose to importance in the 18th century. China was the only other place where such quality and quantity of clay could be found, and it was in Cornwall that William Cookworthy (1705–80) succeeded in replicating the Chinese porcelain in the 18th century. Spoil tips are a prominent feature: on a sunny day they look like snow-covered peaks, meriting the local name the "Cornish Alps".

Environs
The famous **Lost Gardens of Heligan** are an amazing project to restore the extraordinary gardens created by the Tremayne family from the 16th century to World War I.

At the **Wheal Martyn China Clay Museum**, displays evoke the history and human impact of clay and clay quarrying, while nature trails weave through abandoned clay works.

🌳 Lost Gardens of Heligan
Pentewan. **Tel** 01726 845100. **Open** daily. **Closed** 24 & 25 Dec. ▨ ▦ ▨ ▤ ▦ **W** heligan.com

IIII Wheal Martyn China Clay Museum
Carthew. **Tel** 01726 850362. **Open** daily. **Closed** 24 Dec–mid-Jan. ▨ ▦ ltd. ▤ ▦ **W** wheal-martyn.com

• Eden Project

The Eden Project is a global garden for the 21st century, and a dramatic setting in which to tell the fascinating story of plants, people and places. Two futuristic conservatories mimic the environments of warmer climes, the Rainforest Biome (hot and humid) and the Mediterranean Biome (warm and dry). The outer gardens are planted with species that thrive naturally in the Cornish climate. The relationship between humans and nature is interpreted by artists throughout the site. The Core education centre is used for exhibitions, films and workshops. For an aerial view of the Biomes, visitors can ride over them on a 660-m (2,165-ft) zip wire, the longest in England.

Tropical South America
Some plants in this area reach enormous proportions. The leaves of the giant water lily can be up to 2 m (6 ft) across.

West Africa
This section features the Iboga plant, which is central to the African religion Bwiti. Highly hallucinogenic, it is an integral part of initiation ceremonies.

Malaysia
This display features a Malaysian house with a vegetable plot and a paddy field. The star attraction is the Titan arum flower, which grows to 3 m (8 ft) and smells of rotting flesh.

Rainforest Biome
This vast conservatory houses a lush jungle of trees and plants. The dome includes a treetop-level viewing platform and aerial walkway.

Tropical Islands
These islands have many fascinating plants, such as the rare Madagascar Periwinkle (*Catharanthus roseus*), which is used in the treatment of leukaemia.

Building Edenw
Cornwall's declining china clay industry left behind many disused pits and the Eden Project made ingenious use of this industrial landscape. After partly infilling a pit, the massive biomes were constructed using a record 230 miles (370 km) of scaffolding.

Transparent hexagons made
of ultra-light high-tech plastic

Crops and cultivation
The coffee plant (Coffea arabica) is one of the many plants on display that are used in our everyday lives.

The entrance to both the Rainforest and Mediterranean Biomes is via the Link, where the Eden Bakery is located.

The site

Access to the site, with its outdoor and covered Biomes, is via the Visitor Centre.

Rainforest Biome
① Tropical Islands
② Malaysia
③ West Africa
④ Tropical South America
⑤ Crops & cultivation

Mediterranean Biome
⑥ The Mediterranean
⑦ South Africa
⑧ California
⑨ Crops & cultivation

Outdoor Biome
⑩ Pollination

⑪ Cornish crops
⑫ Plants for taste
⑬ Global gardeners
⑭ Beer & brewing
⑮ Rope & fibre
⑯ Hemp
⑰ Steppe & Prairie
⑱ Eco-engineering
⑲ Tea
⑳ Lavender
㉑ Fuel
㉒ Myth & folklore
㉓ Biodiversity & Cornwall
㉔ Play
㉕ Flowers in the making
㉖ Health

㉗ Flowerless garden
㉘ Sense of Memory Garden

| 0 metres | 150 |
| 0 yards | 150 |

Key
🟩 Rainforest Biome
🟨 Mediterranean Biome
⚎ Land Train

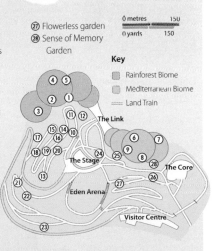

Looking out across the estuary from Fowey to Polruan

⑩ Fowey

Cornwall. 🏘 2,500. 🚇 ℹ 5 South St (01726 833616). 🌐 fowey.co.uk

The river, creeks and gentle waters of the Fowey (pronounced Foy) estuary were probably the inspiration for *The Wind in the Willows*, whose author Kenneth Grahame *(see p238)* spent holidays here. With its tangle of flower-filled streets and seafood restaurants, Fowey can get busy in the summer.

Daphne du Maurier

The period romances of Daphne du Maurier (1907–89) are inextricably linked with the wild Cornish landscape where she grew up. *Jamaica Inn* established her reputation in 1936, and with the publication of *Rebecca* two years later she found herself one of the most popular authors of her day. *Rebecca* was made into a film directed by Alfred Hitchcock, starring Joan Fontaine and Laurence Olivier.

The picturesque charm of the village is undeniable, with its tangle of tiny steep streets and its views across the estuary to Polruan.

The church of **St Fimbarrus** marks the end of the ancient Saint's Way footpath from Padstow, a reminder of the Celtic missionaries who arrived on the shores of Cornwall to convert people to Christianity. A flower-lined path leads to a majestic porch and carved tower. Inside, there are some fine 17th-century memorials to the Rashleigh family whose seat, Menabilly, became Daphne du Maurier's home and featured as Manderley in *Rebecca* (1938).

Jamaica Inn, Bodmin Moor

Environs

For a closer look at the town of **Polruan** and a tour of the busy harbour, there is a number of river trips up the little creeks. At the estuary mouth are the twin towers from which chains were once hung to demast invading ships – an effective form of defence.

A fine stretch of coast leads further east to the picturesque fishing villages of **Polperro**, nestling in a narrow green ravine, and neighbouring **Looe**.

Up-river from Fowey is the tranquil town of **Lostwithiel**. Perched on a hill just to the north are the remains of the Norman **Restormel Castle**.

🏰 Restormel Castle
Lostwithiel. **Tel** 01208 872687.
Open Apr–Oct: daily. 🅿 📷 EH

⑪ Bodmin

Cornwall. 🏘 15,000. 🚆 Bodmin Parkway. 🚌 Bodmin. ℹ Mount Folly Sq, Bodmin (01208 76616). 🌐 bodminlive.com

Bodmin, Cornwall's ancient county town, lies on the sheltered western edge of the great expanse of moorland that shares its name. The history and archaeology of the town and moor are covered by **Bodmin Town Museum**, while **Bodmin Jail**, where public executions took place until 1909, is a gruesome tourist attraction. The churchyard is watered by the ever-gushing waters of a holy spring, and it was here that St Guron established a Christian cell in the 6th century. The **church** is dedicated to St Petroc, a Welsh missionary who founded a monastery here. The monastery has disappeared, but the bones of St Petroc remain, housed in a splendid 12th-century ivory casket in the church.

For a pleasant day out, ride the **Bodmin & Wenford Railway**, a steam train which departs from Bodmin Station, or take part in a Victorian murder trial at **The Courtroom Experience**, run by the tourist office.

South of Bodmin is the **Lanhydrock** estate. Amid its extensive wooded acres and formal gardens *(see p248)* stands the massive Victorian manor house, rebuilt after a fire in 1881, but retaining some Jacobean features. The fine 17th-century plaster ceiling in the Long Gallery depicts scenes from the Bible.

The desolate wilderness of Bodmin Moor is noted for its network of prehistoric field boundaries. The main attraction, however, is the 18th-century **Jamaica Inn**, made famous by Daphne du Maurier's tale of smuggling and romance. Today there is a museum telling the story of smuggling and a room devoted to the author. A 30-minute walk from the Inn, **Dozmary Pool** was reputed to be bottomless until it dried up in 1976. According to legend, the dying King Arthur's sword Excalibur was thrown into the pool.

To the east is **Altarnun**. Its spacious 15th-century church of **St Nonna** is known as the "Cathedral of the Moor".

Bodmin Town Museum
Mt Folly Sq, Bodmin. **Tel** 01208 77067. **Open** Easter–Oct: Mon–Sat, Good Fri. **Closed** public hols.

Bodmin Jail
Berrycombe Rd, Bodmin. **Tel** 01208 76292. **Open** daily. **Closed** 25 Dec. **W** bodminjail.org

Lanhydrock
Bodmin. **Tel** 01208 265950. House: **Open** Mar–Oct: daily. Gardens: **Open** mid-Feb–Oct: daily.

⑫ Padstow

Cornwall. 3,000. North Quay (01841 533449). **W** padstowlive.com

A picturesque little fishing port on the sheltered estuary of the River Camel, chic Padstow is known principally today as a magnet for foodies. Many chefs have followed in the wake of celebrity chef Rick Stein, who opened his first seafood restaurant here in 1975. The daily catch is unloaded at the quayside, behind which cobbled streets are full of boutiques, art galleries and delicatessens. The little **Padstow Museum** displays a range of artifacts including items from the annual Obby Orse (Hobby Horse) May Day ritual. The Elizabethan manor house **Prideaux Place** has been home to the Prideaux-Brune family since 1592. It boasts superb plasterwork and is often used as a film location.

⑬ Tintagel

Cornwall. 1,800. Bossiney Rd (01840 779084). **W** visitboscastle andtintagel.com

The romantic and mysterious ruins of **Tintagel Castle**, built around 1240 by Earl Richard of Cornwall, sit high on a hilltop surrounded by slate cliffs. Access to the castle is via two steep staircases clinging to the cliffside where pink thrift and purple sea lavender abound.

The earl was persuaded to build in this isolated,

The ruins of Tintagel Castle on the north coast of Cornwall

wind-swept spot by the popular belief, derived from Geoffrey of Monmouth's fictitious *History of the Kings of Britain*, that this was the birthplace of the legendary King Arthur.

Large quantities of fine eastern Mediterranean pottery dating from around the 5th century have been discovered, indicating that the site was an important trading centre, long before the medieval castle was built. Whoever lived here, perhaps the ancient Kings of Cornwall, could evidently afford a luxurious lifestyle.

A clifftop path leads from the castle to Tintagel's **church**, which has Norman and Saxon masonry. In Tintagel village the **Old Post Office** is a rare example of a 14th-century restored and furnished Cornish manor house.

Environs
A short distance to the east, **Boscastle** is a pretty village. The River Valency runs down the middle of the main street to the fishing harbour, which is sheltered from the sea by high slate cliffs. Access from the harbour to the sea is via a channel cut through the rocks.

Tintagel Castle
Tintagel Head. **Tel** 01840 770328. **Open** Apr–Oct: daily; Nov–Mar: Sat & Sun. **Closed** 1 Jan, 24–26 Dec. **EH W** english-heritage. org.uk/tintagel

Old Post Office
Fore St. **Tel** 01840 770024. **Open** Mar–Oct: daily.

King Arthur

Historians think the legendary figure of King Arthur has some basis in historical fact. He was probably a Romano-British chieftain or warrior who led British resistance to the Saxon invasion of the 6th century *(see pp50–51)*. Geoffrey of Monmouth's *History of the Kings of Britain* (1139) introduced Arthur to literature with an account of the many legends connected with him – how he became king by removing the sword Excalibur from a stone, his final battle with the treacherous Mordred, and the story of the Knights of the Round Table *(see p174)*. Other writers, such as Alfred, Lord Tennyson, took up these stories and elaborated on them.

King Arthur, from a 14th-century chronicle by Peter of Langtoft

⓮ Bude

Cornwall. ⚏ 9,000. ⓘ Crescent Car Park (01288 354240). ☐ Easter–Oct: Fri. Ⓦ **visitbude.info**

Wonderful beaches around this area make Bude a popular resort for families. The expanse of clean golden sand that attracts visitors today once made Bude a bustling port. Shelly, lime-rich sand was transported along a canal to inland farms where it was used to neutralize the acidic soil. The canal was abandoned in 1880 but a short stretch survives, providing a haven for birds such as kingfishers and herons.

⓯ Clovelly

Devon. ⚏ 440. Tel 01237 431781. Town & Visitors' Centre: **Open** daily. **Closed** 25 & 26 Dec. ⚐ ♿ Visitors' Centre. Ⓦ **clovelly.co.uk**

Clovelly has been renowned as a beauty spot since the novelist Charles Kingsley (1819–75) wrote about it in his stirring story of the Spanish Armada, *Westward Ho!* (1855). The village is privately owned and has been turned into a tourist attraction, with little sign of the flourishing fishing industry to which it owed its birth. It is a charming village with steep, traffic-free cobbled streets rising up the cliff from the harbourside, whitewashed houses and gardens brimming with brightly coloured flowers. There are

Bideford's medieval bridge, 203 m (666 ft) long with 24 arches

superb views from the lookout points and fine coastal paths to explore from the tiny quay.

Hobby Drive is a scenic 3-mile (5-km) approach on foot to the village, running through woodland along the coast. The road was constructed in 1811–29 to give employment to local men who had been made redundant at the end of the Napoleonic Wars *(see pp58–9)*.

⓰ Bideford

Devon. ⚏ 17,000. ☒ ⓘ Burton Art Gallery, Kingsley Rd (01237 477676). Ⓦ **northdevon.com**

Strung out along the estuary of the River Torridge, Bideford grew and thrived on importing tobacco from the New World. Some 17th-century merchants' houses survive in Bridgeland Street, including the splendid bay-windowed house at No. 28 (1693). Beyond is Mill Street, leading to the parish church and the fine medieval bridge. The quay stretches from here

to a pleasant park and a statue that commemorates Charles Kingsley, whose novels helped bring visitors to the area in the 19th century.

Environs

To the west of Bideford, the village **Westward Ho!** was built in the late 19th century and named after Kingsley's popular novel. It is notable for its good surfing and the oldest golf club in England, the Royal North Devon. Rudyard Kipling *(see p167)* was at school here and the hill to the south, known as **Kipling Tors**, was the backdrop for *Stalky & Co* (1899). Also to the west is **Hartland Abbey**, built as a monastery in around 1157, now a family home. The BBC filmed parts of *Sense and Sensibility* here. Visitors can enjoy a museum and gardens.

In **Torridge Valley**, the 180-mile (290km) Tarka Trail follows the route taken by the title character in Henry Williamson's *Tarka the Otter* (1927). Part of the trail runs along a disused railway line beside the Torridge and can be enjoyed by walkers and cyclists. The trail passes close to the magnificent **Rosemoor Garden**. Day trips run from either Bideford or Ilfracombe (depending on the tide) to **Lundy Island**, which is abundant in birds and wildlife.

🌼 **RHS Rosemoor Garden**
Great Torrington. **Tel** 01805 624067. **Open** daily. **Closed** 25 Dec. ⚐ ♿ ⊘ ⌂ Ⓦ **rhs.org.uk/gardens/ rosemoor**

🏛 **Hartland Abbey**
near Bideford. **Tel** 01237 441496. **Open** Apr–Sep: Sun–Thu. ⚐ ♿ limited. ☐ ⌂ Ⓦ **hartland abbey.com**

Boats in the fishing harbour at Clovelly

For hotels and restaurants in this area see pp566–7 and pp591–3

⓱ Appledore

Devon. 🅰 2,800. 🛈 Bideford (01237 477676). 🆆 **appledore.org**

Appledore's remote position at the tip of the Torridge Estuary has helped to preserve its charms intact. Busy boatyards line the long riverside quay, which is also the departure point for fishing trips and ferries to the sandy beaches of Braunton Burrows on the opposite shore. Timeworn Regency houses line the main street that runs parallel to the quay, and behind is a network of narrow cobbled lanes with 18th-century fishermen's cottages. Several shops retain their original bow windows and sell an assortment of crafts, antiques and souvenirs. Local seafood is served in many of the town's pubs and restaurants.

Uphill from the quay is the **North Devon Maritime Museum**, with an exhibition on the experiences of Devon emigrants to Australia and displays explaining the work of local shipyards. The tiny **Victorian Schoolroom**, which is affiliated with the museum, shows various documentary videos on local trades such as fishing and shipbuilding.

🏛 **North Devon Maritime Museum**
Odun Rd. **Tel** 01237 422064.
Open Apr–Oct: 10:30am–5pm. 🅿 🅱 limited. 📷 🆆 **northdevonmaritimemuseum.co.uk**

Colourful fishermen's cottages in a narrow lane, Appledore

A customer making a purchase at Barnstaple's Pannier Market

⓲ Barnstaple

Devon. 🅰 34,000. 🚂 🚌 🛈 The Square (01271 375000). 🆆 **staynorthdevon.co.uk**

Although Barnstaple is an important distribution centre for the whole region, its town centre remains calm due to the exclusion of traffic. The massive glass-roofed **Pannier Market** (1855) has stalls of organic food, much of it produced on local farms. Nearby is **St Peter's Church** with its twisted broach spire, said to have been caused by a lightning strike warping the timbers in 1810.

On the Strand is a wonderful arcade topped with a statue of Queen Anne, now the **Heritage Centre**. This was built as an exchange where merchants traded the contents of their cargo boats moored on the River Taw alongside. Nearby is the 15th-century bridge and the **Museum of Barnstaple and North Devon**, where displays cover local history and the 700-year-old pottery industry, as well as otters and other local wildlife. The Tarka Trail *(see opposite page)* circuits around Barnstaple; 35 miles (56 km) of it can be cycled.

Statue of Queen Anne (1708)

Environs
Just west of Barnstaple, **Braunton "Great Field"** covers over 120 ha (300 acres) and is a well-preserved relic of medieval open-field cultivation. Beyond lies **Braunton Burrows**, one of the most extensive wild-dune reserves in Britain. It is a must for plant enthusiasts who are likely to spot sea kale, sea holly, sea lavender and horned poppies growing in their natural habitat. The sandy beaches and pounding waves at nearby Croyde and Woolacombe, are popular surfing spots, but there are also calmer areas of warm shallow water and rock pools.

Arlington Court and National Trust Carriage Museum, north of Barnstaple, is packed with treasures. It has a collection of horse-drawn vehicles and model ships. The grounds feature magnificent perennial borders and a lake.

🏛 **Museum of Barnstaple and North Devon**
The Square. **Tel** 01271 346747.
Open Mon–Sat. **Closed** 24 Dec–1 Jan. 🅱 ltd. 📷 🆆 **devonmuseums.net**

🚌 **Arlington Court and National Trust Carriage Museum**
Arlington. **Tel** 01271 850296.
Open mid-Feb–Oct: daily; Nov & Dec: Sat & Sun. 🅿 🅱 limited. 💻 📷 🆖

Devonshire Cream Teas

Devonians claim all other versions of a cream tea are inferior to their own. The essential ingredient is Devonshire clotted cream, which comes from Jersey cattle fed on rich Devon pasture. The cream is spread thickly on freshly baked scones, with lashings of homemade strawberry jam. Disputes about whether the cream (Devon) or jam (Cornwall) should be smeared on first can get very passionate.

A typical cream tea with scones, jam and clotted cream

Boats moored in Lynmouth harbour on a bright, sunny day

⓳ Lynton and Lynmouth

Devon. 🔼 2,000. 🚌 ℹ️ Town Hall, Lee Rd, Lynton (01598 752225). 🆆 lynton-lynmouth-tourism.co.uk

Situated at the point where the East and West Lyn rivers meet the sea, Lynmouth is a picturesque, though rather commercialized, village. The pedestrianized main street, lined with shops selling seaside souvenirs, runs parallel to the Lyn, now a canal with high embankments to protect against flash floods. One flood devastated the town at the height of the holiday season in 1952. The scars caused by the flood, which was fuelled by heavy rain on Exmoor, are now overgrown with trees in the pretty **Glen Lyn Gorge**, which leads north out of the village. Sister to Lynmouth is, Lynton, a mainly Victorian town perched on the clifftop 130 m (427 ft) above, giving lovely views across the Bristol Channel to the Welsh coast. It can be reached from the harbour front by a cliff railway (open March to October), by road or by a steep path.

Environs

Lynmouth is an excellent starting point for walks on Exmoor. There is a 2-mile (3-km) trail that leads southeast to tranquil **Watersmeet** *(see p254)*. On the western edge of Exmoor, **Combe Martin** *(see p254)* lies in a sheltered valley. On the main street, lined with Victorian villas, is the 18th-century Pack o' Cards inn, built by a gambler, with 52 windows, one for each card in the pack.

⓴ Exeter

Exeter is Devon's capital, a bustling and lively city with a great deal of character, despite the World War II bombing that destroyed much of its centre. Built high on a plateau above the River Exe, the city is encircled by substantial sections of Roman and medieval wall, and the street plan has not changed much since the Romans first laid out what is now the High Street. Elsewhere the Cathedral Close forms a pleasant green, and there are cobbled streets and narrow alleys which invite leisurely exploration. For shoppers there is a wide selection of big stores and smaller speciality shops.

Exploring Exeter

The intimate green and the close surrounding Exeter's distinctive cathedral were the medieval hub of the city. Nowadays, full of festive crowds watching buskers in the summer, the close features an array of architectural styles. One of the finest buildings is the Elizabethan **Mol's Coffee House**. Among the other notable historic buildings are the opulent Custom House (1681) by **the quay**, and the elegant 18th-century **Rougemont House**, which stands near the remains of a Norman **castle** built by William the Conqueror *(see pp50–51)*.

The port area has been transformed into a tourist attraction with its early 19th-century warehouses converted into craft shops, antique galleries and cafés. Boats can be hired for cruising down the short stretch of canal. The **Quay House Visitor Centre** (www.exeter.gov.uk; open daily Apr–Oct; weekends Nov–Mar) traces the history of Exeter with lively displays and an audio-visual presentation.

🏛️ The Guildhall

High St. **Tel** 01392 665500. **Open** daily; call for times. ♿ 🆆 exeter.gov.uk

Among the historic buildings that survived World War II is the magnificent Guildhall (1330) on the High Street. It is one of Britain's oldest civic buildings and has been a prison, a courthouse, a police station and a place for functions and celebrations. It still serves as the meeting place for the Mayor and the City Council.

⛪ Cathedral Church of St Peter

Cathedral Close. **Tel** 01392 285983. **Open** daily. 📷 ♿ 🚫 📸

Exeter's cathedral is one of the most gloriously ornamented in Britain. Except for the two Norman towers, the cathedral is mainly 14th-century and built in the style known as Decorated because of the swirling geometric patterns of the stonework. The West Front, the largest single collection (66) of medieval figure sculptures in England, includes kings, apostles and prophets.

Among the tombs around the choir is that of Edward II's

Overview of the Cathedral of St Peter in Exeter

treasurer, Walter de Stapledon (1261–1326), who was murdered by a mob in London.

⛪ Underground Passages

Paris St. **Tel** 01392 665887.
Open Jun–Sep: daily; Oct–May: Tue–Sun. 🏛 🐾

Under the city centre lie the remains of Exeter's medieval water-supply system. An excellent video and guided tour explain how the stonelined tunnels were built in the 14th and 15th centuries on a slight gradient in order to bring in fresh water for townspeople from springs outside the town. A heritage centre also explains the history of the remains.

The quay and some of the 19th-century warehouses that are now shops and eateries

🏛 The Quay

Custom House: 46 The Quay. **Tel** 01392 271611 **Open** Apr–Oct: 10am–5pm daily; Nov–Mar: 11am–4pm Sat & Sun. 🍴 🏛 🌐 exeter.gov.uk

Exeter's historic quay has been restored, with early 19th-century warehouses now home to crafts and antique shops, as well as cafés, pubs and restaurants. Boats can be hired for cruising down the canal. In the heart of the quayside is the opulent Custom House. Built in 1680, it now has a visitor centre with lively displays and audio-visual presentations highlighting Exeter's rich history.

⛪ St Nicholas Priory

The Mint. **Tel** 01392 665858. **Closed** for restoration. 🐾 ♿ limited. 🏛

Built in the 12th century, this building has retained many of its original features and rooms. Its history runs from monastic

beginnings and wealthy Tudor residence through to premises for a 20th-century bootmaker and upholsterer.

🏛 Royal Albert Memorial Museum and Art Gallery

Queen St. **Tel** 01392 265858.
Open Tue–Sun. 🍴 ♿ 🏛 🏛

This family-friendly museum has a wonderfully varied collection, including Roman remains, a zoo of stuffed animals, West Country art and a particularly good ethnographic display, including a Samurai warrior. You can discover the city's past in the interactive Making History gallery, and the Finders Keepers display explores the morality of collecting and the story behind the artifacts.

Environs

South of Exeter on the A376, the eccentric **A La Ronde** is a 16-sided house built in 1796 by two spinster cousins, who decorated the interior with shells, feathers and souvenirs gathered while on tours of Europe.

Further east, the unspoilt Regency town of **Sidmouth** lies in a sheltered bay. It boasts an eclectic array of architecture, the earliest buildings dating from the 1820s when Sidmouth became a popular summer resort. Thatched cottages stand opposite huge Edwardian villas, and elegant terraces line the seafront. In summer the town hosts FolkWeek, celebrating music and dance (see p67).

North of Sidmouth lies the magnificent church at **Ottery St Mary**. Built in 1338–42 by Bishop Grandisson, the church

VISITORS' CHECKLIST

Practical Information
Devon. 🗺 125,000.
ℹ Dix's Field (01392 665700).
🌐 visitexeter.com

Transport
✈ 5 miles (8 km) east. 🚆 Exeter St David's, Bonhay Rd; Exeter Central, Queen St. 🚌 Paris St.

is clearly a scaled-down version of Exeter Cathedral, which he had helped build. In the churchyard wall is a memorial to the poet Coleridge, who was born in the town in 1772.

Nearby **Honiton** is famous for its extraordinarily intricate and delicate lace, which you can see in the Honiton Lace Museum.

To the north of Exeter, **Killerton** is home to the National Trust's costume collection. Here, displays of bustles and corsets and vivid tableaux illustrate aristocratic fashions from the 18th century to the present day.

Further north, near Tiverton, is **Knightshayes Court**, a Victorian Gothic mansion, designed by William Burges, with fine gardens of rare shrubs (see p249).

🏛 A La Ronde

Summer Lane, Exmouth. **Tel** 01395 265514. **Open** Feb–Oct: 11am–5pm 🐾 🏛 🏛 🆕 🌐 nationaltrust. org.uk

🏛 Killerton

Broadclyst. **Tel** 01392 881345. House & Garden: **Open** daily. 🐾 ♿ 🏛 🆕

🏛 Knightshayes Court

Bolham. **Tel** 01884 254665. **Open** daily. **Closed** 25 Dec. 🐾 ♿ limited. 🐾 🏛 🆕

Ladram Bay and its sandstone rock stacks, Sidmouth

㉑ Torbay

Torbay. 🚢 🚍 Torquay, Paignton.
🛈 5 Vaughan Parade, Torquay (01803 211211). 🆆 **englishriviera.co.uk**

The seaside towns of Torquay, Paignton and Brixham form an almost continuous resort around the great sweep of sandy beach and blue waters of Torbay. Because of its mild climate, semi-tropical gardens and exuberant Victorian hotel architecture, this popular coastline has been dubbed the English Riviera. In the Victorian era Torbay was patronized by the wealthy. Today, the theme is mass entertainment, and there are plenty of attractions, mostly in and around Torquay.

Torre Abbey includes the remains of a monastery founded in 1196. The mansion dates back to the 17th century, and houses an art gallery and museum, though other rooms have been preserved as they were in the 1920s, when it was still a private residence. **Torquay Museum** nearby covers natural history and archaeology, including finds from **Kents Cavern**, on the outskirts of the town. This is one of England's most important prehistoric sites, and the spectacular caves include displays on people and animals who lived here up to 350,000 years ago.

The charming miniature town of **Babbacombe Model Village** is north of Torquay, while a mile (1.5 km) inland is the lovely village of **Cockington**. It is possible to visit the preserved Tudor manor house, church and thatched cottages and watch craftsmen at work.

In Paignton, the celebrated **Paignton Zoo** teaches children about the planet's wildlife, and from here you can take the steam railway – an ideal way to visit Dartmouth.

Further south beyond Paignton, the pretty town of Brixham was once England's most prosperous fishing port.

🏛 **Torre Abbey**
King's Drive, Torquay. **Tel** 01803 293593. **Open** Mar–Dec: Wed–Sun (Jul–Sep: daily). **Closed** 25 Dec. 🖼 🎫 ♿ 🖥 📷

Bayards Cove, Dartmouth

🏛 **Torquay Museum**
Babbacombe Rd, Torquay. **Tel** 01803 293975. **Open** daily (Nov–Easter: Mon–Sat). **Closed** Christmas week. 🖼 ♿ 🖥 📷 🆆 **torquaymuseum.org**

🏛 **Kents Cavern**
Ilsham Rd, Torquay. **Tel** 01803 215136. **Open** daily. **Closed** 25 Dec. 🖼 🎫 🍴 🖥 🆆 **kents-cavern.co.uk**

🏛 **Babbacombe Model Village**
Hampton Ave, Torquay. **Tel** 01803 315 315. **Open** daily. **Closed** 25 Dec. 🖼 ♿ 🖥

🦓 **Paignton Zoo**
Totnes Rd, Paignton. **Tel** 01803 697500. **Open** daily. **Closed** 25 Dec. 🖼 ♿ 🍴 📷 🆆 **paigntonzoo.org.uk**

㉒ Dartmouth

Devon. 🗠 5,500. 🚍 🛈 Mayors Ave (01803 834224). 🛒 Tue & Fri am. 🆆 **discoverdartmouth.com**

Sitting high on the hill above the River Dart is the **Royal Naval College**, where British naval officers have trained since 1905. Dartmouth has always been an important port and it was from here that English fleets set sail to join the Second and Third Crusades. Some 18th-century houses adorn the cobbled quay of Bayards Cove, while carved timber buildings line the 17th-century Butterwalk, home to **Dartmouth Museum**. To the south is **Dartmouth Castle** (1388).

🏛 **Dartmouth Museum**
Butterwalk. **Tel** 01803 832923. **Open** daily. **Closed** 1 Jan, 25 & 26 Dec. 🖼 📷 🆆 **dartmouthmuseum.org**

🏰 **Dartmouth Castle**
Castle Rd. **Tel** 01803 833588. **Open** daily (Nov–Easter: Sat & Sun). **Closed** 1 Jan, 24–26 Dec. 🖼 📷 EH

Torquay, on the "English Riviera"

For hotels and restaurants in this area see pp566–7 and pp591–3

Stained-glass window in Blessed Sacrament Chapel, Buckfast Abbey

Nearby is the **Buckfast Butterfly Farm and Dartmoor Otter Sanctuary**, and the **South Devon Steam Railway** terminus where steam trains leave for Totnes.

🏛 **Buckfast Abbey**
Buckfastleigh. **Tel** 01364 645500.
Open daily. **Closed** Good Fri, 25–27 Dec. ♿ 🚻 📷 🌐 buckfasttourism.org.uk

🦋 **Buckfast Butterfly Farm and Dartmoor Otter Sanctuary**
Buckfastleigh. **Tel** 01364 642916.
Open daily. 🚻 ♿ 🌐 ottersand butterflies.co.uk

㉕ Burgh Island

Devon. 🚂 Plymouth then taxi.
ℹ The Quay, Kingsbridge (01548 853 195). 🌐 welcomesouthdevon.co.uk

The short walk across the sands at low tide from Bigbury-on-Sea to Burgh Island takes you back to the era of the 1920s and 1930s. It was here that the millionaire Archibald Nettlefold built the luxury **Burgh Island** hotel (see p566) in 1929. Created in Art Deco style with a natural rock sea-bathing pool, this was the exclusive retreat of figures such as the Duke of Windsor and Noël Coward. The restored hotel is worth a visit to see the photographs of its heyday and the Art Deco fittings. You can also explore the island; the **Pilchard Inn** (1336) is reputed to be haunted by the ghost of a smuggler.

㉓ Totnes

Devon. ⛰ 8,000. 🚂 🚌 🚲
🅿 Tue am (Jun–Sep), Fri, Sat.
🌐 englishriviera.co.uk

One of the most ecologically minded towns in the UK, vibrant Totnes is committed to sustainable food, energy and buildings. It is set at the highest navigable point on the River Dart, with a Norman **castle** perched high on the hill above. Linking the two is the steep High Street, lined with bow-windowed Elizabethan houses. Bridging the street is the **Eastgate**, part of the medieval town wall. Life in the town's heyday is explored in the **Totnes Elizabethan Museum**, which also has a room devoted to the mathematician Charles Babbage (1791–1871), who is regarded as the pioneer of modern computers. There is a **Guildhall**, and a **church** with a delicately carved and gilded rood screen. On Tuesdays in the summer, market stall-holders dress in colourful Elizabethan costume.

Environs
A few miles north of Totnes, **Dartington Hall** has 10 ha (25 acres) of lovely gardens and hosts a music school every August, when concerts are held in the timbered 14th-century Great Hall.

🏰 **Totnes Castle**
Castle St. **Tel** 01803 864406. **Open** Apr–Oct: daily, Nov–Mar: Sat & Sun. 📷 🅱

🏛 **Totnes Elizabethan Museum**
Fore St. **Tel** 01803 863821.
Open Apr–Sep: Mon & Tue. 🚻 ♿ limited. 🌐 totnesmuseum.org

🏛 **Guildhall**
Ramparts Walk. **Tel** 01803 862147.
Open Mon–Fri. **Closed** public hols.

🌳 **Dartington Hall Gardens**
Tel 01803 847514. **Open** daily.
🌐 dartington.org

㉔ Buckfastleigh

Devon. ⛰ 3,300. 🚂 ℹ Fore St (01364 644522).

This market town, situated on the edge of Dartmoor (see pp298–9), is dominated by **Buckfast Abbey**. The original abbey, founded in Norman times, fell into ruin after the Dissolution of the Monasteries and it was not until 1882 that a small group of French Benedictine monks set up a new abbey here. Work on the present building was financed by donations and carried out by the monks. The abbey was completed in 1938 and lies at the heart of a thriving community. The fine mosaics and modern stained-glass window are also the work of the monks.

The Art Deco bar in the luxury Burgh Island Hotel

㉖ Plymouth

Plymouth. 🗺 250,000. ✈ 🚢 🚌
🛈 The Mayflower, The Barbican
(01752 306330). 🚢 Mon–Sat.
🌐 **visitplymouth.co.uk**

The tiny port from which Drake,
Raleigh, the Pilgrim Fathers,
Cook and Darwin all set sail on
pioneering voyages has now
grown to a substantial city,
much of it boldly rebuilt after
wartime bombing. Old
Plymouth clusters
around the **Hoe**, the
famous patch of turf
on which Sir Francis
Drake is said to have
calmly finished his
game of bowls as
the Spanish Armada
approached the port
in 1588 (see pp54–5).

Drake's coat of arms

Today the Hoe is a pleasant park
and parade ground surrounded
by memorials to naval men,
including Drake himself.
Alongside is Charles II's **Royal
Citadel**, built to guard the
harbour in the 1660s. On the
harbour is the **National Marine
Aquarium**. Nearby is the

Mayflower Stone and Steps, the
spot where the Pilgrim Fathers
set sail for the New World in
England's third and successful
attempt at colonization in
1620. The popular **Plymouth
Mayflower Exhibition** explores
the story of the *Mayflower* and
the creation of the harbour.
Interactive graphics are used
to tell the tales of merchant
families and emigration to the
New World.

Environs

A boat tour of the
harbour is the best
way to see the
dockyards where
warships have
been built since
the Napoleonic
Wars. There are
also splendid views of various
fine gardens, such as **Mount
Edgcumbe Park** (see p248),
scattered around the coastline.
East of the city, the 18th-century
Saltram House has two rooms
by Robert Adam (see p32) and
portraits by Reynolds, who was
born in nearby Plympton.

Mid-18th-century carved wood
chimneypiece, Saltram House

🏰 **Royal Citadel**
The Hoe. **Open** May–Sep: Tue, Thu
& Sun. 🅿 📷 only. EH 🌐 **english-
heritage.org.uk**

🐟 **National Marine Aquarium**
Rope Walk, Coxside. **Tel** 08448 937938.
Open daily. **Closed** 25 & 26 Dec. 🅿
♿ 🖥 🌐 **national-aquarium.co.uk**

🏛 **Plymouth Mayflower
Exhibition**
3–5 The Barbican. **Tel** 01752 306330.
Open daily (Nov–Apr: Mon–Sat).
🅿 ♿

🏡 **Mount Edgcumbe Park**
Cremyll, Torpoint. 🚢 from Torpoint
car park. **Tel** 01752 822236. House:
Open Apr–Sep: Sun–Thu. Grounds:
Open all year. 🅿 📷 ♿ 🚫 🖥 🏠
🌐 **mountedgcumbe.gov.uk**

🏰 **Saltram House**
Plympton. **Tel** 01752 333500. House:
Open Mar–Dec: daily. **Closed** 25 & 26
Dec. Gardens: **Open** all year. 🅿 📷
♿ limited. 🚫 🖥 🏠 NT

㉗ Buckland Abbey

Yelverton, Devon. **Tel** 01822 853607.
🚌 from Yelverton. **Open** mid-Feb–
Oct & 6–22 Dec: daily; Nov: Fri–Sun.
Closed 25 Dec–mid-Feb. 🅿 ♿ 🚫
🏠 NT 🌐 **nationaltrust.org.uk**

Founded by the Cistercian
monks in 1278, Buckland
Abbey was converted to a
house after the Dissolution of
the Monasteries and became
the home of Sir Francis Drake
from 1581. Many of the
monastic buildings survive
in a garden setting, notably
the 14th-century tithe barn
(see p36). Drake's life is recalled
through paintings and
memorabilia in the house.

Plymouth Harbour as seen from the Hoe

❷❽ Cotehele

St Dominick, Cornwall.
Tel 01579 351346. 🚋 Calstock.
House: Open mid-Mar–Oct: daily.
Grounds: Open daily. 🅿
🚻 limited. 🖉 🗍 🖾 ⚲ NT

Magnificent woodland and
lush river scenery make
Cotehele (pronounced Coteal)
one of the most delightful
spots on the River Tamar and
a rewarding day can be spent
exploring the estate. Far from
civilization, tucked into its
wooded fold in the Cornish
countryside, Cotehele has
slumbered for 500 years. The
main attraction is the house
and valley garden at its centre.
Built mainly between 1489 and
1520, it is a rare example of a
medieval house, set around
three courtyards with a
magnificent open hall, kitchen,
chapel and a warren of private
parlours and chambers. The
romance of the house is enhanced by colourful terraced
gardens to the east, leading via
a tunnel into a richly planted
valley garden. The path
through this garden passes
a large domed medieval
dovecote and descends to a
quay, to which lime and coal
were once shipped, and now
features a restored sailing
barge and a small maritime
museum. There are fine views
up and down the winding
reed-fringed Tamar from
Prospect Tower, and a gallery
on the quayside specializes in
local arts and crafts. The estate
includes a village, working
mill buildings, ancient lime
kilns and workshops.

Medieval dovecote in the gardens
of Cotehele estate

Spanish Armada and British fleets in the English Channel, 1588

Sir Francis Drake

Sir Francis Drake (c.1540–1596) was the first Englishman to
circumnavigate the globe and was knighted by Elizabeth I in 1580.
Four years later he introduced tobacco and potatoes to England,
after bringing home 190 colonists who had tried to establish a
settlement in Virginia. To many, however, Drake was no more than
an opportunistic rogue, renowned for his exploits as a "privateer",
the polite name for a pirate. Catholic Spain was the bitter enemy
and Drake further endeared himself to queen and people by his part
in the victory over Philip II's Armada *(see pp54–5)*, defeated by bad
weather and the buccaneering spirit of the English.

❷❾ Morwellham Quay

Near Tavistock, Devon. **Tel** 01822
832766. 🚋 Gunnislake. **Open** daily.
Closed 25 & 26 Dec. 🅿 🗍 🚻 ltd.
🗍 🖾 🖥 morwellham-quay.co.uk

Morwellham Quay was a
neglected and overgrown
industrial site until 1970, when
members of a local trust began
restoring the abandoned
cottages, schoolhouse, farm-
yards, quay and copper mines
to their original condition.

Today, Morwellham Quay
is a thriving and rewarding
industrial museum, where
you can easily spend a whole
day partaking in the typical
activities of a Victorian village,
from preparing the shire horses
for a day's work, to riding a
tramway deep into a copper
mine in the hillside behind
the village. The museum is
brought to life by characters in
costumes, some of whom give
demonstrations throughout
the day. You can watch, or lend
a hand to the cooper while he
builds a barrel, attend a lesson

Industrial relics at Morwellham Quay
in the Tamar Valley

in the schoolroom, take
part in Victorian playground
games or dress up in 19th-
century hooped skirts,
bonnets, top hats or jackets.
The staff, who convincingly
play the part of villagers, lead
visitors through Victorian life
and impart a huge amount
of information about the
history of this small coppermining community.

30 Dartmoor National Park

The dramatic landscape of central Dartmoor is one of contrasts, providing an impressive variety of striking vistas. The high, open moorlands served as the eerie backdrop for the Sherlock Holmes tale *The Hound of the Baskervilles* (1902), while one of Britain's most famous prisons, Dartmoor Prison, is surrounded by weathered outcrops of stone tors in Princetown. Also dotting the landscape are scores of ancient remains that have survived thanks to the durability of granite. Creating pockets of tranquility, streams tumble through wooded and boulder-strewn ravines forming waterfalls, and thatched cottages nestle in the sheltered valleys and villages around the margins of the moor.

Lydford Gorge
There is a circular 5-km (3-mile) walk through this remote ravine.

St Michael de Rupe
Legend has it that the Devil tried to prevent the construction of this church, perched atop Brent Tor, by moving the stones. Whatever the truth, there has been a church here since the 12th century. Reached by a footpath, there are stunning views over Dartmoor from here.

KEY

① **Dartmoor Prison**

② **The Ministry of Defence** uses much of this area for training but access is available on non-firing days (call 0800 458 4868 to check).

③ **Okehampton** is home to the Museum of Dartmoor Life and a ruined 14th-century castle.

④ **Grimspound** is the impressive remains of a Bronze Age settlement.

⑤ **Dartmeet** marks the confluence of the East and West Dart rivers.

⑥ **Becky Falls** is a 22-m (72-ft) high waterfall set in delightful woodlands.

⑦ **Haytor Rocks** is one of the most remarkable of Dartmoor's many tors.

⑧ **Bovey Tracey** is a small town close to an extensive woodland reserve.

⑨ **Buckfast Abbey** was founded by King Canute in 1018 *(see p295)*.

⑩ **Buckfast Butterfly Farm and Dartmoor Otter Sanctuary** *(see p295)*.

⑪ **South Devon Steam Railway** runs between Buckfastleigh and Totnes.

Meldon

High Willhays
622 m (2000 ft)

A386

Lydford

Mary Tavy ②

River Walkham

Postbridge

Two Bridges

Princetown ①

Tavistock

Gulworthy

A386

Yelverton

River Plym

0 kilometres 5

0 miles 5

Cornwood

Plympton Ivybr

A3

Postbridge
In the centre of the moor and set on the River Dart, the village of Postbridge is a good starting point for walks on the moor. There is a medieval "clapper" bridge here, built to enable pack horses to carry mined tin across the river.

VISITORS' CHECKLIST

Practical Information
Devon. **Map** D5. Dartmoor
National Park Authority Visitor
Centre, Tavistock Rd, Princetown
(01822 890 414). **dartmoor.
gov.uk**. Okehampton Castle:
Castle Lane. **Tel** 01837 52844.
Open Apr–Oct 10am–5pm daily.
Museum of Dartmoor Life:
West St, Okehampton. **Tel** 01837
52295. **Open** Apr–mid-Dec:
10am–3pm Mon–Fri, 10am–
1pm Sat. Castle Drogo:
Drewsteignton. **Tel** 01647 433306.
Open Castle: Mar–Oct: 11am–
5pm daily; Nov–mid-Dec: 11am–
4pm Sat & Sun. Gardens: Mar–Oct:
10am–5:30pm daily; Nov–mid-
Dec: 11am–4pm Sat & Sun.
gardens only. NT

Transport
Exeter, Plymouth, Totnes
then bus.

Castle Drogo
This magnificent early 20th-century mock castle – said to be the last castle built in England – was designed by architect Edwin Lutyens for the grocery magnate Julius Drewe. From the house there are lovely walks through the gorge of the River Teign.

Hound Tor
The remains of this village lie on the eastern edge of Dartmoor. The settlement consists of a cluster of 13th-century stone longhouses – in which the family lived at one end and the animals at the other – on land that was originally farmed in the Bronze Age. It was probably deserted in the early 15th century.

Key
— Major road
Secondary road
Other road

Buckland-in-the-Moor
One of the many picturesque villages on the southeastern side of Dartmoor, Buckland-in-the-Moor features a cluster of pretty thatched stone cottages and a small granite church.

For keys to symbols *see back flap*

THE MIDLANDS

Introducing the Midlands   302–309
The Heart of England   310–333
East Midlands   334–347

The Midlands at a Glance

The Midlands is an area that embraces wonderful landscapes and massive industrial cities. Visitors come to discover the wild beauty of the rugged Peaks, cruise slowly along the Midlands canals on gaily painted narrowboats and explore varied and enchanting gardens. The area encompasses the full range of English architecture from mighty cathedrals and humble churches to charming spa towns, stately homes and country cottages. There are fascinating industrial museums, many in picturesque settings.

Locator Map

Tissington Trail *(see p341)* combines a walk through scenic Peak District countryside with an entertaining insight into the ancient custom of well dressing.

Ironbridge Gorge *(see pp318–19)* was the birthplace of the Industrial Revolution *(see pp352–3)*. Now a World Heritage Site, it is a reminder of the lovely countryside in which the original factories were located.

The Cotswolds *(see pp308–9)* are full of delightful houses built from local limestone, on the profits of the medieval wool trade. Snowshill Manor *(above)* is situated near the unspoilt village of Broadway.

Warrington

Chester

CHESHIRE

Crewe

Stoke-on-Trent

STAFFORD-SHIRE

SHROPSHIRE

Shrewsbury

Telford

Wolverham

THE HEART OF ENGLAND
(See pp310–333)

Birmingham

Ludlow

WORCESTER-SHIRE

Leominster

Stratf upon-A

HEREFORD-SHIRE

Worcester

Hereford

Tewkesbury

Ross-on-Wye

Cheltenham

Gloucester

GLOUCESTER-SHIRE

Cirencester

Stratford-upon-Avon *(see pp328–31)* has many picturesque houses connected with William Shakespeare, some of which are open to visitors. These black-and-white timber-framed buildings, such as Anne Hathaway's house *(left)*, are typical examples of Tudor architecture *(see pp306–7)*.

◀ Edale plateau in the Peak District National Park

Chatsworth House *(see pp338–9)*, a magnificent Baroque edifice, is famous for its gorgeous garden. The Case *(right)*, also known as the "Conservative Wall", is a greenhouse for exotic plants and shrubs. It is also used to grow fruit, including figs, apricots and nectarines.

Worksop

Chesterfield

Lincoln

NOTTINGHAM-
SHIRE

Mansfield

LINCOLNSHIRE

Newark-
on-Trent

Boston

Derby

Nottingham

EAST MIDLANDS
(See pp334–347)

Loughborough

EICESTERSHIRE

Stamford

Leicester

Corby

Coventry

NORTHAMPTON-
SHIRE

VICK-
HE

wick

Northampton

Lincoln Cathedral *(see p345)*, a vast, imposing building, dominates the ancient town. Inside are splendid misericords and the superb 13th-century Angel Choir, which has 30 carved angels.

Burghley House *(see pp346–7)* is a dazzling landmark for miles around in the flat East Midlands landscape, with architectural motifs from the European Renaissance.

0 kilometres	25
0 miles	25

Warwick Castle *(see pp326–7)* is an intriguing mixture of medieval power base and country house, complete with massive towers, battlements, a dungeon and state rooms, such as the Queen Anne Bedroom *(left)*.

Canals of the Midlands

One of England's first canals opened in 1761, built in the northwest by the 3rd Duke of Bridgewater to link the coal mine on his Worsley estate with Manchester's textile factories. This heralded the start of a canal-building boom and, by 1805, a 3,000-mile (4,800-km) network of waterways had been dug across the country, linking into the natural river system. Canals provided the cheapest, fastest way of transporting goods, until competition arrived from the railways in the 1840s. Cargo transport ended in 1963 but today nearly 2,000 miles (3,200 km) of canals are still navigable, for those who wish to take a leisurely cruise on a narrowboat.

The Grand Union Canal (pictured in 1931) is 300 miles (485 km) long and was dug in the 1790s to link London with the Midlands.

Lock-keepers were provided with canalside houses.

Lockside inns cater for narrowboats.

The Farmer's Bridge is a flight of 13 locks in Birmingham. Locks are used to raise or lower boats from one level of the canal to another. The steeper the gradient, the more locks are needed.

Heavy V-shaped timber gates close off the lock.

Water pressing against the gate keeps it shut.

The towpath is where horses pulled the canal boats before engines were used. They were changed periodically for fresh animals.

Narrowboats have straight sides and flat bottoms and are pointed at both ends. Cargo space took up most of the boat, with a small cabin for the crew. Exteriors were brightly painted.

Nº 7 · BILL O TOMS · NEW MARTON LOCK

Midlands Canal Network

The industrial Midlands was the birthplace of the English canal system and still has the biggest concentration of navigable waterways.

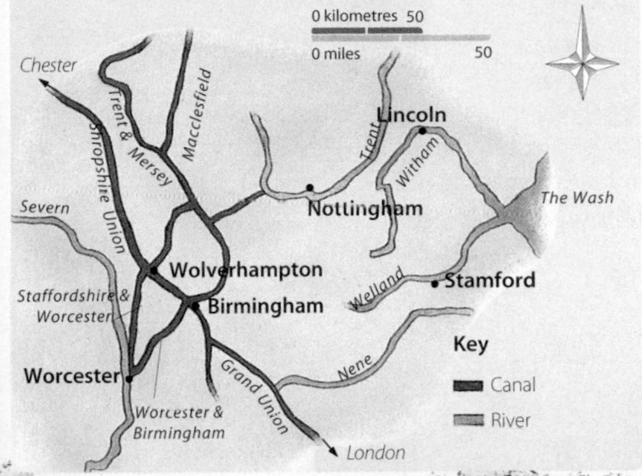

0 kilometres 50
0 miles 50

Chester
Macclesfield
Trent & Mersey
Shropshire Union
Lincoln
Nottingham
Witham
The Wash
Severn
Wolverhampton
Staffordshire & Worcester
Birmingham
Stamford
Welland
Worcester
Grand Union
Nene
Worcester & Birmingham
London

Key
■ Canal
■ River

VISITORS' CHECKLIST

Practical Information
Canalboat holidays: Hoseasons **Tel** 0844 847 1356; Canal Cruising Co: **Tel** 01785 813982 (office hours only); Black Prince Holidays: **Tel** 01527 575115; ABC Leisure Group Ltd: **Tel** 0330 333 0590. Canal museums (phone to check opening times) – National Waterways Museum Gloucester *(see p333)*: **Tel** 01452 318200. The Canal Museum: Stoke Bruerne. **Tel** 01604 862229. National Waterways Museum: Ellesmere Port. **Tel** 0151 3555017.
w canalrivertrust.org.uk

Canal

Footbridge

A windlass fills or lowers water levels.

A balance beam swings the gates open.

Canal Locks

Canals used tunnels, embankments and locks for the speedy transportation of goods across country. Locks were used to convey boats up or down hills.

The Edstone Aqueduct, just north of Stratford-upon-Avon, carries the canal in a cast-iron trough. This is supported on brick piers for 180 m (495 ft), over roads and a busy railway line.

Canal Art

Canalboat cabins are very small and every inch of space is utilized to make a comfortable home for the occupants. Interiors were enlivened with colourful paintings and attractive decorations.

Narrowboats are often decorated with ornamental brass.

Furniture was designed to be functional and to brighten up the cramped cabin.

Water cans were also painted. The most common designs were roses and castles, with local variations in style.

Tudor Manor Houses

Many striking manor houses were built in central England during the Tudor Age *(see pp54–5)*, a time of relative peace and prosperity. The abolition of the monasteries meant that vast estates were broken up and sold to secular landowners, who built houses to reflect their new status *(see pp32–3)*. In the Midlands, wood was the main building material, and the gentry flaunted their wealth by using timber panelling for flamboyant decorative effect.

The decorative moulding on the south wing dates from the late 16th century. Ancient motifs, such as vines and trefoils, are combined with the latest imported Italian Renaissance styles.

The rectangular moat was for decoration rather than defence. It surrounds a recreated knot garden *(see p31)* that was laid out in 1972 using plants known to have been available in Tudor times.

The Long Gallery was one of the last parts to be built (c.1560–62). It has original plasterwork portraying *Destiny* (left) and *Fortune*.

Jetties (overhanging upper storey)

Brickwork chimney

Tudor Mansions and Tudor Revival

There are many sumptuously decorated Tudor mansions in the Midlands. In the 19th century Tudor Revival architecture became a very popular "Old English" style, intended to evoke family pride and values rooted in the past.

Hardwick Hall in Derbyshire, whose huge kitchen is pictured, is one of the finest Tudor mansions in the country. These buildings are known as "prodigy" houses due to their gigantic size.

Charlecote Park, Warwickshire, is a brick mansion built by Sir Thomas Lucy in 1551–59. It was heavily restored in Tudor style in the 19th century, but has a fine original gatehouse. According to legend, the young William Shakespeare *(see pp328–31)* was caught poaching deer in the park.

The Little Parlour was an informal reception room. The biblical scene of *Susannah and the Elders (right)* expressed religious faith and learning.

Entrance

The Great Hall (c.1504–08) is the oldest part of the house, and in Tudor times was the most important. The open-plan hall was the main communal area for dining and entertainment.

Wood panelling

Courtyard

Little Moreton Hall

The Moreton family home *(see p315)* was built between 1504 and 1610 from a number of box-shapes fitted together. Wood panelling and jetties displayed the family's wealth.

The patterned glazing in the great bay window is typically 16th-century: small pieces of locally made glass were cut into various shapes and held in place by lead glazing bars.

Packwood House, Warwickshire, is a timber-framed mid-Tudor house with extensive 17th-century additions. The unusual garden of clipped yew trees dates from the 17th century and is supposed to represent the Sermon on the Mount.

Wightwick Manor, West Midlands, was built in 1887–93. It is a fine example of Tudor Revival architecture and has superb late 19th-century furniture and decorations.

Moseley Old Hall, Staffordshire, has a red-brick exterior concealing its early 17th-century timber frame. The King's Room is where Charles II hid after the Battle of Worcester *(see pp56–7)*.

Building with Cotswold Stone

The Cotswolds are a range of limestone hills running over 50 miles (80 km) in a north-easterly direction from Bath *(see pp262–5)*. The thin soils here are difficult to plough but ideal for grazing sheep, and the wealth engendered by the medieval wool trade was poured into building majestic churches and opulent town houses. Stone quarried from these hills was used to build London's St Paul's Cathedral *(see pp118–19)*, as well as the villages, barns and manor houses that make the local landscape so picturesque.

Arlington Row Cottages in Bibury, a typical Cotswold village, were built in the 17th century for weavers whose looms were set up in the attics.

Windows were taxed and glass expensive. Workers' cottages had only a few, not very large windows made of small panes of glass.

A drip mould keeps rain off the chimney.

The roof is steeply pitched to carry the weight of the tiles. These were made by master craftsmen who would split blocks of stone into sheets by using natural fault lines.

Cotswold Stone Cottage

The two-storey Arlington Row Cottages are asymmetrical and built of odd-shaped stones. Small windows and doorways make them quite dark inside.

Timber lintels and doors

Timber framing was cheaper than stone, and was used for the upper rooms in the roof.

Variations in Stone

Cotswold stone is warmer-toned in the north, pearly in central areas and light grey in the south. The stone seems to glow with absorbed sunlight. It is a soft stone that is easily carved and can be used for many purposes, from buildings to bridges, headstones and gargoyles.

"Tiddles" is a cat's gravestone in Fairford churchyard.

Lower Slaughter gets its name from the Anglo-Saxon word *slough*, or muddy place. It has a low stone bridge over the River Eye.

Cotswold Stone Towns and Villages

The villages and towns on this map are prime examples of places built almost entirely from stone. By the 12th century almost all of the villages in the area were established. Huge deposits of limestone resulted in a wealth of stone buildings. Masons worked from distinctive local designs that were handed down from generation to generation.

① Winchcombe
② Broadway
③ Stow-on-the-Wold
④ Upper and Lower Slaughter
⑤ Bourton-on-the-Water
⑥ Sherborne
⑦ Northleach
⑧ Painswick
⑨ Bibury
⑩ Fairford

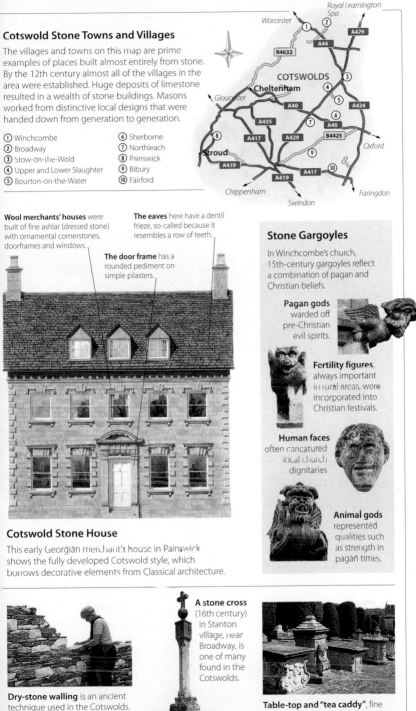

Wool merchants' houses were built of fine ashlar (dressed stone) with ornamental cornerstones, doorframes and windows.

The eaves here have a dentil frieze, so-called because it resembles a row of teeth.

The door frame has a rounded pediment on simple pilasters.

Cotswold Stone House

This early Georgian merchant's house in Painswick shows the fully developed Cotswold style, which borrows decorative elements from Classical architecture.

Stone Gargoyles

In Winchcombe's church, 15th-century gargoyles reflect a combination of pagan and Christian beliefs.

Pagan gods warded off pre-Christian evil spirits.

Fertility figures, always important in rural areas, were incorporated into Christian festivals.

Human faces often caricatured local church dignitaries.

Animal gods represented qualities such as strength in pagan times.

Dry-stone walling is an ancient technique used in the Cotswolds. The stones are held in place without mortar.

A stone cross (16th century) in Stanton village, near Broadway, is one of many found in the Cotswolds.

Table-top and "tea caddy", fine 18th-century tombs, can be found in Painswick churchyard.

THE HEART OF ENGLAND

Cheshire · Gloucestershire · Herefordshire · Shropshire
Staffordshire · Warwickshire · Worcestershire

Britain's great attraction is its variety, and nowhere is this more true than at the heart of the country, where the Cotswold hills, enfolding stone cottages and churches, give way to the flat, fertile plains of Warwickshire. Shakespeare Country borders on the industrial heart of England, once known as the workshop of the world.

Coventry, Birmingham, the Potteries and their hinterlands have been manufacturing iron, textiles and ceramics since the 18th century. In the 20th century these industries declined, and a new type of museum has developed to commemorate the towns' industrial heyday and explain the manufacturing processes that were once taken for granted. Ironbridge Gorge and Quarry Bank, Styal, where the factories are now living museums, are fascinating industrial sites and enjoy beautiful surroundings.

These landscapes may be appreciated from the deck of a narrowboat, making gentle progress along the Midlands canals, to the region on the border with Wales known as the Marches.

Here the massive walls of Chester and the castles at Shrewsbury and Ludlow recall the Welsh locked in fierce battle with Norman barons and the Marcher Lords. The Marches are now full of rural communities served by the peaceful market towns of Ludlow, Leominster, Malvern, Ross-on-Wye and Hereford. The cities of Worcester and Gloucester both have modern shopping centres, yet their majestic cathedrals retain the tranquillity of an earlier age.

Cheltenham has Regency terraces, Cirencester a rich legacy of Roman art and Tewkesbury a solid Norman abbey. Finally, there is Stratford-upon-Avon, where William Shakespeare, the world's greatest dramatist, lived and died.

Barges and narrow boats moored at Diglis Marina, Worcestershire

◀ Gardens behind the house of Mary Arden, Shakespeare's mother

Exploring the Heart of England

In many ways, the heart of England is an idyllic and peaceful landscape, characterized by pretty little market towns with picturesque houses, alongside pubs and churches made from timber and Cotswold stone. The area around Birmingham and Stoke-on-Trent, however – once the industrial hub of England – contrasts sharply. The bleak concrete skyline may not appeal, but the area has a fascinating history that is reflected in its self-confident Victorian art and architecture, and a series of award-winning industrial heritage museums.

Arlington Row: stone cottages in the Cotswold village of Bibury

Sights at a Glance

1. Quarry Bank, Styal
2. Chester
3. Stoke-on-Trent
4. Shrewsbury
5. *Ironbridge Gorge pp318–19*
6. Ludlow
7. Leominster
8. Hereford
9. Ross-on-Wye
10. Ledbury
11. Great Malvern and the Malverns
12. Worcester
13. Birmingham
14. Coventry
16. *Warwick pp325–7*
17. *Stratford-upon-Avon pp328–31*
18. Chipping Campden
19. Tewkesbury
20. Cheltenham
21. Gloucester
22. Cirencester

Walks and Tours

15. *Midlands Garden Tour pp324–5*

Getting Around

The Heart of England is easily reached by train, with mainline rail services to Cheltenham, Worcester, Birmingham, Hereford, Stoke and Coventry. The M5 and M6 motorways are the major road routes but are frequently congested. Long-distance buses provide regular shuttle services to all the major towns and cities. Travelling within the region is best done by car. Rural roads are delightfully empty, although major attractions, such as Stratford-upon-Avon, may be very crowded in the summer.

0 kilometres 10

0 miles 10

For hotels and restaurants in this area see pp567–8 and pp593–4

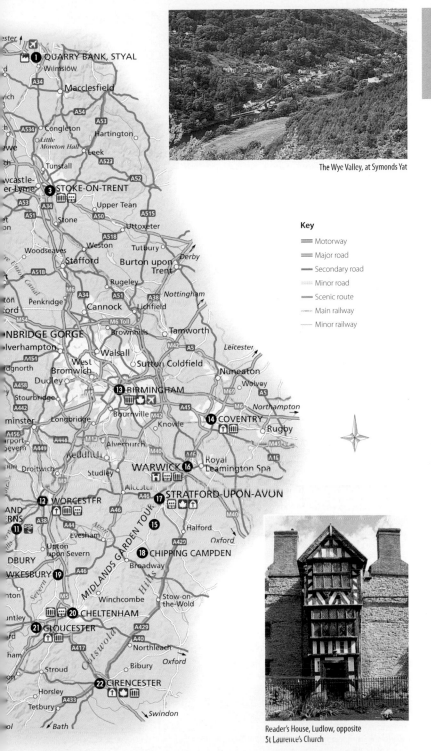

The Wye Valley, at Symonds Yat

Key

━━━ Motorway
━━━ Major road
━━━ Secondary road
┄┄┄ Minor road
━━━ Scenic route
▬▬▬ Main railway
─── Minor railway

Reader's House, Ludlow, opposite
St Laurence's Church

For keys to symbols see back flap

Quarry Bank, a working reminder of the Industrial Revolution

❶ Quarry Bank, Styal

Cheshire. **Tel** 01625 527468. 🚆
Manchester Airport or Wilmslow, then bus. **Open** mid-Feb–Oct: daily; Nov–Feb: Wed–Sun. **Closed** 24 & 25 Dec.
🅿 ♿ limited. 🚻 🏛 NT
Ⓦ **nationaltrust.org.uk**

The history of the Industrial Revolution *(see pp352–3)* is brought vividly to life at Quarry Bank, an early factory now transformed into a museum and private garden. Here, mill master Samuel Greg first used the waters of the Bollin Valley in 1784 to power the "water frame", a machine for spinning raw cotton fibres into thread. By the 1840s, the Greg cotton empire was one of the biggest in Britain, and the mill produced bolts of material to be exported all over the world.

Today the massive old mill buildings have been restored to house a living museum of the cotton industry that dominated the Manchester area for nearly 200 years until it was finally destroyed by foreign competition. The entire process, from spinning and weaving to bleaching, printing and dyeing, is shown through a series of reconstructions, demonstrations and hands-on displays. The weaving shed is full of clattering looms producing textiles. There are fascinating contraptions that demonstrate how water can be used to drive machinery, including an enormous wheel, 50 tons in weight and 7 m (24 ft) high, that is still used to power the looms.

The Greg family realized the importance of having a healthy, loyal and stable workforce. A social history exhibition explains how the mill workers were housed in the purpose-built village of Styal, in spacious cottages which had vegetable gardens and toilets. Details of their wages, working conditions and medical facilities are displayed on information boards.

There are costumed guided tours of the nearby **Apprentice House**. Local orphans lived here, and were sent to work up to 12 hours a day at the mill when they were just 6 or 7 years old. Visitors can try the beds in the house and even sample the medicine they were given. Have a wander, too, around the magnificently restored 1830s glasshouse.

❷ Chester

Cheshire. 🏙 120,000. 🚆 🚌
ℹ️ Town Hall, Northgate St (0845 6477868). 🏛 Mon–Sat.
Ⓦ **visitchester.com**

First settled by the Romans *(see pp48–9)*, who established a camp in AD 79 to defend fertile land near the River Dee, the main streets of Chester are now lined with timber buildings. These are the **Chester Rows**, which, with their two tiers of shops and continuous upper gallery, anticipate today's multistorey shops by several centuries.

Although their oriel windows and decorative timber-work are mostly 19th-century, the Rows were first built in the 13th and 14th centuries, and some of the original buildings are still standing. The façade of the 16th-century **Bishop Lloyd's House** in Watergate Street is the most richly carved in Chester. The Rows are at their most varied and attractive where Eastgate Street meets Bridge Street. Here, views of the cathedral and the town walls give the impression of a perfectly preserved medieval city. This illusion is helped by the Town Crier, who calls the hour and announces news in summer from the Cross, a reconstruction of the 15th-century stone crucifix that was destroyed in the Civil War *(see pp56–7)*.

To the north is the **cathedral**, this present building dates from 1250 onwards and is predominantly Gothic in style. The choir stalls have splendid

Chester's 1897 clock

Examples of the intricate carving on Bishop Lloyd's House, a Tudor building in Watergate Street, Chester

The Chester Rows, where shops line the first-floor galleries

misericords *(see p345)*, with scenes including a quarrelling couple. The lovely gardens are worth a stroll and also host a falconry. The cathedral is surrounded on two sides by the **city walls**, originally Roman but rebuilt at intervals. Visitors can walk the entire circuit but the best stretch is from the cathedral to Eastgate, where a wrought-iron **clock** was erected in 1899. The route to Newgate leads to a **Roman amphitheatre** built in AD 100.

🛈 Chester Cathedral
Abbey Square. **Tel** 01244 324756.
Open daily. 🈂🅰💻📷
W chestercathedral.com

🛈 Roman Amphitheatre
Little St John St. **Tel** 01244 402009.
Open daily. **W** english-heritage.org.uk

❸ Stoke-on-Trent

Stoke-on-Trent. 🅰 250,000. 🚉 🚌
🛈 Potteries Museum and Art Gallery, Bethesda St (01782 236000). 🍴 Mon–Sat. **W** visitstoke.co.uk

From the mid-18th century, Staffordshire became a leading centre for mass-produced ceramics. Its fame arose from the fine bone china and porcelain products of Wedgwood, Minton, Doulton and Spode, but the Staffordshire potteries also make a wide range of utilitarian products such as baths, toilets and wall tiles.

In 1910 a group of six towns – Longton, Fenton, Hanley, Burslem, Tunstall and Stoke – merged to form the conurbation of Stoke-on-Trent, also known as the Potteries. Writer Arnold Bennett (1867–1931) depicted this area as the "Five Towns" in his novels.

The **Gladstone Pottery Museum** is a Victorian complex of workshops, kilns, galleries and an engine house. There are demonstrations of traditional pottery techniques. The **Potteries Museum and Art Gallery** in Hanley has historic and modern ceramics, and items from the Anglo-Saxon "Staffordshire Hoard".

Josiah Wedgwood founded his pottery in 1759. Visitors can see the famous blue jasperware as well as contemporary pieces, and watch demonstrations at the **World of Wedgwood**.

Environs

About 10 miles (16 km) north of Stoke-on-Trent is **Little Moreton Hall** *(see pp306–7)*, a Tudor manor house.

🏛 Gladstone Pottery Museum
Uttoxeter Rd, Longton. **Tel** 01782 237777. **Open** Tue–Sat. **Closed** 24 Dec–2 Jan. 🈂🅰💻📷
W stokemuseums.org.uk/visit/gpm

🏛 Potteries Museum and Art Gallery
Bethesda St, Hanley. **Tel** 01782 232323. **Open** daily. **Closed** 25 Dec–1 Jan. 🅰💻📷 **W** stokemuseums.org.uk/visit/pmag

🏛 World of Wedgwood
Wedgwood Drive, Barlaston. **Tel** 01782 282986. **Open** daily. **Closed** 25 & 26 Dec. 🈂🅰🅰💻📷 **W** worldofwedgwood.com

🏛 Little Moreton Hall
Congleton, off A34. **Tel** 01260 272018. **Open** mid-Feb–Oct: Wed–Sun (Jul & Aug: daily). 🅰 🆖
W nationaltrust.org.uk

Staffordshire Pottery

An abundance of water, marl, clay and easily mined coal to fire the kilns enabled Staffordshire to develop as a ceramics centre; and local supplies of iron, copper and lead were used for glazing.

In the 18th century, pottery became widely accessible and affordable. English bone china, which used powdered animals' bones for strength and translucence, was shipped all over the world, and Josiah Wedgwood (1730–95) introduced simple, durable crockery – though his best-known design is the blue jasperware decorated with white Classical themes. Coal-powered bottle kilns fired the clay until the 1950s Clean Air Acts put them out of business. They have been replaced by electric or gas-fired kilns.

Wedgwood candlesticks, 1785

Timber-framed, gabled mansions in Fish Street, Shrewsbury

❹ Shrewsbury

Shropshire. 🏠 90,000. ✈ 🚌
ℹ️ The Music Hall, The Square (01743 258888). 🛒 Tue, Wed, Fri, Sat. 🎪 Shrewsbury Flower Show (mid-Aug).
🌐 visitshrewsbury.co.uk

Shrewsbury is almost an island, enclosed by a great loop of the River Severn. A gaunt **castle** of red sandstone, built in 1066–74, guards the entrance to the town, standing on the only section of land not surrounded by the river. Such defences were necessary on the frontier between England and the wilder Marches of Wales, whose inhabitants fiercely defied Saxon and Norman invaders (see pp50–51). The castle, rebuilt over the centuries, now houses the Shropshire Regimental Museum.

In AD 60 the Romans (see pp48–9) built the garrison town of Viroconium, modern Wroxeter, 5 miles (8 km) east of Shrewsbury. Finds from the excavations are displayed at **Shrewsbury Museum and Art Gallery**, including a decorated silver mirror from the 2nd century and other luxury goods brought by the Roman army.

The town's medieval wealth as a centre of the wool trade is evident in the many timber-framed buildings found along the High Street, Butcher Row,

Roman silver mirror in Shrewsbury Museum

and Wyle Cop. Two of the grandest High Street houses, **Ireland's Mansions** and **Owen's Mansions**, are named after Robert Ireland and Richard Owen, the wealthy wool merchants who built them in 1575 and 1592 respectively. Similarly attractive buildings in Fish Street frame a view of the **Prince Rupert Hotel**, which was briefly the headquarters of Charles I's nephew, Rupert, in the English Civil War (see pp56–7).

Outside the loop of the river, the **abbey church** survives from the medieval monastery. It has a number of interesting memorials, including one to Lieutenant WES Owen MC, better known as the war poet Wilfred Owen (1893–1918), who taught at the local Wyle Cop school and was killed in the last days of World War I.

Environs
To the south of Shrewsbury, the road to Ludlow passes through the landscapes celebrated in the 1896 poem by A E Housman (1859–1936), *A Shropshire Lad*. Highlights include the bleak moors of **Long Mynd**, with 15 prehistoric barrows, and **Wenlock Edge**, wonderful walking country with glorious, far-reaching views.

🏰 **Shrewsbury Castle**
Castle St. **Tel** 01743 358516.
Open hours vary; call for details.
Closed late Dec–mid-Feb. 🅿️ ♿ 📷

🏛️ **Shrewsbury Museum and Art Gallery**
The Music Hall, Market Sq.
Tel 01743 258885. **Open** Tue–Sun.
Closed 1 Jan, 25 & 26 Dec. 🅿️ ♿ 📷
🌐 shrewsburymuseum.org.uk

❺ Ironbridge Gorge

See pp318–19.

❻ Ludlow

Shropshire. 🏠 10,000. ✈ ℹ️ Ludlow Assembly Rooms, 1 Mill St (01584 875053). 🛒 Mon, Wed, Fri, Sat. 🎪 food (early Sep). 🌐 ludlow.org.uk

Ludlow attracts large numbers of visitors, thanks to its splendid castle, small shops and lovely Georgian and half-timbered Tudor buildings, but perhaps the biggest draw to the town is the quality food on offer. Ludlow is an important area of geological research and the **museum** has fossils of the oldest known animals and plants.

The ruined **castle** is sited on cliffs high above the River Teme. Built in 1086, it was damaged in the Civil War (see pp56–7) and abandoned in 1689. *Comus*, a court masque using music and drama, by John Milton (1608–74), was first performed in the Great Hall here in 1634.

Prince Arthur (1486–1502), elder brother of Henry VIII,

The 13th-century south tower and hall of Stokesay Castle, near Ludlow

died at Ludlow Castle. His heart is buried in **St Laurence Church** at the other end of Castle Square, as are the ashes of the poet A E Housman. The east end of the church backs onto the **Bull Ring**, lined with timber buildings. Two inns vie for attention across the street: **The Bull**, for its Tudor back yard, and **The Feathers**, with its flamboyant façade, whose name recalls the feathers used in arrow-making, once a local industry.

Environs
About 5 miles (8 km) north of Ludlow, in a lovely setting, is **Stokesay Castle**, a fortified manor house with a colourful moated garden.

🏰 Ludlow Castle
Castle Square. **Tel** 01584 873355.
Open daily (Jan & Feb: Sat & Sun only).
🖼 ♿ 🖥 📷 **W** ludlowcastle.com

🏛 Ludlow Museum
Buttercross. **Tel** 0345 678 9024.
Open Call ahead for timings. ♿

🏰 Stokesay Castle
Craven Arms, A49. **Tel** 01588 672544.
Open times vary, call for details. 🖼 📷
📷 EH **W** english-heritage.org.uk

⑦ Leominster

Herefordshire. 🅰 11,000. 🚆
ℹ Corn Sq (01568 616460). 🚌 Fri.
W leominstertourism.co.uk

Farmers come to Leominster (pronounced "Lemster") from all over this rural region to buy supplies. There are two buildings of note in the town, which has been a wool-manufacturing centre for 700 years. In the town centre stands the magnificent Grade II-listed **Grange Court**, carved with bold and bizarre figures in 1633. Nearby is the **priory**, whose imposing Norman portal is carved with an equally strange mixture of mythical birds and beasts. The lions, at least, can be explained: monks believed the name of Leominster was derived from *monasterium leonis*, "the monastery of the lions". In fact, *leonis* probably comes from medieval, rather than Classical Latin, and means "of

The market town of Leominster surrounded by rolling border country

the marshes". The aptness of this description can readily be seen in the lush river valleys that flow around town.

Environs
South of the town, the magnificent gardens and parkland at **Hampton Court Castle** have been restored and include island pavilions and a maze. To the west of the town, along the River Arrow, are the villages of **Eardisland** and **Pembridge**, with their well-kept gardens and timber-framed houses. **Berrington Hall**, 3 miles (5 km) north of Leominster, designed by Henry Holland (1745–1806), is a Neo-Classical house set in grounds by "Capability"

Gatehouse of Stokesay Castle, near Ludlow

Brown. Inside are beautifully preserved ceiling decorations and period furniture.

To the northeast of Leominster is **Tenbury Wells**, which enjoyed brief popularity as a spa in the 19th century. The River Teme flows through it, full of minnows, trout and other fish and beloved by the composer Sir Edward Elgar (*see p321*), who came to seek inspiration on its banks. A few miles south of Tenbury Wells lies **Witley Court and Gardens**. The landscaped gardens contain the splendid Perseus and Andromeda fountain that fires up regularly during the day.

🏰 Hampton Court Castle and Gardens
nr Hope Under Dinmore.
Tel 01568 797777. **Open** Apr–Oct: 10:30am–5pm. 🖼 🍴 ♿ 🚻 📷
W hamptoncourt.org.uk

🏛 Berrington Hall
Berrington. **Tel** 01568 615721.
Open mid-Feb–Oct: 11am–5pm daily; Nov–mid-Feb: Sat & Sun. 🖼
🚻 📷 NT **W** nationaltrust.org.uk

🏰 Witley Court and Gardens
Worcester Rd, Great Witley. **Tel** 01299 896636. **Open** daily. **Closed** 1 Jan, 25 & 26 Dec. 🖼 ♿ 🖥 📷 EH
W english-heritage.org.uk

❺ Ironbridge Gorge

Ironbridge Gorge was one of the most important centres of the Industrial Revolution *(see pp58–9)*. It was here, in 1709, that Abraham Darby I (1678–1717) pioneered the use of inexpensive coke, rather than charcoal, to smelt iron ore. The use of iron in bridges, ships and buildings transformed Ironbridge Gorge into one of the world's great iron-making centres. Industrial decline in the 20th century led to the Gorge's decay, although today it has been restored as an exciting complex of industrial history, with several museums strung along the wooded banks of the River Severn.

VISITORS' CHECKLIST

Practical Information
Shropshire. 🚩 2,900.
ℹ️ Museum of the Gorge (01952 433424). **Open** daily. **Closed** 1 Jan, 24 & 25 Dec. Some sites closed Nov–Apr, call for details.
📷 🎫 by arrangement.
♿ most sites. 🚻 🖥️ 🎁
🔤 **ironbridge.org.uk**

Transport
🚆 Telford then bus (0871 2002233).

🏛 Coalbrookdale Museum of Iron

The history of iron and the men who made it is traced in this remarkable museum. Abraham Darby I's discovery of how to smelt iron ore with coke allowed the mass production of iron, paving the way for the rise of large-scale industry. His original blast furnace forms the museum's centrepiece.

One of the museum's themes is the history of the Darby dynasty, a Quaker family who had a great impact on the Coalbrookdale community.

Ironbridge led the world in industrial innovation, producing the first iron wheels and cylinders for the first steam engine. Cast-iron statues, many of them commissioned for the 1851 Great

Europe (1860), statue in the Museum of Iron

Exhibition *(see pp60–61)*, are among the many Coalbrookdale Company products on display. They include a bronze figure of Andromeda and sculptures of stags and hounds.

One of the Darby family's homes in the nearby village of Coalbrookdale, **Rosehill House** (open during the summer), has been furnished in mid-Victorian style.

🏛 Museum of the Gorge

This partly castellated Victorian building was a warehouse for storing products from the ironworks before they were shipped down the River Severn. The warehouse is now home to the Museum of the Gorge, and has displays illustrating the history of the Severn and the development of the water industry. Until the arrival of the railways in the mid-19th century, the Severn was the main form of transport and communication to and from the Gorge. Sometimes too shallow, at other times in flood, the river was not a particularly reliable means of transportation; by the 1890s river trading had stopped completely.

The highlight of the museum is a wonderful 12-m (40-ft) model of the Gorge as it would have appeared in 1796, complete with foundries, cargo boats and growing villages.

The Museum of Iron, topped by a cast- and wrought-iron clock

Peacock Panel (1928), one of the tile museum's star attractions

🏛 Jackfield Tile Museum

There have been potteries in this area since the 17th century, but it was the Victorian passion for decorative tiles that made Jackfield famous. There were two tile-making factories here – Maw and Craven Dunnill – that produced a tremendous variety of tiles from clay mined nearby. Talented designers created an astonishing range of images. The Jackfield Tile Museum, in the old Craven Dunnill works, has a collection of the decorative floor and wall tiles that were produced here from the 1850s to the 1960s. On certain days, visitors can watch small-scale demonstrations of traditional methods of tile-making in the old factory buildings, including the kilns and the decoration workshops.

Coalport China Museum

In the mid-19th century the Coalport Works was one of the largest porcelain manufacturers in Britain, and its name was synonymous with fine china. Today the china workshops have been converted into a museum, where visitors can watch demonstrations of the various stages of making porcelain, including the skills of pot-throwing, painting and gilding. There is a superb collection of 19th-century china housed in one of the museum's distinctive bottle-shaped kilns. Nearby is the **Tar Tunnel**, an important source of natural bitumen discovered 110 m (360 ft) underground in the 1700s. It once yielded 20,500 litres (4,500 gal) of tar every week. Visitors can still explore part of the tunnel (Apr–Oct). There is also a programme of drop-in creative workshops and events.

Coalport China Museum with its bottle-shaped kiln

Blists Hill Victorian Town

This enormous open-air museum recreates Victorian life in an east Shropshire coalfield town. A group of 19th-century buildings has been reconstructed on the 20-ha (50-acre) site of Blists Hill, an old coal mine that used to supply the ironworks in the Gorge. Here, people in period costume perform tasks such as iron forging.

The site has period housing, a church and even a Victorian school. Visitors can change money into old coinage to buy items from the baker or even pay for a drink in the local pub.

The centrepiece of Blists Hill is a complete foundry that still produces wrought iron. One of the most spectacular sights is the Hay Inclined Plane, which was used to transport canalboats up and down a steep slope. Other attractions include steam engines, a saddlers, a doctors, a chemist, a candlemakers and a sweetshop.

The Iron Bridge

Abraham Darby III (grandson of the first man to smelt iron with coke) cast the world's first iron bridge in 1779, revolutionizing building methods in the process. Spanning the Severn, the bridge is a monument to the ironmaster's skills. The tollhouse on the south bank charts its construction.

Ironbridge Gorge Sights

① Coalbrookdale
   Museum of Iron
② Museum of the Gorge
③ Iron Bridge
④ Jackfield Tile Museum
⑤ Coalport China Museum
⑥ Blists Hill Victorian Town

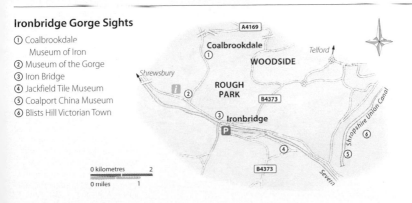

0 kilometres 2
0 miles 1

❽ Hereford

Herefordshire. 59,000. ≋ ☰
🏛 Wed (cattle, general), Sat (general).
🌐 visitherefordshire.co.uk

Once the capital of the Saxon
kingdom of West Mercia,
Hereford is today an attractive
town serving a primarily rural
community. A cattle market is
held here every Wednesday,
and local produce is sold at
the covered market in the town
centre. Almost opposite the
market, the Jacobean timber-
framed **Black and White House**
of 1621 is now a museum of
local history.

In the **cathedral**, only a short
stroll away, interesting features
include the Lady Chapel, in
richly ornamented Early English
style, the *Mappa Mundi* (see
below) and the Chained Library,
whose 1,500 books are tethered
by iron chains to bookcases as
a precaution against theft. The
story of these national treasures
is told through models, original
artifacts and interactive
displays. The best place
for an overall view of
the cathedral is Bishop's
Meadow, south of the
centre, which leads
down to the banks
of the Wye.

Hereford's many
rewarding museums
include the **Hereford
Museum and Art
Gallery**, noted for its
Roman mosaic and for
watercolours by local artists,
and the **Cider Museum**,
where visitors can discover
the history of traditional cider

Hereford's 17th-century Black and White House in the centre of high town

making. This includes exploring
the champagne cellars and
learning how the barrels are
made. There are still around
30 traditional cider-makers
operating in Herefordshire.

Detail of figures on
Kilpeck Church

Environs
During the 12th
century, Oliver de
Merlemond made
a pilgrimage from
Hereford to Spain.
Impressed by several
churches he saw on
the way, he brought
French masons over
to England and
introduced their
techniques to this area. One
result was **Kilpeck Church**,
6 miles (10 km) southwest, full
of splendid carvings including
lustful figures showing their

genitals, tail-biting dragons and
snakes. At **Abbey Dore**, 4 miles
(6 km) west, the Cistercian
abbey church is complemented
by the serene riverside gardens
and tranquil arboretum of
Abbey Dore Court.

🏛 **Black and White House**
High St. **Tel** 01432 260694. **Open**
10am–4pm Tue–Sat. **Closed** 1 Jan,
Good Fri, 25 & 26 Dec . 📷 ♿ limited.
📷 🌐 herefordshire.gov.uk

🏛 **Hereford Museum and
Art Gallery**
Broad St. **Tel** 01432 260692. **Open**
11am–4pm Thu–Sat. **Closed** 1 Jan,
Good Fri, 25 & 26 Dec. ♿ 📷
🌐 herefordshire.gov.uk

🏛 **Cider Museum**
Ryelands St. **Tel** 01432 354207.
Open Mon–Sat. **Closed** 1 Jan,
Good Fri, 25 & 26 Dec . 📷 📷 by
arrangement. ♿ limited. 📷 📷
🌐 cidermuseum.co.uk

❾ Ross-on-Wye

Herefordshire. 10,000. ☰
🏛 Thu, Sat; farmers' market 1st Fri.
🌐 visitrossonwye.com

The fine town of Ross sits on
a cliff of red sandstone above
the water meadows of the River
Wye. There are opportunities
for canoeing and wonderful
views over the river from the
clifftop gardens, given to the
town by a local benefactor,
John Kyrle (1637–1724).

Medieval View

Hereford Cathedral's most
celebrated treasure is the
Mappa Mundi, the Map of
the World drawn in 1290
by a clergyman, Richard of
Haldingham. The world is
depicted here on biblical
principles: Jerusalem is at
the centre, the Garden of
Eden figures prominently
and monsters inhabit the
margins of the world.

Central detail, *Mappa Mundi*

The Wye Valley at Symonds Yat

Kyrle was lauded by the poet Alexander Pope (1688–1744) in his *Moral Essays on the Uses of Riches* (1732) for using his wealth in a practical way, and he came to be known as "The Man of Ross". There is a memorial to Kyrle in **St Mary's Church**.

Environs

Downstream from Ross, the River Wye negotiates a huge, incised meander at **Symonds Yat**. Viewing points and forest walks offer dramatic views across wooded gorges.

Goodrich Castle, 5 miles (8 km) south of Ross, is a 12th-century red sandstone fort on a rock above the river.

🏠 Goodrich Castle
Goodrich. **Tel** 01600 890538.
Open mid-Feb, Apr–Oct: daily, Nov–Mar: Sat & Sun 🅿 🗐 (Apr–Oct). **EH**
W english-heritage.org.uk

❿ Ledbury

Herefordshire. 🔼 9,600. 🚆 🚌
🛈 Ice Bytes, 38 The Homend (0844 567 8650). **W** visitledbury.info

Ledbury's main street is lined with timbered houses, including the **Market Hall**, which dates from 1655. Church Lane, a cobbled lane running up from the High Street, has lovely 16th-century buildings: the **Heritage Centre** and **Butcher Row House** are both now museums. **St Michael and All Angels Church** has a massive detached bell tower, ornate Early English decoration and interesting monuments.

Medieval tile from the Priory at Great Malvern

🏛 Heritage Centre
Church Lane. **Open** Easter–Oct: daily. 🅷

🏛 Butcher Row House
Church Lane. **Tel** 01531 635069.
Open Easter–Oct: daily.

⓫ Great Malvern and the Malverns

Worcestershire. 🔼 37,000. 🚆 🚌
🛈 21 Church St (01684 892289).
🗐 Fri; farmers' market 3rd Sat.
W visitthemalverns.org

The ancient granite rock of the Malvern Hills rises from the plain of the River Severn, its 9 miles (15 km) of glorious scenery visible from afar. Composer Edward Elgar (1857–1934) wrote many of his greatest works here, including the oratorio *The Dream of Gerontius* (1900), inspired by what the diarist John Evelyn (1620–1706) described as "one of the goodliest views in England". Elgar's home was in **Little Malvern**, whose truncated Church of St Giles, set on a steep, wooded hill, lost its nave when the stone was stolen during the Dissolution *(see p355)*. **Great Malvern** is graced with 19th-century buildings akin to Swiss sanitoria: patients would stay at institutions such as Doctor Gulley's Water Cure Establishment. The water gushing from the hillside at St Ann's Well, above the town, is bottled and sold throughout Britain. The town is also home to the famous Morgan cars (call 01684 584580 to arrange a factory visit).

Malvern's highlight is the **Priory**, with its 15th-century stained-glass windows and medieval misericords. The old monastic fishponds below the church form the lake of **Priory Park**. Here a theatre hosts performances of Elgar's music and plays by George Bernard Shaw.

The Malverns range, formed of hard Pre-Cambrian rock

⑫ Worcester

Worcestershire. 🅰 99,000. 🚆 🚌
🛈 High St (01905 726311). 🌐 Mon–
Sat. 🇼 visitworcestershire.org

Worcester is one of many English cities whose character has been transformed by modern development. The architectural highlight is still the **cathedral**, off College Yard, which suffered a collapsed tower in 1175 and a disastrous fire in 1203, before the present structure was started in the 13th century.

The nave and central tower were completed in the 1370s, after building was severely interrupted by the Black Death (see p52), which decimated the labour force. The most recent and ornate addition was made in 1874, when Sir George Gilbert Scott designed the High Gothic choir, incorporating 14th-century carved misericords.

There are many interesting tombs, including King John's, a masterpiece of medieval

Charles I holding a symbol of the Church on Worcester's Guildhall

carving, in front of the altar. Prince Arthur, Henry VIII's brother (see p316), who died at the age of 15, is buried in the chantry chapel south of the altar. Below, the huge Norman crypt survives from the first cathedral (1084).

From the cathedral cloister, a gate leads to College Green and out into Edgar Street with its Georgian houses. Here the **Museum of Royal Worcester** displays Royal Worcester porcelain dating back to 1751. On the High Street, north of the cathedral, the **Guildhall** of 1721 is adorned with statues of Stuart monarchs, reflecting the city's Royalist allegiances. In Cornmarket is **Ye Olde King Charles House**, in which Prince Charles, later Charles II, hid after the Battle of Worcester in 1651.

Some of Worcester's finest timber buildings are found in Friar Street: **The Greyfriars**, built around 1480, has been restored in period style. The **Commandery** was originally an 11th-century hospital. It was rebuilt in the 15th century and used by Charles as a base during the Civil War. Now a museum, it has a fine hammerbeam roof.

Elgar's Birthplace was the home of composer Sir Edward Elgar (see p321) and contains a wealth of memorabilia.

🏛 **Museum of Royal Worcester**
Severn St. **Tel** 01905 21247.
Open Mon–Sat. **Closed** public hols.
🖼 🎫 ♿ 🚻 🏪 🇼 museumof
royalworcester.org

🏠 **The Greyfriars**
Friar St. **Tel** 01905 23571. **Open** mid-Feb–mid-Dec: Tue–Sat. 🖼 NT

🏛 **Commandery**
Sidbury. **Tel** 01905 361821.
Open daily. **Closed** 25 & 26 Dec, early Jan. 🖼 🏪

🏛 **Elgar's Birthplace**
Lower Broadheath. **Tel** 01905 333224. **Open** daily. **Closed** 24 Dec–31 Jan. 🖼 ♿ limited. 🏪 NT

⑬ Birmingham

Birmingham. 🅰 1,037,000. ✈ 🚆 🚌
🛈 New St (0844 888 3883). 🌐 Mon–
Sat. 🇼 visitbirmingham.com

Brum, as it is affectionately known to its inhabitants, grew up as a major centre of the Industrial Revolution in the 19th century. A vast range of manufacturing trades was based in Birmingham leading to the rapid development of grim factories and cramped

Worcester Cathedral, overlooking the River Severn

The Last of England, Ford Madox Brown, Birmingham Art Gallery

housing. Since the clearance of several of these areas after World War II, Birmingham has raised its cultural, architectural and civic profile.

Set away from the massive Bullring shopping centre, Birmingham's 19th-century civic buildings are excellent examples of Neo-Classical architecture. Among them are the **Birmingham Museum and Art Gallery**, where the collection includes outstanding works by Pre-Raphaelite artists such as Edward Burne-Jones (1833–98), who was born in Birmingham, and Ford Madox Brown (1821–93). The museum also organizes some interesting temporary exhibitions of art.

Birmingham's extensive canal system is now used mainly for leisure boating *(see pp304–5)*, and several former warehouses have been converted into museums and galleries. **Thinktank, Birmingham Science Museum** celebrates the city's contribution to the world of railway engines and aircraft, and to the motor trade. The old **Jewellery**

Quarter has practised its traditional crafts since the 16th century – a beautifully preserved workshop recalls the city's glittering jewellery and metalworking heritage and also offers visitors the opportunity to watch demonstrations.

Suburban Birmingham has many attractions, including the **Botanical Gardens** at Edgbaston, and **Cadbury World** at Bournville, where there is a visitor centre dedicated to chocolate (book ahead). Bournville village was built in the 1890s by the Cadbury brothers for their workers and is a pioneering example of a garden suburb.

🏛 Birmingham Museum and Art Gallery
Chamberlain Sq. **Tel** 0121 348 8030.
Open daily. **Closed** 25 & 26 Dec.
♿ 🖥 📷 **w** birmingham
museums.org.uk

🏛 Thinktank
Millennium Point. **Tel** 0121 348 8000.
Open daily. **Closed** 24–26 Dec. ♿
w birminghammuseums.org.uk

🏛 Museum of the Jewellery Quarter
75–80 Vyse St. **Tel** 0121 348 8140.
Open Tue–Sat. 📷 ♿ 🖥 📷
w birminghammuseums.org.uk

🌿 Botanical Gardens
Westbourne Rd, Edgbaston. **Tel** 0121 454 1860. **Open** daily. **Closed** 25 & 26 Dec. 📷 🚗 by appt. ♿ 🚲 📷
w birminghambotanicalgardens.org.uk

🏛 Cadbury World
Linden Rd, Bournville. **Tel** 0844 880 7667. **Open** daily (Nov–Jan: call for details). **Closed** first 3 weeks Jan, 24–26 Dec. 📷 ♿ 🖥
w cadburyworld.co.uk

Stately civic office buildings in Victoria Square, Birmingham

Epstein's *St Michael Subduing the Devil*, on Coventry Cathedral

⓮ Coventry

Coventry. 🚗 330,000. 🚄 🚌
🛈 Bayley Lane (024 7622 5616).
🛒 Mon–Sat. **w** visitcoventryand
warwickshire.co.uk

As an armaments centre, Coventry was a prime target for German bombing raids in World War II, and in 1940 the **cathedral** was almost destroyed. After the war Sir Basil Spence (1907–76) built a modernist-style cathedral alongside the ruins. It includes sculptures by Sir Jacob Epstein and one of the world's largest tapestries, by Graham Sutherland.

The **Herbert Gallery and Museum** has displays on the 11th-century legend of Lady Godiva, who rode naked through the streets of Coventry to gain a pardon for the high taxes imposed by her husband upon his tenants. The **Coventry Transport Museum** has the largest collection of Britain's road transport in the world, including the world's fastest car, Thrust SSC.

🏛 Herbert Gallery and Museum
Jordan Well. **Tel** 024 7623 7521.
Open daily (Sun: pm) 1 Jan. 🖥 📷
w theherbert.org

🏛 Coventry Transport Museum
Hales St. **Tel** 024 7623 4270. **Open** daily.
Closed 1 Jan, 24–26 Dec. ♿ 🖥 📷
w transport-museum.com

⓯ Midlands Garden Tour

The charming Cotswold stone buildings perfectly complement the lush gardens for which the region is famous. This picturesque route from Warwick to Cheltenham is designed to show every type of garden, from tiny cottage plots, brimming with bell-shaped flowers and hollyhocks, to the deer-filled, landscaped parks of stately homes. The route follows the escarpment of the Cotswold Hills, taking in spectacular scenery and some of the prettiest Midlands villages on the way.

Tips for Drivers

Tour length: 35 miles (50 km).
Stopping-off points: Hidcote Manor has excellent lunches and teas; there are refreshments at Kiftsgate Court and Sudeley Castle. Travellers will find a good choice in Broadway, from traditional pubs and teashops to the deluxe Lygon Arms. (See also pp636–7.)

⑨ Cheltenham Imperial Gardens
These colourful public gardens on the Promenade were laid out in 1817–18 to encourage people to walk from the town to the spa (see p332).

⑧ Sudeley Castle
The restored castle is complemented by box hedges, topiary and an Elizabethan knot garden (see p31). Catherine Parr, Henry VIII's widow, died here in 1548.

Winchcombe

CHELTENHAM

⑤ Broadway
In this village, wisteria and cordoned fruit trees cover 17th-century cottages with their immaculate gardens.

⑦ Stanway House
This Jacobean manor has many lovely trees in its grounds and a pyramid above a cascade of water.

⑥ Snowshill Manor
This Cotswold stone manor contains an extraordinary collection, from bicycles to Japanese armour. There are walled gardens and terraces full of *objets d'art* such as this clock (left). The colour blue is a recurrent theme.

① Warwick Castle
The castle's gardens
(see pp326–7) include the
Mound, planted in medieval
style, with grass, oaks, yew
trees and box hedges.

② Anne Hathaway's Cottage
This has a pretty,
informal 19th-century-
style garden *(see p331)*.

③ Hidcote Manor Gardens
Started in the early years of
the 20th century, these
beautiful gardens pioneered
the idea of a garden as a series
of outdoor "rooms" enclosed
by high yew hedges and
planted according to theme.

④ Kiftsgate Court Garden
This charmingly naturalistic garden
lies opposite Hidcote Manor. It has
many rare and unusual plants on a
series of hillside terraces, including
the enormous "Kiftsgate" Rose, nearly
30 m (100 ft) high.

Key

━━━ Motorway

━━━ Tour route

━━━ Other roads

```
0 kilometres        5
0 miles             5
```

⑯ Warwick

Warwickshire. 🚗 30,000. 🚆 🚌 ℹ️
The Courthouse, Jury St (01926 492212).
🗓 Sat. 🌐 visitwarwick.co.uk

Warwick suffered a major fire
in 1694, but some medieval
buildings survived. **St John's
House Museum** in St John's is
a charming Jacobean mansion
housing reconstructions of a
Victorian parlour, kitchen and
classroom. At the west end
of the High Street, a row of
medieval guild buildings was
transformed in 1571 by the Earl
of Leicester, to create the **Lord
Leycester Hospital**, a refuge
for retired soldiers.

The arcaded **Market Hall
Museum** (1670) is part of the
Warwickshire Museum, renowned
for its unusual tapestry map of
the county, woven in 1558.

In Church Street, to the
south of St Mary's Church,
is the **Beauchamp Chapel**
(1443–64). It is a superb example
of Perpendicular architecture
and contains tombs of the Earls
of Warwick. There is a good view
of **Warwick Castle** *(see pp326–7)*
from St Mary's tower.

🏛 **St John's House Museum**
St John's. **Tel** 01926 412132. **Open** Mon–
Sat. **Closed** Nov–Mar: Mon. ♿ limited.

🏛 **Lord Leycester Hospital**
High St. **Tel** 01926 491422. **Open** Tue–
Sun & public hols. **Closed** Good Fri,
25 Dec. Gardens: **Open** same as house
but Easter–Sep only. 📷 ♿ limited.
💻 🌐 lordleycester.com

🏛 **Market Hall Museum**
Market Place. **Tel** 01926 412500.
Open Tue–Sat (Apr–Sep: also Sun).
♿ limited. 📷

The Lord Leycester Hospital, now a
home for ex-servicemen

Warwick Castle

Warwick's magnificent castle is the finest medieval fortress in the country. The original Norman castle was rebuilt in the 13th and 14th centuries, when huge outer walls and towers were added, mainly to display the power of the great feudal magnates, the Beauchamps and, in the 1400s, the Nevilles, the Earls of Warwick. The castle passed in 1604 to the Greville family who, in the 17th and 18th centuries, transformed it into a great country house. In 1978 the owners of Madame Tussauds *(see p108)* bought the castle and set up tableaux of wax portraits to illustrate its history.

Kingmaker
Dramatic displays recreate medieval life as "Warwick the Kingmaker", Richard Neville, prepared for battle in the Wars of the Roses.

Royal Weekend Party
The portrait of the valet is part of the award-winning exhibition on the Prince of Wales's visit in 1898.

KEY

① **Princess Tower**

② **Merlin: The Dragon Tower** houses characters from the BBC TV series *Merlin*, including the great dragon itself.

③ **The Mound** has remains of the motte and bailey castle *(see p490)* and the 13th-century keep.

④ **Ramparts and towers**, of local grey sandstone, were added in the 14th and 15th centuries.

⑤ **The Gatehouse** is defended by portcullises and "murder holes" through which boiling pitch was dropped onto attackers beneath.

⑥ **The Castle Dungeon** is a chilling, live dramatization of plague-ridden medieval Warwick.

⑦ **Caesar's Tower**

⑧ **The Mill and Engine House**

★ **Great Hall and State Rooms**
Medieval apartments were transformed into the Great Hall and State Rooms. A mark of conspicuous wealth, they display a collection of family treasures from around the world.

Warwick Castle, south front, by Antonio Canaletto (1697–1768)

VISITORS' CHECKLIST

Practical Information
Castle Lane, Warwick. **Tel** 0871 265 2000. **Open** from 10am daily. Closing times vary; see website or call for details. **Closed** 25 Dec.
🚗 🅿 ♿ limited. 📷 💻 📱
W warwick-castle.com

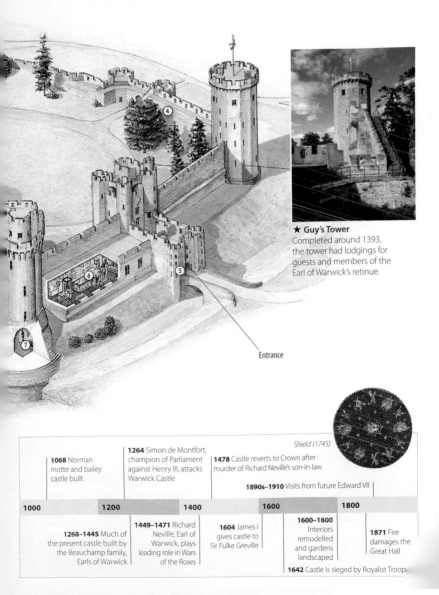

★ **Guy's Tower**
Completed around 1393, the tower had lodgings for guests and members of the Earl of Warwick's retinue.

Entrance

Shield (1745)

1068 Norman motte and bailey castle built

1264 Simon de Montfort, champion of Parliament against Henry III, attacks Warwick Castle

1478 Castle reverts to Crown after murder of Richard Neville's son-in-law

1890s–1910 Visits from future Edward VII

1000	1200	1400	1600	1800

1268–1445 Much of the present castle built by the Beauchamp family, Earls of Warwick

1449–1471 Richard Neville, Earl of Warwick, plays leading role in Wars of the Roses

1604 James I gives castle to Sir Fulke Greville

1600–1800 Interiors remodelled and gardens landscaped

1871 Fire damages the Great Hall

1642 Castle is sieged by Royalist Troops

⑰ Street-by-Street: Stratford-upon-Avon

Situated on the west bank of the River Avon, in the heart of the Midlands, is one of the most famous towns in England. Stratford-upon-Avon dates back to at least Roman times but its appearance today is that of a small Tudor market town, with mellow, half-timbered architecture and tranquil walks beside the tree-fringed Avon. This image belies its popularity as the most visited tourist attraction outside London, with eager hordes flocking to see buildings connected to William Shakespeare and his descendants.

Bancroft Gardens
There is an attractive boat-filled canal basin here and a 15th-century causeway.

★ Shakespeare's Birthplace
This building was almost entirely reconstructed in the 19th century, but in the style of the Tudor original.

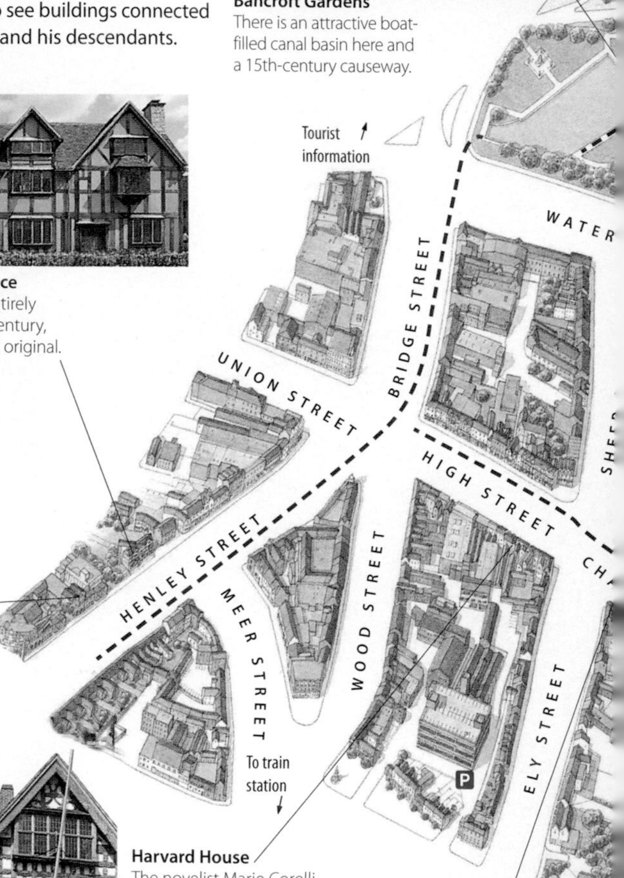

```
0 metres        100
0 yards         100
```

Shakespeare Centre

Tourist information

WATER

BRIDGE STREET

SHEE

UNION STREET

HIGH STREET

CH

HENLEY STREET

MEER STREET

WOOD STREET

ELY STREET

P

To train station

Harvard House
The novelist Marie Corelli (1855–1924) had this house restored. Next door is the 16th-century Garrick Inn.

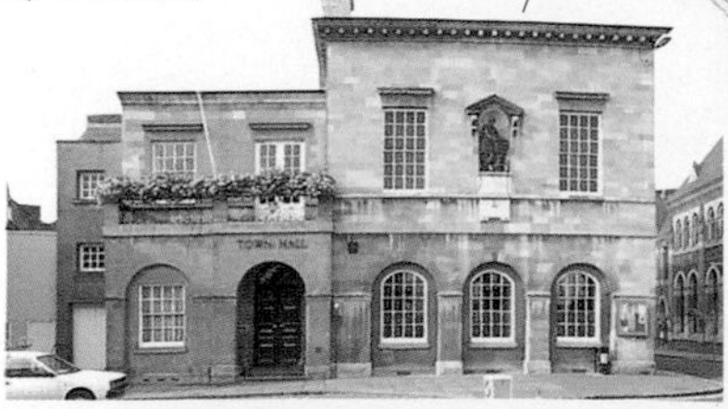

Town Hall
Built in 1767, there are traces of 18th-century graffiti on the front of the building saying "God Save the King".

Royal Shakespeare Theatre and Swan Theatre
Home of the Royal Shakespeare Company (RSC), the Swan Theatre is located on the western bank of the River Avon.

VISITORS' CHECKLIST

Practical Information
Warwickshire. 🏛 25,000.
ℹ Bridgefoot (01789 264293).
🚌 Fri. 🎭 Shakespeare's
Birthday: Apr; Stratford River
Festival: Jul. **W** discover-
stratford.com

Transport
✈ Birmingham, 20 miles (32
km) NW of Stratford-upon-Avon.
🚆 Alcester Rd. 🚌 Bridge St.

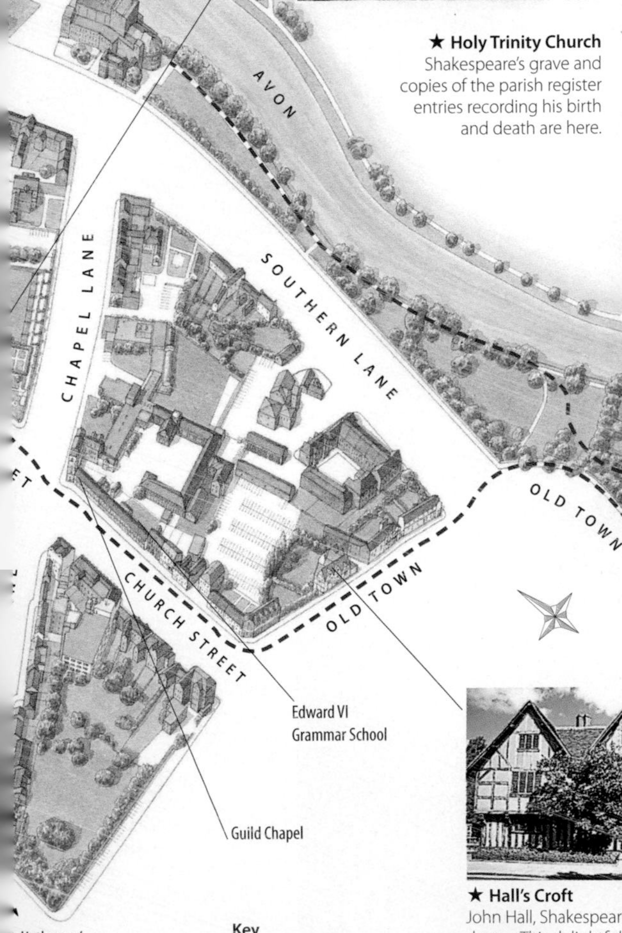

New Place & Nash's House
The foundations of New Place, where Shakespeare died, form the garden beside this house.

★ Holy Trinity Church
Shakespeare's grave and copies of the parish register entries recording his birth and death are here.

AVON

CHAPEL LANE

SOUTHERN LANE

OLD TOWN

CHURCH STREET

OLD TOWN

Edward VI
Grammar School

Guild Chapel

Hathaway's
age

Key
➡ Suggested route

★ Hall's Croft
John Hall, Shakespeare's son-in-law, was a doctor. This delightful house includes an exhibition on medicine in Shakespeare's time

Exploring Stratford-upon-Avon

William Shakespeare was born in Stratford-upon-Avon on St George's Day, 23 April 1564. Admirers of his work have been coming to the town since his death in 1616. In 1847 a public appeal successfully raised the money to buy the house in which he was born. As a result Stratford has become a literary shrine to Britain's greatest dramatist. It also has a thriving cultural reputation as the provincial home of the prestigious Royal Shakespeare Company, whose dramas are usually performed in Stratford before playing a second season in London *(see p156)*.

Around Stratford

The centre of Stratford-upon-Avon has many buildings that are connected with William Shakespeare and his descendants. On the High Street corner is the **Cage**, a 15th-century prison. This was converted into a house where Shakespeare's daughter Judith lived, and is now a shop. At the end of the High Street, the

Town Hall has a statue of Shakespeare on the façade given by David Garrick (1717–79), the actor who in 1769 organized the first Shakespeare festival.

The High Street leads into Chapel Street, where the half-timbered **Nash's House** is a museum of local history. It is also the site of **New Place**, where Shakespeare died in

Anne Hathaway's Cottage, home of Shakespeare's wife

1616. Though the house was demolished in 1759, the knot garden with a deep pool is beautifully preserved. In Church Street opposite, the **Guild Chapel** (1496) has a *Last Judgment* painting (c.1500) on the chancel wall. Shakespeare is thought to have attended the **Edward VI Grammar School** (above the former Guildhall) next door.

A left turn into Old Town leads to **Hall's Croft**, home of Shakespeare's daughter Susanna, which displays 16th- and 17th-century medical artifacts. An avenue of lime trees leads to **Holy Trinity Church**, where Shakespeare is buried. A walk along the river follows the Avon to **Bancroft Gardens**, at the junction of the River Avon and the Stratford Canal.

🏠 Shakespeare's Birthplace

Henley St. **Tel** 01789 204016. **Open** daily. **Closed** 1 Jan, 25 Dec. 🅿️ ♿ limited. 📷 🖥️ shakespeare.org.uk

Bought for the nation in 1847, Shakespeare's Birthplace was restored from its state of disrepair to its original Elizabethan style. Objects associated with Shakespeare's father, John, a glovemaker and wool merchant, are on display. There is a birth room, in which Shakespeare was supposedly born, and another room has a window etched with visitors' autographs, including that of Sir Walter Scott *(see p516)*.

Trinity Church, seen across the River Avon

otels and restaurants in this area see pp567–8 and pp593–4

Harvard House

High St. **Closed** to the public.

Built in 1596, this ornate house was the home of Katherine Rogers, whose son, John Harvard, emigrated to America in 1637. He died the following year, leaving money and a small library to the New College in Cambridge, Massachusetts. They expressed their gratitude by renaming the college in his honour. Harvard never actually lived in this house, however.

Environs

At Shottery, 1 mile (1.5 km) west of Stratford, is **Anne Hathaway's Cottage**, home of Shakespeare's wife before their marriage (see p325). Also worth a visit is **Mary Arden's Farm** in Wilmcote, home of Shakespeare's grandparents and childhood home of his mother, Mary Arden. Activities at the farm include falconry and Tudor music and dance.

🏠 **Anne Hathaway's Cottage**
Cottage Lane. **Tel** 01789 338532. **Open** daily. **Closed** 1 Jan, 25 & 26 Dec. 🐾 📷

🏠 **Mary Arden's Farm**
Station Rd. **Tel** 01789 338535. **Open** Apr–Oct: daily. 🐾 🛍 📷
🌐 shakespeare.org.uk

Kenneth Branagh in *Hamlet*

The Royal Shakespeare Company

The Royal Shakespeare Company is renowned for its new interpretations of Shakespeare's work. It was established in the 1960s as a resident company for the 1932 Shakespeare Memorial Theatre, now the Royal Shakespeare Theatre. It has seen the brightest and best theatrical talent tread its boards, from Laurence Olivier and Vivien Leigh to Helen Mirren and Kenneth Branagh. The RSC also tours, with regular seasons in London, Newcastle and even New York.

Grevel House, the oldest house in Chipping Campden

⑱ Chipping Campden

Gloucestershire. 🗺 2,500.
ℹ High St (01386 841206).
🌐 chippingcampdenonline.org

This perfect Cotswold town is kept in pristine condition by the Campden Society. Set up in the 1920s, the Society has kept alive the traditional skills of stonecarving and repair that make Chipping Campden such a unified picture of golden-coloured and lichen-patched stone. Visitors travelling from the northwest along the B4035 first see a group of ruins: the remains of **Campden Manor**, begun around 1613 by Sir Baptist Hicks, 1st Viscount Campden. The manor was burned by Royalist troops to prevent it being seized by Parliament at the end of the Civil War (see pp56–7), but the almshouses opposite the gateway were spared. They were designed in the form of the letter "I" (representing "J" in Latin), a symbol of the owner's loyalty to King James I.

The town's **Church of St James**, one of the finest in the Cotswolds, was built in the 15th century, financed by merchants who bought wool from Cotswold farmers and exported it at a high profit. Inside the church there are many elaborate tombs, and a magnificent brass dedicated

to William Grevel, describing him as "the flower of the wool merchants of England". He built **Grevel House** (c.1380) in the High Street, the oldest in a fine row of buildings, which is distinguished by a double-storey bay window.

Viscount Campden donated the **Market Hall** in 1627. His contemporary, Robert Dover, founded the "Cotswold Olimpicks", long before the modern Olympic Games had been established. His 1612 version included such painful events as the shin-kicking contest. The games still take place on the first Friday after each Spring Bank Holiday, followed by a torchlit procession into town ready for the Scuttlebrook Wake Fair on the next day. The setting for the games is a spectacular natural hollow on **Dover's Hill** above the town, worth climbing on a clear day for the marvellous views over the Vale of Evesham.

The 17th-century Market Hall in Chipping Campden

Tewkesbury's abbey church overlooks the town, crowded onto the bank of the River Severn

⑲ Tewkesbury

Gloucestershire. ⌂ 11,000.
ℹ Church St (01684 855040).
🛒 Wed, Sat. 🔳 **visittewkesbury.info**

This lovely town sits on the confluence of the rivers Severn and Avon. It has one of England's finest Norman abbey churches, **St Mary the Virgin**, which locals saved during the Dissolution of the Monasteries (*see p355*) by paying Henry VIII £453. Around the church, with its bulky tower and Norman façade, timbered buildings are crammed within the bend of the river. Warehouses are a reminder of past wealth, while the pretty, but redundant, Borough Mill on Quay Street also harks back to a more prosperous age.

Pump Room detail, Cheltenham

Environs
Boat trips run from the river to **Twyning**'s riverside pub, 6 miles (10 km) north.

⑳ Cheltenham

Gloucestershire. ⌂ 115,000. 🚆 🚌
ℹ Clarence St (01241 237431).
🛒 Sun; farmers' market 2nd & last Fri.
🔳 **visitcheltenham.com**

Cheltenham's reputation for elegance was first gained in the late 18th century, when high society flocked to the

spa town to "take the waters", following the example set by George III (*see pp58–9*). Many gracious terraced houses were built in Neo-Classical style, along broad avenues. These survive around the Queen's Hotel, near **Montpellier**, a lovely Regency arcade lined with craft and antique shops, and in the **Promenade**, with its smart department stores and couturiers. A more modern atmosphere prevails in the Regency Arcade, where the star attraction is the 1985 **clock** by Kit Williams: visit on the hour to see fish blowing bubbles over the onlookers' heads. **The Wilson – Cheltenham Art Gallery & Museum** is worth a visit to see its collection of furniture and other crafts made by members of the influential Arts and Crafts Movement (*see p33*), whose strict principles of utilitarian design were laid down by William Morris (*see pp224–5*).

The **Pittville Pump Room** (1825–30), modelled on the Greek Temple of Ilissos in Athens, is frequently used for performances during the town's renowned annual festivals of music (Jul) and literature (Oct).

The event that really attracts the crowds is the Cheltenham

Festival, the country's premier National Hunt race meeting (*see p70*).

🏛 The Wilson – Cheltenham Art Gallery & Museum
Clarence St. **Tel** 01242 237431.
Open daily. **Closed** 1 Jan, 25 & 26 Dec. 🛗 🔲 ♿ 🔳 **cheltenham museum.org.uk**

🏛 Pittville Pump Room
Pittville Park. **Tel** 0844 5762210.
Open daily. **Closed** 1 Jan, 25 & 26 Dec, public hols & frequently for functions: call to check. 🛗
🔳 **cheltenhamtownhall.org.uk**

Fantasy clock, by Kit Williams, in Cheltenham's Regency Arcade

Gloucester Cathedral's nave, lined by huge, impressive stone pillars

㉑ Gloucester

Gloucestershire. 110,000. 28 Southgate St (01452 396572). Fri, Sat. **thecityof gloucester.co.uk**

Gloucester has played a prominent role in the history of England. It was here that William the Conqueror ordered a vast survey of all the land in his kingdom, which was to be recorded in the *Domesday Book* of 1086 *(see p52)*.

The city was popular with the Norman monarchs and in 1216 Henry III was crowned in its magnificent **cathedral**. The solid, dignified nave was begun in 1089. Edward II, who was murdered in 1327 at Berkeley Castle, 14 miles (22 km) to the southwest, is buried in a tomb near the high altar. Many pilgrims came to honour Edward's tomb, leaving behind generous donations, and Abbot Thoky was able to begin rebuilding in 1331. The result was the wonderful east window and the cloisters, where the fan vault was developed and then copied in other churches all over the country.

The impressive buildings around the cathedral include College Court, with its **House of the Tailor of Gloucester** museum, in the house that the children's author Beatrix Potter *(see p371)* used as the setting for her illustrations of that story. A museum complex has been created in the **Gloucester Docks**, part of which is still a port, linked to the Bristol Channel by the Gloucester and Sharpness Canal (opened in 1827). In the old port, and housed in a Victorian warehouse, the **National Waterways Museum Gloucester** relates the history of Britain's canals via a series of interactive galleries. There are boat trips, too.

🏛 **House of the Tailor of Gloucester**
College Court. **Tel** 01452 422856. **Open** Mon–Sat (Sun; pm only). **Closed** public hols. **tailor-of-gloucester.org.uk**

🏛 **National Waterways Museum Gloucester**
Llanthony Warehouse, Gloucester Docks. **Tel** 01452 318200. **Open** daily (Nov–Mar: Tue–Sun). **Closed** 25 Dec. **canalrivertrust. org.uk**

㉒ Cirencester

Gloucestershire. 20,000. Park St (0128 565 4180). Mon–Sat. **cirencester.com**

The town of Cirencester is known as the capital of the Cotswolds. At its heart is a marketplace, and a popular market is held every Monday and Friday. Overlooking the market is the **Church of St John the Baptist**, whose "wineglass" pulpit (1515) is one of the few pre-Reformation pulpits to survive in England. To the west, **Cirencester Park** was laid out by the 1st Earl of Bathurst from 1714, with help from the poet Alexander Pope *(see p321)*.

The mansion is surrounded by a massive yew hedge. Clustering round the park entrance are the 17th- and 18th-century wool merchants' houses of Cecily Hill, built in grand Italianate style. Much humbler Cotswold houses, dating from the same era, are to be found in Coxwell Street.

The **Corinium Museum** is an impressive modern museum. Its fabulous hoard of Roman objects includes a rare tombstone – for a "Bodicacia" – discovered in 2015.

🌳 **Cirencester Park**
Cirencester Park. **Tel** 01285 653135. **Open** daily. **cirencester park.co.uk**

🏛 **Corinium Museum**
Park St. **Tel** 01285 655611. **Open** daily (Sun; pm only). **Closed** 1 Jan, 25 & 26 Dec. **corinium museum.org**

Cirencester's fine parish church, one of the largest in England

Art and Nature in the Roman World

Cirencester was an important centre of mosaic production in Roman days. Fine examples of the local style are shown in the Corinium Museum and mosaics range from mythical subjects, such as Orpheus taming lions and tigers with the music of his lyre, to depictions of

nature, including one of a hare. At Chedworth Roman Villa, 8 miles (13 km) north, a glorious mosaic celebrates the *Four Seasons*. *Winter* shows a peasant, dressed in a woollen hood and a wind-blown cloak, clutching a recently caught hare in one hand and a branch for fuel in the other.

Hare mosaic, Corinium Museum

EAST MIDLANDS

Derbyshire · Leicestershire · Lincolnshire
Northamptonshire · Nottinghamshire

Three very different kinds of landscape greet visitors to the
East Midlands. In the west, wild moors rise to the craggy heights
of the Peak District. These give way to the low-lying plain and
the massive industrial towns at the region's heart. In the east,
hills and limestone villages stretch to the coast.

The East Midlands owes much of its
character to a conjunction of the pastoral
with the urban. The spa resorts, historical
villages and stately homes coexist within
a landscape shaped by industrialization.
Throughout the region there are swathes
of scenic countryside – and grimy
industrial cities.

The area has been settled since
prehistoric times. The Romans mined for
lead and salt here, building a large network
of roads and fortresses. Anglo-Saxon and
Viking influence is found in many of the
place names. During the Middle Ages
profits from the wool industry enabled the
development of towns such as Lincoln,
which still has many fine old buildings.

In the west of the region is the Peak
District, Britain's first national park,
created in 1951. It draws crowds in
search of the wild beauty of the heather-
covered moors, or the wooded dales of
the River Dove. The Peaks are also very
popular with rock climbers and hikers.

The eastern edge of the Peaks
descends through stone-walled
meadows to sheltered valleys. The
Roman spa of Buxton adds a final note
of elegance before the flatlands of
south Derbyshire, Leicestershire and
Nottinghamshire are reached. An area
of coal mines and factories since the
late 18th century, the landscape was
improved greatly by the creation of the
National Forest. This ambitious project
harnesses ancient woodland and
freshly planted areas across a large
swathe of the region.

The steps of the Cascade at Chatsworth House, Derbyshire

◀ Night-time view of the cathedral and Cathedral Square, Lincoln

Exploring the East Midlands

Frequently overlooked by visitors, the East Midlands is actually a region of surprising variety. Numerous well-marked trails pass through the Peak District National Park. There are superb country houses at Chatsworth and Burghley and the impressive historic towns of Lincoln and Stamford to discover.

Lincoln Cathedral towering over half-timbered buildings

Sights at a Glance

1. Buxton
2. *Chatsworth House and Gardens pp338–9*
3. Matlock Bath
6. Nottingham
7. *Lincoln pp344–5*
8. *Burghley House pp346–7*
9. Stamford
10. Northampton

Walks and Tours

4. *Tissington Trail p341*
5. *Peak District Tour pp342–3*

Key

— Motorway
— Major road
— Secondary road
···· Minor road
— Scenic route
⚊ Main railway
— Minor railway
△ Summit

View of Burghley House from the north courtyard

For hotels and restaurants in this area see pp568–9 and pp594–5

Peak District countryside seen from the Tissington Trail

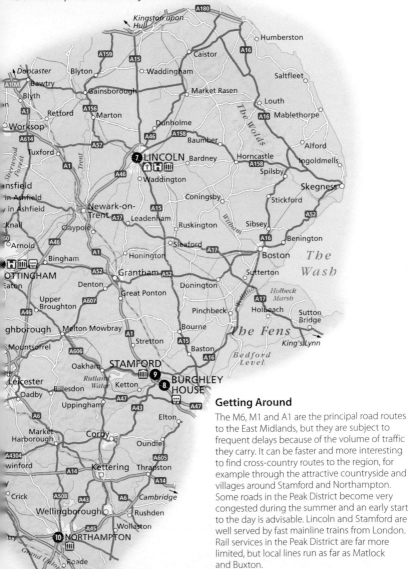

Getting Around

The M6, M1 and A1 are the principal road routes to the East Midlands, but they are subject to frequent delays because of the volume of traffic they carry. It can be faster and more interesting to find cross-country routes to the region, for example through the attractive countryside and villages around Stamford and Northampton. Some roads in the Peak District become very congested during the summer and an early start to the day is advisable. Lincoln and Stamford are well served by fast mainline trains from London. Rail services in the Peak District are far more limited, but local lines run as far as Matlock and Buxton.

For keys to symbols *see back fla*

Buxton Opera House, a late 19th-century building restored in 1979

❶ Buxton

Derbyshire. 👥 24,000. 🚉 🚌
ℹ️ Pavilion Gardens (01298 25106).
🏛️ Tue, Sat. 🌐 **visitbuxton.co.uk**

Buxton was developed as a spa town by the 5th Duke of Devonshire during the late 1700s. It has many fine Neo-Classical buildings, including the **Devonshire Royal Hospital** (1790), originally a stables, at the entrance to the town. The **Crescent** was built (1780–90) to rival Bath's Royal Crescent *(see p262)* and is currently being restored.

The town baths were at the southwest end of the Crescent. Here, a spring where water surges from the ground at a rate of 7,000 litres (1,540 gallons) an hour can be seen. Bottles of Buxton water are for sale but there is also a public fountain at **St Ann's Well**, opposite.

Steep gardens known as the Slopes lead from the Crescent to the small **Museum and Art Gallery**, with geological and archaeological displays. Behind the Crescent, overlooking the **Pavilion Gardens**, is the 19th-century iron and glass Pavilion, and the splendidly restored **Opera House**, where a music and arts festival is held in summer.

🏛️ **Buxton Museum and Art Gallery**
Terrace Rd. **Tel** 01629 533540. **Open** Easter–Sep: Tue–Sun & pub hols; Oct–Easter: Tue–Sat. **Closed** 1 Jan, 24–26 Dec. ♿ 📷 🌐 **derbyshire.gov.uk**

🌿 **Pavilion Gardens**
St John's Rd. **Tel** 01298 23114. **Open** daily. **Closed** Jan & 25 Dec. ♿ 🚫📷 🍴 📷

❷ Chatsworth House and Gardens

Chatsworth is one of Britain's most impressive stately homes. Originally a Tudor mansion built in 1552 by Bess of Hardwick, it was replaced in Baroque style by the 1st Duke of Devonshire between 1687 and 1707. Today the house hosts a particularly fine collection of artwork, including a Sculpture Gallery. The house has a 42-hectare (105-acre) garden, landscaped in the 1760s by "Capability" Brown *(see p30)* and developed by head gardener Joseph Paxton *(see p61)* in the mid-1800s. Alongside some terrific walks and trails, there is a fabulous working farmyard and a woodland playground.

★ Cascade
Water tumbles down the steps of the Cascade, built in 1696 to a French design. From the top, there is a fine view back towards the house.

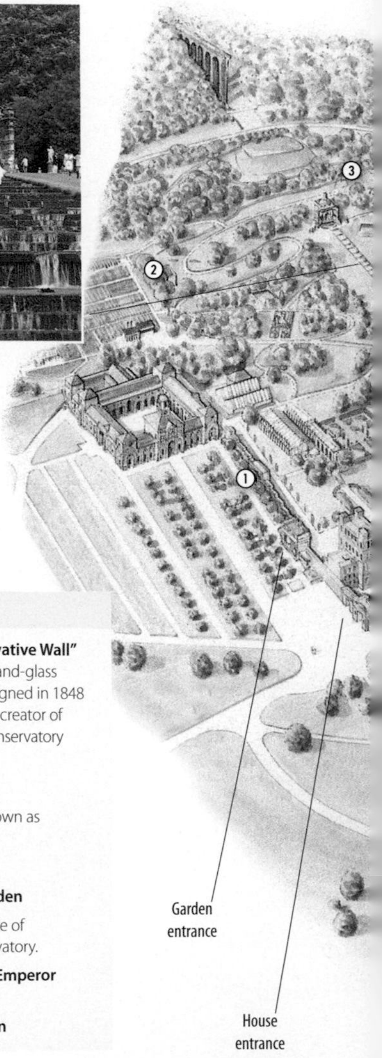

KEY

① **Paxton's "Conservative Wall" (the Case)** is a wood-and-glass conservatory wall designed in 1848 by Joseph Paxton, the creator of Chatsworth's Great Conservatory (now demolished).

② **Summerhouse**

③ **Round ponds**, known as the Spectacles.

④ **Grotto**

⑤ **Paxton's rock garden**

⑥ **The Maze** is the site of Paxton's Great Conservatory.

⑦ **Canal pond with Emperor Fountain**

⑧ **Seahorse Fountain**

Garden entrance

House entrance

South front and canal pond with Emperor fountain

★ **Chapel**
The chapel (1693) is resplendent with art and marble. Highlights include the grand altar, carved out of Derbyshire alabaster, and the stunning murals on the ceiling.

State Rooms
The rooms have fine interiors and superb art, such as this *trompe l'oeil* by Jan van der Vaart (1651–1727).

❸ Matlock Bath

Derbyshire. 🏔 9,500. 🚇
i Matlock Station (01335 343666).
w matlock.org.uk

Matlock was developed as a spa from the 1780s. Interesting buildings include a former hydro-therapy centre (1853) on the hill above the town, now council offices. On the hill opposite is the mock-Gothic Riber Castle.

From Matlock, the A6 winds through the beautiful Derwent Gorge to Matlock Bath. Here, cable cars run to the **Heights of Abraham** pleasure park, with caves, a nature trail and extensive views. Lead mining is the subject of the **Peak District Mining Museum**, and visitors can inspect the old **Temple Mine** nearby. Sir Richard Arkwright's **Cromford Mills** (1771), a World Heritage Site and the first ever water-powered cotton spinning mill, lies at the southern end of the gorge *(see p343)*.

🦌 **Heights of Abraham**
On A6. **Tel** 01629 582365. **Open** Feb–Oct: daily (Mar: Sat & Sun only). 🅿 ♿ limited. ▢ 📷 **w** heightsof
abraham.com

🏛 **Peak District Mining Museum**
The Pavilion, off A6. **Tel** 01629 583834. **Open** Apr–Oct: daily; Nov–Mar: Sat & Sun. **Closed** 25 Dec. 🅿 ♿ ▢ 📷
w peakdistrictleadmining
museum.co.uk

⛏ **Temple Mine**
Temple Rd, off A6. **Tel** 01629 583834.
Open call for details. 🅿 📷

⛏ **Cromford Mills**
Mill Lane, Cromford. **Tel** 01629 823256.
Open daily. **Closed** 25 Dec. 🎫 ♿
🅿 📷 **w** cromfordmills.org.uk

Cable cars taking visitors to the Heights of Abraham

❹ Tissington Trail

See p341.

❺ Peak District Tour

See pp342–3.

❻ Nottingham

Nottinghamshire. 🏔 305,000. 🚇
🚌 *i* Smithy Row (0844 477 5678).
🏪 daily. **w** nottinghamcity.gov.uk

One of Britain's biggest cities, Nottingham is still famed for the legend of Robin Hood and his adversary, the Sheriff of Nottingham. **Nottingham Castle** – not the medieval original – stands on a rock riddled with underground passages and houses a museum, with displays on the city's history, and what was Britain's first municipal art gallery, featuring works by Sir Stanley Spencer (1891–1959) and Dante Gabriel Rossetti (1828–82). At the foot of the castle, Britain's oldest tavern, **Ye Olde Trip to Jerusalem** (1189), is still in business.

Its name may refer to the 12th- and 13th-century crusades, but much of it is 17th-century.

There are several museums nearby, including the **Museum of Nottingham Life**, which describes 300 years of Nottingham's social history, and **Wollaton Hall and Deer Park**, an Elizabethan mansion housing a natural history museum.

Nottingham's redeveloped city centre boasts an award-winning Old Market Square.

Environs
Stately homes within a few miles of Nottingham include the Neo-Classical **Kedleston Hall** *(see pp32–3)*. "Bess of Hardwick", Countess of Shrewbury *(see p338)*, built the spectacular **Hardwick Hall** *(see p306)*.

🏰 **Nottingham Castle and Museum**
Lenton Rd. **Tel** 0115 876 1400.
Open daily. **Closed** 1 Jan, 24–27 Dec. 🅿 🎫 of the caves. ♿ 🅿 📷
w nottinghamcastle.org.uk

🏛 **Wollaton Hall and Deer Park**
Wollaton. **Tel** 0115 876 3100. **Open** daily. **Closed** 25 & 26 Dec. 🎫 fee.
♿ ▢ 📷 **w** wollatonhall.org.uk

🏛 **Museum of Nottingham Life**
Castle Boulevard. **Tel** 0115 876 1400.
Open Sat, Sun & public holidays.
Closed 1 Jan, 24–26 Dec. 🅿 ♿ 📷
w nottinghamcity.gov.uk

🏠 **Kedleston Hall**
Off A38. **Tel** 01332 842191. **Open** Mar–Oct: daily. 🅿 ♿ 🖉 📷 **NTS**

🏠 **Hardwick Hall**
Off A617. **Tel** 01246 850430.
Open mid-Feb–Oct: Wed–Sun.
🅿 ♿ limited. 🖉 📷 **NT**

Robin Hood of Sherwood Forest

England's most colourful folk hero was a legendary bowman, whose adventures are depicted in numerous films and stories. He lived in Sherwood Forest, near Nottingham, with a band of "merry men", robbing the rich to give to the poor. As part of an ancient oral tradition, Robin Hood figured mainly in ballads; the first written records of his exploits date from the 15th century. Today historians think that he was not one person, but a composite of various outlaws who refused to conform to medieval feudal constraints.

Victorian depiction of Friar Tuck and Robin Hood

❹ Tissington Trail

The full-length Tissington Trail runs for 13 miles (22 km), from the town of Ashbourne to Parsley Hay, where it meets the High Peak Trail. This is a short version, taking an easy route along a dismantled railway line around Tissington village and providing good views of the beautiful White Peak countryside. The Derbyshire custom of well dressing, thought to have originated in pre-Christian times, was revived in the region in the early 17th century, when the Tissington village wells were decorated in thanksgiving for deliverance from the plague, in the belief that the fresh water had had a medicinal effect. Well dressing is still an important event in the Peakland calendar, and can be seen in other villages where the water supplies were prone to dry up.

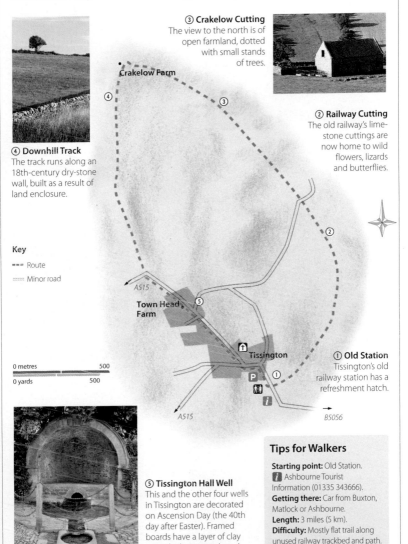

③ **Crakelow Cutting**
The view to the north is of open farmland, dotted with small stands of trees.

Crakelow Farm

④ **Downhill Track**
The track runs along an 18th-century dry-stone wall, built as a result of land enclosure.

② **Railway Cutting**
The old railway's limestone cuttings are now home to wild flowers, lizards and butterflies.

Key

--- Route
=== Minor road

A515

Town Head Farm

⑤

A515

Tissington

0 metres 500
0 yards 500

① **Old Station**
Tissington's old railway station has a refreshment hatch.

B5056

⑤ **Tissington Hall Well**
This and the other four wells in Tissington are decorated on Ascension Day (the 40th day after Easter). Framed boards have a layer of clay into which rice, seeds and flower petals are pressed.

Tips for Walkers

Starting point: Old Station.
ℹ️ Ashbourne Tourist Information (01335 343666).
Getting there: Car from Buxton, Matlock or Ashbourne.
Length: 3 miles (5 km).
Difficulty: Mostly flat trail along unused railway trackbed and path.
Ⓦ visitpeakdistrict.com

❾ Peak District Tour

The Peak District's natural beauty and sheep-grazed crags contrast with the industrial buildings of nearby valley towns. Designated Britain's first National Park in 1951, the area has two distinct types of landscape. In the south are the gently rolling hills of the limestone White Peak. To the north, west and east are the wild, heather-clad moorlands of the Dark Peak peat bogs, superimposed on millstone grit.

⑤ Edale
The high plateau above scenic Edale marks the starting point of the 267-mile (429-km) Pennine Way footpath *(see p40)*.

Tips for Drivers

Tour length: 40 miles (60 km).
Stopping-off points: There are refreshments at Crich Tramway Village and Arkwright's Mill in Cromford. Eyam has good old-fashioned teashops. The Nag's Head in Edale is a charming Tudor inn. Buxton has many pubs and cafés. *(See also pp636–7.)*

⑥ Buxton
This lovely spa town's opera house *(see p338)* is known as the "theatre in the hills" because of its magnificent setting.

⑦ Arbor Low
This stone circle, known as the "Stonehenge of the North", dates from around 2000 BC and consists of 46 recumbent stones enclosed by a ditch.

Key

━━ Tour route
┉┉ Other roads

⑧ Dovedale
Popular Dovedale is one of the prettiest of the Peak District's river valleys, with its stepping stones, thickly wooded slopes and wind-sculpted rocks. Izaak Walton (1593–1683), author of *The Compleat Angler*, used to fish here.

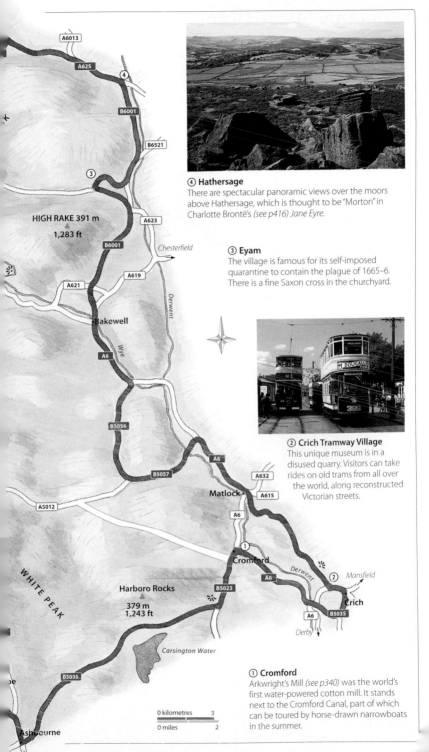

④ Hathersage
There are spectacular panoramic views over the moors above Hathersage, which is thought to be "Morton" in Charlotte Brontë's *(see p416) Jane Eyre.*

③ Eyam
The village is famous for its self-imposed quarantine to contain the plague of 1665–6. There is a fine Saxon cross in the churchyard.

② Crich Tramway Village
This unique museum is in a disused quarry. Visitors can take rides on old trams from all over the world, along reconstructed Victorian streets.

① Cromford
Arkwright's Mill *(see p340)* was the world's first water-powered cotton mill. It stands next to the Cromford Canal, part of which can be toured by horse-drawn narrowboats in the summer.

HIGH RAKE 391 m
1,283 ft

Chesterfield

Bakewell

Matlock

Cromford

Crich

Mansfield

Derby

WHITE PEAK

Harboro Rocks
379 m
1,243 ft

Carsington Water

Ashbourne

Derby

0 kilometres 3
0 miles 2

❼ Street-by-Street: Lincoln

Surrounded by the flat landscape of the Fens, Lincoln rises dramatically on a stone ridge above the River Witham, the three towers of its massive cathedral visible from afar. The Romans *(see pp48–9)* founded the first fortress here in AD 50. By the time of the Norman Conquest *(see p51)*, Lincoln was one of the most important cities in England (after London, Winchester and York). The city's wealth was due to its role in the export of wool from the Lincolnshire Wolds to Europe. Lincoln has managed to retain much of its historic character. Many remarkable medieval buildings have survived, most of which are along the aptly named Steep Hill, leading to the cathedral.

3rd-century Newport Arch

Museum of Lincolnshire Life

WESTGATE

BAILGATE

CASTLE HILL

STEEP HILL

DRURY LANE

MICHAELGATE

Norman House (1180)

★ **Lincoln Castle**
The early Norman castle, rebuilt at intervals, acted as the city prison from 1787 to 1878. The chapel's coffin-like pews served to remind felons of their fate.

Key

— Suggested route

15th-century Stonebow Gate and bus and railway stations

0 metres   100
0 yards   100

Jew's House
Lincoln had a large medieval Jewish community. This mid-12th-century stone house, one of the oldest of its kind, was owned by a Jewish merchant.

For hotels and restaurants in this area see pp568–9 and pp594–5

VISITORS' CHECKLIST

Practical Information
Lincoln. 93,000.
Castle Hill (01522 545458).
visitlincolnshire.com

Transport
Humberside, 30 miles (48 km); E Midlands, 51 miles (82 km).
St Mary St. Melville St.

EASTGATE
MINISTER YARD
POTTERGATE
GREESTONE PLACE
DANESGATE
LINDUM ROAD
NES TERRACE

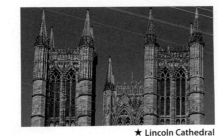

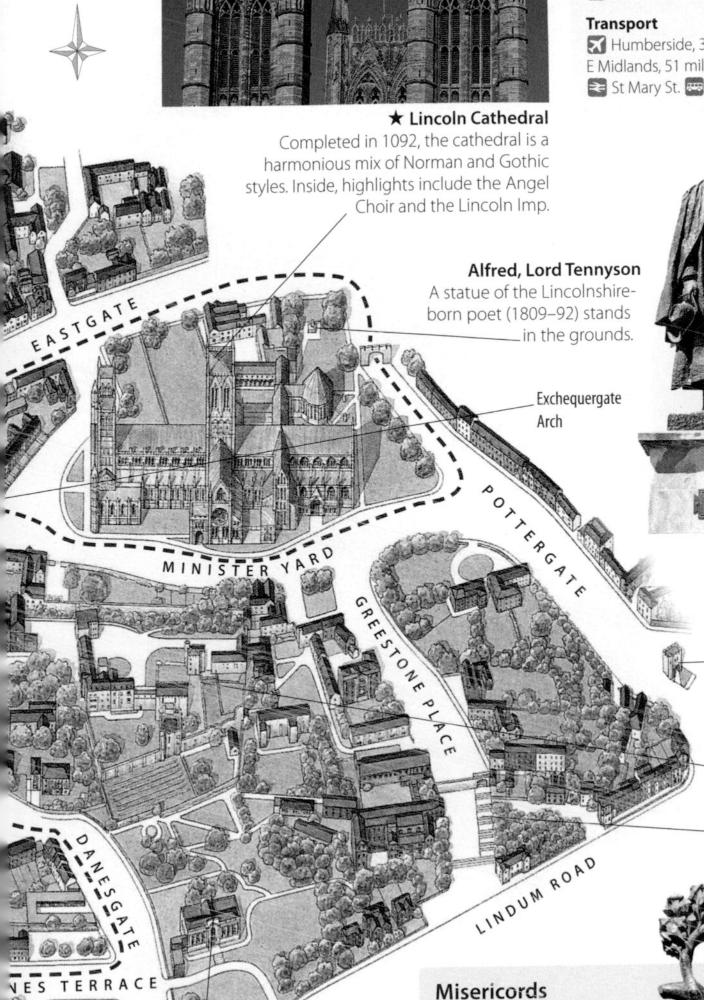

★ Lincoln Cathedral
Completed in 1092, the cathedral is a harmonious mix of Norman and Gothic styles. Inside, highlights include the Angel Choir and the Lincoln Imp.

TENNYSON

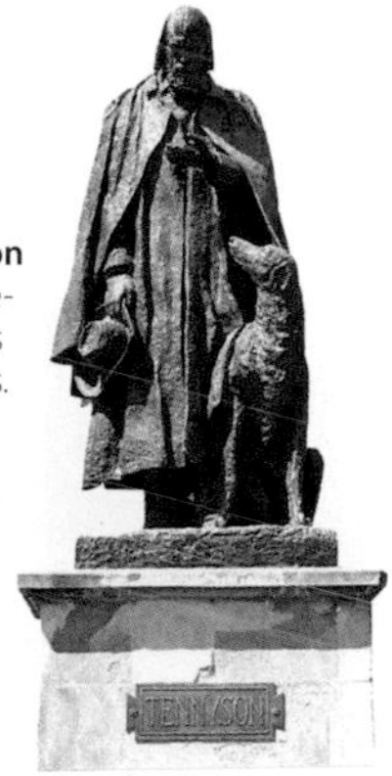

Alfred, Lord Tennyson
A statue of the Lincolnshire-born poet (1809–92) stands in the grounds.

Exchequergate Arch

The 14th-century Pottergate Arch

Victorian Arboretum

Ruins of Medieval Bishop's Palace

Greestone Stairs

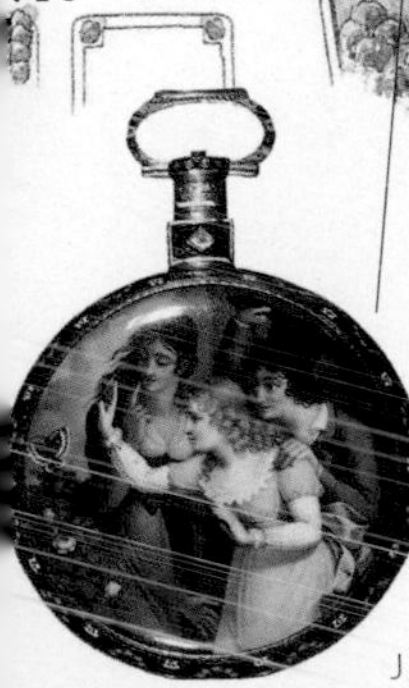

The Collection – Usher Gallery
This is packed with clocks, ceramics and silver. There are paintings by Peter de Wint (1784–1849) and J M W Turner *(see p95)*.

Misericords

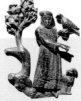

St Francis of Assisi

Misericords are ledges that project from the underside of the hinged seat of a choir stall, which provide support while standing. Lincoln Cathedral's misericords, in the early Perpendicular style canopied choirstalls, are some of the best in England. The wide variety of subjects includes parables, fables, myths, biblical scenes and irreverent images from daily life.

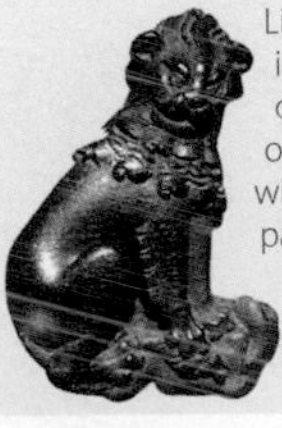

One of a pair of lions

❽ Burghley House

William Cecil, 1st Lord Burghley (1520–98), was Queen Elizabeth I's adviser and confidant for 40 years and built the wonderfully dramatic Burghley House in 1555–87. The roof line bristles with stone pyramids, chimneys disguised as Classical columns and towers shaped like pepper pots, all culminating in a symmetrical pattern when viewed from the west. The surrounding deer park is dotted with lime trees, many of which were planted by "Capability" Brown (see p30) when the park was landscaped in 1760. The interior walls are lavishly decorated with Italian paintings of Greek gods and historical learning activities are available all year in the education centre. The Elizabethan "garden of surprises" features a moss house, swivelling Caesar bust and water jets.

★ **Old Kitchen**
Gleaming copper pans hang from the walls of the fan-vaulted kitchen, little altered since the Tudor period.

North Gate
Intricate examples of 19th-century wrought-iron work adorn the principal entrances.

KEY

① **The Gatehouse**, with its side turrets, is a typical feature of the "prodigy" houses of the Tudor era (see p306).

② **Mullioned windows** were added in 1683 when glass became less expensive.

③ **A chimney** has been disguised as a Classical column.

④ **Cupolas** were very fashionable details, inspired by European Renaissance architecture.

⑤ **The Billiard Room** has many fine portraits inset in oak panelling.

⑥ **Obelisk and clock** (1585)

⑦ **The Great Hall** has a double hammerbeam roof and was a banqueting hall in Elizabethan days.

⑧ **The Heaven Room** features a wine cooler (1710) thought to be the largest in existence.

⑨ **The Fourth George Room**, one of a suite, is panelled in oak stained with ale.

West Front
Featuring the Burghley crest, the West Front was finished in 1577 and formed the original main entrance.

★ **Heaven Room**
Gods tumble from the sky, and satyrs and
nymphs play on the walls and ceiling in this
masterpiece by Antonio Verrio (1639–1707).

★ **Hell Staircase**
Verrio painted the
ceiling to show Hell as
the mouth of a cat
crammed with
tormented sinners. The
staircase, of local stone,
was installed in 1786.

❾ Stamford

Lincolnshire. 🅐 21,000. 🚆 🚌
🛈 27 St Mary's St (01780 755611).
📅 Fri. W southwestlincs.com

Stamford is a showpiece town,
famous for its churches and
Georgian town houses. The
town retains its medieval layout,
with a warren of winding
streets and cobbled alleys.

The spires of the medieval
churches (five survive of the
original eleven) give Stamford
the air of a miniature Oxford.

Barn Hill, leading up from
All Saints Church, is the best
place for a view of Stamford's
Georgian architecture in all its
variety. Below it are Broad Street
and High Street, where the
Public Library is fronted by
Tuscan columns. Inside is
the **Discovering Stamford**
exhibition, which reveals the
town's development through the
ages, as well as the 6-m (20-ft)
Stamford Tapestry, a depiction
of the town's history in wool.

🏛 **Discovering Stamford**
Stamford Library, High St.
Tel 01522 787010. **Open** Mon–
Sat. ♿ W lincolnshire.gov.uk

❿ Northampton

Northamptonshire. 🅐 212,000.
🚆 🚌 🛈 Sessions House, George
Row (01604 367997). 📅 Mon–Sat
(Thu: antiques). W visitnorth
hamptonshire.co.uk

This market town was once
a centre for shoe making, and
the **Museum and Art Gallery**
holds the world's largest
collection of footwear. Among
many fine old buildings is the
Victorian Gothic **Guildhall**.
Six miles west of the town is
Althorp, family home of Diana
Princess of Wales. Visitors can
tour the house and grounds
and see her island resting place.

🏛 **Northampton Museum
and Art Gallery**
Guildhall Rd. **Tel** 01604 838111
Closed until late 2018 ♿ 📷

🏛 **Althorp**
Great Brington (off A428). **Tel** 01604
770107. **Open** May–Jul & Sep: days and
times vary; Aug: daily. **Closed** 31 Aug.
🐾 ♿ 🖥 📷 W althorp.com

NORTHERN ENGLAND

Introducing Northern
England   350–357

Lancashire and the Lakes   358–383

Yorkshire and the
Humber Region   384–417

Northumbria   418–433

Northern England at a Glance

Rugged coastlines, spectacular walks and climbs, magnificent stately homes and breathtaking cathedrals all have their place in the north of England, with its dramatic history of Roman rule, Saxon invasion, Viking attacks and border skirmishes. Reminders of the Industrial Revolution are found in towns such as Halifax, Liverpool and Manchester, contrasting with the dramatic scenery of the Lake District, with its awe-inspiring mountains and lakes.

Locator Map

Hadrian's Wall *(see pp426–7)*, built around AD 120 to protect Roman Britain from the tribes to the north, cuts through rugged Northumberland National Park scenery.

The Lake District *(see pp356–7 and pp358–73)* is a combination of superb peaks, tumbling rivers and falls and shimmering lakes such as Wastwater.

The Yorkshire Dales National Park *(see pp388–90)* creates a delightful environment for walking and touring the farming landscape, scattered with attractive villages such as Thwaite, in Swaledale.

NORTHUMBER

Hexham

Carlisle

NORTHUM
(See pp418–

Cockermouth

Penrith

Whitehaven

Keswick

CUMBRIA

Windermere

Kendal

Barrow-in-Furness

Lancaster

LANCASHIRE AND THE LAKES
(See pp358–83)

Skipt

Blackpool

Blackburn

Burr

Preston

LANCASHIRE

Southport

Rochdale

Bolton

Wigan

Manchester

Liverpool

Stockport

The Walker Art Gallery *(see pp382–3)* in Liverpool is one of the jewels in the artistic crown of the north, with an internationally renowned collection ranging from Old Masters to modern art. Its sculpture includes John Gibson's *Tinted Venus* (c.1851–6).

◄ Sunrise at St Mary's Lighthouse, near Whitley Bay

Durham Cathedral
(see pp432–3), a striking Norman structure with an innovative southern choir aisle and fine stained glass, has towered over the city of Durham since 1093.

Fountains Abbey *(see pp394–5)*, one of the finest religious buildings in the north, was founded in the 12th century by monks who desired simplicity and austerity. Later the abbey became extremely wealthy.

Alnwick

Morpeth

0 kilometres   25

0 miles   25

castle
n Tyne

Sunderland

Durham

HAM

Hartlepool

u Middlesbrough

Darlington

Whitby

hmond

Helmsley

Scarborough

RTH YORKSHIRE

Ripon

YORKSHIRE AND
THE HUMBER REGION
(See pp384–417)

Bridlington

Harrogate

VEST
KSHIRE

York

EAST YORKSHIRE

Leeds

adford

Kingston
upon Hull

Wakefield

dersfield

Scunthorpe

Grimsby

Barnsley

Doncaster

SOUTH
YORKSHIRE

Sheffield

Castle Howard *(see pp402–3)*, a triumph of Baroque architecture, offers many magnificent settings, including this long gallery (1805–10), designed by C H Tatham.

York *(see pp408–413)* is a city of historical treasures, ranging from the medieval to Georgian. Its magnificent minster has a large collection of stained glass and the medieval city walls are well preserved. Other sights include churches, narrow alleyways and notable museums.

The Industrial Revolution in the North

The face of northern England in the 19th century was dramatically altered by the development of the coal mining, textile and shipbuilding industries. Lancashire, Northumberland and the West Riding of Yorkshire all experienced population growth and migration to cities. The hardships of urban life were partly relieved by the actions of several wealthy industrial philanthropists, but many people lived in extremely deprived conditions. Although most traditional industries have now declined sharply or disappeared as demand has moved elsewhere, a growing tourist industry has developed in many of the former industrial centres.

Back-to-backs or colliers' rows, such as these houses at Easington, were provided by colliery owners from the 1800s onwards. They comprised two small rooms for cooking and sleeping, and an outside toilet.

1842 Coal Mines Act prevented women and children from working in harsh conditions in the mines.

1815 Sir Humphrey Davy invented a safety oil lamp for miners. Light shone through a cylindrical gauze sheet which prevented the heat of the flame igniting methane gas in the mine. Thousands of miners benefited from this device.

Coal mining was a family industry in the north of England with women and children working alongside the men.

1750	1800
Pre-Steam	Steam Age
1750	1800

1781 Leeds–Liverpool Canal opened. The building of canals facilitated the movement of raw materials and finished products, and aided the process of mechanization immeasurably.

1830 Liverpool and Manchester railway opened, connecting two of the biggest cities outside London. Within a month the railway carried 1,200 passengers.

Hebden Bridge *(see p416)*, a typical West Riding textile mill town jammed into the narrow Calder Valley, typifies a pattern of workers' houses surrounding a central mill. The town benefited from its position when the Rochdale Canal (1804) and then the railway (1841) took advantage of this relatively low-level route over the Pennines.

Halifax's Piece Hall *(see p417)* is the most impressive surviving example of industrial architecture in northern England. It is the only complete 18th-century cloth market building in Yorkshire. Merchants sold measures of cloth known as "pieces" from rooms lining the cloisters inside.

Saltaire (see p415) was a model village built by the wealthy cloth merchant and mill-owner Sir Titus Salt (1803–76) for the benefit of his workers. Seen here in the 1870s, as well as housing it included facilities such as shops, gardens and sportsfields, almshouses, a hospital, school and chapel. A disciplinarian, Salt banned alcohol and pubs from Saltaire.

George Hudson (1800–71) built the first railway station in York in 1840–42. In the 1840s he owned more than a quarter of the railways in Britain and was known as the "railway king".

Strikes to improve working conditions were common. Violence flared in July 1893 when colliery owners locked miners out of their pits and stopped their pay after the Miners' Federation resisted a 25 per cent wage cut. Over 300,000 men struggled without pay until November, when work resumed at the old rate.

Port Sunlight (see p383) was founded by William Hesketh Lever (1851–1925) to provide housing for workers at his Sunlight soap factory. Between 1889 and 1914 he built 800 cottages. Amenities included a pool.

| 0 | 1900 |

ll Mechanization

| 0 | 1900 |

Power loom weaving transformed the textile industry while creating unemployment among skilled hand loom weavers. By the 1850s, the West Riding had 30,000 power looms, used in cotton and woollen mills. Of 79,000 workers, over half were to be found in Bradford alone.

Joseph Rowntree (1836–1925) founded his chocolate factory in York in 1892, having formerly worked with George Cadbury. As Quakers, the Rowntrees believed in the social welfare of their workers (establishing a model village in 1904), and, with Terry's confectionery (1767), they made a vast contribution to York's prosperity. Today, Nestlé Rowntree makes one of the most popular chocolate bars, the Kit Kat, and York is Britain's chocolate capital.

Furness dry dock was built in the 1890s, when the shipbuilding industry moved north in search of cheap labour and materials. Barrow-in-Furness, Glasgow (see pp520–25) and Tyne and Wear were the new centres.

Northern England Abbeys

Northern England has some of the finest and best preserved religious houses in Europe. Centres of prayer, learning and power in the Middle Ages, the larger of these were designated abbeys and were governed by an abbot. Most were located in rural areas, considered appropriate for a spiritual and contemplative life. Viking raiders had destroyed many Anglo-Saxon religious houses in the 8th and 9th centuries *(see pp50–51)* and it was not until William the Conqueror founded the Benedictine Selby Abbey in 1069 that monastic life revived in the north. New orders, Augustinians in particular, arrived from the Continent and by 1500 Yorkshire had 83 monasteries.

Ruins of St Mary's Abbey today

The Liberty of St Mary was the name given to the land around the abbey, almost a city within a city. Here, the abbey had its own market, fair, prison and gallows – all exempt from the city authorities.

St Mary's Abbey

Founded in York in 1086, this Benedictine abbey was one of the wealthiest in Britain. Its involvement in the wool trade in York and the granting of royal and papal privileges and land led to a relaxing of standards by the early 12th century. The abbot was even allowed to dress in the same style as a bishop, and was raised by the pope to the status of a "mitred abbot". As a result, 13 monks left in 1132, to found Fountains Abbey *(see pp394–5)*.

Gatehouse and St Olave's church

Interval tower

Water tower

Hospitium or guest house

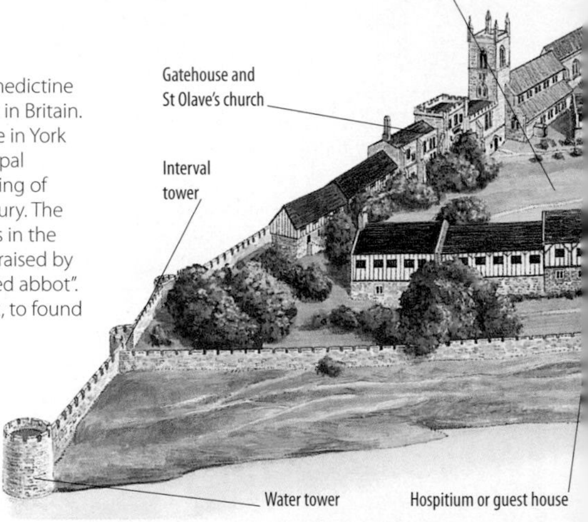

Monasteries and Local Life

As one of the wealthiest landowning sections of society, the monasteries played a vital role in the local economy. They provided employment, particularly in agriculture, and dominated the wool trade, England's largest export during the Middle Ages. By 1387 two-thirds of all wool exported from England passed through St Mary's Abbey, the largest wool trader in York.

Cistercian monks tilling their land

Where to See Abbeys Today

Fountains Abbey *(see pp394–5)*, founded by Benedictine monks and later taken over by Cistercians, is the most famous of the numerous abbeys in the region. Rievaulx *(see p397)*, Byland *(see p396)* and Furness *(see p372)* were all founded by the Cistercians, and Furness became the second wealthiest Cistercian house in England after Fountains. Whitby Abbey *(see p400)*, sacked by the Vikings, was later rebuilt by the Benedictine order. The northeast is famous for its early Anglo-Saxon monasteries at Hexham, Lindisfarne and Jarrow *(see pp422–3)*.

Mount Grace Priory *(see p398)*, founded in 1398, is the best-preserved Carthusian house in England. The former individual gardens and cells of each monk are still clearly visible.

The Dissolution of the Monasteries (1536–40)

By the early 16th century, the monasteries owned one-sixth of all English land and their annual income was four times that of the Crown. Henry VIII ordered the closure of all religious houses in 1536, acquiring their wealth in the process (see pp54–5). This provoked a large uprising of Catholic northerners led by Robert Aske later that year, but the rebellion failed and Aske and others were executed for conspiracy. The dissolution was continued by Thomas Cromwell, the king's chief minister, who became known as "the hammer of the monks".

Thomas Cromwell (c.1485–1549)

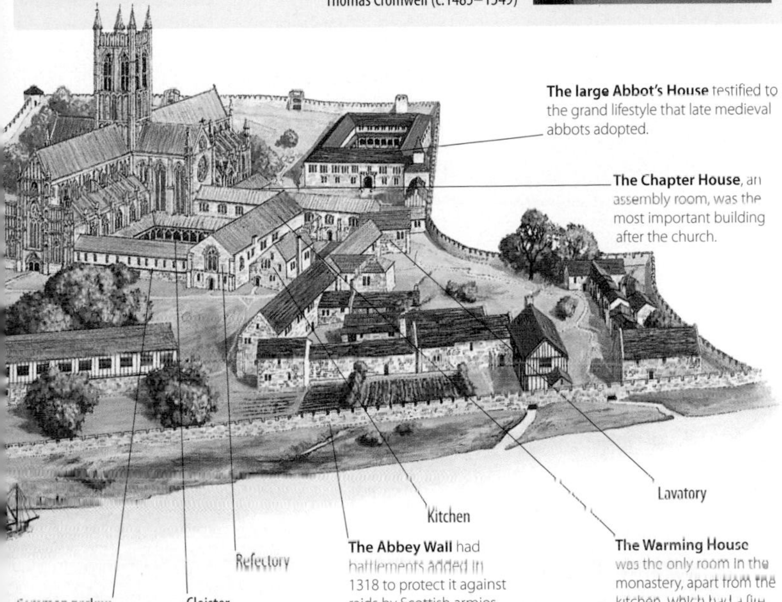

The large Abbot's House testified to the grand lifestyle that late medieval abbots adopted.

The Chapter House, an assembly room, was the most important building after the church.

Lavatory

Kitchen

The Abbey Wall had battlements added in 1318 to protect it against raids by Scottish armies

Refectory

The Warming House was the only room in the monastery, apart from the kitchen, which had a fire.

Common parlour

Cloister

Kirkham Priory, an Augustinian foundation of the 1120s, enjoys a tranquil setting on the banks of the River Derwent, near Malton. The finest feature of the ruined site is the 13th-century gatehouse that leads into the priory complex.

Kirkstall Abbey was founded in 1152 by monks from Fountains Abbey. The well-preserved ruins of this Cistercian house near Leeds include the church, the late Norman chapter house and the abbot's lodging. This evening view was painted by Thomas Girtin (1775–1802)

Easby Abbey lies beside the River Swale, outside the pretty market town of Richmond. Among the remains of this Premonstratensian house, founded in 1155, are the 13th-century refectory and sleeping quarters and 14th-century gatehouse.

The Geology of the Lake District

The Lake District, a UNESCO World Heritage site, contains some of England's most spectacular scenery. Concentrated in just 900 sq miles (231 sq km) are the highest peaks, deepest valleys and longest lakes in the country. Today's landscape has changed little since the end of the Ice Age 10,000 years ago, the last major event in Britain's geological history. But the glaciated hills that were revealed by the retreating ice were once part of a vast mountain chain whose remains can also be found in North America. The mountains were first raised by the gradual fusion of two ancient landmasses which, for millions of years, formed a single continent. Eventually the continent broke into two, forming Europe and America, separated by the widening Atlantic Ocean.

Honister Pass, with its distinctive U-shape, is an example of a glaciated valley, once completely filled with ice.

Geological History

The oldest rock formed as sediment under an ocean called Iapetus. Some 450 million years ago, Earth's internal movements made two continents collide, and the ocean disappear.

1 **The collision** buckled the former sea bed into a mountain range. Magma rose from Earth's mantle, altered the sediments and cooled into volcanic rock.

2 **In the Ice Age**, glaciers slowly excavated huge rock basins in the mountainsides, dragging debris to the valley floor. Frost sculpted the summits.

3 **The glaciers retreated** 10,000 years ago, their meltwaters forming lakes in valleys dammed by debris. As the climate improved, plants colonized the fells.

Radiating Lakes

The diversity of Lake District scenery owes much to its geology: hard volcanic rocks in the central lakes give rise to rugged hills, while soft slates to the north produce a more rounded topography. The lakes form a radial pattern, spreading out from a central volcanic rock zone.

Scafell Pike is the highest peak in England. The peak includes two further points: Broad Crag and Ill Crag.

Great Gable

Old Man Coniston

Coniston Water

Wastwater is the deepest of the lakes. Its southeastern cliffs are streaked with granite scree – the debris formed each year as rock shattered by the winter frost tumbles down during the spring thaw.

Man on the Mountain

The sheltered valley floors with their benign climate and fertile soils are ideal for settlement. Farmhouses, dry-stone walls, pasture and sheep pens are an integral part of the landscape. Higher up, the absence of trees and bracken are the result of wind and a cooler climate. Old mine workings and tracks are the relics of once-flourishing industries.

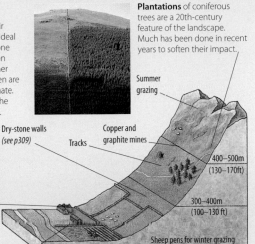

Plantations of coniferous trees are a 20th-century feature of the landscape. Much has been done in recent years to soften their impact.

Summer grazing

Dry-stone walls *(see p309)*

Copper and graphite mines

Tracks

400–500m (130–170ft)

300–400m (100–130 ft)

Sheep pens for winter grazing

Hedges

Slate and other local stone has long been incorporated into buildings: slate roofs, stone walls, lintels and bridges.

Bassenthwaite Lake

Blencathra

Derwent Water

Helvellyn

Ullswater

Place Fell

High Street

Windermere

Skiddaw is composed of slate, formed when the muddy sediment of the ancient ocean floor was altered by extreme pressure.

Striding Edge is a long, twisting ridge which leads to the summit of Helvellyn. It was sharpened by the widening of the valleys on either side caused by the build-up of glaciers.

The Langdale Pikes are remnants of the volcanic activity which once erupted in the area. They are made of hard igneous rocks, known as Borrowdale Volcanics. Unlike the Skiddaw Slates, they have not eroded smoothly, so they leave a craggy skyline.

LANCASHIRE AND THE LAKES

Cumbria · Lancashire

The painter John Constable (1776–1837) declared that the Lake District, now visited by 18 million people annually, had "the finest scenery that ever was". Swathes of rolling hills and mountains, glistening lakes, and ancient woodlands all contribute to this impressive landscape.

Within the 30-mile (45-km) radius of the Lake District lies an astonishing number of fells and lakes. The wild peaks, rolling farmland, placid waters and winding coutry lanes have sunk themselves deep into the national psyche. Today, all looks peaceful, but from the Roman occupation to the Middle Ages, the northwest was a turbulent area, as successive kings and rulers fought over the territory. Historians can revel in the various Celtic monuments, Roman remains, stately homes and monastic ruins.

The magnificent scenery is paramount but is greatly enhanced by local wildlife and the chance to see local culture, such as Cumberland wrestling. And then there are many outdoor activities to enjoy, too.

Lancashire's portfolio of destinations includes the fine county town of Lancaster, Blackpool with its autumn illuminations and fairground attractions, and the peaceful seaside beaches to the south. Inland, the most appealing regions are the Forest of Bowland, a sparse expanse of heathery grouse moor, and the picturesque Ribble Valley. Further south are the industrial conurbations of Manchester and Merseyside. There are many fine Victorian buildings in Manchester, where the industrial quarter of Castlefield has been revitalized. Liverpool, with its restored Albert Dock, is best known as the seaport city of the Beatles. It has a lively club scene and is often used as a film location. Both cities have good art galleries and museums.

Jetty at Grasmere, one of the most popular lakes in the Lake District

◀ View over Keswick to a mist-covered Derwent Water, Lake District National Park

Exploring Lancashire and the Lakes

The Lake District's natural scenery, the result of geological upheavals over millennia *(see pp356–7)*, outweighs any of its man-made attractions. Visitors flock to enjoy the open fells, lakes and the country's highest peak: Scafell Pike, at 978 m (3,210 ft).

The Lakes are most crowded in summer when activities include boat trips and hill walking. The best bases are Keswick and Ambleside, while there are also good hotels on the shores of Windermere and Ullswater and in the Cartmel area.

Lancashire's Bowland Forest, with its picturesque villages, is an attractive place to explore on foot. Further south, the historic town of Lancaster has excellent museums and a castle.

Kayaking on Derwentwater in the Northern Fells and Lakes area

Getting Around

For many, the first glimpse of the Lake District is from the M6 near Shap, but the A6 is a more dramatic route. You can reach Windermere by train, but you need to change at Oxenholme, on the mainline route from Euston to Glasgow. Penrith also has rail services and bus links into the Lakes. La'al Ratty, the miniature railway up Eskdale, and the Lakeside & Haverthwaite railway, which connects with steamers on Windermere, make for enjoyable outings. Regular buses link all the main centres, where excursions are organized. Seasonal minibus services connect some of the more remote passes and valleys.

Lancaster, Liverpool and Manchester are on the main rail and bus routes, and the latter two also have airports. For Blackpool, you may need to change trains in Preston. Wherever you go in the area, one of the best means of getting around is on foot.

For hotels and restaurants in this area see pp569–70 and pp595–7

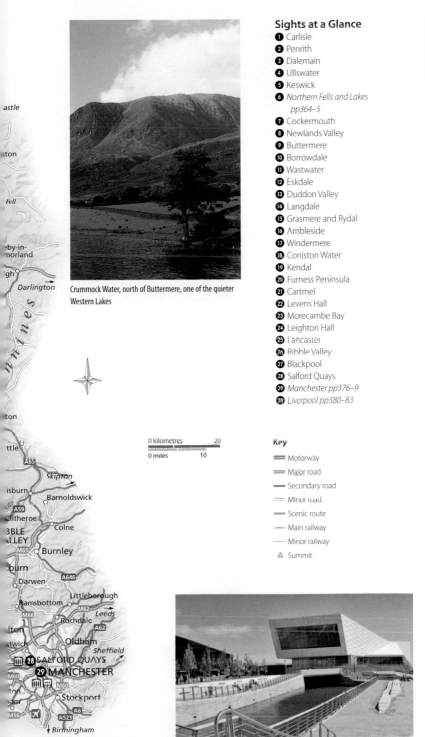

Crummock Water, north of Buttermere, one of the quieter Western Lakes

Sights at a Glance

1. Carlisle
2. Penrith
3. Dalemain
4. Ullswater
5. Keswick
6. *Northern Fells and Lakes pp364–5*
7. Cockermouth
8. Newlands Valley
9. Buttermere
10. Borrowdale
11. Wastwater
12. Eskdale
13. Duddon Valley
14. Langdale
15. Grasmere and Rydal
16. Ambleside
17. Windermere
18. Coniston Water
19. Kendal
20. Furness Peninsula
21. Cartmel
22. Levens Hall
23. Morecambe Bay
24. Leighton Hall
25. Lancaster
26. Ribble Valley
27. Blackpool
28. Salford Quays
29. *Manchester pp376–9*
30. *Liverpool pp380–83*

0 kilometres 20
0 miles 10

Key

━━━ Motorway
━━━ Major road
━━━ Secondary road
╍╍╍ Minor road
━━━ Scenic route
╍╍╍ Main railway
──── Minor railway
△ Summit

The unique façade of the Museum of Liverpool

For keys to symbols *see back flap*

❶ Carlisle

Cumbria. 🏔 110,000. 🚊 🚌
ℹ 40 Scotch St (01228 598596).
Ⓦ discovercarlisle.co.uk

Due to its proximity to the Scottish border, this city has long been a defensive site. Known as Luguvalium by the Romans, it was an outpost of Hadrian's Wall *(see pp426–7)*. Carlisle was sacked and pillaged repeatedly by the Danes, the Normans and border raiders, and suffered damage as a Royalist stronghold under Cromwell *(see p56)*.

Today, Carlisle is the capital of Cumbria. In its centre are the timber-framed Guildhall and market cross, and fortifications still exist in the West Walls, drum-towered gates and its Norman **castle**. The castle tower has a small museum devoted to the King's Own Border Regiment. The cathedral dates from 1122 and features a decorative east window. Carlisle's **Tullie House Museum** recreates the city's past with sections on Roman history and Cumbrian wildlife. Nearby lie the evocative ruins of **Lanercost Priory** (c.1166) and **Birdoswald Roman Fort**.

🏠 Carlisle Castle
Castle Way. **Tel** 01228 591922.
Open Apr–Oct: daily; Nov–Mar: Sat & Sun. **Closed** 1 Jan, 24–26 Dec. 🅿
📷 ♿ limited. 📷 EH **Ⓦ english-heritage.org.uk**

Façade of Hutton-in-the-Forest with medieval tower on the right

🏛 Tullie House Museum
Castle St. **Tel** 01228 618718.
Open daily (Sun: pm only). **Closed** 1 Jan, 25 & 26 Dec 🅿 ♿ 📷 📷 EH
Ⓦ tulliehouse.co.uk

🏠 Lanercost Priory
Nr Brampton. **Tel** 01697 73030.
Open Apr–Sep: daily; Oct: Thu–Mon; Nov–Mar: Sat & Sun. 🅿 ♿ limited.
📷 EH **Ⓦ english-heritage.org.uk**

🏠 Birdoswald Roman Fort
Gilsland, Brampton. **Tel** 016977 47602. **Open** Apr–Oct: daily; Nov–Mar: Sat & Sun. **Closed** 1 Jan, 24–26 & 31 Dec. 🅿 📷 📷 EH **Ⓦ english-heritage.org.uk**

❷ Penrith

Cumbria. 🏔 15,000. **ℹ** Robinson's School, Middlegate (017688 67466). 🛒 Tue, Sat, Sun. **Ⓦ visiteden.co.uk**

Timewarp shopfronts on the market square and a 14th-century **castle** of sandstone are Penrith's main attractions. There are some strange hogback stones in St Andrew's churchyard, allegedly a giant's grave, but more likely Anglo-Viking headstones.

Environs
Just northeast of Penrith at Little Salkeld is the intriguing Bronze Age circle (with 66 tall stones) known as **Long Meg and her Daughters**. Six miles (9 km) northwest of Penrith lies **Hutton-in-the-Forest**. The oldest part of this house is the 13th-century tower. Inside is a magnificent Italianate staircase, a panelled 17th-century Long Gallery, a delicately stuccoed Cupid Room dating from the 1740s, and several Victorian rooms. Outside, you can walk around the walled garden and topiary terraces, or explore the woods.

🏠 Penrith Castle
Ullswater Rd. **Tel** 0370 333 1181.
House: **Open** daily. ♿ grounds. EH
Ⓦ english-heritage.org.uk

🏡 Hutton-in-the-Forest
Off B5305. **Tel** 017684 84449. House: **Open** Apr–Sep: Wed, Thu, Sun & public hols (pm). Grounds: **Open** Apr–Oct: Sun–Fri. 🅿 ♿ limited. 📷 📷
Ⓦ hutton-in-the-forest.co.uk

❸ Dalemain

Penrith, Cumbria. **Tel** 017684 86450. 🚊 🚌 Penrith then taxi. **Open** Apr–Oct: Sun–Thu. 🅿 📷 ♿ limited. 📷 📷 **Ⓦ dalemain.com**

A Georgian façade gives this fine house near Ullswater the impression of architectural unity, but hides a much-altered medieval and Elizabethan

Traditional Cumbrian Sports and Events

Cumberland wrestling is one of the most interesting sports to watch in the summer months. The combatants, often clad in longjohns and embroidered velvet pants, clasp one another in an armlock and attempt to topple each other over. Technique and good balance outweigh physical force. Other traditional Lakeland sports include fell-racing, a gruelling test of speed and stamina up and down local peaks at ankle-breaking speed. Hound-trailing is also a popular sport, in which specially bred hounds follow an aniseed trail over the hills. Sheepdog trials, steam fairs and flower shows take place in summer. The Egremont Crab Fair in September is famous for its face-pulling, or "gurning", competition.

Cumberland wrestlers

Sheep resting at Glenridding, on the southwest shore of Ullswater

structure with a maze of rambling passages. Public rooms include a superb Chinese drawing room with hand-painted wallpaper and a panelled 18th-century drawing room. Several small museums occupy various outbuildings, and the gardens have a fine collection of fragrant shrub roses and a huge silver fir.

Sumptuous Chinese drawing room at Dalemain

❹ Ullswater

Cumbria. 🚂 Penrith. 🅸 Beckside car park, Glenridding (017684 82414).
🆆 **ullswater.com**

Often considered the most beautiful of all Cumbria's lakes, Ullswater stretches from gentle farmland near Penrith to dramatic hills and crags at its southern end. The main western shore road can be very busy.

In summer, two restored Victorian steamers ply regularly from Pooley Bridge to Glenridding. One of the best walks crosses the eastern shore from Glenridding to Hallin Fell and the moorland of Martindale. The western side passes Gowbarrow, where Wordsworth's immortal "host of golden daffodils" bloom in spring (see p370).

❺ Keswick

Cumbria. 🅼 4,800. 🅸 Moot Hall, Market Sq (0845 901 0845).
🆆 **keswick.org**

A tourist destination since the end of the 18th century, Keswick has guesthouses, a summer repertory theatre, outdoor equipment shops and a popular street market. Its most striking central building is the **Moot Hall**, dating from 1813, now housing the tourist office. The town prospered on wool and leather until, in Tudor times, deposits of graphite and copper were discovered. Mining then took over as the main industry and Keswick became an important centre for pencil manufacture. In World War II, hollow pencils were made to hide espionage maps on thin paper. The **Pencil Museum**, housed in a pencil factory, offers a fun insight into the world of pencils.

Among the many fine exhibits at the **Keswick Museum and Art Gallery** are original manuscripts of Lakeland writers, musical stones and other curiosities.

To the east of town lies the ancient stone circle of Castlerigg (see p365), thought to be older than Stonehenge.

🏛 **Pencil Museum**
Carding Mill Lane. **Tel** 017687 73626.
Open 9:30am–5pm daily (Nov–Mar: to 4pm). **Closed** 1 Jan, 25 & 26 Dec.
🄰 🄱 🄳 🄲 🆆 **pencilmuseum. co.uk**

🏛 **Keswick Museum and Art Gallery**
Fitz Park, Station Rd. **Tel** 017687 73263.
Open 10am–4pm daily. ♿ 🄲
🆆 **keswickmuseum.org.uk**

Outdoor equipment shop in Keswick

❻ Northern Fells and Lakes

Many visitors praise this northern area of the Lake District National Park for its scenery and geological interest *(see pp356–7)*. It is ideal walking country, and Derwentwater, Thirlmere and Bassenthwaite provide endless scenic views, rambles and opportunities for water-sports. Large areas surrounding the regional centre of Keswick *(see p363)* are accessible only on foot, particularly the huge mass of hills known as Back of Skiddaw – located between Skiddaw and Caldbeck – or the Helvellyn range, east of Thirlmere.

Lorton Vale
The lush, green farmland south of Cockermouth creates a marked contrast with the more rugged mountain landscapes of the central Lake District. In the village of Low Lorton is the private manor house of Lorton Hall, dating from the 15th century.

KEY

① **The Whinlatter Pass** is an easy route from Keswick to the farmland of Lorton Vale. It gives a good view of Bassenthwaite Lake and a glimpse of Grisedale Pike.

② **Bassenthwaite Lake** is best viewed from the east shore; however, accessibility is limited. Parking is easier on the west side.

③ **Blencathra**, also known as Saddleback because of its twin peaks (868 m; 2,847 ft), is a challenging climb, especially in winter.

④ **Thirlmere** was created as a reservoir to serve Manchester in 1879.

Derwentwater
Surrounded by woodland slopes and fells, this attractive oval lake is dotted with tiny islands. One of these was inhabited by St Herbert, a disciple of St Cuthbert *(see p423)*, who lived there as a hermit until 687. Boats from Keswick provide lake excursions.

The Major Peaks

The Lake District hills are the highest in England. Although they seem small by world standards, the scale of the surrounding terrain makes them look extremely grand. Some of the most important peaks are shown on the following pages. Each peak is regarded as having its own personality. This section shows the Skiddaw fells, north of Keswick.

Blencathra
Skiddaw
Grisedale Pike
Grasmoor
Knott Rigg
Helvellyn
Great Gable
High Street
Wastwater
Screes
Scafell
Hard Knott
The Old Man of Coniston

Key

▬ From ① Blencathra to ② Cockermouth *(see opposite)*

▬ From ③ Grisedale Pike to ④ the Old Man of Coniston *(see pp366–7)*

▬ From ⑤ the Old Man of Coniston to ⑥ Windermere and Tarn Crag *(see pp368–9)*

— National Park boundary

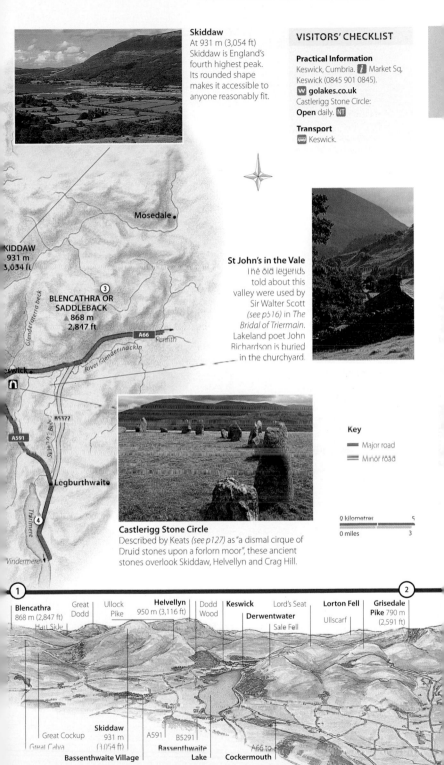

Skiddaw

At 931 m (3,054 ft) Skiddaw is England's fourth highest peak. Its rounded shape makes it accessible to anyone reasonably fit.

St John's in the Vale

The old legends told about this valley were used by Sir Walter Scott *(see p516)* in *The Bridal of Triermain*. Lakeland poet John Richardson is buried in the churchyard.

Key

━━━ Major road
═══ Minor road

0 kilometres 5
0 miles 3

Castlerigg Stone Circle

Described by Keats *(see p127)* as "a dismal cirque of Druid stones upon a forlorn moor", these ancient stones overlook Skiddaw, Helvellyn and Crag Hill.

For keys to symbols *see back flap*

Crummock Water, one of the quieter western lakes

⑦ Cockermouth

Cumbria. 🏠 8,000. 🚂 Workington. 🚌 ℹ️ 4 Kings Arms Lane, off Main St (01900 822634). 🌐 **western-lakedistrict.co.uk**

Brightly coloured terraced houses and restored workers' cottages beside the river make the busy market town of Cockermouth, which dates from the 12th century, an attractive place to visit. The handsome **Wordsworth House**, on Main Street, where the poet was born *(see p370)*, is a must-see. This fine Georgian building still

contains a few of the family's possessions, and is furnished in the style of the late 18th century. Wordsworth mentions the attractive terraced garden, which overlooks the River Derwent, in his *Prelude*. The local parish church contains a Wordsworth memorial window.

Cockermouth **castle** is partly ruined but still inhabited; it is occasionally open to the public, most often during the Cockermouth Festival, which is held in July. Beer fans can visit the **Jennings Brewery** for tours and tastings.

🏛️ **Wordsworth House**
Main St. **Tel** 01900 824805.
Open Mar–Oct: Sat–Thu. 🅿️ 📷
NT 🌐 nationaltrust.org.uk

🏭 **Jennings Brewery**
Castle Brewery. **Tel** 0845 1297190.
Open Mon–Sat. 🔒 Feb–Dec: Thu–Sat.
📷 🌐 jenningsbrewery.co.uk

⑧ Newlands Valley

Cumbria. 🚂 Penrith then bus. 🚌 Cockermouth. ℹ️ Market Sq, Keswick (0845 901 0845). 🌐 lakedistrict.gov.uk

From the gently wooded shores of Derwentwater, the Newlands Valley runs through a scattering of farms towards rugged heights of 335 m (1,100 ft) at the top of a pass, where steps lead to a waterfall, Moss Force. Grisedale Pike, Cat Bells and Robinson all provide excellent fell walks. Local mineral deposits of copper, graphite, lead and even small amounts of gold and silver were extensively mined here from Elizabethan times onwards. The hamlet of **Little Town** was used as a setting by Beatrix Potter *(see p371)* in *The Tale of Mrs Tiggywinkle*.

Kitchen, with an old range and tiled floor, at Wordsworth House

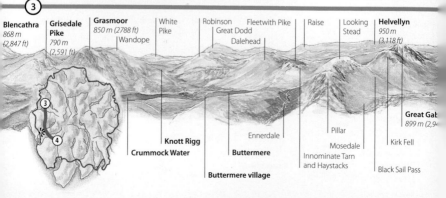

③

| Blencathra 868 m (2,847 ft) | Grisedale Pike 790 m (2,591 ft) | Grasmoor 850 m (2788 ft) Wandope | White Pike | Robinson Great Dodd Dalehead | Fleetwith Pike | Raise | Looking Stead | Helvellyn 950 m (3,118 ft) |

Great Gable 899 m (2,9...

Knott Rigg
Crummock Water

Ennerdale
Buttermere
Buttermere village

Pillar
Mosedale
Innominate Tarn and Haystacks

Kirk Fell
Black Sail Pass

❾ Buttermere

Cumbria. 🚆 Penrith. 🚌 Keswick.
🚌 Penrith to Keswick; Keswick to
Buttermere. 🛈 4 Kings Arms Lane, off
Main St, Cockermouth (01900 822634).

Interlinking with Crummock
Water and Loweswater,
Buttermere and its environs
represent some of the most
appealing countryside in the
region. Often known as the
"western lakes", the three are
remote enough not to become
too crowded. The village of
Buttermere, with its handful
of houses and inns, is a popular
starting point for walks round
all three lakes. Loweswater is
the furthest and therefore the
quietest, surrounded by woods
and hills. Nearby, Scale Force is
the highest waterfall in the Lake
District, plunging 52 m (170 ft).

Buttermere is circled by peaks:
High Stile, Red Pike and Haystacks.
It was at the latter that the ashes
of the celebrated hill-walker and
author of fell walking books,
A W Wainwright, were scattered.

Verdant valley of Borrowdale, a favourite with artists

❿ Borrowdale

Cumbria. 🚆 Penrith. 🚌 Keswick.
🛈 Moot Hall, Keswick (0845 901 0845).

This romantic valley, subject
of many a painter's canvas, lies
beside the densely wooded
shores of Derwentwater under
towering crags. It is a popular
trip from Keswick and a great
variety of walks are possible
along the valley.

The tiny hamlet of **Grange**
is one of the prettiest spots,
where the valley narrows
dramatically to form the "Jaws
of Borrowdale". Nearby Castle
Crag has superb views.

Grange is a good starting
point for an 8-mile (13-km)
walk around Derwentwater
(passing through the town
of Keswick, see p363), or for a
walk or drive south towards
the more open farmland
around Seatoller. If travelling
down by road, look out for
a National Trust sign (see p33)
to the **Bowder Stone**, a
delicately poised block
weighing nearly 2,000
tonnes, which may have
fallen from the crags above
or been deposited by a
glacier millions of years ago.

Two attractive hamlets in
Borrowdale are **Rosthwaite**
and **Stonethwaite**. Also worth
a detour, preferably on foot, is
Watendlath village, off a side
road near the famous beauty
spot of **Ashness Bridge**.

Walking in the Lake District

Typical Lake District stile over
dry-stone wall

Two long-distance footpaths pass
through the Lake District's most
spectacular scenery. The 70-mile
(112-km) Cumbria Way runs from
Carlisle to Ulverston via Keswick
and Coniston. The western section
of the Coast to Coast Walk (see p41)
also passes through this area.
There are hundreds of shorter walks
along lake shores, nature trails as
well as some more challenging
uphill routes. Walkers should stick to
paths to avoid erosion, and check
weather conditions at www.lake
districtweatherline.co.uk.

(4)

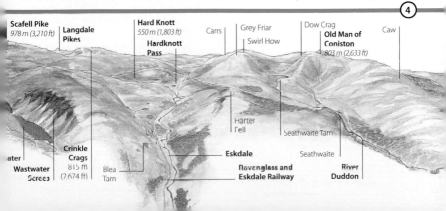

Scafell Pike 978 m (3,210 ft)	Langdale Pikes	Hard Knott 550 m (1,803 ft) Hardknott Pass	Carrs	Grey Friar Swirl How	Dow Crag Old Man of Coniston 803 m (2,633 ft)	Caw

Harter Fell

Seathwaite Tarn

...ater

Wastwater Screes

Crinkle Crags 815 m (2,674 ft)

Blea Tarn

Eskdale

Ravenglass and Eskdale Railway

Seathwaite

River Duddon

Wasdale Head Inn, one of only two buildings at Wasdale Head

⓫ Wastwater

Wasdale, Cumbria. ⚇ Whitehaven.
ℹ Lowes Court Gallery, Egremont (01946 820693).

A silent reflection of truly awesome surroundings, brooding Wastwater is a mysterious, evocative lake. On the northwest side, the road from Nether Wasdale continues. Along its eastern side loom walls of sheer scree over 600 m (2,000 ft) high. Beneath them the water looks inky black, whatever the weather, plunging an icy 80 m (260 ft) from the waterline to form England's deepest lake. You can walk along the scree, but it is an uncomfortable and dangerous scramble. Sailing and power boats are banned, but fishing permits are available from the nearby National Trust campsite.

Wasdale Head offers one of Britain's grandest views: the austere pyramid of Great Gable, centrepiece of a fine mountain range, alongside the huge forms of Scafell and Scafell Pike. The scenery is utterly unspoilt, and the only buildings lie at the far end of the lake: an inn and a tiny church commemorating fallen climbers. Here the road ends, and you must turn back or take to your feet, following signs for Black Sail Pass and Ennerdale, or walk up the grand fells ahead. Wasdale's irresistible backdrop inspired the first serious British mountaineers, who flocked here during the 19th century, insouciantly clad in tweed jackets, carrying little more than a length of rope slung over their shoulders.

⓬ Eskdale

Cumbria. ⚇ Ravenglass then narrow-gauge railway to Eskdale (Easter–Oct: daily; Dec–Feb: check website).
🌐 **ravenglass-railway.co.uk**
ℹ Lowes Court Gallery, Egremont (01946 820693).

The pastoral delights of Eskdale are best encountered by driving the gruelling Hardknott Pass, whose steep gradients make it the most taxing journey in the Lake District, with steep gradients. You can pause below the 393-m (1,291-ft) summit to explore the Roman Hardknott Fort or enjoy the lovely view. As you descend into Eskdale, rhododendrons and pines flourish in a landscape of small hamlets, narrow lanes and gentle farmland. The main settlements are the villages of Boot and Eskdale Green, and Ravenglass, the only coastal village in the Lake District National Park.

Just south of Ravenglass is impressive **Muncaster Castle**, the richly furnished home of the Pennington family. Another way to enjoy the scenery is to take the miniature railway (known as La'al Ratty) from Ravenglass to Dalegarth.

🏠 **Muncaster Castle**
Ravenglass. **Tel** 01229 717614.
Castle: **Open** Apr–Oct: Sun–Fri.
Garden: **Open** Feb–Dec: daily. 📷
🎨 ♿ ground floor and garden.
🍽 🌐 **muncaster.co.uk**

Remains of the Roman Hardknott Fort, Eskdale

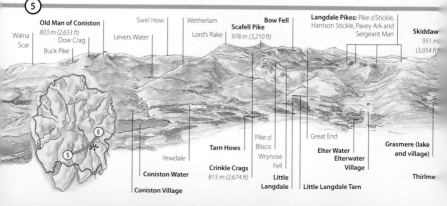

⑤

Walna Scar

Old Man of Coniston
803 m (2,633 ft)
Dow Crag
Buck Pike

Swirl How
Levers Water

Wetherlam
Lord's Rake

Bow Fell
Scafell Pike
978 m (3,210 ft)

Langdale Pikes: Pike o'Stickle, Harrison Stickle, Pavey Ark and Sergeant Man

Skiddaw
931 m (3,054 ft)

⑥

⑤

Yewdale

Coniston Water

Coniston Village

Tarn Hows

Crinkle Crags
815 m (2,674 ft)

Little Langdale

Pike o' Blisco
Wrynose Fell

Great End

Elter Water
Elterwater Village

Little Langdale Tarn

Grasmere (lake and village)

Thirlmere

Seathwaite, in the Duddon Valley, a popular centre for walkers and climbers

⑬ Duddon Valley

Cumbria. ☒ Foxfield, Ulverston.
🛈 The Old Town Hall, Broughton-in-Furness (01229 716115; Easter–Oct: Mon–Sat). ⓦ **duddonvalley.co.uk**

Also known as Dunnerdale, this picturesque tract of countryside inspired 35 of Wordsworth's sonnets (see p370). The prettiest stretch lies between Ulpha and Cockley Beck. In autumn the colours of heather-covered moors and the turning leaves of birch trees are particularly beautiful. Stepping stones and bridges span the river at intervals, the most charming being Birk's Bridge, near Seathwaite. At the southern end of the valley, where the River Duddon meets the sea at Duddon Sands, is the pretty village of Broughton-in-Furness. Note the stone slabs once used for fish in the market square.

⑭ Langdale

Cumbria. ☒ Windermere. 🛈 Market Cross, Ambleside (0844 2250544). ⓦ **golakes.co.uk**

Stretching from Skelwith Bridge, where the Brathay surges powerfully over waterfalls, to the summits of Great Langdale is the two-pronged Langdale Valley. Walkers and climbers throng here to take on Pavey Ark, Pike o'Stickle, Crinkle Crags and Bow Fell. The local mountain rescue teams are the busiest in Britain.

Great Langdale is the more spectacular valley and it is often crowded, but quieter Little Langdale has many attractions too. It is worth completing the circuit back to Ambleside via the southern route, stopping at Blea Tarn. The picturesque spot of **Elter water** was once a site of a gunpowder works. Wrynose Pass, west of Little Langdale, climbs to 390 m (1,281 ft), a warm-up for Hardknott Pass further on. At its top is Three Shires Stone, marking the former boundary of the old counties of Cumberland, Westmorland and Lancashire.

⑥

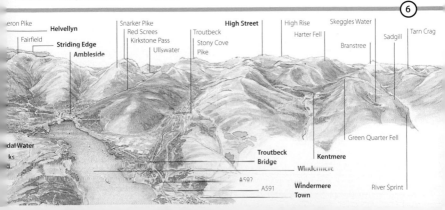

eron Pike
Helvellyn
Fairfield
Striding Edge
Ambleside
Snarker Pike
Red Screes
Kirkstone Pass
Ullswater
Troutbeck
Stony Cove
Pike
High Street
High Rise
Harter Fell
Skeggles Water
Branstree
Sadgill
Tarn Crag
Green Quarter Fell
dal Water
ks
Troutbeck
Bridge
Windermere
A592
A591
Kentmere
Windermere
Town
River Sprint

Rydal Water, one of the major attractions of the Lake District

⓯ Grasmere and Rydal

Cumbria. Grasmere: 🚉 700.
Rydal: 🚉 100. 🚌 Grasmere.
🛈 Central Bldgs, Market Cross,
Ambleside (08442 250544).

The poet William Wordsworth lived in both these villages on the shores of two lakes. Fairfield, Nab Scar and Loughrigg Fell rise steeply above their reedy shores and offer good opportunities for walking. Grasmere is now a sizable settlement and the famous Grasmere Sports attract large crowds every August.

The Wordsworth family is buried in St Oswald's Church, where crowds flock to the annual ceremony of strewing the church's earth floor with fresh rushes. Most visitors head for **Dove Cottage**, where the poet spent his most creative years. The museum in the barn behind includes such artifacts as the great man's socks. The Wordsworths moved to **Rydal Mount** in Rydal in 1813 and lived here until 1850. The grounds contain waterfalls and a summerhouse, and there

are stunning views of Rydal Water and the surrounding fells. Dora's Field nearby is a blaze of daffodils in spring and the Fairfield Horseshoe offers an energetic walk.

🏛 Dove Cottage and the Wordsworth Museum
Off A591 near Grasmere. **Tel** 015394 35544. **Open** daily. **Closed** 24–26 Dec. 🅿️ 🚻 💻 🎁 🌐 wordsworth. org.uk

🏛 Rydal Mount
Rydal. **Tel** 015394 33002. **Open** Mar–Oct: daily; Nov–Feb: Wed–Sun. **Closed** Jan, 25 & 26 Dec. 🅿️ 🚻 ltd. 🎁 🌐 rydalmount.co.uk

🟦 William Wordsworth (1770–1850)

Best known of the Romantic poets, Wordsworth was born in the Lake District and spent most of his life there. After school in Hawkshead and a period at Cambridge, a legacy enabled him to pursue his literary career. He settled at Dove Cottage with his sister Dorothy and in 1802 married an old school friend, Mary Hutchinson. They lived simply, bringing up their children, and enjoying walking and receiving visits from poets such as Coleridge and de Quincey. Wordsworth's prose works include one of the earliest guidebooks to the Lake District.

⓰ Ambleside

Cumbria. 🚉 2,600. 🚌 🛈 Central Buildings, Market Cross (0844 2250544). 🅆 Wed. 🌐 **golakes.co.uk**

Ambleside has good road connections to all parts of the Lakes and is an attractive base, especially for walkers and climbers. Mainly Victorian in character, it has a range of outdoor clothing, crafts and specialist food shops. An enterprising little cinema and a summer classical music festival add life in the evenings. Sights in town are small-scale: the remnants of the Roman fort of Galava, AD 79, Stock Ghyll Force waterfall and **Bridge House**, now a National Trust information centre.

Environs
Within easy reach of Ambleside is the scenic Loughrigg Fell. At nearby Troutbeck is the restored farmhouse of **Townend**, dating from 1626, whose interior gives an insight into Lakeland domestic life.

The tiny Bridge House over Stock Beck in Ambleside

Beatrix Potter and the Lake District

Although best known for her children's stories featuring characters such as Peter Rabbit and Jemima Puddleduck, which she also illustrated, Beatrix Potter (1866–1943) became a champion of conservation in the Lake District after moving there in 1906. She married William Heelis, devoted herself to farming, and was an expert on Herdwick sheep. To conserve her beloved countryside, she donated land to the National Trust.

Cover illustration of *Jemima Puddleduck* (1908)

mills in Cumbria that once served the textiles industry.

Beatrix Potter wrote many of her books at **Hill Top**, the 17th-century farmhouse at Near Sawrey, northwest of Windermere. The house is furnished with many of Potter's possessions and left as it was in her lifetime. The **Beatrix Potter Gallery** in Hawkshead *(see p372)* holds annual exhibitions of her manuscripts and illustrations, and the **World of Beatrix Potter** in Crag Brow brings to life her characters in a fun exhibition.

Townend

Troutbeck, Windermere. **Tel** 015394 32628. **Open** Apr–Oct: Wed–Sun (Sun & bank hol Mon: pm only). **nationaltrust.org.uk**

⑰ Windermere

Cumbria. Windermere. Victoria St. Victoria St (015394 46499) and Glebe Rd, Bowness-on-Windermere (084590 10845).

At over 10 miles (16 km) long, this dramatic watery expanse is England's largest lake. Industrial magnates built mansions around its shores long before the railway arrived. Stately **Brockhole**, now a national park visitor centre, was one such grand estate. When the railway reached Windermere in 1847, it enabled crowds of workers to visit the area on day trips.

Today, a year-round car ferry service connects the lake's east and west shores (it runs between Ferry Nab and Ferry

House), and summer steamers link Lakeside, Bowness and Ambleside on the north–south axis. Belle Isle, a wooded island on which stands a unique round house, is one of the lake's most attractive features, but landing is not permitted. **Fell Foot Park** is at the south end of the lake, and there are good walks on the northwest shore. Northeast of Windermere town is Orrest Head, at 238 m (784 ft) offering terrific views of the area.

Environs

Bowness-on-Windermere on the east shore, is a popular centre. Many of its buildings display Victorian details, and St Martin's Church dates back to the 15th century. The **Blackwell Arts and Crafts House** is one of Britain's most beautiful houses from the early 20th century. It still boasts all of its original features. The **Stott Park Bobbin Mill** is the last working example of over 70 such

Brockhole Visitor Centre
On A591. **Tel** 015394 46601. **Open** daily. **brockhole.co.uk**

Fell Foot Park
Newby Bridge. **Tel** 015395 31273. **Open** daily.

Blackwell Arts and Crafts House
Bowness-on-Windermere. **Tel** 015394 46139. **Open** daily. **blackwell.org.uk**

Stott Park Bobbin Mill
Finsthwaite. **Tel** 01539 531087. **Open** Apr–Oct. Mon–Fri & public hols.

Hill Top
Near Sawrey, Ambleside. **Tel** 015394 36269. House. **Open** Feb–Oct: daily. **nationaltrust.org.uk**

Beatrix Potter Gallery
The Square, Hawkshead. **Tel** 015394 36355. **Open** Feb–Dec: daily. **nationaltrust.org.uk**

World of Beatrix Potter
Crag Brow. **Tel** 015394 88444. **Open** daily. **Closed** 25 Dec. **hop-skip-jump.com**

Boats moored along the shore at Waterhead, near Ambleside, at the north end of Windermere

Peaceful Coniston Water, the setting for Arthur Ransome's novel, *Swallows and Amazons* (1930)

⓲ Coniston Water

Cumbria. 🚆 Windermere then bus. 🚌 Ambleside then bus. 🚹 Coniston car park, Ruskin Ave (01539 441533) 🅦 **conistontic.org**. Coniston Boating Centre: **Tel** 015394 41366. 🅦 **conistonboatingcentre.co.uk**

For the finest view of this lovely lake, you need to climb a little. The 19th-century art critic, writer and philosopher John Ruskin had a fine view from his house, **Brantwood**, where his paintings can be seen today. Contemporary art exhibitions and events take place throughout the year.

An enjoyable excursion is the summer lake trip from Coniston Pier on the National Trust steam yacht, *Gondola*, calling at Brantwood. Alternatively, boats can be hired at the **Coniston Boating Centre**. The lake was the scene of Donald Campbell's fatal attempt on the world water speed record in 1967. The green slate village of Coniston, once a centre for coppermining, now caters for walkers.

Dotted around Coniston Water are **Hawkshead**, a quaint, traffic-free village with timber-framed houses, and Grizedale Forest, scattered with woodland sculptures and popular with mountain bikers. **Tarn Hows** is a landscaped tarn surrounded by woods. Walkers can enjoy a pleasant climb up the 803 m (2,633 ft) Old Man of Coniston.

🏛 Brantwood
Off B5285, near Coniston. **Tel** 015394 41396. **Open** mid-Mar–mid-Nov: daily; mid-Nov–mid-Mar: Wed–Sun. 🅿 🅶 limited. 🍴 🅿 📷 🅦 **brantwood.org.uk**

⓳ Kendal

Cumbria. 🔺 28,600. 🚆 🚹 25 Stramongate (01539 735891). 🅒 Wed, Sat. 🅦 **golakes.co.uk**

A busy market town, Kendal is the administrative centre of the region and the southern gateway to the Lake District. Built in grey limestone, it has an arts centre, the **Brewery**, and a central area which is best enjoyed on foot. **Abbot Hall**, built in 1759, has paintings by Turner and Romney, as well as Gillows furniture. In addition, the hall's stable block contains the **Museum of Lakeland Life**, with occasional workshops demonstrating local crafts and trades. There are dioramas of geology and wildlife in the **Kendal Museum**.

About 3 miles (5 km) south of the town is 14th-century **Sizergh Castle**, with a fortified tower, carved fireplaces and a lovely garden.

Kendal mint cake, the famous Lakeland energy-booster for walkers

🏛 Abbot Hall Art Gallery & Museum of Lakeland Life
Kendal. **Tel** 01539 722464. **Open** Mon–Sat. 🅿 🅾 by arrangement. 🅶 gallery. 🅿 📷 🅦 **abbothall.org.uk**

🏛 Kendal Museum
Station Rd. **Tel** 01539 815597. **Open** Tue–Sat. 📷 🅦 **kendalmuseum.org.uk**

🏰 Sizergh Castle
Off A591 & A590. **Tel** 015395 60951. **Open** Apr–Oct: Sun–Thu. 🅿 🅶 ground floor & grounds. 🅿 📷 🆖 🅦 **nationaltrust.org.uk**

⓴ Furness Peninsula

Cumbria. 🚆 🚌 Barrow-in-Furness. 🚹 Town Hall, Duke St, Barrow-in-Furness (01229 876543). 🅦 **barrowtourism.co.uk**

Barrow-in-Furness is the peninsula's main town. Its **Dock Museum**, built over a Victorian dock where ships were repaired, traces the history of Barrow using interactive displays.

Ruins of the red sandstone walls of **Furness Abbey** remain in the wooded Vale of Deadly Nightshade. It was founded by the Savigniac monks in the mid-12th century and was destroyed during the Reformation. The abbey has a small exhibition of monastic life.

The historic town of Ulverston received its charter in 1280. Stan Laurel, of Laurel and Hardy fame, was born here in 1890. A **museum** dedicated to the pair has a cinema and memorabilia. In the nearby village of Gleaston is the **Gleaston Water Mill**, a 400-year-old, working corn mill.

🏛 Dock Museum
North Rd, Barrow-in-Furness. **Tel** 01229 876400. **Open** Wed–Sun & public hols.
♿ 🖥 📷 🅦 **dockmuseum.org.uk**

🏠 Furness Abbey
Vale of Deadly Nightshade. **Tel** 01229 823420. **Open** Apr–Oct: Thu–Mon; Nov–Mar: Sat & Sun. **Closed** 1 Jan, 24–26 Dec. 📷 ♿ limited. 📷 **EH**
🅦 **english-heritage.org.uk**

🏛 Gleaston Water Mill
Gleaston. **Tel** 01229 869244. **Open** Apr–Sep: Wed–Sun.
🅦 **watermill.co.uk**

🏛 Laurel and Hardy Museum
Upper Brook St, Ulverston. **Tel** 01229 582292. **Open** Easter–Oct: daily; Nov–Easter: Tue & Thu–Sun. **Closed** 25 & 26 Dec. 📷 ♿ 🅦 **laurel-and-hardy.co.uk**

Staircase at Holker Hall

㉑ Cartmel

Cumbria. 🚗 700. 🛈 Main St, Grange-over-Sands (015395 34026).
🅦 **grangeoversands.net**

The highlight of this pretty village is its 12th-century **priory** church, one of the finest Cumbrian churches. The restored church has an attractive east window, a

stone-carved 14th-century tomb and beautiful misericords.

Cartmel also boasts a small racecourse and is known as a centre for gourmet dining. The village has given its name to its surroundings, a hilly district of green farmland with mixed woodland and limestone scars.

A major local attraction is **Holker Hall**, former residence of the Dukes of Devonshire. Inside are lavishly furnished rooms, with fine marble fireplaces and a superb oak staircase. Outside are stunning gardens and a deer park.

🏛 Holker Hall
Cark-in-Cartmel. **Tel** 015395 58328. **Open** Apr–Oct: Wed–Sun. 📷 ♿ limited. 📷 by arrangement.
🖥 📷 🅦 **holker.co.uk**

㉒ Levens Hall

Near Kendal, Cumbria. **Tel** 015395 60321. 🚌 from Kendal or Lancaster. **Open** Easter–early Oct: Sun–Thu. 📷 ♿ gardens only. 🖥 📷
🅦 **levenshall.co.uk**

The outstanding attraction of this Elizabethan mansion is its topiary, but the house itself has much to offer. Built around a 13th-century tower, It contains a fine collection of Jacobean furniture, and watercolours by Peter de Wint (1784–1849). Also

of note are the ornate ceilings, Charles II dining chairs, the earliest example of English patchwork and the gilded hearts on the drainpipes.

The yew and box topiary was designed in 1694 by French horticulturist Guillaume Beaumont.

Box hedges were a common component of geometrically designed gardens of this period.

The 18th-century Turret Clock has a single hand, a common design of the period.

Main entrance

Over 300 years old, the garden's box-edged beds are filled with colourful herbaceous displays.

The complex topiary, shaped into cones, spirals and pyramids, is kept in shape by gardeners. Some specimens are 6 m (20 ft) high.

Morecambe Bay, looking northwest towards Barrow-in-Furness

㉓ Morecambe Bay

Lancashire. 🚆 Morecambe.
🚢 Heysham (to Isle of Man).
ℹ️ Marine Rd (01524 582808).
🌐 **visitmorecambe.co.uk**

The best way to explore
Morecambe Bay is by train
from Ulverston to Arnside.
The track follows a series of low
viaducts across a huge expanse
of glistening tidal flats where
thousands of wading birds
feed and breed. The bay is one
of the most important bird
reserves in the country. On
the Cumbrian side of the
bay, retirement homes have
expanded the sedate Victorian
resort of Grange-over-Sands.
Nearby, Hampsfell and
Humphrey Head Point give
fine views.

㉔ Leighton Hall

Carnforth, Lancashire. **Tel** 01524 734
474. 🚌 to Yealand Conyers (from
Lancaster). **Open** May–Sep: 2–5pm
Tue–Fri & public hols (Aug: also Sun).
🅿️ 🅰️ ♿ ground floor only. 🅿️ 🏠
🌐 **leightonhall.co.uk**

Leighton Hall's estate dates back
to the 13th century, but most
of the building is 19th-century,
including its Neo-Gothic façade.
It is owned by the Gillow family,
of the Lancastrian furniture
business, whose products
have become prized antiques.
Excellent pieces can be seen
here, including a ladies' work-
box inlaid with biblical scenes.
In the afternoons the hall's
large collection of birds of prey
display their aerial prowess.

㉕ Lancaster

Lancaster. 📊 46,000. 🚆 🚌
ℹ️ Meeting House Lane (01524
582394). 🗓️ Mon–Sat. 🌐 **visit
lancaster.org.uk**

The small county town of
Lancaster has a long history
that began when the
Romans named it after their
camp on the other side of
the River Lune. Originally a
defensive site, it developed
into a prosperous port.
Today, its university
and cultural life thrive.
Lancaster Castle
dates back to the
11th century but was
expanded over the years
and was in use as a jail until
2011. It is still used as a Crown
Court. The Shire Hall is decorated
with 600 heraldic shields. Some

Tawny eagle at
Leighton Hall

fragments from Hadrian's
Tower are 2,000 years old.
The nearby priory church
of **St Mary** is on Castle Hill.
Its main features include a
Saxon doorway and carved
14th-century choirstalls. Also
outstanding is the museum
of furniture in the 17th-century
Judge's Lodgings, while the
Maritime Museum contains
displays on the port's history.
The **City Museum**, based in
the old town hall, has exhibits
on the history of Lancaster.
The splendid **Lune Aqueduct**
carries the canal over the River
Lune on five wide arches.
Other attractions are found
in **Williamson Park**, site of the
1907 Ashton Memorial. This folly
was built by linoleum magnate
and politician Lord Ashton.
There are fine views from the
top of this 67-m (220-ft)
domed structure. Opposite
is a tropical butterfly house.

Environs
North of Lancaster, the small
town of **Carnforth**
has some interesting
sights. **Leighton Moss
Nature Reserve** is
the largest reedbed in
the northwest and home
to birds such as bitterns
and bearded tits. The restored
Carnforth Station is the setting
for David Lean's classic film
Brief Encounter, shot here in

Crossing the Sands

Morecambe Bay's sands are very dangerous. Travellers used to
cut across the bay at low tide to shorten the long trail around the
Kent estuary. Many perished as they were caught by rising tides
or quicksand, and sea fogs hid the paths. Locals who knew the bay
became guides, and today you can walk across with a guide from
Kents Bank to Hest Bank near Arnside.

The High Sheriff of Lancaster Crossing Morecambe Sands

1945. Go to www.visitcarnforth. co.uk to find more information on Carnforth sights.

🏰 Lancaster Castle
Castle Parade. **Tel** 01524 64998. **Open** daily. **Closed** 1 Jan, 25 & 26 Dec. 📷 🎬 when court is not in session. 🏛 **W** lancastercastle.com

🏛 Judge's Lodgings
Church St. **Tel** 01524 64637. **Open** Apr–Oct: daily pm. 📷 👶 ♿ limited. 🏛

🏛 Maritime Museum
Custom House, St George's Quay. **Tel** 01524 382264. **Open** daily (Dec–Mar: pm only). **Closed** 1 Jan, Nov, 24–26 & 31 Dec. 📷 ♿ 🎞 🏛 **W** lancashire.gov.uk

🏛 City Museum
Market Sq. **Tel** 01524 64637. **Open** Tue–Sun. **Closed** 24 Dec–2 Jan. ♿ 🏛

🌳 Williamson Park
Wyresdale Rd. **Tel** 01524 33318. **Open** daily. **Closed** 1 Jan, 25 & 26 Dec. 📷 ♿ limited. 🎞 🏛

㉖ Ribble Valley

Lancashire. 🚋 Clitheroe. 🛈 Station Rd, Clitheroe (01200 425566). 🛒 Tue, Thu, Sat. **W** visitribblevalley.co.uk

Clitheroe, a small market town with a hilltop castle, is a good centre for exploring the Ribble Valley's rivers and old villages, such as Slaidburn. Ribchester has a **Roman Museum**, and there is a ruined **Cistercian abbey** at Whalley. To the east is 560-m (1,830-ft) Pendle Hill, with a Bronze Age burial mound at its peak.

🏛 Roman Museum
Ribchester. **Tel** 01254 878261. **Open** daily. 📷 🎬 by arrangement. ♿ 🏛 **W** ribchesterromanmuseum.org

⛪ Whalley Abbey
Whalley. **Tel** 01254 828400. **Open** daily. **Closed** 24 Dec–2 Jan. 📷 ♿ 🎞 🏛 **W** whalleyabbey.co.uk

㉗ Blackpool

Lancashire. 👥 140,000. 🚈 🚋 🚌 🛈 Festival House, Promenade (01253 478222). **W** visitblackpool.com

Blackpool remains a unique experience despite, rather than because of, a major regeneration project on the promenade. A wall of

Coming from the Mill (1930) by L S Lowry (see p379)

amusement arcades, piers, bingo halls and fast-food stalls stretches behind the sands. At night, entertainers strut their stuff under the bright lights. The town attracts thousands of visitors in September and October when Illuminations line the roads for miles. Blackpool's resort life dates back to the 18th century, but it burst into prominence when the railway arrived in 1840, allowing Lancastrian workers to travel to the popular resort.

The iconic, dark red Blackpool Tower, which opened on 14 May 1894

㉘ Salford Quays

Salford. 🚉 Harbour City (from Manchester). 🛈 The Lowry, Pier 8 (0843 208 6000). **W** thequays.org.uk

The Quays, to the west of Manchester city centre (15 minutes by tram), were once the terminal docks for the **Manchester Ship Canal**. After the docks closed in 1982, the area became run down, but since the 1990s a massive redevelopment plan has changed the area dramatically. In 2011, MediaCityUK became the home to major national media outlets, such as the BBC and ITV, who wished to decentralize operations from London. As a consequence, a host of shops, restaurants and cafés sprang up to service the media hub.

There is a wealth of entertainment, leisure and cultural facilities on offer, including **The Lowry** (see p379), the **Manchester United Museum** (see p379), the **Imperial War Museum North** (see p379), the **Salford Museum and Art Gallery** and The Lowry Outlet Mall, as well as a multiplex cinema. There are also various water-based activities and ship-canal cruises.

🏛 Salford Museum and Art Gallery
Peel Park, The Crescent. **Tel** 0161 778 0800. **Open** Tue–Sun pm. **Closed** 25 & 26 Dec.

㉙ Manchester

Manchester dates back to Roman times, when in AD 79, Agricola established the fort called Mamucium. In the late 18th century, the introduction of cotton processing by Richard Arkwright saw the city become an industrial hub, and by 1830, a railway was built to link Manchester and Liverpool. In 1894 the Manchester Ship Canal *(see p375)* opened, allowing cargo vessels inland. The wealth created by the cotton trade helped develop the city, but new buildings contrasted starkly with the slums of the mill-workers. Social discontent led writers, politicians and reformers to espouse liberal or radical causes.

The achievements of football team Manchester United and the international success of bands such as The Smiths, The Stone Roses and Oasis gave Manchester a cachet of cool during the 1980s and 1990s. Devastation caused by an IRA car-bombing of the city centre in 1996 was seized as an opportunity to redevelop the main shopping areas. This regeneration has since spread to other parts of the city, notably the old dockside of Salford Quays.

Exploring Manchester
Manchester is a compact city with much to see in its central areas. The Victorian era of cotton wealth has gifted the city with an imposing heritage of industrial architecture, much of which is providing sites for new development. The former central railway station, for example, is now **Manchester Central**, a huge exhibition and conference complex. Among other fine 19th-century buildings are the dramatic **John Rylands Library** on Deansgate, founded over 100 years ago by the widow of a local cotton millionaire, and the 1856 Renaissance-style **Free Trade Hall**, now the Radisson Edwardian hotel, which stands on the site of the Peterloo Massacre.

The impressive glass Urbis building, home to the National Football Museum

Manchester City Centre

① Free Trade Hall
② Manchester Central
③ John Rylands Library
④ Manchester Town Hall
⑤ Royal Exchange Theatre
⑥ National Football Museum
⑦ Manchester Art Gallery
⑧ Museum of Science and Industry

The Neo-Gothic Town Hall by Alfred Waterhouse

🏛 Manchester Town Hall

Albert Square. **Tel** 0161 827 7661.
Open Mon–Fri. 🎥 👪
🌐 manchester.gov.uk.

Manchester's majestic town hall was designed by Liverpool-born Alfred Waterhouse (1830–1905), an architect who would later find fame with his Natural History Museum in London. Waterhouse won the commission for the building in an architectural competition, his design finding favour for making best use of the awkward triangular site.

The building was completed in 1877 in an English Gothic style with its roots in the 13th century. Tours are available, but visitors can also explore the building on their own. Sign in inside the main entrance, where a statue of Agricola, the Roman general who founded Manchester in AD 79, looks down on passers-by. The highlight is the Great Hall adorned by 12 murals painted by celebrated Pre-Raphaelite artist Ford Madox Brown.

Throughout the building the decoration includes numerous examples of cotton flowers and bees, the latter a symbol of Manchester's industriousness, as well as a brand mark for the city's famous Boddingtons bitter. In the square in front of the town

hall is Manchester's **Albert Memorial**, dedicated to the consort of Queen Victoria, which is similar in style but predates the one in London's Hyde Park.

🏛 Royal Exchange Theatre

St Ann's Square. **Tel** 0161 833 9833. **Open** Mon–Sat. 👪 🖥 🎥 🌐 royal exchange.co.uk

Built in 1729, the Manchester Royal Exchange, as it was then known, was once claimed to be the "biggest room in the world". It was built as the main trading hall of the cotton industry and at the end of the 19th century it was reckoned that over 80 per cent of world trade in cloth was controlled from these premises. During World War II the building was severely damaged by bombs. This coincided with the decline of the country's cotton trade and when the Exchange was rebuilt it was reduced to half its original size. The doors were finally closed to trading in 1968. A daring scheme saw the main hall converted into a theatre in the mid-1970s, with the auditorium enclosed in a high-tech structure supported by the old building's pillars; it nestles like a lunar module beneath the great dome.

The rest of the Exchange building contains an arcade of shops and cafés.

🏛 National Football Museum

Cathedral Gdns. **Tel** 0161 605 8200. **Open** 10am–5pm daily. 👪 ♿ 🖥 🎥 🌐 nationalfootballmuseum. com

The National Football Museum has relocated from its original location in Preston to Manchester. It is housed in a striking, ski slope-shaped glass building, originally the Urbis museum. The visit begins with a glass-elevator ride up the incline, then proceeds down through three staggered floors show casing a huge collection of football memorabilia. A notable object on display is the ball from the 1966 World Cup Final.

Across the plaza from the museum is **Manchester Cathedral**, which largely dates from the 19th century but stands on a site that has been occupied by a church for more than a millennium.

The Peterloo Massacre

In 1819, the working conditions of Manchester's factory workers were so bad that social tensions reached breaking point. On 16 August, 50,000 people assembled in St Peter's Field to protest at the oppressive Corn Laws Initially peaceful, the mood darkened and the poorly trained mounted troops panicked, charging the crowd with their sabres.

Eleven were killed and many wounded. The incident was called Peterloo (the Battle of Waterloo had taken place in 1815). Reforms such as the Factory Act came in later that year.

G Cruikshank's Peterloo Massacre cartoon

Museum of Science and Industry, set in old passenger railway buildings

Manchester Art Gallery

Mosley St & Princess St. **Tel** 0161 235 8888. **Open** Mon–Sun. **Closed** 1 Jan, Good Fri, 24–26 & 31 Dec. **W** manchesterart gallery.org

The original gallery building was designed by Sir Charles Barry (1795–1860) in 1824 and contains a superb collection of British art, notably Pre-Raphaelites such as William Holman Hunt and Dante Gabriel Rossetti. Early Italian, Flemish and French art is also represented, and a number of pieces by contemporary artists are on display.

The gallery has an excellent collection of decorative arts, from the Greeks to Picasso to contemporary craftworkers, in the Gallery of Craft & Design. There is also a changing pro-gramme of special exhibitions in two fantastic galleries on the top floor. Most exhibitions are free, and there is a programme of accompanying events for adults and families.

A lively space called the Clore Art Studio offers a combination of artworks and hands-on activities for children.

The gallery also runs an education programme that includes learning activities with artists, writers and performers.

Museum of Science and Industry

Liverpool Rd. **Tel** 0161 832 2244. **Open** daily. **Closed** 1 Jan, 24–26 Dec. **W** mosi.org.uk

One of the largest science museums in the world, the spirit of scientific enterprise and industrial might of Manchester's heyday is conveyed here. Among the best sections are the Power Hall, a collection of working steam engines, the Electricity Gallery, tracing the history of domestic power, and an exhibition on the Liverpool and Manchester Railway. A collection of planes that made flying history are displayed in the Air and Space Gallery.

Manchester Museum

Oxford Road. **Tel** 0161 275 2648. **Open** daily. **Closed** 1 Jan, 24–26 Dec. **W** museum. manchester.ac.uk

Part of Manchester University, this venerable museum (opened 1885) houses around six million items from all ages and all over the world, but it specializes in Egyptology and zoology. The col-lection of ancient Egyptian artifacts is one of the largest in the country, numbering about 20,000 objects including monumental stone sculpture and mummies, displayed with

Lawrence Alma-Tadema, *Etruscan Vase Painters*, Manchester Art Gallery

their sarcophagi and funerary goods. Funerary masks, tomb models and mummified animals also appear in other sections. The zoological collections number over 600,000 objects, ranging from stuffed animals to a cast of one of the most complete skeletons of a Tyrannosaurus Rex.

The original museum building was designed by Alfred Waterhouse, the same architect responsible for the city's magnifi-cent town hall *(see p377)*.

Whitworth Art Gallery

University of Manchester, Oxford Rd. **Tel** 0161 275 7450. **Open** daily. **Closed** Good Fri, 24 Dec–2 Jan. **W** whitworth. manchester.ac.uk

The Stockport-born machine tool manu-facturer and engineer Sir Joseph Whitworth bequeathed money for this gallery, originally intended to be a museum of industrial art and design that would inspire the city's textile trade. Founded in 1889, it has been a part of the University of Manchester since 1958. The fine red-brick building is from the Edwardian period, while the modern interior dates from the 1960s. A massive redevelopment of the gallery was completed in 2015, doubling the gallery's s pace and providing room for thousands more items from the Whitworth collection.

Jacob Epstein's *Genesis*, Whitworth Art Gallery

The gallery houses a superb collection of drawings, sculpture, contemporary art, textiles and prints. Jacob Epstein's *Genesis* nude sits in the entrance, and there is an important collection of British watercolours by Turner *(see p95)*, Girtin and others. Look out for the Japanese woodcuts and the collection of historic and modern wallpapers, built up from donations from wallpaper manufacturers, as well as through the gallery's active collecting policy.

Exterior of the Imperial War Museum North, designed by Daniel Libeskind to represent a globe shattered by conflict

🏛 Lowry Centre

Pier 8, Salford Quays. **Tel** 0843 208 6000. **Open** daily. Admission free, but donations requested. 👶 ♿ 💻 📷
W thelowry.com

On a prominent site beside the Lowry Ship Canal, the Lowry is a shimmering, silvery arts and entertainment complex that combines two theatres, a restaurant, terrace bars and cafés, art galleries and a shop.

The centre is named after celebrated reclusive artist Laurence Stephen Lowry (1887–1976), who was born locally and lived all his life in the Manchester area. A rent collector by day, in his leisure hours he painted cityscapes dominated by the smoking chimneys of industry beneath heavy, soot-filled skies.

However, he is most famous as a painter of "matchstick men", the term frequently applied to the crowds of slight and ghostly figures peopling his canvases. Some of Lowry's work is displayed in one of the galleries here; another hosts regularly changing temporary exhibitions. A a 20-minute documentary, titled "Meet Mr Lowry", is screened throughout the day.

The centre provides many facilities and activities for children, and is perfect for a family day out.

🏛 Imperial War Museum North

Trafford Wharf Road, Salford Quays. **Tel** 0161 836 4000. **Open** daily. **Closed** 24–26 Dec. 📷 👶 ♿ 💻 📷
W iwm.org.uk

This most striking piece of modern architecture comes courtesy of Daniel Libeskind, the architect nominated to design a replacement for New York's World Trade Center. His Manchester building is a waterfront collision of three great aluminium shards, representing a globe shattered by conflict. Inside, a vast irregular space is used to display a small but well presented collection of military hardware and ephemera, with nine "silos" devoted to exhibits on people's experiences of war.

On the hour the lights are extinguished for an audio-visual display using the angled walls of the main hall.

As visitors leave they are invited to take the elevator up the 55-metre (180-ft) "Air Shard" for views over the city.

🏛 Manchester United Museum

Salford Quays. **Tel** 0161 826 1326. **Open** daily (except match days). Tours must be booked in advance. 🦽 📷
💻 📷 **W** manutd.com

Premier League football (soccer) team Manchester United's ground Old Trafford also includes a purpose-built museum. In addition to the historic displays there is much interactive fun, such as a chance to test your own penalty-taking skills.

The museum tour takes in the dressing rooms, the trophy room and the players' lounge and culminates in a walk down the tunnel, tracing the route taken by players at every home game.

Manchester United Museum on the grounds of Old Trafford football stadium

⑳ Liverpool

Traces of settlement on Merseyside date back to the 1st century. In 1207 "Livpul", a fishing village, was granted a charter by King John. The population was only 1,000 in Stuart times, but during the 17th and 18th centuries Liverpool's westerly seaboard gave it an edge in the lucrative Caribbean slave trade. The first docks opened in 1715 and eventually stretched 7 miles (11 km) along the Mersey. Liverpool's first ocean steamer set out from here in 1840, and would-be emigrants to the New World poured into the city from Europe, including a flood of Irish refugees from the potato famine. Many settled permanently in Liverpool, and a large, mixed community developed. Today, the port still handles great volumes of cargo, but container ships use nearby Bootle docks. Despite economic and social problems, the irrepressible "Scouse" or Liverpudlian spirit re-emerged in the Swinging Sixties, when four local lads stormed the pop scene. Many people still visit Liverpool to pay homage to the Beatles, but the city is also known for its orchestra, the Liverpool Philharmonic, football and its universities. Liverpool's Maritime Mercantile City is one of few British urban areas to be designated a UNESCO World Heritage site.

Liver Bird on the
Royal Liver Building

Victorian ironwork, restored and polished, at Albert Dock

Exploring Liverpool

Liverpool's waterfront by the Pier Head, guarded by the mythical Liver Birds (a pair of cormorants with seaweed in their beaks) on the **Royal Liver Building**, is one of the most easily recognized in Britain. Nearby are the ferry terminal across the River Mersey and the revitalized

Liverpool City Centre

① Beatles Story
② Albert Dock
③ Merseyside Maritime Museum
④ Tate Liverpool
⑤ Museum of Liverpool
⑥ Royal Liver Building
⑦ *The Walker Art Gallery pp382–3*
⑧ World Museum Liverpool
⑨ St George's Hall
⑩ Metropolitan Cathedral of Christ the King

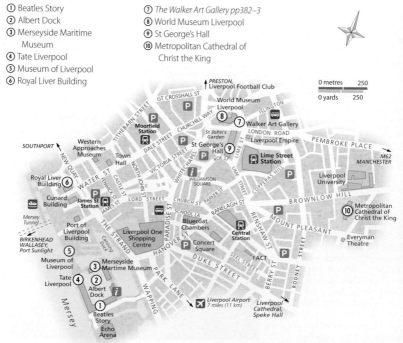

docklands. Other attractions include top-class museums and fine galleries, such as the **Walker** (*see pp382–3*). Liverpool's wealth of interesting architecture includes some fine Neo-Classical buildings, such as the gargantuan **St George's Hall**, and two cathedrals.

🏛 Beatles Story

Albert Dock.
Tel 0151 709 1963.
Open 10am–6pm daily. **Closed** 25 & 26 Dec. 🅿 ♿ 🏠
🅦 beatlesstory.com

In a walk-through exhibition, this museum relates the history of The Beatles' meteoric rise to fame, from their first record, *Love Me Do*, through Beatlemania to their last live appearance together in 1969, and their eventual break-up. One of the highlights is the replica of the Cavern Club, the birthplace of The Beatles. The hits that mesmerized a generation are played throughout the museum. Limited-edition merchandise is on sale in the shop alongside T-shirts and posters.

Albert Dock

🛈 0151 708 7334. **Open** daily. **Closed** 1 Jan. 25 Dec. 🅿 some attractions. ♿ 🅦 **albertdock.com**

There are five warehouses surrounding Albert Dock, all designed by Jesse Hartley in 1846. The docks were closed by 1972, then reopened after a decade of dereliction to house museums, galleries, shops, restaurants, bars and businesses.

🏛 Merseyside Maritime Museum

Albert Dock. **Tel** 0151 478 4499.
Open 10am–5pm daily. **Closed** 1 Jan, 24–26 Dec. ♿ limited. 🅿 🏠
🅦 liverpoolmuseums.org.uk

Ship's bell in the Maritime Museum

Devoted to the history of the Port of Liverpool, this large complex has good sections on shipbuilding and the Cunard and White Star liners. The exhibition on the Battle of the Atlantic in World War II includes models and charts. Another gallery deals with emigration to the New World. The **UK Border Agency National Museum**, also located here, examines the history of customs and excise. Next door is the **International Slavery Museum**, exploring the story of slavery through a range of thought provoking exhibitions. Across the quayside is the rebuilt Piermaster's House and the Cooperage.

🏛 Tate Liverpool

Albert Dock. **Tel** 0151 702 7400.
Open 10am–5pm daily. **Closed** Good Fri, 24–26 Dec. 🅿 some exhibitions. 🍴 🅿 🏠 🅦 tate.org.uk/liverpool

Tate Liverpool has one of the best contemporary art collections outside London. Marked by bright blue and orange panels and arranged over three floors, the gallery was converted from an old warehouse by architect James Stirling. It opened in 1988 as Tate Britain's (*see p95*) first outpost.

Practical Information
Liverpool. 🅜 480,000.
🛈 Albert Dock (0151 233 2008). 🚌 Sun (heritage market). 🏇 Grand National: Apr; Liverpool Show: May; Beatles Week: Aug.
🅦 visitliverpool.com

Transport
✈ 7 miles (11 km) SE Liverpool.
🚆 Lime St. 🚌 Norton St.
🚢 from Pier Head to the Wirral, also sightseeing trips; to Isle of Man & N Ireland.

The striking Museum of Liverpool building on the city's waterfront

🏛 Museum of Liverpool

Pier Head, Albert Dock. **Tel** 0151 478 4545. **Open** 10am–5pm daily. **Closed** 1 Jan, 24–26 Dec. ♿ 🍴 🏠 🅦 liverpoolmuseums. org.uk/mol

The Museum of Liverpool is housed in a stunning building on the waterfront. Inside, visitors are told the story of this famous city, including its contributions to music, popular culture, sport and industry, as well as its role in the wider world. The café, located on the ground floor, has superb views of Albert Dock.

The Beatles

Liverpool has produced many good bands and a host of singers, comedians and entertainers before and since the 1960s. But the Beatles – John Lennon, Paul McCartney, George Harrison and Ringo Starr – were the most sensational, and locations associated with the band, however tenuous, are revered as shrines in Liverpool. Bus and walking tours trace the hallowed ground of the Salvation Army home at Strawberry Fields and Penny Lane (both outside the city centre) as well as the boys' old homes. The most visited site is Mathew Street, near Moorfields Station, where the Cavern Club first throbbed to the Mersey Beat. The original site is now a shopping arcade, but the bricks have been used to create a replica. Nearby are statues of the Beatles and Eleanor Rigby.

Liverpool: The Walker Art Gallery

Founded in 1877 by Sir Andrew Barclay Walker, a local brewer and Mayor of Liverpool, this gallery houses one of the finest art collections in Britain. Paintings range from early Italian and Flemish works to Rubens, Rembrandt, and the work of French Impressionists, such as Degas's *Woman Ironing* (c.1892–5). Among the strong collection of British artists from the 18th century onward are works by Millais and Turner and Gainsborough's *Countess of Sefton* (1769). There is 20th-century art by Hockney and Sickert, and the sculpture collection includes works by Henry Moore and Rodin.

Shells (1878) Albert Joseph Moore painted female figures based on antique statues. Influenced by Whistler (*see p523*), he adopted subtle shading.

Interior at Paddington (1951) Lucian Freud's friend Harry Diamond posed for six months for this picture, intended by the artist to "make the human being uncomfortable".

Big Art for Little Artists Gallery

Ground floor

Façade was designed by H H Vale and Cornelius Sherlock.

Main entrance

First floor

Gallery Guide

All the picture galleries are on the first floor. Rooms 1 and 2 house medieval and Renaissance paintings; Rooms 3 and 4 have 17th-century Dutch, French, Italian and Spanish art. British 18th- and 19th-century works are in Rooms 5–9. Rooms 11–15 display 20th-century and contemporary British art, and Room 10 has Impressionists and Post-Impressionists.

The Sleeping Shepherd Boy (c.1835) The great Neo-Classical sculptor of the mid-19th century, John Gibson (1790–1866), used traditional colours to give his statuary a smooth appearance.

The 7th-century Kingston Brooch in World Museum Liverpool

🏛 World Museum Liverpool

William Brown St. **Tel** 0151 478 4393. **Open** 10am–5pm daily.
Closed 25 & 26 Dec. 🔌 📱 📷
🔲 liverpoolmuseums.org.uk/wml

Six floors of exhibits in this excellent museum include collections of Egyptian, Greek and Roman pieces, and displays on natural history, archaeology, space and time. Highlights include the hands-on Weston Discovery Centre, a planetarium, the Clore Natural History Centre, an aquarium and a Bug House.

🏛 Metropolitan Cathedral of Christ the King

Mount Pleasant. **Tel** 0151 709 9222.
Open 7:30am–6pm daily. Donation.
📱 🔌 📷 🔲 liverpoolmetro cathedral.org.uk

Liverpool's Roman Catholic cathedral rejected traditional forms in favour of a striking modern design. Early plans, drawn up by Pugin and later by Lutyens *(see p33)* in the 1930s, proved too expensive. The final version, brainchild of Sir Frederick Gibberd and built in 1962–7, is a circular building surmounted by a stylized crown of thorns 88 m (290 ft) high. Inside, the stained-glass lantern, designed by John Piper and Patrick Reyntiens, floods the circular nave with diffused blueish light. There is a fine bronze of Christ by Elisabeth Frink (1930–94).

🏛 Liverpool Cathedral

St James' Mount. **Tel** 0151 709 6271.
Open 8am–6pm daily. 📷 🔌 📱 📷
🔲 liverpoolcathedral.org.uk

Although Gothic in style, this building was only completed in 1978. The largest Anglican cathedral in the world, it is a fine red sandstone edifice designed by Sir Giles Gilbert Scott. The foundation stone was laid in 1904 by Edward VII

but, dogged by two world wars, building work dragged on to modified designs. Today, the cathedral also houses works by important 20th- and 21st-century artists.

Environs

Some 3 miles (5 km) northeast of the centre lies Everton, Liverpool's football district, the home of its two major clubs: Liverpool and Everton. Both offer stadium tours, with the much-decorated **Liverpool Football Club** also having a small museum to past successes. A spectacular, richly timbered building dating from 1490, **Speke Hall** lies 6 miles (10 km) east of Liverpool's centre, on the banks of the River Mersey. The oldest parts of the hall enclose a cobbled courtyard dominated by two yew trees, Adam and Eve.

Birkenhead on the Wirral peninsula has been linked to Liverpool by ferry for over 800 years. Now, road and rail tunnels supplement access. The Norman priory church is still in use on Sundays, and stately Hamilton Square was designed from 1825–44 by J Gillespie Graham, one of the architects of Edinburgh's New Town.

On the Wirral side is **Port Sunlight** *(see p353)*, a Victorian garden village built by enlightened soap manufacturer William Hesketh Lever for his factory workers. He also founded the Lady Lever Art Gallery here for his collection of works of art, including Pre-Raphaelite paintings.

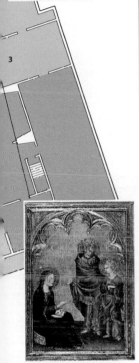

Christ Discovered in the Temple (1342) Simone Martini's Holy Family conveys emotional tension through highly expressive body language.

Key to Floor Plan

- 13th–17th-century European
- 18th–19th-century British, Pre-Raphaelites and Victorian
- Impressionist/Post-Impressionist
- 20th-century and contemporary British
- Sculpture gallery
- Craft and design gallery
- Merseyside people and places
- Special exhibitions
- Non-exhibition space

YORKSHIRE AND THE HUMBER REGION

North Yorkshire · East Yorkshire

With the historic city of York at its heart, this is an area of picturesque moorland and valleys. To the north lie the Yorkshire Dales and the North York Moors; eastwards, a coastline of beaches; and southwards, a landscape of lush meadows.

Yorkshire covers more than 5,000 sq miles (12,950 sq km), making it England's largest county. It's also incredibly diverse. The Dales and Moors in the north both have dramatic scenery that was formed by glaciers in the Ice Age. Farming was the original livelihood, and the dry-stone walls weaving up and down the fells used to divide the land. Imposed on this landscape are the remnants of 19th-century industries; crumbling viaducts are as much a part of the scenery as the grand houses of those who profited from them.

It is the contrasting landscapes that make the area so appealing, ranging from the grandeur of the Humber Bridge to the ragged cliff coast around Whitby,

and the flat expanse of Sunk Island. Along the coast, the grand Humber Bridge overshadows lush and sprawling meadows and a ragtag of reminders of a once-great fishing industry. Beyond the estuary, the seaside becomes far wilder and more beautiful. Here, wide sandy beaches and glorious ragged cliffs fringe bustling harbour towns such as Whitby.

The city of York, where Roman and Viking relics coexist, is the region's foremost attraction. Those in search of a real taste of Yorkshire, however, should head for the countryside. In addition to excellent touring routes, a network of rewarding walking paths ranges from mellow ambles along the Cleveland Way to rocky scrambles over the Pennine Way.

Lobster pots on the quayside at the picturesque fishing port of Whitby

◀ Ribblehead Viaduct on the Settle-to-Carlisle railway line, North Yorkshire

Exploring Yorkshire and the Humber Region

Yorkshire covers a wide area, once made up of three counties or "Ridings". Until the arrival of railways, mining and the wool industry in the 19th century, the county's focus was on farming. Dry-stone walls dividing fields still pepper the northern part of the county, alongside 19th-century mill chimneys and country houses. Among the many abbeys are Rievaulx and the magnificent Fountains. The historic city of York is a major attraction, as are Yorkshire's beaches. The Humber region is characterized by the softer, rolling countryside of the Wolds, and its nature reserves attract enormous quantities of birds.

Rosedale Abbey village in the North York Moors

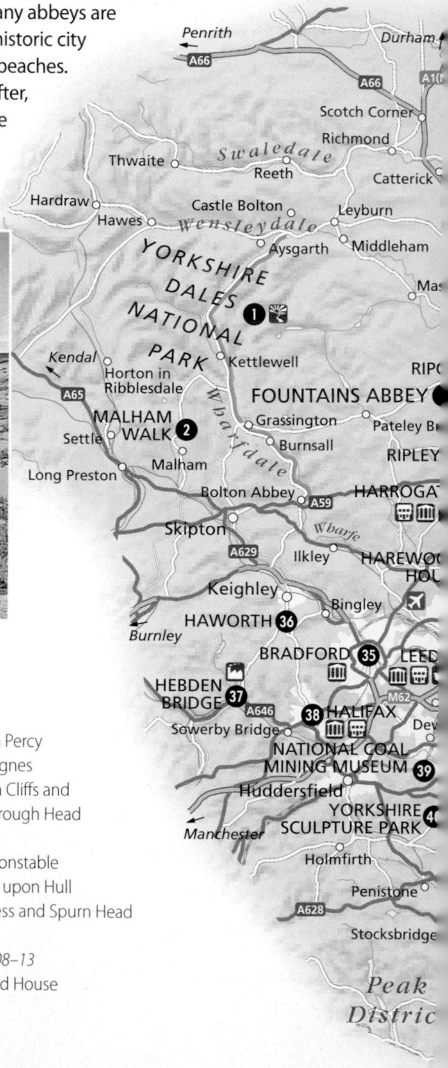

Sights at a Glance

① Yorkshire Dales National Park
  pp388–90
③ Harrogate
④ Knaresborough
⑤ Ripley
⑥ Newby Hall
⑦ Fountains Abbey pp394–5
⑧ Ripon
⑨ Sutton Bank
⑩ Byland Abbey
⑪ Coxwold
⑫ Nunnington Hall
⑬ Helmsley
⑭ Rievaulx Abbey
⑮ Mount Grace Priory
⑯ Hutton-le-Hole
⑰ North York Moors p399
⑱ North Yorkshire Moors Railway
⑲ Whitby p400
⑳ Robin Hood's Bay
㉑ Scarborough
㉒ Castle Howard pp402–3
㉓ Eden Camp

㉔ Wharram Percy
㉕ Burton Agnes
㉖ Bempton Cliffs and
  Flamborough Head
㉗ Beverley
㉘ Burton Constable
㉙ Kingston upon Hull
㉚ Holderness and Spurn Head
㉛ Grimsby
㉜ York pp408–13
㉝ Harewood House
㉞ Leeds
㉟ Bradford
㊱ Haworth
㊲ Hebden Bridge
㊳ Halifax
㊴ National Coal Mining
  Museum
㊵ Yorkshire Sculpture Park
㊶ Magna

Walks

② Malham Walk p391

Map labels: Penrith, Durham, A66, A66, A1, Scotch Corner, Richmond, Swaledale, Thwaite, Reeth, Catterick, Hardraw, Castle Bolton, Leyburn, Hawes, Wensleydale, Aysgarth, Middleham, YORKSHIRE DALES NATIONAL PARK, Mas, Kendal, Horton in Ribblesdale, Kettlewell, RIPC, A65, FOUNTAINS ABBEY, MALHAM WALK, Grassington, Pateley B, Settle, Burnsall, RIPLEY, Malham, Wharfedale, Long Preston, Bolton Abbey, A59, HARROGA, Skipton, Wharfe, A629, Ilkley, HAREWO HOL, Keighley, Bingley, HAWORTH, Burnley, BRADFORD, LEE, HEBDEN BRIDGE, A646, HALIFAX, Sowerby Bridge, Dev, M62, NATIONAL COAL MINING MUSEUM, Huddersfield, YORKSHIRE SCULPTURE PARK, Manchester, Holmfirth, Penistone, A628, Stocksbridge, Peak Distric

0 kilometres 15
0 miles 10

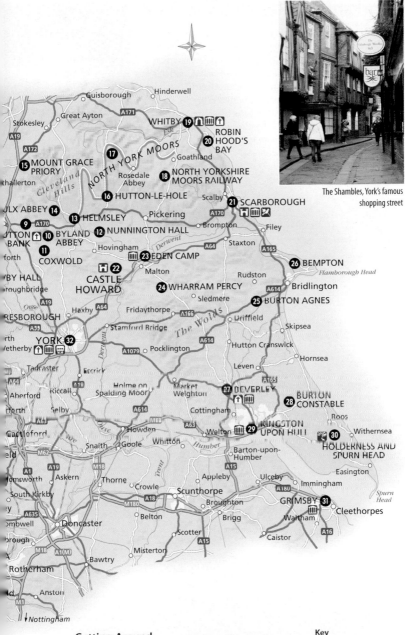

The Shambles, York's famous
shopping street

Getting Around

The area is served by the A1, the M1, the
M62 and the A59. Trains run to York, Leeds
and other cities, and there are train or
coach links between many towns and
hamlets. The Yorkshire Dales and North
York Moors national parks are good for
walkers, and cyclists can enjoy rides
around York and the River Humber.

Key

━━━ Motorway

━━━ Major road

━━━ Secondary road

┅┅┅ Minor road

━━━ Scenic route

━━━ Main railway

─── Minor railway

For keys to symbols *see back flap*

❶ Yorkshire Dales National Park

The Yorkshire Dales is a farming landscape, formed from three principal dales, Swaledale, Wharfedale and Wensleydale, and a number of smaller ones, such as Deepdale. Glaciation in the Ice Age carved out these steep-sided valleys, and this scenery contrasts with the high moorlands. Over 12 centuries of settlement mean the landscape is dotted with cottages, castles and villages, creating a delightful environment to explore. A national park since 1954, the area provides much for visitors seeking rest or recreation.

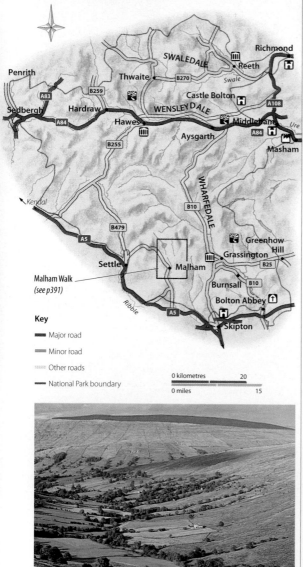

Key

━━━ Major road
═══ Minor road
⋯⋯ Other roads
━━━ National Park boundary

Malham Walk
(see p391)

0 kilometres   20
0 miles   15

The green, rolling landscape of Deepdale, near Dent

For keys to symbols *see back flap*

Monk's Wynd – one of Richmond's narrow, winding streets

Exploring Swaledale

Swaledale's prosperity was founded largely on wool, and it is famous for its herds of sheep that graze on the wild higher slopes even in the harshest weather. The fast-moving River Swale that gives the northernmost dale its name travels from bleak moorland down tumbling waterfalls into the richly wooded lower slopes, passing through the village of Reeth and the town of Richmond.

🏰 Richmond Castle

Tower Street. **Tel** 0870 333 1181.
Open Apr–Sep: daily; Oct: Thu–Mon; Nov–Mar: Sat & Sun. **Closed** 1 Jan, 24–26 Dec. ♿ 🅿 limited. 🏰 EH

Swaledale's main point of entry is the medieval market town of Richmond. Alan Rufus, the Norman 1st Earl of Richmond, began building the castle in 1071, and some masonry probably dates from that time. It has a fine Norman keep, 30 m (100 ft) high with walls 3.3 m (11 ft) thick. An 11th-century arch leads into a courtyard containing Scolland's Hall (1080), one of England's oldest buildings.

Richmond's marketplace was once the castle's outer bailey. Its quaint, narrow streets gave rise to the song *The Lass of Richmond Hill* (1787), written by Leonard McNally for his wife, Frances l'Anson, who was brought up in Hill House, on Richmond Hill. Turner *(see p95)* painted the town many times. The Georgian Theatre (1788) is the only one of its age still surviving.

🏛 Swaledale Folk Museum
Reeth Green. **Tel** 01748 884118. **Open** May–Sep: daily. 🚗 🖥 🏠 **W** swaledalemuseum.org

Reeth, a town that became the centre of the lead-mining industry, houses this museum in a former Methodist Sunday school (1830). Mining and wool-making artifacts (wool from the hardy Swaledale sheep was another mainstay of the economy) and brass band memorabilia are some of the items on show.

🌿 Buttertubs
Near Thwaite, on the B6270 Hawes road, is a series of fluted limestone potholes that became known as the Buttertubs. It is said that farmers on their way to market would lower their butter into the holes to keep it cool.

Buttertubs, near Thwaite

Exploring Wensleydale
The largest of the dales, Wensleydale is famous for its cheese and the television series *All Creatures Great and Small*, based on the books by vet James Herriot, which was filmed there. It is easy walking country for anyone seeking an alternative to major moorland hikes.

🏛 Dales Countryside Museum
Station Yard, Hawes. **Tel** 01969 666210. **Open** 10am–5pm daily. **Closed** 1 Jan, 24–26 Dec. 🚗 🚻 🏠 **W** dalescountrysidemuseum.org.uk

In a former railway goods warehouse in Hawes, capital of Upper Wensleydale, is this fascinating museum, filled with

Barrels at the Theakston Brewery

items from life and industry in the 18th- and 19th-century Upper Dales. These include cheese- and butter-making equipment. Wensleydale cheese was created by monks at nearby Jervaulx Abbey. There is also a rope-making works a short walk away.

Hawes is one of the highest market towns in England, at 259 m (850 ft) above sea level. It is a thriving centre where thousands of sheep and cattle are auctioned each summer.

🌿 Hardraw Force
🚗 at Green Dragon Inn, Hardraw. At the tiny village of Hardraw, nearby, is England's tallest single-drop waterfall, with no outcrops to interrupt its 29 m (96-ft) fall. It became famous in Victorian times when the daredevil Blondin walked across it on a tightrope. Today, you can walk right under it and look through the stream without getting wet.

🌿 Aysgarth Falls
ℹ National Park Centre (01969 662910). **Open** Apr–Oct: daily; Nov–Dec & Feb–Mar: Sat & Sun. 🖥

An old packhorse bridge gives a clear view of the point at which the previously placid River Ure suddenly begins to plunge in foaming torrents over wide limestone shelves. Turner painted the impressive lower falls in 1817.

🏛 Theakston Brewery
Masham. **Tel** 01765 680000. **Open** daily. **Closed** 23 Dec–early Jan. 🚗 🚻 🏠 **W** theakstons.co.uk

The pretty town of Masham is the home of Theakston's brewery, creator of the potent Old Peculier ale. The history of this local family brewery from its origin in 1827 is on display in the visitors' centre.

VISITORS' CHECKLIST

Practical Information
North Yorkshire. ℹ 0300 4560030.
W yorkshiredales.org.uk

Transport
🚆 Skipton. 🚌

Masham village itself has an attractive square once used for sheep fairs, surrounded by 17th- and 18th-century houses.

🏰 Bolton Castle
Castle Bolton, nr Leyburn. **Tel** 01969 623981. **Open** mid-Feb–Oct: daily. 🚗 🖥 🏠 **W** boltoncastle.co.uk

Situated in the village of Castle Bolton, this spectacular medieval fortress was built in 1379 by the 1st Lord Scrope, Chancellor of England. Its most notorious period was from 1568 to 1569 when Mary, Queen of Scots *(see p515)* was held prisoner here by Elizabeth I *(see pp54–5)*.

🏰 Middleham Castle
Middleham, nr Leyburn. **Tel** 01969 623899. **Open** Apr–Sep: daily; Oct: Sat–Wed; Nov–Mar: Sat & Sun. **Closed** 1 Jan, 24–26 Dec. 🚗 🚻 ltd. 🏠 🖥 **W** english-heritage.org.uk

Built in 1170 and later owned by Richard Neville, Earl of Warwick, Middleham Castle is better known as home to Richard III *(see p53)* when he was made Lord of the North. It was once one of the strongest fortresses in the north but became uninhabited during the 15th century, when many of its stones were used for nearby buildings. The keep provides a fine view of the landscape.

Remains of Middleham Castle, once residence of Richard III

Extensive ruins of Bolton Priory, dating from 1154

Exploring Wharfedale

This dale is characterized by gritstone moorland and quiet market towns nestled along meandering sections of river. Many consider Grassington a good point for exploring Wharfedale, but the showpiece villages of Burnsall, overlooked by a 506-m (1,661-ft) fell, and Buckden, near Buckden Pike (701 m/2,302 ft), also make excellent bases.

Nearby are the Three Peaks of Whernside (736 m/2,416 ft), Ingleborough (724 m/2,376 ft) and Pen-y-Ghent (694 m/2,278 ft). They are known for their potholes and tough terrain, but this does not deter keen walkers from attempting to climb them all in one day. If you sign in at the Pen-y-Ghent café at Horton-in-Ribblesdale, at the centre of the Three Peaks, and complete the 20-mile (32-km) course, reaching the summit of all three peaks in less than 12 hours, you can qualify for membership of the Three Peaks of Yorkshire Club.

Burnsall

St Wilfrid's, Burnsall. **Tel** 01756 752575. **Open** Apr–Oct: daily to dusk.

Preserved in St Wilfrid's church graveyard are the original village stocks, gravestones from Viking times and a headstone carved in memory of the Dawson family by sculptor Eric Gill (1882–1940). The village has a five-arched bridge and hosts Britain's oldest fell race every August.

Grassington Folk Museum

The Square, Grassington. **Tel** 01756 753287. **Open** Apr–Oct: 2–4pm daily. limited. **W grassington folkmuseum.org.uk**

This museum is set in two 18th-century lead-miners' cottages. Its exhibits illustrate the domestic and working history of the area, including farming and lead mining.

Bolton Priory

Bolton Abbey, Skipton. **Tel** 01756 718009. **Open** daily. **W bolton abbey.com**

One of the most beautiful parts of Wharfedale is around the village of Bolton Abbey, set in an estate owned by the Duke of Devonshire. While preserving its astounding beauty, its managers have incorporated over 30 miles (46 km) of footpaths, many suitable for the disabled and young families.

The ruins of Bolton Priory, established by Augustinian canons in 1154 on the site of a Saxon manor, are extensive. They include a church, chapter house, cloister and prior's lodging. These all demonstrate the wealth accumulated by the canons through the sale of wool from their flocks of sheep. The priory nave is still used as a parish church. Another attraction of the estate is the "Strid", a point where the River Wharfe surges spectacularly through a gorge, foaming yellow and gradually gouging holes out of the rocks.

Stump Cross Caverns

Greenhow Hill, Pateley Bridge. **Tel** 01756 752780. **Open** mid-Feb–mid-Jan: daily. **Closed** 24 & 25 Dec. **W stumpcrosscaverns.co.uk**

These caves were formed over a period of half a million years: trickles of underground water in time formed intertwining passages of all shapes and sizes. Sealed off in the last Ice Age, the caves were only discovered in the 1850s, when lead miners sank a mine shaft into the caverns.

Skipton Castle

High St. **Tel** 01756 792442. **Open** daily (Sun: pm only). **Closed** 25 Dec. **W skiptoncastle.co.uk**

The market town of Skipton is still one of the largest auctioning and stockraising centres in the north. Its 11th-century castle was almost entirely rebuilt by Robert de Clifford in the 14th century. Beautiful Conduit Court was added by Henry, Lord Clifford, in Henry VIII's reign. The central yew tree was planted by Lady Anne Clifford in 1659 to mark restoration work to the castle after Civil War damage.

Conduit Court (1495) and yew tree at Skipton Castle

❷ Malham Walk

The Malham area, shaped by glacial erosion 10,000 years ago, has one of Great Britain's most dramatic limestone landscapes. The walk from Malham village can take over 4 hours if you pause to enjoy the viewpoints and take a detour to Gordale Scar. Those who are short of time tend to go only as far as Malham Cove. This vast natural amphitheatre, formed by a huge geological tear, is like a giant boot-heel mark in the landscape. Above lie the deep crevices of Malham Lings, where rare flora such as hart's-tongue flourish. Other plants grow in the lime-rich Malham Tarn, said to have provided inspiration for Charles Kingsley's *The Water Babies* (1863). Coot and mallard visit the tarn in summer, as do tufted duck in winter.

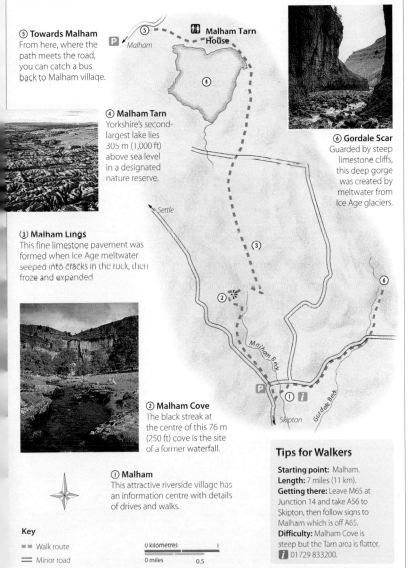

⑤ Towards Malham
From here, where the path meets the road, you can catch a bus back to Malham village.

Malham Tarn House

Malham

④ Malham Tarn
Yorkshire's second-largest lake lies 305 m (1,000 ft) above sea level in a designated nature reserve.

⑥ Gordale Scar
Guarded by steep limestone cliffs, this deep gorge was created by meltwater from Ice Age glaciers.

③ Malham Lings
This fine limestone pavement was formed when Ice Age meltwater seeped into cracks in the rock, then froze and expanded.

Settle

② Malham Cove
The black streak at the centre of this 76 m (250 ft) cove is the site of a former waterfall.

Malham Beck

Gordale Beck

Skipton

① Malham
This attractive riverside village has an information centre with details of drives and walks.

Tips for Walkers

Starting point: Malham.
Length: 7 miles (11 km).
Getting there: Leave M65 at Junction 14 and take A56 to Skipton, then follow signs to Malham which is off A65.
Difficulty: Malham Cove is steep but the Tarn area is flatter.
ℹ 01729 833200.

Key

■ ■ Walk route
═══ Minor road

0 kilometres 1
0 miles 0.5

A 1920s poster advertising the spa town of Harrogate

❸ Harrogate

North Yorkshire. 🗺 76,000. 🚆 🚌
ℹ️ The Royal Baths, Crescent Rd (01423 537300). 🆆 visitharrogate.co.uk

Between 1880 and World War I, Harrogate was the north's leading spa town, with nearly 90 medicinal springs. It was perfect for aristocrats who, after a tiring London season, were able to stop for a health cure before journeying on to grouse-shooting in Scotland.

Today, Harrogate's main attractions are its spa town atmosphere, fine architecture, public gardens and its conven-ience as a centre for visiting North Yorkshire and the Dales.

The naturally welling spa waters may not currently be in use, but you can still go for a Turkish bath in one of the country's most attractive steam rooms. The entrance at the side of the Royal Bath Assembly Rooms (1897) is unassuming, but once inside, the century-old **Harrogate Turkish Baths** are a visual feast of tiled Victoriana.

The town's spa history is recorded in the **Royal Pump Room Museum**. At the turn of the century, the waters were thought to be rich in iron early in the day. So, between 7am and 9am the 1842 octagonal building would have been filled with rich and fashionable people drinking glasses of water. Poorer people could take water from the pump outside. Today you can sample the

waters and enjoy the museum's exhibits, which include a Penny Farthing bicycle.

Harrogate is also known for the rainbow-coloured flowerbeds in **The Stray**, a common space to the south of the town centre, and for the ornamental **Harlow Carr Gardens**, owned by the Royal Horticultural Society. Visitors can enjoy the delicious cakes at **Bettys Café Tea Rooms**.

🏛 **Harrogate Turkish Baths**
The Royal Baths, Crescent Rd.
Tel 01423 556746. **Open** Check website for times (separate times available for women). 🈺
🆆 turkishbathsharrogate.co.uk

🏛 **Royal Pump Room Museum**
Crown Pl. **Tel** 01423 556188. **Open** daily (Sun: pm only). **Closed** 1 Jan, 24–26 Dec. 🈺 ♿ 📷 🆆 harrogate.gov.uk

🏛 **Bettys Café Tea Rooms**
1 Parliament St. **Tel** 01423 814070.
Open daily. **Closed** 1 Jan, 25 & 26 Dec.
🆆 bettys.co.uk

🌺 **RHS Harlow Carr Gardens**
Crag Lane. **Tel** 08452 658070.
Open daily. **Closed** 25 Dec. 🈺
♿ 🅿️ 🖥 🆆 rhs.org.uk

❹ Knaresborough

North Yorkshire. 🗺 15,000. 🚆
🚌 from Harrogate. ℹ️ 9 Castle Courtyard, Market Place (01423 866886). 🅰 Wed.

Perched precipitously above the River Nidd is one of England's oldest towns, mentioned in the Domesday Book of 1086 *(see p52)*. Its historic streets – which link the church, John of Gaunt's ruined castle and the marketplace with the river – are now lined with fine 18th-century houses.

Nearby is **Mother Shipton's Cave**, reputedly England's oldest tourist attraction. It was first opened in 1630 as the birthplace of Ursula Sontheil, a famous local prophetess. Today, people can

Mother Shipton's Cave, Knaresborough, with objects encased in limestone

For hotels and restaurants in this area see p570 and pp597–8

The south front of Newby Hall

view the effect the well near her cave has on objects hung below the dripping surface. Almost any item, from umbrellas to soft toys, will become encased in limestone within a few weeks.

Mother Shipton's Cave
Prophecy House, High Bridge.
Tel 01423 864600. **Open** Easter–Oct: daily; Feb Easter: Sat & Sun.
Closed Nov–Jan. 🏛️ 🎫 📷 📱
W mothershipton.co.uk

❺ Ripley

North Yorkshire. 🚹 250. 🚌 from Harrogate or Ripon. 🚆 Harrogate (01423 537300). **W** harrogate.gov.uk

Since the 1320s, when the first generation of the Ingilby family lived in an early incarnation of **Ripley Castle**, the village has been made up almost exclusively of castle employees. The influence of one 19th-century Ingilby had the most visual impact. In the 1820s, Sir William Amcotts Ingilby was so entranced by a village in Alsace Lorraine that he created a similar one in French Gothic style, complete with an *Hôtel de Ville*. Present-day Ripley has a cobbled market square, and quaint cottages line the streets.

Ripley Castle, with its 15th-century gatehouse, was where Oliver Cromwell *(see p56)* stayed following the Battle of Marston Moor. The 28th generation of Ingilbys live here, and it is open for tours. The attractive grounds contain two lakes and a deer park, as well as more formal gardens.

🏠 Ripley Castle
Ripley. **Tel** 01423 770152. **Open** Apr–Sep: daily; Mar, Oct & Nov: Sat & Sun.
Gardens: **Open** daily all year. **Closed** 1 Jan, 25 & 26 Dec. 🏛️ 🎫 ♿ 📱 📷
W ripleycastle.co.uk

❻ Newby Hall

Near Ripon, North Yorkshire. **Tel** 01423 322583. **Open** Apr Jun & Sep: Tue–Sun; Jul & Aug: daily. 🏛️ ♿ 🎫 📷
W newbyhall.com

Newby Hall stands on land once occupied by the de Nubie family in the 13th century and has been in the hands of the current family since 1748. The central part of the present house was built in the late 17th century, in the style of Sir Christopher Wren.

Visitors will find 25 acres of gardens to explore. Laid out in a series of compartmentalized areas off a main axis, each garden is planted to come into flower during a specific season. There is also a Woodland Discovery Walk, featuring contemporary sculpture.

For children, there is an adventure garden with activities and a miniature railway that runs through the gardens alongside the River Ure. Riverboat rides are also available. Each year a number of special events are staged, including plant fairs, a historic vehicle rally and two craft fairs.

❼ Fountains Abbey

See pp394–5.

❽ Ripon

North Yorkshire. 🚹 17,000. 🚌 from Harrogate. 🚆 Town Hall, Marketplace (0845 389 0178). 🛍️ Thu.
W discoverripon.org

Ripon, a charming small city, is best known for its cathedral and its hornblower, who has announced "the watch" since the Middle Ages. Then, the job of the Wakeman was similar to that of a mayor. Today, a man still blows a horn in the Market Square each evening at 9pm, and every Thursday a handbell is rung to open the market.

The **Cathedral of St Peter and St Wilfrid** is built above a 7th-century Saxon crypt, which is less than 3 m (10 ft) high and just over 2 m (7 ft) wide. It is held to be the oldest complete crypt in England. The cathedral is known for its collection of misericords *(see p345)*, which include both pagan and Old Testament subjects. The architectural historian Sir Nikolaus Pevsner (1902–83) considered the cathedral's West Front the finest in England.

Ripon's **Prison and Police Museum**, housed in the 1686 "House of Correction", looks at police history and the conditions in Victorian prisons.

🏛️ Prison and Police Museum
St Marygate. **Tel** 01765 690799.
Open mid-Feb–Nov: daily pm.
Closed Dec–mid-Feb. 🏛️ ♿ 📷
W riponmuseums.co.uk

Ripon's Wakeman, blowing his horn in the Market Square

❼ Fountains Abbey

Nestling in the wooded valley of the River Skell are the extensive sandstone ruins of Fountains Abbey and the outstanding water garden of Studley Royal. Fountains Abbey was founded by Benedictine monks in 1132 and joined the Cistercian order 3 years later. By the mid-12th century it had become the wealthiest abbey in Britain, though it fell into ruin during the Dissolution *(see p355)*. In 1720, John Aislabie, the MP for Ripon and Chancellor of the Exchequer, developed the land and forest of the abbey ruins. He began work, continued by his son William, on the famous water garden, statuary and Classical temples in the grounds. Studley Royal and the Abbey became a World Heritage Site in 1986.

Fountains Hall
Built by Sir Stephen Proctor around 1604, with stones from the abbey ruins, its design is attributed to architect Robert Smythson. It included a great hall with a minstrels' gallery and an entrance flanked by Classical columns.

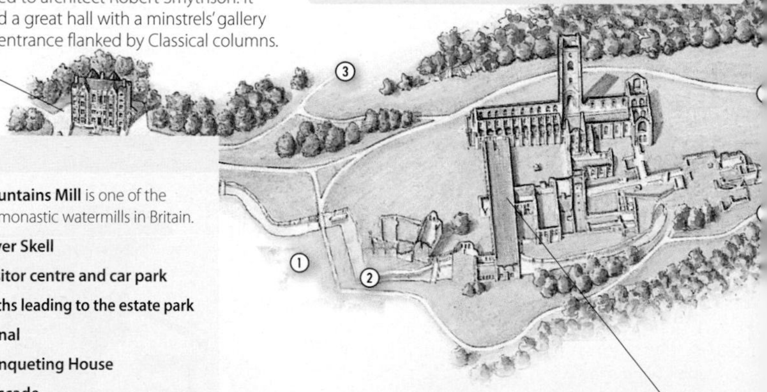

The Abbey

The abbey buildings were designed to reflect the Cistercians' desire for simplicity and austerity. The abbey frequently dispensed charity to the poor and the sick, as well as travellers.

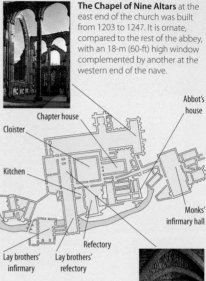

The Chapel of Nine Altars at the east end of the church was built from 1203 to 1247. It is ornate, compared to the rest of the abbey, with an 18-m (60-ft) high window complemented by another at the western end of the nave.

Abbot's house

Chapter house

Cloister

Kitchen

Monks' infirmary hall

Refectory

Lay brothers' infirmary

Lay brothers' refectory

Cellarium and dormitory undercroft, with vaulting 90-m (300-ft) long, was used for storing fleeces, which the abbey monks sold to Venetian and Florentine merchants.

KEY

① **Fountains Mill** is one of the finest monastic watermills in Britain.

② River Skell

③ Visitor centre and car park

④ Paths leading to the estate park

⑤ Canal

⑥ Banqueting House

⑦ Cascade

⑧ Lake

⑨ Footpath to St Mary's Church

⑩ Octagon Tower

⑪ Moon Pond

⑫ **Anne Boleyn's Seat** is a Gothic alcove with a fine view of the abbey. It was built in the late 18th century to replace her statue.

★ **Abbey**
This was built using stones taken from the Skell valley.

St Mary's Church
This sumptuous Victorian Gothic church was built by architect William Burges in 1871–8. Inside, the choirstalls are decorated with multi-coloured carved parrots.

VISITORS' CHECKLIST

Practical Information
Studley Royal Estate, Ripon.
Tel 01765 608888. **Open** 10am–5pm daily (Oct–Mar: to 4pm, or dusk if earlier). **Closed** every Fri in Jan, Nov, Dec; 24 & 25 Dec. 🅿 📷 ♿ ✏ ▣ NT W nationaltrust. org.uk/fountainsabbey

Transport
🚌 from Ripon (May–Sep) or Harrogate.

Temple of Fame
The columns of this domed building are made of hollow timber but look like sandstone.

★ Temple of Piety
This garden house was originally dedicated to Hercules. It was renamed as a symbol of filial piety by William Aislabie after his father's death in 1742.

The 19th-century white horse above Kilburn, seen on one of the walks around Sutton Bank

❾ Sutton Bank

North Yorkshire. ☎ Thirsk.
🛈 Sutton Bank (01845 597426).

Notorious among motorists for its 1 in 4 gradient, which climbs for about 107 m (350 ft), Sutton Bank itself is known for its superb panoramic views. On a clear day you can see across the Vale of York to the Dales *(see pp388–90)*. William Wordsworth and his sister Dorothy stopped here to admire the vista in 1802, on their way to visit his future wife, Mary Hutchinson, at Brompton. The visitor centre, at the top of the Bank, has an interactive exhibition that tells the story of the area's landscape. From here it is a pleasant walk to the white horse above Kilburn.

❿ Byland Abbey

Coxwold, York. **Tel** 01347 868614.
🚌 from York or Helmsley. ☎ Thirsk.
Open Apr–Jun, Sep: Thu–Mon; Jul–Aug: daily; Oct–Mar: Sat & Sun. 🎫
♿ limited. 🇪🇭 🖥 **english-heritage. org.uk**

This Cistercian monastery was founded in 1177 by monks from Furness Abbey in Cumbria. It featured what was then the largest Cistercian church in Britain, 100 m (328 ft) long and 41 m (135 ft) wide across the transepts. The layout of the monastery, including cloisters and the west front of the church, is still visible, as is the green and yellow glazed tile floor. Fine workmanship is shown in carved stone capitals, rich with detail, kept in the small museum.

In 1322 the Battle of Byland was fought nearby, and King Edward II *(see p44)* narrowly escaped capture when the invading Scottish army learned that he was dining with the abbot. In his hurry to escape, the king had to leave many treasures behind, which were looted by the invading soldiers.

⓫ Coxwold

North Yorkshire. 🚗 260. 🛈 49 Market Place, Thirsk (01845 522755).
🖥 **coxwoldvillage.co.uk**

Situated just inside the bounds of the North York Moors National Park *(see p399)*, this charming village nestles at the foot of the Howardian Hills. Its pretty houses are built from local stone, and the 15th-century church has some fine Georgian box pews and an impressive octagonal tower. But Coxwold is best known as the home of author Laurence Sterne (1713–68), whose works

Shandy Hall, home of author Laurence Sterne

For hotels and restaurants in this area see p570 and pp597–8

include *Tristram Shandy* and *A Sentimental Journey*.

Sterne moved here in 1760 as the church curate. He rented a rambling house that he named **Shandy Hall** after a Yorkshire expression meaning eccentric. Originally built as a timber framed, open-halled house in the 15th century, it was modernized in the 17th century and Sterne later added a façade. His grave lies beside the porch at Coxwold's church.

Shandy Hall
Coxwold. **Tel** 01347 868465.
Open May–Sep: Wed & Sun pm.
limited. Gardens: **Open** May–Sep: 11am–4:30pm Sun–Fri.
W laurencesternetrust.org.uk

⑩ Nunnington Hall

Nunnington, Yorkshire. **Tel** 01439 748283. Malton, then bus or taxi. **Open** Feb–Oct: Tue–Sun; Nov–mid-Dec: Sat & Sun. **Closed** mid-Dec–Jan. ground floor. **NT**
W nationaltrust.org.uk

Set in alluring surroundings, this 17th-century manor house is a combination of architectural styles, including features from the Elizabethan and Stuart periods. Both inside and outside, a notable architectural feature is the use of the broken pediment (the upper arch is left unjoined).

Nunnington Hall was a family home until 1952, when Mrs Ronald Fife donated it to the National Trust. A striking

The miniature Queen Anne drawing room at Nunnington Hall

feature is the panelling in the Oak Hall. Formerly painted, it extends over the three-arched screen to the Great Staircase. Nunnington's collection of 22 miniature furnished period rooms is popular with visitors.

A mid-16th-century tenant, Dr Robert Huickes, physician to Henry VIII, is best known for advising Elizabeth I that she should not, at the age of 32, consider having any children.

⑬ Helmsley

North Yorkshire. 1,600. from Malton or Scarborough. Cut Price Bookstore, 11 Market Place (01439 771130). Fri **W visitryedale.co.uk**

This pretty market town is noted for its castle, now an imposing ruin. Built from 1186 to 1227, its main function and strength as a fortress is illustrated by the remaining keep, tower and curtain walls. The original D-shaped keep had one part blasted away in the Civil War *(see p56)* but remains the dominant feature. The walled garden,

situated beneath the castle ruins, was built in 1759 and has a stunning herbaceous border.

Other attractions include the town's church, with its 19th-century murals, and the Helmsley Brewing Co., which produces a range of fine craft beers.

Helmsley church tower

⑭ Rievaulx Abbey

Nr Helmsley, North Yorkshire. **Tel** 01439 790220. Thirsk or Scarborough, then bus or taxi. **Open** Mar & Oct: Wed–Sun; Apr–Sep: daily; Nov–Feb: Sat & Sun. **Closed** 1 Jan, 24–26 Dec. ltd. **EH W english-heritage.org.uk**

Rievaulx is perhaps the finest abbey in the area, due to both its dramatic setting in the steep wooded valley of the River Rye and its extensive remains. It is surrounded by steep banks that form natural barriers against the outside world. Monks of the French Cistercian order from Clairvaux founded this, their first major monastery in Britain, in 1132. The main buildings were finished before 1200. The interior of the chapel, kitchens and infirmary gives an idea of monastic life.

Rievaulx Abbey, painted by Thomas Girtin (1775–1802)

Mount Grace Priory ruins, with farm and mansion in foreground

⑮ Mount Grace Priory

On A19, NE of Northallerton, North Yorkshire. **Tel** 01609 883494. Northallerton then bus. **Open** Apr–Oct: daily; Nov–Mar: Sat & Sun. ground floor, shop & grounds. EH english-heritage.org.uk

Founded by Thomas Holland, Duke of Surrey, and in use from 1398 until 1539, this is the best-preserved Carthusian or charterhouse monastery (see p354) in England. The monks took a vow of silence and lived in solitary cells, each with its own garden and an angled hatch so that he would not even see the person serving his food. They only met at matins, vespers and feast-day services. Attempts at escape by those who could not endure the rigour of the rules were punished by imprisonment.

The ruins of the priory include the former prison, gatehouse and outer court, barns, guest-houses, cells and the church. The 14th-century church, the best-preserved section of the site, is particularly small, as it was only rarely used by the community. A cell has been reconstructed to give an impression of monastic life.

⑯ Hutton-le-Hole

North Yorkshire. 150. Pickering then bus (seasonal service). Ryedale Folk Museum (01751 417367).

This picturesque village is characterized by a spacious green, grazed by roaming sheep, and surrounded by houses, an inn and shops. White wooden fencing lines the village green and grass verges. Its cottages, some with date panels over the doors, are made from limestone, with red pantiled roofs. In the village centre is

Wheelwright's workshop at Ryedale Folk Museum

the excellent **Ryedale Folk Museum**, which records the lifestyle of an agricultural community, from the Iron Age to the 1950s, using ancient artifacts and reconstructed buildings. Visitors can step inside an Iron Age roundhouse, a Tudor manor house, a Victorian cottage and a 19th-century photography studio.

Ryedale Folk Museum
Hutton-le-Hole. **Tel** 01751 417367. **Open** mid-Feb–Nov: daily. ryedalefolkmuseum.co.uk

⑰ North York Moors

See p399.

⑱ North Yorkshire Moors Railway

Pickering & Grosmont, North Yorkshire. **Tel** 01751 472508. **Open** Apr–Oct: daily; Dec–Mar: some weekends (see website). nymr.co.uk

Designed in 1831 by George Stephenson as a route through the North York Moors and linking with the Esk Valley, Pickering and Whitby, this railway was considered an engineering miracle. Due to budget constraints, Stephenson had to lay the route down the mile-long (1.5 km) incline between Goathland and Beck Hole. The area around Fen Bog had to be stabilized using timber, heather, brushwood and fleeces so that a causeway could be built over it. A horse was used to pull a coach along the track at 10 miles (16 km) per hour. After horsepower came steam, and for almost 130 years the railway linked Whitby to the rest of the country. In the early 1960s the line to Pickering was closed, but in 1967 a group of locals began a campaign to relaunch it, and in 1973 it reopened. Today, steam engines run the 24-mile (38-km) line through the scenic heart of the North York Moors, from Pickering via Levisham, Newtondale Halt and Goathland before terminating at Whitby.

⑰ North York Moors

North York Moors National Park covers an area between the cities of Thirsk, Teesside and Scarborough and consists of a landscape of lush green valleys fringed by beautiful moorland. The area had its industrial heyday in the 19th century, when its ironstone, lime and alum were mined for the region's heavy industry. Today, it is tourism that's most significant, with 6 million annual visitors coming for the scenic walking and cycling. Even so, the moors rarely feel crowded.

Mallyan Spout
A footpath leads to this waterfall from Goathland.

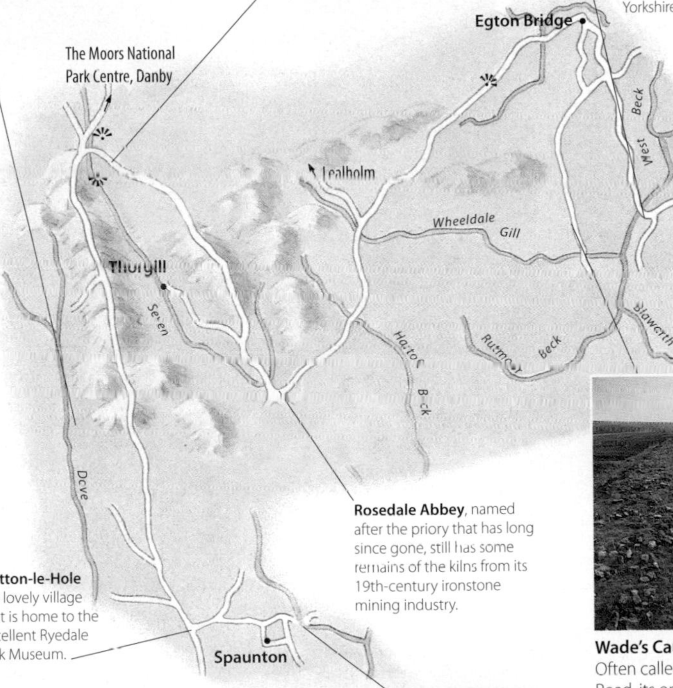

Farndale
During springtime, this area is famous for a profusion of beautiful daffodils.

"Fat Betty" (White Cross) is one of the medieval crosses that are a feature of the Moors.

Goathland is a centre for forest and moorland walks and is a stopping point for the North Yorkshire Moors Railway.

The Moors National Park Centre, Danby

Egton Bridge •

Whitby

↗ Lealholm

Wheeldale Gill

West Beck

Great Fryup Beck

Thorgill •

Seven

Hartof Beck

Rutmoor Beck

Rosedale Abbey, named after the priory that has long since gone, still has some remains of the kilns from its 19th-century ironstone mining industry.

Dove

Hutton-le-Hole is a lovely village that is home to the excellent Ryedale Folk Museum.

Spaunton

Wade's Causeway
Often called the Roman Road, its origins and destination are unknown. Long considered Roman in date, this is now less certain, although it may date from towards the end of the Roman occupation.

VISITORS' CHECKLIST

Practical Information
North Yorkshire. 🛈 Sutton Bank (01845 597426); Moors Centre, Danby (01439 772737).
W northyorkmoors.org.uk

Transport
🚆 Danby. 🚌 Pickering (Easter–Oct).

Lastingham
Lastingham's church, dating from 1078, has a Norman crypt with stone carving.

0 kilometres 2

0 miles ?

For keys to symbols *see back flap*

⑲ Whitby

Whitby's known history dates back to the 7th century, when a Saxon monastery was founded on the site of today's famous 13th-century abbey ruins. In the 18th and early 19th centuries it became an industrial port and shipbuilding town, as well as a whaling centre. In the Victorian era, the red-roofed cottages at the foot of the east cliff were filled with workshops crafting jet into jewellery and ornaments. Today, the tourist shops that have replaced them sell antique and modern pieces crafted from the distinctive black gem.

VISITORS' CHECKLIST

Practical Information
North Yorkshire. 🚗 13,500.
ℹ️ Langborne Rd (01723 383636). 🕐 Tue, Sat. 🎣 Angling Festival: Apr, Jun, Sep; Folk Week: Aug; Whitby Regatta: Aug; Goth Weekend: Nov. 🗑 **discover yorkshirecoast.com**

Transport
✈️ Teeside, 44 miles (70 km) NW Whitby. 🚆 Station Sq.

Exploring Whitby
Whitby is divided into two by the estuary of the River Esk. The Old Town, with its pretty cobbled streets and pastel-hued houses, huddles round the harbour. High above it is St Mary's Church, with a wood interior reputedly fitted by ships' carpenters. The ruins of the 13th-century Whitby Abbey, nearby, are still used as a landmark by mariners. From them you get a fine view over the still-busy harbour, strewn with colourful nets. A pleasant place for a stroll, the harbour is overlooked by an imposing bronze clifftop statue of the explorer Captain James Cook (1728–79), who was apprenticed as a teenager to a Whitby shipping firm.

Lobster pots lining the quayside of Whitby's quaint harbour

Medieval arches above the nave of Whitby Abbey

🏛 Whitby Abbey
Abbey Lane. **Tel** 01947 603568.
Open times vary; call for details.
Closed 1 Jan, 24–26 Dec. 🅿️ ♿
📷 EH 🗑 **english-heritage.org.uk**
The monastery founded in 657 was sacked by Vikings in 870. In the 11th century it was rebuilt as a Benedictine Abbey. The ruins date mainly from the 13th century.

🏛 St Mary's Parish Church
East Cliff. **Tel** 01947 606578. **Open** daily.
Stuart and Georgian alterations to this Norman church have left a mixture of twisted wood columns and maze-like 18th-century box pews. The 1778 triple-decker pulpit has rather avant-garde decor – ear-trumpets used by a Victorian rector's deaf wife.

🏛 Captain Cook Memorial Museum
Grape Lane. **Tel** 01947 601900. **Open** mid-Feb–Oct: daily. 🅿️ ♿ limited.
📷 🗑 **cookmuseumwhitby.co.uk**
The young James Cook slept in the attic of this 17th-century harbourside house when he was apprenticed nearby. The museum has displays of period furniture and watercolours by artists who travelled on his voyages.

🏛 Whitby Museum and Pannett Art Gallery
Pannett Park. **Tel** 01947 602908 (museum), 01947 600933 (gallery).
Open daily. **Closed** 24 Dec– 2 Jan.
🅿️ museum only. ♿ limited. 📷
🗑 **whitbymuseum.org.uk**
The Pannett Park grounds, museum and gallery were a gift of Whitby solicitor Robert Pannett (1834–1920), to house his art collection. Pannett Art Gallery has a collection of 19th and 20th century paintings including works by George Weatherill (1810–1890).

Among the treasures at Whitby Museum are objects illustrating local history, such as jet jewellery, and Captain Cook artifacts. The museum also houses a costume gallery and photography and map collections.

🏛 Caedmon's Cross
East Cliff.
On the path side of the abbey's clifftop graveyard is a cross commemorating Caedmon, an illiterate labourer who worked at the abbey in the 7th century. He experienced a vision that inspired him to compose cantos of Anglo-Saxon religious verse, which are still sung today.

Cross of Caedmon (1898)

⑳ Robin Hood's Bay

North Yorkshire. 🅰 1,400. 🚉
🚌 Whitby. 🇮 Langbourne Rd,
Whitby (01723 383636).

Legend has it that Robin Hood
(see p340) kept his boats here
in case he needed to make a
quick getaway. The village has
a history as a smugglers' haven,
and many houses contain
ingenious hiding places for
contraband. The cobbled main
street is so steep that visitors
need to leave their vehicles in
the car park at the top. In the
village centre, narrow streets
full of colour-washed stone
cottages collect around a
quaint quay. There is a beach
with rock pools that are ideal
for children to play in. At low
tide, the pleasant walk south to
Boggle Hole takes 15 minutes,
but you need to keep an eye
on the tides.

Cobbled alley in the Bay Town area of
Robin Hood's Bay

The fishing port and town of Scarborough nestling round the harbour

㉑ Scarborough

North Yorkshire. 🅰 62,000. 🚉
🚌 🇮 Sandside (01723 383636).
📅 Mon–Sat. 🔲 **discoveryorkshire
coast.com**

The history of Scarborough
as a resort can be traced
back to 1626, when it became
known as a spa. In the Industrial
Revolution (see pp352–3) it was
nicknamed "the Queen of the
Watering Places", but the post-
World War II trend for holidays
abroad has meant fewer
visitors. The town has two
beaches; the South Bay, with
its amusement arcades nearby,
contrasts with the quieter

North Bay. Playwright Alan
Ayckbourn premiers his work
at the Stephen Joseph theatre,
and Anne Brontë (see p416)
is buried in St Mary's Church.

Bronze and Iron Age relics
have been found on the site
of **Scarborough Castle**. The
Rotunda (1828–9), which
underwent a major refurbishment during 2007, was one
of Britain's first purpose-built
museums. Works by the local
artist Atkinson Grimshaw (1876–
93) hang in **Scarborough Art
Gallery**. The **Sea Life and
Marine Sanctuary**'s baby
seals are its main attraction.

🏰 **Scarborough Castle**
Castle Rd. **Tel** 01723 372451.
Open Apr–Sep: daily; Oct: Thu–Mon;
Nov–Mar: Wed–Sun. **Closed** 1 Jan,
24–26 Dec. 🚫 ♿ 🔲 📷 🇪🇭
🔲 **english-heritage.org.uk**

🏛 **Rotunda Museum**
Vernon Rd. **Tel** 01723 353665.
Open Tue–Sun. **Closed** 1 Jan,
25 & 26 Dec. 🚫 📷 🔲 **rotunda
museum.co.uk**

🏛 **Scarborough Art Gallery**
The Crescent. **Tel** 01723 374753.
Open Tue–Sun. **Closed** 1 Jan, 25 &
26 Dec. 🚫 📷 🔲 🔲 **scarborough
artgallery.co.uk**

🐟 **Sea Life and Marine Sanctuary**
Scalby Mills Rd. **Tel** 01723 373414.
Open daily. **Closed** 25 Dec. 🚫 ♿
🔲 📷 🔲 **visitsealife.com**

The Popularity of Swimming

In the 18th century, sea-
bathing came to be seen
as a healthy pastime, and
from 1735 people could
be taken out into the sea in
bathing huts, or "machines".
It was common to bathe
nude, but the Victorians
soon insisted on fully
clothed bathing. The coast
became a popular holiday
destination for 19th-century
workers who travelled from
Britain's industrial heart-
lands on the new steam trains. To meet this demand, seaside resorts
such as Blackpool (see p375) and Scarborough steadily expanded.

Victorian bathing huts in the sea

㉒ Castle Howard

Still owned and lived in by the Howard family, Castle Howard was the work of Charles, 3rd Earl of Carlisle. In 1699, he commissioned Sir John Vanbrugh, a man of dramatic ideas but with no previous architectural experience, to design a palace for him. Vanbrugh's grand designs of 1699 were put into practice by architect Nicholas Hawksmoor *(see p32)*, and the main body of the house was completed by 1712. The West Wing was built in 1753–9, using a design by Thomas Robinson, son-in-law of the 3rd Earl. In the 1980s, Castle Howard was used as the location for the television version of Evelyn Waugh's novel *Brideshead Revisited* (1945) and again in 2008 for a film version.

Temple of the Four Winds
Vanbrugh's last work, designed in 1724, has a dome and four Ionic porticoes. Situated in the grounds at the end of the terrace, it is typical of an 18th-century "landscape building".

Bust of the 7th Earl
J H Foley sculpted this portrait bust in 1870. It stands at the top of the Grand Staircase in the West Wing.

KEY

① **East Wing**

② **The front façade** faces north, which is unusual for the 17th century, while all the state rooms have a southerly aspect, with superb views over the gardens.

③ **North Front**

④ **Antique Passage** is where antiquities collected in the 18th and 19th centuries by the various Earls of Carlisle are displayed. The plethora of mythical figures and gods reflects contemporary interest in Classical civilizations.

⑤ **West Wing**

★ **Great Hall**
Rising 20 m (66 ft), from its 515-sq-m (5,500-sq-ft) floor to the dome, the Great Hall has columns by Samuel Carpenter (1660–1713), wall paintings by Pellegrini and a circular gallery.

Chapel Stained Glass
Admiral Edward Howard altered the chapel in 1870–75. The windows were designed by Edward Burne-Jones and made by William Morris & Co.

VISITORS' CHECKLIST

Practical Information
A64 from York. **Tel** 01653 648333.
House: **Open** Apr–Oct & late Dec:
11am–5pm daily. Grounds: **Open**
10am–4pm daily. 🅿 ♿ 🖥 📷
W **castlehoward.co.uk**

Transport
🚋 York then bus, or Malton
then taxi.

★ **Long Gallery**
Displayed here are paintings and sculptures commissioned by the Howard family, including works by Reynolds and Pannini.

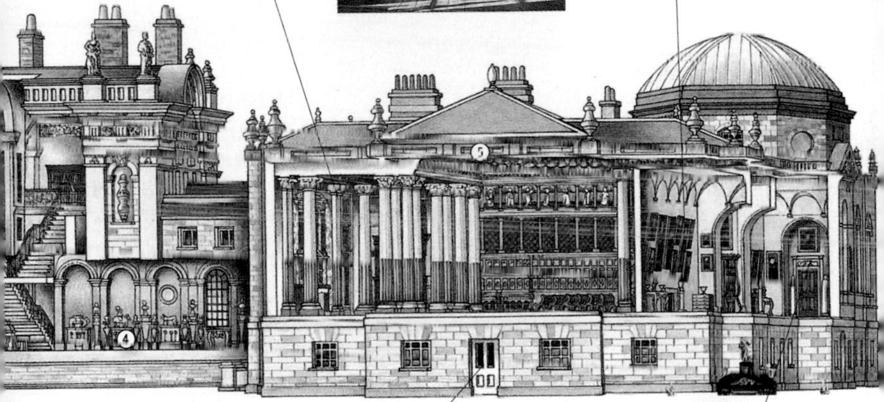

Visitor entrance

Sir John Vanbrugh

Vanbrugh (1664–1726) trained as a soldier, but became better known as a playwright, architect and member of the Whig nobility. He collaborated with Hawksmoor over the design of Blenheim Palace, but his bold architectural vision, later greatly admired, was mocked by the establishment. He died while working on the garden buildings and grounds of Castle Howard.

Museum Room
Items here include this huge 17th-century Delft tulip vase has nozzles shaped like a monster's mouth for cut flowers.

Alabaster carving on the chimneypiece at Burton Agnes

❷❸ Eden Camp

Malton, North Yorkshire. **Tel** 01653 697777. 🚆 Malton then taxi. **Open** daily. **Closed** 24 Dec–12 Jan. 🅿 ♿ 🖥 📷 **W** edencamp.co.uk

This is an unusual, award-winning theme museum that explores military and social history during the World Wars. Italian and German prisoners of war were kept at Eden Camp between 1939 and 1948. Today, some original huts built by Italian prisoners in 1942 are used as part of the museum, with period tableaux and a soundtrack. Each hut adopts a theme to take the visitor through civilian life in wartime, from Chamberlain's radio announcement of the outbreak of hostilities to the coming of peace. Visitors can see the Doodlebug V-1 bomb which crashed outside the Officers' Mess, take tea in the canteen or experience a night in the Blitz. A tour can last for several hours.

❷❹ Wharram Percy

North Yorkshire. **Tel** 0870 333 1181. 🛈 Scarborough (01723 383636). 🚆 Malton then taxi. **Open** daily. 🇪🇭 **W** english-heritage.org.uk

Discovered in 1948, this medieval village site is one of the best-known in England. It was probably founded around the 10th century and flourished between the 12th and 14th centuries, when the Percy family lived here. However, the village suffered during the Black Death (1348–9), and with the price of wool rising, local landowners evicted families to use the land for sheep farming. By around 1500, the village was deserted. Between 1948 and 2012, excavations unearthed evidence of a 30-household community, with two manors and the remains of a medieval church. There is also a millpond with beautiful wild flowers in spring. Wharram Percy is set in a pretty valley, signposted off the B1248 from Burdale, in the heart of the Yorkshire Wolds. About 20 minutes' walk from the car park, it is an ideal picnic stop.

❷❺ Burton Agnes

On A614, near Driffield, East Yorkshire. **Tel** 01262 490324. 🚆 Driffield then bus. **Open** Apr–Oct: daily. 🅿 ♿ limited. 🖥 📷 **W** burtonagnes.com

Of all the grand houses in this area, Burton Agnes Hall is a firm favourite. This is partly because the attractive, red-brick Elizabethan mansion has such a homely atmosphere. One of the first portraits you see in the Small Hall is of Anne Griffith, whose father, Sir Henry, built the house. There is a monument to him in the local church.

Burton Agnes has remained in the hands of the original family and has changed little since it was built, between 1598 and 1610. Visitors enter by the turreted gatehouse, and the entrance hall has a fine Elizabethan alabaster chimney piece. The massive oak staircase is an impressive example of woodcarving from the era.

In the library is a collection of Impressionist and Post-Impressionist art, pleasantly out of character with the rest of the house, including works by André Derain, Renoir and Augustus John. The extensive grounds include a purpose-built play area for children.

❷❻ Bempton Cliffs and Flamborough Head

East Yorkshire. 🚆 Bempton. 🚌 Bridlington. 🛈 Bempton Cliffs Visitor Centre (01262 422212). 🅿 **W** rspb.org.uk

Bempton, which consists of 5 miles (8 km) of steep chalk cliffs between Speeton and Flamborough Head, is the largest breeding seabird colony in England, and is famous for its puffins. The ledges and fissures provide ideal nest-sites for more than 100,000 pairs of

Nesting gannet on the chalk cliffs at Bempton

birds. Today, eight different species, including skinny black shags and kittiwakes, thrive on the Grade I listed *(see p622)* Bempton cliffs. Bempton is the only mainland site of the goose-sized gannet, known for their dramatic fishing techniques. May, June and July are the best bird-watching months.

The spectacular cliffs are best seen from the north side of the Flamborough Head peninsula.

❷ Beverley

East Yorkshire. 🅰 30,000.
🚊 34 Butcher Row (01482 391672).
🛒 Sat. 🆆 **visithullandeast yorkshire.com**

The history of Beverley dates back to the 8th century, when Old Beverley served as a retreat for John, later Bishop of York, who was canonized for his healing powers. Over the centuries Beverley grew as a medieval sanctuary town. Like York, it is an attractive combination of both medieval and Georgian buildings.

The best way to enter Beverley is through the last of five medieval town gates, the

Said to be the inspiration for Lewis Carroll's White Rabbit, St Mary's Church

castellated North Bar (rebuilt 1409–10). The bars were constructed so that market goods had to pass through them and a toll paid.

The skyline is dominated by the twin towers of the magnificent **Beverley Minster**, the resting place of St John of Beverley. The decorated nave is the earliest surviving part of the building, dating back to the early 1300s. It is famous for its 16th-century choirstalls and 68 misericords *(see p345)*.

The minster contains many early detailed stone carvings, including a set of four from about 1308 that illustrate figures with ailments such as toothache and lumbago. On the north side of the altar is the richly carved 14th-century Gothic Percy tomb, thought to be that of Lady Idoine Percy.

Also on the north side is the Fridstol, or Peace Chair, said to date from 924–39, the time of Athelstan. Anyone who sat on it would be granted 30 days' sanctuary. Within the North Bar, **St Mary's Church** has a 13th-century chancel and houses Britain's largest number of medieval stone carvings

Minstrel Pillar in St Mary's Church

of musical instruments. The brightly painted 16th-century Minstrel Pillar is particularly notable. Painted on the panelled chancel ceiling are portraits of monarchs after 1445. On the richly sculpted doorway of St Michael's Chapel is the grinning pilgrim rabbit said to have inspired Lewis Carroll's White Rabbit in *Alice in Wonderland*.

There is a great day out to be had at **Beverley Races**, which holds various theme days throughout the season. Visitors can also enjoy excellent food and drink.

🔼 **Beverley Minster**
Minster Yard. Tel 01482 868540.
Open daily. 🚻 🛒 🅿 🏰
🆆 beverleyminster.org.uk

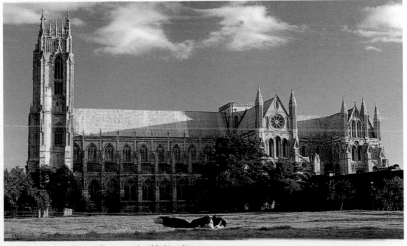
Beverley Minster, one of Europe's finest examples of Gothic architecture

㉘ Burton Constable

Nr Hull, East Yorkshire. **Tel** 01964 562400.
🚆 Hull then taxi. **Open** Easter–Oct:
daily. 🔊 🅿 ♿ 🖥 📷 Ⓦ burton
constable.com

The Constable family have
been landowners since the 13th
century, and have lived at Burton
Constable Hall since work began
on it in 1570. It is an Elizabethan
house, altered in the 18th
century by Thomas Lightholer,
Thomas Atkinson and James
Wyatt. Today, its 30 rooms
include Georgian and Victorian
interiors. It has a fine collection
of Chippendale furniture and
family portraits dating from
the 16th century. Most of the
collections of prints, textiles
and drawings belong to Leeds
City Art Galleries. The family
still lives in the south wing.

Painting of Burton Constable (c.1690) by an anonymous artist

The Prince's Dock in Kingston upon
Hull's restored docks area

㉙ Kingston upon Hull

East Yorkshire. 🏠 260,000. 🚆 🚌
🚍 ℹ 1 Paragon St (01482 223559).
🛍 Mon–Sat. Ⓦ visithullandeast
yorkshire.com

There is a lot more to Hull than
the heritage of a thriving fishing
industry. The restored town
centre docks are attractive,
and Hull's Old Town, laid out in
medieval times, is all cobbled,
winding streets and quaintly
askew red-brick houses. You
can follow the "Seven Seas" Fish
Trail, a path of inlaid metal fishes
on the city's pavements that
illustrates the many different
varieties that have been landed
in Hull, from anchovy to shark.
In Victoria Square is the
Maritime Museum. Built in

1871 as the offices of the Hull
Dock Company, it traces the
city's maritime history. Among
its exhibits are an ornate whale-
bone and vertebrae bench and
a display of complicated rope
knots, such as the Eye Splice
and the Midshipman's Hitch.

Housed in an imposing
Elizabethan building, **Hands
on History** explores Hull's story
through a collection of some
of its families' artifacts.

In the heart of the Old
Town, the **William Wilberforce
House** is one of the surviving
examples of the High Street's
merchants' dwellings. Its first-
floor oak-panelled rooms
date from the 17th century.
As well as examining the
transatlantic slave trade
and contemporary forms of
slavery, exhibits cover West

African culture and the
Wilberforce family.

Nearby is the **Streetlife
Museum of Transport**, Hull's
most popular and noisiest
museum, loved by children. It
features Britain's oldest tramcar.
At the mouth of the River Hull,
The Deep is the world's only
"submarium", in a stunning
building and dramatic setting.
With lots of exciting sea life
and state-of-the-art technology,
it is ideal for families.

🏛 **Maritime Museum**
Queen Victoria Sq. **Tel** 01482 300300.
Open daily (Sun: pm). ♿ 📷
Ⓦ hullcc.gov.uk

🏛 **Hands on History**
South Churchside. **Tel** 01482 300300.
Open 2nd & 4th Sat each month.
Closed 1 Jan, 24–28 Dec. ♿ 📷
Ⓦ hullcc.gov.uk

William Wilberforce (1758–1833)

William Wilberforce, born in Hull to a merchant family, was a natural
orator. After studying Classics at Cambridge, he entered politics
and in 1784 gave one of his
first public addresses in York.
The audience was captivated,
and Wilberforce realized the
potential of his powers of
persuasion. From 1785
onwards, adopted by the Pitt
government as spokesman
for the abolition of slavery,
he conducted a determined
and conscientious campaign.
But his speeches won him
enemies, and in 1792, threats
from a slave-importer meant
that he needed a constant
armed guard. In 1807 his bill
to abolish the lucrative slave
trade became law.

A 19th-century engraving of Wilberforce
by J Jenkins

🏛 **William Wilberforce House**
High St, Hull. **Tel** 01482 300300.
Open daily (Sun: pm only). ♿ ltd. 📷

🏛 **Streetlife Museum of Transport**
High St, Hull. **Tel** 01482 300300.
Open daily (Sun: pm only). ♿ 📷

🐟 **The Deep**
Hull (via Citadel Way). **Tel** 01482
381000. **Open** daily. **Closed** 24 & 25
Dec. 💷 ♿ 🖥 📷 🅿 🌐 thedeep.
co.uk

③⓪ Holderness and Spurn Head

East Yorkshire. 🚆 Hull (Paragon St)
then bus. 🛈 11–17 Newbegin,
Hornsea (01964 536404).

This curious flat area east of
Hull, with straight roads and
delicately waving fields of oats
and barley, in many ways
resembles Holland, except that
its windmills are mostly disused.
Beaches stretch for 30 miles
(46 km) along the coastline.
The main resort towns are
Withernsea and **Hornsea**.

The Holderness landscape
only exists because of erosion
higher up the coast. The sea
washes down tiny bits of rock
which gradually accumulate.
Around 1560, it had begun
to form a sandbank, and by
1669 it was large enough to
be colonized as Sunke Sand.
The last bits of silting mud
and debris joined the island
to the mainland as recently as
the 1830s. Today, you can drive
through the eerie, lush wilderness of Sunk Island on the way
east to Spurn Head. This is
located at the tip of the Spurn

Peninsula, a 3.5-mile (6-km) spit
of land that has also built up as
the result of coastal erosion
elsewhere. Flora, fauna and
birdlife have been protected
here by the Yorkshire Wildlife
Trust since 1960. Walking here
gives the unnerving feeling that
the land could be eroded from
under your feet at any time. A
surprise discovery at the end of
Spurn Head is a tiny community
of pilots and lifeboat crew,
constantly on call to guide ships
into the Humber estuary or help
cope with disasters.

Fishing boat at Grimsby's National
Fishing Heritage Centre

③① Grimsby

NE Lincolnshire. 🏠 88,000. 🚆 🚌
🛈 Grimsby Fishing Heritage Centre
(01472 323111). 🌐 cleethorpes
touristboard.co.uk

Perched at the mouth of the
River Humber, according to
legend Grimsby was founded
in the 9th century by a Danish

fisherman by the name of Grim.
It rose to prominence in the
19th century as one of the
world's largest fishing ports.
Its first dock was opened in
1800 and, with the arrival of
the railways, the town secured
the means of transporting its
catch all over the country. Even
though the traditional fishing
industry had declined by the
1970s, dock area redevelopment
has ensured that Grimsby's
unique heritage is retained.

This is best demonstrated by
the award-winning **Grimsby
Fishing Heritage Centre**, a
museum that recreates the
industry in its 1950s heyday,
capturing the atmosphere of
the period. Visitors sign on as
crew members on a trawler and,
by means of vivid interactive
displays, travel from the back
streets of Grimsby to the Arctic
fishing grounds. On the way,
they can experience the roll
of the ship, the smell of the
fish and the heat of the engine.
The tour ends with a look at
the restored 1950s trawler,
the *Ross Tiger*.

Other attractions in Grimsby
include the shopping street
Abbeygate, a market and a
wide selection of restaurants.
Nearby seaside resorts of
Cleethorpes, Mablethorpe
and Skegness offer miles
of golden sands.

🏛 **Grimsby Fishing Heritage Centre**
Heritage Sq, Alexandra Dock.
Tel 01472 323345. **Open** Tue–Sun.
Closed 1 Jan, 25 & 26 Dec. 💷 📷
♿ 🖥 📷 🌐 nelincs.gov.uk

Isolated lighthouse at Spurn Head, at the tip of Spurn Peninsula

② Street-by-Street: York

The city of York has retained so much of its medieval structure that walking into its centre is like entering a living museum. Many of the ancient timbered houses, perched on narrow, winding streets, such as the Shambles, are protected by a conservation order and much of the centre is pedestrianized. It is close to the railway station which is served by trains from all over the country. The city's strategic position led to its development as a railway centre in the 19th century.

★ York Minster
England's largest medieval church was begun in 1220 *(see pp412–13).*

Stonegate
The medieval red devil is a feature of this street, built over a Roman road.

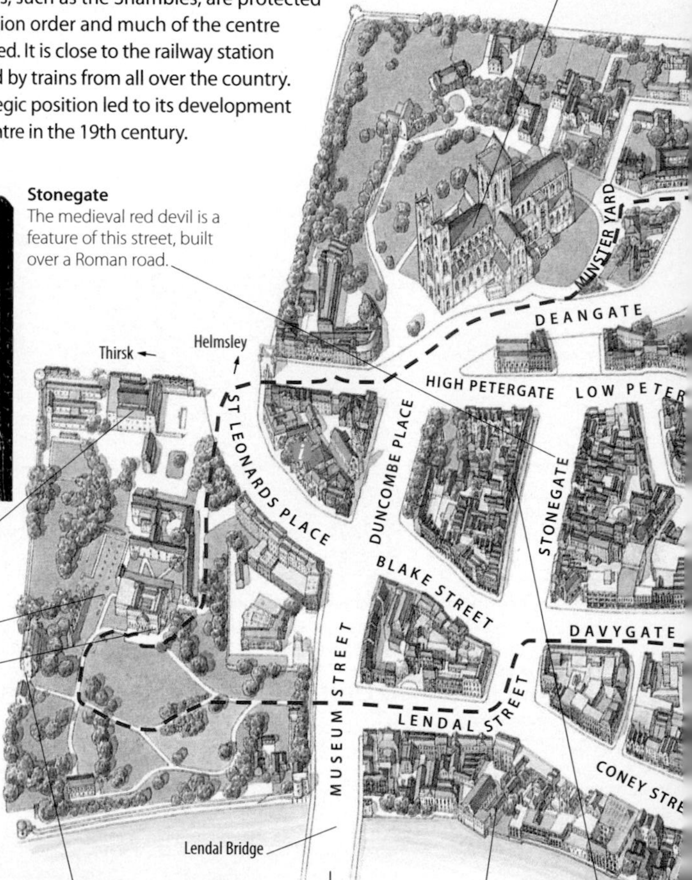

Thirsk ←

Helmsley ↑

DEANGATE

HIGH PETERGATE   LOW PETER

ST LEONARDS PLACE

DUNCOMBE PLACE

BLAKE STREET

STONEGATE

DAVYGATE

MUSEUM STREET

LENDAL STREET

CONEY STRE

York Art Gallery

St Mary's Abbey

Yorkshire Museum is home to some of the most fascinating archaeological finds in the country *(see p410).*

Lendal Bridge

↓
Railway station, long-distance coach stop, National Railway Museum, and Leeds

OUSE

Ye Old Starre Inne is one of the oldest pubs in York.

St Olave's Church
The 11th-century church, next to the gatehouse of St Mary's Abbey *(see pp354–5),* was founded by the Earl of Northumbria in memory of St Olaf, King of Norway. To the left of the church is the Chapel of St Mary on the Walls.

Guildhall
The 15th-century Guildhall, situated beside the River Ouse and rebuilt after bomb damage during World War II, has on its roof this two-headed roof boss.

For hotels and restaurants in this area see p570 and pp597–8

★ Jorvik Viking Centre
The many artifacts on show here illustrate the time when York was a strategic Viking town *(see p410)*. The street names ending in "gate" come from the Danish word *gata*, meaning "street" or "way".

VISITORS' CHECKLIST

Practical Information
York. 205,000. 1 Museum St (01904 550099). Association of Voluntary Guides to the City of York (from Exhibition Sq): Apr–Oct: 10:15am & 2:15pm daily (Jun–Aug: also 6:15pm); Nov–Mar: 10:15am & 1:15pm daily. daily. Jorvik Festival: Feb; Early Music Festival: Jul. avgyork.co.uk visityork.org

Transport
Leeds Bradford, 32 miles (50 km) NW. Station Rd. Station Rd.

WHIP·MA·WHOP·MA·GATE

Whip-ma-whop-ma-gate
York's tiniest street has the city's longest name, which dates from Saxon times and means "neither one thing nor the other".

Merchant Adventurer's Hall, built for a guild in the 14th century, is popular with visitors.

★ York Castle Museum
Converted from two prisons, this museum *(see p410)* features Kirkgate, a Victorian street, and the cell formerly used by highwayman Dick Turpin (1706–39).

Holy Trinity Church

King's Square

Monk Bar

Scarborough

Hull

Clifford's Tower *(see p411)*

Fairfax House *(see p410)*

0 metres 100
0 yards 100

Key
— Suggested route

Exploring York

York's appeal is a result of its many layers of history. A medieval city constructed on top of a Roman one, it was first built in AD 71 as capital of the northern province and was known as Eboracum. It was here that Constantine the Great was made emperor in 306, and reorganized Britain into four provinces. A hundred years later, the Roman army had withdrawn. Eboracum was renamed Eoforwic, under the Saxons, and then became a Christian stronghold. The Danish street names are a reminder that it was a Viking centre from 867, one of Europe's chief trading bases. Between 1100 and 1500 it was England's second city. A highlight in York is the minster (see pp412–13) and the city also boasts 18 medieval churches, 3-mile (4.8-km) long medieval city walls, elegant Jacobean and Georgian architecture and fine museums.

Grand staircase and fine plaster ceiling at Fairfax House

🏛 York Castle Museum

The Eye of York. **Tel** 01904 687687.
Open daily. **Closed** 1 Jan, 25 & 26 Dec.
🅿 ♿ ground floor only. 🔲 📷
🖳 yorkcastlemuseum.org.uk

Housed in two 18th-century prisons, the museum has a fine collection of social history, started by Dr John Kirk of the market town of Pickering. Opened in 1938, its period displays include a Jacobean dining room, a moorland cottage, and a 1950s front room. It also contains an exhibition on the traditions of birth, marriages and death in Britain from 1700 to 2000.

The most famous exhibits include the reconstructed Victorian street of Kirkgate, complete with shopfronts, and the Anglo-Saxon York Helmet, discovered in 1982.

🏛 Jorvik Viking Centre

Coppergate. **Tel** 01904 615505.
Open daily (booking advised).
Closed 24–26 Dec. 🅿 ♿ ring first.
📷 🖳 jorvik-viking-centre.co.uk

This centre is built on the site of the original Viking settlement which archaeologists uncovered at Coppergate. Using new technology, and remains and artifacts from the site, a dynamic vision of 10th-century York is recreated, bringing the Viking world to life. The centre's galleries contain many more fascinating artifacts, from earrings to frying pans, and visitors may handle a few. There is also a display telling the stories of the archaeologists who worked on the site in the 1970s. At the centre's sister attraction, DIG, visitors can take part in an archaeological excavation.

🏛 Yorkshire Museum and St Mary's Abbey

Museum Gardens. **Tel** 01904 687687.
Open daily. 🅿 ♿ 📷
🖳 yorkshiremuseum.org.uk

Yorkshire Museum made the news when it purchased the 15th-century Middleham Jewel for £2.5 million, one of the finest pieces of English Gothic jewellery found this century. Other exhibits include 2nd-century Roman mosaics and an Anglo-Saxon silver gilt bowl. Part of the museum stands in the ruined Benedictine St Mary's Abbey (see pp354–5), a Grade I-listed building.

🚪 Fairfax House

Castlegate. **Tel** 01904 655543.
Open mid-Feb–Dec: daily (Sun: pm only; Mon: tours only). **Closed** Jan–early Feb, 24–26 Dec. 📷 📷 ♿ ltd.
📷 🖳 fairfaxhouse.co.uk

From 1755 to 1762 Viscount Fairfax built this fine Georgian town house for his daughter, Anne. The house was designed by John Carr (see p32), and between 1920 and 1965 it was a cinema and dancehall. It was restored in the 1980s. Today, visitors can see the bedroom of Anne Fairfax (1725–93), and a fine collection of 18th-century furniture, porcelain and clocks.

🏛 National Railway Museum

Leeman Rd. **Tel** 0844 815 3139.
Open daily. **Closed** 24–26 Dec.
♿ 🔲 📷 📷 nrm.org.uk

In what is the world's largest railway museum, nearly 200 years of history are explored using a variety of

Reproduction of Stephenson's *Rocket* (right) and an 1830s first-class carriage in York's National Railway Museum

For hotels and restaurants in this area see p570 and pp597–8

visual aids. Visitors can try wheel-tapping and shunting in the interactive gallery, or find out what made Stephenson's *Rocket* so successful. Exhibits include uniforms, rolling stock from 1797 onwards and Queen Victoria's Royal Train carriage, as well as the very latest rail innovations.

Monk Bar

This is one of York's finest original medieval gates, situated at the end of Goodramgate. It is vaulted on three floors, and the portcullis still works. In the Middle Ages, the rooms above it were rented out, and it was a prison in the 16th century. Its decorative details include men holding stones ready to drop on intruders.

Preparing for a Fancy Dress Ball (1833) by William Etty, York Art Gallery

York Art Gallery

Exhibition Sq. **Tel** 01904 687687. **Open** daily. **W** yorkartgallery.org.uk

This Italianate building of 1879 holds a wide-ranging collection of paintings from western Europe dating from the early 1500s onwards. There is also a large, internationally significant collection of British and foreign studio ceramics. Work by Bernard Leach, William Staite Murray and Shoji Hamada is on display alongside details of the potters themselves and those who collected their work.

In a major redevelopment in 2015, the gallery was expanded to host international shows. The Artists Garden was opened as part of the expansion and hosts contemporary art exhibits.

Clifford's Tower, which was formerly the keep of York Castle

Clifford's Tower

Clifford's St. **Tel** 01904 646940. **Open** daily. **Closed** 1 Jan, 24–26 Dec. **EH** **W** english-heritage. org.uk

William the Conqueror's original wooden castle, sited here, was heavily damaged in 1069. The scene of anti-Jewish riots in 1190, the present tower dates back to the 13th century. Built by Henry III, it was named after the de Clifford family, who were constables of the castle. From the top of the tower there are stunning panoramic views over the city.

DIG – An Archaeological Adventure

St Saviourgate. **Tel** 01904 615505. **Open** daily (book in advance). **Closed** 24 & 25 Dec. **W** digyork.com

Housed in a the restored medieval St Saviour Church, this centre invites visitors to become archaeological detectives and discover how archaeologists have pieced together clues from the past to unravel the history of the Viking age in York.

Merchant Adventurers' Hall

Fossgate. **Tel** 01904 654818. **Open** Mar–Oct: daily; Nov–Feb: Mon–Sat. **Closed** 24 Dec–3 Jan. **W** theyorkcompany.co.uk

Built by a guild of Yorkshire merchants in 1357, this is one of the largest timber-framed medieval buildings in Britain. The Great Hall is probably the best example of its kind in Europe. Among its paintings is an unattributed 17th-century copy of Van Dyck's portrait of Charles I's queen, Henrietta Maria. Below the Great Hall is the hospital, which was used by the guild until 1900, and a private chapel.

Timbered interior of the Merchant Adventurers' Hall

York Minster

The largest medieval Gothic cathedral north of the Alps, and seat of the Archbishop of York, York Minster is 158 m (519 ft) long and 76 m (249 ft) wide across the transepts. It is also home to the largest collection of medieval stained glass in Britain. The word "minster" refers to a missionary teaching church in Anglo-Saxon times. The first minster began as a wooden chapel where King Edwin of Northumbria was baptized in 627. There have been several cathedrals on or near the site, including an 11th-century Norman structure. The present minster was begun in 1220 and completed 250 years later. In 1984, fire damage led to a £2.25 million restoration programme.

Central Tower
This lantern tower was reconstructed in 1420–65 (after partial collapse in 1405) from a design by the master stonemason William Colchester.

South transept entrance

KEY

① **Great East Window**

② **The Quire** has a vaulted entrance with a 15th-century boss of the Assumption of the Virgin.

③ **The 16th-century rose window**

④ **The western towers**, with their 15th-century decorative panelling and elaborate pinnacles, contrast with the simpler design of the north transept. The southwest tower is the minster belfry.

⑤ **West Window**

⑥ **Great West Door**

⑦ **The Nave**, begun in 1291, was severely damaged by fire in 1840. Rebuilding costs were heavy, but it was reopened with a new set of bells in 1844.

★ **Chapter House**
A Latin inscription near the entrance of the wooden-vaulted Chapter House (1260–85) reads: "As the rose is the flower of flowers, so this is the house of houses".

★ **Choir Screen**
Sited between the choir and the nave, this 15th-century stone screen depicts kings of England from William I to Henry VI, and has a canopy of angels.

The Stained Glass of York Minster

York Minster houses the largest collection of medieval stained glass in Britain, some of it dating from the late 12th century. The glass was generally coloured during production, using metal oxides to produce the desired colour, then worked on by craftsmen on site. When a design had been produced, the glass was first cut, then trimmed to shape. Details were painted on with iron oxide-based paint, which was fused to the glass by firing in a kiln. Individual pieces were then leaded together to form the finished window. Part of the fascination of the minster glass is its variety of subject matter. Some windows were paid for by lay donors who specified a particular subject, others reflect ecclesiastical patronage.

Miracle of St Nicholas
(late 12th century) was put in the nave over 100 years after it was made. It shows a Jew's conversion to Christianity.

St John Glimpses God in Majesty
depicts St John gazing through a trapdoor into heaven. God is set in a mandorla, illuminated by lamps.

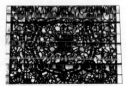

The Five Sisters in the north transept are the largest examples of *grisaille* glass in Britain. This popular 3th-century technique involved creating fine patterning on clear glass and decorating it with black enamel.

St John Sailing to Patmos illustrates the saint's exile to the Greek island where he had several visions. Much original glass is preserved in this piece.

St John the Evangelist, in part of the Great West Window (c.1338), is an example of stickwork, where paint is scraped off to reveal clear glass.

The impressive façade of York Minster in the city centre

㉝ Harewood House

Leeds. **Tel** 0113 218 1010. Leeds then bus. **Open** Apr–Oct: daily. by arrangement.
harewood.org

Designed by John Carr in 1759, Harewood House is the Yorkshire home of the Earl and Countess of Harewood.

The grand Palladian exterior is impressive; the interiors were created by Robert Adam and feature an unrivalled collection of 18th-century furniture made specifically for Harewood by Yorkshire-born Thomas Chippendale (1711–79). There are paintings by Italian and English artists, including Reynolds and Gainsborough, and a vast collection of watercolours.

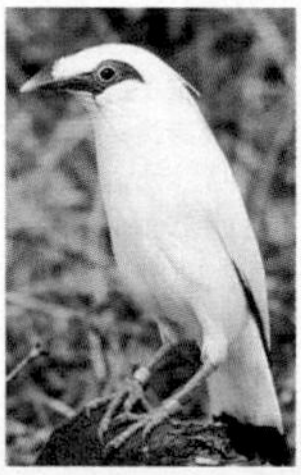
Bali starling, one of Harewood's rare birds

The grounds by "Capability" Brown *(see p30)* include the **Harewood Bird Garden**, a great place for spotting a variety of species that live, breed or visit the area.

㉞ Leeds

Leeds. 775,000.
Headrow (0113 378 6977).
Mon–Sat. **visitleeds.co.uk**

The third largest of Britain's provincial cities, Leeds was at its most prosperous during the Victorian period. An impressive legacy from this era is a series of ornate, covered shopping arcades. Also of note is the **town hall**, designed by Cuthbert Brodrick and opened by Queen Victoria in 1858.

Today, although Leeds is primarily an industrial city, it also boasts a thriving cultural scene. Productions at **The Grand** by Opera North, one of Britain's top operatic companies, are of a superb quality.

The **Leeds Art Gallery** has impressive collections of British 20th-century art and of Victorian paintings, including works by local artist Atkinson Grimshaw (1836–93). Among the late 19th-century French art are works by Signac, Courbet and Sisley. The Henry Moore Institute, added in 1993, is devoted to sculpture from all periods. It comprises a study centre, library, galleries and an archive of material on Moore and other sculptural pioneers.

Housed in a 19th-century woollen mill, the **Armley Mills Museum** explores the industrial heritage of Leeds. Filled with original equipment, recorded sounds and models in 19th-century workers' clothes, it traces the history of the ready-to-wear industry.

The **Leeds City Museum** charts the history of Leeds with ethnographical and archaeological exhibits.

A striking waterfront development by the River Aire has attracted two museums. The **Royal Armouries Museum** is the UK's national museum of arms and armour, home to a vast array of weaponry from around the world. The **Thackray Medical Museum** is an interactive display of medical advances, from a recreated Victorian slum to modern-day challenges.

Aimed at children, **Tropical World** features crystal pools, a rainforest house, butterflies and tropical fish. It's about 3 miles (5 km) northeast of Leeds city centre. There's even more space to let off steam in the huge adjacent Roundhay Park. There is also a farm and a Rare Breeds centre in the grounds of the Tudor-Jacobean **Temple Newsam House**, which has major art and furniture collections inside.

The Grand Theatre
46 New Briggate. **Tel** 0844 848 2700.
leedsgrandtheatre.com

Leeds Art Gallery
The Headrow. **Tel** 0113 247 8256. **Open** Tue–Sun (Sun: pm only). **Closed** public hols.
leedsartgallery.co.uk

Armley Mills Museum
Canal Rd, Armley. **Tel** 0113 378 3173. **Open** Tue–Sun (Sun: pm only), public hols. **Closed** 1 Jan, 25 & 26 Dec.

Leeds City Museum
Millennium Sq. **Tel** 0113 378 5001. **Open** Tue–Sun & public hols.

Royal Armouries
Armouries Drive. **Tel** 0113 220 1999. **Open** daily. **Closed** 24–26 Dec.
royalarmouries.org

Thackray Medical Museum
Beckett St. **Tel** 0113 244 4343. **Open** daily. **Closed** 1 Jan, 24–26 & 31 Dec.
thackraymuseum.org

Tropical World
Canal Gdns, Princes Ave. **Tel** 0113 3957400. **Open** daily. **Closed** 25 & 26 Dec. **roundhaypark.org.uk**

Temple Newsam House
Off A63. **Tel** 0113 336 7461. **Open** Tue–Sun. **Closed** Jan, 25 & 26 Dec.

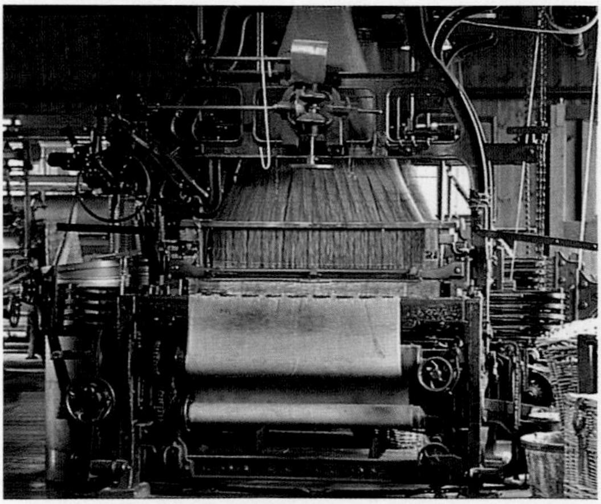
Working loom at the Armley Mills Museum in Leeds

The Other Side (1990–93) by David Hockney, at Bradford's 1853 Gallery in Saltaire

⑤ Bradford

Bradford. ▨ 530,000. ✈ ≋ 🚌
ℹ️ Britannia House, Broadway
(01274 433678). 🛍 Mon–Sat.
🌐 visitbradford.com

In the 16th century, Bradford was a thriving market town, and the opening of its canal in 1774 boosted trade. By 1850, it was the world's capital for worsted (fabric made from closely twisted wool) Many of the city's well-preserved civic and Industrial buildings date from this period, such as the Wool Exchange on Market Street. In the 1800s a number of German textile manufacturers settled in what is now called Little Germany. Their houses are characterized by decorative stone carvings that demonstrated the wealth and standing of the occupants. Another striking tribute to all this wealth is the **Undercliffe Cemetery**, which opened high above the city in 1854 to become a maze of finely decorated obelisks, extravagant mausoleums and giant columns.

The **National Media Museum**, founded in 1983, explores the history of photography, television, gaming, the internet and much more. Interactive television galleries let visitors operate cameras "on set" and read the news; fans of gaming can play on classic arcade machines and consoles

The museum also has three cinemas, including an IMAX screen, and holds two film festivals each year.

The **Cartwright Hall Art Gallery** displays 19th- and 20th-century British art and collections of contemporary art from South Asia. **Bradford Industrial Museum** is housed in an original spinning mill Mill machinery is on display and visitors can also ride on a horse-drawn tram. Saltaire, a Victorian industrial village *(see p353)*, is on the outskirts of the city. Created by Sir Titus Salt for his Salts Mill workers, it was completed in 1873. **Salts Mill** now contains a fascinating exhibition that explores Saltaire's history, while the **1853 Gallery** has the world's largest collection of works by David Hockney, born in Bradford.

🏛 **Undercliffe Cemetery**
127 Undercliffe Lane. **Tel** 01274 642276. **Open** daily. ♿
🌐 undercliffecemetery.co.uk

🏛 **National Media Museum**
Pictureville. **Tel** 0844 8563797.
Open daily. **Closed** 24–26 Dec.
♿ 🅿 📷 🌐 nationalmedia
museum.org.uk

🏛 **Cartwright Hall Art Gallery**
Lister Park. **Tel** 01274 431212.
Open Tue–Sun & public hols. **Closed** Good Fri, 25 & 26 Dec. ♿ 🅿 📷

🏛 **Bradford Industrial Museum**
Moorside Mills, Moorside Rd.
Tel 01274 435900. **Open** Tue–Sun & public hols. **Closed** Good Fri, 25 & 26 Dec. ♿ 📷 🌐 bradford
museums.org

🏛 **Salts Mill and The 1853 Gallery**
Salts Mill, Victoria Rd. **Tel** 01274 531163. **Open** daily. **Closed** 1 Jan, 25 & 26 Dec. ♿ 🅿 🖥 📷
🌐 saltsmill.org.uk

Bradford's Asian Community

Immigrants from the Indian subcontinent originally came to Bradford in the 1950s to work in the mills, but with the decline of the textile industry many began small businesses. By the mid-1970s there were 1,400 such enterprises in the area. Almost one fifth were in the food sector, born out of simple cafés catering for millworkers whose families were far away. As Indian food became more popular, these restaurants thrived, and today there are over 200 in the city serving the spiced dishes of the Indian subcontinent.

A typical Indian curry

Haworth Parsonage, home to the Brontë family, now a museum

㊱ Haworth

Bradford. 🚗 6,400. 🚆 Keighley.
🛈 2–4 West Lane (01535 642329).
🌐 haworth-village.org.uk

The setting of Haworth, in bleak Pennine moorland dotted with farmsteads, has changed little since it was home to the Brontë family. The village boomed in the 1840s, when there were more than 1,200 hand-looms in operation, but it is more famous today for the Brontë connection.

You can visit the **Brontë Parsonage Museum**, home from 1820 to 1861 to novelists Charlotte, Emily and Anne, their brother Branwell and their father, the Reverend Patrick Brontë. Built in 1778–9, the house remains decorated as it was during the 1850s. Eleven rooms, including the children's study and Charlotte's room, display letters, manuscripts, furniture and personal objects.

The nostalgic Victorian **Keighley and Worth Valley Railway** runs from Keighley to Oxenhope and stops at Ingrow West, Damems, Oakworth and Haworth. Parts of *The Railway Children* (1970) were filmed at Oakworth station and the carriages used in the film can be seen at the excellent Rail Story museum at Ingrow West station.

🏛 **Brontë Parsonage Museum**
Church St. **Tel** 01535 642323.
Open daily. **Closed** 24–27 Dec. 🎟
♿ limited. 📷 🌐 bronte.org.uk

Charlotte Brontë's childhood story book, written for her sister, Anne

The Brontë Sisters

Charlotte Brontë (1816–55)

During a harsh, motherless childhood, Charlotte, Emily and Anne retreated into fictional worlds of their own, writing poems and stories. As adults, they had to work as governesses, but still published a poetry collection in 1846. Only two copies were sold, but in the following year Charlotte's *Jane Eyre* became a bestseller, arousing interest in Emily's *Wuthering Heights* and Anne's *Agnes Grey*. After her siblings' deaths in 1848–9, Charlotte published her last novel, *Villette*, in 1852. She married the Reverend Nicholls, her father's curate, in 1854, but died shortly afterwards.

㊲ Hebden Bridge

Calderdale. 🚗 4,500. 🚆 🛈 Butler's Wharf (01422 843831). 🅿 Thu.
🌐 visitcalderdale.com

Hebden Bridge is a delightful South Pennines former mill town, surrounded by steep hills and former 19th-century mills. The houses seem to defy gravity as they cling to the valley sides. Due to the gradient, some houses are made from two bottom floors, and the top two floors form another unit. To separate ownership of these "flying freeholds", an Act of Parliament was devised.

There is a superb view of Hebden Bridge from nearby **Heptonstall**, where the poet Sylvia Plath (1932–63) is buried. The village contains a Wesleyan chapel (1764).

㊳ Halifax

Calderdale. 🚗 82,000. 🚆 🚌
🛈 Northgate (01422 368725).
🅿 Thu–Sat. 🌐 visitcalderdale.com

Halifax's history has been influenced by textiles since the Middle Ages, but today's visual reminders date mainly from the 19th century: stone-built terraced housing and several fine buildings. The wool trade helped to make the Pennines into Britain's industrial backbone.

Until the mid-15th century cloth production was modest, but vital enough to contribute towards the creation of the 13th-century Gibbet Law, which stated that anyone caught stealing cloth could be executed. There is a replica of the gibbet, a forerunner of the guillotine, at the bottom of Gibbet Street. Many of Halifax's 18th- and 19th-century buildings owe their existence to wealthy cloth traders. Sir Charles Barry (1795–1860), architect of the Houses of Parliament, was commissioned by the Crossley family to design the Town Hall. They also paid for the landscaping of the People's Park by the creator of the Crystal Palace, Sir Joseph Paxton (1801–65). Thomas Bradley's

Large Two Forms (1966–9) by Henry Moore at Yorkshire Sculpture Park

18th-century **Piece Hall** was where wool merchants once sold their cloth, trading in one of the 315 "Merchants' Rooms". It has a beautifully restored Italianate courtyard where Halifax's market takes place.

Eureka! is the hands-on National Children's Museum, with exhibits such as the Giant Mouth Machine. **Shibden Hall Museum** is a fine period house, parts of which date to the 15th century.

Environs
The nearby village of **Sowerby Bridge** was an important textile centre from the Middle Ages to the 1960s. Today visitors come to enjoy the scenic canals.

🏛 **Eureka!**
Discovery Rd. **Tel** 01422 330069.
Open Tue–Sun (daily in school hols).
Closed 24–26 Dec. 🖼 🔕 💻
W eureka.org.uk

🏛 **Shibden Hall Museum**
Listers Rd. **Tel** 01422 352246. **Open** Mar–Oct: Sat–Thu; Nov & Dec: Sat–Tue; Jan & Feb: Sat & Sun. **Closed** 24 Dec–2 Jan. 🖼 🏠 💻

㊳ National Coal Mining Museum
Wakefield. **Tel** 01924 848806.
🚆 Wakefield then bus. **Open** daily (last tour 3:15pm – booking advised). Children under 5 not allowed underground. **Closed** 1 Jan, 24–26 Dec. 🖼 🔕 💻 🏠 W ncm.org.uk

Housed in the old Caphouse Colliery, this museum offers the chance to go into a real mine shaft: warm clothing is advised.

An underground tour takes you 137 m (450 ft) down, equipped with a hat and a miner's lamp. Enter narrow seams and see lgas detectors and industrial machines. Displays depict mining from 1820 to the present day.

㊵ Yorkshire Sculpture Park
Wakefield. **Tel** 01924 832631.
🚆 Wakefield then bus. **Open** daily.
Closed 24, 25 & 29–31 Dec. 🔕 💻 🏠
W ysp.co.uk

This is one of Europe's leading open-air galleries: 200 ha (500 acres) of 18th-century parkland dotted with a changing exhibition of the work of Henry Moore, Anthony Caro, Eduardo Chillida, Barbara Hepworth, Antony Gormley and others. The indoor spaces include the ambitious visitor centre, which leads on to the stunning Underground Gallery exhibition space.

㊶ Magna
Rotherham. **Tel** 01709 720002.
🚆 Rotherham Central or Sheffield then bus. **Open** daily. **Closed** 1 Jan, 24–26 & 31 Dec. 🖼 🔕 ✂ 💻 🏠
W visitmagna.co.uk

A former steel works has been imaginatively converted into a huge science adventure centre, with an emphasis on interactive exhibits, noise and spectacle designed to appeal to 4- to 15-year-olds. In the Air, Fire, Water and Earth Pavilions visitors can get close to a tornado, operate real diggers or discover what it's like to detonate a rock face. There are also multi-media displays on the lives of steelworkers and on how a giant furnace operated, as well as a show that features robots with artificial intelligence that evolve and learn as they hunt each other down. There are also two large outdoor areas – Sci-tek, a playground with slides and trampolines, and Aqua-tek (summer only), a water play area.

The Face of Steel display at Magna

NORTHUMBRIA

Northumberland · County Durham

England's northeast is a tapestry of moorland, ruins, castles, cathedrals and delightful villages. With Northumberland National Park and Kielder Water reservoir to the north, a rugged eastern coastline, and the cities of Newcastle and Durham to the south, the area combines a dramatic history with abundant natural beauty.

The empty peaceful hills, rich wildlife and panoramic vistas of Northumberland National Park belie the area's turbulent past. Warring Scots and English, skirmishing tribes, cattle drovers and whisky smugglers have all left traces on ancient routes through the Cheviot Hills. Slicing through the southern edge of the national park is the famous reminder of the Romans' 400-year occupation of Britain, Hadrian's Wall, the northern boundary of their empire.

Conflict between Scots and English continued for 1,000 years after the Romans departed, and even after the 1603 union between the two crowns, which left the border much further north. A chain of massive crenellated medieval castles punctuates the coastline, while other forts that once defended the northern flank of England along the River Tweed lie mostly in ruins. Seventh-century Northumbria was the cradle of Christianity under St Aidan, until its development was stymied by Viking violence from 793 onward, as the Scandinavian invaders raided the monasteries. But a reverence for Northumbrian saints is in the local psyche, and St Cuthbert and the Venerable Bede are both buried in Durham Cathedral. The influence of the Industrial Revolution, concentrated around the mouths of the rivers Tyne, Wear and Tees, made Newcastle upon Tyne the north's main centre for coal mining and shipbuilding. Today, Newcastle is famous for its industrial-heritage attractions and a nightlife centred on the boozy haunts of the Bigg Market. But urban regeneration has also forged intriguing new hip districts here, particularly the Ouseburn, where arts and crafts thrive in studios and galleries and several cheerful bars and clubs entertain after hours.

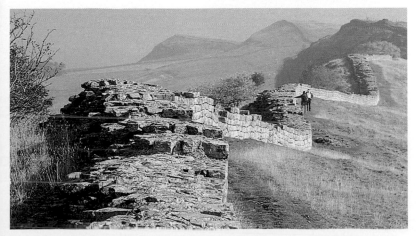

Section of Hadrian's Wall, built by the Romans in about 120, looking east from Cawfields

◀ Antony Gormley's sculpture *Angel of the North*, Gateshead

Exploring Northumbria

Historic sites are plentiful along Northumbria's coast. South of
Berwick-upon-Tweed, a causeway leads to the ruined priory and
castle on Lindisfarne, and there are major castles at Bamburgh,
Alnwick and Warkworth. The hinterland is a region of wide open
spaces, with wilderness in the Northumberland National Park, and
the fascinating Roman remains of Hadrian's Wall at Housesteads
and elsewhere. The glorious city of Durham is dominated by its
castle, cathedral and students, while Newcastle upon Tyne's
main draw is its vibrant nightlife.

Sights at a Glance

1. Berwick-upon-Tweed
2. Lindisfarne
3. Farne Islands
4. Bamburgh
5. Alnwick Castle
6. Warkworth Castle
7. Kielder Water & Forest Park
8. *Cheviot Hills p425*
9. Hexham
10. Corbridge
11. *Hadrian's Wall pp426–7*
12. Newcastle upon Tyne
13. *Beamish Open Air Museum pp428–9*
14. *Durham pp432–3*
16. Middleton-in-Teesdale
17. Barnard Castle

Walks and Tour

15. *North Pennines Tour p431*

The wilderness of Upper Coquetdale in the sparsely
populated Cheviot Hills

For hotels and restaurants in this area see pp570–71 and pp598–9

The rugged coastline of Northumberland, with Bamburgh Castle in the distance

Getting Around

North of Newcastle, the A1068 meets the A1, linking the sights of the Northumbrian coast and continuing on to Scotland. Two scenic inland routes, the A696 and the A68, merge near Otterburn to skirt the Northumberland National Park. A mainline railway links Durham, Newcastle and Berwick, but a car is necessary to explore Northumbria comprehensively.

Key

- ▬▬ Motorway
- ▬▬ Major road
- ▬▬ Secondary road
- ----- Minor road
- ▬▬ Scenic route
- ▬▬ Main railway
- ──── Minor railway
- △ Summit

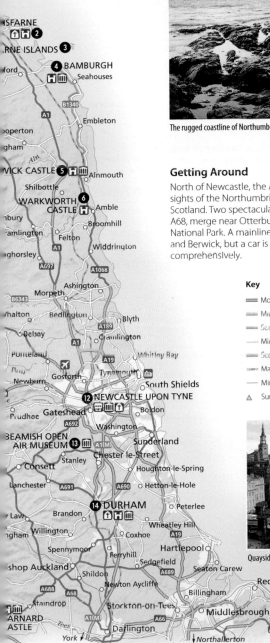

Quayside, Newcastle upon Tyne

Berwick-upon-Tweed's three bridges

❶ Berwick-upon-Tweed

Northumberland. 🏛 12,000. 🚊 ℹ Walkergate (01670 622155). 🛒 Wed, Sat. 🌐 visitnorthumberland.com

Between the 12th and 15th centuries Berwick-upon-Tweed changed hands 14 times in the wars between the Scots and English. Its position, at the mouth of the river which divides the two nations, made the town strategically vital.

The English finally gained permanent control in 1482 and maintained Berwick as a fortified garrison. Ramparts dating from 1555, 1.5 miles (2.5 km) long and 23 ft (7 m) thick, offer superb views over the Tweed. Within the 18th-century barracks are the **King's Own Scottish Borderers Regimental Museum**, an **art gallery**, and **By Beat of Drum**, charting the

history of British infantrymen from the Civil War to World War I.

🏛 **King's Own Scottish Borderers Regimental Museum**
The Barracks. **Tel** 01289 307426. **Open** daily. 🅿 🏛 EH 🌐 english-heritage.org.uk

❷ Lindisfarne

Northumberland. 🚊 Berwick-upon-Tweed then bus. ℹ Walkergate, Berwick-upon-Tweed (01670 622155). 🌐 lindisfarne.org.uk

Twice daily a long, narrow neck of land sinks under the North Sea tide for 5 hours, separating Lindisfarne, or Holy Island, from the mainland. At low tide, visitors stream over the causeway to the island made famous by St Aidan, St Cuthbert and the Lindisfarne Gospels. Nothing remains of the Celtic monks' monastery,

finally abandoned in 875 after successive Viking attacks, but the magnificent arches of the 11th-century **Lindisfarne Priory** are still visible.

After 1540, stones from the priory were used to build **Lindisfarne Castle**, which was restored and made into a private home by Sir Edwin Lutyens (see p33) in 1903. It includes a walled garden by Gertrude Jekyll (see p31).

🏰 **Lindisfarne Castle**
Holy Island. **Tel** 01289 389244. Castle: **Open** Mar–Oct & Feb half-term: Tue–Sun. Gardens: **Open** Tue–Sun all year. Opening times depend on tide – phone to check. 🅿 NT

❸ Farne Islands

Northumberland. 🚢 from Seahouses (Apr–Oct). ℹ Walkergate, Berwick-upon-Tweed (01670 622155); Seafield Rd, Seahouses (01670 625593). NT

There are between 15 and 28 Farne Islands off the coast from Bamburgh, some of them periodically covered by the sea. Nature wardens and lighthouse keepers share them with seals, puffins and other seabirds. Boat tours depart from **Seahouses** harbour and can land on Staple and Inner Farne, site of St Cuthbert's 14th-century chapel, or on Longstone, where Grace Darling's lighthouse is located.

Lindisfarne Castle (1540), the main landmark on the island of Lindisfarne

Celtic Christianity

The Irish monk St Aidan arrived in Northumbria in 635 from the island of Iona, off western Scotland, to evangelize the north of England. He founded the monastery on the island of Lindisfarne, and it became one of the most important centres for Christianity in England. This and other monastic communities thrived in Northumbria, becoming rich in scholarship, although the monks lived simply. It also emerged as a place of pilgrimage after miracles were reported at the shrine of St Cuthbert, Lindisfarne's most famous bishop. But the monks' pacifism made them defenceless against 9th-century Viking raids.

St Aidan's Monastery was added to over the centuries to become Lindisfarne Priory. This 8th-century relic with interlaced animal decorations is from a cross at the site.

The Venerable Bede (673–735), the most brilliant early medieval scholar, was a monk at the monastery of St Paul in Jarrow. He wrote *The Ecclesiastical History of the English People* in 731.

St Aidan (600–651), an Irish missionary, founded a monastery at Lindisfarne and became Bishop of Northumbria in 635. This 1960 sculpture of him, by Kathleen Parbury, is in Lindisfarne Priory grounds.

St Cuthbert (635–87) was the monk and miracle worker most revered of all. He lived as a hermit on Inner Farne (a chapel was built there in his memory) and later became Bishop of Lindisfarne.

Lindisfarne Priory was built by Benedictines in the 11th century, on the site of St Aidan's earlier monastery

The Lindisfarne Gospels

Held in the British Library, this book of richly illustrated portrayals of Gospel stories is one of the masterpieces of the "Northumbrian Renaissance", which left a permanent mark on Christian art and history writing. The work was carried out by monks at Lindisfarne under the direction of Bishop Eadfrith, around 700. Monks managed to save the book and took it with them when they fled from Lindisfarne in 875 after suffering Viking raids. Other treasures were plundered.

Elaborately decorated initial to the *Gospel of St Matthew* (c.725)

Illustration of Grace Darling from the 1881 edition of *Sunday at Home*

❹ Bamburgh

Northumberland. 🚌 400.
🚉 Berwick. ℹ️ Seahouses (01670
625593; Walkergate, Berwick-upon-
Tweed (01670 622155).

Due to Northumbria's history
of hostility against the Scots,
there are more strongholds
and castles here than in any
other part of England. Most
were built from the 11th to the
15th centuries by local warlords,
including Bamburgh's red
sandstone **castle**. Its coastal
position had been fortified
since prehistoric times, but
the first major stronghold
was built in 550 by a Saxon
chieftain, Ida the Flamebearer.

In its heyday between 1095
and 1464, Bamburgh was the
royal castle that was used by
the Northumbrian kings for
coronations. By the end
of the Middle Ages it
had fallen into obscurity,
then in 1894 it was bought
by Newcastle arms tycoon
Lord Armstrong, who
restored it. Works of art are
exhibited in the cavernous
Great Hall, and there
are suits of armour
and medieval artifacts
in the basement.

Bamburgh's other
main attraction is the
tiny **Grace Darling
Museum**, which
celebrates the bravery
of the 23-year-old, who, in 1838,
rowed through tempestuous
seas with her father, the keeper
of the Longstone lighthouse,
to rescue nine people from the
wrecked *Forfarshire* steamboat.

Carrara marble fireplace
(1840) at Alnwick Castle

🏰 **Bamburgh Castle**
Bamburgh. **Tel** 01668 214515. **Open**
daily (Nov–early Feb: Sat & Sun). 🅿️
♿ 🍴 🏠 🌐 bamburghcastle.com

🎞️ **Grace Darling Museum**
Radcliffe Rd. **Tel** 01688 214910.
Open daily (Oct–Easter: closed Mon). ♿

❺ Alnwick Castle

Alnwick, Northumberland.
Tel 01665 511100. 🚉 🚌 Alnmouth.
Open April–Oct: daily. 🅿️ ♿ limited.
🍴 🏠 🌐 alnwickcastle.com

Dominating the pretty market
town of Alnwick on the River
Aln, this castle doubled as
Hogwarts in the first two Harry
Potter movies. It is the main seat
of the Duke of Northumberland,
whose family, the Percys, have
lived here since 1309. This
border stronghold
has survived many
battles, but now sits
peacefully in landscaped
grounds designed by
"Capability" Brown.
The stern medieval
exterior belies the
treasure house within,
furnished in palatial
Renaissance style with
a collection of Meissen
china and paintings
by Titian, Van Dyck
and Canaletto.
The Postern Tower
contains early British
and Roman relics.
The **Regimental Museum of
Royal Northumberland
Fusiliers** is in the Abbot's
Tower. Other attractions
are the Percy state coach
and the dungeon.

❻ Warkworth Castle

Warkworth, nr Amble. **Tel** 01665
711423. 🚉 🚌 518 from Newcastle.
Open Apr–Oct: daily; Nov–mid-Feb:
Sat & Sun. **Closed** 1 Jan, 24–26 Dec.
🏠 🅿️ EH ♿ limited. 🌐 english-
heritage.org.uk

Warkworth Castle sits on a
green hill overlooking the River
Coquet. It was one of the Percy
family homes. Shakespeare's
Henry IV features the castle in
the scenes between the Earl of
Northumberland and his son,
Harry Hotspur. Much of the
present-day castle dates back
to the 14th century. The unusual
turreted, cross-shaped keep is
a central feature of the castle.

Warkworth Castle reflected in
the River Coquet

❼ Kielder Water &
Forest Park

Northumberland. ℹ️ Tower Knowe
Visitor Centre, Kielder (01434 240436).
Open daily. ♿ 🍴 🏠 🌐 visit
kielder.com

One of the top attractions in
Northumberland, Kielder Water
lies close to the Scottish border,
surrounded by spectacular
scenery. With a perimeter of
27 miles (44 km), it is Britain's
largest artificial lake, and has
facilities for sailing, windsurfing,
canoeing, water-skiing and
fishing. In summer, the cruiser
Osprey departs from Leaplish
on trips around the lake.
The Kielder Water Exhibition,
at the Visitor Centre, covers
the history of the valley from
the Ice Age to the present day.

❽ Cheviot Hills

These bare, beautiful moors, smoothed into rounded humps by Ice Age glaciers, form a natural border with Scotland. Walkers and outdoor enthusiasts can explore a near-wilderness unmatched anywhere else in England. This remote extremity of the Northumberland National Park nevertheless has a long and vivid history. Roman legions, warring Scots and English border raiders, cattle drovers and whisky smugglers have all left traces along the ancient routes and tracks they carved out here.

The Cheviots' isolated burns and streams are a stronghold in England for the shy, elusive otter.

Chew Green Camp – known to the Romans as Ad Fines, meaning "towards the last place" – has fine views from the remaining fortified earthworks.

Uswayford Farm track

Byrness

Uswayford Farm
This is perhaps the most remote farm in England and one of the hardest to reach. It is set in deserted moorland.

0 kilometres 5

0 miles 5

The Pennine Way starts in Derbyshire and ends at Kirk Yetholm in Scotland. The final stage (shown here) goes past Byrness, crosses the Cheviots and traces the Scottish border.

Alwinton, a tiny village built mainly from grey stone, is situated beside the River Coquet. It is a starting point for many fine walks in the area, amidst a wild landscape deserted except for sheep.

Key

━━━ Main road

━━━ Secondary road

┅┅┅ Minor road

--- Pennine Way

For keys to symbols see back flap

🄮 Hexham

Northumberland. 🕍 12,000. 🚆
🚌 ⓘ Beaumont St (01670 620450).
🛒 Tue. 🔳 **visitnorthumberland.com**

The busy market town of Hexham was established in the 7th century, growing up around the church and monastery built by St Wilfrid, but the Vikings sacked and looted it in 876. In 1114, Augustinians began work on a priory and abbey on the original church site to create **Hexham Abbey**, which still towers over the market square. The Saxon crypt, built partly with stones from the former Roman fort at Corbridge, is all that remains of St Wilfrid's

Ancient stone carvings at Hexham Abbey

church. The south transept has a 12th-century night stair: stone steps leading from the dormitory. In the chancel is the Frith Stool, a Saxon throne made of sandstone and worn smooth over the centuries by human touch.

Medieval streets, many with Georgian and Victorian shopfronts, spread out from the market square. The 15th-century Moot Hall was once a council chamber and the **Old Gaol** (jail), built in the 1330s, contains a museum of border history.

🄯 Hadrian's Wall

On the orders of Emperor Hadrian, a 73-mile (117-km) wall was erected across northern England to mark and defend the northern limits of the British province and the northwest border of the Roman Empire. The work took two years and was completed in AD 122. Troops were stationed at milecastles along the wall, and large turrets, later forts, were built at 5-mile (8-km) intervals. The wall was abandoned in 383 as the Empire crumbled. In 1987 it was declared a World Heritage Site.

Location of Hadrian's Wall

KEY

① **Carvoran Fort** is probably pre-Hadrianic. Little of the fort survives, but the Roman Army Museum nearby covers the wall's history.

② **Great Chesters Fort** was built facing east to guard Caw Gap, but there are few remains today. To the south and east of the fort are traces of a civil settlement and a bathhouse.

③ **Vindolanda** is the site of several forts. The first timber fort dated from AD 90 and a stone fort was not built until the 2nd century. The museum has a collection of Roman writing tablets that provide details of social history.

④ **Housesteads Settlement** includes the remains of terraced shops or taverns.

⑤ **Carrawburgh Fort**, a 500-man garrison, guarded the Newbrough Burn and North Tynedale approaches.

⑥ **Limestone Corner Milecastle** is sited at the northernmost part of the wall and the foundations of a number of interior buildings can be seen here. It has magnificent views of the Cheviot Hills (*see p425*).

⑦ **Chesters Fort** was a bridgehead over the North Tyne. In the museum are altars, sculptures and inscriptions.

⑧ **Chesters Bridge** crossed the Tyne. The original Hadrianic bridge was rebuilt in 207. The remains of this second bridge abutment can still be seen.

Cawfields, 2 miles (3 km) north of Haltwhistle, is the access point to one of the highest and most rugged sections of the wall. To the east, the wall and a series of milecastles sit on volcanic crags.

⬆ Hexham Abbey

Market Place. **Tel** 01434 602031.
Open 9:30am–5pm daily. 🔲 💻 📷
🅦 hexham-abbey.org.uk

▥ Hexham Old Gaol

Hallgate. **Tel** 01670 624523. **Open** Apr–
Sep: Tue–Sat; Oct, Nov, Feb & Mar:
Tue & Sat. 📷 🔲 📷 🅦 hexham
oldgaol.org.uk

⑩ Corbridge

Northumberland. 🗺 3,500. 🚆
ℹ Hill St (01434 632815).

This quiet town conceals a few
historic buildings made with
stones from the nearby Roman
garrison town of Corstopitum.
These include the Saxon tower of
St Andrew's Church and the 14th-
century fortified tower house
that protected the local clergy.
Excavations of Corstopitum,
now open as **Corbridge Roman
Town–Hadrian's Wall**, have
exposed earlier forts, a well-
preserved granary, temples,
fountains and an aqueduct.

▥ Corbridge Roman Town–
Hadrian's Wall

Tel 01434 632349. **Open** Apr–Oct:
daily; Nov–Mar: Sat & Sun. **Closed** 1
Jan, 24–26 Dec. 📷 🎥 🔲 ltd. 📷 **EH**

The parson's 14th-century fortified tower
house at Corbridge

Housesteads Fort is the best-
preserved site on the wall, with
fine views over the countryside.
The excavated remains include
the commanding officer's house
and a Roman hospital.

| 0 metres | 500 |
| 0 yards | 500 |

**Sewingshields
Milecastle**, with
magnificent views
west to Housesteads,
is one of the best
places for walking. This
reconstruction shows
the layout of a Roman
milecastle on the wall.

Emperor Hadrian (76–138) came to Britain
in 120 to order a stronger defence system.
Coins were often cast to record emperors'
visits, such as this bronze *sestertius*. Until
1971, the British penny was abbreviated
to *d*, short for *denarius*, a Roman coin.

The Wall Coast to Coast

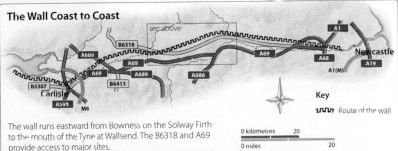

The wall runs eastward from Bowness on the Solway Firth
to the mouth of the Tyne at Wallsend. The B6318 and A69
provide access to major sites.

Key
〰 Route of the wall

| 0 kilometres | 20 |
| 0 miles | 20 |

⑫ Newcastle upon Tyne

⌖ 295,000. ✈ 🚆 🚌 🚢
ℹ Market St (0191 277 8000). 🚌 Sun.
ⓦ **newcastlegateshead.com**

Newcastle owes its name to its Norman **castle**, which was founded in 1080 by Robert Curthose, the eldest son of William the Conqueror *(see p51)*. The Romans had bridged the Tyne and built a fort on the site 1,000 years earlier. During the Middle Ages it was used as a base for English campaigns against the Scots. From the Middle Ages, the city flourished as a coal mining and exporting centre. It was known in the 19th century for engineering, steel production and later as the world's foremost shipyard. The city's industrial era may be over but the home of the "Geordies", as inhabitants of the city are known, has emerged with a reputation for lively nightlife, excellent shops and a thriving arts scene.

The visible trappings of its past are reflected in the magnificent **Tyne Bridge** and in **Earl Grey's Monument**, as well as the grand façades in the city centre thoroughfares, such as Grey Street. The Angel of the North, a major statue and symbol of the area, is located in the nearby town of Gateshead, which is also home to the **Baltic Centre for Contemporary Art**, Sage Gateshead, the international centre for music, and the tilting Gateshead Millennium Bridge.

Bridges crossing the Tyne at Newcastle

🏰 The Castle Keep

St Nicholas St. **Tel** 0191 230 6300. **Open** daily. **Closed** 1 Jan, Good Fri, 24–26 Dec. 🚫 📷
ⓦ **castlekeep-newcastle.org.uk**

Curthose's original wooden "new castle" was rebuilt in stone in the 12th century. Only the thickset, crenellated keep remains intact with its royal apartments, spiral staircases and battlements, from which there are great views of the city and the Tyne. Visitors can explore all four floors of the building, and audio-visuals help tell its story.

---

⑬ Beamish Open Air Museum

This giant open-air museum, spread over 120 hectares (300 acres) of County Durham, recreates an authentic picture of family, working and community life in the northeast in the 19th and early 20th centuries. It includes an Edwardian town and pit village, a working Victorian farm and a Georgian steam railway. A tramway serves the different parts of the museum, which carefully avoids romanticizing the past.

The station, which dates back to 1913, has a platform, a signal box, a wrought-iron footbridge and a goods yard.

Home Farm
This recreates the atmosphere of an old-fashioned farm. Rare breeds of cattle and sheep, more common before the advent of mass breeding, can be seen.

School

Miners' houses were tiny, oil-lit dwellings, backing onto vegetable gardens and owned by the colliery.

Chapel

For hotels and restaurants in this area see pp570–71 and pp598–9

⛪ St Nicholas Cathedral

St Nicholas Sq. **Tel** 0191 232 1939.
Open daily. ♿ 🌐 stnicholas
cathedral.co.uk

This is one of Britain's tiniest cathedrals. Inside, there are remnants of the original 11th-century Norman church on which the present 14th- and 15th-century structure was founded. Its most striking feature is its ornate "lantern tower" – half tower, half spire – of which there are only three others in Britain.

🏛 Bessie Surtees' House

41–44 Sandhill. **Tel** 0191 269 1200.
Open Mon–Fri. **Closed** 24 Dec–
7 Jan, public hols. ♿ limited.
📷 🌐 historicengland.org.uk

The romantic tale of beautiful, wealthy Bessie, who lived here before eloping with penniless John Scott, later Lord Chancellor of England, is told within these half-timbered 16th- and 17th-century houses.

Reredos of the Northumbrian saints in St Nicholas Cathedral

The window through which Bessie escaped now has a blue glass pane.

🏛 Tyne Bridge

Newcastle–Gateshead. **Open** daily. ♿
Opened in 1928, this steel arch was the longest of its type in Britain with a span of 162 m (531 ft). Designed by Mott, Hay and Anderson, it soon became an iconic symbol of the city.

🏛 Earl Grey's Monument

Grey St.
Benjamin Green created this memorial to the 2nd Earl Grey, Liberal Prime Minister from 1830 to 1834.

🏛 Baltic Centre for Contemporary Art

Gateshead. **Tel** 0191 478 1810.
Open daily. 🍴 💻 📷
🌐 balticmill.com

Located on the south bank of the River Tyne, this former grain warehouse has been converted by architect Dominic Williams into a major international centre for contemporary art, one of the biggest in Europe. There are amazing views of Tyneside from its rooftop restaurant.

Beamish Town
The town has a sweet factory, newspaper office, solicitor, dentist and music teacher. There is also a pub.

VISITORS' CHECKLIST

Practical Information
Beamish, County Durham.
Tel 0191 370 4000. **Open** Apr–
Oct: 10am–5pm daily (last adm:
3pm); Nov–Mar: Town and
Colliery Village only 10am–4pm
Tue–Thu, Sat & Sun. 💻 📷
🌐 beamish.org.uk

Transport
🚆 🚌 Newcastle then bus.

The Co-op
This stocked everything a family needed at the turn of the century. A full range of foods available in 1913 is displayed.

Pockerley
Old Hall

The 1825 Railway

Steam Winding Engine

Mahogany Drift Mine
This tunnel driven into coal seams near the surface, was here long before the museum and was worked from the 1850s to 1958. Visitors are given guided tours underground.

Entrance

Houses built by the London Lead Company in Middleton-in-Teesdale

⑭ Durham

See pp432–3.

⑮ North Pennines Tour

See p431.

Cotherstone cheese, a speciality of the Middleton-in-Teesdale area

⑯ Middleton-in-Teesdale

Co. Durham. 🚇 1,100. 🚄 Darlington. ℹ️ Bowlees (03000 262626).

Clinging to a hillside amid wild Pennine scenery on the River Tees is this old lead-mining town. Many of its rows of grey stone cottages were built by the London Lead Company, a paternalistic, Quaker-run organization that influenced every corner of its employees' daily lives.

The company began mining in 1753, and soon it virtually owned the town. Workers were expected to observe strict temperance, send their children to Sunday school and conform to the many company maxims. Today, mining has ceased in

Teesdale, with Middleton standing as a monument to the 18th-century idea of the "company town". The offices of the London Lead Company can still be seen, along with Nonconformist chapels from the era and a memorial fountain made of iron.

The crumbly Cotherstone cow's milk cheese, a speciality of the surrounding dales, is available in local shops.

⑰ Barnard Castle

County Durham. 🚇 5,500. 🚄 Darlington. ℹ️ 3 Horsemarket (03000 262626). 🅦 Wed. 🌐 thisisdurham.com

Barnard Castle, known in the area as "Barney", is a little town full of character, with old shopfronts and a cobbled marketplace overlooked by the ruins of the Norman castle from which it takes its name. The original Barnard Castle was built around 1125–40 by Bernard Balliol, ancestor of the founder of Balliol College, Oxford *(see p226)*. Later, the market town grew up around the fortification.

Today, Barnard Castle is known for the extraordinary French-style château to the east of the town, surrounded by acres of formal gardens. Started in 1860 by the local aristocrat John Bowes and his French wife Josephine, an artist and actress, it was never a private residence, but always intended as a museum and public monument. The château finally opened in 1892, by which time the couple were both dead. Nevertheless, the **Bowes Museum** stands as a monument to their wealth and extravagance.

The museum houses a strong collection of Spanish art, which includes El Greco's *The Tears of St Peter,* dating from the 1580s, and Goya's *Don Juan Meléndez Váldez,* painted in 1797. Clocks, porcelain, furniture, musical instruments, toys and tapestries are among its treasures.

🏛️ **Bowes Museum**
Barnard Castle. **Tel** 01833 690606. **Open** 10am–5pm daily. **Closed** 1 Jan, 25 & 26 Dec. 🎟️ 🎥 (summer). ♿ 🖼️ 📷 🅦 thebowesmuseum.org.uk

The Bowes Museum, a French-style château in Barnard Castle

⓯ North Pennines Tour

Starting just to the south of Hadrian's Wall, this tour explores the South Tyne Valley and Upper Weardale. It crosses one of England's wildest and most remote tracts of moorland, then heads north again. The high ground is mainly blanketed with heather, dotted with sheep or crisscrossed with dry stone walls, a feature of this region. Harriers and other birds of prey hover above, and streams tumble into valleys of tightly huddled villages. Celts, Romans and other settlers have left imprints on the North Pennines, now denoted an Area of Outstanding Natural Beauty.

Sheep sat on the moors

① Haltwhistle
In the Church of the Holy Cross is the tombstone of John Ridley, brother of Protestant martyr Nicholas Ridley, burnt at the stake in 1555.

② Bardon Mill
To the north of Bardon Mill is the Roman fort and civilian settlement of Vindolanda (see p426).

③ Haydon Bridge
There are some delightful walks near this spa town where the painter John Martin was born in 1789. Nearby Langley Castle is worth a visit.

④ Hexham
A pretty old town (see p426), Hexham has a fine abbey.

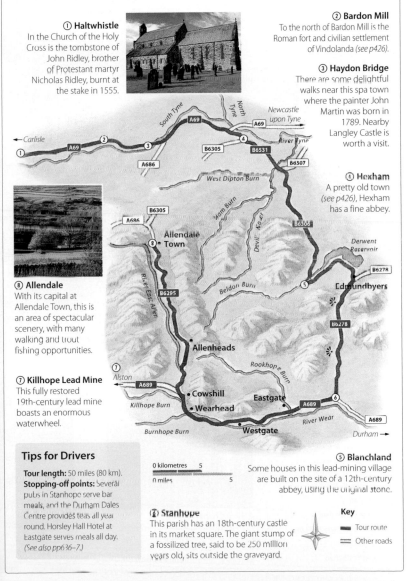

⑧ Allendale
With its capital at Allendale Town, this is an area of spectacular scenery, with many walking and trout fishing opportunities.

⑦ Killhope Lead Mine
This fully restored 19th-century lead mine boasts an enormous waterwheel.

⑤ Blanchland
Some houses in this lead-mining village are built on the site of a 12th-century abbey, using the original stone.

⑥ Stanhope
This parish has an 18th-century castle in its market square. The giant stump of a fossilized tree, said to be 250 million years old, sits outside the graveyard.

Tips for Drivers

Tour length: 50 miles (80 km).
Stopping-off points: Several pubs in Stanhope serve bar meals, and the Durham Dales Centre provides teas all year round. Horsley Hall Hotel at Eastgate serves meals all day. (See also pp636–7.)

0 kilometres 5

0 miles 5

Key
▬ Tour route
═ Other roads

⑭ Durham

The city of Durham was built on Island Hill or "Dunholm" in 995. This rocky peninsula, which defies the course of the River Wear's route to the sea, was chosen as the last resting place for the remains of St Cuthbert. The relics of the Venerable Bede were brought to the site 27 years later, adding to its attraction for pilgrims. Durham Cathedral is known for its striking geometric patterning, while the Castle served as the Episcopal Palace until 1832, when Bishop William van Mildert gave it up and surrendered part of his income to found Britain's third university. The 23-hectare (57-acre) peninsula has many footpaths, views and fine buildings.

★ **Cathedral**
Built from 1093 to 1274, this is an impressive Norman structure.

KEY

① **Prebend's footbridge** was built in 1777. A sculpture by Colin Wilbourn is situated at the "island" end.

② **Old Fulling Mill** is a largely 18th-century building, housing a museum of archaeology.

③ **Town Hall** (1851)

④ **St Nicholas' Church** (1857)

⑤ **University buildings** were built by Bishop John Cosin in the 17th century.

⑥ **Palace Green**

⑦ **Church of St Mary le Bow**

⑧ **Kingsgate Footbridge**, built 1962–3, leads to North Bailey.

⑨ **St Cuthbert's Tomb**

⑩ **South Bailey**

⑪ **College Gatehouse**

⑫ **Church of St Mary the Less**

⑬ **College Green**

⑭ **Monastic Kitchen**

"Our Daily Bread" Window
This modern stained-glass window in the north nave aisle was donated in 1984 by a local department store.

Galilee Chapel
Architects began work on the exotic Galilee Chapel in 1170, drawing inspiration from the Great Mosque of Cordoba in Andalucia. It was altered by Bishop Langley (d. 1437), whose tomb is by the west door.

★ Castle
Begun in 1072, the castle is a fine Norman fortress. The keep, sited on a mound, is now part of the university.

VISITORS' CHECKLIST

Practical Information
County Durham.
🛈 Market Place (03000 262626).
🆆 thisisdurham.com
Cathedral: **Tel** 0191 386 4266.
Open 9:30am–6pm daily (12:45–5:30pm Sun). 🦽 limited. 📺
📷 🆆 durhamcathedral.co.uk
Castle: **Tel** 0191 334 2932.
Open daily (pm only in termtime). 📷 mandatory.

Transport
🚆 Durham.

Tunstal's Chapel
Situated at the end of Tunstal's Gallery, the castle chapel was built around 1542. Its fine woodwork includes this wheelbarrow misericord (see p345).

Castle Gatehouse
Traces of Norman stonework can be seen in the outer arch, while the sturdy walls and upper floors are 18th century, rebuilt in a style dubbed "gothick" by detractors.

Cathedral Architecture

The vast dimensions of the columns, piers and vaults, and the inventive giant lozenge and chevron, trellis and dogtooth patterns carved into the stone columns, are the main innovative features of Durham Cathedral. It is believed that 11th- and 12th-century architects such as Bishop Ranulph Flambard tried to unify all parts of the structure. This can be seen in the south aisle of the nave below.

Ribbed vaults, crisscrossing above the nave, are now common in church ceilings. One of the major achievements of Gothic architecture, they were first built at Durham.

The lozenge shape is a pattern from prehistoric carving, but never before seen in a cathedral.

Chevron patterns on some of the piers in the nave are evidence of Moorish influence.

WALES

Introducing Wales   **436–443**

North Wales   **444–459**

South and Mid-Wales   **460–479**

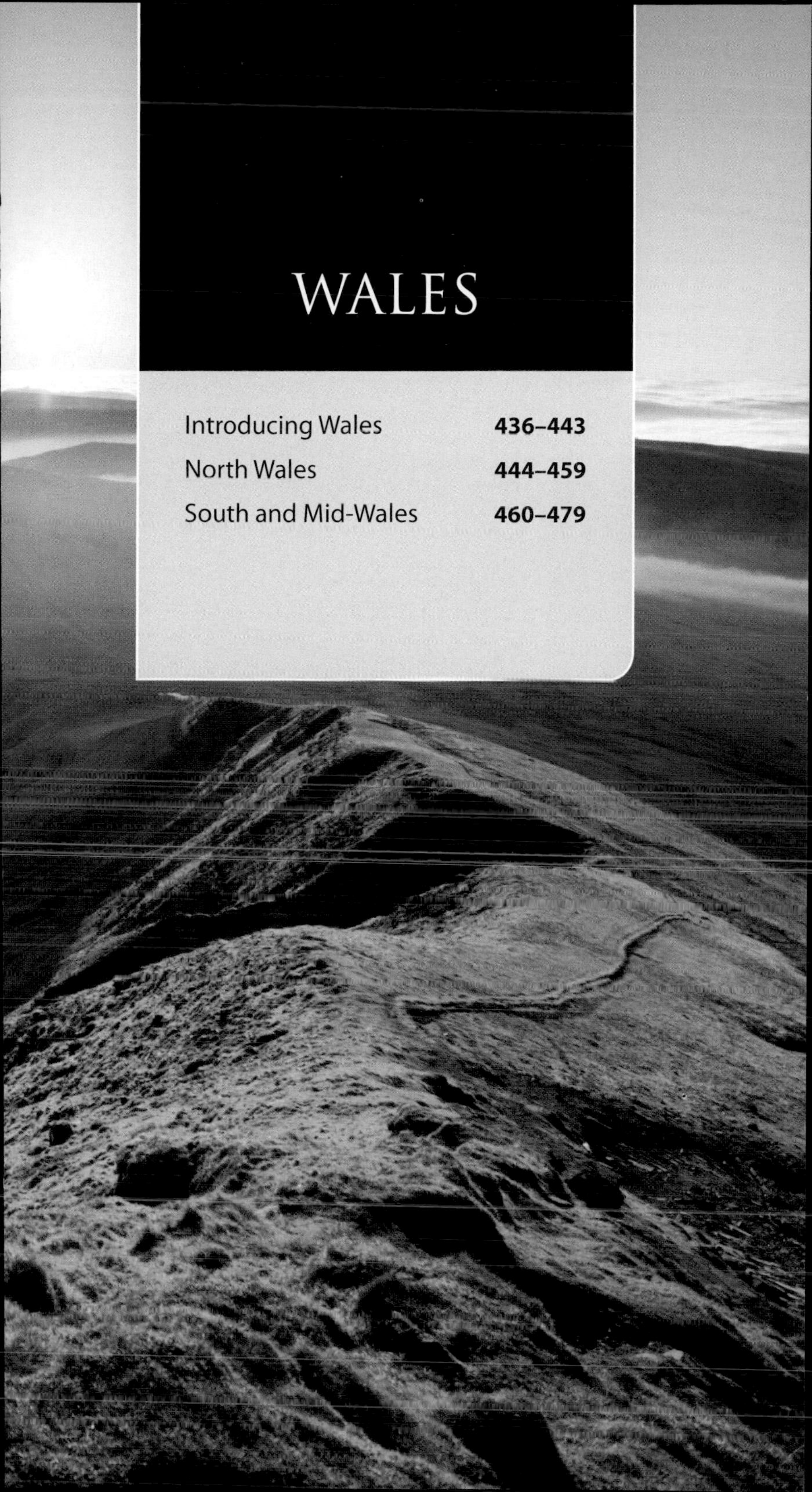

Wales at a Glance

Wales is a country of outstanding natural beauty with varied landscapes. Visitors come to climb dramatic mountain peaks, go walking in the forests, fish in the broad rivers and enjoy the miles of unspoilt coastline. The country's many seaside resorts have long been popular with English holiday-makers. As well as outdoor pursuits there is the vibrant Welsh culture, with its strong Celtic roots, to be experienced. Finally there are many fine castles, ruined abbeys, mansions and a wealth of outstanding industrial heritage.

Beaumaris Castle was intended to be a key part of Edward I's "iron ring" to contain the rebellious Welsh *(see p440)*. Begun in 1295 but never completed, the castle *(see p442)* has a sophisticated defence structure that is unparalleled in Wales.

Holyhead

Bangor

Caernarfon

GWYNE

Porthmadog

Llanberis and Snowdon *(see p455)* is an area famous for dramatic, high peaks, long popular with climbers. Snowdon's summit is most easily reached from Llanberis. Its Welsh name, *Yr Wyddfa*, means "great tomb" and it is the legendary burial place of a giant slain by King Arthur *(see p289)*.

Portmeirion *(see pp458–9)* is a private village whose astonishing buildings seem rather incongruous in the Welsh landscape. The village was created by the architect Sir Clough Williams-Ellis to fulfil a personal ambition. Some of the buildings are assembled from pieces of masonry taken from sites around the country.

Aberystwyth

Aberaeron

CEREDIGIC

Fishguard

St Davids

PEMBROKE-
SHIRE

CARMARTH.
SHIRE

Carmarthen

Pembroke   Tenby

Swan

St Davids is the smallest city in Britain. Its cathedral *(see pp468–9)* is the largest in Wales, with a nave is noted for its carved oak roof and beautiful rood screen. Next to the cathedral is the medieval Bishop's Palace, now a ruin.

◀ Sunrise over Cribyn, as seen from Pen y Fan, in the Brecon Beacons National Park

Conwy Castle guards one of the best-preserved medieval fortified towns in Britain *(see pp450–51)*. Built by Edward I, the castle was besieged and came close to surrender in 1294. It was taken by Owain Glyndŵr's supporters in 1401.

Locator Map

0 kilometres   25
0 miles   25

Conwy

Queensferry

WWY   FLINTSHIRE

Betws-y-Coed   Ruthin

DENBIGH-SHIRE

Wrexham

ORTH WALES
(See pp444–59)

Llangollen

ellau

Welshpool

chynlleth

The Brecon Beacons *(see pp472–3)* is a national park, a lovely area of mountains, forest and moorland in South Wales, which is a favourite with walkers and naturalists. Pen y Fan is one of the principal summits.

POWYS

Llandrindod Wells

OUTH AND
ID WALES
(see pp460–79)

Hay on Wye

andovery

Brecon

Monmouth

Merthyr Tydfil

MONMOUTH-SHIRE

GLAMORGAN

Newport

Cardiff Castle's *(see pp476–7)* Clock Tower is just one of many 19th-century additions by the eccentric but gifted architect William Burges. His flamboyant style still delights and amazes visitors.

gend   Cardiff

Barry

A PORTRAIT OF WALES

Long popular with British holiday-makers, the many charms of Wales are now becoming better known internationally. They include spectacular scenery and a vibrant culture specializing in male-voice choirs, poetry and a passionate love of team sports. Governed from Westminster since 1536, Wales retains its own distinct national identity, and in 1999 it finally gained partial devolution.

Much of the Welsh landmass is covered by the Cambrian Mountain range, which effectively acts as a barrier with England. Wales is warmed by the Gulf Stream and has a mild climate, with more rain than most of Britain. The land is unsuitable for arable farming, but sheep and cattle thrive; the drove roads, along which sheep used to be driven across the hills to England, are now popular walking trails. It is partly because of the rugged terrain that the Welsh have managed to maintain their separate identity and their ancient language.

Welsh is an expansive, musical language, spoken by only 19 per cent of the 3 million inhabitants, but in parts of North Wales it is still the main language of conversation. There is an official bilingual policy: road signs are in Welsh and English, even in areas where Welsh is little spoken. Welsh place names intrigue visitors, being made up of native words that describe features of the landscape or ancient buildings. Examples include *Aber* (river mouth), *Afon* (river), *Fach* (little), *Llan* (church), *Llyn* (lake) and *Nant* (valley).

Wales was conquered by the Romans, but not by the Saxons. The land and the people therefore retained Celtic patterns of settlement and husbandry for six centuries before the Norman Conquest in 1066. This allowed time for the development of a distinctive Welsh nation whose homogeneity continues to this day.

The early Norman kings subjugated the Welsh by appointing "Marcher Lords" to control areas bordering England. A string of massive castles provides evidence of the turbulent years when Welsh insurrection was a constant threat. It was not until 1536 that Wales formally became part of Britain, and it would take nearly 500 years before the Welsh people regained partial autonomy.

Religious non-conformism and radical politics are deeply rooted in Welsh consciousness. St David converted the country to Christianity in the 6th century. Methodism, chapel and teetotalism became firmly entrenched in the Welsh psyche during the 19th century. Even today some pubs stay closed on Sundays. A long-standing oral tradition in Wales has produced many outstanding public speakers, politicians and actors. Welsh labour leaders have played important roles in the British trade union movement and the development of socialism.

Mountain sheep: a familiar sight in rural Wales

A *gorsedd* (assembly) of bards at the eisteddfod

figures and magic were part of the oral tradition of the Dark Ages. They were first written down in the 14th century as the *Mabinogion*, which has inspired Welsh poets up to the 20th century's Dylan Thomas and beyond. The male-voice choirs found in many towns, villages and factories, particularly in the industrial south, express the Welsh musical heritage. Choirs compete in eisteddfods: festivals that celebrate Welsh culture.

In the 19th century, the opening of the South Wales coalfield in Mid-Glamorgan – for a time the biggest in the world – led to an industrial boom, with mass migration from the countryside to the iron- and steelworks. This prosperity was not to last: apart from a brief respite in World War II, the coal industry went into terminal decline, and now only a handful of smaller mines remain open. Today tourism is being promoted in the hope that the wealth generated, by outdoor activities in particular, will be able to take "King Coal's" place

Welsh heritage is steeped in song, music, poetry and legend rather than handicrafts, although one notable exception is the carved Welsh lovespoon – a craft recently revived. The well-known Welsh love of music derives from the ancient bards: minstrels and poets, who may have been associated with the Druids. Bardic tales of quasi-historical

Welsh lovespoon

Conwy's picturesque, medieval walled town, fronted by a colourful harbour

The History of Wales

Wales has been settled since prehistoric times, its history shaped by many factors, from invasion to industrialization. The Romans set up bases in the mountainous terrain, but it was effectively a separate Celtic entity when Offa's Dyke was built as the border with England in 770. Centuries of cross-border raids and military campaigns followed before England and Wales were formally united by the Act of Union in 1535. The rugged northwest, the former stronghold of the Welsh princes, remains the heartland of Welsh language and culture.

Owain Glyndŵr, heroic leader of Welsh opposition to English rule

Ornamental Iron Age bronze plaque from Anglesey

The Celtic Nation

Wales was settled by waves of migrants in prehistoric times. By the Iron Age (see pp46–7), Celtic farmers had established hillforts and a religion, Druidism. From the 1st century AD until the legions withdrew around 400, the Romans built fortresses and roads, and mined lead, silver and gold. During the next 200 years, Wales was converted to Christianity by missionaries from Europe. St David (see pp468–9), the Welsh patron saint, is said to have turned the leek into a national symbol. He persuaded soldiers to wear leeks in their hats to distinguish themselves from Saxons during a 6th-century skirmish.

The Saxons (see pp50–51) failed to conquer Wales, and in 770 the Saxon King Offa built a defensive earthwork along the unconquered territory (see p465). Beyond Offa's Dyke the people called themselves Y Cymry (fellow countrymen) and the land Cymru. The Saxons called the land "Wales" from the Old English wealas, meaning foreigners. It was divided into kingdoms of which the main ones were Gwynedd in the north, Powys in the centre and Dyfed in the south. There were strong trade, cultural and linguistic links among them.

Marcher Lords

The Norman invasion of 1066 (see p51) did not reach Wales, but the border territory ("the Marches") was given by William the Conqueror to three powerful barons based at Shrewsbury, Hereford and Chester. These Marcher Lords made many incursions into Wales and controlled most of the lowlands. But the Welsh princes held the mountainous northwest and exploited English weaknesses. Under Llywelyn the Great (d.1240), North Wales was almost completely

Edward I designating his son Prince of Wales in 1301

independent; in 1267 his grandson, Llywelyn the Last, was acknowledged as Prince of Wales by Henry III.

In 1272 Edward I came to the English throne. He built fortresses and embarked on a military campaign to conquer Wales. In 1283 Llywelyn was killed in a skirmish, a shattering blow for the Welsh. Edward introduced English law and proclaimed his son Prince of Wales (see p448).

Owain Glyndŵr's Rebellion

Welsh resentment against the Marcher Lords continued to grow until it led to rebellion. In 1400 Owain Glyndŵr (c.1350–1416), a descendant of the Welsh princes, laid waste to English-dominated towns and castles. Declaring himself Prince of Wales, he managed to find Celtic allies in Scotland, Ireland, Northumbria and even France. In 1404 Glyndŵr captured Harlech and Cardiff, and formed his first Cynulliad, or parliament, in Machynlleth (see p466). In 1408, however, the French made a truce with the English king, Henry IV. The rebellion then failed and Glyndŵr went into hiding until his death.

Union with England

Wales suffered greatly during the Wars of the Roses *(see p53)*, as Yorkists and Lancastrians tried to gain control of the strategically important Welsh castles. The wars ended in 1485, and the Welshman Henry Tudor, born in Pembroke, became Henry VII. The Act of Union in 1536 and other laws abolished the Marcher Lordships, giving Wales parliamentary representation in London instead. English practices replaced traditional customs and English became the language of the courts and administration. The Welsh language survived, partly helped by the Church and by Dr William Morgan's translation of the Bible in 1588.

Miners from South Wales pictured in 1910

Vernacular Bible, which helped to keep the Welsh language alive

Industry and Radical Politics

The industrialization of south and east Wales began with the development of open-cast coal mining near Wrexham and Merthyr Tydfil in the 1760s. Convenient ports and the arrival of the railways helped the process. By the second half of the 19th century open-cast mines had been superseded by deep pits in the Rhondda Valley.

Living and working conditions were poor for industrial and agricultural workers. A series of "Rebecca Riots" in South Wales between 1839 and 1843, involving tenant farmers (dressed as women) protesting about tithes and rents, was forcibly suppressed. The Chartists, trade unions and the Liberal Party had much Welsh support.

The rise of Methodism *(see p283)* roughly paralleled the growth of industry: 80 per cent of the population was Methodist by 1851. The Welsh language persisted, despite attempts by the British government to discourage its use, which included punishing children caught speaking it.

Wales Today

In the 20th century the Welsh became a power in British politics. David Lloyd George, although not born in Wales, grew up there and was the first British Prime Minister to come from a Welsh family. Aneurin Bevan, a miner's son who became a Labour Cabinet Minister, helped create the National Health Service *(see p63)*.

In 1926 the Welsh Nationalist Party Plaid Cymru was formed. In 1955 Cardiff was recognized as the capital of Wales *(see p474)* and 4 years later the red dragon became the emblem on Wales's new flag. Plaid Cymru won two parliamentary seats at Westminster in 1974, and in a 1998 referendum the Welsh espoused limited home rule. The National Assembly for Wales is housed in the stunning Y Senedd, on the waterfront in Cardiff Bay

The 1967 Welsh Language Act made Welsh lessons compulsory in schools; many TV programmes are broadcast in Welsh, notably on S4C (Sianel 4 Cymru), a Welsh language channel.

The demise of the coal industry led to mass unemployment, though this has been partially alleviated by the spectacular growth in tourism, thanks to initiatives such as the Wales Coast Path. Moreover, the successes of the Welsh national rugby and football teams, allied to the hosting of major world political and sporting events – the NATO summit in 2014 and the Champions League final in 2017, for example – has reinvigorated this proud nation.

Girl in traditional Welsh costume

Castles of Wales

Wales is home to many romantic medieval castles. Soon after the Battle of Hastings, in 1066 *(see p51)*, the Normans turned their attentions to Wales. They built earth and timber fortifications, later replaced by stone castles, initiating a building programme that was continued by the Welsh princes and invading forces. Construction reached its peak during the reign of Edward I *(see p440)*. As the need for security lessened in the later Middle Ages, some castles became stately homes.

The north gatehouse was planned to be 18 m (60 ft) high, providing lavish royal accommodation, but its top storey was never built.

The inner ward contained a hall, granary, kitchens and stables.

The inner wall, with an inner passage, was higher than the curtain wall to permit simultaneous firing.

Rounded towers, with fewer blind spots than square ones, gave better protection.

Arrow slit

Beaumaris Castle

The last of Edward I's Welsh castles *(see p448)*, this perfectly symmetrical, concentric design was intended to combine impregnable defence with comfort. Invaders would face many obstacles before reaching the inner ward.

Moat

Curtain wall

Where to See Welsh Castles

In addition to Beaumaris, in North Wales there are medieval forts at Caernarfon *(see p448)*, Conwy *(see p450–51)* and Harlech *(see p458)*. Edward I also built Denbigh, Flint (near Chester) and Rhuddlan (near Rhyll). In South and Mid-Wales, Caerphilly (near Cardiff), Kidwelly (near Carmarthen) and Pembroke were built between the 11th and 13th centuries. Spectacular sites are occupied by Cilgerran (near Cardigan), Criccieth (near Porthmadog) and Carreg Cennen *(see p472)*. Chirk Castle, near Llangollen, is a good example of a fortress that has since become a stately home.

Caerphilly, 6 miles (10 km) north of Cardiff, is a huge castle with concentric stone and water defences that cover 12 ha (30 acres).

Harlech Castle *(see p458)* is noted for its massive gatehouse, twin towers and the fortified stairway to the sea. It was the headquarters of the Welsh resistance leader Owain Glyndŵr *(see p440)* in 1404–8.

Castell-Y-Bere

This castle at the foot of Cader Idris *(see p458)* was founded by Llywelyn the Great in 1221 *(see p450)*, to secure internal borders rather than to resist the English.

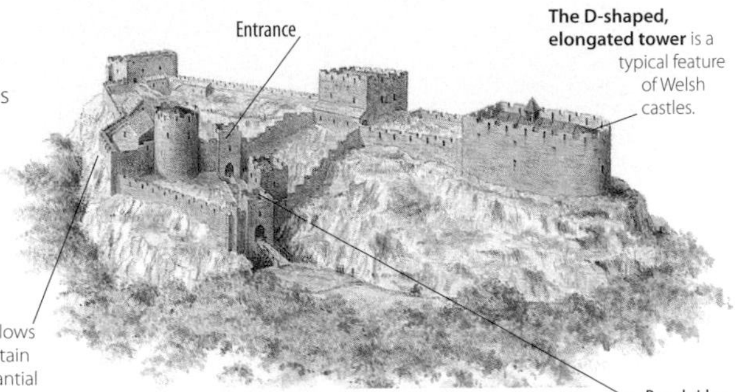

Entrance

The D-shaped, elongated tower is a typical feature of Welsh castles.

The castle's construction follows the shape of the rock. The curtain walls are too low and insubstantial to be of much practical use.

Drawbridge

The Chapel Tower has a beautiful medieval chapel.

Twin-towered gatehouse

The protected dock, on a channel that originally led to the sea, received supplies during sieges.

Edward I and Master James of St George

In 1278 Edward I brought over from Savoy a master stonemason who became a great military architect, James of St George. Responsible for planning and building at least 12 of Edward's fine Welsh castles, James was paid well and awarded a substantial pension, indicating the esteem in which he was held by the king.

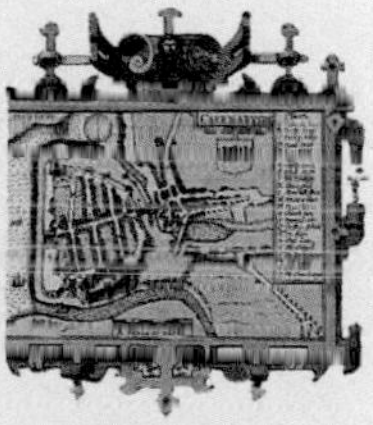

Edward I *(see p440)* was the warrior king whose castles played a key role in the subjugation of the Welsh people.

A plan of Caernarfon Castle illustrates how its position, on a promontory surrounded by water, determined the building's shape and defence.

Caernarfon Castle *(see p448)*, birthplace of the ill-fated Edward II *(see p333)*, was intended to be the official royal residence in North Wales, and has palatial private apartments.

Castell Coch was restored in Neo-Gothic style by Lord Bute and William Burges *(see p476)*. Mock-castles were built by many Victorian industrialists.

Conwy Castle *(see p451)*, like many other castles, required forced labour on a massive scale for its construction.

NORTH WALES

Conwy · Isle of Anglesey · Gywnedd · Denbighshire
Flintshire · Wrexham

North Wales is known primarily for its towering mountains, so beloved of climbers and walkers, but here you'll also find the wonderfully undulating spur of the Llŷn Peninsula. Beyond the mountains, located within the country's social and geographical extremities, there is a rugged coastline and dramatically sited castles to explore.

Defence and conquest have been constant themes in Welsh history. North Wales was the scene of ferocious battles between the Welsh princes and Anglo-Norman monarchs determined to establish English rule. The string of formidable castles that still stand in North Wales are as much a testament to Welsh resistance as to the wealth and strength of the invaders. Several massive fortresses, including Beaumaris, Caernarfon and Harlech, almost surround the rugged high country of Snowdonia, an area that even today maintains an untamed quality.

Sheep and cattle farming are the basis of the rural economy here, though there are also large areas of forestry. Along the coast, tourism predominates. Llandudno, a purpose-built Victorian resort, popularized the sandy northern coastline in the 19th century. The area continues to attract large numbers of visitors, though major development is confined to the narrow coastal strip that lies between Prestatyn and Llandudno, leaving the island of Anglesey and the remote Llŷn Peninsula largely untouched. The Llŷn Peninsula remains one of the strongholds of the Welsh language, along with more isolated inland communities, such as Dolgellau and Bala.

No part of North Wales can truly be called industrial, though there are still remnants of the once-prosperous slate industry in Snowdonia, where the stark, grey quarries provide a striking contrast to the natural beauty of the surrounding mountains. At the foot of Snowdon (the highest mountain in Wales), the villages of Beddgelert, Betws-y-Coed and Llanberis are popular bases for walkers who come to enjoy the spectacular views and lovely scenery of this remote region.

Caernarfon Castle, one of the forbidding fortresses built by Edward I

◄ Fiery sunset over Conwy Harbour

Exploring North Wales

The dominant feature of North Wales is Snowdon, the highest mountain in Wales. Snowdonia National Park extends dramatically from the Snowdon massif south beyond Dolgellau, with its thickly wooded valleys, mountain lakes, moors and estuaries. To the east are the softer Clwydian Hills, and unspoilt coastlines can be enjoyed on Anglesey and the beautiful Llŷn Peninsula.

A lighthouse perched on the sea cliffs of Anglesey

Key

- ━━━ Major road
- ┅┅┅ Minor road
- ━━━ Secondary road
- ━━━ Scenic route
- ┅┅┅ Main railway
- ──── Minor railway
- △ Summit

The peaks and moorland of Snowdonia

For hotels and restaurants in this area see p571 and p599

Getting Around

The main route into North Wales from the northwest of England is the A55, a good dual carriageway that bypasses several places that used to be traffic bottlenecks, including Conwy. The other major route through the region is the A5 Shrewsbury to Holyhead road, which follows a trail through the mountains pioneered by the 19th-century engineer Thomas Telford *(see p451)*. Rail services run along the coast to Holyhead, connecting with ferries across the Irish Sea to Dublin. Scenic branch lines travel from Llandudno Junction to Blaenau Ffestiniog (via Betws-y-Coed) and along the southern Llŷn Peninsula.

Sights at a Glance

1. Caernarfon
2. Beaumaris
3. Conwy *pp450–51*
4. Llandudno
5. Ruthin
6. Llangollen
7. Bala
8. Betws-y-Coed
9. Blaenau Ffestiniog
10. Llanberis and Snowdon
11. Beddgelert
12. Llŷn Peninsula
13. Portmeirion *pp458–9*
14. Harlech
15. Dolgellau
16. Aberdyfi

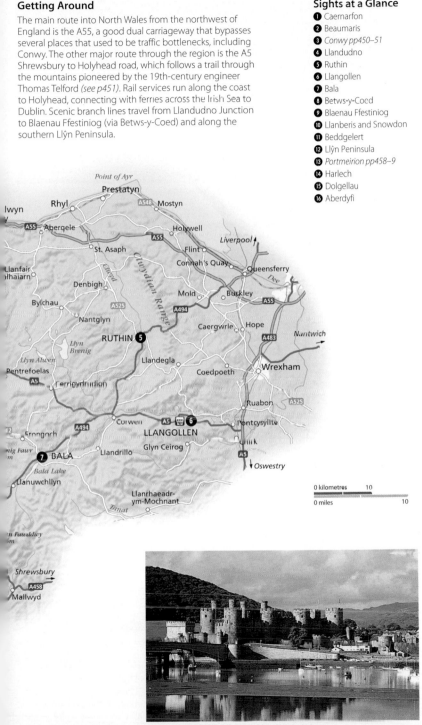

0 kilometres   10

0 miles   10

The imposing castle built at Conwy by Edward I in the 13th century

For keys to symbols *see back flap*

Caernarfon Castle, built by Edward I as a symbol of his power over the conquered Welsh

❶ Caernarfon

Gwynedd. 🚊 10,000. 🚌 ℹ️ Castle Ditch (01286 672232). 🛒 Sat. 🌐 **visitsnowdonia.info**

One of the most famous castles in Wales, Caernarfon Castle, looms over this busy town set at the mouth of the Seiont River. Both town and castle were created after Edward I's defeat of the last native Welsh prince, Llywelyn ap Gruffydd (Llywelyn the Last) in 1283 *(see p440)*. The town walls merge with modern streets that spread beyond the medieval centre to a market square.

Overlooking the town and its harbour, **Caernarfon Castle**

The Investiture

In 1301 the future Edward II became the first English Prince of Wales *(see p440)*, a title since held by the British monarch's eldest son. In 1969 the investiture in Caernarfon Castle of Prince Charles as Prince of Wales drew 500 million TV viewers.

(see p443), with its polygonal towers, was built as a seat of government for North Wales. Caernarfon was a thriving port in the 19th century, and during this period the castle ruins were restored by the architect Anthony Salvin. Today the castle contains the Royal Welch Fusiliers Museum and exhibitions tracing the history of the Princes of Wales and exploring the importance of the castle in Welsh history.

Situated on the hill above the town are the ruins of **Segontium**, a Roman fort built in about AD 78. Local legend claims that the first Christian Emperor of Rome, Constantine the Great, was born here in 280.

🏰 **Caernarfon Castle**
Y Maes. **Tel** 01286 677617. **Open** daily. **Closed** 1 Jan, 24–26 Dec. 🈳 📷 call for details. 🦽 limited. 📷 🌐 **cadw.gov.wales**

🏰 **Segontium**
Beddgelert Rd. **Open** daily. **Closed** 1 Jan, 24–26 Dec. 🦽 limited. 🅽🆃 🌐 **cadw.gov.wales**

❷ Beaumaris

Isle of Anglesey. 🚊 2,000. 🚌 🌐 **visitanglesey.co.uk**

Handsome Georgian and Victorian architecture gives Beaumaris the air of a resort on England's southern coast. The buildings reflect this sailing centre's past role as Anglesey's chief port, before the island was linked to the mainland

by the road and railway bridges built across the Menai Strait in the 19th century. This was the site of Edward I's last, and possibly greatest, **castle** *(see p442–3)*, which was built to command this important crossing to the mainland of Wales.

Ye Olde Bull's Head inn, on Castle Street, was built in 1617. Its celebrated literary patrons have included Dr Samuel Johnson (1709–84) and Victorian novelist Charles Dickens *(see p192)*.

The town's **Courthouse**, was built in 1614, and the restored 1829 **Gaol** preserves its soundproofed punishment room and a huge treadmill for prisoners. Two public hangings took place here. Richard Rowlands, the last victim, protested his innocence and cursed the church clock as he was led to the gallows, declaring that its four faces would never show the same times again. It failed to show consistent times until it had an overhaul in 1980.

🏰 **Beaumaris Castle**
Castle St. **Tel** 01248 810361. **Open** daily. **Closed** 1 Jan, 24–26 Dec. 🈳 🦽 📷 🌐 **cadw.gov.wales**

🏛️ **Courthouse**
Castle St. **Tel** 01248 811691. **Open** Apr–Sep: Sat–Thu. 🈳 🦽 limited. 🌐 **visitanglesey.co.uk**

🏛️ **Gaol**
Steeple Lane. **Tel** 01248 810921. **Open** Apr–Sep: Sat–Thu. 🈳 🦽 limited. 📷 🌐 **visitanglesey.co.uk**

For hotels and restaurants in this area see p571 and p599

Alice in Wonderland

Penmorfa, Llandudno, was the summer home of the Liddells. Their friend, Charles Dodgson (1832–98), would entertain young Alice Liddell with stories of characters such as the White Rabbit and the Mad Hatter. As Lewis Carroll, Dodgson wrote his magical tales in *Alice's Adventures in Wonderland* (1865) and *Through the Looking-Glass* (1871).

One of Arthur Rackham's illustrations (1907) for *Alice in Wonderland*

❸ Conwy

See pp450–51.

Llandudno's crescent-shaped bay

❹ Llandudno

Conwy. 🅰 20,000. 🚆 🚌 🅸 Library Building, Mostyn St (01492 577577). 🆆 visitllandudno.org.uk

Llandudno retains much of the holiday spirit of the 19th century, when the new railways brought crowds to the coast. Its **pier**, the longest in Wales at more than 700 m (2,295 ft), and its canopied walkways recall the seaside holidays in its heyday. The town is also proud of its association with the author Lewis Carroll. Sculptures relating to *Alice in Wonderland* are all over town, including a Mad Hatter on the promenade. The exhibits at the **Llandudno Museum** explore Llandudno's history from Roman times onwards.

Llandudno's cheerful seaside atmosphere owes much to a strong sense of its Victorian roots – unlike many British seaside towns, which embraced the flashing lights and funfairs of the 20th century. To take full advantage of its sweeping beach, Llandudno was built

between its two headlands, Great Orme and Little Orme.

Great Orme, a designated Area of Conservation, and nature reserve, rises to 207 m (670 ft) and has a ski slope and the longest toboggan run in Britain. In the Bronze Age copper was mined here; the **copper mines** and their excavations are open to the public. The **church** on the headland, built from timber in the 6th century by St Tudno, rebuilt in stone in the 13th century, and restored in 1855, is still in use. Local history and wildlife are described in an information centre on the summit.

There are two effortless ways to reach the summit: on the **Great Orme Tramway**, one of only three cable-hauled street tramways in the world (the others are in San Francisco and Lisbon), or by the **Llandudno Cable Car**. Both run from April to October.

🏛 **Llandudno Museum**
Gloddaeth St. **Tel** 01492 876517.
Open 10:30am–1pm, 2–5pm Tue–Sat (from 2:15pm Sun) (Nov–Easter: 1:30–4:30pm Tue–Sat). 🚗 🅿 limited. 📷
🆆 llandudnomuseum.co.uk

⛏ **Great Orme Copper Mines**
Great Orme. **Tel** 01492 870447.
Open mid-Mar–Oct: 9:30am–4:30pm daily. 🚗 🅿 limited. 🖥 📷
🆆 greatormemines.info

❺ Ruthin

Denbighshire. 🅰 5,200. 🚌 🚆 Tue & Sat; Thu (indoor). 🆆 ruthin.com

Ruthin's long-standing prosperity as a market town is reflected in its fine half-timbered medieval buildings, including the NatWest and Barclays banks in St Peter's Square. The former was a 15th-century courthouse and prison, the latter the home of Thomas Exmewe, Lord Mayor of London in 1517–18. **Maen Huail** ("Huail's stone"), a boulder outside Barclays, is said to be where King Arthur *(see p289)* beheaded love rival Huail.

St Peter's Church, on the edge of St Peter's Square, was founded in 1310 and has a Tudor oak ceiling in the north aisle. Next to the Castle Hotel is the **Myddleton Grill** restaurant, whose unusual, Dutch-style dormer windows are known locally as the "eyes of Ruthin".

The "eyes of Ruthin", an unusual feature in Welsh architecture

❸ Street-by-Street: Conwy

Conwy is one of Britain's most underrated historic towns. Until the early 1990s it was famous as a traffic bottleneck, but thanks to a town bypass, its concentration of architectural riches – unparalleled in Wales – can be more readily appreciated. The castle dominates: a brooding, intimidating monument built by Edward I *(see p442)*. But Conwy is set apart from other medieval towns by its amazingly well-preserved town walls. Fortified with 21 towers and three gateways, the walls form an almost unbroken shield around the old town.

Smallest House
This fisherman's cottage on the quayside, just over 3 m (10 ft) high, is said to be the smallest house in Britain.

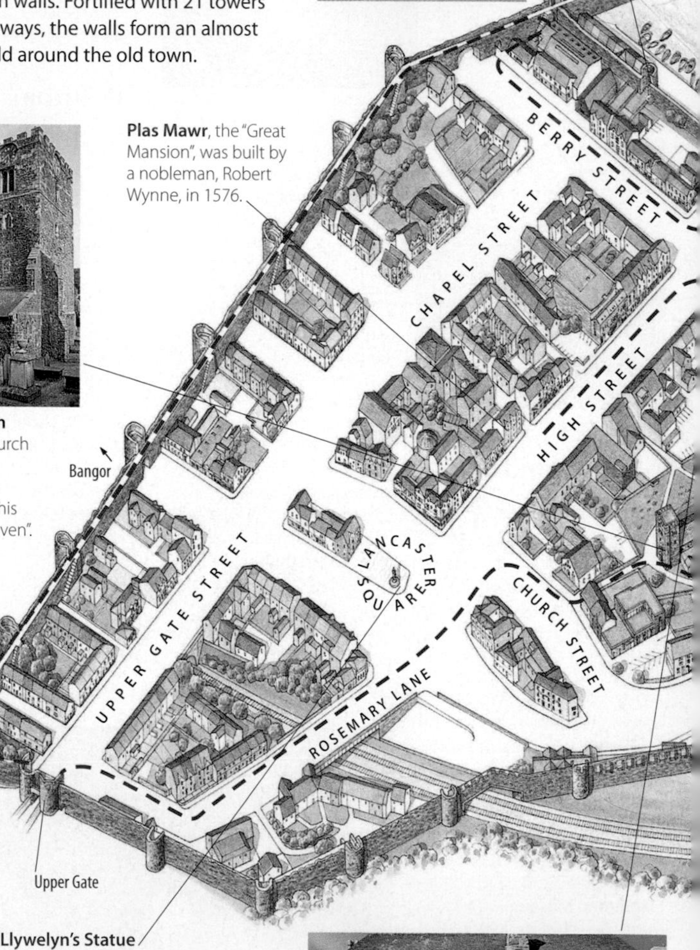

Plas Mawr, the "Great Mansion", was built by a nobleman, Robert Wynne, in 1576.

St Mary's Church
This medieval church is where William Wordsworth was inspired to write his poem "We Are Seven".

Bangor

BERRY STREET

CHAPEL STREET

HIGH STREET

UPPER GATE STREET

LANCASTER SQUARE

ROSEMARY LANE

CHURCH STREET

Upper Gate

Llywelyn's Statue
Llywelyn the Great *(see p440)* was arguably Wales's most successful medieval leader.

Aberconwy House
This restored 14th-century town house was once the home of a wealthy merchant.

Thomas Telford

Thomas Telford (1757–1834) was the gifted Scottish engineer responsible for many of Britain's roads, bridges and canals. The Menai Bridge *(see p448)*, the Pontcysyllte Aqueduct *(see p454)* and Conwy Bridge are his outstanding works in Wales. Telford's graceful bridge at Conwy is as visually appealing as it is useful. Completed in 1826 across the mouth of the Conwy estuary, it was designed in a castellated style to blend with the castle. Before the bridge's construction the estuary could only be crossed by ferry.

VISITORS' CHECKLIST

Practical Information
Conwy. 🚶 8,000. 🌐 conwy.com
ℹ️ Castle Buildings, Rose Hill St (01492 577566). Aberconwy House: **Tel** 01492 592246. **Open** mid-Mar–Oct: 10am–5pm daily; Nov & Dec: 11am–4pm Sat & Sun. **Closed** 25 Dec. 🅿️ 🚻 NT
Conwy Castle: **Tel** 01492 592358. **Open** daily. **Closed** 1 Jan, 24–26 Dec. 🅿️ 🚻 🌐 cadw.gov.wales
Smallest House: **Tel** 01492 573965. **Open** Apr–Oct: daily. 🅿️ 🌐 thesmallesthouse.co.uk

Transport
🚆 Conwy.

Entrance to castle

Railway bridge

Telford's Suspension Bridge

Chester

NEW BRIDGE

CASTLE STREET

CASTLE STREET

EHILL STREET

Key
— Suggested route

0 metres 50
0 yards 50

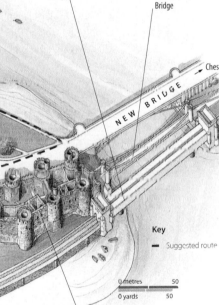

★ **Town Walls**
These remarkably well preserved medieval walls are 1,280 m (4,200 ft) long and over 9 m (30 ft) high.

★ **Conwy Castle**
This atmospheric watercolour, *Conway Castle* (c.1770), is by the Nottingham artist Paul Sandby.

For keys to symbols *see back flap*

Pontcysyllte Aqueduct, built in 1795–1805, carrying the Llangollen Canal

❻ Llangollen

Denbighshire. 🚍 3,500. 🚌
ℹ y Capel, Castle St (01978 860828).
🏪 Tue. 🆆 llangollen.org.uk

Best known for its annual Eisteddfod (festival), this pretty town sits on the River Dee, which is spanned by a 14th-century bridge. The town became notorious in the 1700s, when two Irishwomen, Sarah Ponsonby and Lady Eleanor Butler, the "Ladies of Llangollen", set up house together in the half-timbered **Plas Newydd**. Their unconventional dress and literary enthusiasms attracted such celebrities as the Duke of Wellington (see p166) and William Wordsworth (see p370). The ruins of a 13th-century castle, **Castell Dinas Brân**, occupy the summit of a hill overlooking the house.

Environs

Boats on the **Llangollen Canal** depart from Wharf Hill in summer and cross the spectacular 300-m (1,000-ft) long Pontcysyllte Aqueduct, built by Thomas Telford (see p451) and now a UNESCO World Heritage Site.

🏛 **Plas Newydd**
Hill St. **Tel** 01978 862834. **Open** Apr–Oct: Tue–Sun (Jun–Aug: daily). 🅿
🚻 limited. 🎧 📷 NT

❼ Bala

Gwynedd. 🚍 2,000. 🚌 from Wrexham. ℹ Penllyn, Pensarn Rd (01678 521021). 🆆 visitbala.org

Bala Lake, Wales's largest natural lake, lies between the Aran and Arenig mountains at the fringes

of Snowdonia National Park. It is popular for watersports and has a unique fish called a *gwyniad*, which is related to the salmon.

The little grey-stone town of Bala is a Welsh-speaking community, its houses strung out along a single street at the eastern end of the lake. Thomas Charles (1755–1814), a Methodist Church leader, once lived here. A plaque on his former home recalls Mary Jones, who walked 28 miles (42 km) barefoot from Abergynolwyn to buy a Bible. This led to Charles establishing the Bible Society, providing cheap Bibles to the working classes.

The narrow-gauge **Bala Lake Railway** follows the lakeshore from Llanuwchllyn, 4 miles (6 km) southwest.

❽ Betws-y-Coed

Conwy. 🚍 600. 🚉 ℹ Royal Oak Stables (01690 710426).
🆆 betws-y-coed.co.uk

This village near the peaks of Snowdonia has been a hill-walking centre since the

19th century. To the west are the **Swallow Falls**, where the River Llugwy flows through a wooded glen. The bizarre **Ty Hyll** ("Ugly House") is a *tŷ unnos* ("one-night house"); traditionally, houses erected between dusk and dawn on common land were entitled to freehold rights, and the owner could enclose land as far as he could throw an axe from the door. To the east is **Waterloo Bridge**, built by Thomas Telford to celebrate the victory against Napoleon.

🏛 **Ty Hyll**
Capel Curig. **Tel** 01286 685498.
House: **Open** Mar–Oct: daily.
Grounds: **Open** daily. 🖼 🚻 limited.

The ornate Waterloo Bridge, built in 1815 after the famous battle

◀ Lake in the valley of Nant Gwynant, in Snowdonia National Park

The Snowdonia countryside as seen from Llanberis Pass, on the most popular route to Snowdon's peak

❾ Blaenau Ffestiniog

Gwynedd. 🚇 4,800. 🚌 🅸 Betws-y-Coed (01690 710426). 🏪 Tue (Jun–Sep).

Blaenau Ffestiniog, once the slate capital of North Wales, sits among mountains riddled with quarries. The **Llechwedd Slate Caverns**, overlooking Blaenau, opened to visitors in the early 1970s, marking a new role for the declining industrial town.

On the Deep Mine tour, visitors descend on Britain's steepest passenger railway to the underground chambers, while sound effects recreate the atmosphere of a working quarry. The dangers included landfalls and floods, as well as the more gradual threat of slate dust breathed into the lungs. The Quarry tour, meanwhile, takes visitors on a 4x4 adventure through this remarkable landscape and into numerous huge craters.

There are slate-splitting demonstrations on the surface, a quarryman's cottage and a recreation of a Victorian village to illustrate the cramped and basic living conditions endured by workers between the 1880s and 1945.

The narrow-gauge **Ffestiniog Railway** (see pp456–7) runs from Blaenau to Porthmadog.

🏛 **Llechwedd Slate Caverns**
Off A470. **Tel** 01766 830306. **Open** daily (Jan–mid-Mar: Wed–Sun). 🅟 🅱 except Deep Mine. 🛍 🅿 🆆 **llechwedd-slate-caverns.co.uk**

❿ Llanberis and Snowdon

Gwynedd. 🚇 2,100. 🅸 Electric Mountain Visitor Centre (01286 870765). 🆆 **visitsnowdonia.info**

Snowdon, which at 1,085 m (3,560 ft) is the highest peak in Wales, dominates the vast Snowdonia National Park, whose scenery ranges from this rugged mountain country to moors and sandy beaches.

The easiest route is the 5-mile (8-km) **Llanberis Track**, starting in Llanberis. From Llanberis Pass, the Miners' Track (once used by copper miners) and the Pyg Track are alternative paths.

Walkers should beware of sudden weather changes and dress accordingly. The narrow-gauge **Snowdon Mountain Railway**, which opened in 1896, is another way to reach the summit.

Llanberis was a major 19th-century slate town, with grey terraces hewn into the hills. Other attractions are the 13th-century shell of **Dolbadarn Castle** and above Llyn Peris the **Electric Mountain**, with tours of Dinorwig, Europe's biggest hydro-electric storage station.

🏰 **Dolbadarn Castle**
Off A4086 near Llanberis. **Tel** 01443 336000. **Open** daily. **Closed** 1 Jan, 24–26 Dec.

🅸 **Electric Mountain**
Llanberis. **Tel** 01286 870636. **Open** daily. 🅟 🅲 Easter–Oct only. 🅱 🛍 🅿 🆆 **electric mountain.co.uk**

Britain's Centre of Slate

Welsh slates provided roofing material for Britain's new towns in the 19th century. In 1898, the slate industry employed nearly 17,000 men, a quarter of whom worked at Blaenau Ffestiniog. Foreign competition and new materials later took their toll. Quarries such as Dinorwig in Llanberis and Llechwedd in Blaenau Ffestiniog now survive on the tourist trade.

The art of slate-splitting

For hotels and restaurants in this area see p571 and p599

The village of Beddgelert, set among the mountains of Snowdonia

⑪ Beddgelert

Gwynedd. 🚌 500. 🅸 Canolfan-Hebog (01766 890615).
🌐 beddgelerttourism.com

Beddgelert enjoys a spectacular location in Snowdonia. The village sits on the confluence of the Glaslyn and Colwyn rivers at the approach to two mountain passes: the beautiful Nant Gwynant Pass, which leads to Snowdonia's highest reaches, and the Aberglaslyn Pass, a narrow wooded gorge that acts as a gateway to the sea.

Business was given a boost by Dafydd Pritchard, the landlord of the Royal Goat Hotel, who in the early 19th century adapted an old Welsh legend to associate it with Beddgelert. Llywelyn the Great *(see p440)* is said to have left his faithful hound Gelert to guard his infant son while he went hunting. He returned to find the cradle overturned and Gelert covered in blood. Thinking the dog had savaged his son, Llywelyn slaughtered Gelert, but then discovered the boy, unharmed, under the cradle. Nearby was the corpse of a wolf, which Gelert had killed to protect the child. To support the tale, Pritchard created **Gelert's Grave** (*bedd Gelert* in Welsh) by the River Glaslyn, a mound of stones a short walk south of the village.

Environs

There are many fine walks in the area: one leads south to the Aberglaslyn Pass and along a section of the Welsh Highland Railway (www.festrail.co.uk). The **Sygun Copper Mine**, 1 mile (1.5 km) northeast of Beddgelert, offers self-guided tours of caverns recreating the life of Victorian miners.

🏚 **Sygun Copper Mine**
On A498. **Tel** 01766 890595.
Open mid-Feb–mid-Nov: daily.
🅿 ♿ limited. 🄲 🄿
🌐 syguncoppermine.co.uk

Ffestiniog Railway

The Ffestiniog narrow-gauge railway takes a scenic 14-mile (22-km) route from Porthmadog Harbour to the mountains and the slate town of Blaenau Ffestiniog *(see p455)*. Designed to carry slate from the quarries to the quay, the railway replaced a horse-drawn tramway constructed in 1836, operating on a 60-cm (2-ft) gauge. After closure in 1946, it was reconstructed by volunteers and reopened in sections between 1955 and 1982.

Steam-traction trains were first used on the Ffestiniog Railway in 1863. There are some diesel engines, but most trains on the route are still steam-hauled.

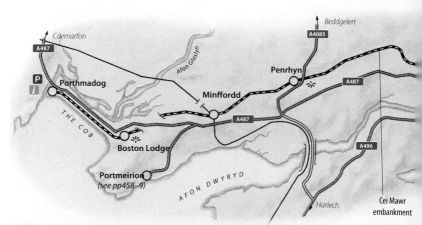

⑫ Llŷn Peninsula

Gwynedd. 🚃 🚌 Pwllheli.
🚢 Aberdaron to Bardsey Island.
ℹ️ Neuadd Dwyfor, Penlan St,
Pwllheli (01758 613000).
🌐 visitsnowdonia.info

This 24-mile (38-km) finger of land points southwest from Snowdonia into the Irish Sea. Although it has popular beaches, notably at Pwllheli, Criccieth, Abersoch and Nefyn, the peninsula's overriding feature is its untamed beauty. Views are at their most dramatic in the far west and along the mountain-backed northern shores.

The windy headland of **Braich-y-Pwll**, to the west of Aberdaron, looks out towards Bardsey Island, the "Isle of 20,000 Saints". This became a place of pilgrimage in the 6th century, when a monastery was founded here. Some of the saints are said to be buried in the churchyard of the ruined

13th-century **St Mary's Abbey**. Close by is **Porth Oer**, a small bay also known as "Whistling Sands" (the sand is meant to squeak, or whistle, underfoot).

East of Aberdaron is the 4-mile (7-km) bay of **Porth Neigwl**, known in English as Hell's Mouth, the scene of many shipwrecks due to the bay's treacherous currents. Hidden in sheltered grounds above Porth Neigwl bay, 1 mile (1.5 km) northeast of Aberdaron, is **Plas-yn-Rhiw**, a

small, medieval manor house with Tudor and Georgian additions and lovely gardens.

The former quarrying village and "ghost town" of **Llithfaen**, tucked away below the sheer cliffs of the mountainous north coast, is now a centre for Welsh language studies.

🏠 Plas-yn-Rhiw
Off B4413. **Tel** 01758 780219.
Open Apr–Jun & Oct: Wed–Mon;
Jul–Sep: daily. 🚫 🔽 limited.
📷 NT

Llithfaen village, now a language centre, on the Llŷn Peninsula

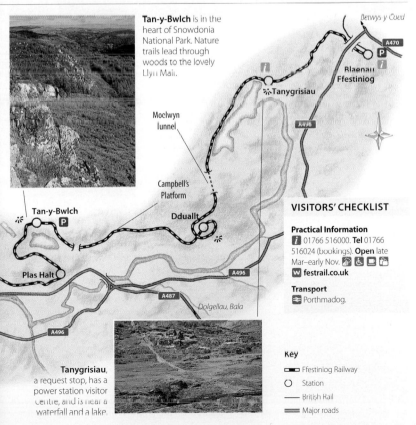

Tan-y-Bwlch is in the heart of Snowdonia National Park. Nature trails lead through woods to the lovely Llyn Mair.

Betwys y Coed

A470

Blaenau Ffestiniog

ℹ️

🚉 Tanygrisiau

A496

Moelwyn Tunnel

Campbell's Platform

Dduallt

Tan-y-Bwlch 🅿️

Plas Halt

A496

A487

Dolgellau, Bala

A496

Tanygrisiau, a request stop, has a power station visitor centre, and is near a waterfall and a lake.

VISITORS' CHECKLIST

Practical Information
ℹ️ 01766 516000. **Tel** 01766 516024 (bookings). **Open** late Mar–early Nov. 🚫 🔽 💻 📷
🌐 festrail.co.uk

Transport
🚃 Porthmadog.

Key
⬛▬⬛ Ffestiniog Railway
◯ Station
—— British Rail
═══ Major roads

For keys to symbols see back flap

⓭ Portmeirion

Gwynedd. **Tel** 01766 770000.
🚋 Minffordd. **Open** daily **Closed**
25 Dec. 🚗 ♿ 🛍️ limited. 📷 🎦 🖼️
📶 🌐 **portmeirion-village.com**

This bizarre Italianate village on a private peninsula at the top of Cardigan Bay was created by Welsh architect Sir Clough Williams-Ellis (1883–1978). He fulfilled a childhood dream by building a village "to my own fancy on my own chosen site". About 50 buildings surround a central piazza, in styles from Oriental to Gothic. Visitors can stay at the luxurious hotel or in one of the charming village cottages. Portmeirion has been an atmospheric location for many films and television programmes, including the popular 1960s television series *The Prisoner*.

Sir Clough Williams-Ellis at Portmeirion

Hercules
This is a life-size 19th-century copper statue near the Town Hall, where a 17th-century ceiling, rescued from a demolished mansion, depicts his legend.

Fountain Cottage is where Noel Coward (1899–1973) wrote *Blithe Spirit*.

The Amis Reunis is a stone replica of a boat that sank in the bay.

Swimming pool

The Portmeirion Hotel
Overlooking the bay, this hotel has a dining room designed by Sir Terence Conran.

⓮ Harlech

Gwynedd. 🗺️ 2,000. 🚋
🌐 **visitharlech.org**

This small town with fine beaches is dominated by **Harlech Castle**, a medieval fortress *(see p442)* built by Edward I between 1283 and 1289. The castle sits on a precipitous crag, with superb views of Tremadog Bay and the Llŷn Peninsula to the west, and of Snowdonia to the north.

When the castle was built, the sea reached a fortified stairway cut into the cliff, so that supplies could arrive by ship, but now the coastline has receded.

Despite its defences, Harlech Castle fell to Owain Glyndŵr *(see p440)* in 1404, and served as his court until its recapture 4 years later. The song *Men of Harlech* is thought to have been inspired by the castle's heroic resistance during an 8-year

siege in the Wars of the Roses *(see p53)*. Access to the towering gatehouse is via a suspended pedestrian bridge. The inner ward is enclosed by massive walls and four round towers.

🏰 **Harlech Castle**
Castle Sq. **Tel** 01766 780552.
Open daily. **Closed** 1 Jan, 24–26 Dec.
🚗 ♿ 🖥️ 📷 🌐 **cadw.gov.wales**

⓯ Dolgellau

Gwynedd. 🗺️ 2,700. 🛈 Eldon Sq
(01341 422888). 🍽️ Fri (livestock).

The dark local stone gives a stern, solid look to this market town, where the Welsh language and customs are still very strong. It lies in the long shadow of the 892-m (2,927-ft) mountain of Cader Idris where, according to legend, anyone who spends a night on its summit will awake a poet or a madman – or not at all.

Dolgellau was gripped by gold fever in the 19th century, when

Harlech Castle's strategic site overlooking mountains and sea

Triumphal Arch

Central Piazza

Lodge

Campanile

Royal
Dolphin
Cottage

Bristol
Colonnade   Viewing platform

The Lady's Lodge
Located next to the Prisoner
Shop, this has a semicircular
mural by Hans Feibusch
above the bay window.

The Pantheon
Built in 1960–61, the Pantheon originally
had a dome made from plywood painted
green, instead of copper, due to a lack of
funds. Its unusual façade is formed by the
upper half of a music room fireplace by
Norman Shaw (see p33).

Dolgellau's grey-stone buildings, dwarfed by the mountain scenery

high-quality gold was
discovered in the Mawddach
Valley nearby. The deposits were
not large enough to sustain an
intensive mining industry for
long. Nevertheless, up until 1999,
small amounts were mined and
crafted locally into fine jewellery.

Dolgellau is a good centre
for walking, whether gentle
strolls through beautiful leafy
countryside or strenuous hikes
across extreme terrain with
dramatic mountain views. The
lovely **Cregennen lakes** are set
high in the hills above the thickly
wooded **Mawddach Estuary**
to the northwest; north are the
harsh, bleak **Rhinog moors**, one
of Wales's last true wildernesses.

🔟 Aberdyfi

Gwynedd. 🚶 1,200. 🚆 ℹ️ Wharf
Gardens (01654 767321).
🌐 **aberdyfi.org**

Perched at the mouth of the
Dyfi Estuary, this little harbour
resort and sailing centre makes
the most of its splendid but
rather confined location, its
houses occupying every yard of
a narrow strip of land between
mountain and sea. In the 19th
century, local slate was exported
from here, and between the
1830s and the 1860s about
100 ships were built in the port.
The Bells of Aberdovey, a song by
Charles Dibdin for his opera
Liberty Hall (1785), tells the
legend of Cantref-y-Gwaelod,
thought to have been located
here, which was protected from
the sea by dykes. One stormy
night, the sluice gates were left
open by Prince Seithenyn, when
he was drunk, and the land
was lost beneath
the waves. The
submerged
church
bells are
said to peal
under the
water to
this day.

Neat Georgian
houses by the
sea, Aberdyfi

SOUTH AND MID-WALES

*Ceredigion · Carmarthenshire · Monmouthshire
Powys · Pembrokeshire*

From the vibrant capital, Cardiff, to its second city, Swansea,
South Wales is the country's most populous area. But it also has
a chunk of wonderful landscape, thanks to the Gower peninsula
and Pembrokeshire, the latter the loveliest stretch of Welsh
coastline. To the north the industrial valleys give way to the wide
hills of the Brecon Beacons and the rural heart of central Wales.

South Wales's coastal strip has been
settled for many centuries. There are
prehistoric sites in the Vale of Glamorgan
and Pembrokeshire. The Romans established a major base at Caerleon, and the
Normans built castles all the way from
Chepstow to Pembroke. In the 18th and
19th centuries, coal mines and ironworks
opened in the valleys of South Wales,
attracting immigrants from all over Europe.
Close communities developed to serve the
growing coal trade, which turned Cardiff
from a sleepy coastal town into the world's
busiest coal exporting port.

The demise of the coal industry has
again changed the face of this area:
spoil heaps have become green hills,
and the valley towns struggle to find
alternative forms of employment.

Coal mines such as Blaenavon's Big Pit are
now tourist attractions; today, many of the
tour guides taking visitors underground
are ex-miners, who can offer a first-hand
glimpse of the hardships of life in mining
communities before the pits closed.

The southern boundary of the
Brecon Beacons National Park marks
the beginning of rural Wales. With a
population sparser than anywhere
in England, this is an area of small
country towns, hill-sheep farms, forestry
plantations and spectacular artificial lakes.

Cardiff, Wales's exciting capital, seems
to have reinvented itself in recent years,
not least in the wholesale redevelopment
of the Bay. South Wales also boasts the
UK's smallest city, St David's, courtesy
of its spectacular cathedral.

Walkers admiring the view at Llyn y Fan Fach, in the Brecon Beacons National Park

◀ The imposing entrance to the Wales Millennium Centre in Cardiff

Exploring South and Mid-Wales

Magnificent coastal scenery marks the Pembrokeshire Coast National Park and cliff-backed Gower Peninsula, while Cardigan Bay and Carmarthen Bay offer quieter beaches. Walkers can enjoy grassy uplands in the Brecon Beacons and gentler country in the leafy Wye Valley. Urban life is concentrated in the southeast of Wales, where old mining towns line the valleys north of Cardiff, the capital.

Cliffs of the Pembrokeshire Coast National Park

Key

═══ Motorway
═══ Major road
─── Secondary road
┄┄┄ Minor road
─── Scenic route
┅┅┅ Main railway
─── Minor railway
△ Summit

Sights at a Glance

1. Powis Castle
2. Knighton
3. Hay-on-Wye
4. Llandrindod Wells
5. Elan Valley
6. Machynlleth
7. Aberystwyth
8. Aberaeron
9. St Davids pp468–9
10. Tenby
11. Swansea and the Gower Peninsula
13. *Brecon Beacons pp472–3*
14. *Cardiff pp474–7*
15. Caerleon
16. Blaenavon
17. Monmouth
18. Tintern Abbey

Walks and Tours

12. *Wild Wales Tour p471*

0 kilometres 15
0 miles 10

The rolling hills near Knighton, on the borderlands between Wales and England

Getting Around

The M4 motorway is the major route into Wales from the south of England, and there are good road links west of Swansea running to the coast. The A483 and A488 give access to Mid-Wales from the Midlands. Frequent rail services connect London with Swansea, Cardiff and the ferry port of Fishguard.

A detail of Cardiff Castle's clock tower, part of the ornate embellishments added in the 19th century

For keys to symbols see back flap

Italianate terraces and formal gardens at Powis Castle, adding a Mediterranean air to the Welsh borderlands

❶ Powis Castle

Welshpool, Powys. **Tel** 01938 551944. 🚆 Welshpool then bus. **Open** daily. House: **Open** Jan & Feb: Sat & Sun; Mar–Dec: daily. Gardens: **Open** daily. **Closed** 25 Dec. 🅿️ 🚽 ♿ limited. 🛗 🍽 🏠 NT W **nationaltrust.org.uk/powis-castle**

Powis Castle – the spelling is an archaic version of "Powys" – has outgrown its military roots. Despite its sham battlements and dominant site, 1 mile (2 km) to the southwest of the town of Welshpool, this red-stone building has served as a country mansion

The richly carved 17th-century Great Staircase

for centuries. It began life in the 13th century as a fortress, built by the princes of Powys to control the border with England.

The castle is entered through one of few surviving medieval features: a gateway, built in 1283 by Owain de la Pole. The gate is flanked by two towers.

The castle's lavish interiors soon banish all thoughts of war. A **Dining Room**, decorated with fine 17th-century panelling and family portraits, was originally designed as the castle's Great Hall. The **Great Staircase**, added in the late 17th century and elaborately decorated with carved fruit and flowers, leads to the main apartments: an early 19th-century library, the panelled **Oak Drawing Room** and the Elizabethan **Long Gallery**, where plasterwork on the fireplace and ceiling date from the 1590s. In the **Blue Drawing Room** there are three 18th-century Brussels tapestries.

The Herbert family bought the property in 1587 and were proud of their Royalist connections; the panelling in the **State Bedroom** bears the royal monogram. Powis Castle was defended for Charles I in the Civil War (see pp56–7), but fell to Parliament in 1644. The 3rd Baron Powis, a supporter of James II, had to flee the country when William and Mary took the throne in 1688 (see pp56–7).

The castle's **Clive Museum** has an exhibition concerning "Clive of India" (1725–74), the general and statesman who helped strengthen British control in India in the mid-18th century. The family's link with Powis Castle was established by the 2nd Lord Clive, who married into the Herbert family and became the Earl of Powis in 1804.

The **gardens** at Powis are among the best-known in Britain, with their series of elegant Italianate terraces, adorned with statues, niches, balustrades, hanging gardens and sinuous mounded yew trees, all stepped into the steep hillside beneath the castle walls. Created between 1688 and 1722, these are the only formal gardens of this period in Britain that have retained their original layout (see pp30–31).

❷ Knighton

Powys. 🚠 3,500. 🚆 ℹ️ Offa's Dyke Centre, West St (01547 528753). 🏪 Sat. 🆆 visitknighton.co.uk

Knighton's Welsh name, Tref y Clawdd ("The Town on the Dyke"), reflects its status as the only original settlement on **Offa's Dyke**. In the 8th century, King Offa of Mercia (central and southern England) constructed a ditch and bank to mark out his territory, and to enable the enforcement of a Saxon law: "Neither shall a Welshman cross into English land without the appointed man from the other side, who should meet him at the bank and bring him back again without any offence being committed." Some of the best-preserved sections of the 6-m- (20-ft-) high earthwork lie in the hills around Knighton. The Offa's Dyke Footpath runs for 177 miles (285 km) along the border between England and Wales.

Knighton is set on a steep hill, sloping upwards from **St Edward's Church** (1877) with its medieval tower, to the summit, where a castle once stood. The main street leads via the market square, which has a 19th-century clock tower, along **The Narrows**, a Tudor street with little shops. **The Old House** on Broad Street is a medieval "cruck" house (curved timbers form a frame to support the roof), with a hole in the ceiling instead of a chimney.

❸ Hay-on-Wye

Powys. 🚠 1,500. ℹ️ Oxford Rd (01497 820144). 🏪 Thu. 🆆 hay-on-wye.co.uk

Book-lovers from all over the world come to this quiet border town in the Black Mountains. Hay-on-Wye has more than 20 second-hand bookshops stocking millions of titles, and in early summer hosts a prestigious Festival of Literature and the Arts. The town's love affair with books began when a bookshop was opened in the 1960s by Richard Booth, who claims the (fictitious) title of King of Independent Hay and lived in Hay Castle, a 17th-century mansion in the grounds of the original 13th-century castle. Now owned by a charitable trust, it remains in a sad state of disrepair, though there are plans for a major renovation. Hay's oldest inn, the 16th-century **Three Tuns** on Bridge Street, is still functioning and has an attractive half-timbered façade.

Environs

Hay-on-Wye sits on the approach to the Black Mountains and is surrounded by rolling hills. To the south are the heights of Hay Bluff and the Vale of Ewyas, with its 12th-century ruins of **Llanthony Priory** (see p473).

❹ Llandrindod Wells

Powys. 🚠 5,300. 🚆 ℹ️ Town Hall, Temple Street (01597 822600). 🏪 Fri.

Llandrindod is a perfect example of a Victorian town, with canopied streets, delicate wrought ironwork, gabled villas, boating lake and

One of Hay-on-Wye's many second-hand bookshops

ornamental parklands, such as the well-tended **Rock Park Gardens**. This purpose-built spa town became Wales's premier inland resort in the 19th century. Its sulphur and magnesium spring waters were taken to treat skin complaints and a range of other ailments.

The town now makes every effort to preserve its Victorian character. During the last full week of August, residents don period costume at the restored 19th-century **Pump Room** in Temple Gardens and cars are banned from the town centre.

The **Radnorshire Museum** traces the town's past as one of a string of 19th-century Welsh spas, which included Builth, Llangammarch and Llanwrtyd, the latter home to a series of quirky festivals.

🏛️ **Radnorshire Museum**
Temple Street. **Tel** 01597 824513.
Open Tue–Sat. **Closed** 1 Jan, 25 & 26 Dec. 📷 ♿

Victorian architecture on Spa Road, Llandrindod Wells

Knighton's clock

Craig Goch, one of the original chain of Elan Valley reservoirs

❺ Elan Valley

Powys. 🚈 Llandrindod. 🛈 Rhayader (01597 810898). 🆆 **elanvalley.org.uk**

A string of spectacular reservoirs, the first of the country's artificial lakes, has made this one of Wales's most famous valleys. **Caban Coch**, **Garreg Ddu**, **Pen-y-Garreg** and **Craig Goch** were created between 1892 and 1903 to supply water to Birmingham, 73 miles (117 km) away. They form a chain of lakes about 9 miles (14 km) long, holding 50 billion litres (13 billion gallons) of water. Victorian engineers selected these high moorlands on the Cambrian Mountains for their high annual rainfall of 1,780 mm (70 in). The choice created bitter controversy and resentment: more than 100 people had to move from the valley that was flooded in order to create Caban Coch.

Unlike their more utilitarian modern counterparts, the dams here were built during an era when decoration was seen as an integral part of any design. Finished in dressed stone, they have an air of grandeur which is lacking in the huge **Claerwen** reservoir, a stark addition built during the early 1950s to double the lakes' capacity. Contained by a 355-m (1,165-ft) dam, it lies 4 miles (6 km) along the B4518 that runs through Elan Valley and offers magnificent views.

The remote moorlands and woodlands surrounding the lakes are an important habitat for wildlife; the red kite can often be seen here. The **Elan Valley Visitors' Centre**, beside the Caban Coch dam, describes the construction of the lakes, as well as the valley's own natural history. **Elan Village**, set beside the centre, is an unusual example of a model workers' village, built during the 1900s to house the waterworks staff. Outside the centre is a statue inspired by the poem "Prometheus Unbound" by Percy Bysshe Shelley *(see p226)*, who stayed in the valley at the mansion of Nantgwyllt in 1810 with his wife, Harriet. The house now lies underneath the waters of Caban Coch, along with the rest of the old village. Among the buildings submerged were the village school and a church.

The trail from Machynlleth to Devil's Bridge, near Aberystwyth

❻ Machynlleth

Powys. 🚈 2,200. 🚉 🛈 Welshpool (01938 552043). 🗓 Wed. 🆆 **midwalesmyway.com**

Half-timbered buildings and Georgian façades appear among the grey-stone houses in Machynlleth. It was here that Owain Glyndŵr, Wales's last native leader *(see p440)*, held a parliament in 1404. The restored Parliament House now contains the **Owain Glyndŵr Centre**.

The ornate **Clock Tower**, in the middle of Maengwyn Street, was erected in 1874 by the Marquess of Londonderry to mark the coming of age of his heir, Lord Castlereagh. The Marquess lived in **Plas Machynlleth**, a 17th-century house in parkland off the main street, which now houses a restaurant and offices.

Environs
In an old slate quarry 2 miles (4 km) to the north, a "village of the future" is run by the **Centre for Alternative Technology**. A water-balanced cliff railway takes summer visitors to view low-energy houses and organic gardens, to see how to make the best of Earth's resources.

🏛 **Owain Glyndŵr Centre** Maengwyn St. **Tel** 01654 702932. **Open** Mar–Dec: daily. 🕭 🏠 🆆 **canolfanglyndwr.org**

🏛 **Centre for Alternative Technology** On A487. **Tel** 01654 705950. **Open** daily. **Closed** early Jan. 🎒 🕭 🅿 🛗 🏠 🆆 **cat.org.uk**

❼ Aberystwyth

Ceredigion. 🚈 14,000. 🚉 🚌 🛈 Terrace Rd (01970 612125). 🆆 **discoverceredigion.co.uk**

This seaside university town claims to be the cultural capital of Mid-Wales. By the standards of this rural area, "Aber" is a big place, with a large student population.

To Victorian travellers, Aberystwyth was the "Biarritz of Wales". There have been no great changes along the promenade, with its gabled hotels, since the 19th century. **Constitution Hill**,

Buskers with a harp and guitar on Aberystwyth's seafront

a steep outcrop at the northern end, can be scaled in summer on the electric **Cliff Railway**, built in 1896. At the top, in a **camera obscura**, a lens projects views of the town. The ruined **Aberystwyth Castle** (1277) is located south of the promenade. In the town centre, the **Ceredigion Museum**, set in a former music hall, traces the history of the town.

To the northeast of the town centre, the **National Library of Wales**, next to the university, has a valuable collection of ancient Welsh manuscripts, as well as copies of every book published in England and Ireland.

Savin's Hotel

When the Cambrian Railway opened in 1864, businessman Thomas Savin put £80,000 into building a new hotel in Aberystwyth for package tourists. The scheme made him bankrupt, but the seafront building, complete with mock-Gothic tower, was bought by campaigners attempting to establish a Welsh university. The "college by the sea" opened in 1872, and is now the University of Aberystwyth.

Mosaics on the college tower

Environs

During the summer the narrow-gauge Vale of Rheidol Railway runs 12 miles (19 km) to **Devil's Bridge**, where a dramatic series of waterfalls plunges through a wooded ravine and a steep trail leads to the valley floor.

🏛 **Ceredigion Museum**
Terrace Rd. **Tel** 01970 633088.
Open Mon–Sat. **Closed** Good Fri, Easter Mon, 25 Dec–2 Jan. 🚻 🅿
W **museum.ceredigion.gov.uk**

❽ Aberaeron

Ceredigion. 🚶 1,500. 🚌 Aberystwyth then bus. 🛈 Pen Cei (01545 570602).
W **discoverceredigion.co.uk**

Aberaeron's harbour, lined with Georgian houses, became a trading port and shipbuilding centre in the early 19th century. Its orderly streets were laid out in pre-railway days, when the ports along Cardigan Bay enjoyed considerable wealth. The last boat was built here in 1994 and its harbour is now full of holiday sailors. The harbour can be crossed via a wooden footbridge.

The town is filled with delis, fishmongers and butchers selling local produce. On the quayside, the Hive honey ice-cream parlour serves world-renowned ice creams to a loyal clientele.

Rows of brightly painted Georgian houses lining the purpose-built harbour at Aberaeron

❾ St Davids

St David, the patron saint of Wales, founded a monastic settlement in this remote corner of southwest Wales in about 550, which became an important Christian shrine. The present cathedral, built in the 12th century, and the Bishop's Palace, added a century later, are set in a grassy hollow below St Davids town, officially Britain's smallest city. The date of St David's death, 1 March, is commemorated throughout Wales.

St Davids' Cathedral, the largest in Wales

Bishop's Palace

The bishop's residence, built between 1280 and 1350 and now in ruins, had lavish private apartments.

Entrance

★ Great Hall

The open arcade and decorated parapet were added by Bishop Gower (1328–47) to unify different sections of the palace.

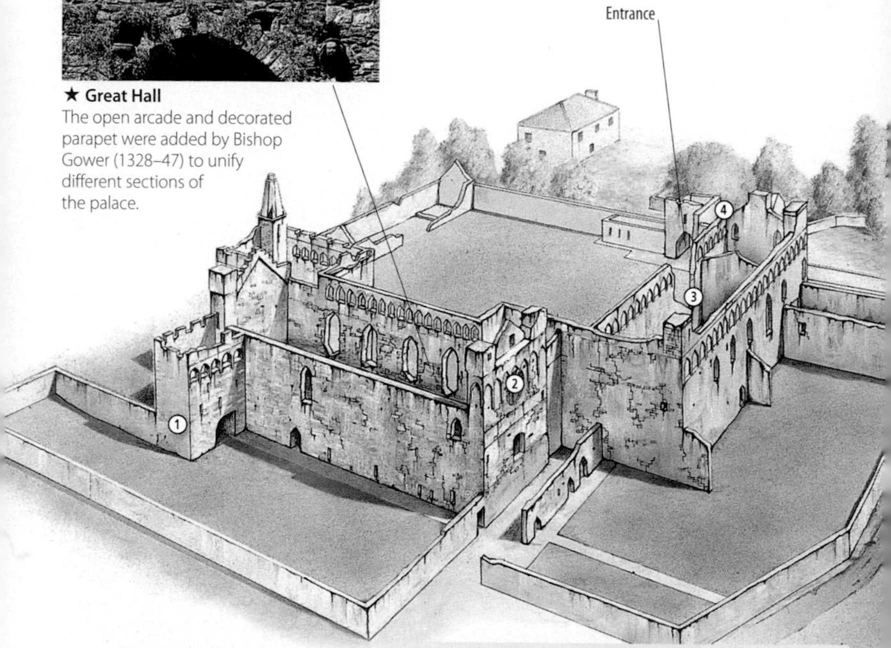

KEY

① Palace latrines

② Rose window

③ **The Bishop's Hall**, smaller than the Great Hall, may have been reserved for private use.

④ **The Private Chapel** was a late 14th-century addition, built, like the rest of the palace, over a series of vaults.

⑤ St Mary's College Chapel

⑥ **Bishop Vaughan's Chapel** has a fine fan-vaulted early Tudor roof.

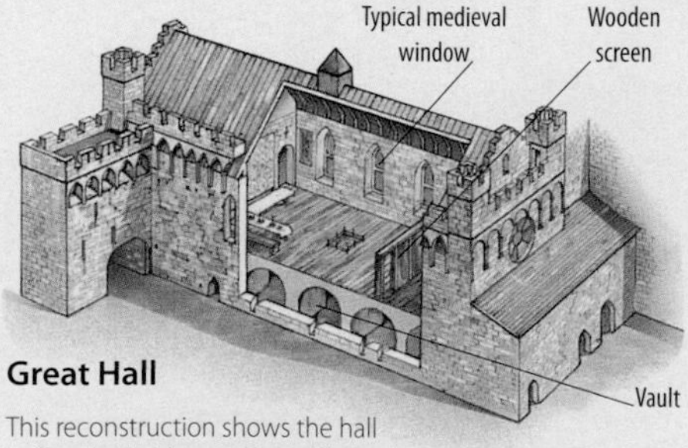

Typical medieval window

Wooden screen

Great Hall

This reconstruction shows the hall before the lead was stripped from the roof. Bishop Barlow, St Davids' first Protestant bishop (1536–48), is thought to have been responsible for the lead's removal.

Vault

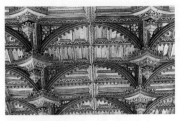

★ Nave Ceiling
The roof of the nave is lowered and hidden by an early 16th-century oak ceiling. A beautiful 14th-century rood screen divides the nave from the choir.

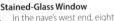

Stained-Glass Window
In the nave's west end, eight panels, produced in the 1950s, radiate from a central window depicting the dove of peace.

Cathedral

St David was one of the founders of the 6th-century monastic movement, so this was an important site of pilgrimage. Three visits here equalled one to Jerusalem.

Entrance

Tower Lantern Ceiling
The medieval roof was decorated with episcopal insignia when restored in the 1870s by Sir George Gilbert Scott.

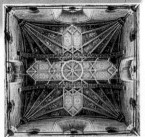

Sixteenth-century Choirstalls
The royal coat of arms on one of the carved choir stalls shows that the sovereign is a member of St Davids' Chapter. There are some interesting misericords (see p345) in these stalls

★ St David's Shrine
A statue of the saint is placed near the shrine. Thought to symbolize the Holy Spirit, a dove is said to have landed on David's shoulder as he spoke to a gathering of bishops.

❿ Tenby

Pembrokeshire. 🚆 5,000. 🚊🚌🚍
ℹ️ Upper Park Road (01437 775603).
🌐 visitpembrokeshire.com

Tenby has successfully
trodden the fine line between
over-commercialization and
popularity, refusing to submit its
historic character to the garish
excesses of some seaside towns.
Georgian houses overlook its
handsome harbour, which is
backed by a well-preserved
medieval clifftop town of narrow
streets and passages. The old
town was defended by a
headland fortress, now ruined,
flanked by two wide beaches
and a ring of 13th-century
walls. These survive to their
full height in places, along
with a fortified gateway,
the **Five Arches**.

The three-storeyed
**Tudor Merchant's
House** is a 15th-
century relic
of Tenby's highly
prosperous
seafaring days,
with original
fireplaces and
chimneys. There
are regular boat
trips from the
harbour to **Caldey Island**,
3 miles (5 km) offshore, home
of a perfume- and chocolate-
making monastic community.

🏛️ Tudor Merchant's House
Quay Hill. **Tel** 01834 842279. **Open** Apr–
Oct: Wed–Mon (Aug: daily); Nov–Dec:
Sat & Sun (Feb half-term: daily). 🐾
🎫 for pre-booked parties. NT

The three-storeyed Tudor Merchant's
House in Tenby

⓫ Swansea and the Gower Peninsula

Swansea. 🚆 240,000. 🚊🚌
🚍🚍 Mon–Sat. 🌐 visitswansea
bay.com

Swansea, Wales's second city, is
set along a wide, curving bay.
The city centre was rebuilt after
heavy bombing in World War II
but, despite the modern
buildings, a traditional Welsh
atmosphere prevails. This is
particularly noticeable in the
excellent food market, full of
Welsh delicacies such as
laverbread (see p581) and
locally caught cockles.

The award-winning
Maritime Quarter
redevelopment has
transformed the old
dock area, and is
worth a visit.
A statue of
copper magnate
John Henry
Vivian (1779–
1855) overlooks
the marina.
The Vivians,
a leading
Swansea
family,
founded
the **Glynn
Vivian Art Gallery**, which has
exquisite Swansea pottery and
porcelain. Archaeology and
Welsh history feature at the
Swansea Museum, the oldest
museum in Wales.

Swansea's most celebrated son,
the poet Dylan Thomas

The life and work of local
poet Dylan Thomas (1914–53)
is celebrated in the **Dylan
Thomas Centre**. A permanent
exhibition, Love the Words,
includes original drafts of his
poems, letters and memorabilia. His statue overlooks the
Maritime Quarter. Thomas
spent his childhood in the
Uplands suburb. His birthplace,
at 5 Cwmdonkin Drive, has
been restored to how it would
have been in 1914, including
his bedroom.

The **National Waterfront
Museum** tells the story of
industry and innovation in
Wales over the past 300 years.
The ultra-modern slate and
glass building incorporates
historic warehouses.

Picturesque fishermen's cottages at the
Mumbles seaside town

Swansea Bay leads to the
Mumbles, a gateway to the
19-mile- (30-km-) long Gower
Peninsula, which in 1956 was
the first part of Britain to be
declared an Area of Outstanding
Natural Beauty. A string of
sheltered, south-facing bays
leads to Oxwich and Port-Eynon
beaches, and the area is popular
with watersports enthusiasts.

The enormous beach at
Rhossili leads to north Gower
and a coastline of low-lying
burrows, salt marshlands and
cockle beds. The peninsula is
littered with ancient sites such
as **Parc Le Breos**, a prehistoric
burial chamber.

Near Camarthen is the
**National Botanic Garden of
Wales**, with gardens and a Great
Glasshouse which contains a
Mediterranean ecosystem.

🏛️ Glynn Vivian Art Gallery
Alexandra Rd. **Tel** 01792 516900.
Open 10am–5pm Tue–Sun.
🐾 🌐 swansea.gov.uk

🏛️ Swansea Museum
Victoria Rd. **Tel** 01792 653763.
Open Tue–Sun & public hols. ♿ ltd.
🐾 🌐 swanseamuseum.co.uk

🏛️ Dylan Thomas Centre
Somerset Pl. **Tel** 01792 463980.
Open daily. ♿ 🌐 dylanthomas.com

🏛️ National Waterfront Museum
Oystermouth Rd. **Tel** 0300 111
2333. **Open** daily. ♿ 🖥️
🌐 museum.wales

🏞️ National Botanic Garden
of Wales
Middleton Hall, Llanarthne.
Tel 01558 667149. **Open** daily.
Closed 24 & 25 Dec. 🐾 ♿ 🚭 🖥️
🐾 🌐 botanicgarden.wales

⑫ Wild Wales Tour

This tour weaves across the Cambrian Mountains' windswept moors, green hills and high, deserted plateaus. New roads have been laid to the massive Llyn Brianne Reservoir, north of Llandovery, and the old drover's road across to Tregaron has a tarmac surface. But the area is still essentially a "wild Wales" of hidden hamlets, isolated farmsteads, brooding highlands and traditional market towns.

⑥ Llanidloes
The town was a centre of religious and social unrest in the 17th and 18th centuries (see p441). There is a rare example of a freestanding Tudor market hall. The medieval church was restored in the late 19th century.

⑤ Elan Valley
This is an area of lakes and important wildlife habitats (see p466).

④ Devil's Bridge
This is a popular, romantic beauty spot with waterfalls, rocks, wooded glades and an ancient stone bridge – built by the Devil, according to legend.

Aberystwyth

③ Strata Florida
This ruined abbey was an important political, religious and educational centre during the Middle Ages.

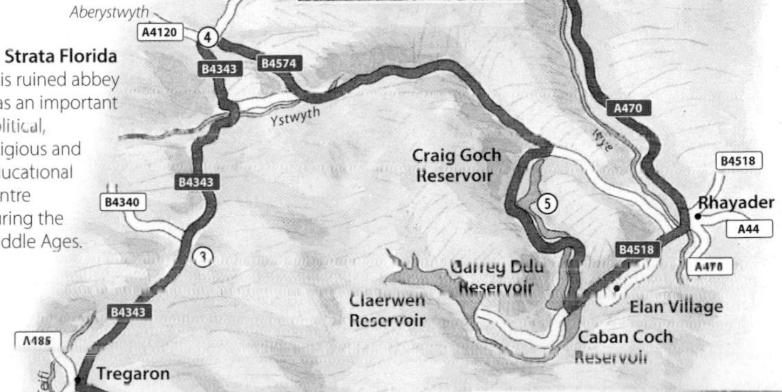

Craig Goch Reservoir

Garreg Ddu Reservoir

Claerwen Reservoir

Elan Village

Caban Coch Reservoir

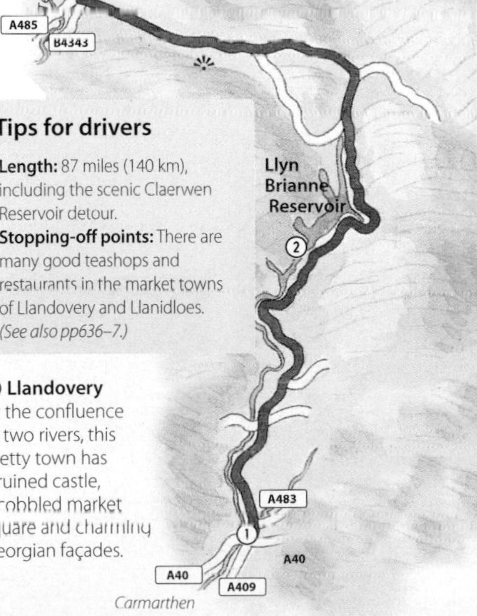

Rhayader

Llangurig

Tips for drivers

Length: 87 miles (140 km), including the scenic Claerwen Reservoir detour.
Stopping-off points: There are many good teashops and restaurants in the market towns of Llandovery and Llanidloes. (See also pp636–7.)

Llyn Brianne Reservoir

Tregaron

① Llandovery
At the confluence of two rivers, this pretty town has a ruined castle, a cobbled market square and charming Georgian façades.

Carmarthen

② Twm Siôn Cati's Cave
This illustration shows the retreat of the 16th-century poet Tom John, a Welsh outlaw who subsequently achieved respectability by marrying an heiress.

Key

▬ Tour route

— Other roads

0 kilometres   5

0 miles   5

⑬ Brecon Beacons

The Brecon Beacons National Park covers 520 sq miles (1,345 sq km), from the Wales–England border almost all the way to Swansea. There are four mountain ranges within the park: the Black Mountain (to the west), Fforest Fawr, the Brecon Beacons and the Black Mountains (to the east). Much of the area consists of high, open country with smooth, grassy slopes on a bedrock of red sandstone. The park's southern rim has limestone crags, wooded gorges, waterfalls and caves. Visitors can enjoy many outdoor pursuits here, from fishing in the numerous reservoirs to pony trekking, caving and walking.

Llyn y Fan Fach
This remote, myth-laden glacial lake is a 4-mile (6-km) walk from Llanddeusant.

Key

▬ Main road

═ Secondary road

═ Minor road

-- Footpath

KEY

① **The Black Mountain**, a largely overlooked wilderness of knife-edged ridges and high, empty moorland, fills the western corner of the National Park.

② **Fforest Fawr** ("Great Forest") is named after an area that was a medieval royal hunting ground.

③ **Brecon** is an old market town with handsome Georgian buildings.

④ **Tretower Castle and Court** comprise a ruined Norman keep and a late-medieval manor house.

⑤ **The Black Mountains** form part of the border with England.

Carreg Cennen Castle
The ruined medieval fortress of Carreg Cennen (see p442) stands on a sheer limestone cliff near the village of Trapp.

Dan-yr-Ogof Caves
A labyrinth of caves runs through the Brecon Beacons. Guided tours of two large caves are offered here.

Hay Bluff
At 677 m (2,221 ft), Hay Bluff looks out across border country. A narrow mountain road climbs from Hay-on-Wye to the Gospel Pass before dropping to Llanthony.

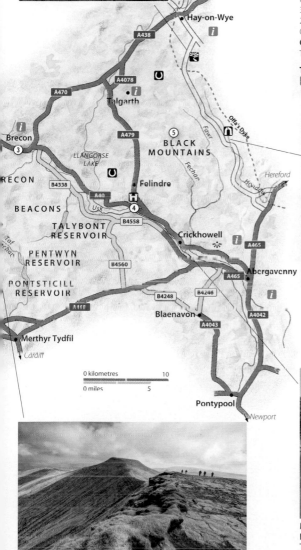

Llanthony Priory
This 12th-century ruin has simply carved but elegant stonework. In the 19th century a small hotel (still open) was built in part of the priory.

Monmouthshire and Brecon Canal
This peaceful waterway, completed in 1812, was once used to transport raw materials between Brecon and Newport. It is now popular with leisure boats.

Pen y Fan
At 886 m (2,907 ft), Pen y Fan is the highest point in South Wales. Its distinctive, flat-topped summit, once a Bronze Age burial ground (see pp46–7), can be reached by footpaths from Storey Arms on the A470.

⑭ Cardiff

Cardiff was first occupied by the Romans, who built a fort here in AD 55 *(see pp48–9)*. Little is known of its subsequent history until Robert FitzHamon *(see p476)*, a knight in the service of William the Conqueror, was given land here in 1093. By the 13th century, the settlement was substantial enough to be granted a royal charter but it remained a quiet country town until the 1830s, when the Bute family, who inherited land in the area, began to develop it as a port. By 1913 this was the world's busiest coal-exporting port, profiting from rail links with the South Wales mines. Its wealth paid for grandiose architecture, while the docklands became a raucous boom town. Cardiff was confirmed as the first Welsh capital in 1955, by which time demand for coal was falling and the docks were in decline. The city has steadily been transformed by urban renewal programmes.

Fireplace detail in the Banqueting Hall, Cardiff Castle

City Hall's dome, adorned with a dragon, the emblem of Wales

Exploring Cardiff

Cardiff is a city with two focal points. The centre, laid out with Victorian and Edwardian streets and gardens, is the first of these. There is a Neo-Gothic castle and Neo-Classical civic buildings, as well as indoor shopping malls and a 19th-century **covered market**. Canopied arcades, lined with shops, lead off the main streets, the oldest being the **Royal Arcade** of 1858. The **Principality Stadium** (on the site of Cardiff Arms Park, the first home of Welsh rugby) opened in 1999 with the Rugby World Cup, and is open for tours most days.

To the south of the centre, the docklands have been transformed into the second focal point by the creation of the freshwater lake and waterfront of Cardiff Bay. **Y Senedd**, which opened in 2006, houses the National Assembly for Wales. Free guided tours are available but booking is essential. Next to the assembly stands the handsome red-brick **Pierhead**. Formerly the headquarters of the Bute Dock Company, it now houses an illuminating exhibition on the history of the docks.

Other attractions in the area are **Techniquest**, a hands-on science museum, and the impressive **Wales Millennium Centre**. A leading cultural venue, it stages a range of arts performances including musicals, ballet and stand-up comedy. It is also home to the Welsh National Opera.

The wooden **Norwegian Church**, now an arts centre, was first erected in 1868 for Norwegian sailors bringing wooden props for use in the coal pits of the South Wales valleys. The building was dismantled and rebuilt as part of the dockland development.

🏛 Craft in the Bay

The Flourish, Lloyd George Ave, Cardiff Bay. **Tel** 029 2048 4611. **Open** 10:30am–5:30pm daily. ♿ ▯
Ⓦ makersguildinwales.org.uk
The Makers' Guild in Wales organizes exhibitions and demonstrations, such as textile weaving and ceramic making, at this extensive craft gallery. On display are a wide variety of crafts.

🏰 Cardiff Castle
See pp476–7.

The entrance to the Wales Millennium Centre

🏛 City Hall and Civic Centre

Cathays Park. **Tel** 029 2087 1727.
Open Mon–Fri. **Closed** public hols.
🅿 ♿ 📶 **cardiffcityhall.com**

Cardiff's Civic Centre of Neo-Classical buildings in white Portland stone is set among parks and avenues around Alexandra Gardens. The City Hall (1905), one of its first buildings, is dominated by its 60-m (200-ft) dome and clock tower. The first-floor Marble Hall is furnished with Siena marble columns and statues of Welsh heroes, among them St David, Wales's patron saint *(see pp468–9)*. The Civic Centre also houses parts of Cardiff University.

🏛 National Museum Cardiff

Cathays Park. **Tel** 0300 111 2333. **Open** Tue–Sun, public hols. **Closed** 1 & 2 Jan, 24 & 25 Dec.
♿ 📷 📶 **museum.wales**

Opened in 1927, the museum occupies an impressive building

Statue of Welsh politician David Lloyd George

with a colonnaded portico and domed roof. Outside stands a statue of David Lloyd George *(see p441)*. The art collection is among the finest in Europe, with works on display by Renoir, Monet and van Gogh.

Environs

Established during the 1940s at St Fagans, on the western edge of the city, the open-air **St Fagans National History Museum** was one of the first of its kind. Buildings from all over Wales, including workers' terraced cottages, farm-houses, a tollhouse, row of shops, chapel and old schoolhouse have been carefully reconstructed within the 40-ha (100-acre) parklands, along with a recreated Celtic village. Visitors can also explore a Tudor mansion which boasts its own beautiful gardens in the grounds.

Llandaff Cathedral lies in a deep, grassy hollow beside

the River Taf at Llandaff, 2 miles (3 km) northwest of the city centre. The medieval cathedral occupies the site of a 6th-century monastic community.

Restored after suffering severe bomb damage during World War II, it was eventually reopened in 1957 with the addition of Sir Jacob Epstein's huge, stark statue, *Christus,* which is mounted on a concrete arch.

🏛 St Fagans National History Museum

St Fagans. **Tel** 0300 111 2333.
Open daily. ♿ ✏ 📷
📶 **museum.wales**

VISITORS' CHECKLIST

Practical Information
Cardiff. 🚹 350,000. 🛈 Wales Millennium Centre (029 2087 7927). 🛏 daily. 🎪 Cardiff Festival: summer. 📶 **visitcardiff.com**

Transport
✈ Rhoose. 🚆 Central Sq. 🚌 Wood St.

Cardiff City Centre

1. Cardiff Market
2. Principality Stadium
3. Y Senedd
4. Pierhead
5. Techniquest
6. Norwegian Church
7. Craft in the Bay
8. Cardiff Castle pp476–7
9. City Hall and Civic Centre
10. National Museum Cardiff

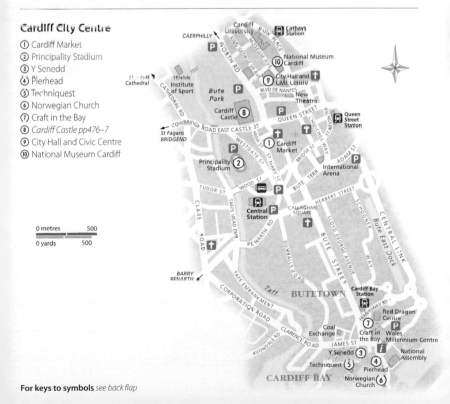

Cardiff Castle

Cardiff Castle began life as a Roman fort, whose remains are separated from later work by a band of red stone. A keep was built within the Roman ruins in the 12th century. Over the following 700 years, the castle passed to several powerful families and eventually to John Stuart, son of the Earl of Bute, in 1776. His great-grandson, the 3rd Marquess of Bute, employed the "eccentric genius" architect William Burges, who created an ornate mansion between 1869 and 1881, rich in medieval images and romantic detail.

Arab Room
The gilded ceiling, with Islamic marble and lapis lazuli decorations, was created in 1881.

★ Summer Smoking Room
This was part of a complete bachelor suite in the Clock Tower, which also included a Winter Smoking Room.

KEY

① **Clock Tower**

② **Herbert Tower**

③ **The Octagon Tower**, also called the Beauchamp Tower, is the setting for Burges's Chaucer Room, decorated with themes from the *Canterbury Tales (see p191)*.

④ **The Bute Tower** had a suite of private rooms added in 1873, including a dining room, bedroom and sitting room.

Main entrance to apartments

AD 55 Roman fort constructed

1107 Castle inherited by Mabel FitzHamon, whose husband is made Lord of Glamorgan

1183 Castle damaged during Welsh uprising

1423–49 Beauchamp family adds the Octagon Tower and Great Hall ceiling

1445–1776 Castle passes in turn to Nevilles, Tudors and Herberts

1869 3rd Marquess of Bute begins reconstruction

| 1000 | 1200 | 1400 | 1600 | 1800 |

1093 First Norman fort built by Robert FitzHamon of Gloucester

1308–1414 Despenser family holds castle

1776 Bute family acquires the castle

1947 The castle is gi⟨ in trust to⟩ city of Car⟨⟩

Chaucer Room wall detail

For hotels and restaurants in this area see pp571–2 and pp599–600

VISITORS' CHECKLIST

Practical Information
Castle St, Cardiff. **Tel** 029 2087 8100. **Open** Mar–Oct: 9am–6pm daily; Nov–Feb: 9am–5pm daily. **Closed** 1 Jan, 25 & 26 Dec. **W** cardiffcastle.com

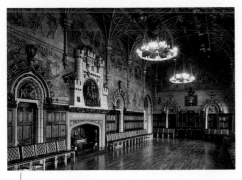

★ Banqueting Hall
Detailed murals, finely crafted ceiling and castellated fireplace all contribute to the elaborate decor of this magnificent hall.

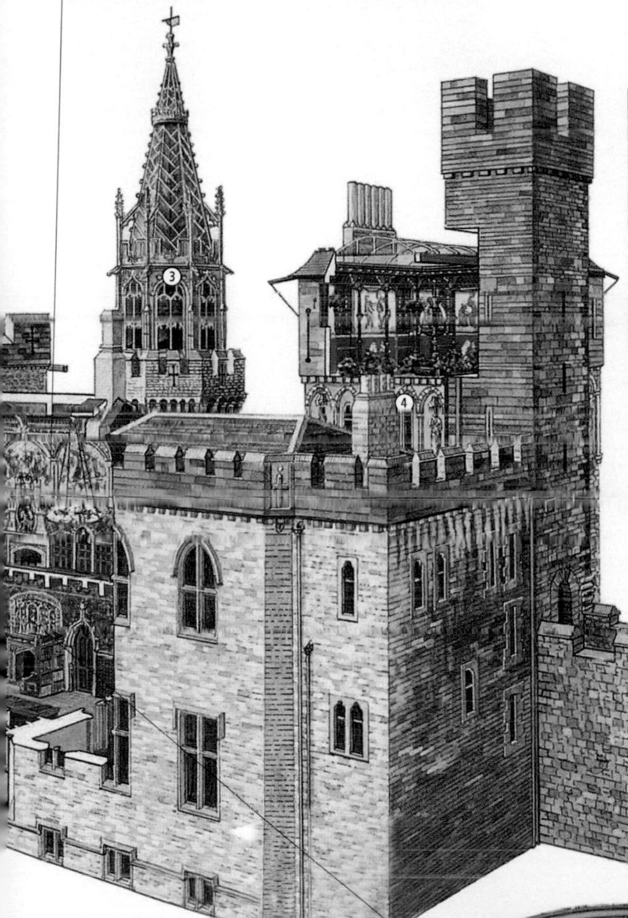

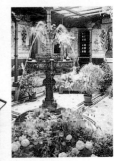

★ Roof Garden
Using tiles, shrubs and a central fountain, Burges aimed to create a Mediterranean feel in this indoor garden, turning it into the crowning glory of the castle's apartments.

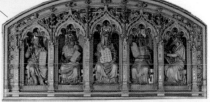

★ Library
Carved figures representing ancient characters of Greek, Assyrian, Hebrew and Egyptian alphabets decorate the library's chimneypiece.

Remains of Caerleon's amphitheatre, built in the 2nd century

❶ Caerleon

Newport. 🚊 9,500. 🛈 John Frost Sq, Newport (01633 842962).
W newport.gov.uk

Together with York (see pp408–13) and Chester (see pp314–15), Caerleon was one of only three fortress settlements in Britain built for the Romans' elite legionary troops. From AD 74 Caerleon (Isca to the Romans, after the River Usk, which flows beside the town) was home to the 2nd Augustan Legion, which had been sent to Wales to crush the native Silures tribe. The remains of their base now lie between the modern town and the river.

An altar at the National Roman Legion Museum

The excavations at Caerleon are of great social and military significance. The Romans built not just a fortress for their crack 5,500-strong infantry division but a complete town to service their needs, including a stone amphitheatre. Judging by the results of the excavation work carried out since archaeologist Sir Mortimer Wheeler unearthed the amphitheatre in 1926, Caerleon is one of the largest and most important Roman military sites in Europe. The defences enclosed an area of 20 ha (50 acres), with 64 rows of barracks, arranged in pairs, a hospital and a bathhouse complex.

Outside the settlement, the amphitheatre's large stone foundations have survived in an excellent state of preservation.

Six thousand spectators could enjoy the blood sports and gladiatorial combat.

More impressive still is the fortress baths complex, which opened to the public in the mid-1980s. The baths were designed to bring every home comfort to an army posted to barbaric Britain. The Roman troops could take a dip in the open-air swimming pool, play sports in the exercise yard or covered hall, or enjoy a series of hot and cold baths.

Nearby are the foundations of the only Roman legionary barracks on view in Europe. The many excavated artifacts, including a collection of engraved gemstones, are displayed at the **National Roman Legion Museum**.

🏛 **National Roman Legion Museum**
High St. **Tel** 0300 111 2333.
Open Mon–Sat, Sun (pm only).
Closed 1 Jan, 24–26 Dec. ♿ 📷
W museum.wales

Big Pit National Coal Museum, a reminder of a vanished industrial society

❶ Blaenavon

Torfaen. 🚊 6,350. 🛈 World Heritage Centre, Church Rd (01495 742333).
W visitblaenavon.co.uk

Commercial coal mining has now all but ceased in the South Wales valleys – an area that was once gripped by the search for its "black gold". Though coal is no longer produced at **Big Pit** in Blaenavon, the **National Coal Museum** provides a vivid reminder of this tough industry. The Big Pit closed in 1980 and opened three years later as a museum. Visitors follow a marked route around the mine's surface workings to the miners' baths, the blacksmith's forge, the workshops and the engine house. There is also a replica of an underground gallery, where mining methods are explained. But the climax of the visit is beneath the ground. Kitted out with helmets, lamps and safety batteries, visitors descend by cage 90 m (300 ft) down the mineshaft and then are guided by ex-miners on a tour of the underground workings and pit ponies' stables.

Across the valley from Big Pit stand the 18th-century smelting furnaces and workers' cottages that were once part of the **Blaenavon Ironworks**, and which are now a museum.

🏛 **Big Pit National Coal Museum**
Blaenavon. **Tel** 0300 111 2333.
Open daily. 📷 ♿ phone first. 🖥 📷
W museum.wales

🏛 **Blaenavon Ironworks**
North St. **Tel** 01495 792615.
Open daily (Nov–Mar: Thu–Sat).
Closed 1 Jan, 24–26 Dec. 📷 🖥 📷
W cadw.gov.wales

❶ Monmouth

Monmouthshire. 🚊 10,000. 🚌 🛈 Shire Hall (01600 775257). 🔔 Fri, Sat. **W** visitmonmouthshire.com

This market town, which sits at the confluence of the Wye and Monnow rivers, has many historical associations. The 11th-century castle, behind Agincourt Square, is in ruins but the **Regimental Museum**, beside it, remains open to the

Monnow Bridge in Monmouth, once a watchtower and jail

public. The castle was the birthplace of Henry V *(see p53)* in 1387. Statues of Henry V (on the façade of Shire Hall) and Charles Stewart Rolls stand in the square. Rolls, born at nearby Hendre, was the co-founder of Rolls-Royce cars.

Lord Horatio Nelson *(see p58)* visited Monmouth in 1802. An excellent collection of Nelson memorabilia, gathered by Lady Llangattock, mother of Charles Rolls, is displayed at the **Nelson Museum**.

Monmouth was the county town of the old Monmouthshire. The wealth of elegant Georgian buildings, including the elaborate **Shire Hall**, which dominates Agincourt Square, reflects its former status. Visitors are free to wander around the old courtroom, while in the foyer there's a fascinating little collection of local archaeological finds. The most famous architectural feature in Monmouth is **Monnow Bridge**, a narrow 13th-century gateway on its western approach, thought to be the only surviving fortified bridge gate in Britain.

For a lovely view over the town, climb the Kymin, a 256-m (840-ft) hill crowned by a **Naval Temple** built in 1801.

🏰 Monmouth Castle and Regimental Museum
The Castle. **Tel** 01600 772175. **Open** Apr–Oct: 2–5pm daily. 🚻 📷
W monmouthcastlemuseum.org.uk

🏛 Nelson Museum
Priory St. **Tel** 01600 710630. **Open** daily (Sun: pm only). 🚻 📷

🔵 Tintern Abbey

Monmouthshire. **Tel** 01291 689251. 🚃 Chepstow then bus. **Open** daily **Closed** 1 Jan, 24–26 Dec. 🚻 🚻 📷
W cadw.gov.wales

Ever since the 18th century, travellers have been enchanted by Tintern's setting in the steep and wooded Wye Valley and by the majestic ruins of its abbey. Poets were often inspired by the scene. Wordsworth's sonnet, "Lines composed a few miles above Tintern Abbey", embodied his romantic view of landscape:

once again
Do I behold these steep and
*   lofty cliffs,*
That on a wild, secluded
*   scene impress*
Thoughts of more deep
*   seclusion*

The abbey was founded in 1131 by Cistercian monks, who cultivated the surrounding lands (now forest), and it developed into an influential religious centre. By the 14th century this was the richest abbey in Wales, but along with other monasteries it was dissolved in 1536. Its skeletal ruins are now left roofless and exposed, the soaring arches and windows giving them a poignant grace and beauty.

Tintern Abbey in the Wye Valley, formerly a thriving centre of religion and learning, now a romantic ruin

SCOTLAND

Introducing Scotland   **482–493**

The Lowlands   **494–527**

The Highlands
and Islands   **528–553**

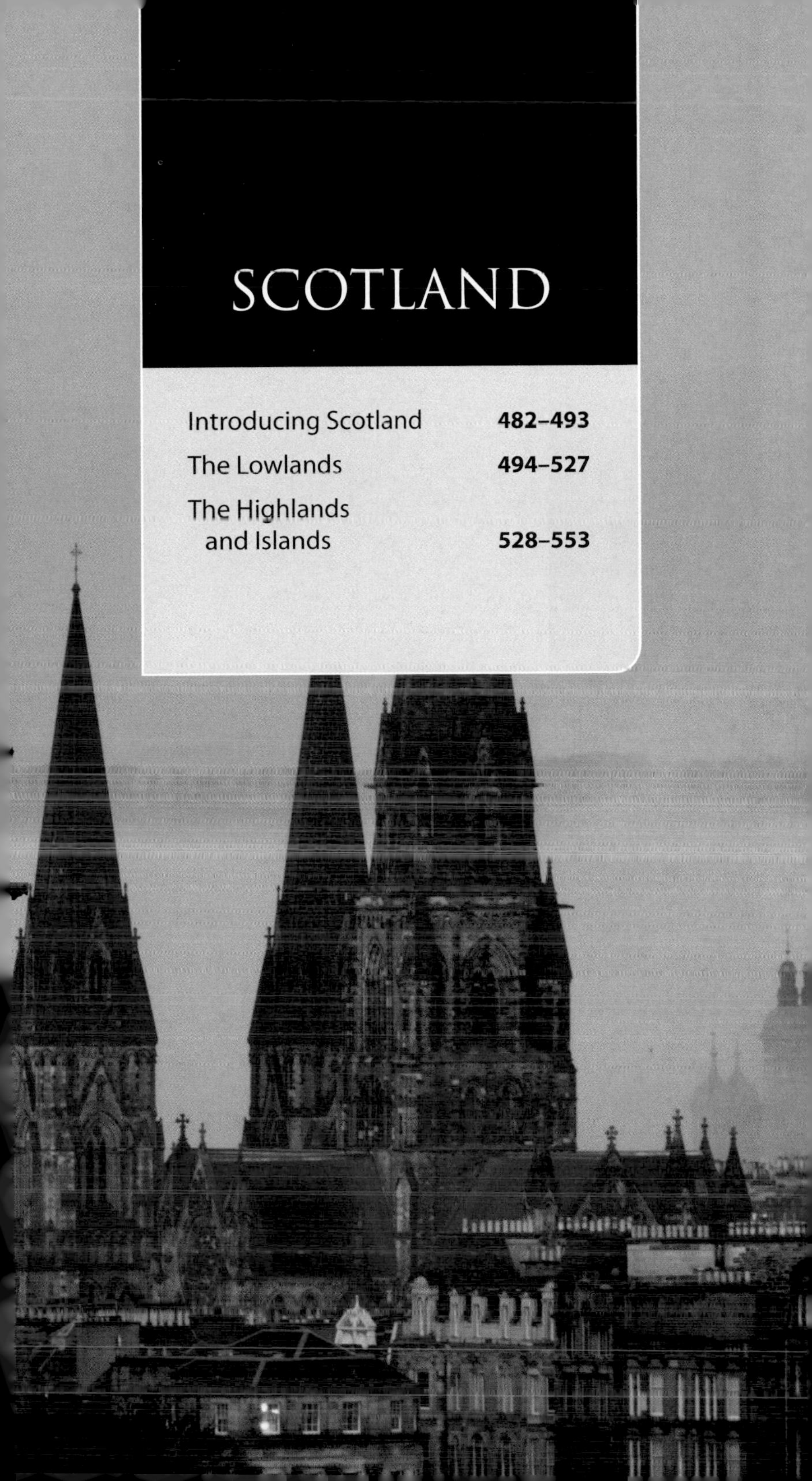

Scotland at a Glance

Stretching from the rich farmlands of the Borders to a chain of
isles only a few degrees south of the Arctic Circle, the Scottish
landscape has a diversity without parallel in Britain. As you
travel northwest from Edinburgh, the land becomes more
mountainous and its archaeological treasures more
numerous. In the far northwest, Scotland's earliest
relics stand upon the oldest rock on Earth.

Stornoway

Isle of Skye *(see
pp534–5)*, renowned
for its dramatic
scenery, has one
of Scotland's most
striking coastlines.
On the east coast,
a stream plunges
over Kilt Rock, a
cliff of hexagonal
basalt columns
named after its
likeness to the
item of Scottish
national dress.

Tarbert

Ullapoo

Lochmaddy

Uig

HIGHLAN

Kyle of
Lochalsh

Mallaig

Fort Wil

Tobermory

Oban

Inverary

*ARGYLL
AND BUTE*

Greenock

P

The Trossachs *(see pp498–9)* are a beautiful range of hills
straddling the border between the Highlands and the
Lowlands. At their heart, the forested slopes of Ben Venue
rise above the still waters of Loch Achray.

AYRS

Campbeltown

Ayr

*DUMF
AN
GALLO*

Stranraer

Culzean Castle *(see pp526–7)*
stands on a cliff's edge on the
Firth of Clyde, amid an extensive
country park. One of the jewels
of the Lowlands, Culzean is a
magnificent showcase of work
by the Scottish-born architect
Robert Adam *(see p32)*.

◀ Tower of the Balmoral Hotel in Edinburgh

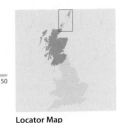

Locator Map

The Cairngorms *(see pp548–9)* cover an area prized for its beauty and diversity of wildlife, though there are also many historical relics to be found, such as this early 18th-century arch at Carrbridge.

Royal Deeside *(see pp544–5)* in the Grampians has been associated with British royalty since Queen Victoria bought Balmoral Castle in 1852.

Edinburgh *(see pp508–15)* is the capital of Scotland. Between its medieval castle and the Palace of Holyroodhouse stretches the Royal Mile – a concentration of historic sights, ranging from the old Scottish Parliament buildings to the house of John Knox. Georgian terraces predominate in the New Town.

The Kelvingrove Art Gallery and Museum *(see pp524–5)* in Glasgow is Scotland's premier museum and art gallery. Inside its grand Spanish Baroque-style shell, it houses one of Europe's great civic art collections.

A PORTRAIT OF SCOTLAND

From the grassy hills of the Borders to the desolate Cuillin Ridge of Skye, the landscape of Scotland is breathtaking in its variety. Lonely glens, sparkling lochs and ever-changing skies give the land a strong and robust character, which is reflected in the qualities of the Scottish people. Tough and self-reliant, they have made some of Britain's finest soldiers, its boldest explorers and most astute industrialists.

The Scots are proud of their separate identity and their own systems of law and education and in 1998 voted overwhelmingly for their own parliament. Many Scots welcomed this as a partial reversal of the 1707 Act of Union that united the English and Scottish parliaments, though a 2014 referendum fell short of demanding full independence for Scotland. Some would reason that it was the presence of many non-Scots living in Scotland that tipped the balance, but the Scots are not a homogeneous people. The main division is between traditionally Gaelic-speaking Highlanders, and the Lowlanders who spoke Scots, a now extinct form of Middle English. Today, though Gaelic survives (chiefly in the Western Isles), most people speak regional dialects or richly accented English. Many Scottish surnames derive from Gaelic: the prefix "mac" means "son of". A Norse heritage can be found in the far north, where Shetlanders celebrate the Viking fire festival, Up Helly Aa.

A hammer-thrower at the Braemar Games

In the 16th century, a suspicion of authority and dislike of excessive flamboyance attracted many Scots to the Presbyterian Church, with its absence of bishops and its stress on simple worship. The Presbyterian Church of Scotland was established in 1690, though a substantial Catholic minority remained which today predominates in the crofting (small-scale farming) communities of the Western Isles. Now sparsely populated, the Isles preserve a rural culture that once dominated the Highlands, a region that is the source of much that is distinctively Scottish. The clan system originated there, as did the tartans, bagpipes and such unique sports as tossing the caber – a large tree trunk. Highland sports, along with traditional dances, are still performed at annual games (see p68).

Edinburgh bagpiper

Resourcefulness has always been a prominent Scottish virtue, and Scotland has produced a disproportionately high number of Britain's geniuses. James Watt designed the first effective steam engine to power the Industrial Revolution, while Adam Smith became the 18th century's most influential economist. In the 19th century, James Simpson discovered the

The Viking festival, Up Helly Aa, in Lerwick, Shetland

A traditional stone croft on the Isle of Lewis

by Scots, while Andrew Carnegie created one of 19th-century America's biggest business empires.

With some of the harshest weather conditions in Europe, it is perhaps less surprising that Scotland has bred numerous explorers, including polar explorer William Speirs Bruce and African missionary David Livingstone.

There is also a strong intellectual and literary tradition, from the 18th-century philosopher David Hume, through novelists Sir Walter Scott (see p516) and Robert Louis Stevenson, to the poetry of Robert Burns.

anaesthetic qualities of chloroform, James Young developed the world's first oil refinery and Alexander Bell revolutionized communications by inventing the telephone. The 20th century saw one of the greatest advances in medicine with the discovery of penicillin by Alexander Fleming.

The Scots are also known for business acumen, and have always been prominent in finance: both the Bank of England and the Royal Bank of France were founded

Detail of Edinburgh's Festival Fringe office

With a population density only one-fifth that of England and Wales, Scotland has vast tracts of untenanted land which offer numerous outdoor pleasures. It is richly stocked with game, and the opening of the grouse season on 12 August is a highlight of the social calendar. Fishing and hill-walking are popular and in winter thousands flock to the Cairngorms and Glencoe for skiing. Though the weather may be harsher than elsewhere, the Scots will claim that the air is purer – and that enjoying rugged conditions is what distinguishes them from their soft southern neighbours.

The blue waters of Loch Achray in the heart of the Trossachs, north of Glasgow

The History of Scotland

Since the Roman invasion of Britain, Scotland has been resistant to foreign domination. The Romans never conquered here, and when the Scots extended their kingdom to its present boundary in 1018, a long era of conflict with England began. A union with the "auld enemy" was finally accepted: first with the union of crowns, and then with the Union of Parliament in 1707. Over the years, the trend has been towards increased separation, with the inauguration of a Scottish Parliament in 1999 and a narrowly defeated vote for full independence in 2014.

An elaborately carved Pictish stone at Aberlemno, Angus

Early History

There is much evidence in Scotland of important prehistoric population centres, particularly in the Western Isles, which were peopled mostly by Picts who originally came from the Continent. By the time Roman Governor Julius Agricola invaded in AD 81, there were at least 17 independent tribes for him to contend with.

The Romans reached north to the Forth and Clyde valleys, but the Highlands deterred them from going further. By 120, they had retreated to the line where the Emperor Hadrian had built his wall to keep the Picts at bay (not far from today's border). By 163 the Romans had retreated south for the last time. The Celtic influence began when Gaels arrived from Ireland in the 6th century, bringing the Gaelic language with them.

The Picts and Gaels united to become Scots under Kenneth McAlpin in 843.

The English Claim

The Norman kings regarded Scotland as their territory but seldom pursued the claim. William the Lion of Scotland recognized English sovereignty by the Treaty of Falaise (1174), though English control never spread to the northwest. In 1296 William Wallace, supported by the French (the start of the Auld Alliance, which lasted two centuries), began the long war of independence. During this bitter conflict, Edward I seized the sacred Stone of Destiny from Scone (see p502), and took it to Westminster Abbey. The war lasted more than 100 years. Its great hero was Robert the Bruce, who defeated the English in 1314 at Bannockburn. The English held the upper hand after that, even though the Scots would not accept their rule.

The Road to Union

The seeds of union between the crowns were sown in 1503 when James IV of Scotland married Margaret Tudor, daughter of Henry VII. When her brother, Henry VIII, came to the throne, James sought to assert independence but was defeated and killed at Flodden Field in 1513. His granddaughter, Mary, Queen of Scots (see p515), married the French Dauphin in order to cement the Auld Alliance and gain assistance in her claim to the throne of her English cousin, Elizabeth I. She had support from Catholics wanting to see an end to Protestantism in England and Scotland. However, fiery preacher John Knox won support for the Protestants and the Presbyterian tradition was established in the

John Knox statue in Edinburgh

Bruce in Single Combat at Bannockburn (1906) by John Hassall

mid-16th century. Mary's Catholicism led to the loss of her Scottish throne in 1568, and her subsequent flight to England, following defeat at Langside. Finally, after nearly 20 years of imprisonment she was executed for treason by Elizabeth in 1587.

Union and Rebellion

On Elizabeth I's death in 1603, Mary's son, James VI of Scotland, succeeded to the English throne and became James I, king of both countries. Thus the crowns were united, though it was 100 years before the formal Union of Parliaments in 1707. During that time, religious differences within the country reached boiling point. There were riots when the Catholic-influenced Charles I restored bishops to the Church of Scotland and authorized a new prayer book. This culminated in the signing of the 1638 National Covenant, a document that condemned Catholic doctrines. Though the Covenanters were suppressed, the Protestant William of Orange took over the English throne in 1688 and the crown passed out of Scottish hands.

In 1745, Bonnie Prince Charlie *(see p535)*, a descendant of the Stuart kings, tried to seize the throne from the Hanoverian George II. He marched far into England, but was driven back and defeated at Culloden *(see p541)* in 1746.

Articles of Union between England and Scotland, 1707

Industrialization and Social Change

In the late 18th and 19th centuries, technological progress transformed Scotland from a nation of crofters to an industrial powerhouse.

The factories on Clydeside, manufacturing the world's greatest ships

In the notorious Highland Clearances *(see p539)*, from the 1780s on, landowners ejected tenants from their smallholdings and gave the land over to livestock. The first ironworks was established in 1760 and was soon followed by coal mining, steel production and shipbuilding on the Clyde. Canals were cut, railways and bridges built.

A strong socialist movement developed as workers sought to improve their conditions. Keir Hardie, an Ayrshire coal miner, in 1892 became the first socialist elected to parliament, and in 1893 founded the Independent Labour Party. The most enduring symbol of this time is the spectacular Forth rail bridge *(see p506)*.

A flowering of original thinkers also emerged in Scotland in the 18th century, most notably the philosopher David Hume, the economist Adam Smith and the "Bard of Humanity", Robert Burns.

Scotland Today

Although the status of the country appeared to have been settled in 1707, a strong nationalist sentiment remained and was heightened by the Depression, which had severe effects on heavily industrialized Clydeside and inspired the formation of Scottish National Party, which advocated self-rule. The Nationalists asserted themselves in 1950 by stealing the Stone of Scone from Westminster Abbey.

The discovery of North Sea oil in 1970 sparked more nationalism, which led to the creation of a Scottish Parliament in 1999. In 2014, a referendum on independence returned a "no" vote. However, more than 44 per cent of voters said "yes" and the aftermath saw a huge increase in the membership of the Scottish National Party and a historic win of 56 seats at the 2015 general election. New independence initiatives were further stoked by Britain's 2016 referendum on membership of the European Union. In contrast to their English neighbours, 62 per cent of Scots voted to remain part of the EU. All this suggests that the debate is far from over.

A North Sea oil rig, helping to provide prosperity in the 1970s

Clans and Tartans

The clan system, by which Highland society was divided into tribal groups led by autocratic chiefs, can be traced to the 12th century, when clans were already known to wear the chequered wool cloth later called tartan. All members of the clan bore the name of their chief, but not all were related by blood. Though they upheld high standards of hospitality, the clansmen had to be warriors to protect their herds. After the Battle of Culloden *(see p541)*, all clan lands were forfeited to the Crown, and the wearing of tartan was banned for nearly 100 years.

The Mackays, also known as the Clan Morgan, won lasting renown during the Thirty Years War.

The MacLeods are of Norse heritage. The clan chief still lives in Dunvegan Castle, Skye *(see p534)*.

The MacDonalds were the most powerful of all the clans, holding the title Lords of the Isles.

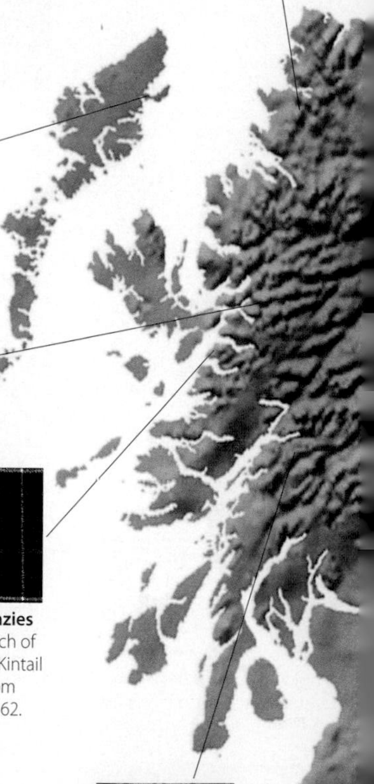

Clan Chief

The chief was the clan's patriarch, judge and leader in war, commanding absolute loyalty from his clansmen, who gave military service in return for his protection. The chief summoned his clan to do battle by sending a runner across his land bearing a burning cross.

Bonnet with eagle feathers, clan crest and plant badge.

Basket-hilted sword

Dirk

Sporran, or pouch, made of badger's skin.

Feileadh-mor, or "great plaid" (the early kilt), wrapped around waist and shoulder.

The Mackenzies received much of the lands of Kintail *(see p538)* from David II in 1362.

The Campbells were a widely feared clan who fought the Jacobites in 1746 *(see p541)*.

The Black Watch, raised in 1729 to keep peace in the Highlands, was one of the Highland regiments in which the wearing of tartan survived. After 1746, civilians were punished by exile for up to 7 years for wearing tartan.

The Sinclairs came from France in the 11th century and became Earls of Caithness in 1455.

The Frasers came to Britain from France with William the Conqueror *(see p51)* in 1066.

George IV, dressed as a Highlander, visited Edinburgh in 1822, the year of the tartan revival. Many tartan "setts" (patterns) date from this time, as the original ones had been lost.

The Gordons were famously good soldiers; the clan motto is "by courage, not by craft".

The Stuarts were Scotland's royal dynasty. Their motto was "no one harms me with impunity".

The Douglas clan were prominent in Scottish history, though their origin is unknown.

Plant Badges

Each clan had a plant associated with its territory. It was worn on the bonnet, especially on the day of battle.

Scots pine was worn by the MacGregors of Argyll.

Rowan berries were worn by the Clan Malcolm.

Ivy was worn by the Clan Gordon of Aberdeenshire.

Spear thistle, now a national symbol, was a Stuart badge.

Cotton grass was worn by the Clan Henderson.

Clan Territories

The territories of 10 prominent clans are marked here with their clan tartans. Dress tartans tend to be colourful, while hunting tartans are darker.

Highland Clans Today

Once the daily dress of the clansmen, the kilt is now largely reserved for formal occasions. The one-piece *feileadh-mor* has been replaced by the *feileadh-beag*, or "small plaid", made from approximately 7 m (23 ft) of material with a double apron fastened at the front with a silver pin. Though they exist now only in name, the clans are still a source of pride for Scots, and many still live in areas traditionally belonging to their clans. Many visitors to Britain with Scots ancestry *(see p35)* can trace this to the Highlands.

Traditional Highland dress

Evolution of the Scottish Castle

There are few more evocative sights in the British Isles than a Scottish castle on an island or at a lochside. These formidable retreats, often in remote settings, were essential all over the Highlands, where incursions and strife between the clans were common. From the earliest Pictish *brochs (see p47)* and Norman-influenced motte and bailey castles, the distinctively Scottish stone tower-house evolved, first appearing in the 13th century. By the mid-17th century fashion had become more important than defence, and there followed a period in which numerous huge Scottish palaces were built.

Detail of the Baroque façade, Drumlanrig

Motte and Bailey

These castles first appeared in the 12th century. They stood atop two adjacent mounds enclosed by a wall, or palisade, and defensive ditches. The higher mound, or motte, was the more strongly defended as it held the keep and chief's house. The lower bailey was where the people lived. Of these castles little more than earthworks remain today.

Keep, with chief's house, lookout and main defence

All that remains today of Duffus Castle, Morayshire

Duffus Castle (c.1150) was atypically made of stone rather than wood. Its fine defensive position dominates the surrounding flatlands north of Elgin.

Bailey enclosing dwellings and storehouses

Motte of earth or rock, sometimes partially man-made

Early Tower-House

Designed to deter local attacks rather than a major assault, the first tower-houses appeared in the 13th century, though their design lived on for 400 years. They were built initially on a rectangular plan, with a single tower divided into three or four floors. The walls were unadorned, with few windows. Defensive structures were on top, and extra space was made by building adjoining towers. Extensions were vertical where possible, to minimize the area open to attack.

Crenellated parapet for sentries

Featureless, straight walls with arrow slits for windows

Claypotts Castle (c.1570) with uniquely projecting garrets above its towers

Small, inconspicuous doorway

Braemar Castle (c.1630), a conglomeration of extended towers

Neidpath Castle, standing upon a steep rocky crag above the River Tweed, is an L-shaped tower-house dating from the late 14th century. Once a stronghold for Charles II, its walls still bear damage from a siege conducted by Oliver Cromwell (see p56).

Later Tower-House

Though the requirements of defence were being replaced by those of comfort, the style of the early tower-house remained popular. By the 17th century, wings for accommodation were being added around the original tower (often creating a courtyard). The battlements and turrets were kept more for decorative than defensive reasons.

Drum Castle *(see p545)*, a 13th-century keep with a mansion house extension from 1619

Priest's room with secret access   The original 15th-century tower-house

Round angle tower, containing stairway

A 16th-century horizontal extension

Traquair House *(see p517)*, by the Tweed, is reputedly the oldest continuously inhabited house in Scotland. The largely unadorned, roughcast exterior dates to the 16th century, when a series of extensions were built around the original 15th-century tower-house.

Decorative, corbelled turret

Blair Castle *(see p547)*, incorporating a medieval tower

Classical Palace

By the 18th century, the defensive imperative had passed and castles were built in the manner of country houses, rejecting the vertical tower-house in favour of a horizontal plan (though the building of imitation fortified buildings continued into the 19th century with the mock-Baronial trend). Outside influences came from all over Europe, including Renaissance and Gothic revivals, and echoes of French châteaux.

Dunrobin Castle (c.1840), Sutherland

Larger windows due to a reduced need for defence

Balustrades instead of battlements

Decorative cupola

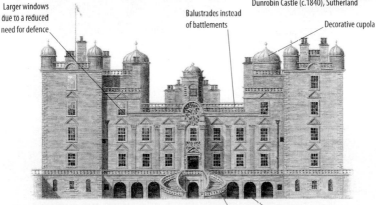

Drumlanrig Castle *(see p518)* was built in the 17th century. There are many traditional Scots aspects as well as such Renaissance features as the decorated stairway and façade.

Renaissance-style colonnade

Baroque horseshoe stairway

The Flavours of Scotland

At its best, Scottish food is full of the natural flavour of the countryside. Served with few sauces or spices, the meat is lean and tasty. Beef doesn't get better than Aberdeen Angus, the lamb is full flavoured, and the venison superb. Scottish salmon and trout are renowned, but there are also excellent mussels, lobster and crabs. Wheat does not grow here, so oatcakes and bannocks (flat, round loaves) replace bread. The Scots have a sweet tooth, not just for cakes and shortbread but also for toffee and butterscotch.

Smoked salmon

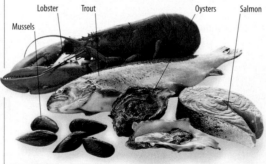

Pedigree Aberdeen Angus cattle grazing the Scottish moors

The Lowlands

The pasturelands of southern Scotland nourish dairy cattle and sheep, producing cheeses such as Bonnet, Bonchester and Galloway Cheddar. To accompany them are summer fruits such as loganberries, tayberries and strawberries that ripen in the Carse of Gowrie beside the River Tay. Oats, the principal cereal, appear in much Scottish cookery, from porridge to oatcakes. Pearl barley is also a staple, used in Scotch broth (made with mutton and vegetables) or in a milk pudding. Oats are also used in the making of haggis, a round sausage of sheep or venison offal – the "chieftain o' the puddin' race", as the poet Robert Burns described it. It is often served with "neeps and tatties" (mashed swede and potato).

The Highlands

From the Highlands comes wonderful game, including grouse, partridge, capercaillie (a large type of grouse) and deer. Fish are smoked around the coast, the west coast producing kippers, the east coast Finnan haddock, notably Arbroath Smokies. Smoked white fish is the main ingredient of Cullen Skink, a soup served on Burns Night.

Mussels | Lobster | Trout | Oysters | Salmon

Selection of fresh Scottish fish and seafood

Traditional Scottish Food

Kippers (oak-smoked herrings) are one way to start the day in Scotland, and porridge – traditionally served with salt rather than sugar – is another, although oatcakes or some other kind of griddled scone are usually present. A bowl of porridge would once last all week, just as one-pot Scotch broths bubbled in iron cauldrons over peat fires for days. Sometimes broths were made with kale or lentils, or they might contain an old boiling fowl and leeks, in which case they were known as cock-a-leekie. Any leftover meat went into making stovies, a potato and onion hash. The evening meal in Scotland is traditionally "high tea", taken in the early evening, which might start with smoked fish, cold meats and pies, followed by shortbread, fruit cake or drop scones, all washed down with cups of tea.

Oats

Haggis with neeps and tatties
This is the definitive Scottish dish, traditionally served on Burns Night (25 January).

How Whisky is Made

Traditionally made from just barley, yeast and stream water, Scottish whisky (from the Gaelic *usquebaugh*, or the "water of life") takes a little over 3 weeks to produce, though it must be given at least 3 years to mature. Maturation usually takes place in oak casks, often in barrels previously used for sherry. The art of blending was pioneered in Edinburgh in the 1860s.

Barley grass

1 Malting is the first stage. Barley grain is soaked in water and spread on the malting floor. With regular turning the grain germinates, producing a "green malt". Germination stimulates the production of enzymes, which turn the starches into fermentable sugars.

2 Drying of the barley halts germination after 12 days of malting. This is done over a peat fire in a pagoda-shaped malt-kiln. The peat-smoke gives flavour to the malt and eventually to the mature whisky. The malt is gleaned of germinated roots and then milled.

3 Mashing of the ground malt, or "grist", occurs in a large vat, or "mash tun", which holds a vast quantity of hot water. The malt is soaked and begins to dissolve, producing a sugary solution called "wort", which is then extracted for fermentation.

4 Fermentation occurs when yeast is added to the cooled wort in wooden vats, or "wash-backs". The mixture is stirred for hours as the yeast turns the sugar into alcohol, producing a clear liquid called "wash".

5 Distillation involves boiling the wash twice so that the alcohol vaporizes and condenses. In copper "pot stills", the wash is distilled – first in the "wash still", then in the "spirit still". Now purified, with an alcohol content of 57 per cent, the result is young whisky.

6 Maturation is the final process. The whisky mellows in oak casks for a legal minimum of 3 years. Premium brands give the whisky a 10- to 15-year maturation, though some are given up to 50 years.

Traditional drinking vessels, or *quaichs*, made of silver

Blended whiskies are made from a mixture of up to 50 different single malts

Single malts vary according to regional differences in the peat and stream water used

THE LOWLANDS

Clyde Valley · Central Scotland · Fife · The Lothians
Ayrshire · Dumfries and Galloway · The Borders

Scotland's Lowlands are not the ideal place to seek out Scottish clichés: heathery mountains, lone pipers, shaggy cattle, distilleries and kilts. These come from Highland culture. Instead, the Lowlands are Scotland's business end, where commerce and industry of the great cities of Edinburgh and Glasgow have built the pillars of a proud nation. Even so, it's not all urban here, with the Lowlands also famed for bucolic countryside and lovely stretches of coast.

Being close to the English border, the Scottish Lowlands inevitably became the crucible of Scottish history. For centuries after the Romans built the Antonine Wall *(see p48)* across the Forth–Clyde isthmus, the area was engulfed in conflict. The Borders are scattered with castles, and the ramparts of Stirling Castle overlook no fewer than seven different battlefields.

The ruins of medieval abbeys, such as Melrose, also bear witness to the dangers of living on the invasion route from England, though the woollen trade founded by their monks still flourishes in Peebles and Hawick.

North of the Borders lies Edinburgh, the cultural and administrative capital of Scotland. With its Georgian squares dominated by a medieval castle, it is one of Europe's most elegant cities. While the 18th and 19th centuries saw a great flowering of the arts in Edinburgh, the city of Glasgow became a merchant city second only to London. Fuelled by James Watt's development of the steam engine in the 1840s, Glasgow became the cradle of Scotland's Industrial Revolution, which created a prosperous cotton industry and launched the world's greatest ships.

Both cities retain this dynamism today: Edinburgh annually hosts the world's largest arts festival, and Glasgow is acclaimed as a model of post-industrial renaissance.

A juggler performing at the Edinburgh Festival, an annual arts extravaganza

◀ The Old Town quarter of Edinburgh, with the castle in the background

Exploring the Lowlands

The Lowlands are traditionally all the land south of the fault line stretching northeast from Loch Lomond to Stonehaven. Confusingly, they include plenty of wild upland country. The wooded valleys and winding rivers of the borders give way to the stern hills of the Cheviots and Lammermuirs. Fishing villages cling to the rocky east coast, while the Clyde coast and its islands are dotted with holiday towns. Inland lies the Trossachs, a romantic area of mountain, loch and woodland east of Loch Lomond that is a magnet for walkers *(see p40)* and well within reach of Glasgow.

Loch Katrine seen from the Trossachs

Sights at a Glance

1 The Trossachs pp498–9
2 Stirling pp500–501
3 Doune Castle
4 Perth
5 Glamis Castle
6 Dundee
7 St Andrews
8 East Neuk
9 Falkland Palace
10 Dunfermline
11 Culross
12 Linlithgow Palace
13 Falkirk Wheel
14 Hopetoun House
15 Forth Bridges
16 Edinburgh pp508–15
17 St Abb's Head
19 Melrose Abbey
20 Abbotsford House
21 Traquair House
22 Biggar
23 Pentland Hills
24 New Lanark
25 Glasgow pp520–25
26 Sanquhar
27 Drumlanrig Castle
28 Threave Castle
29 Whithorn
30 Culzean Castle pp526–7
31 Burns Cottage

Walks and Tours

18 Tour of the Borders p507

Key

🟰 Motorway
🟰 Major road
━ Secondary road
┄ Minor road
━ Scenic route
⤙ Main railway
━ Minor railway
△ Summit

Getting Around

Access to the Lowlands from the south is made easy by the M74 to Glasgow or A702 to Edinburgh which connect the region to the M6 in England. Other motorways lead to Edinburgh, Glasgow, Stirling and Perth, north of which A roads feed the Highlands. Glasgow, Edinburgh and Glasgow Prestwick have international airports. Ferries from Ardrossan provide access to the Isle of Arran.

0 kilometres   20
0 miles   20

Edinburgh Castle viewed from Princes Street

For keys to symbols see back flap

① The Trossachs

Combining the ruggedness of the Grampians with the pastoral tranquillity of the Borders, this beautiful region of craggy hills and sparkling lochs is the colourful meeting place of the Lowlands and Highlands. The Trossachs are home to a wide variety of wildlife, including the golden eagle, peregrine falcon, red deer and wildcat. Numerous writers have been inspired by the area, including Sir Walter Scott *(see p516)*, who made it the setting for several of his novels. It was also the home of Scotland's folk hero, Rob Roy, who was so well known that, in his own lifetime, he was fictionalized in *The Highland Rogue* (1723), a novel attributed to Daniel Defoe.

Loch Katrine
The setting of Sir Walter Scott's *Lady of the Lake* (1810), this freshwater loch can be explored on the Victorian steamer SS *Sir Walter Scott*, which cruises from the Trossachs Pier.

Loch Lomond
Britain's largest freshwater lake was immortalized in a ballad composed by a local Jacobite soldier, dying far from home. He laments that though he will return home before his companions who travel on the high road, he will be doing so on the low road (of death).

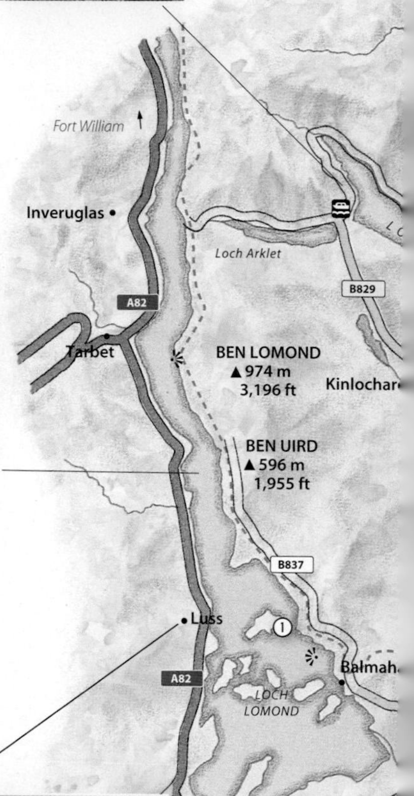

Key

▰▰ Main road

▭▭ Secondary road

▭▭ Minor road

– – Footpath

```
0 kilometres        5
0 miles             5
```

Map labels:
Fort William
Inveruglas •
Loch Arklet
B829
A82
Tarbet
BEN LOMOND
▲ 974 m
3,196 ft
Kinlochard
BEN UIRD
▲ 596 m
1,955 ft
B837
• Luss ①
Balmaha
LOCH LOMOND
A82
A82
• Balloch
↓ Glasgow

KEY

① **The West Highland Way** is a good trail through the area for walkers and cyclists *(see p40).*

② **The Duke's Pass**, between Callander and Aberfoyle, affords some of the finest views in the area.

③ **Rob Roy's grave**

Luss
With its exceptionally picturesque cottages, Luss is one of the prettiest villages in the Lowlands. Surrounded by grassy hills, it occupies one of the most scenic parts of Loch Lomond's western shore.

Inchmahome Priory
Mary, Queen of Scots *(see p515)* was hidden in this island priory to escape the armies of Henry VIII *(see p516)*.

Callander
This is the most popular town from which to explore the Trossachs and has a helpful information centre.

Rob Roy (1671–1734)

Robert MacGregor, known as Rob Roy (Red Robert) for the colour of his hair, grew up as a herdsman near Loch Arklet. After a series of harsh winters, he took to raiding richer Lowland properties to feed his clan, and was declared an outlaw by the Duke of Montrose who then burned his house to the ground. After this, Rob's Jacobite *(see p541)* sympathies became inflamed by his desire to avenge the crime. Plundering the duke's lands and repeatedly escaping from prison earned him a reputation similar to England's Robin Hood *(see p340)*. He was pardoned in 1725 and spent his last years freely in Balquhidder, where he is buried.

Queen Elizabeth Forest Park
There are woodland walks through this vast tract of countryside, home to black grouse and red deer, between Loch Lomond and Aberfoyle.

For keys to symbols *see back flap*

The 17th-century town house of the Dukes of Argyll, Stirling

❷ Stirling

Stirling. 🏘 45,800. 🚄 🚌
ℹ️ St John St (01786 475019).
W **visitstirling.org**

Situated between the Ochil Hills and the Campsie Fells, Stirling grew up around its castle, historically one of Scotland's most important fortresses. Below the castle the Old Town is still protected by the original 16th-century walls, built to keep Mary, Queen of Scots safe from Henry VIII. The medieval **Church of the Holy Rude**, on Castle Wynd, where the infant James VI was crowned in 1567, has one of Scotland's few surviving hammerbeam oak roofs. The ornate façade of **Mar's Wark** is all that remains of a grand palace which was commissioned in 1570 by the 1st Earl of Mar, though never completed. It was destroyed by the Jacobites (see p541) in 1746. Opposite stands the beautiful 17th-century town house of the Dukes of Argyll.

Environs

Two miles (3 km) south, the **Battle of Bannockburn Visitor Centre** stands by the field where Robert the Bruce defeated the English (see p486). After the battle, he dismantled the castle so it would not fall back into English hands. A bronze statue commemorates the man who is an icon of Scottish independence.

ℹ️ **Battle of Bannockburn Visitor Centre**
Glasgow Rd. **Tel** 01786 812664.
Open Mar–Oct: 10am–5:30pm daily; Nov–Feb: 10am–5pm daily. **Closed** 1 & 2 Jan, 25 & 26 Dec 🅿️ ♿ NTS

Stirling Castle

Rising high on a rocky crag, this magnificent castle, which dominated Scottish history for centuries, now remains one of the finest examples of Renaissance architecture in Scotland. Legend says that King Arthur (see p289) wrested the original castle from the Saxons, but there is no evidence of a castle before 1124. The present building dates from the 15th and 16th centuries and was last defended, against the Jacobites (see p541), in 1746. From 1881 to 1964 the castle was a depot for recruits into the Argyll and Sutherland Highlanders, though now it serves no military function.

Entrance

KEY

① **Forework**

② **Prince's Tower**

③ **The King's Old Building** houses the Regimental Museum of the Argyll and Sutherland Highlanders.

④ **Nether Bailey**

⑤ **The Great Hall**, built in 1500, has been restored to its former splendour.

⑥ **The Elphinstone Tower** was made into a gun platform in 1714.

Robert the Bruce
In the esplanade, this modern statue shows Robert the Bruce sheathing his sword after the Battle of Bannockburn in 1314.

★ **Palace**
The restored interiors of the royal apartments contain the Stirling Heads. These Renaissance roundels depict 38 figures, thought to be contemporary members of the royal court.

VISITORS' CHECKLIST

Practical Information
Castle Esplanade, Stirling.
Tel 01786 450000. **Open** 9:30am–6pm daily (Oct–Mar: to 5pm).
Closed 25 & 26 Dec. 🅿 except museum. 🎫 ♿ limited. 🔄 📷
📷 🆆 stirlingcastle.gov.uk

★ **Chapel Royal**
Seventeenth-century frescoes by Valentine Jenkins adorn the chapel, reconstructed in 1594.

Grand Battery
Seven guns stand on this parapet, built in 1708 during a strengthening of defences following the revolution of 1688 (see p57).

Stirling Battles

At the highest navigable point of the Forth and holding the pass to the Highlands, Stirling occupied a key position in Scotland's struggles for independence. Seven battlefields can be seen from the castle; the 67 m (220-ft) Wallace Monument at Abbey Craig recalls William Wallace's defeat of the English at Stirling Bridge in 1297, foreshadowing Bruce's victory in 1314 (see p486).

The Victorian Wallace Monument

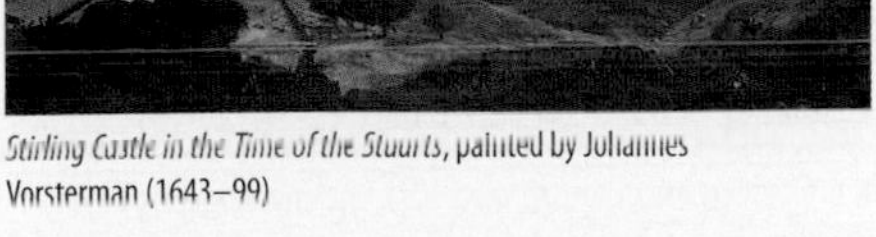

Stirling Castle in the Time of the Stuarts, painted by Johannes Vorsterman (1643–99)

Perth seen from the east across the Tay

❸ Doune Castle

Doune, Stirling. **Tel** 01786 841742.
🚆 🚌 Stirling then bus. **Open** Apr–
Sep: 9:30am–5:30pm daily; Oct–Mar:
9:30am–4:30pm daily; (last adm: 30
mins before closing). 🅿 ♿ limited.
W historicenvironment.scot

Constructed as a residence
for Robert, Duke of Albany,
the son of King Robert II of
Scotland, in the 14th century,
Doune Castle was a Stuart
stronghold until it fell into ruin
in the 18th century. Now fully
restored, it is one of the most
complete castles of its time
and offers a unique insight
into the royal household.

The Gatehouse, once a self-
sufficient residence, leads to the
central courtyard off which is
the Great Hall. Complete with its
reconstructed open-timber roof,
minstrels' gallery and central
fireplace, the Hall adjoins the
Lord's Hall and Private Room.
A number of private stairways
and narrow passages reveal the
ingenious ways the royal family

tried to hide during times of
danger. The castle was the
setting for the 1975 film *Monty
Python and the Holy Grail*.

❹ Perth

Perthshire. 🏔 47,200. 🚆 🚌
ℹ West Mill St (01738 450600).
W perthshire.co.uk

Once the capital of medieval
Scotland, Perth's rich heritage is
reflected in several of its buildings. It was in the **Church of
St John**, founded in 1126,
that John Knox *(see p486)*
delivered many of his fiery
sermons. The Victorianized
Fair Maid's House, on North
Port, is one of the oldest houses
in town (c.1600) and was the
fictional home of the heroine
of Sir Walter Scott's *(see p516)*
The Fair Maid of Perth (1828).

In **Balhousie Castle**, the
Museum of the Black Watch
commemorates the first
Highland regiment, while
the **Perth Museum & Art**

Gallery on George Street has
displays on local industry and
exhibitions of Scottish art.

Environs
Two miles (3 km) north of Perth,
the Gothic mansion of **Scone
Palace** stands on the site of
an abbey destroyed in 1559.
Between the 9th and 13th
centuries, Scone guarded the
sacred Stone of Destiny *(see
p486)*, now kept in Edinburgh
Castle *(see pp510–11)*. Some of
Mary, Queen of Scots' *(see p515)*
embroideries are on display.

🏠 **Balhousie Castle**
RHQ Black Watch, Hay St. **Tel** 01738
638152. **Open** 10am–4pm daily.
W theblackwatch.co.uk

🏛 **Perth Museum & Art Gallery**
78 George St. **Tel** 01738 632488.
Open 10am–5pm Tue–Sat (Apr–Oct:
daily). ♿ **W** culturepk.org.uk

🏠 **Scone Palace**
A93 to Braemar. **Tel** 01738 552300.
Open Apr–Oct: 10am–4pm daily
(May–Sep: to 5pm). 🅿 ♿
W scone-palace.co.uk

❺ Glamis Castle

Forfar, Angus. **Tel** 01307 840393. 🚆
🚌 Dundee then bus. **Open** Apr–Oct:
11am–5:30pm daily (last adm: 4:30pm).
🅿 📷 **W** glamis-castle.co.uk

With the pinnacled fairy-tale
outline of a Loire chateau, the
imposing medieval towerhouse
of **Glamis Castle** began as a
royal hunting lodge in the
11th century but underwent

Glamis Castle with statues of James VI (left) and Charles I (right)

For hotels and restaurants in this area see p572 and pp600–602

extensive reconstruction in the 17th century. It was the childhood home of Queen Elizabeth the Queen Mother, and her former bedroom can be seen, with its youthful portrait by Henri de Laszlo (1878–1956).

Many rooms are open to the public, including Duncan's Hall, the oldest in the castle. The castle also features in the Shakespeare play *Macbeth*.

❻ Dundee

Dundee City. 🚠 150,000. ✈ ⇄
🚌 *i* 16 City Sq (01382 527527).
🏪 farmers' market 3rd Sat of month (May–Oct). **W** angusanddundee.co.uk

Famed for its three Js of jam, jute mills and journalism – see the statues of publisher DC Thomson's *Beano* and *Dandy* comicbook characters near the grand venue of Caird Hall – Dundee was a hub of creative industries and science. Today, the city is undergoing major restoration and development. The **V&A Museum of Design**, opened in 2018, promises to inject new energy into the city by charting Scotland's outstanding design heritage inside a cutting-edge building by the Japanese architect Kengo Kuma.

On the River Tay is the royal research ship *Discovery*, built here in 1901 for Captain Scott's first voyage to the Antarctic. Audiovisual shows and displays describe the captain and crew's heroic journey. Over at Victoria

View of St Andrews over the ruins of the cathedral

Dock is **HMS *Unicorn*** (1824), Britain's oldest warship still afloat. The **McManus Galleries**' collection of Dundee-related art and artifacts is housed in a splendid Victorian Gothic building and gives an excellent insight into the city and its people.

A walk along the riverside takes you to the Tay Rail Bridge, the second on this site; the first collapsed in 1879, one of the worst engineering disasters in history.

🏛 V&A Museum of Design
Victoria Docks. **Tel** 01382 305665.
Open daily. 👤 **W** vandadundee.org

🏛 *Discovery*
Discovery Point. **Tel** 01382 309060.
Open daily (Sun pm only). 🅿 👤
W rrsdiscovery.com

🏛 HMS *Unicorn*
Victoria Docks, City Quay. **Tel** 01382 200900. **Open** Apr–Oct: daily, Nov–Mar: Thu–Sun. 🅿 👤 limited.
W frigateunicorn.org

🏛 McManus Galleries
Albert Sq. **Tel** 01382 307200.
Open 10am–5pm Mon–Sat, 12:30–4:30pm Sun. 👤 **W** mcmanus.co.uk

❼ St Andrews

Fife. 🚠 17,000. ⇄ Leuchars. 🚌 Dundee. *i* 70 Market St (01334 472021). **W** standrews.co.uk

Scotland's oldest university town and one-time ecclesiastical capital, **St Andrews** is now a mecca for golfers from all over the world. Its three main streets and numerous cobbled alleys, full of crooked housefronts, dignified university buildings and medieval churches, converge on the venerable ruins of the 12th-century **cathedral**. Once the largest in Scotland, the cathedral was later pillaged for stones to build the town. **St Andrew's Castle** was built for the bishops of the town in 1200 and its dungeon can still be seen. The **British Golf Museum** tells how the city's Royal and Ancient Golf Club became the ruling arbiter of the game, and to the west, the city's golf courses are open for a modest fee.

🏰 St Andrew's Castle
The Scores. **Tel** 01334 477196.
Open Apr–Sep: 9:30am–5:30pm daily; Oct–Mar: 10am–4pm daily.
Closed 1 & 2 Jan, 25 & 26 Dec. 🅿
👤 **W** historicenvironment.scot

🏛 British Golf Museum
Bruce Embankment. **Tel** 01334 460 046. **Open** Jan–Mar: 10am–4pm daily, Apr–Oct: 9.30am–5pm daily, Nov–Dec: 10am–4pm daily 🅿 👤 👶

The Ancient Game of Golf

Mary, Queen of Scots at St Andrews in 1563

Scotland's national game was pioneered on the sandy links around St Andrews. The earliest record dates from 1457, when golf was banned by James II on the grounds that it was interfering with his subjects' archery practice. Mary, Queen of Scots *(see p515)* enjoyed the game and was berated in 1568 for playing straight after the murder of her husband Darnley.

The central courtyard of Falkland Palace, bordered by rose bushes

❽ East Neuk

Fife. 🚆 Leuchars. 🚌 Glenrothes and Leuchars. 🛈 70 Market Street, St Andrews (01334 472021).

A string of pretty fishing villages scatters the shoreline of the **East Neuk** (the eastern "corner") of Fife, stretching from Earlsferry to Fife Ness. Much of Scotland's medieval trade with Europe passed through these ports, a connection reflected in the Flemish-inspired crow-stepped gables of many of the cottages. Although the herring industry has declined and the area is now a peaceful holiday centre, the sea still dominates village life. Until the 1980s, fishing boats were built at St Monans, a charming town of narrow twisting streets.

Pittenweem is the base for the East Neuk fishing fleet. The town is also known for **St Fillan's Cave**, the retreat of a 9th-century hermit whose relic was used to bless the army of Robert the Bruce (*see p486*) before the Battle of Bannockburn. A church

stands among the cobbled lanes and colourful cottages of **Crail**; the stone by the church gate is said to have been hurled to the mainland from the Isle of May by the Devil.

Several 16th- to 19th-century buildings in the village of Anstruther contain the **Scottish Fisheries Museum** which records the area's history with the aid of interiors, boats and displays on whaling. From the village you can take a trip to the nature reserve on the **Isle of May**, which teems with seabirds and grey seals. The statue of Alexander Selkirk in **Lower Largo** recalls the local boy whose adventures inspired Daniel Defoe's *Robinson Crusoe* (1719). Disagreeing with his captain, he was dumped on a desert island for four years.

🏛 **Scottish Fisheries Museum**
St Ayles, Harbourhead, Anstruther. Tel 01333 310628. **Open** Apr–Sep: 10am–5:30pm Mon–Sat (Oct–Mar: to 4:30pm), 11am–5pm Sun (Oct–Mar: from noon). **Closed** 1 & 2 Jan, 25 & 26 Dec. 🅿 🚹 🅦 scotfishmuseum.org

❾ Falkland Palace

Falkland, Fife. **Tel** 01337 857397. 🚆 🚌 from Ladybank. **Open** Mar–Oct: 11am–5pm Mon–Sat, 1–5pm Sun. 🅿 🚻 ♿ 🏠 NTS 🅦 nts.org.uk

This stunning Renaissance palace was designed as a hunting lodge for the Stuart kings. Although its construction was begun by James IV in 1500, most of the work was carried out by his son, James V, in the 1530s. Under the influence of his two French wives he employed French workmen to redecorate the façade of the East Range with dormers, buttresses and medallions, and to build the beautifully proportioned South Range. The palace fell into ruin during the years of the Commonwealth (*see p56*) and was occupied briefly by Rob Roy (*see p499*) in 1715.

After buying the estates in 1887, the 3rd Marquess of Bute became the Palace Keeper and restored it. The richly panelled interiors are filled with superb furniture and portraits of the Stuart monarchs. The royal tennis court is the oldest in Britain.

❿ Dunfermline

Fife. 🏠 50,500. 🚆 🚌 🛈 1 High St (01383 720999). 🅦 visitdunfermline.com

Scotland's capital until 1603, Dunfermline is dominated by the ruins of the 12th-century abbey and palace. In the 11th century, the town was the seat of King Malcolm III, who founded a priory on the present site of the **Abbey Church**. With its Norman nave and 19th-century choir, the church contains the tombs of 22 Scottish kings and queens, including Robert the Bruce (*see p486*).

The ruins of King Malcolm's **palace** soar over the beautiful gardens of Pittencrieff Park. Dunfermline's most famous son, philanthropist Andrew Carnegie (1835–1919), had been forbidden entrance to the park as a boy. After making his fortune, he bought the entire Pittencrieff estate and gave it

The Palace Keeper

Due to the size of the royal household and the necessity for the king to be itinerant, the office of Keeper was created by the medieval kings who required custodians to maintain and replenish the resources of their many palaces while they were away. Now redundant, it was a hereditary title and gave the custodian permanent and often luxurious lodgings.

James VI's bed in the Keeper's Bedroom, Falkland Palace

to the people of Dunfermline. He was born in the town, though moved to Pennsylvania in his teens. There he made a vast fortune in the iron and steel industry. The **Carnegie Birthplace Museum** is still furnished as it was when he lived there, and tells the story of his meteoric career.

🏛 **Carnegie Birthplace Museum**
Moodie St. **Tel** 01383 724302. **Open** Mar–Nov: 10am–5pm Mon–Sat; 2–5pm Sun. 🚻 📷 ⓦ carnegie birthplace.com

The 12th-century Norman nave of Dunfermline Abbey Church

⑪ Culross

Fife. 🚏 400. 🚆 Dunfermline. 🚌 Dunfermline. ℹ️ The Palace (01383 880359). Palace: **Open** Apr–Aug: 11am–5pm Wed–Mon (Jul & Aug: daily); Sep–Oct: 11am–4pm Sat Mon. Garden: **Open** 10am–6pm (or dusk if earlier). 📷 🏷 ltd. 📷 NTS 🎵 Music & Arts: Jun.

An important religious centre in the 6th century, the town of Culross is said to have been the birthplace of St Mungo in 514. Now a beautifully preserved 16th- and 17th-century village, Culross prospered in the 16th century with the growth of its coal and salt industries, most notably under Sir George Bruce. He took charge of the Culross colliery in 1575 and created a drainage system called the "Egyptian Wheel", which cleared a mile-long (1.5-km) mine beneath the River Forth.

During its subsequent decline Culross stood unchanged for over 150 years. The National Trust for Scotland began restoring the town in 1932 and now provides a guided tour, which starts at the **Visitors' Centre**.

Built in 1577, Bruce's **palace** has the crow-stepped gables, decorated windows and red pantiles typical of the period. The interior retains its original early 17th-century painted ceilings. Crossing the Square, past the **Oldest House**, dating from 1577, head for the Town House to the west. Behind it, a cobbled street known as the Back Causeway (with its raised section for nobility) leads to the turreted **Study**, built in 1610 as a house for the Bishop of Dunblane. The main room is open to visitors and should be seen for its original Norwegian ceiling. Continuing northwards to the ruined abbey, fine church and Abbey House, don't miss the Dutch-gabled **House with the Evil Eyes**.

The 16th-century palace of industrialist George Bruce, Culross

⑫ Linlithgow Palace

Linlithgow, West Lothian. **Tel** 01506 842896. 🚆 🚌 **Open** Apr–Sep: 9:30am–5:30pm daily; Oct–Mar: 10am–4pm daily. **Closed** 1 & 2 Jan, 25 & 26 Dec. 📷 🏷 limited. ⓦ historicenvironment.scot

On the edge of Linlithgow Loch stands the former royal palace of **Linlithgow**. Today's remains are mostly the palace of James I in 1425. The scale of the building is demonstrated by the 28 m (94 ft) long Great Hall with its huge fireplace and windows. Mary, Queen of Scots (*see p515*), was born here in 1542.

⑬ Falkirk Wheel

Lime Rd, Falkirk. **Tel** 08700 500208 (booking line). 🚆 Falkirk. **Open** Feb–Nov: Boat trips from 3 daily trips Wed–Sat in winter to 5 trips in summer. Visitor Centre: 10am–5:30pm daily (Nov–Mar: Wed–Sun). 📷 boat trip. 📷 📷 ⓦ thefalkirkwheel. co.uk

This impressive boat lift is the first ever to revolve, and the centrepiece of Scotland's canal regeneration scheme. Once important for commercial transport, the Union and the Forth and Clyde canals were blocked by several roads in the 1960s. Now the Falkirk Wheel gently swings boats between the two waterways, creating an uninterrupted link between Glasgow and Edinburgh. Visitors can ride the wheel on boats that leave from the Visitor Centre.

The rotating Falkirk Wheel boat lift

⑭ Hopetoun House

West Lothian. **Tel** 0131 331 2451.
🚆 Dalmeny then taxi. **Open** Apr–
Sep: 10:30am–5pm (last adm: 4pm).
▨ ◫ for groups – book ahead.
♿ ltd. 🖥 🏠 W **hopetoun.co.uk**

Extensive parklands by the Firth
of Forth, designed in the style
of Versailles, and the setting for
one of Scotland's finest stately
homes. The original house
was built by 1707; it was later
absorbed into William Adam's
grand extension. The dignified,
horseshoe-shaped plan and
lavish interiors represent
Neo-Classical 18th-century
architecture at its finest. The
drawing rooms, with their
Rococo plasterwork and highly
ornate mantelpieces, are
particularly impressive. The
Marquess of Linlithgow, whose
family still occupies part of the
house, is a descendant of the
1st Earl of Hopetoun, for whom
the house was built.

A wooden panel above the main stair,
depicting Hopetoun House

⑮ Forth Bridges

Edinburgh. 🚆 Dalmeny, North
Queensferry. 🚍 South Queensferry.

The small town of South
Queensferry is dominated by
the three great bridges that
span the mile (1.5 km) across
the River Forth to North Queensferry. The spectacular rail bridge,
the first major steel-built bridge
in the world, was opened in
1890 and remains one of the
greatest engineering achievements of the late Victorian era.

The shattered crags and cliffs of St Abb's Head

Its massive cantilevered sections
are held together by more than
6.5 million rivets, and the
painted area adds up to some
55 hectares (135 acres). The
saying "like painting the Forth
Bridge" has become a byword
for nonstop, repetitive
endeavour. The bridge also
inspired *The Bridge* (1986) by
writer Iain Banks (1954–2013).
There are plans to perch a
viewing platform atop the
101-m (330-ft) rail bridge,
    The neighbouring road bridge
was the largest suspension
bridge outside the USA when
it opened in 1964. In 2017
a second road bridge, the
strikingly futuristic Queensferry
Crossing, was completed.
    South Queensferry got its
name from the 11th-century
Queen Margaret *(see p511)*,
who used the ferry here on her
journeys between Edinburgh
and the royal palace at
Dunfermline *(see p504)*.

⑯ Edinburgh

See pp508–15.

The huge, cantilevered Forth Rail Bridge, seen from South Queensferry

⑰ St Abb's Head

Scottish Borders. 🚆 Berwick-upon-
Tweed. 🚍 from Edinburgh. NTS

The jagged cliffs of St Abb's Head,
rising 91 m (300 ft) from the
North Sea near the southeastern
tip of Scotland, offer a spectacular
view of thousands of seabirds
wheeling and diving below. This
80-ha (200-acre) nature reserve is
an important site for cliff-nesting
seabirds and becomes, during
the May to June breeding
season, the home of more than
50,000 birds, including fulmars,
guillemots, kittiwakes and
puffins, which throng the
headland near the fishing village
of St Abbs. The village has one
of the few unspoiled working
harbours on Britain's east coast.
A clifftop trail begins at the
Visitors' Centre, where displays
include identification boards
and a touch table where young
visitors can get to grips with
wings and feathers.

ℹ **Visitors' Centre**
St Abb's Head. **Tel** 01890 771443.
Open Apr–Oct: 10am–5pm daily. ◫

⑱ A Tour of the Borders

Because of their proximity to England, the Scottish Borders are scattered with the ruins of many buildings destroyed over the centuries in the conflicts between the two nations. Most poignant of all are the Border abbeys, whose magnificent architecture bears witness to their former spiritual and political power. Founded during the 12th-century reign of David I, the abbeys were torn down by Henry VIII (*see p516*).

② **Kelso Abbey**
The largest of the Border abbeys, Kelso was once the most powerful ecclesiastical establishment in Scotland.

① **Floors Castle**
The largest inhabited castle in Scotland, this is the Duke of Roxburghe's ancestral home and was built in the 18th century by William Adam.

⑥ **Melrose Abbey**
Once one of the richest abbeys in Scotland, it is here that Robert the Bruce's heart is buried (*see p516*).

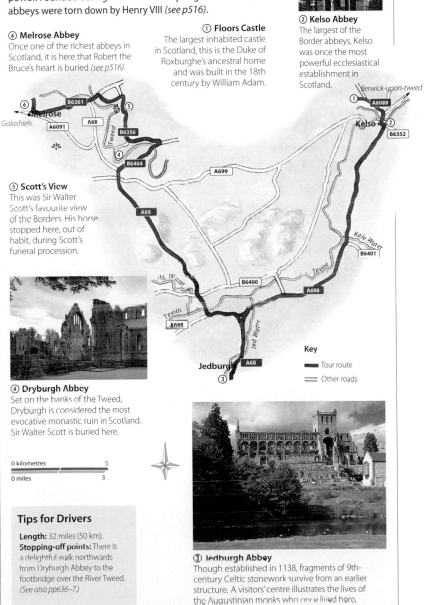

⑤ **Scott's View**
This was Sir Walter Scott's favourite view of the Borders. His horse stopped here, out of habit, during Scott's funeral procession.

④ **Dryburgh Abbey**
Set on the banks of the Tweed, Dryburgh is considered the most evocative monastic ruin in Scotland. Sir Walter Scott is buried here.

0 kilometres 5
0 miles 3

Key
▬▬ Tour route
═══ Other roads

Tips for Drivers

Length: 32 miles (50 km).
Stopping-off points: There is a delightful walk northwards from Dryburgh Abbey to the footbridge over the River Tweed. (*See also pp636–7.*)

③ **Jedburgh Abbey**
Though established in 1138, fragments of 9th-century Celtic stonework survive from an earlier structure. A visitors' centre illustrates the lives of the Augustinian monks who once lived here.

⑯ Edinburgh

With its striking medieval and Georgian districts, overlooked by the extinct volcano of Arthur's Seat and, to the northeast, Calton Hill, Edinburgh is widely regarded as one of Europe's most handsome capitals. The city is famous for the arts (it was once known as "the Athens of the North"), a pre-eminence reflected in its hosting every year of Britain's largest arts extravaganza, the Edinburgh Festival *(see p513)*. Its museums and galleries display the riches of many cultures.

Exploring Edinburgh

Edinburgh falls into two main sightseeing areas, divided by Princes Street, the city's most famous thoroughfare and its commercial centre. The Old Town straddles the ridge bet-ween the castle and the Palace of Holyroodhouse, with most of the city's medieval history clustered in the alleys of the Grassmarket and Royal Mile areas. The New Town, to the north, evolved after 1767 when wealthy merchants expanded the city beyond its medieval walls. This district contains Britain's finest concentration of Georgian architecture.

🏛 National Gallery of Scotland

The Mound. **Tel** 0131 624 6200. **Open** 10am–5pm Fri–Wed (Aug: to 6pm), 10am–7pm Thu. 📷 for special exhibitions. 📷 by appt. 🦽 🖵 🆆 nationalgalleries.org

One of Britain's finest art galleries, the National Gallery of Scotland is worth visiting for its 15th- to 19th-century

British and European paintings alone, though plenty more can be found to delight the art-lover. Highlights among the Scottish works include portraits by Allan Ramsay and Henry Raeburn, such as the latter's *Reverend Robert Walker Skating on Duddingston Loch* (c.1800). The Early German collection includes Gerard David's almost comic-strip treatment of the *Three Legends of Saint Nicholas* (c.1500). Works by Raphael, Titian and Tintoretto accompany southern European paintings such as Velázquez's *An Old Woman Cooking Eggs* (1620) and there's an entire room devoted to *The Seven Sacraments* (c.1640) by Nicholas Poussin.

The Weston Link is an underground complex that connects the gallery with the Royal

Raeburn's Rev. Robert Walker Skating on Duddingston Loch

Scottish Academy. It contains a lecture theatre/cinema, shop, restaurant, café, and an education room.

🏚 Georgian House

7 Charlotte Sq. **Tel** 0844 493 2118. **Open** Mar & Nov: 11am–4pm daily; Apr–Oct: 10am–5pm daily; (last adm: 30 minutes before closing). 📷 🦽 limited. 🆖🆃🆂 🆆 nts.org.uk

In the heart of the New Town, Charlotte Square is a superb example of Georgian architecture, its north side, built in the 1790s, being a masterwork by the architect Robert Adam *(see p32)*. The Georgian House at No. 7 has been furnished and repainted in its original 18th-century colours, providing a memorable introduction to the elegance of wealthy New Town life. In stark contrast, "below stairs" is the household staff's living quarters, demonstrating how Edinburgh's working class lived and worked.

🏛 Scottish National Portrait Gallery

1 Queen St. **Tel** 0131 624 6200. **Open** 10am–5pm daily (to 7pm Thu) Aug: 10am–6pm daily. 📷 by appointment. 🦽 🆆 nationalgalleries.org

The Scottish National Portrait Gallery provides a unique visual history of Scotland told through the portraits of those who created it, from Robert the

The view from Dugald Stewart Monument on Calton Hill, looking west towards the castle

For hotels and restaurants in this area see p572 and pp600–602

The magnificent Great Hall at the Scottish National Portrait Gallery

Bruce *(see p486)* to Queen Anne. Portraits of other famous Scots include Robert Burns *(see p519)* by Alexander Nasmyth. The collection of memorabilia include Mary, Queen of Scots' *(see p515)* jewellery and a silver travelling canteen left by Bonnie Prince Charlie *(see p535)*. There is also an emphasis on photography at the gallery, such as the display of Alexander Hutchinson's moving record of the lost

community of St Kilda, and Scottish art, as well as a dynamic exhibition programme.

🏛 National Museum of Scotland

Chambers Rd. **Tel** 0300 123 6789. **Open** 10am–5pm daily. **Closed** 25 Dec. 📷 ♿ 🎥 free. 🚫 **w** nms.ac.uk

This purpose-built museum houses the Scottish collections of the National Museums of Scotland. Exhibitions tell the story of Scotland, the land and its people, dating from its geological beginnings right up to the exciting events of today.

The museum's key exhibits include the famous medieval *Lewis Chessmen*, *Pictish Chains*, known as Scotland's earliest crown jewels, and the *Ellesmere* railway locomotive. A huge Tyrannosaurus rex skeleton guards the entrance to the natural world galleries, and the 1930s Schmidt telescope is the centrepiece of the Earth and

Space gallery. There is also a special exhibition gallery that houses temporary displays.

🚌 Greyfriars Bobby

Near the gateway to Greyfriars Church stands the statue of a Skye terrier. It commemorates the dog who is said to have guarded the grave of his master, John Gray, for 14 years. The people of Edinburgh cared for Bobby until his death in 1872.

Statue of Greyfriars Bobby, near Greyfriars Church

Edinburgh City Centre

① National Gallery of Scotland
② Georgian House
③ Scottish National Portrait Gallery
④ National Museum of Scotland
⑤ Greyfriars Bobby
⑥ *Edinburgh Castle pp510–11*
⑦ Gladstone's Land
⑧ Parliament House
⑨ St Giles Cathedral
⑩ Museum of Childhood
⑪ Palace of Holyroodhouse
⑫ Our Dynamic Earth

Edinburgh Castle

Standing upon the basalt core of an extinct volcano, Edinburgh Castle is an assemblage of buildings dating from the 12th to the 20th centuries, reflecting its changing role as fortress, royal palace, military garrison and state prison. Though there is evidence of Bronze Age occupation of the site, the original fortress was built by the 6th-century Northumbrian King Edwin, from whom the city takes its name. The castle was a favourite royal residence until the Union of Crowns *(see p487)* in 1603, after which the king resided in England. After the Union of Parliaments in 1707, the Scottish regalia were walled up in the Royal Palace for over a hundred years. The castle is now the zealous possessor of the so-called Stone of Scone, a relic of ancient Scottish kings, which was seized by the English in 1296 from Scone Palace, Perthshire, and not officially returned until 1996.

Scottish Crown
On display in the palace, the crown was restyled by James V of Scotland in 1540.

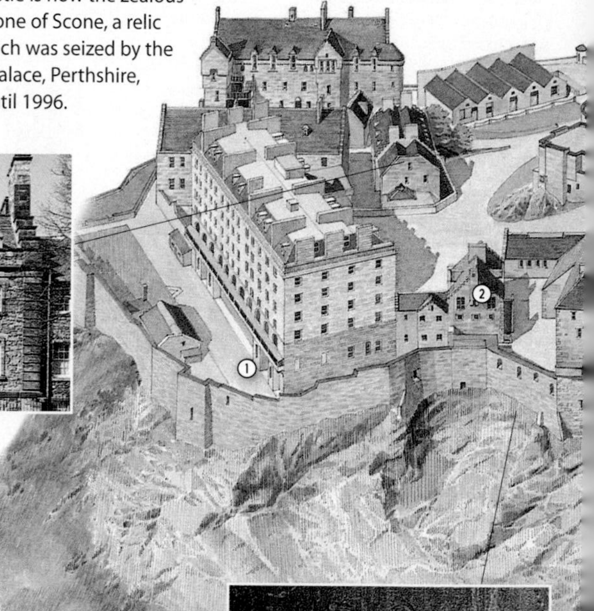

Governor's House
Complete with Flemish-style crow-stepped gables, this building was constructed for the governor of the castle in 1742. It can only be viewed from the outside as it is still reserved for ceremonial use.

Vaults
This French graffiti, dating from 1780, recalls the many prisoners who were held in the vaults during the wars with France in the 18th and 19th centuries.

Mons Meg

Positioned outside St Margaret's Chapel, the siege gun (or *bombard*) Mons Meg was made in Belgium in 1449 for the Duke of Burgundy, who gave it to his nephew, James II of Scotland. It was used by James against the Douglas family in their stronghold of Threave Castle *(see p519)* in 1455, and later by James IV against Norham Castle in England. After exploding during a salute to the Duke of York in 1682, it was kept in the Tower of London until being returned to Edinburgh in 1829 at Sir Walter Scott's request.

KEY

① **Old Back Parade**

② **Military Prison**

③ **The Half Moon Battery** was built in the 1570s as a platform for the artillery defending the northeastern wing of the castle.

④ **The Esplanade** is the location of the Military Tattoo *(see p513)*.

Argyle Battery
This fortified wall commands a spectacular view to the north, beyond the city's Georgian district of New Town.

VISITORS' CHECKLIST

Practical Information
Castle Hill. **Tel** 0131 225 9846.
Open 9:30am–6pm daily (Oct–Mar: to 5pm; last adm: 1 hr before closing). **Closed** 25 & 26 Dec.
book tickets online to avoid queuing.
w edinburghcastle.gov.uk

★ Royal Palace
Mary, Queen of Scots
(see p515) gave birth to James VI
in this 15th-century palace,
where the Scottish regalia
are on display.

Entrance

Royal Mile

★ Great Hall
With its restored open-timber roof, the Hall dates from the 15th century and was the meeting place of the Scottish parliament until 1639.

St Margaret's Chapel
This stained-glass
window depicts Malcolm
III's saintly queen, to
whom the chapel is
dedicated. Probably built
by her son, David I, in the
early 12th century, the
chapel is the castle's
oldest existing building

Exploring the Royal Mile: Castlehill to High Street

The Royal Mile is a stretch of four ancient streets (from Castlehill to Canongate) that formed the main thoroughfare of medieval Edinburgh, linking the castle to the Palace of Holyroodhouse. Confined by the city wall, the "Old Town" grew upwards, with some tenements climbing to 20 storeys. It is still possible, among the 66 alleys and closes off the main street, to get a sense of the city's medieval past.

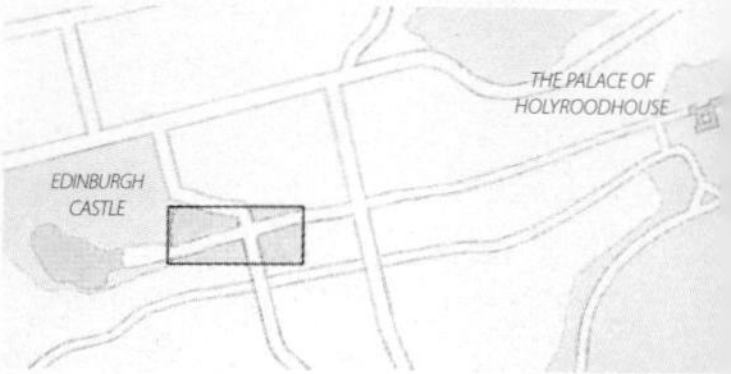

THE PALACE OF HOLYROODHOUSE

EDINBURGH CASTLE

Locator Map

Gladstone's Land is a preserved 17th-century merchant's house.

Scotch Whisky Heritage Centre introduces visitors to Scotland's national drink.

The Camera Obscura contains an observatory from which to view the city, plus optical illusions and giant kaleidoscopes.

LAWNMARKET

Edinburgh Castle

CASTLEHILL

Lady Stair's House
This 17th-century house contains a museum devoted to the life and work of Burns, Scott *(see p516)* and Stevenson.

The "Hub" (c.1840) has the city's highest spire.

🏠 Gladstone's Land

477B Lawnmarket. **Tel** 0131 226 5856. **Open** Easter–Oct: 10am–5pm daily (last adm: 30 mins before closing). 🏠 ✉ ♿ 🏛 🌐 nts.org.uk

This 17th-century merchant's house provides a window on life in a typical Old Town house before overcrowding drove the rich to the Georgian New Town. "Lands", as they were known, were tall, narrow buildings erected on small plots of land. The six-storey Gladstone's Land was named after Thomas Gledstanes, the merchant who built it in 1617. The house still has its original arcade booths on the street front and a painted ceiling with fine Scandinavian floral designs. Though extravagantly furnished, it also contains reminders of the less salubrious side of the old city, such as the wooden overshoes which had to be worn in the dirty streets. A chest in the beautiful Painted Chamber is said to have been given by a Dutch sea captain to a Scottish merchant who saved him from a shipwreck. A similar house, Morocco Land, can be found on Canongate *(see p515)*.

🏠 Parliament House

Parliament Sq, High St. **Tel** 0131 348 5000. **Open** 9am–5pm Mon–Fri. **Closed** public hols. ♿ limited.

This majestic Italianate building was constructed in the 1630s for the Scottish parliament but has been home to the Court of Session and the Supreme Court since the Union of Parliaments *(see p487)* in 1707. It is worth seeing, as much for the spectacle of its gowned and wigged advocates as for the stained-glass window in its Great Hall, commemorating the inauguration of the Court of Session by James V, in 1532.

The bedroom of Gladstone's Land

For hotels and restaurants in this area see p572 and pp600–602

The Signet Library has a lavish interior; it was described by George IV as the "finest drawing room in Europe".

St Giles Cathedral
A bagpiping angel can be found on the arched entrance to the Chapel of the Thistle.

BANK STREET

HIGH STREET

GEORGE IV BRIDGE

Rib-vaulting in the Thistle Chapel, St Giles Cathedral

The City Chambers were designed by John Adam in the 1750s.

The Heart of Midlothian is an arrangement of granite cobblestones on the former site of the city jail.

Parliament House was built in 1639. The Scottish parliament convened here from 1640 until 1707.

Charles II Statue

🏛 St Giles Cathedral
Royal Mile. **Tel** 0131 225 9442.
Open May–Sep: 9am–7pm Mon–Fri, 9am–5pm Sat, 1–5pm Sun; Oct–Apr: 9am–5pm Mon–Sat, 1–5pm Sun.
Closed 1 & 2 Jan, 25 & 26 Dec.
🅿 donation. ♿ 🆆 stgiles cathedral.org.uk

Officially the High Kirk (church) of Edinburgh, it is ironic that St Giles has become known as a cathedral. Though it was twice the seat of a bishop in the 17th century, it was from here that John Knox *(see p486)* directed the Scottish Reformation with its emphasis on individual worship freed from the authority of bishops. A tablet marks the place where Jenny Geddes, a stallholder from a local market, scored a victory for the Covenanters *(see p487)* by hurling her stool at a preacher

reading from an English prayer book in 1637.

The Gothic exterior is dominated by a 15th-century tower. Inside, the impressive Thistle Chapel can be seen, with its elaborate rib-vaulted roof

and carved heraldic canopies. The chapel honours the knights, past and present, of the Order of the Thistle. The carved royal pew in the Preston Aisle is used by the Queen when she stays in Edinburgh.

Edinburgh International Festival

Every year, for three weeks in late summer *(see p67)*, Edinburgh hosts one of the world's most important arts festivals, with every available space (from theatres to street corners) packed with performers. It has been held in Edinburgh since 1947 and brings together the best in international contemporary theatre, music, dance and opera. The alternative Festival Fringe balances the classic productions with a host of innovative performances. The most popular event is the Edinburgh Military Tattoo, held on the Castle Esplanade – a spectacle of Scottish infantry battalions marching to pipe bands. Other city-wide events include the Edinburgh Book Festival and Edinburgh Film Festival.

Street performer at the Edinburgh Festival Fringe

Exploring the Royal Mile: High Street to Canongate

The second section of the Royal Mile passes two monuments to the Reformation: John Knox House and the Tron Kirk. The latter is named after a medieval *tron* (weighing beam) that stood nearby. The Canongate was once an independent district, owned by the canons of the Abbey of Holyrood, and sections of its south side have been restored. Beyond Morocco's Land, the road stretches for the final half-mile (800 m) to the Palace of Holyroodhouse.

Locator Map

HIGH STREET

SOUTH BRIDGE STREET

The Mercat Cross marks the city centre. It was here that Bonnie Prince Charlie *(see p535)* was proclaimed king in 1745.

The Tron Kirk was built in 1630 for the Presbyterians who left St Giles Cathedral when it came under the Bishop of Edinburgh's control.

The entrance to the Palace of Holyroodhouse, seen from the west

🏛 Museum of Childhood

42 High St. **Tel** 0131 529 4142. **Open** 10am–5pm Thu–Mon (from noon Sun). **Closed** 25–27 Dec. ♿ limited. 🌐 edinburghmuseums.org.uk

This lovely museum is not merely a toy collection but a magical insight into childhood. Founded in 1955 by a city councillor, Patrick Murray (who claimed to enjoy eating children for breakfast), it was the first museum in the world to be devoted to the history and theme of childhood. The collection includes medicines, school books and prams, as well as galleries full of old toys. With its nickelodeon, antique slot machines and the general enthusiasm of visitors, this has been called the world's noisiest museum.

🏰 Palace of Holyroodhouse

East end of Royal Mile. **Tel** 0131 556 5100. **Open** Apr–Oct: 9:30am–6pm; Nov–Mar: 9:30am–4:30pm daily. **Closed** 25 & 26 Dec and during royal visits. 📷 ♿ limited. 🌐 royalcollection.org.uk

The Queen's official Scottish residence, the Palace of Holyroodhouse is named after the "rood", or cross, which King David I is said to have seen between the antlers of a stag he was hunting here in 1128. The present palace was built in 1529 to accommodate James V and his French wife, Mary of Guise, though it was remodelled in the 1670s for Charles II. The Royal Apartments (including the Throne Room and Royal Dining Room) are used for investitures and banquets whenever the Queen visits the palace. A chamber in the James V Tower is associated with the unhappy reign of Mary, Queen of Scots. It was here, in 1566, that she saw the murder of her trusted Italian secretary, David Rizzio, by her jealous husband, Lord Darnley. She had married Darnley a year earlier in Holyroodhouse chapel. Bonnie Prince Charlie held court here in 1745 during the Jacobite *(see p541)* uprising.

An 1880 automaton of the Man on the Moon, Museum of Childhood

John Knox House
The oldest house in the city, dating from 1490, was the home of John Knox *(see p486)* in the 1560s. He is said to have died in an upstairs room.

Morocco Land is a reproduction of a 17th-century tenement house. It takes its name from the statue of a Moor that adorns the entrance.

Morocco Land

The Palace of Holyroodhouse

CANONGATE

MUSEUM OF CHILDHOOD

Museum of Childhood
This lively museum, popular with young and old alike, is packed with toys and games from across generations.

Moubray House was to be the signing place of the Treaty of Union In 1707 *(see p487)*, until a mob forced the authorities to retreat to another venue.

🏛 Our Dynamic Earth
Holyrood Rd. **Tel** 0131 550 7800
Open 10am–5:30pm daily (to 6pm Jul & Aug). 🅿 Ⓦ **dynamicearth.co.uk**

Housed in an eye-catching spiked tent with a translucent roof, this visitor attraction holds exhibitions that are both educational and entertaining, and perfect for children as well as adults. Beginning with the Big Bang, it takes visitors on a journey through time, culminating in the present day. A range of natural events are recreated, including volcanic eruptions, tidal waves and earthquakes. State-of-the-art lighting and interactive elements bring alive extinct dinosaurs and recreate tropical downpours. Visitors find themselves standing on shaking floors and flying over prehistoric Scottish glaciers. The exhibition also raises important questions about the future and the impact of climate change.

The establishment has a 360-degree full dome film theatre that screens a variety of movies throughout the year. There is also a café that serves hot meals.

🏛 Scottish National Gallery of Modern Art One and Two
75 Belford Rd. **Tel** 0131 624 6200.
Open 10am–5pm daily (Aug: to 6pm). 🚻 Ⓦ **nationalgalleries.org**

Housed in a 19th-century school to the northwest of the city centre, the Modern One gallery features most European and American 20th-century greats, from Vuillard and Picasso to Magritte and Lichtenstein. Work by John Bellany can be found among the Scottish painters. Sculpture by Henry Moore is on display in the grounds. The adjacent Modern Two gallery showcases Dada and Surrealist art.

Mary, Queen of Scots (1542–87)

Born only days before the death of her father, James V, the young Queen Mary spent her childhood in France, after escaping Henry VIII's invasion of Scotland *(see p516)*. A devout Catholic, she married the French Dauphin, and then made claims on the English throne. This alarmed Protestants throughout England and Scotland, and when she returned as a widow to Holyroodhouse, aged 18, she was harangued for her faith by John Knox *(see p486)*. In 1567 she was accused of murdering her second husband, Lord Darnley. Two months later, when she married the Earl of Bothwell (also implicated in the murder), rebellion ensued. She lost her crown and fled to England where she was held prisoner for 20 years, before being charged with treason and beheaded at Fotheringhay.

The ruins of Melrose Abbey, viewed from the southwest

⑲ Melrose Abbey

Abbey Street, Melrose, Scottish Borders.
Tel 01896 822562. **Open** 9:30am–4pm
daily (Apr–Sep: to 5:30pm; last adm: 30
mins before closing). **Closed** 1 & 2 Jan,
25 & 26 Dec. ♿ ⬆ limited.
🌐 **historicenvironment.scot**

The rose-pink ruins of this
beautiful Border abbey *(see
p507)* bear testimony to the
hazards of standing in the path
of successive English invasions.
Built by David I in 1136 for
Cistercian monks from Yorkshire,
and replacing a 7th-century
monastery, Melrose was
repeatedly ransacked by English
armies, notably in 1322 and
1385. The final blow, from
which none of the abbeys
recovered, came in 1545
during Henry VIII's destructive

Scottish policy known as the
"Rough Wooing". This resulted
from the failure of the Scots
to ratify a marriage treaty
between Henry VIII's son and
the infant Mary, Queen of
Scots *(see p515)*. What remains
of the abbey are the outlines of
cloisters, the kitchen and other
monastic buildings, and the
shell of the abbey church with
its soaring east window and
profusion of medieval carvings.
The rich decorations on the
south exterior wall include a
gargoyle shaped like a pig
playing the bagpipes.

An embalmed heart, found
here in 1920, is probably that
of Robert the Bruce *(see p486)*,
who had decreed that his heart
be taken on a crusade to the
Holy Land. It was returned to

Melrose after its bearer, Sir
James Douglas *(see p519)*,
was killed in Spain.

⑳ Abbotsford House

Galashiels, Scottish Borders. **Tel** 01896
752043. 🚌 from Galashiels. **Open**
Apr–Oct: 10am–5pm daily; Mar & Nov:
10am–4pm daily. ♿ ⬆ ⬆ limited.
🌐 **scottsabbotsford.co.uk**

Few houses bear the stamp
of their creator so intimately
as Abbotsford House, the home
of Sir Walter Scott for the last
20 years of his life. He bought
a farm here in 1811, known
as Clarteyhole ("dirty hole"
in Scots), though he soon
renamed it Abbotsford,
after the monks of Melrose
Abbey who used to cross the
River Tweed nearby. He later
demolished the house to
make way for today's turreted
building, funded by the sales
of his novels.

Scott's library contains
more than 9,000 rare books
and his collections of historic
relics reflect his passion for
the heroic past. An extensive
array of arms and armour
includes Rob Roy's broadsword
(see p499). Stuart mementoes
include a crucifix that belonged
to Mary, Queen of Scots and
a lock of Bonnie Prince
Charlie's *(see p535)* hair. The
small study in which he wrote
his *Waverley* novels can be
visited, as can the room,
overlooking the river, in
which he died in 1832.

Sir Walter Scott

Sir Walter Scott (1771–1832) was
born in Edinburgh and trained as
a lawyer. He is best remembered
as a champion and literary figure
of Scotland, whose poems and
novels (most famously his *Waverley*
series) created enduring images of
a heroic wilderness filled with tales
of the clans. His orchestration, in
1822, of the state visit of George IV
to Edinburgh *(see p489)* was an
extravaganza of Highland culture
that helped re-establish tartan as
the national dress of Scotland. He
served as Clerk of the Court in Edinburgh's Parliament House *(see p512)*
and for 30 years was Sheriff of Selkirk in the Scottish Borders, a place
he loved. He put the Trossachs *(see pp498–9)* firmly on the map with
the publication of the *Lady of the Lake* (1810). His final years were
spent writing to pay off a £114,000 debt following the collapse of his
publisher, of which he was a financial partner, in 1827. He died with
his debts paid, and was buried at Dryburgh Abbey *(see p507)*.

The Great Hall at Abbotsford, adorned
with arms and armour

㉑ Traquair House

Peebles, Scottish Borders. **Tel** 01896 830 323. 🚌 from Peebles. **Open** Apr–Sep: 11am–5pm daily; Oct: 11am–4pm daily; Nov: 11am–3pm Sat & Sun. 🅿️ 🅶 limited. 🅆 **traquair.co.uk**

As Scotland's oldest continuously inhabited house, Traquair has deep roots in Scottish religious and political history, stretching back over 900 years. Evolving from a fortified tower to a stout-walled 17th-century mansion (*see p491*), the house was a Catholic Stuart stronghold for 500 years. Mary, Queen of Scots (*see p515*) was among the many monarchs to have stayed here and her bed is covered by a counterpane she made herself. Family letters and engraved Jacobite (*see p541*) drinking glasses are among relics recalling the period of the Highland rebellions.

Mary, Queen of Scots' crucifix, Traquair House

After a vow made by the 5th Earl, Traquair's Bear Gates (the "Steekit Yetts"), which closed after Bonnie Prince Charlie's (*see p535*) visit in 1745, will not reopen until a Stuart again ascends the throne. A secret stairway leads to the Priest's Room, which attests to the problems faced by Catholic families until Catholicism was legalized in 1829. Traquair House Ale is still produced in the 18th-century brewhouse.

㉒ Biggar

Clyde Valley. 🚉 2,300. 🚆 Lanark, Ladyacre Rd (01555 668249).

This typical Lowland market town has a number of museums worth visiting. The **Museum of Biggar and Upper Clydesdale** boasts a reconstructed Victorian street, complete with a milliner's, printer's and a village library, while the grimy days of the town's industrial past are recalled at the **Gasworks Museum**, with its collection of engines, gaslights and appliances. Established in 1839 and preserved in the 1970s, the Biggar Gasworks is the only remaining rural gasworks in Scotland.

🏛️ **Museum of Biggar and Upper Clydesdale**
High St. **Tel** 01899 221050. **Open** Apr–Oct: 11am–5pm Tue–Sat, 1–5pm Sun; Nov–Mar: 10am–5pm Sat, 1–5pm Sun. 🅿️ 🅶

🏛️ **Gasworks Museum**
Gasworks Rd. **Tel** 01899 221070. **Open** Jun–Sep: 2–5pm daily.

㉓ Pentland Hills

The Lothians. 🚉 Edinburgh, then bus. 🅸 Flotterstone Information Centre, off A702 (0131 529 2401).

The Pentland Hills, stretching for 16 miles (26 km) southwest of Edinburgh, offer some of the best hill-walking country in the Lowlands. Leisurely walkers can saunter along the many signposted footpaths, while the more adventurous can take the chairlift at the Hillend dry ski slope to reach the higher ground leading to the 493-m (1,617-ft) hill of Allermuir. Even more ambitious is the classic scenic route along the ridge from Caerketton to West Kip.

To the east of the A703, in the lee of the Pentlands, stands the exquisite and ornate 15th-century **Rosslyn Chapel**. It was originally intended as a church, but after the death of its founder, William Sinclair, it was also used as a burial ground for his descendants. The delicately wreathed Apprentice Pillar recalls the legend of the apprentice carver who was killed by the master stone-mason in a fit of jealousy at his pupil's superior skill.

🏰 **Rosslyn Chapel**
Roslin. **Tel** 0131 4402159. **Open** daily (Sun: pm only). 🅿️ 🅤 🅆 **rosslynchapel.com**

Details of the decorated vaulting in Rosslyn Chapel

The 18th-century tenements of New Lanark on the banks of the Clyde

24 New Lanark

Clyde Valley. 190. Lanark. Horsemarket, Ladyacre Rd (01555 668249). daily.

Situated by the falls of the River Clyde, the village of New Lanark was founded in 1785 by the industrial entrepreneur David Dale. An ideal location for water-driven mills, the village became Britain's largest cotton producer by 1800. Dale and his successor, Robert Owen, were philanthropists whose reforms proved that commercial success need not undermine the wellbeing of the workforce. Now a museum, New Lanark is a window onto working life in the early 19th century. Films tell the story of New Lanark and Robert Owen's progressive ideals, and how they are as relevant today as they were in the 1820s.

Environs

15 miles (24 km) north, Blantyre has a memorial to the famous Scottish explorer David Livingstone.

New Lanark

New Lanark Visitor Centre. **Tel** 01555 661345. **Open** 10am–5pm daily (Nov–Mar: to 4pm). groups only, by appointment. **newlanark.org**

David Livingstone

Scotland's great missionary doctor and explorer was born in Blantyre, where he began his working life as a mill boy at the age of ten. Livingstone (1813–73) made three epic journeys across Africa from 1840, promoting "commerce and Christianity". He became the first European to see Victoria Falls and died in 1873 while searching for the source of the Nile. He is buried in Westminster Abbey *(see pp96–7)*.

25 Glasgow

See pp520–25.

26 Sanquhar

Dumfries & Galloway. 2,100. 64 Whitesands, Dumfries (01387 253862).

Now of chiefly historic interest, the town of Sanquhar played a key role in the history of the Covenanters *(see p487)*. In the 1680s, two declarations opposing the rule of bishops were pinned to the Mercat Cross, the site of which is now marked by a granite obelisk. One protest was led by a local teacher, Richard Cameron, whose followers became the Cameronian regiment. The town's Georgian **Tolbooth** was designed by William Adam *(see p552)* in 1735 and houses a local interest museum and tour centre. The post office, opened in 1763, is the oldest in Britain, predating the mailcoach service.

27 Drumlanrig Castle

Thornhill, Dumfries & Galloway. **Tel** 01848 331555. Dumfries then bus. **Open** Castle: Easter–Aug: 11am–5pm daily. Grounds: Apr–Sep: 10am–5pm daily; Nov–Mar: 11am–4pm Sat & Sun. **drumlanrig.com**

Rising squarely from a grassy platform, the massive fortress-palace of **Drumlanrig** *(see p491)* was built from pink sandstone

The Baroque front steps and doorway of Drumlanrig Castle

between 1679 and 1691 on the site of a 15th-century Douglas stronghold. Its formidable multi-turreted exterior contains a priceless collection of art treasures, including paintings by Holbein and Rembrandt, as well as Jacobite relics such as Bonnie Prince Charlie's camp kettle and sash. The emblem of a crowned and winged heart, shown throughout the castle, recalls Sir James, the "Black Douglas", who bore Robert the Bruce's *(see p486)* heart while on crusade. After being mortally wounded he threw the heart at his enemies with the words "forward brave heart!"

The sturdy island fortress of Threave Castle on the River Dee

㉘ Threave Castle

Castle Douglas, Dumfries & Galloway. **Tel** 07711 223101. ▨ Dumfries. **Open** Apr–Sep: 10am–4:30pm daily; Oct: 10am–3:30pm daily. ▨
W **historicenvironment.scot**

This menacing giant of a tower, a 14th-century Black Douglas stronghold standing on an island in the Dee, commands the most complete medieval riverside harbour in Scotland. Douglas's struggles against the early Stuart kings culminated in his surrender here after a two-month siege in 1455 – but only after James II had brought the cannon Mons Meg *(see p510)* to batter the castle. Threave was dismantled after Protestant Covenanters *(see p487)* defeated its Catholic defenders in 1640. Inside the

tower, only the shell of the kitchen, great hall and domestic levels remain. Over the 15th-century doorway is the "gallows knob", which the owners are said never lacked its noose. A small boat ferries visitors to and from the castle.

㉙ Whithorn

Dumfries & Galloway. ▨ 900. ▨ Stranraer. ▨ ℹ Dashwood Sq, Newton Stewart (01671 402431). W **visitdumfriesandgalloway.co.uk**

The earliest site of continuous Christian worship in Scotland, Whithorn (meaning "white house") takes its name from the white chapel built here by St Ninian in 397. Though nothing remains of his chapel, a guided tour of the archaeological dig reveals evidence of Northumbrian, Viking and Scottish settlements dating from the 5th to the 19th centuries. A visitors' centre, **The Whithorn Story**, provides information on the excavations and contains a collection of carved stones. One, dedicated to Latinus, dates to 450, making it Scotland's earliest Christian monument.

▥ The Whithorn Story
The Whithorn Trust, 45–47 George St. Tel 01988 500508. **Open** Apr–Oct: 10:30am–5pm daily. ▨
W **whithorn.com**

㉚ Culzean Castle

See pp526–7.

Robert Burns surrounded by his creations, by an unknown artist

㉛ Burns Cottage

Robert Burns Birthplace Museum: Alloway, South Ayrshire. **Tel** 01292 443700. ▨ Ayr, then bus. **Open** 10am–5pm daily. **Closed** 25 Dec–3 Jan. ▨ ▨ ▨ W **burnsmuseum. org.uk**

Robert Burns (1759–96), Scotland's favourite poet, was born and spent his first seven years in this small thatched cottage in Alloway. Built by his father, the restored cottage still contains much of its original furniture. A modern museum displays many of Burns's manuscripts along with early editions of his works. Much of his poem *Tam o' Shanter* (1790) is set in Alloway, which commemorates him with elegant monuments on the outskirts of the village.

Burns became a celebrity following the publication in 1786 of the Kilmarnock Edition of his poems. Scots everywhere gather to celebrate Burns Night *(see p69)* on his birthday, 25 January.

Scottish Textiles

Weaving in the Scottish Borders goes back to the Middle Ages, when monks from Flanders established a thriving woollen trade with the Continent. Cotton became an important source of wealth in the Clyde Valley during the 19th century, when hand loom weaving was overtaken by power-driven mills. The popular Paisley patterns were based on Indian designs.

A colourful pattern from Paisley

㉕ Glasgow

Though its Celtic name, *Glas cu*, means "dear green place",
Glasgow is more often associated with its industrial past,
and once enjoyed the title Second City of the Empire (after
London). Glasgow's architectural standing as Scotland's finest
Victorian city reflects its era of prosperity, when ironworks,
cotton mills and shipbuilding were fuelled by Lanarkshire
coal. The city rivals Edinburgh *(see pp508–15)* in the arts,
with galleries such as the Kelvingrove *(see pp524–5)* and
the Burrell Collection; it also has a fine Science Centre
on the Clyde's revitalized south bank.

Glasgow's medieval cathedral viewed
from the southwest

Exploring Glasgow

Glasgow is a city of contrasts
with relics of its grimy industrial
past standing alongside glossy
new and restored buildings.
The deprived East End, with its
busy weekend market, "the
Barras", is held by the restored
18th-century Merchant City
and Victorian George Square.
The more affluent West End
prospered in the 19th century as
a retreat for wealthy merchants
escaping the industrialized
Clydeside, and it is here that
restaurants, bars, parks and
Glasgow University can be
found. On the south side, next

to affluent Pollokshields, is Pollok
Country Park, site of the Burrell
Collection. An underground
rail network and a good bus
system make it easy to travel
around the city.

🏛 Glasgow Cathedral

2 Castle St. **Tel** 0141 552 8198.
Open Apr–Sep: 9:30am–5:30pm
Mon–Sat, 1–5pm Sun; Oct–Mar:
10am–4pm Mon–Sat, 1–4:30pm Sun.
♿ 🆆 glasgowcathedral.org.uk

As one of the only cathedrals
to escape destruction during
the Scottish Reformation *(see
pp486–7)* – by adapting itself
to Protestant worship – this is

a rare example of an almost
complete 13th-century church. It
was built on the site of a chapel
founded by the city's patron
saint, St Mungo, a 6th-century
bishop of Strathclyde. According
to legend, Mungo placed the
body of a holy man named
Fergus on a cart yoked to two
wild bulls, telling them to take it
to the place ordained by God. In
the "dear green place" at which
the bulls stopped he built his
church. The cathedral is on two
levels. The crypt contains the

Glasgow City Centre

① Glasgow Cathedral
② Glasgow Necropolis
③ St Mungo Museum of
   Religious Life and Art
④ Provand's Lordship

⑤ People's Palace
⑥ Willow Tea Room
⑦ Tenement House
⑧ Glasgow Science Centre
⑨ Riverside Museum
⑩ Hunterian Art Gallery
⑪ *Kelvingrove Art Gallery
   and Museum pp524–5*

tomb of St Mungo, surrounded by an intricate forest of columns that end in delicately carved rib-vaulting. The Blackadder Aisle, reputed to have been built over a cemetery blessed by St Ninian (see p519), has a ceiling thick with decorative bosses.

Glasgow Necropolis
Cathedral Sq. **Open** daily. ltd.
glasgownecropolis.org

Behind the cathedral, the reformer John Knox (see p486) surveys the city from his Doric pillar overlooking a Victorian cemetery. It is filled with crumbling monuments to the dead of Glasgow's wealthy merchant families.

The Glasgow Necropolis, where an estimated 50,000 people are buried

St Mungo Museum of Religious Life and Art
2 Castle St. **Tel** 0141 276 1625.
Open 10am–5pm Tue–Thu & Sat, 11am–5pm Fri & Sun. by appt.

Situated in the cathedral precinct, this museum is a world first. The main exhibition illustrates religious themes with

Exterior of St Mungo Museum of Religious Life and Art

superb artifacts, including a 19th-century dancing Shiva and an Islamic painting entitled the *Attributes of Divine Perfection* (1986) by Ahmed Moustafa. Other religious paintings on display include *Crucifixion VII* (1988) by Scottish artist Craigie Aitchison. An exhibition on religion in Glasgow throws light on the life of the missionary David Livingstone (see p518). Outside, you can visit Great Britain's only permanent Zen Buddhist garden.

Provand's Lordship
3 Castle St. **Tel** 0141 2761625.
Open 10am–5pm Tue–Thu & Sat, 11am–5pm Fri & Sun. glasgowlife.org.uk

Now a museum, Provand's Lordship was built as a canon's house in 1471, and is the city's oldest surviving house.

VISITORS' CHECKLIST

Practical Information
City of Glasgow. 605,000.
Gallery of Modern Art
(0141 287 3005). Sat, Sun.
peoplemakeglasgow.com

Transport
Argyle St (Glasgow Central). Buchanan St.

Its low ceilings and austere wooden furnishings create a vivid impression of life in a wealthy 15th-century household. It is thought that Mary, Queen of Scots (see p515) may have stayed here in 1566 when she made a visit to see her cousin and husband, Lord Darnley.

People's Palace
Glasgow Green. **Tel** 0141 276 0795.
Open 10am–5pm Tue–Thu & Sat, 11am–5pm Fri & Sun. **Closed** 1 & 2 Jan, 25 & 26 Dec.
glasgowmuseums.com

This Victorian sandstone structure was built in 1898 as a cultural museum for the people of Glasgow's East End. It houses everything from temperance tracts to trade-union banners, suffragette posters to comedian Billy Connolly's banana-shaped boots, providing a social history of the city from the 12th century to the present day. A conservatory at the back contains an exotic winter garden.

Winter-garden conservatory at the People's Palace, Glasgow Green

Mackintosh's interior of the Willow Tea Room

🎫 Willow Tea Room
119 Sauchiehall St (also 97 Buchanan St). **Tel** 0141 332 8446. **Open** 9:30am–5pm Mon–Sat, 11:30am–4:30pm Sun. 📷 W **willowtearooms.co.uk**

This is the sole survivor of a series of delightful tearooms created by Charles Rennie Mackintosh in 1904 for the celebrated restaurateur Miss Kate Cranston. Everything from the high-backed chairs to the tables and cutlery was his design. In particular, the 1904 Room de Luxe sparkles with silver furniture and flamboyant leaded glass work. The No. 97 Buchanan Street branch opened in 1997, and recreates Cranston's original Ingram Street Tea Rooms. It features painstaking replicas of Mackintosh's light and airy White Dining Room and atmospheric Chinese or "Blue" Room.

🎫 Tenement House
145 Buccleuch St. **Tel** 0141 333 0183. **Open** Apr–Oct: 1–5pm daily (Jul & Aug: from 11am). 📷 🎴 by appointment. NTS W **nts.org.uk**

Less a museum than a time capsule, the Tenement House is an almost undisturbed record of life in a modest Glasgow flat in a tenement estate during the early 20th century. Glasgow owed much of its vitality and neighbourliness to tenement life, though these Victorian and Edwardian apartments were to earn a bad name for poverty and overcrowding, and many have now been pulled down. The Tenement House was first owned by Miss Agnes Toward, who lived here from 1911 until 1965. It remained largely unaltered and, since Agnes threw very little away, it is now a treasure trove of social history. The parlour, previously used only on formal occasions, has afternoon tea laid out on a white lace cloth. The kitchen, with its coal-fired range and box bed, is filled with the tools of a vanished era, such as a goffering iron for crisping waffles, a washboard and a stone hot-water bottle.

Agnes's lavender water and medicines are still in the bathroom, as though she had left for a minute 70 years ago and forgotten to return home.

🏛 Glasgow Science Centre
50 Pacific Quay. **Tel** 0141 420 5000 **Open** Apr–Oct: 10am–5pm daily; Nov–Mar: 10am–3pm Wed–Fri (to 5pm Sat & Sun). 🎴 W **glasgowsciencecentre.org**

The centrepiece of an impressive £75 million millennium project, Glasgow's glass and titanium Science Centre is located on the south bank of the River Clyde. The centre has three huge floors full of interactive puzzles, optical illusions, scientific and craft areas aimed at entertaining and educating kids. Big hits include mind control games and Madagascan hissing cockroaches. There's also an IMAX theatre that projects gigantic 3D and 2D films (some are feature length). The 127-m (417-ft) revolving tower, Scotland's tallest freestanding structure, provides striking views of central Glasgow and beyond.

🏛 Riverside Museum
Pointhouse Quay. **Tel** 0141 287 2720. **Open** 10am–5pm Mon–Thu & Sat, 11am–5pm Fri & Sun. 🎴 ♿ 📷 🎴 W **glasgowlife.org.uk**

Model ships and ranks of gleaming Scottish-built steam engines, cars and motorcycles recall the 19th and early 20th centuries, when Glasgow's supremacy in shipbuilding, trade and manufacturing made her the "second city" of the British Empire. Old Glasgow's transition into a modern city can be seen through fascinating footage of the town in the cinema and

Charles Rennie Mackintosh
Glasgow's most celebrated designer, Charles Rennie Mackintosh (1868–1928) entered Glasgow School of Art at 16. After his first big break with the Willow Tea Room, he became a leading figure in the Art Nouveau movement, developing a unique style that borrowed from Gothic and Scottish Baronial designs. He believed a building should be a fully integrated work of art, creating furniture and fittings that complemented the overall construction. The Glasgow School of Art, designed by Mackintosh in 1896 but lost to a terrible fire in 2014, epitomized this design theory. Unrecognized in his lifetime, Mackintosh's work is now widely imitated. Its characteristic straight lines and flowing detail are the hallmark of early 20th-century Glasgow style, in all fields of design from textiles to architecture.

A Mackintosh floral design

For hotels and restaurants in this area see p572 and pp600–602

Peasants Hunting Rabbits with Ferrets (c.1450–75), The Burrell Collection

through a series of three street reconstructions covering 1890–1930, 1930–60 and 1960–80. Don't miss the *Tall Ship Glenlee*, berthed just outside the museum on the River Clyde.

⬛ Hunterian Art Gallery
82 Hillhead St. **Tel** 0141 330 4221. **Open** 10am–5pm Tue–Sat, 11am–4pm Sun. **Closed** 24 Dec–5 Jan & public hols. 🚻 limited. 📷
W gla.ac.uk/hunterian

Built to house a number of paintings bequeathed to Glasgow University by a former student, physician Dr William Hunter (1718–83),

Whistler's *Sketch for Annabel Lee* (c.1869), Hunterian Art Gallery

the Hunterian Art Gallery contains Scotland's largest print collection and works by major European artists stretching back to the 16th century. A selection of work by Charles Rennie Mackintosh is supplemented by a complete reconstruction of No. 6 Florentine Terrace, where he lived from 1906 to 1914. A major collection of 19th- and 20th-century Scottish art includes work by William McTaggart (1835–1910), but the gallery's most famous pieces of work are by the painter James McNeill Whistler (1834–1903).

⬛ The Burrell Collection
2060 Pollokshaws Rd. **Tel** 0141 287 2550. **Open** 10am–5pm Mon–Thu & Sat, 11am–5pm Fri & Sun.
W glasgowmuseums.com

Due to reopen in 2020 after extensive refurbishment, the Burrell Collection was given to Glasgow in 1944 by Sir William Burrell (1861–1958), a shipping magnate. It instantly become the jewel in Glasgow's cultural crown, with objects of major importance from numerous fields. The sleek building was purpose-built in 1983 and is best appreciated in the sun,

when the collection's 600 medieval stained-glass panels blaze with colour.

The 9,000-piece collection also includes ancient Middle Eastern, Greek and Roman treasures; 150 tapestries including the *Bible Tapestry* from 16th-century Germany, Chinese ceramics and superb Oriental embroideries and carpets, and even Old Masters such as Rembrandt's *Self-Portrait* (1632).

🏛 Pollok House
2060 Pollokshaws Rd. **Tel** 0141 616 6410. **Open** Apr–Dec: 10am–5pm daily. **Closed** 1 & 2 Jan, 25 & 26 Dec.
📷 **NTS** **W** nts.org.uk

Pollok House is Glasgow's finest 18th-century domestic building and contains one of Britain's best collections of Spanish paintings. The Neo-Classical central block was finished in 1750, the sobriety of its exterior contrasting with the exuberant plasterwork within. The Maxwells have lived at Pollok since the mid-13th century, but the male line ended with Sir John Maxwell, who added the grand entrance hall in the 1890s and designed most of the terraced gardens and parkland beyond.

Hanging above displays of the family silver, porcelain, hand-painted Chinese wall-paper and Jacobean glass, the Stirling Maxwell collection is strong on British and Dutch schools, and includes William Blake's *Sir Geoffrey Chaucer and the Nine and Twenty Pilgrims* (1745) and William Hogarth's portrait of James Thomson, who wrote the words to *Rule Britannia*.

Spanish 16th- to 19th-century art predominates: El Greco's *Lady in a Fur Wrap* (1541) hangs in the library, while the drawing room contains works by Francisco de Goya and Esteban Murillo. In 1966 Anne Maxwell Macdonald gave the house and 146 ha (361 acres) of parkland to the City of Glasgow. The park was subsequently chosen as the site for the city's fascinating Burrell Collection

Glasgow: Kelvingrove Art Gallery and Museum

Housed in a grand Spanish Baroque building in Glasgow's West End, the Kelvingrove deservedly ranks among Scotland's most popular civic art collections. Its 8,000 item collection includes many pieces of international significance which span from ancient Middle-Eastern cultures to notable European and Scottish art. But the museum is equally rewarding for its insights into Glasgow's evolution from its medieval beginnings, through its 19th and 20th-century economic and cultural transformation, to the 2010 Commonwealth Games, which the city hosted.

Entrance to the Kelvingrove

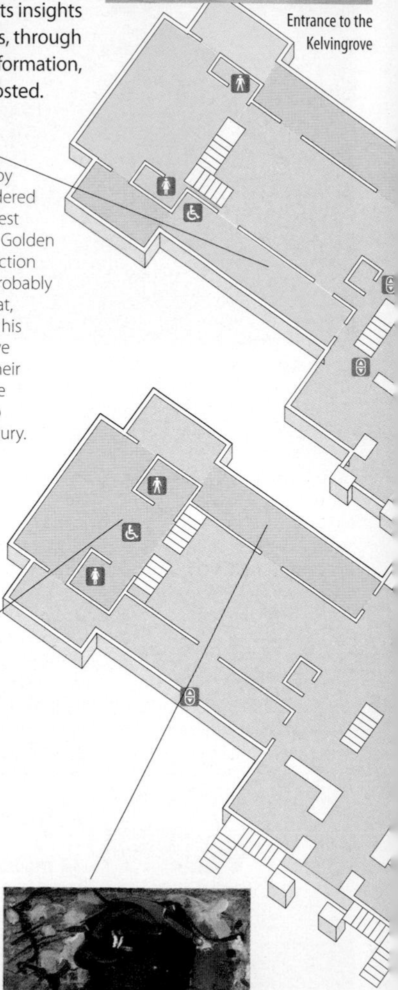

Man in Armour
This fine painting by Rembrandt, considered by many the greatest artist of the Dutch Golden Age, is a bold depiction of a young man, probably Alexander the Great, weighed down by his armour. Kelvingrove curators voted it their favourite piece. The work dates back to the mid- 17th century.

Miss Cranston's Tearoom
Between 1900–21 the venerable Charles Rennie Mackintosh (1868–1928) was the sole designer for Catherine Cranston's tearoom empire. These beautiful interiors are of both artistic and social significance.

Key to Floorplan

- Scottish Art and Design
- Dutch and French Art
- Every Picture Tells a Story
- Scottish History
- Arms and Armour
- Natural History
- World Cultures
- Ancient Egypt

Japanese Lady with a Fan
This was painted in 1894 by Glasgow Boy George Henry in Tokyo. It plays on ukiyo-e, a type of Japanese art that uses woodblock printing, and emphasises colour and patterning – partly by having the sitter look away.

For hotels and restaurants in this area see p572 and pp600–602

Christ of Saint John
Salvador Dalí's surrealist painting was first displayed in 1952. With its unusual angle of the Crucifixion, it demands attention. It has attracted admiration, criticism and controversy.

VISITORS' CHECKLIST

Practical Information
Argyle St, G3 8AG. **Tel** 0141 276 9599. **Open** 10am–5pm Mon–Thu & Sat, 11am–5pm Fri & Sun. **Closed** 1 & 2 Jan, 25–26 & 31 Dec.
w **glasgowlife.org.uk/ museums/kelvingrove**

Transport
Partick Station. 2, 3, 77.

First Floor

Ancient Egypt
Egyptian wonders abound in the Ancient Egypt gallery, including the obligatory mummies and tombs. The coffin and mummy of Egyptian lady Ankhesnefer date back to 610 BC. Her mummified body has remained undisturbed since her funeral and burial approximately 2,500 years ago.

Gallery Guide
The main collections and galleries are set out on the ground and first floors. Highlights on the ground floor are the excellent Scottish Art and Design galleries, while on the first floor the Dutch and French collections are particularly fine. On the lower ground floor a temporary gallery space is reserved for major touring exhibitions, the cafe and the main gift shop.

Argyle St Entrance

Ground Floor

Spitfire
The Spitfire LA 198 602, City of Glasgow Squadron, hangs dramatically from the ceiling of the West Court, soaring above the bodies of stuffed giraffes and wild cats. It is recognized as the best-restored warplane of its kind in the UK.

⊛ Culzean Castle

Standing on a cliff's edge in an extensive parkland estate, the 15th-century keep of Culzean (pronounced Cullayn), home of the Earls of Cassillis, was remodelled between 1777 and 1792 by the architect Robert Adam *(see p32)*. Restored in the 1970s, it is now a major showcase of his later work. The grounds became Scotland's first public country park in 1969 and, with farming flourishing alongside ornamental gardens, they reflect both the leisure and everyday activities of a great country estate.

View of Culzean Castle (c.1815), by Nasmyth

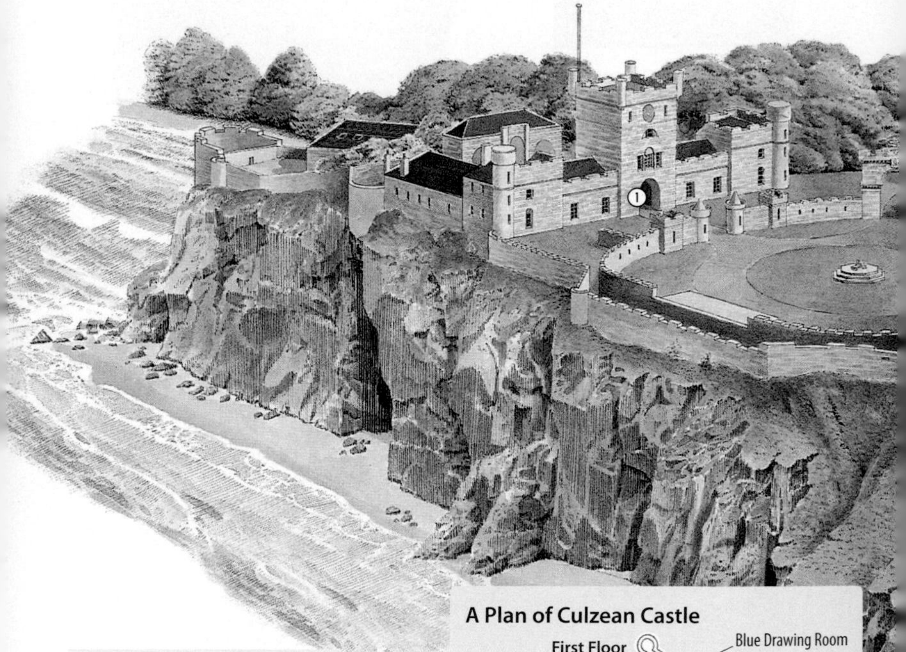

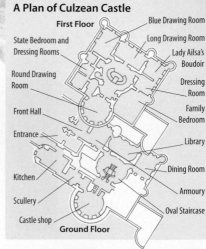

KEY

① **The clock tower**, fronted by the circular carriageway, was originally the coach house and stables. The clock was added in the 19th century. Today the buildings are used for residential and educational purposes, and also house a gallery and exhibition space.

② **The State Bedroom** contains mid-18th-century furnishings, including a 1740s gentleman's wardrobe.

③ **The Eisenhower Office** has mementoes of the general's life. He was given the top floor of Culzean in gratitude for his role in World War II.

④ **Carriageway**

A Plan of Culzean Castle

First Floor

Blue Drawing Room
Long Drawing Room
Lady Ailsa's Boudoir
State Bedroom and Dressing Rooms
Round Drawing Room
Dressing Room
Front Hall
Family Bedroom
Entrance
Library
Kitchen
Dining Room
Scullery
Armoury
Oval Staircase
Castle shop

Ground Floor

Armoury
Displayed on the walls is a world-famous collection of flintlock pistols, used by the British Army and Militia between the 1730s and 1830s.

VISITORS' CHECKLIST

Practical Information
4 miles (6 km) West of Maybole.
Tel 01655 884455. Castle: **Open**
Apr–Oct: 10:30am–5pm daily
(last adm: 4pm). Grounds:
Open 9am–dusk daily. 🐾 📷
♿ 🚻 🏠 ⛴ 🌐 nts.org.uk/
Property/Culzean-Castle-and-
Country-Park

Transport
🚆 Ayr then bus.

Fountain Court
This sunken garden is a good place to begin a tour of the grounds to the east.

★ **Round Drawing Room**
With its authentically restored 18th-century colour scheme, this elegant saloon perches on the cliff's edge 46 m (150 ft) above the Firth of Clyde. The carpet is a copy of the one designed by Adam.

★ **Oval Staircase**
Illuminated by an overarching skylight, the staircase, with its Ionic and Corinthian pillars, is considered one of Adam's finest achievements.

THE HIGHLANDS AND ISLANDS

*Aberdeenshire · Moray · Argyll & Bute · Perth & Kinross
Shetland · Orkney · Western Isles · Highlands · Angus*

Most of the symbols of Scottishness – clans and tartans, whisky and porridge, bagpipes and heather – originate in the Highlands and have come to represent the popular image of Scotland as a whole. But for many centuries the Gaelic-speaking, cattle-raising Highlanders had little in common with their southern neighbours.

Clues to the non-Celtic ancestors of the Highlanders lie scattered across the Highlands and Islands in the form of stone circles, brochs and cairns, some over 5,000 years old. In the 6th century, the Gaelic-speaking Celts arrived from Ireland, along with St Columba who brought Christianity. The fusion of the religion with Viking culture in the 8th and 9th centuries produced St Magnus Cathedral in the Orkney Isles.

For over 1,000 years, Celtic Highland society was founded on a clan system of loyal groups built from close families, dependent on a feudal chief. However, the clans were systematically broken up by England after 1746, following the defeat of the Jacobite attempt on the British crown, led by Bonnie Prince Charlie *(see p535)*.

The Highlands began to be considered favourably in the early 19th century, largely due to Sir Walter Scott, whose novels and poetry depicted the majesty and grandeur of a country previously considered merely poverty-stricken and barbaric. Another great popularizer was Queen Victoria, whose passion for Balmoral helped to establish the trend for acquiring Highland sporting estates. But beneath the sentimentality lay harsh economic realities that drove generations of Highlanders to seek a new life overseas.

Today, over half the inhabitants of the Highlands and Islands still live in communities of less than 1,000, but population figures are stable, as the growth of tourism helps supplement existing fishing and whisky businesses.

A wintry dawn over the Cairngorms, the home of Britain's only free-ranging herd of reindeer

◄ The Ring of Brodgar, a stone circle on the Mainland, the largest island in Orkney

Exploring the Highlands and Islands

The classic route into the Highlands is along the Tay Valley via the sedate Perthshire towns of Dunkeld and Pitlochry. Further north, the scenery rears up into the magnificent mountains and glens of the Cairngorms. This naturally leads into Speyside, a valley famed for its many whisky distilleries. Meanwhile, the city of Inverness, even further north, serves as the launch pad for the rest of the Highlands, though the key route is along the Great Glen to Loch Ness and town the of Fort William, which is the gateway to Ben Nevis and Glencoe.

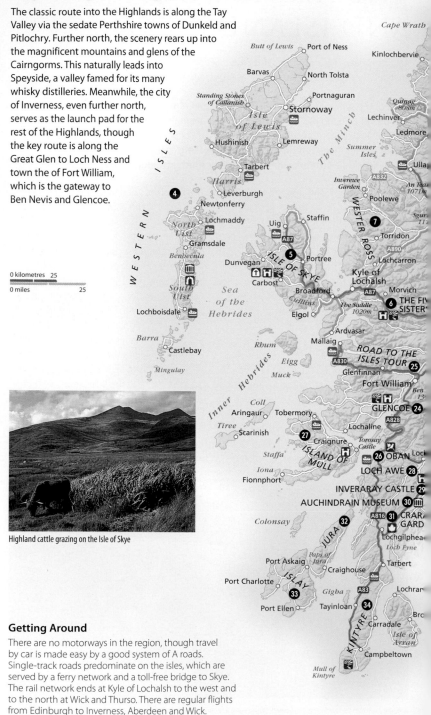

Highland cattle grazing on the Isle of Skye

Getting Around

There are no motorways in the region, though travel by car is made easy by a good system of A roads. Single-track roads predominate on the isles, which are served by a ferry network and a toll-free bridge to Skye. The rail network ends at Kyle of Lochalsh to the west and to the north at Wick and Thurso. There are regular flights from Edinburgh to Inverness, Aberdeen and Wick.

For hotels and restaurants in this area see pp572–3 and pp602–3

Key

- ▬▬ Motorway
- ▬▬ Major road
- ▬▬ Secondary road
- ═══ Minor road
- ∷∷∷ Scenic route
- ▬▬ Main railway
- ─── Minor railway
- △ Summit

Colour-washed houses at the harbour of Tobermory, Mull

Sights at a Glance

❶ Shetland Islands
❷ Orkney Islands
❸ John o'Groats
❹ Western Isles p533
❺ Isle of Skye pp534–5
❻ The Five Sisters
❼ Wester Ross
❽ Dornoch
❾ Strathpeffer
❿ The Black Isle
⓫ Loch Ness
⓬ Inverness
⓭ Culloden
⓮ Fort George
⓯ Cawdor Castle
⓰ Elgin
⓱ Aberdeen pp542–4
⓳ Dunkeld
⓴ Pitlochry
㉒ Blair Castle

㉓ The Cairngorms pp548–9
㉔ Glencoe
㉕ Oban
㉖ Island of Mull
㉗ Loch Awe
㉘ Inveraray Castle
㉚ Auchindrain Museum
㉛ Crarae Gardens
㉜ Jura
㉝ Islay
㉞ Kintyre

Walks and Tours

⓲ Royal Deeside Tour pp544–5
㉑ Killiecrankie Walk p546
㉕ Road to the Isles Tour
    pp550–51

❶ Shetland Islands

Shetland. 🔼 23,000. ✈🚢 from Aberdeen and Stromness on the mainland; Orkney. 🛈 Lerwick (01595 693434). 🌐 shetland.org

Lying six degrees south of the Arctic Circle, the rugged Shetland Islands are Britain's most northerly territory and were, with Orkney, part of the kingdom of Norway until 1469. In the main town of Lerwick, this Norse heritage is remembered during the ancient midwinter festival Up Helly Aa (see p484), in which costumed revellers set fire to a replica Viking longship. In town, the **Shetland Museum** tells the story of a people dependent on the sea and includes the discovery of North Sea oil and gas in the 1970s.

An Iron Age tower, **Mousa Broch**, can be visited on its isle by boat from Sandwick. There is more ancient history at Jarlshof, where a museum has exhibits on sprawling seafront ruins that span 3,000 years.

A boat from Lerwick sails to the Isle of Noss, where grey seals bask beneath sandstone cliffs crowded with Shetland's seabirds – a spectacle best seen between May and June. Otters and killer whales might also be spotted.

🏛 Shetland Museum
Hay's Dock, Lerwick. **Tel** 01595 695057. **Open** daily (Sun: pm only). 🌐 shetlandmuseumandarchives. org.uk

❷ Orkney Islands

Orkney. 🔼 21,000. ✈🚢 from Gills Bay, Caithness; John o'Groats (May–Sep); Scrabster, Aberdeen. 🛈 West Castle St, Kirkwall (01856 872856). 🌐 visitorkney.com

The fertile Isles of Orkney are remarkable for their wealth of prehistoric monuments, which places them among Europe's most treasured archaeological sites. In the town of Kirkwall, the sandstone **St Magnus Cathedral** stands amid a charming core of narrow streets. Its many interesting tombs include that of its 12th-century patron saint.

The Shetland Seabird Isles

Millions of migrant and local birds can be admired on these islands. More than 20 species of seabirds regularly breed here, and over 340 different species have been recorded passing through Fair Isle, one of the world's great staging posts. Inaccessible cliffs – such as Noss and Hermaness on Unst – provide security at vulnerable nesting times for huge colonies of gannets, guillemots, puffins, kittiwakes, fulmars and razorbills. Species found here but in few other UK locations include great skuas and storm petrels.

Puffin

Razorbills

Great skua

Black guillemot

Fulmar

Nearby, the early 17th-century **Earl's Palace** is widely held to be one of Scotland's finest Renaissance buildings. To the west of Kirkwall lies Britain's most impressive chambered tomb, the cairn of **Maes Howe**. Dating from 2000 BC, the tomb has runic graffiti on its walls believed to have been left by Norsemen returning from the crusades in 1150.

Nearby, the great **Standing Stones of Stenness** may have been associated with Maes Howe rituals, though they still remain a mystery. Further west, on a bleak heath, stands the Bronze Age **Ring of Brodgar**.

Another archaeological treasure can be found in the Bay of Skail: the complete Stone Age village of **Skara Brae**. It was unearthed by a storm in 1850, after lying buried for 4,500 years.

The Norman façade of St Magnus Cathedral, Orkney

Further south, the town of Stromness was a vital centre of Scotland's herring industry in the 18th century. Its story is told in the local museum, while the **Pier Arts Centre** displays British and international art.

🏛 Earl's Palace
Palace Rd, Kirkwall. **Tel** 01856 721205. **Open** daily. ♿ limited. 🌐 historicenvironment.scot

🏛 Pier Arts Centre
Victoria St, Stromness. **Tel** 01856 850209. **Open** 10:30am–5pm Tue–Sat. 🌐 pierartscentre.com

❸ John o'Groats

Highland. 🔼 300. ✈🚢🚌 Wick 🚌 John o'Groats to Burwick, Orkney (May–Sep). 🛈 Thurso (01847 893155).

Some 876 miles (1,409 km) north from Land's End, Britain's most northeasterly mainland village faces Orkney, 8 miles (13 km) across the turbulent Pentland Firth. The village takes its name from 15th-century Dutchman John de Groot, who, to avoid accusations of favouritism, is said to have built an octagonal house here with one door for each of his eight heirs. The spectacular cliffs and rock stacks of Duncansby Head lie a few miles further east.

❹ Western Isles

Western Scotland ends with this remote chain of islands, some of the oldest rock on Earth. Almost treeless landscapes are divided by countless waterways, the western, windward coasts edged by miles of white sandy beaches. For centuries the eastern shores, composed largely of peat bogs, have provided the islanders with fuel. Man has been here for 6,000 years, living off the sea and the thin turf, though such monuments as an abandoned Norwegian whaling station on Harris attest to the difficulties in commercializing the islanders' traditional skills. Gaelic, part of an enduring local culture, is widely spoken.

The Blackhouse, a traditional croft on Lewis

The Uists, Benbecula and Barra

Western Isles. 🏔 3,600. ✈ Barra, Benbecula. 🚢 Uig (Skye), Oban. 🚢 Oban, Mallaig, Kyle of Lochalsh. 🚌 🛈 Lochmaddy, North Uist (01876 500321); Castlebay, Barra (01871 810336). 🅦 visithebrides.com

After the dramatic scenery of Harris, the lower-lying, largely waterlogged southern isles may seem an anticlimax, though they nurture secrets well worth discovering. Long, white, sandy beaches fringe the Atlantic coast, edged with one of Scotland's natural treasures: the lime-rich soil known as *machair*. During the summer months, the soil is covered with wild flowers.

From **Lochmaddy**, North Uist's main village, the A867 crosses 5 miles (5 km) of causeway to Benbecula, the island from which Flora MacDonald smuggled Bonnie Prince Charlie *(see p535)* to the Isle of Skye. Another causeway leads to South Uist, with its golden beaches renowned as a National Scenic Area. From Lochboisdale, a ferry sails to the tiny Isle of Barra. The ferry docks in Castlebay, affording an unforgettable view of **Kisimul Castle**, the ancestral stronghold of the MacNeils of Barra.

The monumental Standing Stones of Callanish in northern Lewis

Lewis and Harris

Western Isles. 🏔 21,000. ✈ Stornoway. 🚢 Uig (Skye), Ullapool. 🛈 Stornoway, Lewis (01851 703088). 🅦 visithebrides.com
The Blackhouse: **Tel** 01851 710395.
Open Apr–Sep: 9:30am–5:30pm Mon–Sat, Oct–Mar: 10am–4pm Mon, Tue & Thu–Sat. 🅿 🅿 🅿 🅿

Forming the largest landmass of the Western Isles, Lewis and Harris are a single island, though Gaelic dialects differ between the two parts. From **Stornoway**, with its bustling harbour and colourful house fronts, the ancient **Standing Stones of Callanish** are only 16 miles (26 km) to the west. Just off the road on the way to Callanish are the ruins of **Carloway Broch**, a Pictish *(see p486)* tower over 2,000 years old. The more recent past can be explored at Arnol's **Blackhouse** – a showcase of crofting life as it was until only 50 years ago.

South of the rolling peat moors of Lewis, a range of mountains marks the border with Harris, which one enters by passing Aline Lodge at the head of Loch Seaforth. Only a little less spectacular than the "Munros" (peaks over 914 m, 3,000 ft) of

the mainland and the Isle of Skye *(see pp534–5)*, the mountains of Harris are a paradise for the hill walker and, from their summits on a clear day, the distant Isle of St Kilda can be seen, 50 miles (80 km) to the west.

The ferry port of Tarbert stands on a slim isthmus separating North and South Harris. Some local weavers of the famous Harris Tweed still follow the old tradition of using plants to make their dyes.

From the port of Leverburgh, close to the southern tip of Harris, a ferry can be taken to the island of North Uist, where a causeway has been built to Berneray.

The remote and sandy shores of South Uist

❺ Isle of Skye

The largest of the Inner Hebrides, Skye can be reached by the bridge linking Kyle of Lochalsh and Kyleakin. A turbulent geological history has given the island some of Britain's most varied and dramatic scenery. From the rugged volcanic plateau of northern Skye to the ice-sculpted peaks of the Cuillins, the island is divided by numerous sea lochs, so that the sea is never more than 8 km (5 miles) away. North of Dunvegan are small caves and white beaches, while limestone grasslands predominate in the south, where the hillsides, grazed by sheep and cattle, are scattered with the ruins of crofts abandoned during the Clearances *(see p539)*. Historically, Skye is best known for its association with Bonnie Prince Charlie.

Dunvegan Castle
For over seven centuries, Dunvegan Castle has been the seat of the chiefs of Clan MacLeod. It contains the Fairy Flag, a fabled piece of magic silk treasured for its magical protection in battle.

0 kilometres   10
0 miles   5

Cuillins
Britain's finest mountain range is within walking distance of Sligachan, and in summer a boat sails from Elgol to the desolate inner sanctuary of Loch Coruisk. As he fled across the surrounding moorland, Bonnie Prince Charlie is said to have claimed: "Even the Devil shall not follow me here!"

KEY

① Grave of Flora MacDonald

② Kilt Rock

③ **Luib** has a beautiful thatched cottage, preserved as it was 100 years ago.

④ **Bridge to mainland**

⑤ **Otters** can be seen from the haven in Kylerhea.

⑥ **Armadale Castle Gardens and**

Museum of the Isles houses the Clan Donald visitor centre.

⑦ **Loch Coruisk**

⑧ **The Talisker Distillery** produces one of the best Highland malts, often described as "the lava of the Cuillins".

⑨ **Skeabost** has the ruins of a chapel associated with St Columba. Medieval tombstones can be found in the graveyard.

Key
━━ Major road
═══ Minor road
═══ Narrow lane

Quiraing

A series of landslides has exposed the roots of this volcanic plateau, revealing a fantastic terrain of spikes and towers. They are easily explored off the Uig to Staffin road.

The Storr

The erosion of this basalt plateau has created the Old Man of Storr, a monolith rising to 49 m (160 ft) by the Portree road.

Portree

With its colourful harbour, Portree (meaning "port of the king") is Skye's main town. It received its name after a visit by James V in 1540.

Kilchrist Church

This ruined pre-Reformation church's last service was held in 1843. It once served Skye's most populated areas, though the surrounding moors are now deserted.

Bonnie Prince Charlie

The last of the Stuart claimants to the Crown, Charles Edward Stuart (1720–88), came to Scotland from France in 1745 to win the throne. After marching as far as Derby, his army was driven back to Culloden, where it was defeated. Hounded through the Highlands for 5 months, he escaped to Skye, disguised as the maidservant of a woman called Flora MacDonald, from Uist. From the mainland, he sailed to France in September 1746, and would eventually die in Rome. Flora was buried in 1790 at Kilmuir, on Skye, wrapped in a sheet taken from the bed of the "bonnie" (handsome) prince.

The prince, disguised as a maidservant

Rugged sea cliff and lighthouse on the west coast of Skye ▶

The western side of the Five Sisters of Kintail, seen from above Loch Duich

❻ The Five Sisters

Skye & Lochalsh. 🚋 Kyle of Lochalsh.
🚌 Glenshiel. 🛈 Bayfield Road,
Portree, Isle of Skye (01478 612992).
Ⓦ **visithighlands.com**

Dominating one of Scotland's most haunting regions, the awesome summits of the Five Sisters of Kintail rear into view at the northern end of Loch Cluanie as the A87 enters Glen Shiel. The **Visitor Centre** at Morvich offers ranger-led excursions in the summer. Further west, the road passes **Eilean Donan Castle**, connected by a bridge. A Jacobite *(see p541)* stronghold, it was destroyed in 1719 by English warships. In the 19th century it was restored and now contains Jacobite relics.

🏰 **Eilean Donan Castle**
Off A87, nr Dornie. **Tel** 01599 555202.
Open Feb–Dec: 10am–4pm daily
(Mar–Oct: to 6pm). 🅿
Ⓦ **eileandonancastle.com**

❼ Wester Ross

Ross & Cromarty. 🚋 Achnasheen,
Strathcarron. 🛈 Ullapool (01854
612486). Ⓦ **visithighlands.com**

Leaving the village of Lochcarron to the south, the A890 enters the northern Highlands and the great wilderness of Wester Ross. The Torridon Estate includes some of the oldest mountains on Earth (Torridonian rock is over 600 million years old), and is

home to red deer, wild cats and wild goats. Peregrine falcons and golden eagles nest in the towering sandstone mass of Liathach, above the village of Torridon with its breathtaking views over Applecross to Skye. The **Torridon Countryside Centre** provides guided walks in season and information on the region's natural history. The estate is open all year.

To the north, the A832 cuts through the Beinn Eighe National Nature Reserve. Here, remnants of the ancient Caledonian pine forest still stand on the banks and isles of Loch Maree.

Along the coast, exotic gardens thrive in the warming currents of the Gulf Stream, most impressive being **Inverewe Garden**, created in 1862 by Osgood Mackenzie (1842–1922). May and June are the months to see the display of azaleas and rhododendrons; visit in July and August for the herbaceous borders.

Typical Torridonian mountain scenery in Wester Ross

🏛 **Torridon Countryside Centre**
Torridon. **Tel** 01445 791221.
Open Apr–Sep: 10am–5pm Sun–Fri.
Estate: **Open** daily all year. 🅿 ♿ NTS
Ⓦ **nts.org.uk**

🌺 **Inverewe Garden**
Off A832, near Poolewe. **Tel** 01445
712952. **Open** daily. 🅿 ♿ NTS
Ⓦ **nts.org.uk**

❽ Dornoch

Sutherland. 🚹 1,200. 🚋 Golspie, Tain.
🛈 Castle Wynd, Inverness (01463
252401). Ⓦ **visithighlands.com**

With its first-class golf course and extensive sandy beaches, **Dornoch** is a popular holiday resort, which retains its peaceful atmosphere. Now the parish church, the medieval cathedral was all but destroyed in a clan dispute in 1570; it was finally restored in the 1920s for its 700th anniversary. A stone at the beach end of River Street marks the place where Janet Horne, the last woman to be tried in Scotland for witchcraft, was executed in 1722.

Environs
Twelve miles (19 km) northeast of Dornoch is the stately Victorianized pile of **Dunrobin Castle** *(see p491)*, magnificently situated in a great park with formal gardens overlooking the sea. Since the 13th century, this has been the seat of the Earls of Sutherland. Many of its rooms are open to visitors. A steam-powered fire engine

is among the miscellany of objects on display.

South of Dornoch stands the town of **Tain**. A place of pilgrimage for medieval kings, it became an administrative centre of the Highland Clearances. **Tain Through Time**, a heritage centre, tells the town's story.

🏠 Dunrobin Castle
Near Golspie. **Tel** 01408 633177. **Open** Apr, May, Sep & Oct: 10:30am–4:30pm daily (from noon Sun); Jun–Aug: 10am–5pm daily. Falconry displays: 11:30am & 2pm. 🅿 **W** dunrobincastle.co.uk

🏛 Tain Through Time
Tower St. **Tel** 01862 894089. **Open** Apr–Oct: 10am–5pm Mon–Fri (Jun–Aug: also Sat). 🅿 ♿ 📷 **W** tainmuseum.org.uk

The serene parish church in the town of Dornoch

🟠 Strathpeffer

Ross & Cromarty. 🗺 1,500. 🚆 Dingwall, Inverness. 🚌 Inverness. 🛈 Castle Wynd, Inverness (01463 252401).

Standing 5 miles (8 km) from the Falls of Rogie, this popular town still has something of the refined charm for which it was known in Victorian times, when it flourished as a spa resort. The grand hotels and gracious layout of Strathpeffer recall the days when royalty from all over Europe used to flock to the mineral-laden springs, believed to have curative powers. But today, one of the biggest attractions is the local pipe band and dancers who perform in the square every Saturday in summer (May–Sep: 8.30pm).

The shores of the Black Isle in the Moray Firth

🔟 The Black Isle

Ross & Cromarty. 🚆 🚌 Inverness. 🛈 Castle Wynd, Inverness (01463 252401).

Though the drilling platforms in the Cromarty Firth are reminders of how oil has changed the local economy, the peninsula of the Black Isle is still largely composed of farmland and fishing villages. **Cromarty** was an important port town in the 1700s, with thriving rope and lace industries. Many of its merchant houses still stand; the museum in the **Cromarty Courthouse** offers heritage tours. The **Hugh Miller Museum** is dedicated to the theologian and geologist Hugh Miller (1802–56), who was born here. **Fortrose** has a ruined 14th-century cathedral, while a stone on Chanonry Point commemorates the Brahan Seer, a 17th-century prophet burned alive in a tar barrel by the Countess of Seaforth after he foresaw her husband's infidelity. Chanonry Point is also renowned as a great spot for bottlenose dolphin-watching. For Celtic and Pictish art, visit **Groam House Museum** in Rosemarkie.

🏛 Cromarty Courthouse
Church St, Cromarty. **Tel** 01381 600 418. **Open** Apr–Sep: noon–4pm Sun–Thu. 🅿 **W** cromarty-courthouse.org.uk

🏠 Hugh Miller Museum
Church St, Cromarty. **Tel** 01381 600 245. **Open** mi-Apr–Sep: daily; Oct: Tue, Thu & Fri (pm). 🅿 ♿ limited. **NTS**

🏛 Groam House Museum
High St, Rosemarkie. **Tel** 01463 811883. **Open** Jan–Mar: 2–4pm Fri–Sun; Apr–Oct: 11am–4:30pm Mon–Fri, 2–4:30pm Sat & Sun.

The Highland Clearances

During the heyday of the clan system (see p488), tenants paid their clan chiefs for their land in the form of military service. However, with the decline of the clans after the Battle of Culloden (see p541) and the decision that farming sheep was more profitable than agriculture, landowners began to demand a financial rent their tenants were unable to afford and the land was then bought up by Lowland and English farmers. In what became known as "the year of the sheep" (1792), thousands of tenants were evicted to make way for sheep. Many emigrated to Australia, America and Canada. Ruins of their crofts can still be seen in Sutherland and Wester Ross.

The Last of the Clan (1865) by Thomas Faed

The ruins of Urquhart Castle on the western shore of Loch Ness

⓫ Loch Ness

Inverness. 🚆 🚌 Inverness.
ℹ️ Castle Wynd, Inverness (01463
252401). 🌐 visithighlands.com

At 24 miles (39 km) long, one
mile (1.5 km) at its widest and
up to 305 m (1,000 ft) deep,
Loch Ness fills the northern
half of the Great Glen fault
from Fort William to Inverness.
It is joined to lochs Oich and
Lochy by the 22-mile (35-km)
Caledonian Canal, designed
by Thomas Telford *(see p451)*.

The Loch Ness Monster

First sighted by St Columba
in the 6th century, "Nessie" has
attracted increasing attention
since ambiguous photographs
were taken in the 1930s.
Though serious investigation
is often undermined by
hoaxers, sonar techniques
continue to yield enigmatic
results: plesiosaurs, giant eels
and too much whisky are the
most popular explanations.
Nessie appears to have a close
relative in the waters of Loch
Morar *(see p550)*.

On the western shore,
the A82 passes the ruins of
the 16th-century **Urquhart
Castle**, which was blown up
by government supporters
in 1692 to prevent it falling
into Jacobite hands. A short
distance west, **Loch Ness
Centre and Exhibition**
explores the loch's
environment and the
famous legend.

🏰 Urquhart Castle
Nr Drumnadrochit.
Tel 01456 450551.
Open 9:30am–6pm
daily (Oct–Mar: to
4:30pm; last adm:
45 mins before closing).
🅿️ ♿ 🏠 🌐 **historic
environment.scot**

🏛️ Loch Ness Centre and Exhibition
Drumnadrochit. **Tel** 01456 450573.
Open Nov–Easter: 10am–3:30pm
daily; Easter–Oct: 9:30am–5pm daily.
🅿️ ♿ 🖥️ 🏠 🌐 **lochness.com**

⓬ Inverness

Highland. 🏘️ 47,000. 🚆 🚌
ℹ️ Castle Wynd (01463 252401).
🌐 visitscotland.com

As the Highland capital,
Inverness makes an ideal base
from which to explore the
surrounding countryside.
The Victorian castle dominates
the town centre, the oldest
buildings of which are found
in nearby Church Street. Today
the castle is used as law courts.

The **Inverness Museum and
Art Gallery** provides a good
introduction to the history
of the Highlands with exhibits
including a lock of Bonnie
Prince Charlie's *(see p535)*
hair and a fine collection of
Inverness silver. The **Scottish
Kiltmaker Visitor Centre**
explores the history and
tradition of Scottish kilts,
while those in
search of tartans
and knitwear
should visit
Ben Wyvis Kilts.
Jacobite Cruises run
a variety of year-round
cruises along the
Caledonian Canal
and on to Loch Ness.
The unfolding scenery

Kilt-maker with royal
Stuart tartan

makes this a tranquil way to
spend a sunny afternoon.

🏛️ Museum and Art Gallery
Castle Wynd. **Tel** 01463 237114.
Open Tue–Sat (Nov–Mar: Tue–Thu,
pm only). ♿ 🌐 **inverness.
highland.museum**

🏠 Ben Wyvis Kilts
Highland Rail House, Station Square.
Tel 01463 715448. **Open** daily. ♿
🌐 **benwyviskilts.co.uk**

🏛️ Scottish Kiltmaker Visitor Centre
Huntly St. **Tel** 01463 222781.
Open daily. 🅿️ 🌐 **highland
houseoffraser.com**

Jacobite Cruises
Glenurquhart Road. **Tel** 01463
233999. **Open** daily. 🅿️ ♿
🌐 **jacobite.co.uk**

⑬ Culloden

Inverness. 🚂 🚌 Inverness. NTS
W nts.org.uk/culloden

A desolate stretch of moorland, Culloden looks much as it must have done on 16 April 1746, the date of the last battle to be fought on British soil *(see p487)*. Here the Jacobite cause, under Bonnie Prince Charlie's *(see p535)* leadership, finally perished beneath the onslaught of Hanoverian troops led by the Duke of Cumberland. The battle is explained in the **NTS Visitor Centre**.

Environs
A mile (1.5 km) or so east are the the **Clava Cairns**, outstanding Neolithic burial sites.

ℹ️ **NTS Visitor Centre**
On the B9006 east of Inverness. **Tel** 01463 796090. **Open** Apr–Oct: 9am–5:30pm daily; Nov–Dec & Feb– Mar. 10am–4pm daily. **Closed** 24 Dec–1 Feb. 🅿️ 🚻 NTS W nts.org.uk

⑭ Fort George

Inverness. **Tel** 01667 460232. 🚂
🚌 Inverness, Nairn. **Open** Apr–Sep. 9:30am–5:30pm daily (Oct–Mar. to 4pm). **Closed** 25 & 26 Dec. 🅿️ 🚻 🚻
W historicenvironment.scot

One of the finest examples of European military architecture, Fort George stands on a wind-swept promontory jutting into the Moray Firth, ideally located to fend off the Highlanders. Completed in 1769, the fort was built after the Jacobite risings to discourage further rebellion in the Highlands and has

The Jacobite Movement

The first Jacobites (mainly Catholic Highlanders) were the supporters of James II of England (James VII of Scotland), who was deposed by the "Glorious Revolution" of 1688 *(see p57)*. With the Protestant William of Orange on the throne, the Jacobites' desire to restore the Stuart monarchy led to the uprisings of 1715 and 1745. The first, in support of James VIII, the "Old Pretender", ended at the Battle of Sheriffmuir (1715). The failure of the second uprising, with the defeat at Culloden, saw the end of Jacobite hopes and led to the end of the clan system and the suppression of Highland culture for over a century *(see pp488–9)*.

James II, by Samuel Cooper (1609–72)

The drawbridge on the eastern side of Cawdor Castle

remained a military garrison ever since. The Fort houses the **Regimental Museum of the Highlanders**, and some of its barracks rooms reconstruct the conditions of the common soldiers stationed here more than 200 years ago. The **Grand Magazine** contains an outstanding collection of arms and military equipment. The battlements also make an excellent place from which to spot dolphins in the Moray Firth.

⑮ Cawdor Castle

On B9090 (off A96). **Tel** 01667 404401. 🚂 Nairn, then bus. 🚌 from Inverness. **Open** May–Sep: 10am– 5:30pm daily. 🅿️ 🚻 gardens & ground floor only. 🚫 W cawdor castle.com

With its turreted central tower, moat and drawbridge, Cawdor Castle is one of the most romantic stately homes in the Highlands. Though the castle is famed for its links to Shakespeare's Macbeth, it is not historically proven that he, or King Duncan, came here

An ancient holly tree preserved in the vaults is said to be the one under which, in 1372, Thane William's donkey, laden with gold, stopped for a rest during its master's search for a place to build a fortress. According to legend, this was how the site for the castle was chosen. Now, after 600 years of continuous occupation (it is still the home of the Thanes of Cawdor), the house is a treasury of family history, containing a number of rare tapestries and portraits by the 18th-century painters Joshua Reynolds (1723–92) and George Romney (1734– 1802). Furniture in the Pink Bedroom and Woodcock Room includes work by Chippendale and Sheraton. In the Old Kitchen, the huge Victorian cooking range stands as a shrine to below-stairs drudgery. The grounds provide nature trails and a nine-hole golf course.

A contemporary picture, *The Battle of Culloden* (1746), by D Campbell

⑯ Elgin

Moray. 🏘 23,100. 🚆 🚌 ℹ️ Castle Wynd, Inverness (01463 252401).

With its cobbled marketplace and crooked lanes, the popular holiday centre of Elgin still retains much of its medieval layout. The 13th-century **cathedral** ruins next to King Street are all that remain of one of Scotland's architectural triumphs, the design of its tiered windows reminiscent of the cathedral at St Andrews (see p503). Once known as the Lantern of the North, the cathedral was severely damaged in 1390 by the Wolf of Badenoch (the son of Robert II) in revenge for his excommunication by the Bishop of Moray. Worse damage came in 1576 when the Regent Moray ordered the stripping of its lead roofing. Among the remains is a Pictish cross-slab in the nave, and a basin in a corner where one of Elgin's benefactors, Andrew Anderson, was kept as a baby by his homeless mother. Next to the cathedral are the **Biblical Gardens**, containing all 110 plants mentioned in the Bible, the **Elgin Museum**, which has anthropological displays, and the **Moray Motor Museum** with over 40 vehicles exhibited.

🏛 Elgin Museum
1 High St. **Tel** 01343 543675. **Open** Apr–Oct: 10am–5pm Mon–Fri; 11am–4pm Sat. 🐾 ♿ limited. 📷 **W** elginmuseum.org.uk

🏛 Moray Motor Museum
Bridge St, Bishopmill. **Tel** 01343 544933. **Open** Apr–Oct: 11am–5pm daily. 🐾 ♿ **W** moraymotormuseum.org

Details of the central tower of Elgin Cathedral

⑰ Aberdeen

Scotland's third largest city and Europe's offshore oil capital, Aberdeen has prospered since the discovery of petroleum in the North Sea in 1970. The seabed has now yielded over 100 oilfields. Widely known as the Granite City, its rugged outlines are softened by sumptuous year-round floral displays in its public parks and gardens, the Duthie Park Winter Gardens being one of the largest indoor gardens in Europe. The picturesque village of Footdee, which sits at the end of the city's 2-mile (3-km) beach, has good views back to the busy harbour.

The spires of Aberdeen, rising behind the city harbour

Exploring Aberdeen
The mile-long (1.5 km) Union Street bisects the city centre, ending to the east at the **Mercat Cross**. The cross stands in Castlegate, the one-time site of the city castle. From here the cobbled Shiprow winds southwest, passing Provost Ross's House (see p544) on its way to the harbour and fish market. A bus can be taken a mile (1.5 km) north of the centre to Old Aberdeen which, with its peaceful medieval streets and wynds, seems like a separate village. Driving is restricted in some streets.

🏛 Aberdeen Art Gallery
Schoolhill. **Tel** 03000 200293. **Open** 10am–5pm Thu–Sat, 1–4pm Sun. ♿ **W** aagm.co.uk

Housed in a Neo-Classical building, purpose-built in 1884, the Art Gallery has a wide range of exhibitions, with an emphasis on contemporary work. A fine collection of Aberdonian silver can be found among the decorative arts on the ground floor, and is the subject of a video presentation. A permanent collection of 18th- to 20th-century fine art features such names as Toulouse-Lautrec, Reynolds and Zoffany. Several of the works were bequeathed in 1900 by a local granite merchant, Alex Macdonald. He commissioned many of the paintings in the Macdonald Room, which displays 92 self-portraits by British artists. Occasionally poetry readings, music recitals and films take place.

⛪ St Nicholas Kirk
Union St. **Tel** 01224 643494. **Open** noon–4pm Mon–Fri. ♿ **W** kirk-of-st-nicholas.org.uk

Aberdonian silver in the Art Gallery

Founded in the 12th century, St Nicholas is Scotland's largest parish church. Though the present structure dates from 1752, many relics of earlier incarnations can be seen inside. After being damaged during the Reformation, the interior was divided into two. A chapel in the East Church contains iron rings used to secure witches in the 17th century, while in the West Church there are some embroidered panels attributed to one Mary Jameson (1597–1644).

🏛 Provost Skene's House

Guestrow. **Tel** 01224 641086.
Closed for ongoing redevelopment
work – check website for details.
🌐 aagm.co.uk

Once the home of Sir George
Skene, a 17th-century provost
(mayor) of Aberdeen, the
house was built in 1545.
Inside, an exhibition tells the
story of local people who
had a global impact – from
sporting heroes to Nobel-
winning scientists.

VISITORS' CHECKLIST

Practical Information
City of Aberdeen. 🔼 230,000.
ℹ️ Marischal College,
Broad St. (01224 269180).
🌐 aberdeen-grampian.com

Transport
✈️ 🚆 🚌 Guild St.

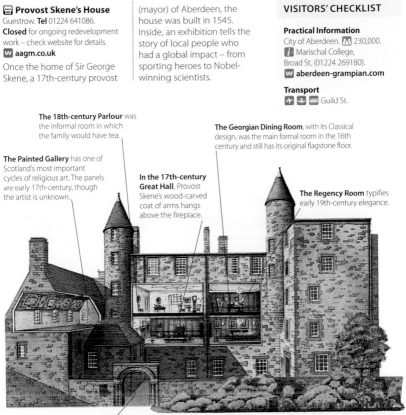

The 18th-century Parlour was the informal room in which the family would have tea.

The Painted Gallery has one of Scotland's most important cycles of religious art. The panels are early 17th-century, though the artist is unknown.

In the **17th-century Great Hall**, Provost Skene's wood-carved coat of arms hangs above the fireplace.

The Georgian Dining Room, with its Classical design, was the main formal room in the 16th century and still has its original flagstone floor.

The Regency Room typifies early 19th-century elegance.

Entrance

Aberdeen City Centre

① Aberdeen Art Gallery
② St Nicholas Kirk
③ Provost Skene's House
④ St Andrew's Cathedral
⑤ Mercat Cross
⑥ Maritime Museum

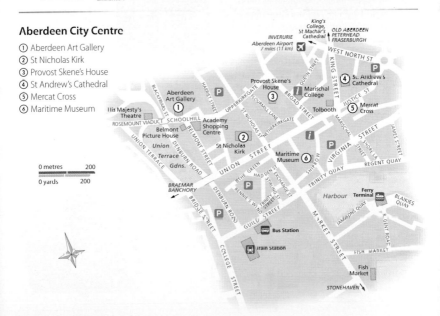

0 metres 200
0 yards 200

For keys to symbols *see back flap*

🏛 St Andrew's Cathedral
King St. **Tel** 01224 640119.
Open mid-Jun–early Sep: 11am–4pm
Tue–Fri. 📷 by appointment. ♿

The Mother Church of the
Episcopal Communion in
America, St Andrew's has a memorial to Samuel Seabury, the first
Episcopalian bishop in the United
States, who was consecrated in
Aberdeen in 1784. Coats of arms
adorn the ceiling above the
north and south aisles, contrasting colourfully with the white
walls and pillars. They represent
the American States and local
Jacobite (see p541) families.

🏛 Maritime Museum
Shiprow. **Tel** 01224 337700.
Open 10am–5pm Mon–Sat, noon–
3pm Sun. ♿ 📱 📷 🖥 **w** aagm.co.uk

Overlooking the harbour is
Provost Ross's House, which
dates back to 1593 and is one of
the oldest residential buildings
in the city. This museum traces
the history of Aberdeen's
seafaring tradition. Exhibitions

cover shipwrecks, rescues,
shipbuilding and the oil installations off Scotland's east coast.

The elegant lantern tower of the chapel
at King's College

🏛 King's College
College Bounds, Old Aberdeen.
Tel 01224 272137. Chapel:
Open 10am–3:30pm Mon–Fri. ♿

King's College was founded in
1495 as the city's first university.

The interdenominational chapel
(the only part of the college
open to the public), in the past
consecutively Catholic and
Protestant, has a lantern tower
rebuilt after a storm in 1633.
Stained-glass windows
by Douglas Strachan add a
contemporary touch to the
interior, which contains a 1540
pulpit, later carved with the
heads of Stuart monarchs.

🏛 St Machar's Cathedral
The Chanonry. **Tel** 01224 485988.
Open 9:30am–4:30pm daily
(10am–4pm winter). ♿

Dominating Old Aberdeen,
the 15th-century edifice of
St Machar's is the oldest
granite building in the city.
The stone-work of one arch
dates as far back as the 14th
century. The impressive nave
now serves as a parish church
and its magnificent oak ceiling
is adorned with the coats of
arms of 48 popes, emperors
and princes of Christendom.

🔘 Royal Deeside Tour

Since Queen Victoria's purchase of the
Balmoral estate in 1852, Deeside has
been known as the summer home of the
British Royal Family, though it has been
associated with royalty since the time
of Robert the Bruce (see p486). This route
follows the Dee, formerly a prolific salmon
river, through some magnificent
Grampian scenery.

④ **Muir of Dinnet
Nature Reserve**
An information centre
on the A97 provides
an excellent starting
point for exploring
this beautiful mixed
woodland area,
formed by the
retreating glaciers
of the last Ice Age.

⑥ **Balmoral**
Bought by Queen Victoria for
30,000 guineas in 1852, after
its owner choked to death on a
fishbone, the castle was rebuilt
in the Scottish Baronial style at
Prince Albert's request.

⑤ **Ballater**
The old railway town of
Ballater has royal warrants
on many of its shopfronts. It
expanded as a 19th-century
spa town, its waters
reputedly providing a
cure for tuberculosis.

The ruins of the beautifully situated
Dunkeld Cathedral

The **Little Houses** lining
Cathedral Street were the
first to be rebuilt, and are
fine examples of imaginative
restoration. The ruins of the
14th-century **cathedral** enjoy
an idyllic setting on shady
lawns beside the Tay, against
a backdrop of steep, wooded
hills. The choir is used as the
parish church and its north wall
contains a Leper's Squint: a hole
through which lepers could see
the altar during mass. It was
while on holiday in the Dunkeld
countryside that Beatrix Potter
(see p371) found the location
for her Peter Rabbit stories.

resorts in Europe. In early
summer, salmon swim up
the ladder built into the
Power Station Dam, on their
way to spawning grounds
up-river. There is a viewing
chamber here to see them.
Above the ladder are fine
views of Loch Faskally, an
artificial reservoir. Walking
trails from here lead to the
pretty gorge at Killiecrankie
(see p546). The tasting tours
at **Edradour Distillery** give
an insight into traditional
whisky-making (see p493).
Scotland's famous **Festival
Theatre** puts on a summer
season with a programme
that changes daily.

⑲ Dunkeld

Perth & Kinross. 🚹 1,200. 🚆 Birnam.
🚌 ℹ️ The Cross (01350 727688).
🌐 perthshire.co.uk

Situated by the River Tay, this
ancient and charming village
was all but destroyed in the
1689 Battle of Dunkeld, a
Jacobite (see p541) defeat.

⑳ Pitlochry

Perth & Kinross. 🚹 2,600. 🚆 🚌
ℹ️ 22 Atholl Rd (01796 472215).
🌐 perthshire.co.uk

Surrounded by pine-forested
hills, Pitlochry became famous
after Queen Victoria (see p60)
described it as one of the finest

🎭 **Festival Theatre**
Port-na-Craig. **Tel** 01796 484626.
Open daily. 🎫 📷 ♿ 🌐 pitlochry.
org.uk

🏭 **Edradour Distillery**
Pitlochry, off A924. **Open** Apr–Oct:
Mon–Sat. 🎫 📷 ♿ limited. 📷
🌐 edradour.co.uk

Tips for Drivers

Tour length: 60 miles (111 km).
Stopping-off points: Crathes
Castle café (May–Sep: daily);
Station Restaurant, Ballater (food
served all day). (See also pp636–7)

① Drum Castle
This impressive 13th-century keep
was granted by Robert the Bruce
to his standard bearer in 1323,
in gratitude for his services.

③ Banchory
This town used to be known for its lavender fields. From
the 18th-century Brig o' Feugh, salmon can be seen.

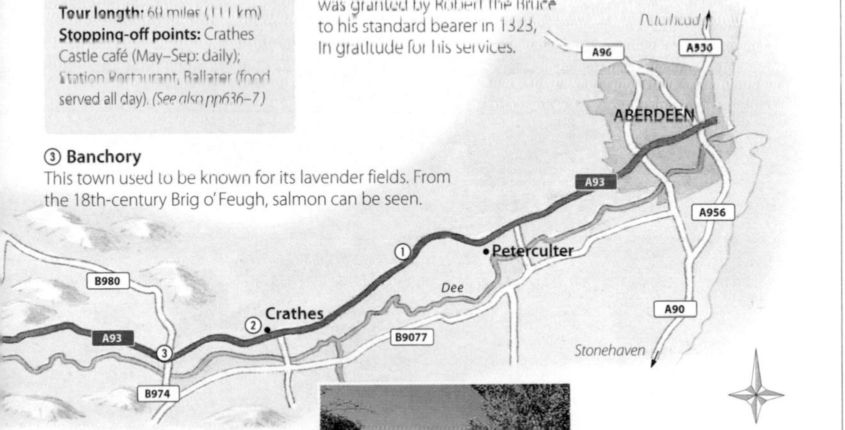

② Crathes Castle and Gardens
This is the family home
of the Burnetts, who were
made Royal Foresters of
Drum by Robert the Bruce.
Along with the title, he
gave Alexander Burnett
the ivory Horn of Leys,
which is still on display.

Peterhead

A96   A930

ABERDEEN

A93

A956

Peterculter

Dee

A90

Crathes

B9077

Stonehaven

B980

A93

B974

Key
━━ Tour route
══ Other roads

0 kilometres   5
0 miles   4

㉑ Killiecrankie Walk

In an area famous for its scenery and historical connections, this circular walk offers typical Highland views. The route is fairly flat, though ringed by mountains, and follows the River Garry south to Loch Faskally, meandering through a wooded gorge, passing the Soldier's Leap and a Victorian viaduct. There are several good picnic spots along the way. Returning along the River Tummel, the walk crosses one of Queen Victoria's favourite Highland areas, before doubling back along the rivers to complete the circuit.

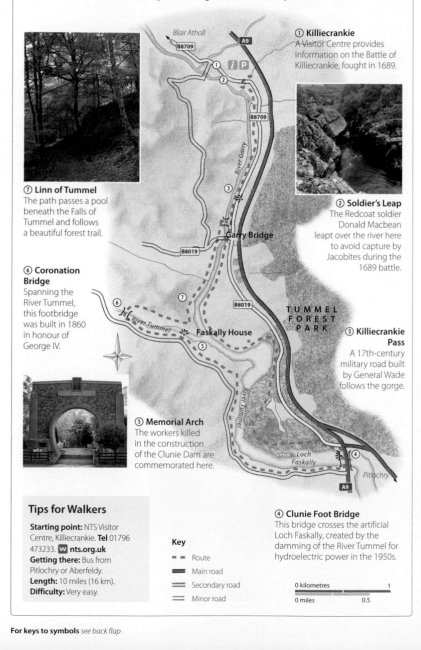

① **Killiecrankie**
A Visitor Centre provides information on the Battle of Killiecrankie, fought in 1689.

② **Soldier's Leap**
The Redcoat soldier Donald Macbean leapt over the river here to avoid capture by Jacobites during the 1689 battle.

③ **Killiecrankie Pass**
A 17th-century military road built by General Wade follows the gorge.

⑦ **Linn of Tummel**
The path passes a pool beneath the Falls of Tummel and follows a beautiful forest trail.

⑥ **Coronation Bridge**
Spanning the River Tummel, this footbridge was built in 1860 in honour of George IV.

⑤ **Memorial Arch**
The workers killed in the construction of the Clunie Dam are commemorated here.

④ **Clunie Foot Bridge**
This bridge crosses the artificial Loch Faskally, created by the damming of the River Tummel for hydroelectric power in the 1950s.

Tips for Walkers

Starting point: NTS Visitor Centre, Killiecrankie. **Tel** 01796 473233. **W** nts.org.uk
Getting there: Bus from Pitlochry or Aberfeldy.
Length: 10 miles (16 km).
Difficulty: Very easy.

Key

–– Route
▬ Main road
═ Secondary road
═ Minor road

0 kilometres 1
0 miles 0.5

The Three Sisters, Glencoe, in late autumn

㉒ Blair Castle

Blair Atholl, Perthshire. **Tel** 01796
481207. 🚉 Blair Atholl. **Open** Apr–
Oct: 9:30am–5:30pm daily. **Closed**
1 & 2 Jan, 25–27 Dec. 🅿 ♿ limited.
W blair-castle.co.uk

This rambling, turreted castle
has been altered so often in its
700 year history that it provides
a unique insight into the history
of Highland aristocratic life.
The 18th- century wing has a
display containing the gloves
and pipe of Bonnie Prince
Charlie *(see p535)*, who spent

two days here gathering
Jacobite *(see p541)* support.
Family portraits cover 300
years and include paintings
by such masters as Johann
Zoffany and Sir Peter Lely.
Sir Edwin Landseer's *Death
of a Stag in Glen Tilt* (1850)
was painted nearby.

In 1844 Queen Victoria
visited the castle and conferred
on its owners, the Dukes of
Atholl, the distinction of being
allowed to maintain a private
army. The Atholl Highlanders
still flourish.

㉓ The Cairngorms

See pp548–9.

㉔ Glencoe

Highland. 🚉 Fort William.
🚌 Glencoe. 🛈 15 High St, Fort
William (0139 770 1801).

Renowned for its awe inspiring
scenery and savage history,
Glencoe was compared by
Dickens to "a burial ground of
a race of giants". The precipitous
cliffs of Buachaille Etive Mor
and the knife-edged ridge
of Aonach Eagach (both over
900 m; 3,000 ft) present a
formidable challenge even
to experienced mountaineers.

Against a dark backdrop of
craggy peaks and the River
Coe, the Glen offers superb hill
walking in the summer. Stout
footwear, waterproofs and
attention to safety warnings
are essential. Details of routes,
ranging from the easy half-hour
between the **NTS Visitor Centre**
and Signal Rock (from which the
signal was given to commence
the massacre) to a stiff 6-mile
(10-km) haul up the Devil's
Staircase, can be had from the
Visitor Centre. Guided walks
are offered in summer by the
NTS Ranger service.

🛈 **NTS Visitor Centre**
Glencoe. **Tel** 01855 811307. **Open** daily.
🅿 ♿ ltd 🆖 **W** glencoe-nts.org.uk

The Massacre of Glencoe

In 1692, the chief of the Glencoe MacDonalds was five days
late in registering an oath of submission to William III, giving the
government an excuse to root out a nest of Jacobite *(see p541)*
supporters. For 10 days 130 soldiers, captained by Robert Campbell,
were hospitably entertained by the unsuspecting MacDonalds. At
dawn on 13 February, in a terrible breach of trust, the soldiers fell
on their hosts, killing some 38 MacDonalds. Many more died in
their wintry mountain hideouts.
The massacre, unsurprisingly,
became a political scandal,
though there was to be
no official reprimand
for three years.

Detail of *The Massacre of
Glencoe* by James
Hamilton

㉓ The Cairngorms

Rising to a height of 1,309 m (4,296 ft), the Cairngorm mountains form the highest landmass in Britain. Cairn Gorm itself is the site of one of Britain's first ski centres, and the weather station at its summit provides regular reports, essential in an area known for sudden changes in conditions. Any walkers here should follow the mountain code without fail. If walking is not your thing, the funicular railway that climbs Cairn Gorm offers superb views over the Spey Valley. Many estates in the valley have centres that introduce the visitor to Highland land use.

Strathspey Steam Railway This line between Aviemore and Broomhill dates from 1863.

Highland Wildlife Park
Driving through this park, the visitor can see bison, wolves and wild boar. All of these animals were once common in the Highlands.

Inverness
Nairn
A938 Carrbridge
B9153
Boat of Garten
A9
Aviemore
Coylumbridge
A9 B9152 Spey
LOCH AN EILEIN
Kincraig
LOCH INSH
Kingussie
Newtonmore
B970
Tolvah
Feshie
BRAERIACH
1,295 m (4,248 ft)
LOCH EINICH
Perth

0 kilometres 5
0 miles 5

KEY

① **Aviemore**, the commercial centre of the Cairngorms, provides buses to the ski area 9 miles (13 km) away.

② **The Cairngorm Reindeer Centre** organises walks in the hills among Britain's only herd of reindeer.

③ **Ben MacDhui**, is Britain's second highest peak, after Ben Nevis.

Rothiemurchus Estate
Highland cattle can be seen among at Rothiemurchus. A visitor centre provides guided walks and describes life on a Highland estate.

For hotels and restaurants in this area see pp572–3 and pp602–3

Loch Garten Osprey Centre
Ospreys now thrive in this reserve in Abernethy Forest, which was established in 1959 to protect the first pair seen in Britain for 50 years.

VISITORS' CHECKLIST

Practical Information
The Highlands. 7 The Parade, Aviemore (01479 810930).
Cairngorm Reindeer Centre, Loch Morlich. **Tel** 01479 861228. **Open** daily.
W **cairngormreindeer.co.uk**
Highland Wildlife Park: **Tel** 01540 651270. **Open** daily (weather permitting).
W **highlandwildlifepark.org**
Rothiemurchus Visitor Centre: **Tel** 01479 812345. **Open** daily.
W **rothiemurchus.net**
Loch Garten Osprey Centre: **Tel** 01479 831476. **Open** daily.
Skiing: **Tel** 01479 861261.
W **rspb.org.uk**

Transport
Aviemore.

Skiing and Funicular Railway
During the winter, chairlifts and tows provide access to more than 28 ski runs on Cairn Gorm's northern flanks. Scotland's only funicular railway also operates here.

Flora of the Cairngorms
With mixed woodland at their base and the summits forming a sub-polar plateau, the Cairngorms present a huge variety of flora. Ancient Caledonian pines (once common in the area) survive in Abernethy Forest, while arctic flowers flourish in the heights.

The Cairngorm plateau holds little life except lichen (Britain's oldest plant), wood rush and cushions of moss campion, which is often completely covered with pink flowers.

Shady corries are important areas for alpine plants such as arctic mouse-ear, hare's foot sedge, mountain rock-cress and alpine speedwell.

Pinewoods occupy the higher slopes, revealing purple heather as they become sparser.

Mixed woodland covers the lower ground, which is carpeted with heather and deergrass.

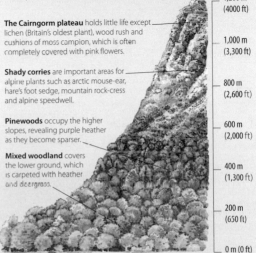

An idealized section of the Cairngorm plateau

1,200 m (4000 ft)
1,000 m (3,300 ft)
800 m (2,600 ft)
600 m (2,000 ft)
400 m (1,300 ft)
200 m (650 ft)
0 m (0 ft)

Key
Major road
Minor road
Narrow lane
Footpath

Grantown-on-Spey
Broomhill — A95
B970 — Nethy Bridge
LOCH GARTEN
LOCH RLICH
CAIRN GORM 1,245 m (4,081 ft)
BEN MACDHUI 1,309 m (4,296 ft)
CAIRNGORM MOUNTAINS

㉕ Road to the Isles Tour

This scenic route passes vast mountain corridors, breathtaking beaches of white sand and tiny villages, to reach the town of Mallaig, one of the ferry ports for the isles of Skye, Rum and Eigg. As well as the stunning scenery, the area is steeped in Jacobite history *(see p541)*.

Tips for Drivers

Tour length: 45 miles (72 km).
Stopping-off points: Glenfinnan NTS Visitors' Centre (01397 722250) describes the Jacobite risings and serves refreshments; the Old Library Lodge, Arisaig *(see p573)*, has good food. *(See also pp636–7.)*

⑦ Mallaig
The Road to the Isles ends at Mallaig, an active little fishing port with a very good harbour and one of the ferry links to Skye *(see pp534–5)*.

⑥ Morar
The road continues through Morar, an area renowned for its white sands; Loch Morar is rumoured to be the home of a 12-m (40-ft) monster known as Morag.

⑤ Prince's Cairn
On the shores of Loch Nan Uamh, a cairn marks the spot from which Bonnie Prince Charlie finally left Scotland for France in 1746.

㉖ Oban

Argyll & Bute. 🚹 8,600. 🚢 🚌 🚃
ℹ️ North Pier (01631 563122).
🌐 **oban.org.uk**

Located on the Firth of Lorne and commanding a magnificent view of the Argyll coast, the port of Oban is busy with travellers on their way to Mull and the Western Isles *(see p533)*.

Dominating the skyline is McCaig's Tower, an unfinished Victorian imitation of the Colosseum in Rome. It is worth making the 10-minute climb from the town centre for the sea views alone. Attractions in the town include working centres for glass, pottery and whisky; the Oban distillery produces one of the country's finest malt whiskies *(see p493)*. The **Scottish Sealife Sanctuary** rescues injured and orphaned seals and has displays of underwater life. Car ferries depart for Barra and South Uist, Mull, Tiree and Colonsay islands.

Dunstaffnage Castle, 3 miles (5 km) north of Oban, was the 13th-century stronghold of the MacDougalls. It has atmospheric ruins, a chapel and the "new house" where Flora MacDonald *(see p535)* is believed to have been imprisoned in 1746.

🏛 Scottish Sealife Sanctuary
Barcaldine. **Tel** 01631 720386.
Open Apr–Oct: daily; Nov–Mar: Fri–Mon. **Closed** 25 Dec. 🅿️ ♿ 🚻 📷
🌐 **sealsanctuary.co.uk**

🏰 Dunstaffnage Castle
Dunbeg, off A85. **Tel** 01631 562465.
Open daily. **Closed** Nov–Mar: Thu & Fri. 🅿️ 📷 🌐 **historicenvironment. scot**

㉗ Island of Mull

Argyll & Bute. 🚹 2,800. 🚢 from Oban, Kilchoan, Lochaline. ℹ️ The Pier, Craignure (01680 812377).

Most roads on this easily accessible Hebridean island follow the sharply indented rocky coastline, affording wonderful sea views. On a promontory in the east lies **Duart Castle**, home of the chief of Clan Maclean. Visitors can see the Banqueting Hall and State Rooms in the 13th-century keep. Its dungeons once held prisoners from a Spanish Armada galleon sunk by a

Looking out to sea across Tobermory Bay, Mull

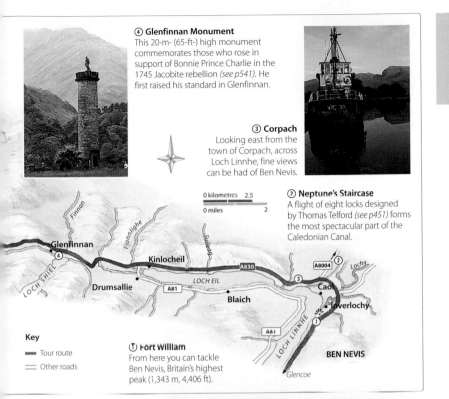

④ Glenfinnan Monument
This 20-m- (65-ft-) high monument commemorates those who rose in support of Bonnie Prince Charlie in the 1745 Jacobite rebellion *(see p541)*. He first raised his standard in Glenfinnan.

③ Corpach
Looking east from the town of Corpach, across Loch Linnhe, fine views can be had of Ben Nevis.

② Neptune's Staircase
A flight of eight locks designed by Thomas Telford *(see p451)* forms the most spectacular part of the Caledonian Canal.

0 kilometres 2.5
0 miles 2

Key

— Tour route

= Other roads

① Fort William
From here you can tackle Ben Nevis, Britain's highest peak (1,343 m, 4,406 ft).

BEN NEVIS

Maclean in 1588. The attractive riverside village of Dervaig houses a fascinating heritage centre.

Environs

From Fionnphort, a ferry goes to **Iona**, where St Columba *(see p529)* began his mission in Scotland in 563. North of Iona, the Isle of Staffa should be visited for its magnificent **Fingal's Cave**.

🏠 Duart Castle
Off A849, near Craignure. **Tel** 01680 812309. **Open** Apr: 11am–4pm Sun–Thu; May–Oct: 10:30am–5pm daily.
🅰 Ⓦ duartcastle.com

㉘ Loch Awe

Argyll & Bute. 🚆 🚌 Dalmally.
ℹ Inveraray (01499 302063).
Ⓦ loch-awe.com

One of the longest of Scotland's freshwater lochs, Loch Awe fills a 25-mile (40-km) glen in the southwestern Highlands. A short drive east from the village of Lochawe leads to the

The ruins of Kilchurn Castle on the shore of Loch Awe

lochside remains of **Kilchurn Castle**, abandoned after being struck by lightning in the 18th century. Dwarfing the castle is the huge bulk of Ben Cruachan, whose summit can be reached by the narrow Pass of Brander, in which Robert the Bruce *(see p486)* fought the Clan MacDougal in 1308. From the A85, a tunnel leads to the cavernous Cruachan Power Station. Near the village of

Taynuilt, the preserved Lorn Furnace at Bonawe is a reminder of the iron-smelting industry that caused the destruction of much of the area's woodland in the 18th and 19th centuries.

Marked prehistoric cairns are found off the A816 between Kilmartin and Dunadd. The latter boasts a 6th-century hillfort from which the Stone of Destiny *(see p486)* originated.

The pinnacled, mock Gothic exterior of Inveraray Castle

㉙ Inveraray Castle

Inveraray, Argyll & Bute. ⊟ Dalmally. 🚌 from Glasgow. **Tel** 01499 302203. **Open** Apr–Oct: 10am–5:45pm daily. 🔲 📷 🚻 limited. 🔲 📷 🅦 **inveraray-castle.com**

This multi-turreted mock Gothic palace is the family home of the powerful Clan Campbell, who have been the Dukes of Argyll since 1701. The castle was built in 1745 by architects Roger Morris and William Adam on the ruins of a 15th-century castle, and the conical towers added later, after a fire in 1877. Magnificent interiors, designed by Robert Mylne in the 1770s, form the backdrop to a huge collection of Oriental and European porcelain, Regency furniture and portraits by Ramsay, Gainsborough and Raeburn. The Armoury Hall features a display of weaponry collected by the Campbells to fight the Jacobites (see p541).

㉚ Auchindrain Museum

Inveraray, Argyll & Bute. **Tel** 01499 500235. 🚌 Inveraray then bus. **Open** Apr–Oct: 10am–5pm daily (last adm: 4pm); Nov–Apr: Mon–Fri, weather permitting. 📷 🚻 limited. 📷 🅦 **auchindrain.org.uk**

The first open-air museum in Scotland, Auchindrain illuminates the working life of the kind of farming community that was typical of the Highlands until the late 19th century. Originally comprising some 20 thatched buildings, the site was communally farmed by its tenants until the last one retired in 1962. Visitors can wander through

the buildings, many of which combine living space, kitchen and cattle shed under one roof. Some are furnished with box beds and old rush lamps. The homes of Auchindrain are a fascinating memorial to the time before the transition from subsistence to commercial farming.

An old hay turner at the open-air Auchindrain Museum

㉛ Crarae Gardens

Crarae, Argyll & Bute. **Tel** 01546 886614. 🚌 Inveraray then bus. Garden: **Open** 9:30am–sunset daily. Visitor Centre: **Open** Apr–Sep: 10am–5pm daily; Oct: 10am–5pm Thu–Mon. 📷 🚻 limited. NTS 🅦 **nts.org.uk**

Considered the most beguiling gardens in the western

Highlands, the **Crarae Gardens** were created in the 1920s by Lady Grace Campbell. She was the aunt of explorer Reginald Farrer, whose specimens from Tibet were the beginnings of a collection of exotic plants. The gardens are nourished by the warmth of the Gulf Stream and high rainfall. Although there are many unusual Himalayan rhodo-dendrons flourishing here, the gardens are also home to exotic plants from countries ranging from New Zealand to the USA. Plant collectors still contribute to the gardens, which are best seen in spring and early summer against the blue waters of Loch Fyne.

㉜ Jura

Argyll & Bute. 🚶 200. 🚌 from Kennacraig to Islay, then Islay to Jura. 🅸 The Square, Bowmore, Islay (01496 305165).

Barren, mountainous and overrun by red deer, the Isle of Jura has only one road, which connects the single village of Craighouse to the Islay ferry. Though walking is restricted during the stalking (deer-hunting) season between August and October, the island offers superb hill walking, especially on the slopes of the three main peaks, known as the Paps of Jura. The tallest of these is Beinn An Oir at 784 m (2571 ft). Beyond the island's northern tip are the notorious whirlpools of Corryvreckan. The novelist George Orwell (who came to the island to write his final novel, *1984*) nearly

Jetty extending in the waters of Ardlussa Bay, on the Isle of Jura

For hotels and restaurants in this area see pp572–3 and pp602–3

Mist crowning the Paps of Jura, seen at sunset across the Sound of Islay

lost his life here in 1946 when he fell into the water. A legend tells of Prince Breackan who, to win the hand of a princess, tried to keep his boat anchored in the whirlpool for three days, held by ropes made of hemp, wool and maidens' hair. The prince drowned when a single rope, containing the hair of a girl who had been untrue, finally broke.

⊕ Islay

Argyll & Bute. 🚌 3,300. 🚢 from Kennacraig. 🚉 The Square, Bowmore (01496 305165).

Islay (pronounced "Eye-luh") is the home of respected Highland single malt whiskies Lagavulin and Laphroaig. Most of the island's distilleries produce heavily peated malts with a distinctive tang of the sea. The Georgian village of Bowmore has the island's oldest distillery and a circular church designed to minimize the Devil's possible lurking places. The **Museum of Islay Life** in Port Charlotte contains fascinating information on social and natural history. Seven miles (11 km) east of Port Ellen stands the Kildalton Cross. A block of local green stone adorned with Old Testament scenes, it is one of the most impressive 8th-century

Celtic crosses in Britain. Worth a visit for its archaeological and historical interest is the medieval stronghold of the Lords of the Isles, **Finlaggan**. Islay's beaches support a variety of birdlife, some of which can be observed at the RSPB reserve at Gruinart.

🏛 Museum of Islay Life
Port Charlotte. **Tel** 01496 850358.
Open Apr–Sep: Mon–Fri. 🈲 ♿
🌐 **islaymuseum.org**

⊕ Kintyre

Argyll & Bute. 🚌 6,000. 🚢 Oban. 🚉 Campbeltown. 🚉 MacGinnon House, The Pier, Campbeltown (01586 556162).

A long, narrow peninsula stretching far south of Glasgow, Kintyre has superb views across to the islands of Gigha, Islay and Jura. The 9-mile (14-km) Crinan Canal, opened in 1801,

is a delightful inland waterway, its 15 locks bustling with pleasure craft in the summer. The town of Tarbert (meaning "isthmus" in Gaelic) takes its name from the neck on which it stands, which is narrow enough to drag a boat across between Loch Fyne and West Loch Tarbert. This feat was first achieved by the Viking King Magnus Barfud who, in 1198, was granted by treaty as much land as he could sail around.

Travelling south past Campbeltown, the B842 ends at the headland known as the Mull of Kintyre, which was made famous when former Beatle Paul McCartney popularized a traditional pipe tune of the same name. Westward lies the Isle of Rathlin, where Robert the Bruce *(see p486)* learned patience in his struggles against the English by watching a spider weaving a web in a cave.

Fishing boats and yachts moored at Tarbert harbour, Kintyre

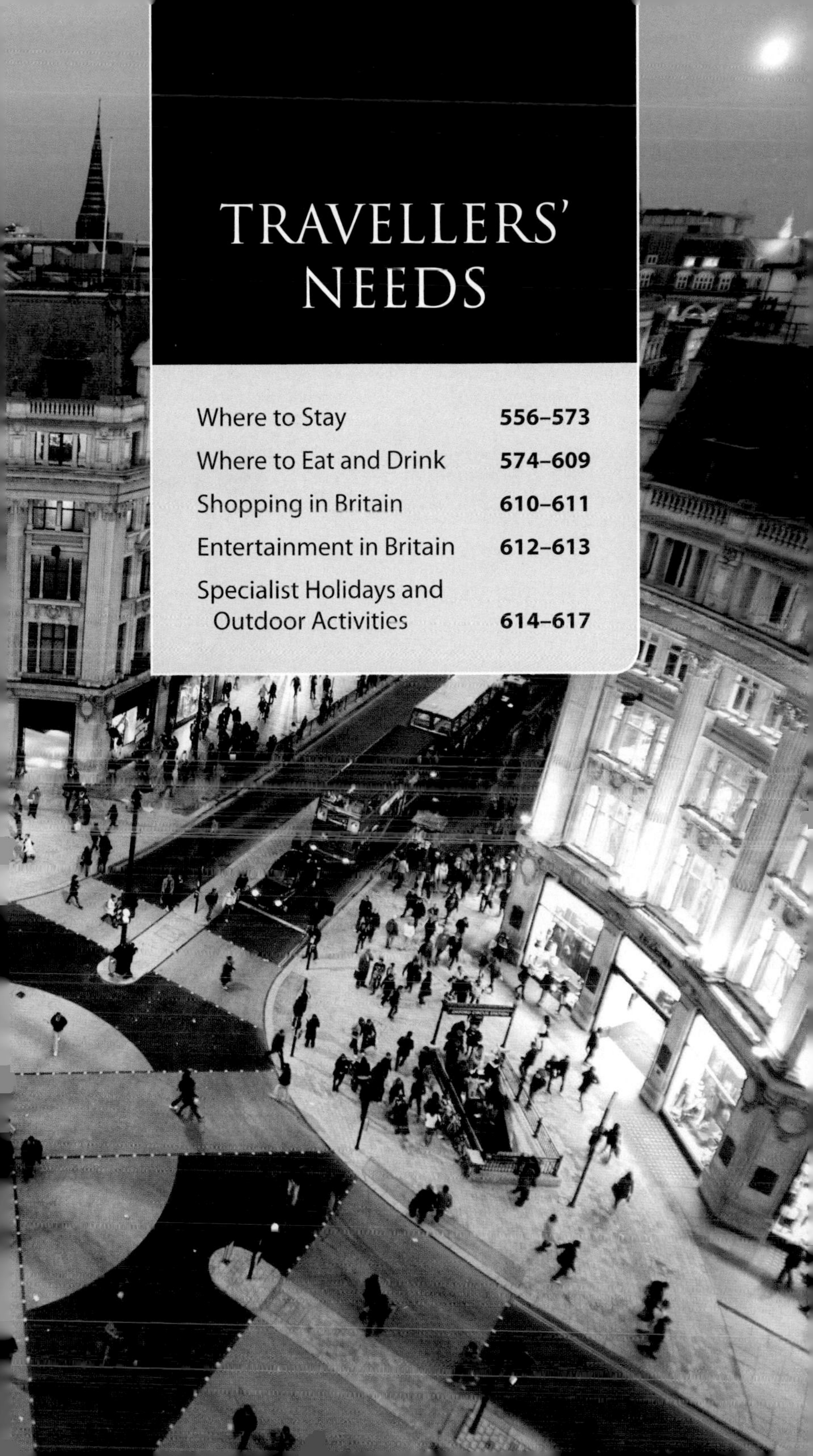

TRAVELLERS' NEEDS

Where to Stay   556–573

Where to Eat and Drink   574–609

Shopping in Britain   610–611

Entertainment in Britain   612–613

Specialist Holidays and
    Outdoor Activities   614–617

WHERE TO STAY

Whatever your budget or accommodation preferences, you should easily be able to find an establishment to suit your needs from the large choice given in the hotel listings on pages 560–73. These include places to stay at all price points, from modest budget venues to palatial and super-luxurious five-star establishments. All the hotels selected are among the best of their kind, perhaps with a distinctive character, or are exceptional in terms of hospitality, facilities or value for money. Location is another prime consideration for inclusion: all the hotels and guesthouses listed make convenient touring bases for one or more of the destinations featured in this book, or have attractive or interesting settings, which are enjoyable in their own right.

On the next few pages we outline some of the types of accommodation available across Great Britain, along with various aspects of choosing, booking and paying for your stay.

Country-House Hotels

The quintessentially British country-house hotel has proliferated in the past few decades. Individual examples vary widely, but the best are usually set in buildings of architectural or historic interest, filled with antiques or high-quality traditional furnishings. They generally have extensive grounds but are not always in deeply rural locations. Some of the best in the country are found in the Cotswolds.

Comfort, even luxury, is assured, along with good food and service – frequently with a very high price tag. Many country-house hotels also offer extensive spa or health club facilities. Some of these hotels are still owned and personally managed by resident proprietors; others belong to groups or chains.

Boutique and Designer Hotels

This fashionable, design-conscious type of hotel is found around the country. Revelling in innovative architecture, funky decor and high-tech gadgetry, many exude an air of uncluttered minimalism, and some have outstanding restaurants. Chains like **Malmaison** or **Hotel du Vin** are also included in this category. Popular with the budget-conscious traveller, the boutique B&B is a spin-off of the trend.

Hotel Groups

Newer hotel groups have taken the place of many of the long-established names, providing standardized accommodation at all price levels in most parts of Great Britain. The majority of chain

The front entrance of The Royal Crescent, Bath *(see p565)*

hotels lie in accessible, convenient locations. Though lacking in individuality, they are efficiently run, and they usually represent good value for money. They also frequently offer bargain deals and reduced rates, depending on the time of year.

Budget chains offering no-frills, motel-lodge-style accommodation include **Ibis**, **Travelodge** and **Premier Inn**; further up the scale are mid-market chains like **Holiday Inn**, **Novotel**, **Marriott** and **Radisson Blu**. Some of these hotels have corporate deals and will offer cheaper rates at the weekend.

Also found throughout the country are well-known, independently owned franchise hotels, including **Best Western** and **Pride of Britain**.

A River View suite at The Savoy, London, offers panoramic views of the Thames *(see p560)*

◀ Diagonal pedestrian crossing at Oxford Circus, London

Elegantly furnished room at Urban Beach Hotel, a boutique hotel in Bournemouth *(see p565)*

Inns and Pubs with Rooms

The coaching inn is a familiar sight in Britain. Many of these fine old hostelries date from the 18th century, though some are even older, and they usually have reliable restaurants, traditional decor and a warm and friendly atmosphere.

Other types of pubs or inns now also offer accommodation and good food, and many have become very welcoming to families. Britain's best inns are comfortable and have the usual modern amenities, and bear comparison with any good hotel. Gastropubs, informal eateries serving exceptional food, sometimes offer stylish accommodation at reasonable prices.

Guesthouses and B&Bs

The bed-and-breakfast is probably the best-known type of budget accommodation in Great Britain. These establishments are generally family-owned private homes or farmhouses. Accommodation and facilities can be simple (bedrooms may not have TV, telephones or en-suite bathrooms, for example), but the best can be quite sophisticated. Prices include breakfast – generally a traditional British fry up but other options, such as cereals, fruit and yogurt, are usually available as well.

A few B&Bs are reluctant to accept credit cards or travellers' cheques, or may charge a premium for doing so. It is advisable to have some alternative method of payment, preferably cash. Any regional tourist office should be able to supply a list of local registered B&Bs on request, though they cannot make specific recommendations and may charge a fee or a commission for making bookings on your behalf. Travel websites such as www.visitengland.com serve as a good resource, as does the **London Bed and Breakfast Agency**.

Hotel Gradings

Partially successful attempts have been made to harmonize the confusing and often conflicting systems of accommodation classification used by the various tourist boards and motoring organizations, such as the AA and RAC. In England, hotel gradings are based on a system of one to five stars awarded for facilities and service: the more stars, the more luxurious you can expect your hotel to be. Guesthouses and B&Bs are also graded with one to five stars, a quality score that is based on various aspects of the accommodation, including cleanliness and hospitality. Special awards (gold and silver, ribbons, rosettes and so on) are given for excellence in certain categories, such as an exceptional breakfast or a warm welcome.

Scotland and Wales have their own separate quality-based gradings.

The modern Champagne Bar at Gilpin Lodge, Windermere *(see p570)*

Prices and Bookings

Some hotels just quote room rates; others may quote a B&B or half-board (dinner, bed and breakfast) rate per person. Rates are generally inclusive of Value Added Tax (VAT) and service, but some top-range hotels make additional charges; most charge hefty single-person supplements.

The cost of a standard en-suite double room in a London hotel including breakfast averages £130 per night, but at the top end of the scale, a suite can cost around £3,000. The summer months and key events hike up hotel prices even further.

Outside London, expect to pay an average of £100 per night for the same. Standard B&B accommodation is typically under £50 per person per night, but again there is wide variation, with boutique B&Bs operating more like hotels. A B&B in London typically costs around £100 for a double room per night, including breakfast.

Most hotels request confirmation by email and a deposit in advance (a credit card number will generally do). Email bookings are now commonplace, and most hotels have an online booking facility on their website. Bargains can be found on sites including www.laterooms.com and www.lastminute.com. Websites such as Expedia, Kayak and Travelocity are cheaper ways of booking, especially for a room and a flight together.

The luxurious drawing room at Middlethorpe Hall, York *(see p570)*

Any hotel booking is a legally binding contract. If you don't show up, the full cost of your stay may be charged. Most hotels will refund your deposit if they are able to re-let the room, but some will charge a penalty, depending how late you cancel. Most travel insurance policies cover cancellation charges for pre-booked UK hotel stays of more than two days, if there is a satisfactory reason.

Watch out for hidden extras. Telephone charges from hotel rooms have a high mark-up, and rates quoted per unit do not always indicate clearly how much time you get for your money.

There is no need to tip staff unless they go out of their way to perform some exceptional duty.

Roadside sign for a bed-and-breakfast

Self-Catering

Self-catering has many attractions, especially for families on a budget. With the arrival of the "unhotel" concept, self-catering has become a popular way to travel. Sites like **Airbnb** and **One Fine Stay** offer apartments and homes to rent directly from their owners, giving the chance to live like a local. The range of places to let for holiday rentals is huge, from luxury apartments to log cabins or converted farm buildings. Properties full of character are available from conservation organizations such as the **Landmark Trust**, which restores buildings of historic or architectural interest and makes them available for short-term lets, and **English Heritage** and the **National Trust** *(see p33)*, which have a number of holiday cottages on their estates. They tend to be popular, so book ahead.

Annually updated self-catering guides are a useful source of listings, and Sawdays.co.uk is a particularly good font of information. Tourist offices can supply up-to-date regional lists and may also offer a booking service.

Confirm what is included in the price (cleaning, electricity and so on), and check whether any extra fees, deposits or insurance charges will be added to the bill.

Caravanning, Camping and Motor Homes

Most of Britain's campsites and caravan parks open only for about 6 months of the year (typically from Easter to

A traditionally decorated bedroom at Judges Country House, Yarm *(see p570)*

October), but you will need to make reservations in advance. Helpful organizations include the **Camping and Caravanning Club** and the **Caravan and Motorhome Club**, which publish lists of their member parks and operate their own grading systems.

Camping or caravanning pitches typically cost around £20 per night. For a list of sites, check www.pitchup.com, www.coolcamping.com or the **Forest Holidays** website.

Motor homes give greater freedom to explore at your own pace and a wider choice of places to stay, including most campsites and caravan parks. Some operators will let guests pick up their vehicle directly from an airport or ferry terminal.

Disabled Travellers

All the UK's tourist boards, including **Visit England**, **Visit Wales** and **Visit Scotland**, provide information about disabled access in their accommodation and sightseeing

Campsite in Ogwen Valley, Snowdonia

guides. The Visit England website also has an Accessible England section detailing accessible attractions and transport, and runs the National Accessible Scheme for accommodation. The scheme grades properties approved under the **Tourism for All** initiative for various categories of disability. **Disability Rights UK** also publishes an annual holiday guide.

Recommended Hotels

The accommodation options that follow have been selected

across a wide range of prices for their excellent facilities, good location and value. There are five-star country-house retreats and rooms with stunning sea or country views, as well as character hotels that are full of charm, boutique city hotels and the humble B&B.

For the best in each region, look out for hotels designated as DK Choices. These offer something unique: perhaps a stunning location, a compelling history or a special atmosphere.

For map references for London listings see pp131–151.

DIRECTORY

Boutique and Designer Hotels

Hotel du Vin
Tel 0819 130345.
W hotelduvin.com

Malmaison
Tel 08719 430350.
W malmaison.com

Hotel Groups

Best Western
Tel 08457 767676.
W bestwestern.co.uk

Holiday Inn
W holidayinn.com

Ibis
W ibis.com

Marriott
W marriott.com

Novotel
W novotel.com

Premier Inn
W premierinn.com

Pride of Britain
Tel 0808 163 9207.
W prideofbritain
hotels.com

Radisson Blu
W radissonblu.com

Travelodge
W travelodge.co.uk

Guesthouses and B&Bs

London Bed and Breakfast Agency
Tel 020 7586 2768.
W londonbb.com

Self-Catering

Airbnb
W airbnb.co.uk

English Heritage
Tel 0370 333 1181.
W english-heritage.
org.uk

Landmark Trust
Tel 01628 825925.
W landmarktrust.org.uk

National Trust
Tel 0344 800 2070
W nationaltrust
holidays.org.uk

National Trust for Scotland
Tel 0131 458 0200.
W nts.org.uk

One Fine Stay
Tel 020 3588 0600
W onefinestay.com

Caravanning, Camping and Motor Homes

Camping and Caravanning Club
Tel 08451 307633.
W campingand
caravanningclub.co.uk

Caravan and Motorhome Club
W caravanclub.co.uk

Forest Holidays
Tel 08451 308223.
W forestholidays.co.uk

Disabled Travellers

Disability Rights UK
Ground floor, CAN
Mezzanine, 49–51 East Rd,
London, N1 6AH.
Tel 020 7250 8181.
W disabilityrightsuk.
org

Tourism for All
7a Pixel Mill,
44 Appleby Rd, Kendal,
Cumbria, LA9 6ES.
Tel 08451 249971.
W tourismforall.org.uk

Visit England
W visitengland.com

Visit Wales
W visitwales.com

Visit Scotland
W visitscotland.com

Where to Stay

London

West End and Westminster

Lime Tree ££
B&B Map 18 E2
135–137 Ebury St, SW1W 9QU
Tel *020 7730 8191*
W limetreehotel.co.uk
This attractively furnished and comfortable, family-run B&B is in a convenient location. The rooms are individually decorated.

The Athenaeum £££
Luxury Map 10 E4
116 Piccadilly, W1J 7BJ
Tel *020 7499 3464*
W athenaeumhotel.com
An established hotel brought up to date with spacious bedrooms and family-friendly apartments.

Claridge's £££
Luxury Map 10 E2
49 Brook St, W1K 4HR
Tel *020 7629 8860*
W claridges.co.uk
One of London's greats. Seamless service and understated luxury in a superb Art Deco hotel. Perfect for a special occasion.

DK Choice

The Dorchester £££
Luxury Map 10 D3
Park Lane, W1K 1QA
Tel *020 7629 8888*
W dorchestercollection.com
London's Art Deco grand dame, overlooking Hyde Park, is the hotel of choice for A-list movie stars. The bath in which Elizabeth Taylor signed her $1m contract for *Cleopatra* (1963) is preserved, but the rest of the hotel has been gorgeously refurbished. Savour the famous and delectable after-noon tea in the dining room.

The Goring £££
Historic Map 18 E1
15 Beeston Place, SW1W 0JW
Tel *020 7396 9000*
W thegoring.com
A great English institution with liveried doormen, private gardens and crackling fires on winter days. The Duchess of Cambridge stayed here before her wedding.

The Orange £££
Character Map 18 D2
37 Pimlico Rd, SW1W 8NE
Tel *020 7881 9844*
W theorange.co.uk
Calls itself a "Public House and Hotel", but really it's a rustic restaurant with four snug en-suite bedrooms.

The Ritz £££
Luxury Map 10 F3
150 Piccadilly, W1J 9BR
Tel *020 7493 8181*
W theritzlondon.com
A treat with its gilded dining room and modernized yet stunning Louis XVI-style bedrooms. Don't miss its famous afternoon tea.

St James's Hotel and Club £££
Luxury Map 10 F4
7–8 Park Place, SW1A 1LS
Tel *020 7316 1600*
W stjameshotelandclub.com
Town house with its own art collection and Michelin-starred restaurant. Close to designer shops.

The Savoy £££
Luxury Map 11 C2
Strand, WC2R 0EU
Tel *020 7836 4343*
W fairmont.com
Famed for its Art Deco American bar, this is luxury at its best with elegantly decorated rooms. Has six acclaimed restaurants and bars on site.

The Stafford London £££
Character Map 10 F4
16–18 St James's Place, SW1A 1NJ
Tel *020 7493 0111*
W thestaffordlondon.com
A class act, this hotel boasts traditional country-house decor and an American bar.

W £££
Boutique Map 11 A2
10 Wardour St, W1D 6QF
Tel *020 7758 1000*
W wlondon.co.uk
The ultimate in cool, this global brand hotel has ontemporary, colourful rooms set within a glass exterior. On-site spa and private cinema.

The Wellesley £££
Luxury Map 10 D5
11 Knightsbridge, SW1X 7LY
Tel *020 7235 3535*
W thewellesley.co.uk
No expense spared, this self-consciously stylish hotel even offers free Rolls-Royce transfers.

South Kensington and Hyde Park

Hyde Park Rooms £
B&B Map 9 A1
137 Sussex Gardens, W2 2RX
Tel *020 7723 0225*
W hydeparkrooms.com
No-frills rooms, some with shared bathrooms, all kept spick and span. Fill up on the generous breakfasts.

The Ampersand ££
Boutique Map 17 A2
10 Harrington Rd, SW7 3ER
Tel *020 7589 5895*
W ampersandhotel.com
This restored Victorian hotel has bright, cheerful interiors inspired by music, science and nature. The on-site restaurant, Apero, serves tasty Mediterranean cuisine.

Rhodes ££
B&B Map 9 A1
195 Sussex Gardens, W2 2RJ
Tel *020 7262 0537*
W rhodeshotel.com
Welcoming family-run B&B in a charming Georgian building with contemporary rooms.

The Savoy hotel, London, seen from the south bank of the River Thames

Elegant bar in The Halkin by COMO

Belgraves £££
Luxury **Map** 18 D1
20 Chesham Place, SW1X 8HQ
Tel *020 7858 0100*
W thompsonhotels.com
New York "boho" in Belgravia, with a bold, eclectic design, and a retractable roof over the terrace.

The Capital £££
Luxury **Map** 9 C5
22–24 Basil St, SW3 1AT
Tel *020 7589 5171*
W capitalhotel.co.uk
This is an intimate place that offers the luxury and service of a grand hotel.

The Gore £££
Boutique **Map** 8 F5
190 Queen's Gate, SW7 5EX
Tel *020 7584 6601*
W gorehotel.com
The Gore explodes with character. All the bedrooms are unique. Great offers are usually available online.

The Halkin by COMO £££
Boutique **Map** 10 D5
5 Halkin St, SW1X 7DJ
Tel *020 7333 1000*
W comohotels.com
Smiling service, fresh flowers, soft lighting and exquisite beds. Michelin-starred restaurant on site.

The Levin £££
Boutique **Map** 9 C5
28 Basil St, SW3 1AS
Tel *020 7589 6286*
W thelevinhotel.co.uk
Smart and stylish, with well-presented bedrooms. Eye-catching designs throughout.

Mandarin Oriental Hyde Park £££
Luxury **Map** 9 C5
66 Knightsbridge, SW1X 7LA
Tel *020 7235 2000*
W mandarinoriental.com
Blending old with new, this renowned hotel has fireplaces and mahogany furniture.

Royal Garden £££
Luxury **Map** 8 D5
2–24 Kensington High St, W8 4PT
Tel *020 7937 8000*
W royalgardenhotel.co.uk
A 1960s hotel well suited to families. Go for a room with an unrivalled park view.

Regent's Park and Bloomsbury

Ridgemount Hotel £
B&B **Map** 3 A5
65–67 Gower St, WC1E 6HJ
Tel *020 7636 1141*
W ridgemounthotel.co.uk
Old-school family-run B&B, with a small garden. Modestly furnished, this is great value for the location.

Montagu Place ££
Boutique **Map** 9 C1
2–3 Montagu Place, W1H 2ER
Tel *020 7467 2777*
W montagu-place.co.uk
Choose from a selection of "comfy", "swanky" or "fancy" rooms at this intimate hotel.

No. 5 Doughty Street ££
Apartments **Map** 4 D4
5 Doughty St, WC1N 2PL
Tel *020 7014 0240*
W blueprintlivingapartments.com
Modern studio and one-bedroom apartments with all comforts, at reasonable rates. Full kitchens.

Rough Luxe ££
B&B **Map** 3 C3
1 Birkenhead St, WC1H 8BA
Tel *020 7837 5338*
W roughluxe.co.uk
A quirky B&B with original art and conscientious service.

The Arch £££
Designer **Map** 9 C2
50 Great Cumberland Place, W1H 7FD
Tel *020 7724 4700*
W thearchlondon.com
Cleverly converted from a terrace of town houses, The Arch offers individually decorated rooms that feature hand-painted wallpaper. Popular bar and laid-back dining.

Charlotte Street £££
Boutique **Map** 11 A1
15–17 Charlotte St, W1T 1RJ
Tel *020 7806 2000*
W firmdalehotels.com
Favourite of media folk, with lively public areas and a private cinema. Stylish, in a refreshingly modern English way.

Durrants £££
Character **Map** 10 D1
26–32 George St, W1H 5BJ
Tel *020 7935 8131*
W durrantshotel.co.uk
A privately owned English classic, with tasteful rooms. Panelled entrance and snug bar.

DK Choice

The Langham £££
Luxury **Map** 10 E1
1c Portland Place, W1B 1JA
Tel *020 7636 1000*
W langhamhotels.com
This grand Victorian hotel has opulent rooms, handsome bathrooms and a stunning spa and pool. The Landau restaurant is in a striking oval room, and the cocktail bar, Artesian, is one of the capital's most romantic.

The City and Southwark

Boundary Rooms ££
Designer **Map** 6 D4
2–4 Boundary St, E2 7DD
Tel *020 7729 1051*
W boundary.london
Terence Conran's hotel exudes great style. Each room is different. Pick a suite with a terrace.

The Hoxton ££
Designer **Map** 5 C4
81 Great Eastern St, EC2A 3HU
Tel *020 7550 1000*
W thehoxton.com
This is a very hip place with ultra-cool, sleek and comfy rooms. There's also the buzzy Hoxton Grill restaurant, bar and lounge.

Kennington B&B ££
B&B **Map** 20 F3
103 Kennington Park Rd, SE11 4JJ
Tel *020 7735 7669*
W kenningtonbandb.com
A family-run B&B in a lovingly restored Georgian town house. Comfortable bedrooms with contemporary decor.

For more information on types of hotels *see pages 556–7*

London Bridge ££
Boutique **Map** 13 B4
8–18 London Bridge St, SE1 9SG
Tel *020 7855 2200*
w londonbridgehotel.com
Captivating modern lobby, smart rooms, gym and restaurants. Close to museums and galleries.

The Montcalm at The Brewery London City ££
Designer **Map** 5 B4
52 Chiswell St, EC1Y 4SA
Tel *020 7614 0100*
w themontcalmlondoncity.co.uk
Chic, modern hotel created out of a London brewery once visited by George III. Butler service.

The Rookery ££
Boutique **Map** 4 F5
12 Peter's Ln, Cowcross St, EC1M 6DS
Tel *020 7336 0931*
w rookeryhotel.com
Three restored 18th-century houses crammed with curiosities. Rooms have antique beds. Open fires downstairs.

Shoreditch Rooms ££
Designer **Map** 6 D4
Ebor St, E1 6AW
Tel *020 7739 5040*
w shoreditchhouse.com
The Shoreditch Rooms is set within a warehouse imaginatively renovated in New England style.

The Zetter Townhouse ££
Boutique **Map** 4 E2
49–50 St John's Square, EC1V 4JJ
Tel *020 7324 4444*
w thezettertownhouse.com
Get toothpaste and champagne from the same vending machine at this cool, playful hotel.

King's Wardrobe by BridgeStreet £££
Apartments **Map** 12 F2
6 Wardrobe Place, EC4V 5AF
Tel *020 7792 2222*
w bridgestreet.com
Flagship building with comfortable, well-equipped

Comfortable furnishings at the London Bridge Hotel

apartments ranging from studios to three bedrooms. The minimum stay varies from 3 to 30 days, based on the time of year.

Further Afield

Avo £
Boutique
82 Dalston Lane, E8 3AH
Tel *020 3490 5061*
w avohotel.com
DVDs for rent, memory foam beds and a host of extras at this trendy hotel. Great value for money.

Hotel 55 £
Boutique
55 Hanger Lane, W5 3HL
Tel *020 8991 4450*
w hotel55-london.com
A stylish hotel with neutral colours, Indian art, immaculate bathrooms and a restful garden.

The Victoria Inn £
B&B
72–79 Choumert Rd, SE15 4AR
Tel *020 7639 5052*
w victoriainnpeckham.com
This gastropub is equipped with sunny and stylish rooms. There are also bunks and a jungle-themed playroom for kids.

The Alma ££
Boutique
499 Old York Rd , SW18 1TF
Tel *020 8870 2537*
w almawandsworth.com
Victorian tavern, now a pub-restaurant with 23 stylishly decorated rooms.

Cannizaro House ££
Historic
Westside Common, Wimbledon, SW19 4UE
Tel *020 8879 1464*
w hotelduvin.com
A 300-year-old country house with stunning park views. Boasts a history of well-known guests such as Lord Tennyson and Oscar Wilde.

Fox and Grapes ££
Boutique
9 Camp Rd, SW19 4UN
Tel *020 8619 1300*
w foxandgrapeswimbledon.co.uk
Chic getaway above a French-owned gastropub. Three snug en suite rooms available.

High Road House ££
Boutique
162–170 Chiswick High Rd, W4 1PR
Tel *020 8742 1717*
w highroadhouse.co.uk
Scandinavian-inspired rooms in a Georgian town house. There is also a brasserie downstairs.

Premier Suites London Limehouse £££
Rooms with a view
John Nash Mews, Limehouse Lock, 602 Commercial Rd, E14 7HS
Tel *020 7199 6255*
w premiersuiteslondon.eu
Cheerful living areas and well-equipped granite kitchens with views of Docklands.

The Downs and Channel Coast

ARUNDEL: The Town House ££
Historic
65 High St, West Sussex, BN18 9AJ
Tel *01903 883847*
w thetownhouse.co.uk
This elegant Regency building overlooks Arundel Castle. The rooms are elegant, and there is an excellent restaurant on the ground floor that has a stunning Florentine ceiling.

BRIGHTON: Hotel Una ££
Boutique
55–56 Regency Square, East Sussex, BN1 2FF
Tel *01273 820464*
w hotel-una.co.uk
Luxurious, individually decorated rooms and breakfast in bed at no extra cost.

CANTERBURY: Cathedral Lodge £
Designer
The Precincts, Kent, CT1 2EH
Tel *01227 865350*
w canterburycathedrallodge.org
This modern lodge in the grounds
of Canterbury Cathedral has
stylish rooms.

DK Choice

CHICHESTER:
Lordington House ££
B&B
Lordington, West Sussex, PO18 9DX
Tel *01243 375862*
w sawdays.co.uk/britain/
england/sussex/lordington-house
A quintessentially English
country house with Edwardian-
style bedrooms and well-kept
gardens. Arrive to tea and cake
and enjoy a game of croquet on
the lawn in summer.

HASTINGS: Swan House ££
B&B
Hill St, East Sussex, TN34 3HU
Tel *01424 430014*
w swanhousehastings.co.uk
Half-timbered 1490 guesthouse.
Serves gourmet breakfasts
sourced from local suppliers.

HEVER: Hever Castle B&B ££
Character
The Astor Wing, Hever Castle, TN8 7NG
Tel *01732 061000*
w hevercastle.co.uk
Luxury B&B with access to
the castle and a golf course.
Childhood home of Anne Boleyn.

LEWES: The Shelleys ££
Boutique
135–136 High St, East Sussex,
BN7 1XS
Tel *01273 472361*
w the-shelleys.co.uk
Family-run hotel in a Grade-II
listed building. Luxurious rooms
decorated in Georgian style.

PORTSMOUTH: The George £
Historic
84 Queen St, Hampshire, PO1 3HU
Tel *02392 753885*
w thegeorgehotel.org.uk
Pastel rooms with wooden
beams. Public bar serves cask
ales and home-cooked meals.

PORTSMOUTH: Number Four
Boutique Hotel ££
Boutique
69 Festing Rd, Southsea, Hampshire,
PO4 0NQ
Tel *02392 008444*
w number4hotel.co.uk
This plush designer hotel is
walking distance from the town
and seafront. Quality restaurant.

ROCHESTER: Sovereign £
Character
29 Medway Bridge Marina, Manor
Lane, Kent, ME1 3HS
Tel *01634 400474*
w thesovereignbb.co.uk
Stay on this charmingly renovated
1930s Rhine cruising ship.
Colourful and bright rooms.

SEAVIEW: Priory Bay Hotel £££
Luxury
Priory Drive, Isle of Wight, PO34 5BU
Tel *01983 613146*
w priorybay.com
Period buildings in an estate
surrounded by woodland. Yurts
and thatched cottages available.

SOUTHAMPTON: Hotel
Terravina ££
Boutique
174 Woodlands Rd, Woodlands,
Hampshire, SO40 7GL
Tel *02380 293784*
w hotelterravina.co.uk
Rain showers, fluffy bath robes
and handmade toiletries provided
at this chic and stylish hotel.

WHITSTABLE: Sleeperzzz
Guesthouse £
B&B
30 Railway Ave, Kent, CT5 1LH
Tel *01227 636975*
w sleeperzzz.net
Simple and pleasant B&B near
the town centre. Bright decor
and hearty English breakfasts.

WINCHELSEA: Strand House £
Historic
Tanyards Lane, East Sussex, TN36 4JT
Tel *01797 226276*
w thestrandhouse.co.uk
Old Tudor house providing full
Sussex breakfasts, packed lunches,
afternoon tea and evening meals.

WINCHESTER: Lainston
Country House ££
Luxury
Woodman Lane, Sparsholt,
Hampshire, SO21 2LT
Tel *01962 776088*
w lainstonhouse.com
A 17th-century country house
with sprawling parkland, ruins of
a historic chapel and fine dining.

East Anglia

ALDEBURGH: Laurel
House £
B&B
23 Lee Rd, Suffolk, IP15 5EY
Tel *01728 452775*
w laurel-house.net
Two supremely stylish rooms in
a Victorian house. Continental
breakfast with fresh fruit.

CAMBRIDGE: Madingley
Hall £
Historic
Madingley, Cambridgeshire,
CB23 8AQ
Tel *01223 746222*
w madingleyhall.co.uk
Grand 16th-century country
house with functional and
modern rooms. Superb gardens.

CAMBRIDGE: The Varsity
Hotel & Spa £££
Luxury
Thompson's Lane, Cambridgeshire,
CB5 8AQ
Tel *01223 306030*
w thevarsityhotel.co.uk
Situated on the River Cam with
spa, gym and roof terrace. Rooms
have picture windows.

LITTLE DOWNHAM:
Anchor £
Boutique
25 Main St, Cambridgeshire,
CB6 2ST
Tel *01353 699333*
w littledownhamanchor.co.uk
This hotel has minimal but
attractive rooms. The bar serves
cask ales and local gin.

LOWESTOFT: Britten
House £
Rooms with a view
21 Kirkley Cliff Rd, Suffolk, NR33 0DB
Tel *01502 573950*
w brittenhouse.co.uk
Birthplace and family home of
Benjamin Britten. Traditional
Victorian town house with
original features and sea views.

NORWICH: The Old
Rectory ££
Country House
103 Yarmouth Rd, Norfolk, NR7 0HF
Tel *01603 700772*
w oldrectorynorwich.com
This B&B in a beautiful Grade-II
listed Georgian country house
has elegant rooms and an
excellent candlelit restaurant.

Picturesque exterior of the Swan House
B&B, Hastings

For more information on types of hotels *see pages 556–7*

SOUTHWOLD: The Crown ££
Historic
*The Street, Westleton, Suffolk,
IP17 3AD*
Tel *01728 648777*
w westletoncrown.co.uk
A traditional Suffolk coaching
inn with local ales, log fires,
terraced gardens and
comfortable rooms.

**SOUTHWOLD: Sutherland
House** ££
Character
56 High St, Suffolk, IP18 6DN
Tel *01502 724544*
w sutherlandhouse.co.uk
Choose a room with a sleigh
bed, a fresco ceiling or a slipper
bath in this charming 15th-
century house.

Thames Valley

**BANBURY: Banbury Cross
Bed & Breakfast** £
B&B
*1 Broughton Rd, Oxfordshire,
OX16 9QB*
Tel *01295 266048*
w banburycrossbandb.co.uk
Award-winning B&B with
traditional rooms in a Victorian
house. Extensive breakfast menu.

**GREAT MILTON: Le Manoir
aux Quat' Saisons** £££
Luxury
Church Rd, Oxfordshire, OX44 7PD
Tel *01844 278881*
w belmond.com
Opulent hotel in a lush garden
setting with Raymond Blanc's
Michelin-starred restaurant and
cookery school. Rooms are very
pricey, starting at £570.

MARLOW: Kenton House £
B&B
*4 Kenton Close, Buckinghamshire,
SL7 1DU*
Tel *01628 486536*
w marlow-bedandbreakfast.co.uk
The elegant open-plan kitchen/
living room here overlooks an
attractive garden. The breakfasts
offered are huge.

OXFORD: Keble College ££
Historic
Keble College, Oxfordshire, OX1 3PG
Tel *01865 272727*
w keble.ox.ac.uk
Unique opportunity to stay
in a historic college building.
Breakfast is served in the Great
Hall. Rooms can be booked
two to three months in advance
and are only available during
vacations; check website for
full details.

The grand Gold Room at Fleuchary House, St Albans

OXFORD: Old Bank Hotel £££
Luxury
92–94 High St, Oxfordshire, OX1 4BJ
Tel *01865 799599*
w oldbank-hotel.co.uk
Beautifully converted bank, with
a fine collection of art and free
use of bicycles.

ST ALBANS: Fleuchary House £
Boutique
*29 Upper Lattimore Rd, Hertfordshire,
AL1 3UA*
Tel *01727 766764*
w 29stalbans.com
This boutique B&B offers
immaculate and elegant rooms,
as well as bountiful breakfasts.

DK Choice

**STOKE POGES:
Stoke Park** £££
Historic
Park Rd, Buckinghamshire, SL2 4PG
Tel *01753 717172*
w stokepark.com
This gleaming white five-star
mansion hotel is full of antiques
and paintings and has three
restaurants and a swimming
pool. Plenty of opportunities for
golf, tennis and spa treatments.
Close to Windsor and Heathrow.

UFFINGTON: The Fox & Hounds £
Historic
High St, Oxfordshire, SN7 7RP
Tel *01367 820680*
w uffingtonpub.co.uk
Quiet ground-floor rooms with
beamed pub, friendly locals and
good beer. Lovely views.

WANTAGE: Court Hill Centre £
Character
Court Hill, Oxfordshire, OX12 9NE
Tel *01235 760253*
w courthill.org.uk
Five barns converted into bunk-
houses with beamed rooms.
Enjoy stunning views over the
Vale of the White Horse.

**WINDSOR:
The Old Farmhouse** £
Historic
Oakley Green, Berkshire, SL4 4LH
Tel *01753 850411*
w theoldfarmhousewindsor.com
A 15th-century half-timbered
hotel in a garden setting.
Traditionally furnished rooms.

Wessex

**ABBOTSBURY:
The Abbey House** £
B&B
Church St, Dorset, DT3 4JJ
Tel *01305 871330*
w theabbeyhouse.co.uk
Small and friendly B&B with cosy
rooms and a picturesque garden.
No children under 12.

**AVEBURY:
The Lodge Avebury** ££
B&B
High St, Wiltshire, SN8 1RF
Tel *01672 539023*
w aveburylodge.co.uk
Antique-filled B&B with views of
Avebury's ancient stones from
the rooms. Vegetarian food.

Cosy bedroom at Le Manoir aux
Quat' Saisons, Great Milton

BATH: Apsley House Hotel ££
B&B
141 Newbridge Hill, Somerset, BA1 3PT
Tel 01225 336966
W apsley-house.co.uk
Apsley House is a 12-roomed Georgian house that is set in its own gardens. Four-poster beds and great service.

BATH: The Queensberry ££
Boutique
7 Russel St, Somerset, BA1 2AF
Tel 01225 447928
W thequeensberry.co.uk
Gorgeous, romantic rooms and a modern Mediterranean restaurant. Run by a husband and wife team.

DK Choice

BATH: The Royal Crescent £££
Luxury
16 Royal Crescent, Somerset, BA1 2LS
Tel 01225 823333
W royalcrescent.co.uk
This opulent Relais & Châteaux hotel has high-ceilinged rooms, a fantastic candlelit spa and a gourmet restaurant. Step into the very best of the Georgian era while enjoying modern amenities. Private garden cottages are also available.

BOURNEMOUTH: The Chocolate Boutique Hotel £
Boutique
5 Durley Rd, Dorset, BH2 5JQ
Tel 01202 556857
W thechocolateboutiquehotel. co.uk
Novelty hotel in a tree-lined area. Chocolate-themed rooms and chocolate making lessons.

BOURNEMOUTH: Miramar ££
Rooms with a view
East Overcliff Drive, Dorset, BH1 3AL
Tel 01202 556581
W miramar-bournemouth.com
A large three-star hotel close to the beach so expect sea views. Good for families.

BOURNEMOUTH: Urban Beach Hotel ££
Boutique
23 Argyll Rd, Boscombe, Dorset, BH5 1EB
Tel 01202 301509
W urbanbeach.co.uk
Award-winning family-friendly hotel with a bistro. Breakfast included. It is conveniently located near the beach.

BRIDPORT: The Bull Hotel ££
Boutique
34 East St, Dorset, DT6 3LF
Tel 01308 422878
W thebullhotel.co.uk
Lavish 16th-century former coaching inn bathed in modern glamour. There is also a popular pub on site.

BRISTOL: Brooks Guesthouse £
B&B
St Nicholas St, BS1 1UB
Tel 0117 930 0066
W brooksguesthousebristol.com
This bright B&B behind St Nick's market is a real find. An option is to stay in one of four rooftop retro caravans. Excellent breakfast included.

BRISTOL: The Bristol Camper Company £
Camping
Carpenter's Farm, Yatton, BS21 6TL
Tel 01275 340170
W thebristolcampercompany.co.uk
Hire an up-to-date VW camper van and explore the West Country. Weekly or part-week hire only.

BRISTOL: Hotel du Vin ££
Boutique
The Sugar House, Lewins Mead, BS1 2NU
Tel 0117 925 5577
W hotelduvin.com/bristol
Classy hotel in a beautifully restored 18th-century sugar warehouse, with a bar, brasserie and romantic rooms.

BRUTON: At the Chapel ££
Boutique
High St, Somerset, BA10 0AE
Tel 01749 814 070
W atthechapel.co.uk
Eight luxury rooms in a former chapel. Enjoy freshly baked croissants for breakfast.

CORSHAM: Guyers House Hotel ££
Country House
Pickwick, Wiltshire, SN13 0PS
Tel 01249 713399
W guyershouse.com
Surrounded by beautiful gardens, this hotel offers tennis, croquet and candlelit dinners.

HINTON ST GEORGE: Lord Poulett Arms £
Boutique
High St, Somerset, TA17 8SF
Tel 01460 73149
W lordpoulettarms.com
A 17th-century inn with lovely chic rooms featuring antique bedheads, roll-top baths and an excellent restaurant.

LACOCK: Sign of the Angel ££
B&B
6 Church St, Chippenham, Wiltshire, SN15 2LB
Tel 01249 730230
W signoftheangel.co.uk
This 15th-century pub and B&B offers home-cooked meals, antique carved beds and a fire. Ideal for a romantic weekend.

LONGLEAT: The Bath Arms ££
Boutique
Horningsham, Warminster, Wiltshire, BA12 7LY
Tel 01985 844308
W batharms.co.uk
Character-packed pub with 16 rooms in the heart of the Longleat estate. Dog- and family-friendly. Good base for parties.

LYME REGIS: Hix Townhouse ££
B&B
1 Pound St, Dorset, DT7 3HT
Tel 01297 442499
W hixrestaurants.co.uk
Boutique B&B with luxurious touches and a breakfast hamper of delicious local produce.

LYME REGIS: Hotel Alexandra ££
Boutique
Pound St, Dorset, DT7 3HZ
Tel 01297 442010
W hotelalexandra.co.uk
Some rooms here have views of the beach and the Cobb (harbour), while others offer views of Lyme or the gardens. Two self-catering family cottages also available.

MALMESBURY: The Rectory ££
Luxury
Crudwell, Wiltshire, SN16 9EP
Tel 01666 577194
W therectoryhotel.com
Boutique Cotswolds hotel in a good location with bright rooms, a walled garden and outdoor pool.

Welcoming façade of The Chocolate Boutique Hotel in Bournemouth

For more information on types of hotels *see pages 556–7*

Traditional furnishings in the lounge area at Bovey Castle, Dartmoor

POOLE: Hotel du Vin ££
Boutique
The Quay, Thames St, Dorset, BH15 1JN
Tel *01202 785570*
w hotelduvin.com
Virginia creeper-clad Georgian-house hotel, with signature bistro, wine cellar and tasting room.

SALISBURY: Howard's House Hotel ££
Boutique
Teffont Evias, Wiltshire, SP3 5RJ
Tel *01722 716392*
w howardshousehotel.co.uk
Classic country-house hotel with modern bedrooms. Great for shooting and fishing breaks.

SALISBURY: St Ann's House ££
B&B
33–34 St Ann St, Wiltshire, SP1 2DP
Tel *01722 335657*
w stannshouse.co.uk
Four-star Georgian house with cathedral views. Close to train station. Large breakfast menu.

STUDLAND: The Pig on the Beach ££
Boutique
Manor House, Manor Rd, Dorset, BH19 3AU
Tel *01929 450288*
w thepighotel.com
Country-house hotel with great views, beautiful furnishings, a restaurant and spa treatments.

TISBURY: The Beckford Arms ££
B&B
8-10 Fonthill Gifford, Wiltshire, SP3 6PX
Tel *01747 870385*
w beckfordarms.com
Stylish traditional pub with simple bedrooms and two larger lodges. Close to Stonehenge.

WELLS: The Crown at Wells £
B&B
Market Place, Somerset, BA5 2RP
Tel *01749 673457*
w crownatwells.co.uk
A 15th-century coaching inn with four-poster beds and a characterful pub. Family rooms.

Devon and Cornwall

BABBACOMBE BEACH: The Cary Arms £££
Boutique
South Devon, TQ1 3LX
Tel *01803 327110*
w caryarms.co.uk
Beachfront hotel with New England striped linen, gastropub food and activities for kids.

BARNSTAPLE: Broomhill Art Hotel ££
Designer
Muddiford, North Devon, EX31 4EX
Tel *01271 850262*
w broomhillart.co.uk
Six-room hotel in a modern sculpture park. Weekend rates include breakfast and dinner.

BIGBURY-ON-SEA: Burgh Island £££
Luxury
South Devon, TQ7 4BG
Tel *01548 810514*
w burghisland.com
Art Deco hotel on its own private island accessible by water tractor. A favourite of Agatha Christie.

BODMIN MOOR: Ekopod ££
Character
St Clether, Launceston, Cornwall, PL15 8QJ
Tel *01566 880248*
w ekopod.co.uk
Four eco-friendly pods, each sleeping two, with kitchen and bathroom. Minimum three nights.

BOSCASTLE: The Old Rectory ££
Historic
St Juliot, Cornwall, PL35 0BT
Tel *01840 250225*
w stjuliot.com
Victorian house where Thomas Hardy once stayed, with green credentials and lovely gardens. Breakfast eggs from the hens.

DK Choice

CAMELFORD: Belle Tents ££
Family
Owl's Gate, Davidstow, Cornwall, PL32 9XY
Tel *01840 261556*
w belletentscamping.co.uk
This cluster of candy-coloured luxury tents in a private dell near Tintagel is a great base for a family holiday with a twist. Tents have beds and kitchens in wooden sheds, and there is a fire pit and shared bar tent for the evening. Open May to September only, with a two-night minimum stay.

CHAGFORD: Gidleigh Park £££
Luxury
Devon, TQ13 8HH
Tel *01647 432367*
w gidleigh.co.uk
Tudor-house hotel famed for fine dining. Spa suites available. A river flows through the gardens.

CHILLINGTON: The White House £££
Boutique
Devon, TA7 2JX
Tel *01548 580505*
w whitehousedevon.com
Georgian house near the coast, with slow suppers, croquet on the lawn and modern luxury rooms.

CLOVELLY: The Red Lion ££
Rooms with a view
The Quay, Devon, EX39 5TF
Tel *01237 431237*
w stayatclovelly.co.uk
This seaside hotel overlooking the ancient harbour has rooms in marine colours and offers in-room spa treatments.

DARTMOOR: Bovey Castle £££
Luxury
North Bovey, Dartmoor National Park, Devon, TQ13 8RE
Tel *08444 740077*
w boveycastle.com
This is a large castle hotel with lavish furnishings, a golf course and spa. Great views to the Moor.

FOWEY: The Old Ferry Inn ££
Rooms with a view
Bodinnick, Cornwall, PL23 1LX
Tel *01726 870237*
w oldferryinn.co.uk
This welcoming 17th-century inn near the Bodinnick/Fowey river crossing offers hearty meals.

FOWEY: The Old Quay House ££
Rooms with a view
28 Fore St, Cornwall, PL23 1AQ
Tel *01726 833302*
w theoldquayhouse.com
Modern boutique hotel overlooking boats on the estuary. Great terrace at the back.

The beautifully situated Howard's House Hotel, Salisbury

HONITON: The Pig at Combe ££
Boutique
Gittisham, Devon, EX14 3AD
Tel *01404 540400*
W thepighotel.com
An Elizabethan mansion in a lush
valley with beautifully furnished
rooms and three cottages.

LIFTON: The Arundell Arms ££
Luxury
1 Fore St, Devon, PL16 0AA
Tel *01566 784666*
W arundellarms.com
Country hotel ideal for fishing
and shooting. Self-catering
cottages are also available.

**MAWGAN PORTH: Bedruthan
Steps** ££
Family
Trenance, Cornwall, TR8 4BU
Tel *01637 860860*
W bedruthan.com
Bright and colourful hotel with
a great café, beach and superb
family facilities.

DK Choice

**MAWGAN PORTH:
The Scarlet** £££
Rooms with a view
Tredragon Rd, Cornwall, TR8 4DQ
Tel *01637 861800*
W scarlethotel.co.uk
This luxury hotel overlooking
the sands of Mawgan Porth is
the UK's first five star eco hotel.
Enjoy cream teas, cider and spa
facilities, including a seaweed
hot-tub experience. No children.

**MOUSEHOLE: The Old
Coastguard Hotel** ££
Rooms with a view
The Parade, Cornwall, TR19 6PR
Tel *01736 731222*
W oldcoastguardhotel.co.uk
Seaside hotel in an old fishing
village: 15 traditional rooms with
glorious sea views.

**MULLION: The Polurrian Bay
Hotel** ££
Family
Polurrian Bay, Cornwall, TR12 7EN
Tel *01326 240421*
W polurrianhotel.com
Family-friendly hotel overlooking
the sea. Crèche, spa, cinema room,
tennis court and indoor pool.

**NEWQUAY: Watergate Bay
Hotel** £££
Boutique
Watergate Bay, Cornwall, TR8 4AA
Tel *01637 860543*
W watergatebay.co.uk
Large contemporary hotel facing
the Atlantic, with an infinity
pool and lots of beach events

**PENZANCE: The Artist
Residence** ££
B&B
20 Chapel St, Cornwall, TR18 4AW
Tel *01736 365664*
W arthotelcornwall.co.uk
Fun and hip guesthouse in a
Georgian mansion with bright
art on the walls. Conveniently
close to the seafront.

PENZANCE: The Cove £££
Boutique
*Lamorna Cove, Cornwall,
TR19 6XH*
Tel *01736 731411*
W thecovecornwall.com
The eight self-catering boutique
apartments here are centred
around a pool.

ROCK: St Enodoc's £££
Boutique
Rock, Cornwall, PL27 6LA
Tel *01208 863394*
W enodoc-hotel.co.uk
A relaxed hotel overlooking
the Camel estuary. There are
Cornish paintings on the walls
and a restaurant on the terrace.

SALCOMBE: South Sands £££
Rooms with a view
Bolt Head, Devon, TQ8 8LL
Tel *01548 845900*
W southsands.com
This beachfront boutique hotel
offers estuary views and is well
placed for guests who wish to
explore South Devon.

**SAUNTON:
Saunton Sands Hotel** £££
Family
Braunton, North Devon, EX33 1LQ
Tel *01271 890 212*
W sauntonsands.co.uk
Classic family hotel overlooking
Saunton's sand dunes. Baby-
sitting is available, along with a
playroom and surfing lessons.

ST IVES: Headland House ££
B&B
*Headland Rd, Carbis Bay, Cornwall,
TR26 2NS*
Tel *01736 79664*
W headlandhousehotel.co.uk
Soothing nautical colours and
super-king-size beds feature in
this Edwardian house with sea
views, a garden and a snug bar.

ST MAWES: Hotel Tresanton £££
Luxury
*27 Lower Castle Rd, Cornwall,
TR2 5DR*
Tel *01326 270055*
W tresanton.com
Super-glamorous hotel over-
looking the sea. There are thirty
rooms in addition to two small
cottages on the grounds.

Estuary view of the picturesque Old Quay
House, Fowey

TAVISTOCK: Hotel Endsleigh £££
Luxury
Milton Abbot, Devon, PL19 0PQ
Tel *01822 870000*
W hotelendsleigh.com
Former hunting and fishing
lodge set in Repton-designed
gardens. Country chic interiors.

ZENNOR: The Gurnard's Head ££
Boutique
Near Zennor, Cornwall, TR26 3DE
Tel *01736 796920*
W gurnardshead.co.uk
Gastropub with rooms in a wild
and exciting spot. The Sunday
Sleepover includes Sunday
lunch, dinner and breakfast.

The Heart of England

BIRMINGHAM: La Tour ££
Boutique
Albert St, West Midlands, B5 5JE
Tel *0121 718 8000*
W hotel-latour.co.uk
Sleek and classy hotel with
executive rooms and suites and
Marco Pierre White's sparkling
Chophouse restaurant.

**BOURTON-ON-THE-WATER:
Cranbourne House** ££
B&B
*Moore Rd, Cheltenham,
Gloucestershire, GL54 2AZ*
Tel *01451 821883*
W cranbournehousebandb.co.uk
A Cotswolds stone house
featuring rain showers, antique
French beds and a lounge
with log fire.

CHELTENHAM: The Bradley £
Boutique
*19 Royal Parade, Bayshill Rd,
GL50 3AY*
Tel *01242 519077*
W thebradleyhotel.co.uk
Family-run Regency town house.
Antique furnished rooms with
contemporary comforts

For more information on types of hotels *see pages 556–7*

Outdoor tables in a lovely riverside garden at Edgar House, a deluxe hotel in Chester

CHELTENHAM: Number 4 at Stow ££
Boutique
Fosseway, Stow-on-the-Wold, Gloucestershire, GL54 1JX
Tel *01451 830297*
W hotelnumberfour.co.uk
Housed in a 1500s building with flagstone floors, oak beams and pine beds. Home-baked goodies.

CHESTER: Edgar House £££
Luxury
22 City Walls, CH1 1SB
Tel *01244 347007*
W edgarhouse.co.uk
Fine Georgian house right on the city walls overlooking the river, with sumptuous rooms.

COVENTRY: Coombe Abbey Hotel ££
Historic
Brinklow Rd, Warwickshire, CV3 2AB
Tel *024 7645 0450*
W coombeabbey.com
Set in a 12th-century former abbey amid parkland, gardens and a lake. Superb antiques inside.

HEREFORD: Castle House ££
Luxury
Castle St, HR1 2NW
Tel *01432 356321*
W castlehse.co.uk
Castle House offers individually styled rooms in a Georgian mansion and nearby townhouse.

IRONBRIDGE: Library House £
Historic
11 Severn Bank, Telford, TF8 7AN
Tel *01952 432299*
W libraryhouse.com
Next to the iconic Iron Bridge, this is the former village library with three rooms and pretty gardens.

MALVERN: Cannara B&B £
B&B
147 Barnards Green Rd, WR14 3LT
Tel *01684 564418*
W cannara.co.uk
Large Victorian house with four intimate rooms, some affording lovely views of the Malvern Hills.

MORETON-IN-MARSH: Manor House ££
Character
High St, GL56 0LJ
Tel *01608 650501*
W cotswold-inns-hotels.co.uk
Lovely conversion of a 16th-century coaching inn. Smart rooms overlook walled gardens.

DK Choice

PAINSWICK: Cardynham House ££
Historic
Tibbiwell St, Gloucestershire, GL6 6XX
Tel *01452 814006*
W cardynham.co.uk
All the beamed rooms in this 16th-century wool merchant's house have individual character and four-poster beds. Arabian Nights is red and sultry, Dovecote crisp and white. The Pool Room comes with a private pool.

ROSS-ON-WYE: Norton House £
B&B
Old Monmouth Rd, Whitchurch, Herefordshire, HR9 6DJ
Tel *01600 890046*
W norton-house.com
Traditional rooms offer old-fashioned charm and thoughtful touches like fresh fruit and flowers.

SHREWSBURY: Old House Suites £
Historic
20 Dogpole, Shropshire, SY1 1ES
Tel *07813 610904*
W theoldhousesuites.com
Two suites in a half-timbered 1480 building. Log fires in rooms and breakfast in the library.

STRATFORD-UPON-AVON: Twelfth Night Guesthouse £
B&B
13 Evesham Place, Warwickshire, CV37 6HT
Tel *01789 414595*
W twelfthnight.co.uk
Victorian villa with bright rooms. A short walk from Royal Shakespeare Company theatres.

WORCESTER: Holland House £
B&B
210 London Rd, WR5 2JT
Tel *01905 353939*
W holland-house.me.uk
Victorian terraced house in the centre of the city, with well-equipped rooms. Friendly service and quality breakfasts.

East Midlands

BAKEWELL: Hassop Hall Hotel ££
Luxury
Hassop Rd, Derbyshire, DE45 1NS
Tel *01629 640488*
W hassophallhotel.co.uk
Historic hotel in picturesque village of Hassop with comfortable rooms and gardens.

BUXTON: Griff House Bed & Breakfast £
B&B
2 Compton Rd, Derbyshire, SK17 9DN
Tel *01298 23628*
W griffhousebuxton.co.uk
Late-Victorian property with bright rooms. Breakfast includes homemade bread.

LINCOLN: The Castle Hotel ££
Boutique
Westgate, Lincolnshire, LN1 3AS
Tel *01522 538801*
W castlehotel.net
Designer rooms and bathrooms with drench showers and full-size bathtubs. A luxury apartment too.

DK Choice

MATLOCK: Glendon Guesthouse £
B&B
7 Knowleston Place, Derbyshire, DE4 3BU
Tel *01629 584732*
W glendonbandb.co.uk
This welcoming guesthouse has four-poster, double, twin and family en-suite rooms, and a lounge with views of Knowleston Gardens. Luxury touches include Egyptian cotton linen and towels. Home-made sausages and free-range eggs feature on the breakfast menu. Little touches throughout make this extra-special.

NOTTINGHAM: Mama's Inn £
Boutique
124–126 Mansfield Rd, NG1 3HL
Tel *0115 779 9262*
W mamasinn.co.uk
Occupying two Victorian villas, Mama's is both opulent and eccentric – one room even has a telephone-booth wardrobe.

Sunny outdoor terrace at the Bridge Hotel, Buttermere

STAMFORD: The Bull & Swan £
Boutique
St Martins, Lincolnshire, PE9 2LJ
Tel *01780 766412*
W thebullandswan.co.uk
Historic and charming inn with chic rooms, local ales and great pub food.

Lancashire and the Lakes

AMBLESIDE: Waterhead £££
Boutique
Waterhead, Cumbria, LA22 0ER
Tel *08458 504503*
W englishlakes.co.uk
Situated on the shores of Lake Windermere, this town house hotel has an on-site restaurant serving modern regional food.

ARMATHWAITE: Drybeck Farm £
Character
Cumbria, CA4 9ST
Tel *07854 523012*
W drybeckfarm.co.uk
Experience "glamping" in traditional Mongolian yurts or a gypsy caravan on this working farm.

BLACKPOOL: The Kenley £
B&B
29 St Chads Rd, Cumbria, FY1 6BP
Tel *01253 346447*
W kenleyhotel.co.uk
Boutique B&B with contemporary kitsch styling. Breakfast includes local black pudding.

BORROWDALE: Borrowdale Gates Hotel £
Rooms with a view
Grange, Cumbria, CA12 5UQ
Tel *08458 332524*
W borrowdale-gates.com
Victorian country house in the hamlet of Grange with fell views and wooded grounds.

BOWNESS-ON-WINDERMERE: Linthwaite House ££
Rooms with a view
Crook Rd, Cumbria, LA23 3JA
Tel *01539 488600*
W linthwaite.com
Views of Windermere and the fells are one of the highlights at this swish country-house hotel. Stylish rooms and fine dining.

BUTTERMERE: Bridge Hotel ££
Rooms with a view
Cumbria, CA13 9UZ
Tel *01768 770252*
W bridge-hotel.com
Set in the rolling hills of the Lake District, this splendid stone hotel has cheery, floral-themed rooms and two bars.

COCKERMOUTH: Six Castlegate £
B&B
6 Castlegate, Cumbria, CA13 9EU
Tel *01900 826786*
W sixcastlegate.co.uk
This refurbished Georgian town house features simple but smart rooms with luxury towels and linen.

CONISTON: Bank Ground Farm £
Family
East of the Lake, Cumbria, LA21 8AA
Tel *01539 441264*
W bankground.com
Lakefront farm with a 15th-century B&B and self-catering cottages. Idyllic views.

GRANGE OVER SANDS: Broughton House £
B&B
Field Broughton, Cumbria, LA11 6HN
Tel *01539 536439*
W broughtonhousecartmel.co.uk
Pick from cosy bedrooms in the B&B or try "glamping" in a yurt with an accompanying cabin.

GRASMERE: Grasmere Hotel ££
Rooms with a view
Broadgate, Cumbria, LA22 9TA
Tel *01539 435277*
W grasmerehotel.co.uk
A refurbished Victorian country house with comfortable, stylish rooms and great views of the surrounding countryside.

IREBY: Overwater Hall ££
Luxury
Cumbria, CA7 1HH
Tel *01768 776566*
W overwaterhall.co.uk
An 18th-century country house with sprawling gardens and woodland, and opulent rooms with floral furnishings.

KENDAL: Crosthwaite House £
Rooms with a view
Crosthwaite, Cumbria, LA8 8BP
Tel *01539 568264*
W crosthwaitehouse.co.uk
Bright rooms and a spacious lounge at this pretty B&B. Self-catering cottages also available.

KESWICK: Oakthwaite House £
B&B
35 Helvellyn St, Cumbria, CA12 4EP
Tel *01768 772398*
W oakthwaite-keswick.com
Late Victorian stone town house in a quiet neighbourhood. Tasteful rooms and views of crags and fells.

LANCASTER: The Stork Inn £
Boutique
Corricks Lane, Conder Green, LA2 0AN
Tel *01524 751234*
W thestorkinn.com
Whitewashed country inn with attractive rooms, tasty traditional food and good real ales.

LIVERPOOL: The Nadler ££
Boutique
29 Seel St, L1 4AU
Tel *0151 7052626*
W base2stay.com
Boldly styled rooms in the UNESCO-protected RopeWalks area. Good value and service.

MANCHESTER: Didsbury House ££
Luxury
Didsbury Park, Didsbury, M20 5LJ
Tel *0161 4482200*
W eclectichotels.co.uk
Victorian villa in leafy suburb of Didsbury with comfortable, individually styled rooms.

MORECAMBE: Yacht Bay View Hotel £
Rooms with a view
359 Marine Rd, Lancashire, LA4 5AQ
Tel *01524 414481*
W yachtbay.co.uk
Located on Morecambe's promenade. Superior doubles and singles have sea views.

Typical double bedroom at the Waterhead hotel, Ambleside

For more information on types of hotels *see pages 556–7*

ULLSWATER: Rampsbeck Country House Hotel £££
Luxury
Watermillock, Cumbria, CA11 0LP
Tel *01768 486442*
W rampsbeck.co.uk
Antique-bedecked bedrooms in this country house dating from the 1700s.

WASDALE HEAD: Wasdale Head Inn ££
Historic
Gosforth, Cumbria, CA20 1EX
Tel *01946 726229*
W wasdale.com
Famous walkers' inn beside England's highest peak and deepest lake. Well-worn and welcoming, with hearty food.

DK Choice

WINDERMERE: Gilpin Lodge £££
Luxury
Crook Rd, LA23 3NE
Tel *01539 488818*
W thegilpin.co.uk
This supremely stylish hotel combines a warm welcome with haute cuisine and contemporary comforts. The garden suites make the most of the sylvan environs, while other rooms are located in the venerable old lodge itself.

WINDERMERE: Holbeck Ghyll £££
Luxury
Holbeck Lane, Cumbria, LA23 1LU
Tel *01539 432375*
W holbeckghyll.com
Luxurious country-house hotel with lake and fell views, a superb gourmet restaurant and a spa.

Yorkshire and the Humber Region

AMPLEFORTH: Shallowdale House £££
Rooms with a view
North Yorkshire, YO62 4DY
Tel *01439 788325*
W shallowdalehouse.co.uk
Award-winning 1960s B&B overlooking the countryside. Traditional floral decor.

BRADFORD: Dubrovnik Hotel £
Boutique
3 Oak Ave, West Yorkshire, BD8 7AQ
Tel *01274 543511*
W dubrovnik.co.uk
Former mill owner's home in leafy suburbs. Family-run and has great weekend deals.

The pretty Ivy-clad exterior of Holdsworth House, Halifax

GUISBOROUGH: Gisborough Hall £
Country House
Whitby Lane, North Yorkshire, TS14 6PT
Tel *08448 799149*
W macdonaldhotels.co.uk
A grand, ivy-clad Victorian mansion. Some rooms have four-poster beds, others roll-top baths.

HALIFAX: Holdsworth House ££
Country House
Holdsworth Rd, West Yorkshire, HX2 9TG
Tel *01422 240024*
W holdsworthhouse.co.uk
Jacobean manor with some period rooms. Breakfast made with locally sourced produce.

HARROGATE: The Grafton ££
Boutique
Franklin Mt, North Yorkshire, HG1 5EJ
Tel *01423 508491*
W graftonhotel.co.uk
Historic hotel stylishly refurbished in red and black. Range of luxurious rooms and suites.

HELMSLEY: Feversham Arms ££
Luxury
1–8 High St, North Yorkshire, YO62 5AG
Tel *01439 770766*
W fevershamarmshotel.com
Former coaching inn with individually styled rooms, a swimming pool and a spa. Excellent gourmet food.

LEEDS: Malmaison Leeds £
Character
1 Swine Gate, West Yorkshire, LS1 4AG
Tel *0844 693 0654*
W malmaison-leeds.com
Sophisticated bar, brasserie and 100 funky rooms and suites in the city's former tramways office.

PICKERING: White Swan ££
Country House
Market Pl, North Yorkshire, YO18 7AA
Tel *01751 472288*
W white-swan.co.uk
Old-fashioned inn with fireplaces and real ales. Choose from "treat", "vintage" and "hideaway" rooms.

SCARBOROUGH: Wrea Head Country House Hotel £££
Country House
Barmoor Lane, Scalby, North Yorkshire, YO13 0PB
Tel *01723 371190*
W wreaheadhall.co.uk
Mock-Tudor Victorian house with panelled rooms and roll-top baths. Popular restaurant.

WHITBY: Broom House ££
Country House
Broom House Lane, Egton Bridge, YO21 1XD
Tel *01947 895279*
W egton-bridge.co.uk
Good base for exploring the North York moors. Comfortable, modern rooms.

YARM: Judges Country House Hotel ££
Luxury
Kirklevington Hall, Cleveland, North Yorkshire, TS15 9LW
Tel *01642 789000*
W judgeshotel.co.uk
Glorious country mansion with bags of Victorian charm. Period rooms are fitted with modern amenities.

DK Choice

YORK: Middlethorpe Hall £££
Luxury
Bishopthorpe Rd, Yorkshire, YO23 2GB
Tel *01904 641241*
W middlethorpe.com
Superb mansion built in 1699 amid acres of manicured gardens and mature parkland. Antiques and artworks abound in ten bedrooms in the house and 19 in cottages around the stable block. Guests can dine in a beautiful panelled dining room.

Northumbria

CROOKHAM: Coach House £
B&B
Cornhill-on-Tweed, Northumberland, TD12 4TD
Tel *01890 820293*
W coachhousecrookham.com
Pleasant, comfortable rooms in a complex of renovated 17th-century farm buildings.

DARLINGTON: Headlam Hall   ££
Country House
Headlam, County Durham, DL2 3HA
Tel *01325 730790*
Ⓦ headlamhall.co.uk
Grand 17th-century mansion with impressive spa. Some rooms have private balconies.

HEXHAM: Battlesteads Hotel   ££
Character
Wark on Tyne, Northumberland, NE48 3LS
Tel *01434 230209*
Ⓦ battlesteads.com
Pleasant, family-friendly hotel and restaurant. Real ales and a seven-course menu using local and home-grown ingredients.

MORPETH: Macdonald Linden Hall Golf & Country Club   ££
Country House
Longhorsley, Northumberland, NE65 8XF
Tel *08448 799084*
Ⓦ macdonaldhotels.co.uk/linden
Large country house surrounded by private grounds. Spa, health club and 18-hole golf course.

DK Choice

NEWCASTLE UPON TYNE: Hotel du Vin   ££
Boutique
City Rd, Northumberland, NE1 2BE
Tel *00447 304259*
Ⓦ hotelduvin.com/newcastle
This friendly, stylish hotel on the banks of the River Tyne has 42 imaginatively crafted rooms with stunning bathrooms and great views. There is a bistro and wine-tasting room, as well as a courtyard for alfresco dining.

North Wales

BEAUMARIS: Ye Olde Bull's Head Inn and Townhouse   ££
Character
Castle St, Isle of Anglesey, LL58 8AP
Tel *01248 810329*
Ⓦ bullsheadinn.co.uk
A 15th-century inn with a prized restaurant. Cheerful and modern bedrooms in the town house.

BEDDGELERT: Sygun Fawr   £
Country House
Rooms with a view
Gwynedd, LL55 4NE
Tel *01766 890258*
Ⓦ sygunfawr.co.uk
Rural 17th-century manor house with oak beams and fireplaces. Superb on-site restaurant.

Enjoy afternoon tea in the drawing room at Bodysgallen Hall, Llandudno

HARLECH: Gwrach Ynys   £
B&B
Ynys, Talsarnau, Gwynedd, LL47 6TS
Tel *01766 781199*
Ⓦ gwrachynys.co.uk
Quiet guesthouse overlooking Snowdonia National Park. Cosy, modern bedrooms.

LLANABER: Llwyndu Farmhouse   ££
Country House
Barmouth, Gwynedd, LL42 1RR
Tel *01341 280144*
Ⓦ llwyndu-farmhouse.co.uk
Retaining its 17th-century charm, this farmhouse offers fine wines and local beers – and spectacular views of the bay.

LLANDUDNO: Bodysgallen Hall   ££
Luxury
Conwy, Gwynedd, LL30 1RS
Tel *01492 584466*
Ⓦ bodysgallen.com
Set in a 17th-century walled garden with an award-winning restaurant and bistro. Superb spa.

LLANGOLLEN: The Wild Pheasant Hotel   £
Family
Berwyn Rd, Denbighshire, LL20 8AD
Tel *01978 860629*
Ⓦ wildpheasanthotel.co.uk
Charming historic rural inn with a spa. Terrific dining options and plenty of activities nearby.

DK Choice

PENMAENPOOL: Penmaenuchaf Hall   £££
Country House
Dolgellau, Gwynedd, LL40 1YB
Tel *01341 422129*
Ⓦ penhall.co.uk
Delightful Victorian house with 8 ha (20 acres) of landscaped gardens, an oak panelled restaurant, a library, drawing room and a morning room for guests to relax in. Mountain-biking, fishing, walking, golf and cycling excursions are available as well.

PORTMEIRION: Portmeirion   ££
Character
Gwynedd, LL48 6ER
Tel *01766 770000*
Ⓦ portmeirion-village.com
A fantasy village built by Clough Williams-Ellis. Elegantly decorated rooms, some with sea views.

RUTHIN: Ruthin Castle Hotel   ££
Historic
Denbighshire, LL15 2NU
Tel *01824 702664*
Ⓦ ruthincastle.co.uk
Luxurious 13th-century castle with opulent bedrooms and a spa in the woodlands.

South and Mid-Wales

ABERGAVENNY: Angel Hotel   £
Character
15 Cross St, NP7 5EN
Tel *01873 857121*
Ⓦ angelabergavenny.com
This old coaching inn now keeps plush rooms. It is renowned for its afternoon teas.

ABERYSTWYTH: Gwesty Cymru   £
Boutique
19 Marine Terrace, SY23 2AZ
Tel *01970 612252*
Ⓦ gwestycymru.com
Modern twist on traditional Welsh boarding house. The stylish rooms have oak and slate furnishings.

CARDIFF: St David's Hotel & Spa   ££
Luxury
Havannah St, CF10 5SD
Tel *02920 454045*
Ⓦ thestdavidshotel.com
Luxury spa hotel with large, comfortable rooms, many with private decks overlooking the bay.

CRICKHOWELL: Gliffaes Country House   ££
Country House
Powys, NP8 1RH
Tel *01874 730371*
Ⓦ gliffaeshotel.com
Victorian house with period rooms giving views of the gardens.

For more information on types of hotels *see pages 556–7*

DK Choice

LLANTHONY: Llanthony Priory £
Historic
Monmouthshire, NP7 7NN
Tel *01873 890487*
🆆 llanthonyprioryhotel.co.uk
Rooms in this ruined 12th-century Augustinian priory are off a stone spiral staircase. It's a great base for walking the Black Mountains and the vaulted undercroft bar serves real ale. There's a minimum two-night stay and bathrooms are shared.

ST DAVIDS: The Waterings £
B&B
Anchor Drive, Pembrokeshire, SA62 6BW
Tel *01437 720876*
🆆 waterings.co.uk
A strong maritime theme runs through this ex-marine research centre with en-suite bathrooms.

TENBY: Fourcroft Hotel ££
Family
North Beach, Pembrokeshire, SA70 8AP
Tel *01834 842886*
🆆 fourcroft-hotel.co.uk
Smart rooms overlook the old fishing harbour here, and there's an on-site restaurant and bar.

TINTERN: Parva Farmhouse Guesthouse £
Rooms with a view
Chepstow, Monmouthshire, NP16 6SQ
Tel *01291 689411*
🆆 parvafarmhouse.co.uk
Stone farmhouse and restaurant on the banks of River Wye. Cosy lounge and comfortable rooms.

The Lowlands

DUNDEE: Apex City Quay Hotel & Spa £
Rooms with a view
1 West Victoria Dock Rd, DD1 3JP
Tel *08453 650000*
🆆 apexhotels.co.uk
The best hotel in Dundee sits on the waterfront. Modern rooms, some with views of the River Tay.

EDINBURGH: Classic Guesthouse ££
B&B
50 Mayfield Rd, EH9 2NH
Tel *01316 675847*
🆆 classicguesthouse.co.uk
Comfortably furnished Victorian house. Free Wi-Fi and full Scottish breakfast with vegetarian options available.

EDINBURGH: Dalhousie Castle Hotel £££
Historic
Bonnyrigg, EH19 3JB
Tel *01875 820153*
🆆 dalhousiecastle.co.uk
Experience a night in a castle at this 14th-century hotel. The on-site restaurant is excellent, and there is also a health spa.

GLASGOW: Malmaison ££
Boutique
278 W George St, G2 4LL
Tel *01415 721000*
🆆 malmaison.com
This former church in the heart of Glasgow is now part of a trendy hotel chain. Efficient, welcoming and central.

GLASGOW: Cameron House £££
Country House
Loch Lomond, G83 8QZ
Tel *08712 224681*
🆆 cameronhouse.co.uk
Grand rooms with stunning loch views. There is also a great spa, golf and attentive service. Guests can arrive by seaplane.

DK Choice

GLASGOW: Hotel du Vin at One Devonshire Gardens £££
Boutique
One Devonshire Gardens, G12 0UX
Tel *08447 364256*
🆆 hotelduvin.com
Housed in a quintet of Victorian town houses, this hotel emphasizes opulence, from its spacious and unique rooms through to the whisky bar and restaurant. Service is impeccable.

PEEBLES: Cringletie House ££
Country House
Edinburgh Rd, EH45 8PL
Tel *01721 725750*
🆆 cringletie.com
This country castle set in vast grounds exudes traditional luxury. Great service, and dog-friendly.

PERTH: Parklands ££
Rooms with a view
2 St Leonard's Bank, Perthshire, PH2 8EB
Tel *01738 622451*
🆆 theparklandshotel.com
Smart, simple en-suite rooms with park views. Fine dining and informal bistro.

ST ANDREWS: Old Course Hotel £££
Luxury
Fife, KY16 9SP
Tel *01334 474371*
🆆 oldcoursehotel.co.uk
One of the world's top golf hotels overlooks the celebrated course. Excellent food, service and spa.

STIRLING: The Stirling Highland Hotel ££
Family
Spittal St, Stirlingshire, FK8 1DU
Tel *01786 272727*
🆆 stirlinghighlandhotel.co.uk
Well-presented bedrooms with modern decor. Less than a mile away from Stirling Castle.

The Highlands and Islands

ABERDEEN: Malmaison Aberdeen £
Boutique
49–53 Queens Rd, Aberdeenshire, AB15 4YP
Tel *08446 930649*
🆆 malmaison.com
This is another great branch of the hotel chain, boasting spacious rooms with big bathrooms and well-stocked mini bars.

ACHILTIBUIE: Summer Isles Hotel ££
Rooms with a view
Ross-shire, IV26 2YG
Tel *01854 622282*
🆆 summerisleshotel.co.uk
Romantic hideaway with views over the Summer Isles and the Hebrides. Elegant en-suite rooms. Seafood restaurant.

The cosy restaurant in the Parva Farmhouse Guesthouse, Tintern

Key to Price Guide *see page 560*

ARDEONAIG: Ardeonaig
Hotel & Restaurant   ££
Luxury
Near Killin, South of Loch Tay, FK21 8SU
Tel *01567 820351*
w ardeonaighotel.co.uk
Historic inn with comfortable
rooms, African-style luxury huts
and cottage suites.

ARDUAINE: Loch Melfort
Hotel & Restaurant   £££
Rooms with a view
Oban, Argyll, PA34 4XG
Tel *01852 200233*
w lochmelfort.co.uk
Beautiful and peaceful three-star
hotel with views of the west coast.
Standard but spotless rooms.

ARISAIG: Old Library
Lodge & Restaurant   ££
Character
Inverness-shire, PH39 4NH
Tel *01687 450651*
w oldlibrary.co.uk
A well-run B&B and restaurant
in 200-year-old stables; right on
the waterfront.

AVIEMORE: Macdonald
Aviemore Highland Resort   ££
Character
Inverness-shire, PH22 1PN
Tel *0844 8799152*
w macdonaldhotels.co.uk
Four hotels and 18 wooden
lodges for all budgets. Pool,
restaurants and a 3D cinema.

BARRA: Castlebay Hotel   £
Rooms with a view
Castlebay, HS9 5XD
Tel *01871 810223*
w castlebay-hotel.co.uk
Charming hotel with pleasant
en-suite rooms. Lovely views of
Kisimul Castle and Vatersay Island.

COLL: Coll Hotel   ££
Rooms with a view
Ariangour, PA78 6SZ
Tel *01879 230334*
w collhotel.com
Well-appointed lochside hotel
with epic views of the Treshnish
Isles, Staffa, Iona and Jura.

DK Choice

ERISKA: Isle of Eriska Hotel,
Spa & Island   ££
Luxury
Benderloch, Argyll, PA37 1SD
Tel *01631 720371*
w eriska-hotel.co.uk
An enchanting country house
on a private island with grand
bedrooms and fine dining. Self-
catering lodging is also on offer.
Badgers roam the grounds, and
seals swim in the nearby waters.

The harbourside Plockton Inn & Seafood Restaurant, Plockton

DUNKELD: Royal Hotel   £
Historic
Atholl St, Perthshire, PH8 0AR
Tel *01350 727322*
w royaldunkeld.co.uk
The Royal is a good-value hotel
with simple rooms. Built around
1815, it maintains traditional
decor and furnishings.

FORT AUGUSTUS:
The Lovat   ££
Family
Inverness-shire, PH32 4DU
Tel *01456 490000*
w thelovat.com
Relaxed, eco-friendly accommodation is offered here, on the
southern tip of Loch Ness. Good
for families.

FORT WILLIAM: Inverlochy
Castle   £££
Luxury
Torlundy, Perthshire, PH33 6SN
Tel *01397 702177*
w inverlochycastlehotel.com
This is one of Scotland's finest
luxury hotels, decked out
with antiques. Boasts Queen
Victoria as a former guest.

INVERNESS: Beach
Cottage B&B   £
B&B
3 Alturlie Point, Inverness, IV2 7HZ
Tel *01463 237506*
w beachcottageinverness.co.uk
Watch dolphins swimming in the
Moray Firth from this renovated
18th-century fisherman's cottage.
The breakfasts are made using
local produce.

MULL: Highland Cottage   ££
Luxury
*24 Breadalbane St, Tobermory,
Argyll, PA75 6PD*
Tel *01688 302030*
w highlandcottage.co.uk
Individually styled, luxuriously
furbished rooms can be found
at Highland Cottage. Innovative
modern Scottish cuisine is served
in the restaurant.

ORKNEY ISLANDS:
The Foveran   ££
Family
Kirkwall, St Ola, KW15 1SFUK
Tel *01856 872389*
w foveranhotel.co.uk
The Foveran is a family-run
restaurant that also offers B&B
accommodation. The rooms are
pretty, with en-suite bathrooms.

PITLOCHRY: East Haugh
Country House Hotel &
Restaurant   ££
B&B
Pitlochry, Perthshire, PH16 5TE
Tel *01796 473121*
w easthaugh.co.uk
This family-run hotel offers
comfortable rooms with lush
fabrics and period features.
Restaurant on site.

PLOCKTON: Plockton Inn &
Seafood Restaurant   ££
Rooms with a view
Innes St, Ross-shire, IV52 8TW
Tel *01599 544222*
w plocktoninn.co.uk
Traditional inn with tasteful
bedrooms (some with stunning
sea views). Great dinners to be
had in the restaurant.

SHETLAND ISLANDS:
Skeoverick   £
B&B
Tingwall, ZE2 9SE
Tel *01595 840403*
w valleybandb.co.uk
Welcoming B&B in a quiet
countryside location, just a
20-minute drive from Lerwick.
Spacious en-suite rooms and
great breakfasts.

SPEYSIDE: Craigellachie   £
Country House
Victoria St, Banffshire, AB38 9SR
Tel *01479 841641*
w craigellachieguesthouse.co.uk
Delightful country house in a
riverside location. Be sure to make
use of the superb restaurant and
the Quaich whisky bar.

WHERE TO EAT AND DRINK

Great Britain's restaurant scene is booming. Gastropubs, street wagons, Michelin-starred restaurants and designer beach cafés, as well as a wave of celebrity chefs, are all making eating out in the UK a mouthwatering prospect. British chefs are today among the most innovative in the world, and national recipes – in the best cases using local and seasonal produce, along with foraged fruit, vegetables and herbs – are worth trying. Modern approaches combine fresh ingredients with influences from around the world. Pub fare has perhaps undergone the greatest transformation, with a wide variety of food found in all kinds of pubs. Gastropubs in particular focus on quality cuisine. On any budget, it is possible to eat well at most times of day in the larger towns. Less elaborate but well-prepared, affordable food is available in all types of restaurants and cafés. The restaurant listings on pages 582–603 feature some of the very best places, as well as those with a reliable track record.

Types of Cuisine

The choice seems endless in large cities, particularly in London. Cuisines from all over the world are represented, including Thai, Tex-Mex, Turkish, Tuscan and Tandoori, as well as infinite variations of Indian and Italian food. There are many more less common styles of cooking, too, such as Ethiopian, Polish, Peruvian, Caribbean and Pacific Rim.

Outside the major cities the food scene is more limited, but creative cooking can be found in the most rural areas, and more and more AA-Rosette-awarded pubs and restaurants are popping up. Destination restaurants such as Le Manoir de Quat' Saisons are found outside major cities and are worth making a special pilgrimage for.

The vague term "Modern European cuisine" adopted by many restaurants disguises a diverse collection of culinary styles. The spectrum ranges from French to Asian recipes, loosely characterized by the clever use of fresh, high-quality ingredients, cooked simply with a wide range of seasonings.

Nostalgic yearnings for British food have produced a revival of hearty traditional dishes such as steak and kidney pie and treacle pudding (see p580), though "Modern British" cooking adopts a lighter, more innovative approach. The likes of celebrity chef Heston Blumenthal have encouraged an experimental, often scientific, style of cookery, with unexpected flavours and ingredients complementing each other.

Breakfast

The traditional British breakfast starts with cereal and milk, followed by bacon, eggs, sausage and tomato, perhaps with fried black pudding (see p581) in the north and Scotland. It is finished off with toast and marmalade, washed down with tea. Or you can just have black coffee and fruit juice, with a croissant or selection of pastries (continental breakfast). The price of breakfast is often included in hotel and B&B tariffs in Britain.

Lunch

The most popular lunchtime food includes sandwiches, salads, baked potatoes with fillings, and Ploughman's lunches (see p580). A traditional Sunday lunch of roast chicken, lamb, pork or beef is served in

Bibendum, offering sophisticated French cuisine in London (see p584)

The bar and dining area at Rick Stein in Poole, Dorset *(see p591)*

most pubs and many restaurants. Reasonably priced set lunches can often make dining in up-market and Michelin-starred restaurants much more affordable.

Afternoon Tea

No visitor should miss the experience of a proper British afternoon tea. Some of the most extravagant teas are offered by country-house and top London hotels, such as the Ritz or Brown's. The area that is best known for the classic "cream tea" is the West Country; these always include scones spread with clotted cream and jam. Wales, Scotland, Yorkshire and the Lake District also offer tasty teas with regional variations; in the north, a slice of apple pie or fruitcake may be served hot with a piece of Wensleydale cheese on top.

Dinner

In the evening, grander restaurants and hotels offer elaborately staged meals, sometimes billed as five or six courses (though one may be simply a sorbet, or coffee with *petits fours*). Tasting menus, which can sometimes have up to 20 courses, are a great way to sample the best a restaurant has to offer, if you have the time and budget

In comparison with much of Europe, people in the UK eat early. Dinner is typically around 8pm in restaurants and hotels, although it can be taken as early as 6pm. In smaller towns and villages, it can be difficult to find an evening meal after 10pm.

Places to Eat

Eating venues are extremely varied, with brasseries, bistros, wine bars, tearooms, tapas bars and theatre cafés competing with the more conventional cafés and restaurants. Many pubs also serve excellent food, often at reasonable prices *(see pp604–9)*. Some of the finest restaurants are located in grand hotels.

Brasseries, Cafés and Wine Bars

Cafés and brasseries are popular in Britain, often staying open all day, serving coffee, snacks and fairly simple dishes, along with a selection of beers and wines. Alcoholic drinks, however, may only be available at certain times of day. The atmosphere is usually young and urban, with decor to match.

Wine bars are similar to brasseries but with a better selection of wines, which may include English varieties *(see p164)*. Some bars have a good range of ciders and real ales as well *(see p578)*.

The outside eating area at The Winking Prawn in Salcombe, Devon *(see p593)*

Restaurants with Rooms and Hotels

Restaurants with rooms are a new breed of small establishments offering a handful of bedrooms and usually excellent food. They tend to be expensive, though the best can be unparalleled, and frequently in a rural location. Many hotel restaurants happily serve non-residents. Hotels serving a high standard of food are also included on pages 560–73.

Restaurant Etiquette

As a rule of thumb, the more expensive the restaurant, the more formal the dress code, though very few restaurants expect men to wear a jacket and tie. Call ahead to check.

A total smoking ban in public places was implemented throughout the UK in 2007. However, smoking outside is still permitted.

The vegetarian restaurant Mildreds, in London *(see p582)*

Flowers adorning the dining area at Clos Maggiore, London *(see p583)*

Alcohol

Britain's laws concerning the sale of alcohol, the "licensing laws", were once among the most restrictive in Europe. Now they are much more relaxed, with some places operating extended opening hours, especially at weekends. Some establishments, however, may only serve alcohol at set times with food. Some unlicensed restaurants operate a "Bring Your Own" policy; a corkage fee is often charged. It is illegal to sell alcohol to under-18s.

Vegetarian Food

Britain's restaurants are keen to offer vegetarian alternatives and welcome non-meat eaters. An increasing number of places serve only vegetarian meals, and most offer at least one vegetarian option. Those who want a wider choice could seek out South Indian and other restaurants that have a tradition of vegetarian cuisine.

Fast-Food and Chain Restaurants

Fast food usually costs well under £10. Apart from the ubiquitous fish and chip shop, there are many fast-food chains, as well as some more up-market

options such as Pizza Express and Zizzi. Other chains offering good-value, quality food, as well as facilities for children, include Ask, Giraffe, Byron and Leon. Budget cafés, nicknamed "greasy spoons", serve inexpensive food, often in the form of endless variations of the breakfast fry-up *(see p580)*.

Booking Ahead

It is always safer to book a table before making a special trip to a restaurant; city restaurants can be very busy, and some famous establishments can be fully booked a month or more in advance. Fridays, Saturdays and Sunday lunchtimes are particularly busy.

Softly lit dining room at Fifteen Cornwall restaurant, Newquay *(see p593)*

Checking the Bill

All restaurants are required by law to display their current prices outside the door. These amounts include Value Added Tax (VAT), currently at 20 per cent. Service and cover charges (if any) are also specified.

Wine is always pricey in Britain, and extras such as coffee or bottled water can be disproportionately expensive.

A service charge (usually 10–12.5 per cent) is often automatically added to the bill. If you feel that the service has been poor, you are entitled to subtract this service charge. If no service charge has been added, you are expected to add 10–12.5 per cent to the bill. This tip can often be added when paying with a card machine.

Look out for additional charges: some restaurants add a "cover charge" for bread and butter, and so on. Most restaurants accept credit cards.

Mealtimes

Breakfast may be as early as 6:30am in a city business hotel (most hoteliers will make special arrangements if you have to check out early for some reason) or as late as 10:30am in relaxed country-house hotels. Some hoteliers, however, insist on serving breakfast at 9am sharp. In some city restaurants it is possible to find breakfast all day. The American concept of Sunday brunch is becoming increasingly popular in more urban hotels, restaurants and cafés.

Lunch in restaurants and pubs is usually served between noon and 2:30pm. Try to arrive in time to order the main course before 1:30pm, or you may find choice restricted. Most tourist areas have plenty of cafés, fast-food outlets and coffee bars where you can have a snack at any time of day.

Traditional afternoon tea is served between 3pm and 5pm. Dinner is usually served from 6pm until 10pm; some places stay open later. In guesthouses or small hotels, dinner may be served at a specific time. In cities, restaurants are sometimes closed on Sunday evenings and on Mondays.

Children

The continental norm of dining out *en famille* is welcomed in Britain, and visiting a restaurant may no longer entail endless searches for a babysitter, although after 8pm, it is not usual to see small children in restaurants.

Many places welcome junior diners, and some actively encourage families, at least during the day or early evening. Formal restaurants sometimes cultivate a more adult ambience at dinnertime, and some impose age limits. If you want to take young children to a restaurant, check ahead.

Italian, Spanish, Indian or fast-food restaurants and ice-cream parlours nearly always welcome children and sometimes provide special menus or high chairs for them. Even traditional English pubs, which were once a strictly adult preserve, accommodate families and may provide special rooms or play areas. The places that welcome and cater for children are indicated in the pub guide (see pp604–9).

Food box delivery at organic Riverford Field Kitchen, Buckfastleigh *(see p592)*

Disabled Access

Restaurant facilities in Great Britain could be better for disabled visitors, but things are slowly improving. Modern premises usually take account of mobility problems, but it's always best to check first if you have special needs. The website www.openbritain.net has information on accessible cafés and restaurants.

Picnics

Eating outside is becoming more popular in Britain, though it is more likely that you will find tables outside pubs (in the form of a beer garden) than outside restaurants. An inexpensive option is to make up your own picnic; most towns have good delicatessens and bakeries where you can collect provisions. Look out for street markets to pick up fresh fruit and local cheeses at bargain prices.

Department stores such as Marks & Spencer and super-markets including Sainsbury's and Waitrose often sell an excellent range of pre-packed sandwiches and snacks; large towns usually have several sandwich bars to choose from. Your hotel or guesthouse may also be able to provide a packed lunch. Ask for it the night before.

Recommended Restaurants

The restaurants in this guide have been chosen across a wide price range for their atmosphere, location and good food. With such an eclectic mix of restaurants on offer, the listings showcase the best of their kind. They include no-frills seafood shacks, characterful pubs, Indian curry houses, cafés and Michelin starred restaurants in country-house estates. In a gastropub you can expect beautifully presented food in a casual pub environment. Places serving Modern British food offer dishes that are contemporary versions of traditional classics, whereas Traditional British will be hearty portions of staple fare, such as puddings, pies and stews.

The entries highlighted as DK Choice have been chosen for their exceptional features, which may include a celebrity chef, sensational food, an unusual or spectacular location, or a great atmosphere. All DK Choice eateries offer a memorable dining experience.

Eating alfresco at Grasmere in the Lake District

The Traditional British Pub

Every country has its bars, but Britain is famous for its pubs, or "public houses". Ale was brewed in England in Roman times – mostly at home – and by the Middle Ages inns and taverns were brewing their own beers. The 18th century was the heyday of the coaching inn as stage coaches brought more custom. In the 19th century came railway taverns for travellers and "gin palaces" for the new industrial workers. Today, pubs come in all styles and sizes, serving food as well as drink *(see pp604–9)*. Gastropubs see as much emphasis placed on food as on the beer selection, revitalizing English classics.

Early 19th-century coaching inn – also a social centre and post office

The Victorian Pub

A century ago, many pubs in towns and cities had smart interiors, which contrasted with the poor housing of their patrons.

Pint glasses (containing just over half a litre) are used for beer.

The Red Lion pub name is derived from Scottish heraldry *(see p34)*.

Elaborately etched glass is a feature of many Victorian interiors.

Pub games, such as cribbage, bar billiards, pool and dominoes, are part of British pub culture. Here some regular customers are competing against a rival pub's darts team.

Beer gardens outside pubs are popular with families in summer.

Old-fashioned cash register contributes to the period atmosphere of the bar.

Pewter tankards, seldom used by drinkers today, add a traditional touch.

What to Drink

Draught bitter is the most traditional British beer. Brewed from malted barley, hops, yeast and water, and usually matured in a wooden cask, it varies from region to region. In the north of England the sweeter mild ale is popular, and lagers served in bottles or on tap are also widely drunk. Stout, made from black malt, is another variation. Pale ales are increasingly popular everywhere.

Beer pump

Draught bitter is drunk at cellar temperature.

Draught lager is a light-coloured, carbonated beer.

Guinness is a thick, creamy Irish stout.

Pavement tables, crowded with city drinkers during the summer months

A village pub, offering a waterside view and serving drinks in the garden

Pub Signs

Early medieval inns used vines or evergreens as signs – the symbol of Bacchus, the Roman god of wine. Soon pubs acquired names that signalled support for monarchs or noblemen, or celebrated victories in battle. As many customers could not read, pub signs had vivid images.

The George may derive from one of the six English kings of that name, or, as here, from England's patron saint.

Bottles of spirits are ranged behind the bar.

Glass lamps imitate the Victorian style.

The Bat and Ball celebrates cricket, and may be sited near a village green where the game can be played.

Wine, once rarely found in pubs, is now commonplace.

The Green Man is a figure from pagan mythology, possibly the basis for the legend of Robin Hood (see p340).

A deep-toned mahogany bar forms part of the traditional decor.

The Magna Carta sign commemorates and illustrates the "great charter" signed by King John in 1215 (see p52).

Draught beer, served from pumps or taps, comes from national and local brewers.

Optics dispense spirits in precise measures.

The Bird in Hand refers to the ancient country sport of falconry, traditionally practised by noblemen.

Mild may be served by the pint or in a half-pint tankard (as above).

Popular mixed drinks are gin-and-tonic and Pimm's with lemonade.

The Flavours of Great Britain

A rich agriculture that provides meat and dairy products, as well as fruit, vegetables and cereals, gives the British table a broad scope. Traditional dishes – cooked breakfasts, roast beef, fish and chips – are famous, but there is much more on offer, varying from region to region. Many towns give their names to produce and dishes. Seasonal choices include game and seafood, while other produce can be seen at the increasingly popular farmers' markets. Britons still have a penchant for pies and puddings, and most regions have cakes and buns they can call their own. Scotland has its own distinctive cuisine *(see p492)*.

Asparagus

Local fresh beetroot on sale at a greengrocer's shop

Central and Southern England

All tastes are catered for in the metropolis, and the surrounding countryside has long been given over to its demands. The flat lands of East Anglia provide vegetables and root crops; the South Downs have been shorn by sheep; geese have made Nottingham famous; and the county of

Kent is known as "the Garden of England" for its glorious orchards and its fields of soft fruits. From around the coast come Dover sole, Whitstable oysters (popular since Roman times) and the Cockney favourites, cockles and whelks. The game season runs from November to February, and pheasant is often on the menu.

West of England

The warmest part of England is renowned for its classic cream teas, the key ingredient provided by its dairy herds. In Cornwall, pasties have long been a staple. Once eaten by tin miners and filled with meat at one end and jam the other, to give two courses in one, they are now generally made with

Selection of fine, farm-produced British cheeses

Cornish Yarg
Montgomery Cheddar
Cider-washed Celtic Promise
Dorstone goat's-milk cheese
Cropwell Bishop Stilton
Ewe's-milk Wigmore

Traditional British Food

Though many traditional dishes, such as Lancashire hotpot, beef Wellington and even fish and chips, can be harder to hunt down than tapas, pizza or chicken tikka masala, other reliable regulars remain popular. Among them are shepherd's pie (minced lamb topped with mashed potatoes), steak and kidney pie (beef and kidney in gravy baked in a pastry crust), game pie and "bangers and mash" (sausages with mashed potatoes and onion gravy). For pudding there is a variety of trifles, pies, tarts and crumbles, often eaten with custard, as well as a lighter summer pudding of seasonal fruit. A "full English breakfast" is a fry-up of sausages, eggs, bacon, tomatoes, mushrooms and bread, perhaps with black pudding or laverbread. Lunchtime snacks include a "ploughman's lunch" of cheese and pickles with a "doorstep" of bread.

Dover sole This is the most tasty flatfish, best served simply grilled with lemon, spinach and new potatoes.

Apples

Display of British breads at a local farmers' market

meat and vegetables. The clear waters around the peninsula offer up such seafood as sardines, mackerel and crab in abundance, and many of the region's best restaurants specialize in fish. Bath gives its name to special biscuits and buns.

North of England

Cumberland sausage, Lancashire hotpot, Goosnargh duck and Yorkshire pudding – the names tell you exactly where the food on your plate originated. These are the staples, but restaurants these days are creating new dishes from old, such as trout with black (blood) pudding, and even being adventurous with "mushy" peas. Bradford, with its large Asian community, is one of the best places to eat Indian food.

Wales

The green hills and valleys of Wales are grazed by sheep, producing lamb that is simply roasted and eaten with mint sauce – a favourite all over Britain. The grass is good for dairy products, too, including white, crumbly Caerphilly.

A Cornish fishmonger displays a locally caught red mullet

Cheese is the principal ingredient of Welsh rarebit (pronounced rabbit), made with cheese grilled on toast and occasionally augmented with beer. Look out for prize-winning Welsh Black beef – prime fillets are often accompanied by horseradish sauce. The Irish Sea provides plenty of fish, but there is also freshwater trout and salmon. A curiosity of the South Wales seashore is laver, a kind of sea spinach, which is mixed with oatmeal and fried in small cakes called *bara lawr*, or laverbread, to be served with sausage and bacon for breakfast.

British Cheeses

Caerphilly Fresh, white, mild cheese from Wales.

Cheshire Crumbly, silky and full-bodied cheese.

Cheddar Often imitated, never bettered; the best comes from the West Country.

Double Gloucester Mellow flavoured, smooth and creamy.

Sage Derby Flavoured with green veins of sage.

Stilton The king of British cheeses, a strong, blue-veined cheese with a creamy texture. Popular at Christmas.

Wensleydale Young, moist and flaky-textured, with a mild, slightly sweet flavour.

Cornish mackerel The ideal partner for this rich fish is a piquant sauce made from English gooseberries.

Roast beef Horseradish sauce is a traditional accompaniment, as are crisp Yorkshire puddings made of batter.

Welsh lamb with leeks The leek is the national vegetable of Wales, and perfectly complements roast lamb.

Where to Eat and Drink

London

West End and Westminster

Belgo Centraal £
Belgian **Map** 11 B2
50 Earlham St, WC2H 9LJ
Tel *020 7813 2233*
Bustling and quirky restaurant –
and one of the largest in the city.
Team the excellent lobster with
a delicious Trappist beer.

Princi £
Italian **Map** 11 A2
135 Wardour St, W1F 0UT
Tel *020 7478 8888*
A stylish Milan import, serving
homemade bread, wood-fired
pizzas and delicious pastries.

Regency Café £
Traditional British **Map** 19 A2
17–19 Regency St, SW1P 4BY
Tel *020 7821 6596* **Closed** *Sun*
An authentic 1950s "caff" that was
featured in a couple of movies.
Try the heavenly hash browns
and eggs Benedict for breakfast.

Sagar £
Vegetarian **Map** 11 C2
31 Catherine St, WC2B 5JS
Tel *020 7836 6377*
Freshly made curries, delicious
crispy *dosas* (rice batter crepes)
and great-value *thalis* (selection
of dishes) make this Indian
restaurant a vegetarian favourite.

Soho Joe £
Italian **Map** 11 A1
22–25 Dean St, W1D 3RY
Tel *07534 134398*
Thin-crust pizzas are the star of
the show at this great-value
Italian joint. Fantastic pastas,
burgers and sandwiches on the
menu as well. Great ambience.

Al Duca ££
Italian **Map** 11 A3
4–5 Duke of York St, SW1Y 6LA
Tel *020 7839 3090* **Closed** *Sun*
Classic Italian dishes are given a
modern twist using the freshest
of ingredients at this popular and
busy eatery.

Andrew Edmunds ££
European **Map** 11 A2
46 Lexington St, W1F 0LW
Tel *020 7437 5708* **Closed** *Sun
dinner*
Quirky and romantic restaurant
featuring imaginative dishes on
its daily-changing menu.

Barshu ££
Chinese **Map** 11 B2
28 Frith St, W1D 5FL
Tel *020 7287 8822*
Dishes from the Sichuan province
dominate the menu. Try the
Chengdu street snacks.

Bocca di Lupo ££
Italian **Map** 11 A2
12 Archer St, W1D 7BB
Tel *020 7734 2223*
Chef Jacob Kennedy specializes
in robust and rare regional
recipes at this small restaurant.

Haozhan ££
Chinese **Map** 11 A2
8 Gerrard St, W1D 5PJ
Tel *020 7434 3838*
A world away from the standard
sweet-and-sour staples, Haozhan
serves superb cuisine made with
the finest seasonal ingredients.

Hard Rock Café ££
American **Map** 10 E4
150 Old Park Lane, W1K 1QZ
Tel *020 7514 1700*
Savour American classic at this
legendary restaurant with a
fascinating collection of rock
memorabilia.

Mildreds ££
Vegetarian **Map** 11 A2
45 Lexington St, W1F 9AN
Tel *020 7494 1634* **Closed** *Sun*
Inspired vegetarian cuisine fit to
convert the most confirmed
carnivore. Try porcini and ale pie.

Noura ££
Lebanese **Map** 18 E1
16 Hobart Pl, SW1W 0HH
Tel *020 7235 9444*
Classy looks and a tempting
menu at this popular flagship.
Exceptional mezes and kebabs.

El Pirata ££
Tapas **Map** 10 E4
5–6 Down St, W1J 7AQ
Tel *020 7491 3810* **Closed** *Sat
lunch & Sun*
Lively restaurant, with all the classic
Spanish and Portuguese favourites.
Great special set lunch menu.

Terroirs ££
French **Map** 11 B3
5 William IV St, WC2N 4DW
Tel *020 7036 0660* **Closed** *Sun*
An impressive selection of
biodynamic wines teamed with
exquisite cuisine including pork,
snails, lentils and mushrooms.
Reminiscent of a Parisian bar.

Thai Pot ££
Thai **Map** 11 B2
1 Bedfordbury, WC2N 4BP
Tel *020 7379 4580* **Closed** *Sun*
Relish Thai staples full of fragrant
flavour and fresh ingredients.
Dashes of warm colour jazz up
the contemporary decor.

The Wolseley ££
European **Map** 10 F3
160 Piccadilly, W1J 9EB
Tel *020 7499 6996*
A Wolseley motor car showroom
from the 1920s makes a stunning
home for this glamorous café-
restaurant. Try the rib-eye steak.

Vasco and Piero's Pavilion ££
Italian **Map** 11 A2
15 Poland St, W1F 8QE
Tel *020 7437 8774* **Closed** *Sat
lunch & Sun*
Delicious homemade pasta,
some dishes featuring truffles
when in season. Try Umbrian
specialities such as pork and lentils.

The beautifully lit interiors of Bocca di Lupo

Atelier de Joël Robuchon £££
French **Map** 11 B2
13–15 West St, WC2H 9NE
Tel 020 7010 8600
Get a front row seat at the
Japanese-inspired counter in this
two-Michelin-starred restaurant
serving fantastic French food.

Bentley's Oyster Bar and Grill £££
Seafood **Map** 10 F3
11 Swallow St, W1B 4DG
Tel 020 7734 4756
Serving delectable seafood since
1916. Chef Richard Corrigan's
inventive creations keep Bentley's
firmly on the map.

Le Caprice £££
European **Map** 10 F3
Arlington House, Arlington St, SW1A 1RJ
Tel 020 7629 2239
This restaurant serves flavourful
bistro food complemented by
classic decor and attentive service.

Cecconi's £££
Italian **Map** 10 F3
5a Burlington Gardens, W1S 3EP
Tel 020 7434 1500
Sample virtuoso versions of
classic dishes at Cecconi's. Gets
busy at peak times so come early.

DK Choice

Clos Maggiore £££
European **Map** 11 B2
33 King St, WC2E 8JD
Tel 020 7379 9696
Book in advance for a table in
the courtyard, with its blossom-
laden branches, for a magical,
romantic evening. French
regional food inspires the
modern European cooking.

Le Gavroche £££
French **Map** 10 D2
43 Upper Brook St, W1K 7QR
Tel 020 7408 0881 **Closed** *Sat lunch,
Sun & public hols*
A byword for luxury and excep-
tional haute cuisine. Great service
and a well-priced set lunch.

Murano £££
European **Map** 10 E3
20 Queen St, W1J 5PP
Tel 020 7495 1127 **Closed** *Sun*
Murano serves modern European
cuisine with a bias towards Italian
flavours. Nothing on the menu
disappoints – from the amuse-
bouche to petits fours.

Nobu £££
Japanese **Map** 10 E4
*Metropolitan Hotel W1, 19 Old Park
Lane, W1K 1LB*
Tel 020 7447 4747
Beautifully prepared sashimi,

Elegant dining area at the sophisticated Murano, London

tempura and other excellent
contemporary Japanese dishes.
Great place for celebrity spotting.

Nopi £££
European **Map** 11 C2
21–22 Warwick St, W1B5NE
Tel 020 7494 9584
Renowned British-Israeli cookery
writer Yotam Ottolenghi brings his
trademark touch of the Middle
Eastern to sharing dishes here, full
of exciting aromas and textures.

The Ritz Restaurant £££
Modern British **Map** 10 F3
150 Piccadilly, W1J 9BR
Tel 020 7493 8181
The perfect place to sample
exquisite classic cuisine from
the seasonally changing menu.
Spectacular decor.

Rules £££
Traditional British **Map** 11 C2
35 Maiden Lane, WC2E 7LB
Tel 020 7836 5314
Robust British food such as rib
of beef, oysters and game at
London's oldest restaurant,
established in 1798. Procures
game from its own country estate.

Veeraswamy £££
Indian **Map** 10 F3
*Victory House, 99 Regent St,
W1B 4RS*
Tel 020 7734 1401
This London institution, opened
in 1926, offers contemporary
and classic Indian dishes in lush
interiors that evoke a palace.

South Kensington and Hyde Park

Byron £
American **Map** 7 C5
222 Kensington High St, W8 7RG
Tel 020 7361 1717
One of many branches across the
city. Burgers are made from
quality, freshly minced beef,

Café Mona Lisa £
Italian **Map** 16 E5
417 King's Rd, SW10 0LR
Tel 020 7376 5447
Popular neighbourhood café
with friendly service and warm
interiors. Delicious Italian fare,
with daily specials displayed on
a chalkboard.

The Abingdon ££
European **Map** 15 C1
54 Abingdon Rd, W8 6AP
Tel 020 7937 3339
A converted pub with a refined
feel and great brasserie-style
food. Ask to be seated at a booth.

DK Choice

Assaggi ££
Italian **Map** 7 C2
39 Chepstow Pl, W2 4TS
Tel 020 7792 5501 **Closed** *Sun*
Hidden away above a pub, this
alluring restaurant is a worthy
addition to the burgeoning
foodie scene. The bright room
reflects the vivid colours of chef
Nino Sassu's native Sardinia.
Sample from an extensive
menu of superb regional
specialities. Be sure to make
a reservation in advance.

The Belvedere ££
European **Map** 7 B5
*Off Abbotsbury Rd, Holland Park,
W8 6LU*
Tel 020 7602 1238
Enjoy modern European food in
a sumptuous former ballroom
overlooking beautiful gardens.

Buona Sera Jam ££
Italian **Map** 17 A4
289 King's Rd, SW3 5EW
Tel 020 7352 8827 **Closed** *Mon
lunch*
A lively trattoria that is great
for families. Climb miniature
ladders to reach the top tier
tables and enjoy terrific pasta,

E&O ££
Asian **Map** 7 A2
14 Blenheim Crescent, W11 1NN
Tel *020 7229 5454*
Amid glossy decor, E&O serves delicious tempura, sushi and specials such as pad thai.

Gallery Mess ££
European **Map** 17 C2
Saatchi Gallery, Duke of York's HQ, King's Rd, SW3 4RY
Tel *020 7730 8135*
A desirable lunch spot after an exhibition. Ask for a table in the airy cloister, which overlooks a leafy square.

Jak's ££
Mediterranean **Map** 17 B2
77 Walton St, SW3 2HT
Tel *020 3393 1796*
Savour a range of healthy organic dishes and tempting desserts in a spacious, bare-brick basement.

Kensington Place ££
Seafood **Map** 7 C4
201 Kensington Church St, W8 7LX
Tel *020 7727 3184*
This famous goldfish-bowl brasserie serves fantastic beer-battered fish and chips.

The Levin Hotel ££
European **Map** 9 C5
28 Basil St, SW3 1AS
Tel *020 7589 6286*
A genteel basement brasserie with delectable food and the feel of a modern European tearoom.

Babylon at the Roof Garden £££
Modern British **Map** 10 D5
99 Kensington High St, W8 5SA
Tel *020 7368 3993*
Dine al fresco on the terrace at this fashionable restaurant overlooking the "hanging gardens." Themed areas with trees, flamingos and a fish-stocked stream. Book in advance.

Bibendum £££
French **Map** 17 A2
Michelin House, 81 Fulham Rd, SW3 6RD
Tel *020 7581 5817*
Michelin House's Art Nouveau stained glass makes for a stunning backdrop to this airy first-floor dining room. Come for the fantastic seasonal French cuisine and assiduous service.

Dinner by Heston Blumenthal £££
Modern British **Map** 9 C5
Mandarin Oriental Hyde Park, 66 Knightsbridge, SW1X 7LA
Tel *020 7201 3833*
London's most hyped restaurant showcases this celebrity chef's inspired take on historic British

Formal dining at Restaurant Gordon Ramsay, London

cuisine. Meteoric prices, but an unforgettable dining experience.

Hunan £££
Chinese **Map** 18 D2
51 Pimlico Rd, SW1W 8NE
Tel *020 7730 5712* **Closed** *Sun*
Pick a handful of small dishes from the Taiwanese-style menu.

Marcus £££
Modern British **Map** 10 D5
The Berkeley Hotel, Wilton Pl, SW1X 7RL
Tel *020 7235 1200* **Closed** *Sun*
An elegant dining room with a modern menu of delectable dishes by a superstar chef.

Restaurant Gordon Ramsay £££
French **Map** 17 C4
68 Royal Hospital Rd, SW3 4HP
Tel *020 7352 4441* **Closed** *Sat & Sun*
Standards remain high at this three-Michelin-starred shrine to haute cuisine. Very expensive, but the menu is truly exciting.

Zuma £££
Japanese **Map** 9 B5
5 Raphael St, SW7 1DL
Tel *020 7584 1010*
Spot the celebrities at this cool joint. They're drawn – like everyone – by tasty robata-grilled dishes, tempura, nigiri sushi and sashimi.

Regent's Park and Bloomsbury

Gem £
Turkish **Map** 4 F1
265 Upper St, N1 2UQ
Tel *020 7359 0405*
True to its name, Gem is a great little place serving fragrant meze at bargain prices in a charming white-painted room decorated with Kurdish farm implements.

DK Choice

Golden Hind £
Traditional British **Map** 10 E1
73 Marylebone Lane, W1U 2PN
Tel *020 7486 3644* **Closed** *Sun*
A welcoming no-frills family-run place with no alcohol licence but a minimal corkage fee. Established in 1914, Golden Hind has been expanded by its current Greek owners. The homemade fishcakes with the obligatory mushy peas are an enticing alternative to their famous fish and chips.

Galvin Bistrot de Luxe ££
French **Map** 1 C5
66 Baker St, W1U 7DJ
Tel *020 7935 4007*
A popular high-class bistro that serves classic French cuisine and a wide choice of wines. Saturday lunches are excellent value.

The House of Ho ££
Vietnamese **Map** 11 A1
1 Percy St, W1T 1DB
Tel *020 7323 9130* **Closed** *Sun*
Stop by for a drink in the romantic top-floor bar and then descend to the candlelit restaurant to enjoy well-crafted and innovative French-Vietnamese dishes.

Ottolenghi ££
Mediterranean **Map** 4 F1
287 Upper St, N1 2TZ
Tel *020 7288 1454* **Closed** *Sun dinner*
Ottolenghi's designer space is complemented by divine, healthy cuisine served at communal tables. An innovative take on Mediterranean cuisine.

Orrery £££
French **Map** 2 D5
55–57 Marylebone High St, W1U 5RB
Tel *020 7616 8000*
Outstanding modern French cuisine, served in a converted stable block. Grab a table by the stylish arched windows.

Pied à Terre £££
French **Map** 3 A5
34 Charlotte St, W1T 2NH
Tel *020 7636 1178* **Closed** *Sun*
Known for its adventurous and impeccable food. A refined yet friendly place with a comfortable dining room. Attentive staff.

Roka £££
Japanese **Map** 3 A5
37 Charlotte St, W1T 1RR
Tel *020 7580 6464*
Sit at the wooden counter of this goldfish-bowl restaurant to savour delicious sushi and watch the chefs at the robata grill.

The City and Southwark

Cây Tre £
Vietnamese   **Map** 5 A4
301 Old St, EC1V 9LA
Tel *020 7729 8662*
Authentic and high-quality dishes, including pho and seafood platters. They also serve delicious Cornish scallops and anchovied chicken wings.

Clerkenwell Kitchen £
Modern British   **Map** 4 E4
27–31 Clerkenwell Close, EC1R 0AT
Tel *020 7101 9959*   **Closed** *Sat & Sun; dinner*
Home-style cooking using organic produce, with attentive service. Modern brick-and-wood surroundings. A great place for lunch.

Lahore Kebab House £
Pakistani   **Map** 14 E1
2–10 Umberston St, E1 1PY
Tel *020 7481 9737*
Spiced curries and kebabs will set the taste buds tingling in this warehouse style space. Bring your own alcohol.

Leon Spitalfields £
European   **Map** 6 D5
3 Crispin Pl, E1 6DW
Tel *020 7247 4369*   **Closed** *Sun dinner*
Healthy "superfood" salads and Mediterranean-inspired fast food in a colourful space. Part of a chain. Great option for families.

Anchor and Hope ££
Modern British   **Map** 12 F4
36 The Cut, SE1 8LP
Tel *020 7928 9898*   **Closed** *Mon lunch & Sun dinner*
Come with a large appetite for gutsy fare: braised venison, calves' brains, and pumpkin risotto. Tables are first-come-first-served, so either arrive early or enjoy a drink in the bar while you wait.

Brawn ££
French   **Map** 6 E3
49 Columbia Rd, E2 7RG
Tel *020 7729 5692*   **Closed** *Mon lunch & Sun dinner*
Big, bold flavours can be found in abundance here: think venison pie and grilled duck hearts.

Le Café du Marché ££
French   **Map** 4 F5
22 Charterhouse Sq, EC1M 6DX
Tel *020 7600 1609*   **Closed** *Sat lunch & Sun*
This family-run French hideaway offers accomplished classic cooking teamed with a simple, stylish ambience. The menu changes regularly. Great jazz nights.

Champor-Champor ££
Thai/Malaysian   **Map** 13 C4
62–64 Weston St, SE1 3QJ
Tel *020 7403 4600*
Translating as "mix and match", this place is known for its exotic decoration and eclectic, wonderful Thai and Malaysian cuisine.

The Peasant ££
Modern British   **Map** 4 E2
240 St John St, EC1V 4PH
Tel *020 7336 7726*
Finely executed brasserie cooking in an agreeable Victorian dining room. First-rate pub food in the cavernous bar below.

Vanilla Black ££
Vegetarian   **Map** 12 E1
17–18 Tooks Court, EC4A 1LB
Tel *020 7242 2622*   **Closed** *Sun*
Sophisticated vegetarian cuisine in an elegant setting. Try the goat's cheese and cauliflower millefeuille and smoked paprika fudge.

Vinoteca ££
European   **Map** 4 E2
7 St John St, EC1M 4AA
Tel *020 7253 8786*   **Closed** *Sun*
An extensive wine list and excellent modern European food ensure a steady crowd at this Farringdon wine bar.

L'Anima £££
Italian   **Map** 5 C5
1 Snowden St, EC2A 2DQ
Tel *020 7422 7000*   **Closed** *Sat lunch & Sun*
Francesco Mazzei's food is as elegant as the minimalist setting at L'Anima. Stunning regional dishes with wines to match.

The Chancery £££
European   **Map** 12 E1
9 Cursitor St, EC4A 1LL
Tel *020 7831 4000*   **Closed** *Sat lunch & Sun*
Loin of venison, halibut, pigeon and slow-cooked pork belly are typically on the frequently changing menu.

Galvin La Chapelle £££
French   **Map** 6 D5
35 Spital Sq, E1 6DY
Tel *020 7299 0400*
Housed in a converted school hall, this restaurant offers a remarkable and varied menu of French specialities. There is also a good Sunday roast lunch menu. Friendly and attentive service.

Hawksmoor £££
Steakhouse   **Map** 14 E1
157 Commercial St, E1 6BJ
Tel *020 7426 4850*
Hawksmoor is, quite simply, a carnivore's delight. Feast on succulent steaks prepared from traditionally reared Longhorn cattle, dry aged and cooked on a charcoal grill.

DK Choice

Oxo Tower Restaurant and Brasserie £££
European   **Map** 12 E3
Oxo Tower Wharf, Barge House St, SE1 9GY
Tel *020 7803 3888*
The delectable cuisine and international wine list at Oxo is complemented by breathtaking eighth-floor views: colourful by day, glittering by night. Choose between the relaxed brasserie and sophisticated restaurant, both superbly run by Harvey Nichols. Picturesque terrace seating in the summer.

Further Afield

Anarkali £
Indian
303–305 King St, W6 9NH
Tel *020 8748 1760*
A Hammersmith restaurant in a class of its own. Unique, subtle spicing and a great choice for vegetarians. Try the delicious home-made *Rafique* sauce. Delightful service.

City views at the Oxo Tower Restaurant and Brasserie, London

For more information on types of restaurants *see pages 575–6*

Exemplary food served in a casual setting at The Curlew, Bodiam

The Greenwich Union £
Modern British
56 Royal Hill, SE10 8RT
Tel *020 8692 6258*
A local landmark, this pub showcases a unique range of beers. Menus recommend ale pairings for each delicious dish.

Safi £
Persian
70 Askew Rd, W12 9BJ
Tel *020 8834 4888*
Great-value, authentic Persian food in a cosy setting. Expect flavour-laden stews, quality cuts of meat and flatbread baked in the clay oven by the front door.

Emile's £££
European
98 Felsham Rd, Putney, SW15 1DQ
Tel *020 8789 3323* **Closed** *Sun; lunch*
A Putney treasure: good, simple food in an unfussy room. A black-board, brought to the table, displays the seasonal menu.

Enoteca Turi £££
Italian
87 Pimlico Rd, Belgravia, SW1W 8PH
Tel *020 8785 4449* **Closed** *Sun*
Run by a dedicated couple, this restaurant offers a convivial and relaxed atmosphere, wholesome food and expertly selected wine.

Indian Zing £££
Indian
236 King St, Hammersmith, W6 0RF
Tel *020 8748 5959*
Contemporary Indian cuisine, prepared with panache at this up-market gem. Noteworthy wine list.

Jin-Kichi £££
Japanese
73 Heath St, NW3 6UG
Tel *020 7794 6158* **Closed** *Mon & Tue after public hols*
A piece of Tokyo in Hampstead, with a grill, sublime sushi, well-spaced seating and efficient service.

Tatra £££
Polish
24 Goldhawk Rd, W12 8DH
Tel *020 8749 8193* **Closed** *Mon–Fri lunch*
Located in Shepherd's Bush, Tatra blends the most appetizing tastes from Eastern Europe. Don't miss the flavoured vodka at dinner.

The Wells £££
Modern British
30 Well Walk, NW3 1BX
Tel *020 7794 3785*
Stop to grab a light snack or a meal in the warmly decorated dining room of this splendid gastropub.

DK Choice

Chez Bruce £££
Modern British
2 Bellevue Rd, Wandsworth, SW17 7EG
Tel *020 8672 0114*
Chez Bruce is renowned for its top-notch food, wine and service. The classic cuisine on offer here has French overtones with the emphasis on offal, fish and remarkable flavour combinations. Specialities include home-cured charcuterie and bread, slow-cooked braises, and warm and cold salads.

Gaucho £££
Steakhouse
64 Heath St, Hampstead, NW3 1DN
Tel *020 7431 8222*
This stylish chain restaurant has hearty steaks cooked on a genuine Argentine barbecue. Bright decor and cheerful ambience.

The Downs and Channel Coast

ALFRISTON: Wingrove House £££
Modern British
High St, East Sussex, BN26 5TD
Tel *01323 870276* **Closed** *Mon–Wed lunch*
Set in a 19th-century colonial-style house, this restaurant serves traditional English dishes. Try the delicious Sussex lamb roast.

ARUNDEL: The Bay Tree £££
European
19a–21 Tarrant St, Town Centre, West Sussex, BN18 9DG
Tel *01903 883679*
Housed in a beautiful 16th-century timber-framed building, the Bay Tree offers excellent contemporary cuisine made with high-quality organic produce.

BIDDENDEN: The West House £££
Modern British
28 High St, Ashford, TN27 8AH
Tel *01580 291341* **Closed** *Sun dinner & Mon*
Set in a 15th-century weaver's cottage, this Michelin-starred family-run restaurant gives British classics a modern twist.

BODIAM: The Curlew £££
Modern British
Junction Rd, East Sussex, TN32 5UY
Tel *01580 861394* **Closed** *Mon*
Michelin-starred restaurant with a casual setting and an emphasis on organic and biodynamic wines.

BRIGHTON: Tookta's Café £
Thai
30 Spring St, East Sussex, BN1 3EF
Tel *01273 748071* **Closed** *Sun*
Small café with endearingly chic decor and a contemporary and individual take on Thai cuisine.

BRIGHTON: The Gingerman £££
European
21a Norfolk Sq, East Sussex, BN1 2PD
Tel *01273 326688* **Closed** *Mon*
This small, intimate restaurant is delightfully unpretentious both in looks and cuisine. The food is full flavoured and created from fresh, high-quality ingredients.

CANTERBURY: Kathton House £££
European
6 High St, Sturry, Kent, CT2 0BD
Tel *01227 719999* **Closed** *Sun & Mon*
Up-market restaurant focusing on local and seasonal produce. Try the rack of Kentish lamb.

CHICHESTER: El Castizo £
Tapas
24 St Pancras, Victoria Court, West Sussex, PO19 7LT
Tel *01243 788988* **Closed** *Sun & Mon*
This affable vaulted restaurant serves traditional Spanish tapas, seafood and vegetarian dishes flavoured with imported cheese.

CUCKFIELD: Ockenden Manor £££
European
Ockenden Ln, West Sussex, RH17 5LD
Tel *01444 416111*
Set in an attractive Elizabethan manor house, this restaurant has excellent food and great views.

EASTBOURNE: La Locanda del Duca £
Italian
26 Cornfield Terrace, East Sussex, BN21 4NS
Tel *01323 737177* **Closed** *25 & 26 Dec*
Sample a variety of Italian dishes and a good selection of wines in a relaxed atmosphere.

EMSWORTH: 36 on the Quay £££
European
47 South St, Hampshire, PO10 7EG
Tel *01243 375592* **Closed** *Sun &
Mon; two weeks Jan, one week May,
one week Oct*
Overlooking the bay in the
fishing village of Emsworth,
36 on the Quay serves excellent
Michelin-starred European
cuisine. The five-course lunch
tasting menu is great value.

HASTINGS: Café Maroc £
Moroccan
37 High St, East Sussex, TN34 3ER
Tel *07500 774017* **Closed** *lunch;
dinner Mon–& Tue*
Bring your own wine to this small,
authentic Moroccan restaurant.
Great tagines and delicious lemon-
infused chicken.

**HORSHAM: The Pass at South
Lodge Hotel** £££
Modern British
Brighton Rd, West Sussex, RH13 6PS
Tel *01403 891711* **Closed** *Mon & Tue*
Michelin-starred restaurant in a
luxurious country-house hotel.
The menu features unusual flavour
combinations and ingredients.

**ISLE OF WIGHT: The Pilot
Boat Inn** £
Modern British
Station Rd, Bembridge, PO35 5NN
Tel *01983 872077* **Closed** *Sun dinner*
This pub looks like a boat and is
worth visiting for the fresh sea-
food, including Bembridge crab.

**LYMINGTON:
The Elderflower** £££
Fine dining
4–5 Quay St, Hampshire, SO41 3AS
Tel *01590 676908* **Closed** *dinner Sun
& Mon*
Imaginative and beautifully
presented food with clever
French touches is the hallmark of
this central Lymington restaurant.

PETERSFIELD: JSW £££
Modern British
20 Dragon St, Hampshire, GU31 4JJ
Tel *01730 262030* **Closed** *Wed lunch;
Sun–Tue dinner*
Housed in a 17th-century
coaching inn, JSW prepares
local seasonal fare. The tasting
menus are superb. There are
also excellent vegetarian options
and an extensive wine list.

**PORTSMOUTH: Spice
Merchants** £
Indian
44 Osborne Rd, Southsea, PO5 3LT
Tel *023 9282 8900* **Closed** *lunch*
This small and convivial Indian
restaurant has a menu of authentic
recipes. Eat in or take away.

ROCHESTER: Topes ££
Modern British
60 High St, Kent, ME1 1JY
Tel *01634 845270* **Closed** *Sun
dinner; Mon & Tue*
Excellent British food made
with fresh seasonal produce
brought in daily. The restaurant
is housed in a 15th-century
building.

SWANLEY: Fahims £
Indian
9 High St, Kent, BR8 8AE
Tel *01322 836164*
Great blending of herbs and
spices at this Indian and
Bangladeshi place. Try the
bargain £10 buffet on Sunday.

DK Choice

**WHITSTABLE: Wheelers
Oyster Bar** ££
Seafood
8 High St, Kent, CT5 1BQ
Tel *01227 273311* **Closed** *Wed*
The longest-established
restaurant in seaside Whitstable,
Wheelers has a short menu that
changes seasonally: there are
six starters, six main courses and
six desserts. Bring your own
wine and dine in the Oyster
Parlour or Seafood Bar, or order
something to take away.

WINCHELSEA: The Ship £
Grill
Sea Rd, East Sussex, TN36 4LH
Tel *01797 226707* **Closed** *Sun–Tue
dinner*
Enjoy picturesque views of the
surroundings while dining on
delicious grilled meats in this
bright, cheerful place.

**Winchester:
Kyoto Kitchen** £
Japanese
*70 Parchment St, Hampshire,
SO23 8AT*
Tel *01962 890895*
Specializing in sushi and sashimi,
Kyoto Kitchen provides a good

introduction to Japanese
cuisine. Great presentation
and polite service.

WINCHESTER: Chesil Rectory ££
Modern British
1 Chesil St, Hampshire, SO23 0HU
Tel *01962 851555*
Enjoy classic contemporary
dishes, sourced from local
suppliers, in this charming 15th-
century timber-framed building.

East Anglia

DK Choice

ALDEBURGH: Regatta ££
Seafood
171 High St, Suffolk, IP15 5AN
Tel *01728 452011*
Long a feature of the seaside
town of Aldeburgh, Regatta
has a cheerful nautical theme,
with a metal ship adorning the
exterior. In summer the focus
is on local seafood, though
vegetarian and meat dishes are
also available. Don't miss the
scallops and lobster dishes.

**BURY ST EDMUNDS: Maison
Bleue** ££
French
30 Churchgate St, Suffolk, IP33 1RG
Tel *01284 760623* **Closed** *Sun
& Mon*
Exquisitely presented French
cuisine in an elegant setting.
Try the Wester Ross salmon
or Devonshire duck and
French cheeses.

**CAMBRIDGE: Ristorante
Il Piccolo Mondo** ££
Italian
*85 High St, Bottisham,
Cambridgeshire, CB25 9BA*
Tel *01223 811434* **Closed** *Sun–Tue*
Restaurant in an old Victorian
village school, serving tasty
gnocchi, risotto and pasta.

Dine on traditional Indian and Bangladeshi cuisine at Fahims, Swanley

For more information on types of restaurants *see pages 575–6*

CAMBRIDGE: The Oak Bistro ££
British
6 Lensfield Rd, Cambridgeshire, CB2 1EG
Tel *01223 323361* **Closed** *Sun & public hols*
Try the fillet of sea bream or the rump of lamb at this bistro with a great walled garden to dine in.

CHELMSFORD: Olio ££
Italian
37 New London Rd, Essex, CM2 0ND
Tel *01245 269174* **Closed** *Mon*
A little corner of Italy in Essex. Traditionally made specialty pizzas topped with artisan cheeses and meats. Steak, chicken and veal are also on the menu.

COLCHESTER: Mehalah's £
Seafood
East Rd, East Mersea, Essex, CO5 8TQ
Tel *012063 82797* **Closed** *dinner*
A modest venue serving stand-out seafood, including oysters and scallops, alongside local ales.

CROMER: Constantia Cottage Restaurant ££
Greek
The High St, East Runton, Norfolk, NR27 9NX
Tel *01263 512017* **Closed** *Sun*
A long-established restaurant with a cheerful ambience and occasional live music. Try classics such as *souvlaki* (Greek kebab) and *stifado* (beef and onion stew).

ELY: Peacocks Tearoom £
Café
65 Waterside, Cambridgeshire, CB7 4AU
Tel *01353 661100* **Closed** *Mon & Tue*
An attractive award-winning tea-room with a lush garden, serving quiches, soup and sandwiches along with tea and cake.

HOLT: Morston Hall £££
European
Morston, Norfolk, NR25 7AA
Tel *01263 741041* **Closed** *Jan; Dec 25*
Enjoy modern fare in a lovely countryside setting. Good wine list.

The refined orangery dining room at Morston Hall, Holt

HUNTINGDON: Old Bridge Hotel Restaurant ££
Modern British
1 High St, Cambridgeshire, PE29 3TQ
Tel *01480 424300*
Savour premium English cuisine in an 18th-century, ivy-clad town house with scenic views. Refined presentation and service.

IPSWICH: Alaturka £
Turkish
9 Great Colman St, Suffolk, IP4 2AA
Tel *01473 233448* **Closed** *Sun & lunch*
Alaturka features modern decor and traditional Turkish cuisine, including dishes cooked in clay pots. Finish with sweet baklava.

KING'S LYNN: Market Bistro ££
Modern British
11 Saturday Market Pl, Norfolk, PE30 5DQ
Tel *01553 771483* **Closed** *Sun & Mon; Tue lunch*
Serves everything from home-smoked fish and meat to delicious desserts. Sample local produce such as Cromer crabs.

LOWESTOFT: Desmond's £
Café
221b London Rd, Suffolk, NR33 0DS
Tel *07968 636647* **Closed** *Sun*
A pleasant café during the week, Desmond's serves excellent stone-baked pizza at weekends.

MALDON: El Guaca £
Mexican
122 High St, Essex, CM9 5ET
Tel *01621 852009*
Try classic fajitas and nachos at this warm, friendly and efficient Maldon joint.

NEWMARKET: Khobkun £
Thai
160 High St, Suffolk, CB8 9AQ
Tel *01638 660646*
Fragrant, spicy food delicately prepared and beautifully served. Wines by the bottle and Thai beer.

NORWICH: Moorish Falafel Bar £
Vegetarian
17 Lower Goat Lane, Norfolk, NR2 1EL
Tel *01603 622250*
A little place with a big reputation, offering filling falafel burgers, salad pittas and homemade lemonade.

PETERBOROUGH: Prévost £££
Fine dining
20 Priestgate, Cambridgeshire, PE1 1JA
Tel *01733 313623* **Closed** *Sun–Tue*
Set menus of three, five or nine courses are cooked before you. Creative Nordic touches and excellent selection of cocktails.

SOUTHWOLD: Sutherland House ££
Seafood
56 High St, Suffolk, IP18 6DN
Tel *01502 724544* **Closed** *Mon (except public hols)*
The superb dining room is the perfect setting to enjoy acclaimed dishes such as English snails, pan-fried Suffolk lamb and bread-and-butter pudding.

SWAFFHAM: Rasputin £
Russian
21–22 Plowright Pl, Norfolk, PE37 7LQ
Tel *01760 724725* **Closed** *Sun, Mon; lunch*
A surprising find in East Anglia, serving authentic Russian food. Modern decor with the odd Russian flourish.

Thames Valley

ABINGDON: The White Hart ££
Gastropub
Main Rd, Fyfield, Oxfordshire, OX13 5LW
Tel *01865 390585* **Closed** *Sun dinner; Mon*
Timber-framed gastropub where many ingredients are sourced from the kitchen garden. Great homemade bread and pasta.

BANBURY: Sheesh Mahal £
Indian
43 South Bar, Oxfordshire, OX16 9AB
Tel *01295 266489*
Stylish Indian restaurant housed in a handsome mansion and serving succulent meat dishes.

BEACONSFIELD: The Royal Standard of England ££
Traditional British
Forty Green, Buckinghamshire, HP9 1XT
Tel *01494 673382*
One of England's oldest pubs, this jovial place serves up British staples such as steak-and-kidney pie and sausage and mash.

CHINNOR: Sir Charles Napier £££
European
Spriggs Alley, Oxfordshire, OX39 4BX
Tel *01494 483011* **Closed** *Sun dinner & Mon*
This Michelin-starred pub goes beyond pub fare to offer dishes such as Orkney scallops and suckling pig. Lovely garden.

CHIPPING NORTON: Wild Thyme ££
Modern British
10 New St, Oxfordshire, OX7 5LJ
Tel *01608 645060* **Closed** *Sun & Mon*
Set in an attractive old Cotswold stone building. Fantastic Cornish monkfish and rare-breed pork feature on the menu.

Country house setting of French fine-dining restaurant L'Ortolan, Reading

COOKHAM: The White Oak £
European
The Pound, Maidenhead, Berkshire, SL6 9QE
Tel *01628 523043* **Closed** *Sun dinner*
Stylish pub with a range of choices, with good quality set meals and bar snacks.

GREAT MISSENDEN: La Petite Auberge £££
French
107 High St, Buckinghamshire, HP16 0BB
Tel *01494 865370* **Closed** *Sun, Mon; lunch*
This tiny bistro has a great atmosphere, with quintessential French classics on the menu.

HEMEL HEMPSTEAD: Chiangmai Cottage £
Thai
80 High St, Hertfordshire, HP1 3AQ
Tel *01442 263426*
With charmingly rustic decor, this little place offers great pad thai and lightly spiced dishes. Good service and a cheerful atmosphere.

HENLEY-ON-THAMES: Shaun Dickens at The Boathouse £££
Modern British
Station Rd, Oxfordshire, RG9 1AZ
Tel *01491 577937* **Closed** *Mon & Tue*
Savour modern British food in a stunning riverside setting. Week-end breakfasts, plus vegetarian choices and tasting menus.

MARLOW: The Coach £
Gastropub
3 West St, Buckinghamshire, SL7 2LS
You'll find winning combinations, such as hare with mushroom ketchup, at this relaxed pub established by chef Tom Kerridge. No bookings taken.

MARLOW: Vanilla Pod ££
French
31 West St, Buckinghamshire, SL7 2LS
Tel *01628 898101* **Closed** *Sun & Mon*
Every dish is prepared by the chef-patron of this small restaurant in the former home of T S Eliot.

NEWBURY: The Halfway Bistro ££
Gastropub
Bath Rd, West Berkshire, RG20 8NR
Tel *01488 608 115* **Closed** *Sun dinner*
The Halfway takes pub food to a classy level with mains such as slow-braised beef with fresh herbs.

OXFORD: Everest £
Nepalese
14/–151 Howard St, Oxfordshire, OX4 3AZ
Tel *01865 251555*
Everest serves authentic Nepalese cuisine prepared from the freshest of ingredients.

OXFORD: Cherwell Boathouse ££
Modern British
Bardwell Rd, Oxfordshire, OX2 6ST
Tel *01865 515978*
Long-established family restaurant on the banks of the Cherwell serving classic dishes, alfresco in summer. Good wine list.

READING: Mya Lacarte £
Modern British
5 Prospect St, West Berkshire, RG4 8JB
Tel *01189 463400* **Closed** *Sun*
This restaurant gives an interesting twist to traditional British cuisine and uses quality seasonal ingredients.

DK Choice

READING: L'Ortolan £££
French
Church Lane, Shinfield, West Berkshire, RG2 9BY
Tel *01189 888500* **Closed** *Sun & Mon*
Located in a former vicarage, this Michelin-starred restaurant features French classics with a contemporary twist. The service is excellent and knowledgeable sommeliers recommend suitable wine pairings. There are also affordable set lunch menus and elaborate tasting menus.

ST ALBANS: L'Olivo £
Italian
135 Marford Rd, Wheathampstead, Hertfordshire, AL4 8NH
Tel *01582 834145* **Closed** *Sun & Mon; lunch*
The chic decor provides the perfect setting for sampling delectable southern Italian fare, from handmade pasta to seafood.

WATFORD: Tarboush £
Lebanese
57 Market St, Hertfordshire, WD18 0PR
Tel *01923 248898*
The Middle East comes to Watford with a shisha garden and authentic Lebanese cuisine – at reasonable prices, too.

WINDSOR: Al Fassia £
Moroccan
27 St Leonard's Rd, West Berkshire, SL4 3BP
Tel *01753 855370* **Closed** *lunch Mon–Fri*
Relish home-cooked tagines and couscous specials teamed with beer from Casablanca at this richly decorated restaurant.

WOBURN: Paris House £££
Modern British
Woburn Safari Park, London Rd, Bedfordshire, MK17 9QP
Tel *01525 290692* **Closed** *Sun dinner; Mon & Tue*
At this acclaimed destination restaurant, diners can choose from the six-, eight- or ten-course menus on offer.

WOODSTOCK: La Galleria ££
Italian
2 Market Pl, Town Centre, OX20 1TA
Tel *01993 813381* **Closed** *Mon*
This up-market restaurant dishes up traditional Italian fare. Staff give a warm welcome.

Wessex

AVEBURY: Circles Café £
Café
Wiltshire, SN8 1RF
Tel *01672 539250*
These National Trust tearooms are great for relaxing with tea and homemade cake after a trip to the stones.

BATH: The Circus ££
Modern British
34 Brock St, BA1 2LN
Tel *01225 466020*
The Circus offers and all-day menu of dishes ranging from crumpets to wild boar and Yorkshire rhubarb. The lively ambience fits the name of the place.

The stylish seating area at Urban Reef, Bournemouth

BATH: Acorn Vegetarian Kitchen ££
Vegetarian
2 North Parade Passage, Somerset, BA1 1NX
Tel *01225 446059*
Vegetarian restaurant serving innovative small dishes. Sunday roasts and cocktails are popular.

BATH: The Marlborough Tavern ££
Gastropub
35 Marlborough Buildings, Somerset, BA1 2LY
Tel *01225 423731* **Closed** *Sun dinner*
Relaxed, friendly pub, close to the Royal Crescent, focusing on local and quality ingredients. Good selection of beers and wines.

BATH: Menu Gordon Jones ££
Fine Dining
2 Wellsway, Somerset, BA2 3AQ
Tel *01225 480871* **Closed** *Sun*
Friendly fine dining, with superb ingredients and plenty of surprises: Dorset snails or Cornish gull eggs maybe?

BOURNEMOUTH: Chez Fred £
Traditional British
10 Seamoor Rd, Dorset, BH4 9AN
Tel *01202 761023* **Closed** *Sun lunch*
Bournemouth's favourite fish-and-chips spot, with delicious sustainable cod and haddock to eat in or take away.

BOURNEMOUTH: Urban Reef ££
Café
The Overstrand, Undercliff Drive, Boscombe, Dorset, BH5 1BN
Tel *01202 443960*
Café by day and restaurant by night, right on the beach, serving anything from pancakes to Dorset rock oysters and wasabi.

BOURNEMOUTH: West Beach ££
Seafood
Pier Approach, Dorset, BH2 5AA
Tel *01202 587785*
Kid-friendly beachfront bistro. Great seafood platters, Poole Bay lobster and local mussels, plus Dorset beef. Book ahead.

BRADFORD-ON-AVON: Fat Fowl and the Roost ££
Mediterranean
Silver St, Wiltshire, BA15 1JX
Tel *01225 863111*
This family-friendly café by day transforms into a quality eatery by night. Great tapas.

BRIDPORT: Hive Beach Café £
Café
Beach Rd, Burton Bradstock, Dorset, DT6 4RF
Tel *01308 897070*
Popular café overlooking the shingle beach and honey-coloured cliffs. Great seafood and West Country ice creams.

BRIDPORT: Watch House Café £
Café
West Bay, Dorset DT6 4EN
Tel *01308 459330*
Breezy harbourside café serving hearty breakfasts and lunchtime pizzas from its wood-fired oven.

BRISTOL: Maitreya Social £
Vegetarian
89 St Marks Rd, Easton, BS5 6HY
Tel *0117 951 0100* **Closed** *Tue–Thu lunch; Sun & Mon*
Friendly, buzzing restaurant, showcasing local art and serving innovative vegetarian and vegan dishes with tasty dressings.

BRISTOL: Rocotillos £
Café
1 Queen's Rd, Clifton Triangle, Clifton, BS8 1EZ
Tel *0117 929 7207*
A 1950s-style diner on Clifton Triangle, popular with students and local workers. Great burgers, chips and ice-cream milkshakes.

BRISTOL: Thali Café £
Indian
1 Regents St, Clifton, BS8 4HW
Tel *0117 974 3793*
A Bristol landmark, the Thali Café is a kitsch Indian café serving traditional *thalis*. Takeaways, too.

BRISTOL: Riverstation Restaurant ££
Modern British
The Grove, Bristol BS1 4RB
Tel *0117 914 4434*
Savour the views of the harbour from this modern restaurant, where local and seasonal produce is used for tasty dishes.

BRUTON: At the Chapel ££
Pizzeria
28 High St, Somerset, BA10 0AE
Tel *01749 814070*
Set in a converted chapel, this place serves delicious wood-fired-oven pizzas and seasonal salads. Bakery and wine store on site.

CHIPPENHAM: Lucknam Park £££
Fine Dining
Colerne, Wiltshire, SN14 8AZ
Tel *01225 742777* **Closed** *Mon & Tue*
Exquisite Michelin-starred and locally sourced fine dining in the 17th-century Lucknam Park Hotel.

EASTON GREY: Whatley Manor £££
Fine Dining
Malmesbury, Wiltshire, SN16 0RB
Tel *01666 822888* **Closed** *Mon & Tue*
Home to the Michelin-starred Dining Room, which is known for its legendary food and afternoon tea. For more casual dining, try Grey's brasserie (open daily).

GLASTONBURY: Rainbow's End £
Vegetarian
17b High St, Somerset, BA6 9DP
Tel *01458 833896*
Glastonbury's original vegetarian café serves homemade meals and cakes and has a salad bar. Vegan and wheat-free dishes available.

ISLE OF PURBECK: Shell Bay Seafood Restaurant ££
Seafood
Ferry Rd, Swanage, Dorset, BH19 3BA
Tel *01929 450363*
Arrive by boat, ferry or car at this stunning restaurant and bistro on the edge of the Isle of Purbeck. Superb seafood dishes.

LACOCK: The Bell £
Traditional British
The Wharf, Bowden Hill, Wiltshire, SS15 2PJ
Tel *01249 730308*
Award-winning country pub on the outskirts of Lacock, serving traditional pub classics.

LACOCK: Sign of the Angel ££
Traditional British
6 Church St, Wiltshire, SN15 2LB
Tel *01249 730230* **Closed** *Sun & Mon*
Enjoy a cream tea or meal at this ancient coaching inn that lights log fires in winter.

LONGLEAT: The Bath Arms ££
Modern British
Horningsham, Warminster, Wiltshire, BA12 7LY
Tel *01985 844308*
Set on the edge of the Longleat estate, The Bath Arms offers fabulous pub food plus a dining room that serves local cuisine and drinks.

**LYME REGIS: Hix Oyster &
Fish House** ££
Seafood
Cobb Rd, DT7 3JP
Tel *01297 446910* **Closed** *Nov–Feb:
Mon & Tue*
With a panoramic view of the bay,
this restaurant specializes in oyster
and salmon snacks, as well as
plenty of local fish dishes.

**MALMESBURY: The Potting
Shed** ££
Modern British
Crudwell, Wiltshire, SN16 9EW
Tel *01666 577833*
Vegetables and herbs go straight
from the garden to the plate at
this beamed Cotswold pub.
Good choice of wines and port.

POOLE: Courtyard Tea Rooms £
Café
18a High St, Dorset, DH15 1DT
Tel *01202 670358* **Closed** *Nov–Mar:
Mon & Tue*
Sit in the intimate courtyard for
soups, snacks, quiches or a light
lunch. Excellent selection of black
and green teas.

POOLE: Sandbanks Beach Café £
Café
*Banks Rd, Sandbanks, Dorset,
BH13 7QQ*
Tel *01202 708621*
Beachside café in an up-market
area, serving fish and chips,
burgers, tea and cakes.

POOLE: Rick Stein ££
Seafood
10–14 Banks Rd, Dorset, BH13 7QB
Tel *01202 283000*
Classic seafood dishes such as crab
salad and *fruits de mer* accompany
the great views across the bay.

PORLOCK: The Big Cheese £
Café
High St, Somerset, TA24 8PT
Tel *01643 862773* **Closed** *Sun*
A delightful café and purveyor of
fine local cheeses. Try the cheese
platters, ploughman's or a coffee.

**ROWDE: The Rowdey Cow
Farm Café** £
Café
*Lower Farm, Devizes Rd, Devizes,
Wiltshire, SN10 2LX*
Tel *01380 829666*
Fun for the whole family, with
cows grazing nearby. Homemade
ice cream, soups and sandwiches.

SALISBURY: Hox Brasserie £
Indian
155 Fisherton St, Wiltshire, SP2 7RP
Tel *01722 341600*
This restaurant and takeaway,
specializing in traditional South
Indian dishes, is a local favourite.

SALISBURY: Wagamama £
Asian
8–10 Bridge St, Wiltshire, SP1 2LX
Tel *01722 412165*
Japanese-inspired dining is the
order of the day at this chain
restaurant. Good for families.
Takeaway is available.

SALISBURY: Charter 1227 ££
Modern British
*6–7 Ox Row, The Market Place,
Wiltshire, SP1 1EU*
Tel *01722 333118* **Closed** *Sun & Mon*
Stylish, top-rated restaurant
overlooking Salisbury's marketplace. Delicious modern British
and European fare.

**SHEPTON MALLET:
Kilver Court** £
Café
Kilver St, Somerset, BA4 5NF
Tel *01749 340363*
The two cafés at Kilver Court
serve sandwiches, spelt flat
breads and salads, as well as
a range of heartier dishes.

SHERBORNE: The Bakery Café £
Café
1 The Green, Dorset, DT9 3HZ
Tel *01935 813264* **Closed** *Sun*
This charming bakery offers
great-value delicious bread, cakes
and pizzas. Popular with kids.

**SHERBORNE: The Rose and
Crown at Trent** ££
Gastropub
Trent, Dorset, DT9 4SL
Tel *01935 850776*
A 14th-century rural pub just
outside Sherborne. It's worth
making a detour for its fine food
and charming country appeal.
Fantastic Sunday lunch.

**STUDLAND: The Pig on
the Beach** ££
Modern British
*Manor House, Manor Rd, Dorset,
BH19 3AU*
Tel *01929 450288*
Vegetables, fruit and herbs from
the walled garden alongside local

fish and meat are served in a
lovely conservatory restaurant.

WEYMOUTH: Fish 'n' Fritz £
Traditional British
9 Market St, Dorset, DT4 8DD
Tel *01305 766386*
Fish 'n' Fritz has fantastic,
award-winning fish and chips
to take away or eat on site.
There is also a great kids' menu.

**WEYMOUTH:
Crab House Café** ££
Café
*Ferrymans Way, Portland Rd, Wyke
Regis, Dorset, DT4 9YU*
Tel *01305 788867* **Closed** *Mon
& Tue*
Glorious café overlooking Chesil
Beach that serves the best fresh
crabs and oysters from the
nearby beds. The menu changes
twice daily. Children welcome.

DK Choice

**WRINGTON:
The Ethicurean** ££
Modern British
*Barley Wood Walled Garden,
Somerset, BS40 5SA*
Tel *01934 863713* **Closed** *Mon*
The Ethicurean is an outstanding
café-restaurant overlooking
the Mendip Hills. It serves
dynamic and experimental
organic food and is worth the
trek, especially in autumn.
Delicious coffee and sticky
toffee apple cake.

Devon and Cornwall

BARNSTAPLE: Terra Madre ££
Mediterranean
Muddiford, Devon, EX31 4EX
Tel *01271 850262* **Closed** *Sun
dinner; Mon & Tue*
Fantastic Mediterranean slow food
restaurant in a sculpture garden.
Local organic produce and good
vegetarian and vegan options.

Looking out to the harbour from Riverstation Restaurant, Bristol

For more information on types of restaurants *see pages 575–6*

BIGBURY: The Oyster Shack £
Seafood
Milburn Orchard Farm, Stakes Hill,
Devon, TQ7 4BE
Tel *01548 810878* **Closed** *Sun dinner*
Cheerful venue serving truly
great local seafood with a
Mediterranean twist. Set menus
and a friendly atmosphere.

DK Choice

BUCKFASTLEIGH: Riverford
Field Kitchen ££
Café
Wash Barn, Devon, TQ11 0JU
Tel *01803 762074*
Get a genuine taste of the
southwest: Riverford's great
family-friendly restaurant serves
simple weekday meals and
indulgent weekend feasts.
Bookings essential.

BUDE: The Beach Restaurant ££
Modern British
Summerleaze Crescent, Cornwall,
EX23 8HJ
Tel *01288 389800*
Chic restaurant with a lovely
terrace for sunset views and
cocktails and great seafood dishes.

CHAGFORD: Gidleigh Park £££
Fine Dining
Gidleigh Park, Devon, TQ13 8HH
Tel *01647 432367*
Head chef Michael Wignall serves
a feast of complex British delights
at this two-Michelin-starred
restaurant. Book well ahead.

CROYDE: Sandleigh Tea
Rooms £
Café
Moor Lane, Devon, EX33 1PA
Tel *01271 890930*
These National Trust tearooms,
tucked around the corner from
the surf beach, are great for a
proper Devon cream tea.

DARTMOUTH: Rockfish £
Seafood
8 South Embankment, Devon,
TQ6 9BH
Tel *01803 832800*
This Mitch Tonks-run takeaway
and restaurant serves award-
winning, top-quality fish and
South Devon crab sandwiches.

DARTMOUTH: The Seahorse £££
Seafood
5 South Embankment, Devon,
TQ6 9BH
Tel *01803 835147* **Closed** *Sun & Mon*
Another fantastic Mitch Tonks-
run fish restaurant specializing in
seafood with the likes of cuttlefish,
squid, turbot, sole and mussels
on the menu. Extensive wine list.

EXETER: Darts Farm £
Café
Bridge Hill, Topsham, Devon, EX3 0QH
Tel *01392 878201*
Ingredients come straight from
the farm shop to the table. All-
day breakfasts, daily specials and
cream teas are offered.

EXETER: Jack in the Green ££
Gastropub
Rockbeare, Devon, EX5 2EE
Tel *01404 822240*
This cheerful pub serves nicely
presented food that makes the
most of Devon produce.

EXMOUTH: River Exe Café £
Traditional British
The Docks, Devon
Tel *07761 116103* **Closed** *Nov–Mar*
Book a water taxi to this floating
restaurant for local seafood, fish
and chips, burgers and pizza.

FALMOUTH: Gylly Beach Café £
Café
Cliff Rd, Cornwall, TR11 4PA
Tel *01326 312884*
Stylish beach café serving big,
delicious Cornish meals. Music
every Sunday night, with roasts in
winter and barbecues in summer.

FALMOUTH: The Wheelhouse ££
Seafood
Upton Slip, Cornwall, TR11 3DQ
Tel *01326 318050* **Closed** *Sun–Tue*
This crab and oyster bar has no
menu but serves great seafood
combinations. Bookings essential.

FOWEY: Sam's on the Beach £
Café
14 Polkerris, Par, Cornwall, PL24 2TL
Tel *01726 812255*
Part of a Cornish mini-chain, this
branch in the old lifeboat station
serves pizza, lobster and a fusion
of Cornish and Mediterranean fare.

Beautiful estuary views from the dining
room at Q Restaurant, Fowey

FOWEY: Q Restaurant £££
Bistro
28 Fore St, Cornwall, PL27 1AQ
Tel *01726 833302*
Up-market but relaxed restaurant
with fabulous views. Serves Fowey
River oysters, local scallops,
venison and Cornish cheeses.

HELSTON: Croust House £
Café
Tregellas Barton Farm, St Keverne,
Cornwall, TR12 6NX
Tel *01326 280479*
Homemade breakfasts and
lunches include soups, salads,
burgers, ice creams and pizzas.

HELSTON: Kota ££
Asian
Harbour Head, Porthleven, Cornwall,
TR13 9JA
Tel *01326 562407* **Closed** *Sun &*
Mon; out of season: Sun–Tue
In a lovely harbourside setting,
this restaurant serves delicious
Asian fusion food. *Kota* is the
Maori word for "shellfish".

ILFRACOMBE: 11 The Quay ££
Café
11 The Quay, Devon, EX34 9EQ
Tel *01271 868090*
This Damien Hirst-owned chic
café-bar serves local seafood and
pasta dishes, with a more refined
dining room upstairs.

KINGSBRIDGE: Millbrook Inn ££
Gastropub
South Pool, Devon, TQ7 2RW
Tel *01548 531581* **Closed** *Dec–Feb:*
Mon dinner
Millbrook is an award-winning
traditional inn with a British menu
specializing in nose-to-tail eating.

MAWGAN PORTH: Bedruthan
Steps Wild Café ££
Brasserie
Trenance, Cornwall, TR8 4BU
Tel *01637 861212*
This sophisticated, bright café
serves pizzas, burgers and three-
course meals. Family friendly.

MAWGAN PORTH: The Scarlet £££
Fine Dining
Tredragon Rd, Cornwall, TR8 4DQ
Tel *01637 861800*
Up-market restaurant with views
of the beach and sea. Enjoy
delicious Cornish food and wines.

MOUSEHOLE: The Old
Coastguard £
Modern British
The Parade, Penzance, Cornwall,
TR19 6PR
Tel *01736 731222*
Brasserie-style restaurant serving
plenty of fresh fish, local game and
dairy produce, and a Sunday roast.

Key to Price Guide *see page 582*

The spacious interior of The Scarlet, Mawgan Porth

NEWQUAY: Fifteen Cornwall £££
Seafood
Watergate Bay, Cornwall,
TR8 4AA
Tel *01637 861000*
Celebrity chef Jamie Oliver's
restaurant perched on the cliffs
serves fantastic seafood with rich
Mediterranean flavours.

OKEHAMPTON: Lewtrenchard
Manor £££
Fine Dining
Lewdown, Devon, EX20 4PN
Tel *01566 783222*
Exquisite fine-dining restaurant
in a country house on Dartmoor.
Some of the best local produce
cooked in innovative ways.

PADSTOW: St Petroc's ££
Fine Dining
4 New St, Cornwall, PL28 8EA
Tel *01841 532700*
Tucked away on a back street,
St Petroc's serves Mediterranean-
inspired, bistro-style dishes in a
charming rustic building.

DK Choice

PADSTOW: The Seafood
Restaurant £££
Seafood
Riverside, Cornwall, PL28 8BY
Tel *01841 532700*
Rick Stein's restaurant, opened
in 1975, has an international
reputation for superb seafood
dishes exquisitely cooked. Sit
at the central bar and watch
sashimi and oysters being
prepared before you. Menus
change according to what is
caught on the day. No children
under three.

PENZANCE: The Victoria Inn ££
Gastropub
Perranuthnoe, Cornwall, TR20 9NP
Tel *01736 710309* **Closed** *Sun*
dinner
A 12th-century inn serving award-
winning food, fine wine, cider and
Cornish lager. Good for families.

PLYMOUTH: River Cottage
Canteen £
Bistro
Royal William Yard, Cornwall, PL1 3QQ
Tel *01752 252702*
Housed in the Royal Navy's former
victualling depot, this bistro
serves seasonal and organic
food, with plenty of local fish.

PLYMOUTH:
Barbican Kitchen ££
Modern British
Plymouth Gin Distillery, 60 Southside
St, Devon, PL1 2LO
Tel *01752 604448* **Closed** *Sun*
This busy brasserie in the famous
gin distillery serves up plenty of
steaks and burgers along with its
fish dishes, all locally sourced.

PORT ISAAC: Restaurant
Nathan Outlaw £££
Fine Dining
6 New Rd, Cornwall, PL29 3SB
Tel *01208 880895* **Closed** *lunch Wed*
& Thu; Sun–Tue
An outstanding seafood tasting
menu is served at this glossy
two-Michelin-starred restaurant.
Vegetarian menu available if
booked in advance.

SALCOMBE: The Winking
Prawn ££
Café
North Sands, Devon, TQ8 8LD
Tel *01548 842326*
Fun beach café and barbecue
restaurant overlooking North
Sands. Range of seafood, snacks,
ice cream and cream teas on offer.

SHALDON: Ode Café £
Café
Ness Cove, Devon, TQ14 0HP
Tel *01626 873427*
Stylish café serving sourdough
pizzas, soups, salads and ice
creams. Microbrewery on site.

ST IVES: Tate St Ives Café £
Café
Porthmeor Beach, Cornwall, TR26 1TG
Tel *01736 791122* **Closed** *Mon*
Light-filled café in the Tate St Ives

art gallery. Sample the luscious
cakes and light bites, often
sourced from Cornwall.

ST IVES: Porthminster
Beach Restaurant and Café ££
Café
Porthminster Beach, Cornwall,
TR26 2EB
Tel *01736 795352* **Closed** *dinner*
Sun–Wed; Nov–Mar: Mon
Café by day, restaurant by night,
this places serves award-winning
seafood with Mediterranean and
Asian touches.

SOUTH MILTON:
The Beachhouse £
Seafood
Kingsbridge, Devon, TQ7 3JY
Tel *01548 561144* **Closed** *dinner*
Sun–Thu exc school hols
Hearty breakfasts, crab
sandwiches and daily specials
such as sardines on sourdough
are served at this popular
beachside shack.

TAVISTOCK: Hotel Endsleigh £££
Fine Dining
Milton Abbot, Tamar Valley, Devon,
PL19 0PQ
Tel *01822 870000*
The elegant restaurant within
the luxurious Hotel Endsleigh
serves delicious meals including
scallops, venison, soufflés and
opera cake. Good lunch deals.

TORQUAY: The Elephant £££
Fine Dining
3–4 Beacon Hill, Devon, TQ1 2BH
Tel *01803 200044* **Closed** *Sun*
& Mon
Michelin-starred restaurant
and brasserie set within a two-
storey Georgian town house.
Great tasting menu. Reservations
are essential.

ZENNOR: The Gurnard's
Head ££
Pub
St Ives, Cornwall, TR26 3DE
Tel *01736 796928*
This cosy pub with rooms serves
fresh local food, with a short
seasonal menu based on what is
best on the day. Kids welcome.

The Heart of England

BIRMINGHAM: Purnell's £££
Modern British
55 Cornwall St, West Midlands,
B3 2DH
Tel *0121 212 9799* **Closed** *Sun & Mon*
Outstanding Michelin-starred
restaurant; try the roast loin of
veal with scorched squid and
shallot purée.

BIRMINGHAM: Simpsons £££
French
20 Highfield Rd, Edgbaston, B15 3DU
Tel *0121 454 3434*   **Closed** *Mon*
A stylish place where the emphasis
is on high-quality ingredients
and beautiful presentation.

DK Choice

BOURTON-ON-THE-HILL:
Horse and Groom £
Modern British
Bourton-on-the-Hill, GL56 9AQ
Tel *01386 700413*   **Closed** *Sun;*
25 & 31 Dec
Horse and Groom is a multi-
award-winning Gloucestershire
pub where the daily-changing
blackboard menu features
anything from beer-battered
fillet of hake to Dexter beef and
ale pie. The honey-coloured
building itself is part of the
draw, as is the convivial outside
seating and picturesque kitchen
garden. Friendly staff and
beautiful surroundings.

BOURTON-ON-THE-WATER:
The Croft Restaurant £
Traditional British
Victoria St, Gloucestershire, GL54 2BX
Tel *01451 821132*
An all-day restaurant serving full
English breakfasts through to
meaty mains: steak and ale pie,
bangers and mash, and burgers.

CHELTENHAM: Daffodil ££
Modern British
18–20 Suffolk Parade, GL50 2AE
Tel *01242 700055*   **Closed** *Sun*
An Art Deco cinema transformed
into a lively restaurant. The Afternoon Matinee Tea is great fun, as
are cocktails from the Circle Bar.

CHELTENHAM: Prithvi ££
Indian
37 Bath Rd, Gloucestershire, GL53 7HG
Tel *01242 226229*   **Closed** *Mon*
A sophisticated take on Indian

The lamp-lit garden at The Mad Turk,
Stamford

cuisine – for example, stone bass
with a clementine jus.

CHESTER: Upstairs at the Grill ££
Grill
70 Watergate St, Cheshire, CH1 2LA
Tel *01244 344883*
Manhattan-style steakhouse and
cocktail bar, with fabulous steaks
and lobster and Sunday roasts.

CHIPPING CAMPDEN: Eight Bells £
Traditional British
Church St, Gloucestershire, GL55 6JG
Tel *01386 840371*
An ancient pub, rebuilt using
original stone and timbers in the
17th century. Hearty English food
made with seasonal produce.

CIRENCESTER: Piazza Fontana £
Italian
30 Castle St, Gloucestershire, GL7 1QH
Tel *01285 643133*   **Closed** *Sun*
Popular pizza joint serving up
Sardinian wine alongside pizzas
and calzones. Great tiramisu.

CIRENCESTER: Jesse's ££
Modern British
The Stableyard, Black Jack St, GL7 2AA
Tel *01285 641497*   **Closed** *Sun &*
Mon dinner
This intimate bistro has a little
courtyard and serves the best
seasonal foods. Enjoy a chilled
sherry and Cotswold game terrine.

COVENTRY: Rising Café £
Café
Priory St, CV1 5FB
Tel *0247 652 1235*   **Closed** *Sun*
This 1940s-style café/diner in the
cathedral grounds offers super
breakfasts and baked treats.

IRONBRIDGE: Restaurant
Severn ££
French
33 High St, Telford, Shropshire TF8 7AG
Tel *01952 432233* **Closed** *Mon & Tue*
Classic French food incorporating
modern British trends. Produce
comes from the restaurant's farm.

MALVERN: The Inn at Welland £
Gastropub
Drake St, Welland, Worcestershire,
WR13 6LN
Tel *01684 592317*   **Closed** *Mon*
Modernized country inn where
posh pub food hits the mark.
Excellent Sunday roasts, Waldorf
salad and cheese platters.

MORETON-IN-MARSH:
The Spice Room £
Indian
3 Oxford St, Gloucestershire, GL56 0LA
Tel *01608 654204*
Long-established Indian eatery
in a quintessential Cotswolds
town. Try the Jingra Roshi platter.

ROSS-ON-WYE: Eagle Inn £
Traditional British
Broad St, Herefordshire, HR9 7EA
Tel *01989 562625*
A traditional friendly pub with
filling burgers and steaks. They also
do smaller portions of the mains.

SHREWSBURY: La Dolce Vita ££
Italian
35 Hill's Lane, Shropshire, SY1 1QU
Tel *01743 249126* **Closed** *Mon & Tue*
Traditional but contemporary
Italian food. Lovely atmosphere
and friendly service.

STOW-ON-THE-WOLD:
Cutler's Restaurant ££
Modern British
Fosseway, Gloucestershire, GL54 1JX
Tel *01451 830297* **Closed** *Sun dinner*
Located in the boutique Number
Four Hotel, Cutler's fuses the
modern and the traditional in
its roast meat and fish dishes.

STRATFORD-UPON-AVON:
The Opposition Bistro £
Bistro
13 Sheep St, Warwickshire, CV37 6EF
Tel *01789 269980*   **Closed** *Sun*
except public hols
A timber-framed interior provides
a great atmosphere for good
bistro standards.

WORCESTER: Burgerworks £
American
12 Friar St, Worcestershire, WR1 2LZ
Tel *01905 27770*   **Closed** *Mon*
Chicken and lamb are on the menu,
along with burgers using beef
from grass-fed Hereford cattle.

East Midlands

DK Choice

ASHBOURNE: Lighthouse ££
Modern British
The Rose and Crown, New Rd,
Boylestone, Derbyshire, DE6 5AA
Tel *01335 330658* **Closed** *Sun–Tue*
Elegant, classic British food with
a distinct French influence, for
example truffle stuffed quails
with asparagus, and bresse
chicken with leek hollandaise.
There are seasonal tasting menus
and a six-course set menu. An
exquisite dining experience.

BAKEWELL: Piedaniel's ££
French
Bath St, Derbyshire, DE45 1BX
Tel *01629 812687* **Closed** *Sun & Mon*
Attractive dining room serving
elaborate French cuisine, such as
rabbit rillettes and crêpes suzette.

BASLOW: Fischer's £££
Modern British
Calver Rd, Derbyshire, DE45 1RR
Tel *01246 583259*
A handsome 1907 house with
a kitchen garden. Try the
Derbyshire lamb, Scottish hand-
dived scallops or Cornish crab.

BUXTON: The Knight's Table £
Traditional British
*Leek Rd, Quarnford, Derbyshire,
SK17 0SN*
Tel *01298 23695* **Closed** *Mon & Tue*
Ancient Peak District pub with
open fires and stone-paved floors.
Old favourites such as steak and
ale pie on the menu.

BUXTON: Carriages Bar &
Restaurant ££
Modern British
*Newhaven, near Hartington,
Derbyshire, SK17 0DU*
Tel *01298 84528* **Closed** *Sun dinner,
Wed*
This rather unique restaurant is
located inside a railway carriage
and offers juicy steaks, venison
burgers and pasta dishes.

DERBY: The Exeter Arms £
Traditional British
Exeter Pl, Derbyshire, DE1 2EU
Tel *01332 605323*
Cosy pub serving well-cooked fish
and chips, smoked meats and
steaks. Good choice of ales.

GLOSSOP: Ayubowan £
Sri Lankan
46–50 High St, Derbyshire, SK13 8BH
Tel *01457 865168* **Closed** *Mon*
Authentic Sri Lankan food with a
modern twist. Elegant interiors
featuring bold Asian artworks.

ILKESTON: Durham Ox £
Traditional British
Durham St, Derbyshire, DE7 8FQ
Tel *0115 854 7107* **Closed** *Mon & Tue*
An inn founded in 1780, once the
town gaol. Try the lamb and mint
pie or beef bourguignon.

LEICESTER: Sapori ££
Italian
40 Stadon Rd, Leicestershire, LE7 7AY
Tel *0116 236 8900* **Closed** *Sun
dinner; Mon*
Sapori's head chef, from Torre del
Greco in Italy, whips up fantastic
creations like rabbit ragout with
black olives and dark chocolate.

LINCOLN: The Bronze Pig £££
Traditional British
4 Burton Rd, LN1 3LB
Tel *01522 524817* **Closed** *Sun dinner;
Mon & Tue*
Welcoming restaurant run by an
Irishman and a Sicilian who give
a European twist to British dishes.

The interior of Burgerworks, Worcester

MANSFIELD: BB's Italian
Restaurant £
Italian
*1 Bridge St, Nottinghamshire,
NG18 1AL*
Tel *01623 622940* **Closed** *Sun
& Mon*
An unglamorous exterior, but
great food and warm service.
Delicious pizzas and puddings.

MATLOCK: The Balti £
Indian
*256 Dale Rd, Matlock Bath,
Derbyshire, DE4 3NT*
Tel *01629 55069* **Closed** *Tue*
Attentive waiters serve reliably
good Indian food at this Peak
District restaurant.

NOTTINGHAM: La Rock ££
French
*4 Bridge St, Sandiacre,
Nottinghamshire, NG10 5QT*
Tel *0115 939 9833* **Closed** *Mon &
Tue; 26 Dec–15 Jan, 25 July–15 Aug*
Combines traditional styles with
cutting-edge French cuisine.
Artistic presentation.

NORTHAMPTON: Sophia's ££
Mediterranean
54 Bridge St, NN1 1PA
Tel *01604 250654* **Closed** *Sun*
This warm, welcoming trattoria
serves pasta and pizza dishes, as
well as meat and fish mains.

STAMFORD: The Gallery
Restaurant £
Modern British
*New College Stamford, Drift Rd,
Lincolnshire, PE9 1XA*
Tel *01780 484340*
Fine gourmet dinners and simpler
lunch specials cooked by aspiring
chefs at New College Stamford.

STAMFORD: The Mad Turk ££
Turkish
*8–9 St Paul's St, Lincolnshire,
PE9 2BE*
Tel *01780 238001* **Closed** *Sun*
Dine on meze and chicken shish
kebabs at this popular Turkish
place with a lamp-lit garden.

Lancashire and
the Lakes

AMBLESIDE: Zeffirellis £
Vegetarian
Compston Rd, Cumbria, LA22 9AD
Tel *015394 33845.*
Book ahead at this hugely
popular vegetarian pizza joint.
Attached cinema and jazz bar.

AMBLESIDE: Eltermere Inn
Restaurant ££
Modern British
Elterwater, Cumbria, LA22 9HY
Tel *015394 37207*
Dishes are created from local
ingredients and inventive recipes.
Enjoy views of Elterwater Lake
and Loughrigg Fell.

AMBLESIDE: Fellini's ££
Vegetarian
Church St, Cumbria, LA22 0BT
Tel *015394 32487*
A stylish modern vegetarian
restaurant attached to a small,
state-of-the-art cinema.

AMBLESIDE: The Old Stamp
House Restaurant £££
Modern British
Church St, Cumbria, LA22 0BU
Tel *01539 432775* **Closed** *Sun & Mon*
Heavy on the use of shellfish,
this restaurant serves Cumbrian-
inspired food. Local ingredients
are used whenever possible.

BOOTLE: The Byre Tearooms ££
Traditional British
Millstones Barn, Millom, LA19 5TJ
Tel *01229 718757* **Closed** *Mon*
This gem of a place serves
Cumbrian specialities such as
pork and apple loaf, as well
as tasty homemade cakes.

BOWNESS ON WINDERMERE:
Jintana Thai Restaurant £
Thai
Lake Rd, Cumbria, LA23 3BJ
Tel *015394 45002*
Enjoy traditional dishes of Jintana
Thai's own specialties.

For more information on types of restaurants *see pages 575–6*

BOWNESS-ON-WINDERMERE:
Porto Restaurant ££
European
3 Ash St, Cumbria, LA23 3EB
Tel *015394 48242*
Refined dining in a boutique
setting. Try the Porto Pig Plate and
twice-baked sticky toffee soufflé.

BRAITHWAITE: The Restaurant
at The Cottage in the Wood ££
Modern British
Magic Hill, Whinlatter Forest,
near Keswick, Cumbria CA12 5TW
Tel *01768 778409* **Closed** *Sun & Mon*
Enjoy breathtaking views while
tucking into beautifully presented food. The menu makes
the most of local produce.

BROUGHTON-IN-FURNESS:
Beswicks Restaurant ££
French
Langholme House, The Square,
Cumbria, LA20 6JF
Tel *01229 716285* **Closed** *Sun & Mon*
The changing menu features up
to five courses, with options for
vegetarians and those with
special dietary needs.

BROUGHTON-IN-FURNESS:
The Blacksmiths Arms ££
Pub
Broughton Mills, near Bowness-on-
Windermere, Cumbria, LA20 6AX
Tel *01229 716824*
One of the Lakes' characteristic
ancient inns, serving fantastic
local beef and Herdwick lamb.

DK Choice

CARTMEL: L'Enclume £££
Modern British
Cavendish St, Cumbria, LA11 6PZ
Tel *015395 36362*
An ancient building with rough
lime-washed walls and low
beams is the rustic setting for
some extraordinary food.
Savour local cuisine, partly
foraged, and presented with
lots of attention to detail.

COCKERMOUTH: Quince &
Medlar ££
Vegetarian
13 Castlegate, Cumbria, CA13 9EU
Tel *01900 823579* **Closed** *Sun & Mon*
Elegantly presented dishes
include wasabi-baked beets and
a wild mushroom filo cup.

GRANGE-OVER-SANDS: The
Hare and Hounds Restaurant ££
Gastropub
Bowland Bridge, Cumbria, LA11 6NN
Tel *015395 68333*
Great gastropub with a cosy log
fire. Try the local black pudding
gâteau or lamb hot pot.

Oak-beamed restaurant at The Dining Room, Grasmere

GRASMERE: The Dining Room ££
Modern British
Broadgate, Cumbria, LA22 9TA
Tel *015394 35217*
Enjoy fine dining at this hotel
restaurant where patrons relax in
the lounge until the first course
is ready. Local and homemade
produce used when possible.

GRASMERE: Jumble Room ££
European
Langdale Rd, Cumbria, LA22 9SU
Tel *015394 35188* **Closed** *Tue*
Long-established and lavishly
decorated restaurant with an
eclectic European menu.

KENDAL: Baba Ganoush
Canteen £
Middle Eastern
Unit 4, Berrys Yard, 27 Finkle St,
Cumbria, LA9 4AB
Tel *01539 738210* **Closed** *Sun & Mon*
Canteen-style restaurant. Great
risotto, cassoulet, slow-roasted
meat and vegetarian meze boards.

KESWICK: A Taste of Thailand £
Thai
Shemara Guest House, 27 Bank St,
Cumbria, CA12 5JZ
Tel *017687 73936*
Savour exquisitely presented
northern Thai food in this
Lakeland guesthouse.

KESWICK: Morrels Restaurant £
Traditional British
34 Lake Rd, Cumbria, CA12 5DQ
Tel *017687 72666* **Closed** *Mon*
Light, modern bistro-style place.
Try a starter of asparagus with
walnut, and move on to braised
daube of beef on root mash.

LIVERPOOL: Shiraz £
Turkish
19 North John St, Merseyside,
L2 5QU
Tel *0151 236 8325*
The food is robust but well
presented. Try the Turkish classic
barbecue meat grills, served with
a selection of salads.

LIVERPOOL: Pushka ££
Modern British
16 Rodney Street, Liverpool L1 2TE
Tel *0151 708 8698*
Unpretentious, smart family-run
place serving delicious daily
specials off a small menu focused
on local seasonal produce.

MANCHESTER: The Pavilion 2 ££
Bangladeshi
231 Spotland Rd, Rochdale,
Lancashire, OL12 7AG
Tel *01706 526666*
Specializes in balti curries and
tandoori. Great banquet-style
meals for big groups.

MANCHESTER: Teppanyaki
Chinatown ££
Japanese
58/60 George Street, M1 4HF
Tel *0161 228 2219*
This great spot in Manchester's
Chinatown offers authentic
teppanyaki and has well-priced
set menus – all served in stylish,
Japanese surroundings.

MORECAMBE BAY:
Aspect Bar & Bistro ££
Bistro
320–323 Marine Rd Central,
Lancashire, LA4 5AA
Tel *01524 416404*
Delicious tapas, as well as mains.
Try the fish platter. Great views.

WINDERMERE: Grey Walls
Steakhouse and Restaurant ££
Steakhouse
Elleray Rd, Cumbria, LA23 1AG
Tel *015394 43741* **Closed** *Sun–Wed*
Folks come here for the local ales
and hearty steak dished up at
this typical British pub.

WINDERMERE: Hooked ££
Seafood
Ellerthwaite Sq, Cumbria, LA23 1DP
Tel *015394 48443* **Closed** *Mon*
An eclectic little seafood
restaurant with influences from
the Mediterranean, Southeast
Asia and Australia.

Key to Price Guide *see page 582*

WINDERMERE: Holbeck Ghyll £££
Fine dining
Holbeck Lane, Cumbria, LA23 1LU
Tel *015394 32375*
Michelin-starred for 12 years, this is one of the best restaurants in the area. Great views.

WINDERMERE: Miller Howe £££
European
Rayrigg Rd, Cumbria, LA23 1EY
Tel *015394 42536*
This family-owned hotel has impressive lake views. The food on offer is both imaginative and well presented.

Yorkshire and the Humber Region

ASENBY: Crab and Lobster ££
Seafood
Crab Manor, Dishforth Rd, Thirsk, North Yorkshire, YO7 3QL
Tel *01845 577286*
Old-fashioned seafood diner decorated with antiques. Jazz music on Sundays. Try their signature dish: lobster Thermidor.

BIRDFORTH: The Corner Cupboard ££
Bistro
Easingwold, North Yorkshire, YO26 4NW
Tel *01349 301495* **Closed** *Mon*
The tearooms serve food ranging from café items such as scones and tea cakes to heavy lamb curries. Adjoining gift shop sells vintage items.

BOLTON ABBEY: The Devonshire Arms Brasserie ££
Modern British
Skipton, North Yorkshire, BD23 6AJ
Tel *01756 710710*
Enjoy British and French cuisine in a coaching inn dating back to 1753. Informal atmosphere.

BOROUGHBRIDGE: The Dining Room £££
Modern British
20 St James Sq, North Yorkshire, YO51 9AR
Tel *01423 326426* **Closed** *Mon*
Cosy and popular brasserie that uses locally sourced produce to create dishes that are full of flavour. Fine selection of wines and champagne.

BRADFORD: Mughals £
Pakistani
790 Leeds Rd, BD3 9TY
Tel *01274 733324*
Choose from an array of dishes at one of the best South Asian restaurants in town.

EAST WITTON: The Blue Lion ££
Traditional British
Near Leyburn, North Yorkshire, DL8 4SN
Tel *01969 624273*
Housed in an old coaching inn. Traditional fish and meat dishes dominate. Extensive wine list and hand-drawn real ales at the bar.

FERRENSBY: The General Tarleton Inn ££
Seafood
Boroughbridge Rd, nr Knaresborough, North Yorkshire, HG5 0PZ
Tel *01423 340284*
This 18th-century coaching inn is renowned for its seafood Thermidor. Local produce used.

HARROGATE: Drum and Monkey ££
Seafood
5 Montpellier Gardens, North Yorkshire, HG1 2TF
Tel *01423 502650* **Closed** *Sun*
Locally sourced fish served in an old dining club. Try the scallops with cheese and garlic butter or the fisherman's pie.

HARROGATE: The Sportsman's Arms ££
Modern British
Wath-in-Nidderdale, Pateley Bridge, North Yorkshire, HG3 5PP
Tel *01423 711306*
A charming converted farmhouse and barn. Relish fresh, seasonal fish and seafood brought from Whitby, along with local lamb, duck and guinea fowl.

HARROGATE: The Yorke Arms ££
Modern British
Ramsgill-in-Nidderdale, Pateley Bridge, North Yorkshire, HG3 5RL
Tel *01423 755243*
Come here for Michelin starred dining in a 17th-century shooting lodge. Seasonal meat, fish and game dishes.

ILKLEY: Box Tree ££
French
35–37 Church St, West Yorkshire, LS29 9DR
Tel *01943 608484* **Closed** *Mon*
Michelin-starred restaurant serving modern French dishes. Don't miss the hand-dived scallops served with truffle oil.

LEEDS: Sous le Nez en Ville ££
French
The Basement, Quebec House, Quebec St, West Yorkshire, LS1 2HA
Tel *0113 244 0108* **Closed** *Sun*
This is an excellent, traditional French restaurant. Try the fabulous fillet steak stuffed with shallot.

RIPLEY: The Boar's Head ££
Modern British
Harrogate, North Yorkshire, HG3 3AY
Tel *01423 771888*
A former coaching inn with a restaurant and bistro. Seasonal fish, meat and game on offer.

ROBINS HOOD'S BAY: Wayfarer Bistro ££
Bistro
Station Rd, near Whitby, North Yorkshire, YO22 4RL
Tel *01947 880240* **Closed** *Mon*
Sample excellent seafood along with chargrilled steaks and vegetarian choices.

SCARBOROUGH: AZ Restaurant ££
Turkish
89 Columbus Ravine, YO12 7QU
Tel *01723 366180*
This friendly place, located just outside the town centre, serves quality Turkish cuisine including superb aubergine and lamb dishes.

SHEFFIELD: Zeugma £
Turkish
146 London Rd, South Yorkshire, S2 4LT
Tel *0114 2582223*
Watch *cop shish* (marinated lamb) or *kaburga* (spare ribs) cooking over charcoal. Bring your own wine for a small corkage fee.

DK Choice

SHEFFIELD: Greenhead House £££
Traditional British
84 Burncross Rd, Chapeltown, South Yorkshire, S35 1SF
Tel *0114 2469004* **Closed** *Sun–Tue*
Located in a lovely 17th-century house with an open fire, intimate dining room and walled garden. The husband-and-wife team at the helm offer a traditional British menu, with delicious sea bass, quail and beef dishes.

The innovative dishes at Miller Howe, Windermere

For more information on types of restaurants *see pages 575–6*

STOKESLEY: Chapter's ££
Modern British
*27 High St, Middlesbrough,
North Yorkshire, TS9 5AD*
Tel *01642 711888* **Closed** *Sun dinner*
Choose between gourmet dining
in the stylish restaurant or more
casual fare in the bar brasserie.

**SUTTON-ON-THE-FOREST:
The Rose and Crown Inn** ££
Traditional British
Main St, North Yorkshire, YO61 1DP
Tel *01347 811333*
This village inn restaurant uses
fantastic, locally sourced beef
and fish. Try the roast on Sundays.

WHITBY: The Magpie Café £
Traditional British
14 Pier Rd, North Yorkshire, YO21 3PU
Tel *01947 602058*
Historic merchant's house turned
café. Eight kinds of fish and chips.

YORK: Walmgate Ale House £
Bistro
*25 Walmgate, North Yorkshire,
YO1 9TX*
Tel *01904 629222*
A converted saddler's shop, this
informal bistro has homemade
light bites and speciality beers.

**YORK: The Blue Bicycle
Restaurant** ££
Seafood
34 Fossgate, North Yorkshire, YO1 9TA
Tel *01904 673990*
Housed in a former 19th-century
brothel, this restaurant serves
great seafood.

YORKSHIRE DALES: Angel Inn ££
Gastropub
*Hetton, Skipton, North Yorkshire,
BD23 6LT*
Tel *01756 730263*
Angel Inn has a charming interior
of wooden beams and log fires.
Eat in the restaurant or in the
informal bar-brasserie.

Northumbria

DURHAM: Finbarr's ££
Bistro
*Aykley Heads House, Aykley Heads,
County Durham, DH1 5TS*
Tel *0191 307 7033*
A popular brasserie in an18th-
century farmhouse. Dine in
the courtyard during summer.

GATESHEAD: Six Restaurant ££
Modern British
*Baltic Centre for Contemporary Art,
Gateshead Quays, South Shore Rd,
Tyne and Wear, NE8 3BA*
Tel *0191 440 4948*
Splendid views of the Tyne from
this converted flour mill. Good
service in the stylish dining room.

**GREAT WHITTINGTON:
Queens Head Inn** £
Chinese
*Corbridge, Newcastle upon Tyne,
Tyne and Wear, NE19 2HP*
Tel *01434 672267* **Closed** *Mon*
This early 17th-century coaching
inn near Hadrian's Wall may be
classically English, but the food
is full of Oriental flavour.

**HEXHAM: Valley
Connection 301** £
Bangladeshi
Market Pl, Northumberland, NE46 3NX
Tel *01434 601234* **Closed** *Mon*
At this Bangladeshi gem, ask
for Mr Daraz's *bhuna gosht* (stir-
fried lamb) and *bongo po* curry
(king prawns).

HEXHAM: General Havelock Inn ££
Traditional British
*9 Ratcliffe Rd, Haydon Bridge,
Northumberland, NE47 6ER*
Tel *01434 684376* **Closed** *Mon*
This riverside inn offers traditional
seasonal cuisine. Ask for the
chef's signature Cullen skink, a
rich smoked haddock chowder.

DK Choice
**MATFEN: Matfen Hall
Country House Hotel** ££
Traditional British
Northumberland, NE20 0RH
Tel *0116 188 6500*
This beautifully restored 19th-
century mansion has a two-
AA-Rosette dining room in the
library and print rooms. Less
formal dining can be found in
the conservatory bistro, with
pub fare served in the keeper's
lodge. The Sunday lunches are
particularly excellent.

**NEWCASTLE UPON TYNE:
The Cherry Tree** £
Modern British
9 Osborne Rd, Jesmond, NE2 2AE
Tel *0191 239 9924*
The imaginative menu features
Bury black pudding, Ingram
Valley lamb and grilled halibut.
Good-value set lunches and early
evening menus.

**NEWCASTLE UPON TYNE:
Paradiso** £
Italian
*1 Market Lane, Tyne and Wear,
NE1 6QQ*
Tel *0191 221 1240* **Closed** *Sun*
This stylish Italian restaurant has
exposed brickwork and the food
has unexpected influences from
Africa and Asia.

**NEWTON AYCLIFFE:
The County** ££
Modern British
*13 The Green, Darlington, County
Durham, DL5 6LX*
Tel *01325 312273*
Experience contemporary dining
with traditional British dishes
given a modern twist. There is a
good range of New World wines
and real ales.

**NEWTON AYCLIFFE: Redworth
Hall Hotel** ££
Fine Dining
Redworth, County Durham, DL5 6NL
Tel *01388 770600*
Built in 1693, the expansive
Redworth Hall has an elegant
dining room. The English and
European seasonal menu
features high-quality ingredients.

**ROMALDKIRK: The Rose and
Crown Inn** ££
Traditional British
Barnard Castle, Co. Durham, DL12 9EB
Tel *01833 650213*
This charming 18th-century
stone-built coaching inn has
a classic restaurant, as well as a
less formal, rustic brasserie to
choose from.

Picturesque exterior of the seafood restaurant The Blue Bicycle, York

Views over Mount Snowdon at Castle Cottage, Harlech

YARM: Chadwicks ££
European
*High Lane, Maltby, Middlesbrough,
TS8 0BG*
Tel *01642 590300* **Closed** *Mon*
A bustling restaurant offering
pizzas and pasta at lunchtime,
with a more formal evening
menu. Enthusiastic staff and a
good atmosphere.

North Wales

ABERDYFI: Penhelig Arms ££
Traditional British
27–29 Terrace Rd, Gwynedd, LL35 0LT
Tel *01654 767215*
Small, friendly restaurant overlooking the Dyfi Estuary. Locally
sourced fish and meat feature in
some intriguing Indian dishes.

**BEAUMARIS: Ye Olde Bull's
Head Inn** ££
Traditional British
Castle St, Isle of Anglesey, LL58 8AP
Tel *01248 810329*
This 15th-century coaching inn
has the gorgeous Loft restaurant
for fine dining and the Brasserie
for simpler fare.

BEDDGELERT: Hebog ££
Welsh
LL55 4UY
Tel *01766 890400*
Smart, rustically furnished café/
bistro offering mouthwatering
fare such as pork tenderloin
with apple mousse wrapped
in Parma ham.

DOLGELLAU: Mawddach ££
Welsh
*Maesygarnedd, Llanelltyd,
Gwynedd, LL40 2TA*
Tel *01341 421752* **Closed** *Sun dinner,
Mon & Tue*
The stunning views here are
the perfect accompaniment to
exquisite food. Try the duck
breast with Parmesan polenta
and spiced aubergine.

**DOLGELLAU: Penmaenuchaf
Hall** £££
Modern British
Penmaenpool, Gwynedd, LL40 1YB
Tel *01341 422129*
Sample award-winning simple
but elegant cuisine in a beautiful
garden room with Gothic
windows and views of Snowdon.

HARLECH: Castle Cottage ££
Welsh
Y Llech, Gwynedd, LL46 2YL
Tel *01766 780479*
Award-winning restaurant with
rooms. The traditional Welsh
menu features lobster, sea bass
and black bream plus venison
from the Brecon Beacons.

**LLANBEDROG: Glyn-Y-Weddw
Arms** £
Traditional British
Abersoch Rd, Pwllheli, LL53 7TH
Tel *01758 740212*
Low-key village pub serving
delicious homemade goodies and
succulent steaks. Sip on a draught
ale in their beer garden.

DK Choice

LLANDRILLO: Tyddyn Llan £££
Modern British
*Llandrillo, near Corwen,
Denbighshire, LL21 0ST*
Tel *01490 440264*
Concealed within an elegant
Georgian house, Tyddyn Llan is
one of Wales's few Michelin-
starred restaurants. Chef Bryan
Webb conjures up memorable
dishes like loin of venison with
port sauce and baked goat's
cheese; there are also six- and
nine-course taster menus.

**LLANDUDNO: Forte's
Restaurant** £
Café
69 Mostyn St, Conwy, LL30 2NN
Tel *01492 877910*
A lunch venue that doubles as an
ice-cream parlour. Choose from a

delicious range of sundaes, all
made with the house ice cream.

LLANDUDNO: The Seahorse ££
Seafood
7 Church Walks, Conwy, LL30 2HD
Tel *01492 875315*
Intimate bistro downstairs and
Victorian dining room upstairs
serving daily fish specials from set
menus. Try the chef's fish platter.

**LLANGEFNI: Noëlle's at
Tre-Ysgawen Hall** ££
Traditional British
Capel Coch, Isle of Anglesey, LL77 7UR
Tel *01248 750750*
Lemon sole with shellfish mousse
is one of the options on the
excellent menu here. There's a
great wine list too. Afternoon tea is
served in the hotel drawing room.

LLANGOLLEN: The Corn Mill £
Traditional British
Dee Lane, Denbighshire, LL20 8NN
Tel *01978 869555*
Family-friendly restaurant inside
a heritage building. Children can
fill up on haddock and chips,
while the grown-ups check out
the sea trout and pork belly.

**PORTMEIRION: The Hotel
Portmeirion** ££
Welsh
Gwynedd, LL48 6ET
Tel *01766 772440*
The hotel's beautiful dining room
was designed by Terence Conran
and overlooks a stunning estuary.

PWLLHELI: Plas Bodegroes £££
Modern British
Nefyn Rd, Gwynedd, LL53 5TH
Tel *01758 612363* **Closed** *Mon*
This highly rated establishment
offers inventive dishes such as
braised pork cheek with crispy
ham hock and black pudding.

RUTHIN: Manorhaus ££
Welsh
10 Well St, Denbighshire, LL15 1AH
Tel *01824 704830* **Closed** *Sun & Mon*
Stylish restaurant with rooms in
a listed Georgian stone building.
The seasonal menu features salt
marsh Welsh lamb, Menai
mussels and Welsh whiskies.

South and Mid-Wales

**ABERAERON: The Hive Bar
and Grill** £
American
Cadwgan Pl, Dyfed, SA46 0BU
Tel *01545 570445*
Enjoy harbour views while feasting
on succulent burgers, ribs and.
Try the honey ice cream.

For more information on types of restaurants *see pages 575–6*

BRECON: Felin Fach Griffin ££
Welsh
Felin Fach, Powys, LD3 OUB
Tel *01874 620111*
Warm, well-regarded inn-style restaurant with seasonal food like Bwlch venison with artichoke.

BRIDGEND: Eliot Restaurant ££
Modern British
Coed-y-Mwstwr Hotel, Coychurch, CF35 6AF
Tel *01656 860621*
The daily *table d'hôte* menu at Eliot includes dishes such as lamb rump with chips, and duck breast with sherry sauce. Great views.

BUILTH WELLS: The Drawing Room £££
Welsh
Cwmbach, Powys, LD2 3RT
Tel *01982 552493*
A five-star restaurant with rooms in a Georgian country house. Delicious local beef and lamb.

CARDIFF: Café Città £
Italian
4 Church St, CF10 1BG
Tel *02920 224040* **Closed** *Sun*
Marvellous family-run restaurant serving the city's finest pizzas, calzones and pizzottos.

CARDIFF: Ffresh £
Welsh
Wales Millennium Centre, Bute Pl, Cardiff Bay, CF10 5AL
Tel *02920 636465*
Stylish restaurant and bar with great pre-show menus; try the fillet of cod with chickpea salad.

DK Choice

CARDIFF: Le Monde ££
Seafood
60–62 St Mary St, CF10 1FE
Tel *029 2038 7376*
Le Monde may be dark as a dive bar, but it has the best fish. The sea bass in rock salt is a house speciality, but the atmosphere and the downtown location make this brasserie unmissable.

CRICKHOWELL: Nantyffin Cider Mill ££
Welsh
Brecon Rd, Powys, NP8 1SG
Tel *01873 810775* **Closed** *Mon & Tue*
Pretty country restaurant in a converted mill. Try the slow-cooked pork belly with cider gravy.

HAVERFORDWEST: The Shed Fish and Chip Bistro £
Seafood
Porthgain, Pembrokeshire, SA62 5BN
Tel *01348 831518*
Specializes in locally caught

Sophisticated dining area at Andrew Fairlie at Gleneagles, Auchterarder

fish and shellfish. This quayside bistro also has a takeaway menu.

HAVERFORDWEST: Wolfscastle Country Hotel ££
Welsh
Wolfscastle, Pembrokeshire, SA62 5LZ
Tel *01437 741225*
An old riverside vicarage with panoramic views and a menu featuring hake, monkfish and halibut, as well as Welsh beef, lamb and duck.

HAY-ON-WYE: Tomatitos Spanish Bar £
Spanish
38 Lion St, HR3 5AA
Tel *01497 820772*
This lively restaurant and bar serves a wide range of freshly prepared tapas such as chorizo cooked in cider. Great fun.

LLANWRTYD WELLS: Lasswade Country House Hotel & Restaurant ££
Welsh
Station Rd, Powys, LD5 4RW
Tel *01591 610515*
This award-winning restaurant in an Edwardian country-house hotel has built a strong reputation for its use of locally sourced, organic produce.

DK Choice

LLYSWEN: Llangoed Hall Hotel £££
Traditional British
Brecon, Powys, LD3 0YP
Tel *01874 754525*
When Sir Bernard Ashley took over this ancient hall, he set out to recreate the Edwardian country-house weekend in all its comfort and grandeur. The afternoon tea at Llangoed is a real treat, but lunch and dinner are even better, in a beautiful candlelit dining room. Book well in advance to ensure a fantastic dining experience.

PEMBROKE: George Wheeler Restaurant ££
Welsh
Old Kings Arms Hotel, Main St, Pembrokeshire, SA71 4JS
Tel *01646 683611*
This award-winning restaurant showcases some of the best of Wales's local produce. Try the Welsh cockles with laverbread and bacon.

SWANSEA: Hanson at The Chelsea Restaurant ££
Seafood
17 St Mary St, SA1 3LH
Tel *01792 464068* **Closed** *Sun*
Award-winning fish restaurant Hanson offers great locally caught sea bass, as well as Swansea smoked salmon and Gower lamb.

SWANSEA: Munch ££
Welsh
650 Mumbles Rd, Mumbles, SA3 4EA
Tel *01792 362244* **Closed** *Sun–Tue*
This gorgeous restaurant offers contemporary Welsh dishes such as lamb and rosemary pie with marsh samphire.

SWANSEA: Verdi's ££
Café
Knab Rock, SA3 4EN
Tel *01792 369135* **Closed** *Nov–Feb*
Glass-fronted Italian café serving the best pizza this side of Naples, as well as pasta and focaccia. Tasty desserts include tiramisu and Turkish delight ice cream.

The Lowlands

ABERLADY: Ducks Inn ££
Scottish
Main St, Longniddry, EH32 0RE
Tel *01875 870682*
Legendary Edinburgh restaurateur Malcolm Duck is the man behind this destination dining venue. There is a modern fine-dining restaurant and a relaxed bistro.

DK Choice

AUCHTERARDER: Andrew Fairlie at Gleneagles £££
Scottish
Perthshire, PH3 1NF
Tel *01764 694267* **Closed** *Sun*
The grand Gleneagles Hotel is the setting for Scotland's only two-Michelin-starred restaurant. Chef Andrew Fairlie works his magic on locally sourced produce and creates dishes that have an international twist. Try the smoked lobster and roast Anjou squab.

BALQUHIDDER: Monachyle Mhor £££
Scottish
Lochearnhead, Stirling, FK19 8PQ
Tel *01877 384 622*
Chef Tom Lewis grows his own vegetables and herbs, as well as rearing livestock. The sublime five-course *table d'hôte* menu here makes the most of this produce.

CUPAR: The Peat Inn ££
Scottish **Map** E4
Fife, near St Andrews, KY15 5LH
Tel *01334 840206* **Closed** *Sun & Mon*
Michelin-starred rural retreat. The menu expertly utilizes local produce such as salmon, langoustine and beef. Come here to savour the multi-course tasting menu.

DUNDEE: Jute Café Bar £
Café
152 Nethergate, DD1 4DY
Tel *01382 909246*
The café at the Dundee Contemporary Arts centre serves light lunches, as well as a three-course evening meal. For main, try the steak; for dessert, the chocolate torte.

Outdoor tables at the popular pizzeria La Favorita, Edinburgh

EDINBURGH: David Bann £
Vegetarian
56–58 St Mary's St, EH1 1SX
Tel *0131 556 5888*
Stylish fine-dining restaurant with delicious vegetarian dishes such as leek, tarragon and butternut squash risotto. Try the tartlet made with Ardrahan smoked cheese and slow-dried tomatoes.

EDINBURGH: La Favorita £
Italian
321 Leith Walk, EH6 8SA
Tel *0131 554 2430*
A strong contender for the city's best pizzeria, the bustling La Favorita offers doughy delights served with an infinite range of toppings. Save space for an ice-cream treat afterwards.

EDINBURGH: Orocco Pier £
International
17 High St, South Queensferry, EH30 9PP
Tel *0870 118 1664*
Choose from the sumptuous pub fare at Antico Café Bar or feast on seafood in the Samphire Bar and Grill. Offers sweeping views of the Forth estuary and its bridges.

EDINBURGH: Contini Ristorante ££
Italian
103 George St, EH2 3ES
Tel *0131 225 1550*
Edinburgh's grandest Italian restaurant, Contini guarantees authentic pasta dishes. A great place for lunch, dinner or just a quick snack.

EDINBURGH: Galvin Brasserie de Luxe ££
Brasserie
Princes St, EH1 2AB
Tel *0131 222 8988*
This swish brasserie in the hotel Caledonian is a real treat for lovers of French cuisine. It features a crustacean bar and superb wine list. Great-value set menus.

EDINBURGH: Jeremy Wares ££
Scottish
Macdonald Houston House Hotel, Uphall, West Lothian, EH52 6JS
Tel *0844 879 9043*
Jeremy Wares's signature modern Scottish cooking in the romantic Houston House features local Perthshire venison, Borders lamb and Scottish beef.

EDINBURGH: Kyloe Restaurant & Grill ££
International
1–3 Rutland St, EH1 2AE
Tel *0131 229 3402*
Choose from a variety of steak cuts at this carnivore's heaven

Located in the Rutland Hotel, it offers fine views of the castle.

EDINBURGH: Ondine ££
Seafood
2 George IV Bridge, EH1 1AD
Tel *0131 226 1888*
Inspirational cooking based on sustainable sourcing by chef Roy Brett. Try the heavenly shellfish platter served on ice (French-style) or warmed with garlic butter.

EDINBURGH: Spoon ££
Café
6a Nicolson St, EH8 9DH
Tel *0131 623 1752* **Closed** *Sun*
This modern, arty café serves the finest vegetarian breakfast in the city, as well as a good carnivore's version. Great place for lunch.

EDINBURGH: Stac Polly ££
Scottish
29–33 Dublin St, EH3 6NL
Tel *0131 556 2231*
Stac Polly serves dependable and modern Scottish cooking. Excellent steak with black pudding and white fish dishes.

EDINBURGH: Restaurant Martin Wishart £££
French
54 The Shore, Leith, EH6 6RA
Tel *0131 553 3557* **Closed** *Sun & Mon*
This restaurant offers a truly memorable experience for lovers of French food: classic cooking with sublime use of Scottish ingredients. Excellent service.

EYEMOUTH: Mackays of Eyemouth £
Traditional British
20–24 High St, Berwickshire, TD14 5EU
Tel *01890 751142*
Tuck into a fish supper or binge on lobster and chips at Mackays, while watching local fishing boats head out to sea.

GLASGOW: Café Gandolfi £
Café
64 Albion St, G1 1NY
Tel *0141 552 6813*
A city institution and part of the Gandolfi mini-empire. Come here for the great breakfasts, light lunches or substantial dinners.

GLASGOW: The Chippy Doon the Lane £
Traditional British
84 Buchanan St, McCormick Lane, G1 3AJ
Tel *0141 225 6650*
Relaxed restaurant serving excellent monkfish tails, hake and lemon sole, cod and haddock

The tasteful dining room at the Boath House, Auldearn

GLASGOW: Bistro du Vin ££
Scottish
One Devonshire Gardens, G12 0UX
Tel 08447 364256
A fine-dining restaurant housed in the stately Hotel du Vin. Serves Scotland's finest red meat and fish. Try the seven-course tasting menu.

GLASGOW: City Merchant ££
Seafood
97–99 Candleriggs, G1 1NP
Tel 01415 531577
The fine steak and seafood are complemented by the elegant Art Deco surroundings. Most items come from Scotland but are prepared with Gallic touches.

HADDINGTON:
The Waterside Bistro £
Scottish
1–5 Waterside, East Lothian, EH41 4AT
Tel 01620 825674
Set on the banks of the River Tyne, this welcoming, family-run bistro serves well-sourced local produce. Great for families with kids.

INVERARNAN: The Drover's Inn £
Scottish
Arrochar, G83 7DX
Tel 01301 704234
Great pub food such as steak pies and haggis, in a space that has barely changed in the last 300 years.

LAUDER: Black Bull Hotel £
Traditional British
Market Pl, Berwickshire, TD2 6SR
Tel 01578 722208
Traditional pub serving quality food in a Georgian dining room or a cosy bar-lounge. Dishes include fish and chips and chunky burgers. Good kids' menu.

PEEBLES: Coltman's
Delicatessen & Kitchen £
Café
71–73 High St, EH45 8AN
Tel 01721 720405
Charming deli and restaurant with

views over the River Tweed. Sandwiches, platters and dishes with an international flavour. Good three-course set menu.

STANLEY: Ballathie House ££
Scottish
Kinclaven, Perth, PH1 4QN
Tel 01250 883268
The best of Scottish produce, such as Pittenweem langoustines and Perthshire venison, are given a modern twist in this elegant restaurant. Wonderful desserts.

The Highlands and Islands

ABERDEEN: The Silver Darling ££
Seafood
Pocra Quay, North Pier, Aberdeenshire, AB11 5DQ
Tel 01224 576229 **Closed** Sun
Fresh seafood is expertly cooked, often by using traditional French techniques. Choose from a range of French wines, and enjoy magnificent sea views.

ABOYNE: At the Sign of the Black Faced Sheep £
Café
Ballater Rd, Aberdeenshire, AB34 5HN
Tel 01339 887311
Lovely coffee shop and food emporium. Tasty sandwiches and sun-dried tomato scones are popular menu choices. Attractive collection of crockery on display.

ACHILTIBUIE: Summer
Isles Hotel ££
Seafood
Ullapool, Ross-shire, IV26 2YG
Tel 01854 622282
The award-winning restaurant at the Summer Isles Hotel delivers exceptional seafood dishes. Diners enjoy views of the sea and surrounding mountains.

APPLECROSS: Applecross Inn £
Seafood
Wester Ross, IV54 8LR
Tel 01520 744262
Locally caught seafood, such as huge Applecross prawns and plump lobster, served in generous portions at this restaurant and inn.

ARDEONAIG: Ardeonaig
Hotel & Restaurant ££
Scottish
South Loch Tay Side, Killin, FK21 8SU
Tel 01567 820400 **Closed** Mon & Tue
Pleasantly appointed dining room overlooking Loch Tay. An enticing menu features dishes such as venison loin and hay smoked salmon.

AULDEARN: Boath House £££
Scottish
Nairn, IV12 5TE
Tel 01667 454896
The award-wining food at the luxurious Boath House hotel is one of its main attractions. The six-course tasting menu showcases seasonal produce.

BADACHRO: Badachro Inn £
Pub
Gairloch, Ross-shire, IV21 2AA
Tel 01445 741255
Friendly local pub serving bar lunches and evening meals. Jacket potatoes, panini and sandwiches feature alongside fresh seafood, Scottish beef and lamb.

COLL: Gannet Restaurant ££
Seafood
Arinagour, PA78 6SZ
Tel 01879 230334
This waterfront restaurant, in the Coll Hotel, overlooks the harbour and boasts fresh, delicious seafood from around the island. Try the lobster with homemade spaghetti.

FINDHORN: The Bakehouse £
Café
91–92 Forres, IV36 3YG
Tel 01309 691826
Known for its organic produce. The menu includes tasty pork and venison burgers, and jacket potatoes with a variety of fillings.

FORT WILLIAM: Lime Tree ££
Scottish
The Old Manse, Achintore Rd, Inverness-shire, PH33 6RQ
Tel 01397 701806
Highly praised hotel-restaurant known for its warm welcome and excellent food. Specialities include pan seared Glenfinnan venison, mackerel, West Coast crab and smoked haddock.

Key to Price Guide *see page 582*

FORT WILLIAM: Inverlochy Castle £££
Scottish
Torlundy, Inverness-Shire, PH33 6SN
Tel *01397 702177*
The three regal dining rooms at Inverlochy Castle make for a truly memorable experience. Do not miss the hot cranachan soufflé.

GLENCOE: Clachaig Inn £
Scottish
Argyll, PH49 4HX
Tel *01855 811252*
Characterful old inn set in the centre of Glencoe. Hearty pub food, fine ales and a range of malt whiskies to choose from.

INVERIE: The Old Forge £
Scottish
Knoydart, Mallaig, Inverness-shire, PH41 4PL
Tel *01687 462267*   **Closed** *Wed, Nov–Feb*
The most remote pub in Britain is a good place to try white fish and shellfish culled from around the Knoydart Peninsula.

INVERNESS: Rocpool Restaurant ££
Brasserie
1 Ness Walk, Inverness-hire, IV3 5NE
Tel *01463 717274*
This stylish eatery has lovely river views and offers modern British classics. Relish dishes such as Parma ham salad served with balsamic roasted purple figs and baked Parmesan brûlée.

ISLE OF SKYE: The Three Chimneys £££
Scottish
Colbost, Dunvegan, IV55 8ZT
Tel *01470 511258*
Enjoy a superb dining experience in a spectacular location at this converted stone croft run by the self-taught, visionary chef Shirley Spear. The seasonal menu features local produce. Book ahead.

KILBERRY: The Kilberry Inn ££
Modern British
Tarbert, Argyll and Bute, PA29 6YD
Tel *01880 770223*   **Closed** *Mon*
This award-winning inn serves flawless dishes created with local ingredients such as surf clam with spaghetti, white wine and cream. Warm and cosy atmosphere.

DK Choice

KINLOCHLEVEN: Lochleven Seafood Café ££
Seafood
Onich, Fort William, Inverness-shire, PH33 6SA
Tel *01855 821048*
Heaven for seafood lovers, Lochleven Seafood Café serves large scallops, delicious oysters and an unparalleled shellfish platter, with refreshing white wines to ease them down. Outside tables in summer have splendid views of Loch Leven and Pap of Glencoe. Call to check opening times.

KYLESKU: Kylesku Hotel £
Scottish
Lairg, Sutherland, IV27 4HW
Tel *01971 502231*
Spacious bar-lounge in a former coaching inn. Serves quality meals including creel-caught lobster, langoustine and crab. Scottish meats and fish on offer as well.

MULL: Highland Cottage ££
Scottish
24 Breadalbane St, Tobermory, Argyll, PA75 6PD
Tel *01688 302030*
The award-winning menu at this place is packed with dishes made from fresh, quality local produce. Intimate dining room. Good wine list.

OBAN: Waterfront Fishouse Restaurant ££
Seafood
1 Railway Pier, PA34 4LW
Tel *01631 563110*
Plump langoustines, large king scallops and local lobster are on the menu at this waterfront restaurant. Spectacular views over the beautiful Oban bay.

PLOCKTON: Plockton Inn & Seafood Restaurant ££
Seafood
Innes St, Ross-shire, IV52 8TW
Tel *01599 544222*
Award-winning, traditional inn and restaurant in the picturesque village of Plockton, serving seafood platters, local beef, lamb and game. Vegetarian options.

PORT APPIN: The Airds Hotel & Restaurant £££
French
Argyll and Bute, PA38 4DF
Tel *01631 730236*
The modern French fine-dining menu here uses local Scottish produce. Savour hand-dived scallops, slow-poached chicken and Mallaig halibut.

SCRABSTER: The Captain's Galley £££
Seafood
The Harbour, Caithness, KW14 7UJ
Tel *01847 894999*   **Closed** *Sun & Mon*
Set in a former ice house and salmon bothy with exposed brickwork, this place has a dozen different fresh fish on the menu.

SHETLAND ISLANDS: Frankie's Fish and Chips £
Traditional British
Brae, Shetland, ZE2 9QJ
Tel *01806 522700*
Award-winning fish-and-chip restaurant on Shetland's mainland. Fresh sustainable fish, with some unusual treats such as scallops and blue mussels.

TROON: MacCallum's of Troon Oyster Bar ££
Seafood
Harbourside, Ayrshire, KA10 6DH
Tel *01292 319339*   **Closed** *Mon*
Seafood restaurant known for its exemplary dishes. Delicacies include lemon sole with capers, prawn tempura and Cullen skink (white fish soup).

TYNDRUM: The Real Food Café £
Café
Perthshire, FK20 8RY
Tel *01838 400235*
Arguably the best fish and chips in Scotland. Enjoy a large or small fish supper, and finish with excellent coffee and cakes.

Enjoy views across the North Sea at Frankie's Fish and Chips, Shetland

For more information on types of restaurants *see pages 575–6*

British Pubs

No tour of Britain could be complete without some exploration of its public houses. These are a great social institution, descendants of centuries of hostelries, ale houses and stagecoach halts. Some have colourful histories, and occupy a central role in the community, staging quiz nights, live music or folk dancing. Many of those listed below are lovely buildings, or have particularly attractive settings. Most serve a variety of beers, spirits and wine by the glass, and non-alcoholic drinks.

A "free house" is independent and will stock several leading regional beers, but most pubs are "tied" – this means that they are owned by a brewery and only stock that brewery's selection.

Many pubs offer additional attractions such as beer gardens with picnic tables. Traditional pub food and more varied gastropub cuisine is often served at lunchtime and increasingly in the evenings as well. Traditional pub games take many forms, including cribbage, pool, skittles, dominoes and darts.

London

Bloomsbury: Lamb
94 Lamb's Conduit St, WC1.
Tel *020 7405 0713.* **Map** *3 C5*
Victorian pub with lovely cut-glass "snob screens" and theatrical photographs. Small rear courtyard.

Covent Garden: Lamb and Flag
33 Rose St, WC2.
Tel *020 7497 9504.* **Map** *11 B2*
Traditional Georgian pub always busy with drinkers crammed into its cosy spaces. Charles Dickens was a former patron.

City: Black Friar
174 Queen Victoria St, EC4.
Tel *020 7236 5474.* **Map** *12 F2*
Eccentric inside and out, with intriguing Art Nouveau decor. Saved from demolition by Sir John Betjeman.

City: Ye Olde Cheshire Cheese
145 Fleet St, EC4.
Tel *020 7353 6170.* **Map** *12 E1*
Authentic 17th-century inn that evokes Dickens's London. Try for a spot near one of the open fires.

Hammersmith: Dove
19 Upper Mall, W6. **Tel** *020 8748 9474.*
One of west London's most attractive riverside pubs – you can watch rowing crews from the terrace.

Hampstead: Spaniards Inn
Spaniards Rd, NW3. **Tel** *020 8731 8406.*
Famous Hampstead landmark dating from the 16th century, once part of a tollgate.

Kensington: Windsor Castle
114 Campden Hill Rd, W8.
Tel *020 7243 8797.* **Map** *7 C4*
A civilized Georgian inn with oak furnishings and open fires. The walled garden attracts well-heeled crowds in summer. Hearty food.

Southwark: George Inn
77 Borough High St, SE1.
Tel *020 7407 2056.* **Map** *13 B4*
Quaint coaching inn with galleried courtyard. Rooms ramble upstairs and downstairs, and the overspill sits outside. Morris dancers may be seen performing here at times *(see p124).*

Southwark: Anchor
34 Park St, SE1.
Tel *0207407 1577.* **Map** *13 B3*
Historic riverside pub with traditional interior and a pavement terrace looking down on the Thames and traditional interior.

The Downs and Channel Coast

Alciston: Rose Cottage Inn
Alciston nr Polegate. **Tel** *01323 870377.*
In a creeper-covered cottage, this rural Sussex pub with beamed ceilings and open fires is decorated in rustic style. Local ales and ciders. The busy kitchen cooks up satisfying meals, such as curry and fish pie.

Brighton: Market Inn
Market St. **Tel** *01273 329483.*
Once home to the Prince of Wales's chimney sweep, this is now something of an institution, spilling out onto The Lanes in the summer.

Charlton: The Fox Goes Free
Charlton near Chichester.
Tel *01243 811461.*
This lovely 16th-century inn serves local ales and cider straight from barrels. Full à la carte menu and great selection of bar meals. Low beams, inglenook fireplace and bread oven add to the charm.

Ditchling: The Bull Hotel
2 High St. **Tel** *01273 843147.*
Housed in a 14th-century building, the main bar is large, rambling and pleasantly traditional with characterful old wooden floorboards, beams and furniture, and a blazing fire.

Faversham: White Horse Inn
The Street, Boughton.
Tel *01227 751343.*
Chaucer gave this place a passing mention in *The Canterbury Tales.* Among hop gardens and orchards, this genial country pub resounds with echoes from the past. Low-beamed ceilings and log fires create a cosy atmosphere. Thirteen en-suite bedrooms.

Isle of Wight: The Wight Mouse Inn
Church Place, Chale.
Tel *01983 730431.*
This pub draws in the locals with its range of real ales. Live music on Saturdays, good sunsets and views to the Needles.

Lewes: Six Bells Inn
Chiddingly, nr Lewes.
Tel *01825 872227.*
Once a stopover for stagecoaches, this cosy drop-in now does a fine job of reviving weary ramblers and thirsty locals. Supposedly haunted by Sara French, hanged in 1852 after serving her husband an onion pie seasoned with arsenic. Folk and blues music on Tuesdays.

Romsey: The Star Inn
East Tytherley, near Romsey.
Tel *01794 340225.*
Popular watering hole on the edge of the New Forest, overlooking the village cricket pitch. Curry-and-pint nights on Wednesdays. Three cottage bedrooms available.

Rye: The Mermaid
Mermaid St. **Tel** *01797 223065.*
Dating from 1136, this is one of the country's oldest inns. Constructed from old ship timbers, The Mermaid is an evocative slice of England's nautical history. Sit by the open fire and spot the celebrities having a quiet drink.

Walliswood: The Scarlett Arms
Horsham Rd. **Tel** *01306 627243.*
Handsome inn with flagstone
bar, wooden benches and a
grand inglenook fireplace. The
staff make the experience all
the more congenial. Occasional
live music in the summer.

East Anglia

Bardwell: The Six Bells at Bardwell
Bardwell, Bury St Edmunds.
Tel *01359 250820.*
This village green charmer, dating
from the 1500s, is surrounded by
countryside and offers superb food
and peaceful accommodation.

Cambridge: The Mill
14 Mill Lane. **Tel** *01223 311829.*
This cosy pub on the banks of the
River Cam has a radiogram, vinyl
records and a selection of board
games for winter days, as well as
outside seating in summer and
classic pub food all year round.

Great Yarmouth: The Nelson Head
Horsey. **Tel** *01493 393378.*
Traditional, unpretentious red-brick
country pub, close to the beach and
the winter seal colony of Horsey.
There's a good selection of ales
and ciders and home-cooked food.
Popular with walkers.

Itteringham: The Walpole Arms
The Common. **Tel** *01263 587258.*
Oak beamed and brick-walled inn
that has been serving locally brewed
ales since the 1700s. The restaurant
is also highly regarded.

Norfolk: Red Lion
44 Wells Rd, Stiffkey. **Tel** *01328 830552.*
The oldest parts of this pub have a
few beams, aged flooring tiles or
bare boards, and big open fires.
A back gravel terrace has seats and
tables for enjoying seafood and real
ale on a sunny day, and there are
some pleasant walks nearby. There
are 10 eco-friendly rooms available.

Norwich: The Fat Cat
49 W End St. **Tel** *01603 624364.*
Rightly famed for its extensive real
ale selection, the multi-award-
winning Fat Cat has a well-stocked
bar and lively local clientele.

Ringstead: The Gin Trap Inn
6 High St. **Tel** *01485 525264.*
Close to the Norfolk coastline and
just on the edge of the Ringstead
Downs nature reserve, this 17th-
century country pub features hand-
pumped real ales, specialist gins and
cosy log fires. The restaurant has a
devoted following. Four en-suite
rooms available.

Saffron Walden: Queen's Head Inn
High St, Littlebury.
Tel *01799 520365.*
Attractive coaching inn with a
relaxed, family ambience. Stocks a
decent selection of ales and has a
good wine list. There are six en-
suite rooms.

Southwold: The Crown Hotel
High St. **Tel** *01502 722275.*
The pub remains the star of this
converted hotel, though the chic
restaurant is becoming a firm local
favourite. Excellent selection of
wines at the bar.

Stowmarket: The Buxhall Crown
Mill Rd, Buxhall.
Tel *01449 736521.*
Local real ales take pride of place
in this old village pub that also
does a roaring trade in home-
cooked food with locally sourced
ingredients. Good list of wine by
the glass.

Thames Valley

Aylesbury: The King's Head
*Kings Head Passage, Market Sq,
Buckinghamshire.*
Tel *01296 718812.*
A small oasis in the heart of a
pretty market town, this airy
pub has award-winning food and
ales and a courtyard for whiling
away long summer afternoons.

Bedford: The Park
98 Kimbolton Rd, Bedfordshire.
Tel *01234 273929.*
This warm and friendly pub built
in the 1900s has exposed beams
and brickwork. Good, wholesome
food on offer.

Chipping Norton: The Falkland Arms
*Great Tew, Chipping Norton,
Oxfordshire.* **Tel** *01608 683653.*
Award-winning cask ales and a
wonderful atmosphere. You can try
beer before you buy at this traditional
gem of a place.

Faringdon: The Trout Inn
*Tadpole Bridge, Buckland Marsh,
near Faringdon.*
Tel *01367 870382.*
Always busy and bustling, this
17th-century pub boasts a riverfront
garden where customers can savour
local dishes.

Great Hormead: The Three Tuns
High Street, Hertfordshire.
Tel *01763 289405.*
A traditional thatched and
beamed village pub with a cosy
open fire in winter and a patio in
summer. Hearty and reasonably
priced food.

Leighton Buzzard: The Five Bells
Station Road, Stanbridge, Bedfordshire.
Tel *01525 210224.*
A traditional pub surrounded by
picturesque countryside. Locally
sourced pub classics are served,
with barbecues in the summer
months. Seasonal cask ales and
fine wines.

Oxford: The Bear Inn
6 Alfred St. **Tel** *01865 728164.*
The oldest pub in Oxford (1242) is
famed for its quirky collection of ties
that dates back to the early 1900s,
representing clubs in the Oxford
area. The pub serves real ale and
good home-cooked food.

Oxford: The White Horse
52 Broad St. **Tel** *01865 204801.*
This cosy pub has loads of character,
with pictures of old sports stars on
the walls and a great range of beers.

Watton-at-Stone: The Bull
113 High St, Herts. **Tel** *01920 831032.*
Sit around the open-hearth fire at
this 15th-century inn, or in the
picturesque garden.

Windsor: The Two Brewers
34 Park St. **Tel** *01753 855426.*
Flourishing since 1792, this small
and quirky pub just outside Windsor
Great Park serves good wine, beer
and food. Sunday roasts are popular.

Wessex

Abbotsbury: Ilchester Arms
Market St, Dorset. **Tel** *01305 873841.*
A prominent landmark in this quaint
village, the 18th-century stone inn
serves local produce at breakfast,
and afternoon teas and dinners.

Bath: The Bell
103 Walcot St, Bath, Avon.
Tel *01225 460426.*
Splendid little pub, renowned for
its live music. Soak in the friendly
atmosphere while sampling its
organic beers and tasty sandwiches
and snacks.

Bridport: Shave Cross Inn
Shave Cross, Marshwood Vale, Dorset.
Tel *01308 868358.*
Award-winning inn with fine ales,
as well as English, Caribbean and
international food. Five modern
rooms are available.

Bristol: Llandoger Trow
King St. **Tel** *01179 261650.*
Dating from 1664, this black-and-
white timber-framed building is said
to have inspired the Admiral Benbow
Inn in R L Stevenson's *Treasure Island*.
Convivial atmosphere, real ales and
an upstairs restaurant.

Pensford: Carpenter's Arms
Stanton Wick, near Pensford, Somerset.
Tel *01761 490202.*
Overlooking the lovely Chew Valley,
this welcoming pub is set among a
row of miners' cottages. It has an
excellent menu and a comprehensive wine list.

Salisbury: Haunch of Venison
1 Minster St, Salisbury, Wiltshire.
Tel *01722 411313.*
The severed, mummified hand of
an 18th-century card player is on
display (along with more pleasant
antiques) at this 650-year-old pub.
The restaurant is great for a good
meal. Keep an eye out for the
resident ghost.

Salisbury: The New Inn
41/47 New St, Wiltshire.
Tel *01722 326662.*
Low-beamed ceilings and intimate
interior lighting inside. There are
fine views of the cathedral spire
opposite. The menu is broad and
vegetarian-friendly.

Devon and Cornwall

Dawlish: The Mount Pleasant
Mount Pleasant Rd, Dawlish Warren,
Devon. **Tel** *01626 863151.*
This pub is renowned for its views
over Exmouth from the dining area.
Drinkers visit once and become loyal
customers for years, relishing the
warm ambience and superb value.

Exeter: The Bridge Inn
Bridge Hill, Topsham, Devon.
Tel *01392 873862.*
With its pink exterior, you can't miss
this riverside pub, run by the same
family since 1899. Its several rooms
with fireplaces are snug in winter,
while the garden is gorgeous
on sunny days. They serve drinks
and bar snacks through a hatch
in the corridor.

Falmouth: Pandora Inn
Restronguet Creek, Mylor Bridge, near
Falmouth, Cornwall. **Tel** *01326 372678.*
Medieval pub with a thatched roof
by the waterside. Full of cosy corners,
low ceilings, panelled walls and a
variety of maritime memorabilia.

Helston: Blue Anchor
50 Coinage Hall, Cornwall.
Tel *01326 562821.*
One of the oldest inns in the country,
this place serves beers from its own
brewery. There's a skittle alley and
live music.

Knowstone: Masons Arms Inn
South Molton, Devon. **Tel** *01398 341231.*
An atmospheric Grade II listed
cottage that is full of character.

The decor includes farm tools and
a bread-oven fireplace. Delicious
restaurant food and friendly hosts.

Lynton: Fox and Goose
Parracombe, Barnstaple.
Tel *01598 763239.*
A friendly and welcoming pub/B&B
with very good food and beer. The
log fire, plank ceiling and assorted
mounted antlers and horns give a
proper Exmoor feel to the place.
Serves real ale and local cider.

Newton Abbot: Two Mile Oak
Totnes Rd, Devon. **Tel** *01803 812411.*
An old coaching inn with a beamed
lounge and an alcove just for two.
A mix of wooden tables and chairs,
and a fine winter log fire.

Penzance: The Pirate Inn
Alverton Rd, Alverton, Cornwall.
Tel *01736 366094.*
Warm and cosy in winter, and
plenty of outside seating in summer,
this is a friendly stop for beer and
food. Pizza on Saturdays, folk music
on Tuesdays.

Porthleven: Harbour Inn
Commercial Rd, Cornwall.
Tel *01326 573876.*
Watch the sun go down and sip
a top-quality pint as you sit by
Porthleven's harbour. Two hundred
years old, this pub retains its original
character, the modern sofas and
coffee tables notwithstanding.

Saltash: Rod and Line
Church Rd, Tideford, Cornwall.
Tel *01752 851323.*
This friendly old Cornish pub is set
just off the main A38 road. Popular
with locals, it has a single bar with
a log fire. The interesting menu
features local seafood.

Tavistock: The Cornish Arms
15 West St, Devon.
Tel *01822 612145.*
The last coaching inn before Cornwall,
this pub serves St Austell beers,
well-chosen wine and an excellent
range of food.

The Heart of England

Alderminster: The Bell
Warwickshire. **Tel** *01789 450414.*
Smart 18th-century coach inn just
4 miles (6 km) from Stratford-upon-
Avon, The Bell also boasts a high-
class restaurant. Great views over
Stour Valley from the garden
and conservatory.

Armscote: The Fuzzy Duck
Imington Rd. **Tel** *01608 682293.*
This atmospheric bar-restaurant
(and B&B) is perfect for a light

supper or relaxing drink. Sit out
on the lawns during summer.
The bar has an open fire in winter.

Ashleworth: Queen's Arms
The Village, Gloucestershire.
Tel *01452 700395.*
Sixteenth-century inn with a
noticeable Victorian makeover,
this pub features wood-beamed
ceilings and antique furnishings.
The fantastic kitchen serves
traditional pub food as well as
more international flavours.

Bickley Moss: Cholmondeley Arms
Malpas, Cheshire.
Tel *01829 720300.*
The menu in this family-friendly
pub includes the very best
of traditional local cuisine.
Children will love the desserts –
baked syrup sponge, black cherry
Pavlova, bakewell tart, ice creams
and sorbets. Accommodation
is also available.

Bretforton: Fleece Inn
Near Evesham.
Tel *01386 831173.*
This real-ale pub with its half-
timbered façade is a National
Trust property. Beautifully located
in the Vale of Evesham. Rooms
available. Parking in village square.

Chester: Pheasant Inn
High Burwardsley, Tattenhall.
Tel *01829 770434.*
Popular country pub with splendid
views across the Cheshire Plain to
Wales. It's invariably packed on
sunny days, when you're just as
likely to find as many dogs here
as people.

Farnborough: Inn at Farnborough
Near Banbury. **Tel** *01295 690615.*
A Grade II listed free house from the
1700s and now an inn. The menu
features delicious local cuisine,
including sumptuous organic
steak burgers. Large garden
and conservatory.

Shrewsbury: Armoury
Welsh Bridge, Victoria Quay.
Tel *01743 340525.*
This converted 18th-century
warehouse, with views over the
river, is a popular venue. Go early
if you want to enjoy a leisurely sit-
down meal.

Welford-on-Avon: The Bell Inn
Near Stratford-upon-Avon,
Warwickshire. **Tel** *01789 750353.*
This lovely 17th-century country
pub, just a short distance southwest
of Stratford-upon-Avon, serves
wonderful real ale and traditional bar
food. There is a delightful seating
area in the garden.

East Midlands

Alderwasley: The Bear Inn
Belper, Derbyshire. **Tel** *01629 822585.*
Friendly country pub with real olde-
worlde charm, The Bear Inn serves a
good range of real ales and delicious
food. Popular with locals and visitors
alike. Ten rooms are also available.

Bakewell: Packhorse Inn
Main St, Little Longstone.
Tel *01629 640471.*
This has been a welcome stop for
weary travellers since 1787. The pub
sits off what is known today as the
Monsal Trail, a popular route with
walkers, runners, and cyclists. Great
real ales and locally sourced food.

Hathersage: Plough Inn
*Leadmill Bridge, Hope Valley,
Derbyshire.* **Tel** *01433 650319.*
Enjoying an idyllic location on
the banks of River Derwent, the
16th-century Plough Inn is set on
nine acres of private parklands and
offers the perfect summer stop off.
Fabulous food, great views and six
en suite rooms.

Lyddington: Old White Hart
51 Main St, Rutland.
Tel *01572 821 703.*
Charming country inn with an
award-winning à la carte menu.
The Old White Hart has lovingly
retained the oak-beamed ceilings,
exposed brick walls and open fires
of the renovated 17th-century
stone building.

Mumby: Red Lion
Hogsthorpe Rd, Lincolnshire.
Tel *01507 490391.*
Run by the local Bateman's Brewery,
this pub is an excellent choice to
sample the flavours of Lincolnshire.
On the menu are traditional dishes
prepared with locally sourced
ingredients.

Nottingham: Cock and Hoop
25 High Pavement, Nottingham.
Tel *0115 948 4414.*
This traditional Victorian Ale House
offers a friendly, civilised retreat
where punters can enjoy superb
real ale and excellent wines. The
restaurant serves excellent British
home cooking. Small dogs welcome.

Stamford: The George of Stamford
71 St Martins, Lincolnshire.
Tel *01780 750750.*
One of England's most famous
coaching inns, the George's bar,
restaurant and rooms are all rich in
history. Other than the award-
winning restaurant menu, there are
also more informal pub food choices
served in the ivy-covered courtyard
and in the York Bar.

Tideswell: Anchor Inn
4 Lanes End, Derbyshire.
Tel *01298 871371.*
This warming hostelry makes for
a great pit stop following a walk in
the Peaks. A roaring log fire and
good old-fashioned hospitality are
complemented by a wide selection
of delicious local ales. Dogs are
welcome, too.

Lancashire and the Lakes

Ambleside: The Britannia Inn
Elterwater, Cumbria.
Tel *015394 37210.*
This traditional inn began life
as a farmhouse and cobbler's.
Standing on the village green
and surrounded by stunning
scenery, it is a delightful place to
unwind after a day's walk. There
are also en-suite rooms.

Clitheroe: The Shireburn Arms
Hurst Green, Lancashire.
Tel *01254 826678.*
Located in a picturesque village,
this characterful 17th-century inn
was one of author J R R Tolkien's
favourite haunts. Takes its name
from the family who built Stonyhurst
College and nearby almshouses.

Downham: Assheton Arms
Downham, Lancashire.
Tel *01200 441227.*
Previously known as The George
and Dragon, this pub was renamed
following the elevation of the local
squire, Ralph Assheton, to Lord
Clitheroe. Facing the old church in a
pretty village of stone cottages, it
has even been featured in films and
television series. Specialities on the
menu include seafood and stone-
cooked steaks.

Hawkshead: Queen's Head Hotel
Main St, Cumbria.
Tel *01539 436271.*
Situated at the heart of one
of the prettiest Lake District
villages. The superb food ranges
from simple sandwiches at the bar
to full meals in the restaurant.
William Wordsworth was schooled
in this village.

Hawkshead: Tower Bank Arms
Near Sawrey, Hawkshead, Cumbria.
Tel *01539 436334.*
Standing in a picturesque village,
this 17th-century inn is very close
to Hill Top, where the legendary
children's author Beatrix Potter
once lived. It even features in
one of her well-known stories,
The Tale of Jemima Puddle-Duck.
There are four rooms for guests
wishing to stay.

Liverpool: Ship and Mitre
133 Dale St, Merseyside.
Tel *0151 236 0859.*
Close to the city centre, this
traditional pub has a reputation
for serving a wide range of
real ales. Hot food served daily.
Pub quiz on Thursdays.

Lonsdale: Snooty Fox Tavern
Main St, Kirkby Lonsdale, Cumbria.
Tel *01524 271308.*
A listed Jacobean coaching inn in
the centre of the town, which lies
in the picturesque Lune Valley.
Its rambling bars and cobbled
courtyard exude a traditional
British charm.

Manchester: Lass o' Gowrie
36 Charles St.
Tel *0161 273 6932.*
Famous for its cask ales, this lively
pub is popular with students.
The menu features a Sunday roast.
Entertainment comes in the form
of live music and comedy nights.

Yorkshire and Humberside

Askrigg: Kings Arms
Market Place, North Yorkshire.
Tel *01969 650113.*
Fans of James Herriot's *All Creatures
Great and Small* will recognize this
as "The Drover's Arms". There is a
broad menu of appetizing food
and five real ales on tap in the bar.

Driffield: Wellington Inn
*19 The Green, Lund, Driffield, East
Yorkshire.* **Tel** *01377 217294.*
Just north of the minster town
of Beverley, this attractive pub
overlooks a charming village green.
Its fine food and friendly service
have won it an enviable reputation.

Flamborough: The Seabirds
Tower St, Flamborough, East Yorkshire.
Tel *01262 850242.*
Near the bird sanctuary on the
chalk cliffs of Flamborough Head,
this pub is popular with locals and
walkers. The specialities on the menu
revolve around locally sourced fish,
but there's a range of other dishes
on offer too.

Lancaster: The Game Cock Inn
The Green Austwick, North Yorkshire.
Tel *01524 251226.*
Close to the Yorkshire "Three Peaks",
this 17th century coaching inn
is the focal point of the tiny village.
The award-winning food is home-
cooked by a French chef, and the
menus offer a range of options –
everything from a simple snack to
an elaborate dinner. Dog friendly
and rooms available.

Leyburn: The Blue Lion
E Witton, Leyburn, North Yorkshire.
Tel *01969 624273.*
An 18th-century coaching and
drover's inn within a charming
Wensleydale village, it retains many
original features. Open fires warm the
rooms in winter. The food is traditional,
but often with an unusual twist.

Pickering: New Inn
Cropton, Pickering, North Yorkshire.
Tel *01751 417330.*
With an award-winning brewery in
the backyard, it's no wonder that this
popular pub on the edge of the Moors
can get busy. The warren of rooms
includes several characterful dining
areas. Brewery tours are available.

Skipton: The Red Lion Hotel
By the Bridge, Burnsall, North Yorkshire.
Tel *01756 720204.*
Before the bridge was built across
the Wharfe at Burnsall, this 16th-
century inn used to operate a ferry
across the river. Today, it has a reputation for fine food and a wide range
of real ales and wine. Dogs welcome.

Northumbria

Barnard Castle: The Morritt Arms
*Greta Bridge, Barnard Castle, County
Durham.* **Tel** *01833 627232.*
Located between Carlisle and
London, this 17th-century stone
farmhouse eventually became
a coaching inn. Dickens stayed
here while writing *Nicholas Nickleby.*
A mural by local artist John
Gilroy depicts Dingley Dell from
The Pickwick Papers.

Consett: Lord Crewe Arms
*Blanchland, near Consett, County
Durham.* **Tel** *01434 675469.*
Built in 1160 as the abbot's house,
this delightful hotel faces an unusual
enclosed cobbled square at the
heart of a pretty village. Dine in
the formal restaurant or opt for
the more casual style and menu
in the bar. Dog friendly. Accommodation available.

Craster: Jolly Fisherman
*Haven Hill, near Alnwick,
Northumberland.* **Tel** *01665 576461.*
Unassuming local pub with lovely
sea views. Homemade crab soup
and seafood are specialities.

Haltwhistle: Black Bull
Market Sq, Northumberland.
Tel *01434 320463.*
Cluttered and cosy, with a roaring
fire, this lovely pub on the southern
edge of Kielder Forest serves hearty
traditional pub food and good real
ales. The cheerful service adds to
the warm atmosphere.

Hedley on the Hill: The Feathers Inn
Stocksfield, Northumberland.
Tel *01661 843607.*
This family-run pub serves traditional
British fare and is popular with
foodies. There is always a good
selection of vegetarian dishes and at
least four guest ales on tap at the bar.

Hexham: Dipton Mill Inn
Dipton Mill Rd, Northumberland.
Tel *01434 606577.*
Originally an 18th-century mill, this
family-run pub lies beside Dipton
Burn in a wooded valley. The
characterful bar stocks a range
of beers brewed next door, and
serves homemade food.

Kielder Water: The Pheasant Inn
*Stannersburn, Falstone,
Northumberland.* **Tel** *01434 240382.*
This farmhouse, dating back to
the 1600s, has functioned as a pub
since the 18th century. Popular with
visitors to Kielder Water and the
surrounding forest. Meals are served
at the bar, with the dining room
opening for Sunday lunch and
evening dinner.

Newton: Cook and Barker Inn
Morpeth, Northumberland.
Tel *01665 575234.*
Once a forge, this inn got its
name from its first proprietors,
a Captain Cook who married a
Miss Barker. Guests can dine à la
carte in the restaurant, where
the original fireplace and well
remain. Hearty pub meals can
be ordered at the bar. There is also
accommodation available.

Seahouses: The Olde Ship Inn
Northumberland. **Tel** *01665 720200.*
Situated above the tiny fishing
harbour with a view across Farne
Islands. Interesting nautical
memorabilia decorate the bars
and there's a pleasant beer garden.
Accommodation is also available.

North Wales

Caernarfon: Black Boy Inn
Northgate St. **Tel** *01286 673604.*
This venerable pub has been
welcoming visitors for centuries,
and it remains a great place to
down tools. It has a couple of low-
beamed bars from where the finest
beers in town are served.

Capel Curig: Bryn Tyrch Inn
Conwy. **Tel** *01690 720223.*
Pretty country inn in the heart of
Snowdonia National Park, this is a
popular stopping-off point for
walkers and climbers. Traditional
Welsh cuisine. Great views of Mount
Snowdon from the bar.

Glanwydden: Queen's Head
Llandudno. **Tel** *01492 546570.*
This bustling village pub has
a great bar menu. Tables fill
quickly so it is wise to arrive
early. Great range of real ales.

Maentwrog: Grapes Hotel
Blaenau Ffestiniog, Gwynedd.
Tel *01766 590365.*
Said to be haunted, this Grade II
listed coaching inn serves fine
ales and homemade food in
a stunning setting. Pitch pine
pews, exposed stone walls and
a roaring fire in winter all add
to the effect.

Holywell: The Black Lion
Babell, Flintshire.
Tel *01352 720239.*
The Black Lion can trace its roots
back to the 13th century. Today
this quiet country pub, near the
A55, is popular with diners and
real ale enthusiasts.

Mold: Glasfryn
Raikes Lane, Sychdyn.
Tel *01352 750500.*
Pretty village pub known for its
theatre-going clientele (Theatre
Clwyd is just next door), Glasfryn
is a converted farmhouse pub
with a warm welcome. Good
menu and wine list.

Nant Gwynant: Pen-y-Gwryd
Gwynedd.
Tel *01286 870211.*
Hotel with a bustling pub in the
shadow of Mount Snowdon. It is
here that the 1953 Everest team
holed up while training for the
ultimate ascent. Popular with
walkers for its prime location,
it also serves great food and drink.

Overton Bridge: Cross Foxes Inn
Erbistock, Wrexham, Clwyd.
Tel *01978 780380.*
Fabulous food in a fabulous
setting, Cross Foxes Inn, on the
banks of the River Dee, is a very
welcoming 18th-century coaching
inn with a distinctive dining room.
Good choice of real ales.

South and Mid-Wales

Aberaeron: Harbourmaster
Pen Cei, Ceredigion.
Tel *01545 570755.*
Fabulous hotel-pub overlooking
the town's picturesque harbour.
This blue-washed building serves
tasty seafood such as Cardigan Bay
crab and lobster, Aberaeron
mackerel and several other such
freshly caught delicacies in its
restaurant. Also has 13 rooms.

Aberystwyth: Halfway Inn
Devils Bridge Rd, Pisgah.
Tel *01970 880631.*
Halfway between Aberystwyth
and Devil's Bridge (hence the
name), this large inn has steadily
built a strong reputation for its
fine food and fabulous real ale.
Designated restaurant area away
from the bar.

Brecon: Griffin at Felin Fach
Felin Fach, Brecon.
Tel *01874 602111.*
Comfy leather sofas piled with
soft cushions, roaring log fires in
winter, and a gorgeous garden
for summer drinking and dining,
the Griffin has it all. Food and ales
are locally sourced (many
ingredients are home-grown)
and there's a great choice of
fine wines, sherries and spirits
too. Seven beautifully furnished
and comfortable rooms complete
the picture.

Cardiff: City Arms
12 Quay St. **Tel** *02920 641913.*
A good old-fashioned boozer
right opposite the Principality
Stadium, this pub is heaving
on rugby match days. The beers
are mostly from the nearby Brains
brewery, but there's also a selection
of guest ales.

East Aberthaw: Blue Anchor
Barry, S Glamorgan.
Tel *01446 750329.*
This refurbished, thatched pub
in the seaside town of Barry is
just 10 miles (16 km) from
Cardiff. It has a friendly little bar
as well as an elegant restaurant
serving superior cuisine. Estuary
walks nearby.

Hay-on-Wye: The Pandy Inn
Dorstone, Herefordshire.
Tel *01981 550273.*
A picturesque pub with rooms just
over the border in Herefordshire,
the Pandy Inn boasts a long and
illustrious history. Supposedly
the oldest pub in the county, it
played host to Oliver Cromwell
during the 17th-century Civil War.
The restaurant serves wholesome,
filling and tasty food. Dogs are
welcome, too.

Pembroke Ferry: Ferry Inn
Pembroke Dock.
Tel *01646 682947.*
This early 17th-century inn serves
delicious seafood in a prime
location overlooking the harbour.
The extensive waterfront terrace
is a perfect setting for languid
summer dining. Check out the
specials board for locally caught fish.
Roast dinners are served on Sunday.

Penallt: Boat Inn
Lone Lane. **Tel** *01600 712615.*
With a stunning location on the
banks of the River Wye, the beer
garden at the Boat Inn is a great
place to relax with a chilled drink
on a warm summer's day. Bar food is
available. Access is via a footbridge.

Swansea: King Arthur Hotel
Reynoldston, Gower. **Tel** *01792 390775.*
The real appeal of this handsome
old pub is the sweeping green,
which is invariably populated by
sheep. But the beer and food are
both very decent, too. A great spot
in warmer weather.

Tintern: The Rose & Crown Inn
Monmouth Rd, Monmouthshire.
Tel *01291 689254.*
On the banks of the River Wye, in
a designated Area of Outstanding
Natural Beauty, the Rose & Crown
dates back to at least 1835. Walkers
and dogs welcome.

Usk: Nag's Head
Twyn Sq. **Tel** *01291 672820.*
Atmospheric village pub with
an extensive menu that is very
reasonably priced for the size
of the portions. This warmly
welcoming establishment places
an emphasis on the homemade
food, but there is also a terrific
selection of real ales.

The Lowlands

Dunblane: Sheriffmuir Inn
nr Bridge of Allan and Dunblane.
Tel *01786 823285.*
This middle-of-nowhere former
coaching inn still has the trappings
of an old pub but has also become
a trendy restaurant worth finding.
Good food at good prices.

Edinburgh: Bennets Bar
8 Leven St. **Tel** *0131 229 5143.*
Ever popular, this venue's one-
time ordinary "pubness" is rapidly
becoming exotic: big old mirrors,
a mix of ages, drinks in pint pots
and cheap lunches.

Edinburgh: Café Royal Circle Bar
West Register St. **Tel** *0131 556 1884.*
This atmospheric pub features
tiled portraits of Scottish worthies
and ornate chandeliers. Sink
back into one of the comfortable
leather chairs for a drink before
making your way to the oyster bar
and restaurant.

Elie: Ship Inn
The Harbour, Fife. **Tel** *01333 330 246.*
This quayside pub offers nautical
decor and appealing views. It also
hosts barbecues in the summer.

Glasgow: Horseshoe
17–21 Drury St.
Tel *0141 248 6368.*
A busy Victorian pub with a long
bar and plenty of period features,
the Horseshoe offers good-value
bar snacks. There is also karaoke
in the evenings.

Isle of Whithorn: Steam Packet
Dumfries & Galloway.
Tel *01988 500 334.*
Superb setting on a lovely
harbour. Pleasant eating areas
and a good selection of real ales.
Boat trips from the harbour.

The Highlands and Islands

Applecross: Applecross Inn
Shore St, Wester Ross, Highlands.
Tel *01520 744262.*
Spectacularly located beyond
Britain's highest mountain pass,
this pub overlooks the Isle of
Skye. Local seafood is served,
and there is live music once
a week in season.

Dundee: Fisherman's Tavern
10–16 Fort St, Broughty Ferry, Tayside.
Tel *01382 775941.*
Choose between award-winning
real ales and the extensive selection
of malts, or savour a little of both.
Good seafront and views of the
Tay Rail Bridge. Rooms available

Isle of Skye: Praban Bar at Eilean
Iarmain
Isle Ornsay, Isle of Skye.
Tel *01471 833332.*
Welcoming hotel bar. Lots of malts
and real local ales, as well as good
bar food. Gorgeous setting, too.

Loch Lomond: Oak Tree Inn
Balmaha (E side)
Tel *01360 870357.*
Traditional stone inn with a
well-stocked bar, restaurant and
B&B accommodation. Sit by the
roaring fires in winter and snack
on the tasty bar food that is
served all day.

Portsoy: The Shore Inn
The Old Harbour, Banffshire.
Tel *01261 842831.*
An 18th-century seafaring inn
nestled in a picturesque harbour.
Traditional cask ale and a real
open fire.

Ullapool: Ferry Boat Inn
Shore St, Highland.
Tel *01854 612366.*
Good whiskies, bar lunches
and fine views over the harbour.
Coal fires and big windows
overlooking the loch.

SHOPPING IN BRITAIN

While the West End of London (*see pp152–5*) is undeniably the most exciting place to shop in Britain, many of the regional towns and cities offer nearly as wide a range of goods. Moreover, regional shopping can be less stressful, less expensive, and remarkably varied, with craft studios, farm shops, street markets and factory outlets adding to the enjoyment of bargain-hunting. Britain is famous for its country clothing: wool, waxed cotton and tweed are all popular, along with classic prints such as Liberty or Laura Ashley, and tartan. Other particularly British goods include antiques, floral soaps and scents, porcelain, glass and local crafts.

A selection of goods for sale at a stall in Norwich Market

Shopping Hours

In general, shops in Britain open during the week from 9am or 10am, and close after 5pm or 6pm. Many town centre shops open on Sundays. Some stores all around the country open late on Thursdays – until 8pm outside the big cities and as late as 10pm in London's West End. Village shops may close at lunchtime, or for one afternoon each week. Market days vary from town to town.

How to Pay

Most large shops all over the UK accept well-known credit cards such as Mastercard and VISA. Charge cards such as American Express or Diners Club are widley accepted, but markets and some small shops do not take credit cards. Travellers' cheques can be used in larger stores, though exchange rates for non-sterling cheques may be poor. Take your passport with you for identification. Few places accept cheques drawn on foreign banks. Cash is still the most popular way to pay for small purchases.

Rights and Refunds

If something you buy is defective, you are entitled to a refund, provided you have kept your receipt as proof of purchase and return the goods in the same condition as when you bought them, preferably in the same packaging. This may not always apply to sale goods clearly marked as seconds, imperfect, or shop-soiled. Inspect these carefully before you buy. You do not have to accept a credit note in place of a cash refund.

Annual Sales

Sales take place during January, and in June and July, when nearly every shop cuts prices to get rid of old stock. But you may find special offers at any time of the year. Some shops begin winter sales just before Christmas. Department stores and fashion houses have some excellent bargains for keen shoppers; one of the most prestigious sales is at Harrods (*see p101*), where queues form long before opening time.

Street stalls set out in the summertime in Brighton

VAT and Tax-Free Shopping

Value added tax (VAT) is charged on most goods and services sold in Britain – exceptions are food, books and children's clothes. It is usually included in the advertised price. Visitors from outside the European Union who stay less than three months may claim this tax back. Take your passport with you when you go shopping. You must complete a form in the shop when you buy goods and give a copy to the customs authorities when you leave the country. You may have to show your goods as proof of purchase. If you arrange to have goods shipped from the store, VAT should be deducted before you pay.

Out-of-Town Shopping Centres

These large complexes, built in the style of North American malls, have also opened around Britain. The advantages of car access and cheap parking are undeniable, and most centres are accessible by public transport too. The centres usually feature popular high street stores, with facilities such as cafés, crèches, restaurants and cinemas.

Department Stores

A few big department stores, such as Harrods, are only found in London, but others have provincial branches. John Lewis, for example, has shops all over the country. It sells a huge range of fabrics, clothing and household items, combining

Shoppers wandering up and down Stonegate, York

quality service with good value. Marks & Spencer, with branches in most towns and cities in Britain, is famed for its good-value clothing and pre-prepared food. Debenhams is another well-known general store with inexpensive clothing and home furnishings. Habitat is a reputable supplier of modern furniture. The sizes of all these stores, and the range of stock they carry, differs from region to region.

Clothes Shops

Once again, the larger cities such as London, Manchester, Birmingham and Bristol have the widest range, from *haute couture* to cheap and cheerful ready-made items. Shopping for clothing in the regions, however, can often be less tiring. Many towns popular with tourists – Oxford, Bath and York for instance – have independently owned clothes shops where you are likely to receive a more personal service. Or you could try one of the chain stores in any high street, such as Laura Ashley or Next for smart, reasonably priced clothes, and Topshop, Oasis and H&M for younger and cheaper fashions.

Supermarkets and Food Shops

Supermarkets are a good way to shop for food. The range and quality of items is usually excellent. Several large chains compete for market share, and as a result prices are generally lower than in smaller shops. Sainsbury's, Tesco, Asda, Morrisons and Waitrose are some of the national names. The smaller food shops in town centres such as bakeries, greengrocers and farm shops, may give you a more interesting choice of regional produce, and a more personal service.

Souvenir, Gift and Museum Shops

Buying presents is a must for most travellers. Most reputable large stores can arrange freight of high-value items. If you want to buy things you can carry back in your suitcase, the choice is wide. You can buy attractive, well-made, portable craft items all over the country, especially in areas tourists are likely to visit. For slightly more unusual presents, have a look in museum shops or at the gifts available in National Trust *(see p33)* and English Heritage *(see p622)* properties.

Second-hand and Antique Shops

A visit to any of Britain's stately homes will reveal a passion for antiques and there are many interesting artifacts to be found in second-hand shops. Most towns have an antique or bric-a-brac (miscellaneous second-hand items) shop or two. Look out for auctions – tourist information centres *(see p621)* can help you to locate them. You may like to visit a car boot sale or charity shop in the hope of picking up a bargain.

Markets

Large towns and cities usually have a central covered market which operates most weekdays, selling everything from fresh produce to pots and pans. The information under each town entry in this guide lists market days. Many towns hold weekly markets in the main square, while farmers' markets have become increasingly popular and are a good place to source fresh, organic produce from British farms.

Browsers at stalls at Covent Garden Market, London

ENTERTAINMENT IN BRITAIN

London is without a doubt the entertainment capital of Britain *(see pp156–9)*, with countless shows, films and concerts to choose from, but many regional theatres, opera houses and concert halls have varied programmes too. Edinburgh, Manchester, Leeds, Birmingham and Bristol, in particular, have a lot to offer and there are a number of summer arts festivals around the country, such as those at Bath and Aldeburgh *(see p67)*. Ticket prices vary but are usually cheaper outside the capital and when booked in advance.

Sources of Information

In London, check the listings magazines, such as *Time Out*, or the *Metro or Evening Standard*, London's morning and evening newspapers (all free). All of the high-brow newspapers *(see p631)* provide comprehensive arts reviews and listings of the cultural events and shows throughout the country. Local newspapers, libraries and tourist offices *(see p621)* can supply details of regional events. Specialist magazines such as *NME* give up-to-date news of the pop music scene and are available from any newsagent.

Theatres

Britain has an enduring theatrical tradition dating back to Shakespeare *(see pp328–9)* and beyond. All over the country, amateurs and professionals tread the boards in auditoriums, pubs, clubs and village halls. Production and performance standards are generally high, and British actors have an international reputation. London is the place to enjoy theatre at its most varied and glamorous. The West End alone has more than 50 theatres *(see p156)* ranging from elaborate Edwardian to Modernist-style buildings such as the National Theatre on the South Bank.

In Stratford-upon-Avon, the Royal Shakespeare Company presents a year-round programme of Shakespeare, as well as avant-garde and experimental plays. Bristol also has a long dramatic tradition: its Theatre Royal *(see p260)* is the oldest working theatre in Britain. Some of the best productions outside the capital can be found at the West Yorkshire Playhouse in Leeds, the Royal Exchange in Manchester *(see p377)* and the Traverse in Edinburgh. Open-air theatre ranges from the free street entertainment found in many city centres, to student performances in the grounds of university colleges, or a production at Cornwall's clifftop amphitheatre, the Minack Theatre *(see p280)*. Every fourth year, York also stages a series of open-air medieval mystery plays called the York Cycle. Perhaps the liveliest theatrical tradition in Britain is the Edinburgh Festival *(see p513)*.

Ticket availability varies from show to show. For a midweek matinee, you may be able to buy a ticket at the door, but for the more popular West End shows tickets may have to be booked weeks or months in advance. You can book through agencies and some travel agents, and most hotels will organize tickets for you. Booking fees are often charged. Beware of tickets offered by touts *(see p71)* – these may be counterfeit. There are no age restrictions in Britain's theatres.

Street entertainer

Music

The country has a diverse musical repertoire that can be found in a variety of venues. Church choral music is a national tradition, and many churches and cathedrals host concerts. London, Manchester, Birmingham, Liverpool, Bristol and Bournemouth, amongst others, all have their own excellent orchestras.

Rock, jazz, folk and country concerts are often staged in pubs and clubs around the country. Wales has a strong musical tradition; northern England is known for its booming brass bands; and Scotland is renowned for its famous bagpipers *(see p484)*.

The Buxton Opera House, the Midlands

Cinemas

The latest films can be seen in any large town. Check the local papers or the tourist office to find out what is on.

Luxurious multi-screen cinemas have now taken over from the smaller, single-screen cinemas. In larger cities a more diverse range of films is often on offer, including foreign-language productions. These tend to be shown at arts or repertory cinemas. Mainstream English-language films are usually shown by the big chains. Age limits apply to certain films. Young children are allowed to see any feature film which is graded with a U (universal) or PG (parental guidance) certificate. Cinema prices vary widely; some are cheaper at off-peak times, such as Mondays or in the afternoons. For new releases it is advisable to book in advance.

The multiplex Vue West End cinema, Leicester Square, London

Clubs

Most cities have some sort of club scene, though London has many of the most famous venues in the country (see p158). These may feature live music, discos, or DJ or dance performances. Some clubs (or specific club nights) insist on dress codes or are members only, and most have doormen, or "bouncers". Brighton and Bristol are also well known for their lively clubs.

Dance

This covers a multitude of activities: everything from classical ballet and house music to traditional English Morris dancing or the Scottish Highland fling, which you may come upon in pubs and villages around the country.

Dance halls are rarer than they were, but ballroom dancing is alive and well. Other dance events you may come across are ceilidhs (pronounced "kay-lee"), which is Celtic dancing and music, dinner or tea dances and square dancing.

Birmingham is home to the Birmingham Royal Ballet and is the best place to see performances outside London. Avant-garde contemporary dance is also performed.

Gay Scenes

Most large communities will have some gay meeting places, mostly bars and clubs. You can find out about them from publications such as the free *Pink Paper* or *Gay Times* on sale in some newsagents, and in gay bars and clubs. London's gay scene centres on Soho (see p84) with its many European-style cafés and bars. Outside London, the most active gay scenes are in Manchester and Brighton. The annual Gay Pride is the largest free outdoor festival in Europe.

Children

London offers children a positive goldmine of fun, excitement and adventure, though it can be expensive. From the traditional sights to something more unusual such as a discovery centre, London has a wide range of activities, many interactive, to interest children of all ages. The weekly magazine *Time Out* has details of children's events.

Outside London, activities for children range from nature trails to fun fairs. The local tourist office or library will have information on things to do with children.

Pirate Ship, Chessington World of Adventures, Surrey

Theme Parks

Theme parks in Britain are enjoyed by children of all ages. **Alton Towers** has conventional rides plus a motor museum. **Chessington World of Adventures** is a huge complex south of London. Based on a zoo, it includes ten themed areas, such as Forbidden Kingdom and Pirates Cove. **Legoland** in Windsor, west of London, is fantastic for younger children. **Thorpe Park**, not far from Legoland or Chessington, is a large, watery theme park with roller-coasters. Not for the faint-hearted, it is aimed at older children and adults.

SPECIALIST HOLIDAYS AND OUTDOOR ACTIVITIES

A wide variety of special interest holidays and courses are on offer in Britain, where you can learn a new sport or skill, practise an activity you enjoy, or simply have fun and meet people. If you prefer less structured activities, there are numerous options to choose from, such as walking in Britain's national parks, pony trekking in Wales, surfing in Cornwall or skiing in Scotland. There are also several spectator sports for those who like to watch rather than participate, including Premier League football, Test Match cricket and historic horse races.

Arvon Foundation writing week at Totleigh Barton in Devon

Special Interest Holidays

The advantage of going on a special interest holiday or residential course in Britain, is that you can attend a course alone, and yet have plenty of congenial company – most people are delighted to meet others who share their interests. Whatever your passion or if you are looking to try something new, you are likely to find a holiday package that suits your needs.

Centres such as **Wye Valley Art Centre** in Gloucestershire and **West Dean College**, West Sussex, offer engaging residential courses in arts and crafts. These can range from familiar activities such as drawing and painting to more esoteric subjects such as mosaic art and glass engraving. Those interested in writing can enrol at the **Arvon Foundation**, which organizes week-long courses in fiction, poetry, songwriting and TV drama at three rural retreats in Devon, Shropshire and West Yorkshire. The **Ashburton Cookery School** in Devon and **Cookery at the Grange** in Somerset offer fun cookery courses with lots of hands-on involvement. Non-carnivores might try the **Vegetarian Society Cookery School** in Cheshire, which has innovative cookery courses catering to chefs at all levels – from complete beginners to talented amateurs.

Companies such as **Hidden Britain Tours**, **Inscape Tours** and the **Back-Roads Touring Company** provide themed holidays. History lovers can opt for a tour of King Arthur's Country or Shakespeare's England. Other tours designed for motor enthusiasts, garden lovers or fans of rock and roll are also available.

Prices for these holidays include expert guidance, transport, entry fees to attractions, and accommodation, which could be anything from a farmhouse to a medieval castle.

Walking

Walking is a popular activity in Britain and a network of long-distance footpaths and shorter routes crisscrosses the country *(see pp40–41)*. It is an excellent way to experience the spectacular variety of the British landscape, either by yourself or with a group. An advantage is that most routes are away from major tourist sites and often pass through picturesque villages that are off the beaten track.

The **Ramblers** is Britain's main walking organization, and its website provides useful information on most routes and walking areas. It also publishes a range of books, including their excellent *Short Walks* guides, covering all the most popular walking regions in Britain, with first-class maps and detailed route instructions.

There is no shortage of companies providing guided and self-guided holidays for walkers. The cost of these holiday packages should cover accommodation, transport

Walking on Holyhead Mountain near South Stack Anglesey, Wales

and detailed route guides.
Ramblers' Walking Holidays
offers guided group walks
through some of the country's
most splendid landscapes.
Sherpa Expeditions has a
variety of self-led walks. Pick a
challenging 15-day coast-to-
coast walk, or a more leisurely
ramble along the South Downs
Way. Individual companies
will advise you on the level of
fitness required and the type
of clothing and footwear that
will be needed.

If you are planning to walk
on your own, especially in
remote areas, remember that
it is essential to not only be
well equipped, but to also
leave details of your route
with someone.

A trio of cyclists mountain biking in
verdant Yorkshire

Cycling

The country's tranquil lanes,
bridleways and designated
tracks are perfect for cyclists
who want to explore the back
roads of Britain. Depending on
your level of fitness, you may
opt for demanding routes
through mountainous areas
such as the magnificent West
Highland Way in Scotland (*see
p498*). Those who would like to
take it easy can enjoy a relaxed
tour along Devon's lanes and
take the opportunity to stop
off for a delicious cream tea.

Country Lanes Cycle Centre
offers half a dozen self-guided
cycling tours around the Lake
District and the northwest of
England. The price includes
an experienced leader, high
quality bicycle equipment,

accommodation, meals,
baggage transfer and maps.
Compass Holidays and
Wheely Wonderful Cycling
concentrate on self-led tours,
with routes throughout the
country. They also provide
bicycles, accommodation,
detailed route maps (including
details of pubs, cafés and
places of interest along
the way) and appropriate
luggage transport. Such self-
guided cycling holidays are
ideal for families or groups
of friends.

If you wish to organize your
own cycling holiday, contact
the **Cycling UK**, which is
Britain's main recreational
cycling body, and **Sustrans**,
the organization responsible
for the National Cycle Network.
Both can provide a wealth of
information about cycling in
Britain, including advice on
matters such as bringing a
bike into the country, taking
your bike on the train and
the rules of the road. *Cycling
in the UK*, the official guide
book for the National Cycle
Network, has route details
and maps for many of the
best rides, and offers tips on
how to hire a bike and what
to do along the way.

Horse Riding and
Pony Trekking

There are good riding centres
in most parts of Britain, but
certain areas are especially
suitable for this invigorating
activity. The best of these
locations include the New
Forest (*see p172*), the South
Downs (*see p185*), the Yorkshire
Dales National Park (*see pp388–
90*) and the Brecon Beacons
on the border between Wales
and England (*see pp472–3*).

Pony trekking holidays are
also becoming very popular,
and generally include basic
training, a guide, meals and
accommodation. These
vacations are perfect for novice
riders and children since the
ponies are very well-trained and
rarely proceed above a canter.
The **British Horse Society** has
information on where to ride as

Horse riders taking a leisurely trek along
a country bridleway

well as a list of approved riding
schools that offer training.
National park information
offices can also provide details
of the many equestrian centres
that organize riding holidays in
or around national parks.

Golf

Over a quarter of Britain's 2,000-
odd golf clubs are in Scotland,
which is unsurprising given that
the ancient game was invented
here. The first formal club was
established in Edinburgh in 1744.

Today, the best-known clubs
are Carnoustie and St Andrews
in Scotland, Royal St George's in
England and Celtic Manor in
Wales. These high-profile clubs
only admit players above a
certain handicap. Most other
clubs, however, are more
relaxed and welcome visitors.

Green fees vary greatly, as do
the facilities offered by various
clubs. Some clubs may ask to
see a valid handicap certificate
before they allow a player on
the course. Failing that, a letter
of introduction from a home
club may be sufficient.

Specialist operators such as
Golf Vacations UK and **Great
Golf Holidays** can smooth the
way to the first hole considerably
by arranging golf packages. They
will organize travel and accommodation, reserve tee times and
pay the green fees. They will
also help you get temporary
membership of a club if required.

If you wish to go it alone, the
Golf Club of Great Britain can
provide information on where
to play. They have an affiliated
website for nonresidents of
the UK.

Surfing

The best areas for surfing are in the West Country and South Wales. Tuition is available at many resorts, and equipment can be hired.

The **Surfing England** website is able to help you locate a surf club or a surf school and it maintains a calendar of surfing events around the country. Other companies that offer good surfing courses include **Surf South West** in Devon and the **Welsh Surfing Federation Surf School** in South Wales.

Sailing boats on the beautiful blue waters of Cardigan Bay, Wales

Boating and Sailing

The British are extremely enthusiastic about boating and sailing. The country's network of rivers, lakes and canals offer great boating sites and there are many excellent choices. The Isle of Wight and the south coast are full of pleasure crafts. Several inland areas such as the Lake District *(see pp358–73)* are among the most widely favoured. Canal cruising is also popular *(see p641)* and the Norfolk Broads *(see p202)* provide one of the best inland boating experiences. Check with the **Broads Authority** for details.

Sailing courses are readily available. The **Royal Yachting Association** can provide lists of approved courses and training centres around Britain. One of the most trusted is Dorset's **Weymouth & Portland National Sailing Academy**, which has a range of courses to suit all ages and levels of ability. The **Falmouth School of Sailing** in Cornwall is a privately owned

sailing and powerboat school, which conducts lessons in the enclosed, safe waters of the Fal Estuary. Courses include basic "taster sessions" and one-to-one tuition for adults and children, as well as group lessons.

Skiing

Facilities for skiing are limited in the UK, especially since the weather for snow is rather unreliable. However, Scotland does have a range of challenging slopes. **Ski Scotland**, the official ski website of the Scottish Tourist Board, has information about ski packages, accommodation, up-to-date weather conditions and details of the main ski areas, including the Cairngorms and the Nevis Range. **Snowsport Scotland**, the governing body for all Scottish snowsports, provides information on other snow-based activities such as Nordic skiing and snowboarding.

Fishing

Fishing, both on the sea and in rivers, is one of Britain's most popular participatory sports. Regulations, however, are strict and can be rather complicated. It is advisable to check for details about rod licences, close seasons and other restrictions at tourist offices or tackle shops, or with the **Angling Trust** in Leominster.

The best game fishing (trout and salmon) is in the West Country, the northeast, Wales and Scotland. There are several specialist websites that have practical information about arranging fishing holidays.

Anglers fishing from the pier at Portsmouth Harbour

Spectator Sports

Football (soccer) is a passion for a large section of the population. The English Premier League, governed by the **Football Association**, is home to some of the world's top clubs, including **Manchester United** *(see p379)*, **Arsenal** and **Chelsea**. The domestic football season runs from August to May. Tickets for Premier League games can be expensive and difficult to obtain, but it is worth attempting to get hold of returned or unsold tickets directly from the clubs.

The main tennis event of the year is Wimbledon, held at the **All England Lawn Tennis Club (AELTC)** in London. This event takes place in the last week of June and the first week of July. The tournament sparks off a period of tennis fever in England, especially when British players such as Andy Murray progress in the competition. Most tickets for Centre Court are allocated by a public ballot. Check the AELTC website for ticket information. Around 6,000 tickets are available on the day of play (payment by cash only), except for the final four days of the tournament.

There are two codes of rugby: rugby league and rugby union. The latter is administered by **Rugby Football Union**. Both have popular professional leagues, with rugby league dominant in the north of England and rugby union teams primarily drawn from the south.

Cricket, the English national game, is played from April to September. Tickets for county matches are relatively cheap. International test matches are played on historic grounds such as **Surrey County Cricket Club's** ground at The Oval in London, and the **Yorkshire County Cricket Club** at Headingley in Leeds.

Horseracing, both steeple-chasing and flat-racing, is very popular, and betting is big business. The Grand National is the best-known steeplechase and runs at **Aintree Racecourse** in early April. The main flat-race meeting is the famous **Royal Ascot** event, which takes place in Berkshire towards the end of June.

DIRECTORY

Special Interest Holidays

Arvon Foundation
42A Buckingham Palace Rd, London, SW1.
Tel 020 7324 2554.
W arvonfoundation.org

Ashburton Cookery School
Old Exeter Rd, Ashburton, Devon, TQ13. **Tel** 01364 652784. W ashburton cookeryschool.co.uk

Back-Roads Touring Company
107 Power Rd, London, W4. **Tel** 020 8987 0990.
W backroadstouring. co.uk

Cookery at the Grange
The Grange, Whatley, Frome, Somerset, BA11.
Tel 01373 836099.
W cookeryatthegrange. co.uk

Hidden Britain Tours
28 Chequers Rd, Basingstoke, Hampshire, RG21 7PU. **Tel** 01256 814222. W hidden britaintours.co.uk

Inscape Tours
12a Castlebar Hill, London, W5. **Tel** 020 8566 7509.
W inscapetours.co.uk

Vegetarian Society Cookery School
The Vegetarian Society, Parkdale, Dunham Rd, Altrincham, Cheshire, WA14. **Tel** 0161 925 2000.
W vegsoccookery school.org

West Dean College
West Dean, Chichester, W Sussex, PO18. **Tel** 01243 811301.
W westdean.org.uk

Wye Valley Art Centre
Llandogo, Monmouth-shire, NP25. **Tel** 01594 530214. W wyearts. co.uk

Walking

Ramblers
2nd Floor, Camelford Hse, 87–90 Albert Embankment, London, SE1. **Tel** 020 7339 8500.
W ramblers.org.uk

Ramblers' Walking Holidays
Lemsford Mill, Lemsford Village, AL8. **Tel** 01707 818470. W ramblers holidays.co.uk

Sherpa Expeditions
1B Osiers Rd, Wandsworth, London, SW18. **Tel** 0800 008 7741. W sherpa expeditions.com

Cycling

Compass Holidays
Cheltenham Spa Railway Station, Queens Rd, Cheltenham, GL51.
Tel 01242 250642.
W compass-holidays. com

Country Lanes Cycle Centre
Railway Station Precinct, Windermere, Cumbria, LA23. **Tel** 015394 44544.
W countryaneslake district.co.uk

Cycling UK
Parklands, Railton Rd, Guildford, GU2.
Tel 01483 238301.
W cyclinguk.org

Sustrans
National Cycle Network Centre, 2 Cathedral Sq. College Green, Bristol, BS1. **Tel** 0117 926 8893.
W sustrans.org.uk

Wheely Wonderful Cycling
Petchfield Farm, Elton, Ludlow, Shropshire, SY8.
Tel 01568 770755.
W wheelywonderful cycling.co.uk

Horse Riding and Pony Trekking

British Horse Society
Abbey Park, Stareton, Kenilworth, Warwickshire, CV8. **Tel** 02476 840500.
W bhs.org.uk

Golf

Golf Club of Great Britain
338 Hook Rd, Chessington, Surrey, KT9. **Tel** 020 8391 4000. W golfclubgb.co.uk

Golf Vacations UK
Tel 01228 598098.
W golfvacationsuk.com

Great Golf Holidays
Tel 01892 544872.
W greatgolfholiday. com

Surfing

Surf South West
PO Box 39, Croyde, N Devon, EX33.
Tel 01271 890400.
W surfsouthwest.com

Surfing England
The Yard, Caen St, Braunton, Devon, EX33.
Tel 07429 208283.
W surfingengland.org

Welsh Surfing Federation Surf School
The Barn, The Croft, Llangennith, Swansea, SA3. **Tel** 01792 386426.
W surfschool.wsf.wales

Boating and Sailing

Broads Authority
Yare House, 62–64 Thorpe Rd, Norwich, NR1.
Tel 01603 610734.
W broads-authority. gov.uk

Falmouth School of Sailing
Grove Place, Falmouth, Cornwall, TR11. **Tel** 01326 211311. W falmouth-school-of-sailing.co.uk

Royal Yachting Association
RYA House, Ensign Way, Southampton, Hampshire, SO31. **Tel** 023 8060 4100. W rya.org.uk

Weymouth & Portland National Sailing Academy
Osprey Quay, Portland, Dorset, DT5. **Tel** 01305 866 000. W wpnsa.org.uk

Skiing

Ski Scotland
W skiscotland.com

Snowsport Scotland
South Gyle, Edinburgh, EH12. **Tel** 0131 625 4405.
W snowsportscotland. org

Fishing

Angling Trust
6 Rainbow St, Leominster, Herefordshire, HR6.
Tel 0844 770 0616.
W anglingtrust.net

Fisheries.co.uk
W fisheries.co.uk

Fishing Info
W fishinginfo.co.uk

Spectator Sports

Aintree Racecourse
Ormskirk Rd, Aintree, Liverpool, L9. **Tel** 0151 523 2600. W aintree. thejockeyclub.co.uk

All England Lawn Tennis Club (AELTC)
Church Rd, Wimbledon, SW19. **Tel** 020 8944 1066.
W wimbledon.com

Arsenal FC
Emirates Stadium, Hornsey Rd, London, N7.
Tel 020 7619 5000.
W arsenal.com

Chelsea FC
Stamford Bridge, Fulham Rd, London, SW6.
Tel 0871 984 1955.
W chelseafc.com

Football Association
Wembley Stadium, London, HA9. **Tel** 0800 169 1863. W thefa.com

Manchester United
Old Trafford, Manchester, M16. **Tel** 0161 868 8000.
W manutd.com

Royal Ascot
Ascot Racecourse, Ascot, Berkshire, SL5. **Tel** 0844 346 3000. W ascot.co.uk

Rugby Football Union
Rugby Rd, Twickenham, Middlesex, TW1.
Tel 020 8892 8877.
W englandrugby.com

Surrey County Cricket Club
The Kia Oval, Kennington, London, SE11. **Tel** 0044 375 1845. W kiaoval.com

Yorkshire County Cricket Club
Headingley Carnegie Cricket Ground, Leeds, LS6. **Tel** 0871 971 1222.
W yorkshireccc.com

SURVIVAL GUIDE

Practical Information   620–631

Travel Information   632–643

PRACTICAL INFORMATION

Every year, millions of people from all over the world seek out what the British often take for granted: the country's ancient history, colourful pageantry, spectacularly varied countryside and idyllic coastline. The range of facilities on offer to visitors has improved considerably in recent years. Be aware that prices vary across Britain, and regional differences can be very noticeable. London, not surprisingly, is the most expensive city, and the knock-on effect extends to most of southern England, Britain's most affluent region. Food, accommodation, entertainment, transport and consumer items in shops are generally cheaper in other parts of the country. It is always advisable to plan your trip before you travel to make the most of your time in the country and to get an idea of when is the best time to visit, what to take, how to get around, where to find information and what to do if things go wrong.

Weymouth Beach, Dorset, on a busy public holiday weekend

When to Go

Britain's temperate climate does not produce many temperature extremes (see pp72–3). However, weather patterns shift constantly, and the climate can vary widely in places only a short distance apart. Since it is impossible to predict rain or shine reliably in any season, be sure to pack a mix of clothes for warm and cool weather and an umbrella, irrespective of when you visit. Always get an up-to-date weather forecast before you set off on foot to remote mountain areas or moorland. Walkers can be surprised by the weather, and the Mountain Rescue services are often called out due to unexpectedly severe conditions. Weather reports can be found on television and radio, or in newspapers and online. They can also be provided by phone.

A sign for the Mountain Rescue

Britain's towns and cities are all-year destinations, but many attractions are open only between Easter and October. The main school holiday months, July and August, and public holidays (see p69) are always busy, and some hotels are full around Christmas. Spring and autumn offer a good compromise with reasonably good weather and a relative lack of crowds.

Visas and Passports

A valid passport is required to enter Britain. Visitors from the European Union (EU), the United States, Canada, New Zealand and Australia do not need visas to enter the country. Citizens of some countries may require a visa; details can be found on the **UK Visas and Immigration** (UKVI) pages of the UK government website, gov.uk.

The UK is not signed up to the Schengen open-borders agreement operated by most EU countries. Hence, visitors arriving from France or any other Schengen country must still pass through immigration checks when entering the UK. Travellers from the USA, Canada, Australia, New Zealand and a few other non-EU countries entering the UK for tourism, as well as business or study trips of less than six months, don't need a visa, but the UKVI advises that you bring the documents needed to apply for a visa, to show to officers at the UK border

(more details on UKVI web pages). Citizens of most other non-EU countries will need a visa, depending on the reason for the trip, in keeping with the points-based immigration system.

Britain is scheduled to leave the European Union in 2019, so check the latest visa requirements with your British embassy before you travel.

Travel Safety Advice

Visitors can get up-to-date travel safety information from the **Foreign and Common-wealth Office** in the UK, the **State Department** in the US and the **Department of Foreign Affairs and Trade** in Australia.

Customs Information

Britain is part of the European Union (until 2019), so anyone who arrives here from a member country can pass through a blue channel if they have already cleared customs in that country. Travellers entering from outside the EU have to pass through customs channels. Go through the green channel if you have nothing to declare, and use the red channel if you have goods to declare. If you are unsure of importation restrictions, go through the red channel.

On departure, non-EU residents can apply for a VAT refund on goods bought in Britain (see p610). However, random checks are still made to detect entry of prohibited goods, particularly drugs, indecent material and weapons.

◀ Beech trees in autumn in the Cotswolds, Gloucestershire

Never carry luggage or parcels through customs for someone else. For most EU citizens there is no limit to the amount of excise goods (such as tobacco or alcohol) that can be brought into Britain, if these are for your own use. This legislation does not apply to some new member states; check if you are unsure.

Britain is free of rabies, and no live animals may be imported without a permit. Any animals found will be impounded and may be put down.

Tourist Information

Tourist information is available in many towns and public places, including airports and main rail and coach stations, and some places of historical interest. Look out for the tourist information symbol, which can indicate anything from a large and busy central tourist bureau to a simple kiosk or even just an information board in a parking area.

Tourist offices will be able to help you on almost anything in their area, including places of interest and guided walks. Both the regional and national tourist boards produce comprehensive lists of local attractions and registered accommodation options. A range of leaflets is generally available for free at tourist offices, but a charge may be made for more detailed maps and booklets. For route planning, consider the excellent large-format motoring atlases produced by both the RAC and the AA (see p637). For rural exploration, Ordnance Survey maps are excellent (www.ordnancesurvey.co.uk).

It's wise to book accommodation well in advance of your visit. **VisitBritain** is a good resource for this. Out of season, you should have few problems booking transport, restaurants or even theatre performances at short notice, but in the high season, if you have set your heart on a luxury hotel, popular West End show or specific

tour, you should try to book in advance. Contact VisitBritain in your country, or see a travel agent for advice and general information.

Opening Hours

Outside of London and other main cities, some businesses and shops still close on Sundays, even though trading is legal. During the week, opening hours are generally from 9 or 10am until 5 or 5:30pm. Shop hours may include a late opening one evening a week, usually Thursday. In big city centres, particularly London, shops often open longer – until 7pm and seven days a week.

Museums in London tend to operate late opening hours one day a week, while those outside the capital may have shorter hours, sometimes closing in the morning or for one day a week, often on Mondays.

On public holidays, also known as bank holidays in Britain, banks, offices and some shops, restaurants and attractions close, and transport networks may run a limited number of services.

The most common English tourist information sign

Admission Prices

Admission fees for museums and sights vary widely, from under £10 to well over £15 for the more popular attractions. Many of the major national museums are free, although donations are

encouraged. The same is true of a few local authority museums and art galleries. Some sights are in private hands, run either as a commercial venture or on a charitable basis. Stately homes open to the public may still belong to the gentry who have lived there for centuries; a charge is usually made to offset the enormous costs of upkeep. Some of these houses, such as Woburn Abbey (see p234), have added safari parks or garden centres to attract larger numbers of visitors.

Britain's thousands of small parish churches are among the country's greatest architectural treasures. None of these churches charges an entrance fee, although you may find that some are locked because of vandalism. Increasingly, many of the great cathedrals may charge a visitor entry fee

Reductions are often available for groups, senior citizens, children and students. Proof of eligibility will be required when purchasing a ticket. Visitors from overseas may buy an English Heritage Overseas Visitor Pass, which gives access to more than 100 sights including Stonehenge (see pp266–7). This is also available as a Family Pass covering two adults and up to three children, aged 5–15. The pass can be bought online at english-heritage.org.uk and from VisitBritain offices abroad. In the UK, it is sold at the Britain Visitor Centre in Lower Regent Street in London, as well as at some ports of entry and tourist information centres across Britain.

A Cotswolds church, one of hundreds of parish churches open to the public free of charge

ENGLISH HERITAGE

The sign and symbol of
English Heritage

Heritage Organizations

Many of Britain's historic
buildings, parks and gardens,
not to mention vast tracts of
countryside and coastline, are
cared for by associations such
as **English Heritage** EH, the
National Trust NT or the
National Trust for Scotland NTS.
Entrance fees for these sights
are often quite steep, so if you
wish to visit several of them
during your stay, it may be
worth taking out an annual
membership, which allows
free access to any of these
properties for a calendar year.
Be aware that many may be
closed in winter.

Many of the National Trust's
properties are "listed", meaning
that they are recognized as
having special architectural
or historical interest and are
therefore protected from
alterations and demolition.
This guide identifies EH, NT
and NTS properties at the
beginning of each entry.

Disabled Travellers

The facilities on offer for
disabled visitors in Britain are
steadily improving. Recently

designed or newly renovated
buildings and public spaces
provide lifts and ramps for
wheelchair access (this
information is given in the
headings for each entry in this
guide); specially designed
toilets; grab rails; and, for the
hearing-impaired, earphones.
Buses are also becoming
increasingly accessible, and,
if given advance notice, train,
ferry or bus staff will help any
disabled passengers. Visit www.
disabledpersons-railcard.co.uk
for details of the Disabled
Persons Railcard and to
apply for a card.

Many banks, theatres and
museums now provide aids
for the visually or
hearing-impaired.
Specialist tour
operators, such
as **Tourism for All**,
cater for physically
disabled visitors.

Hertz (see p637)
offers hand-controlled
vehicles for hire at no
extra cost to the standard
car hire fees. In order to use
any of the disabled parking
spaces, you need to display a
special badge in your car.

For more general information
on facilities for disabled
travellers, visit www.openbritain.
net or contact **Disability Rights
UK**. This association also
publishes a book that carries
a wealth of information for

**Disabled Persons
Railcard**

disabled holiday-makers:
There and Back. It is a comprehensive guide to non-local
travel that pays particular
attention to the links between
the different methods of
transport, whether by air,
rail, road or sea.

Travelling with
Children

Britain offers a wealth of
activities and fun days out for
those travelling with children.
The VisitBritain website
(see p625) is a great resource
offering ideas, tips and useful
information for the family.

Peak holiday times – Easter,
July and August –
and half-term
school holidays
have most to
offer in terms
of entertainment
for children.
There is always
something child-
friendly going
on at Christmas, too, like
pantomimes and winter
skating rinks. It is worth
checking the websites of
individual museums and art
galleries, because these often
host child-centred events at
key times of year. A couple of
useful websites for information
on things to do with children
are dayoutwiththekids.co.uk
and letsgowiththekids.co.uk.

Discounts for children or
family tickets are available
for travel, theatre shows and
other forms of entertainment.

Choose a hotel that
welcomes children, or opt
for self-catering quarters with
hard-wearing furnishings and
lots of room in which to run
around. Many hotels now
provide baby-sitting or baby-
listening services, and may
offer reductions or even free
accommodation for very
young children.

Most restaurants are very
welcoming of younger
patrons, and will provide
high chairs and special
children's menus (see p577).
Italian eateries are often the
most friendly and informal,

The Natural History Museum, London, offers a great family day out (see p104)

Sheltered Praa Sands Beach, popular with families, in Penzance, Cornwall

but even the traditional British pub, once resolutely child-free, has relented, with beer gardens and family rooms. Under-18s are not permitted near the bars, nor are they allowed to buy or consume alcohol. The over-16s however, are permitted to consume wine, beer or cider with a table meal provided the alcohol is bought by an adult.

Baby-changing facilities are often provided at larger shops, department stores and shopping centres, as well as at most large museums and art galleries. For those who don't want to travel with all the paraphernalia necessary for their offspring (baby food, nappies, sunscreen), many shops will deliver everything you need for your trip directly to your accommodation if you order online – try johnlewis.com, mothercare.com, or tesco.com.

Student Travellers

Full-time students with a valid International Student Identity Card (ISIC) are often entitled to discounts on things such as travel, entrance fees and sports facilities. North American students can also get medical cover, though it may be very basic (see p627). ISICs can be bought from **STA Travel**, the **National Union of Students** or online. Proof of student status is required.

A **Hostelling International** card enables you to stay in Britain's youth hostels. Those who are exploring the wilder regions of Britain can find affordable sleeping quarters in camping barns (dormitory-style bunkhouses). Though spartan, they cost very little. The YHA website (www.yha.org.uk) has a full list of camping barns across Britain. Outside of term time, accommodation is also available at many of the university halls

of residence, such as the **University of London**. This is a good way of staying in city centres on a tight budget.

US and Canadian students interested in working in Britain should contact **BUNAC**, a student club that organizes exchange schemes.

International Student Identity Card

Tipping, Smoking and Alcohol

In Britain it is normal to tip taxi drivers and waiting staff in restaurants. Between 10 and 15 per cent is standard. Many restaurants automatically add a service charge to the bill, so do check before leaving a tip. It is not customary to leave a tip when buying a drink in a pub or bar.

Smoking is now forbidden in all of Britain's public indoor spaces, including pubs, restaurants, nightclubs, transport systems, taxis, theatres and cinemas. For advice on smoking-related issues, contact **ASH** (Action on Smoking and Health). It is illegal to buy cigarettes if you are under the age of 18.

Age restrictions also apply in pubs and bars, where you must be over 18 to be served alcohol. Some bars are for over-21s only, and patrons may be asked for identification before being served.

The privately owned, family-friendly Hever Castle (see p193)

A wide variety of tomatoes being sold on a stall at London's Borough Market

Public Toliets

Although some old-style supervised public toilets still exist, these have been largely replaced by the modern, freestanding, coin-operated "superloos". Main railway stations usually have toilet facilities for which there is sometimes a small charge. Young children should never use these facilities on their own.

Clock at the Royal Observatory, Greenwich (see p129)

Time

During the winter months, Britain is on Greenwich Mean Time (GMT), which is 5 hours ahead of Eastern Standard Time and 10 hours behind Sydney. From late March until late October, the clocks go forward 1 hour to British Summer Time (BST) (equivalent to Central European Time).

At any time of year, to check the correct time, contact the automated Speaking Clock 24-hour service by dialling 123 on a BT landline (note that there is a charge for this service).

Electricity

The voltage in Britain is 220/240 AC, 50 Hz. Electrical plugs have three rectangular pins and take fuses of 3, 5 and 13 amps. Visitors from abroad will need an adaptor for appliances that have been brought from home, such as laptops, hairdryers and phone chargers. Most hotels will have two-pronged European-style sockets for shavers only.

Conversion Chart

Britain is officially metric, in line with the rest of Europe. However, imperial measures are still in use, especially for road distances, which are measured in miles. Imperial pints and gallons are 20 per cent larger than US measures.

Imperial to Metric

1 inch = 2.5 centimetres
1 foot = 30 centimetres
1 mile = 1.6 kilometres
1 ounce = 28 grams
1 pound = 454 grams
1 pint = 0.6 litres
1 gallon = 4.6 litres

Metric to Imperial

1 millimetre = 0.04 inch
1 centimetre = 0.4 inch
1 metre = 3 feet 3 inches
1 kilometre = 0.6 mile
1 gram = 0.04 ounce
1 kilogram = 2.2 pounds

Responsible Travel

Like many European countries, Britain is striving to go green and is making a concerted effort to reduce emissions and waste. While most rubbish is still sent to landfill sites, there are recycling facilities in every town and city, and the amounts of household waste are gradually diminishing.

Many holiday properties across the country publish their green policies, showing how they minimize energy use. Some lodgings even offer discounts to guests arriving by public transport or on foot, particularly in heavily congested areas such as national parks. These themselves vary in the environmental schemes they operate, but all are committed to encouraging green tourism.

Green Tourism is a national scheme that has vetted more

Stalls selling fresh, colourful produce at a farmers' market

than 2,000 places to stay in England, Scotland and Wales, from small B&Bs to luxury five-star hotels, as well as about 500 visitor attractions. The scheme requires owners to provide details on more than 145 criteria, ranging from energy and waste control to use of transport and local produce. A qualified environmental auditor visits each property and allocates an award based on the standards met. There are also more than 20 regional accommodation certification schemes across Britain. Visit their website for information on sustainable options available to visitors. Another green accommodation solution is the great outdoors. Campsites are located across Britain, and pitches are available from around £20 per night. Note, however, that sites are often fairly far from the main towns and may not be served by public transport.

Organic and fair-trade products can be bought at most supermarkets. Many towns and cities hold a weekly food market, and farmers' markets are also on the increase. These stock locally sourced produce, and shopping here is a great way to give back to the local economy. Visit farma.org.uk to find your nearest farmers' market. When in rural areas, look out for farm shops that stock fresh products from local farms. "Slow Food" fairs are held occasionally across the country. These tend to last several days and are a great opportunity for small vendors to set up stalls and for visitors to sample food from sustainable sources.

DIRECTORY

Visas and Passports

UK Visas and Immigration
W gov.uk/browse/visas-immigration

Travel Safety Advice

UK
Foreign and Commonwealth Office.
W gov.uk/foreign-travel-advice

US
US Department of State
W travel.state.gov

Australia
Department of Foreign Affairs and Trade.
W smartraveller.gov.au

Embassies and Consulates

Australian High Commission
Australia House, Strand, London WC2.
Tel 020 7379 4334.
W uk.embassy.gov.au

Canadian High Commission
Macdonald House, Grosvenor Square, London W1.
Tel 020 7258 6600.
W canadainternational.gc.ca

New Zealand High Commission
New Zealand House, 80 Haymarket, London SW1. Tel 020 7930 8422.
W mfat.govt.nz

United States Embassy
24 Grosvenor Sq, London W1
(due to move to Nine Elms, SW8, in 2018).
Tel 020 7499 9000.
W uk.usembassy.gov

Tourist Information

VisitBritain
W visitbritain.com

Regional Tourist Boards

Cumbria
Tel 01539 822222.
W golakes.co.uk

East of England
Tel UK: 0333 320 4202; International: +44 1953 888021. W visiteastof england.com

East Midlands
W eastmidlands tourism.com

London
Tel 0870 156 6366.
W visitlondon.com

Northumbria
W visitnortheast england.com

Northwest
W visitnorthwest.com

Scotland
Tel 0845 859 1006.
W visitscotland.com

Southeast
W visitsoutheast england.com

Southwest
Tel 0117 230 1262.
W swtourism.org.uk

Wales
Tel 0870 830 0306.
W visitwales.com

Yorkshire and the Humber Region
W yorkshire.com

Heritage Organizations

English Heritage
Tel 0870 333 1181.
W english-heritage.org.uk

National Trust
Tel 0844 800 1895.
W nationaltrust.org.uk

National Trust for Scotland
Tel 0131 458 0200.
W nts.org.uk

Disabled Travellers

Disability Rights UK
Tel 020 7250 8181.
W disabilityrightsuk.org

Tourism for All
Tel UK: 0845 124 9971; International: +44 1539 726 111.
W tourismforall.org.uk

Student Travellers

BUNAC
Priory House, 6 Wrights Lane, London, W8 6TA.
Tel 020 7870 9570.
W bunac.org

Hostelling International
Tel 01707 324170.
W hihostels.com

National Union of Students
Tel 0845 521 0262.
W nus.org.uk

STA Travel
Priory House, 6 Wrights Lane, Kensington, London, W8.
Tel 0333 321 0099.
W statravel.co.uk

University of London
Malet St, London, WC1.
Tel 020 7862 8880.
W housing.lon.ac.uk

Responsible Travel

Green Leaf Tourist Scheme
W www.thenewforest.co.uk/accommodation/green-leaf-accommodation.aspx

Green Tourism
W green-tourism.com

Personal Security and Health

Britain is a densely populated country that, like any other, has its share of social problems. However, it is very unlikely that you will come across any violence. If you do encounter difficulties, do not hesitate to contact the police for help. Britain's National Health Service can be relied upon for both emergency and routine treatment. Note that you may have to pay if your country has no reciprocal arrangement with Britain.

Police car

Ambulance

Police

The sight of a traditional bobby walking the streets is now less common than that of the police patrol car, but the old-fashioned police constable does still exist, particularly in rural areas and patrolling city centres.

Unlike in many other countries, the police force in Britain does not carry guns, however there are specially trained Firearms Officers.

If you are lost, ask a policeman or woman – they are courteous, approachable and helpful. Traffic wardens may also be able to help you with directions. If you have been the victim of a robbery or an assault, contact the police by dialling 999 or 101 for non-emergencies. All Britain's major cities have community police support officers, who patrol the city streets working alongside the police. They are able to deal with anti-social behaviour, can offer advice on crime prevention and can also help you with directions and information.

What to be Aware of

Britain is not a dangerous place for visitors, and it is most unlikely that your stay will be blighted by crime. Due to terrorist threats, there are occasional security alerts, especially on the Underground, but these are mainly false alarms often due to people accidentally leaving a bag or parcel unattended. Always cooperate with the authorities if your bag has to be searched or if you are asked to evacuate a building.

Make sure that your possessions are adequately insured before you arrive, and never leave them unattended in public places. Keep your valuables concealed (particularly mobile phones), especially in crowded places.

Pickpockets love markets, busy shops and all modes of transport during rush hour. Keep handbags on your lap, never on the floor or on the back of your chair. It is advisable not to carry too much cash or jewellery with you. Take what you need for the day, and leave the rest in your hotel safe instead. It is also advisable not to leave any valuables on display in your hotel room.

At night, try to avoid deserted and poorly lit places such as back streets and car parks.

Begging is an increasingly common sight in many British cities, and foreign visitors are targets for hard-luck stories. Requests for money are usually polite, but any abuse should be reported to the police immediately.

In an Emergency

The police, fire and ambulance services are on call 24 hours a day and can be reached by dialling 999. Along the coastal areas, this number will also put you in touch with Britain's voluntary coastguard rescue service, the **Royal National Lifeboat Institute (RNLI)**. Calls are free from any public or private phone, but they should be made only in real emergencies.

Female police constable   Traffic police officer   Male police constable

Lost and Stolen Property

If you lose anything or have something stolen, report it at the nearest police station as soon as you are able. A written report from the local police is required to make a claim on your insurance for any theft. All of the main bus and rail stations have lost property offices. For property lost on national rail services, you will need to contact the individual trainline operator. In London, if you lose anything on buses, Underground or DLR trains, or in taxis (black cabs), it should eventually reach the Transport for London Lost Property Office in Baker Street. You can also enquire about lost items online through the **Tfl** website (under "Useful Contacts").

Medical Treatment

You can buy a wide range of over-the-counter drugs in Britain. **Boots** is the best-known chemist, with branches in most towns. Many medicines, however, are available only with a doctor's prescription. If you are likely to need medication, either bring it with you or ask your doctor to write out the generic (as opposed to the brand) name of the drug. If you are entitled to an NHS prescription, you will be charged a standard rate; if not, you will be charged the full cost of the drug. Do ask for a receipt for any insurance claim.

Some pharmacies are open until midnight; contact your local hospital for a list. You can call the **NHS 111 Service,** a 24-hour helpline or, for emergencies, go to a hospital A&E department. In an emergency, dial 999 for assistance.

If you need to see a dentist while staying in Britain, be aware that you will have to pay. The cost varies, depending on your entitlement to NHS treatment and whether you can find an NHS dentist to treat you (many dental practices no longer take on NHS patients). Emergency dental treatment is available in some hospitals. To find NHS and private dentists near you, see the **British Dental Association (BDA)** website.

Pharmacy sign

Health Insurance

It is sensible to take out travel insurance to cover cancellation or curtailment of your holiday, theft or loss of money and possessions, and the cost of any medical treatment, which may include emergency hospital care, repatriation and specialists' fees. This is particularly important for visitors from outside the European Union. Emergency medical treatment in a British NHS casualty ward is free, but any kind of additional medical care could prove very expensive.

Those with a European Health Insurance Card (EHIC) are entitled to free treatment under the NHS. This applies to visitors from EU and European Economic Area (EEA) countries, as well as some Commonwealth countries, such as Australia and New Zealand. Be aware, though, that certain benefits covered by medical insurance will not be included. North American and Canadian health plans or student identity cards (see p623) may give you some protection against costs, but do always check the small print.

DIRECTORY

Police and Emergencies

Police, Fire and Ambulance services
Tel 999.

Accident and Emergency (A&E) Departments
For your nearest unit, visit nhs.uk or thephonebook.bt.com

Ploice Non-Emergency Service
Tel 101 (24 hours).

Royal National Lifeboat Institution (RNLI)
W rnli.org

Lost and Stolen Property

Transport for London (Tfl) Lost Property Office
200 Baker St, NW1.
Tel 0343 222 1234.
Open 6:30am–4:30pm Mon–Fri.
W tfl.gov.uk

Medical Treatment

Boots
W boots.com

British Dental Association (BDA)
W bda.org

NHS
W nhs.uk
To locate a hospital, look under "Find and choose services".

NHS 111 Service
Tel 111 (24-hour health information and nurse led advice).

A Boots branch in Leeds

Banking and Currency

The high-street banks usually offer the best rates of currency exchange, though commission fees vary. However, if you do find yourself having to use one of the many privately owned bureaux de change found at nearly every major airport, train station and tourist area, take care to check the commission and minimum charges before completing any transaction.

ATMs outside a branch of Lloyds, one of Britain's high-street banks

Bureaux de Change

Private bureaux de change may be more conveniently located and have more flexible opening hours than banks. However, rates of exchange vary and commission charges can be high, so it is always worth shopping around.

Travelex, **American Express** and **Chequepoint** all have branches throughout Britain and usually offer good exchange facilities, as do many of the main branches of the Post Office (www.postoffice.co.uk). It is also possible to order your currency in advance on the Post Office website. Marks & Spencer (www.marksandspencer.com) has bureaux de change in more than 110 of its stores across the UK.

Banks

Every large town and city in Britain has a branch of at least one of these five high-street banks: Barclays, Lloyds, HSBC, NatWest and Royal Bank of Scotland.

Banking hours vary but the majority are open 9am to 5:30pm Monday to Friday. Most main branches open on Saturday mornings, too. All banks close on public holidays *(see p69)*.

If you run out of funds, it is possible to have money wired from your country to your nearest British bank. Branches of Travelex and American Express will also do this for you. North American visitors can get cash dispatched through **Western Union** to a bank or post office. Remember to take along your passport as proof of identity.

ATMs

Most banks have a cash dispenser, or ATM, from which you can obtain money with a credit card and your personal identification number (PIN). Cash machines can also be found in some supermarkets, post offices, petrol stations, train stations and London Underground stations. Some of the most modern ATMs have on-screen instructions in several languages. Some make a charge for cash withdrawals (typically £1.50 per transaction). American Express cards may be used at all cash-dispensing machines, but there is a 2 per cent handling charge for each transaction.

There have been some incidences of card crime at ATMs; be vigilant and cover the keypad with your hand when entering your PIN.

Credit Cards

Credit cards are widely used throughout Britain. Indeed, a credit card is necessary in order to rent a car and for some hotel bookings. However, many small shops, guest-houses, markets and cafés may not accept them or have a minimum spend, so always check in advance of your purchase. Cards that are accepted are usually displayed on the windows of the establishment. Britain uses the "chip and PIN" system instead of a signature. You will need a four-digit PIN, so ask your bank for one before you leave.

Currency Cards

Pre-paid currency cards are becoming increasingly popular, since they are both economical and user-friendly. Before you leave home, load the card

---

British Banks

High-street banks have branches in most of Britain's towns and cities. Many will also offer currency-exchange facilities, but proof of identity may be required.

HSBC logo

Royal Bank of Scotland logo

Barclays Bank logo

National Westminster logo

DIRECTORY

American Express
Tel 01273 696 933.
Ⓦ americanexpress.com/uk

Caxton FX
Ⓦ caxtonfx.com

Chequepoint
Tel 020 7244 1252.
Ⓦ chequepoint.com

Travelex
Ⓦ travelex.co.uk

Western Union
Tel 0808 234 9168.
Ⓦ westernunion.com

with money from your bank account, which will be fixed at that day's exchange rate. You can then use the card to buy goods or withdraw cash from an ATM when in Britain. You can also cancel it if it is lost or stolen. Look out, however, for additional charges. Currency cards are issued by several companies, including Travelex and **Caxton FX**.

Currency

Britain's currency is the pound sterling (£), divided into 100 pence (p). You may bring in and take out as much cash as you like. Scotland has its own pound sterling notes. These represent the same value as an English note and can

A Scottish one pound (£1) bank note

be used elsewhere in Britain, but usually accepted reluctantly. The Scottish £1 note is not accepted outside Scotland.

Traveller's cheques are no longer widely used – they incur hefty charges, are rarely accepted and have been superseded by cards.

Banknotes

English notes are produced in denominations of £5, £10, £20 and £50. Some shops may refuse the larger notes, so always try to get small denominations.

£50 note

£20 note

£10 note

£5 note

Coinage

Coins currently in use are £2, £1, 50p, 20p, 10p, 5p, 2p and 1p.

2 pounds (£2)

1 pound (£1)

50 pence (50p)

20 pence (20p)

10 pence (10p)

5 pence (5p)

2 pence (2p)

1 penny (1p)

Communications and Media

The mobile phone is king in the UK, and there is a plethora of mobile-phone operators, networks and phone shops to meet demand. Wi-Fi is common and provided for free in numerous public institutions and commercial spaces. With well over half the population regularly accessing the internet via their mobile phone, internet cafés are largely a thing of the past. While there are still a few surviving examples of the famous red telephone boxes, these are mainly defunct.

Mobile Phones

Mobile phones are widespread in Britain. The four biggest networks are **Vodafone**, **O2**, **EE** and **Three**, but there are at least another dozen service providers. Every high street has at least one mobile-phone shop, most commonly run by one of the four major networks. The UK network uses the 900 or 1800 GSM system, so visitors from the United States (where the system is 800 or 1900 MHz band) will need to acquire a tri- or quad-band set. Contact your service provider for details. You may need to inform your network operator in advance of your trip, so that the "roaming" facility can be enabled. When abroad, you will be charged for the calls you receive, as well as for the calls you make; in addition, you have to pay a substantial premium for the international leg of the call.

It is easier and cheaper to purchase a SIM card locally and top it up with credit. This will allow you to use the local mobile-phone networks, though you can only do this if your handset is not locked to a specific network.

Alternatively, you could buy a brand new phone and top up with a pay-as-you-go card. Make sure the phone you buy can accept international calls. Check that your insurance policy covers you in case your phone gets stolen, and keep your network operator's helpline number handy for emergencies.

Useful Dialling Codes

The following services exist to help you find or reach a specific phone number. You will be charged more for enquiries if calling from a mobile phone.

BT Directory Enquiries
Tel 118 500
(charge applies).

International Directory Enquiries
Tel 118 505
(charge applies).

International Operator
Tel 155
(free).

Operator Assistance
Tel 100.

Overseas Calls
Tel 00 followed by country code: Australia (61), Canada (1), Ireland (353), New Zealand (64), South Africa (27), United States (1).

Yellow Pages
Tel 118 247 (charge applies).
w yell.com
Provides services in any area, as well as maps and driving directions.

Public Telephones

You can use a payphone with coins or a card. All payphones accept 10p, 20p, 50p and £1 pieces; the newer ones also accept £2 coins. The minimum cost of a call is 60p. Phone cards are more convenient than coins and can be bought from newsagents and post offices. If you use a credit card, note that it carries a minimum charge and that your calls will be charged at a higher rate.

Internet

Free Wi-Fi is commonplace throughout the UK and is available in airports, hotels, B&Bs, pubs, cafés, museums and libraries and on some trains. The Cloud is a free Wi-Fi service provider used in many public locations including train stations and shopping malls. The service only requires you to log in for access and does not have a data allowance (fair usage policy applies).

Between them, the mobile-phone operators provide over 90 per cent of the UK with 3G coverage, but a 4G signal is still often difficult to come by. Access to 4G is very uneven, with much greater availability in London and relatively poor access in rural areas, particularly in Wales and parts of the Southwest. However, download speeds in London are often not as high as in other regions, due to the number of users attempting to access the network, though

Traveller using free Wi-Fi at a London underground station

speeds are, of course, also dependent on the network provider. A 2016 survey conducted by OpenSignal and consumer watchdog Which? found that EE had the fastest average download speeds (27.9 Mbps), followed by Three (24.4 Mbps), Vodafone (17.9 Mbps) and O2 (16.1 Mbps).

Postal Services

Stamps can be bought at many outlets, including supermarkets and petrol stations. When writing to a British address, always include the postcode, which can be obtained from **Royal Mail** (royalmail.com). Within the UK, letters and postcards can be sent either first or second class; second-class mail is cheaper and takes a day or two longer. The price of postage depends on the size and weight of your letter. For more details, visit the Royal Mail website or take your letter/parcel to any post office.

In more isolated areas, as well as in larger towns and cities, there are often small branches in newsagents, grocery stores and general information centres. In many villages, the post office is also the only shop.

Post offices are usually open from 9am to 5:30pm Monday to Friday, and until 12:30pm on Saturday.

Post boxes can be found throughout cities, towns and villages in Britain. They may be either freestanding boxes or wall safes, but they are always painted bright red.

Air letters go by Royal Mail's airmail service anywhere in the world. On average, it takes three days for them to reach cities in Europe, and four to six days for other destinations. Royal Mail also offers an express airmail service called **Airsure**, available from all post office branches.

Parcelforce Worldwide offers courier-style services to most destinations and is comparable in price to **DHL**, **Crossflight**, **Expressair** or **UPS**.

Newspapers and Magazines

British national newspapers fall into two categories: quality papers, such as *The Times*, *The Daily Telegraph* and *The Guardian*; and those heavy on gossip, such as *The Sun* or the *Daily Mirror*. The weekend newspapers, more expensive than dailies, are packed with supplements of all kinds, including sections on the arts, entertainment, travel, listings and reviews. Free newspapers, with an emphasis on news and celebrity gossip, are given away, morning and evening, at main railway stations in major cities such as London and Manchester.

Post box

Specialist periodicals on just about every topic are available from newsagents. For in-depth analysis of current events, buy *The Economist*, *New Statesman* or *The Spectator*, while *Private Eye* offers a satirical look at public figures. A few foreign magazines and newspapers are available in large towns, often at main train stations, but mostly in London. Popular papers such as the *International Herald Tribune* and the *New York Times* are widely.

Television and Radio

The state-run BBC (British Broadcasting Corporation) has nine national TV channels, ten national and numerous regional radio stations and a reputation for making some of the world's best television. Its traditional commercial rivals include ITV, Channel 4 and Five. ITV is known for its soap

Some of Britain's national newspapers

DIRECTORY

Mobile Phones

EE
W ee.co.uk

O2
W o2.co.uk

Three
W three.co.uk

Vodafone
W vodafone.co.uk

Postal Services

Airsure (Royal Mail)
Tel 08457 740 740.
W royalmail.com

Crossflight
Tel 01753 776 000.
W crossflight.com

DHL
Tel 0844 248 0844.
W dhl.co.uk

Expressair
Tel 033 3320 2120.
W expressair.co.uk

Parcelforce Worldwide
Tel 0344 800 4466.
W parcelforce.com

Royal Mail
Tel 08457 740 740.
W royalmail.com

UPS
Tel 00457 877 877.
W ups.com

operas and game shows; Channel 4 offers art films, documentaries and offbeat chat shows; and Five relies on US imports and TV movies.

There are also dozens of free-to-view digital TV channels (depending on area), including Sky News and BBC News, and many homes and hotels have hundreds of British and international channels via digital subscription services.

The BBC's radio stations range from pop music (Radio 1) to the current affairs network Radio 4. There are many local commercial radio stations.

Full TV and radio schedules appear in newspapers and listings magazines, as well as online and in the *Radio Times*, a weekly publication.

TRAVEL INFORMATION

Britain is an international gateway for both air and sea traffic, which translates into a variety of options in terms of travel. Visitors benefit from a large selection of air carriers linking Britain to the rest of Europe, North America and Australasia. Coach travel is a cheap, if rather slow, form of transport from Europe, while travelling by train has been transformed thanks to the Channel Tunnel. It takes less than two and a half hours from

Paris to London on Eurostar. Travelling within Britain is also easy. There is an extensive network of roads to all parts of the country, and hiring a car can be a convenient way of travelling around. The railway network is efficient and far-reaching, especially around London. Travelling by coach is the cheapest option. The coach network reaches most areas but can be slow. If time is short, air travel is possible, if expensive.

Eurostar trains at St Pancras International Station, London

Travelling Around Britain

Choosing the best form of transport depends on where and when you want to go, although the quickest and most convenient methods can be the most expensive. The website www.rome2rio.com lists a number of alternative ways of getting to your chosen destination.

Distances between any two points within mainland Britain are relatively small, so air travel usually makes sense only between the extremes, such as London to Edinburgh.

Train travel is the best option if you want to visit Britain's major cities, though fares, especially at peak times, can be expensive. If you plan to do much travelling within Britain, invest in a rail pass (see p638). You can buy one before you arrive in the UK; a number of schemes cater for overseas visitors. **BritRail** offers several options, from a few days' to two weeks' worth of rail travel.

Coaches (see p640) cover a wide number of UK destinations and are cheaper than trains, but they take longer and may be less comfortable.

For a touring holiday, hiring a car (see p637) is easier than relying on public transport. Car rental can be arranged at major airports, large train stations and city centre outlets. Small local firms often undercut the large operators in price but may not be as reliable or convenient. To get the best deals, book from abroad.

For detailed exploration of smaller areas, such as Britain's national parks, you may prefer more leisurely forms of transport such as bike, narrowboat or horse. Sometimes there are picturesque local options, like the rowing-boat ferry between Southwold and Walberswick on the Blyth Estuary (see p206). Larger car ferries travel to Britain's islands.

Taxis (see pp642–3) are available at all main coach and train stations; without a car you will avoid the stress of driving in congested city centres.

Green Travel

With congestion charges in London and limited parking in most urban areas, driving in British cities is not recommended. Instead, make use of the country's extensive public transport network.

Covering a lot of ground without a car is possible, although this does take careful planning to ensure you catch all of your connections. Most areas are served by trains and/or buses, and services tend to be fairly regular. Travelling around the countryside without private transport, however, can be difficult, because bus services can be infrequent (particularly on Sundays). It may be sensible to hire a car.

Trains in Britain can be overcrowded at peak times, and they are often expensive, although booking tickets in advance can bring the cost down. The GroupSave ticket scheme allows discounted rail travel for groups of three or four, and various other discounts are available with a travel card.

The National Trust (see p622) offers some incentives, including discounted entry, to those who use public transport when visiting some of their sites.

The National Cycle Network provides more than 20,000 km (12,430 miles) of cycle paths across Britain. A bike can be taken on most off-peak trains, but you may have to book a spot for it. Check before you travel. For more information on the National Cycle Network and other environmentally friendly travel options, contact **Sustrans**.

Arriving by Sea, Rail and Coach

Irrespective of how you are travelling from Europe, you will have to cross the English Channel or the North Sea. Ferry services operate from a number of ports on the European mainland and have good link-ups with international coaches, with services from most European cities to Britain. The Channel Tunnel means there is a nonstop rail link between Europe and Britain. Prices among the ferries and the tunnel services remain competitive, and both options are good green alternatives to flying.

Ferry Services from Europe

A complex network of car and passenger ferry services links over a dozen British ports to ports in northern and southern Europe.

Ferries can be convenient and economical for those travelling by car or on foot. Fares vary according to the season, time of travel and duration of stay. Early booking means big savings – a Dover–Calais return crossing can cost as little as £22. The shortest crossings are not always the cheapest, since you often pay a premium for faster journeys.

Crossing Times

Crossing times vary from just over an hour on the shortest routes to a full 24 hours on services from Spain and Scandinavia. If you take an overnight sailing, it is often worth paying extra for sleeping quarters to avoid feeling exhausted when you arrive. The fastest route between France and England is Calais to Dover (ferries no longer connect Boulogne direct to any English port), taking around 90 minutes

with **DFDS** or **P&O Ferries**. Four ferry companies connect the two countries, with **Brittany Ferries** and **Condor Ferries** operating various routes to and from Portsmouth, Plymouth and Poole.

Seaport Bureaucracy

Visitors from outside the EU should allow plenty of time for immigration control and customs clearance at British seaports *(see p620)*.

Channel Tunnel

Thanks to the Channel Tunnel, there is access to Britain via **Eurostar** and **Eurotunnel** with French and Belgian high-speed rail networks. These trains reach speeds of up to 186 mph (300 km/h). The cost is comparable to flying but the train is more convenient and less environmentally damaging. Typically, a one-way ticket from London to Paris costs about £110 but can be as low as £29.

Passengers on buses and in cars board a freight train

Eurotunnel logo

run by Eurotunnel that takes 35 minutes to travel between Calais and Folkestone. For those travelling by rail there are about 40 scheduled passenger-only Eurostar services, operated by the French, Belgians and British. They run direct services from Brussels, Paris, Lille and Calais to Ashford, Ebbsfleet and St Pancras *(see p109)* in London. There are two passenger tunnels and one service tunnel, both lying 25–45 m (82–147 ft) below the seabed.

International Coach Travel

Although coach (bus) travel is considerably cheaper than other forms of travel, it is not the most comfortable. If you have a lot of spare time and want to stop off en route, however, it can be convenient. Once you have paid for your ticket, you will not have to pay extra for the ferry or the Channel Tunnel.

DIRECTORY

Green Travel

Sustrans
W sustrans.org.uk

Sea, Rail and Coach Information

BritRail
W britrail.com

Brittany Ferries
Tel 0330 159 7000.
W brittany-ferries.co.uk

Condor Ferries
W condorferries.co.uk

DFDS
W dfdsseaways.co.uk

European Rail Travel
Tel 08448 484 078.
W raileurope.com

Eurostar
Tel 03432 186186.
W eurostar.com

Eurotunnel/Le Shuttle
Tel 08443 35 35 35.
W eurotunnel.com

P&O Ferries
W poferries.com

Rome2rio
W rome2rio.com

Ferry arriving at Dover

Arriving by Air

Britain has about 130 licensed airports, only a handful of which deal with long-haul traffic. The largest one, London's Heathrow, is the world's busiest international airport and one of Europe's main routing points for international air travel. Heathrow is served by most of the world's leading airlines, with direct flights from nearly all major cities. Other international airports include Gatwick and Stansted in London, Manchester, Glasgow, Newcastle, Birmingham and Edinburgh. Smaller airports, such as London City, Bristol, Norwich and Cardiff, have daily flights to Europe. Strict anti-terrorist measures are in force at all airports.

A British Airways 747 jet at Heathrow Airport

British Airports

Most of Britain's largest and best-known airports have excellent facilities, including 24-hour banking, shops, cafés, hotels and restaurants. Security is strict at all British airports, so it may take some time to get through passport control and customs. It is important never to leave your luggage unattended.

For visitors to London, Heathrow, Gatwick or Stansted are equally convenient. If you plan to visit northern England, there are many flights direct to Birmingham,

Leeds-Bradford, Newcastle and Manchester, while for Scotland you can fly to Glasgow or Edinburgh.

Heathrow has five terminals and other airports tend to have more than one. Before you fly, check with the airport from which terminal your flight leaves.

During severe weather conditions in the winter months, your flight may be diverted to another airport. If this happens, the airline will organize transportation to get you back to your original destination.

Airlines

British Airways has flights to most of the world's important destinations. Other British international airlines include **Virgin Atlantic**, with routes from the USA and the Far East, **Flybe**, which flies from Western Europe's main cities, and **Ryanair** and **easyJet**, which fly from Europe and North Africa.

American airlines offering scheduled services to Britain include **Delta**, **United Airlines** and **American Airlines**. From Canada, the main carrier is **Air Canada**. From Australasia, the national carriers **Qantas** and **Air New Zealand** vie with several Far Eastern rivals, including Emirates.

Transport from the Airport

Britain's international airports lie some way from the city centres, but transport to and from them is efficient. The most convenient form of door-to-door travel is a taxi, but it is also the most expensive. In addition, taxis can be slow if there is road congestion. This is also a problem with buses or coaches, although they are a lot cheaper.

Heathrow and Newcastle airports are linked to the city centres by the Underground, which is efficient, quick and cheap. Visitors to London arriving at Heathrow can also take the Heathrow Express, the

Airport	ℹ️ Information	Distance to City Centre	Taxi Fare to City Centre	Public Transport to City Centre
Heathrow	08443 351 801	14 miles (23 km)	£40–£45	Rail: 15 mins Tube: 45 mins
Gatwick	08448 920 322	28 miles (45 km)	£75	Rail: 30 mins Bus: 70 mins
Stansted	08443 351 803	37 miles (60 km)	£80	Rail: 45 mins Bus: 75 mins
Manchester	08712 710 711	10 miles (16 km)	£15–£16	Rail: 15 mins Bus: 30 mins
Birmingham	08712 220 072	8 miles (13 km)	£12–£15	Bus: 30 mins
Newcastle	08718 821 121	5 miles (8 km)	£22	Metro: 20 mins Bus: 20 mins
Glasgow	08444 815 555	8 miles (13 km)	£17–£20	Bus: 20 mins
Edinburgh	08444 81 89 89	8 miles (13 km)	£17–£18	Bus: 25 mins

Terminal 5 at Heathrow Airport

fast train to Paddington Station (www.heathrowexpress.com or 0845 600 1515). Trains run every 15 minutes from 5am until around midnight, taking 15 minutes from Terminals 1, 2 and 3, and 21 minutes from Terminal 5. Terminal 4 requires a change of train and takes a total of 23 minutes. (The Crossrail service between Heathrow T4 and Paddington is due to begin in May 2018.) Those arriving at Gatwick can take the Gatwick Express to London Victoria (www.gatwick express.com or 0845 850 15 30). Trains run every 15 minutes and take 30 minutes. Stansted and Manchester also have regular express trains that are not too expensive and are a reliable method for travelling into the heart of the city.

Signs for express railway services to London

National Express coaches (see p640) provide direct connections from major airports (London's Heathrow, Gatwick and Stansted, Luton, Birmingham, Liverpool, Manchester, Coventry, East Midlands and Bristol) to many British destinations. They also have a regular service between Gatwick and Heathrow.

Choosing a Ticket

Finding the right flight at the right price can be difficult. Promotional fares do come up, and it is always worth checking

with the airlines. Other good ways to find the cheapest flight are to consult a package operator or use one of the fare aggregator websites, such as **Skyscanner** or **Cheapflights**. Even if you enjoy independent travel, it may be worth considering a package, since sometimes car rental or rail travel is included, and this can be cheaper than arranging it yourself once in Britain.

Fares are usually seasonal, the most expensive falling between June and September. The best deals can be had from November to April, excluding Christmas – if you want to travel then, be sure to book well in advance.

APEX (Advance Purchase Excursion) fares are often the best value, though they must be booked up to a month ahead and are subject to restrictions. Charter flights offer even cheaper seats but are not usually flexible.

Budget airlines such as easyJet and Ryanair offer exceptionally cheap flights if booked long enough in advance. Always buy discount fares from a reputable operator.

Students, the under-26s, senior citizens and frequent travellers may obtain a discount through student travel agencies. Children also travel at cheaper rates.

Travelling Within Britain by Air

Internal air travel in Britain only makes sense over long distances, where it can save a great deal of time – for example, London to Scotland, or to one of the many offshore islands. Fares can be expensive, but if you book well ahead, they can be up to three times cheaper than if you just turn up at the airport. The British Airways shuttle flights that operate between London and cities such as Glasgow, Edinburgh and Manchester are very popular with business travellers. At peak times of the day, flights leave every hour, while at other times there is usually a flight every two hours. Even on domestic flights, security is strict.

DIRECTORY

Airlines

Air Canada
W aircanada.com

Air New Zealand
W airnewzealand.co.uk

American Airlines
W americanairlines.co.uk

British Airways
W britishairways.com

Delta
W delta.com

easyJet
W easyjet.com

Flybe
W flybecom

Qantas
W qantas.com

Ryanair
W ryanair.com

United Airlines
W united.com

Virgin Atlantic
W virgin-atlantic.com

Choosing a Ticket

Skyscanner
W skyscanner.net

Cheapflights
W cheapflights.co.uk

Travelling Around by Car

The most startling difference for most foreign motorists is that in Britain you drive on the left, with corresponding adjustments at roundabouts and junctions. Distances are measured in miles. Once you adapt, rural Britain is an enjoyable place to drive, though traffic density in towns and at busy holiday times can cause long delays – public holiday weekends near the south coast can be particularly horrendous. An extensive network of toll-free motorways and trunk roads makes travelling around the country quite straightforward.

The A30 dual carriageway running through Cornwall

What You Need

To drive in Britain you need a current driving licence with an international driving permit, if required. You must also carry proof of ownership or a rental agreement in your vehicle, plus any insurance documents.

Roads in Britain

Rush hour can last from 8 to 9:30am and from 5 to 7pm on weekdays in the cities; at these times, traffic can grind to a halt.

A good map is vital and the AA or RAC motoring atlases are good resources. For exploration of more rural areas, the Ordnance Survey series is the best. Most hire cars will include GPS. Motorways are marked with an "M" followed by their identifying number. "A" roads, sometimes dual carriageways (that is, with two lanes in each direction), are main routes, while "B" roads are secondary roads. The latter are often less congested and more enjoyable. Rural areas are criss-crossed by a web of tiny lanes.

Road Signs

Signs are mostly standardized in line with Europe. Directional signs are colour-coded: blue for motorways, green for major routes and white for minor routes. Brown signs indicate places of interest. Advisory or warning signs are usually triangles in red and white, with easy-to-understand pictograms. Watch for electronic notices on motorways that warn of roadworks, accidents or patches of fog.

Level crossings, found at railway lines, often have automatic barriers. If the lights are flashing red, it means a train is coming and you must stop.

The UK Highway Code Manual, available from the Department for Transport section of the gov.uk website, is an up-to-date guide to all the current British driving regulations and traffic signs.

Rules of the Road

Speed limits are 20–40 mph (50–65 km/h) in built-up areas and 70 mph (110 km/h) on motorways or dual carriageways. Look out for speed signs on other roads. It is compulsory to wear seatbelts in Britain. Drink-driving penalties are severe; see the UK Highway Code Manual for legal limits. It is illegal to use a mobile phone while driving unless it is operated hands-free.

Parking

Parking meters operate during working hours (usually 8am–6:30pm Mon–Sat). Be sure to keep a supply of coins for them. Some cities have "park and ride" schemes, where you can take a bus from an out-of-city car park into the centre. Other towns have parking schemes where you buy a card at the tourist office or newsagents, fill in your parking times and display it on your dashboard. Avoid double red or yellow lines at all times; single lines sometimes mean you can park in the evenings and at weekends, but check

Distance Chart

London

Distance in miles
Distance in kilometres

London	Aberdeen	Birmingham	Bristol	Cardiff	Dover	Edinburgh	Exeter	Liverpool	Manchester	Newcastle	Oxford	York
492 / 792	**Aberdeen**											
111 / 179	**411** / 658	**Birmingham**										
114 / 182	**490** / 784	**88** / 101	**Bristol**									
150 / 241	**493** / 789	**102** / 164	**44** / 70	**Cardiff**								
74 / 119	**563** / 901	**185** / 298	**189** / 302	**228** / 367	**Dover**							
372 / 599	**121** / 194	**290** / 467	**369** / 590	**373** / 600	**442** / 711	**Edinburgh**						
170 / 272	**565** / 904	**164** / 262	**75** / 120	**120** / 192	**244** / 342	**444** / 710	**Exeter**					
198 / 317	**792** / 492	**90** / 144	**161** / 258	**165** / 264	**270** / 432	**214** / 342	**237** / 380	**Liverpool**				
184 / 296	**333** / 533	**81** / 130	**162** / 258	**173** / 278	**257** / 414	**213** / 343	**238** / 381	**34** / 54	**Manchester**			
274 / 441	**228** / 365	**204** / 328	**288** / 461	**301** / 484	**343** / 552	**107** / 172	**364** / 582	**155** / 248	**131** / 211	**Newcastle**		
56 / 90	**473** / 757	**63** / 101	**70** / 112	**104** / 166	**129** / 206	**353** / 565	**141** / 226	**153** / 245	**144** / 230	**254** / 406	**Oxford**	
194 / 310	**307** / 491	**129** / 206	**217** / 347	**231** / 397	**264** / 422	**186** / 297	**292** / 467	**97** / 155	**65** / 104	**82** / 131	**174** / 278	**York**

signs carefully. Traffic wardens will not hesitate to ticket, clamp or tow away your car. If in doubt, find a car park. Outside urban areas and popular tourist zones, parking is much easier. Look out for signs with a blue "P", indicating parking spaces. Never leave any valuables or luggage in your car: thefts are common, especially in cities.

Petrol

Large supermarkets often have the best deals; look out for branches of Asda, Morrisons or Sainsbury's with petrol stations. Motorway service areas and rural or isolated regions are generally more expensive. Petrol is sold in three grades: diesel, LRP (lead replacement petrol) and unleaded. Most modern cars in Britain use unleaded petrol, and any vehicle you hire will probably do too. Unleaded and diesel are cheaper than LRP. Most petrol stations in Britain are self-service, but the instructions at pumps are easy to follow.

Breakdown Services

Britain's major motoring organizations are the **AA** (Automobile Association) and the **RAC** (Royal Automobile Club). They provide a comprehensive 24-hour breakdown assistance for members, as well as many other motoring services. Both offer reciprocal assistance for members of overseas motoring organizations – before leaving home, check to see if you are covered. You can contact the AA or RAC from the roadside SOS phones found on motorways. **Green Flag** is the other major rescue service in Britain.

A small petrol station in Goathland, North Yorkshire

Most car-hire agencies have their own cover, and their charges include membership of the AA, the RAC or Green Flag. Be sure to ask the rental company for the service's emergency number.

If you are not a member of an affiliated organization, you can still call out a rescue service, although it will be expensive. Always follow the advice given on your insurance policy or rental agreement. If you have an accident that involves injury or another vehicle, call the police as soon as possible (see p627).

The Environmental Transport Association gives advice on reducing the impact of carbon emissions, as well as offering a number of ethical breakdown services.

Car Hire

Hiring a car in Britain can be expensive. Details of car-hire companies at Britain's airports are on the VisitBritain website (see p625). All the well-known car-rental firms, such as **Avis**, **Hertz**, **Europcar**, **easyCar** and **Budget**, operate in Britain, but small local firms may undercut their rates. It is illegal to drive without third-party insurance, and it is advisable to take out fully comprehensive insurance. Most companies require a credit card number; if not, you may have to part with a substantial cash deposit. You will need your driving licence and a passport to pick up your car. Most companies will not hire cars to novice drivers, and may have age limits (normally 21–74). Automatic cars are also usually available for hire. If you are touring Britain for three weeks or more, you may find a leasing arrangement cheaper than hiring. Remember to add insurance costs when you check rental rates.

Hitchhiking and Ride-Sharing

It is not advisable to hitchhike in Britain, and there is a risk in hitchhiking alone, especially for a woman. If you must, stand

DIRECTORY

Breakdown

AA
Tel 0800 085 2721.
W theaa.com

RAC
Tel 01922 437000.
W rac.co.uk

Car Hire

Avis
Tel 0808 284 0014.
W avis.co.uk

Budget
Tel 0808 284 4444.
W budget.co.uk

easyCar
W easycar.com

Europcar
Tel 0871 384 9900.
W europcar.co.uk

Hertz
Tel 0207 026 00 77.
W hertz.co.uk

General Information

AA Disability Helpline
Tel 0800 262 050

AA Road Watch Traffic News
Tel 0906 888 4322.

Department for Transport
W gov.uk

Environmental Transport Association
W eta.co.uk

Green Flag
Tel 0800 051 0636.
W greenflag.com

Weather
W metoffice.gov.uk

near a busy exit road junction. In rural or walking areas like the Lake District, tired hikers may well be offered a lift. It is illegal to hitch on motorways or their approach roads.

Lift-sharing is now a common practice. The website www.gumtree.com has a large section for lift-seekers; www.blablacar.co.uk is another reliable ride-sharing website.

Travelling Around by Rail

Britain has a privatized rail network that covers the whole of the country, serving more than 2,500 stations. Divided into regional sections, the system is generally efficient and reliable. Parts of the network are occasionally closed for repairs, mostly at weekends, so check with your local station or online before travelling. Journeys across the country may involve a number of changes, since most lines radiate from London, which has seven major terminals. There is also a rail link with continental Europe on Eurostar, from St Pancras International station in London and Ebbsfleet and Ashford in Kent *(see p633).*

The concourse at Liverpool Street Station, London

Tickets

Large travel agents and all railway stations sell train tickets. First-class tickets cost about one-third more than standard fares, and buying a return fare is sometimes cheaper than buying two singles.

Allow plenty of time to buy your ticket, and always ask about any special offers or reduced fares. An Advance ticket is usually cheaper than one bought on the day, but often has restrictions on your ability to change or cancel your journey.

Consumers can buy tickets directly from the rail provider, National Rail or a third-party website, such as thetrainline.com, which is the most popular of these and worth checking first. At raileasy.co.uk, you may find discounted tickets in advance. Virgin Trains cover much of the UK, and there are no booking fees.

Inspectors can levy on-the-spot fines if you do not have a valid ticket, so buy a ticket before boarding the train at all times. Many stations have automatic ticket machines. Ticket offices in rural areas may close at weekends, so if you are unable to buy a ticket a conductor on board will sell you one.

Rail Passes

If you plan to do a lot of train travel around Britain, it is worth buying a rail pass. This can be purchased from many agents abroad, such as **Rail Europe**. National Rail's All Line Rail Rover gives adults unlimited travel throughout England, Scotland and Wales for 7 or 14 days. For many trips, a Family & Friends Railcard or Network Railcard

saves one-third on adult and 60 per cent off kids' (aged 5–15) fares. A Young Person's Railcard offers discounts to 16- to 25-year-olds or full-time students attending a UK educational establishment. The Senior Rail Card entitles those over the age of 60 to a discount of one-third on most fares. There are special passes for London transport, too, and a pass that covers London, Oxford, Canterbury and Brighton. Children aged 5 to 15 pay half fare; those under the age of 5 travel free. Disabled travellers qualify for many discounts.

Keep a passport-sized photograph handy for buying passes. If you have a pass, make sure you always show it when you buy a ticket.

General Tips

Britain's fastest and most comfortable trains are those on the mainline routes. These are very popular services and get booked up quickly. It is always advisable to reserve your seat in advance, especially if you want to travel at peak times, such as Friday evenings. Mainline trains have dining cars and airconditioning, and they are fast – travelling to Edinburgh from London, for example, takes just over 4 hours.

Porters are rare at British stations, although trolleys are often available for passengers to help themselves. If you are disabled and need help, call **National Rail Enquiries** to book Passenger Assistance at least 24 hours ahead of your journey. A yellow line above a train window indicates a first-class compartment. Note that even if the train is full, you cannot sit

Mainline train at platform

Reconditioned steam trains on the tracks in North Yorkshire

in the first-class area without paying the full fare.

Trains sometimes split en route, each section proceeding to different destinations, so always check which section you should be on. Trains stop for only a minute at each station, and doors close 30 seconds before the train is due to depart, so gather your belongings in advance and be ready to get on and off.

Some stations are a little way from town centres, but they are usually well signposted and mostly on a bus route. Trains on Sundays and public holidays can be slower and less frequent than normal.

Scenic Train Rides

After motor transport made many rural railways redundant in the mid-20th century, some picturesque sections of track, as well as many old steam engines, were rescued and restored to working order by enthusiasts. These services are often privately run; the local tourist office, railway station ticket office or travel agents can provide you with more information. This is one of the best ways to enjoy Britain's spectacular scenery. Most of the lines are short – around 20 miles (32 km) – but cover some of the prettiest parts of the country. Lines include the Ffestiniog Railway (see pp456–7) in North Wales; the North York Moors Railway (see p398); the Strathspey Steam Railway in the Cairngorm Mountains of the Scottish Highlands (see p548) and the La'al Ratty Railway in Cumbria.

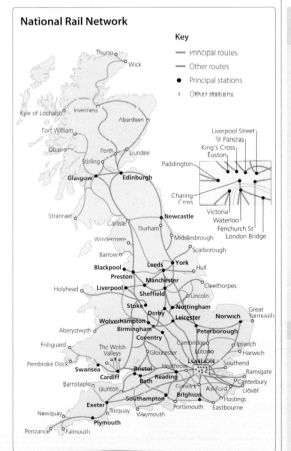

National Rail Network

Key

— Principal routes
— Other routes
● Principal stations
¡ Other stations

DIRECTORY

UK Rail Companies

East Midlands Train
Tel 03457 125 678 (bookings).
W eastmidlandstrains.co.uk

Great Western Railway
Tel 03457 000 125.
W gwr.com

Rail Europe
Tel 08448 485 848 (UK);
1-800-622-8600 (USA);
1 800-361-7245 (Canada).
W raileurope.com

Thameslink
Tel 03450 264 700.
W thameslinkrailway.com

Virgin Trains
Tel 0344 556 5650 (bookings).
W virgintrains.co.uk

General Tips

Lost Property
Tel 0343 222 1234 (for London Transport) or contact the relevant train company.

National Rail Enquiries
Tel 03457 48 49 50.
W nationalrail.co.uk

Travelling by Coach and Bus

In Britain, the word "coach" refers to a long-distance express bus as well as those used for sightseeing excursions. What the British refer to as "buses" are the vehicles that operate on regular routes with scheduled stops in or between villages, towns and cities. Many coach services duplicate rail routes but are generally cheaper. Journey times, however, are longer and much less predictable on crowded roads. Modern coaches are comfortable, sometimes with refreshments and toilets on board. Some intercity routes, especially at weekends, are so popular that it is a good idea to buy tickets in advance, which guarantees you a seat. For ideas on places to visit by coach or bus consult the VisitBritian website.

National Coach Network

There are many regional coach companies, but the largest British coach operator is **National Express**, with a nationwide network of more than 1,200 destinations. Always book ahead for the more popular routes. The company offers a number of discounts, such as their £5 Funfares (£1 booking fee), which are available online, to over 50 destinations. **Megabus** offers tickets to destinations all over Britain from as little as £1 (50p booking fee). As you would expect, you will need to book early, and the less popular destinations and travel times have the best deals.

The **Oxford Tube** and **X90 Oxford** run frequent, wheelchair-friendly services between Oxford and London, while **Scottish Citylink** is a major operator running regular services between London, the north and Scotland. Some services run from Heathrow, Gatwick and Stansted airports. Allow plenty of time to buy your ticket before boarding.

Discounts are available for full-time students and anyone under 25. The over-50s qualify for a discount coach card, saving up to 30 per cent on many fares.

Coach Tours

Coach tours covering a variety of destinations and suitable for all interests and age groups are available. Some include a tour guide. They may last anything from a couple of hours to two weeks or more, touring coast or countryside and stopping at places of interest. Some are highly structured, organizing every break en route; others leave you to sightsee or shop at your own pace. You can opt for a prearranged route, or commission your own itinerary for a group. The **VisitBritain** website has lots of inspiration on planned tours available to visitors. Any large town will have a selection of coach companies. Check the local Yellow Pages (see p630), ask at the local tourist office or contact the **Coach Tourism Association**. You can also book coach trips direct from overseas through a specialist travel agent.

Seaside resorts and tourist sites are destinations for many day trips, especially in high season. In some of the more popular rural areas, such as the Lake District, special small coaches operate for ease of movement. You can book these in advance, or just turn up before the coach leaves, but the tour is likely to be fully booked, especially in high season. The local tourist information point or travel agent will be able to tell you where these trips leave from, the cost and may even sell you tickets. It is customary to tip the guide after your tour.

Regional Buses

Regional bus services are run by a number of companies, some private and some operated by local authorities. Services to remote areas tend to be sporadic and expensive, with some buses running just once a week and many isolated villages having no service at all. Only a few rural buses are equipped for wheelchairs.

As a rule, the further you get from a city, the fewer the buses and the more expensive the fare. On the plus side, local buses can be a pleasant and often sociable way of travelling around Britain's lovely countryside.

Most buses run with just one operator – the driver. All drivers prefer you to have the correct fare, so always keep a selection of coins handy. Some routes do not operate on Sundays and public holidays; those that do offer a much reduced service. Always check routes, schedules and fares at the local tourist office or bus station before you depart on a bus to avoid becoming stranded somewhere remote with no return transport.

A National Express coach

Travelling Britain's Coasts and Waterways

Britain has thousands of miles of inland waterways and hundreds of islands scattered along its beautiful coastline. Cruising along a canal in the Midlands countryside or travelling on one of the small local ferries to a remote Scottish island are both wonderful experiences. Canal boats can be hired, and scores of ferries run between Britain's offshore islands. For information on Britain's canals, rivers and lakes and to book accommodation, a boat or a hotel boat, visit the Canal & River Trust website.

A barge moored on the Welsh Backs in Bristol

Canals

As industrial production grew in the 18th century, it became vital to find a cheap and effective way of transporting heavy loads. Canals fulfilled this need, and a huge network was built, linking most industrial areas with the country's sea ports.

The arrival of the railways and their influence on freight movement made most canals redundant. However, there are still some 2,000 miles (3,200 km) of canals, most in the old industrial heartland of the Midlands.

Today these canals lure travellers who are content to cruise on old-fashioned, slow narrowboats, taking their time to enjoy the views and the canal-side inns, originally built to satisfy the bargees' thirsts and to supply stabling for the barge horses. These canal holidays can be very relaxing if you have the time.

To hire a narrow boat, book with a specialist firm such as **Canal Holidays** or **Drifters**, or contact **Canal & River Trust**. The **Canal Junction** website has maps, tour suggestions and a directory of boat hire firms. **Hotel Boating** offers skippered tours.

Local Ferries

Britain's local ferries can offer anything from a 10-minute river journey to a 7-hour sea cruise.

Many of Scotland's ferries are operated by **Caledonian MacBrayne**. They sail to lots of different destinations, such as the Isle of Skye to the Kyle of Lochalsh, or the 5-hour journey from Oban to Lochboisdale in the Western Isles. They offer a variety of different ticket types, from unlimited rover tickets for a specific period of time, to island-hop passes or all-inclusive coach tour and ferry tickets. Not all the island ferries take cars.

River ferries make an interesting alternative to the more usual forms of transport. The ferry across the Mersey, between Liverpool and Birkenhead, is still used by many commuters. London's river trips, such as the one that runs from Westminster to Tower Bridge, offer a different perspective on the city and make a change from tubes, buses and cars. Local tourist centres can give you information about ferry routes and timetables in their area.

A car ferry travelling from Oban to Lochboisdale

DIRECTORY

Travelling within Cities

Urban public transport in Britain is efficient and can be fun. Fares are reasonable, especially compared to the expense of parking a car. Most of the larger cities have good bus services. London, Newcastle and Glasgow also have an underground system, while Edinburgh, Manchester and Nottingham have trams. Taxis are available at every train station and at ranks in city centres. The best way to see many cities is on foot, but whatever transport you opt for, try to avoid the rush hours from 8am to 9:30am and 5pm to 6:30pm.

Double-decker buses on the Strand, in London

Local Buses

Buses come in all shapes and sizes, with automatic doors and comfortable interiors. They include driver-operated double-deckers, the Routemaster buses and even smaller single-deckers that are able to weave in and out of traffic more easily. The old "big red bus" with a conductor still exists in London, but only as Heritage route number 15 through the City.

On most buses you pay the driver as you enter. They will not always accept notes, so keep a few pound coins handy. Credit cards are not accepted. On London buses you can only pay with contactless or Oyster cards If you are exploring a city by bus, a daily pass is a good idea. Many of the larger cities have daily or weekly passes that can be used on all public transport in that city; these can often be bought from newsagents. Check with the tourist office for schedules and fares.

Night services are available only in major cities, from about 11pm until early morning. Day passes are valid on these until 4:30am. In London,

night buses are prefixed with the letter "N", and most of them pass through Trafalgar Square. Be on your guard when travelling alone late at night, when there may be few other passengers on board, and sit downstairs, near the driver.

At some stops, called request stops, the driver will not halt unless you signal that you want to get on or off. If you want to board, raise your arm as the bus approaches; if you want to get off, ring the bell once before your stop. Destinations are shown on the front of buses. If you are not sure which stop you need, ask the driver or conductor to alert you and stay on the lower deck. Always keep your ticket until the end of the journey in case an inspector gets on board. They can impose an on-the-spot fine if you are without a valid ticket.

Cities have bus lanes, intended to bypass car traffic jams during the rush hours. These can be effective, but your journey could still take a long time. Schedules are hard to keep to, so regard timetables as advisory.

Driving

Driving in city centres is increasingly discouraged. London has a congestion charge – if you drive or park within the congestion zone from Monday to Friday (7am to 6pm), you will be charged a £11.50 fee to pay online before midnight that day. Not paying the charge will lead to a large fine. See **Transport for London**'s website for more information. Other cities are considering similar steps to keep drivers out of the centres. Parking in city centres is also strictly controlled to prevent congestion (see pp636–7).

Taxis

In large towns, taxis can be found at taxi ranks and train stations. Some operate by radio, so you have to phone. The local Yellow Pages (see p630), pubs, restaurants and hotels will all have a list of taxi numbers. Prices are usually regulated. Always ask the price before you start your journey if there is no taxi meter. If you are not sure ask the local tourist information point the usual rate charged to specific desintations.

The famous London black cabs are almost as much of an institution as the big red buses. These are the safest cabs to use in London since all the drivers are licensed and have undergone strict tests. All licensed cabs must display a "For hire" sign, which is lit up whenever they are free.

The newer cab designs are equipped to carry wheelchairs. If a cab stops for you in London, it must by law take you anywhere within a radius of 6 miles (10 km) so long as it is within the Metropolitan Police District. This includes most of London and Heathrow Airport. All licensed cabs have meters that start ticking as soon as the driver accepts your

One of London's black cabs

custom. The fare will increase minute by minute or for each 311 m (1,020 ft) travelled. Most drivers expect a tip of between 10 and 15 per cent of the fare. If you have a complaint, note the serial number found in the back of the cab.

Do not use unlicensed minicabs – they may be mechanically unsound or even uninsured. Never accept an unbooked minicab ride in the street. Mobile phone apps such as **Uber** allow you to book a taxi using your phone location and pay safely and conveniently through the app with a credit or debit card.

Guided Bus Tours

Most major tourist cities offer sightseeing bus tours. Weather permitting, a good way to see the cities is from an open-topped double-decker bus. Private tours can be arranged with many companies. Contact the local tourist information centre for more details.

Trams

Trams are making a comeback throughout Britain in clean, energy-efficient and more modern guises. One of the best tram schemes in Britain is Manchester's Metrolink. The oldest tramway is in Blackpool, which opened in 1885.

A tram running along Blackpool's famous promenade

London Underground

The Underground network in London, known as the Tube, has more than 270 stations, each of which is marked with the London Underground logo. The only other cities with an underground system are Newcastle and Glasgow. Newcastle's system is limited to the city centre, while Glasgow's skirts around the centre. Both run the same hours as London's, and are a reliable way to get around.

London tube trains run every day, except Christmas Day, from about 5:30am until just after midnight, and there are five lines now running 24 hours on Fridays and Saturdays. Fewer trains run on Sundays and public holidays. Note that the tube can get very crowded during rush hour.

London's tube lines are colour coded and maps are posted at every tube station, while maps of the central section are found in each train. Most tube journeys between central destinations in London can be completed with only one or two changes of line.

Tickets are bought at the station, but many travellers use an Oyster card, a prepaid electronic card that can be topped up for use on buses, trains and the tube. Using an Oyster card is by far the cheapest way of travelling on London Transport's tubes and buses. For information on how to get one, see the Transport for London website. Oyster cards can be purchased from abroad or you can use contactless credit or debit cards for each journey. There are similar electronic card schemes in other major British cities, such as Oxford.

A London Underground sign outside a station

An Oyster card

Cycling

Cycling is one of the greenest ways of getting around town. Even small towns have some-where you can hire bikes (see

Cyclists stopped at a red light on a London street

tfl.gov.uk for London, or cycle hireinfo.com for the rest of the UK). Cyclists may not use motorways or their approach roads, nor can they ride on pavements, footpaths or pedestrianized zones. Many city roads have cycle lanes and their own traffic lights. You can take a bike on most trains; see the National Rail website *(see p639)* for details. Never leave your bike unlocked, and always wear a helmet.

Walking

Once you get used to traffic on the left, Britain's cities can be safely and enjoyably explored on foot. Instructions written on the road will tell you from which direction you can expect the traffic to come.

There are two types of pedestrian crossing: striped zebra crossings and push-button crossings at traffic lights. At a zebra crossing, traffic should stop for you, but at push-button crossings, cars will not stop until the lights change in your favour. More and more cities and towns are creating traffic-free zones in the city centre for pedestrians.

DIRECTORY

Transport for London
Tel 0343 222 1234
(voice-activated service).
🌐 tfl.gov.uk

Uber
🌐 get.uber.com/go

General Index

Page numbers in **bold** refer to main entries

A

A La Ronde (Exmouth) 293
Abbey Mill (Bradford-on-Avon) 251
Abbeys and priories
  Abbey Dore 320
  Bath Abbey 245, 263, **264**
  Battle Abbey 185
  Beaulieu Abbey 172
  Bolton Priory **390**
  Buckfast Abbey **295**, 298
  Buckland Abbey **296**
  Bury St Edmunds Abbey 210
  Byland Abbey **396**
  Cartmel Priory 373
  Castle Acre Priory 199
  Christchurch Priory 275
  Dryburgh Abbey 507
  Dunfermline Abbey 504, 505
  Easby Abbey 355
  Fountains Abbey 54, 351, **394–5**
  Furness Abbey 372, 373
  Glastonbury Abbey 257
  Hartland Abbey 290
  Hexham Abbey 426, 427
  Inchmahome Priory 499
  Jedburgh Abbey 507
  Kelso Abbey 507
  Kirkham Priory 355
  Kirkstall Abbey 355
  Lanercost Priory 362
  Lindisfarne Priory 422, 423
  Llanthony Priory 465, 473
  Malvern Priory 321
  Melrose Abbey 507, **516**
  Mount Grace Priory 354, **398**
  Northern England **354–5**
  Rievaulx Abbey **397**
  St Mary's Abbey (Llŷn Peninsula) 457
  St Mary's Abbey (York) **354–5**, **410**
  St Michael's Mount 282–3
  St Nicholas Priory (Exeter) **293**
  Sherborne Abbey 272
  Shrewsbury Abbey 316
  Strata Florida 471
  Tewkesbury Abbey 332
  Tintern Abbey 16, **479**
  Torre Abbey 294
  Westminster Abbey (London) 12, 77, 92, **96–7**
  Whalley Abbey 375
  Whitby Abbey **400**
Abbot Hall Art Gallery and Museum of Lakeland Life (Kendal) 372
Abbotsbury 14, 36, **272**
  hotels 564
  pubs 605
Abbotsford House **516**
Aberaeron 16, **467**
  pubs 608
  restaurants 599
Aberdeen **542–4**
  hotels 572
  map 543
  restaurants 602
Aberdeenshire see Highlands and Islands
Aberdyfi **459**
  restaurants 599
Abergavenny, hotels 571
Aberlady, restaurants 600

Aberystwyth 16, **466–7**
  hotels 571
  pubs 609
Abingdon, restaurants 588
Abney Park Cemetery (London) 78
Aboyne, restaurants 602
Achiltibuie
  hotels 572
  restaurants 602
Achray, Loch 485
Act of Union (1535) 54, 440, 441
Act of Union (1707) 43, 57, 484, 486, 487
Adam, James 32
Adam, John 513
Adam, Robert 29, 59
  Audley End 212–13
  Bowood House 259
  Bury St Edmunds 210
  Culzean Castle 482, 526, 527
  Georgian House (Edinburgh) 508
  Harewood House 414
  Kedleston Hall 32–3
  Kenwood House (London) 128
  Pulteney Bridge (Bath) 263
  Saltram House 296
  Syon House (London) 130
Adam, William 506, 507, 518, 552
Admission prices 621
The Adoration of the Magi (Rubens) 219
Afternoon tea 575, 577
  Devonshire cream teas 291
Agincourt, Battle of (1415) 53
Agricola, Julius 48, 486
Ai Weiwei 125
Aidan, St 50, 422, 423
Air travel **634–5**
Aislabie, John 394
Aislabie, William 394, 395
Aitchison, Craigie 521
Alban, St 49
Albert, Prince Consort
  Albert Memorial (London) 101, **104–5**
  Balmoral 544
  Great Exhibition 61, 99, 100
  Manchester 377
  Osborne House 166, 172
  Victoria and Albert Museum (London) 102
  Windsor Castle 240
Albert Dock (Liverpool) 15, **381**
Albert Memorial (London) 101, **104–5**
Alciston, pubs 604
Alcohol 576, 623
  see also pubs
Aldeburgh **206–7**
  hotels 563
  restaurants 587
Aldeburgh Festival 67, **207**
Alderminster, pubs 606
Alderwasley, pubs 607
Aldrich, Henry 230
Alexander Keiller Museum (Avebury) 267
Alfred the Great, King 51, 184, 225, 251, 272
Alfriston 185
  restaurants 586
Alice in Wonderland (Carroll) **449**
All Souls College (Oxford) 53, **230**
Allendale 431
Alma-Tadema, Lawrence 95
  Etruscan Vase Painters 378
Alnwick Castle 15, **424**
Altarnun 289
Althorp 347

Alton Towers 613
Alwinton 425
The Ambassadors (Holbein) 87
Ambleside 15, **370–71**
  hotels 569
  pubs 607
  restaurants 595
Ambulances 627
American Museum (Bath) **265**
Amigoni, Jacopo 216
Ampleforth, hotels 570
Ancestry, tracing 35
Ancient House (Ipswich) 207
Angel of the North (Gormley) 418
Anglesey 446
  see also North Wales
Anglesey Abbey **212**
Anglo-Saxon Kingdoms **50–51**
Angus see Highlands and Islands
Anne, Queen 45, 58, 291, 509
  Bath 264
  Blenheim Palace 221, 232, 233
  death 105
  Hampton Court 177
  Kensington Gardens (London) 105
Anne of Cleves House (Lewes) 184
Anne Hathaway's Cottage (Stratford-upon-Avon) 325, 331
The Annunciation (Lippi) 86
Antiques for Everyone (Birmingham) 66
Antiques shops 611
  London 154, 155
Antonine Wall 48, 495
Applecross
  pubs 609
  restaurants 602
Appledore 14, **291**
Aquariums
  The Deep (Kingston upon Hull) 406, 407
  National Marine Aquarium (Plymouth) 296
  Sea Life Centre (Brighton) 179
Arbor Low 342
Architecture 29
  building with Cotswold stone **308–9**
  Durham Cathedral 433
  Georgian architecture 58–9
  rural architecture **36–7**
  Scottish castles **490–91**
  stately homes **32–3**
  Tudor manor houses **306–7**
Ardeonaig
  hotels 573
  restaurants 602
Arduaine, hotels 573
Argyll, Dukes of 500, 552
Argyll and Bute see Highlands and Islands
Arisaig, hotels 573
Aristocracy **34–5**
Arkwright, Sir Richard 59, 340, 343, 376
Arlington Court 291
Arlington Row Cottages (Bibury) 308
Armathwaite, hotels 569
Armley Mills Museum (Leeds) 414
Armscote, pubs 606
Armstrong, Lord 424
Arnolfini Portrait (Van Eyck) 86
Art
  canal boats 305
  courses 614, 617
  shops 154, 155
  see also Museums and galleries

Arthur, King 51, 251, **289**
  Dozmary Pool 289
  Glastonbury 257
  Ruthin 449
  Snowdon 436
  Stirling Castle 500
  Tintagel 277, 289
  Winchester 174
Arthur, Prince 316–17, 322
The Arts 28–9
Arts and Crafts movement 225, 332
Arundel
  Castle **176**
  hotels 562
  restaurants 586
Asenby, restaurants 597
Ashbourne, restaurants 594
Ashleworth, pubs 606
Ashmole, Elias 228
Ashmolean Museum (Oxford) 226, **228**
Ashness Bridge 367
Asian community, Bradford **415**
Aske, Robert 355
Askrigg, pubs 607
Asquith, Henry 62
Astor, Nancy 166
Astor, William Waldorf 193
At the Theatre (Renoir) 87
Athelhampton 249
Athelhampton House 273
Athelstan, King of Wessex 405
Atholl, Dukes of 547
Atholl Gathering and Highland Games
  66
Atkinson, Thomas 406
ATMs 628
Auchindrain Museum **552**
Auchterarder, restaurants 601
Audley End **212–13**
Augustine, St 50, 190
Auld Alliance 486
Auldearn, restaurants 602
Austen, Jane
  Bath 262, 264
  grave 174
  Jane Austen Centre (Bath) 262, **264**
  Jane Austen's House (Chawton)
    166, 176
Autumn 68
Avebury 14, 46, 47, **267**
  hotels 564
  restaurants 589
Aviemore 548
  hotels 573
Awe, Loch 17, **551**
Ayckbourn, Alan 28, 401
Aylesbury, pubs 605
Ayrshire see Lowlands (Scotland)
Aysgarth Falls **389**

B
Babbacombe
  hotels 566
  Model Village 294
Babbage, Charles 295
Back of the New Mills (Crome) 205
The Backs (Cambridge) 13, 214, 216
Bacon, Francis 84, 95, 205
Bacon, Sir Francis 236
Badachro, restaurants 602
Bakewell
  hotels 568
  pubs 607
  restaurants 594

Bala **454**
Balhousie Castle (Perth) 502
Ballater 544
Ballet 613
  London 158
Balliol, Bernard 430
Balmoral 17, 483, 529, 544
Balquhidder, restaurants 601
Baltic Centre for Contemporary Art
  (Newcastle upon Tyne) 15, 428, **429**
Bamburgh **424**
  Castle 421
Banbury **224**
  hotels 562
  restaurants 588
Banchory 545
Bancroft Gardens (Stratford-upon-Avon)
  328, 330
Bank holidays 69
Bankes, Sir John 274
Bankes family 275
Banking **628**
Banks, Iain 485
Bankside Power Station (London) **125**
Banksy 261
Bannockburn, Battle of (1314) 53, 500
Banqueting House (London) 93, **94**
Barbican Concert Hall (London) 158, 159
Bardon Mill 431
Bardwell, pubs 605
Bargate (Southampton) 173
Barlow, Bishop of St Davids 468
Barnard Castle **430**
  pubs 608
Barnstaple **291**
  hotels 566
  restaurants 591
Barra 533
  hotels 573
Barrie, J M 105
Barrow-In-Furness 353, 372
Barry, Sir Charles
  Houses of Parliament (London) 94
  Manchester Art Gallery 378
  Town Hall (Halifax) 416
Barry, E M 84
Baslow, restaurants 595
Bassenthwaite 364
Bateman's (Burwash) 167
Bath 10, 14, 25, 49, 245, **262–5**
  hotels 565
  International Music Festival 67
  pubs 605
  restaurants 589–90
  street-by-street map 262–3
Bath, Marquesses of 270
Bathurst, 1st Earl 333
Battersea Park (London) 79
Battle Abbey 185
Battle of Bannockburn Visitor Centre
  500
The Battle of Culloden (Campbell) 541
Beachy Head 168, 184
Beaconsfield, restaurants 589
Beaker People 46, 47
Beale, Gilbert 238
Beale Park 238
Beamish Open Air Museum 11, 15,
  428–9
The Beatles 64, 380, **381**
  The Beatles Story (Liverpool) **381**
  International Beatleweek (Liverpool) 67
Beauchamp family 326, 327, 476
Beaulieu **172**

Beaumaris **448**
  Castle 436, 442–3, 448
  hotels 571
  restaurants 599
Beaumont, Guillaume 373
Becket, St Thomas à 52–3, 190, 191
Becky Falls 298
Bed-and-breakfast 557, 559
Beddgelert **456**
  hotels 571
  restaurants 599
Bede, the Venerable 419, 423, 432
Bedford, pubs 605
Bedford, Dukes of 234
Bedford Square (London) 109
Bedfordshire see Thames Valley
Bedingfeld, Sir Edmund 199
"Beefeaters" 122, 123
Beer **578–9**
Belfast, HMS (London) **121**
Bell, Alexander 485
Bell, Vanessa 167
Bellany, John 515
Bellini, Giovanni 228
Bempton Cliffs **404–5**
Ben MacDhui 548
Ben Nevis 17, 551
Benbecula 533
Bennett, Arnold 315
Bere Regis 273
Berkeley Castle 333
Berkshire see Thames Valley
Bermondsey Market (London) 153
Berrington Hall 317
Berwick Street market (London) 153
Berwick-upon-Tweed **422**
Bess of Hardwick 338, 340
Bessie Surtees House (Newcastle upon
  Tyne) **429**
Beth Chatto Garden (Colchester) 209
Betjeman, John 109
Betty's Café Tea Rooms (Harrogate) 392
Betws-y-Coed 16, **454**
Bevan, Aneurin 441
Beverley **405**
Bibury 308, 312
Bickley Moss, pubs 606
Biddenden, restaurants 586
Bideford **290**
Big Ben (London) 80, 93, 94
Big Pit National Coal Museum
  (Blaenavon) 461, **478**
Bigbury-on-Sea
  hotels 566
  restaurants 592
Biggar **517**
Birdforth, restaurants 597
Birdoswald Roman Fort 362
Birds 38–9
  Bempton Cliffs 404–5
  Harewood Bird Garden 414
  Loch Garten Osprey Centre 549
  St Abb's Head 506
  Shetland seabirds 532
  Swannery (Abbotsbury) 272
  see also Wildlife
Birkenhead 383
Birmingham **322–3**
  airport 634
  events 66
  hotels 567
  restaurants 593–4
Bishop's Palace (St David's) 460
Bishop's Palace (Wells) 256–7

Bistros 575
Black Death 52, 53, 211, 322
The Black Isle **539**
Black Mountain 472
Black Mountains 16, 465, 472
Black Watch 488
Black and White House (Hereford) 320
Blackmore, R D 254
Blackpool **375**
  hotels 569
  Illuminations 68
Blackwell Arts and Crafts House
  (Bowness-on-Windermere) 371
Bladud, King 264
Blaenau Ffestiniog **455**
Blaenavon **478**
Blair Atholl, festivals 66
Blair Castle 491, **547**
Blake, Peter 95
Blake, William 95, 523
Blakeney Marshes 201
Blanchland 431
Blencathra 364
Blenheim Palace 13, 32, 162, 221,
  232–3
Blickling Hall **202**
Blists Hill Victorian Town (Ironbridge
  Gorge) **319**
Bloomsbury (London) **109**
  see also Regent's Park and Bloomsbury
Bloomsbury Group 107, 109, **167**, 184
Bloomsbury Square (London) 109
Blumenthal, Heston 29
Boatbuilding (Constable) 208
Boats
  boating and sailing 616
  canals 304, 305, 641
  ferries 633, 641
  Jacobite Cruises 540
  punting on the Cam 216
  Thames boating tours 239
Bodiam, restaurants 586
Bodiam Castle **186**
Bodleian Library (Oxford) 13, **231**
Bodley, Thomas 231
Bodmin **288–9**
Bodmin Moor, hotels 566
Boer War 61
Boleyn, Anne
  Blickling Hall 202
  execution 122
  Fountains Abbey 394
  Hever Castle 193
Bolton Abbey, restaurants 597
Bolton Castle **389**
Bolton Priory **390**
Book shops, London 154, 155
Booth, Richard 465
Bootle, restaurants 595
Borders (Scotland)
  A Tour of the Borders 507
  see also Lowlands (Scotland)
Boroughbridge, restaurants 597
Borromini, Francesco 118
Borrowdale **367**
  hotels 569
Boscastle 14, **289**
  hotels 566
Bosham 175
Bossanyi, Erwin 190
Bosworth, Battle of (1485) 53
Botallack Mine 280
Bothwell, Earl of 515
Botticelli, Sandro, *Venus and Mars* 77
Boucher, François 109

Boudica 48, **199**
  Colchester 209
  St Albans 236
Bourgeois, Louise 125
Bournemouth **275**
  hotels 565
  restaurants 590
Bourton-on-the-Hill, restaurants 594
Bourton-on-the-Water
  hotels 567
  restaurants 594
Bovey Tracey 298
Bow Fell 369
Bowder Stone 367
Bowes Museum (Barnard Castle) **430**
Bowness-on-Windermere 371
  hotels 569
  restaurants 595–6
Bowood House 259
Box Hill 176
Boyle, Danny 29
Boyne, Battle of the (1690) 57
Bradford **415**
  hotels 570
  restaurants 597
Bradford-on-Avon 251, **259**
  restaurants 590
Bradley, Thomas 416–17
Braemar Castle 490
Braemar Gathering 68, 71, 484
Braich-y-Pwll 457
Braithwaite, restaurants 596
Bramber 184
Branagh, Kenneth 331
Brancusi, Constantin, *Fish* 125
Brantwood (Coniston) 372
Brasseries 575
Braunton Burrows 291
Braunton "Great Field" 291
Brawne, Fanny 127
Breakdown services 637
Breakfast 574, 576–7
Brecon 472
  pubs 609
  restaurants 600
Brecon Beacons 16, 434–5, 437, 461,
  472–3
Brecon Jazz 67
Brent Tor 298
Bretforton, pubs 606
Brick Lane market (London) 153
Bridge House (Ambleside) 370
Bridge of Sighs (Cambridge) 214, 217
Bridge of Sighs (Oxford) 227
Bridgend, restaurants 600
Bridgewater, 3rd Duke of 304
Bridport
  hotels 565
  pubs 605
  restaurants 590
Brighton 11, 13, 170, **178–83**
  festivals 66, 68, 69
  hotels 562
  pier 178, 180–81
  pubs 604
  restaurants 586
  Royal Pavilion 13, 163, 179, 182–3
  street-by-street map 178–9
Brighton Festival 66
Bristol 14, **260–61**
  hotels 565
  map 261
  pubs 605
  restaurants 590
Bristol Museum and Art Gallery **261**
British Broadcasting Corporation (BBC)
  29

British Empire 27, 43, 60
British Figure Skating and Ice Dance
  Championships 71
British Golf Museum (St Andrews) 503
British Grand Prix 71
British Library (London) **109**
British Museum (London) 77, 106,
  110–11
British Open Golf Championship 71
Britten, Benjamin 207
Brixham 294
Brixton Market (London) 153
Broadlands 166
The Broads **202**
  windmills 203
Broadstairs 167
Broadway 324
Brockhole Visitor Centre (Windermere)
  371
Brodrick, Cuthbert 414
Brompton Oratory (London) **101**
Brontë, Anne 401, **416**
Brontë, Charlotte 343, **416**
Brontë, Emily **416**
Brontë Parsonage Museum (Haworth)
  416
Broughton-in-Furness, restaurants 596
Brown, "Capability" 30
  Alnwick Castle 424
  Audley End 212
  Berrington Hall 317
  Blenheim Palace 233
  Bowood House 259
  Burghley House 346
  Chatsworth House 338
  Harewood House 414
  Longleat House 270
  Petworth House 176
  Stowe 234
Brown, Ford Madox 53, 377
  The Last of England 323
Brownsea Island 275
Bruce, Sir George 505
Bruce, William Speirs 485
Bruce in Single Combat at Bannockburn
  (Hassall) 486
Brunel, Isambard Kingdom 260, 261
Bruton
  hotels 565
  restaurants 590
Buckfast Abbey **295**, 298
Buckfast Butterfly Farm and Dartmoor
  Otter Sanctuary 295, 298
Buckfastleigh **295**
  restaurants 592
Buckingham, Dukes of 234
Buckingham Palace (London) 76, **90–91**
Buckinghamshire *see* Thames Valley
Buckinghamshire, 2nd Earl of 202
Buckland Abbey **296**
Buckland-in-the-Moor 279, 299
Buckler's Hard 172
Bude **290**
  restaurants 592
Building materials 37
Builth Wells
  festivals 67
  restaurants 600
Bunker Hill, Battle of (1775) 58
Bunyan, John 235
Bureaux de change 628
Burford **224**
Burges, William
  Cardiff Castle 437, 476–7
  Castell Coch 443
  Fountains Abbey 395
Burgh Island **295**

The Burghers of Calais (Rodin) 92
Burghley, William Cecil, 1st Lord 346
Burghley House 303, 336, **346–7**
Burlington, 3rd Earl of 130
Burlington Arcade (London) 88
Burlington House 32
"The Burlington House Cartoon"
  (Leonardo da Vinci) 86
Burne-Jones, Sir Edward 323, 403
Burning of the Clocks (Brighton) 69
Burns, Robert 69, 485, 487, 509
  Burns Cottage **519**
  Burns Night 69
Burnsall **390**
Burrell, Sir William 523
Burrell Collection (Glasgow) **523**
Burton Agnes **404**
Burton Constable **406**
Bury St Edmunds **210–11**
  restaurants 587
Buses 640, 641
  from airports 634–5
  guided tours 643
  local buses 642
Butcher Row House (Ledbury) 321
Bute, 3rd Marquess of 476, 504
Butler, Lady Eleanor 454
Buttermere **367**
  hotels 569
Buttertubs **389**
Buxton **338**, 342
  hotels 568
  restaurants 595
Byland Abbey **396**
Byron, Lord 35

C

Caban Coch 466
Cabot, John 54, 260
Cadbury, George 353
Cadbury World (Bournville) 323
Caedmon's Cross (Whitby) **400**
Caerleon **478**
Caernarfon **448**
  pubs 608
Caernarfon Castle 443, 445, 448
Caernarfonshire *see* North Wales
Caerphilly Castle 442
Caesar, Julius 48, 265
Cafés 575
Cairngorms 11, 17, 483, 529, **548–9**
Caldey Island 470
Callander 499
Camber Sands 189
Cambrian Mountains 471
Cambridge 13, 194, 196, **214–19**
  festivals 67
  hotels 563
  pubs 605
  restaurants 587–8
  street-by-street map 214–15
Cambridge University 163, **216–17**
Cambridgeshire *see* East Anglia
Camden (London) **128**
Camden Lock Market (London) 128, 153
Camden Passage (London) 153
Camelford, hotels 568
Cameron, David 65
Camilla, Duchess of Cornwall 65, 239
Campbell, Colen 32, 270
Campbell, D, *The Battle of Culloden* 541
Campbell, Donald 372
Campbell, Lady Grace 552
Campbell clan 488, 552
Campden, Sir Baptist Hicks, 1st Viscount 331

Campden Manor (Chipping Campden) 331
Camping 558–9
Canaletto, Antonio 424
  Entrance to the Arsenal 234
  Goodwood House 175
  Wallace Collection (London) 109
  Warwick Castle 327
Canals 59, **641**
  Caledonian Canal 540, 551
  Canals of the Midlands **304–5**
  Falkirk Wheel **505**
  Industrial Revolution 352
  Leeds-Liverpool Canal 352
  Llangollen Canal 454
  Manchester Ship Canal 375, 376
  Monmouthshire and Brecon Canal 473
Canterbury **190**
  Cathedral 163, **190–91**
  hotels 563
  restaurants 586
  Thomas Becket 52
Canterbury Festival 68
Canterbury Heritage Museum 190
Canterbury Roman Museum 190
Canute, King 51
  Bosham 175
  Buckfast Abbey 298
  Bury St Edmunds 210
Canynge, William 260
Capel Curig, pubs 608
Caravanning 558–9
Cardiff 16, **474–7**
  hotels 571
  map 475
  pubs 609
  restaurants 600
Cardiff Castle 16, 437, 463, **476–7**
Cardigan Coast 16
Carfax Tower (Oxford) **228**
Carisbrooke Castle 172
Carlisle **362**
Carlisle, Earls of 402
Carloway Broch 533
Carlyle, Thomas 126
Carnegie, Andrew 485, 504–5
  Carnegie Birthplace Museum
    (Dunfermline) 505
Carnforth 374
Caro, Anthony 417
Carol concerts 69
Caroline of Ansbach, Queen 105
Caroline of Brunswick, Queen 183
Carpenter, Samuel 402
Carr, John 32, 410, 414
Carrawburgh Fort 426
Carrick Roads 284
Carroll, Lewis 229, 405, **449**
Cars **636–7**
  driving in cities 642
  hiring 632, 637
  racing 71
  see also Tours by car
Cartier International Polo 71
Cartmel **373**
  restaurants 596
Cartwright Hall Art Gallery (Bradford) 415
Carvoran Fort 426
Cash dispensers 628
Castell Coch 443
Castell-y-Bere 443
Castle Acre Priory 199
Castle Drogo 33, 299
Castle Howard 32, 351, **402–3**
Castle Museum (Norwich) **204–5**
Castlereagh, Lord 466
Castlerigg Stone Circle 47, 363, 365

Castles
  Aberystwyth 467
  Alnwick 15, **424**
  Arundel **176**
  Balhousie (Perth) 502
  Balmoral 17, 483, 529, 544
  Bamburgh 421, **424**
  Beaumaris 436, 442–3, **448**
  Berkeley 333
  Blair 491, **547**
  Bodiam **186**
  Bolton **389**
  Braemar 490
  Bramber 184
  Caernarfon 443, 445, **448**
  Caerphilly 442
  Camber 189
  Cardiff 16, 437, 463, **476–7**
  Carisbrooke 172
  Carlisle 362
  Carreg Cennen 472
  Castell Coch 443
  Castell Dinas Brân 454
  Castell y Bere 443
  castle life 53
  Cawdor **541**
  Claypotts 490
  Cockermouth 366
  Colchester 209
  Conwy 16, 437, 443, 447, 451
  Corfe 274
  Crathes 545
  Culzean 482, **526–7**
  Dartmouth 294
  Dolbadarn 455
  Doune 17, **502**
  Dover 186, 187
  Drum 491, 545
  Drumlanrig 490, 491, **518–19**
  Duart 550, 551
  Duffus 490
  Dunrobin 491, 538–9
  Dunstaffnage 550
  Dunster 14, 254
  Dunvegan 534
  Durham 433
  Edinburgh 17, 191, 197, **510–11**
  Eilean Donan 538
  Exeter 292
  Finlaggan (Islay) 553
  Floors 507
  Framlingham **207**
  Glamis **502–3**
  Goodrich 321
  Guildford 176
  Harlech 16, 442, 458
  Helmsley 397
  Hever **193**
  Inverary 17, **552**
  Kilchurn 551
  Kisimul 533
  Lancaster 374, 375
  Leeds 67, 171, **192**
  Lewes 184
  Lincoln 344
  Lindisfarne 422
  Ludlow 316–17, 317
  Middleham **399**
  Monmouth 478–9
  Muncaster 368
  Neidpath 490
  Newcastle upon Tyne 428
  Nottingham 340
  Orford 207
  Oxford 229
  Pendennis 285
  Penrith 362

Castles (cont.)
Portchester 173
Powis **464**
Restormel 288
Richmond **388–9**
Ripley 393
Rochester 192
St Andrews 503
Scarborough 401
Scottish castles **490–91**
Sherborne 272
Shrewsbury 316
Sizergh 372
Skipton **390**
Stirling 17, **500–501**
Stokesay 316, 317
Sudely 324
Taunton 256
Threave **519**
Tintagel 14, 289
Totnes 295
Tower of London 12, 77, **122–3**
Tretower 472
Urquhart 17, 540
Warkworth Castle **424**
Warwick 303, 325, **326–7**
Welsh castles **442–3**
Winchester 174
Windsor 162, 220, 221, 239, **240–41**
see also Palaces; Stately homes
Cathedrals
Aberdeen **544**
Beverley Minster 405
Bristol **261**
Bury St Edmunds 210
Canterbury 163, **190–91**
Chester 314–15
Chichester 175
Coventry 323
Dunkeld 545
Durham 351, 419, **432–3**
Edinburgh **513**
Elgin 542
Ely 163, **198–9**
Exeter **292–3**
Glasgow **520–21**
Gloucester 333
Hereford 320
Kirkwall 532
Lincoln 303, 334, 336, **345**
Liverpool Anglican **383**
Llandaff 475
Manchester 377
Metropolitan Cathedral of Christ the
King (Liverpool) **383**
Newcastle upon Tyne **429**
Norwich **204**
Peterborough 198
Ripon 393
Rochester 192
St Albans **237**
St Andrews 503
St Davids 16, 436, 469
St Paul's (London) 12, 77, 114,
118–19
Salisbury 14, 245, **268–9**
Southwark (London) 12, **124**
Truro 285
Wells 245, **256–7**
Winchester 27, 162, **174–5**
Worcester 322
York Minster 408, **412–13**
Catherine of Aragon 54
tomb of 198
Catherine the Great, Empress of Russia
202
Cavell, Edith, grave of 204

Caves
Cheddar Gorge 258
Dan-yr-Ogof Caves 472
Fingal's Cave 551
Gelert's Cave (Beddgelert) 456
Kents Cavern 294
Llechwedd Slate Caverns (Blaenau
Ffestiniog) 455
Mother Shipton's Cave
(Knaresborough) 392–3
St Fillan's Cave (East Neuk) 504
Stump Cross Caverns **390**
Wookey Hole 256, 257
Cawdor Castle **541**
Cawfields 426
Cecil, Robert 235
Cedd, St 213
Celts
chalk figures 225
Christianity 423
in Scotland 486, 529
in Wales 438, 440
Cemeteries
Glasgow Necropolis **521**
London 78
The Cenotaph (London) 93
Center for Alternative Technology
(Machynlleth) 466
Central Hall (London) 92
Cenwulf 51
Ceramics
Coalport China Museum 319
Jackfield Tile Museum (Ironbridge
Gorge) 318
Museum of Royal Worcester
(Worcester) 322
Staffordshire pottery 315
World of Wedgwood (Barlaston) 315
Ceredigion Museum (Aberystwyth) 467
Cerne Abbas 14, **273**
Chagall, Marc 175
Chagford
hotels 566
restaurants 592
Chalk figures **225**
Cerne Abbas 273
Long Man of Wilmington 185
Sutton Bank 396
White Horse of Uffington 47, 225
Chamberlain, Neville 93
Chambers, William 84
Chanctonbury Ring 184
Changing of the Guard 90, **91**
Channel Coast *see* Downs and
Channel Coast
Channel Tunnel 65, 633
Chapman, John 199
Charlecote Park 306
Charles I, King 45, 130
Banqueting House (London) 94
Bodiam Castle 186
Carisbrooke Castle 172
Civil War 56
execution 56–7, 122
marriage 89
Powis Castle 464
and Scotland 487
Charles II, King 45, 178
Audley End 212
Crown Jewels 122
Great Fire of London 121
Holyroodhouse (Edinburgh) 514
The Mall (London) 89
Moseley Old Hall 307
Newmarket 211
Plymouth 296
Restoration 56, 57

Charles II, King (cont.)
Windsor Castle 240
Worcester 322
Charles, Prince of Wales
investiture 448
weddings 64, 65, 239
Charles, Thomas 454
Charles Dickens Museum (London) 109
Charleston (Lewes) 167, 184
Charlie, Bonnie Prince 58, 487, **535**
Abbotsford House 516
Battle of Culloden 541
Blair Castle 547
Drumlanrig Castle 519
Glenfinnan Monument 551
Holyroodhouse (Edinburgh) 514
Inverness 540
Jacobite Rebellion 529
Prince's Cairn 550
Skye 533, 534
Traquair House 517
Charlotte, Princess 65
Charlotte, Queen 109
Charlotte Square (Edinburgh) 59
Charlton, pubs 604
Charterhouse School (Godalming) 24
Chartists 441
Chartwell 167, **193**
Chatham 192
Chatsworth House 303, 335, **338–9**
Chatto, Beth 209
Chaucer, Geoffrey **191**
Canterbury Tales 28, 53, 191
memorial to 97
Chawton 166, 176
Cheddar Gorge 10, 14, 250, **258**
Chedworth Roman Villa 333
Cheere, John 270
Cheese 580, 581
Cheddar 258
Chelmsford, restaurants 588
Chelsea (London) **126**
Chelsea Flower Show 66
Chelsea Physic Garden (London) 126
Cheltenham 28, **332**
hotels 567–8
restaurants 594
Cheltenham Gold Cup 70
Cheltenham Imperial Gardens 324
Cheshire *see* Heart of England
Chesil Beach 246, 272
Chessington World of Adventures 613
Chester 16, **314–15**
hotels 568
pubs 606
restaurants 594
Chesters Bridge 426
Chesters Fort 426
Cheviot Hills 420, **425**
Chew Green Camp 425
Cheyne Walk (London) 126
Chichester **175**
hotels 563
restaurants 586
Children **622–3**
entertainment 613
in restaurants 577
Chillida, Eduardo 417
Chillington, hotels 566
Chinatown (London) 27, **84**
Chinese New Year 69
Chinnor, restaurants 588
Chippendale, Thomas 59
Burton Constable 406
Cawdor Castle 541
Harewood House 414
Stourhead House 271

Chippenham, restaurants 590
Chipping Campden **331**
  restaurants 594
Chipping Norton
  pubs 605
  restaurants 588
Chiswick (London) **130**
Chiswick House (London) 130
The Choice of Hercules (Poussin) 271
Cholmondeley Ladies 77
Christ Church College (Oxford) 13, 227,
  230
Christ Discovered in the Temple (Martini)
  383
Christ of St John of the Cross (Dalí) 525
Christchurch Mansion (Ipswich) 207
Christchurch Priory 275
Christianity, Celtic **423**
Christmas 69
Church of England 54
Churches
  architecture **36–7**
  Brompton Oratory (London) **101**
  Holy Trinity Church (Bosham) 175
  Kilpeck Church 320
  Queen's Chapel (London) 89
  St Bartholomew-the-Great (London)
    116–17
  St James Garlickhythe (London) 114
  St James's (London) 88
  St Margaret's (London) 92
  St Mary Abchurch (London) 115
  St Mary Radcliffe (Bristol) **260**
  St Mary the Virgin (Oxford) 13, **229**
  St Mary-le-Bow (London) 114
  St Mary's Parish Church (Whitby) **400**
  St Michael's (St Albans) **236**
  St Nicholas Cole Abbey (London) 114
  St Nicholas Kirk (Aberdeen) **542**
  St Paul's Church (London) 82, 83
  St Peter Mancroft (Norwich) **205**
  St Peter's-on-the-Wall (Maldon) 213
  St Stephen Walbrook (London) 115, **116**
  St Thomas Becket (Rye) 189
  Temple Church (London) 116
  Wimborne Minster 275
  wool churches 211
  see also Abbeys and priories;
    Cathedrals; individual places by name
Churchill, Sir Winston 64
  Blenheim Palace 232
  Chartwell 167, 193
  Churchill War Rooms (London) 92, **93**
  World War II 63
Chysauster 282–3
Cider
  Cider Museum (Hereford) 320
  Somerset **256**
Cinema *see* Film
Cinque Ports 185, **186**, 188
Cirencester **333**
  restaurants 594
Cissbury Ring 184
City Hall (London) **121**
The City and Southwark (London)
  112–25
  area map 113
  The City street-by-street 114–15
  hotels 561–2
  pubs 604
  restaurants 585
City Hall (Cardiff) **475**
Civic Centre (Cardiff) **475**
Civil War 43, 56, 209
Claerwen reservoir 466
Clans **488–9**, 539
Class structure 27–8

Claude Lorrain 245
Claudius, Emperor 48, 187, 209
Claydon House (Winslow) 166
Claypotts Castle 490
Clergy House (Alfriston) 185
Cley Windmill 201
Clifford, Lady Anne 390
Clifford, Lord Henry 390
Clifford, Robert de 390
Clifford's Tower (York) **411**
Clifton Suspension Bridge (Bristol) **261**
Climate **72–3**, 620
Clitheroe, pubs 607
"Clive of India", Clive Museum (Powis
  Castle) 464
Cliveden House 13, 166
Cliveden Reach 239
Clothes
  in restaurants 575
  shops 154, 155, 611
Clovelly 14, **290**
  hotels 566
Clubs **613**
  London 158–9
Clunie Foot Bridge (Loch Faskally) 546
Clyde Valley *see* Lowlands (Scotland)
Clydeside 487
Coach travel 632, 633, 640, 641
  from airports 635
Coalbrookdale Museum of Iron **318**
Coalport China Museum **319**
Coast-to-Coast Walk 41, 367
Coats of arms 34
The Cobb (Lyme Regis) 253, 274
Cobbett, William 164
Cockermouth **366**
  hotels 569
  restaurants 596
Cockington 294
Coggeshall 209
Colchester **209**
  restaurants 588
Colchester, William 412
Coleridge, Samuel Taylor 293, 370
Colet, John 54
Coll
  hotels 573
  restaurants 602
College of Arms (London) 34, 114
Colman's Mustard **205**
Columba, St 529
  Iona 50, 551
  Loch Ness Monster 540
  Skye 534
Columbia Road market (London) 153
Combe Martin 14, 254, 292
Coming from the Mill (Lowry) 375
Commandery (Worcester) 322
Communications **630–31**
Compton Acres (Bournemouth) 275
Coniston, hotels 569
Coniston Water **372**
Conran, Sir Terence 458
Conservative Party 64, 65
Consett, pubs 608
Constable, John
  Boatbuilding 208
  Christchurch Mansion (Ipswich) 207
  Constable Walk 13, **208**
  Fitzwilliam Museum (Cambridge) 218
  The Hay Wain 87, 208
  Lake District 359
  Salisbury Cathedral 245
  Tate Britain (London) 95
Constantine the Great, Emperor 49, 448
Consulates 625
Conversión chart 624

Conwy 10, 16, 439, 444
  Castle 437, 443, 447, 451
  street-by-street map 450–51
Conwy (county) *see* North Wales
Conwy Castle (Sandby) 451
Cook, Captain James
  Captain Cook Memorial Museum
    (Whitby) **400**
  Pitt Rivers Museum (Oxford) 229
  Plymouth 296
  Whitby 400
Cookery courses 614, 617
Cookham 239
  restaurants 589
Cooper, Samuel, *James II* 541
Corbridge **427**
Corelli, Marie 328
Corfe Castle **274**
Corinium Museum (Cirencester) 333
Cornhill on Tweed, pubs 608
Cornish Seal Sanctuary (Helston) 284
Cornwall **276–89**
  climate 72
  hotels 566–7
  map 278–9
  Penwith tour 280
  pubs 606
  restaurants 591–3
  smugglers **284**
Coronation Bridge (River Tummel) 546
Corpach 591
Corpus Christi College (Cambridge) **216**
Corpus Christi College (Oxford) **231**
Corsham 14, **259**
  hotels 565
Cotehele 248, **297**
Cotman, John Sell 205
Cotswold Wildlife Park 224
Cotswolds 13, 14, 221, 302, 618–19
  Midlands garden tour 324–5
  stone buildings 308–9
Countryside **38–9**
Courbet, Gustave 414
Courtauld Gallery (London) 84
Courthouse (Beaumaris) 448
Covenanters 487, 513
Covent Garden (London) 12
  markets 153
  pubs 604
  street-by-street map 82–3
Coventry **323**
  hotels 568
  restaurants 594
Coward, Noël 295, 458
Cowes Week 71
Coxwold **396–7**
Crabbe, George 207
Craft in the Bay (Cardiff) **474**
Craft courses 614, 617
Cragside 33
Craig Goch 466
Cranmer, Thomas, Archbishop, Martyrs'
  Memorial (Oxford) 226, 229
Crarae Gardens **552**
Craster, pubs 608
Crathes Castle and Gardens 545
Credit cards 628
  in hotels 558
  in restaurants 576
  in shops 610
Cregennen lakes 459
Cribyn 434–5
Crich Tramway Village 343
Cricket 71, 159, 616
Crickhowell
  hotels 571
  restaurants 600

Crime 626
Crimean War 60
Crinkle Crags 369
Cromarty 539
Crome, John 205
  Back of the New Mills 205
Cromer, restaurants 588
Cromford Mills 340, 343
Cromwell, Oliver 45, 56
  Carlisle 362
  Ely Cathedral 198
  Huntingdon 212
  Peterborough 198
  Ripley Castle 393
Cromwell, Thomas 355
Crookham, hotels 570
Croquet 159
Crown Jewels **122**
Croyde, restaurants 592
Crufts Dog Show 66
Cruikshank, G 377
Crummock Water 361
Cuckfield, restaurants 586
Cuckmere Haven 185
Cuillins 534
Culbone 254
Culloden, Battle of (1746) 17, 58, 487, **541**
Culross **505**
Culture 28–9
Culzean Castle 482, **526–7**
Cumberbatch, Benedict 28
Cumberland, Duke of 541
Cumbria *see* Lake District
Cumbria Way 367
Cupar, restaurants 601
Currency **628–9**
Currency cards 628–9
Curthose, Robert 428
Curzon, Lord 186
Curzon family 32
Custom House (King's Lynn) 201
Customs information 620–21
Cuthbert, St 364, 423
  Lindisfarne 422
  tomb of 419, 432
Cuthburga 275
Cutty Sark 129
Cuyp, Albert 218
Cycling 61, **615**, 617, 632
  in cities 643

D

D-Day Museum (Portsmouth) 173
Dahl, Roald, Roald Dahl Museum
  (Great Missenden) 234
Dale, David 518
Dalemain **362–3**
Dales Countryside Museum (Hawes) **389**
Dales Way 41
Dalí, Salvador, *Christ of St John of the
  Cross* 525
Dan-yr-Ogof Caves 472
Danby, Earl of 228
Danby, Francis 261
Dance **613**
  London 158
Dance, George the Elder 115
Darby, Abraham I 318
Darby, Abraham III 319
Darling, Grace 422, 424
Darlington, hotels 571
Darnley, Lord 514, 515
Dartington Hall 295
Dartmeet 298
Dartmoor
  hotels 566
  National Park 10, 14, 244, **298–9**

Dartmouth **294**
  restaurants 592
Darts 71
Darwin, Charles 167, 296
David I, King of Scotland
  Border abbeys 507
  Holyroodhouse 514
  Melrose Abbey 516
  St Margaret's Chapel (Edinburgh)
    511
David, Gerard 508
David, St 438, 440, 468, 475
Davy, Sir Humphry 282, 352
Dawlish, pubs 606
de la Pole, Owain 464
de Montfort, Simon 184, 327
de Morgan, William 225
de Quincey, Thomas 84, 370
de Wint, Peter 345, 373
Dean's Yard (London) 92
Dedham Church 208
The Deep (Kingston upon Hull) 406,
  407
Deepdale 388
Deeside tour **544–5**
Defoe, Daniel
  Cheddar Gorge 258
  The Highland Rogue 498
  Robinson Crusoe 260, 504
Degas, Edgar 382
Denbighshire *see* North Wales
Dench, Judi 28
Dennis Severs House (London) 129
Dentists 627
Department stores 610–11
  London 152
Depression 62, 63, 487
Derain, André 404
Derby, restaurants 595
Derby Day (Epsom) 70
Derbyshire *see* East Midlands
Derwent Gorge 340
Derwentwater 358, 360, 364
Design Museum (London) 126
Despenser family 476
Destailleur, Gabriel-Hippolyte 234
Devil's Bridge 467, 471
Devil's Dyke 185
Devon **277–9**, **290–99**
  climate 72
  Devonshire cream teas 291
  hotels 566–7
  map 278–9
  pubs 606
  restaurants 591–3
Devonshire, Dukes of 338, 373, 390
Dialling codes 630
Diana, Princess of Wales
  Althorp 347
  Kensington Gardens (London) 105
  Kensington Palace (London) 105
  Spencer House (London) 88
  wedding 64
Dibdin, Charles 459
Dickens, Charles **192**, 547
  Beaumaris 448
  Bleak House (Broadstairs) 167
  Bloomsbury (London) 107
  Charles Dickens Birthplace Museum
    (Portsmouth) 173
  Charles Dickens Museum (London)
    109
  George Inn (London) 124
  Great Yarmouth 203
  DIG – An Archaeological Adventure
    (York) **411**
  Dinner 575, 577

Directory enquiries 630
Disabled travellers **622**, 625
  in hotels 559
  in restaurants 577
Discovery (Dundee) 503
Disraeli, Benjamin 61
Dissolution of the Monasteries 54, 105,
  332, **355**, 507
Distance chart 22, 636
Ditchling, pubs 604
Dock Museum (Barrow-in-Furness)
  372, 373
Docklands (London) 65, **128–9**
Dolbadarn Castle 455
Dolgellau **458–9**
  restaurants 599
Domesday Book 36, 52, 184, 333, 392
Dorchester 14, **273**
Dornoch **538–9**
Dorset *see* Wessex
Dorset County Museum (Dorchester)
  273
Douglas, Sir James ("Black Douglas")
  516, 519
Douglas family 489, 510
Doune Castle 17, **502**
Dove Cottage and the Wordsworth
  Museum (Grasmere) 370
Dovedale 342
Dover **187**
Dover, Robert 331
Down House (Downe) 167
Downham, pubs 607
Downing Street (London) 92, **93**
Downs and Channel Coast **168–93**
  climate 73
  The Downs **185**
  hotels 562–3
  map 170–71
  pubs 604–5
  restaurants 586–7
  wildlife 38
Doyle, Sir Arthur Conan 298
  Sherlock Holmes Museum (London)
    108
Dozmary Pool 289
Drake, Sir Francis 55, 296, **297**
Dress code 575
Driffield, pubs 607
Druids 266
Drum Castle 491, 545
Drumlanrig Castle 490, 491, **518–19**
Dryburgh Abbey 507
du Maurier, Daphne **288**
Duart Castle (Mull) 550, 551
Duchêne, Achille 232
Duddon Valley **369**
Duffus Castle 490
Duke's Pass 498
Dumfries and Galloway *see* Lowlands
  (Scotland)
Dunblane, pubs 609
Dundee **503**
  hotels 572
  pubs 609
  restaurants 601
Dunfermline **504–5**
Dungeness 186–7
Dunkeld 17, **545**
  hotels 573
Dunkery Beacon 255
Dunrobin Castle 491, 538–9
Dunstaffnage Castle 550
Dunster 14, 254
Dunvegan Castle 534
Dunwich **206**
Durdle Door 247, 274

Durham 15, **432–3**
 Cathedral 351, 419
 restaurants 598
Durham, County see Northumbria
Dysart, Elizabeth Countess of 130

E

Eardisland 317
Earl Grey's Monument (Newcastle
 upon Tyne) **429**
Earl's Palace (Kirkwall) 532
Early Music Festival (Brighton) 68
Easby Abbey 355
Easington 352
East Aberthaw, pubs 609
East Anglia **194–219**
 climate 73
 hotels 563–4
 map 196–7
 North Norfolk coastal tour 13, 200–201
 pubs 605
 restaurants 587–8
 wool trade **211**
East End (London) **128–9**
East India Company 55
East Lambrook Manor 249
East Midlands **334–47**
 climate 73
 hotels 568–9
 map 336–7
 pubs 607
 restaurants 594–5
East Neuk **504**
East Street market (London) 153
East Witton, restaurants 597
Eastbourne **184–5**
 restaurants 586
Easter 69
Easton Grey, restaurants 590
Edale 300–301, 342
Eden Camp **404**
Eden Project 14, **286–7**
Edinburgh 11, 17, 480–81, 483, **508–15**
 airport 634
 Castle 17, 494, 497, **510–11**
 Festival 17, 28, 67, 495, **513**
 Festival Fringe 67
 hotels 572
 map 509
 pubs 609
 restaurants 601
 Royal Mile 17, **512–15**
Edinburgh, Duke of 35
Edmund, St 210
Edradour Distillery (Pitlochry) 545
Edstone Aqueduct 305
Edward I, King 44, 53
 Beaumaris Castle 436, 442
 Caernarfon Castle 445, 448
 Conwy Castle 437, 447
 Eleanor crosses 229
 Harlech Castle 458
 Leeds Castle 192
 and Scotland 486
 Tower of London 122
 Welsh castles 440, 442, 443
 Winchelsea 189
Edward II, King 44, 448
 Byland Abbey 396
 Caernarfon Castle 443
 tomb of 292, 333
Edward III, King 44
 Order of the Garter 34
 Windsor Castle 241
 wool trade 211
Edward IV, King 44
 "Princes in the Tower" 122, 123

Edward V, King 44
Edward VI, King 42, 44, 55
 Leeds Castle 192
 Sherborne School 272
Edward VII, King 45
 Anglican Cathedral (Liverpool) 383
 Sandringham 201
 Warwick Castle 326, 327
Edward VIII, King (Duke of Windsor)
 45, 63, 295
Edward, the Black Prince, tomb of 191
Edward the Confessor, King 51
 Crown Jewels 122
 Wimborne Minster 275
Edwin, King of Northumbria 412, 510
Eilean Donan Castle 538
Eisenhower, Dwight D 526
Elan Valley **466**, 471
Eleanor, Queen 237
Electric Mountain (Llanberis) 455
Electricity 624
Elgar, Sir Edward 317, 321
 birthplace 322
Elgin **542**
Elgin, Lord 110
Eliasson, Olafur 125
Elie, pubs 609
Eliot, George 126
 tomb of 128
Eliot, T S
 Cheyne Walk (London) 126
 memorial to 97
 Russell Square (London) 109
Elizabeth I, Queen 43, 45, 54–5, 260, 346
 childlessness 397
 Epping Forest 213
 and Francis Drake 297
 Hatfield House 221, 235
 Ipswich 207
 Knole 192
 and Mary, Queen of Scots 486–7
 Spanish Armada 55
Elizabeth II, Queen 45
 Buckingham Palace (London) 90–91
 coronation 64, 90
 Diamond Jubilee 65
 Edinburgh 513, 514
 Golden Jubilee 91
 Honours List 35
 Madame Tussaud's (London) 108
 Windsor Castle 240
Elizabeth, the Queen Mother 503
Elizabeth of York 174
Elizabethan House Museum (Great
 Yarmouth) 203
Elterwater 15, 369
Ely 13, **198–9**
 Cathedral 163, **198–9**
 restaurants 588
Ely, Reginald 218
Embankment Galleries (London) 84
Embassies 625
Embassy World Snooker
 Championships (Sheffield) 70
Emergencies 626, 627
Emirates Air Line Cable Car (London) 129
Emmanuel College (Cambridge) **216**
Emsworth, restaurants 587
England **74–433**
 climate 72–3
 food and drink 580–81
 hotels 560–71
 London 74–159
 Midlands 300–47
 Northern England 348–433
 pubs 604–8
 restaurants 582–99

England (cont.)
 Southeast England 160–241
 West Country 242–99
English Heritage 558, 559, 622, 625
Entertainment **612–13**
 London 156–9
Entrance to the Arsenal (Canaletto) 234
Environmental issues
 holidays 624–5
 travel 632, 633
Epping Forest **213**
Epstein, Sir Jacob
 Genesis 378
 Llandaff Cathedral 475
 St Michael Subduing the Devil 323
 Tate Britain 95
Erasmus 217
Eriska, hotels 573
Erpingham, Sir Thomas 204
Eskdale **368**
Essex see East Anglia
Ethelwulf, King 184
Etiquette, restaurants 575
Eton College 13, **239**
Etruscan Vase Painters (Alma-Tadema) 378
Etty, William, Preparing for a Fancy Dress
 Ball 411
Eureka! (Halifax) 417
European Show Jumping
 Championships 71
European Union 25, 64
Eurostar 633
Eurotunnel 633
Evelyn, John 321
Exeter **292–3**
 pubs 606
 restaurants 592
Exmewe, Thomas 449
Exmoor National Park 14, 242–3, 244,
 254–5
Exmouth, restaurants 592
Exmouth, restaurants 592
Fyam 343
Eyemouth, restaurants 601

F

FA Cup Final 70
Faed, Thomas, The Last of the Clan 539
Fairfax, Sir Thomas 397
Fairfax, Viscount 410
Fairfax House (York) **410**
Fairhaven, Lord 212
Falkirk Wheel **505**
Falkland, Lord 224
Falkland Arms Pub (Great Tew) 224
Falkland Palace **504**
Falklands War 64
Falmouth **284–5**
 pubs 606
 restaurants 592
Faringdon, pubs 605
Farmer's Bridge (Birmingham) 304
Farnborough, pubs 606
Farndale 399
Farne Islands **422**
Farrer, Reginald 552
Fashion 29, 64, 154
Fast food 576
"Fat Betty" (White Cross) 399
Faversham, pubs 604
Fawkes, Guy 68, 85, 184
Fell Foot Park (Newby Bridge) 371
Fen Bridge (Constable walk) 208
The Fens **200**
 windmills 203
Ferrensby, restaurants 597
Ferries 633, **641**
Festival of Britain (1951) 64

Festivals and events 28, **66–9**
Ffestiniog Railway 16, 455, **456–7**
Fields 39
Fife *see* Lowlands (Scotland)
Film 29, **613**
  festivals 68
  London 157
Findhorn, restaurants 602
Fingal's Cave 551
Finlaggan Castle (Islay) 553
Fire service 627
The First Marriage (Hockney) 95
Fish (Brancusi) 125
Fishbourne Roman Palace 48–9, 175
Fishing **616**, 617
FitzHamon, Robert 474, 476
Fitzherbert, Mrs 182, 183
Fitzwilliam Museum (Cambridge) 13, **218**
The Five Sisters **538**
Flag Fen Bronze Age Centre
  (Peterborough) 198
Flambard, Ranulph, Bishop of Durham 433
Flambards Experience (Helston) 284
Flamborough, pubs 607
Flamborough Head **404–5**
Flaxman, John 84, 211
Fleming, Alexander 485
Flintshire *see* North Wales
Flitcroft, Henry 234, 270
Flodden, Battle of (1513) 54
Floors Castle 507
Flowers
  The Countryside 38–9
  Development of the Modern Pansy 31
  Flora of the Cairngorms 549
  Gardens through the Ages 30–31
Foley, J H 402
Foley, John 105
Folk Festival (Cambridge) 67
Fontaine, Joan 288
Food and drink 29
  Asian 415
  Colman's Mustard 205
  cookery courses 614, 617
  Devonshire cream teas 291
  The Flavours of Britain 580–81
  The Flavours of Scotland 492
  The Garden of England 164–5
  pubs 604–9
  shops 611
  Somerset cider 256
  whisky 493
  see also Restaurants
Football 70, 159, 616, 617
  Liverpool Football Club 383
  Manchester United Museum
    (Salford Quays) 375, **379**
  National Football Museum
    (Manchester) **377**
Forbes, Stanhope 282
Forestry Commission 559
Forster, E M 167
Fort Amherst 192
Fort Augustus, hotels 573
Fort George **541**
Fort William 551
  hotels 573
  restaurants 602–3
Forth Bridges **506**
Fortnum and Mason (London) 88,
  152, 153
Fortrose 539
Foster, Norman 29, 121, 205
Fountains Abbey 54, 351, **394–5**
Fowey **288**
  hotels 566
  restaurants 592

Fox Talbot Museum (Lacock) 259
Fragonard, Jean Honoré 10
Framlingham Castle **207**
Frampton, George 105
Fraser clan 489
Freud, Anna 127
Freud, Lucian 28
  Interior at Paddington 382
  Tate Britain (London) 95
Freud, Sigmund 127
Freud Museum (London) 127
Frink, Elisabeth 268, 383
Frith, William Powell 95
Frobisher, Martin 55
Fruit, The Garden of England 164–5
Furness Peninsula **372–3**
Furry Dancing Festival (Helston) 66

G

Gaelic language 26, 484
Gaels 486
Gainsborough, Thomas
  Anglesey Abbey 212
  Bath 262, 264
  Blickling Hall 202
  Christchurch Mansion (Ipswich)
    207
  Gainsborough's House (Sudbury)
    167, 210
  Harewood House 414
  Mr and Mrs Andrews 167
  Petworth House 176
  Tate Britain (London) 95
  Walker Art Gallery (Liverpool) 382
Galleries *see* Museums and galleries
Gaol (Beaumaris) 448
The Garden of England **164–5**
Gardens *see* Parks and gardens
Gargoyles, stone **309**
Garreg Ddu 466
Garrick, David 330
Gateshead 428
  restaurants 598
Gatwick Airport 634
Gay and lesbian meeting places **613**
Gelert's Cave (Beddgelert) 456
General Strike (1926) 63
Genesis (Epstein) 378
Geoffrey of Monmouth 289
Geology of the Lake District **356–7**
George I, King 45, 58
  Lamb House (Rye) 188
George II, King 45
  Jacobite Rebellion 487
  Marble Hill House (London) 130
George III, King 45, 59
  Cheltenham 332
  Weymouth 272
  Windsor Great Park 239
George IV, King 45, 59
  Buckingham Palace (London) 90
  Coronation Bridge 546
  Edinburgh 489, 513, 516
  and Mrs Fitzherbert 183
  Royal Pavilion (Brighton) 163, 178,
    179, 182
  Windsor Castle 240, 241
George V, King 45, 240
George VI, King 45
George, Prince 65
George Inn (London) 12, **124**
Georgian Britain **58–9**
Georgian House (Bristol) **261**
Georgian House (Edinburgh) **508**
"The Gherkin" (London) 65
Giacometti, Alberto 205
Gibberd, Sir Frederick 383

Gibbons, Grinling
  Blenheim Palace 232
  Hampton Court 177
  Petworth House 176
  St Mary Abchurch (London) 115
  St Paul's Cathedral (London) 119
Gibbs, James
  King's College (Cambridge) 218
  Radcliffe Camera (Oxford) 231
  Senate House (Cambridge) 216
Gibson, John
  The Sleeping Shepherd Boy 382
  Tinted Venus 350
Gift shops 611
  London 154, 155
Gilbert and George 95
Gill, Eric 390
Gfilbert and George 95
Girtin, Thomas 355
  Rievaulx Abbey 397
Gladstone, William Ewart 61
Gladstone Pottery Museum (Stoke-
  on-Trent) 315
Gladstone's Land (Edinburgh) **512**
Glamis Castle **502–3**
Glanwydden, pubs 608
Glasgow 11, 17, **520–25**
  airport 634
  hotels 572
  Jazz Festival 67
  map 520
  pubs 609
  restaurants 601–2
Glasgow Necropolis **521**
Glasgow School of Art 522
Glasgow Science Centre **522**
Glastonbury 10, 14, **257**
  restaurants 590
Glastonbury Festival 67
Gleaston Water Mill 372–3
Glen Lyn Gorge 292
Glencoe 17, **547**
  restaurants 603
Glencoe Massacre (1692) 57, **547**
Glendurgan 248, 285
Glenfinnan Monument 551
Glenridding 363
Globe Theatre (London) 54, 112, **124**
Glorious Revolution (1688) 57, 541
Glossop, restaurants 595
Gloucester **333**
Gloucester, Humphrey, Duke of 231
Gloucestershire *see* Heart of England
Glynde Place 184
Glyndebourne Festival Opera Season 66
Glyndŵr, Owain 440
  Conwy Castle 437
  Harlech Castle 442, 458
  Machynlleth 466
Glynn Vivian Art Gallery (Swansea) 470
Goathland 399
Godiva, Lady 323
Gold Cup Humber Powerboat
  Championships 71
Golf 71, **503**, **615**, 617
Goodrich Castle 321
Goodwood House 175
Gordale Scar 391
Gordon clan 489
Gormley, Antony 417
  Angel of the North 418
Gower, George 55
Gower, Bishop Henry 468
Gower, John 124
Gower Peninsula **470**
Goya, Francisco de 430, 523
Graham, J Gillespie 383
Grahame, Kenneth 238, 288

Grand National (Aintree) 70
Grand Union Canal 304
Grandisson, Bishop of Exeter 293
Grange-in-Borrowdale 367
Grange-over-Sands
  hotels 569
  restaurants 596
Grant, Duncan 167
  Vanessa Bell at Charleston 167
Grasmere 15, **370**
  hotels 569
  restaurants 596
Grassington Folk Museum **390**
Grays Antiques market (London) 153
Great Autumn Flower Show (Harrogate)
  68
SS Great Britain **260**
Great Chesters Fort 426
Great Dixter 186
Great Exhibition (1851) 60–61, 99, 100
Great Fire of London (1666) 57
  Monument 121
Great Gable 368
Great Glen 17
Great Hall and Visitor Centre
  (Winchester) 174
Great Hormead, pubs 605
Great Langdale 369
Great Malvern **321**
Great Milton, hotels 564
Great Missenden, restaurants 589
Great Orme 449
Great Plague (1665-6) 57
Great Tew **224**
Great Whittington, restaurants 598
Great Yarmouth **203**
  pubs 605
El Greco 230, 430, 523
Green, Benjamin 429
Green Park (London) 79
Green tourism 624–5
Green travel 632, 633
Greenwich (London) **129**
Greenwich Market (London) 153
Greenwich Park (London) 79
Greg, Samuel 314
Gresham, Sir Thomas 115
Grevel, William 331
Grevel House (Chipping Campden) 331
Greville, Sir Fulke 327
Greville family 326
Grey, 2nd Earl 429
Greyfriars Bobby **509**
The Greyfriars (Worcester) 322
Griffith, Sir Henry 404
Grimes Graves **198–9**
Grimsby **407**
Grimshaw, Atkinson 401, 414
Grimspound 298
Grimsthorpe, pubs 607
Guesthouses 557, 559
Guildford **176**
Guildhall (Exeter) **292**
Guildhall (Norwich) **205**
Guildhall (Totnes) 295
Guildhall (York) 408
Guisborough, hotels 570
Gunpowder Plot (1605) 56
Guy Fawkes Night 68, 184

H
Haddington, restaurants 602
Hadrian, Emperor 48, 426, 427
Hadrian's Wall 11, 15, 48, 350, 419,
  426–7, 486
Halifax 352, **416–17**
  hotels 570

Hall, John 329
Hals, Frans 109, 218
Haltwhistle 431
  pubs 608
Ham House (London) 130
Hamada, Shoji 411
Hambledon Mill 238
Hamilton, James, *The Massacre of*
  Glencoe 547
Hamilton, Richard 95
Hammersmith, pubs 604
Hampshire *see* Downs and Channel
  Coast
Hampstead (London) **127**
  pubs 604
Hampstead Heath (London) 79, **128**
Hampton Court 55, 169, **177**
  Flower Show 67
  Privy Garden 30
Hampton Court Castle (Leominster)
  317
Handel, George Frederick 218
Hands on History (Kingston upon Hull)
  406
Hardknott Fort 368
Hardknott Pass 369
Hardraw Force **389**
Hardwick Hall 306, 340
Hardy, Thomas **273**
  Hardy's Cottage (Dorchester) 14, 273
Hare, David 28
Harewood House 32, **414**
Harlech **458**
  Castle 16, 442
  hotels 571
  restaurants 599
Harlow Carr Gardens 392
Harold II, King 175
  Battle of Hastings 50, 51, 185
Harris, Isle of **533**
Harrods (London) **101**, 152, 153
  Christmas Parade 69
Harrogate **392**
  festivals 68
  hotels 570
  restaurants 597
Hartland Abbey 290
Hartley, Jesse 381
Hartnett, Angela 29
Harvard, John 216, 331
Harvard House (Stratford-upon-Avon)
  331
Harvest Festivals 68
Harvey Nichols (London) 152, 153
Hassall, John, *Bruce in Single Combat*
  at Bannockburn 486
Hastings **185**
  hotels 563
  restaurants 587
Hastings (1810) (Turner) 8–9
Hastings, Battle of (1066) 43, 50, 51, **185**
Hatfield House 57, 221, **235**
Hathaway, Anne 325, 331
Hathersage 343
  pubs 607
Haverfordwest, restaurants 600
Hawes 389
Hawkins, John 55
Hawkshead 372
  pubs 607
Hawksmoor, Nicholas 32
  Blenheim Palace 232
  Castle Howard 402
Haworth **416**
Hay Bluff 473
Hay Festival 67
The Hay Wain (Constable) 87, 208

Hay-on-Wye 10, 16, 28, **465**
  pubs 609
  restaurants 600
Haydon Bridge 431
Haytor Rocks 10, 14, 298
Heacham 195
Health **626–7**
Heart of England **310–33**
  climate 72
  hotels 567–8
  map 312–13
  pubs 606
  restaurants 593–4
  A Week in Wales and the West 10, **16**
Heathrow Airport 634
Hebden Bridge 352, **416**
Hebrides 534
Heddon's Mouth 254
Hedley on the Hill, pubs 608
Heights of Abraham 340
Helmsley **397**
  hotels 570
Helplines 627
Helston **284**
  festivals 66
  pubs 606
  restaurants 592
Helvellyn 357
Hemel Hempstead, restaurants 589
Henderson, Fergus 29
Hengist 225
Hengistbury Head 275
Henley-on-Thames 11, 13, 238
  Henley Royal Regatta 67, 70
  restaurants 589
Henrietta Maria, Queen
  portrait of 411
  Queen's Chapel (London) 89
  Queen's House (London) 129
Henry I, King 44, 117
Henry II, King 44, 52
  coat of arms 44
  Dover Castle 187
  Orford Castle 207
  Rosa Mundi 237
  Windsor Castle 240, 241
Henry III, King 44, 327
  Clifford's Tower (York) 411
  Gloucester 333
  Lewes 184
  and Wales 440
  Westminster Abbey (London) 97
Henry IV, King 44, 440
Henry V, King 44
  Battle of Agincourt 53
  Monmouth Castle 479
  Portchester Castle 173
Henry VI, King 44
  All Souls College (Oxford) 230
  Eton College 239
  King's College (Cambridge) 218
  St Albans 236
Henry VII, King 44, 441
  King's College (Cambridge) 218
  Richmond Palace (London) 130
  Tudor rose 34
  Westminster Abbey (London) 96
Henry VIII, King 42, 43, 44
  Camber Castle 189
  Church of England 54
  Dissolution of the Monasteries 97,
    105, 332, **355**, 507
  Epping Forest 213
  Falmouth 285
  Hampton Court 177
  King's College (Cambridge) 215
  Knole 192

Henry VIII, King (cont.)
  Leeds Castle 192
  Mary Rose 173
  Melrose Abbey 516
  navy 54
  portraits 218
  St James's Palace (London) 88
  St Michael's Mount 282
  and Scotland 486, 515
  Trinity College (Cambridge) 217
  wives 122
Henry, George, *Japanese Lady with a Fan*
  524
Henry Wood Promenade Concerts 67
Heptonstall 416
Hepworth, Barbara 28, **281**
  Barbara Hepworth Museum and
    Sculpture Garden (St Ives) 281
  Tate Britain (London) 95
  Two Forms (Divided Circle) 281
  Yorkshire Sculpture Park 417
Heraldry **34–5**
Herbert, St 364
Herbert family 464, 476
Herbert Gallery and Museum
  (Coventry) 323
Hereford **320**
  hotels 568
Herefordshire *see* Heart of England
Hereward the Wake 52, 198
Heritage organizations 622, 625
Heron, Patrick 244
  St Ives Harbour 281
Herriot, James 389
Hertford, Marquesses of 108
Hertforshire *see* Thames Valley
Hervey, Bishop Lord Arthur 257
Herzog and de Meuron 125
Hestercombe Garden 256
Hetton, restaurants 598
Hever, hotels 563
Hever Castle **193**
Hexham **426–7**, 431
  hotels 571
  pubs 608
  restaurants 598
Hidcote Manor Gardens 325
*The High Sheriff of Lancaster Crossing
  Morecambe Sands* (anon) 374
Highgate (London) **128**
  Cemetery 78, 128
Highland Games 66
Highland Wildlife Park 548
Highlands and Islands **528–53**
  climate 73
  The Flavours of Scotland 492
  Highland Clearances 487, **539**
  hotels 572–3
  map 530–31
  pubs 609
  restaurants 602–3
  A Week in Scotland 11, **17**
Hill, Octavia 33
Hill Top (Near Sawrey) 15, 371
Hinton St George, hotels 565
Historic Dockyard (Chatham) 192
History **42–65**
  Scotland 486–7
  Wales 440–41
Hitchcock, Alfred 288
Hitchhiking 637
Hoare, Henry 270, 271
Hobart, Sir Henry 202
Hobbema, Meindert 218
Hockney, David 28
  The First Marriage 95
  The Other Side 415

Hockney, David (cont.)
  Tate Britain (London) 95
  Walker Art Gallery (Liverpool) 382
Hodgkin, Howard 95
Hogarth, William 59, 95
  Pollok House (Glasgow) 523
  Portrait of Richard James 218
  St Bartholomew-the-Great (London) 117
  Sir John Soane's Museum (London) 116
Hogmanay 69
Holbein, Hans 240
  The Ambassadors 87
Holburne of Menstrie, William 264
Holburne Museum of Art (Bath) **264**
Holderness **407**
Holidays, public 69
Holker Hall 373
Holkham Hall 32, **201**
Holland, Henry
  Berrington Hall 317
  Royal Pavilion (Brighton) 182, 183
  Woburn Abbey 32, 234
Holland House (London) 126
Holland Park (London) 78, **126–7**
Hollytrees Museum (Colchester) 209
Holmes, Sherlock 108
Holt, restaurants 588
Holy Trinity Church (Bosham) 175
Holyroodhouse (Edinburgh) 17, **514**
Holywell, pubs 608
Holywell Music Room (Oxford) **229**
Honister Pass 356
Honiton 293
  hotels 567
Honours List 35
Hood, Robin **340**, 401
Hoover, William 63
Hopetoun House **506**
Hops and hop picking **164–5**
Hornsea 407
Horse Guards (London) 93
Horse racing 70, 616, 617
  Newmarket 211
Horse riding **615**, 617
Horse of the Year Show 68, 71
Horsham, restaurants 587
Hospital of St Cross (Winchester) 175
Hospitals 627
Hotels **556–73**
  boutique and designer 556, 559
  children in 622
  country-house 556
  Devon and Cornwall 566–7
  Downs and Channel Coast 562–3
  East Anglia 563–4
  East Midlands 568–9
  gradings 557
  groups 556, 559
  Heart of England 567–8
  Highlands and Islands 572–3
  Lancashire and the Lakes 569–70
  London 560–62
  Lowlands 572
  North Wales 571
  Northumbria 570–71
  prices and bookings 558
  restaurants 575
  South and Mid-Wales 571–2
  Thames Valley 564
  Wessex 564–6
  Yorkshire and the Humber Region 570
Hound Tor 299
House of the Tailor of Gloucester
  (Gloucester) 333
Houses of Parliament (London) 28, 80, **94**
  State Opening of Parliament 68
  street-by-street map 93

Housesteads Fort 426, 427
Housman, A E 316, 317
Howard, Catherine 122
Howard, Sir Ebenezer 62
Howard, Admiral Edward 403
Howard, Lord 55
Howard family 402–3
Hoy, Chris 35
Hudson, George 353
Hughes, Thomas 225
Huguenots 128
Hull **406–7**
Humber Region **384–417**
  hotels 570
  map 386–7
  pubs 607–8
  restaurants 597–8
Hume, David 485, 487
Hundred Years' War 53
Hunstanton Cliffs 200
Hunt, Charles, *Life Below Stairs* 33
Hunt, Leigh 126
Hunt, William Holman 378
Hunterian Art Gallery (Glasgow)
  17, **523**
Huntingdon **212**
  restaurants 588
Hutchinson, Mary 370, 396
Hutton-in-the-Forest 362
Hutton-le-Hole **398**, 399
Hyde Park (London) 76, 79, **105**
  see also South Kensington and
    Hyde Park

I
i360 (Brighton) 178
Ice skating 71
Iceni **199**
Icknield Way 41
Ickworth House 210–11
Ideal Home Show (London) 66
Ightham Mote 192–3
Ilfracombe, restaurants 592
Ilkeston, restaurants 595
Ilkley, restaurants 597
Immigration 27, 64, 620
  Bradford's Asian community 415
Imperial War Museum North (Salford
  Quays) 375, **379**
Inchmahome Priory 499
Industrial Revolution 58
  Birmingham 322
  The Industrial Revolution in the North
    352–3
  Ironbridge Gorge 318–19
  Quarry Bank Mill, Styal 314
  Scotland 484, 495
Ingilby, William Amcotts 393
Inns, accommodation 557
Insurance
  health 627
  travel 626
Interior at Paddington (Freud) 382
International Beatleweek (Liverpool) 67
International Eisteddfod 67, 454
International Sheepdog Trials 68
International Slavery Museum
  (Liverpool) 381
Internet **630–31**
Inverarnan, restaurants 602
Inverary Castle 17, **552**
Inverewe Garden 538
Inverie, restaurants 603
Inverness 11, 17, **540**
  hotels 573
  restaurants 603
Iona 551

Ipswich **207**
 restaurants 588
Iraq War 65
Ireby, hotels 569
Ireland, Robert 316
Ironbridge Gorge 10, 16, 302, **318–19**
 hotels 568
 restaurants 594
Islay **553**
Isle of Mull see Mull
Isle of Skye see Skye
Isle of Wight **172**
 Coastal Path 41
 Music Festival 67
 pubs 604
 restaurants 587
Isles of Scilly 283
Islington (London) **128**
Itineraries **10–17**
 Two Days in London **12**
 A Week in Northern England 11, **15**
 A Week in Scotland 11, **17**
 A Week in Southeast England 11, **13**
 A Week in Southwest England 10, **14**
 A Week in Wales and the West 10, **16**
Itteringham, pubs 605

J

Jack the Ripper 85
Jackfield Tile Museum (Ironbridge Gorge) **318**
Jacobite Movement 487, 529, **541**
 Battle of Culloden 58, 541
 Glencoe Massacre 57, 547
Jamaica Inn (Bodmin Moor) 288
James I, King 45, 55, 56, 487
 Audley End 212
 Banqueting House (London) 94
 birth 511
 Campden Manor 331
 Epping Forest 213
 Falkland Palace 504
 Hyde Park (London) 105
 Newmarket 211
 Stirling 500
 Trinity College (Cambridge) 217
James I, King of Scotland 505
James IV/VI, King, Warwick Castle 327
James II (Cooper) 541
James II, King of Scotland 503, 510, 519
James II/VII, King 45, 56, 57
 Jacobite Movement 541
 Knole 192–3
 Monmouth Rebellion 256
James III/VIII (the "Old Pretender") 541
James IV, King of Scotland 486, 504, 510
James V, King of Scotland 512
 Edinburgh Castle 510
 Falkland Palace 504
 Holyroodhouse (Edinburgh) 514
James, Henry 126
James of St George **443**
Japanese Lady with a Fan (Henry) 524
Jazz
 festivals 67
 London 158–9
Jedburgh Abbey 507
Jeffreys, Judge **256**
Jekyll, Gertrude 31
 Hestercombe Garden 256
 Lindisfarne Castle 422
Jenkins, J 406
Jenkins, Valentine 501
Jennings Brewery (Cockermouth) 366
Jermyn Street (London) 89
Jesus College (Cambridge) **216**
Jewellery Quarter (Birmingham) 323

Jew's House (Lincoln) 344
John, King 44
 Beaulieu 172
 Liverpool 380
 Magna Carta 52, 221, 237, 239
 tomb of 322
John, Augustus 404
John, Elton 35
John, Tom 471
John of Beverley, St 405
John of Gaunt 392
John Lewis (London) 152, 153
John o'Groats **532**
Johnson, Dr Samuel 448
Jones, Sir Horace 120
Jones, Inigo 29, 57
 Banqueting House (London) 93, 94
 Covent Garden Piazza (London) 83
 Queen's Chapel (London) 89
 Queen's House (London) 129
 St Paul's Church (London) 82, 83
 Wilton House 269
Jones, Mary 454
Jorvik Viking Centre (York) 15, 409, **410**
Joseph of Arimathea, St 257
Jubilee and Apple Market (London) 153
Judge's Lodgings (Lancaster) 374, 375
Jura **552–3**

K

Kandinsky, Wassily 125
Katrine, Loch 496, 498
Keats, John 127, 218, 365
Keats House (London) 127
Kedleston Hall 32–3, 340
Keighley and Worth Valley Railway 416
Keir Hardie, James 487
Kelmscott **224–5**
Kelso Abbey 507
Kelvingrove Art Gallery and Museum (Glasgow) 17, 483, **524–5**
Kendal **372**
 hotels 569
 restaurants 596
Kennedy, Joseph Jr 206
Kenneth McAlpin, King of Scotland 51, 486
Kensal Green Cemetery (London) 78
Kensington (London) see South Kensington
Kensington Gardens (London) 12, 79, **105**
Kensington Palace (London) **105**
Kent see Downs and Channel Coast
Kent, William 32, 105
Kents Cavern 294
Kenwood House (London) 128
Keswick 358, **363**
 hotels 569
 restaurants 596
Kew (London) **130**
Kew Gardens (London) 78, 130
Keynes, J M 167
Kielder Water **424**
 pubs 608
Kiftsgate Court Garden 325
Kilberry, restaurants 603
Kilchrist Church 535
Killerton 293
Killhope Lead Mine 431
Killiecrankie Walk **546**
Kilpeck Church 320
Kilts 488–9, 540
Kimmeridge 274
King, Bishop Oliver 264
King's College (Aberdeen) **544**
King's College (Cambridge) 13, 215, **218–19**

King's College Choir (Cambridge) 219
King's Lynn **200–201**
 restaurants 588
King's Own Scottish Borderers Regimental Museum (Berwick-upon-Tweed) 422
King's Road (London) 126
Kings and queens **44–5**
Kingsbridge, restaurants 592
Kingsley, Charles 290
Kingston Lacy 275
Kingston upon Hull **406–7**
Kinlochleven, restaurants 603
Kinski, Nastassja 273
Kintyre **553**
Kipling, Rudyard 167, 290
Kirk, Dr John 410
Kirkham Priory 355
Kirkstall Abbey 355
Kirkwall 532
Kitaj, R B 95
Knaresborough **392–3**
Knebworth House **235**
Kneller, Sir Godfrey 233
Knighton 463, **465**
Knights Templar 116
Knightshayes Court 249, 293
Knole **192–3**
Knot gardens 31
Knowstone, pubs 606
Knox, John
 Church of Saint John (Perth) 502
 John Knox House (Edinburgh) 515
 St Giles Cathedral (Edinburgh) 513
 statues of 486, 521
Kylesku, restaurants 603
Kynance Cove 284
Kyrle, John 320–21

L

La Lines Latin Music Festival (London) 66
Labour Party 65
Lacock 14, **259**
 hotels 565
 restaurants 590
Laguerre, Louis 233
Lainé, Elle 234
Lake District 11, 15, 350, **358–73**
 climate 72
 geology 356–7
 hotels 569–70
 major peaks 364–9
 map 360–61
 Northern Fells and Lakes 364–5
 pubs 607
 restaurants 595–7
 traditional Cumbrian sports 362
 walking in 367
Lake Village Museum (Glastonbury) 257
Lamb and Flag (London) 82, 604
Lancashire 359, **374–83**
 climate 72
 hotels 569
 map 360–61
 pubs 607
 restaurants 595–6
Lancaster **374–5**
 hotels 569
 pubs 607
Landmark Trust 558, 559
Land's End 246, 278, 280
Landscape **38–9**
Landseer, Sir Edwin 547
Lanercost Priory 362
Lanfranc, Archbishop of Canterbury 190
Langdale 15, **369**
Langdale Pikes 357

Langley, Bishop of Durham 432
Languages
  Gaelic 26, 484
  Welsh 26, 438, 441
Lanhydrock 248, **288**, 289
Lanyon Quoit 280
Large Two Forms (Moore) 417
The Last of the Clan (Faed) 539
The Last of England (Brown) 323
Lastingham 399
Laszlo, Henri de 503
Latimer, Bishop Hugh, Martyrs'
  Memorial (Oxford) 226, 229
Lauder, restaurants 602
Lauderdale, Duke and Duchess of 130
Laurel and Hardy Museum (Ulverston)
  372, 373
Lavenham **210**
Lawrence, Sir Thomas 261
Layer Marney Tower 209
Leach, Bernard 281, 411
Ledbury **321**
Leeds **414**
  hotels 570
  restaurants 597
Leeds Castle 171, **192**
  Classical Concert 67
Legoland 613
Leicester, restaurants 595
Leicestershire *see* East Midlands
Leigh, Mike 29
Leigh, Vivien 331
Leighton, Lord 127
Leighton Buzzard, pubs 605
Leighton Hall **374**
Leighton House (London) 127
Leighton Moss Nature Reserve 374
Leith Hill 176
Lely, Sir Peter 547
Leominster 16, **317**
Leonardo da Vinci 240
  "The Burlington House Cartoon" 86
  Queen's Gallery (London) 91
Lerwick 532
Levens Hall **373**
Lever, William Hesketh 353, 383
Lewes **184**
  hotels 563
  pubs 604
Lewis, Isle of 485, **533**
Lewis, Wyndham 95
Leyburn, pubs 608
Liberty (London) 152, 153
Libeskind, Daniel 379
Life Below Stairs (Hunt) 33
Lifton, hotels 567
Lightholer, Thomas 406
Limestone Corner Milecastle 426
Lincoln
  Cathedral 303, 334, 336
  hotels 568
  restaurants 595
  street-by-street map 344–5
Lincoln College (Oxford) **230**
Lincolnshire *see* East Midlands
Lindisfarne 50, 51, **422**, 423
Lindisfarne Gospels **423**
Lindow Man 111
Linley Sambourne House (London)
  126–7
Linlithgow, Marquess of 506
Linlithgow Palace **505**
Linn of Tummel 546
Lippi, Fra Filippo, *The Annunciation* 86
Literature 28
Little Downham, hotels 563
Little Hall (Lavenham) 210

Little Langdale 369
Little Malvern 321
Little Moreton Hall **306–7**, 315
Little Town 366
Liverpool 15, 359, 361, **380–83**
  festivals 67
  hotels 569
  map 380
  pubs 607
  restaurants 596
  Walker Art Gallery 382–3
Liverpool and Manchester railway 352
Livingstone, David 485, **518**, 521
Lizard Peninsula **284**
Llanaber, hotels 571
Llanbedrog, restaurants 599
Llanberis 436, **455**
Llandaff Cathedral 475
Llandovery 471
Llandrillo, restaurants 599
Llandrindod Wells **465**
Llandudno **449**
  hotels 571
  restaurants 599
Llanelli, restaurants 599
Llangollen 16, **454**
  hotels 571
  International Eisteddfod 67, 454
  restaurants 599
Llanidloes 471
Llanthony Priory 465, 473
  hotels 572
Llanwrtyd Wells, restaurants 600
Llechwedd Slate Caverns (Blaenau
  Ffestiniog) 455
Llithfaen 457
Lloyd, Christopher 186
Lloyd George, David 441, 475
Lloyd's Building (London) **120**
Llŷn Peninsula **457**
Llyn y Fan Fach 461, 472
Llyswen, restaurants 600
Llywelyn the Great 440
  Beddgelert 456
  Castell-y-Bere 443
  statue of 450
Llywelyn the Last 440, 448
Loch Garten Osprey Centre 549
Loch Ness Monster 17, **540**
Lochmaddy 533
Lombard Street (London) 115
Lomond, Loch 17, 498
  pubs 609
London **74–159**
  cemeteries 78
  The City and Southwark 112–25
  The City street-by-street 114–15
  climate 73
  congestion charge 642
  Covent Garden street-by-street 82–3
  entertainment **156–9**
  festivals 66–9
  Further afield 126–30
  hotels 560–62
  map 21
  parks and gardens 78–9
  Piccadilly and St James's street-by-
    street 88–9
  pubs 604
  Regent's Park and Bloomsbury 106–11
  restaurants 582–6
  shops and markets **152–5**
  South Kensington and Hyde Park
    98–105
  South Kensington street-by-street
    100–101
  squares 79

London (cont.)
  Street Finder 131–51
  travel 642–3
  Two Days in London **12**
  West End and Westminster 80–97
  Whitehall and Westminster street-
    by-street 92–3
London Coliseum (London) 158, 159
London Dungeon **85**
London Eye 12, **84–5**
London Film Festival 68
London Marathon 70
London to Brighton Veteran Car Rally 68
London Underground 28, 60, **643**
Londonderry, Marquess of 466
London's Transport Museum 83, **84**
Long, Charles 241
Long, Richard 95
Long Man of Wilmington 184
Long Meg and her Daughters 362
Long Mynd 316
Longleat
  hotels 565
  restaurants 590
Longleat House **270**
Lonsdale, pubs 607
Looe 288
Lord Leycester Hospital (Warwick) 325
Lord Mayor's Show (London) 68
Lord Nelson pub (Burnham Market) 200
Lorton Vale 364
Loseley Park 176
Losinga, Bishop of Norwich 204
Lost Gardens of Heligan 248, 285
Lost/stolen property 627, 639
Lostwithiel 288
Lothians *see* Lowlands (Scotland)
Lower Slaughter 308
Lowestoft **203**
  hotels 563
  restaurants 588
Lowlands (Scotland) **494–527**
  climate 73
  The Flavours of Scotland 492
  hotels 572
  map 496–7
  pubs 609
  restaurants 600–602
  A Week in Scotland 11, **17**
Lowry, L S 379
  Coming from the Mill 375
Lowry Centre (Salford Quays) 375, **379**
Lucy, Sir Thomas 306
Ludlow 16, 313, **316–17**
Luib 534
Lullingstone Roman Villa 49
Lulworth Cove 274
Lunch 574–5, 577
Lundy 290
Luss 498
Lutyens, Sir Edwin 383
  Castle Drogo 33, 299
  Great Dixter 186
  Hestercombe Garden 256
  Lindisfarne Castle 422
  Queen Mary's Dolls' House 240
Lyddington, pubs 607
Lydford Gorge 298
Lyme Regis 253, **274**
  hotels 565
  restaurants 591
Lymington, restaurants 587
Lymouth 14, 255, **292**
Lynton **292**
  pubs 606
Lytton, 1st Earl of 235
Lytton, Lord 235

M

M-Shed (Bristol) **260**
McCartney, Paul 553
  see also The Beatles
MacDonald, Flora 533, 534, 535, 550
MacDonald clan 488, 547
Machynlleth 16, **466**
Mackay clan 488
McKellen, Ian 28
Mackenzie, Osgood 538
Mackenzie clan 488
Mackintosh, Charles Rennie **522**, 523, 524
Maclean clan 550
MacLeod clan 488
McNally, Leonard 388
McTaggart, William 523
Madame Tussaud's (London) **108**
Madame Tussaud's (Warwick Castle) 326
Madonna and Child (Michelangelo) 88
Maeldune Centre (Maldon) 213
Maentwrog, pubs 608
Maes Howe 532
Magazines 631
  London 154, 155
Magdalen College (Oxford) **230**
Magdalene College (Cambridge) **217**
Magna (Rotherham) **417**
Magna Carta 52, 221, 237, 239, 268
Magnus, St 532
Magnus Barfud, King 553
Maiden Castle 47, 273
Major, John 65
Malcolm III, King of Scotland 504
Maldon **213**
  restaurants 588
Malham 391
Malham Cove 391
Malham Lings 391
Malham Tarn 391
Malham Walk **391**
The Mall (London) **89**, 91
Mallaig 550
Mallyan Spout 399
Malmesbury
  hotels 565
  restaurants 591
Malvern
  hotels 568
  restaurants 594
Malverns **321**
Man in Armour (Rembrandt) 524
Manchester 15, 359, **376–9**
  airport 634
  hotels 569
  map 376
  pubs 607
  restaurants 596
Manchester Art Gallery **378**
Manchester Museum **378**
Manchester Ship Canal 375, 376
Manchester Town Hall **377**
Manchester United Museum (Salford Quays) 375, **379**
Manifold Valley 2–3
Manor houses, Tudor **306–7**
Mansfield, restaurants 595
Mansfield, Isaac 233
Mansion House (London) 115
Mantegna, Andrea 177
Mappa Mundi **320**
Maps
  Aberdeen 543
  Bath street-by-street 262–3
  Borders tour 507
  Brecon Beacons 472–3
  Brighton street-by-street 178–9
  Bristol 261

Maps (cont.)
  Cairngorms 548–9
  Cambridge street-by-street 214–15
  Cardiff 475
  Cheviot Hills 425
  clans and tartans 488–9
  climate 72–3
  Constable Walk 208
  Conwy street-by-street 450–51
  Cotswold stone towns and villages 309
  Dartmoor National Park 298–9
  Devon and Cornwall 278–9
  Downs and Channel Coast 170–71
  East Anglia 196–7
  East Midlands 336–7
  Edinburgh 509
  Europe 19
  Exmoor National Park 254–5
  Ffestiniog Railway 456–7
  Glasgow 520
  Great Britain 18–19
  Hadrian's Wall 427
  Heart of England 312–13
  Highlands and Islands 530–31
  houses of historical figures 166–7
  Ironbridge Gorge 319
  Isle of Skye 534–5
  Killiecrankie Walk 546
  Lancashire and the Lakes 360–61
  Lincoln street-by-street 344–5
  Liverpool 380
  London: at a Glance 76–7
  London: Central London *see* inside back cover
  London: The City and Southwark 113
  London: The City street-by-street 114–15
  London: Covent Garden street-by-street 82–3
  London: Further Afield 126
  London: Greater London 21, 76
  London: parks and gardens 78–9
  London: Piccadilly and St James's street-by-street 88–9
  London: Regent's Park and Bloomsbury 107
  London: South Kensington and Hyde Park 99
  London: South Kensington street-by-street 100–101
  London: Street Finder 131–51
  London: useful bus routes *see* inside back cover
  London: West End and Westminster 81
  London: Whitehall and Westminster street-by-street 92–3
  Lowlands 496–7
  Malham Walk 391
  Manchester 376
  Midlands 302–3
  Midlands canal network 305
  Midlands garden tour 324–5
  national rail network 639
  North Norfolk coastal tour 200–201
  North Pennines tour 431
  North Wales 446–7
  North York Moors 399
  Northern England 350–51
  Northern Fells and Lakes 364–5
  Northumbria 420–21
  Ordnance Survey 40
  Orkney Islands 19, 23, 531
  Oxford street-by-street 226–7
  Peak District tour 342–3
  Penwith tour 280
  Regional Great Britain 20–23
  road maps 636

Maps (cont.)
  Road to the Isles tour 550–51
  Royal Deeside tour 544–5
  Rye street-by-street 188–9
  Scotland 482–3
  Shetland Islands 19, 23, 531
  South and Mid-Wales 462–3
  Southeast England 162–3
  Stratford-upon-Avon street-by-street 328–9
  Thames Valley 222–3
  Thames Valley tour 238–9
  Tissington Trail 341
  The Trossachs 498–9
  Wales 436–7
  Walkers' Britain 40–41
  Wessex 252–3
  West Country 244–5
  West Country Gardens 248–9
  Wild Wales tour 471
  York street-by-street 408–9
  Yorkshire Dales 388
  Yorkshire and the Humber Region 386–7
Mar, 1st Earl of 500
Marble Hill House (London) 130
Marcher Lords 440, 441
Marchesa Maria Grimaldi (Rubens) 275
Marconi, Guglielmo 62
Margaret, Queen of Scotland 506, 511
Margaret of Anjou 216
Margate **187**
Maritime Museum (Aberdeen) **544**
Maritime Museum (Kingston upon Hull) 406
Maritime Museum (Lancaster) 374, 375
Market Hall (Chipping Campden) 331
Market Hall Museum (Warwick) 325
Markets 153, 611
  Camden Lock Market (London) 128, 153
  Covent Garden Piazza and Central Market (London) **83**
Marlborough 267
Marlborough, 1st Duke of 221, 232–3
Marlow 221, 223
  hotels 564
  restaurants 589
Marney, Sir Henry 209
Marshland 39
Martello towers 186
Martin, John 431
Martini, Simone, *Christ Discovered in the Temple* 383
Martyrs' Memorial (Oxford) 226, **229**
Marx, Karl 107
  tomb of 128
Mary I, Queen 44, 5, 54
  Framlingham Castle 207
  Protestant martyrs 55, 116, 184, 229
  tomb of 210
Mary II, Queen 45, 56, 177
Mary, Queen, consort of George V 240
Mary, Queen of Scots 54, 55, 486–7, **515**
  Abbotsford House 516
  Bolton Castle 389
  Edinburgh Castle 511
  golf 503
  Holyroodhouse (Edinburgh) 514
  Inchmahome Priory 499
  Linlithgow Palace 505
  Oxburgh Hall 199
  Provand's Lordship (Glasgow) 521
  "Rough Wooing" 516
  Scone Palace 502
  Stirling 500
  Traquair House 517
Mary Arden's Farm 310, 331

Mary of Guise 514
Mary Rose 54, 173
Mary Rose Museum (Portsmouth) 173
Masham 389
The Massacre of Glencoe (Hamilton) 547
Matfen, restaurants 598
Matisse, Henri 125
Matlock 340
  hotels 568
  restaurants 595
Matlock Bath **340**
Maumbury Rings 273
Maundy Thursday 66
Mawddach Estuary 459
Mawgan Porth
  hotels 567
  restaurants 592
Max Gate (Dorchester) 273
May, Isle of 504
Mayflower 56, 172–3, 296
Media **631**
Melrose Abbey 507, **516**
Memorial Arch (Clunie Dam) 546
Memorial to the Great Exhibition
  (London) 100
Merchant Adventurers Hall (York) 409,
  411
Mercia 50
Merionethshire *see* North Wales
Merlemond, Oliver de 320
Merry Maidens 280
Merseyside Maritime Museum
  (Liverpool) **381**
Merton College (Oxford) **231**
Methodism **283**, 441
Methuen, Lady 259
Metropolitan Cathedral of Christ the
  King (Liverpool) **383**
Michelangelo
  Madonna and Child 88
  Windsor Castle 240
Mid-Wales **460–79**
  climate 72
  hotels 571–2
  map 462–3
  pubs 608–9
  restaurants 599–600
  A Week in Wales and the West 10, **16**
  Wild Wales tour 471
Middle Ages **52–3**
Middleham Castle **389**
Middleton, Catherine 65
Middleton-in-Teesdale **430**
Midlands **300–47**
  building with Cotswold stone **308–9**
  Canals of the Midlands 304–5
  East Midlands 334–47
  Heart of England 310–33
  map 20–21, 302–3
  Midlands garden tour 13, 324–5
  Tudor manor houses 306–7
Midnight Mass 69
Mildert, William van, Bishop of Durham
  432
Mileage chart 22, 636
Millais, Sir John Everett
  Ashmolean Museum (Oxford) 228
  Ophelia 60
  Tate Britain (London) 95
  Walker Art Gallery (Liverpool) 382
Miller, Hugh 539
Milton, John 235, 316
Minack Theatre 280
Minehead 254
Ministry of Defence 298
Minsmere Reserve 206
Minster Lovell Hall (Swinbrook) 224

Mirren, Helen 28, 331
Misericords **345**
Miss Cranston's Tearoom 524
Mobile phones 630, 631
Modigliani, Amedeo 205
Mold, pubs 608
Mompesson House (Salisbury) **269**
Monarchy 28, **44–5**
  royal coat of arms 34
Monasteries **354**
  Dissolution of 54, 105, 332, **355**, 507
Monet, Claude 218
Money **628–9**
Monk Bar (York) **411**
Monmouth **478–9**
Mons Meg **510**, 519
Montacute House 249, 272
Montgomery, Viscount 35
Montrose, Duke of 499
Monument (London) 12, **121**
Moore, Albert Joseph, *Shells* 382
Moore, Henry 28
  Large Two Forms 417
  Leeds Art Gallery 414
  Recumbent Figure 95
  Sainsbury Centre for Visual Arts
    (Norwich) 205
  St Stephen Walbrook (London) 115, 116
  Scottish National Gallery of Modern
    Art (Edinburgh) 515
  Tate Britain (London) 95
  Walker Art Gallery (Liverpool) 382
  Yorkshire Sculpture Park 417
Moorland 38
Moot Hall (Aldeburgh) 206–7
Morar 550
Moray *see* Highlands and Islands
More, Sir Thomas 54, 126
Morecambe Bay **374**
  hotels 569
  restaurants 596
Moreton family 307
Moreton-in-Marsh
  hotels 568
  restaurants 594
Morgan, Dr William 441
Morpeth, hotels 571
Morris, Roger 552
Morris, William 332
  Castle Howard 403
  Jesus College (Cambridge) 216
  Kelmscott 224–5
  Peterhouse (Cambridge) 217
Morwellham Quay **297**
Mosaics, Roman 333
Moseley Old Hall 307
Mother Shipton's Cave (Knaresborough)
  392–3
Motor homes 559
Motor racing 71
Mott, Hay and Anderson 429
Motte and bailey castles 490
Mount Edgcumbe Park 248, 296
Mount Grace Priory 354, **398**
Mountbatten, Earl 35, 166
Mousa Broch 532
Mousehole 282
  hotels 567
  restaurants 592
Moustafa, Ahmed 521
Moyse's Hall (Bury St Edmunds) 210, 211
Mr and Mrs Andrews (Gainsborough) 167
Muir of Dinnet Nature Reserve 544
Mull, Isle of **550–51**
  hotels 573
  restaurants 603
Mullion, hotels 567

The Mumbles 470
Mumby, pubs 607
Muncaster Castle 368
Mungo, St 505, 520–21
Murillo, Esteban 523
Museums and galleries
  admission prices 621
  shops in 611
  1853 Gallery (Bradford) 415
  Abbot Hall Art Gallery and Museum
    of Lakeland Life (Kendal) 372
  Aberdeen Art Gallery **542**
  Aldeburgh Museum 207
  Alexander Keiller Museum (Avebury)
    267
  American Museum (Bath) **265**
  Anne of Cleves House (Lewes) 184
  Armley Mills Museum (Leeds) 414
  Arnolfini (Bristol) 260
  Ashmolean Museum (Oxford) 226, **228**
  At-Bristol 260
  Auchindrain Museum **552**
  Baltic Centre for Contemporary Art
    (Newcastle upon Tyne) 15, 428, **429**
  Barbara Hepworth Museum and
    Sculpture Garden (St Ives) 281
  Beamish Open Air Museum 11, 15,
    428–9
  The Beatles Story (Liverpool) **381**
  Beatrix Potter Gallery (Hawkshead) 371
  Big Pit National Coal Museum
    (Blaenavon) 461, **478**
  Birmingham Museum and Art Gallery
    323
  Black and White House (Hereford) 320
  Blackhouse Museum (Arnol) 533
  Blackwell Arts and Crafts House
    (Bowness-on-Windermere) 371
  Blaenavon Ironworks 478
  Blists Hill Victorian Town (Ironbridge
    Gorge) **319**
  Bodmin Jail 288, 289
  Bodmin Town Museum 288, 289
  Bowes Museum (Barnard Castle) **430**
  Bradford Industrial Museum 415
  Brantwood (Coniston) 372
  Brighton Museum and Art Gallery 178
  Bristol Museum and Art Gallery **261**
  British Golf Museum (St Andrews) 503
  British Museum (London) 77, 106,
    110–11
  Brontë Parsonage Museum (Haworth)
    416
  Brunel's SS Great Britain (Bristol) **260**
  Buckler's Hard 172
  Burns Cottage **519**
  The Burrell Collection (Glasgow) **523**
  Butcher Row House (Ledbury) 321
  Buxton Museum and Art Gallery 338
  Cadbury World (Bournville) 323
  Canterbury Heritage Museum 190
  Canterbury Roman Museum 190
  Captain Cook Memorial Museum
    (Whitby) **400**
  Carnegie Birthplace Museum
    (Dunfermline) 505
  Cartwright Hall Art Gallery (Bradford)
    415
  Castle Museum (Colchester) 209
  Castle Museum (Norwich) **204–5**
  Center for Alternative Technology
    (Machynlleth) 466
  Ceredigion Museum (Aberystwyth) 467
  Charles Dickens Birthplace Museum
    (Portsmouth) 173
  Charles Dickens Museum (London) 109
  Christchurch Mansion (Ipswich) 207

Museums and galleries (cont.)
Churchill War Rooms (London) 92, **93**
Cider Museum (Hereford) 320
City Museum (Lancaster) 374, 375
Clive Museum (Powis Castle) 464
Coalbrookdale Museum of Iron **318**
Coalport China Museum **319**
Coggeshall Grange Barn 209
The Collection – Usher Gallery
(Lincoln) 345
Corbridge Roman Town - Hadrian's
Wall 427
Corinium Museum (Cirencester) 333
Courtauld Gallery (London) 84
Coventry Transport Museum 323
Craft in the Bay (Cardiff) **474**
Crich Tramway Village 343
Cromarty Courthouse 539
Cromwell Museum (Huntingdon) 212
Custom House (King's Lynn) 201
D-Day Museum (Portsmouth) 173
Dales Countryside Museum (Hawes)
389
Dartmouth Museum 294
Dennis Severs House (London) 129
Design Museum (London) 126
DIG – An Archaeological Adventure
(York) **411**
Discovering Stamford 347
Discovery (Dundee) 503
Dock Museum (Barrow-in-Furness)
372, 373
Dorset County Museum (Dorchester)
273
Dove Cottage and the Wordsworth
Museum (Grasmere) 370
Dylan Thomas Centre (Swansea) 470
Eden Camp **404**
Elgar's Birthplace (Worcester) 322
Elgin Museum 542
Elizabethan House Museum (Great
Yarmouth) 203
Embankment Galleries (London) 84
Eureka! (Halifax) 417
Falmouth Art Gallery 285
Fitzwilliam Museum (Cambridge)
13, **218**
Flambards Experience (Helston) 284
Fox Talbot Museum (Lacock) 259
Freud Museum (London) 127
Gainsborough's House (Sudbury)
167, 210
Gasworks Museum (Biggar) 517
Georgian House (Bristol) **260**
Gladstone Pottery Museum (Stoke-
on-Trent) 315
Glasgow Science Centre **522**
Glynn Vivian Art Gallery (Swansea) 470
Grace Darling Museum (Bamburgh) 424
Grassington Folk Museum **390**
Grimsby Fishing Heritage Centre 407
Groam House Museum (Rosemarkie)
539
Hands on History (Kingston upon
Hull) 406
Helston Museum 284
Herbert Gallery and Museum
(Coventry) 323
Hereford Museum and Art Gallery 320
Heritage Centre (Ledbury) 321
Hexham Old Gaol 426–7
Historic Dockyard (Chatham) 192
HMS Belfast (London) **121**
Holburne Museum of Art (Bath) **264**
Hollytrees Museum (Colchester) 209
House of the Tailor of Gloucester
(Gloucester) 333

Museums and galleries (cont.)
Hugh Miller Museum (Cromarty) 539
Hunterian Art Gallery (Glasgow) 17, **523**
Imperial War Museum North (Salford
Quays) 375, **379**
International Slavery Museum
(Liverpool) 381
Inverness Museum and Art Gallery
17, 540
Jackfield Tile Museum (Ironbridge
Gorge) **318**
Jane Austen Centre (Bath) 262, **264**
Jorvik Viking Centre (York) 15, 409, **410**
Judge's Lodgings (Lancaster) 374, 375
Keats House (London) 127
Kelvingrove Art Gallery and Museum
(Glasgow) 17, 483, **524–5**
Kendal Museum 372
Keswick Museum and Art Gallery 363
King's Own Scottish Borderers
Regimental Museum (Berwick-upon-
Tweed) 422
Lady Lever Art Gallery (Port Sunlight)
383
Lake Village Museum (Glastonbury)
257
Laurel and Hardy Museum (Ulverston)
372, 373
Leeds Art Gallery 414
Leeds City Museum 414
Linley Sambourne House (London)
126–7
Little Hall (Lavenham) 210
Lizard Lighthouse Heritage Centre 284
Llandudno Museum 449
Llechwedd Slate Caverns (Blaenau
Ffestiniog) 455
Loch Ness Centre and Exhibition
17, **540**
London Dungeon **85**
London's Transport Museum 83, **84**
Lowestoft Museum 203
Lowry Centre (Salford Quays) 375, **379**
Ludlow Museum 316, 317
Lyme Regis Museum 274
M-Shed (Bristol) **260**
McManus Galleries (Dundee) 503
Madame Tussaud's (London) **108**
Madame Tussaud's (Warwick Castle)
326
Maeldune Centre (Maldon) 213
Magna (Rotherham) **417**
Manchester Art Gallery **378**
Manchester Museum **378**
Manchester United Museum (Salford
Quays) 375, **379**
Maritime Museum (Aberdeen) **544**
Maritime Museum (Kingston upon
Hull) 406
Maritime Museum (Lancaster) 374, 375
Market Hall Museum (Warwick) 325
Mary Rose Museum (Portsmouth) 173
Merseyside Maritime Museum
(Liverpool) **381**
Moray Motor Museum (Elgin) 542
Morwellham Quay **297**
Moyse's Hall (Bury St Edmunds) 210, 211
Museum of Barnstaple and North
Devon 291
Museum of Biggar and Upper
Clydesdale 517
Museum of Childhood (Edinburgh)
514, 515
Museum of the Gorge (Ironbridge
Gorge) **318**
Museum of the History of Science
(Oxford) **228**

Museums and galleries (cont.)
Museum of Islay Life 553
Museum of the Isles 534
Museum of the Jewellery Quarter
(Birmingham) 323
Museum of Liverpool 361, **381**
Museum of London **117**
Museum of London, Docklands 129
Museum of Norwich **205**
Museum of Nottingham Life 340
Museum of Oxford **229**
Museum of Royal Worcester
(Worcester) 322
Museum of Science and Industry
(Manchester) **378**
Museum of Somerset (Taunton) 256
National Coal Mining Museum
(Wakefield) **417**
National Football Museum
(Manchester) **377**
National Gallery (London) 12, 77, **86–7**
National Gallery of Scotland
(Edinburgh) 17, **508**
National Horseracing Museum
(Newmarket) 211
National Maritime Museum (London)
129
National Maritime Museum Cornwall
(Falmouth) 285
National Media Museum (Bradford) 415
National Motor Museum (Beaulieu) 172
National Museum Cardiff 16, **475**
National Museum of Scotland
(Edinburgh) **509**
National Portrait Gallery (London)
12, **85**
National Railway Museum (York)
410–11
National Roman Legion Museum
(Caerleon) 478
National Trust Assembly Rooms and
Fashion Museum (Bath) **264**
National Trust Carriage Museum
(Barnstaple) 291
National Waterfront Museum
(Swansea) 470
National Waterways Museum
(Gloucester) 333
Natural History Museum (London)
12, 98, 100, **104**
Nelson Museum (Monmouth) 479
New Lanark 518
No. 1 Royal Crescent (Bath) **264**
North Devon Maritime Museum
(Appledore) 291
Northampton Museum and Art
Gallery 347
The Old Operating Theatre (London)
121
Our Dynamic Earth (Edinburgh) **515**
Owain Glyndŵr Centre (Machynlleth)
466
Oxford Castle Unlocked **229**
Oxford University Museum of Natural
History **229**
Padstow Museum 289
Peak District Mining Museum
(Matlock Bath) 340
Pencil Museum (Keswick) 363
Penlee House Gallery and Museum
(Penzance) 282, 283
People's Palace (Glasgow) **521**
Perth Museum and Art Gallery 502
Pier Arts Centre (Stromness) 532
Pitt Rivers Museum (Oxford) **229**
Plymouth Mayflower Exhibition 296
Poldark Mine 284

Museums and galleries (cont.)
Pollok House (Glasgow) **523**
Poole Museum 274, 275
Port Sunlight Museum and Garden Village 383
Portsmouth Historic Dockyard 173
Potteries Museum and Art Gallery (Hanley) 315
Powell-Cotton Museum (Margate) 187
Priest's House Museum (Wimborne Minster) 275
Prison and Police Museum (Ripon) 393
Provand's Lordship (Glasgow) **521**
Quarry Bank Mill (Styal) **314**
Queen's Gallery (London) 90, **91**
Radnorshire Museum (Llandrindod Wells) 465
The Red House (Aldeburgh) 207
Regimental Museum (Monmouth) 478–9
Regimental Museum of the Highlands (Fort George) 541
Regimental Museum of Royal Northumberland Fusiliers (Alnwick Castle) 424
Riverside Museum (Glasgow) **522–3**
Roald Dahl Museum (Great Missenden) **234**
Roman Baths (Bath) **264–5**
Roman Museum (Ribchester) 375
Rotunda Museum (Scarborough) 401
Royal Academy (London) **85**, 88
Royal Albert Memorial Museum and Art Gallery (Exeter) **293**
Royal Armouries (Leeds) 414
Royal Cornwall Museum (Truro) 285
Royal Observatory Greenwich (London) 129
Royal Pump Room Museum (Harrogate) 392
Russell-Cotes Art Gallery and Museum (Bournemouth) 275
Rydal Mount (Rydal) 370
Ryedale Folk Museum (Hutton-le-Hole) 398
Sainsbury Centre for Visual Arts (Norwich) **205**
St Fagans National History Museum (Cardiff) **475**
St John's House Museum (Warwick) 325
St Mungo Museum of Religious Life and Art (Glasgow) **521**
Salford Museum and Art Gallery 375
Salisbury Museum **269**
Salt's Mill (Leeds) 415
Scarborough Art Gallery 401
Science Museum (London) 12, 100, **104**
Scottish Fisheries Museum (East Neuk) 504
Scottish Kiltmaker Visitor Centre (Inverness) 540
Scottish National Gallery of Modern Art One and Two (Edinburgh) **515**
Scottish National Portrait Gallery (Edinburgh) **508–9**
Sea City Museum (Southampton) 173
Sherlock Holmes Museum (London) **108**
Shetland Museum (Lerwick) 532
Shibden Hall Museum (Halifax) 417
Shrewsbury Museum and Art Gallery 316
Sir John Soane's Museum (London) **116–17**
Somerset Rural Life Museum (Glastonbury) 257
Southwold Museum 206

Museums and galleries (cont.)
Stott Park Bobbin Mill (Finsthwaite) 371
Stranger's Hall (Norwich) **205**
Streetlife Museum of Transport (Kingston upon Hull) 406, 407
Sutton Hoo 207
Swaledale Folk Museum (Reeth Green) **389**
Swansea Museum 470
Swiss Cottage (Osborne House) 172
Tain Through Time 539
Tate Britain (London) 77, **95**
Tate Liverpool 11, **381**
Tate Modern (London) 12, **125**
Tate St Ives 281
Techniquest (Cardiff) 474
Tenement House (Glasgow) 17, **522**
Thackray Medical Museum (Leeds) 414
Thinktank, Birmingham Science Museum 323
Tom Brown's School Museum (Uffington) 225
Torquay Museum 294
Torridon Countryside Centre 538
Totnes Elizabethan Museum 295
Tullie House Museum (Carlisle) 362
Turner Contemporary (Margate) 187
UK Border Agency National Museum (Liverpool) 381
HMS *Unicorn* (Dundee) 503
V&A Design Museum (Dundee) 503
V&A Museum of Childhood (London) 129
Verulamium Museum (St Albans) **236**
Victoria and Albert Museum (London) 12, 76, 101, **102–3**
Walker Art Gallery (Liverpool) 350, 381, **382–3**
Wallace Collection (London) **108–9**
Wells & Mendip Museum (Wells) 256
Westgate Museum (Winchester) 174
Wheal Martyn China Clay Museum 285
Whitby Museum and Pannett Art Gallery **400**
The Whithorn Story 519
Whitworth Art Gallery (Manchester) **378**
William Wilberforce House (Kingston upon Hull) 406, 407
The Wilson, Cheltenham Art Gallery and Museum 332
Wordsworth House (Cockermouth) 366
World of Beatrix Potter (Windermere) 371
World Museum Liverpool **383**
World of Wedgwood (Barlaston) 315
York Art Gallery **411**
York Castle Museum 409, **410**
Yorkshire Museum (York) 408, **410**
Yorkshire Sculpture Park **417**
Music **612**
festivals 67, 68
London 158–9
The Music Lesson (Vermeer) 90
Mylne, Robert 552

N
Nant Gwynant 452–3, 456
pubs 608
Napoleon I, Emperor 59
Waterloo Bridge (Betws-y-Coed) 454
Napoleon III, Emperor 241
Nash, John 29, 59
Buckingham Palace (London) 90
Regent's Park (London) 109
Royal Mews (London) 91
Royal Opera Arcade (London) 89
Royal Pavilion (Brighton) 163, 182–3

Nash, Paul 84
Nash, Richard "Beau" **265**
Nasmyth, Alexander 509
View of Culzean Castle 526
National Botanic Garden of Wales 470
National Coal Mining Museum (Wakefield) **417**
National Football Museum (Manchester) **377**
The National Forest 335
National Gallery (London) 12, 77, **86–7**
National Gallery of Scotland (Edinburgh) 17, **508**
National Health Service 63
National Horseracing Museum (Newmarket) 211
National Library of Wales (Aberystwyth) 467
National Marine Aquarium (Plymouth) 296
National Maritime Museum (London) 129
National Maritime Museum Cornwall (Falmouth) 285
National Media Museum (Bradford) 415
National Motor Museum (Beaulieu) 172
National Museum Cardiff 16, **475**
National Museum of Scotland (Edinburgh) **509**
National parks
Brecon Beacons 16, 437, 461, **472–3**
Dartmoor 14, 244, **298–9**
Exmoor 14, 242–3, 244, **254–5**
Lake District 364–5
North York Moors 15, **399**
Northumberland 425
Peak District 2–3, **342–3**
Pembrokeshire Coast 10, 16, 462
Snowdonia 16, 446, 452–3, 455
Yorkshire Dales 350
National Portrait Gallery (London) 12, **85**
National Railway Museum (York) **410–11**
National Roman Legion Museum (Caerleon) 478
National Stud (Newmarket) 211
National Theatre (London) 156, 157
National Trust 32, **33**, 558, 559, 622, 625
National Trust Assembly Rooms and Fashion Museum (Bath) **264**
National Trust Carriage Museum (Barnstaple) 291
National Trust for Scotland 559, 622, 625
National Waterfront Museum (Swansea) 470
National Waterways Museum (Gloucester) 333
Natural History Museum (London) 12, 98, 100, **104**
Nature reserves *see* Wildlife
Neal Street (London) 82
Neal's Yard (London) 82
The Needles 170, 172
Neidpath Castle 490
Nelson, Admiral Lord Horatio 58
Battle of Trafalgar 59
coat of arms 35
HMS *Victory* 173
Lord Nelson pub (Burnham Market) 200
Monmouth 479
Neptune's Staircase (Caledonian Canal) 551
Ness, Loch **540**
Nettlefold, Archibald 295
Neville family 326, 476
New Change (London) 114
New College (Oxford) **230**
New Forest **172**, 252

New Lanark **518**
New Year 69
Newbury, restaurants 589
Newby Hall **393**
Newcastle upon Tyne 15, 60, 421, **428–9**
    airport 634
    hotels 571
    restaurants 598
Newlands Valley **366**
Newlyn 280, 281, 282
Newlyn School 282
Newman, John Henry 101
Newmarket **211**
    restaurants 588
Newquay
    hotels 567
    restaurants 593
Newspapers 29, 631
Newton, Sir Isaac 56
    statue of 217
Newton Abbot, pubs 606
Newton Aycliffe, restaurants 598
Nicholson, Ben 95, 218, 281
Nicolson, Harold 193
Nightingale, Florence 60, 166
Ninian, St 519, 521
Norfolk see East Anglia
Norfolk, Dukes of 176
Norfolk, Earl of 207
Norfolk Coast Path 41
Norfolk Lavender 200
Normans 50–51
    castles 52
    invasion of Britain 438, 442
    and Scotland 486
North Devon Maritime Museum
    (Appledore) 291
North Downs Way 41
North Pennines tour 15, **431**
North Sea oil 487
North Uist 533
North Wales **444–59**
    climate 72
    hotels 571
    map 446–7
    pubs 608
    restaurants 599
    A Week in Wales and the West 10, **16**
North York Moors 15, **399**
North Yorkshire Moors Railway **398**
Northampton **347**
    restaurants 595
Northamptonshire see East Midlands
Northern England **348–433**
    abbeys 354–5
    The Industrial Revolution in the North
        352–3
    Lancashire and the Lakes 358–83
    map 22–3, 350–51
    Northumbria 418–33
    A Week in Northern England 11, **15**
    Yorkshire and the Humber Region
        384–417
Northumberland see Northumbria
Northumberland, Dukes of 130, 424
Northumberland National Park 425
Northumbria 15, 50, 51, **418–33**
    climate 73
    hotels 570–71
    map 420–21
    pubs 608
    restaurants 598–9
Norwich **204–5**
    hotels 563
    pubs 605
    restaurants 588
Norwich School 205

Nothe Fort (Weymouth) 273
Notting Hill (London) **127**
Notting Hill Carnival 67
Nottingham **340**
    hotels 568
    pubs 607
    restaurants 595
Nottingham Goose Fair 68
Nottinghamshire see East Midlands
Nunnington Hall **397**

O

The O2 (London) 129, 158, 159
Oare 254
Oast houses 164–5
Oban **550**
    restaurants 603
Offa, King of Mercia 50, 237, 465
Offa's Dyke 440, 465
Offa's Dyke Footpath 40, 465
Okehampton 298
    restaurants 593
Old Merchant's House (Great Yarmouth)
    203
The Old Operating Theatre (London)
    121
Old Post Office (Tintagel) 289
Old Royal Naval College (London) 129
Old Sarum 267, 268
The Old Ship Hotel (Brighton) 178
Old Spitalfields market (London) 153
Old Vic (London) 156, 157
Oliver, Isaac 235
Olivier, Laurence 28, 288, 331
Olympic Games 64, 65, 129
Omega Workshops 167
One Canada Square (London) 65
Open-air theatre, London **157**
Opening hours 621
    shops 610
Opera **158**
    Royal Opera House (London) 83, **84**
Ophelia (Millais) 60
Ordnance Survey maps 40
Oxford Castle 207
Orkney Islands **532**
    hotels 573
    maps 19, 23, 531
Orton, Joe 128
Orwell, George 128, 552–3
Osborne House 166, **172**
Osmund, St 268
The Other Side (Hockney) 415
Ottery St Mary 293
Our Dynamic Earth (Edinburgh) **515**
Outdoor activities **614–17**
Overbecks 248
Overton Bridge, pubs 608
Owen, Richard 316
Owen, Robert 518
Owen, Wilfred 316
Oxburgh Hall and Garden 199
Oxford 11, 13, 160–61, 221, **226–31**
    hotels 564
    pubs 605
    restaurants 589
    street-by-street map 226–7
    student life 230
Oxford and Cambridge Boat Race
    66, 70
Oxford Castle Quarter **229**
Oxford Circus (London) 554–5
Oxford University 13, 162, **230–31**
Oxford University Museum of Natural
    History (Oxford) **229**
Oxfordshire see Thames Valley
Oyelowo, David 28

P

Packwood House 307
Padstow **289**
    restaurants 593
Paignton 277, 294
Paignton Zoo 294
Paine, Tom 199
Painswick 309
    hotels 568
Palaces
    Bishop's Palace (St David's) 468
    Bishop's Palace (Wells) 256–7
    Blenheim Palace 13, 32, 162, 221,
        232–3
    Buckingham Palace (London)
        76, **90–91**
    Culross Palace 505
    Dunfermline Palace 504
    Earl's Palace (Kirkwall) 532
    Falkland Palace **504**
    Hampton Court 30, 55, 159, **177**
    Holyroodhouse (Edinburgh) 17, **514**
    Kensington Palace (London) **105**
    Linlithgow Palace **505**
    St James's Palace (London) 88
    Scone Palace 502
    Scottish classical palaces 491
    see also Castles; Stately homes
Pall Mall (London) 89
Palladio, Andrea 130
Palmerston, Lord 217
Pangbourne 238
Pannett, Robert 400
Pannini, Paolo 403
Pansies 31
Parbury, Kathleen 423
Paris, Matthew 44
Parking 636–7
Parks and gardens
    Abbey Dore Court 320
    Abbotsbury Sub-Tropical Gardens 272
    Anglesey Abbey 212
    Anne Hathaway's Cottage (Stratford-
        upon-Avon) 325, 331
    Armadale Castle Gardens 534
    Athelhampton House 249, 273
    Bancroft Gardens (Stratford-upon-
        Avon) 328, 330
    Battersea Park (London) 79
    Beale Park 238
    Beth Chatto Garden (Colchester) 209
    Biblical Gardens (Elgin) 542
    Blenheim Palace 232, 233
    Botanical Gardens (Edgbaston) 323
    Chatsworth House 335, **338–9**
    Chelsea Physic Garden (London) 126
    Cheltenham Imperial Gardens 324
    Cirencester Park 333
    Compton Acres (Bournemouth) 275
    Cotehele 248, **297**
    Crarae Gardens **552**
    Crathes Castle and Gardens 545
    Dartington Hall Gardens 295
    East Lambrook Manor 249
    Eden Project 14, **286–7**
    Fell Foot Park (Newby Bridge) 371
    Gardens of the Rose **237**
    Gardens through the Ages **30–31**
    Glendurgan 248, 285
    Great Dixter 186
    Green Park (London) 79
    Greenwich Park (London) 79
    Hampstead Heath (London) 79, **128**
    Hampton Court 177
    Hampton Court Castle Gardens
        (Leominster) 317
    Hestercombe Garden 256

Parks and gardens (cont.)
Hidcote Manor Gardens 325
Holland Park (London) 78, **126–7**
Hyde Park (London) 76, 79, **105**
Inverewe Garden 538
Kensington Gardens (London) 12, 79, **105**
Kew Gardens (London) 78, 130
Kiftsgate Court Garden 325
Knightshayes Court 249, 293
Lanhydrock 248, **288**, 289
Levens Hall **373**
London **78–9**
Lost Gardens of Heligan 248, 285
Midlands garden tour 13, **324–5**
Montacute House 249
Morrab Gardens (Penzance) 282
Mount Edgcumbe Park 248, 296
National Botanic Garden of Wales 470
Newby Hall **393**
Overbecks 248
Oxburgh Hall and Garden 199
Parnham 249
Pavilion Gardens (Buxton) 338
Powis Castle **464**
Priory Park (Great Malvern) 321
Queen Elizabeth Forest Park 499
Queen Elizabeth Park (London) 129
Regent's Park (London) 79, 107
RHS Harlow Carr Gardens 392
RHS Rosemoor Garden 290
RHS Wisley 176
Richmond Park (London) 78, 130
Russell Square Gardens (London) 79
St James's Park (London) 79
Seven Sisters Country Park 185
Sissinghurst Castle Garden 193
Snowshill Manor 324
Stanway House 324
Stourhead 245, 249, **270–71**
Stowe **234**
Studley Royal **394–5**
Sudely Castle 324
Trebah 285
Trelissick 248, 285
Trengwainton 248, 280
Trewithen 248, 285
Tropical World (Leeds) 414
University Botanic Garden (Cambridge) **217**
University of Oxford Botanic Garden **228**
Waddesdon Manor 234
Warwick Castle 325
West Country gardens **248–9**
Williamson Park (Lancaster) 374, 375
Windsor Great Park 239
Witley Court and Gardens 317
Woburn Abbey **234**
Parliament (London) *see* Houses of Parliament
Parliament Hill (London) 128
Parliament House (Edinburgh) **512**
Parnham 249
Parr, Catherine 324
Parracombe 254
Passes, rail 638
Passports 620, 625
Pavey Ark 369
Pavilion Gardens (Buxton) 338
Paxton, Sir Joseph 61, 338, 416
Paycocke's (Coggeshall) 209
Peak District 2–3, 335, 337
  Peak District tour 342–3
  Tissington Trail 341
Peak District Mining Museum (Matlock Bath) 340

Peasants Hunting Rabbits with Ferrets (tapestry) 523
Peasants' revolt (1381) 53, 122
Peddars Way 41
Peebles
  hotels 572
  restaurants 602
Peers of the realm 35
Pellegrini, Giovanni Antonio 402
Pembridge 317
Pembroke, Earls of 269
Pembroke, restaurants 600
Pembroke College (Cambridge) **216**
Pembroke Ferry, pubs 609
Pembrokeshire Coast National Park 10, 16, 462
Pembrokeshire Coastal Path 40
Pen y Fan 10, 16, 473
Pen-y-Garreg 466
Penallt, pubs 609
Pencil Museum (Keswick) 363
Pendennis Castle (Falmouth) 285
Penlee House Gallery and Museum (Penzance) 282, 283
Penmaenpool, hotels 571
Penn, William 235
Pennines
  North Pennines tour 431
  Pennine Way 40, 342, 425
Penrith **362**
Pensford, pubs 606
Penshurst Place 193
Pentland Hills **517**
Pentre Ifan 46
Penwith tour **280**
Penzance **282–3**
  hotels 567
  pubs 606
  restaurants 593
People's Palace (Glasgow) **521**
Pepys, Samuel 217
Percy family 424
Personal security **626–7**
Perth **502**
  hotels 572
Perth and Kinross *see* Highlands and Islands
Peter the Great, Tsar 202
Peter Jones (London) 152, 153
Peter of Langtoft 289
Peterborough **198**
  restaurants 588
Peterhouse (Cambridge) **217**
Peterloo Massacre (1819) **377**
Petersfield, restaurants 587
Petroc, St 288
Petrol 637
Petticoat Lane market (London) 153
Petworth House 13, 26, **176**
Pevsner, Sir Nikolaus 393
Pharmacies 627
Philip II, King of Spain 55, 297
Piano, Renzo 121
Covent Garden Piazza and Central Market (London) **83**
Picasso, Pablo
  Ashmolean Museum (Oxford) 228
  Manchester Art Gallery 378
  Sainsbury Centre for Visual Arts (Norwich) 205
  Scottish National Gallery of Modern Art One and Two (Edinburgh) 515
  Tate Modern (London) 125
Piccadilly (London), street-by-street map 88–9
Piccadilly Circus (London) **85**, 89
Piccadilly Crafts (London) 153

Pickering
  hotels 570
  pubs 608
Picnics 577
Picts 486
Piece Hall (Halifax) 352, 417
Pike o'Stickle 369
Pilgrim Fathers 56, 57, 173, 296
Piper, John 383
Pitlochry 17, **545**
  hotels 573
Pitt Rivers Museum (Oxford) **229**
Pittville Pump Room (Cheltenham) 332
Plaid Cymru 441
Plas Newydd 454
Plas-yn-Rhiw 457
Plath, Sylvia 416
Plockton
  hotels 573
  restaurants 603
Plymouth **296**
  restaurants 593
Polanski, Roman 273
Police 626, 627
Politics 27–8
Pollok House (Glasgow) **523**
Polo 71, 159
Polperro 288
Polruan 288
Ponsonby, Sarah 454
Pontcysyllte Aqueduct 454
Pony trekking **615**, 617
Poole **274–5**
  hotels 566
  restaurants 591
Pop music, London 158–9
Pope, Alexander 321, 333
Porlock 255
  restaurants 591
Port Appin, restaurants 603
Port Isaac, restaurants 593
Port Sunlight 353, 383
Porth Neigwl 457
Porth Oer 457
Porthleven, pubs 606
Portmeirion 10, 16, 436, **458–9**
  hotels 571
  restaurants 599
Portobello Road (London) **127**, 153
Portrait of Richard James (Hogarth) 218
Portree 535
Portsmouth **173**
  hotels 563
  restaurants 587
Portsoy, pubs 609
Postal services **631**
Postbridge 298
Potter, Beatrix **371**
  Beatrix Potter Gallery (Hawkshead) 371
  Dunkeld 545
  Hill Top (Near Sawrey) 371
  House of the Tailor of Gloucester (Gloucester) 333
  Newlands Valley 366
  World of Beatrix Potter (Windermere) 371
The Potteries 315
Potteries Museum and Art Gallery (Hanley) 315
Poundbury Camp 273
Poussin, Nicolas 245, 508
  The Choice of Hercules 271
Powell-Cotton Museum (Margate) 187
Powis Castle **464**
Praxiteles 176
Pre-Raphaelites 95, 224–5, 378

Prehistoric Britain **46–7**
Arbor Low 342
Avebury 14, 46, 47, **267**
Carloway Broch 533
Castlerigg Stone Circle 47, 363, 365
Cerne Abbas 14, 273
Chanctonbury Ring 184
Cissbury Ring 184
Flag Fen Bronze Age Centre
(Peterborough) 198
Great Orme Copper Mines 449
Grimes Graves **198–9**
Grimspound 298
Hillside Chalk Figures **225**
Kents Cavern 294
Lake Village Museum (Glastonbury) 257
Long Man of Wilmington 185
Long Meg and her Daughters 362
Long Mynd 316
Maes Howe 532
Maiden Castle 47, 273
Maumbury Rings 273
Mousa Broch 532
Old Sarum 267, 268
Parc Le Breose 470
Pentre Ifan 16
Penwith tour 280
Poundbury Camp 273
Ring of Brodgar 528, 532
Rollright Stones 224
Silbury Hill 266
Skara Brae 47, 532
Standing Stones of Callanish 533
Standing Stones of Stenness 532
Stonehenge 10, 14, 47, 245, **266–7**
Uffington Castle 225
Vale of the White Horse **225**
Wayland's Smithy 225
West Kennet Long Barrow 266–7
White Horse of Uffington 47, **225**
Wiltshire's prehistoric sites 266–7
Preparing for a Fancy Dress Ball (Etty) 411
Presbyterian Church 484, 486
Prideaux Place (Padstow) 289
Priestley, Joseph 260
Priest's House Museum (Wimborne
Minster) 275
Prince's Cairn (Road to the Isles tour)
550
"Princes in the Tower" 122, **123**
Principality Stadium (Cardiff) 16, 474
Priories *see* Abbeys and priories
Prison and Police Museum (Ripon) 393
Pritchard, Dafydd 456
Proctor, Sir Stephen 394
Provand's Lordship (Glasgow) **521**
Provost Skene's House (Aberdeen) **543**
Public conveniences 624
Public holidays 69
Pubs 26, **604–9**
accommodation in 557
signs 579
traditional British pub **578–9**
Pugin, A W N 383
Punting on the Cam **216**
Purbeck, Isle of **274**
restaurants 590
Puritans **235**
Pwllheli, restaurants 599

Q
Quarry Bank Mill (Styal) **314**
Queen Elizabeth Forest Park 499
Queen Elizabeth Park (London) 129
Queen Elizabeth's Hunting Lodge
(Epping Forest) 213
Queen's Chapel (London) **89**

Queens' College (Cambridge) 215,
216–17
Queen's College (Oxford) **230**
Queen's Gallery (London) 90, **91**
Queen's House (London) 129
Quex Park (Margate) 187
Quiraing 535

R
Rackham, Arthur 238, 449
Radcliffe Camera (Oxford) 160–61, 223,
227, **231**
Radcot Bridge 225
Radio 29, 631
Raeburn, Henry, *Rev. Robert Walker
Skating on Duddingston Loch* 508
Rahere 117
Rail travel 632, 633, **638–9**
Bala Lake Railway 454
Bodmin & Wenford Railway 288
Cliff Railway (Aberystwyth) 467
Ffestiniog Railway 455, **456–7**
from airports 634–5
Industrial Revolution 352, 353
Keighley and Worth Valley Railway
416
National Railway Museum (York)
410–11
North Yorkshire Moors Railway **398**
Ravenglass & Eskdale Railway 368
Romney, Hythe & Dymchurch Light
Railway 187
scenic train rides 639
Settle-to-Carlisle Railway 384
Snowdon Mountain Railway 455
South Devon Steam Railway 295, 290
Strathspey Steam Railway 548
Rainfall 72–3
Raleigh, Sir Walter 55, 296
Ramsay, Allan 508
Raphael 228
Reading, restaurants 589
Real tennis 159
Rebecca, Biagio 213
"Rebecca Riots" 441
Reculver Fort 187
Recumbent Figure (Moore) 95
Redmayne, Eddie 28
Referendum 2016 (European Union)
64, 65
Regent Street Christmas Lights 68
Regent's Park (London) 79, 107, **109**
Regent's Park and Bloomsbury
(London) 79, **106–11**
area map 107
hotels 561
pubs 604
restaurants 584–5
Regimental Museum (Monmouth)
478–9
Regimental Museum of the Highlands
(Fort George) 541
Regimental Museum of Royal
Northumberland Fusiliers (Alnwick
Castle) 424
Reilly, Michael 84
Religious organizations 625
Rembrandt van Rijn
Burrell Collection (Glasgow) 523
Kenwood House (London) 128
Man in Armour 524
Queen's Gallery (London) 91
Walker Art Gallery (Liverpool) 382
Wallace Collection (London) 109
Remembrance Day 68
Renoir, Pierre Auguste 218, 404
At the Theatre 87

Responsible travel **624–5**
Restaurants **574–603**
chain 576
children in 622–3
Devon and Cornwall 591–3
Downs and Channel Coast 586–7
East Anglia 587–8
East Midlands 594–5
The Flavours of Britain **580–81**
food scene 574
The Heart of England 593–4
Highlands and Islands 602–3
in hotels 575
Lancashire and the Lakes 595–7
London 582–6
Lowlands 600–602
North Wales 599
Northumbria 598–9
with rooms 575
South and Mid-Wales 599–600
Thames Valley 588–9
Wessex 589–91
Yorkshire and the Humber Region
597–8
see also Food and drink
Restormel Castle 288
*Rev. Robert Walker Skating on
Duddingston Loch* (Raeburn) 508
Reynolds, Sir Joshua
Castle Howard 403
Cawdor Castle 541
Harewood House 414
Ickworth House 211
Saltram House 296
Woburn Abbey 234
Reyntiens, Patrick 383
Rhinog moors 459
Ribble Valley **375**
Ribblehead Viaduct 384
Richard I, King 44
coat of arms 34
statue of 92
Richard II, King 44, 225
Richard III, King 44
Middleham Castle 389
"Princes in the Tower" 123
Wars of the Roses 53
Richard, Earl of Cornwall 289
Richard of Haldingham 320
Richardson, John 365
Richborough Roman Fort 187
Richmond (London) **130**
Richmond (Yorkshire) **388–9**
Richmond Park (London) 78, 130
Richter, Gerhard 125
Ride sharing 637
The Ridgeway 41
Ridley, John 431
Ridley, Nicholas 431
Martyrs' Memorial (Oxford) 226, 229
Rievaulx Abbey **397**
Rievaulx Abbey (Girtin) 397
Ring of Brodgar 528, 532
Ringstead, pubs 605
Ripley **393**
restaurants 597
Ripon **393**
Ritz, César 85, 88
Ritz Hotel (London) **85**, 88
Riverside Museum (Glasgow) **522–3**
Rizzio, David 514
Road signs 636
Road to the Isles tour 17, **550–51**
Roald Dahl Museum **234**
Rob Roy 498, **499**
Abbotsford House 516
Falkland Palace 504

Robert the Bruce 509
  Battle of Bannockburn 486, 500
  Drum Castle 545
  heart 507, 516, 519
  Pass of Brander 551
  Rathlin 553
  St Fillan's Cave (East Neuk) 504
  tomb of 504
Robin Hood's Bay **401**
  restaurants 597
Robinson, Thomas 402
Rochester **192**
  hotels 563
  restaurants 587
Rock, hotels 567
Rock music, London 158–9
Rodin, Auguste, *The Burghers of Calais*
  92, 382
Rogers, Richard 29, 120
"The Rokeby Venus" (Velázquez) 87
Rollright Stones 224
Rolls, Charles Stewart 479
Romaldkirk, restaurants 598
Roman Britain 25, **48–9**
  Antonine Wall 48, 495
  Bath 49, 263, 264–5
  Birdoswald Roman Fort 362
  Boudica and the Iceni **199**
  Caerleon 478
  Carlisle 362
  Chedworth Roman Villa 333
  Chester 314, 315
  Chew Green Camp 425
  Chysauster 282–3
  Cirencester 333
  Dorchester 273
  Fishbourne Roman Palace 48–9, 175
  Hadrian's Wall 11, 15, 48, 350, 419,
    426–7, 486
  Hardknott Fort 368
  Lincoln 344
  Lullingstone Roman Villa 49
  Ribchester 375
  Richborough Roman Fort 187
  Roman Theatre (St Albans) **236**
  Scotland 486
  Segontium (Caernarfon) 448
  Shrewsbury 316
  Verulamium (St Albans) **236**
  Wade's Causeway 399
  Wales 440
  York 410
Romney, George 232, 541
Romney, Hythe & Dymchurch Light
  Railway 187
Romney Marsh **186–7**
Romsey, pubs 604
Rosedale Abbey 386, 399
Rosemoor Garden, RHS 290
Ross-on-Wye **320–21**
  hotels 568
  restaurants 594
Rossetti, Dante Gabriel
  Ashmolean Museum (Oxford) 228
  Kelmscott 224
  Manchester Art Gallery 378
  Nottingham Castle 340
  Tate Britain (London) 95
Rosslyn Chapel 517
Rosthwaite 367
Rothiemurchus Estate 548
Rothko, Mark 125
Rothschild, Baron Ferdinand de 234
Rotunda Museum (Scarborough) 401
Roubiliac, Louis François 217
Rowde, restaurants 591
Rowing 70

Rowntree, Joseph 353
Roxburghe, Duke of 507
Royal Academy of Arts (London) **85**, 88
  Summer Exhibitions 67
Royal Albert Hall (London) 100, **104–5**,
  158, 159
Royal Albert Memorial Museum and Art
  Gallery (Exeter) **293**
Royal Armouries (Leeds) 414
Royal Ascot 70, 616, 617
Royal Citadel (Plymouth) 296
Royal coat of arms 34
Royal College of Music (London) 100
Royal Cornwall Museum (Truro) 285
Royal Deeside 11, 17, 483
  tour 17, **544–5**
Royal Exchange (London) 115
Royal Exchange Theatre (Manchester)
  377
Royal Highland Show (Ingliston) 67
Royal Hospital (London) 126
Royal Liver Building (Liverpool) 380
Royal Mews (London) **91**
Royal Mile (Edinburgh) 17, **512–15**
Royal National Eisteddfod 67
Royal Naval College (Dartmouth) 294
Royal Observatory Greenwich (London)
  129
Royal Opera Arcade (London) 89
Royal Opera House (London) 83, **84**,
  158, 159
Royal Pavilion (Brighton) 13, 163, 179,
  182–3
Royal Pump Room Museum (Harrogate)
  392
Royal Shakespeare Company 156, **331**
Royal Tunbridge Wells **193**
Royal Welsh Show (Builth Wells) 67
Rubens, Peter Paul 382
  The Adoration of the Magi 219
  Banqueting House (London) 94
  Marchesa Maria Grimaldi 275
  Samson and Delilah 86
Rugby 70, 71, 159, 616, 617
Runnymede 239
Rupert, Prince 316
Rural architecture **36–7**
Ruskin, John 372
Russell Square (London) 109
Russell Square Gardens (London) 79
Russell-Cotes Art Gallery and Museum
  (Bournemouth) 275
Ruthin **449**
  hotels 571
  restaurants 599
Rydal **370**
Rye
  pubs 604
  street-by-street map 188–9
Ryedale Folk Museum (Hutton-le-Hole)
  398
Rysbrack, Michael 232

S
Sackville, Thomas 192
Sackville-West, Vita 167, 192, 193
Sadler's Wells (London) 158, 159
Safety **626–7**
  travel safety advice 620, 625
Saffron Walden, pubs 605
Sailing 71, **616**, 617
Sainsbury Centre for Visual Arts
  (Norwich) **205**
St Abb's Head **506**
St Albans **236–7**
  hotels 564
  restaurants 589

St Anderew's Cathedral (Aberdeen) **544**
St Andrews **503**
  hotels 572
St Aubyn, Colonel John 282
St Austell **285**
St Bartholomew-the-Great (London)
  116–17
St Davids 16, 436, **468–9**
  Cathedral 16, 436, 469
  hotels 572
St Fagans National History Museum
  (Cardiff) **475**
St Fillan's Cave (East Neuk) 504
St George's Day 66
St Giles Cathedral (Edinburgh) **513**
St Ives 14, 244, 276, **281**
  hotels 567
  restaurants 593
  St Ives Festival 68
St Ives Harbour (Heron) 281
St James Garlickhythe (London) 114
St James's (London), street-by-street
  map 88–9
St James's Church (London) 88
St James's Palace (London) 88
St James's Park (London) 79
St James's Square (London) 89
St John's College (Cambridge) 214, **217**
St John's College (Oxford) **231**
St John's House Museum (Warwick) 325
St John's, Smith Square (London) 158, 159
St John's in the Vale 365
St Leger, Sir Anthony 192
St Machar's Cathedral (Aberdeen) **544**
St Margaret's Church (London) 92
St Martin in the Fields (London) 158, 159
St Martin's Theatre (London) 82
St Mary Abchurch (London) 115
St Mary Radcliffe (Bristol) **260**
St Mary the Virgin Church (Oxford)
  13, **229**
St Mary-le-Bow (London) 114
St Mary's Abbey (York) **354–5**, **410**
St Mary's House (Bramber) 184
St Mary's Lighthouse (Whitley Bay) 348–9
St Mawes, hotels 567
St Michael Subduing the Devil (Epstein) 323
St Michael's Church (St Albans) **236**
St Michael's Mount **282–3**
St Mungo Museum of Religious Life
  and Art (Glasgow) **521**
St Nicholas Cole Abbey (London) 114
St Nicholas Kirk (Aberdeen) **542**
St Nicholas Priory (Exeter) **293**
St Pancras International (London) 61, **109**
St Patrick's Day 66
St Paul's Cathedral (London) 12, 77,
  118–19
  street-by-street map 114
St Paul's Church (London) 82
St Peter Mancroft Church (Norwich) **205**
St Peter's-on-the-Wall (Maldon) 213
St Stephen Walbrook (London) 115, **116**
Salcombe
  hotels 567
  restaurants 593
Sales 152, 610
Salford Quays **375**
Salisbury 14, **268–9**
  Cathedral 245
  hotels 566
  pubs 606
  restaurants 591
Salisbury, Marquess of 35
Salt, Sir Titus 353, 415
Saltaire 353, 415
Saltash, pubs 606

Saltram House 296
Salt's Mill (Leeds) 415
Salvin, Anthony 448
Sambourne, Edward Linley 126–7
Samson and Delilah (Rubens) 86
Sandby, Paul, *Conwy Castle* 451
Sandringham **201**
Sanquhar **518**
Saunton, hotels 567
Savin, Thomas **467**
Scafell Pike 356, 368
Scale Force 367
Scarborough **401**
　hotels 570
　restaurants 597
Science Museum (London) 12, 100, **104**
Scilly Isles 283
Scone Palace 502
Scotland 25–6, **480–553**
　castles 490–91
　clans and tartans 488–9
　climate 73
　food and drink 492
　Highlands and Islands 528–53
　history 486–7
　hotels 572–3
　Lowlands 494–527
　map 22–3, 482–3
　portrait of 484–5
　pubs 609
　referendum 65, 487
　restaurants 600–603
　A Week in Scotland 11, **17**
　whisky 493
Scott, Sir George Gilbert
　Anglican Cathedral (Liverpool) 383
　Bath Abbey 264
　Martyrs' Memorial (Oxford) 229
　St Davids Cathedral 469
　Worcester Cathedral 322
Scott, Sir Giles Gilbert 125
Scott, Captain Robert 503
Scott, Sir Walter 330, 485, **516**
　Abbotsford House 516
　grave 507
　Highlands and Islands 529
　Mons Meg 510
　Perth 502
　St John's in the Vale 365
　Scott's View 507
　The Trossachs 498
　Wayland's Smithy 225
Scottish Fisheries Museum (East Neuk) 504
Scottish National Gallery of Modern Art
　One and Two (Edinburgh) **515**
Scottish National Party 487
Scottish National Portrait Gallery
　(Edinburgh) **508–9**
Scottish Parliament 65
Scottish Sealife Sanctuary (Oban) 550
Scrabster, restaurants 603
Scrope, 1st Lord 389
Sea-Life and Marine Sanctuary
　(Scarborough) 401
Seabury, Samuel 544
Seahouses 422
　pubs 608
Seathwaite 369
Seaview, hotels 563
Secondhand shops 611
Segontium (Caernarfon) 448
Self-catering accommodation 558, 559
Selfridges (London) 152, 153
Selkirk, Alexander 260, 504
Selworthy 254
Senate House (Cambridge) **216**

Serpentine (London) 105
Seven Dials (London) 82
Seven Sisters 13, 184–5
Severs, Dennis 129
Severus, Septimius 49
Sewingshields Milecastle 427
Seymour, Jane 42
Seymour-Conway family 108
Shaftesbury **272**
Shakespeare, William 28, 54, 55
　Charlecote Park 306
　Glamis Castle 503
　grave 329, 330
　Great Bed of Ware 102
　Henry IV 424
　Macbeth 503, 541
　monument to 124
　Royal Shakespeare Company 331
　Shakespeare's Birthplace (Stratford-
　　upon-Avon) 328, **330**
　Shakespeare's Globe (London) 12,
　　112, **124**
　Stratford-upon-Avon 302, 311, 330
　Westminster Abbey (London) 97
Shaldon, restaurants 593
Shandy Hall (Coxwold) 397
The Shard (London) 75, **121**
Sharington, Sir William 259
Shaw, George Bernard 107, **237**, 321
Shaw, Norman 33, 459
Sheffield, restaurants 597
Sheldon, Gilbert, Archbishop of
　Canterbury 229
Sheldonian Theatre (Oxford) 226, **229**
Shelley, Percy Bysshe **226**, 466
Shells 247
Shells (Moore) 382
Shephard, Ernest 238
Shepton Mallet, restaurants 591
Sheraton, Thomas 541
Sherborne **272**
　restaurants 591
Sherlock, Cornelius 382
Sherlock Holmes Museum (London)
　108
Sherwood Forest 340
Shetland Islands **532**
　hotels 573
　maps 19, 23, 531
　restaurants 603
　seabirds 532
　Up Helly Aa 404, 532
Shibden Hall Museum (Halifax) 417
Shipping at the Mouth of the Thames
　(Turner) 95
Shoe shops, London 154, 155
Shopping **610–11**
　London 152–3
Show jumping 71
Shrewsbury **316**
　hotels 568
　pubs 606
　restaurants 594
Shropshire *see* Heart of England
Sickert, Walter Richard 95, 382
Sidmouth 293
　Folk Week 67
Siever, Robert William 78
Signac, Paul 414
Signs
　long-distance footpaths 41
　pub 579
Silbury Hill 266
Simonsbath 254
Simpson, James 484–5
Simpson, Wallis 63
Sinclair clan 489

Sir John Soane's Museum (London)
　116–17
Sisley, Alfred 414
Sissinghurst Castle Garden 193
Six Nations Rugby Union 70
Skara Brae 47, 532
Skeabost 534
Skene, Sir George 543
Sketch for Annabel Lee (Whistler) 523
Skiddaw 357, 365
Skiing 549, **616**, 617
Skinners' Hall (London) 115
Skipton
　Castle **390**
　pubs 608
Sky Garden (London) **120**
Skye, Isle of 17, 482, 530, **534–7**
　pubs 609
　restaurants 603
Slate **455**
The Sleeping Shepherd Boy (Gibson)
　382
Sloane, Sir Hans 110, 126
Sloane Square (London) 126
Smirke, Robert 110
Smith, Adam 484, 487
Smoking 623
　in restaurants 575
Smugglers, Cornwall **284**
Smythson, Robert 394
Snooker 70
Snowdon 436, **455**
Snowdonia National Park 16, 446,
　452–3, 455
Snowshill Manor 302, 324
Soane, Sir John 116
Society 27
Soho (London) **84**
Soldier's Leap (Killiecrankie Walk) 546
Somerleyton Hall 203
Somerset *see* Wessex
Somerset House (London) **84**
Somerset Rural Life Museum
　(Glastonbury) 257
Sonning Bridge 239
South Devon Steam Railway 295, 298
South Downs Way 41
South Kensington and Hyde Park
　(London) **98–105**
　area map 99
　hotels 560–61
　pubs 604
　restaurants 583–4
　South Kensington street-by-street
　　100–101
South Milton, restaurants 593
"South Sea Bubble" (1720) 58
South Uist 533
South Wales **460–79**
　climate 72
　hotels 571–2
　map 462–3
　pubs 608–9
　restaurants 599–600
　A Week in Wales and the West 10, **16**
South West Coast Path 254
Southampton **172–3**
　hotels 563
Southbank Centre (London) 158, 159
Southeast England **160–241**
　Downs and Channel Coast 168–93
　East Anglia 194–219
　The Garden of England 164–5
　houses of historical figures 166–7
　map 162–3
　Thames Valley 220–41
　A Week in Southeast England 11, **13**

Southwark (London) *see* The City and Southwark
Southwark Cathedral (London) 12, **124**
Southwest Coastal Path 40, 246
Southwold 13, **206**
  hotels 564
  pubs 605
  restaurants 588
Souvenir shops 611
  London 154, 155
Sowerby Bridge 417
Spacey, Kevin 156
Spanish Armada (1588) 43, 54–5, 296, 297, 550
Speaker's Corner (London) 105
Special needs 622, 625
Specialist holidays **614–17**
Spectator sports **616**, 617
Speed limits 636
Speke Hall (Liverpool) 383
Spence, Sir Basil 323
Spencer, 1st Earl 88
Spencer, Sir Stanley 218, 340
  Swan Upping 239
Spencer House (London) 88
Speyside, hotels 573
Spinnaker Tower (Portsmouth) 173
Sports 29
  London 159
  spectator 616, 617
  The Sporting Year 70–71
  traditional Cumbrian sports 362
Spring 66
Spurn Head **407**
Squares, London 79
Staffa, Isle of 551
Staffordshire *see* Heart of England
Staffordshire pottery **315**
Stained glass (York Minster) **413**
Staite Murray, William 411
Stamford **347**
  hotels 569
  pubs 607
  restaurants 595
Standen 33
Standing Stones of Callanish 533
Standing Stones of Stenness 532
Stanhope 431
Stanley, restaurants 602
Stanpit Marsh 275
Stansted Airport 634
Stanton 309
Stanway House 324
Stapledon, Walter de 293
State Opening of Parliament 68
Stately homes **32–3**
  Althorp 347
  Anglesey Abbey **212**
  Arlington Court 291
  Athelhampton House 249, 273
  Audley End **212–13**
  Berrington Hall 317
  Blickling Hall **202**
  Bowood House 259
  Buckland Abbey **296**
  Burghley House 303, 336, **346–7**
  Burlington House 32
  Burton Agnes **404**
  Burton Constable **406**
  Castle Drogo 33, 299
  Castle Howard 32, 351, **402–3**
  Charlecote Park 306
  Chartwell 167, **193**
  Chatsworth House 303, **338–9**
  Chiswick House (London) 130
  Claydon House (Winslow) 166
  Cliveden House 13, 166

Stately homes (cont.)
  Corsham Court 259
  Cotehele **297**
  Cragside 33
  Dalemain **362–3**
  Fountains Hall 394
  Glynde Place 184
  Goodwood House 175
  Great Dixter 186
  Ham House (London) 130
  Hardwick Hall 306, 340
  Harewood House 32, **414**
  Hatfield House 57, 221, **235**
  Hay Castle 465
  Hever Castle **193**
  Holker Hall 373
  Holkham Hall 32, **201**
  Holland House (London) 126
  Hopetoun House **506**
  houses of historical figures 166–7
  Hutton-in-the-Forest 362
  Ickworth House 210–11
  Ightham Mote 192–3
  Kedleston Hall 32–3, 340
  Kelmscott Manor **224–5**
  Kenwood House (London) 128
  Kingston Lacy 275
  Knebworth House **235**
  Knole **192**
  Lacock Abbey 259
  Lanhydrock 248, **288**, 289
  Layer Marney Tower 209
  Leighton Hall **374**
  Levens Hall **373**
  Little Moreton Hall **306–7**, 315
  Longleat House **270**
  Loseley Park 176
  Marble Hill House (London) 130
  Minster Lovell Hall (Swinbrook) 224
  Montacute House 249, 272
  Moseley Old Hall 307
  Muncaster Castle 368
  Newby Hall **393**
  Nunnington Hall **397**
  Osborne House 166, **172**
  Oxburgh Hall 199
  Packwood House 307
  Penshurst Place 193
  Petworth House 13, 26, **176**
  Plas Newydd 454
  Plas-yn-Rhiw 457
  Prideaux Place (Padstow) 289
  Queen's House (London) 129
  Quex Park (Margate) 187
  Royal Pavilion (Brighton) 13, 163, 179, **182–3**
  St Michael's Mount 282–3
  Saltram House 296
  Sandringham **201**
  Sizergh Castle 372
  Snowshill Manor 302
  Somerleyton Hall 203
  Speke Hall 383
  Spencer House (London) 88
  Standen 33
  Stokesay Castle 316, 317
  Stourhead House 271
  Stowe House 221, **234**
  Stratfield Saye 166
  Syon House (London) 130
  Temple Newsam House (Leeds) 414
  Traquair House 491, **517**
  Uppark House 185
  Waddesdon Manor 221, **234**
  Wightwick Manor 307
  Wilton House 269
  Woburn Abbey 32, 221, **234**

Stately homes (cont.)
  Wollaton Hall and Deer Park (Nottingham) 340
  see also Castles; Palaces
Stephen, King 44
Stephenson, George 398, 410
Sterne, Laurence 396–7
Stevenson, Robert Louis 485
Steyning 13, **184**
Stiffkey, pubs 605
Stirling 17, **500**
  Castle 17, **500–501**
  hotels 572
Stirling, James 381
Stirling Castle in the Time of the Stuarts (Vorstermann) 501
Stoke Poges, hotels 564
Stoke-by-Nyland 211
Stoke-on-Trent **315**
Stokesay Castle 316, 317
Stokesley, restaurants 598
Stone, Nicholas 228
Stone buildings, Cotswolds **308–9**
Stone circles *see* Prehistoric Britain
Stone of Destiny 486, 502, 510, 551
Stonehenge 10, 14, 47, 245, **266–7**
Stonethwaite 367
Stoppard, Tom 28
Stornoway 533
The Storr 535
Story, Waldo 232
Stott Park Bobbin Mill (Finsthwaite) 371
Stour, River 208
Stourhead 245, 249, **270–71**
Stow-on-the-Wold, restaurants 594
Stowe 221, **234**
Stowmarket, pubs 605
Strachan, Douglas 189, 544
Stranger's Hall (Norwich) **205**
Strata Florida 471
Stratfield Saye 166
Stratford-upon-Avon 11, 13, 302, 311, **328–31**
  hotels 568
  restaurants 594
  street-by-street map 328–9
Strathpeffer **539**
Strathspey Steam Railway 548
Street, G E 261
Streetlife Museum of Transport (Kingston upon Hull) 406, 407
Striding Edge 357
Stromness 532
Stuart, John 476
Stuart Britain **56–7**
Stuart clan 489
Stubbs, George 175, 264
Student travellers **623**, 625
Studland Bay 274
  hotels 566
  restaurants 591
Studley Royal 394–5
Stump Cross Caverns **390**
Sudely Castle 324
Suffolk *see* East Anglia
Suffolk, 1st Earl of 212, 213
Suffragettes 62
Summer 67
Summerson, John 270
Sunshine 72–3
Supermarkets 611
Surfing **616**, 617
Surrey *see* Downs and Channel Coast
Surrey, Thomas Holland, Duke of 398
Surtees, Bessie 429
Sussex *see* Downs and Channel Coast
Sutherland, Earls of 538

Sutherland, Graham 84
  Chichester Cathedral 175
  Coventry Cathedral 323
Sutton Bank **396**
Sutton Hoo **207**
Sutton-on-the-Forest, restaurants 598
Swaffham **199**
  restaurants 588
Swaledale **388–9**
Swaledale Folk Museum (Reeth Green) **389**
Swallow Falls (Betws-y-Coed) 16, 454
Swan Upping (Spencer) 239
Swanage 274
  restaurants 590
Swanley, restaurants 587
Swansea **470**
  pubs 609
  restaurants 600
Swimming **401**
Swiss Cottage (Osborne House) 172
Sygun Copper Mines 456
Symonds Yat 313, 321
Syon House (London) 130

T

Tain 539
Talbot, William Henry Fox 259
Talisker Distillery 534
Tan-y-Bwlch 457
Tanygrisiau 457
Tar Tunnel (Ironbridge Gorge) 319
Tarn Hows 372
Tarr Steps 254
Tartans **488–9**, 540
Tate Britain (London) 77, **95**
Tate Liverpool 11, **381**
Tate Modern (London) 12, **125**
Tate St Ives 281
Tatham, C H 351
Taunton **256**
Tavistock
  hotels 567
  pubs 606
  restaurants 593
Taxes, Value Added Tax (VAT) 576, 610
Taxis 632, **642–3**
  from airports 634
Techniquest (Cardiff) 474
Telephones **630**, 631
Television 29, 631
Telford, Thomas **451**
  Caledonian Canal 540
  Neptune's Staircase 551
  Pontcysyllte Aqueduct 454
  Waterloo Bridge (Betws-y-Coed) 454
Temperatures 72–3
Temple (London) **116**
Temple Mine (Matlock Bath) 340
Temple Newsam House (Leeds) 414
Tenbury Wells 317
Tenby 16, **470**
  hotels 572
Tenement House (Glasgow) 17, **522**
Tennis 70, 159, 616
Tennyson, Alfred, Lord 289, 345
Teresa, Mother 35
Terrorism 65
Tettersells, Nicholas 178
Tewkesbury **332**
Textiles, Scottish **519**
Thackray Medical Museum (Leeds) 414
Thames Path 41
Thames Valley 13, **220–41**
  climate 72
  hotels 564
  map 222–3

Thames Valley (cont.)
  pubs 605
  restaurants 588–9
  Touring the Thames 238–9
Thatcher, Margaret 28, 64, 65
Theakston Brewery (Masham) **389**
Theatre 28, **612**
  Festival Theatre (Dunkeld) 545
  The Grand Theatre (Leeds) 414
  London 156–7
  Open Air Theatre (Regent's Park) 108
  Royal Exchange Theatre (Manchester) **377**
  Royal Opera House (London) 83, **84**
  Royal Shakespeare Theatre and Swan Theatre (Stratford-upon-Avon) 329
  Shakespeare's Globe (London) 12, 112, **124**
Theft 626
Theme parks **613**
Thermae Bath Spa 14, **265**
Thetford 199
Thinktank, Birmingham Science Museum 323
Thirlmere 364
Thoky, Abbot 333
Thomas, Dylan 84, 439
  Dylan Thomas Centre (Swansea) 470
Thomson, James 523
Thornhill, Sir James 232
Thorpe Park 613
Threave Castle **519**
Thynne, John 270
Tickets
  air 635
  entertainment 612
  London Underground 643
  rail 638
  sporting events 71
Tideswell, pubs 607
Tijou, Jean 110
Time 624
Tintagel 10, 14, **289**
Tinted Venus (Gibson) 350
Tintern
  hotels 572
  pubs 609
Tintern Abbey 16, **479**
Tipping 623
  in restaurants 576
Tisbury, hotels 566
Tissington, festivals 66
Tissington Trail 302, 337, **341**
Titanic 173
Tithe Barn (Bradford-on-Avon) 259
Titian
  Alnwick Castle 424
  Fitzwilliam Museum (Cambridge) 218
  Ickworth House 211
  Petworth House 176
  Wallace Collection (London) 109
Tobermory 531
Togidubnus 49
Toilets, public 624
Tolpuddle Martyrs 60
Tom Brown's School Museum (Uffington) 225
Torbay **294**
Torquay 279, 294
  restaurants 593
Torridge Valley 290
Torridon Countryside Centre 538
Totnes **295**
Tourism for All 559, 622, 625
Tourist information 621, 625

Tours by car
  Midlands garden tour 13, 324–5
  North Norfolk coastal tour 200–201
  North Pennines tour 431
  Peak District tour 342–3
  Penwith tour 280
  Road to the Isles tour 17, 550–51
  Royal Deeside tour 17, 544–5
  A Tour of the Borders 507
  Touring the Thames 238–9
  Wild Wales tour 471
Toward, Agnes 522
Tower Bridge (London) 12, 74–5, **120**
Tower houses 490–91
Tower of London 12, 77, **122–3**
Townend (Troutbeck) 370–71
Tradescant, John 228, 235
Trafalgar, Battle of (1805) 59
Trains *see* Rail travel
Trams 643
Traquair House 491, **517**
Travel **632–43**
  air 634–5
  bus 640, 641, 642
  car 636–7
  in cities 642–3
  coach 632, 633, 640, 641
  coasts and waterways 641
  cycling 643
  Devon and Cornwall 279
  Downs and Channel Coast 171
  East Anglia 197
  East Midlands 337
  ferries 633, 641
  Heart of England 312
  Highlands and Islands 530
  Lancashire and the Lakes 360
  London 642–3
  London Underground 643
  Lowlands 497
  North Wales 447
  Northumbria 421
  rail 632, 633, 638–9
  safety advice 620, 625
  South and Mid-Wales 464
  taxis 632, 642–3
  Thames Valley 222
  Wessex 252
  Yorkshire and the Humber Region 387
Traveller's cheques 628
  in shops 610
Trebah 205
Trelissick 248, 285
Tremayne family 285
Trengwainton 248, 280
Trewithen 248, 285
Trinity College (Cambridge) **217**
Trinity College (Oxford) **231**
Troon, restaurants 603
Trooping the Colour 67
Tropical World (Leeds) 414
The Trossachs 482, 485, **498–9**
Truro **285**
Tube *see* London Underground
Tudno, St 449
Tudor manor houses **306–7**
Tudor Merchant's House (Tenby) 470
Tudor Renaissance **54–5**
Tullie House Museum (Carlisle) 362
Tunbridge Wells **193**
Turkish Baths (Harrogate) 392
Turner, J M W
  Ashmolean Museum (Oxford) 228
  Cheyne Walk (London) 126
  The Collection – Usher Gallery (Lincoln) 345
  Hastings (1810) 8–9

Turner, J M W (cont.)
Petworth House 176
Shipping at the Mouth of the Thames 95
Turner Bequest 95
Turner Contemporary (Margate) 187
Walker Art Gallery (Liverpool) 382
Turpin, Dick 409
Tussaud, Madame 108
Twenty20 cricket final 71
Twm Siôn Cati's Cave 471
Two Forms (Divided Circle) (Hepworth) 281
Twombly, Cy 125
Twyning 332
Ty Hyll (Betwys-y-Coed) 454
Tyler, Wat 116
Tyndrum, restaurants 603
Tyne Bridge (Newcastle upon Tyne) **429**

U

Uffington 225
hotels 564
The Uists 533
UK Border Agency National Museum
(Liverpool) 381
Ullapool, pubs 609
Ullswater **363**
hotels 570
Underground Passages (Exeter) **293**
HMS *Unicorn* (Dundee) 503
University Botanic Garden (Cambridge)
217
University of Oxford Botanic Garden **228**
Up Helly Aa (Shetland) 484, 532
Uppark House 185
Upper Coquetdale 420
Upper Swarford 222
Urquhart Castle 17, 540
Usk, pubs 609
Uswayford Farm 425

V

V&A Design Museum (Dundee) 503
V&A Museum of Childhood (London) 129
Vale, H H 382
Vale of the White Horse **225**
Valley of Rocks (Exmoor) 254
Value Added Tax (VAT) 576, 610
Van der Plas, Pieter 235
Van der Vaart, Jan 339
Van Dyck, Sir Anthony
Alnwick Castle 424
Merchant Adventurers' Hall (York) 411
Petworth House 176
Wallace Collection (London) 109
Wilton House 269
Van Eyck, Jan, *Arnolfini Portrait* 86
Vanbrugh, Sir John 32, **403**
Blenheim Palace 232, 233
Castle Howard 402
Stowe 234
Vanessa Bell at Charleston (Grant) 167
Vegetarian food 576
Velázquez, Diego 508
"The Rokeby Venus" 87
Venus and Mars (Botticelli) 77
Vermeer, Johannes, *The Music Lesson* 90
Verrio, Antonio 347
Verulamium (St Albans) **236**
Victoria, Queen 45, 60–61, 235
Balmoral 483, 529, 544
Blair Castle 547
Buckingham Palace (London) 90
Crown Jewels 122
Kensington Palace (London) 105
Killiecrankie 546
Osborne House 166, 172
Pitlochry 545

Victoria, Queen (cont.)
Royal Pavilion (Brighton) 182, 183
Victoria and Albert Museum (London)
102
Victoria and Albert Museum (London)
12, 76, **102–3**
street-by-street map 101
Victorian Britain **60–61**
HMS *Victory* 173
View of Culzean Castle (Nasmyth) 526
Vikings 50, 51, 354, 529
Up Helly Aa (Shetland) 484, 532
York 410
Vindolanda 426
Viñoly, Rafael 120
Visas 620, 625
Visit England 559
VisitBritain 621, 625
Visit Scotland 559
Visit Wales 559
Vivian, John Henry 470
Vorstermann, Johannes, *Stirling Castle in the Time of the Stuarts* 501
Vorticists 95

W

Waddesdon Manor 221, **234**
Wade, General 546
Wade's Causeway 399
Wainwright, A W 367
Walberswick 206
Wales 25–6, **434–79**
castles 442–3
climate 72
food and drink 581
history 440–41
hotels 571–2
map 20, 436–7
North Wales 444–59
portrait of 438–9
pubs 608–9
restaurants 599–600
South and Mid-Wales 460–79
A Week in Wales and the West 10, **16**
Wales Millennium Centre (Cardiff) 16,
460, **474**
Walker, Sir Andrew Barclay 382
Walker, William **175**
Walker Art Gallery (Liverpool) 350, 381,
382–3
Walking **614–15**, 617
in cities 643
Constable Walk **208**
Killiecrankie Walk 546
Lake District 367
Malham Walk 391
Tissington Trail 341
Walkers' Britain 40–41
Wallace, Sir Richard 109
Wallace, William 486, 501
Wallace Collection (London) **108–9**
Walliswood, pubs 605
Walpole, Sir Robert 58, 92
Walsingham, Alan de 198
Walton, Izaak 174, 342
Wanamaker, Sam 124
Wantage, hotels 564
Warkworth Castle **424**
Warner Bros. Studio Tour – The Making
of Harry Potter **237**
HMS *Warrior* 173
Wars of the Roses 53, 236, 441
Warwick **325–7**
Warwick, Earls of 325, 326–7
Warwick, Richard Neville, Earl of 326,
327, 389
Warwick Castle 303, 325, **326–7**

Warwick Castle (Canaletto) 327
Warwickshire *see* Heart of England
Wasdale Head 368
hotels 570
Washington, George 265
Wastell, John 218
Wastwater 356, **368**
Waterfalls
Aysgarth Falls **389**
Becky Falls 298
Devil's Bridge 467, 471
Hardraw Force **389**
Mallyan Spout 399
Scale Force 367
Swallow Falls (Betws-y-Coed) 16, 454
Waterhouse, Alfred 377, 378
Waterloo, Battle of (1815) 59
Watersmeet 254, 292
Watford, restaurants 589
Watt, James 58, 484, 495
Watteau, Antoine 109
Watton-at-Stone, pubs 605
Waugh, Evelyn 128, 402
Wayland's Smithy 225
Wealdon Hall House (Sussex) 36
Weather **72–3**
information 637
when to go 620
Webb, Aston 90, 103
Webb, Philip 33, 225
Wedgwood, Josiah 315
Welford-on-Avon, pubs 606
Well-dressing festivals (Tissington) 66, 341
Wellington, Duke of 59, 166, 454
Wells 14, 245, **256–7**
hotels 566
Wells-next-the-Sea 197, 201
Welsh Assembly 65
Welsh language 26, 438, 441
Welwyn Garden City 62–3
Wenlock Edge 316
Wensleydale **389**
Wesley, John 205, 230, **283**
Wessex 14, 50, 51, **250–75**
hotels 564–6
map 252–3
pubs 605–6
restaurants 589–91
A Week in Southwest England 10, **14**
West Country **242–99**
climate 72
coastal wildlife 246–7
Devon and Cornwall 276–99
map 244–5
Wessex 250–75
West Country gardens 248–9
West End and Westminster (London)
80–97
area map 81
hotels 560
restaurants 582–3
Whitehall and Westminster street-
by-street 92–3
West Highland Way 40, 498
West Kennet Long Barrow 266–7
Wester Ross **538**
Western Isles 17, **533**
Westgate Museum (Winchester) 174
Westminster (London)
street-by-street 92–3
see also West End and Westminster
Westminster Abbey (London) 12, 77,
96–7
street-by-street map 92
Westminster Pier (London) 93
Westward Ho! 290
Westwood, Vivienne 29

Weymouth **272–3**
restaurants 591
Whalley Abbey 375
Wharfedale **390**
Wharram Percy **404**
Wheal Martyn China Clay Museum 285
Wheelchair access *see* Disabled travellers
Wheeler, Sir Mortimer 478
Whinlatter Pass 364
Whisky **493**
Whistler, James McNeill, *Sketch for Annabel Lee* 523
Whitby 11, 15, 29, 385, **400**
Abbey **400**
hotels 570
restaurants 598
Whitchurch Mill 238
White Horse of Uffington 47, **225**
Whitehall (London), street-by-street 92–3
Whithorn **519**
pubs 609
Whitstable
hotels 563
restaurants 587
Whitworth, Sir Joseph 378
Whitworth Art Gallery (Manchester) **378**
Widecombe-in-the-Moor 26
Wightwick Manor 307
Wigmore Hall (London) 158, 159
Wilberforce, William **406**
Wilbourn, Colin 432
Wilde, Oscar 184
Wildlife
Braunton Burrows 291
Brownsea Island 275
Buckfast Butterfly Farm and Dartmoor Otter Sanctuary 295, 298
Cairngorm Reindeer Centre 548
Cornish Seal Sanctuary (Helston) 284
Cotswold Wildlife Park 224
The Countryside 38, 9
Elan Valley 460
Highland Wildlife Park 548
Leighton Moss Nature Reserve 374
Longleat House Safari Park 270
Minsmere Reserve 206
Muir of Dinnet Nature Reserve 544
St Abb's Head 506
Scottish Sealife Sanctuary (Oban) 550
Sea-Life and Marine Sanctuary (Scarborough) 401
West Country Coastal Wildlife **246–7**
Woburn Safari Park 234
see also Birds; Flowers; Zoos
Wilfrid, St 426
William II, King 44
death 172
William III, King 45, 56
Battle of the Boyne 57
Glencoe Massacre (1692) 547
Hampton Court 177
Hyde Park (London) 105
Jacobite Movement 541
and Scotland 487
William IV, King 45, 105
William, Prince 65
William the Conqueror, King 44, 175
Battle Abbey 185
Battle of Hastings 50, 51, 185
coronation 96
Domesday Book 333
Exeter 292
Gloucester 333
Lewes 184
Selby Abbey 354
Tower of London 122
and Wales 440

William the Conqueror, King (cont.)
Winchester 174
Windsor Castle 240
York 411
William the Lion, King of Scotland 486
Williams, Dominic 429
Williams, Kit 332
Williams-Ellis, Sir Clough 436, 458
Williamson, Henry 290
Williamson, Matthew 29
Williamson Park (Lancaster) 374, 375
Willow Tea Room (Glasgow) 17, **522**
Willy Lott's Cottage 208
The Wilson, Cheltenham Art Gallery and Museum 332
Wilson, Colin St John 109
Wilton 269
Wilton House 269
Wiltshire *see* Wessex
Wimbledon Lawn Tennis Tournament 67, 70
Wimborne Minster **275**
Winchcombe 309
Winchelsea **189**
hotels 563
restaurants 587
Winchester 11, 13, **174–5**
Cathedral 27, 162, 174–5
hotels 563
restaurants 587
Windermere 15, **371**
hotels 570
restaurants 596–7
Windmills **203**
Windsor 11, 13, **239–41**
Castle 162, 220, 221, 239, **240–41**
hotels 564
pubs 605
restaurants 589
Windsor, Duke of (Edward VIII) 45, 63, 295
Winmau World Masters Darts Championships 71
Winter 69
Wisley, RHS 176
Withernsea 407
Witley Court and Gardens 317
Woburn Abbey 32, 221, **234**
Woburn, restaurants 589
Wolf of Badenoch 542
Wollaton Hall and Deer Park (Nottingham) 310
Wolsey, Cardinal
Christ Church College (Oxford) 230
Hampton Court 177
Ipswich 207
Wood, John the Elder 245, 260, 262
Woodstock, restaurants 589
Woodville, Elizabeth 216
Wookey Hole 256, 257
Wool trade **211**
Woolf, Virginia 167
Worcester **322**
hotels 568
restaurants 594
Worcestershire *see* Heart of England
Wordsworth, Dorothy 370, 396
Wordsworth, William **370**
Dove Cottage and the Wordsworth Museum (Grasmere) 370
Duddon Valley 369
Plas Newydd 454
Rydal Mount (Rydal) 370
St John's College (Cambridge) 217
Sutton Bank 396
Tintern Abbey 479

Wordsworth, William (cont.)
Ullswater 363
Wordsworth House (Cockermouth) 366
World War I 62
World War II 62, 63
Churchill War Rooms (London) 92, **93**
D-Day Museum (Portsmouth) 173
World of Wedgwood (Barlaston) 315
Worthing 184
Wren, Sir Christopher 29, 57, 113, **119**
Christ Church College (Oxford) 230
Emmanuel College (Cambridge) 216
Guildhall (Windsor) 239
Hampton Court 177
Monument (London) 121
Old Royal Naval College (London) 129
Pembroke College (Cambridge) 216
Royal Hospital (London) 126
St James Garlickhythe (London) 114
St James's Church (London) 88
St Mary Abchurch (London) 115
St Nicholas Cole Abbey (London) 114
St Paul's Cathedral (London) 114, 118–19
St Stephen Walbrook (London) 115, 116
Sheldonian Theatre (Oxford) 226, 229
Swanage Town Hall 274
Wrexham (county) *see* North Wales
Wrington, restaurants 591
Wyatt, James 406
Wyatville, Sir Jeffry 240
Wycliffe, John 53
Wye Valley 313, 321
Wykeham, William of 230

Y
Yarm
hotels 570
restaurants 599
Ye Olde Fighting Cocks (St Albans) 336
Yeomen Warders (Tower of London) 123
York 11, 15, 351, 387, **408–13**
hotels 570
restaurants 598
street-by-street 408–9
York Minster 15, 408, 412–13
York, Duke of 264
York Castle Museum 409, **410**
Yorkshire **384–417**
climate 73
hotels 570
map 386–7
pubs 607–8
restaurants 597–8
Yorkshire Dales National Park 350, **388–91**
map 388
restaurants 598
Yorkshire Museum (York) 408, **410**
Yorkshire Sculpture Park **417**
Young, James 485
Ypres Tower (Rye) 189

Z
Zennor 280
hotels 567
restaurants 593
Zoffany, Johann 547
Zoos
Bristol Zoo Gardens 260
Paignton Zoo 294
Tropical World (Leeds) 414
ZSL London Zoo 108
ZSL Whipsnade Zoo 235
see also Aquariums; Wildlife

Acknowledgments

Dorling Kindersley would like to thank the following people whose contributions and assistance have made the preparation of this book possible.

Main Contributor

Michael Leapman was born in London in 1938 and has been a professional journalist since he was 20. He has worked for most British national newspapers and now writes about travel and other subjects for several publications, among them *The Independent, Independent on Sunday, The Economist and Country Life*. He has written 11 books, including the award-winning *Companion Guide to New York* (1983, revised 1995) and *Eyewitness Travel Guide to London*. In 1989 he edited the widely praised *Book of London*.

Additional Contributors

Amanda Clark, Paul Cleves, Laura Dixon, Damian Harper, James Henderson, Lucy Juckes, John Lax, Marcus Ramshaw, Nick Rider, Victoria Trott.

Additional Illustrations

Christian Hook, Gilly Newman, Paul Weston.

Design and Editorial

Managing Editor Georgina Matthews
Senior Art Editor Sally Ann Hibbard
Deputy Editorial Director Douglas Amrine
Deputy Art Director Gaye Allen
Production David Proffit
Picture Research Ellen Root, Rhiannon Furbear, Susie Peachey
DTP Designer Ingrid Vienings
Map Co-ordinators Michael Ellis, David Pugh
Researcher Pippa Leahy
Revisions Team Ashwin Adimari, Emma Anacootee, Eliza Armstrong, Sam Atkinson, Chris Bagshaw, Lydia Baillie, Josie Barnard, Moerida Belton, Kate Berens, Sonal Bhatt, Hilary Bird, Louise Boulton, Julie Bowles, Nick Bruno, Roger Bullen, Robert Butt, Chloe Carleton, Divya Chowfin, Deborah Clapson, Louise Cleghorn, Elspeth Collier, Gary Cross, Cooling Brown Partnership, Lucy Cowie, Richard Czapnik, Deshphal Singh Dabas, Caroline Elliker, Guy Dimond, Nicola Erdpresser, Mariana Evmolpidou, Danny Farnham, Joy Fitzsimmons, Fay Franklin, Ed Freeman, Janice Fuscoe, Melissa Graham, Richard Hammond, John Harrison, Mohammed Hassan, Charlie Hawkings, Andy Hayes, Kaberi Hazarika, Martin Hendry, Andrew Heritage, Kate Hughes, Shobhna Iyer, Annette Jacobs, Gail Jones, Cincy Jose, Rupanki Kaushik, Sumita Khatwani, Steve Knowlden, Rahul Kumar, Nic Kynaston, Esther Labi, Kathryn Lane, Pippa Leahy, Darren Longley, Carly Madden, Alison McGill, Caroline Mead, James Mills Hicks, Rebecca Milner, Kate Molan, Elaine Monaghan, Natalie Morrison, George Nimmo, Matthew Norman, Mary Ormandy, Catherine Palmi, Garima Pandey, Helen Peters, Marianne Petrou, Chez Picthall, Clare Pierotti, Andrea Powell, Mani Ramaswamy, Mark Rawley, Jake Reimann, Marisa Renzullo, Carolyn Ryden, David Roberts, Sands Publishing Solutions, Mary Scott, Ankita Sharma, Azeem Siddiqui, Claire Smith, Meredith Smith, Alison Stace, Hollie Teague, Priyanka Thakur, Gillian Thomas, Hugh Thompson, Simon Tuite, Conrad Van Dyk, Karen Villabona, Mary Villabona, Christian Williams, Alice Wright.

Additional Photography

Max Alexander, Peter Anderson, Apex Photo Agency: Stephen Bere, Deni Bown, June Buck, Simon Burt, Lucy Claxton, Michael Dent, Philip Dowell, Tim Draper, Mike Dunning, Chris Dyer, Andrew Einsiedel, Gaizka Elordi, Philip Enticknap, Jane Ewart, DK Studio/Steve Gorton, Frank Greenaway, Alison Harris, Stephen Hayward, John Heseltine, Nigel Hicks, Sean Hunter, Ed Ironside, Dave King, Neil Mersh, Laurie Noble, Robert O'Dea, Ian O'Leary, Stephen Oliver, Vincent Oliver, Roger Phillips, Rough Guides: Tim Draper/Lydia Evans/Diana Jarvis/Suzanne Porter/Paul Whitfield, Kim Sayer, Karl Shone, Helena Smith, Chris Stevens, Jim Stevenson, Clive Streeter, Harry Taylor, Conrad Van Dyk, David Ward, Mathew Ward, Alan Williams, Stephen Wooster, Nick Wright, Colin Yeates.

Photographic and Artwork Reference

Christopher Woodward of the Building of Bath Museum, Franz Karl Freiherr von Linden, Gendall Designs, NRSC Air Photo Group, The Oxford Mail and Times, and Mark and Jane Rees.

Photography Permissions

Dorling Kindersley would like to thank the following for their assistance and kind permission to photograph at their establishments:
Banqueting House (Crown copyright by kind permission of Historic Royal Palaces); Cabinet War Rooms; Paul Highnam at English Heritage; Dean and Chapter of Exeter Cathedral; Gatwick Airport Ltd; Heathrow Airport Ltd; Thomas Woods at Historic Scotland; Provost and Scholars Kings College; Cambridge; London Transport Museum; Madame Tussaud's; National Museums and Galleries of Wales (Museum of Welsh Life); Diana Lanham and Gayle Mault at the National Trust; Peter Reekie and Isla Roberts at the National Trust for Scotland; Provost Skene House; Saint Bartholmew the Great; St James's Church; London St Paul's Cathedral; Masters and Wardens of the Worshipful Company of Skinners; Provost and Chapter of Southwark Cathderal; HM Tower of London; Dean and Chapter of Westminster; Dean and Chapter of Worcetser Cathedral: and all the other churches, museums, hotels, restaurants, shops, galleries and sights too numerous to thank individually.

Picture Credits

a = above; b = below/bottom; c = centre; f = far; l = left; r = right, t = top.

Works of art have been reproduced with the permission of the following copyright holders: © ADAGP, Paris and DACS, London 2011: 175tr; © Alan Bowness, Hepworth Estate 281bl; *Fish* Constantin Brancusi © ADAGP, Paris and DACS, London 2011 © The Estate of Patrick Heron/DACS, London 2011: 244cl; Barbara Hepworth © Bowness/Paul Melling 281crb; © David Hockney: *The First Marriage (A Marriage of Styles I)* 1962, oil on canvas 1829–2140 mm, 95tr; *The Other Side* 1990–93, oil on 2 canvases, 72 x 132 in, 415t; © Estate of Stanley Spencer/DACS, London 2011 239t; © Angela Verren-Taunt/DACS, London 2011: 281br.

The work of Henry Moore, *Large Two Forms,* 1966, illustrated on page 417b, *Recumbent Figure* 1938 illustrated on page 95c has been reproduced by permission of the Henry Moore Foundation.

The publishers would like to thank the following individuals, companies and picture libraries for permission to reproduce their photographs:

123RF.com: Roman Babakin 85br, flik47 103cra, ladyligeia 522tl, Michael Lane 39tr; **Roman Abbot Hall Art Gallery and Museum**, Kendal: 374br(d); **Aberdeen Art Galleries** 542br; **Aberdeen and Grampian Tourist Board** 483cr; **Action Plus:** 484ca; David Davies 71cra; Peter Tarry 70cla, 71bl; **Airport Express Alliance:** 687c; Printed by kind permission of **Mohamed Al Fayed:** 101tr; **Alamy Stock Photo:** ACORD 10 341bl; Action Plus Sports images 711c; Peter Adams Photography 14b, 418; AM Corporation 249crb; Jenny Bailey 552br; BANANA PANCAKE 220, 434–5; chris brignell 299tl; Kevin Britland 248cl; Gina Calvi 377tl; Paul Carstairs 78bl; CBW 334; Bertrand Collet 492cla; Greg Balfour Evans 24; BlueSkyStock/Chris Rose 470bl; Ian M Butterfield (Sussex) 188br; Emma Durnford 238cl; eye35.pix 411tr; f8 images 598bl; gkphotography 581tl; GRANT ROONEY PREMIUM 179bl; Nick Higham 379br; Holmes Garden Photos 433cra; Brian Jannsen 324bl; John Peter Photography 499cr; Tim Jones 282cr; B. O'Kane 635tl; andy lane 100cl; Lenscap 178clb; LOOK Die Bildagentur 180–81; Nick Maslen 575tr; keith morris 439tl; PAINTING 524cla; Jeremy Pardoe 616bc; The Photolibrary Wales 455br, 581c; PRISMA ARCHIVO 103br; redsnapper 448cl; Seb Rogers 615cl; Sheree Sedgbeer 299br; Neil Setchfield 580cl; Slawek Staszczuk 179cra; Mark Thomas 178cla; Nick Turner 461bc; Urbanmyth 509tl, 525br; ; **American Museum**, Bath: 265ca; **Ancient Art and Architecture Collection:** 46cb, 48cla, 48cb, 49cra, 49clb, 50br, 52clb, 55cra, 239br, 443ca; **The Archive & Business Records Centre**, University of Glasgow: 487tr; **T & R Annan and Sons:** 522br(d); **Ashmolean Museum**, Oxford: 51tc; **Association of Train Operating Companies:** 622cr; **Barnaby's Picture Library:** 64ca; **Beamish Open Air Museum:** 428bl, 429c, 429crb, 429bc; **BFI London IMAX Cinema Waterloo:** Richard Holttum 157c; **Blenheim Palace:** 232tr, 233tl, 233bl; **Boath House:** 602tl; **Bocca di Lupo:** 582bl; **Bodysgallen Hall:** 571tr; **Bridge Hotel:** 569tl; **Bridgeman Art Library, London and New York:** 239tl, 191tc, 39cal; Agnew and Sons, London 327tl; Bibliotheque Nationale, Paris *Neville Book of Hours* 326t(d); Birgmingham

City Museums and Gallery 323tl; Bonham's, London, *Portrait of Lord Nelson with Santa Cruz Beyond*, Lemeul Francis Abbot 58cb(d); Bradford Art Galleries and Museums 53clb; British Library, London, *Pictures and Arms of English Kings and Knights* 8t(d), 43t(d), *The Kings of England from Brutus to Henry* 34bl(d), *Stowe manuscript* 44ca(d), *Calendar Anglo-Saxon Miscellany* 50–51t(d), 50–51b(d), *Decrees of Kings of Anglo-Saxon and Norman England* 51cb, 53bl(d), *Portrait of Chaucer*, Thomas Occleve 53br(d), *Portrait of Shakespeare*, Droeshurt 55bl(d), *Chronicle of Peter of Langtoft* 289bl(d), *Lives and Miracles of St Cuthbert*, 423cl(d), 423cr(d), *Lindisfarne Gospels* 423br(d), *Commendatio Lamentabilis intransitu Edward IV* 440bc(d). *Histoire du Roy d'Angleterre Richard II* 541bl; Christies, London 449tc; Claydon House, Bucks, *Florence Nightingale*, Sir William Blake Richmond 166tr; Department of Environment, London 52tr; City of Edinburgh Museums and Galleries, *Chief of Scottish Clan*, Eugene Deveria 488bl(d); Fitzwilliam Museum, University of Cambridge, *George IV as Prince Regent*, Richard Cosway 183tc, 216bl, Giraudon/ Musee de la Tapisserie, with special authorization of the city of Bayeux 51br,185bc; Guildhall Library, Corporation of London, *The Great Fire*, Marcus Willemsznik 57bl(d), *Bubbler's Melody* 58bc(d), *Triumph of Steam and Electricity*, The Illustrated London News 61tc(d), *Great Exhibition, The transept from Dickenson's Comprehensive Pictures* 60–61; Harrogate Museum and Art Gallery, North Yorkshire 392tl; Holburne Museum and Crafts Study Centre, Bath 57tl; Imperial War Museum, *London Field Marshall Montgomery*, J Worsley 35cb(d); Kedleston Hall, Derbyshire 32br; Lambeth Palace Library, London, *St Alban's Chronicle* 53tc; Lever Brothers Ltd, Cheshire 353cra; Lincolnshire County Council, Usher Gallery, Lincoln, *Portrait of Mrs Fitzherbert after Richard Cosway* 183tc; London Library, *The Barge Tower from Ackermann's World in miniature*, F Scoberl 59tc; Manchester Art Gallery, UK, *Etruscan Vase Painters* 1871, Sir Lawrence Alma-Tadema 378bc; Manchester City Art Galleries 377bc; David Messum Gallery, London 451br; National Army Museum, London, *Bunker's Hill*, R Simkin 58ca; National Gallery, London, *Mrs Siddons the Actress*, Thomas Gainsborough 167cra; National Museet, Copenhagen 50ca; Phillips, the International Fine Art Auctioneers, *James I*, John the Elder Decritz 56bl(d); Private Collections: 34ca(d), 52–3, 59ca, 59bl, 60clb, Vanity Fair 61la, 167tl, *Armada, map of the Spanish and British Fleets*, Robert Adam 297tl, 426b; Royal Geographical Society, London 167cr(d); Smith Art Gallery and Museum, Stirling 501bl; Tate Gallery, London: 60crb; Thyssen-Bornemisza Collection, Lugo Casta, *King Henry VIII*, Hans Holbein the Younger 54bc(d); Victoria and Albert Museum, London 60b, 101ca, 208tl, 355crb, 397bl, *Miniature of Mary Queen of Scots, by a follower of Francois Clouet* 313bl, 341tl(d), Walker Art Gallery, Liverpool 382cla; Westminster Abbey, London, *Henry VII Tomb effigy*, Pietro Torrigiano 34br(d), 44bc(d); The Trustees of the Weston Park Foundation, *Portrait of Richard III*, Italian School 53ca(d); Christopher Wood Gallery, London, *High Life Below Stairs*, Charles Hunt 37cr(d); **Britich Airways** Adrian Meredith 624cla; **British Library Board**: Cotton Faustina BVII folio 85 53crb, 113cl; © **The British Museum**: 46c, 47crb, 77tl, 110–11 all except 111tr and 111bl; © **The Bronte Society**: 416 all; **Burgerworks/KFD Photography (Katie Foulkes)**: 595tr; **The Burrell Collection, Glasgow**: 523tl; **Cadogan Management**: 88bl; CADW – Welsh Historic Monuments (Crown Copyright): 478tl; **Cairngorm Mountain**: 549c; **Camera Press**: Cecil Beaton 96bc; **Cardiff City Council**: 476tr, 477tl, 477cr; **Fkb Carlson**: 579bl; **Castle Cottage**: 599tl; **Castle Howard Estate Ltd**: 402ca, 403br; Trustees of the **Chatsworth Settlement**: 339br; **Chocolate Boutique Hotel**: 565br; **Clos Maggiore**: 576t; **Colin de Chaire**: 201c; **Collections**: Liz Stares 34tr, Yuri Lewinski 377tl; **Burton Constable**: 406tr; **Corbis**: Atlantide Phototravel 98; Richard Bowden/Loop Images 348–9; Matt Cheetham/ Loop Images 554–5; Neale Clark/Robert Harding World Imagery 460; Kathy Collins 310; Ashley Cooper 15tl; Alan Copson/info@awl-images. com/JAI 384, 480–81; Alan Copson/JAI 74–5; Alan Copson/Robert Harding World Imagery 2–3; Julian Elliott/Robert Harding World Imagery 618–19; Eurasia Press/Steven Vidler 441br; Krista Ewert/Design Pics/Design Pics 194; John Harper 61cr; Nigel Hicks/Purestock/ Superstock 300–301; Craig Joiner/LOOP IMAGES/Loop Images 242–3; John Heseltine 115br; Angelo Hornak 121bc; Eric Nathan/Loop Images 160–61; Ocean 80, 494; Sebastian Wasek/Loop Images 250; Doug Corrance: 489b; **John Crook**: 175b; **The Curlew**: 586tl; **Dean & Chapter of Westminster**: 97tc; **1805 Club**: 35tc; **1853 Gallery, Bradford**: 415t; **The Dining Room at Oak Bank Hotel**: 596tr; **Dorling Kindersley**: Max Alexander/London Transport Museum 83c; **Dreamstime.com**: 489br; Acceleratorhams 170bl, 288tl, 293br; Laurence Agron 64br; Alanjeffery 189bc; Alexaranda 71bc; Alexirina27000 264cl; Steve Allen 39cl, 104tl, 439b; Allouphoto 4cr; Altezza 92cl; Andyfox0c0uk 10cla; Anizza 12bc; Anthony Baggett 154tr; Arenaphotouk 253br; Atgimages 71cla; Anthony Baggett 79cra; Darren Baker 184br; Alan Barr 274bl;

Bcnewell 16bl; Felix Bensman 77cra, 102clb; Philip Bird 191c; Richard Bowden 39bc; John Braid 490cr; Dan Breckwoldt 93bl; Anthony Brown 473bl; Jurate Buiviene 521cl; Burnstuff2003 407b; Lenise Calleja 624t; Richie Chan 109br; Claudiodivizia 82bl, 260tr, 260cl; Clickos 187b, 286br; Fernando Comet 29tl; James Copeland 627bl; Jan Csernoch 114bl; Danielal 78cl; Davidmartyn 39br, 311b; Kristof Degreef 78br; Chris Dorney 214cl; Drumist 532tr; Kevin Eaves 5cl; Exflow 104br; Featureflash 35br; Alexey Fedorenko 27tr, 179crb, 610bc; Michael Foley 83tl; Filip Fuxa 187tc; Georgesixth 381cr, 521b; Milan Gonda 185cr; Helen E. Grose 38bc; Haphand 292br; Hdanne 246bl; Heathpt1 184tc; Patricia Hofmeester 196bl; Helen Hotson 188tr, 201br, 203tr, 252bl, 271tl, 298cl; Darren Howe 290bl; Wei Huang 82cl; Irishka777 78tr, 79crb; Irstone 611br; Françoise De Valera James 65br; Attila Jandi 532c, 532ftr; Valerijs Jegorovs 192t, 245bl; Richard Jemmett 170tr; Johnhill118 387tr; Emma Jones 524tr; Jorisvo 189tl; Aliaksandr Kazlou 611tl; 9Hans Klamm 16tr; Georgios Kollidas 35c; Elena Kramarenko 433tl; Leisyan 31c; Edyta Linek 31crb; Nicky Linzey 246cla; Lymey 283c, 293cl; Madrabothair 153tr; Maigi 85cl; Petr Malohlava 425cra; Marco Manieri 70bl; Sarah Marchant 165cb; Martinmates 79tr; Martin Meehan 271c; Mikelane45 39tl, 39tl (1), 39tc; Stephen Minkler 39cb; Chris Moncrieff 201tr; Mrloz 30 31tc; Murdock2013 108bl; Adina Nani 111br; Virgil Naslenas 70bc; Derrick Neill 335b; Nicku 192bl; Nigel Nudds 270ca; Nui7711 76br; Ohmaymay 190c; Patrickwang 11c, 251b; John Pavel 38cb (1), Photographyfirm 165cb (1); Enrico Della Pietra 259c; Pjhpix 68tl; Prestong 375bc; Ariadna De Raadt 25b; Rkaphotography 67br; Paul Rookes 165cb (2); Patrick Rowney 271bl; Sgar80 509c; Sharpshot 263br; Victoria Simmonds 261cr; Michael Smith 38bc (1); Nikolay Stoimenov 39clb; Dmytro Strelbytskyy 540bl; Swisshippo 97cr; TasFoto 188bl; Graham Taylor 39tc (1); Simon Taylor 630br; Rudolf Tepfenhart 521tc; Thawats 549tc; Ugo Toldi 623tr; Toldiu74 622bl; Tt 39cb (1); Ints Vikmanis 93c; Leon Viti 31cra; Keith Wheatley 171br; Whiskybottle 38clb, 38cb, 38br, 39bl, 299cr; Paul Wishart 83bc; Ian Woolcock 272tl, 275br, 281t, 298bc, 623t; Tom Wurl 286clb; Bahadir Yeniceri 298tr; **Eden Project**: 287tl; **Edgar House**: 568tl; **English Heritage**: 130b, 212cb, 213cb, 267bc, 354br, 355bc, 423tr, 423c; Avebury Museum 46cla; Devizes Museum 46br, drawing by Frank Gardiner 427clb, Salisbury Museum 46bl, 46bc, Skyscan Balloon Photography 47tl, 266crb, 398tl, 427cla **English Life Publications Ltd**, Derby: 346tr, 347tl, 347bc; **Et Archive**: 45tc, 45cr, 56clb, 57clb, 62crb, 166clb; Bodleian Library, Oxford 52cb; British Library, London 52cla; Devizes Museum 46cl, 47bc; Imperial War Museum, London 62clb(d), 63br; Labour Party Archives 64bc; London Museum 47cla; Magdalene College 34cla; National Maritime Museum, London 43tl, Stoke Museum Staffordshire Polytechnic 45bc; **Mary Evans Picture Library**: 578tr, 44hr, 45tl, 45cl, 45clb, 45br, 48bl, 48br, 50clb, 51ca, 55tl, 55crb, 55br, 57crb, 58bl, 59br, 62ca, 63ca, 63cb, 63cr, 108tc, 124br, 167br, 191cr, 199br, 210crb, 226bl, 232br, 236c, 235cb, 235bc, 235br, 238bl, 283tr, 340bc, 357r, 357cb, 404l, 451tl, 496hr, 502bl, 516bl, 519clb, 510tr, 525br **Fahims**: 587br; **Andrew Fairlie at Gleneagles**: 600tl; **Falkirk Wheel**: 505bl; **La Favorita**: 601bl; **Paul Felix**: 239ca; **Fifteen Cornwall**: 576bc; **Fishbourne Roman Villa**: 49tc; **Fleuchary House**: 564tr; **Louis Flood**: 488bc; **Foreign and British Bible Society**: Cambridge University Library 441cl, **Fotolia**. Zechal 276, Frankie's Fish & Chips. 603br. **Getty Images**. 45cra, 65cr, 625tc; Gonzalo Azumendi 106; Bettmann 232br; Mike Caldwell 452–3; Alan Copson 221bc; DEA PICTURE LIBRARY 87cb, 87br; Fine Art 86tr, 87tc; Cate Gillon 362bc; Bill Heinsohn 528; Heritage Images 86cl; Hulton Archive 403bc; joe daniel price 444; Peter Macdiarmid 157tl; Photo 12 86bc, 87cr; Print Collector 87c, 102cl; Terry Roberts Photography 536–7; Science & Society Picture Library 65bc, 401bl; Stringer/Central Press 63tc; Stringer/Hulton Archive 35cl; Stringer/IAN KINGTON 70c; Stringer/Ernest H. Mills 237br; Stringer/ Harry Shepherd 164tr; Stringer/Haywood Magee 64bl; Stringer/Michael Ochs Archives 381br; Stringer/Topical Press Agency 166cla; Matthew Stockman 70crb; Travel Ink 677tc; Universal History Archive 86clb, 354bl; Ivan Vdovin 191bl; Wirelmage/Samir Hussein 65tr; **Gilpin Lodge**: 557br; Art Gallery & Museum, Kelvingrove 523tr, 539br, 547b(d); Saint Mungo Museum of Religious Life and Art 525tl; **Glasgow Museums, Art Gallery & Museums**: 524clb, 525tl, 525cr; Art Gallery & Museum, Kelvingrove 523tr 539br; **John Glover**: 66cr, 164cb, 209br; **The Halkin by COMO**: 561tl; **Robert Harding Picture Library**: 186t, 552t, 626cr; Jan Baldwin 291bl; Michael Botham 40crb; C Bowman 613tr; Nelly Boyd 378tl; Lesley Burridge 308tr; Martyn F Chillman 309bc; 204hr, 329ca; Eurasia /Jtr; Nigel Francis 223br; Robert Francis 16 / b; Paul Freestone 230b; Sylvain Gradadom 303tc; Brian Harrison 533br; Van der Hars 542cra; Michael Jenner 49br, 533cla; Christopher Nicholson 257tl; B O'Connor 41ca; Jenny Pate 165bc; Rainbird Collection 51crb; Roy Rainsford 41bl, 172tl, 302clb, 342cl, 372l, 390tl, 479b; Michael Short 309br; James Strachen 388bl; Julia K Thorne 490bl; Adina Tovy 65tl,

490br; Andy Williams 238br, 350cl, 436tr; Adam Woolfitt 28tc, 48tr, 49crb, 291cra, 309bl, 443bl, 548tr; **Harewood House:** 414c; **Paul Harris:** 66cl, 305bl(d), 342bl, 371b, 615tr; **Harrogate International Centre:** 393br; **Crown copyright is reproduced with the permission of the Controller of HMSO:** 77br, 122br, 122tr; **Cathedral Church of the Blessed Virgin Mary and St Ethelbert in Hereford:** 320bc; **Hertfordshire County Council:** Bob Norris 62–3, 63clb; John Heseltine 111tr, 254cla, 254tr, 473tl; **Historic Royal Palaces** (Crown Copyright): 4crb, 30cl, 123tl, 177 all; **Historic Scotland** (Crown Copyright): 501cra, 510tr, 510cl; **Holdsworth House:** 570tc; **Peter Hollings:** 352clb; **Barry J. Holmes/Glastonbury:** 67tr; **Angelo Hornak Library:** 412bc, 412br; Reproduced by permission of the **Clerk of Records, House of Lords:** 487bl; **Howard's House Hotel:** 566br; **Hulton-Deutsch Collection:** 30ca, 57ca, 58cl, 60c, 61crb, 62tc, 62bl, 166cla, 173tl, 304tr, 352cla, 353crb, 441tr, 499br; **Hunterian Art Gallery:** 523bl; **Hutchison Library:** Bernard Gerad 485tl; **Hutton in the Forest:** Lady Inglewood 362tr; **Images Colour Library:** 47cr, 225br, 238tr, 254clb, 255br, 340tr, 342cla, 343tr, 357cr, 638cl; Horizon/Robert Estall 442cb; Lanscape Only 41cr, 369t, 443br; **Imperial War Museum North:** 379t; **Ironbridge Museum:** 319cl; **ISIC:** 623cr; **iStockphoto.com:** duncan1890 50cb; **Jarrold Publishers:** 217tc, 308bc; **Michael Jenner:** 344bl, 532bc; **Jorvik Viking Centre,** York: 409tc; Judges Country House: 558bl. **Frank Lane Picture Agency:** 404br(d); W Broadhurst 258bl; Michael Callan 246clb; **Image courtesy of the Leach Pottery:** Matthew Tyas 281c; **Lincolnshire County Council:** Usher Gallery, Lincoln: c 1820 by William Ilbery 345bl; **Llangolen International Musical Eisteddfod** 454cra; **London Ambulance Service:** 626cra; **London Bridge Hotel:** 562tr; **London Transport Museum:** 84tl; **Longleat House:** 270tl; **The Lowry Collection,** Salford: *Coming From the Mill,* 1930, L.S. Lowry 375tr. **Mad Turk:** 594bl; **Magna:** 417br; **Maldom Millenium Trust:** 213tr; **Mansell Collection,** London: 35clb, 56cla, 59crb, 265tr, 353clb, 406br; **Alison McGill:** 169b; **Nick Meers:** 26t; **Metropolitan Police Service:** 679t; **Middlethorpe Hall:** 558tr; **Mildreds:** 575br; **Archie Miles:** 244ca; **Simon Miles:** 356tr; **Minack Theatre:** Murray King 280bl; **Mirror Syndication International:** 91bc; **Morston Hall:** 588bl; **Murano:** 583tr; **Museum of Childhood,** Edinburgh: 514bc; **Museum of London:** 48crb, 117tr; **National Express Ltd:** 640bl; **National Fishing Heritage Centre,** Grimsby: 407c; **National Gallery of Scotland:** *The Reverend Walker Skating on Duddingston Loch,* Sir Henry Raeburn 508c(d); **National Library Of Wales:** 440tr, 443cr(d), 471crb; Board of Trustees of the **National Museums and Galleries on Merseyside:** Liverpool Museum 383tc; Walker Art Gallery 350bc, 382tr, 382br, 383cl; **National Museums Liverpool:** Mills Media 361br; **National Museum of Wales:** 440cla; By courtesy of the **National Portrait Gallery,** London: *First Earl of Essex,* Hans Peter Holbein 355tr(d); **National Tramway Museum,** Crich: 343cr; **National Trust Images:** John Bethell 283br; **National Trust Photographic Library:** 395tl, 395br, 397tr, 624bl; *Bess of Hardwick (Elizabeth, Countess of Shrewsbury),* Anon 338tr(d); Mathew Antrobus 306br, 394cl, 395bl; Oliver Benn 33br, 297bl, 394br; John Bethell 307tr; Nick Carter 259br; Prudence Cumming 271br Martin Dohrn 54crb; Andreas Von Einsidedel 33bl, 306clb, 307cra; Roy Fox 275tr; Jerry Harpur 248tr, 248bc; Derek Harris 248clb; Nadia MacKenzie 32cla; Nick Meers 270br, 676bl; Rob Motheson 296tr; Ian Shaw 464t; Richard Surman 307bl, 366clb; Rupert Truman 307br; Andy Tryner 306bl; Charlie Waite 396t; Jeremy Whitaker 307bc, 464b; Mike Williams 306cla, 396c; George Wright 248crb, 296cla; **National Trust for Scotland:** 482br, 504bc, 512bl, 526tr, 527tl, 527br; Lindsey Robertson 527bl; **National Waterways Museum at Gloucester:** 305bc, 305br; **NHPA:** Martin Garwood 399cla; Daniel Heuclin 286cl; **Network Photographers:** Laurie Sparham 484bl; **Norfolk Museums Service:** Norwich Castle Museum 205br; **Old Quay House:** 567tr, 592bc; **Orient Express Hotels:** Paul Wilkinson 564br; **L'Ortolan:** 589tl; **OXO Tower Restaurant/Harvey Nichols:** 585br; **'PA' News Photo Library:** John Stillwell 65cr. **Palace Theatre Archive:** 156cl; **Parva Farmhouse**

Guesthouse: 572br; **Planet Earth Pictures:** David Phillips 31cra; **Plockton Inn:** 73tr; **Portmeirion Ltd:** 458cr, 458cl; **The Post Office:** 511bl; **Press Association:** Martin Keene 66bl; **Public Record Office** (Crown Copyright): 52b. **Restaurant Gordon Ramsay:** 584tc; **Rob Reichenfeld:** 304br; **RBS Group:** 628bl, 628cb; **Rex Features Ltd:** 35ca, 240cl; Barry Beattie 263c; Peter Brooke 682br; Nils Jorgensen 34cb; Eileen Kleinman 665br; Hazel Murray 65tl; Tess, Renn-Burrill Productions 273c; Tim Rooke 68cr; **Riverford Field Kitchen:** 577tc; **Riverstation Restaurant:** 591br; **Royal Academy Of Arts,** London: 88cla; **Royal Collection** © 1995 Her Majesty Queen Elizabeth II: *The Family of Henry VIII,* Anon 42(d), 89cr, 90tr, 90clb, 91tl, 240br, 241tl(d), 241tr, *George IV, in full Highland dress,* Sir David Wilkie 489tc; David Cripps 91cr; **Royal Crecent Hotel, Bath:** 556cra; **Royal Pavilion & Museums, Brighton & Hove:** 178c, 182tr, 182c, 183cl, 183cr; **Royal Shakespeare Theatre Company:** 329tl; Donald Cooper 331cl(d). **St. Alban's Museums:** Verulamium Museum 236bl; **Sartaj Balti House:** Clare Carnegie 415br; **The Savoy:** 556bl, 560bl; **The Scarlet Hotel:** 593tl; **Scottish National Portrait Gallery:** on loan from the collection of the Earl of Roseberry, *Execution of Charles I,* Unknown Artist 56–7; **Shakespeare Birthplace Trust:** Amy Murrell 302bl; **Skyscan Balloon Photography:** 266cl; **Southbank Press Office:** 158tl; **Still Moving Pictures:** Wade Cooper 487br; Derek Laird 486cla; Robert Lees 69t; STB 548br, 549cr, Paisley Museum 519br, Paul Tomkins 533tr; SJ Whitehorn 499tl; **David Tarn:** 393tl; **Tony Stone Images:** 578–9; Richard Elliott 68b; Rob Talbot 357cla; **Superstock:** Adam Burton/Robert Harding Picture Library 358; Malcome Park/Loop Images 168; Prisma 411bl; Lizzie Shepherd/Robert Harding Picture Library 112; **Swan House/Fotoseeker:** Grant Scott 563br; © **Tate Britain:** 77bl, 95all, ; © **Tate Modern:** 125tr, 125cr, 125br; © **Tate St. Ives:** 281br; **Rob Talbot:** 357crb; **Transport for London:** 643crb; **Troika Photos Limited:** Michael Walter 632cla; **Urban Beach Hotel:** 557tl; **Urban Reef Café:** 590tl; **Urbis:** 376c; courtesy of the Board of Trustees of the **Victoria and Albert Museum, London:** 102clb, 103tc, 103crb; **The View from the Shard:** 121tr; **Charlie Waite:** 553t; © **Wales Tourist Board:** 437cr, 438bl, 442–3, 472br, 473cra, 473br; Roger Vitos 472tr, 472cb; **The Wallace Collection,** London: 108br; **David Ward:** 529b, 547t; **Frederick Warne & Co:** 371tc(d); © **Warwick Castle:** 327cra; Courtesy of the Trustees of **The Wedgwood Museum,** Barlaston, Staffordshire, England: 315bc; **West Midlands Police:** 626bl, 626br, 626tr; **Dean and Chapter of Westminster:** 96cla, 97bl; Tony Middleton 96clb; **Jeremy Whitaker:** 232cla; **Whitworth Art Gallery,** University of Manchester: courtesy of Granada Television Arts Foundation 378c; **Christopher Wilson:** 408bl; **Wilton House Trust:** 269btl **Woburn Abbey** – by kind permission of the Marquess of Tavistock and Trustees of the Bedford Estate: 54–5, 234tl; **York Castle Museum:** 409crb; **York Art Gallery:** 411cl; **Dean & Chapter York Minster:** Peter Gibson 413cla, 413ca, 413cr; Jim Korshaw 412tr; **York Minster (Chapter of York):** 413cl/c/bc; **Yorkshire Sculpture Park:** Jerry Hardman Jones 417t.

Front Endpaper: Alamy Images: Peter Adams Photography Ltd Rtr; BANANA PANCAKE Rbr; CBW Rcra; **Corbis:** Neale Clark/Robert Harding World Imagery Lcb; Kathy Collins Rcl; Alan Copson/info@awl-images. com/JAI Rca; Krista Ewert/Design Pics/Design Pics Rcrb; Ocean Rcb; Sebastian Wasek/Loop Images Lbc; **Fotolia:** Zechal Lbl; **Getty Images:** Bill Heinsohn Lcla; joe daniel price Lclb; **Superstock:** Adam Burton/ Robert Harding Picture Library Rtc; Malcom Park/Loop Images Rbc.

Back Endpaper: Corbis: Atlantide Phototravel Lbl; Ocean Lbr; **Getty Images:** Gonzalo Azumendi Ltl; **Superstock:** Lizzie Shepherd/Robert Harding Picture Library Rbl.

Cover: Front main image and spine – **Robert Harding Picture Library:** Adam Burton; Back image – **Dreamstime.com:** Arndale.

All other images © Dorling Kindersley. For further information see www.DKimages.com